MW00562263

NATIONAL GEOGRAPHIC
American
GOVERNMENT

Acknowledgments

Grateful acknowledgment is given to the authors, artists, photographers, museums, publishers, and agents for permission to reprint copyrighted material. Every effort has been made to secure the appropriate permission. If any omissions have been made or if corrections are required, please contact the Publisher.

Special thanks to Program Consultant Roger Miller.

Photographic Credits

Cover: trekandshoot/Getty Images; Scott Rothstein/iStock/Getty Images; **Title Page:** trekandshoot/Getty Images; **Page iii:** Collection of the Supreme Court of the United States; **Page 1:** Mark Thiessen/National Geographic Image Collection

Acknowledgments and credits continue on page R73.

For product information and technology assistance, contact us at Customer & Sales Support, 888-915-3276

For permission to use material from this text or product, submit all requests online at **www.cengage.com/permissions**

Further permissions questions can be emailed to **permissionrequest@cengage.com**

National Geographic Learning | Cengage
200 Pier 4 Blvd., Suite 400
Boston, MA 02210

National Geographic Learning, a Cengage company, is a provider of quality core and supplemental educational materials for the PreK–12, adult education, and ELT markets. Cengage is a leading provider of customized learning solutions with employees residing in nearly 40 different countries and sales in more than 125 countries around the world. Find your local representative at NGL.Cengage.com/RepFinder.

Visit National Geographic Learning online at NGL.Cengage.com

Visit our corporate website at **www.cengage.com**

ISBN: 978-0-357-10903-8

Printed in the United States of America.

Print Number: 06
Print Year: 2023

DEDICATION

Before Ruth Bader Ginsburg became a notorious Supreme Court Justice, she was a teacher.

And before she was a teacher, she was a student.

Ginsburg studied at two of the finest law schools during a time in history when her mere presence in these male-dominated institutions challenged social norms. When she graduated from Columbia Law at the top of her class in 1959, she struggled to find work as a lawyer because she was a woman and a mother. After being rejected for a Supreme Court clerkship on the basis of gender, Ginsburg chose instead to begin her law career as a professor, teaching for nearly two decades at Rutgers School of Law and Columbia Law School while doggedly advocating for women's legal rights. Appointed to the Supreme Court by President Bill Clinton in 1993—the second woman ever to sit on the highest court in the United States—Ginsburg fought fiercely and fairly for gender equality for nearly three decades. "So often in life, things that you regard as an impediment turn out to be great, good fortune," said Ginsburg in 2012, referring to the events that shaped her own career path.

Justice Ginsburg died on September 18, 2020, shortly before the release of this U.S. Government book. We dedicate it to her—a legal pioneer whose tenacity has inspired generations of learners, educators, advocates, and policy-makers. Thank you, Justice Ginsburg, for teaching us that education is power; women's rights are human rights; and equity benefits all of society.

UNIT 1

Foundations of the American System 2

CHAPTER 1
THE PRINCIPLES OF AMERICAN GOVERNMENT 4

1.1 What Are Government and Politics? 5
1.2 Different Systems of Government 10
National Geographic Magazine: These Are the World's Happiest Places 15
1.3 American Representative Democracy 16
1.4 American Political Philosophies 27

CHAPTER 1 REVIEW 34

CHAPTER 2
THE BEGINNINGS OF AMERICAN GOVERNMENT 36

2.1 Government in the English Colonies 37
2.2 The Rebellion of the Colonists 42
2.3 Independence and Revolution 47
National Geographic Online: The Letter That Won the American Revolution ... 52
2.4 The Confederation of States 53
2.5 Drafting and Ratifying the Constitution 57

CHAPTER 2 REVIEW 66

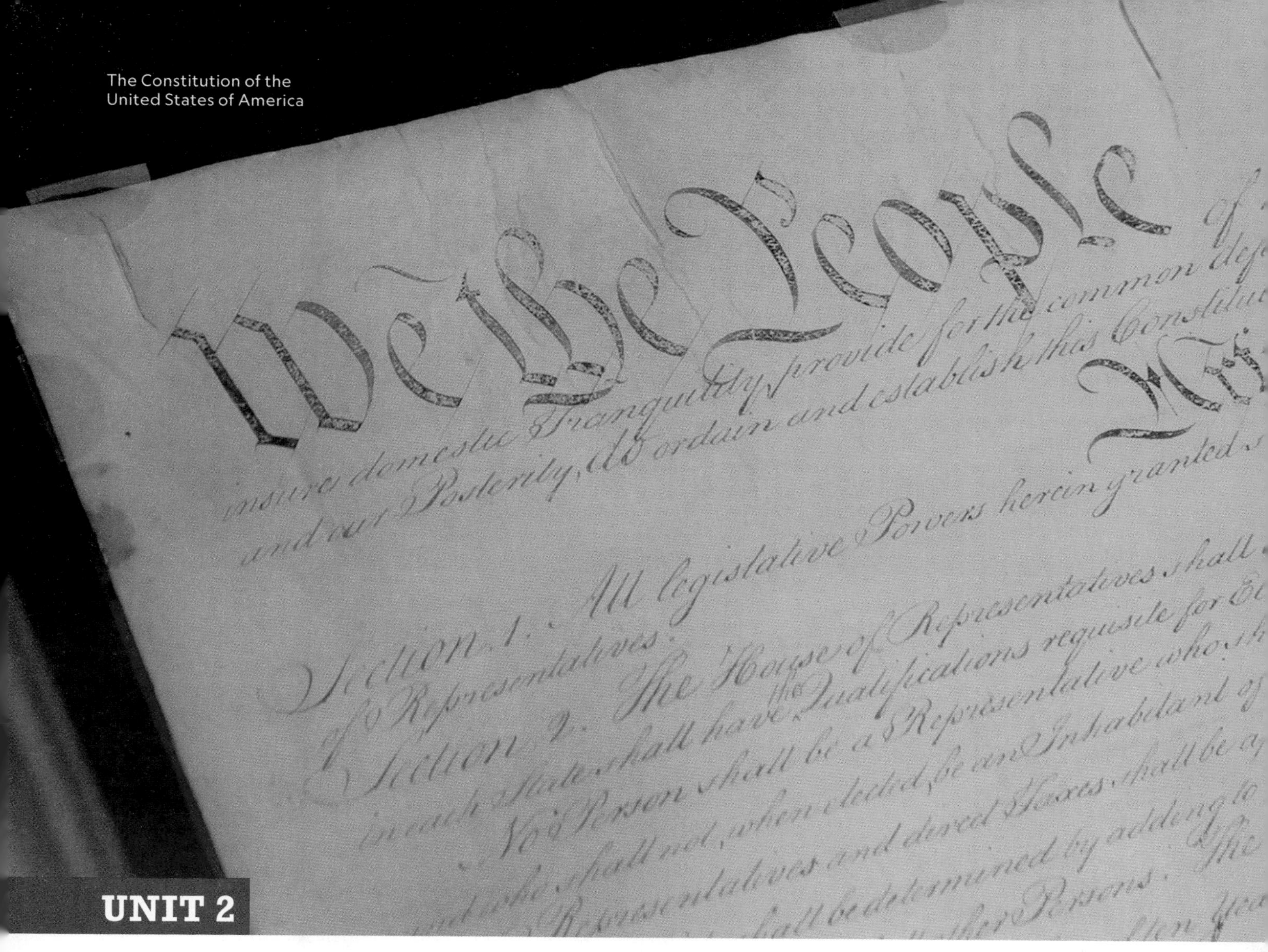

The Constitution and Federalism 68

CHAPTER 3
THE CONSTITUTION 70

- **3.1** Overview of the U.S. Constitution 71
- **3.2** Popular Sovereignty, Republicanism, Limited Government, and Rule of Law 76
- *National Geographic* Magazine: President Abe Lincoln 150 Years After His Death 81
- **3.3** Federalism, Separation of Powers, Checks and Balances, and Individual Rights 82
- **3.4** Amending the Constitution 86
- **3.5** Analyzing the Amendments 90
- **3.6** Putting the Constitution to Work 98
- Supreme Court Feature: *Marbury* v. *Madison,* 1803 101

CHAPTER 3 REVIEW 104

CHAPTER 4
FEDERALISM 106

- **4.1** What Is Federalism? 107
- **4.2** The Constitutional Division of Powers 111
- **4.3** Federal-State Relationships 117
- Supreme Court Feature: *McCulloch* v. *Maryland,* 1819 118
- Supreme Court Feature: *Gibbons* v. *Ogden,* 1824 123
- **4.4** Federalism Today 124
- *National Geographic* Magazine: Inside the New Battle for the American West 129

CHAPTER 4 REVIEW 132

March on Washington,
August 28, 1963, Washington, D.C.

UNIT 3

Civil Liberties and Civil Rights 134

CHAPTER 5
CIVIL LIBERTIES 136

5.1 The Constitutional Basis of Our Civil Liberties .. 137
5.2 Freedom of Religion 142
Supreme Court Feature: *Engel* v. *Vitale,* 1962 145
Supreme Court Feature: *Lemon* v. *Kurtzman,* 1971 146
National Geographic Magazine: Why Do Many Reasonable People Doubt Science? 150
5.3 Freedom of Expression 151
Supreme Court Feature: *Schenck* v. *United States,* 1919 155
Supreme Court Feature: *Texas* v. *Johnson,* 1989 156
5.4 Freedom of Assembly and Petition 159
National Geographic Online: How the Environment Has Changed Since the First Earth Day 163
5.5 Due Process Under the Law 164
Supreme Court Feature: *Mapp* v. *Ohio,* 1961 166
Supreme Court Feature: *Miranda* v. *Arizona,* 1966 167
Supreme Court Feature: *Gideon* v. *Wainwright,* 1963 168
5.6 The Right to Privacy 169
Supreme Court Feature: *Roe* v. *Wade,* 1973 171
CHAPTER 5 REVIEW 176

CHAPTER 6
CITIZENSHIP AND CIVIL RIGHTS 178

6.1 Citizenship in the United States 179
Supreme Court Feature: *Dred Scott* v. *Sandford,* 1857 180
6.2 Civil Rights and African Americans 186
Supreme Court Feature: *Plessy* v. *Ferguson,* 1896 189
National Geographic Magazine: Why Do We See So Many Things as 'Us vs. Them'? 196
6.3 Women's Rights 197
Supreme Court Feature: *R.G. and G.R. Harris Funeral Homes, Inc.* v. *Equal Employment Opportunity Commission,* 2020 203
National Geographic Magazine: For These Girls, Danger Is a Way of Life 206
6.4 Extending Civil Rights 207
Supreme Court Feature: *Hernandez* v. *Texas,* 1954 210
Supreme Court Feature: *Korematsu* v. *United States,* 1944 213
6.5 Beyond Equal Protection —Affirmative Action 219
Supreme Court Feature: *Regents of the University of California* v. *Bakke,* 1977 220
Supreme Court Feature: *Grutter* v. *Bollinger,* 2003 222
CHAPTER 6 REVIEW 224

U.S. Capitol Building, Washington, D.C.

UNIT 4

The Legislative Branch 226

CHAPTER 7
THE STRUCTURE OF CONGRESS .. 228

7.1 A Bicameral Legislature 229
7.2 The House of Representatives 232
Supreme Court Feature: *Baker* v. *Carr,* 1962 236
National Geographic Online: Deb Haaland: "Why Not Me? Why Not Now?" 239
7.3 The Senate 240
7.4 Congressional Leadership and Committees . 242
7.5 Congressional Elections 246
Supreme Court Feature: *Reynolds* v. *Sims,* 1964 247

CHAPTER 7 REVIEW 250

CHAPTER 8
THE POWERS OF CONGRESS 252

8.1 Enumerated Powers of Congress 253
Supreme Court Feature: *United States* v. *Lopez,* 1995 256
8.2 Inherent and Implied Powers of Congress.... 259
8.3 Non-Legislative Powers of Congress 264
National Geographic Magazine: Scenes From the Japanese Internment Resonate Today 269

CHAPTER 8 REVIEW 270

CHAPTER 9
THE LEGISLATIVE PROCESS 272

9.1 Introducing and Passing Laws 273
9.2 Conference Committees and Presidential Action 280
9.3 The Budgeting Process 284
National Geographic Magazine: The New Face of Hunger 289

CHAPTER 9 REVIEW 290

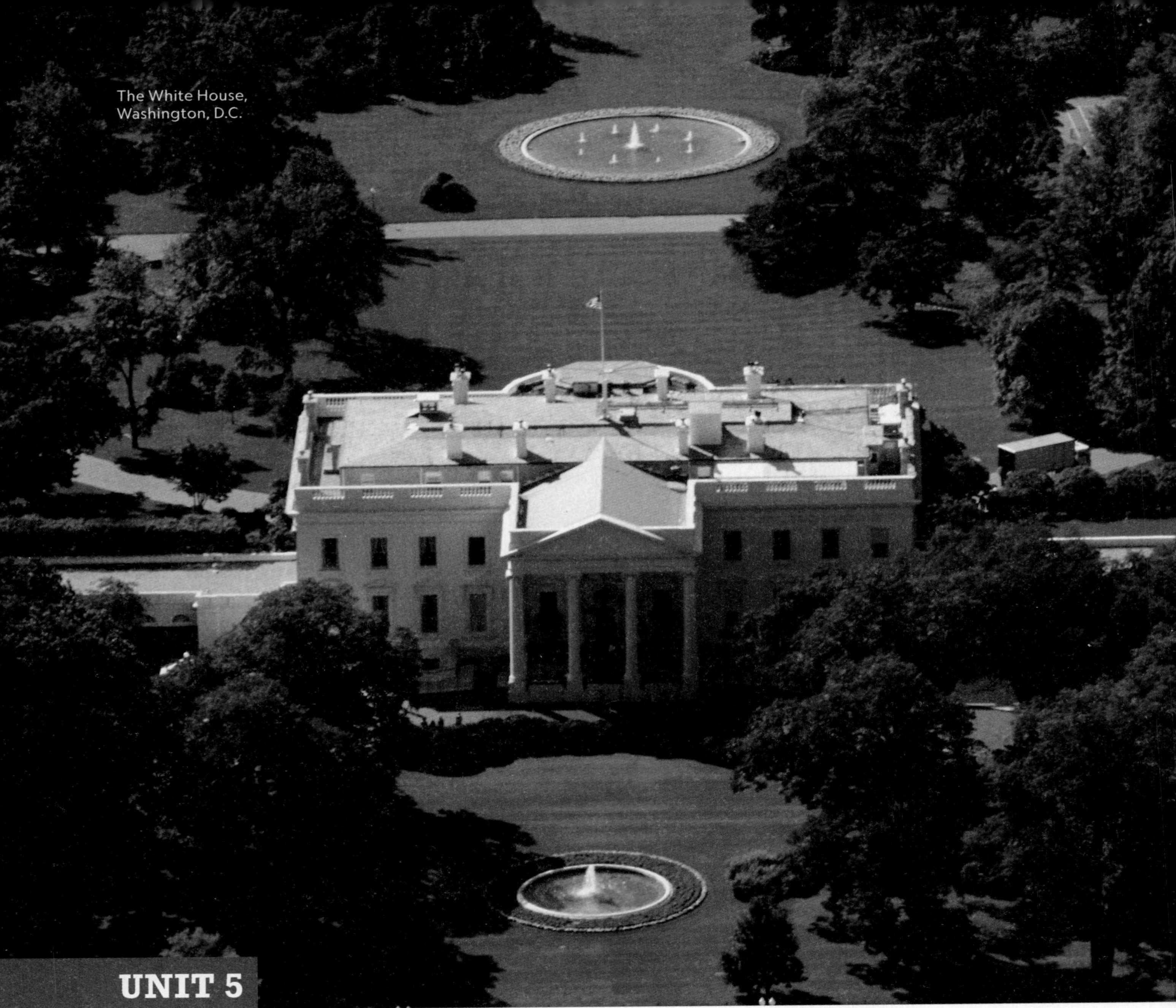

The White House, Washington, D.C.

The Executive Branch

The Executive Branch 292

CHAPTER 10
THE PRESIDENCY 294

10.1 The Roles of the President 295
National Geographic Magazine: 50 Years of Wilderness 302
10.2 Presidential Powers 303
10.3 The President and Congress 311
10.4 Organization of the Executive Branch 315

CHAPTER 10 REVIEW 322

CHAPTER 11
THE BUREAUCRACY 324

11.1 The Nature of Bureaucracy 325
11.2 The Structure of the Federal Bureaucracy 332
11.3 The Growth of the Federal Bureaucracy 340
11.4 Curbing Waste and Improving Efficiency 345
National Geographic Online: What Trump's Shrinking of National Monuments Actually Means 346

CHAPTER 11 REVIEW 354

U.S. Supreme Court building, Washington, D.C.

UNIT 6

The Judicial Branch 356

CHAPTER 12
THE AMERICAN COURT SYSTEM 358

12.1 Origins and Sources of American Law 359
Supreme Court Feature: *Brown* v. *Board of Education of Topeka,* 1954 361
12.2 The Federal Court System 367
12.3 Other Trial Courts 371
National Geographic Magazine: They Are Watching You—and Everything Else on the Planet 375

CHAPTER 12 REVIEW 376

CHAPTER 13
THE SUPREME COURT 378

13.1 Jurisdiction of the Supreme Court 379
13.2 Federal Judicial Appointments 383
13.3 The Courts as Policymakers 388
Supreme Court Feature: *Loving* v. *Virginia,* 1967 391
National Geographic Magazine: The Many Colors of Matrimony 393
13.4 The Role of Federal Courts 394
Supreme Court Feature: *Masterpiece Cakeshop, Ltd.* v. *Colorado Civil Rights Commission,* 2018 399

CHAPTER 13 REVIEW 400

2016 Republican National Convention, Cleveland Ohio, July 21, 2016

The Politics of Democracy 402

CHAPTER 14
POLITICAL PARTIES AND INTEREST GROUPS 404

14.1 Political Parties, Then and Now 405
- *National Geographic* Magazine: How Latinos Are Shaping America's Future 413

14.2 Our Two-Party System 414
14.3 Third Parties in American Politics 421
14.4 What Are Interest Groups? 424
14.5 What Interest Groups Do 435

CHAPTER 14 REVIEW 442

CHAPTER 15
THE ELECTORAL PROCESS 444

15.1 How We Nominate Candidates 445
15.2 Nominating Presidential Candidates 450
15.3 How We Elect Candidates 457
15.4 The Modern Political Campaign 460
- Supreme Court Feature: *Bush* v. *Gore*, 2000 461
- National Geographic Online: Election Maps Can Be Misleading—Here's a Solution 462

15.5 Financing Political Campaigns 468
- Supreme Court Feature: *Citizens United* v. *Federal Election Commission*, 2010 471
- Supreme Court Feature: *McCutcheon* v. *Federal Election Commission*, 2014 472

CHAPTER 15 REVIEW 474

CHAPTER 16
VOTING AND VOTING RIGHTS 476

16.1 Who Gets to Vote? 477
16.2 The Struggle for Voting Rights 480
- Supreme Court Feature: *Shelby County* v. *Holder*, 2013 485
- *National Geographic* Magazine: A Century After Women's Suffrage, the Fight for Equality Isn't Over 487

16.3 The Process of Voting 488
16.4 Understanding Voter Behavior 493
16.5 Public Opinion Polls 502

CHAPTER 16 REVIEW 508

White House Press Briefing Room, Washington D.C.

UNIT 8

Government in Action: Public Policy 510

CHAPTER 17

GOVERNMENT AND DOMESTIC POLICY 512

17.1 The Policymaking Process 513
17.2 Economic Policy, Budgeting, and Taxes 516
17.3 Health-Care Policy 523
Supreme Court Feature: *National Federation of Independent Business* v. *Sibelius*, 2012 527
17.4 Energy and the Environment 529
National Geographic Magazine: This Refuge May Be the Most Contested Land in the U.S. 535

CHAPTER 17 REVIEW 536

CHAPTER 18

GOVERNMENT AND FOREIGN POLICY 538

18.1 Who Makes Foreign Policy? 539
18.2 A Short History of American Foreign Policy 543
18.3 Global Challenges 548
National Geographic Magazine: A Thawing Arctic Is Heating Up a New Cold War 556
18.4 Diplomacy and International Economics 557

CHAPTER 18 REVIEW 566

CHAPTER 19

GOVERNMENT, POLITICS, AND THE MEDIA 568

19.1 Media in a Democracy 569
19.2 Politics, Television, and Radio 576
19.3 The Power of the Internet and Social Media 583
National Geographic Online: The Internet Is Drowning 589

CHAPTER 19 REVIEW 590

Texas Capitol Rotunda, Austin, Texas

UNIT 9

State and Local Government

State and Local Government 592

CHAPTER 20
STATE GOVERNMENTS 594

20.1 State Constitutions 595
20.2 State Legislative Branches 600
National Geographic Online: How Geography Shaped American History, Law, and Politics 607
20.3 State Executive Branches 608
20.4 State Judicial Systems 614

CHAPTER 20 REVIEW 622

CHAPTER 21
LOCAL GOVERNMENTS 624

21.1 Municipal Governments 625
National Geographic Magazine: Cities, Businesses, and Citizens Can Save the Planet 631
National Geographic Online: Tough, Cheap, and Real, Detroit Is Cool Again 632
21.2 County, Township, and Tribal Governments 633
National Geographic Magazine: Native Lands 637
21.3 State and Local Government Finances 638

CHAPTER 21 REVIEW 644

Resources Table of Contents R1
Citizenship Handbook R2
Vocabulary Words by Chapter R44
English Glossary R46
English Academic Vocabulary R53
Spanish Glossary R54
Spanish Academic Vocabulary R62
Index R63

FEATURES AND VISUALS

SUPREME COURT FEATURES

Marbury v. *Madison*, 1803 ... 101
McCulloch v. *Maryland*, 1819 ... 118
Gibbons v. *Ogden*, 1824 ... 123
Engel v. *Vitale*, 1962 ... 145
Lemon v. *Kurtzman*, 1971 ... 146
Schenck v. *United States*, 1919 ... 155
Texas v. *Johnson*, 1989 ... 156
Mapp v. *Ohio*, 1961 ... 166
Miranda v. *Arizona*, 1966 ... 167
Gideon v. *Wainwright*, 1963 ... 168
Roe v. *Wade*, 1973 ... 171
Dred Scott v. *Sandford*, 1857 ... 180
Plessy v. *Ferguson*, 1896 ... 189
R.G. & G.R. Harris Funeral Homes, Inc. v. *Equal Employment Opportunity Commission*, 2020 ... 203
Hernandez v. *Texas*, 1954 ... 210
Korematsu v. *United States*, 1944 ... 213
Regents of the University of California v. *Bakke*, 1977 ... 220
Grutter v. *Bollinger*, 2003 ... 222
Baker v. *Carr*, 1962 ... 236
Reynolds v. *Sims*, 1964 ... 247
United States v. *Lopez*, 1995 ... 256
Brown v. *Board of Education of Topeka*, 1954 ... 361
Loving v. *Virginia*, 1967 ... 391
Masterpiece Cakeshop, Ltd. v. *Colorado Civil Rights Commission*, 2018 ... 399
Bush v. *Gore*, 2000 ... 461
Citizens United v. *Federal Election Commission*, 2010 ... 471
McCutcheon v. *Federal Election Commission*, 2014 ... 472
Shelby County v. *Holder*, 2013 ... 485
National Federation of Independent Business v. *Sebelius*, 2012 ... 527

NATIONAL GEOGRAPHIC FEATURES

These Are the World's Happiest Places ... 15
The Letter That Won the American Revolution ... 52
President Abe Lincoln 150 Years After His Death ... 81
Inside the New Battle for the American West ... 129
Why Do Many Reasonable People Doubt Science? ... 150
How the Environment Has Changed Since the First Earth Day ... 163
Why Do We See So Many Things as 'Us vs. Them'? ... 196
For These Girls, Danger Is a Way of Life ... 206
Deb Haaland: "Why Not Me? Why Not Now?" ... 239
Scenes from the Japanese Internment Resonate Today 269
The New Face of Hunger ... 289
50 Years of Wilderness ... 302
What Trump's Shrinking of National Monuments Actually Means ... 346
They are Watching You—and Everything Else on the Planet ... 375
The Many Colors of Matrimony ... 393
How Latinos Are Shaping America's Future ... 413
Election Maps Can Be Misleading—Here's a Solution ... 462
A Century After Women's Suffrage, the Fight for Equality Isn't Over ... 487
This Refuge May Be the Most Contested Land in the U.S. ... 535
A Thawing Arctic Is Heating Up a New Cold War ... 556
The Internet Is Drowning ... 589
How Geography Shaped American History, Law, and Politics ... 607
Cities, Businesses, and Citizens Can Save the Planet ... 631
Tough, Cheap, and Real, Detroit Is Cool Again ... 632
Native Lands ... 637

SPECIAL FEATURES

The Electoral College ... 79
Admitting New States ... 112
The American Civil Liberties Union ... 141
Scopes "Monkey Trial" ... 148
Deferred Action for Childhood Arrivals (DACA) ... 183
American Gallery: Women in Politics ... 205
The Filibuster ... 279
Team of Rivals ... 316
How to Make a FOIA Request ... 350
Whistleblowers Time Line ... 352
Supreme Court Justices ... 385
Justice Ruth Bader Ginsburg, Advocate for Equality ... 387
What's in a Name? ... 626

INFOGRAPHICS AND DIAGRAMS

The Traditional Political Spectrum ... 31
Structure of the Government Under the Articles of Confederation ... 54
Weaknesses of Government Under the Articles ... 55
3 Branches of U.S. Government ... 73
The Electoral and Popular Votes for President in 2016 ... 79

The Balance of Power Under Federalism 83
Checks and Balances 84
The Federal Court System 98
National and State Powers Under Federalism 116
U.S. Congressional Districts, 2010 234
How a Bill Becomes a Law 277
The Budget Process in Congress 287
The Iron Triangle 330
Issue Network: The Environment 331
Organization of the Federal Government 333
Organization of the Federal Court System 369
Originalism and Modernism: A Case Study 392
Road to the Presidency 454
Typical Presidential Campaign Organization 463
Voting by Groups in the 2016 Presidential Election 499
The Policymaking Process 513
How Interest Rates Affect the Economy and Inflation 518
Fracking 533
Standard Steps in a Criminal Case 616
Structure of State Courts 620
Municipal Government Structures 627

CHARTS, GRAPHS, AND TABLES

U.S. Defense Spending, 1950–2020 8
Party Identification of U.S. Voters, 1992–2018 22
Party Identification of Voters in Presidential Elections, 2000–2016 35
Free and Enslaved Population by State, 1790 59
Changing House Representation in Selected States, 1850–2000 60
Ratification of the U.S. Constitution, by State 67
Overview of the U.S. Constitution 74
The Electoral and Popular Votes for President in 2016, Bar Graph 79
Provisions of the U.S. Bill of Rights 92
Governmental Units in the United States, 2012 109
Sources of Revenue for State and Local Governments, 2015 128
Federal Grants to State and Local Governments, FY 2018 (estimated) 133
Who Do Americans Trust with Their Data? 174
African Americans Serving in Congress, 1999–2021 193
Women's and Men's Experience of Workplace Discrimination 200
U.S. Minorities, 2000 and 2019 207
Hispanic Origins, 2017 208
Sources of Asian Immigration, 2014 212
Standing Committees in the 116th Congress, 2019–2020 245
Seats in the U.S. House or Representatives, Selected States, 1960–2010 234
Political Action Committee (PAC) Spending, 2017–2018 249
Total PAC Contributions to Candidates by Party, 2000–2018 251
Federal Minimum Wage, 1970–2020 262
Average Number of Votes Against Confirmed Federal Judges, 1960–2018 266
Projected Budget Impact of Laws Enacted by Congress in 2015 271
Cloture Motions Filed and Invoked, 1921–2018 278
Budget Expenditures by Function, Fiscal Year 2019 285
Number of People Represented by Each House Member and House Size, 1790–2010 291
Constitutional Duties of the President of the United States 298
The Roles and Activities of the President of the United States 301
The 15 Executive Departments 315
Presidential Vetoes and Control of Congress, 1993–2009 323
Selected Independent Executive Agencies 335
Selected Independent Regulatory Agencies 337
Selected Government Corporations 338
Civilian Employment in Executive Branch since 1940 342
Major Components of Federal Spending, 2018 343
Government Employees as a Percentage of U.S. Population, 1960–2017 355
Criminal and Civil Law 364
Trial Court Caseloads 377
Supreme Court Opinions, 1955 to 2020 380
Public Opinion of the Supreme Court, 1991–2018 395
Levels of Confidence, 2018 398
Judicial Ideologies of Justice Antonin Scalia and Fellow Justices 401
Reasons Independents Don't Join a Major Party, 2016 412
Top Lobbying Groups, 2018 428
Amount Spent on Lobbying, 1998–2018 428
PAC and Super PAC Contributions to Federal Candidates, 1980–2018 435
Direct Lobbying Techniques 436
Voting for House of Representatives, 2018 Midterm Elections 443
Total Cost of Federal Elections, 1998–2018 469
Groups Making Independent Campaign Expenditures, 2017–2018 Election Cycle 473
Campaign Contribution Limits for 2020 475
Voting Restrictions Enacted, 2011–2018 486
Federal Elections: Percent Voting Absentee, by Mail, and Early, 2004–2018 492
Telephone Survey Response Rates, 1997–2017 503
Final Poll Results for the 2016 Presidential Election 506
Opinions on the Voting Rights Act, 1965 and 2015 509

Federal Income Tax Rates for Unmarried Persons, Tax Year 2020 ... 521
Net Public Debt as a Percentage of the Gross Domestic Product (GDP) ... 522
Health Status of Selected Developed Countries, 2016 ... 524
Opinions on Role U.S. Should Play in World Affairs ... 567
Decline of the Daily Newspaper, 1957–2017 ... 570
Free and Paid Advertising for/by Candidates for the 2016 Presidential Nominations (through February 2016) ... 579
Selected Top Media Companies (by Total Revenue), 2012–2018 ... 584
States that Limit Terms for State Legislators, 2020 ... 598
Lower Houses of State Legislatures ... 602
Upper Houses of State Legislatures ... 602
Governors Who Later Served as President, 1900–Present ... 608
Public Trust and Confidence in Different Government Bodies, September 2018 ... 623
Sources of State and Local Government Revenue, 2017 ... 640
State and Local Government Direct Spending, 2016 ... 641

TIME LINES

Key Dates in Establishing Government Under the U.S. Constitution ... 85
Ratification of Amendments to the U.S. Constitution ... 93
Incorporation of the Bill of Rights ... 142
Selected Immigration Legislation ... 181
Whistleblowers Time Line ... 352
U.S. Political Parties Running Presidential Candidates ... 407
Extending the Right to Vote ... 482
North Korea Weapons Negotiations, 1985–2019 ... 560
The Internet and New Media ... 591

MAPS

The 2020 Election ... 24
The 1964 Election ... 30
The 1984 Election ... 30
Growth of Colonial Settlement ... 40
U.S. Population by State, 1790 ... 59
The Electoral and Popular Votes for President in 2016 ... 79
Death Penalty by State, 2018 ... 177
Latinos as a Share of State Population, 2018 ... 209
U.S. Congressional Districts, 2010 ... 234
Maryland's Third Congressional District ... 237
Share of Federal Land in Each State ... 261
U.S. Courts of Appeals and U.S. District Courts ... 369
2020 Presidential Election Results ... 410
2020 Presidential Election Results in Minnesota ... 411
States with Right-to-Work Laws, 2020 ... 431
Electoral Vote Counts, 2012, 2016, and 2020 ... 459
Traditional Electoral Vote Map ... 462
Cartogram Electoral Vote Map ... 462
Federal Reserve System ... 537
ISIS Control in Syria and Iraq, 2015 and 2018 ... 553
Authority for Drawing District Lines ... 603
Party Control of State Government, 2019 ... 604
State Sales Tax Rates, 2019 ... 639
Public School Spending per Student by State, 2016 ... 642
San Patricio Municipal Water District ... 645

DIGITAL HANDBOOKS IN MINDTAP

Citizenship Handbook
U.S. Presidents Handbook
Supreme Court Cases Handbook

FOREWORD

Susan Goldberg, Editor in Chief
National Geographic Magazine

The ideas and issues that make the news in the United States today—the ideas we feel most strongly about, the issues that can turn a casual conversation into a heated discussion—frequently connect to principles put in place centuries ago by the Framers of the U.S. Constitution.

An instructional program on American government relies on a foundation that can be found in tradition and history, even as it reaches into the norms of contemporary society. That's why we cover these issues on the pages of *National Geographic* magazine. Whether it's exploring race or gender, balancing respect for individual needs with legislating for the common good, or tackling the threat of climate change, it takes a deep understanding of how we got here to be able to think with intention about how to find the path forward.

As you read *American Government,* you'll find a National Geographic article aligned with every chapter. We hope you'll discover that the modern perspectives offered by National Geographic enrich your study of our government and make evident the critical need for the grounded decisions and positive action that will impact your future. Yours will be the generation that leads the way.

Susan Goldberg, Editor in Chief
National Geographic Magazine

Foundations of the American System

UNIT 1 OVERVIEW

Chapter 1 The Principles of American Government

Chapter 2 The Beginnings of American Government

CRITICAL VIEWING The architects of American government drew on ideas of government that dated to ancient Greece and Rome. Similarly, the designers of the U.S. Capitol, completed in the 1860s, looked to the classical past for inspiration. How do you think the architecture and art of the Capitol Rotunda are meant to affect the legislators and visitors who pass under it?

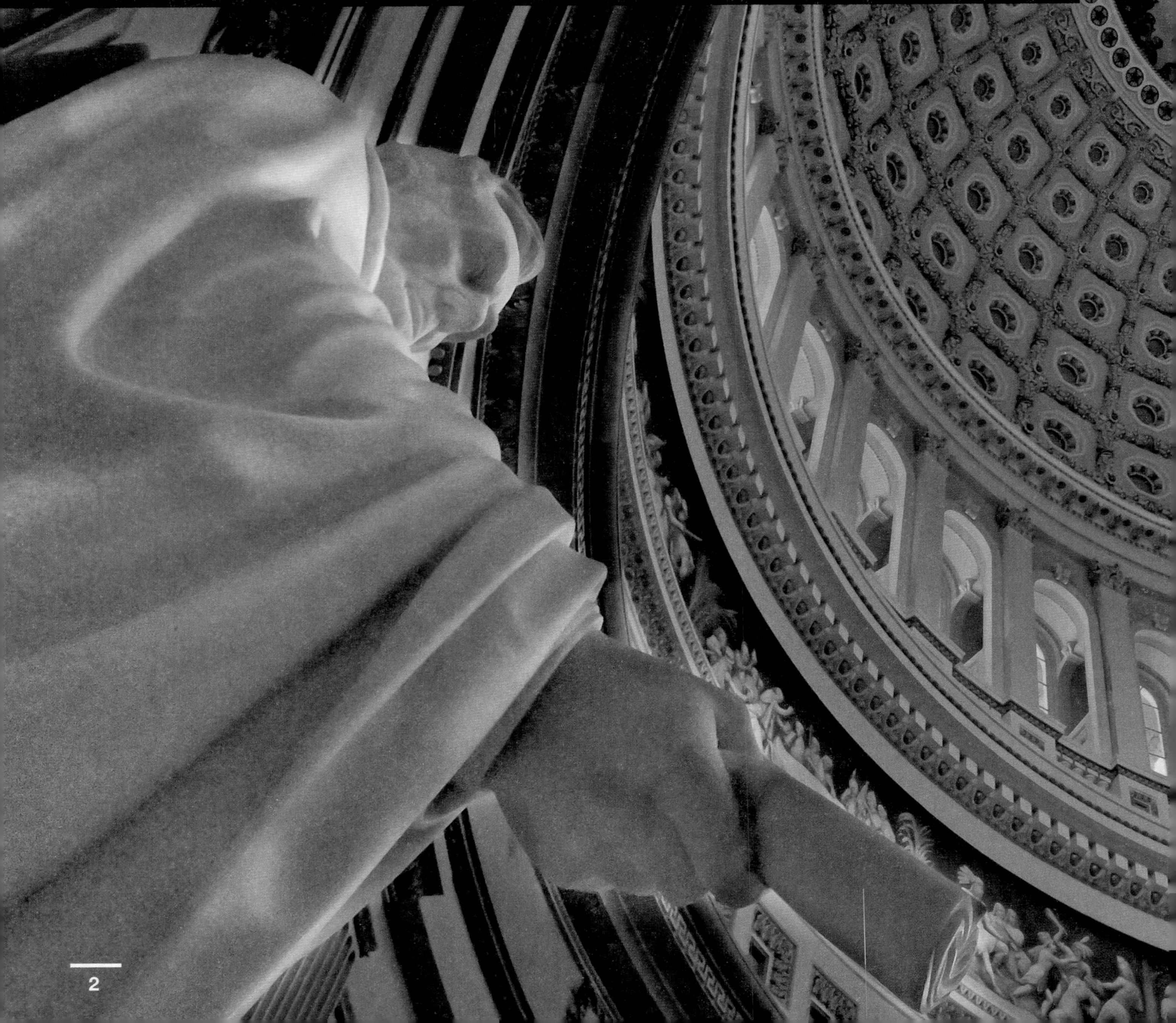

"Upon this point all . . . will agree, that the happiness of society is the end [goal] of government."

—John Adams, *Thoughts on Government (1776)*

CHAPTER 1

The Principles of American Government

LESSONS

1.1 What Are Government and Politics?

1.2 Different Systems of Government

National Geographic Magazine: These Are the World's Happiest Places

1.3 American Representative Democracy

1.4 American Political Philosophies

CRITICAL VIEWING A member of the Standing Rock Sioux Tribe in North Dakota attaches signs about voting to a bus that will take tribal members to the polls in 2018. What does the act of voting represent for so many Americans?

LESSON **1.1**

What Are Government and Politics?

Government is part of everyday life in the United States, even for high school students. Most American students attend schools run and funded by local government. They ride or walk on roads or sidewalks paid for with money collected by local, state, or national government. They live in a nation protected by a government-funded military. They need to pass a test to get a government-issued license to drive a car, and when they drive, they have to obey traffic laws passed by a government. If they work, taxes are taken out of their paychecks to help pay for all that government.

Defining Government and Politics

So who actually made those traffic laws? How was the money collected in order to run those schools and build those roads? And who made sure the money was spent the way it was supposed to be? In other words, what is government? **Government** consists of the individuals and groups that make society's rules and possess the power and authority to guarantee that these rules are followed.

The process of making and enforcing these rules isn't necessarily smooth and easy. People disagree about what the rules should be, who gets to make them, and how they should be enforced. Politics is the arena in which those disagreements are confronted and resolved. This is why most formal definitions of politics assume that social conflict—disagreements about a society's priorities—is inevitable, or impossible to avoid. Think of how often there is news of marches or rallies to protest a social issue. Think of how often people complain about government actions or decisions on social media. Disputes are inevitable because a society's resources are limited, while people's wants are unlimited. Should resources be used to support schools or a strong military? Who should receive such benefits as health care and higher education? Activities aimed at resolving conflicts over the distribution of society's scarce resources are the essence of **politics**. In the words of political scientist Harold Lasswell, politics is the process of determining "who gets what, when, and how" in a society.

In the United States, that process of determining how to use resources—and for whom—is strongly influenced by the actions and wishes of the people. As President Franklin D. Roosevelt once said, "The ultimate rulers in our democracy are . . . the voters of this country." Voters have this power because the United States is a representative democracy in which voters elect people to represent them. Those elected representatives make government decisions, but the voters influence their decisions. Voters can push their representatives to address particular issues or take a particular stand. If enough voters disapprove of the decisions a representative makes, they can vote that person out of office at the next election.

Politics might seem like distant activities that happen only in the halls of power or around elections. But politics is something every American can take part in at any time. When people call or write to elected officials and express their views on an issue, they are taking part in politics. When people act to support a cause

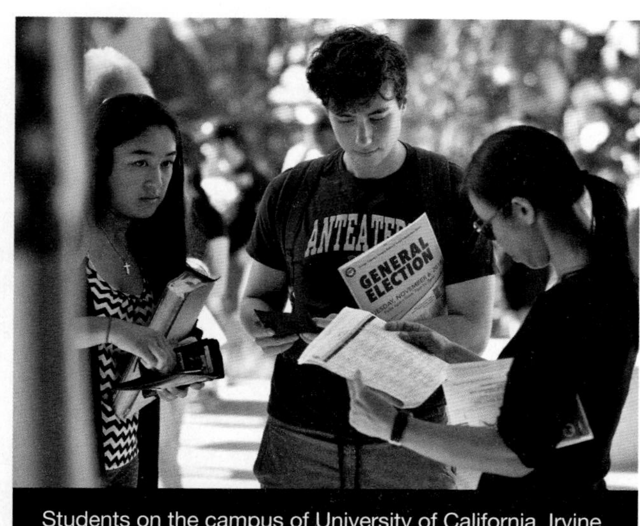

Students on the campus of University of California, Irvine, prepare to vote in the November 2018 midterm election.

they believe in, they are taking part in politics. When people discuss issues with friends and neighbors, that, too, is politics. Each action contributes to the broader conversation by which Americans decide how to use resources.

HISTORICAL THINKING

1. **MAKE GENERALIZATIONS** Why does politics involve conflict?
2. **MAKE CONNECTIONS** How do politics and government each influence the other? Give an example.

Purposes of Government

Government, then, is the people and institutions that make a society's rules. But what is the point of those rules? What are those people and institutions trying to achieve? In general, most governments serve at least three essential purposes. The first one was touched on earlier—governments resolve conflicts. Second, they provide public services. Third, they defend the country and its people against attacks.

RESOLVING CONFLICTS People have lived together in groups for thousands of years, but none of these groups has ever been entirely free of social conflict. Disputes over how to distribute resources inevitably arise. As you saw earlier, the source for this conflict is the clash between limited resources and unlimited wants. Some people will get more of these resources, and some will get less. But how does a society determine who gets more and who gets less? Just as important—how does it convince those who get less to accept their situation? This is where governments step in.

Governments need to resolve conflicts so order can be maintained. Governments do this by using their power, or their ability to get someone to do something he or she would not otherwise do. Power can be wielded in a variety of ways. Governments can use persuasion or rewards to encourage people to act in certain ways. For example, a state government may reduce taxes on a company that builds a factory or warehouse in

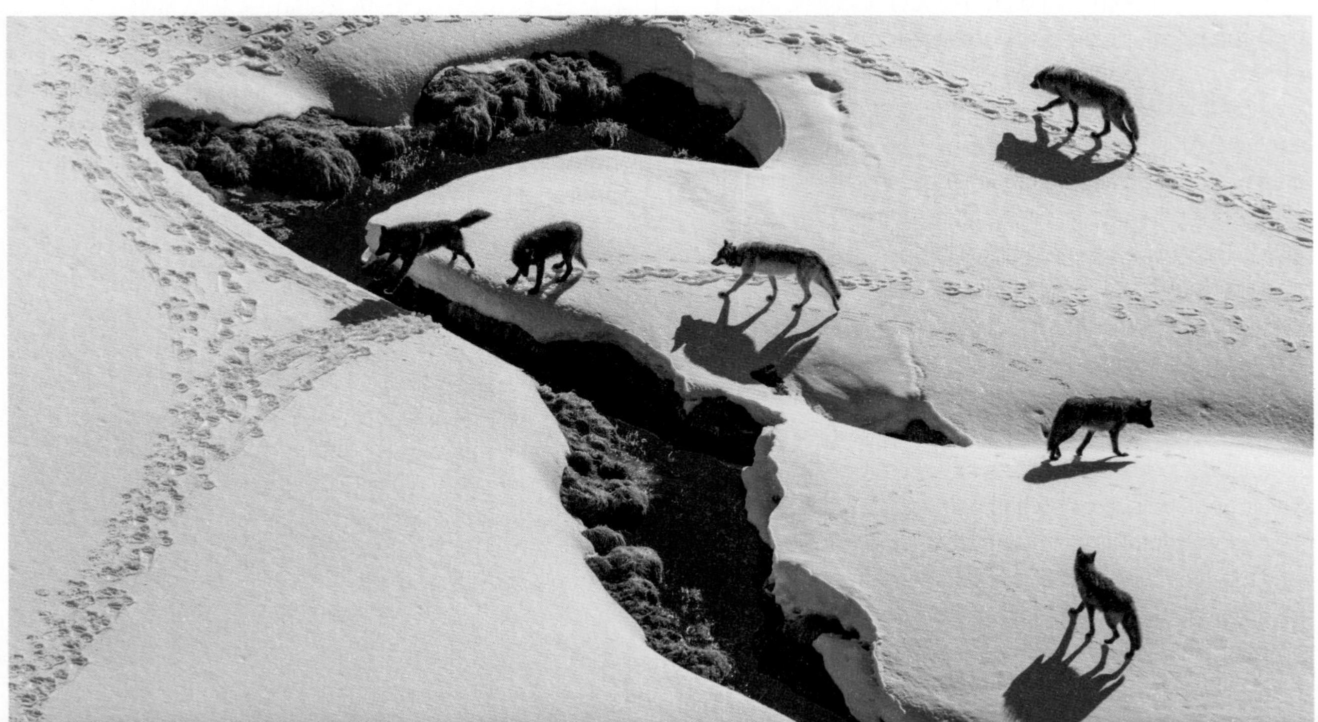

Gray wolves, killed off in the region a century ago, have been reintroduced to Yellowstone National Park in recent decades by the Department of the Interior. Ranchers fearing for the safety of their livestock waged a legal battle against the gray wolf program, but a federal court upheld the reintroduction in 2000, affirming the authority of the Department of the Interior to take this step.

the state. Governments may also use or threaten to use force to get people to do what governments want them to do. Dictators often use punishments such as seizing property or putting people in prison to coerce people into obeying laws.

Even in a representative democracy like the United States, fear of punishment can encourage people to obey the law. One reason drivers do not drive above the speed limit, for example, is that they don't want to pay a fine for speeding. Most Americans pay their taxes on time because they don't want to face fines for failing to do so.

The power of governments typically depends on their authority. If people refuse to recognize a government, its power is useless. **Authority** is the legitimate, or valid, right to use power. When a government has authority, people accept its legal and moral right to wield its power. Power and authority are central to the ability of a government to make and enforce laws and regulations.

Governments also develop court systems to make final decisions when conflicts arise. When a government is legitimate, these court decisions are widely accepted. Each year, the United States Supreme Court rules on some of the most highly controversial questions and issues in the country. Because of that court's high stature and authority, even groups that work for outcomes contrary to its decisions accept them as law. For example, the Second Amendment to the U.S. Constitution states, "A well regulated Militia, being necessary to the security of a free State, the right of the people to keep and bear Arms, shall not be infringed."

In recent years, the Supreme Court has heard cases concerning whether that amendment grants individuals, as well as state and national militia, the right to own firearms. As the Court has considered these cases, groups on both sides of the issue have filed papers stating their position. Groups that want laws to control gun ownership, such as Everytown for Gun Safety, argue one way. The National Rifle Association (NRA), which lobbies on behalf of gun owners, argues differently. Yet when the Court affirmed in 2008 and again in 2010 that the right to bear arms applies to individuals, both sides accepted the Court's decisions.

PROVIDING PUBLIC SERVICES Another key purpose of governments is to provide **public services**, important services that individuals cannot provide for themselves. For example, no one person can pay for all the roads and education, or provide all the clean air and water, he or she needs. Governments undertake projects that most individuals would not or could not carry out on their own, such as building airports and sewer systems. Every public service, from cutting the grass in local parks to maintaining an effective police department, costs money. Governments have the responsibility to determine how much to spend on these services and how best to cover these costs.

The people who benefit from these services can vary from one type of service to another. Services like fire fighting and prevention or environmental programs benefit society as a whole. Everyone feels more secure knowing that their lives and property are protected or that the water from their faucets is safe to drink. Other types of services are targeted to benefit specific parts of the population, however. For example, public schools serve children and their families. Schools are funded by taxpayer dollars, even though not all taxpayers have children in schools. Similarly, the Social Security Disability Insurance program provides some income to people whose ability to work is limited because they have a disability. Working Americans contribute to the program through a tax, regardless of whether they ever become disabled.

Government involvement in the overall economy is another public service. The U.S. government passes laws that give inventors the right to benefit from their inventions. It sets rules and regulations that determine how companies can be organized and operate. To protect workers, the government passes laws about safety in the workplace. To protect consumers, it makes laws to ensure that food is safe to eat. The government plays a big role in promoting the growth of the economy so individuals and businesses can prosper.

Economic growth is not always a sure thing, though. The government may also be expected to provide protection from hardship in bad times. In 2008, this objective became extremely important when the country was mired in a severe economic downturn called the Great Recession. Many companies went out of business, and millions of people lost their jobs.

The United States, along with the rest of the world, faced an even greater challenge in 2020. A **pandemic**, an outbreak of a disease that affects a large number of people over a wide area, forced some state and local governments to mandate the closure of many businesses in order to lower rates of infection. Unemployment rates in the United States reached their highest levels since the Great Depression of the 1930s.

DEFENDING THE COUNTRY Governments have historically given very high priority to a third purpose of government—protecting the country. Matters of national security and defense demand considerable time, effort, and expense. The Constitution of the United States gives the national government the exclusive power to conduct relations with foreign countries, which involve everything from discussing possible treaties to declaring and carrying out war.

The U.S. government provides for the common defense and national security with its Army, Navy, Marines, Air Force, and Coast Guard. The departments of State, Defense, and Homeland Security contribute to this defense network. Agencies like the Central Intelligence Agency, the Federal Bureau of Investigation, and the National Security Agency also play vital roles in this effort.

Attacks by foreign countries are not the only threat that governments face, however. Since the terrorist attacks on the World Trade Center and the Pentagon on September 11, 2001, preventing terrorist attacks has become a priority of the U.S. government. Terrorists often act independently of any foreign country. They may be inspired by the ideas of a terrorist group or leader even if they are not supported by a foreign group or government. For example, in 2017 a man believed to have been inspired by the ideas of the terrorist group the Islamic State (also known as ISIS) drove a truck onto a New York City bike path, killing 8 people and injuring at least 12 others. But that same year another man with no ties to a terrorist group opened fire on a crowd attending an outdoor concert in Las Vegas, killing nearly 60 people and wounding hundreds more. This event makes clear that terrorist acts are not the only domestic threats governments must worry about.

In recent decades, governments have also confronted another type of terrorism: cyberattacks. These attacks on computer-based systems or information can threaten national security in a variety of ways. Government or business systems can be hacked to get private information. They can also be damaged through the use of computer viruses and other tools. Governments now need to watch constantly for signs of such attacks on their own computer systems or the systems of companies or private groups.

U.S. Defense Spending, 1950–2020

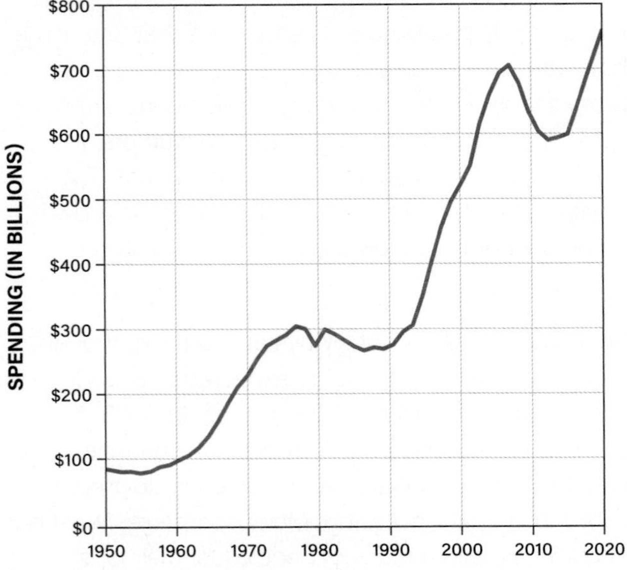

Source: Government Publishing Office **Note:** 2018-2020 are estimates

HISTORICAL THINKING

3. **MAKE INFERENCES** Justices on the U.S. Supreme Court are not elected by the people. How might this fact affect how Americans view the authority of Court decisions?
4. **EVALUATE** Is the national park system a government service that benefits society as a whole or only parts of the population? Explain.
5. **INTERPRET GRAPHS** How has defense spending changed since the government has made preventing terrorism a higher priority?

The State

Governments are a key characteristic of the political units called states. In the United States, most people are used to thinking of the word *state* as meaning one

CRITICAL VIEWING Statues in Abu Simbel Temple in Egypt commemorate Ramses II, who, like other Egyptian pharaohs, claimed a divine right to rule. Note the people on the lowest platform of the temple to give you a sense of the size of these statues. How would these statues help substantiate the pharaoh's claim that Egypt's gods supported his rule?

of the 50 constituent units that make up the country as a whole. But the word *state* is also a synonym for what people commonly think of as a country. That is what political scientists mean when they use the term.

CHARACTERISTICS OF A STATE A state has four defining characteristics. One is a government. A state also requires territory, or a recognized geographic area with formal boundaries that belongs only to that state. A population, or a group of people who live within the governed territory, is the third requirement for a state. Finally, a state is defined by its **sovereignty**—a concept that is directly linked to government. When a state is sovereign, it has the absolute authority to govern itself. In other words, a state is autonomous. It, and it alone, is responsible for its government.

THEORIES OF THE ORIGIN OF STATES How did states come into being? In general, political scientists focus on four theories to explain the origins of states.

The first of these theories, evolutionary theory, looks back thousands of years to explain how the earliest political structures formed. According to this theory, the first governments arose when early humans shifted from hunting and gathering to farming and formed agricultural communities. They formed governments because they needed some sort of central organization. In this view, farming led to larger, more complex societies requiring decisions about use of resources like land and water and the crops farmers produced.

The second theory of state origin is called force theory. In force theory, one group of people or an existing state takes control of a government by force. For example, military leaders may seize control of their own country's government and put themselves in power. This violent change of leadership is called a *coup*, a French word meaning "stroke" that suggests a swift seizure of power. In other cases, a group of rebels may revolt against the existing government and seize power.

The third theory for how states originate is the **divine right theory**, the idea that the ruler of the state is granted the authority to do so by God or gods. Divine right was used to claim authority in ancient times. For instance, the pharaohs of ancient Egypt claimed the right to rule was given to them by the gods. The divine right theory also appeared in the 16th century in

Europe, when kings and queens claimed they had the divine right to rule with almost unquestioned authority.

The fourth theory of state origin developed as a reaction to the divine right theory. It arose during the intellectual movement called the Enlightenment, which began in the 17th century. Thinkers of the Enlightenment emphasized the use of reason in individual behavior and social institutions. According to **social contract theory**, people agree to obey a common set of rules and give up some of their freedom in return for security. According to this theory, governments began in the distant past, when people lived without laws in what Enlightenment thinkers called a state of nature. They entered into a social contract for their own safety and that of their property. By agreeing with others to obey the same laws, they protected themselves from harm. On the other hand, each individual gave up some freedom of action in the process.

Enlightenment thinkers used social contract theory in different ways. Some used it to explain the origin of a monarchy. They replaced the divine right theory by justifying the monarch's power based on the idea that the people—once upon a distant time—had consented to the monarch's rule. Others used the theory to claim that the individuals who entered into that contract had rights that the government had to recognize and protect.

HISTORICAL THINKING

6. **EVALUATE** Which characteristics of what political scientists call a state does each of the 50 states in the United States have, and which does each one lack?
7. **DRAW CONCLUSIONS** How is the role of government leadership in a state formed by force different from the leadership in a state where the social contract theory is accepted?

LESSON 1.2 Different Systems of Government

As you have read, government involves people making decisions to achieve certain goals. But who exactly makes those decisions? One of the most meaningful ways to classify the various systems of government around the world is by answering that simple—but important—question: Who gets the power to make the rules people must obey? An equally important question is: How do those people get the power to make the rules?

Undemocratic Systems

The form of a country's government is influenced by a number of factors. They include the country's history, its customs and values, and its geography and resources. Given all the possible ways these factors can come together, no two countries have exactly the same form of government. Still, political scientists have found that many governments have enough in common that they can be grouped into two broad categories—democratic and undemocratic. In democratic governments, the people are the ultimate source of power. The voters in these countries choose the leaders and lawmakers. Those leaders are expected to consider the people's needs and wishes when they make laws and regulations. In undemocratic countries, the people have no such role. In these countries, leaders gain the power by other means.

As you learned in the last lesson, the United States is a representative democracy. For most Americans, democracy may seem like the model for all governments. Yet until the birth of modern democracy in the United States in the 18th century, nearly all governments were **authoritarian**, governments in which the people must obey leaders who are not required to answer to the people. Authoritarian leaders determine what the laws are and how they shall be enforced. There is no legal process by which the people can hold their leaders accountable. The only option is a revolt or seizure of power. A government in which such power is held by a single person or a group of individuals with no accountability to the people is called an **autocracy**.

MONARCHIES Authoritarian leaders can take power in two ways—through traditional means or by force. One form of autocracy, known as a monarchy, is government by a king or queen, an emperor or empress, or a person with some other aristocratic title. Monarchs usually gain power through inheritance from a parent or another relative. Most monarchs are examples of authoritarian leaders who take power through traditional means.

As you read earlier, monarchs of 16th-century Europe justified their rule through the theory of divine right. They claimed they were given the right to power and authority by God. As absolute monarchs, they claimed unlimited power. In today's world, the king of Saudi Arabia and the sultan of Oman are examples of absolute monarchs. Yet most monarchies today are constitutional monarchies. In these nations, the power of the monarch is limited, or checked, by elected leaders.

Today, most constitutional monarchs are merely ceremonial leaders. That is the case, for example, in Spain, Sweden, and the United Kingdom. These monarchs are called heads of state. In that role, they attend official events, such as the opening of an important new building. They also represent the country to the rest of the world. But in a constitutional monarchy, kings and queens have no real power. A different person—often a prime minister or another elected official—serves as the head of government.

In 2006, Jigme Khesar Namgyel Wangchuck became the fifth king of Bhutan after his father, the fourth king, abdicated, or stepped down voluntarily. At age 28, the new king became the youngest reigning monarch in the world. Bhutan is a constitutional monarchy. The king serves as the head of state, but has no real power.

DICTATORSHIPS Like monarchies, dictatorships are undemocratic. Unlike monarchies, **dictatorships** are governments formed by an individual or a group whose power is not supported by tradition. Generally, dictators gain power by seizing it, often through a military takeover or as a result of the actions of a mass political party. Adolf Hitler, for example, gained power in Germany in 1933 as the leader of the Nazi Party. While a dictator is often a single individual, such as Hitler or Nicolas Maduro of Venezuela, dictatorial power can also be exercised by a group, such as the Communist Party of China. Dictators aren't accountable to anyone other than themselves.

Some dictatorships are **totalitarian**, which means the dictatorship sets the goals and controls almost all aspects of a country's social and economic life. The government controls what types of industries and businesses people can run, how much money workers can earn, and what products they can use that money to buy. Totalitarian states also try to control ideas and opinions. They limit the books and news sources citizens can read, the movies they can watch, and the social media they can use, usually with the goal of benefiting only themselves and their supporters. Many rules, in fact, are in place to ensure that the leaders hold on to their power. Examples of totalitarian governments include Hitler's Nazi regime in Germany from 1933 to 1945 and Joseph Stalin's dictatorship in the Soviet Union (of which Russia was

ВПЕРЕД, К ПОБЕДЕ КОММУНИЗМА!

CRITICAL VIEWING This 1952 poster with a slogan that translates to "Forward to the victory of communism!" is one of many propaganda pieces created by the Communist government under Joseph Stalin, shown in the foreground. The Soviet Union became a military superpower during Stalin's regime, which lasted from the 1920s to 1953. How do you think totalitarianism influenced the military growth of the Soviet Union?

the most important part) from 1929 to 1953. A current example of a totalitarian dictator is North Korea's Kim Jong Un.

While monarchs generally inherit power and dictators gain it in other ways, this distinction is not hard and fast. North Korea's Kim Jong Un, for example, though a dictator, gained power by inheriting it. He succeeded his father, Kim Jong Il, as Supreme Leader when the latter died in 2011, just as a prince would succeed his father, the king. Kim didn't take the title of a monarch, however, so the government is considered a dictatorship. Likewise, throughout history, some individuals have seized control of a monarchy just as some dictators seize power. But because they took the title of king or emperor and passed that title to their children, they are considered monarchs.

HISTORICAL THINKING

1. **MAKE CONNECTIONS** How might this textbook be different if you were using it in a country with an undemocratic government?
2. **DRAW CONCLUSIONS** How do you think the rise of more democratic governments has affected the authority of monarchs?

Democratic Systems

A **democracy** is a form of government in which the supreme political authority rests with the people. In fact, the word *democracy* comes from the Greek *demos*, meaning "the people," and *kratia*, meaning "rule." Democratic governments are based on a key idea: Government exists through the consent of the people and reflects the will of the majority. Though not widely practiced until recent centuries, this idea first took root thousands of years ago.

THE FIRST DIRECT DEMOCRACY The democracy we are familiar with in the United States is adapted to a nation of over 330 million people spanning six time zones. The first democracies, established about 2,500 years ago in Athens and several other ancient Greek city-states, were much simpler affairs. For starters, they were direct democracies, with voters participating directly in government decision-making. Every adult male Athenian citizen took part in the governing assembly and voted on all major issues.

The Athenian form of direct democracy demanded a high level of participation. Since citizens were both the governed and the governing, they could be sure that their decisions reflected their wants and needs. This complete reliance on the people makes Athenian democracy sound ideal. But the system had a serious flaw. Most residents in the Athenian city-state—including women who were citizens, children, foreigners, and enslaved people—could not vote. As a result, they had no say in government decisions. Therefore, the earliest democracy was rule by only some of the people.

DIRECT DEMOCRACY TODAY Clearly, direct democracy as a form of government is feasible only in small communities where citizens can meet regularly to decide key issues and make laws. For this reason, pure direct democracy as it existed in ancient Greece is not found in any nation today. Modern countries have too much land and too many people for all citizens to meet, speak their minds, and vote on every issue. Governments of some New England towns and certain parts of Switzerland use direct democracy, however. Some countries use direct democracy as part of their democratic process, as well. According to the Global Forum on Modern Direct Democracy, roughly 80 percent of the world's nations have held a popular vote on a national issue since 1980.

Some American states also include processes that come close to direct democracy. For example, an **initiative** is a process that allows citizens to vote measures into law or recommend measures to the legislature. Some states also allow for **referendums**, a process in which voters have the power to approve a new law or remove an existing law. In both cases, the measures in question are placed on a ballot, and a simple majority of votes decides the issue. There are several categories of each of these types of ballot measures:

- **Direct initiative:** Citizens collect a minimum number of signatures to put a proposed measure on the ballot. If the majority votes in favor of the measure, it becomes a law.
- **Indirect initiative:** Citizens collect a minimum number of signatures to put a proposed measure before the state legislature. If the legislature doesn't pass the measure, it can then be put on the ballot for citizens to decide.
- **Required referendum:** The state constitution requires that a certain measure must be placed on the ballot and approved by the people to be enacted. This may be the case with any changes made to the constitution.
- **Legislative referendum:** The state legislature votes to have a measure put on the ballot for the people's approval before it can become law.
- **Veto referendum:** Citizens collect a minimum number of signatures in order to put an existing law on the ballot. Voters then decide whether to keep or abolish the law.
- **Recall:** Citizens have the power to remove an elected official from office before his or her term of office has ended. Much like a veto referendum, people must collect a minimum number of signatures to put the recall question on the ballot. If a majority votes in favor of the recall, the official is removed from office.

HISTORICAL THINKING

3. **EVALUATE** In what way did Athenian democracy fall short of our present standards?

4. **COMPARE AND CONTRAST** What are two differences between a legislative referendum and a veto referendum?

In 2018, over 1 million people demonstrated in Barcelona, Spain, in support of independence for Catalonia, an autonomous region in northeast Spain. Barcelona is the capital city of Catalonia. A majority of voters cast ballots in favor of independence in a 2017 referendum there, but the Spanish central government declared the referendum illegal.

Republic and Representative Democracy

The ancient Greeks served as an inspiration for the leaders who formed American government, but the Framers of the American government knew there were times when the Athenians had been swayed by an eloquent speaker or a popular leader to make bad decisions. The Framers worried that rule by the people could spiral out of control. Left unchecked, majorities might ignore the rights of those in the minority. Fearful of a system of government that would collapse into mob rule, the Framers of the Constitution turned to the Roman Republic.

Rome's government consisted of appointed executives and three representative bodies whose members were chosen by different social classes. Taken as a whole, the various bodies were meant to represent the desires of the people—or, at least, of male citizens. Neither women who were citizens nor enslaved residents had a voice. But the powers and responsibilities of each body depended on its makeup. The Senate, whose members typically came from the most privileged social class, was the most powerful of the bodies. Even though it could not propose legislation—a power reserved to the popular assemblies made up of the less privileged—the Senate controlled Rome's finances and directed its foreign policy.

This elaborate structure appealed to the Framers of the U.S. Constitution for two reasons. It placed decision-making power in the hands of representatives, not directly with the people, and it dispersed the various functions of government, rather than concentrating them in a single body or person. In the United States, then, the will of the people is expressed through the individuals that the people elect to act as representatives. These representatives are responsible to the people for their conduct and can be voted out of office.

The Framers called American government a republic. A **republic** is a specific type of representative democracy with an elected head of state rather than a king or queen. As you read earlier, constitutional monarchies have the monarch as head of state and an elected official as head of government. The head of state and the head of government in the United States are combined in one person, the president.

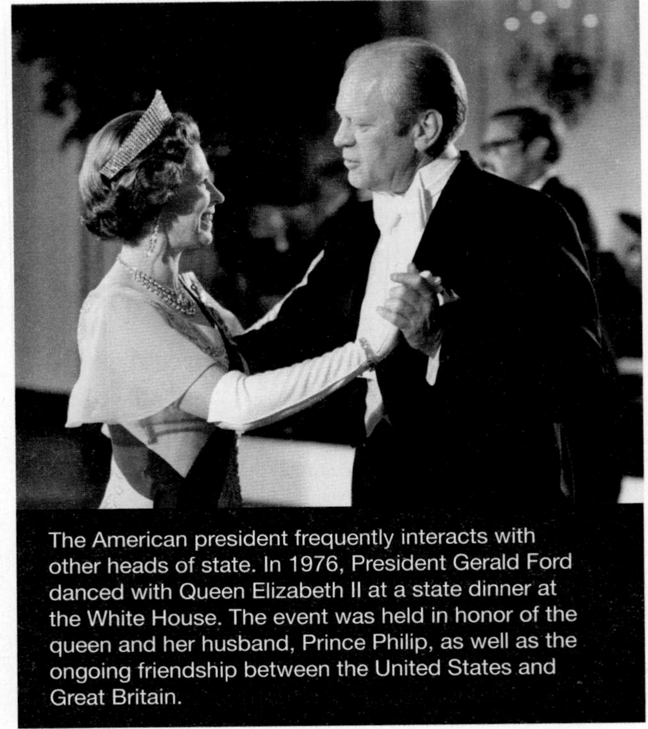

The American president frequently interacts with other heads of state. In 1976, President Gerald Ford danced with Queen Elizabeth II at a state dinner at the White House. The event was held in honor of the queen and her husband, Prince Philip, as well as the ongoing friendship between the United States and Great Britain.

The United States has a presidential democracy. Brazil and the Philippines have this form of government as well. In a presidential democracy, the making of laws and the execution, or carrying out, of the laws are handled by two different yet equally powerful branches of government. Congress has the power to make laws, and the president has the power to carry them out. In a parliamentary democracy, laws are created and executed by a single branch. In Britain, for example, the prime minister is the head of government and has the power to carry out the laws. That official, unlike the president, is also a member of the legislature, called Parliament. Countries with parliamentary systems include Canada, India, and Japan.

HISTORICAL THINKING

5. **CATEGORIZE** Why was it so important to the Framers that the United States become a republic and not just a representative democracy?
6. **COMPARE AND CONTRAST** Explain the difference between a presidential democracy and a parliamentary democracy.

Danish teens joyously dive from a platform into Copenhagen's harbor. The Danish government provides recreational facilities across the country, which encourages exercise and helps Danes stay physically fit.

These Are the World's Happiest Places

by Dan Buettner ***National Geographic*** **Magazine, November 2017**

How happy are you? Each year, researchers from around the world ask this question in a variety of ways as they compile the annual World Happiness Report, which ranks 156 countries by their happiness level. As Dan Buettner explains in "These Are the World's Happiest Places," levels of pleasure, purpose, and pride are consistently found to be high in the countries that rank the happiest.

Buettner profiles three countries—Costa Rica, Denmark, and Singapore—that consistently rate high for happiness to reveal what makes their people so happy year after year. In Costa Rica, the secret might be a clear correlation between lifestyle and pleasure. Both Costa Rica's government and society stress the ideas of contentment and generosity, and universal health care with a focus on preventative medicine helps support these ideas. In Denmark, the national government, funded by high taxes, covers the costs of every Dane's health, education, and other social needs so citizens have the freedom to pursue their personal purpose in whatever career and hobby appeal to them. In Singapore, government and national values promote harmony and hard work, and the government gives subsidies that reward career dedication and increased economic status—ideas that emphasize that country's focus on personal pride.

When it comes to the United States, Buettner reports that residents of Boulder, Colorado, experience the highest levels of happiness. Boulder's top spot on the national happiness index is typically explained by its residents' appreciation of their local environment and focus on living healthfully. As Buettner describes, factors like these are tied to a loose formula for happiness:

> *The researchers who publish the annual World Happiness Report found that about three-quarters of human happiness is driven by six factors: strong economic growth, healthy life expectancy, quality social relationships, generosity, trust, and freedom to live the life that's right for you. These factors don't materialize by chance; they are intimately related to a country's government and its cultural values. In other words the happiest places incubate happiness for their people.*

Access the full version of "These Are the World's Happiest Places" by Dan Buettner through the Resources Menu in MindTap.

THINK ABOUT IT How does the relationship between government and citizens factor into the happiness

LESSON
1.3 American Representative Democracy

A defendant stands and faces a group of 12 men and women in a courtroom. Her fate depends on whether those people think she committed a crime or not. As the head of the jury rises to read the verdict, the defendant takes a deep breath. Dramas similar to this one take place in courtrooms across the country every day. One of the most sacred rights cherished by Americans is the right to be judged by a jury of ordinary people, people much like themselves. Where did that right come from? Strange as it may sound, it dates back to a confrontation with the king of England more than 900 years ago.

The Building Blocks of American Democracy

In writing the U.S. Constitution in 1787, the Framers incorporated two basic principles of government: limited government and representative government, ideas that began evolving in England centuries earlier. The Framers combined those English traditions with the ideas of more recent political thinkers to make a completely new form of "government by the people."

THE ENGLISH LEGACY OF LIMITED GOVERNMENT Back in the early Middle Ages, English kings had few limits to their power. This began to change in 1215, when King John was confronted by a large group of nobles, or members of the land-owning upper class, who were angry over the increased demands for payments to the king and his refusal to recognize their authority over their own subjects. These nobles forced the king to accept limits to his power that were written into a document called the Magna Carta, or the Great Charter. For instance, the Magna Carta provided for a trial by a jury of one's peers, or equals. It also prohibited the taking of a free man's life, liberty, or property except through due process of law. Additionally, the charter forced the king to obtain the nobles' approval for any taxes he imposed on them. The Magna Carta was a contract between the king and his subjects that channeled some authority away from the monarch and to the people he had previously ruled without check.

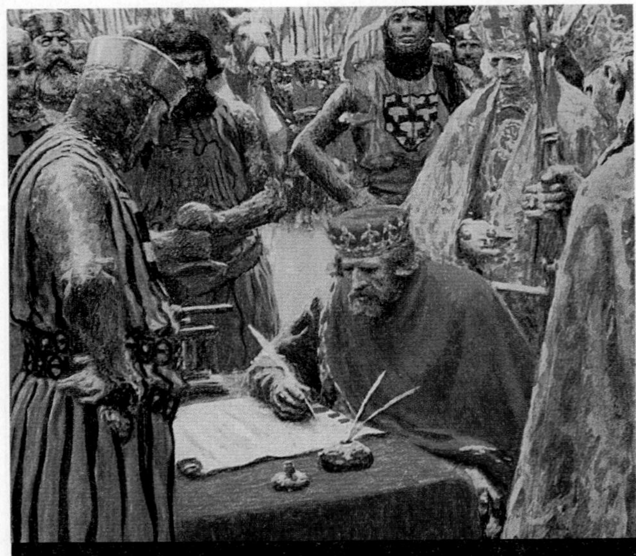

CRITICAL VIEWING In this lithograph celebrating the Magna Carta, King John is shown reluctantly signing that document. Why do you think the Magna Carta is still considered such an important document, more than 800 years after its signing?

The importance of the Magna Carta to England cannot be overemphasized. This key document established the principle of **limited government**, a government whose powers and actions are restricted by a system of laws. A limited government has some form of checks and safeguards to ensure that leaders serve public rather than private interests. Nonetheless, the Magna Carta did not benefit all English people. Like Athenian democracy, it had limited scope. Many of the rights it named applied only to the nobility. Nobles wanted to protect themselves—not the peasants whose labor they depended on. Still, the document was a breakthrough. It formed the basis for future constitutional government for England and eventually the United States.

THE ENGLISH LEGACY OF REPRESENTATIVE GOVERNMENT As you have read, in a representative government, people elect individuals to make governmental decisions. Usually, these representatives are elected to their offices for specific periods of time. England had a representative assembly that became larger in size and power in the centuries following adoption of the Magna Carta. By the 14th century, this assembly—called Parliament—had broken into two units. The House of Commons was made up of representatives chosen by ordinary, or common, people. The House of Lords was made up of nobles and top officials of the church.

In 1689, the English Parliament took another significant step in extending the concepts of limited and representative government by passing the English Bill of Rights. This document included three key ideas. First, the king or queen was barred from interfering with elections to Parliament. Second, the monarch was forbidden from collecting taxes or maintaining an army without Parliament's approval. Third, any king or queen could rule only with the consent of Parliament.

The Framers were deeply familiar with this Bill of Rights and the tradition of limited government that developed first in England and then in Britain after 1707, when England and Scotland were joined to form Great Britain. These concepts would eventually become part of the American system of government.

PHILOSOPHICAL INFLUENCES In addition to these traditions, some of the Framers were influenced by Judeo-Christian teachings, such as biblical accounts of the Ten Commandments, a set of laws that Moses is said to have delivered to the ancient Israelites. The Framers also looked at the writings of legal thinker William Blackstone. His landmark work, *Commentaries on the Laws of England,* published earlier in the 18th century, was a study of common law, or decisions in actual cases. The Framers admired Blackstone's analysis of **precedent**, or earlier court decisions that furnish examples or authority for deciding later cases.

The Framers also turned to the works of political philosophers who wrote about social contract theory, which you read about earlier. Chief among the thinkers they drew on was John Locke (1632–1704). He argued that people are born with natural rights to life, liberty, and property. The main purpose of government, he said, was to protect those rights. If government failed to do so, it was not holding up its end of the social contract and the people would be justified, or proven right, in moving to abolish that government. Locke's idea of natural rights influenced the underlying political values of the new United States of America.

HISTORICAL THINKING

1. **ANALYZE CAUSE AND EFFECT** How did the Magna Carta, written in 1215, influence American government more than 500 years later?
2. **FORM AND SUPPORT OPINIONS** Who benefits most from the social contract, the governed or the government? Explain.

Principles of American Representative Democracy

In a representative democracy, people elect leaders to government office. In the United States, those officials are then responsible for making and carrying out the laws based on five key principles of American representative democracy:

- **Equality in voting:** Citizens must have equal opportunities to express their preferences about policies and leaders.
- **Individual freedom:** Individuals must have the greatest amount of freedom possible without interfering with the rights of others.
- **Equal protection of the law:** The law must treat all people the same way by following the same procedures.
- **Majority rule and minority rights:** The majority should rule, but the rights of those in the minority must be protected.
- **Voluntary consent to be governed:** The people collectively agree to be governed by the rules made by their representatives.

These principles frame many American political issues, past and present. Given that, it is only natural that these principles are also at the heart of many American political conflicts. Why? Americans may agree on these principles but they do not always agree on how they should be put into practice. For example, how is the principle of minority rights applied if minorities face lingering inequality due to

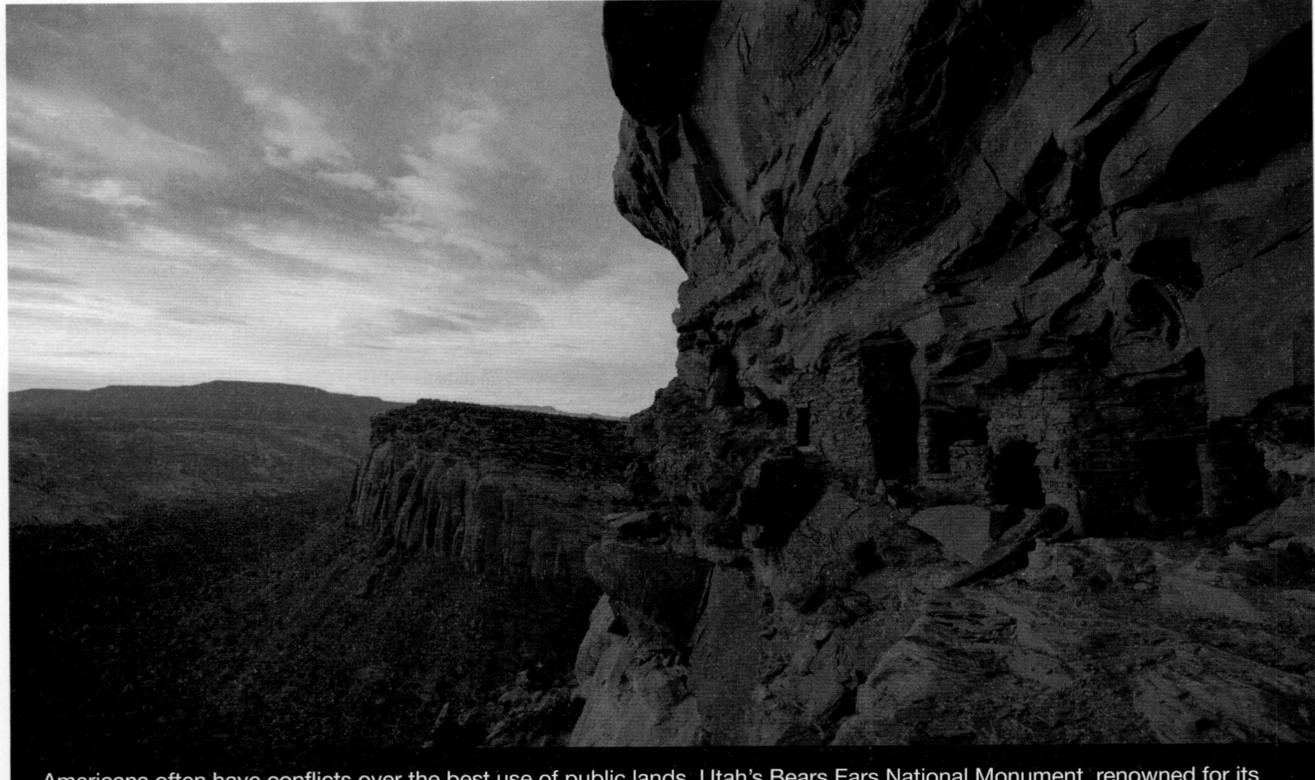

Americans often have conflicts over the best use of public lands. Utah's Bears Ears National Monument, renowned for its beauty and cultural significance to many Native Americans, was named a national monument by President Barack Obama in 2016 in response to urging from conservation groups. Obama's designation sparked controversy because it barred new mining activity. In 2017, President Donald Trump vastly reduced the acreage designated for the monument, an action that angered many, including those hoping to protect the minority rights of Native Americans.

past injustices? Should they receive some preferential treatment in college admissions, for example? Likewise, the principle of individual freedom means that people can post their thoughts and feelings on the internet. Does that include the right to post hateful, racist comments?

Resolving these conflicts is what politics is all about. While rarely a straightforward task, Americans can often reach acceptable solutions to these conflicts. They do so by drawing on their common political heritage.

HISTORICAL THINKING

3. **DRAW CONCLUSIONS** Given the principle of individual freedom, why do groups organizing protests often have to obtain a permit before holding a rally or march in a public space?
4. **MAKE CONNECTIONS** How is the principle of individual freedom related to the idea of limited government?

American Political Values

From its beginnings, the United States has had a population made up of groups with different traditions, religious views, and languages. The United States has been defined less by any one culture in our diverse population than by the ideas that make up our political culture. For example, more Americans share an appreciation for free speech and free assembly than they do a common ethnic background. Even in the country's earliest days, as the Constitution was being written, Americans knew what standards and rights were most important to them.

A **political culture** can be defined as a set of ideas, values, and ways of thinking about government and politics. The ideals and standards that constitute American political culture are embodied in the Declaration of Independence and carried out through the Constitution. They include the rights to liberty, equality, and property, which are fundamental political values shared by most Americans. Each of these rights is just what it sounds like—and much more. Of course, the meanings of these values can be defined quite differently by different people. These differences can produce sharp conflict in the political arena.

LIBERTY What is liberty? Is it being free of external controls or restrictions? In the United States, the Constitution—specifically, the **Bill of Rights**—sets forth basic civil liberties, and they are very broad. They include the right to speak freely on any topic and issue. People cannot govern themselves unless they are free to voice their opinions. As a result, freedom of speech is more than a right. It is a fundamental requirement for a true democracy to function. The exercise of freedom of speech can be as simple as a comment you send to another person in a text, or it can be a beautiful and complex work of art.

But the protection of civil liberties does not grant a person the license to do whatever he or she pleases whenever he or she wants. If people were allowed to do whatever they wished without regard for the rights or liberties of others, chaos would result.

Think about texting while driving. Each person with a driver's license has the right to drive a car. Everyone has the right to send text messages as well. But practicing those rights at the same time can seriously endanger others. For that reason, 48 states, the District of Columbia, and three U.S. territories have passed laws banning drivers from texting. That example helps clarify the definition of liberty. **Liberty** is the freedom of individuals to believe, act, and express themselves as they choose so long as doing so does not infringe on the rights of other individuals in the society.

Americans have differing ideas of when—and how—the concept of liberty should be applied. These differences in opinion have resulted in some of the country's most heated and prolonged political debates. In modern times, these debates have revolved around questions such as, Should employers be free to set the wages and working conditions of their employees? A belief in liberty unites Americans—but it can also divide them.

EQUALITY The goal of **equality**, or the state of being equal, has long been a central ideal of American government and political culture. Over 240 years ago, the Declaration of Independence stated, "We hold these Truths to be self-evident, that all Men are created equal." The Constitution that followed would emphasize equal protection under the law.

But what, exactly, does equality mean? Does equality simply mean political equality—the right to vote and run for political office? Over the centuries, amendments to the Constitution have tweaked this understanding of equality to some degree. For example, it took many, many decades before changes to the Constitution ended slavery and guaranteed the right to vote to people of all races and women.

But does equality mean more than just political rights? Does it mean that individuals should have equal opportunities to education, housing, and employment? Most Americans believe that all persons should have

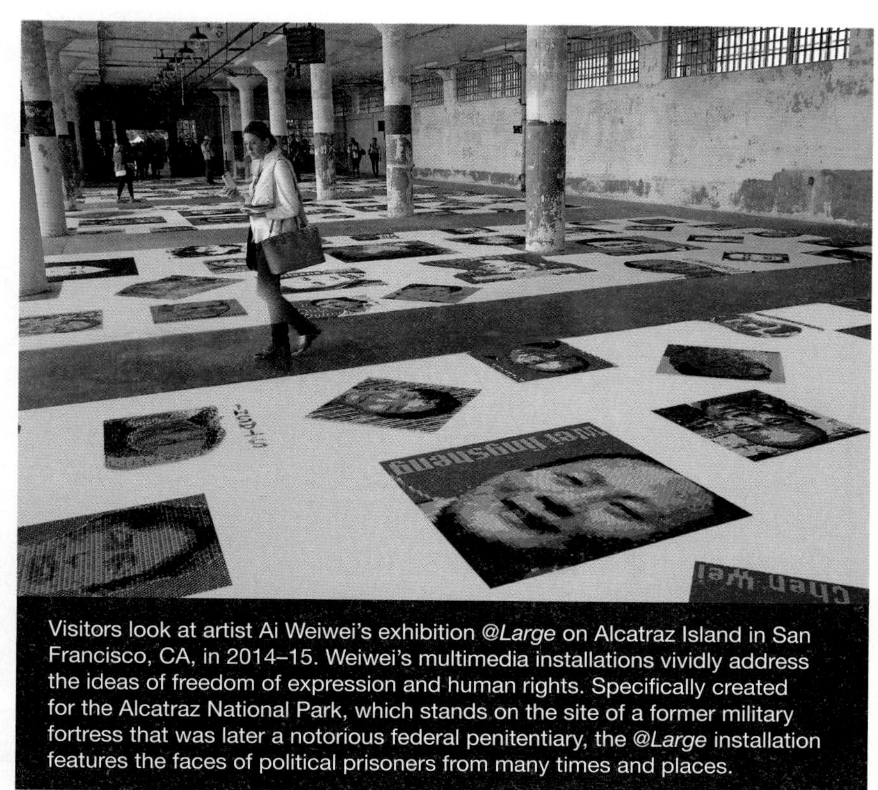

Visitors look at artist Ai Weiwei's exhibition *@Large* on Alcatraz Island in San Francisco, CA, in 2014–15. Weiwei's multimedia installations vividly address the ideas of freedom of expression and human rights. Specifically created for the Alcatraz National Park, which stands on the site of a former military fortress that was later a notorious federal penitentiary, the *@Large* installation features the faces of political prisoners from many times and places.

the opportunity to fulfill their potential. Still, few hold that it is the government's responsibility to eliminate all the economic and social differences that lead to unequal opportunities. Some Americans see efforts to achieve this kind of equality as incompatible with the value of liberty.

PROPERTY John Locke called the rights to life, liberty, and property "natural rights." The Declaration of Independence refers to the "unalienable rights" of life, liberty, and the pursuit of happiness. For Americans, combining these two lists of rights works quite well, since owning property and the pursuit of happiness are often closely related. Americans place a great value on home ownership, on material possessions, and on business success. Property gives people wealth, and wealth gives people political power and the liberty to do what they want—but again, within limits.

Private property in America is not limited to personal possessions such as automobiles and houses. Property also consists of assets that can be used to create and sell goods and services, from factories to farms to shops. Private ownership of wealth-producing property is at the heart of the **free enterprise system**. Under that system, individuals create private businesses that operate for profit with limited government oversight. The free enterprise system also involves free markets. That is, people have the right to freely buy and sell goods, services, and financial investments without undue constraint by the government. Capitalism—the economic system in which free enterprise exists—enjoys widespread support in the United States.

The question of what counts as undue constraint has been an important issue in U.S. politics since the late 19th century. After the Great Depression of the 1930s, the size of government and its oversight role grew tremendously. Since then, Americans have approached the question of the proper relationship between capitalism and the government in different ways. You will read more about the conflicting views of government's role in the economy in the next lesson.

HISTORICAL THINKING

5. **IDENTIFY MAIN IDEAS AND DETAILS** Paraphrase the meaning of "unalienable rights," then give an example of one of these rights.
6. **MAKE CONNECTIONS** What is the relationship between equality and liberty in American government?

Partisanship and a Divided Electorate

Debates over the size of government, over the meaning of equal treatment, or when one person's rights impinge on another person's liberty are ongoing. As a result, most people identify with the political

CRITICAL VIEWING This 1982 political cartoon depicts the problem of salary and wage disparity between men and women. How do you think American history has contributed to unequal pay for women?

American free enterprise has often inspired and enabled huge advances in technology. In 2012, high-school freshman Jack Andraka, now a National Geographic Explorer, won the Intel International Science and Engineering Fair grand prize for inventing a sensor that can detect early-stage pancreatic cancer—a device with the potential to advance medical technology and improve lives.

party that best reflects their views in each debate. Political parties organize to win elections, operate the government, and determine policy. Thomas Jefferson acknowledged the inevitable presence of these parties in a letter he wrote in 1798:

> *In every free and deliberating society there must, from the nature of man, be opposite parties and violent dissensions and discords; and one of these [parties], for the most part, must prevail over the other for a longer or shorter time.*

Historically, the United States has had two main political parties. Today, those parties are the Republicans and the Democrats. Members of these parties tend to view the basic American values in deeply different ways. A quick glance at any U.S. newspaper or television news channel is enough to see how so many issues fall along party lines. Public opinion polls report that increasing numbers of Republicans and Democrats consider the other party to be not merely misguided, but a danger to the country. **Partisanship**, or the strong attachment of people to a political party and the ideals and standards it promotes, plays a major role in American politics. At the same time, it is also clear that Americans are nearly evenly divided. The percentages of registered voters who see themselves as closely aligned with each party are fairly close to each other, as are the number of those who see themselves as independents not connected to either party.

PARTY LINES IN THE 21ST CENTURY Elections from 2000 to the present demonstrate just how evenly divided voters are. In 2000, for example, Republican George W. Bush won the presidency with just one more vote than he needed in the electoral college. (You'll read more about the role of the electoral college in presidential elections in another chapter.)

Since that year, support for the two major parties has swung back and forth, sometimes dramatically. The years 2006 and 2008 were very good for Democrats. Analysts think the first result stemmed from public dissatisfaction with the war in Iraq. The second was likely because of the economic crisis that struck during President Bush's last year in office. Republicans, in turn, enjoyed a banner year in 2010, based in part on the view that President Barack Obama and the Democrats were going too far to enact their party platform.

As you can see, voting behavior is closely tied to the performance of the leaders from the political parties. If voters believe one of the two major parties is doing something right, that party's candidates will fare better in the next election. The reverse is also true, however. When voters think the party in power is taking the country in the wrong direction, they typically turn to the other party, in hopes of a change. In the 2016 presidential election, many disillusioned voters turned to someone they believed was a new kind of candidate: Republican Donald J. Trump.

THE 2016 PRESIDENTIAL ELECTION Trump was an unprecedented presidential candidate. His background, campaign style, and positions on the issues were quite different from those of past Republican candidates. For years, a core Republican goal had been to cut taxes. At the same time, Republican leaders wanted to cut government programs. Some even spoke of making changes to Social Security and Medicare, programs people pay into during their working years and that provide income and health-care benefits after retirement. Many Republican voters saw these programs as benefits they had earned through the taxes they had paid into the funds.

In his 2016 campaign, Trump pledged to protect Social Security and Medicare while promising to revitalize the American economy. Trump did best in areas with large numbers of White voters without college educations. These people, commonly known as members of the White working class, felt an economic pinch. They saw their jobs disappearing and their wages shrinking, and they were angry. Possibly as a result, they were under greater stress. They were more likely to suffer from poor health, and death rates were well above the national average. Many of these voters had traditionally voted for Democratic candidates, but by 2016, they thought the Democrats had abandoned them. Trump's promise to "make America great again" energized this group of voters.

Two issues united Trump voters: immigration and trade. Many Americans believed increased immigration created competition for jobs. They claimed that low-skilled immigrants drove wages down and that highly skilled immigrants took job opportunities from well-educated citizens. Trump promised to clamp down on immigration, using some of the most inflammatory language ever used by a major party candidate. He also blamed foreign trade for the dramatic drop in manufacturing jobs. He pledged to take tough positions with American trading partners to protect American jobs—and to encourage companies to create new jobs.

While Democratic presidential candidate Hillary Rodham Clinton won the popular vote by a margin of 2.1 percent, Trump carried the electoral college, which decides who is president. Trump won by capturing traditional Republican states in the South and West, but he also won Pennsylvania and states in the industrial Midwest. In these states, traditionally Democratic voters concerned about immigration and jobs voted with traditional Republican voters to elect Trump. His victory put Republicans in control of the government, as the party also had majorities in the House and Senate. For the first time since December 2010, one party was in full control of the national government.

THE 2020 ELECTION These trends saw yet another reversal in the 2018 midterm election. With voter turnout at its highest level in more than four decades, Democrats won 40 seats to achieve a majority in the House. But early in 2020, the COVID-19 pandemic reached the United States. By election day, November 3, 2020, the pandemic had killed more than 232,000 Americans, and rates of infection were continuing to climb. Efforts to control the pandemic had led to high rates of unemployment, hunger, and business failures.

A series of highly publicized police-involved deaths of African Americans prompted widespread protests

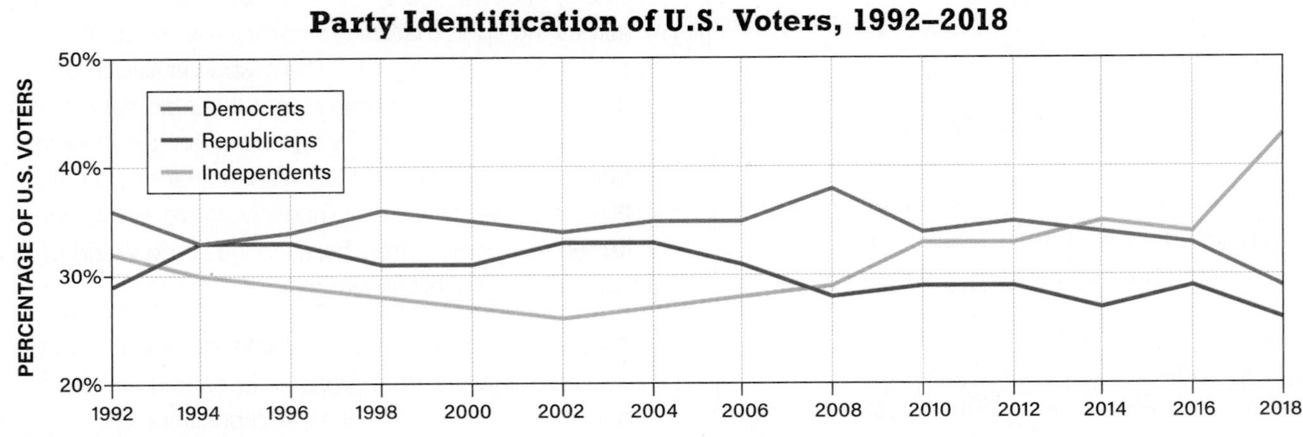

SOURCE: Pew Research Center; Gallup

President-elect Joe Biden and Vice President-elect Kamala Harris interact with their family members after addressing the nation from the Chase Center on November 7, 2020, in Wilmington, Delaware. After a contentious election battle against incumbent Republican president Donald Trump and four days of counting the large number of mail-in ballots in key battleground states, the Associated Press called the race for Democratic candidate Biden.

under the Black Lives Matter banner throughout the country during the 2020 election season. Many Americans joined these protests to express their concerns about racial inequality, but some people saw these protests as a threat to peace. The failing economy, the continued pandemic, and concerns about social injustice led many to expect exactly what the polls predicted by the fall of 2020—a landslide victory for Trump's Democratic opponent, Joe Biden, and his vice-presidential running mate, Kamala Harris, as well as Democratic majorities in Congress. But just as in 2016, the polls were inaccurate.

The COVID-19 pandemic made many voters anxious about voting in person, so large numbers of people voted by mail for the first time. Turnout of the eligible voting population was the highest it had been in more than 100 years. The Biden-Harris ticket received about 80 million popular votes, more than any presidential team in U.S. history, and won 306 electoral votes. The Trump-Pence team received the second-highest number of popular votes in history—nearly 74 million—and 232 electoral votes.

In a break with decades of tradition, no winner was announced on election night. The large numbers of mail-in ballots had to be opened and counted. It took several days before the Associated Press, which uses an unbiased set of mathematical projections once it has adequate verifiable data, determined that Biden and Harris had achieved the minimum of 270 electoral votes to win the election.

The Biden-Harris ticket flipped Wisconsin, Michigan, and Pennsylvania—states that had voted Republican in 2016—back to the Democratic column. Two states—Arizona and Georgia—that supported Republican candidates in 2012 and 2016 also added their electoral votes to the Biden victory. But the margin of victory that pollsters predicted for Democrats overall, whether in the presidential race or in congressional contests, never materialized. Even so, Biden's electoral vote victory of 306 was slightly higher than Trump's 2016 win of 304 electoral votes.

ALLEGATIONS OF FRAUD

Traditionally, defeated candidates call their victorious opponents to congratulate them and then address the people who donated to or worked on their campaigns, many as volunteers, to thank them for their support. They typically remind everyone that in a democratic system, even those who are disappointed in the result of an election recognize the importance of a peaceful continuation or transition of power.

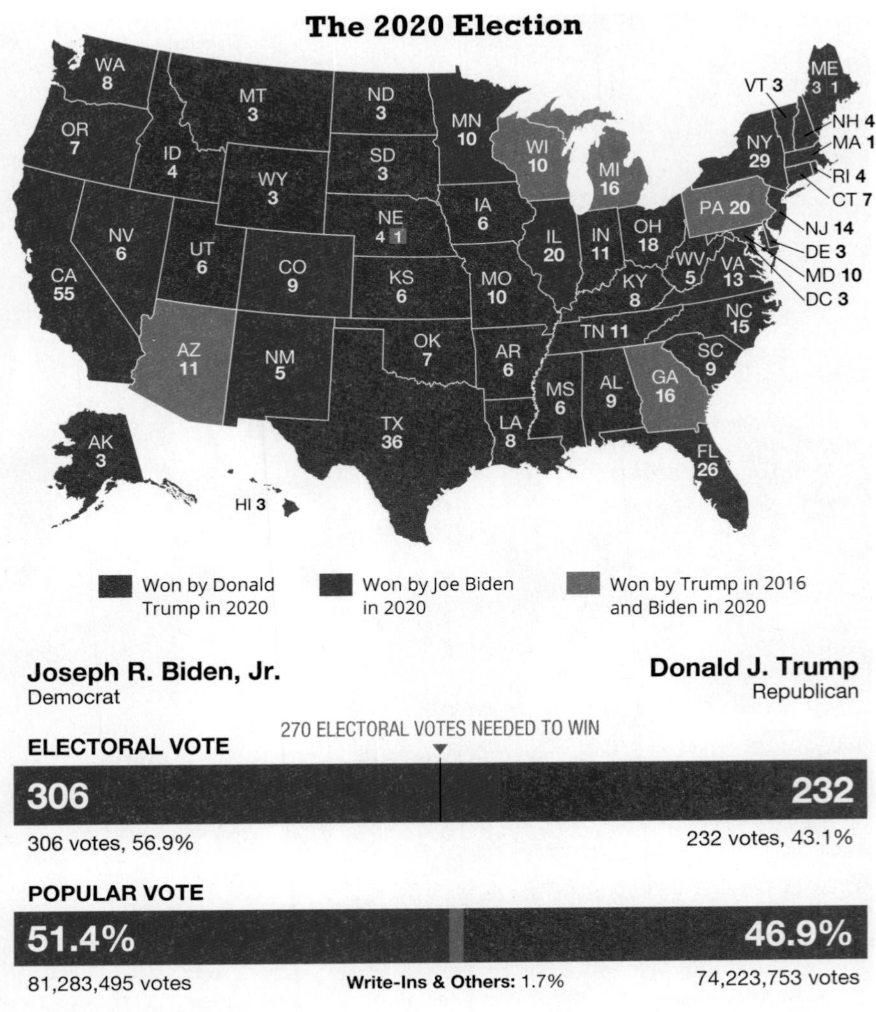

This did not happen in 2020. Instead of conceding and urging unity, Trump claimed voter fraud. He launched a series of legal challenges, most of which were thrown out by the courts. Federal prosecutors denied any evidence of fraud, and election officials in states where Biden won, as well as in states where Trump won, attested that there had been no evidence of fraud. Social media flagged posts in which Trump claimed the election was rigged or fraudulent. He fired a Department of Homeland Security director after the department stated that the 2020 election was "the most secure in U.S. history." In early December, Trump's attorney general, William Barr, announced that there was no evidence of fraud that could have changed the outcome of the election.

In a normal transition of power, an outgoing administration provides incoming officials with vital information about U.S. security, both domestic and international. A delay or interruption to this process places the national security of the United States at risk. More than two weeks after the election was called for Biden, the Trump administration began this transition process. Even then, Trump refused to concede, claiming victory and complaining of voter fraud despite overwhelming evidence to the contrary.

President Trump's rhetoric ultimately had dire consequences. On January 6, 2021, the ceremonial procedure of counting electoral votes in Congress was violently disrupted by a mob of Trump supporters who stormed the U.S. Capitol—incited by comments made by the president and members of Congress. Hours later, after the attempted insurrection was stopped and the Capitol secured, democracy prevailed as members of the House and Senate reconvened on-site and, at 3:42 a.m. on January 7, confirmed Joe Biden's win in the 2020 presidential election. Five people, including a police officer, died as a result of the Capitol riot.

HISTORICAL THINKING

7. **MAKE GENERALIZATIONS** What generalizations can you make about party politics in American government over the past two decades?
8. **INTERPRET GRAPHS** Based on the graph, how has voter identification varied in the past 15 years between independent voters and those belonging to either of the major parties?
9. **SUMMARIZE** How did Donald Trump forge a victory in the 2016 presidential campaign?

Political Values in a Changing Society

The elections of 2016 and 2020 are examples of how changes within American society can influence politics and, as a result, how the government functions. From the time of the earliest European settlers, America's people have had widely differing origins. Some groups, including White European immigrants, have had an easier time being accepted than other groups, including Native Americans, African Americans, and Hispanic Americans, who have a background in Spanish-speaking cultures of Central and South America. In the late 20th century, many Americans recognized this diversity. They came to believe that society should embrace **multiculturalism**, or the belief that the many cultures that make up American society should remain distinct and be protected by laws. That began to shift in the early 21st century.

POLITICAL IMPACT OF POPULATION SHIFTS The racial and ethnic makeup of the United States has changed dramatically since the late 20th century. It is likely to continue to change, based on population trends. Already, non-Hispanic Whites are a minority in California. For the nation as a whole, non-Hispanic Whites are likely to be in the minority by 2050.

The effect of this growing diversity on modern politics is uncertain. Some groups of Hispanics and Asian American immigrants are more likely to vote for Democrats than Republicans. If that continues, their growing share in the population will give a substantial boost to the Democratic Party. In recent elections, however, this benefit has been counteracted by another effect. Donald Trump's 2016 presidential campaign showed that many White Americans worry that immigrants threaten traditional American culture.

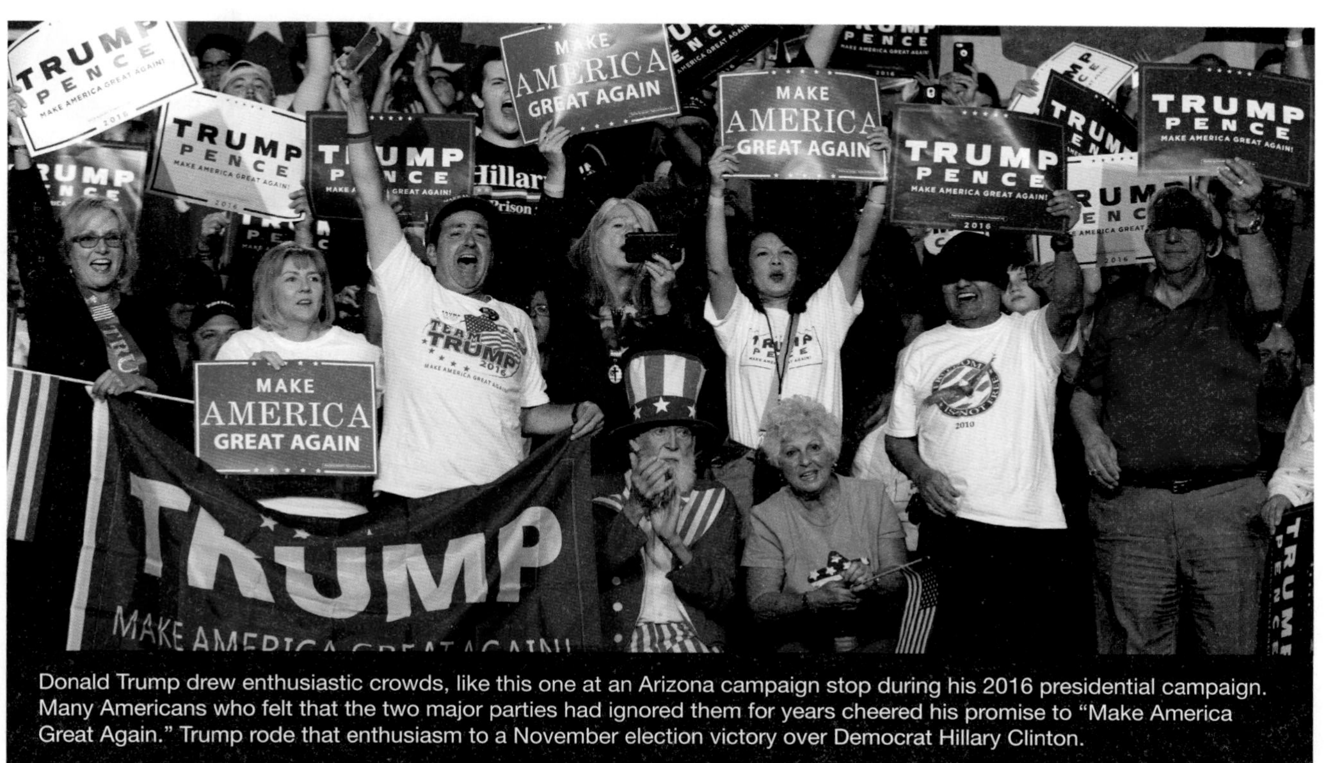

Donald Trump drew enthusiastic crowds, like this one at an Arizona campaign stop during his 2016 presidential campaign. Many Americans who felt that the two major parties had ignored them for years cheered his promise to "Make America Great Again." Trump rode that enthusiasm to a November election victory over Democrat Hillary Clinton.

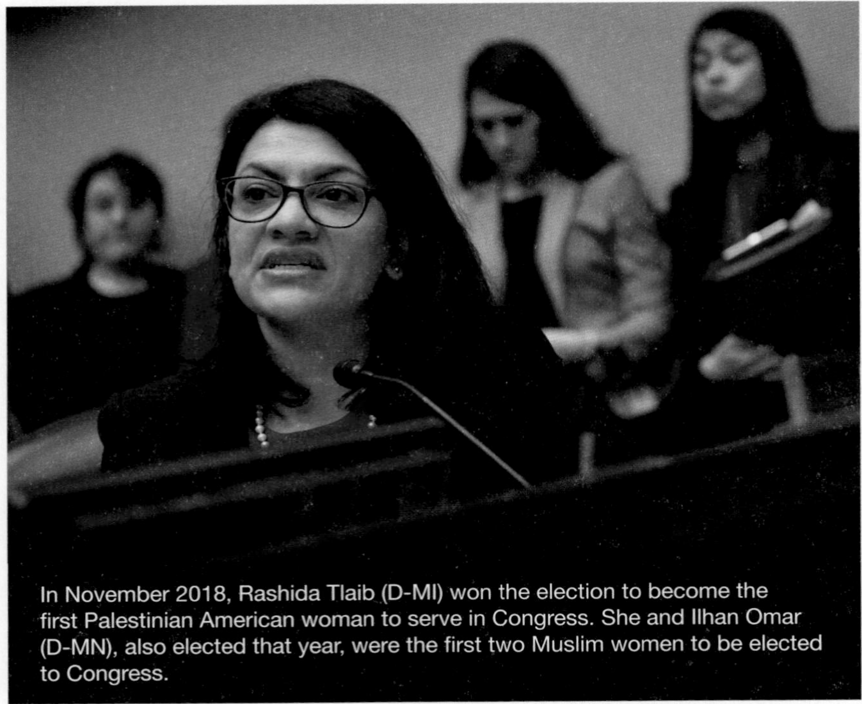

In November 2018, Rashida Tlaib (D-MI) won the election to become the first Palestinian American woman to serve in Congress. She and Ilhan Omar (D-MN), also elected that year, were the first two Muslim women to be elected to Congress.

As a result, a growing number of non-Hispanic Whites—especially older ones—have been drawn to the Republican Party. Once again, people's views of the meaning of American political values are at odds. These debates center on such questions as the meaning of equality and whose civil liberties are protected.

Another change in recent decades has been growing participation by women in politics. While women make up 51 percent of the U.S. population, the percentage of elected officials who are female is far lower. As of 2018, only 20 percent of seats in Congress were held by women. In state legislatures, women hold 25.5 percent of seats. By fall of 2018, however, a record number of women had won nominations in Congressional primaries. Many of these candidates ran on platforms of change and increased openness in politics.

In 2010, Americans aged 65 or above made up 13 percent of the total population. By 2040, that figure is expected to exceed 21 percent. These numbers mean growing numbers of retired people collecting Social Security, Medicare, and private pensions. At the same time, the percentage of working adults in the population will decline. Those reverse trends point to an economic problem. Workers pay the taxes that fund Social Security, Medicare, and pension programs. If the share of people getting those benefits goes up, and the share of workers funding them goes down, trouble looms. This is one area where immigration can help. New and younger workers from other countries can earn the wages that will fund those programs.

THE POLITICS OF CRIME Crime rates have fallen dramatically in recent decades. For example, the murder rate peaked at 10.2 people per 100,000 in 1980. By 2014, it was at 4.5 per 100,000, almost an all-time low. Since 2014, the murder rate appears to have gone up slightly, but it remains far below what it was in the 1980s and 1990s. The recent uptick is partly due to increased crime in a limited number of neighborhoods in cities such as Baltimore and Chicago, not the country as a whole.

In fact, digging further into crime statistics reveals that crime rates overall are down among minority youth and up among middle-aged Whites. California has the most complete statistics. According to a recent report, in 2008, about as many middle-aged White people were arrested for felonies, which are serious crimes, as young people of color in California. By 2014, more than twice as many middle-aged Whites were arrested as were young people of color. Death rates for rural Whites are up as well—by 48 percent among White women ages 35 to 39—at a time when death rates for every other group are falling. These increases may be due to the growing problem of drug and alcohol abuse among rural Whites, another sign of the cultural and economic crisis that helped elect Donald Trump.

HISTORICAL THINKING

10. **SYNTHESIZE** Explain how shifting racial and ethnic demographics can affect party politics.
11. **MAKE CONNECTIONS** Why is it important for the U.S. population to keep growing as it ages?

LESSON 1.4

American Political Philosophies

It is nearly impossible to follow current events without hearing the terms *liberal* and *conservative* used to describe politicians and the policies they favor. But what do these labels mean, and what do they imply? There's another important set of questions too. Are these the only two positions that people can take politically? Are there Americans who see things differently?

What Is Ideology?

Liberals and conservatives follow two different political ideologies. In a general sense, ideology refers to any system of beliefs that shapes a person's ideas, views, and actions. More specifically, **political ideology** is a system of political ideas that are rooted in religious or philosophical beliefs about human nature, society, and government. Over time, political ideologies have developed to adjust to more recent political concerns.

These days, conservatives are typically associated with the Republican Party. Liberals are typically associated with the Democratic Party. When they were first coined, however, those labels meant just what they sound like. Conservatives were people who wished to conserve, or keep, what they considered to be traditional social and political habits and institutions. Liberals were those who wanted to be free from tradition to establish new policies and practices.

In today's politics, these simple definitions of liberalism and conservatism are incomplete—and a bit misleading. Both terms mean much more. They describe only general attitudes, not actual positions on concrete issues. And those positions can change over time. Some positions once considered liberal are now seen as conservative. Even what seem to be core, or basic, beliefs, such as the proper amount of government involvement in the lives of citizens, can shift, depending on the issue at hand. Conservatives generally want less government involvement in the economy, for example. But they may be more willing to accept a greater government role on what they consider moral issues, such as abortion or same-sex marriage. Likewise, liberals may call for less government oversight of individuals' private lives but greater oversight of big business and what they see as civil rights issues.

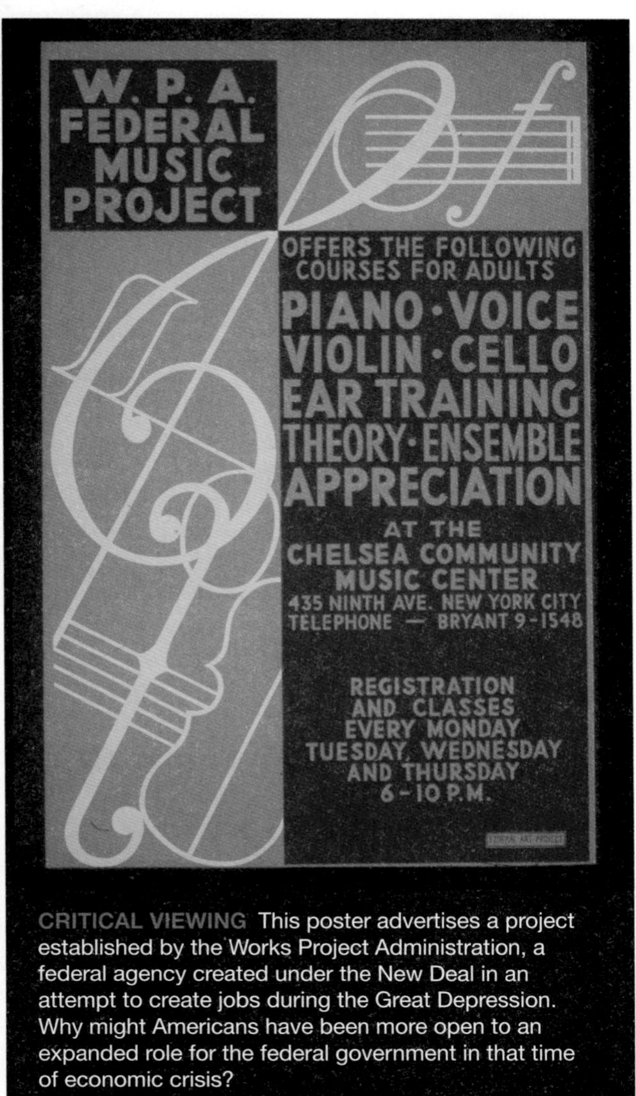

CRITICAL VIEWING This poster advertises a project established by the Works Project Administration, a federal agency created under the New Deal in an attempt to create jobs during the Great Depression. Why might Americans have been more open to an expanded role for the federal government in that time of economic crisis?

HISTORICAL THINKING

1. **IDENTIFY MAIN IDEAS AND DETAILS** Why is it difficult to define precisely what comprises the conservative or liberal ideology?

Ronald Reagan ran in the 1980 presidential election as a movement conservative firmly opposed to big government. Reagan is shown here at the 1984 Republican National Convention where he accepted his party's nomination and began his successful run for re-election.

Conservatism

Conservatism in the United States is generally the view that government should play a limited role in economic affairs and in helping individuals, while supporting what many Americans see as traditional values and lifestyles. Uniting these two beliefs is an opposition to what conservatives call big government.

The onset of the Great Depression in 1929 brought on a crisis in the banking industry, an enormous decline in industrial output, and a staggeringly high unemployment rate. By 1933, nearly one-quarter of American workers were out of work. Intent on addressing this economic crisis, President Franklin D. Roosevelt launched the New Deal. This series of programs created government jobs, restructured how banking was monitored, and put many other attempted recovery measures into place—all of which involved the government in the American economy to an extent previously unknown.

In response to Roosevelt's sweeping actions, conservatives saw a need to protect a key tradition. They believed they had to protect free enterprise, the system in which individuals and businesses are free to engage in economic activity with a minimum of government interference. The New Deal had given conservatives an organizing principle: opposition to big government.

THE CONSERVATIVE MOVEMENT The conservative movement in the 1950s and 1960s broadened the ideological scope of conservatism beyond the preservation of free enterprise. Previously, conservatives who wanted to protect free enterprise could be dismissed as trying to protect their personal wealth or power. Once the conservative movement embraced social concerns, it was no longer just about self-interest, but about society as a whole.

The conservative movement attracted millions of followers and emerged as a major political force in 1964. That year, Arizona senator Barry Goldwater won the Republican presidential nomination. Goldwater promised to cut taxes, reduce government spending, restrict the scope of government, and promote "a spiritual awakening." He was soundly defeated by Texas Democrat Lyndon B. Johnson. In 1980, however, Republican Ronald Reagan of California ran on a set of ideas largely similar to those of Goldwater. As Reagan put it, "government is not the solution to our problem; government is the problem." He became the first movement conservative to win the White House.

CONSERVATISM TODAY A key element in conservative thinking is the belief that the less government, the better. Conservatives believe that the distribution of social and economic benefits among people should take place with little or no government involvement. They believe that individuals and families should take responsibility for their own economic circumstances. Private charities and religious organizations, not the government, should assist the needy or those in difficult circumstances.

As in the past, conservatism today values traditions. Conservatives also value order and what they define as family values and patriotism. Conservatism has always included those who want society and the government to reflect their religious values. Christian conservatives remain an important part of the conservative movement today.

When Donald Trump was elected to the presidency in 2016, he and his supporters promoted many ideas that were within this conservative ideology. But some of these beliefs and policies depart from post-1950s conservatism. For example, President Trump placed tariffs on foreign trade, whereas traditional conservatism placed a high value on free trade. This is an example of how conservatism, like most political ideologies, is changing over time.

HISTORICAL THINKING

2. **ANALYZE CAUSE AND EFFECT** Why was the formation of the conservative movement in the 1950s and 1960s important to the conservative ideology itself?
3. **MAKE INFERENCES** How would conservatives likely react to new legislation proposing expansion of social benefit programs like Medicaid, which provides medical care for poor people? Why do you think so?

Liberalism

Modern American **liberalism**, a set of political beliefs that advocate government intervention to promote general well-being and protection of civil rights, followed a similar time line to that of modern conservatism. Like conservatism, liberalism's roots lie in the New Deal, though it championed the very programs that conservatives found so worrying. Liberalism took on its modern form in the 1960s under President Lyndon B. Johnson, who introduced a program he called the Great Society. While the New Deal pioneered Social Security to help the elderly, the Great Society created Medicare, which covers many of the health-care costs of older Americans, and Medicaid, which funds health care for the poor. Both programs represented huge extensions of government's role in the economy and in the lives of ordinary Americans.

Conservatives commonly accuse liberals of valuing big government for its own sake. Liberals counter that big government is necessary to promote the common welfare. Moreover, programs like Medicare and Medicaid reflect liberalism's belief that many individuals face social and economic difficulties resulting from social inequities rather than their own actions. Government, liberals believe, has a duty to try to level the playing field for such people. The 2010 Affordable Care Act, which aimed to ensure health care for all Americans, was a logical extension of liberalism's view of government.

Yet liberal and conservative attitudes are not set in stone in the United States, even though you may hear people talk as though they are. As you can see from the maps, a liberal Democrat, Lyndon B. Johnson, won the presidency by a huge margin in 1964. Just a generation later, however, in 1984, conservative Republican Ronald Reagan of California won the presidency by an even larger victory.

CIVIL RIGHTS AND OTHER VALUES In the 1960s, liberals in the Democratic Party strongly supported the civil rights movement. Many conservatives in the party, however, continued to support laws that segregated African Americans. Eventually, liberal Democrats won control of the party. White southern Democrats who felt the push for civil rights was going too far joined the Republican Party. From 1968 on, the southern

The 1964 Election

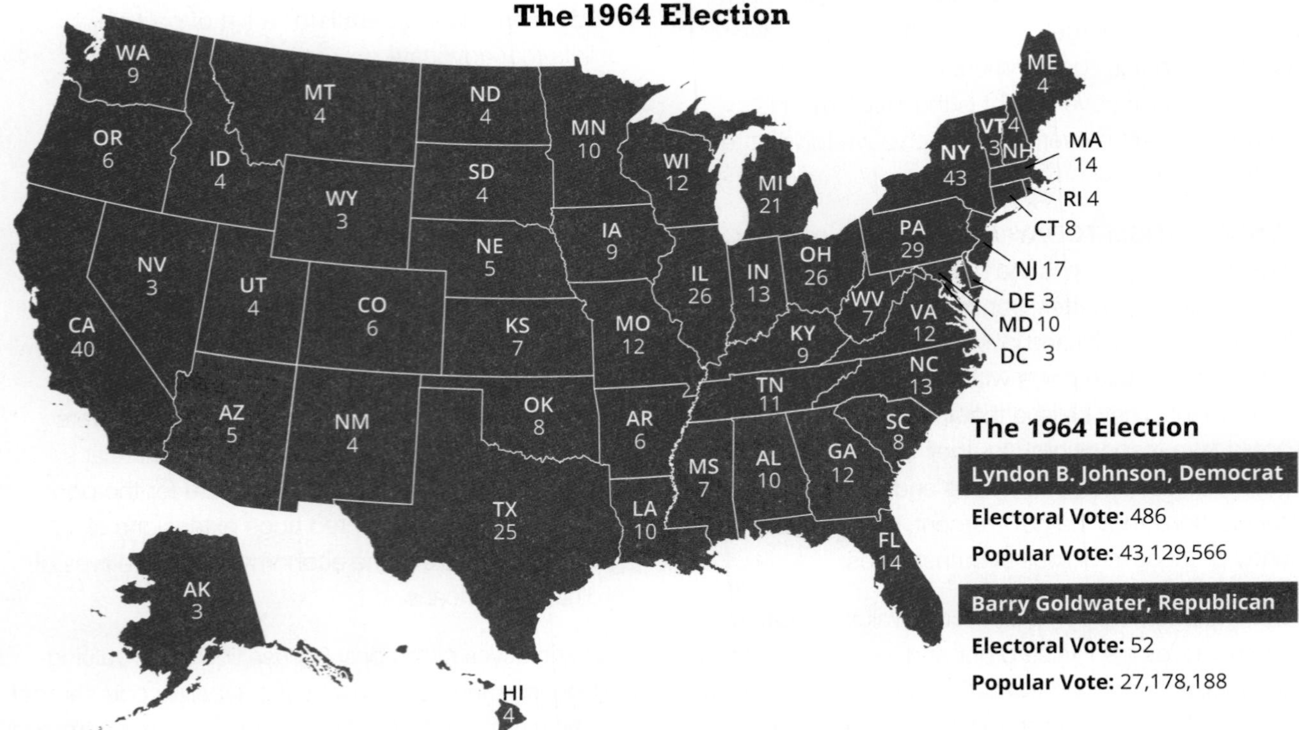

SOURCE: National Archives

The 1984 Election

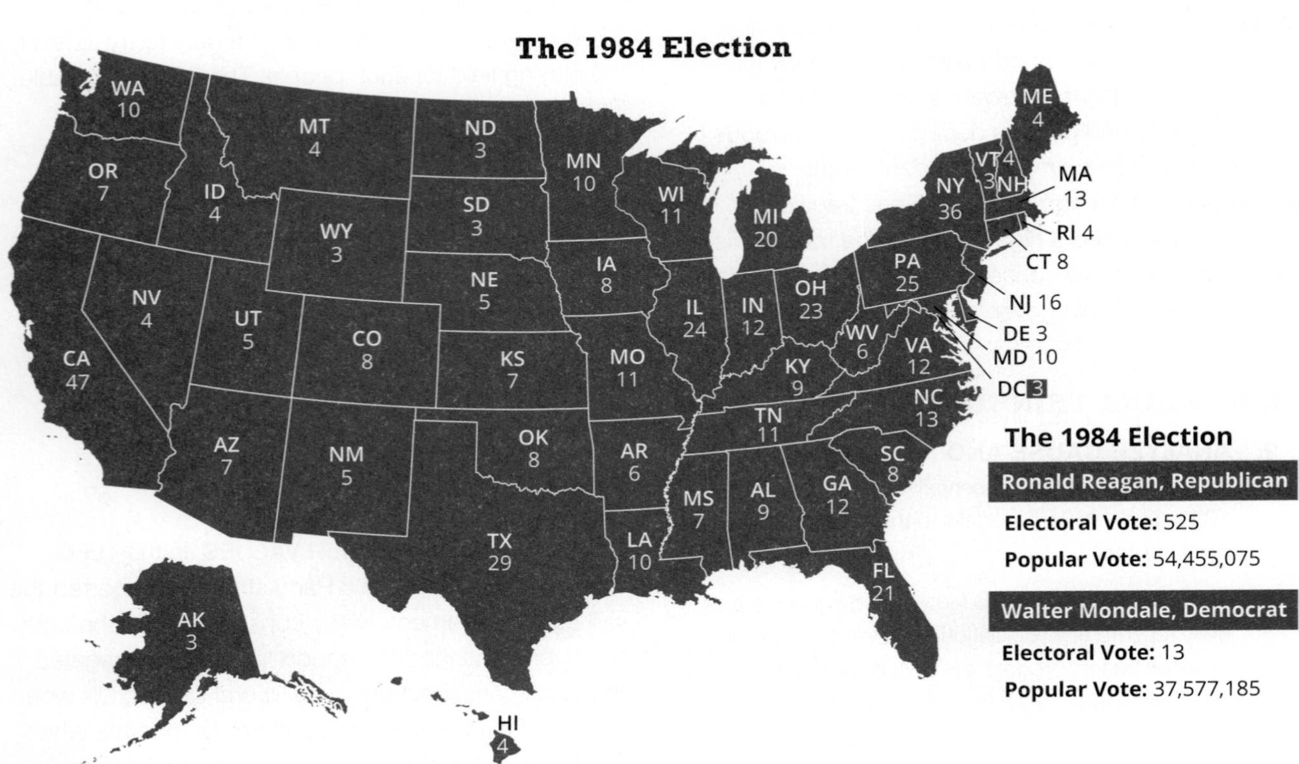

SOURCE: National Archives

states became increasingly Republican and liberals embraced a commitment to protecting and promoting the rights of minorities.

Liberal ideology includes several other key beliefs. For example, liberals tend to be more skeptical of American military intervention than conservatives. This attitude arose in response to the Vietnam War, in which over 50,000 Americans died in a failed effort to stop the spread of communism in that country. Liberals argued that the war was misguided, and they were reluctant to embrace subsequent military interventions in its aftermath. In recent years, that distrust has declined, and a school of so-called liberal interventionists have argued that American military power can protect the rights and lives of vulnerable people around the world.

Liberals also strongly favor the separation of church and state. They generally think the government should avoid laws that suggest approval of the beliefs or values of any religion. For example, liberals oppose laws that might limit the rights of members of the LGBTQ community. This position puts them in opposition to Christian conservatives, who are more likely to favor such laws.

LIBERALISM TODAY The failure of liberal programs to solve all the problems they aimed to fix has led many liberals to adopt the label "progressive." This term dates back to the early 1900s. Originally, progressivism was a loose collection of reform efforts targeting problems resulting from the rapid growth of American industrial wealth and city populations. Progressives hoped to address such problems as workplace safety and overcrowded tenements, or apartment blocks. Progressives today believe in the use of government policies to ensure safe and healthy places to live and work. They also push for equal rights for members of minority groups.

HISTORICAL THINKING

4. **COMPARE AND CONTRAST** How did the New Deal lead to the rise of both conservatism and liberalism?
5. **INTERPRET MAPS** Using the maps of the 1964 and 1984 presidential elections, what can you infer about the unsuccessful political party in each election?
6. **SYNTHESIZE** How does the idea of a national health-care system guaranteeing coverage for all Americans align with the liberal ideology?

Beyond Conservatism and Liberalism

There are positions more extreme than either liberal or conservative and there is also a middle ground between these two ideologies. While Democrats fall more heavily on the liberal end of the political spectrum and Republicans fall more on the conservative side, some members of both parties can be found in the moderate middle. (See chart.) The numbers of moderates within each party are shrinking, however. In the past, there were more conservative Democrats and more liberal Republicans than there are now.

MODERATES Those who classify themselves as **moderates** do not fully embrace either liberalism or conservativism. They may vote for either Republicans or Democrats, although in public opinion polls Democrats are about twice as likely as Republicans to identify themselves as moderates. A large number of moderates describe themselves as independent, and they often register to vote with that label. These people might favor government involvement in some areas but not in others.

the TRADITIONAL POLITICAL SPECTRUM

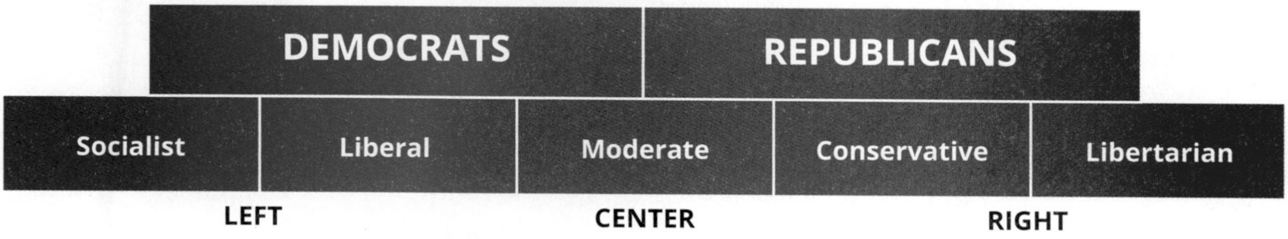

DEMOCRATS			REPUBLICANS	
Socialist	Liberal	Moderate	Conservative	Libertarian
	LEFT	CENTER	RIGHT	

For example, conservatives typically support restrictions on abortion, while liberals tend to feel that women should have the right to choose whether or not to have an abortion. Many liberals believe that the government ought to guarantee jobs for everyone; conservatives generally reject this idea. But plenty of Americans support restrictions on abortion and favor government jobs programs. Others oppose government involvement in both issues. These people often form their own personal brand of political ideology, based on their own social, cultural, economic, and religious beliefs.

Many other voters are liberal on economic issues even as they favor conservative positions on social ones. They support government intervention to promote economic fairness, like liberals. But they may also support laws that favor traditional moral values, like conservatives. Many low-income people appear in this group. A large number of African Americans and Hispanics of many income levels do as well.

There is currently no political party for people who fall in the middle of the political spectrum. It is not surprising, then, that recent polls show that an increasing number of people wish that there was a third major political party in the center of the political spectrum. That feeling seems to ebb and flow according to the popularity of the two major parties' candidates.

SOCIALISM To the left of liberalism on the traditional ideological spectrum lies **socialism**. This ideology, which advocates a system in which the welfare of the community, rather than profits, drives the economy, has had relatively few adherents in the United States. But in recent decades, a growing number of Democrats and independents are pursuing policies that they describe with this label. One of them is Vermont senator Bernie Sanders, a self-described democratic socialist, who tried, and failed, to become the Democratic presidential candidate in 2016 and again in 2020.

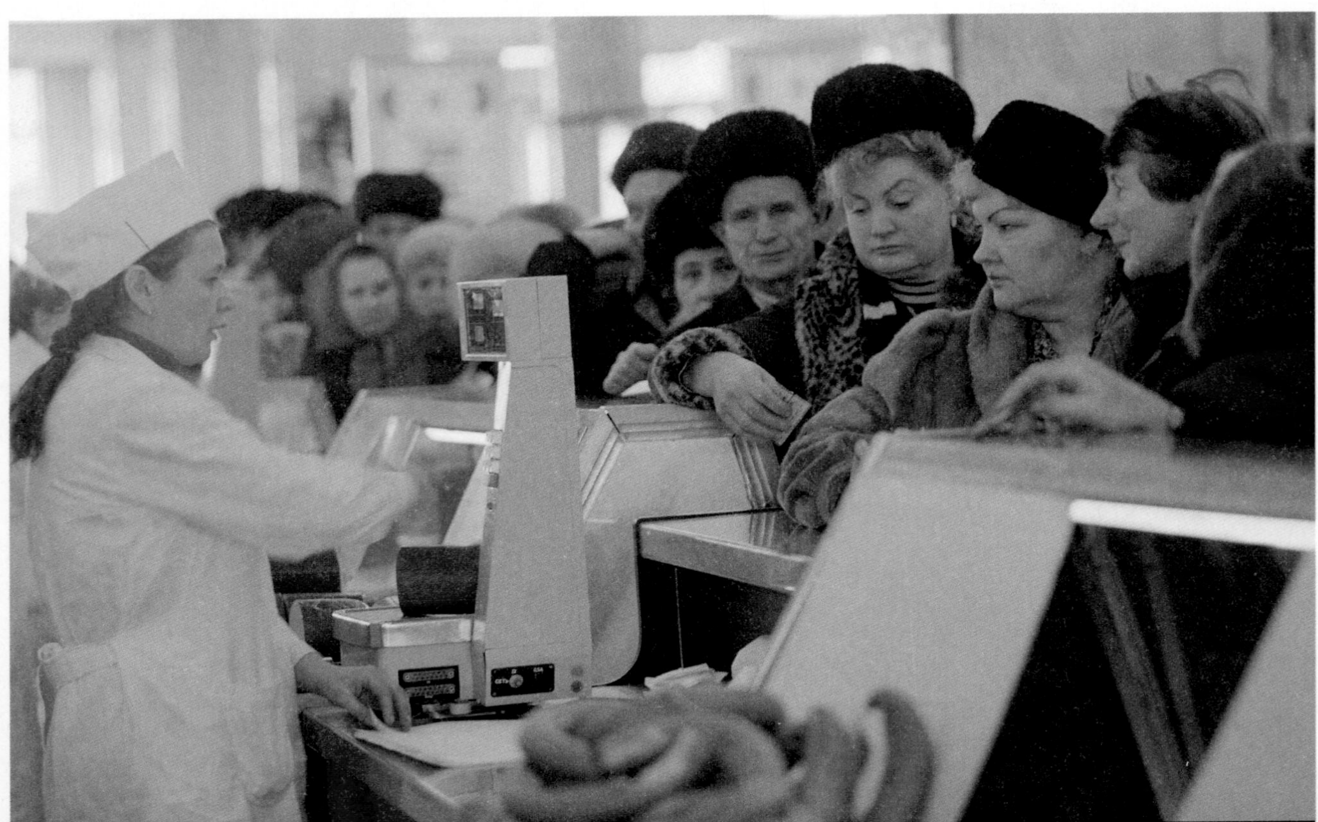

Purely communist economies find it difficult to provide sufficient consumer goods. In the former Soviet Union, consumers frequently had to wait in long lines only to find few goods actually for sale, fueling anger and ultimately undermining support for communism.

In much of the world, however, the main left-of-center party comes from the socialist tradition. Members of such parties are often called social democrats. They believe in egalitarianism, or the idea that all people deserve equal social and economic opportunity. Their commitment to this idea is stronger than that of American liberals, and they are more willing than liberals to accept a large role for government. In the first half of the 20th century, most socialists called for the government to own and run all major businesses. Few social democrats endorse such ideas today, however, and social democrats have played a leading role in the governments of countries such as Germany and Sweden.

In the 20th century, **communism**, a system of government in which the state owns and controls all capital and natural resources, was adopted in large parts of the world. Followers of this movement, called Communists, seized the government in Russia, renaming the country the Soviet Union. They set up a brutal dictatorship and supported the formation of similar governments in other countries. Communism largely collapsed around 1990. Although communists remain in power in China and a few other countries today, most of these governments have found that economic growth is difficult in a purely communist economy. For this reason, China has opened its economy to allow some capitalist businesses to operate.

LIBERTARIANISM The conservative side of the ideological spectrum also has a more extreme position. **Libertarianism** is an ideology that involves opposition to almost all government regulation of the economy and of people's personal behavior. It even objects to the government collecting income tax to fund public programs if they are not required by the Constitution. While socialism is weaker in the United States than in the rest of the world, libertarianism is fairly strong in this country.

Many ardent conservatives share the economic perspectives of libertarians. What distinguishes libertarians is that they also oppose government involvement in issues of personal behavior. Libertarians, then, object to laws that restrict abortions or limit the rights of LGBTQ individuals. In these beliefs, libertarians have more in common with liberals than they do with conservatives. For most people, however, economic issues remain more important, and for this reason, most libertarians ally with conservatives and support the Republican Party.

HISTORICAL THINKING

7. **ANALYZE VISUALS** Look at the model of the political spectrum. Knowing what you do now of various political ideologies, where would you place yourself on the spectrum? Explain.
8. **DRAW CONCLUSIONS** Which group of voters do you think would find a third major political party most appealing? Why?

CHAPTER 1

THE PRINCIPLES OF AMERICAN GOVERNMENT

Review

VOCABULARY

For each pair of vocabulary words, write one sentence that demonstrates the connection between the words.

1. politics; government
2. divine right theory; social contract theory
3. authoritarian; democracy
4. initiative; referendum
5. political ideology; political culture
6. liberty; equality

MAIN IDEAS

Answer the following questions. Support your answer with evidence from the chapter.

7. What are the four characteristics of a state? **LESSON 1.1**
8. What are the main purposes of government? **LESSON 1.1**
9. Why did the Framers favor a representative democracy rather than direct democracy? **LESSON 1.2**
10. How is the parliamentary democracy found in Great Britain different than the presidential democracy of the United States? **LESSON 1.2**
11. Why was the Magna Carta important? **LESSON 1.3**
12. What is the relationship between limited government and representative government? **LESSON 1.3**
13. What are the five key principles that underlie American government? **LESSON 1.3**
14. Explain what political culture is in your own words. **LESSON 1.3**
15. What are the fundamental beliefs of conservatism today? **LESSON 1.4**
16. What are the fundamental beliefs of liberalism today? **LESSON 1.4**

HISTORICAL THINKING

Answer the following questions. Support your answer with evidence from the chapter.

17. **DRAW CONCLUSIONS** How does the authority of a government contribute to social order?
18. **IDENTIFY MAIN IDEAS AND DETAILS** How do the public services provided by government vary in terms of who benefits from them?
19. **MAKE CONNECTIONS** What is the relationship between capitalism and liberty?
20. **MAKE PREDICTIONS** What is required for bipartisanship, or cooperative action by members of both political parties?
21. **ANALYZE CAUSE AND EFFECT** What made Donald Trump's campaign and election different from earlier Republican presidential campaigns?
22. **DESCRIBE** How can demographic trends affect the outcome of elections?
23. **MAKE INFERENCES** Why does socialism typically not align well with American government principles?

INTERPRET VISUALS

Study the table. Then answer the questions.

24. How would you characterize the role of independent voters over the last five U.S. presidential elections?

25. Presidential candidates are always very familiar with previous voter participation rates. Predict how the candidates in the 2016 race might have used some of the data in this table.

Party Identification of Voters in Presidential Elections, 2000–2016

YEAR	REPUBLICAN	DEMOCRAT	INDEPENDENT
2000	35%	39%	26%
2004*	37%	37%	26%
2008	32%	39%	29%
2012**	32%	38%	29%
2016	33%	37%	31%

*Republican candidate was the incumbent. **Democratic candidate was the incumbent. SOURCE: Roper Center, Cornell University

ANALYZE SOURCES

In *The Second Treatise on Government* (1690), John Locke wrote about the "state of nature" and political societies. Read the excerpt from this work below and answer the question that follows.

> If man in the state of nature be so free, as has been said; if he be absolute lord of his own person and possessions, equal to the greatest, and subject to no body, why will he part with his freedom? . . . To which it is obvious to answer, that though in the state of nature he hath such a right, yet the enjoyment of it is very uncertain, and constantly exposed to the invasion of others: for all being kings as much as he, . . . the enjoyment of the property he has in this state is very unsafe, very unsecure. This makes him willing to quit a condition, which, however free, is full of fears and continual dangers: and it is not without reason, that he seeks out, and is willing to join in society with others . . . for the mutual preservation of their lives, liberties and estates.

26. According to Locke, what is the state of nature like, and how does that explain why a person sacrifices some personal freedom to consent to obey the laws made by a government?

CONNECT TO YOUR LIFE

27. **ARGUMENT** Imagine that people in your state have collected enough signatures for a ballot initiative banning clubs that allow only women or only men as members. How would you vote on this issue? Think about what you have learned about the key principles and political values that form the basis of American government. Then write three paragraphs explaining your support or opposition to such a ban.

TIPS

- Develop a strong thesis statement that expresses your view on this matter.
- Anticipate what those on the other side of the issue will argue. Then address that opposition.
- Use information from the chapter to support your argument, including key vocabulary.
- Organize each part of your argument logically, moving from point to point with strong transitions. Address the principles of individual freedom and the political value of liberty in your argument.
- Include a conclusion that states your opinion clearly and briefly revisits each supporting detail of your argument.

CHAPTER 2

The Beginnings of American Government

LESSONS

2.1 Government in the English Colonies

2.2 The Rebellion of the Colonists

2.3 Independence and Revolution

National Geographic Online:
The Letter That Won the American Revolution

2.4 The Confederation of States

2.5 Drafting and Ratifying the Constitution

CRITICAL VIEWING The town of Canterbury, New Hampshire, is governed by the townspeople. They meet annually in a town meeting, a form of government established in New England during colonial times. The Canterbury Town Hall also serves as a polling place for national elections, such as presidential primaries. Why would it be important to have a central building in which to conduct government business?

LESSON 2.1

Government in the English Colonies

When the first English settlers arrived in North America in the 1600s, they faced a daunting challenge. With the English king and his officers far away, the colonists had to figure out how to govern themselves. What rules would they live by—and who would make those rules? English political traditions influenced these colonists, but most of their political ideas came from the colonists' own experiences.

The Constitution and American History

The principles of government set forth in the United States Constitution had their origins in the beginnings of American history. A **constitution** is a set of rules that establishes the framework of a government and the powers of that government. When the Framers of the Constitution met in Philadelphia in 1787, they brought with them some valuable political assets. One was their English political heritage, which you read about earlier. Another was the knowledge they gained from wide reading in philosophy, political science, law, and history. Finally, they benefited greatly from the hands-on political experience they had acquired during the colonial era. Their knowledge and experience made it possible for them to write a constitution to meet not only their own needs but also those of future Americans.

Native Americans had lived in North America for well over 10,000 years when, in the 1500s, European countries began to establish colonies on the continent. Colonies are settlements, or a group of settlements, under the rule of a government based elsewhere. Several countries, including France, Germany, the Netherlands, Spain, and Sweden, started colonies in the present-day United States. By 1770, the 13 colonies that would soon form the government of the United States of America were all under British rule. These colonies had a mix of people, including more than a half million people of African origin. They, or their ancestors, had been brought to the colonies against their will. Most of them lived and worked in slavery. A much smaller number of African Americans were free. While African Americans generally had no voice in the government of the colonies, they had a significant impact on the economy, society, and culture of colonial America.

HISTORICAL THINKING

1. **MAKE INFERENCES** Why might the writers of the U.S. Constitution have benefited from reading the political and legal history of earlier societies?

Government in the First English Settlements

Though under the ultimate control of the English crown, the English colonies weren't founded by the English government. The original settlers were not employees of the king. There were no staffs of professional bureaucrats responsible for laying out towns, setting up courts, and plotting out roads. Colonies were business ventures established by private individuals and private trading companies. Explorers had claimed vast swaths of land for the English king, who then gave a charter, or legal agreement, to a colony's founder that said, in effect, "I'm giving you this chunk of America. Make it profitable. But don't expect a lot of help from us. Good luck."

The rulers of England had little to do with those early colonies. It took two months for a ship to cross the Atlantic, so colonists had to create their own laws and institutions. They drew on what they knew of the traditions of English common law and the English constitution to create systems of **self-government**, or government that was under the control of the people who lived in the colonies rather than of a distant ruler.

THE VIRGINIA COLONY The first permanent English settlement in North America was Jamestown, in what is now Virginia. Founded by the Virginia Company in

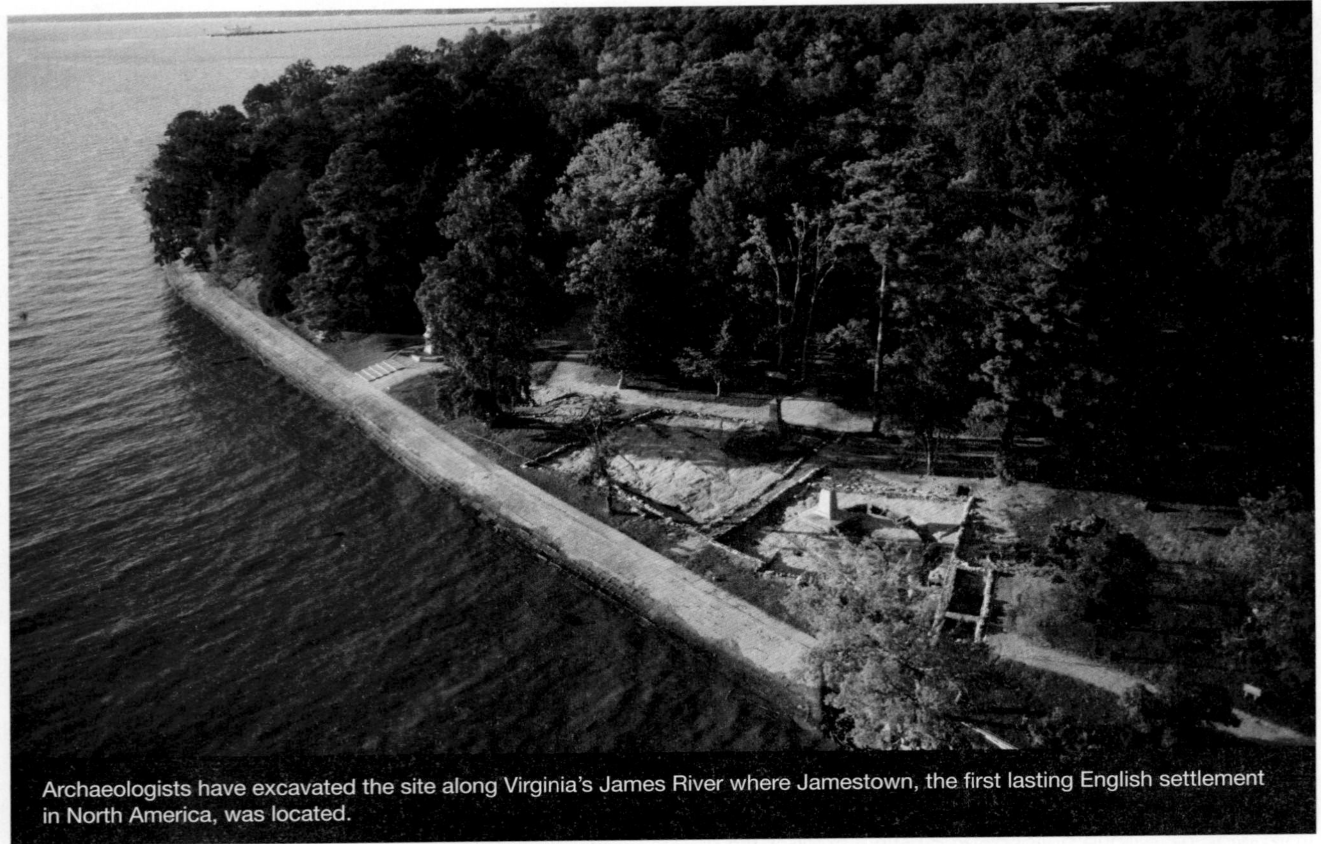
Archaeologists have excavated the site along Virginia's James River where Jamestown, the first lasting English settlement in North America, was located.

1607, the colony began as a venture to look for gold and silver and a route to the Pacific. A governing council of seven men chosen by company officials in England made rules for the colony. The settlers found no precious metals or route to the Pacific, but in time, despite disease, starvation, and attacks by Native Americans, they found something that proved extremely valuable—the soil and climate in Virginia were ideal for growing tobacco. Soon, colonists were shipping large quantities of tobacco back to England. As the colony became successful, it grew and needed more structure. In 1619, Virginia settlers formed the Virginia House of Burgesses, the first elected **legislature**, or lawmaking body, in the colonies. At first, its responsibilities were limited. But over time, the powers of the House of Burgesses grew and expanded. A number of men who would influence the early United States—Patrick Henry, George Washington, Thomas Jefferson, and James Madison—would receive their training in the workings of government in the Virginia House of Burgesses.

PLYMOUTH COLONY Plymouth, Massachusetts, the first New England colony, was founded in 1620. Like Jamestown, Plymouth was also ostensibly a commercial venture. Many of its settlers, however, were more interested in finding a place where they could worship as they wished than they were in making money for themselves or the British crown. These were Pilgrims, a group of English Protestants who wanted to separate themselves from the Church of England and escape the official church's control. They were Separatists who believed that each congregation, or group that worships together, should determine its own practices.

The Pilgrims had planned to settle within the area granted to the Virginia colony, but their ship, the *Mayflower*, was blown off course. By settling in New England, outside the land given to the Virginia Company, the Pilgrims were not bound by the charter that governed Virginia. Leaders of the Pilgrims feared that some settlers might decide they were no longer subject to any rules. These leaders decided that some form of governmental authority was needed. So they drafted an agreement aboard the *Mayflower* that almost all the male passengers signed.

This agreement, known as the **Mayflower Compact**, was essentially a social contract, which you read about earlier. In the Mayflower Compact, the signers stated their goal to "combine ourselves together into a civil Body Politick." They agreed to "enact, constitute, and frame, such just and equal Laws, Ordinances, Acts, Constitutions, and Offices, from time to time, as shall be thought most meet [proper] and convenient for the general Good of the Colony." They also pledged to obey those laws. The Mayflower Compact was the first agreement in the new American colonies to set out the basic rules for governing.

MORE COLONIES, MORE CONSTITUTIONS English settlers established a second colony in New England, the Massachusetts Bay Colony, in 1630. Its founders, known as the Puritans, also wanted religious freedom to worship as they saw fit. Unlike the Pilgrims, the Puritans didn't want to separate themselves from the Church of England. Instead, they wanted to purify it of what they saw as the inappropriate trappings of Roman Catholicism. They thought this would be easier to do in North America, far from the church leaders back in England. By the 1640s, more than 10,000 Puritans (and 10,000 non-Puritans) had settled in Boston and surrounding communities to form what is now Massachusetts. Under the original colonial charter, the governing body of the colony should have been officers of the company who remained in England. But the Puritans wanted more control over their own affairs. They moved their company to Massachusetts and gave the power of governing to local representatives, who established a government with an elected governor, council, and legislature.

Government in the Massachusetts Bay Colony was organized around the principles of Puritanism and was closely linked to the religious ideals of Puritanism. Only members of Puritan congregations could vote, and Puritanism was the official religion of the colony. In 1636, a group of Puritans who objected to the leadership of Massachusetts Bay Colony formed three settlements in present-day Connecticut. Three years later, in 1639, the people of these communities developed America's first written constitution, called the Fundamental Orders of Connecticut. The document declared that laws would be made by an assembly of elected representatives

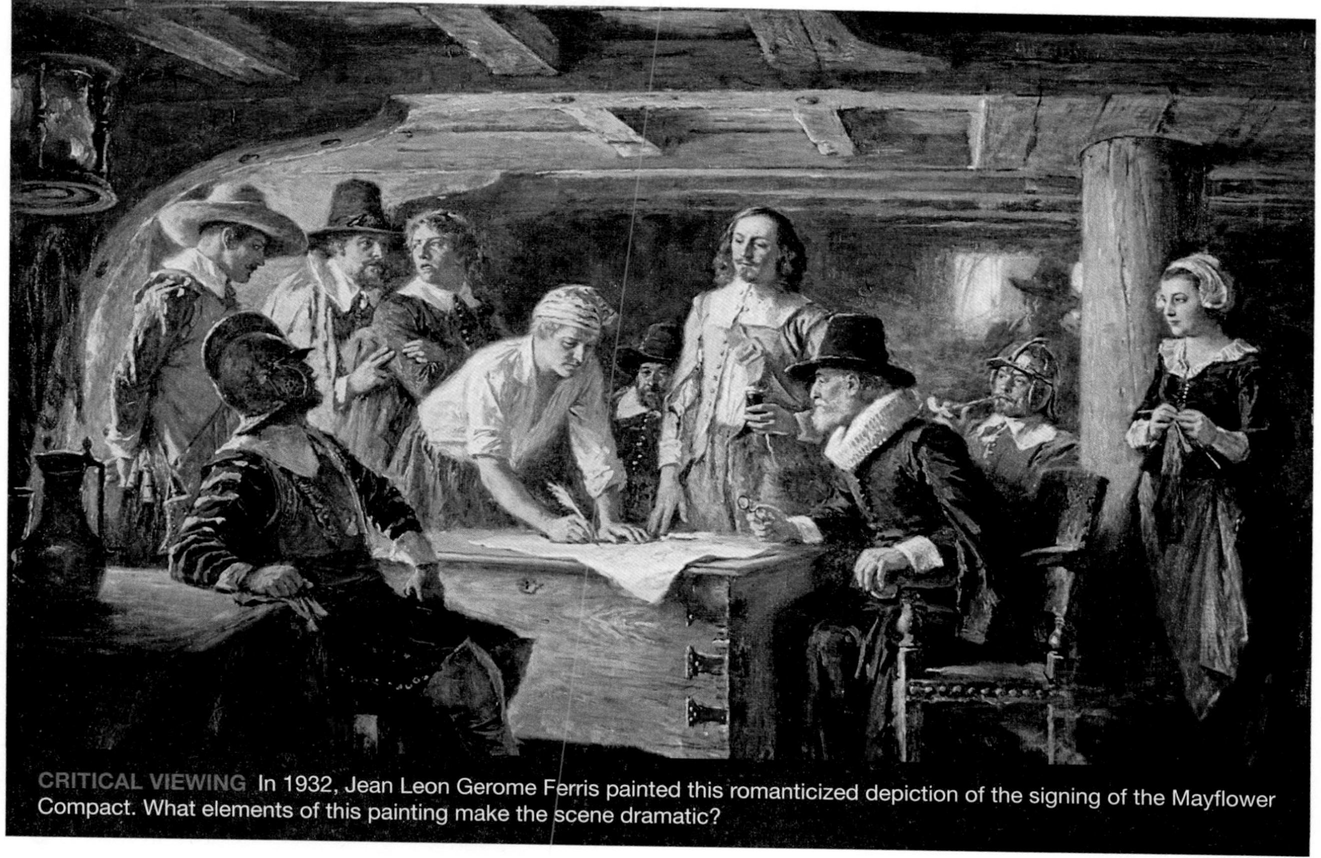

CRITICAL VIEWING In 1932, Jean Leon Gerome Ferris painted this romanticized depiction of the signing of the Mayflower Compact. What elements of this painting make the scene dramatic?

from each town. The document also provided for the popular election of a governor and judges. At about this time, other refugees from Massachusetts settled communities such as Newport, in present-day Rhode Island.

In 1641, colonists in Massachusetts adopted a set of rules called the Body of Liberties that protected individual rights. For instance, one rule declared that no man could be arrested or punished unless he had been found to violate a law duly passed by the colony. Another offered "the same justice and law" to all people in the colony. These liberties didn't extend to enslaved people. In fact, the Massachusetts Body of Liberties was the first legal code to recognize and sanction slavery in North America.

Farther south and some decades later, William Penn, proprietor of the colony of Pennsylvania, with its capital in Philadelphia, wrote a Frame of Government that colonial representatives adopted in 1683. This constitution formed a government that included a governor named by Penn, a council to advise the governor, and an assembly chosen by settlers. In addition, Penn issued a Charter of Privileges in 1701. This document established principles that were later included in the U.S. Constitution and Bill of Rights. The first of these was a protection of the right to follow the religion of one's choice. As the charter put it, no person shall "be compelled to frequent or maintain any religious Worship, Place or Ministry, contrary to his or their Mind." That right was not absolute but was limited to Christians. Still, in a period of religious strife, it showed unusual tolerance. Penn was a Quaker, a member of a group of religious radicals who faced persecution in England, and his constitution underscored the importance of this right by promising it "shall be kept and remain, without any Alteration, inviolably [protected from violation] forever." Penn's charter also gave those accused of a crime the right to call witnesses and have legal counsel.

Other colonies also adopted their own constitutions. Settlements grew along the Chesapeake Bay and the Atlantic seaboard in what became Baltimore, Maryland, and Charleston, South Carolina. By 1733, when Savannah, Georgia, was established in the last of the 13 colonies, each had its own framework of government.

Growth of Colonial Settlement

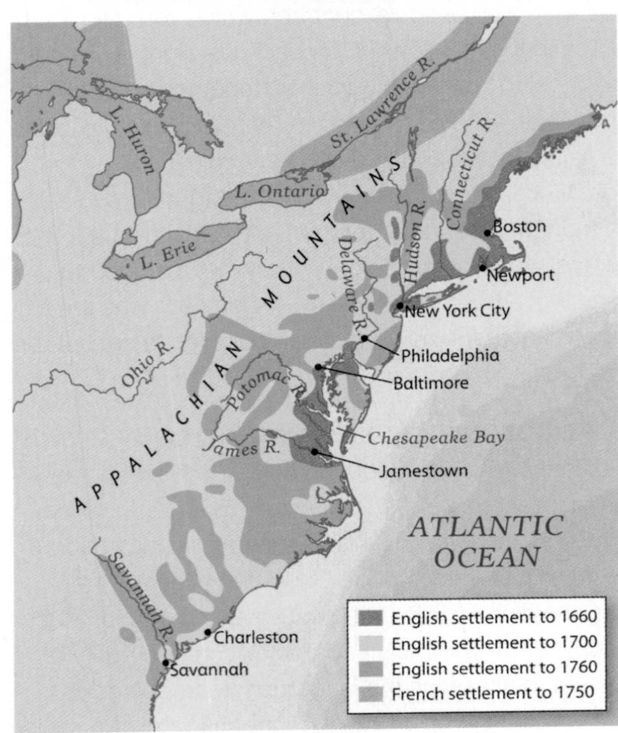

HISTORICAL THINKING

2. **MAKE CONNECTIONS** What values of the American political system are expressed in the Mayflower Compact?
3. **FORM AND SUPPORT OPINIONS** Were the Fundamental Orders of Connecticut a social contract? Why or why not?
4. **COMPARE AND CONTRAST** How did the rights of colonists in Pennsylvania differ from those in Massachusetts?
5. **INTERPRET MAPS** Based on the map Growth of Colonial Settlement, why were British colonists concerned about the size and location of French settlements along the St. Lawrence River?

Colonial Legislatures

By the time of the American Revolution, all the colonies involved in the movement for independence had legislatures. Many had been in existence for more than 100 years. These legislatures carried out the daily business of colonial government, usually along with

CRITICAL VIEWING Virginians moved their capital to the city of Williamsburg in 1704. The House of Burgesses—the colonial legislature—met in this structure after it was built in the 1750s. How does this building show the growth of Virginia from its beginnings in Jamestown?

royal governors appointed by the king. The assemblies of legislators consisted of colonists who often tried to check, or limit, the power of royal governors. Sometimes they refused to grant money to pay the governor a salary. Other times they voted against the governor's proposed projects. Colonial government was marked by tensions between the executive power of the governor and the legislative power of the assemblies, a tension that left its mark on Americans' political views.

Through their participation in colonial governments, the colonists gained crucial political experience. Colonial leaders became familiar with the practical problems of governing. They learned how to build coalitions among groups with diverse interests and how to make compromises. Indeed, by the time of the American Revolution in 1776, Americans had developed their own unique and complex political system.

Those who gained this experience in self-governing were somewhat few in number, however. Voting was generally limited to adult White males who owned property, which excluded most of the population. Those elected to leadership positions tended to be the wealthy and prominent. For these reasons, only a small sector of the colonial population had political experience. Still, these people used their knowledge to quickly establish state governments after declaring independence from Britain in 1776. Eventually, they were able to set up a national government as well.

HISTORICAL THINKING

6. **EVALUATE** How democratic were the colonial governments? Explain your answer.
7. **MAKE PREDICTIONS** How do you think the experience with royal governors shaped the political views of colonial Americans? Explain your answer.

LESSON 2.2

The Rebellion of the Colonists

When Great Britain defeated France in the Seven Years' War in 1763, British colonists in North America celebrated. By 1776 thousands of Americans were reading—and agreeing with—a pamphlet that boldly proclaimed, "It is the interest of America to be separated from Britain." The shift in perspective resulted directly from a long series of events that soured relations between the colonists and the British government. But beneath those events lay a deeper cause: Over the decades, colonists had come to feel that they were not British, but something different—they were Americans.

Seeds of Conflict

Ironically, one of the events that drove a wedge between Americans and the British government was the very event that colonists had celebrated—the end of the Seven Years' War (1756–1763). This conflict between Britain and France was often called the French and Indian War by Americans. Prior to that war, the French had held vast stretches of territory in North America, including land in what is now eastern Canada and the Mississippi River Valley. Both the British and the French claimed areas along the Ohio River and Great Lakes regions as well, and British colonists who settled west of the Appalachian Mountains faced attacks from the French and their Native American allies.

CRITICAL VIEWING In 1754, as the French and Indian War began in the colonies, Benjamin Franklin published what may be the first American political cartoon. What message was Franklin sending to people of the different colonies?

The colonists hoped the British victory in the Seven Years' War would open more land to settlement, but that hope was quickly dashed by the **Proclamation of 1763**. As part of the peace treaty with Native Americans, the proclamation banned or greatly restricted colonists from settling on land west of the Appalachians. Many colonists were angered by the treaty. Some ignored the proclamation and moved to western lands despite the ban.

The end of the war had another effect. To pay its war debts and finance the defense of its large North American empire, Britain needed money. The British government decided to exercise more direct control over colonial trade and imposed **taxes**, legal requirements for individuals or businesses to pay funds to the government, on the American colonists. Then, as now, taxes became a source of resentment, especially since colonists had no representatives in Parliament who could vote for or against these taxes.

The war also inspired the growth of a sense of identity separate from the British. Having fought alongside British forces, the colonists began to view the British differently than they had before. They were shocked by cruel punishments used to enforce discipline among British troops, and they felt they deserved more credit for the victory in war. The British, in turn, had little good to say about the colonists. They considered them uncivilized and undisciplined and did not think the colonists had played much of a role in the victory. More and more, the colonists began to use the word "American" to describe themselves.

HISTORICAL THINKING

1. **DRAW CONCLUSIONS** What can you conclude about Americans' attitudes toward British law from the response to the Proclamation of 1763?
2. **EVALUATE** Why might results of the British victory in the Seven Years' War be referred to as mixed?

The Sugar and Stamp Acts

Even though the colonists started to think of themselves as Americans at this time, they primarily thought of themselves as citizens of their individual colonies. They were New Yorkers or Virginians more than they were Americans, but this mindset began to change when Parliament started taxing all the colonies as a group. Resistance to taxation helped spur intercolonial cooperation.

THE SUGAR ACT One of the first taxes the British Parliament passed to raise money was the Sugar Act of 1764, which placed a duty, or import tax, on sugar from French and Dutch colonies. The goal was to protect British sugar producers by making foreign sugar more expensive. To prevent smuggling, customs houses were established to enforce the law and collect taxes. Some colonists, particularly in Massachusetts, vigorously opposed the sugar duty on the grounds that it had been approved by British Parliament and not the colonial assemblies. Worse still, the Sugar Act declared that anyone charged with trying to avoid the law could be tried in a court in British Canada. American colonists protested that these provisions stripped Americans of their basic right to trial by a jury of their peers.

The British saw the sugar duty as a way to raise money, but the Americans saw it as a violation of their basic rights. The Sugar Act sparked an organized resistance. Leaders in Massachusetts boycotted, or refused to buy, certain British imports, including luxury fabrics. They coordinated their resistance with leaders in other colonies. Colonists wrote scores of letters to British Parliament, expressing their anger. Leaders of the resistance waited anxiously for the royal government's response.

THE STAMP ACT OF 1765 In the midst of the turmoil caused by the Sugar Act, Parliament provoked the Americans further. In 1765 it passed the Stamp Act, which imposed taxes directly on the colonists by taxing everyday items. Under the Stamp Act, all legal documents, newspapers, and even playing cards had to be printed on specially stamped paper purchased from the British government. The purpose of the tax was to pay the costs of keeping British troops stationed in America. From the British perspective, it was only fair that the colonists pay the tax. The funds helped support the costs incurred by the British government in defending its American territories.

The Stamp Act angered the colonists even more than the Sugar Act. Many in the colonies argued that "taxation without representation is tyranny." They thought any tax imposed by Parliament violated the principle of representative government, because Americans were not represented in the British Parliament. Britain's leaders thought only people living in the British Isles could be represented in Parliament. In their view, though the American colonists could not send a representative to Parliament, they were subjects of the British crown and had to obey British law.

In October 1765, **delegates**, or chosen representatives, from 9 of the 13 colonies attended a meeting in New York called the Stamp Act Congress. The delegates prepared a declaration of rights and grievances, or complaints, which they sent to King George III. This action marked the first time that a majority of the

This teapot protesting the Stamp Act was made in England for sale in the American market sometime between 1766 and 1770, shortly after the Stamp Act was repealed. Many British citizens sympathized with the colonists' complaint about the tax. The other side of the teapot says: "America, Liberty Restored."

colonies had joined together to oppose actions by the British government.

At the same time, popular protests arose against the Stamp Act. Some colonists attacked the property of other colonists who had been chosen to collect the stamp tax. Others attacked the tax collectors themselves, forcing them to resign. Groups that took a leading role in these protests called themselves the Sons of Liberty.

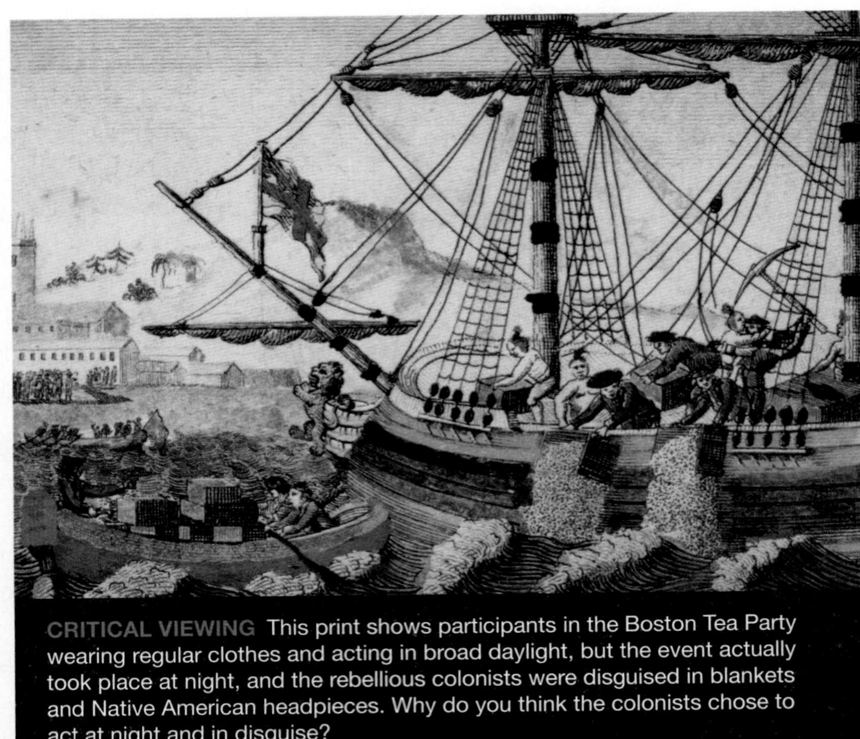

CRITICAL VIEWING This print shows participants in the Boston Tea Party wearing regular clothes and acting in broad daylight, but the event actually took place at night, and the rebellious colonists were disguised in blankets and Native American headpieces. Why do you think the colonists chose to act at night and in disguise?

In the face of American resistance, the British Parliament repealed, or canceled, the Stamp Act in 1766. Parliament also took two other steps. First, it extended the duty on sugar to imports of British sugar, not just foreign sugar. Second, it passed the Declaratory Act. That law stated that Parliament had the "full power and authority to make laws . . . to bind the colonies and people of America." With this act, Parliament made its view of who held the power clear to the American colonists.

HISTORICAL THINKING

3. **COMPARE AND CONTRAST** How did American and British views on the Sugar Act differ?
4. **EVALUATE** Do you think the phrase "taxation without representation is tyranny" was an accurate description of the situation the colonists faced? Explain your answer.
5. **MAKE INFERENCES** What might the British government have hoped to gain by passing the Declaratory Act?

New Taxes and Growing Protests

Soon, Parliament passed more new laws designed to bind the colonies tightly to the government. In 1767 Parliament imposed taxes on glass, paint, lead, and other items. In response, people throughout the colonies boycotted all British goods. As the *Massachusetts Gazette* proclaimed, "the whole continent from New England to Georgia seems firmly fixed."

Colonists were further enraged after Parliament passed the Quartering Act in 1765. This law required Americans to raise funds for the food, housing, and transportation of British troops. When New York's colonial legislature refused to do so, Parliament passed the Suspending Act, which ordered that any laws passed by the New York assembly would be invalid until the assembly passed a law to pay for the troops. Staring at the loss of self-government, the New York assembly passed a law to raise the money. Americans grew angrier as they saw their right of self-government eroded by British power.

The protests from colonists and complaints from British merchants who were hurt by the boycotts eventually led Parliament to repeal duties on glass, paper, paint, and other manufactured goods. A tax on tea remained, however. Americans responded by smuggling, or illegally importing, tea without paying the tax. They also increased their efforts to band together. The Boston town government formed what it called a Committee of Correspondence to make public statements and communicate with the other colonies. Colonists in dozens of other Massachusetts towns also formed committees, as did people in other colonies.

In 1773 Parliament passed the Tea Act. The act had two goals: to make British tea the only tea that could be sold in the colonies and to reassert its authority to tax the colonies. In response, American tea agents in several colonies refused to accept British tea when it arrived at the ports. In Massachusetts, however, the royal governor allowed three tea ships to enter Boston Harbor. On December 16, 1773, under cover of darkness, about 60 men disguised as Mohawk Indians climbed aboard the ships and dumped more than 340 chests of British tea into Boston Harbor in what is now known as the Boston Tea Party.

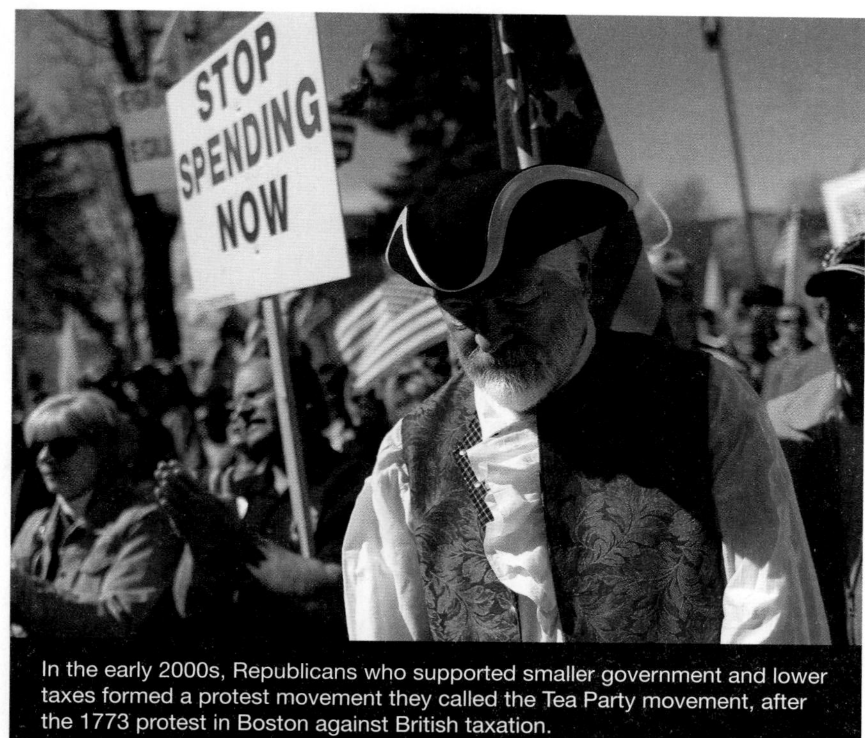

In the early 2000s, Republicans who supported smaller government and lower taxes formed a protest movement they called the Tea Party movement, after the 1773 protest in Boston against British taxation.

The British government retaliated. In 1774 Parliament passed four laws called the Coercive Acts. Coercive means the use of power to force obedience. One law closed Boston Harbor, preventing trade from moving into and out of the city. Another placed the government of Massachusetts under direct British control. A third required the colony to house British troops. The last ordered that trials for certain crimes must be held in other colonies—or in Britain. Leaders across the colonies labeled the laws the "Intolerable Acts." They saw the laws as an unjustified assault on the rights of all Americans.

HISTORICAL THINKING

6. **EVALUATE** What cherished American value was threatened by the Suspending Act?
7. **FORM AND SUPPORT OPINIONS** Why do you think the British effort to ease tensions in the late 1760s and early 1770s did not work?

The First Continental Congress

On September 5, 1774, delegates from 12 of the 13 colonies—Georgia was the exception—gathered at a meeting in Philadelphia called the First Continental Congress. A **congress** is a conference or meeting held to discuss important issues. The delegates sent a petition, a document that asks someone in power to take an action, to King George III asking for the repeal of the Coercive Acts. The Congress also called for a continued boycott of British goods. Further, it declared that if Parliament didn't act, Americans would stop exporting goods to Britain.

To enforce the boycott and other acts of resistance, the delegates to the First Continental Congress urged cities and towns to form committees of "safety" or "observation." These committees organized militias, or groups of armed citizens, held special courts, and suppressed the opinions of those who remained loyal to the British crown. Committee members spied on neighbors and reported those who violated the boycott to newspapers. Publishers printed these names, and the guilty parties were harassed and ridiculed.

HISTORICAL THINKING

8. **SYNTHESIZE** How can the actions of the First Continental Congress be seen as sending mixed messages about the protection of colonists' rights?

The Second Continental Congress

The British government condemned the actions of the Congress as open acts of rebellion. It responded with stricter and more repressive measures. The British sent ships to North America to blockade American ports, preventing trade with other nations. The government also ordered General Thomas Gage—the military governor of Massachusetts—to shut down protests. In the spring of 1775, Gage sent troops to seize military supplies in towns near Boston. On April 19, 1775, these British soldiers in their red jackets, known as Redcoats, clashed with colonial militia. Though war hadn't yet been declared, the fighting in the towns of Lexington and Concord marked the first battles of the American Revolution.

Less than a month later, delegates from all 13 colonies gathered in Pennsylvania for the Second Continental Congress. The Congress immediately assumed the powers of a central government. It took control of the militia gathered around Boston. It also named George Washington, a Virginia delegate who had some military experience, as the army's commander in chief.

Despite these steps, the delegates to the Second Continental Congress still hoped to reach a peaceful settlement. They issued a declaration stating that "we [the Congress] have not raised armies with ambitious designs of separating from Britain, and establishing independent States." At about the same time, the Congress issued a statement called the Olive Branch Petition. In it, the delegates pledged loyalty to King George III and asked him to resolve the situation by repealing the laws the Americans objected to. But rather than offering a peaceful settlement, King George III declared that the colonies were in rebellion, or open opposition.

HISTORICAL THINKING

9. **SEQUENCE** What events between the meetings of the First and Second Continental Congresses showed that the situation had worsened?

10. **MAKE PREDICTIONS** What do you think will happen as a result of King George III's response to the Olive Branch Petition?

COMMON SENSE;

ADDRESSED TO THE

INHABITANTS

OF

AMERICA,

On the following interefting

SUBJECTS.

I. Of the Origin and Defign of Government in general, with concife Remarks on the Englifh Conftitution.

II. Of Monarchy and Hereditary Succeffion.

III. Thoughts on the prefent State of American Affairs.

IV. Of the prefent Ability of America, with fome mifcellaneous Reflections.

Man knows no Mafter fave creating HEAVEN,
Or thofe whom choice and common good ordain.
THOMSON.

PHILADELPHIA;
Printed, and Sold, by R. BELL, in Third-Street.
MDCCLXXVI.

Thomas Paine galvanized many Americans to join the push for independence with his 1776 pamphlet *Common Sense*. He donated the money from sales of the pamphlet to the American cause.

Paine's *Common Sense*

Public debate about the problems with Britain continued to rage, but the stage had been set for declaring independence. One of the most rousing arguments in favor of independence was presented by Thomas Paine. A former English tax collector who was fired for his political opinions, he moved to Philadelphia in 1774. Soon after the battles of Lexington and Concord, Paine wrote a highly influential pamphlet called *Common Sense*.

The pamphlet was published in Philadelphia in January 1776. In it, Paine addressed the crisis using "simple fact, plain argument, and common sense." He attacked every argument that favored loyalty to the king, mocking George III as a "royal brute." Paine contended that America could survive on its own and no longer needed its British connection. He wanted the American colonies to become a new republic that would be a model in a world in which other nations were oppressed by powerful kings. Paine's arguments were not new, but his wit and eloquence made *Common Sense* persuasive:

> *"A government of our own is our natural right: and when a man seriously reflects on the precariousness [instability] of human affairs, he will become convinced, that it is infinitely wiser and safer, to form a constitution of our own in a cool and deliberate manner, while we have it in our power, than to trust such an interesting event to time and chance."*

Many historians regard Paine's *Common Sense* as the single most important publication of the American Revolution. More than 500,000 copies were sold within a few months of publication. Paine's work put the idea of independence in the forefront of colonists' minds. Above all, *Common Sense* removed the final emotional barrier to independence. That effect was profound, as John Adams would say later: "What do we mean by the Revolution? The War? That was no part of the Revolution. It was only an effect and consequence of it. The Revolution was in the minds of the people."

HISTORICAL THINKING

11. **MAKE CONNECTIONS** What principle does Thomas Paine use as the basis for his call for independence?
12. **MAKE INFERENCES** What does John Adams mean when he says that the American Revolution "was in the minds of the people"?

LESSON 2.3 Independence and Revolution

In 1776 Thomas Jefferson wrote the now familiar phrase: "We hold these Truths to be self-evident, that all Men are created equal, that they are endowed by their Creator with certain unalienable [absolute] Rights, that among these are Life, Liberty, and the Pursuit of Happiness." Jefferson expressed truths that, in his mind, were "self-evident" because he believed the rights of Americans had been violated and they were entitled to proclaim their independence. Jefferson's ringing words inspired many who followed, starting with the French revolutionaries of 1789. In 1848 Elizabeth Cady Stanton adapted the words of the Declaration to demand equal rights for women. Nearly 100 years later, in 1945, Vietnamese nationalists quoted them in their assertion of independence from France.

The Declaration of Independence

By June 1776 the Second Continental Congress was taking steps to break with Britain. The Congress had already voted to restrict British trade from passing through American ports. The Congress had also told the colonies to establish new state governments separate from British colonial governments. Yet Congress had stopped short of taking the formal step of declaring independence. On June 7, 1776, it inched closer.

THE LEE RESOLUTION Acting on instructions from the patriot government of Virginia, Richard Henry Lee placed a resolution before the Congress:

> *RESOLVED, That these United Colonies are, and of right ought to be, free and independent States, that they are absolved [released] from allegiance [loyalty] to the British Crown, and that all political connection between them and the state of Great Britain is, and ought to be, totally dissolved.*

Congress postponed consideration of Lee's resolution until a formal statement of independence could be drafted. On June 11 the delegates named a Committee of Five to draft a declaration that would present to the world the American case for independence. Among the five were John Adams of Massachusetts and Benjamin Franklin of Pennsylvania. Thomas Jefferson of Virginia, who became the main author of the resulting document, the Declaration of Independence, was also part of this group.

JEFFERSON'S ARGUMENT FOR INDEPENDENCE Adopted on July 4, 1776, the **Declaration of Independence**, in which Americans declared they were a nation separate from Great Britain, is one of the world's most famous documents. This event has been celebrated throughout the history of the United States on Independence Day, the 4th of July, with fireworks and patriotic tributes. In the Declaration, Jefferson began by stating that Americans had found it "necessary" to declare independence so they could gain the "equal station [status] to which the Laws of Nature and of Nature's God entitle them." The declaration, he said, was an attempt to explain why they found it necessary to do so. Jefferson identified certain rights as "unalienable," and he declared that a government derives, or gains, its authority to govern through the consent of those who are governed:

> *That to secure these Rights, Governments are instituted [set up] among Men, deriving their just Powers from the Consent of the Governed, that whenever any Form of Government becomes destructive of these Ends [of securing rights], it is the Right of the People to alter or to abolish it, and to institute new Government.*

English thinker John Locke's ideas provided the philosophical basis on which a revolution could be justified. Locke had written of the people's right to rebel against a government that did not protect their natural rights. Jefferson drew on these ideas in his defense of independence.

Jefferson then moved to particulars: "The history of the present King of Great Britain is a history of repeated injuries," he wrote. He lists dozens of grievances against the actions of George III and the British government. The main body of the Declaration provides detailed support for the claim that the king had failed to protect Americans' natural rights. The final paragraph adopts the words of the Lee Resolution to formally declare independence.

Before adopting Jefferson's Declaration, Congress debated it. In that debate, the delegates made compromises. For example, Jefferson addressed the trade that brought enslaved Africans to North America. Though Jefferson himself was an enslaver, he blamed the king for the slave trade. He called slavery "a cruel war against human nature." He even denounced it as "violating [the] most sacred rights of life and liberty" of enslaved Africans. Other delegates who enslaved people objected. The passage was deleted in order to win approval of the Declaration.

JUNETEENTH Conflicts over slavery continued in the United States, leading to secession and war. On January 1, 1863, in the midst of the Civil War, President Abraham Lincoln issued the Emancipation Proclamation. This document decreed that all enslaved people in the Confederate states would be "forever free" from slavery. For some, the edict had an immediate impact. As the Union army advanced through the South, tens of thousands of Black people crossed Union lines to seize their freedom. Many formerly enslaved men joined the Union army. Not everyone heard the news, however, or was able to claim the promised freedom. It was June 19, 1865, before many in Texas learned that they were no longer enslaved. People celebrated. Many walked away from the plantations where they had been held captive for years.

African Americans in Texas continued to celebrate Black independence on June 19, year after year. Over the decades, observances of the holiday, which became known as Juneteenth, spread through the nation. During some periods of history, when laws barred African Americans from public displays, these

Protesters in Brooklyn carry pictures of George Floyd, whose murder by police sparked protests throughout the nation, at a Juneteenth rally on June 19, 2020. The Juneteenth observance, also known as Emancipation Day, recognizes the day in 1865 when enslaved people in rural Texas learned they were free.

independence celebrations took place in private. At other times, such as during the Civil Rights movement of the 1960s, the events became larger. In 1980, Texas became the first state to recognize Juneteenth as a state holiday. In 2020, Black Lives Matter organizers raised the visibility of the holiday, and as of that year, 47 states and the District of Columbia recognized the holiday in some way. To many Americans, June 19 is a truer Independence Day than July 4.

HISTORICAL THINKING

1. **MAKE INFERENCES** Why might the government of Virginia be referred to as a "patriot government"?
2. **MAKE CONNECTIONS** Which of Jefferson's passages relates to Locke's idea that the people have the right to overthrow a government?
3. **SYNTHESIZE** What phrases in the Declaration of Independence justify the passage condemning slavery that was deleted by the Congress?

From Colonies to States

In May 1776 the Second Continental Congress had directed each of the colonies to form "such government as shall . . . best be conducive to [contribute to] the happiness and safety" of their people. Before long, all 13 colonies had created constitutions. Eleven of these constitutions were completely new. Two states, Rhode Island and Connecticut, made minor modifications to old royal charters. All the constitutions called for limited government, or a government whose powers and actions are limited by a system of laws.

One way to limit government was through the **separation of powers**, a political idea that spreads government functions and powers among different branches of government. French philosopher Baron de Montesquieu promoted this idea, maintaining that separating powers allows each branch of the government to check, or limit, the powers of the other branches. You will read more about the separation of powers and checks and balances in another chapter.

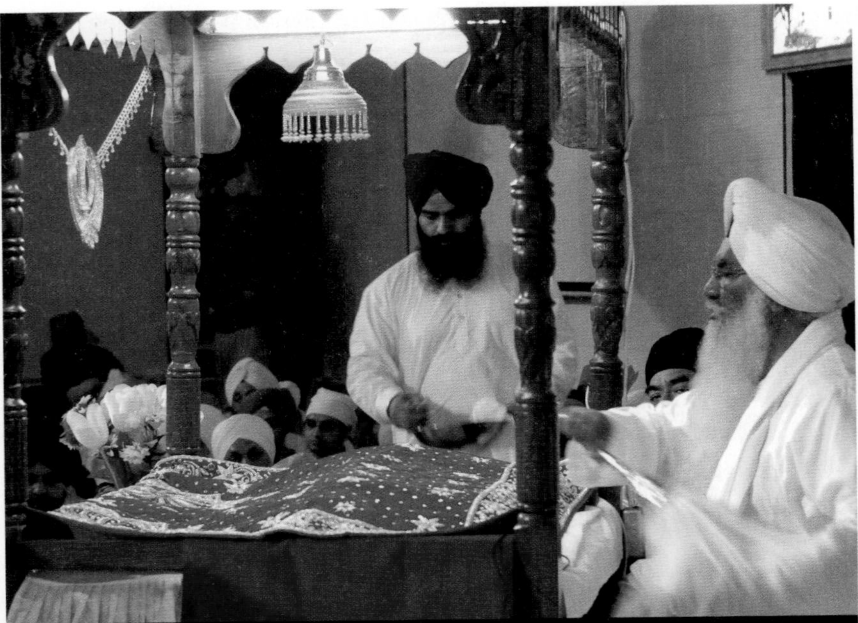
Sikhs in Wisconsin gather to pray after an attack on a Sikh temple in that state resulted in the deaths of six people. One of the protections guaranteed by many of the first state constitutions was freedom of religion.

Another way to limit government was to include a bill of rights. Seven of the new constitutions contained bills, or lists, of rights that defined citizens' civil liberties. Virginia's bill of rights—written by George Mason and James Madison—was the first to be adopted, in June 1776. It protected such rights as trial by jury in criminal cases, freedom of the press, and the free exercise of religion. Some states that did not have a separate bill of rights had constitutions that provided guarantees of civil liberties and other rights. New Jersey, for example, declared that the "right of trial by jury shall remain confirmed . . . without repeal, forever." That state's constitution also protected the right of people to follow the religion of their choice.

HISTORICAL THINKING

4. **MAKE INFERENCES** Why did leaders in Congress and the states see the need for written constitutions?
5. **FORM AND SUPPORT OPINIONS** How does having a bill of rights contribute to limited government?

Republicanism

At the time of the Revolution, many Americans feared a strong central government. Their recent experiences under the British crown led them to oppose a government that resembled a monarchy in any way. Instead, they wanted a form of democracy in which the people elect representatives who make and carry out the laws—a republic. Most patriots—those who supported a break with Britain—were republicans. (That is, they wanted to form a republic. They were not members of the Republican Party formed nearly a century later.) They were suspicious not only of executive power in their states but also of a strong central government.

REPUBLICANISM IN ACTION In places where opposition to royal power was particularly strong, citizens created strong legislatures and avoided placing too much power in the hands of any individual leader. Pennsylvania, for example, had no single governor but rather a 12-person executive council. Members of the council were chosen by voters, but the president and vice president of the council were chosen by the legislature. Even in those states with a governor, the executive branch was extremely weak.

State constitutions reflected republican ideas in other ways. One was by embracing **popular sovereignty**, the idea that the people hold the ultimate power of government. As the Pennsylvania Constitution put it, "all power is . . . derived from, the people." Others had similar expressions. The people's power was demonstrated in their right to elect government officials. In some states, officials had to seek popular, or the people's, approval by facing frequent elections. In Georgia and New Jersey, elections for the legislature were held every year.

In practice, popular sovereignty was limited by the fact that not everyone enjoyed the right to vote. In most states, men needed to own property to be able to vote. Pennsylvania was the exception, giving the right to vote to "Every freemen of the full age of twenty-one Years . . . ." In most states, the right to vote was limited to men. New Jersey's constitution, however, had broader language. It said that "all inhabitants . . . of full age [who reached adulthood]" could vote as long as they owned a certain amount of property. That wording allowed women and free African Americans to vote in the state if they met the property requirement. (New Jersey later limited the right to vote to White males.)

AUTHORITY OF STATES AND NATIONALISM The republican spirit was so strong that it threatened the ability of the new nation to win the Revolutionary War. During the war, the Congress in Philadelphia served as the central government. Fear of a too-strong central government led the states to be slow in sending Congress the funds it needed to supply General Washington's army. In fairness, the states had difficulty raising money, in part because they were reluctant to tax their people. Disputes over taxes, after all, had led to the Revolution in the first place.

The state-centered view contrasted with the nationalist sentiments of many leaders. John Adams of Massachusetts, a fierce advocate of independence, was a nationalist. In 1775 he had been the one to propose that Congress create a national army and place Washington in charge. Washington himself was a nationalist, as was Alexander Hamilton, the young man from New York who was one of Washington's closest aides. Nationalists favored an effective central authority. While some early leaders, such as Thomas Jefferson, held both republican and nationalist views, the tension between these two perspectives would continue beyond the end of the war. Like most political leaders of the period, those who favored the authority of the states were men of property and standing. Many republicans were small farmers, however, who tended to be less wealthy and prominent than those who held nationalist views. Significantly, this group, which favored the authority of the states, represented a majority of the voters in every state.

HISTORICAL THINKING

6. **ANALYZE CAUSE AND EFFECT** Why were political leaders typically "men of property and standing"?
7. **SYNTHESIZE** How does John Adams's idea of creating an army with a Virginian in command reflect a nationalist spirit?

CRITICAL VIEWING After George Washington had the newly issued Declaration of Independence read to his troops, a group of soldiers and civilians who were inspired by the document and the ideals of republicanism and popular sovereignty pulled down a statue of King George III. The event is portrayed in this 1859 painting by artist Johannes Adam Simon Oertel. Why do you suppose the artist portrayed some members of the crowd as worried about what is taking place?

An anonymous print depicts an imagined meeting between Captain Nathan Hale and General George Washington. Historians do not know whether Hale ever actually met Washington in person.

The Letter That Won the American Revolution

by Nina Strochlic **National Geographic Online, July 3, 2017**

In the winter of 1777, the Continental Army was losing its fight for independence. The British held New York City, a crucial port, and the Continental Congress had been driven out. In the face of Britain's superior military power, Continental Army commander George Washington's only hope was to find out what the enemy was up to. His effort to recruit officers willing to go behind British lines foundered when the sole volunteer—Nathan Hale—was captured by the British and hanged as a spy in September 1776.

Washington realized that he needed more than an individual volunteer. He needed an organization. In "The Letter That Won the American Revolution," writer Nina Strochlic tells the story of the founding of America's first spy network, which began with a February 1777 letter from Washington offering Nathaniel Sackett $50 a month to lead a spy ring. As Washington said in his letter, he hoped to gain the "advantage of obtaining the earliest and best Intelligence of the designs of the Enemy."

Eventually, these efforts led to the creation of the Culper Spy Ring, a group of childhood friends from Long Island that included a New York City shop owner, a traveling trader, and a boat captain. The group hid messages in hollow feather quills, delivered messages to secret locations, and employed elaborate codes and invisible ink to expose enemy spies and destroy a British counterfeiting plan meant to undermine the American economy. It was skilled, resourceful, and resilient:

Washington's espionage experiment paid off. In 1781 the British surrendered, thanks in part to the intelligence gathered by the Culper Ring and their networks. "Washington didn't really out-fight the British. He simply out-spied us," a British intelligence officer allegedly said after the war.

Washington paid for the entire operation out of his own pocket, though Congress reimbursed him after the war. Yet even he never knew exactly who was part of the intelligence network, and the very existence of the spying operation was unknown to historians until the 1900s.

Access the full version of "The Letter That Won the American Revolution" by Nina Strochlic through the Resources Menu in MindTap.

THINK ABOUT IT What does the fact that Washington had to pay for the spy network himself suggest about the American ideas of government and republicanism during the Revolutionary War?

LESSON

2.4 The Confederation of States

Americans fought a bloody war to win their independence. But just three years after the end of the war, the states and their citizens were heavily in debt. In Massachusetts, the government tried to raise money by imposing heavy taxes. Those who could not pay had their property seized by the courts. In September 1786 several hundred Massachusetts farmers, led by former Revolutionary War captain Daniel Shays, attacked a courthouse in Springfield, forcing it to close. By January Shays's forces, which had grown to around 1,200, stormed a national government arsenal in Springfield. Many feared the United States was about to collapse. Would the American experiment in republican government end in its infancy?

The Articles of Confederation

The Second Continental Congress created a national government in the face of widespread fears of a strong central government. In addition, the idea of an American identity was not yet fully formed. Many people were loyal to their state, first and foremost, whether their state was Connecticut, Pennsylvania, North Carolina, or another state. Congress needed to organize a national government strong enough to override state-centered fears and to create a national spirit, all while fighting a war against a powerful foe.

Influenced by republican ideas and these strong state loyalties, the delegates to the Second Continental Congress formed a committee to draft a plan of **confederation**, or a voluntary association of independent states. Under that plan, the central government had the power to undertake only a limited number of activities. The plan didn't allow the central government to place many restrictions on the states. States could still govern most affairs as they saw fit.

On November 15, 1777, the Second Continental Congress agreed on a draft of the plan, the **Articles of Confederation**. Final approval from all 13 states was not won until March 1, 1781, however. On that date, the official name of the national legislature became the Confederation Congress. The Articles of Confederation served as the nation's first national constitution. It was an important step in the creation of the American governmental system.

THE STRUCTURE OF GOVERNMENT The Articles of Confederation established the Congress of the Confederation as the sole central governing body. This congress was **unicameral**, meaning it had one legislative house. The assembly was made up of representatives from the various states. Although each state could send from two to seven representatives to the Congress, each state, no matter what its population, had only one vote in Congress. The states wanted to protect their sovereignty—or their authority to act independently. This right was an important part of the Articles of Confederation. Article II stated: "Each State retains its sovereignty, freedom, and independence, and every power, jurisdiction, and right, which is not by this Confederation expressly delegated to the United States in Congress assembled."

The new government had no executive branch. The Congress named a president to preside over its meetings, but that official had no powers to direct government activity. And the Articles didn't establish any national court system.

POWERS UNDER THE ARTICLES The Congress had the sole power to wage war and make peace under the Articles of Confederation. Only the national government could send or receive ambassadors to other countries or sign treaties on most matters with those countries. The Congress also had the power to settle disputes between states.

Congress used its foreign policy powers to achieve an important wartime objective. As the war raged on, it sent diplomats to France and other European rivals of Great Britain. Loans from these nations provided vital financial support to the Patriots' cause. After an American victory at the Battle of Saratoga, in New

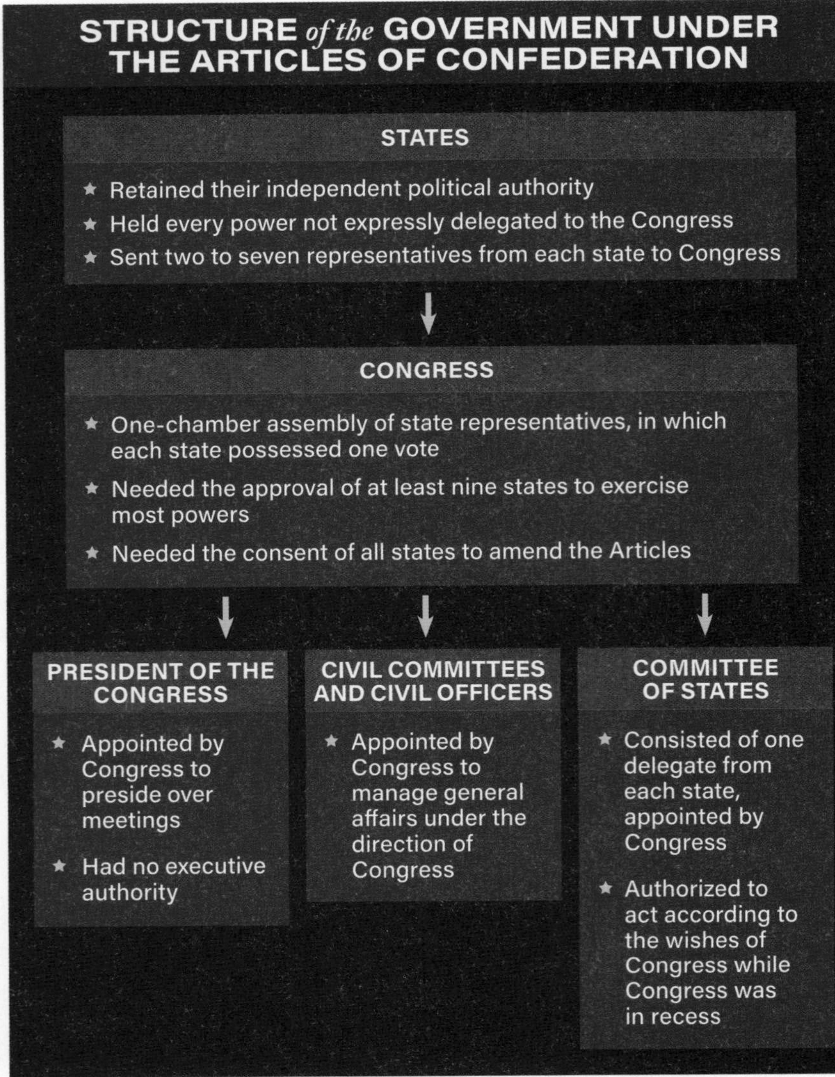

York, in late 1777, France agreed to an alliance. Later, France sent money and military supplies that were essential to the American victory.

STRUCTURE of the GOVERNMENT UNDER THE ARTICLES OF CONFEDERATION
STATES
★ Retained their independent political authority
★ Held every power not expressly delegated to the Congress
★ Sent two to seven representatives from each state to Congress
CONGRESS
★ One-chamber assembly of state representatives, in which each state possessed one vote
★ Needed the approval of at least nine states to exercise most powers
★ Needed the consent of all states to amend the Articles
PRESIDENT OF THE CONGRESS
★ Appointed by Congress to preside over meetings
★ Had no executive authority
CIVIL COMMITTEES AND CIVIL OFFICERS
★ Appointed by Congress to manage general affairs under the direction of Congress
COMMITTEE OF STATES
★ Consisted of one delegate from each state, appointed by Congress
★ Authorized to act according to the wishes of Congress while Congress was in recess

The Confederation Congress had another major achievement. It settled states' conflicting claims to many of the western lands. In three laws called the Northwest Ordinances, it set forth how those lands would be divided and settled. In the 1787 law, it established a basic pattern for the government of new territories and allowed for the addition of new states from this area. That law also banned slavery from the area, a move that would have a lasting impact on the nation's history.

Most important, the Confederation Congress won the war. Its agents negotiated the 1783 peace treaty with Britain that recognized American independence. That treaty also granted to the United States all the territory from the Atlantic Ocean to the Mississippi River and from the Great Lakes and Canada to what is now northern Florida.

WEAKNESSES UNDER THE ARTICLES In spite of these accomplishments, the central government created by the Articles of Confederation was weak. The Congress had no power to raise revenue for the army or to force the states to meet military quotas. Essentially, this meant that the new government didn't have the power to enforce its laws. Even passing laws was difficult because the Articles of Confederation provided that nine states had to approve any law before it was enacted. If the members of Congress had ideas about changing the Articles of Confederation, they faced an uphill fight: The legislatures of every single state—without exception—had to approve any change.

Money remained a major problem for the Congress throughout this period. Congress took out loans to finance the war, and it imposed taxes on the states in order to repay them. It couldn't force the states to pay their share. Furthermore, Congress had no power to regulate paper money. States issued their own paper money, which Congress could not control. The central government printed paper money, too, but because the Congress had difficulty obtaining funds to back its money, that currency lost value.

In spite of its problems, the Articles of Confederation proved to be a good first draft for the U.S. Constitution. In fact, at least half of the text of the Articles would later appear in the Constitution. The Articles were an experiment that tested some of the principles of government set forth in the Declaration of Independence. Some historians argue that without the experience of government under the Articles, it would have been difficult, if not impossible, to arrive at the compromises that were necessary to create the Constitution.

WEAKNESSES *of* GOVERNMENT UNDER THE ARTICLES	
LIMITS ON THE CENTRAL GOVERNMENT	**RESULT**
Congress could not force the states to meet military quotas.	The central government could not draft soldiers to form a standing army.
Congress could not regulate commerce between the states or with other nations.	Each state was free to tax goods imported from other states, resulting in economic quarrels between the states and with other nations.
Congress could enter into treaties but could not enforce them.	The states were not forced to respect treaties, and many states entered treaties independent of Congress.
Congress could not directly tax the people.	The central government had to rely on the states to collect taxes, which the states were reluctant to do.
Congress had no power to enforce its laws.	The central government depended on the states to enforce its laws, which they rarely did.
Any amendment to the Articles required approval by all 13 states.	In practice, the powers of the central government could not be changed.
There was no national judicial system.	Most disputes among the states could not be settled by the central government.
There was no national executive branch.	Coordinating the work of the central government was almost impossible.

HISTORICAL THINKING

1. **MAKE INFERENCES** Why was each group of state representatives in the Confederation Congress given only one vote?
2. **ANALYZE VISUALS** Under the Articles of Confederation, how did government operate when the Congress was in recess?
3. **INTERPRET CHARTS** Based on the information in the diagram showing the weaknesses of the United States government under the Articles of Confederation, which weakness do you think was the most damaging? Why?

A Time of Crisis—the 1780s

For all intents and purposes, the Revolutionary War ended on October 19, 1781. On that day, a major British army surrendered at Yorktown, Virginia, to combined American and French forces. Scattered fighting continued, and it took two more years before the parties signed a peace treaty, but with the defeat at Yorktown, the British government essentially gave up fighting. Still, peace with Britain didn't signal the end of conflict within the new nation. The states bickered among themselves and refused to support the new central government. As George Washington stated, "We are one nation today and thirteen tomorrow. Who will treat [make agreements with] us on such terms?"

Indeed, the national government couldn't prevent the various states from entering into agreements with foreign powers, despite the danger that such agreements could present to national survival. When Congress proved reluctant to admit Vermont into the Union as a new state, Britain began negotiations with leaders in Vermont with the aim of annexing, or joining, the district to Canada. Likewise, the governor of Louisiana—ruled by Spain—sought to detach the area that is now Alabama, Mississippi, and Tennessee from the United States.

The states also competed with each other economically. They increasingly taxed each other's imports and at times even prevented trade across state lines. By 1784 the new nation was suffering from a serious economic crisis. States printed their own money at dizzying rates. Having more money in circulation made that money worth less, which led to **inflation**, or an overall rise in prices. In response,

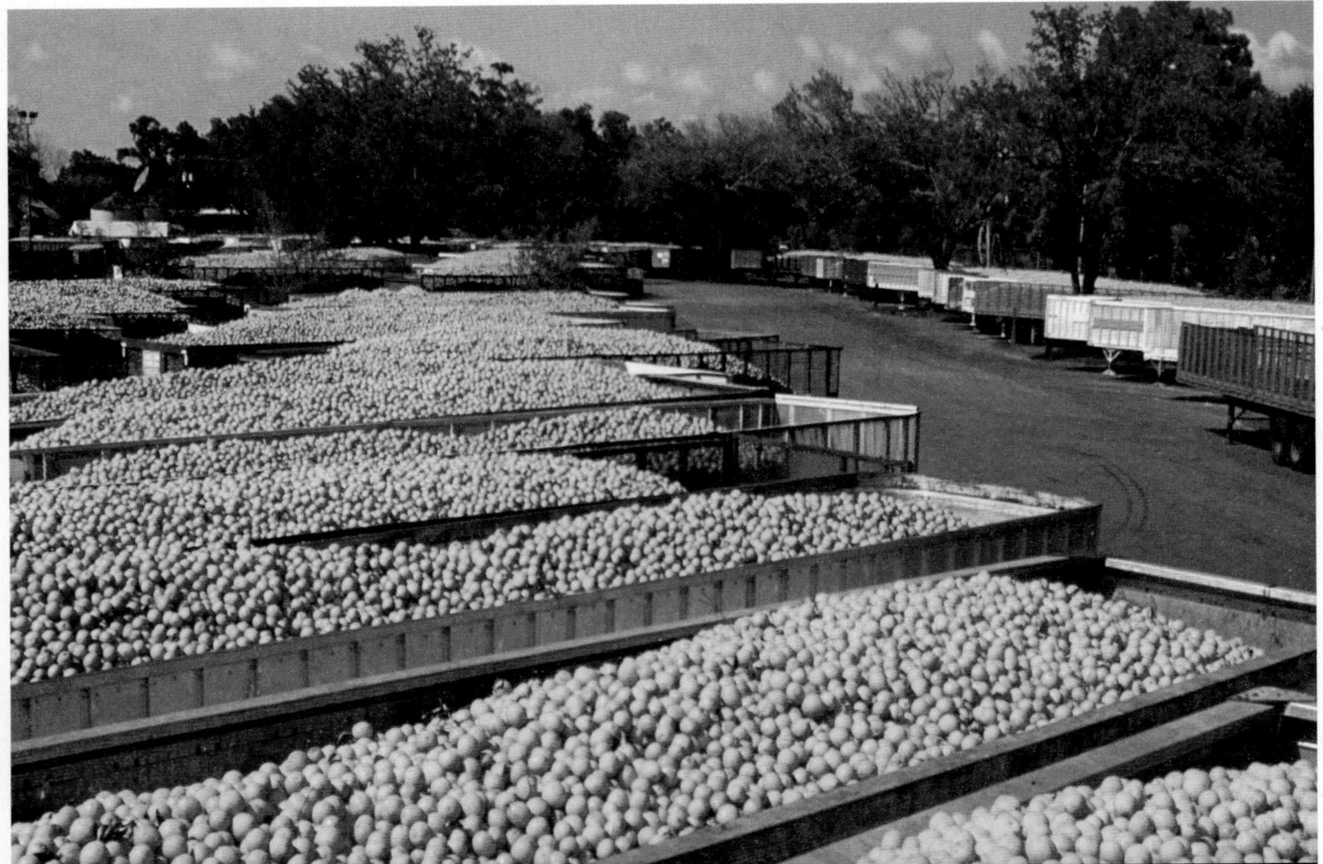

The free flow of goods across state lines was difficult under the Articles of Confederation because each state could enact its own laws about the movement of goods. Today, goods such as Florida oranges can be sold throughout the nation.

banks stopped lending money. Worse, they called in old loans, forcing borrowers to pay off their debts. Those who couldn't pay their debts were often thrown into prison. Many of those debtors were small farmers who had fought in the war.

INTERNAL REBELLION As you read earlier, Shays's Rebellion broke out in the fall of 1786. It continued to grow in intensity and lasted into the winter, when it was stopped by a volunteer army of soldiers paid by Boston merchants. Similar disruptions occurred throughout most of the New England states and in some other areas as well. The revolts frightened many Americans, including many political and business leaders. More and more Americans began to support creation of a true national government.

HISTORICAL THINKING

4. **MAKE INFERENCES** Under the Articles of Confederation, why did the ability of state governments to work out their own treaties with foreign governments pose dangers to the nation?
5. **ANALYZE CAUSE AND EFFECT** Why would business owners raise prices simply because more money was in circulation?
6. **MAKE INFERENCES** Why would the participation of Revolutionary War veterans like Shays contribute to the impact of the revolt?
7. **CAUSE AND EFFECT** What did Hamilton and Madison do to advance their goal of creating a stronger central government?
8. **SYNTHESIZE** Based on provisions of the Articles of Confederation, what challenge might the members of the Philadelphia meeting face in carrying out their stated objective?

The Annapolis Meeting

After trying to resolve a dispute with Maryland about water rights in 1785, the Virginia legislature asked other states to send representatives to a meeting in Annapolis, Maryland, on September 11, 1786. The meeting's purpose was to consider extending national authority to matters of interstate commerce, or trade among the states. Only 5 of the 13 states sent delegates, however. With so few states in attendance, it was not possible to address the issue effectively. Two of the individuals who did come were Alexander Hamilton of New York and James Madison of Virginia, both of whom favored a strong central government. They persuaded the other delegates to call for a convention in Philadelphia in May of the following year.

The Confederation Congress at first was reluctant to give its approval to the Philadelphia convention. By mid-February 1787, however, seven states had named delegates to the Philadelphia meeting. Finally, on February 21, the Congress called on all the states to send delegates to Philadelphia "for the sole and express purpose of revising the Articles of Confederation." The people who attended that meeting took a far more dramatic action. That Philadelphia meeting became the Constitutional Convention.

CRITICAL VIEWING A print made around 1850 depicts the violence and upheaval that marked Shays's Rebellion decades earlier. How did scenes like this echo events from the years before the American Revolution?

LESSON 2.5

Drafting and Ratifying the Constitution

Imagine what would happen today if political and business leaders from across the nation met for months behind closed doors to discuss possible changes to the American government. Think about the reactions if those in the secret meeting solicited no opinions from the people or from existing bodies of government. Many Americans would demand to know what those leaders were planning. They might also insist on being involved in the process.

The Delegates to the Constitutional Convention

In February 1787 the Confederation Congress reluctantly agreed to call for a meeting in Philadelphia to suggest changes to the Articles of Confederation. Although the meeting was supposed to start on May 14, 1787, few of the delegates had actually arrived in Philadelphia by that date. The convention formally opened on May 25, after 55 of the 74 delegates had arrived. The meeting took place in the East Room of the Pennsylvania State House, the building now known as Independence Hall. Some delegates were quite familiar with this room. It was the same one where the Declaration of Independence had been debated and signed. Only Rhode Island did not send any delegates.

The size of Mount Vernon—George Washington's Virginia home—reflects the wealth of most members of the Constitutional Convention. Washington inherited the estate from his father in 1754 and spent the next 45 years remodeling and enlarging it in line with the latest architectural fashions in England.

Feelings in that state ran strong against creating a more powerful central government.

Among the delegates to this Constitutional Convention were some of the nation's best-known leaders. George Washington was present, as were fellow Virginians James Madison and George Mason. Washington's former aide, Alexander Hamilton of New York, was there as well. You might remember that Madison and Hamilton had worked together the previous autumn to convince delegates at the meeting in Annapolis to agree to a Constitutional Convention. Robert Morris, James Wilson, and Benjamin Franklin of Pennsylvania also attended. Franklin, who was 81 years old, had to be carried to the convention on a portable chair. (Wheelchairs had been invented, but were not widely used.)

Some notable leaders were absent. Thomas Jefferson and John Adams were serving as ambassadors in Europe and could not attend. Patrick Henry did not attend because he "smelt a rat." Henry, from Virginia, strongly favored a republican system with a weaker central government. Another republican who opposed a strong national government was Sam Adams, who had helped stoke anti-British feeling in Massachusetts in the 1760s and 1770s. He had not been sent by his home state.

For the most part, the delegates were from the wealthy class. Thirty-three delegates were lawyers, three were physicians, eight were important business owners, six owned large plantations, and at least 19 owned enslaved African Americans. They were highly educated, with nearly half of the delegates having graduated from college at a time when many adults could not read or write. Twenty-one had fought in the Revolutionary War. The delegates were also experienced political leaders. Forty had been members of the Confederation Congress, and seven had served as governors of their respective states. More significantly, 15 had taken part in drafting the constitutions for their states.

In other words, the convention was an assembly of **elites**, or the most privileged and powerful members of society. No ordinary farmers or merchants were present. One historian pointed out that many of those attending had loaned money to the government under the Articles and might have feared it would not be repaid. While later historians have rejected this view, it is certainly true that the delegates were men of property and wealth.

HISTORICAL THINKING

1. **EVALUATE** Which feature of the delegates' backgrounds do you think made them the most qualified to draft the Constitution? Explain your answer.

The Virginia Plan and the New Jersey Plan

The delegates chose the widely respected George Washington to preside over the meeting. At the next meeting, they agreed that—as in the Confederation Congress—each state would have one vote. A few days later, they agreed that they would hold their discussions in strict secrecy. This, James Madison said, would ensure the "freedom of discussion" required to be effective.

THE VIRGINIA PLAN Madison had spent months studying and reviewing European political theory before coming to the Philadelphia convention. The result of this reading and thinking was a set of proposals that came to be called the Virginia Plan. Madison is called the "father of the Constitution" because he played such a central role in writing the document. On the third day of the convention, Governor Edmund Randolph of Virginia presented the Virginia Plan. This was a masterful political stroke on the part of Madison and the Virginia delegation. Virginia's proposals immediately set the agenda for the remainder of the convention. The 15 resolutions contained in the Virginia Plan proposed an entirely new national government.

The plan called for the following:

- A **bicameral**, or two-chamber, legislature including a larger chamber (or arm) to be chosen by the people and a smaller chamber to be chosen by the elected members of the larger chamber. The number of representatives would be in proportion to each state's population. This lawmaking body would have the power to void, or make inoperative, any state laws.
- A national executive branch, to be elected by the legislature
- A national court system, to be created by the legislature

The delegates quickly agreed on the three-part structure for the government. They also agreed on a bicameral legislature. Then the discussion grew more heated. Since representation in the Congress was based on state population, the Virginia Plan gave more influence to states with more people—like Virginia. The states with smaller populations did not like this plan. They were used to the system in the Confederation Congress, where each state had only one vote. After two weeks of debate on other issues, the smaller states offered their own plan—the New Jersey Plan.

U.S. Population by State, 1790

STATE	FREE	ENSLAVED
New Hampshire	141,727	158
Massachusetts (with Maine)	475,327	0
Rhode Island	67,877	948
Connecticut	235,182	2,746
New York	318,796	21,324
New Jersey	172,716	11,423
Pennsylvania	430,636	3,737
Delaware	50,207	8,887
Maryland	216,692	103,036
Virginia	454,983	292,627
North Carolina	293,179	100,572
South Carolina	141,979	107,094
Georgia	53,284	29,264

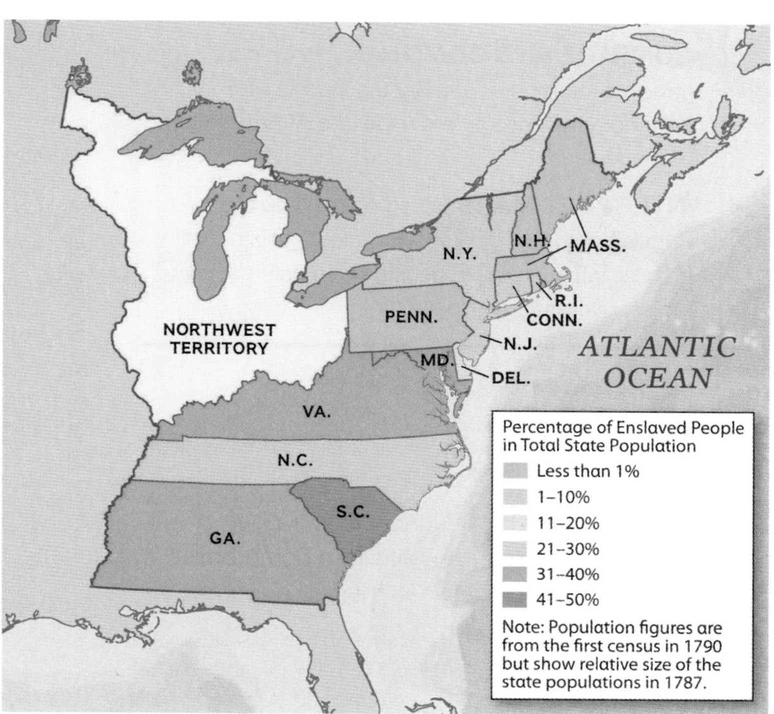

THE NEW JERSEY PLAN William Paterson of New Jersey presented an alternative plan favorable to the less populous states. He argued that because each state had an equal vote under the Articles of Confederation, the convention had no power to change this arrangement. The New Jersey Plan proposed the following:

- Congress would be able to regulate trade and impose taxes.
- Each state would have only one vote.
- Acts of Congress would be the supreme law of the land.
- An executive office of more than one person would be elected by Congress.
- The executive would appoint a national supreme court.

Most delegates were unwilling to consider the New Jersey Plan. When the Virginia Plan was brought up again, however, delegates from the smaller states threatened to walk out, putting the convention in danger of dissolving without devising a solution to the nation's problems.

HISTORICAL THINKING

2. **FORM AN OPINION** Were the delegates right in deciding to make their discussions secret? Explain your answer.
3. **COMPARE AND CONTRAST** How did the government to be created by the Virginia Plan differ from the government under the Articles of Confederation?
4. **INTERPRET MAPS** Based on the map U.S. Population by State, 1790, how did Virginia benefit from including enslaved people when determining representation in the House?

The Compromises

In June two delegates from Connecticut, Roger Sherman and Oliver Ellsworth, offered a compromise that broke the deadlock between the two opposing groups. Compromises on other disputed issues followed.

THE GREAT COMPROMISE Sherman and Ellsworth's plan, which has become known as the **Great Compromise** (or the Connecticut Compromise), set different rules for representation in the two houses of the new legislature, or law-making body of government.

- In the House of Representatives, the number of representatives from each state would be determined by the number of people in that state. In other words, the House would establish proportional representation based on the number of people in each state.
- In the Senate, each state would have a number of members equal to that of other states.

The Great Compromise gave something to both sides. The number of representatives in the House would be based on population. Therefore, states with larger populations would have more representatives in the House than states with fewer people, yet each state would have an equal number of senators in the Senate. The delegates debated the details for several days and finally settled on a plan that gave each state two senators to be chosen by the state legislatures. Members of the House of Representatives, however, would be elected by the people. The Great Compromise thus resolved the small-state/large-state controversy.

Changing House Representation in Selected States, 1850–2000

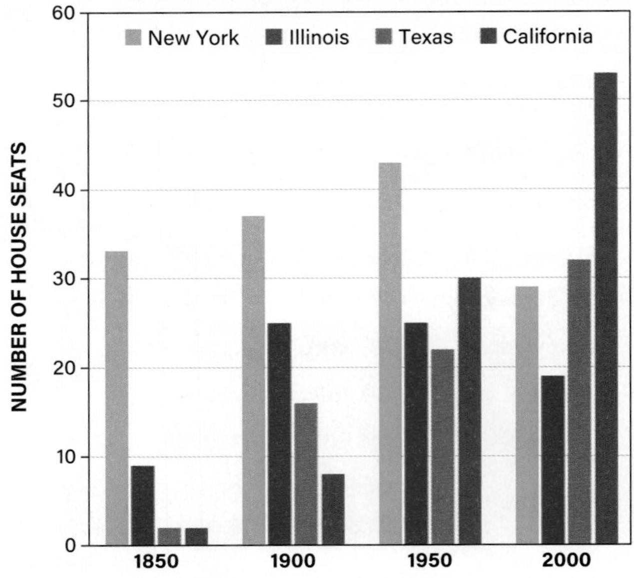

SOURCE: U.S. House of Representatives, Office of the Historian

THE THREE-FIFTHS COMPROMISE Another small-state/large-state controversy that simmered among the convention's delegates involved how a state's population would be counted for representation. Although slavery was legal in parts of the North, most slaves and slave owners lived in the South. Many of the southern states, where enslaved people made up around 40 percent of the population, feared the power of states like Massachusetts and Pennsylvania that had larger populations. Southern delegates wanted enslaved people counted as part of their populations so they could increase their number of congressional representatives (even though enslaved people could not vote). Delegates from the larger northern states opposed this plan—it meant they would lose their advantage of having a greater number of votes in the House of Representatives.

Pennsylvania's James Wilson suggested a way to break the impasse. The delegates adopted his idea and settled on the Three-Fifths Compromise. This was an agreement that stated that the number of representatives would be determined by adding to "the total number of free persons" "three fifths of all other Persons." Enslaved people were never mentioned, although these were the people who were intended by the term "other Persons." (The method adopted for computing representation also excluded "Indians not taxed" from the count.)

SLAVE IMPORTATION The Three-Fifths Compromise didn't satisfy everyone at the Constitutional Convention. Many delegates wanted slavery to be banned completely in the United States. Southern delegates wouldn't accept such a provision, however. The delegates compromised on this question by agreeing that Congress could prohibit **slave importation**, or the business of bringing slaves into the country, beginning in 1808. As a result, the slave trade, which brought money into the North as well as the South, continued without limits or restrictions for another 20 years.

The issue of slavery itself was never really addressed by the delegates to the Constitutional Convention, though they did include a clause requiring that no person "held in Service or Labour in one State" (in other words, enslaved people) could be discharged or freed after escaping to another state and had to be delivered, or returned, to the person "to whom such Service or Labour may be due."

Today, many people wonder why the Framers didn't ban slavery outright as they created the Constitution. Certainly, many of the delegates thought that slavery was morally wrong and that the Constitution should ban it entirely. On the one hand, many Americans regard the Framers' failure to deal with the slavery issue as a betrayal of the Declaration of Independence, which proclaimed that "all Men are created equal." On the other hand, it seems possible that if antislavery delegates had insisted on banning slavery, delegates from southern states most likely would have walked out of the convention, and there would have been no Constitution to ratify.

BANNING EXPORT TAXES The South's economic health depended in large part on its export of agricultural products. Southerners feared that the northern majority in Congress might impose taxes on these exports. This fear led to yet another compromise. Southerners agreed to let Congress have the power to regulate interstate commerce, or trade across state lines, as well as commerce with other nations. In exchange, the Constitution guaranteed that no export taxes would be imposed. Today, the United States is one of the few countries that doesn't tax its exports.

HISTORICAL THINKING

5. **COMPARE AND CONTRAST** What did both large states and small states gain and lose from the Great Compromise?
6. **ANALYZE CAUSE AND EFFECT** How would states with active shipping industries that carried trade goods—like those in New England—benefit from the ban on export taxes?
7. **INTERPRET GRAPHS** Based on the graph of changing House representation, what can you conclude about population change in these states from 1950 to 2000?

Finalizing the Constitution

The Great Compromise was reached by mid-July. Still to be determined was the makeup of the executive branch and the judiciary. One of the weaknesses of the Confederation had been the lack of an independent executive authority and a court system.

THE EXECUTIVE AND JUDICIAL BRANCHES The delegates remedied the first problem by creating the office of the president. The convention made the president the commander in chief of the army and navy and of the state militias when called into national service. The president was also given extensive appointment powers, although Senate approval was required for major appointments. Why were delegates willing to risk having a strong executive despite lingering concerns over what Americans had seen as King George III's abuse of power? It was widely understood that George Washington would be chosen as the first president, and the delegates trusted that he would not abuse the powers of the office.

CRITICAL VIEWING Andrew Johnson, who became president after Abraham Lincoln's assassination in 1865, was the first president to face impeachment. After impeachment by the House of Representatives, he escaped removal from office by just one vote in the U.S. Senate. What does the fact that tickets were issued for the impeachment trial suggest about that event?

In a time when letters and newspapers traveled slowly beyond cities, delegates feared that citizens in more remote areas would not have sufficient information to make informed decisions about candidates for president. To keep the important office of president from being selected by a direct vote from poorly or uninformed voters, they decided that members of an **electoral college**, a group of electors selected in each state, would officially elect the president and vice president. You'll read more about how this works later.

Another problem under the Confederation was the lack of a **judiciary**, or system of courts and judges, that was independent of the state courts. The Constitution established the United States Supreme Court but left to Congress the power of establishing "inferior," or lower, courts that would review cases before they went to the Supreme Court.

Finally, the Framers wanted to be sure that there was a way to remove dishonest or corrupt leaders. The Constitution provides that an official suspected of committing "Treason, Bribery, or other high Crimes and Misdemeanors" may be **impeached**—charged with wrongdoing—by the House of Representatives. An official who has been impeached by the House is then tried by the Senate. If found guilty of the charges by a two-thirds vote in the Senate, the official can be removed from office and prevented from ever assuming another government post.

THE FINAL DRAFT IS APPROVED A five-delegate Committee of Detail worked out the details on the executive and judicial branches and finished other remaining work. In August the committee presented a rough draft of the whole document to the convention, and on September 17, 1787, after months of work, the final draft of the Constitution was approved by 39 of the remaining 42 delegates. Many of the 74 delegates had had to leave before the convention was over. Three—Edmund Randolph and George Mason of Virginia and Elbridge Gerry of Massachusetts—objected to the new government for various reasons and refused to sign.

HISTORICAL THINKING

8. **MAKE INFERENCES** How might including the possibility of impeachment reassure delegates worried about the power of a president?
9. **MAKE PREDICTIONS** What reasons do you think Randolph, Mason, and Gerry had to object to the Constitution?

Federalists and Antifederalists

When the Second Continental Congress drafted the Articles of Confederation, all 13 states had to **ratify**, or formally approve, it. That process took nearly four years. The Constitutional Convention delegates didn't want ratification to take such a long time, given the crisis they believed the country faced. They also remembered how difficult it had been to amend the Articles, since amendments required the approval of all 13 states. They didn't want one state to be able to hold things up. They decided that the Constitution would take effect once 9 states ratified it, and assumed that all 13 would ratify once 9 did. They hoped that setting the requirement at nine would ensure a decision relatively quickly.

But ratification set off a national debate of unprecedented proportions. The battle was fought chiefly by two opposing groups. **Federalists** favored a strong central government and the new Constitution. **Antifederalists** opposed a strong central government and the new Constitution.

The federalists had several advantages in this debate. For one thing, their name clearly stated what it was they favored—a strong **federal** government—in other words, a national government that shared power with state governments. This left the opposing side with the "anti" label, which told people what they were against but not what they favored.

In addition, more federalists had attended the Constitutional Convention and thus were familiar with the arguments both in favor of and against various constitutional provisions. Only a few antifederalists had actual knowledge of those discussions because they hadn't attended the convention. The federalists also had time, funding, and prestige on their side. Their numbers included impressive political thinkers and writers, such as John Marshall, Alexander Hamilton, John Jay, and James Madison. The federalists could communicate with one another more readily because many were bankers, lawyers, and merchants who lived in urban areas, where communication was easier. Accordingly, the federalists organized a campaign to get each other elected as delegates to each state's ratifying convention.

THE FEDERALISTS ARGUE FOR RATIFICATION Hamilton enlisted Jay and Madison to help him write newspaper columns in support of the new Constitution. In less than a year, these three men wrote a series of 85 essays. Although they were written to convince New Yorkers of the federalist cause, they were printed in newspapers throughout the states. Collectively, they are known as the Federalist Papers, or *The Federalist*.

In general, the essays attempted to address fears expressed by the Constitution's critics. One fear was that the rights of those in the minority would not be protected under a strong central government. Many critics also feared that a republican form of government would not work in a nation the size of the United States. Various groups, or factions, would struggle for power, they said, and chaos would result. Madison responded to this argument in Federalist No. 10, which has become a classic in political theory. Among other things, Madison argued that the nation's size was actually an advantage in controlling factions. In a large nation, he said, there would be so many diverse interests and factions that no one faction would be able to gain control of the government.

Another concern was whether the Constitution created a republic. Madison answered this charge in Federalist No. 39. He argued that there were two key requirements for a government to be considered a republic. First, it had to be "derived from the great body of the society" rather than by a chosen few. Second, officials must be chosen "directly or indirectly" by the people. He then outlined how the various federal officials were chosen in this way. He also compared their terms of office to the terms of comparable officials in state government. Essentially, he was saying "if the state constitutions are republican, then so is the U.S. Constitution, because it has similar rules."

Critics of the Constitution warned that the strong central government would abuse its power. Madison responded with Federalist No. 51, in which he outlined the benefit of the separation of powers into three branches. The abuse of power, he said, is "guarded against by a division of the government into distinct and separate departments." It is further prevented, Madison argued, through creation of the federal system. Dividing power between the state and federal governments, Madison said, offers "a double security . . . to the rights of the people."

THE ANTIFEDERALISTS' RESPONSE Perhaps the greatest advantage the antifederalists had was

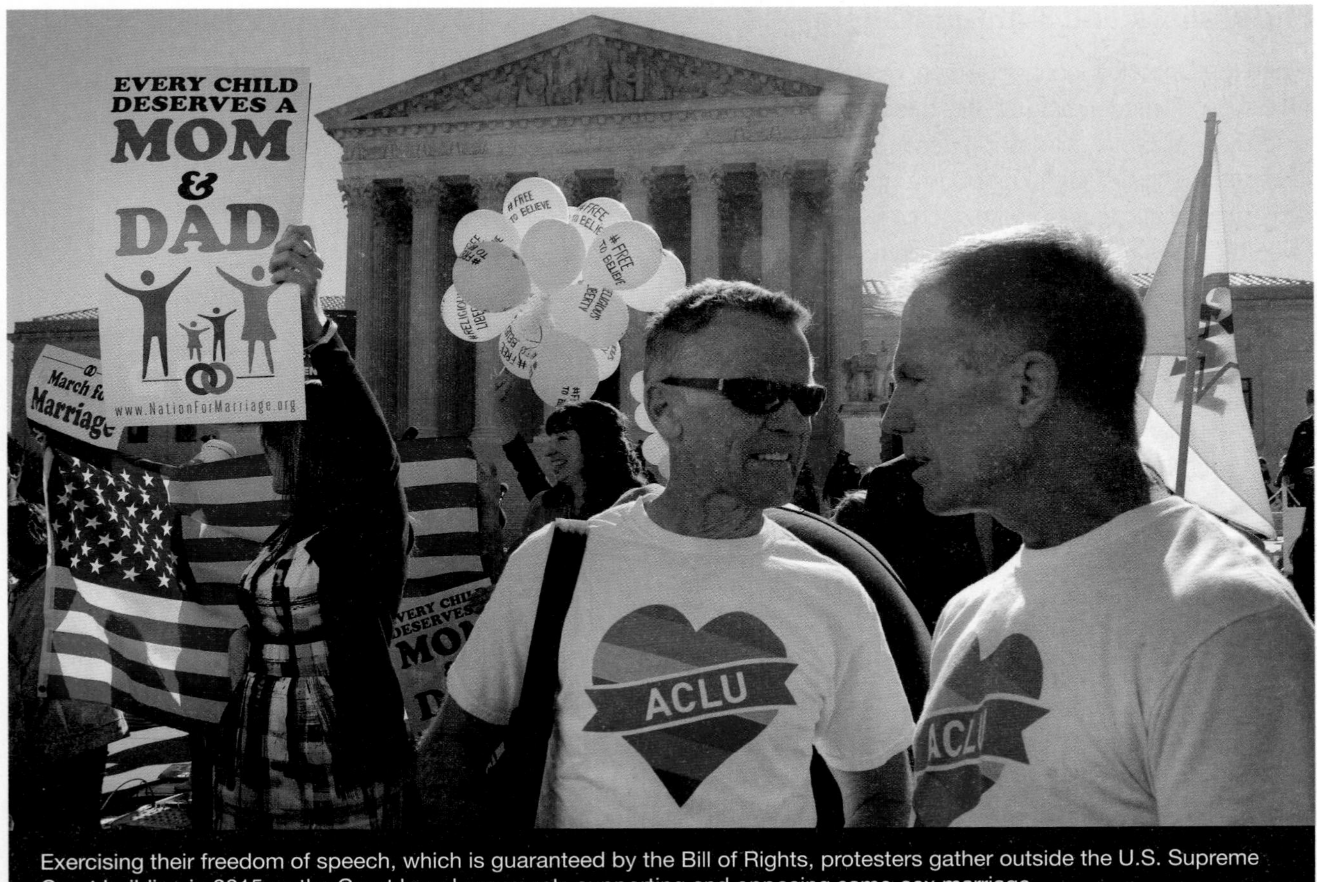

Exercising their freedom of speech, which is guaranteed by the Bill of Rights, protesters gather outside the U.S. Supreme Court building in 2015 as the Court heard arguments supporting and opposing same-sex marriage.

that they represented those who supported the government structure created by the Articles of Confederation. Usually, it is more difficult to change things than it is to keep what is already known and understood. The antifederalists also had some notable and influential leaders. Among them were such patriots as Patrick Henry and Samuel Adams. Patrick Henry said of the proposed Constitution, "I look upon that paper as the most fatal plan that could possibly be conceived to enslave a free people."

In response to the Federalist Papers, the antifederalists published their own essays attacking the new document. Many antifederalists contended that the Constitution had been written by aristocrats who would keep themselves in power. As Elbridge Gerry wrote, "There is no provision for a rotation [of officials], nor anything to prevent the perpetuity [continuance] of office in the same hands for life." Antifederalists also feared that the Constitution created an overly powerful central government that would limit personal freedom. Gerry, for example, complained that "There is no security in the proferred [proposed] system, either for the rights of conscience or the liberty of the Press."

The antifederalists argued vigorously that the Constitution needed a bill of rights. They warned that without a bill of rights, a strong national government might take away the important freedoms won during the American Revolution. Federalists argued that the Constitution did not threaten these rights, but they finally promised to add a bill of rights to the Constitution as the first order of business under the new government. This promise turned the tide in favor of the Constitution.

HISTORICAL THINKING

10. **IDENTIFY MAIN IDEAS AND DETAILS** What was the purpose of the Federalist Papers?
11. **MAKE PREDICTIONS** Which state do you think would be least likely to ratify the Constitution? Why?

Ratification

In 1787 Delaware, Pennsylvania, and New Jersey quickly voted to ratify the Constitution. Georgia and Connecticut followed with approval early the next year. Though antifederalists formed the majority in Massachusetts, a successful campaign by Federalists led to ratification by that state on February 6, 1788. The promise of a bill of rights helped convince enough members of the state convention to vote to ratify.

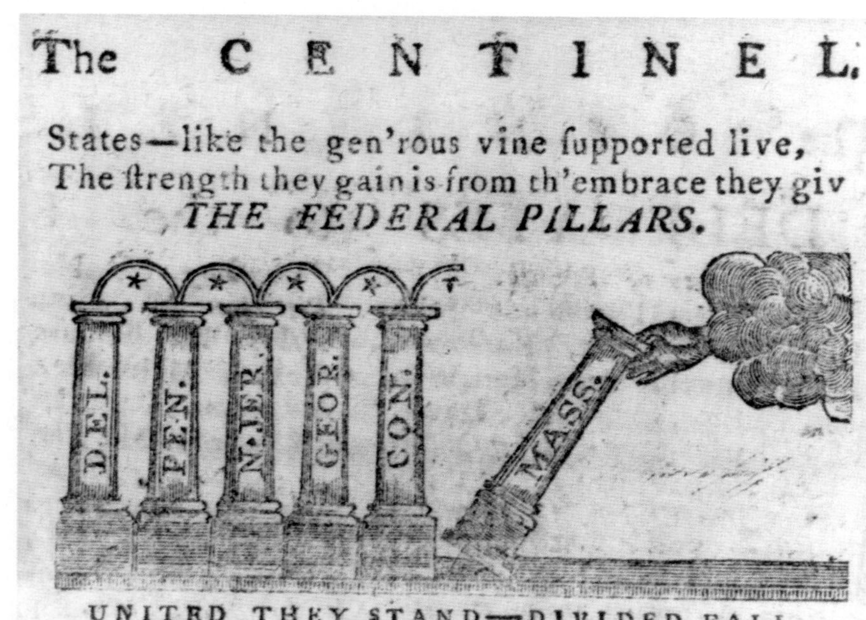

The CENTINEL.
States—like the gen'rous vine ſupported live,
The ſtrength they gain is from th'embrace they giv
THE FEDERAL PILLARS.
DEL.
PEN.
N.JER.
GEOR.
CON.
MASS.
UNITED THEY STAND—DIVIDED FALL.

CRITICAL VIEWING This 1788 cartoon commented on the process of ratifying the Constitution. What details reveal which side of the ratification debate the cartoonist is taking?

Following Maryland and South Carolina, New Hampshire became the ninth state to ratify the Constitution on June 21, 1788, putting the Constitution into effect. New York and Virginia had not yet ratified, however. Without them, the Constitution would have no true power because they were the two most populous states. Again, the promise to add a bill of rights helped secure ratification in those states in the summer of 1788. North Carolina waited until November 21, 1789, to ratify the Constitution, and Rhode Island did not ratify until May 29, 1790.

Some historians have called the Constitution an aristocratic document that lacked majority support. It is impossible to conclusively say what most Americans thought of the Constitution, however, because the great majority of adults did not have the right to vote.

Enslaved African Americans and women could not vote. Nor could Native Americans. Furthermore, free men generally could not vote unless they held sufficient property. A typical voting requirement in several states was the possession of land or other property worth 40 British pounds. At the time, this sum would buy about 100 acres of average U.S. farmland. Today, an acre of farmland in the United States is worth on average about $3,000. Many of the men who could not vote, it has been argued, were strong republicans, or antifederalists who might have opposed a strong central government.

Still, support for the Constitution seems to have been widespread in all social classes. Both rich and poor Americans were troubled by the weakness of the national government under the Articles of Confederation. In the end, the Constitution was ratified by all 13 state conventions. It has certainly gained the support and allegiance of Americans during its more than two centuries of operation.

HISTORICAL THINKING

12. **DRAW CONCLUSIONS** Why was it important that New York and Virginia ratify the Constitution?
13. **SEQUENCE** How long did it take for the Constitution to be ratified, and how long did it take for all 13 states to ratify it?

CHAPTER 2

THE BEGINNINGS OF AMERICAN GOVERNMENT

Review

VOCABULARY

Use each of the following vocabulary words in a sentence that shows an understanding of the term's meaning.

1. constitution
2. self-government
3. separation of powers
4. popular sovereignty
5. confederation
6. inflation
7. elites
8. bicameral
9. electoral college
10. federal

MAIN IDEAS

Answer the following questions. Support your answer with evidence from the chapter.

11. How did Pennsylvania make a point of protecting religious freedom early in its formation? **LESSON 2.1**
12. Why did the British want to raise revenue after the end of the French and Indian War? **LESSON 2.2**
13. Which British laws passed during the 1760s and 1770s threatened Americans' right to self-government? **LESSON 2.2**
14. What significant compromise was made when the Second Continental Congress debated Jefferson's draft of the Declaration of Independence? **LESSON 2.3**
15. How were the constitutions of Pennsylvania and New Jersey different from those of other states in terms of voting rights? **LESSON 2.3**
16. Why was it difficult for the Confederation Congress to fix the problems caused by the Articles of Confederation? **LESSON 2.4**
17. What were the three major provisions of the Northwest Ordinance of 1787? **LESSON 2.4**
18. Why were most of the delegates to the Constitutional Convention part of the elite? **LESSON 2.5**
19. What four compromises were key to the decisions of the Constitutional Convention? **LESSON 2.5**
20. How did James Madison set the agenda for the debates at the Constitutional Convention? **LESSON 2.5**

HISTORICAL THINKING

Answer the following questions. Support your answer with evidence from the chapter.

21. **SYNTHESIZE** How did the Mayflower Compact represent an example of the ideas John Locke wrote about in *Two Treatises on Government*?
22. **COMPARE AND CONTRAST** How did Americans and the British differ in their views about representation in Parliament?
23. **MAKE CONNECTIONS** How did Jefferson's list of grievances against King George III in the Declaration of Independence relate to the ideas of John Locke?
24. **FORM AND SUPPORT OPINIONS** Was Shays's Rebellion only an economic problem or a political problem? Explain your answer.
25. **IDENTIFY MAIN IDEAS AND DETAILS** What were the main objections of antifederalists to the Constitution?

INTERPRET VISUALS

Study the table below. Then answer the questions.

Ratification of the U.S. Constitution, by State

STATE	VOTES FOR RATIFICATION	VOTES AGAINST RATIFICATION
Delaware	30	0
Pennsylvania	46	23
New Jersey	38	0
Georgia	26	0
Connecticut	128	40
Massachusetts	187	168
Maryland	63	11
South Carolina	149	73
New Hampshire	57	47
Viginia	89	79
New York	30	27
North Carolina	194	77
Rhode Island	34	32

SOURCE: Natalie Bolton and Gordon Lloyd, "Ratification of the Constitution of the United States," TeachingAmericanHistory

26. In which states was ratification easiest to achieve, and in which states was it hardest?

27. States are listed in the order in which they voted. Did the voting for ratification generally become easier or more difficult over time? How do you explain the change?

ANALYZE SOURCES

Author and educator Noah Webster wrote an essay expressing his view of the U.S. Constitution during the debate over ratification. It included this statement:

> The separation of the legislature divides the power—checks—restrains—amends the proceedings—at the same time, it creates no division of interest, that can tempt either branch to encroach upon the other, or upon the people. In turbulent times, such restraint is our greatest safety—in calm times, and in measures obviously calculated for the general good, both branches must always be unanimous.

28. Based on this statement, do you think Webster was a federalist or an antifederalist? Why?

29. How might the other side have responded to this passage?

CONNECT TO YOUR LIFE

30. **EXPLANATORY** Describe how the compromises made during the Constitutional Convention affect life in the United States today. Look for a news story on a reputable site or in a reliable publication about a conflict either between the two houses of Congress or between a state and the federal government. Write a short essay to describe how this conflict arose as a result of the compromises made during the convention.

TIPS

- Review the lesson on compromises made during the Constitutional Convention that led to the situation you want to describe.
- Think about how today's situation might have been different if the compromise had turned out differently. For example, what if a unicameral legislature had been created or if state governments had kept more power?
- Write a clear thesis statement to describe the conflict you want to discuss.
- Explain how the compromises of the late 1780s led to the present-day situation.
- Offer a view as to how things might have gone differently and then offer an opinion as to whether the current situation is an improvement over the alternative or not.
- Use two or three vocabulary terms in your essay.

2 The Constitution and Federalism

UNIT 2 OVERVIEW

Chapter 3 The Constitution

Chapter 4 Federalism

CRITICAL VIEWING The original U.S. Constitution, in four pages, is held for all Americans to see in four metal cases housed in the Rotunda of the National Archives Building in Washington, D.C. The document is flanked by original copies of the Declaration of Independence and Bill of Rights. What is the value of preserving historical documents?

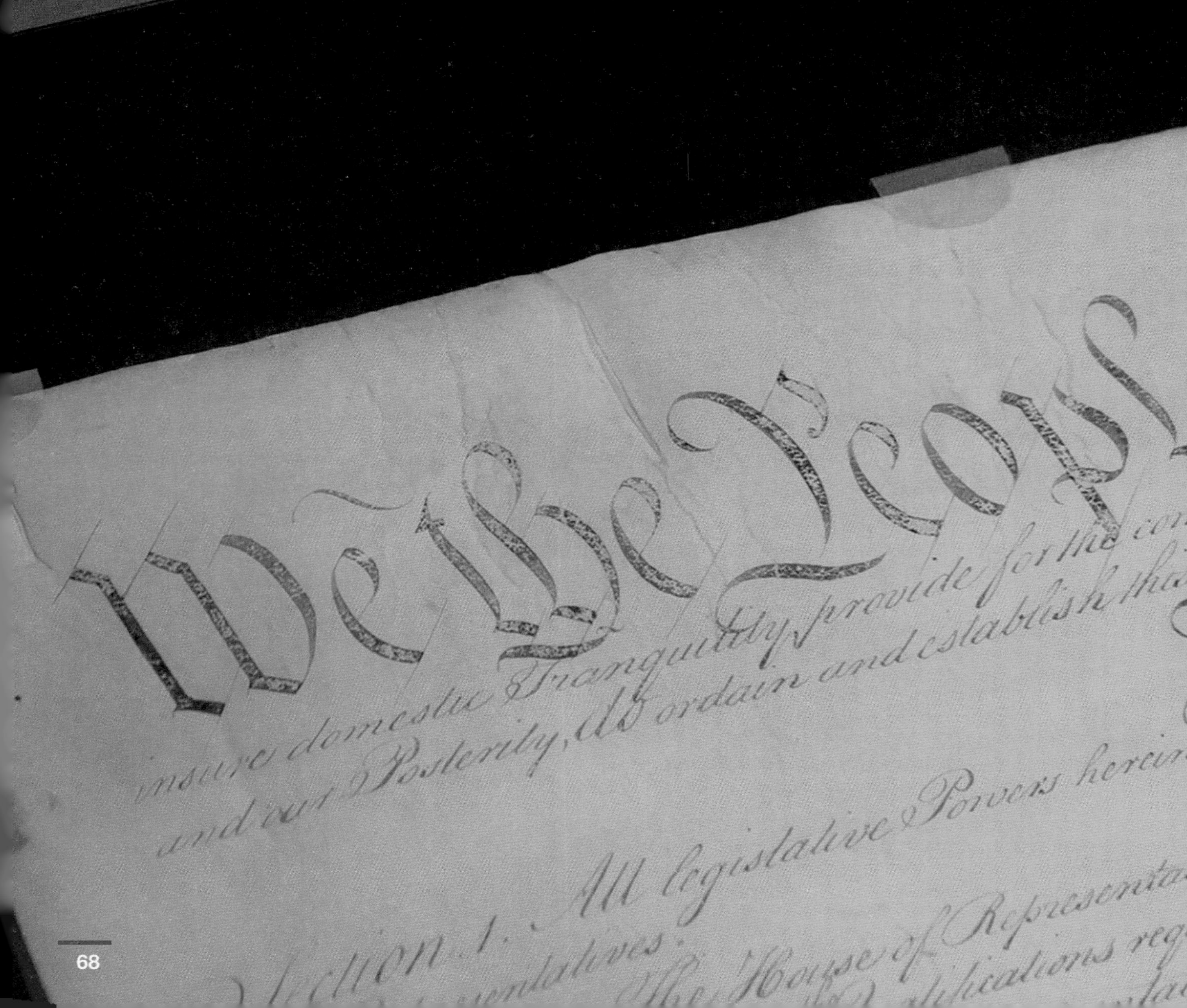

[The Constitution's] language is "we the people". . . not we the high, not we the low, but we the people.

—Frederick Douglass

CHAPTER 3

The Constitution

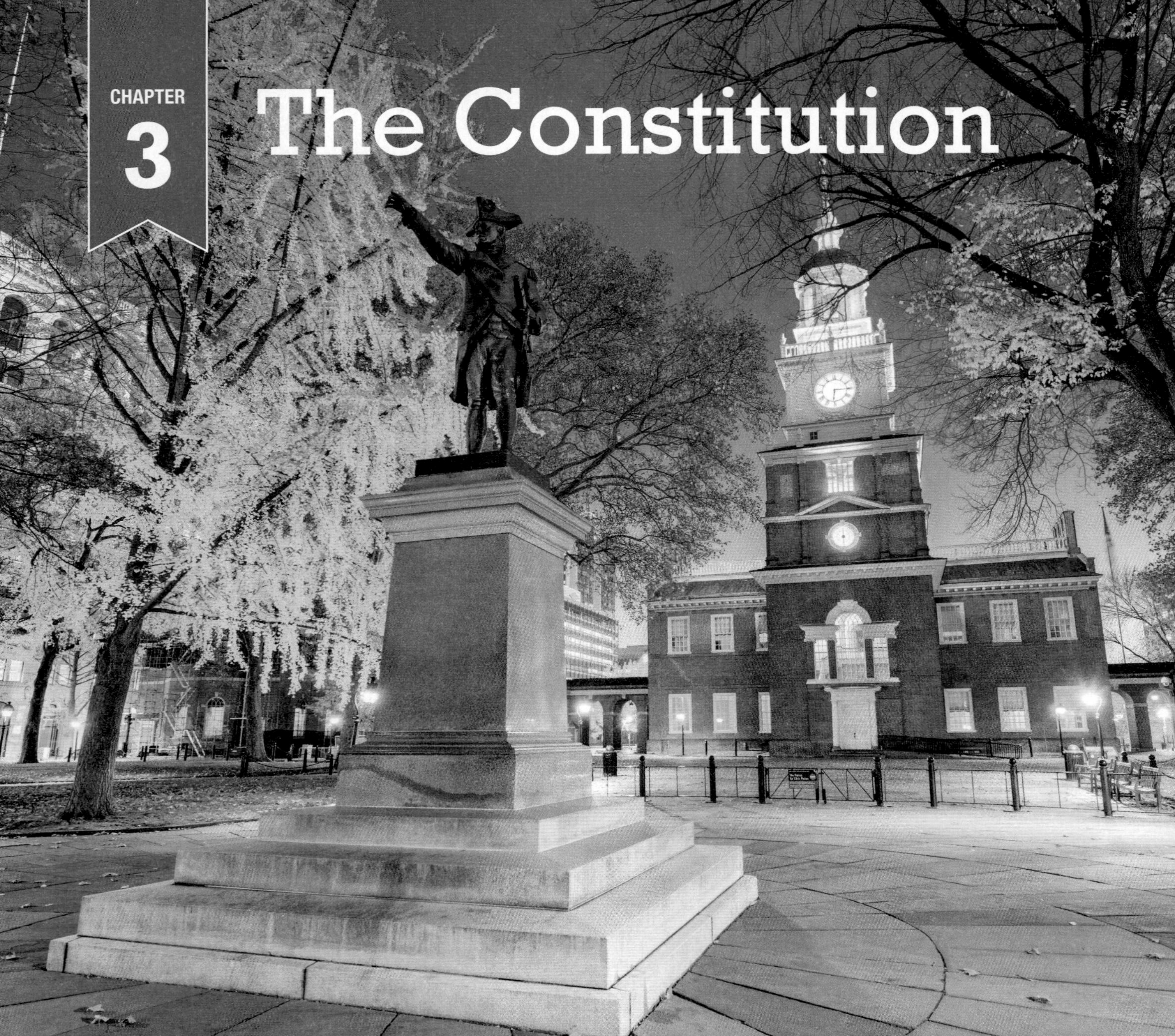

LESSONS

3.1 Overview of the U.S. Constitution

3.2 Popular Sovereignty, Republicanism, Limited Government, and Rule of Law

National Geographic **Magazine:** President Abe Lincoln 150 Years After His Death

3.3 Federalism, Separation of Powers, Checks and Balances, and Individual Rights

3.4 Amending the Constitution

3.5 Analyzing the Amendments

3.6 Putting the Constitution to Work

CRITICAL VIEWING Built in the 1730s as the Pennsylvania State House in Philadelphia, Independence Hall was used by the Second Continental Congress, which approved the Declaration of Independence in 1776, and by the Constitutional Convention, whose delegates wrote the U.S. Constitution in 1787. The building is now known as the birthplace of America. What does that designation say about those two documents?

LESSON
3.1 Overview of the U.S. Constitution

In 1787, Americans faced a crisis. Creating a new nation required many decisions—and lots of money. The Articles of Confederation didn't give any single body the power to make those decisions or raise that money. The national Congress was too weak to make decisions affecting the whole country, and it couldn't collect taxes to fund the government. The individual states didn't want to give up power, and Americans remembered very well their fight to rid themselves of the tyranny of Great Britain. They were suspicious of a strong central government.

Purposes of the U.S. Constitution

The **Framers**, as the delegates to the Constitutional Convention are called today, met in Philadelphia. They faced a difficult challenge—how to create a government that was powerful enough to do what it needed to do but not so powerful that it threatened the liberties of the people. They had been charged with the task of revising the Articles of Confederation. But working behind closed doors, they threw out the Articles and offered something completely new. With remarkable vision, they created in the Constitution a new government structure based on ideas such as popular sovereignty, limited government, and individual rights, principles that would become key to the American identity.

The Framers created a blueprint for a new government that devotes most of its space to describing the three branches of the government—the legislative, executive, and judiciary—and to spelling out the powers and responsibilities of those branches. It also lays out general rules for how government officials will be chosen.

The Framers needed to justify their decision to create a completely new plan for government, as well as explain their purpose in writing the Constitution, so they began the document with a **preamble**, or short introductory statement. The Preamble to the U.S. Constitution reads as follows:

> *We the People of the United States, in Order to form a more perfect Union, establish Justice, insure domestic Tranquility, provide for the common defence, promote the general Welfare, and secure the Blessings of Liberty to ourselves and our Posterity, do ordain and establish this Constitution for the United States of America.*

We can break the Preamble into two sections. The opening and closing phrases state *who* is doing this and *what* they are doing—"We the People" are creating a "Constitution for the United States of America." The middle section explains *why* they are doing it—"in Order to form a more perfect Union, establish Justice, insure domestic Tranquility, provide for the common defence, promote the general Welfare, and secure the Blessings of Liberty."

This middle section can also be broken down into parts. The first part explains why the Framers were taking the radical step of creating a new government. They hoped "to form a more perfect Union." The new government, therefore, was meant to be more complete and better suited to its purpose than that created by the Articles of Confederation. In short, the Framers were saying that they were fixing a broken system. The rest of the middle section outlines what the Framers saw as the proper goals of government. By establishing justice and ensuring domestic tranquility, the new government would create an orderly, fair society where people could live safely and securely. By providing for the common defense, the new government would protect the people from external threats. By promoting the general welfare, the new government would help people achieve what the Declaration called "the pursuit of happiness." The last purpose, to "secure the Blessings of Liberty to ourselves and our Posterity," makes two important points. First, the Framers showed their commitment to the goal of protecting individual freedom that was a driving force behind the American Revolution. Second, they stated their intention that this new government would be a lasting one.

It was important for the Framers to put this new framework of government in writing. The British constitution, in contrast, is **uncodified**. In other words, it is not collected in a single written code of law. It is a mixture of custom, case law based on previous legal decisions, and several historic documents, including the Magna Carta (1215) and the English Bill of Rights (1689). The British constitution grew over the centuries as new elements were added and circumstances changed. The Framers, however, were forming a new government for a new country in a single act of creation. They needed to spell out how that government would be structured and how the different parts would work together.

By describing their ideas in a single written document, the Framers let other Americans—including future generations—know what they had in mind. In addition, the Framers believed the British government had abused its power and taken away their rights. Stating the limits on government power in writing provided some protection against the new government doing the same. Finally, the Framers were following American precedents, or earlier examples. In the Mayflower Compact of 1620, the first settlers in Massachusetts agreed in writing to obey the laws they made. During the Revolution, each state had written its own constitution. And they were replacing a written document, the Articles of Confederation, so it made sense to write out this new plan for government in a single document.

HISTORICAL THINKING

1. **MAKE INFERENCES** Why did the Framers decide to create an entirely new document rather than revise the Articles of Confederation?
2. **IDENTIFY MAIN IDEAS AND DETAILS** Why did the Framers choose to put the Constitution in writing, rather than leaving it uncodified like the British constitution?

A family looks at the pages of the U.S. Constitution inside the Rotunda for the Charters of Freedom of the National Archives in Washington, D.C.

Organization of the U.S. Constitution

The Constitution created a federal system, one that divides power and responsibilities between the states and the national (also known as the federal) government. Following the Preamble, the Constitution is divided into seven major sections called articles. Each article focuses on a specific aspect of the new government.

Article I outlines the structure, composition, and powers of the **legislative branch**, the part of the federal government responsible for making the laws. The legislature, called the U.S. Congress, is bicameral, or consisting of two bodies, or chambers. Those chambers are the House of Representatives and the Senate. Article I lays out the qualifications for membership in each chamber. It also identifies the presiding officers of each chamber, details the powers specific to each chamber, and sets the rules for the sessions of Congress. Article I, Section 7, explains how a bill becomes a law. Article I, Section 8, lists the powers of Congress. For example, one of the powers given to Congress is the exclusive power to print and coin money.

Article II creates a new **executive branch**, the part of the government responsible for carrying out the laws. The executive branch of the federal government includes the president, vice president, and the executive departments such as the Department of Defense. Article II, Section 1, states the qualifications of the president and vice president. The section also describes the method for electing these two leaders. Article II, Section 2, spells out the powers of the president—including the power to appoint federal officials and judges. It also discusses the president's relationship to Congress, and explains the president's role in working with other countries. It also explains how the president, and all other officers of the federal government, may be impeached and removed from office. The Constitution gives Congress the power to impeach, or to charge and try a public official for crimes that might result in removal, which is another example of the checks and balances the Framers built into the new government.

3 BRANCHES of U.S. GOVERNMENT
LEGISLATIVE BRANCH
House of Representatives (435 members, based on state population)
Senate (100 members, 2 per state)
Congressional support offices
RESPONSIBILITY: To make laws
EXECUTIVE BRANCH
President
Vice President
Cabinet departments (15 departments)
Other executive agencies and bureaus
RESPONSIBILITY: To carry out laws
JUDICIAL BRANCH
U.S. Supreme Court (9 justices)
U.S. Courts of Appeal (13 courts)
U.S. District Courts (94 courts)
Other specialized courts
RESPONSIBILITY: To interpret laws

Article III describes the **judicial branch**, the part of the government chiefly responsible for interpreting the laws and resolving controversies. This article states that there will be a national Supreme Court responsible for hearing certain types of cases, and that Congress has the power to create other courts as needed. The Framers were very specific about the lengths of the terms of federal judges. Article III states that federal judges will have lifetime appointments—in other words, they can serve until they choose to retire or they die in office, though Congress can remove them for serious misconduct. The point of this provision was to ensure that judges make their rulings based solely on the

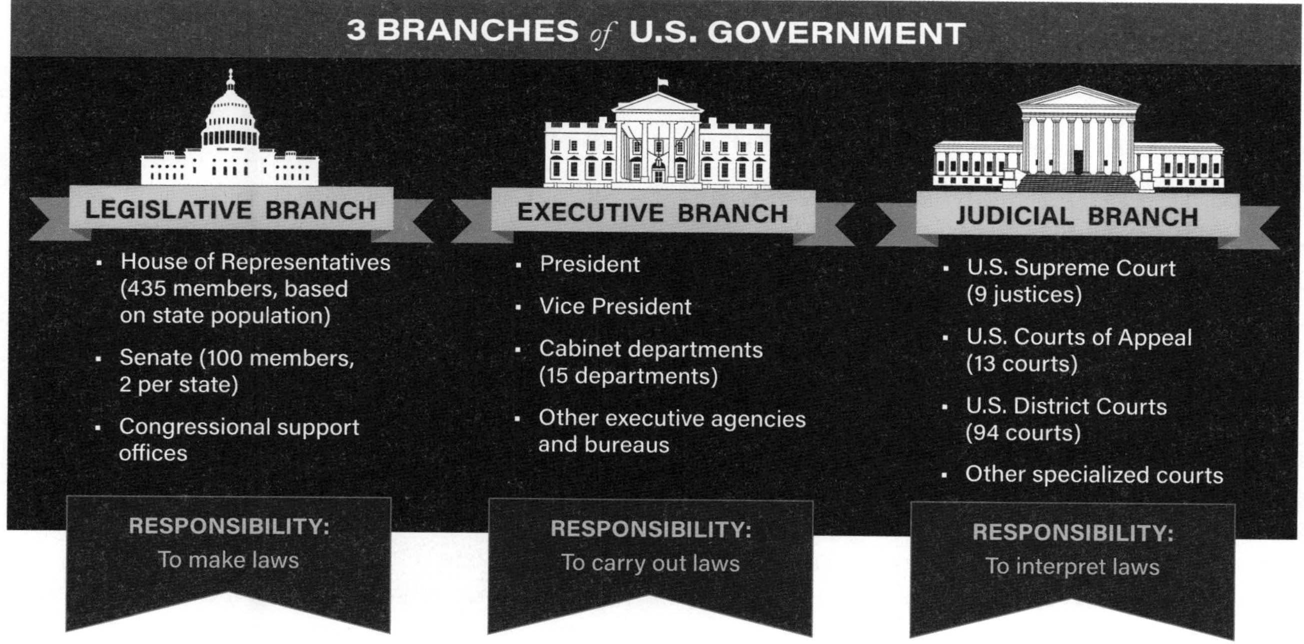

law and would not be influenced by the need to seek approval from the voters or anyone else.

Article IV covers relations among the states. It calls on the states to recognize each other's laws and treat citizens of other states fairly. This article also looks to the future growth of the country. It gives Congress the power to set up territories, and it lays out rules for admitting those territories as new states. Finally, it guarantees that all states will have a republican form of government, meaning one in which voters have the power to choose their own representatives.

Article V explains how to add **amendments**, or formal changes to the Constitution made by constitutional procedure. It provides two methods for proposing amendments and two methods to ratify, or formally approve, them. The Framers allowed for amendments because they did not want to tie the hands of future generations. Yet they did not want making changes to be too easy, either. They made the amendment process difficult enough to prevent frivolous changes or those favored by only a small minority. At the same time, they made the process easier than it had been under the Articles of Confederation.

Article VI includes the **supremacy clause**, which states that the Constitution and federal laws "shall be the supreme Law of the Land." This may seem obvious today, but it struck at the very heart of what the Framers were doing. The laws of the Confederation Congress were often ignored by the states, which at times viewed them as little more than requests. Article VI emphasized the importance of the Constitution by requiring that all officeholders—state and federal—swear to uphold the Constitution when taking office. It also states that "no religious Test" shall ever be required of anyone in order to hold office.

Finally, Article VII spells out the method by which the Constitution would take effect—after ratification by 9 of the 13 states. By requiring approval from only 9 states, the Framers hoped to persuade states to ratify it early. They also hoped to prevent any states that withheld approval from demanding special favors in return for that approval. While Article VII says that only 9 states needed to ratify the Constitution, the Framers believed that all 13 would eventually do so. And they did, though two states delayed for a long time. North Carolina and Rhode Island did not ratify it until George Washington had been sworn in as president and the First Congress had taken office.

Overview of the U.S. Constitution

ARTICLE	SUMMARY OF CONTENTS
Article I	Legislative branch
Article II	Executive branch
Article III	Judicial branch
Article IV	Relations among states and formation of new states
Article V	Process for amending the Constitution
Article VI	Constitution and federal laws as supreme law of the land
Article VII	Ratification process for the Constitution

These articles set up the government structure the Framers thought was needed to meet their goals for the Constitution. Creating a federal court system provides a mechanism for seeking justice. It also protects people's liberties. With more powers, the central government would be able to do a better job of ensuring domestic tranquility and promoting the general welfare. Creating an executive who was commander in chief of the armed forces gave the government a greater ability to provide for the common defense.

HISTORICAL THINKING

3. **MAKE INFERENCES** What can you infer about the Framers' thinking about the three branches from the fact that the Constitution defines the legislative power first?
4. **ANALYZE VISUALS** What parts of each branch of the government shown in the diagram are not actually found in the Constitution?
5. **COMPARE AND CONTRAST** What are two ways that the government set up by the Constitution differs from the government under the Articles of Confederation?

Principles of the U.S. Constitution

The United States Constitution is built on eight key principles. These principles reflect the Framers' ideas of what is required for a just, effective government.

- **Popular sovereignty**—The ultimate power in a democracy rests with the people.
- **Republicanism**—The people exercise their sovereignty through elected representatives rather than voting directly on laws.
- **Limited government**—The Constitution limits government power to safeguard the rights of the people. The Framers included rules that prevented one individual from having too much power and made sure that one branch could not dominate government. Finally, they tried to make sure that the majority could not take away the rights of a minority.
- **Rule of law**—Under the Constitution, the people are governed by laws, not rulers. No person is above the law, and the law applies equally to all. Only then can justice be achieved.
- **Federalism**—Government power is divided between the national, or federal, government and the state governments. This creates a stronger central government while still preserving state power in some areas.
- **Separation of powers**—Government power is spread among executive, legislative, and judicial branches.
- **Checks and balances**—The Constitution grants each branch certain powers to check, or limit, the power of other branches to prevent tyranny and a concentration of power in any one branch.
- **Individual rights**—The Framers believed individuals have basic rights that no government can take away without due process of law. Having seen freedoms curtailed by the British, the Framers wanted to ensure that the new government would be prevented from depriving people of their rights.

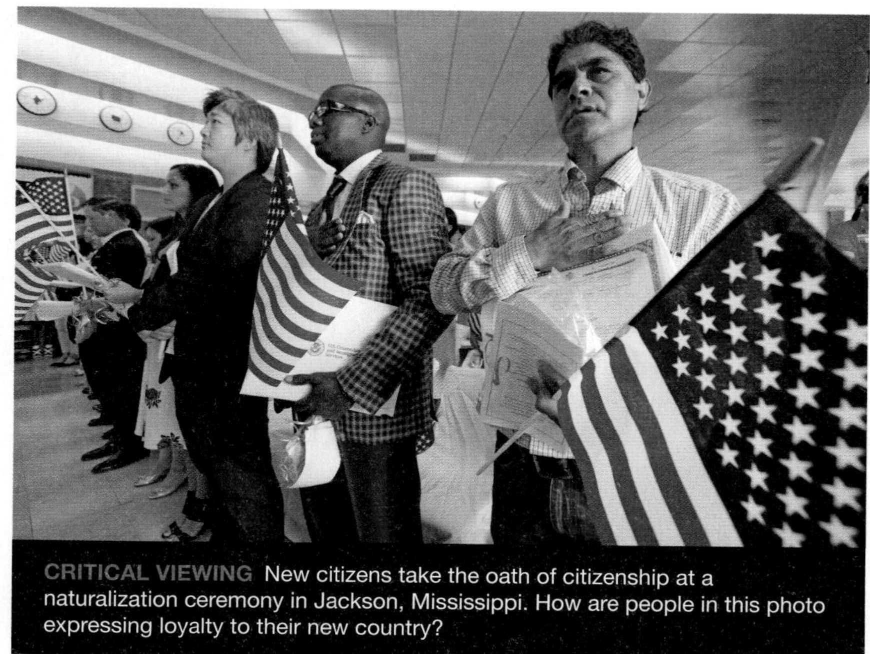

CRITICAL VIEWING New citizens take the oath of citizenship at a naturalization ceremony in Jackson, Mississippi. How are people in this photo expressing loyalty to their new country?

These principles form the bedrock of American identity. They were expressed first in the Declaration of Independence. For example, the Declaration announced the determination of a free people to seize the power of governing their lives for themselves. They also appear in the statement that "all men are created equal" and have rights to "life, liberty, and the pursuit of happiness." The Constitution gave these ideas shape and substance. They continue to unite all Americans, old and new, regardless of race or ethnicity, religion, gender, or place of birth. Each year in the 2010s, from 600,000 to nearly 800,000 people born in another country became naturalized citizens. They swore an oath of **allegiance**, or loyalty, and promised to "support and defend the Constitution and laws of the United States of America." In taking that oath, they became Americans and adopted the principles of the Constitution and the Declaration of Independence embodied in the United States today.

HISTORICAL THINKING

6. **CATEGORIZE** The U.S. Supreme Court building has "Equal Justice Under Law" engraved on it. Which principle does that phrase represent?
7. **MAKE CONNECTIONS** Which other principles of the Constitution are related to the principle of limited government?

LESSON 3.2 Popular Sovereignty, Republicanism, Limited Government, and Rule of Law

Early in November of every even-numbered year, Americans go to the polls to cast their ballots for members of the House of Representatives as well as for state and local officials. In some years, they vote for one of their U.S. senators. Every four years, they can vote for president. When they cast these votes, they demonstrate two principles of the Constitution. Their votes reflect popular sovereignty—the idea that the people are the ultimate source of the government's power. And they choose the people who will represent them, putting republicanism into action.

Popular Sovereignty

The words that begin the Preamble reflect a fundamental point about American government. The U.S. Constitution is written to express the intentions of "We the People." Of course, "the people" did not actually write the Constitution, but the Framers believed they were expressing the will of the people. The focus on "the people" in the Preamble contrasts sharply with the beginning of the Articles of Confederation. That document formed a "perpetual Union between the states." In other words, the Articles of Confederation were an agreement among the states. The Constitution is an act of and for the people.

The opening of the Preamble reflects the principle of popular sovereignty, based on the idea that the people of a country hold the ultimate power. The people form a government and decide on the powers that government can exercise. If the government exercises powers beyond those granted by the Constitution, it is acting illegally.

This principle reflects the thinking of English political philosopher John Locke. In Locke's view of the social contract, the people become the fundamental source of authority when they agree to join together and live under a common set of laws. Through their consent, they give authority to the government that makes the laws. Locke's ideas influenced Thomas Jefferson as he wrote the Declaration of Independence, because Locke argued that a ruler who did not uphold the social contract could be overthrown. Without the people, the government has no power, and the main task of the government is to meet the needs of the people. Abraham Lincoln explained this idea years later in the Gettysburg Address. The fundamental principle of American government under the Constitution, he said, is "government of the people, by the people, for the people."

HISTORICAL THINKING

1. **COMPARE AND CONTRAST** How does the idea of popular sovereignty in the Constitution contrast with the view of the national government under the Articles of Confederation?
2. **MAKE CONNECTIONS** How does the right "to throw off" a tyrannical government that Jefferson stated in the Declaration of Independence connect to the principle of popular sovereignty?

Republicanism

While the Framers believed that the people were the source of power, they also worried about having the people govern directly. As a result, they established a republic, a form of representative democracy in which the people elect representatives who make and carry out the laws.

In establishing a republic, the Framers were guided by precedent. As colonists, Americans had elected officials for local town and county governments. They had also elected members of the assemblies that passed laws for the colonies. Still, the Framers' decision to form a republic stemmed from more than

Newly elected members of the House of Representatives gather for a group photo on the steps of the U.S. Capitol in 2018 in the midst of orientation sessions.

precedent. They believed a republic would be more effective in protecting people's liberties.

In Federalist No. 10, James Madison explains the advantages of **republicanism** with two strong arguments. First, he says representative democracy acts as a safeguard against the dangers of what he calls **"faction,"** by which he meant a group of people working together because they had a common interest that might or might not be at odds with the interests of most other people. He saw factions as one of the greatest dangers facing popular government. He worried that a united faction would act in its own interest, ignoring the interests of others or the greater good. Madison believed that in a direct democracy—in which the people themselves make the laws—there was a greater risk that one faction could seize control of government. But in a representative democracy, he believed voters would select the wisest people, who would be moved by "patriotism and love of justice," to represent them and pursue the common good.

Second, Madison argued that a republican form of government was well suited to a country the size of the United States. In his view, the larger the republic, the greater the number of wise leaders there would be. And since there were more of them, there was a higher likelihood that those wise people would be elected to public office. Furthermore, a large republic would have a greater collection of competing interests. That is, a large republic will have more factions than a small republic and each faction will find it more difficult to become strong enough to dominate the others. In other words, the best way to solve the problem of factions was to have more of them.

For Madison, then, the chief value of a republic was that it was more stable, effective, and capable of protecting the liberties of the people. Madison was not alone in recognizing the value of republicanism. The Patriots who fought in the American Revolution saw themselves as republicans. So, too, did many of the Framers. Recall that in Article IV, Section 4, they included a guarantee that every state would have a republican form of government.

But how could republicanism be squared with the idea of popular sovereignty? The answer was simple: in a republic, the people retain the ultimate authority and power; they merely loan it to their elected representatives. And they maintain control over those representatives through elections. That is why the Framers made members of the House of Representatives stand for election every two years. They wanted the House of Representatives to be the people's house, elected by the people. This was a departure from the way the Confederation Congress was organized. Members of that body were chosen by the state legislatures.

At the same time, the Framers hedged their bets. They were concerned about the vulnerability of the people to a **demagogue**, a leader who makes use of popular prejudices and false claims and promises in order to gain power. These leaders appeal to passion rather than reason and are more interested in gaining power than in working for the common good. For this reason, the Framers did not give the people the power to choose all government officials. Members of the Senate would be chosen by each state's legislature, not directly by the people. This method of electing senators remained in effect until 1913, when the 17th Amendment was ratified, establishing the current system of direct election of senators by the people.

HISTORICAL THINKING

3. **FORM AND SUPPORT AN OPINION** Write a statement agreeing or disagreeing with Madison's ideas about factions. Explain your reasoning.

4. **IDENTIFY MAIN IDEAS AND DETAILS** Explain why the Framers had people vote for members of the House of Representatives every two years.

Limited Government

The government the Framers created embodied the principle of limited government, or a government whose powers and actions are limited by a system of laws. The Framers drew this concept from the ideas of such Enlightenment thinkers as Locke. But they also derived lessons from their own experience with the British government prior to the American Revolution. For example, in 1767, Parliament passed a law that suspended New York's colonial assembly until New Yorkers agreed to pay for the housing of British troops. Several years later, to punish Massachusetts, Parliament passed a law that took away the colony's charter and banned town meetings without British approval. Americans saw these laws as outrageous acts depriving them of their right to self-government. They were determined to form a government that could not abuse its powers.

The Framers wove the principle of limited government throughout the Constitution. Articles I, II, and III, for example, list the powers of each branch of the national government. At the same time, the Constitution lists actions government cannot take. For example, Article I, Section 9, says "no Bill of Attainder or ex post facto Law shall be passed." A bill of attainder is a law that directs punishment at a particular individual or group. The Framers saw such laws as unfairly punishing a person or group without giving them the benefit of a trial. An ex post facto law is one that makes a legal action illegal after it has been taken or increases the punishment for a crime after the crime has been committed. The Framers thought both situations were unjust. By preventing Congress from making such laws, they limited its power.

These limits on the power of government did not necessarily protect the rights of individuals. Several states insisted on a Bill of Rights as a condition for their ratification of the Constitution. Therefore, Congress proposed a series of amendments to protect individual liberties a few months after the new government was formed. These first 10 amendments to the Constitution protect basic civil liberties from government action. The limits placed on government power by the Bill of Rights are among the most cherished features of the U.S. Constitution.

Limited government has remained a guiding principle of the Constitution. The 22nd Amendment, ratified in 1951, set a **term limit**, or a maximum number of terms that a person is allowed to hold office, on the presidency. In 1992, the 27th Amendment gained ratification. It said that if Congress voted to give itself a pay raise, the raise couldn't take effect until after the next election. In effect, the voters would have the chance to replace their representatives if they thought the raise wasn't merited.

HISTORICAL THINKING

5. **ANALYZE CAUSE AND EFFECT** How did experience with British colonial rule lead to the desire for limited government in the United States?

6. **DRAW CONCLUSIONS** How would placing term limits on an office limit the power of the person in that role?

The Rule of Law

Another important principle of the Constitution is the rule of law. This is the simple but profound idea that no one, including government officials, is above the law. The ability of a democracy to survive rests on the willingness of the people and their leaders to obey the rule of law. A nation's written constitution may guarantee numerous rights and liberties for its citizens. Yet, unless the government enforces those rights and liberties, the law does not rule the nation. Rather, the government decides what the rules will be.

The rule of law extends to the highest office of the land. Article II, Section 4, states that government officials can be removed from office. For that to happen, they must first be formally charged with crimes or misconduct in the House of Representatives, the first stage of the impeachment process. This happens if a majority of the House finds the official has committed "Treason, Bribery, or other high Crimes and

The Electoral and Popular Votes for President in 2016

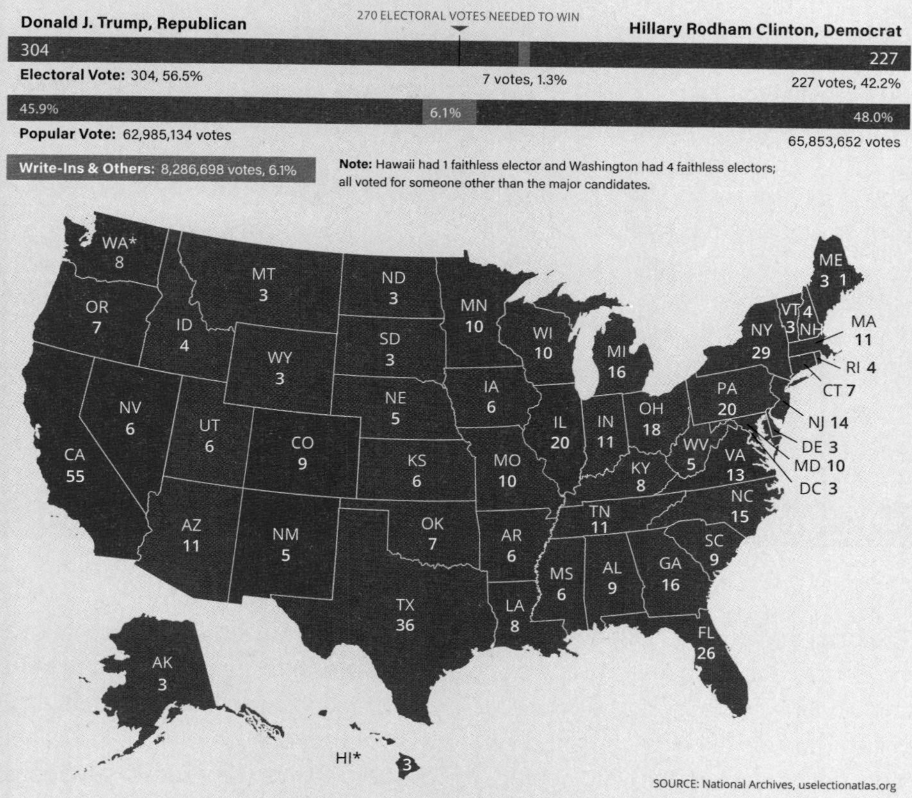

The Electoral College

The Framers also removed the office of president from direct election by the people. They invented the electoral college to make the final choice. It works this way: The political parties in each state and in the District of Columbia choose slates of potential electors who pledge to vote for the party's eventual presidential candidate. In most states, the presidential candidate who wins the popular vote gets all the electoral votes. (Nebraska and Maine sometimes split their electoral votes.)

The number of electors in each state equals the number of people serving the state in the U.S. Congress. So, for instance, a state like Montana, with only one member of the House, gets three electoral votes—two for its senators and one for the House member. California and Texas, the states with the largest populations, had 55 and 38 electoral votes respectively in 2016. To win the presidency, a candidate must have a majority of the electoral votes.

Currently, the threshold for victory is 270 electoral votes. Because most electoral votes from most states are awarded on a winner-take-all basis, a candidate can win the nationwide popular vote by racking up large margins in some states but still lose the presidency. That has happened a number of times, including in both 2000 and 2016. The proportions of the total popular and electoral votes that candidates win can be very different. In 2016, Hillary Clinton won 48 percent of the popular vote and Donald Trump had just over 46 percent. (Third-party candidates made up the difference.) Trump, however, won 57 percent of the electoral votes while Clinton had only 43 percent.

The National Popular Vote Interstate Compact, which would guarantee that the presidential candidate who won the most popular votes would be elected in the electoral college, has been introduced in all 50 states and the District of Columbia. Passage in jurisdictions controllng 270 electoral votes—a majority—would put the bill in effect nationwide.

CRITICAL VIEWING The right to demonstrate for a cause, such as urging officials to consider scientific evidence in creating government policies, is enshrined in the Bill of Rights. What details in this photograph from the April 22, 2017, March for Science in Washington, D.C., indicate that this group is well organized?

Misdemeanors." The official who is impeached is then put on trial, with the Senate acting as the jury. If two-thirds of the senators find the official guilty, he or she is removed from office. The idea of impeachment drew on British legal history dating back to the 14th century. It had been used by Parliament to remove from office government ministers who were seen as corrupt or incompetent. The Framers' decision that even the chief executive could be removed from office reflected their deep belief that no person was above the law.

In 1974, the U.S. Supreme Court ruling in *United States* v. *Nixon* reflected the principle of rule of law. President Nixon refused to turn over tape recordings of conversations he had with aides who had been charged with crimes related to his campaign on the grounds of **executive privilege**. This is a president's claim to withhold information from Congress and the courts in order to safeguard the internal deliberations of the executive branch. Nixon claimed that his private conversations with aides were protected by this principle. The Supreme Court unanimously ruled against the president, saying that executive privilege didn't apply to a criminal matter. Even the president, the court said, had to obey the law.

Presidents since Nixon, both Democrat and Republican, have continued to assert executive privilege, particularly in dealings with Congress. Usually, the two branches arrive at a compromise, allowing Congress to exercise its oversight functions while preserving a president's right to confidential deliberations with close advisers. In 2019, for example, a congressional committee investigating potentially illegal dealings with Russia subpoenaed Donald McGahn, former counsel to President Trump. The president blocked McGahn from testifying, citing executive privilege. A U.S. Appeals Court recognized Congress's oversight powers and right to enforce its subpoena in August 2020, but additional challenges by the executive branch continued.

The concept of the rule of law applies to the criminal justice system as well. Police officers, for example, must follow strict standards set out in the Bill of Rights about how they obtain evidence when they investigate a crime. They also have to treat people they suspect of a crime in ways that meet certain standards. If they violate those standards, the courts can overturn a conviction. In this way, the Bill of Rights aims to ensure equal justice to all.

HISTORICAL THINKING

7. **MAKE CONNECTIONS** How are the constitutional bans on bills of attainder and ex post facto laws examples of the rule of law?

8. **DESCRIBE** How did the Supreme Court's decision in *United States* v. *Nixon* show the principle of the rule of law?

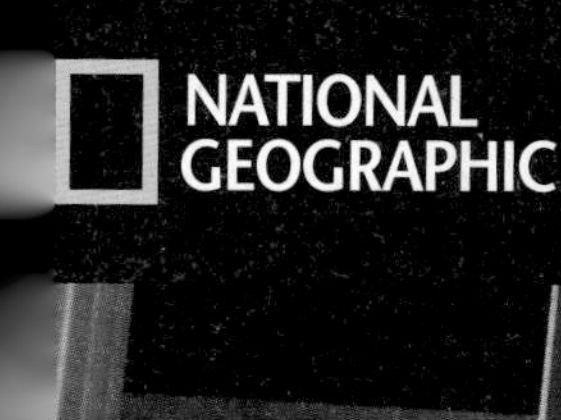

Sculptor Daniel Chester French designed the 19-foot statue of Lincoln that sits in the Lincoln Memorial in hopes of portraying the president's strength and compassion. To execute the work, he hired in 1918 the six brothers of the Piccirilli family, who came from a New York family highly skilled in working marble and needed four years to complete the carving.

President Abe Lincoln 150 Years After His Death

by Adam Goodheart ***National Geographic*** **Magazine, April 2015**

Abraham Lincoln took what the Framers of the U.S. Constitution envisioned for their country to heart. The founding principles on which the Constitution is built—such as individual rights and rule of law—were key to Lincoln's political philosophy. He was not part of the founding generation, but he revived and added to the legacy of the founding principles as the Great Emancipator and Savior of the Union.

In the *National Geographic* article, "President Abe Lincoln 150 Years After His Death," writer Adam Goodheart describes the impact Lincoln had and still has on the United States. He focuses on how Lincoln's assassination just after the Civil War profoundly affected the American public and how tensions Americans faced then—between the North and the South and concerning individual rights—still exist today. As Goodheart travels the old railroad route that Lincoln's funeral train followed, he reports current American stories of gay activism, racism, gun ownership, allegiance to the Confederacy, and disenchantment with being a soldier.

Despite the fact these tensions still exist, Goodheart finds that "to follow the route of Lincoln's train is to discover how much his spirit still pervades the nation he loved and saved." At one point on the journey, Goodheart rests on a bench that straddles the old boundary between slave and free states—the Mason-Dixon Line—and reflects:

> *Earth's most impassable barriers—as Lincoln the lawyer knew, as Lincoln the writer knew—are often those formed not of walls and trenches, nor even of mountains and oceans, but of laws and words. At this spot, as at no historic site I've visited, I feel the terrible arbitrariness of slavery. But Lincoln also knew that a line made of laws and words, no matter how formidable, could be erased with new laws and words. He made this line cease to exist. No wonder newly freed African Americans lined the sides of these tracks throughout the first day of his funeral journey.*

Access the full version of "President Abe Lincoln 150 Years After His Death" by Adam Goodheart through the Resources Menu in MindTap.

THINK ABOUT IT What connections can you make between the presidency of Abraham Lincoln and the

LESSON 3.3

Federalism, Separation of Powers, Checks and Balances, and Individual Rights

Are people basically concerned about the public good? Or are they basically selfish? James Madison thought people tended to be selfish when it came to politics. How, then, could the Framers make a government that prevented people in power from promoting their own interests at the expense of others? They did it by dividing power. Principles such as the separation of powers and checks and balances prevent each branch of the federal government from abusing its power.

Federalism

While the Framers believed ultimate sovereignty rested with the people, they had to confront the practical problem of whether the states or the national government would have the day-to-day decision-making powers. Under the Articles of Confederation, the states had most of that power. The national government did not have enough power to get things done. Seeking a better balance in the Constitution, the Framers adopted the principle of **federalism**, the distribution of power in a government between a central authority and the constituent units, in this case the national government and state governments. They assigned some powers exclusively to the national government and other powers exclusively to the states. There were some powers that both the national and state governments would possess, but only in their respective areas.

NATIONAL POWERS Compared to the Articles of Confederation, the Constitution gives the national government a robust collection of powers. For starters, the Constitution declares that it and the laws created by the national government are supreme. That is, they take precedence over conflicting state laws. The Constitution gives Congress the sole power to coin money. Under the Articles, both state and national governments could issue money. The Constitution gives Congress the power to collect taxes. Under the Articles, the best that the Confederation Congress could do was to ask the states for contributions, but it could not force them to pay.

The Constitution gives Congress the power to regulate **commerce**, or business activities, between the states themselves and between the states and foreign countries. Under the Articles, states were free to lay tariffs on goods from other states, discouraging the free flow of goods. The last sentence of Section 8 of Article 1 is the **necessary and proper clause**, often referred to as the *elastic clause* because it gives elasticity to our constitutional system by stating that Congress can make "all laws which shall be necessary and proper" for carrying out its delegated powers. (Delegated powers are those powers expressly given to the federal government.) As you will read later in this chapter, the necessary and proper clause, as it is called, amounted to an invitation for Congress to enlarge the scope of its activities, not to mention its powers, over the years.

STATE POWERS If you searched the Constitution for a mention of specific powers given to the states, you wouldn't find many. (The 21st Amendment is an exception. It gives states the power to regulate the sale of alcohol.) The delegates at the Constitutional Convention didn't think they needed to spell those powers out, so you'd have better luck looking for powers denied the states, explicitly or implicitly. The delegates knew the states already had considerable powers, so they focused on defining the powers of the national government, and that sometimes meant denying powers to the states. Moreover, the delegates assumed that powers not given to the national government remained with the states.

When the Constitution went to the states for ratification, however, many people voiced concern that the national government envisioned by the new plan would be too powerful. To address concerns that the Constitution would allow the national government to amass power at the expense of the state governments, the First Congress added the Tenth Amendment. This

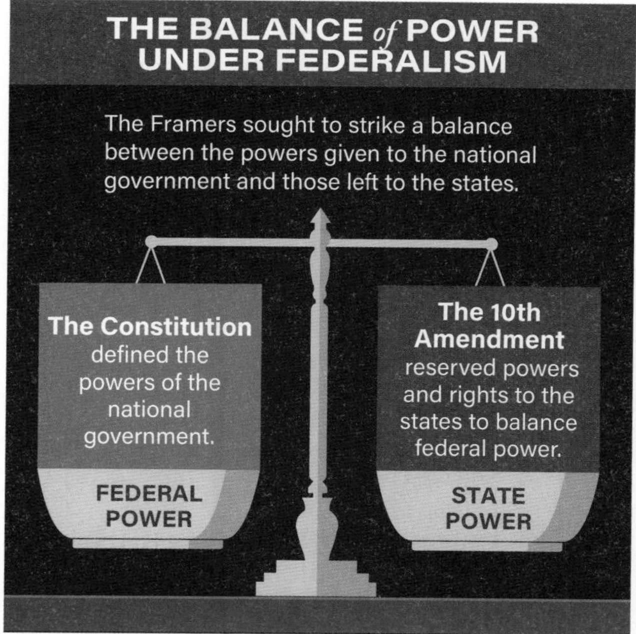

amendment says that "The powers not delegated to the United States by the Constitution, nor prohibited by it to the States, are reserved to the States respectively, or to the people." That leaves to the states everything from regulating businesses operating within state borders to creating schools; from licensing automobiles to determining how much smog those automobiles can generate; from establishing cities and towns to building roads and bridges—and much more besides.

THE BALANCE of POWER UNDER FEDERALISM
The Framers sought to strike a balance between the powers given to the national government and those left to the states.
The Constitution defined the powers of the national government.
FEDERAL POWER
The 10th Amendment reserved powers and rights to the states to balance federal power.
STATE POWER

HISTORICAL THINKING

1. **FORM AND SUPPORT OPINIONS** Explain why you agree or disagree with Madison's beliefs about what motivates people in politics.
2. **ANALYZE VISUALS** Based on the diagram, what are the two mechanisms by which the Constitution distributes power under federalism?
3. **SYNTHESIZE** How do you think small states would react to a constitution based on the principle of federalism? Explain your answer.

Separation of Powers

The Framers feared concentrating too much power in any one place. In creating a federal system, they divided power between the national and state governments. In creating a federal government with three branches, they prevented any person or group from holding too much power in the national government. They did so by giving different branches of government separate powers. They also tried to make sure these branches were co-equal.

This decision was based on the work of French political philosopher the Baron Charles de Montesquieu. In his book *The Spirit of Laws,* he set forth the principle of separation of powers, or the idea of dividing government power into distinct branches to ensure that no one branch can dominate the others. He viewed the powers of government as legislative, executive, and judicial, and argued that these powers must be separated to prevent tyranny.

Montesquieu's writing greatly influenced the Framers, especially Madison. According to Madison, once the government has the ability to control its citizens, it is important to "oblige it to control itself." To force the government to "control itself," Madison devised what is known today as the Madisonian Model. This scheme separates the powers of the national government into the different branches you've already read about. The legislative branch (Congress) passes laws. The executive branch, headed by the president, administers and carries out the laws. The judicial branch, the courts, interprets the laws. By separating the powers of government, the Framers tried to keep any one branch from dominating the others.

HISTORICAL THINKING

4. **DESCRIBE** How does the Madisonian Model prevent the concentration of power?
5. **EVALUATE** Do you agree or disagree with Montesquieu's—and Madison's—view of the three types of governmental power? Explain.

Checks and Balances

Along with the separation of powers, the Framers adopted another of Montesquieu's ideas. They formed a system of **checks and balances**, in which each of the branches of government has the ability to limit the power of the other two. The purpose is to ensure that no one group or branch of government could control

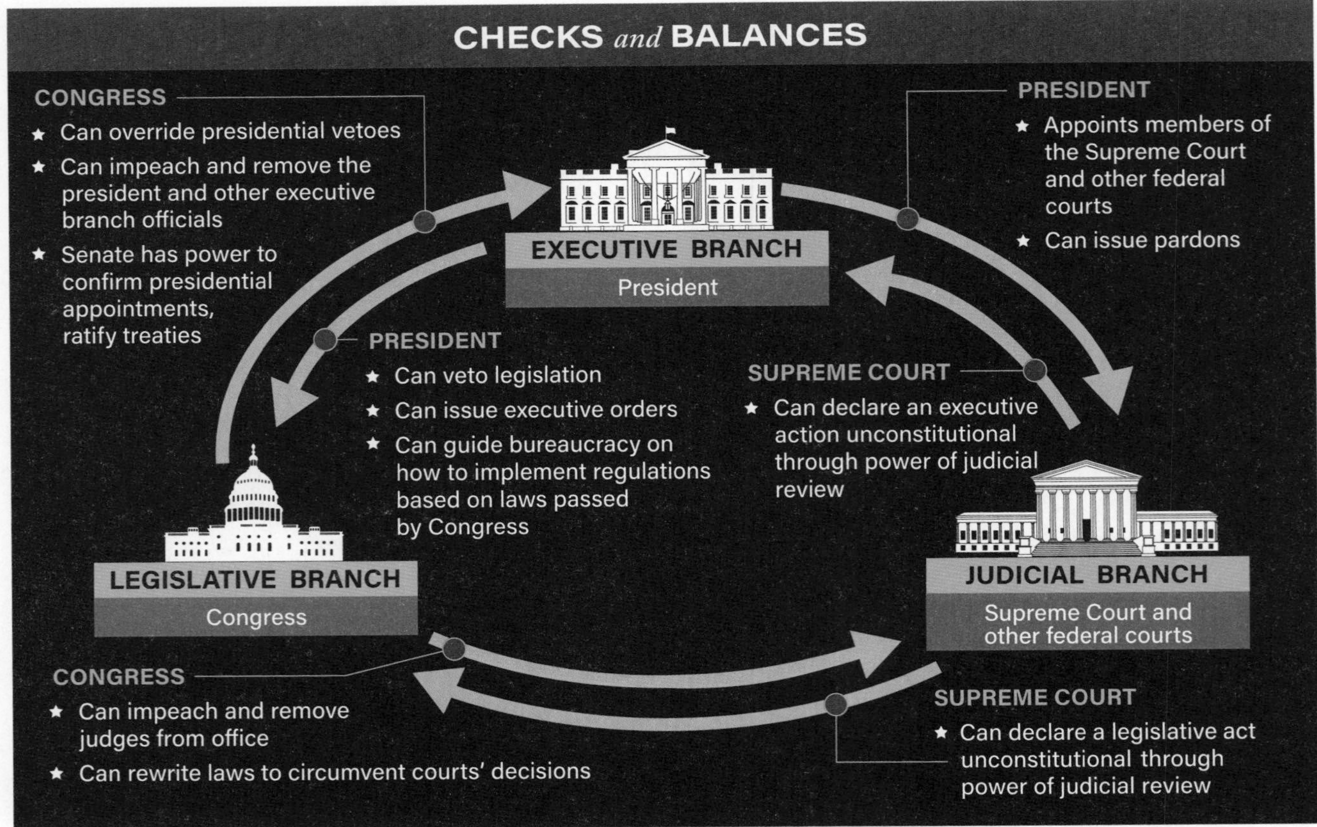
CHECKS and BALANCES
CONGRESS
Can override presidential vetoes
Can impeach and remove the president and other executive branch officials
Senate has power to confirm presidential appointments, ratify treaties
EXECUTIVE BRANCH
President
PRESIDENT
Appoints members of the Supreme Court and other federal courts
Can issue pardons
PRESIDENT
Can veto legislation
Can issue executive orders
Can guide bureaucracy on how to implement regulations based on laws passed by Congress
SUPREME COURT
Can declare an executive action unconstitutional through power of judicial review
LEGISLATIVE BRANCH
Congress
JUDICIAL BRANCH
Supreme Court and other federal courts
CONGRESS
Can impeach and remove judges from office
Can rewrite laws to circumvent courts' decisions
SUPREME COURT
Can declare a legislative act unconstitutional through power of judicial review

the others. Even though each branch of government is independent of the others, it can also check the actions of the others. This principle also ensures limited government.

As the diagram shows, the president checks Congress by holding the power of veto, which is the ability to reject bills and return them to Congress for reconsideration. Congress, in turn, has a check on the president through the veto override. This is the power to cancel a presidential veto if two-thirds of each chamber of Congress votes to approve a bill that had been vetoed. In addition, the Senate must approve the president's nominations for major positions in the executive branch. The judicial branch can check the other branches with its power to say that laws passed by Congress or actions taken by the president are **unconstitutional**, or in violation of the rules set forth in the Constitution. (You'll learn more about how the judicial branch claimed that power later in this chapter.) In turn, the president and the Senate have some control over the judicial branch. The president has the power to appoint federal judges, but only after the Senate approves the judges the president nominates.

Among the other checks and balances built into the American system are staggered terms of office. Members of the House of Representatives serve for two years, members of the Senate for six, and the president for four. By staggering these terms of office, the Framers made it difficult for officials to form controlling factions. For instance, two years after a president is elected, the people vote once again for every member of the House of Representatives. They also elect a third of the Senate at that time. If people disapprove of the job a president is doing, they can elect members of Congress who are likely to limit the president's ability to carry out an agenda.

The terms of office of federal judges are another example of these checks and balances. Since they have lifetime appointments, judges are free from undue political influence or pressures, but their power is checked by Congress, which can impeach and remove federal judges for misconduct. You'll read about many other checks and balances, and how the different branches of government employ them to advance their goals, in later chapters of this book.

HISTORICAL THINKING

6. **DRAW CONCLUSIONS** How does the system of checks and balances help ensure that power is divided among the three branches of the federal government?
7. **ANALYZE VISUALS** What are the checks that the legislative branch has on the judicial branch?
8. **MAKE CONNECTIONS** How are principles such as the separation of powers and checks and balances related to the principle of limited government?

Individual Rights

The principle of individual rights is founded on the Enlightenment idea of natural rights, which comes from the belief that every human being has basic human rights. In the Declaration of Independence, Jefferson referred to these rights as "unalienable," meaning they could not be taken or given away. He included among them the rights of "Life, Liberty, and the Pursuit of Happiness."

One reason the Framers wished to prevent excessive government power was to protect the individual rights of citizens. They had seen these rights threatened by King George and the British Parliament. For example, in the 1760s, the British began to aggressively use writs of assistance. These search warrants allowed the authorities to enter any home to search for smuggled goods. This kind of generalized search warrant went against tradition. Americans believed the police should have a specific warrant for a specific location belonging to a particular person suspected of specific crimes. They saw these writs as abuses of power.

The Framers provided some protections of basic rights. For example, Article I, Section 9, states that the right of habeas corpus cannot be suspended, or taken away. This right, from Latin words meaning "you should have the body," prevents the government from holding someone in custody in secret. If challenged, the government has to admit that it is holding a person. It also has to charge anyone being held with a specific crime.

Many of the state constitutions written during the American Revolution contained bills of rights protecting

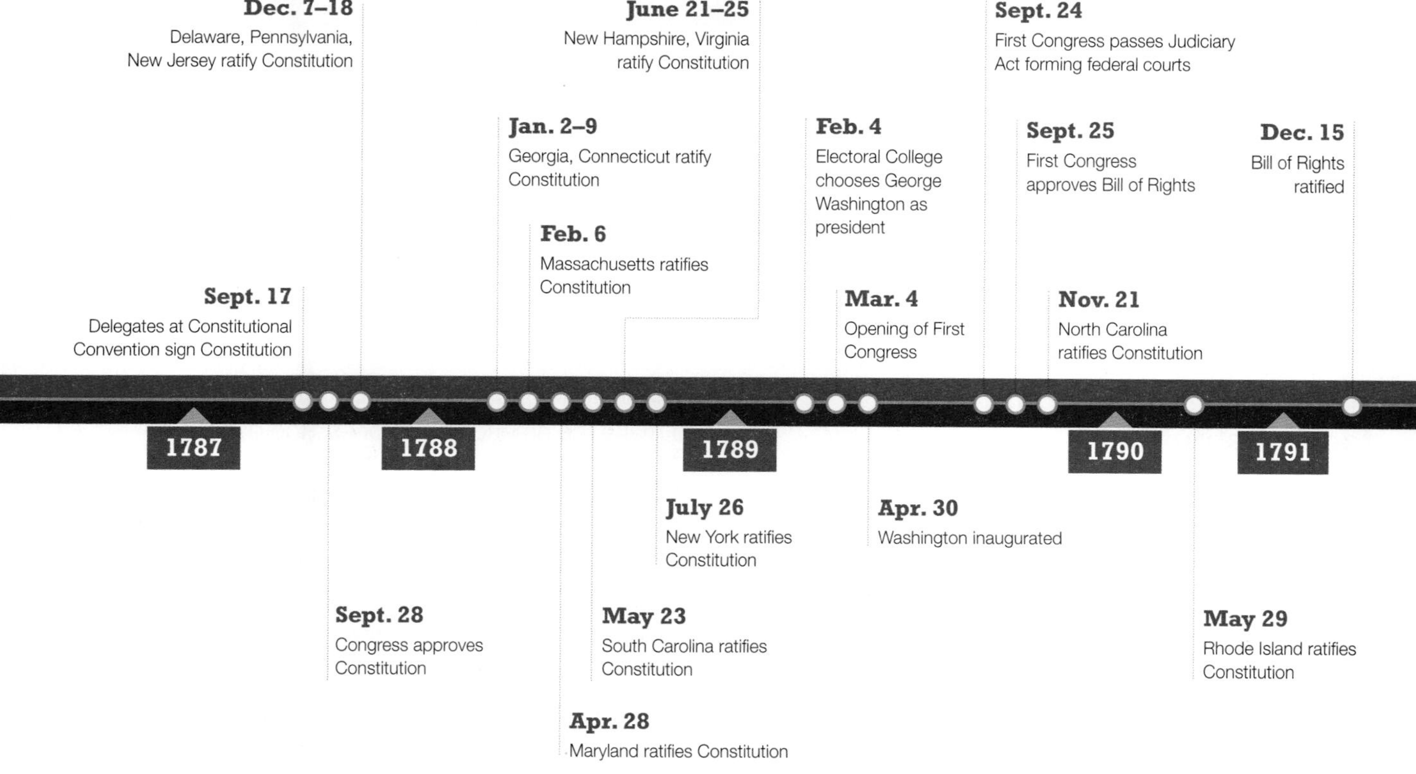

Key Dates in Establishing Government Under the U.S. Constitution
Sept. 17
Delegates at Constitutional Convention sign Constitution
Sept. 28
Congress approves Constitution
Dec. 7–18
Delaware, Pennsylvania, New Jersey ratify Constitution
1787
1788
Jan. 2–9
Georgia, Connecticut ratify Constitution
Feb. 6
Massachusetts ratifies Constitution
Apr. 28
Maryland ratifies Constitution
May 23
South Carolina ratifies Constitution
June 21–25
New Hampshire, Virginia ratify Constitution
July 26
New York ratifies Constitution
1789
Feb. 4
Electoral College chooses George Washington as president
Mar. 4
Opening of First Congress
Apr. 30
Washington inaugurated
Sept. 24
First Congress passes Judiciary Act forming federal courts
Sept. 25
First Congress approves Bill of Rights
Nov. 21
North Carolina ratifies Constitution
1790
May 29
Rhode Island ratifies Constitution
1791
Dec. 15
Bill of Rights ratified

basic individual freedoms. When the Framers drafted the Constitution, they debated whether to include a similar statement of rights. They were concerned that if they protected certain rights, it would be assumed that any rights not mentioned were not protected. Some delegates to the Convention also argued that a national bill of rights was not necessary because the states' bills of rights provided protection.

The absence of a bill of rights became a major sticking point in the debate over ratification of the Constitution, however. After five states quickly voted to ratify it, Massachusetts threatened to block approval without the promise of a national bill of rights. In February 1788, federalists promised to add a national bill of rights to the document. Massachusetts then ratified it, followed by Maryland and South Carolina, and by the end of May, the Constitution had met the nine-state threshold to take effect. But Virginia and New York—the two most populous states—had not yet voted. The full success of the new government required approval from these states, and again, the promise to add a bill of rights helped secure ratification in those two states, along with New Hampshire, in June and July of 1788.

The First Congress convened on March 4, 1789. That June, James Madison introduced 12 amendments to the Constitution, and Congress approved them three months later. The first two amendments were not approved by the states at the time (though the second was incorporated into the Constitution in 1992). The other 10 were officially added to the Constitution on December 15, 1791. These 10 amendments are known collectively as the U.S. Bill of Rights. You will read more about the Bill of Rights and the ways in which the courts have struggled to interpret them later in this chapter.

HISTORICAL THINKING

9. **ANALYZE CAUSE AND EFFECT** Why was the Bill of Rights added to the Constitution?
10. **MAKE CONNECTIONS** How does the creation of the Bill of Rights help fulfill the goals of the Constitution stated in the Preamble?
11. **INTERPRET TIME LINES** How much time passed between the opening of the First Congress and ratification of the Constitution by North Carolina and Rhode Island?

LESSON 3.4 Amending the Constitution

When the Constitution was written, 18-year-olds didn't have the right to vote. But a constitutional amendment passed in 1971 gave them that right. Some amendments have added new rules to the Constitution. Others have changed or replaced provisions in the original document. The 21st amendment repealed an earlier amendment, the 18th. Every amendment to the Constitution has the same force of law as the original articles in the Constitution.

A Process for Changing the Constitution

The Framers included a process for changing, or amending, the Constitution because they were realistic. Though they had crafted the Constitution with great care and after long deliberation, they knew they weren't infallible; in other words, they weren't without shortcomings and might make mistakes. Nor could they anticipate every eventuality future leaders would have to face. In short, they knew that changes to the Constitution were inevitable. But they were careful not to make the amendment process too easy.

DIFFICULTY OF AMENDING THE CONSTITUTION

The Framers knew that if the new government was to function well, it needed to have some stability. Making the amendment process too easy might undermine that stability, so the Constitution lays out a two-step amendment process—formal proposal and ratification—and requires a **supermajority**, or a majority (such as two-thirds or three-fourths) that is greater than a simple majority, at each step for passage of an amendment. A two-thirds vote is required in the proposal stage and a three-fourths vote in the ratification stage.

A look at the record of proposed amendments that have made it into the Constitution shows that these steps are more like high hurdles. Since the Constitution was adopted in 1789, more than 11,000 amendments have been introduced in Congress. Yet, in all that time, only 27 proposed amendments have actually become a part of our Constitution. That is a success rate of less than three-tenths of one percent.

Even though the process is difficult, it is easier than it was under the Articles of Confederation. Under the Articles, an amendment required unanimous approval by all the states. The Framers thought unanimous approval could allow a minority to check the will of the majority, so in the Constitution, they set the bar for ratification a bit lower.

REASONS FOR AMENDING THE CONSTITUTION

Amendments have been adopted for many different reasons. The first 10 amendments to the Constitution, known today as the Bill of Rights, were added to ensure the protection of certain basic rights. As you have read, they also fulfilled promises made during the ratification process.

Other amendments have been added to fix problems in the Constitution that arose over time. The 12th Amendment, for example, fixed a problem with the way electoral votes were cast for president and vice president. Under the Constitution, the president and vice president are not elected by popular vote. Instead, they are voted on by **electors**, people chosen in each state to vote on behalf of that state. As originally

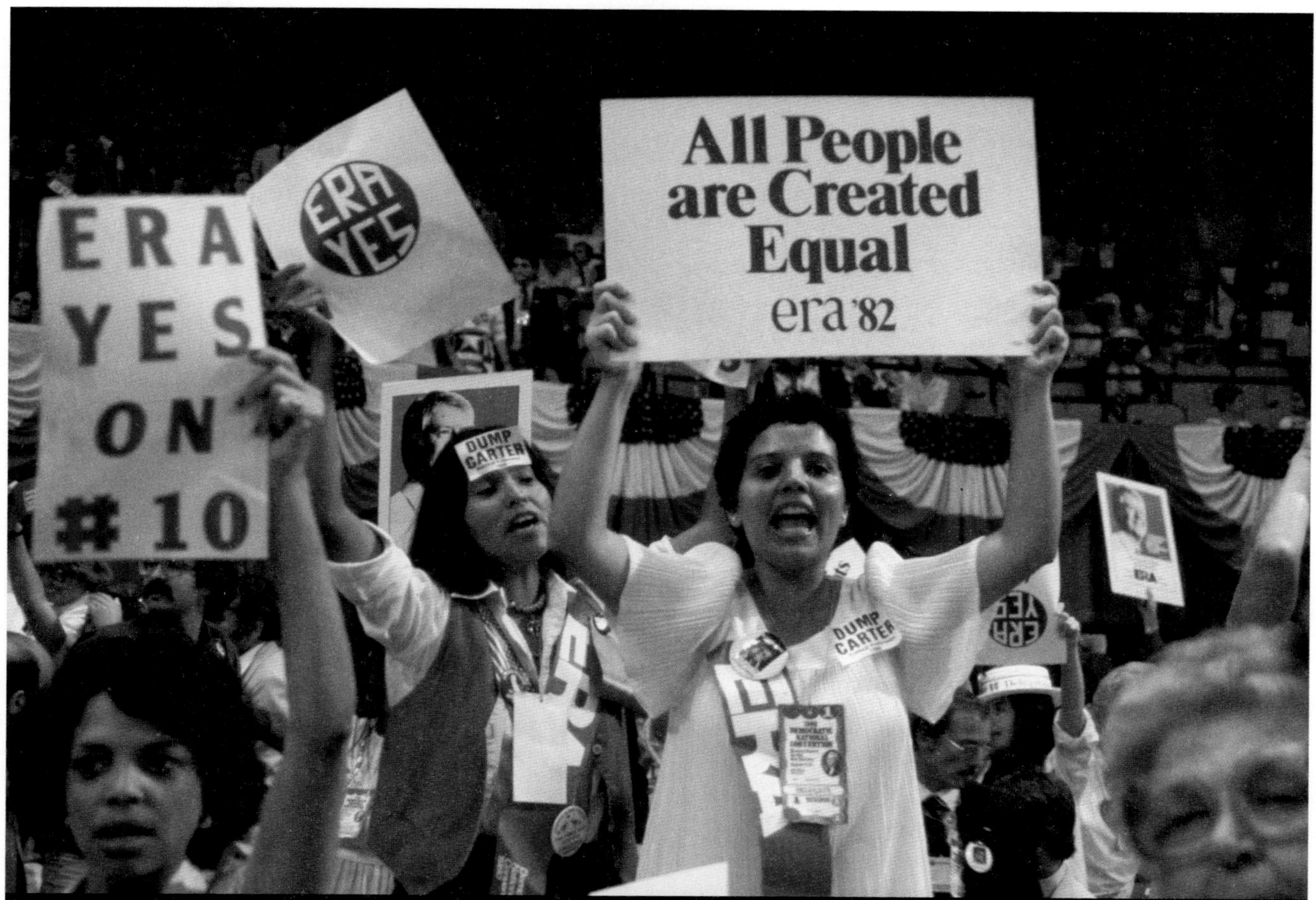

In the 1970s, Congress approved the equal rights amendment (ERA), which would have banned discrimination on the basis of sex. After the ERA won ratification in several states, the effort slowed, prompting these women at a New York rally to urge a renewed effort to push for ratification. Many advocates wore buttons and clothing with the distinctive ERA YES graphic. Virginia became the 38th state to ratify the amendment in January of 2020, long after the 1982 deadline for ratification.

written, the Constitution said that the person with the most electoral votes becomes president, and the person with the next highest number becomes vice president. The election of 1800 revealed flaws in these rules, however, when the electoral vote ended in a tie. The 12th Amendment changed the rules so that electors voted specifically for one person to be president and for another as vice president.

Two later amendments were added to fix other issues related to the presidency. The 22nd Amendment set a limit on the number of terms a president could serve. George Washington, the first president, only served two terms. Many people viewed Washington's action as an unwritten rule that later presidents should follow. In the 1930s and 1940s, though, Franklin D. Roosevelt won election to four terms as president. A few years after his last term, the 22nd Amendment was ratified to put a two-term cap on the presidency. The 25th Amendment, proposed and ratified following the assassination of President John F. Kennedy, clarified how the office would be filled if a president could not serve either temporarily or permanently. It also provided a process for naming a new vice president when that office became vacant.

Other amendments have recognized fundamental rights. The three amendments approved after the Civil War, for example, included protections for the rights of African Americans in the Constitution. The 13th Amendment ended slavery across the United States in 1865. It also made obsolete a clause in Article IV, Section 2, that had allowed the capture and return of enslaved African Americans who had escaped to a free state. The 14th Amendment proclaimed African Americans to be U.S. citizens in 1868. The 15th Amendment, ratified in 1870, stated that the right to vote could not be denied on account of "race, color, or previous condition of servitude."

As American ideas of democracy changed, three amendments further expanded voting rights. When it was ratified in 1920, the 19th Amendment ended a decades-long struggle by acknowledging the right of women to vote. The 26th Amendment extended the same right to persons 18 years and older in 1971. The 23rd Amendment, ratified in 1961, allocated three electoral votes to the District of Columbia. For the first time, citizens living in the nation's capital had a voice in presidential elections.

HISTORICAL THINKING

1. **IDENTIFY MAIN IDEAS AND DETAILS** What balance did the Framers try to reach in crafting the amendment process?
2. **MAKE INFERENCES** Based on the 15th, 19th, and 26th amendments, who had voting rights under the Constitution as it was originally written?

Proposing an Amendment

Article V of the Constitution lays out two ways to propose an amendment:

1. *A proposed amendment is introduced in Congress and wins approval of two-thirds of both the Senate and the House of Representatives. All of the 27 existing amendments have been proposed in this way.*
2. *An amendment can be proposed at a national amendment convention called by Congress at the request of two-thirds of the state legislatures.*

By having Congress propose amendments, the first method simply followed the process established in the Articles of Confederation. But why did the Framers set out a second method? The answer is that they didn't

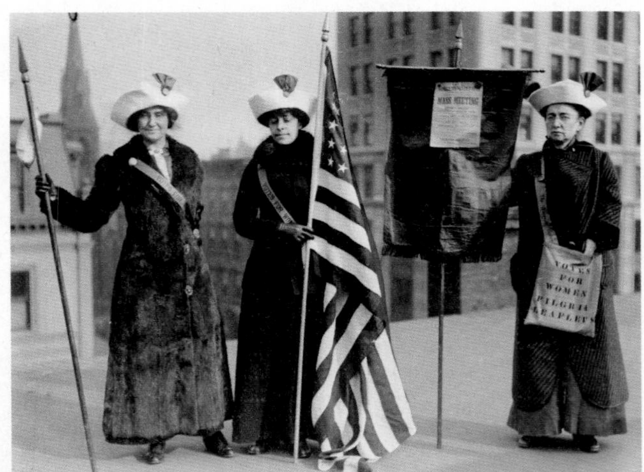

CRITICAL VIEWING These suffragists were among the thousands of women who campaigned for the right to vote before the 19th Amendment was ratified. Based on what you see in this photo and the photo on the previous page, how did women differ in their approach to calling for change between the 1910s and 1970s?

want the amendment power to be the exclusive power of Congress. They wanted to give the states a role. If a reform was needed but for some reason members of Congress didn't choose to act on that need, the states could take action. In practice, this second method has never been used.

While never used, the option of a national convention to propose amendments has appealed to some Americans at different times. There were calls for such a convention in the 1970s and 1980s, for instance, by those who wanted an amendment requiring the federal government to balance its budget. The legislatures in several states passed resolutions calling for such a convention. Some later rescinded their resolutions, however, in response to warnings from constitutional scholars who argued against holding a new constitutional convention.

The scholars gave several reasons for their concerns. First, the convention would be able to make its own rules—including what amendments it proposed and even how many states would be needed to ratify them. In other words, such a convention could go well beyond the original charge. In fact, it could do what the Constitutional Convention did—create a new form of government. Second, the convention's actions would not be subject to any outside control, including that of the courts. Third, special interests could exert considerable influence over a convention, meaning its actions could potentially reflect the agenda of a small group of people rather than the popular will.

Of course, any amendments proposed by such a convention would still need to be ratified. That process could act as a check on a convention going too far. But if the convention reduced the number of states needed for approval, it could potentially change American government in a radical way.

HISTORICAL THINKING

3. **COMPARE AND CONTRAST** How is the process for proposing an amendment under the Articles of Confederation similar to and different from the process described in the Constitution?
4. **MAKE CONNECTIONS** Why do those opposed to calling a national convention to amend the Constitution point to the Constitutional Convention as an example?

Ratifying an Amendment

Just as there are two ways to propose an amendment, there are also two methods of ratifying an amendment:

1. *Three-fourths of the state legislatures vote in favor of the proposed amendment. This method—the traditional one—has been used 26 times.*
2. *The states can call special state conventions to vote on a proposed amendment. If three-fourths of these conventions approve it, the amendment is ratified. This method has been used only once—to ratify the 21st Amendment.*

The traditional method continued the practice under the Articles of giving the state legislatures the power to give final approval of an amendment. The second option, allowing state legislatures to call for ratifying conventions, makes ratification more democratic. It permits the people to take part in ratification, as they would choose the delegates to attend a state convention.

TIME LIMITS FOR RATIFICATION Unless explicitly called for, amendments don't need to be ratified in a set amount of time. The amendment that set the record for the fastest ratification was the 26th, which gave 18-year-olds the right to vote. Congress proposed it on March 23, 1971, and the required number of states ratified it on July 7, 1971—less than four months later. In contrast, the 27th Amendment, requiring that no increase to congressional pay could take effect until after the election following passage of the pay raise, was proposed as part of the Bill of Rights in 1789 but was not ratified until 1992—more than 200 years later.

The 18th Amendment—which banned the manufacture and sale of alcoholic beverages—was the first to set a time limit on ratification. That limit was seven years, which the amendment easily met. In fact, it was approved by three-quarters of the states in just 13 months. It took even less time—a mere nine months—to approve the 21st Amendment, which repealed the 18th. Most later amendments have had a time limit as well. In some cases, the limit is specified in the text of the amendment. At other times, it's placed in the resolution that Congress passes when it sends the amendment to the states.

AMENDMENTS THAT FAILED RATIFICATION Some amendments have been proposed multiple times but have never made it through the two steps. Some were never approved by Congress. Others were approved by the Senate and House but fell short of ratification by three-quarters of the states. Notable examples of failed amendments include:

- **The equal rights amendment (ERA):** First proposed in 1923, this amendment states, "Equality of rights under the law shall not be denied or abridged by the United States or by any state on account of sex." It was approved by Congress in 1972, but only 35 states—three short of the 38 needed—had ratified it by 1982, the date established by Congress as a deadline for its ratification. Three additional states—Nevada, Illinois, and Virginia—ratified the amendment in 2017, 2018, and 2020, but the missed deadline makes the amendment unlikely to be adopted.
- **Electoral college reform amendments:** More than 700 proposals have been introduced in Congress to abolish or change the electoral college. As explained earlier, electors are the voters who actually choose the president and vice president. Each candidate has a slate of electors. In most states, electoral votes are awarded on a winner-takes-all basis. The candidate who wins the popular vote in the state gets all the electoral votes. Some proposals have called for electoral votes to be cast proportionately based on candidates' shares of the popular vote in the state rather than allowing the winner-takes-all approach. Others call for doing away with the electoral college completely. Under these proposals, the winner of the national popular vote would become the president. None of these ideas have ever passed through both houses of Congress to be sent to the states, however.
- **Line-item veto amendment:** Conservatives have called for an amendment giving the president a line-item veto as a way to curb government spending. This would let the president veto one or more parts of a spending bill while approving the bill as a whole. In a 1996 law, Congress gave the president this power, but the Supreme Court later ruled the law unconstitutional. Because the court rejected the law, an amendment is needed for the president to receive this power. While popular among those who wish to restrain federal spending, a proposal for a line-item veto amendment has not yet made it through Congress.

HISTORICAL THINKING

5. **IDENTIFY PROBLEMS AND SOLUTIONS** Why did the Framers make it more difficult for the states to ratify a constitutional amendment than for Congress or a national convention to propose one?
6. **COMPARE AND CONTRAST** Historically, how has the use of the two processes for ratification compared to the use of the two processes for proposing an amendment?
7. **DRAW CONCLUSIONS** Because the Supreme Court overturned a law allowing the line-item veto, a constitutional amendment is required in order to give the president that power. What does that indicate about the role of the Supreme Court in the U.S. constitutional system?

LESSON 3.5 Analyzing the Amendments

Most of the 27 amendments were ratified during major historical periods. The first 12 were adopted during the early days of the republic as the country adapted to the new Constitution. Several others were ratified shortly after the Civil War as part of the process of dismantling the institution of slavery. The Progressive Era, a period of reform and social change in the early 20th century, ushered in several amendments. The 1960s and 1970s, another era of significant reform, brought about a new group of amendments. When will the next period of amendment creation come?

The Bill of Rights

In the closing days of the Constitutional Convention, Virginia delegate George Mason rose to protest that the Constitution the convention was drafting didn't include a list of individual rights. At first, his fellow delegates ignored him, but as opponents of the Constitution cited the absence of a bill of rights as a reason to reject the new plan, Mason's concern began to attract more notice. Even Thomas Jefferson weighed in from his post as minister to France in favor of a bill of rights.

James Madison sorted through more than 200 recommendations from the states and selected 19 of them. He then drafted the amendments and submitted them to the First Congress. In September of 1789, Congress approved 12 of Madison's proposed amendments. By 1791, 10 of those 12 had been ratified and added to the Constitution. Those 10 amendments make up the U.S. Bill of Rights.

THE REVOLUTION AND THE BILL OF RIGHTS

The Bill of Rights is largely a restatement of rights found in the English common law tradition. But for Americans of the 1790s, the need to protect these rights grew out of their experiences during the American Revolution.

The First Amendment's protection of freedom of the press, for example, reflected the role that newspapers and pamphlet writers like Thomas Paine had played in promoting the rebellion against Britain. Likewise, the First Amendment's right to petition the government for redress of grievances grew out of the protests against the Stamp Act and other acts of the British parliament that had been the sparks of rebellion.

The Second Amendment, which protects the right to bear arms in order to support a "well regulated Militia," also reflected recent history. Militia troops—units of citizen-soldiers—were vital to American victories in the Revolution from Lexington and Concord in 1775 to Yorktown in 1781.

The Third Amendment struck closest to home. It prevented the government from quartering, or housing, troops in people's homes in peacetime. It reflected the anger Americans felt when forced to house British troops in their homes before and during the Revolution.

NEED TO INTERPRET THE BILL OF RIGHTS

The language of the Bill of Rights may seem clear and direct, but it is also open to interpretation. For instance, the First Amendment uses 16 words to guarantee religious freedom: "Congress shall make no law respecting an establishment of religion, or prohibiting the free exercise thereof." In other words, under the Bill of Rights, religious freedom includes both freedom from religion and freedom of religion. First, no official religion can be imposed on Americans. Constitutional scholars call the first part of this statement the **establishment clause**, which provides that Congress cannot establish any national religion. At the same time, each person is free to follow whatever religion he or she chooses. That is known as the "free exercise clause." While both clauses may seem clear, people can disagree about how the language applies in specific situations. The courts are called on to settle these disagreements.

Take the establishment clause. The Framers believed that recognizing a single, official religion would be unfair to those who practiced other religions. Some scholars interpret the establishment clause very narrowly as prohibiting the government only from naming one religion as an official religion. Others interpret it more broadly, arguing that the establishment clause requires a complete separation of church and state. Both sides can find support in the writings of the Framers and others at the time the First Amendment was written. The U.S. Supreme Court has had to draw fine lines tailored to specific situations. On the one hand, the Court ruled that it is unconstitutional for a public school official to recite a prayer at a school function. On the other hand, the Court has ruled that it is permissible for students themselves to say prayers while on school grounds.

Likewise, the Court has been called on to determine what sorts of government actions amount to limits on the free exercise of religion. In *Wisconsin* v. *Yoder* (1972), some followers of the Amish religion objected to a Wisconsin law requiring them to send children to school until they were 16. They argued that courses that were taught after eighth grade included ideas that contradicted Amish religious beliefs. The U.S. Supreme Court decided in favor of the Amish. It said that the law violated their right to freely exercise their religion.

Provisions of the Bill of Rights

AMENDMENT	TOPIC	KEY PROVISIONS
First	Basic rights	• Protects religious freedom • Protects freedom of speech • Protects freedom of the press • Protects the right to assemble • Protects the right to petition the government
Second	Basic rights	• Establishes the right to bear arms
Third	Basic rights	• Bans laws requiring quartering of troops in peacetime
Fourth	Criminal justice	• Bans "unreasonable searches and seizures" • Requires that search warrants be based on "probable cause" and identify the person, places, and things to be searched
Fifth	Criminal justice	• Requires that charges for major crimes be brought by a grand jury • Protects individuals from "double jeopardy"—being tried more than once on the same charge • Allows individuals not to testify against themselves • Guarantees "due process" in criminal cases • Bars the taking of private property for a public purpose "without just compensation"
Sixth	Criminal justice	• Guarantees the right to a speedy and public trial • Guarantees trial by impartial jury in the appropriate jurisdiction • Requires that an accused person be informed of charges against him or her • Guarantees a defendant's right to face and examine witnesses for the prosecution • Guarantees a defendant's right to be represented by an attorney
Seventh	Civil justice	• Grants the right to trial by jury in civil cases
Eighth	Criminal justice	• Bans excessive bail or fines • Bans "cruel and unusual punishment"
Ninth	General rights	• Establishes the existence of individual rights beyond those specifically stated
Tenth	General power	• Reserves to the states or the people any powers not given to the federal government by the Constitution

Finding the line between what the Constitution allows and what it doesn't can be very complex. Does the Constitution, for example, allow the use of public money to fund religious schools? In *Zelman* v. *Simmons-Harris* (2002), the Supreme Court ruled in favor of a **voucher program**, in which states provide parents with public money to pay for the education of their children at the schools of their choice. The Court ruled that because the choice of schools lies with the parents, the state is not favoring religion if parents use public funds to pay tuition at a religious school. In some states, however, voucher programs run afoul of the Blaine Amendment. This was a proposed constitutional amendment introduced in 1875 by Senator James Blaine. It explicitly banned the use of tax dollars to aid religious schools. The Blaine Amendment was never approved by Congress and is not part of the U.S. Constitution, but many states incorporated this ban into their state constitutions.

LIMITS TO RIGHTS IN THE BILL OF RIGHTS The Bill of Rights does not provide absolute protection of rights. Even the freedom of speech—one of the most cherished rights—has limits. For instance, laws can ban "fighting words," which incite people to commit violence. Freedom of the press can also be limited. For example, news media can be prevented from publishing detailed information about the location and number of troops in time of war. Of course, people can challenge government actions that they think wrongly take away their rights. They can bring a lawsuit against the government action. In that case, the courts will decide the case by listening to both sides, looking at past court decisions, and making a ruling.

HISTORICAL THINKING

1. **IDENTIFY** Which amendment in the Bill of Rights protects the right of people to stage a demonstration in Washington, D.C., in support of a bill pending before Congress?
2. **INTERPRET TABLES** Defendants often "plead the Fifth" in real-life and fictionalized trials. Which provision of the Fifth Amendment do you think they are calling on when they do this?
3. **EVALUATE** The language of constitutional amendments like the First Amendment is open to interpretation. Do you think that is good or bad?

The 11th to the 15th Amendments

After the Bill of Rights, the pace of changes to the Constitution slowed down. In the next 80 years, only 5 amendments were ratified. Two were passed within 15 years of the Constitution's ratification by the states. Both of those corrected defects that emerged as the new government found its footing. Then, for more than 60 years, no new amendments were ratified.

The 11th Amendment arose when a citizen of South Carolina brought a lawsuit against the state of Georgia in federal court. Political leaders feared that this action would open the door to more such lawsuits. The 11th Amendment, ratified in 1795, bans lawsuits in federal court brought by an individual from one state or from a foreign country against another state.

The 12th Amendment was written to correct a flaw in the rules for choosing a president. As originally written, the Constitution gave the presidency to the person with the most electoral votes and the vice presidency to the person with the second most votes. Electors didn't have to indicate if they wanted one candidate to be the president and another to be vice president. That proved problematic in the fourth presidential election, however.

In 1800, Thomas Jefferson and Aaron Burr both ran from the same political party and received the same number of electoral votes. The members of their

Ratification of Amendments to the U.S. Constitution

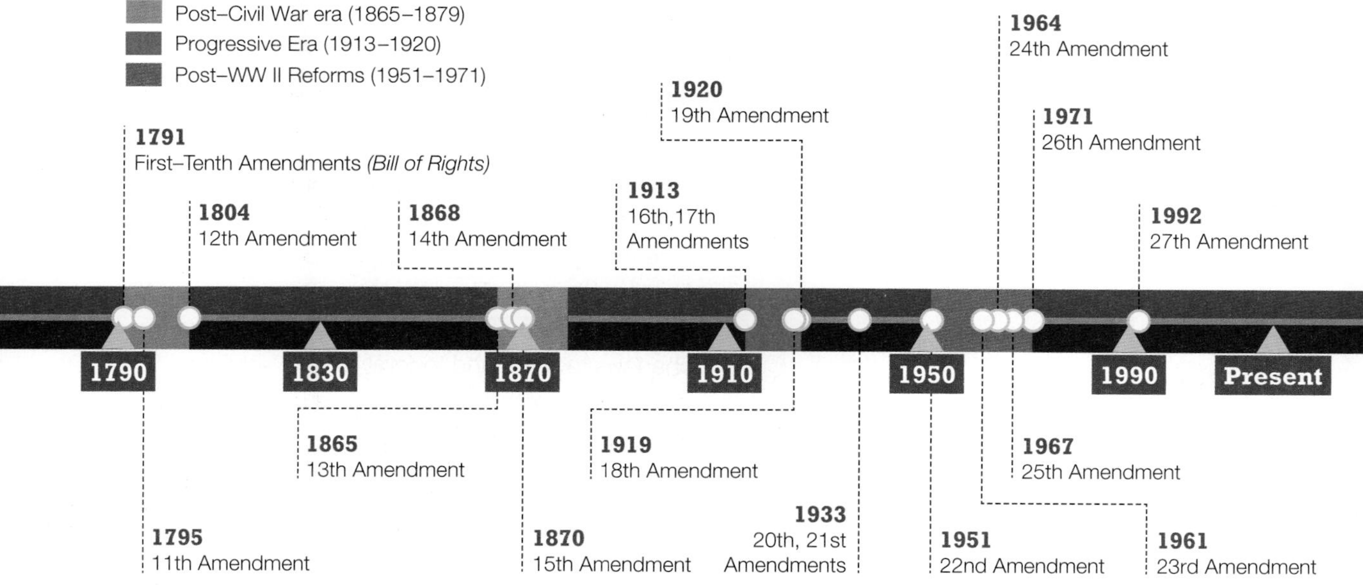

political party had clearly meant for Jefferson to be president and Burr to be vice president. Burr, however, refused to say that he would not accept the presidency. The result was settled in the House of Representatives, as provided by the Constitution. House members gave Jefferson more votes, making him president, and Burr, the runner-up, became vice president. But the tie showed that the system of casting electoral votes had problems. The 12th Amendment fixed the problem by having electors vote separately for president and vice president. It was ratified in 1804.

The next three amendments arose as a result of the Civil War and the conflict over slavery. As originally written, the Constitution had allowed slavery. By 1804, the northern states had abolished slavery. As the nation expanded, many southerners wanted new territories to allow slavery, despite the objections of northerners. The conflict over the spread of slavery led to the Civil War between the Union states and southern states that had left the United States to form the Confederated States of America, or the Confederacy.

The Union victory in the Civil War led to the 13th, 14th, and 15th amendments. The 13th Amendment, ratified in 1865, abolished slavery in the United States. The 14th, ratified in 1868, provided that all people born in the United States were citizens. Its primary aim was to grant citizenship to African Americans who had been enslaved. The 15th, as you read earlier, stated that the right to vote could not be denied on the basis of race. It was ratified in 1870.

The subsequent history of these amendments shows how events can shape the meaning of the Constitution. In the latter half of the 1800s, racial discrimination led to state laws that made it nearly impossible for African Americans, especially in the South, to exercise their voting rights. For nearly 100 years, therefore, the 15th Amendment shrank into insignificance.

In the early 20th century, however, the 14th Amendment underwent a major expansion in significance. Section 1 of the amendment contains what is called the "due process" clause. It says, "no state shall . . . deprive any person of life, liberty, or property, without due process of law." Starting in 1925, the Supreme Court used the due process clause to rule that various parts of the Bill of Rights applied to state government as well as the national government. This idea is called *incorporation.* Through the due process clause, the Bill of Rights is incorporated, or made to apply, to the states. For example, in 1963, the Supreme Court decided that Sixth Amendment protections for those accused of crimes applied to the state courts as well as the federal courts. As a result of this decision, *Gideon* v. *Wainwright*, anyone being tried for committing a crime in state court has the right to an attorney. If that person cannot afford an attorney, the state government has to provide one.

Meanwhile, the 13th Amendment, which banned involuntary servitude as well as slavery, was invoked to end **peonage**, the use of laborers bound in servitude because of debt, in *Bailey* v. *Alabama* in 1911. Congress has also drawn on the 13th Amendment to support portions of the Hate Crimes Prevention Act of 2009 and the Trafficking Victims Protection Act.

HISTORICAL THINKING

4. **INTERPRET TIME LINES** In which period were the most amendments added to the Constitution?
5. **MAKE CONNECTIONS** How has the 12th Amendment affected the way political parties nominate candidates for national office in presidential election years in our own time?
6. **ANALYZE CAUSE AND EFFECT** How did changes in state laws affect the 15th Amendment?
7. **DESCRIBE** How did the doctrine of incorporation change the meaning of the Bill of Rights?

The 16th to the 21st Amendments

The 16th to the 19th amendments were all proposed and ratified during the **Progressive Era**, a period of political reform in the early 1900s. Reformers of this time thought businesses and corporations had gained too much power. They also thought government needed to be more democratic. They pushed for changes to state and federal laws to advance these goals, and they succeeded in passing four amendments to the Constitution.

The 16th Amendment, approved by the states in 1913, gave the federal government the power to

With her family looking on, Republican Marsha Blackburn (TN) takes the oath of office of a U.S. senator from Vice President Mike Pence in January 2019. The 17th Amendment, ratified in 1913, changed the constitutional provision that called for state legislatures to name senators to require their direct election by the people. Blackburn won election to her first term in the Senate in November 2018.

collect an income tax from individuals. Until this time, almost all of the government's **revenue**, or income, came from **tariffs**, which are fees imposed by a government on imported or, in some countries, exported goods. (The Constitution bans Congress from imposing tariffs on exports from any state, but import tariffs are allowed.) That source was increasingly inadequate to meet the needs of an expanding federal government taking on greater responsibilities. The federal government had invoked an emergency tax on incomes, as well as many other taxes, to finance the Civil War, but efforts to continue a federal tax on income ran aground in 1895, when the Supreme Court ruled such a tax unconstitutional. The 16th Amendment allowed Congress to collect income taxes, thus providing adequate funding to the government. It also spoke to the desire of progressives to restore a sense of fairness to American society. Industrialization had made some business leaders very wealthy. An income tax was a way to make the wealthy contribute something to the larger good.

The 17th Amendment is the only amendment that has changed the structure of Congress, and it resulted from Progressive Party efforts to reform government. Prior to the amendment's ratification, senators were chosen by state legislatures, many of which were viewed as corrupt and easily manipulated by big business. In addition, they often had trouble getting things done, so some senate seats were unfilled for years. The 17th Amendment changed that, requiring that senators be elected directly by the voters of their states. It was approved in 1913. Since 1914, all senators have been elected by the people of their state, making senators more responsive to the people they represent.

With the 19th Amendment, progressives made government more democratic by stating that women had the right to vote. The fight for women's **suffrage**, or the right to vote, began in the mid-1800s but saw little success for many years. It gained some momentum in the late 1800s when a few western states gave women the right to vote. But the movement finally achieved national success in 1920 when the 19th Amendment was approved. From then on, women have had the right to vote.

Other reformers of the era pushed for a ban on alcoholic beverages. They argued that many social ills, from poverty to abuse of women and children, were caused or worsened by alcohol addiction. They gained victory with ratification of the 18th Amendment in 1919. It made the manufacture and sale of alcoholic beverages illegal. The period that followed is called Prohibition.

The ratification of the 18th Amendment marked the end of the era of progressive reform. Prohibition itself proved to be a failure. The demand for alcohol did not go away. Instead, the law made criminals of anyone who had a beer or a glass of wine. Worse still, criminal gangs gained control of alcohol sales. Competition among gangs led to violence that left scores dead, horrifying ordinary citizens. As a result, a movement to end Prohibition spread across the country. In December 1933, the states approved the 21st Amendment, which repealed the 18th Amendment. The 21st Amendment is the only amendment that repeals an earlier amendment.

About a year earlier, in January 1933, the states had ratified the 20th Amendment, the so-called lame duck amendment. *Lame duck* is a term for an elected official serving the remainder of a term after deciding not to seek re-election or having been defeated for re-election. The 20th Amendment moved the date to begin sessions of Congress to January 4. Likewise, the date for a presidential inauguration was moved from March to January 20.

The delay between election and the start of a representative's term under the original Constitution was partly to allow lawmakers time to get from their home states to Washington, D.C., in an era when travel was slow. It also resulted from the timing of the ratification of the Constitution itself, which set the government in motion in March of an odd-numbered year. Since Congressional sessions started in December, and elections are held in even-numbered years, a newly elected member of Congress didn't get down to work until 13 months after being elected. Even more troubling, there were long periods when many of those serving in Congress had been voted out of office, but still had the power to pass laws as lame ducks. Worse, lawmakers who were leaving Congress could trade their votes on bills congressional leaders wanted with no fear of punishment by voters in the next election. Efforts to change the December start date began soon after ratification of the Constitution, but it wasn't until January 23, 1933, that the amendment was ratified.

HISTORICAL THINKING

8. **DESCRIBE** How did the 16th, 17th, 18th, and 19th amendments reflect the Progressive Era's interest in reform?
9. **ANALYZE CAUSE AND EFFECT** What unintended consequences of the 18th Amendment led to the 21st Amendment?

The 22nd to the 27th Amendments

The most recent six amendments were added to the Constitution between 1951 and 1992. Several of them address issues connected to the presidency and voting rights.

Two amendments ratified in the two decades after World War II focused on the presidency. Franklin Roosevelt had broken a long-standing tradition, set by George Washington, of presidents serving only two terms. He ran for and won the presidency four times. Many Americans accepted Roosevelt's break with tradition because his third and fourth elections in 1940 and 1944 came during World War II, a time of crisis. He died a few months into his fourth term, however, and after the war, many Americans wanted to return to the two-term limit. They feared the consequences of one person having executive power for more than eight years. The 22nd Amendment, ratified in 1951, made the two-term limit part of the Constitution. It also

Gerald Ford (right) became vice president in 1973. He was nominated by President Richard Nixon after Vice President Spiro Agnew's resignation and confirmed by Congress under the terms of the 25th Amendment. The following year, Nixon resigned, and Ford became president. He then nominated Nelson Rockefeller (left) as vice president. Rockefeller's confirmation in December of 1974 marked the first time both president and vice president had not been elected by the people.

stated that a vice president who served as president for at least two years after the death or departure of a president could be elected to only one full term as president.

Tragedy triggered another amendment. After President Kennedy was assassinated in 1963, the president died in office and a vice president became president for the second time in 20 years. (Harry Truman had become president when Franklin Roosevelt died in 1945.) Americans worried about the fact that the office of the vice president was once again vacant. They were also concerned about the lack of leadership that would occur if a president became seriously ill or unable to function. That had happened in the 1950s, when President Dwight Eisenhower had a heart attack. The 25th Amendment, ratified in 1967, addressed these issues. It provided that:

- If the office of the vice president becomes vacant, the president can appoint a new vice president. That person must be approved by a majority vote of both houses of Congress.
- If a president becomes temporarily unable to serve, the vice president can carry out the duties of the office until the president can return.

Other amendments from this period came in response to the civil rights movement. Under the Constitution, the District of Columbia—the federal district that serves as the nation's capital—had no electoral votes because it is not a state. By 1960, however, the District had more than 700,000 people—a larger population than that of several states. Because the district had no electoral votes, its residents had no voice in the election of the president. Since more than half the city's population was African American, the ability of D.C. voters to have their votes count in presidential elections was seen as a civil rights issue. In 1963, the 23rd Amendment gave three electoral votes—the minimum for the smallest state—to the District of Columbia.

The 24th Amendment tried to fulfill the broken promise of the 15th Amendment. As you will recall, the earlier amendment said that the right to vote could not be denied on the basis of race, but African Americans were not always able to exercise that right. In the late 1800s and early 1900s, White southerners passed laws to prevent African Americans from voting. Among them were laws that required voters to pay a **poll tax**, which is a tax of a fixed amount per person levied on adults and often linked to the right to vote. This tax blocked African Americans from voting because many did not have enough money for that tax. White voters who didn't have the money for the tax were excused from the tax by other laws. The push to secure basic rights for African Americans that resulted from the civil rights movement led to action against poll taxes. When it was ratified in 1964, the 24th Amendment outlawed poll taxes.

The 26th Amendment, discussed earlier, arose in response to the bitter divisions caused by the Vietnam War. Young men 18 to 21 years old were being drafted to fight in that war, but since the voting age was 21, most of them could not vote for or against leaders making decisions about the war. This situation was widely seen as unfair, and the 26th Amendment, which gave those who were 18 and older the right to vote, was ratified in 1971 as a result.

The most recent amendment has roots that extend back to James Madison's original proposed amendments. The 27th Amendment had been part of the proposed Bill of Rights he submitted back in 1789. It provides that, should Congress pass a law raising the salary of members of Congress, the increase would not take effect until the next newly elected Congress took office. Only six states ratified it in the late 1700s. While one more state ratified the amendment in the 19th century, no further action was taken. A new push to ratify the amendment arose in the 1980s, when public opinion about Congress was highly unfavorable, and more states approved it. The 27th Amendment finally became part of the Constitution in 1992.

HISTORICAL THINKING

10. **ANALYZE CAUSE AND EFFECT** How did the civil rights movement lead to passage of the 24th Amendment?
11. **FORM AND SUPPORT OPINIONS** What would be an argument in favor of the 27th Amendment?

LESSON 3.6

Putting the Constitution to Work

Whatever their aspirations and dreams for the nation they were creating, the Framers probably never imagined a country with the population and economic clout of the United States today. Yet they created a framework with the strength and flexibility to allow Congress, the courts, and presidents to fill in the details to create a complex federal government to meet the needs of a changing nation. That's why, for better or worse, the United States government of the 21st century is quite different from the government the Framers originally outlined.

Clarifying the Constitution Through Laws

Congress has generally relied on two clauses in Article I, Section 8, of the Constitution—the necessary and proper clause and the commerce clause—to clarify the Constitution and expand the powers of Congress.

ORGANIZING THE JUDICIAL BRANCH For example, Article III, Section 1, says that the judicial power of the United States (meaning the federal government) shall be placed in a Supreme Court and in "such inferior federal Courts as the Congress may from time to time ordain [order] and establish." In other words, the Framers left the details to Congress. The First Congress spent the majority of its first session crafting the Judiciary Act of 1789. This law set up the federal court system, which you'll learn more about in a later unit.

The Judiciary Act of 1789 created three levels of federal courts—district courts, circuit courts, and the U.S. Supreme Court. The district courts are trial courts, where evidence is heard and juries or judges decide cases. The Supreme Court also functions as a trial court with certain types of cases, though in this case the justices—and not a jury—decide the case. Each circuit court and the Supreme Court is an **appellate court**, a court devoted to the hearing of appeals of decisions of lower courts.

Appeals are made by parties that lose a case and believe they were treated unfairly. Appeals must be based on the application of the law or the procedures followed before or during the trial. They are not based on the facts of a case. Allowing losers to appeal a result helps ensure that due process of law, as guaranteed in the Fifth Amendment, is followed. For instance, a person convicted of a crime might appeal on the grounds that police did not follow correct procedure in gathering evidence. The appeals court

the FEDERAL COURT SYSTEM

 U.S. SUPREME COURT	• **Composition:** Chief Justice, eight associate justices • **Type of court:** hears most cases on appeal; court of original jurisdiction in some cases • Highest court in land • Four justices must agree to hear a case • Decisions issued by majority vote of justices
 U.S. COURT OF APPEALS	• **13 total:** 12 in regions plus Court of Appeals for the Federal Circuit • **Type of court:** appellate (appeals from decisions in District Courts and administrative courts) • Court of Appeals for Federal Circuit hears appeals on patent law and from U.S. Court of International Trade and U.S. Court of Federal Claims • Cases decided by majority vote of panel of three judges
 U.S. DISTRICT COURT	• **94 total:** (at least one in each state plus one in D.C.), organized into 12 areas • **Two special courts:** U.S. Court of International Trade and U.S. Court of Federal Claims • **Type of court:** trial • Decisions made by judge or jury

must examine how evidence was gathered and decide if it fits the rules police are supposed to follow.

The Judiciary Act of 1789 divided the country into districts, creating one court for each district. It also organized the districts into circuits. Each circuit court handles appeals based on decisions made in the district courts within its circuit. Appeals to circuit court decisions go to the U.S. Supreme Court, which can decide whether or not to hear a case.

Federal courts hear both criminal and civil cases. In criminal cases, the government charges that one or more people broke a law. The government has to prove that those accused of the crime are guilty. Civil cases are legal disputes between two or more parties. They result from lawsuits that arise when one party claims it has been injured by another party.

The Judiciary Act of 1789 also created important judicial officers. It established the office of attorney general of the United States, who is the highest officer in the Department of Justice. The act also created the position of U.S. attorney. These attorneys represent the government in district courts. For example, a U.S. attorney presents the case against someone accused of a crime. If a citizen brings a lawsuit against the federal government, the U.S. attorney presents the case on behalf of the government.

Congress retains the power to define and redefine the federal judiciary. To take one example, Congress has altered the number of justices of the Supreme Court six times. Set originally at 6 in 1789, the number was dropped to 5 in 1801, returned to 6 in 1802, boosted to 7 in 1807, increased to 9 in 1837, and expanded to 10 in 1863 before being reduced again to 7 in 1866. The Judiciary Act of 1869 set the number at its current 9. In 1937, President Franklin D. Roosevelt proposed a plan to add as many as six more justices to the Supreme Court, but Congress rejected the plan.

CONGRESSIONAL POWER AND THE ELASTIC CLAUSE Much of what we think of as the federal government—including executive departments such as the Department of Defense and executive agencies such as NASA—sprang from one clause in the Constitution. Article I, Section 8, Clause 18, gives Congress the power to "make all Laws which shall be necessary and proper for carrying into Execution the foregoing powers." In other words, if a law can reasonably be linked to one of the powers explicitly given to Congress in the Constitution, the Supreme Court has ruled, the law is necessary. Not surprisingly, this clause's tremendous flexibility has earned it the nickname of the *elastic clause* because Congress has used it to stretch its powers to meet what it argues are new needs.

CONGRESSIONAL POWER AND THE COMMERCE CLAUSE Article I also includes the **commerce clause**, a clause of the Constitution that gives Congress the power to "regulate commerce with foreign Nations, and among the several states." Congress has used this power to set international trade policies by placing tariffs, or taxes, on goods imported from another country. Congress has also used the power to regulate **interstate commerce**, or the sale, purchase, or trade of goods between states, to pass laws with far-reaching impact.

Throughout the 1800s and into the early 1900s, the courts limited the use of the commerce clause to regulating the movement of goods. Starting in the early 1900s, Congress began to use the clause to extend the federal government's reach, and the courts have ruled in favor of this effort. For example, in the early 1900s consumers grew alarmed at news reports and books that described unsanitary conditions in factories that processed food and drugs. This concern prompted Congress to pass the Pure Food and Drug Act and the Meat Inspection Act in 1906. The Pure Food and Drug Act was challenged by a company that sold canned eggs containing a harmful ingredient. The company said that the way food is processed was not a matter of interstate commerce. The Supreme Court upheld the Pure Food and Drug Act in 1911, however, on the grounds that the law was aimed at preventing the transportation of harmful products.

In the 1960s the definition of interstate commerce was broadened once again, this time to further the cause of civil rights legislation. Part of the Civil Rights Act of 1964 was based on the commerce clause. Title II of the law barred motels, restaurants, and other establishments from discrimination on the basis of race. When the federal government moved to force an Atlanta, Georgia, hotel to obey this law, the hotel filed an appeal. But in 1964, the Supreme Court ruled in favor of the government. The Court decision pointed out that the hotel was near two interstate highways and

CRITICAL VIEWING In a Progressive Era political cartoon, Theodore Roosevelt is shown holding a "muck-rake." Investigative journalists of the time were known as *muckrakers* for their work in digging up dirt or scandals regarding powerful people and institutions. Muckraking investigations led Roosevelt to champion passage of the Pure Food and Drug and Meat Inspection Acts. What job is the cartoonist portraying as repugnant in this cartoon?

that most of its customers came from outside Georgia. Since these customers had traveled across state lines, the hotel was engaged in interstate commerce.

HISTORICAL THINKING

1. **FORM AND SUPPORT OPINIONS** Why might the Framers have left creation of the federal court system up to Congress?
2. **DRAW CONCLUSIONS** How does the appeals process help ensure that the justice system is fair and treats people equally?
3. **INTERPRET CHARTS** Based on the chart, which federal courts have original jurisdiction and which have appellate jurisdiction?
4. **DESCRIBE** What does the name *elastic clause* imply about this power of Congress?

Court Decisions

The courts have also played a role in shaping the meaning of the Constitution. They do this through the process of **judicial review**, a constitutional doctrine that gives the federal courts the power to annul legislative or executive acts which the judges declare to be unconstitutional. The Constitution does not specifically grant this judicial review power to the courts. Article III, however, gives the courts the power to hear "all cases … arising under this Constitution."

The U.S. Supreme Court claimed the power of judicial review in the case of *Marbury* v. *Madison* (1803). The case arose from a feature in the Judiciary Act of 1789. That law gave the Supreme Court the power to issue writs of *mandamus*. These writs are court orders that force an official in the executive branch to carry out an action. In a unanimous decision written by Chief Justice John Marshall, the Supreme Court ruled that Congress violated the Constitution in giving the Court the power to issue writs of *mandamus*. Ironically, in stripping the Court of one power, Marshall and the other justices were claiming a far greater power—the power of federal courts to review, and strike down, acts of Congress. Marshall was unequivocal in his assertion of judicial power: "It is emphatically the province and duty of the Judicial Department to say what the law is." (You will read more about *Marbury* v. *Madison* in Chapter 4.)

The Supreme Court is not the only federal court that can exercise judicial review. A federal court of appeal can rule a law or executive action unconstitutional. But such a decision applies only to the region of the United States where that court is located. Only the U.S. Supreme Court can determine if a law or action does—or does not—apply to the whole country.

The Supreme Court can also exercise judicial review over state laws. The supremacy clause of the U.S. Constitution, in Article VI, says the Constitution and laws passed by Congress are the "supreme Law of the Land." That means they overrule state laws. If a state law conflicts with a federal law, the Supreme Court can strike down the state law.

Decided: February 24, 1803, 4–0

Majority: Chief Justice John Marshall wrote the opinion of the Court, which ruled that the law that would compel Madison to deliver commissions to duly appointed judges was unconstitutional. (Two justices recused themselves from the decision due to illness.)

In the final hours of his presidency, John Adams signed commissions for several federal judgeships. He wanted to stack the judiciary with people who believed, like him, in a strong central government before the offices could be filled by those who, like incoming president Thomas Jefferson, favored a weaker federal government. But not all the commissions were delivered before Jefferson took the oath of office and became president, and Jefferson ordered the acting secretary of state not to deliver those remaining commissions. Based on powers vested in the Supreme Court by the Judiciary Act of 1789, William Marbury and three other men who were denied their office demanded that the Court order Secretary of State James Madison to deliver their commissions.

Chief John Marshall faced a dilemma. If he ruled in Marbury's favor, Jefferson could defy the Court. Unable to force the president to act, the Supreme Court would be rendered irrelevant. If he found in Madison's favor, however, he would appear to be yielding to executive authority. Marshall found a clever third path.

The Court, according to Marshall, had to decide three issues. Do the men whose commissions were never delivered have a rightful claim to their positions? If they do, do the laws provide them with a remedy? If so, does the Supreme Court have the power to provide that remedy?

On the first point, Marshall ruled in favor of the four men—the commissions had been properly issued. Jefferson's failure to deliver them was an act "violative of a vested [guaranteed] legal right." On the second point, too, he ruled for the four petitioners. Any individual whose rights have been violated can call on the courts to remedy the situation.

On the third point, though, Marshall delivered a twist. The Judiciary Act of 1789 gave the Supreme Court original jurisdiction in cases like this one. In doing so,

William Marbury was a well-respected and successful businessman. He was also a staunch supporter of John Adams and the Federalist Party. In the election of 1800, he had worked hard to swing Maryland's votes to Adams. If he had succeeded, Adams would have won re-election.

Marshall said, it violated Article III of the Constitution, which set the rules for the Court's jurisdiction. The Constitution is the supreme law of the land, he wrote; and "a law repugnant to the Constitution is void." Who is to say when laws violate the Constitution? Marshall had a ready answer: "It is emphatically the province and duty of the Judicial Department to say what the law is." This is the power of judicial review. Interestingly, the Judiciary Act of 1789 is the only law declared unconstitutional in Marshall's tenure as Chief Justice.

THINK ABOUT IT In what way does this decision create a hierarchy of law?

HISTORICAL THINKING

5. **SYNTHESIZE** Why is *Marbury* v. *Madison* such an important Supreme Court decision?
6. **COMPARE AND CONTRAST** Why does a circuit court decision on whether a law is constitutional have less of an impact than a decision by the U.S. Supreme Court?

Executive Actions

Presidents have also found ways to enlarge the scope of executive branch power under the Constitution. They have issued executive orders and entered into executive agreements. Perhaps most dramatically, they have sent U.S. troops into foreign conflicts despite the Constitution placing the power to declare war solely with Congress. That use of executive power has been challenged by Congress at times.

EXECUTIVE ORDERS Starting with George Washington, presidents have issued executive orders. These presidential directives have the force of law until another president cancels or revokes them or the courts overturn them. Article II of the Constitution, which describes the executive branch, doesn't mention executive orders. Nonetheless, all presidents have issued such orders. They base their claim to this power on the Article II statement that the president "shall take Care that the Laws be faithfully executed." These orders frequently come under criticism as abuses of executive power. They can be challenged in the courts, and the Supreme Court has ruled some orders unconstitutional.

President George Washington issued the first executive order just a few months after he took office. He used it simply to ask the heads of the executive departments to send him a report on their department's activities.

In one of his more than 1,000 executive orders, Theodore Roosevelt proclaimed the Grand Canyon a national monument in 1908. Eleven years later, Congress passed a law making it a national park.

Some orders address minor matters, such as the location of a post office. Others can have a major impact. Abraham Lincoln's Emancipation Proclamation was an executive order that freed enslaved African Americans in states that had seceded from the United States during the Civil War.

Early presidents issued only a handful of these orders. It was not until the late 1800s that presidents regularly signed 100 or more executive orders during their term in office. President Theodore Roosevelt signed 1,081 executive orders. President Franklin Delano Roosevelt holds the record, having issued more than 3,720 orders over his 4 terms.

EXECUTIVE AGREEMENTS Presidents sometimes sign agreements with leaders of foreign countries. These are called *executive agreements*. They differ from formal treaties because, unlike treaties, they do not need approval by a vote of two-thirds of the U.S. Senate. They also differ from treaties because they may not apply after the term of the president who signed them. Of course, the next president can extend the agreement. Presidents claim the right to enter into these agreements on the basis of their power to carry out the country's foreign policy. In some cases, Congress passes a law that gives a president power to work out an agreement with another country on a specific matter.

WAR POWERS Article I, Section 8, Clause 11, clearly states that Congress has the power to declare war. Yet many presidents have committed troops to action in foreign countries without a declaration of war from Congress. Sometimes, these actions are brief and cost little in money or lives. In 1983, President Ronald Reagan sent troops to the tiny island of Grenada in an action that lasted only a few days. Other actions are longer lasting. Four presidents oversaw the American military presence in South Vietnam during the Vietnam War without a formal declaration of war.

Starting in 1965, President Lyndon Johnson ordered a massive build-up of American forces in Vietnam. That presence—in which more than 2.5 million Americans had served by 1973—prompted a debate over the war powers of the president and the Congress. Johnson claimed that the Gulf of Tonkin Resolution, passed by Congress in 1964 to give him the power to fight back against any attacks on U.S. forces in Vietnam, allowed him to send hundreds of thousands of troops into the war. As the war dragged on, critics said this resolution did not authorize as large a military response as Johnson had ordered.

In 1973, Congress passed the War Powers Resolution. It has several parts. The act requires a president to consult Congress before sending U.S. armed forces into an area where combat is taking place or may take place. A president can send troops somewhere to respond to an emergency, but the act puts a 60-day limit on such an action unless Congress formally approves the use of troops. Another part of the act states that the president must withdraw troops immediately if both houses of Congress pass a resolution requiring it. Congressional resolutions do not have the force of law, however, and the president does not have to sign them. But just as a president does not have to sign a resolution because it is not a law, neither can a president veto a resolution calling for the withdrawal of troops.

Though Congress tried to reclaim some power with this act, presidents have continued to commit troops without congressional approval. Some actions—like Reagan's in Grenada—were too brief to trigger the 60-day limit. On other occasions, presidents have sought congressional approval of military action but they may couch the request in language that implies that the president does not require that approval. For example, in 1990 Iraq invaded Kuwait, one of its neighbors. President George H.W. Bush wanted to send troops to Saudi Arabia, a U.S. ally in the region, to protect it from an Iraqi invasion. He said he did not need authorization from Congress because he was responding to a call for action by the United Nations. He did, however, request a congressional resolution supporting the action and he received it.

HISTORICAL THINKING

7. **MAKE INFERENCES** Why would a president say he did not need Congress to authorize him to send troops but that he would welcome the support of Congress?
8. **COMPARE AND CONTRAST** How do executive orders differ from laws in both process and effect?

CHAPTER 3

THE CONSTITUTION Review

VOCABULARY

Use each of the following vocabulary words in a sentence that shows an understanding of the term's meaning.

1. Preamble
2. allegiance
3. faction
4. demagogue
5. federalism
6. commerce
7. supermajority
8. revenue
9. tariff
10. suffrage
11. appellate court
12. judicial review

MAIN IDEAS

Answer the following questions. Support your answer with evidence from the chapter.

13. What are two ways the U.S. Constitution fulfills the goals for the document stated in the Preamble? **LESSON 3.1**
14. How is the principle of popular sovereignty related to the Preamble of the Constitution? **LESSON 3.2**
15. Identify one check that each branch of the federal government has on another branch and explain how it works as a check on the powers of that branch. **LESSON 3.3**
16. What is the amendment process under the Constitution? **LESSON 3.4**
17. How does the power of judicial review increase the power of the federal judiciary? **LESSON 3.6**

HISTORICAL THINKING

Answer the following questions. Support your answer with evidence from the chapter.

18. **FORM AND SUPPORT OPINIONS** Why did the Framers see the need to have a written constitution, rather than an unwritten one, such as the British constitution?
19. **ANALYZE CAUSE AND EFFECT** How does the fact that federal judges have lifetime appointments help make them independent and contribute to the power of the federal judiciary?
20. **SYNTHESIZE** How did the Framers use republican government to make the principle of popular sovereignty workable in a large country?
21. **MAKE CONNECTIONS** How is the principle of the rule of law connected to the principles of limited government and individual rights?
22. **IDENTIFY** Which principles of the U.S. Constitution is the Bill of Rights most closely connected to? Why?
23. **SYNTHESIZE** How have court decisions involving incorporation made the 14th Amendment significant for all Americans?
24. **ANALYZE CAUSE AND EFFECT** Why has each branch of the federal government been able to claim and use powers not specifically granted in the Constitution?

INTERPRET VISUALS

Study the political cartoon below. Then answer the questions.

25. What is the cartoonist saying about the government's responsibility towards Americans regarding freedom of speech?

26. What is the cartoonist saying about the difficulties that Americans sometimes have regarding freedom of speech?

ANALYZE SOURCES

In Federalist No. 39, James Madison wrote about the republican form of government created by the U.S. Constitution. Read the excerpt from the essay and answer the questions that follow.

> [W]e may define a republic to be ... a government which derives all its powers directly or indirectly from the great body of the people, and is administered by persons holding their offices during pleasure [for as long as people want them in office], for a limited period, or during good behavior. It is essential to such a government that it be derived from the great body of the society, not from ... a favored class of it.... It is *sufficient* for such a government that the persons administering it be appointed, either directly or indirectly, by the people; and that they hold their appointments by either of the tenures [conditions] just specified.

27. What principles of the U.S. Constitution is Madison writing about in Federalist No. 39?

28. What are two examples of how these principles are carried out in the Constitution?

CONNECT TO YOUR LIFE

29. **ARGUMENT** Which principle of the U.S. Constitution do you think is most important to the ability of that government to meet the goals of the Constitution as set forth in the Preamble? Give examples from the structure of the government or the powers and responsibilities of the different branches—and of the federal and state governments—to explain your ideas.

TIPS

- Reread the Preamble and the discussion of the goals it establishes for the Constitution.
- Review the structure of the government under the Constitution and the discussion of the powers of the different branches.
- Be sure that you have a clear statement of your response to the essay prompt.
- In your introduction, present the organization that your written response will follow.
- Cite specific details from the Constitution to support your ideas.
- End with a conclusion that restates your point and explains how your argument supported it.

CHAPTER 4
Federalism

LESSONS

4.1 What Is Federalism?

4.2 The Constitutional Division of Powers

4.3 Federal–State Relationships

4.4 Federalism Today

National Geographic Magazine:
Inside the New Battle for the American West

CRITICAL VIEWING In the federal system of government, power is divided between the national government and the individual states. Some powers are shared, but most powers are distinct, and in many situations, the national and state governments must cooperate to solve problems. During the coronavirus pandemic in 2020, members of the Michigan National Guard assembled beds at a convention center being converted to an emergency hospital by the U.S. Army Corps of Engineers. How does this effort reflect the federal system of the United States?

LESSON
4.1 What Is Federalism?

Like all Americans, you are governed by the national government as well as by your state and local governments. For example, the national government regulates farms that produce the food you eat. State governments license truckers who transport food to your grocery store. Local governments provide the permits the grocery store needs to do business. These different levels of government work together—usually!—in a federal system of government.

Shared Powers of Government

In 1787, at the Constitutional Convention, the Framers knew what they had to do. The national government was too weak to govern effectively, so they strengthened it. At the same time, they reserved important decision-making powers for the states. The result was a federal system of government, or federalism, a system in which the powers held by government are shared between the national government and the states.

Most countries have national, or central, governments as well as subnational (or below the national level) units, such as states or provinces. But that does not make their systems federal. For a system to be truly federal, the national and state powers must be specified and limited. As you have read, the Constitution of the United States meets this criterion. It sets forth certain powers that can be exercised by the national government. All other powers are "reserved," in the language of the Tenth Amendment, to the states or to the people.

Sharing power has not been easy. The broad language of the Constitution leaves much room for debate over the proper balance between national and state authority. Federalism ensures that neither the national government nor the state governments have all the power. But it does not provide equal power to both. The Constitution clearly states in Article VI that the Constitution is the "supreme law of the land" and that the laws of every state are bound by the laws of the national government. In other words, no state can make a law that violates the laws set forth by the national government under the rules established by the Constitution.

Over time, the national government has increased its power. President Ronald Reagan, who favored shifting power to the states, said:

> *The Founding Fathers saw the federalist system as constructed something like a masonry wall. The states are the bricks, the national government is the mortar. . . . Unfortunately, over the years, many people have increasingly come to believe that Washington is the whole wall.*

The national government, although it is expanding, is still just a part of the federal system of government. But the term *federal government* can be confusing. When people talk of the federal government, they mean the national government based in Washington, D.C. They are not referring to the federal system of government, which is made up of both the national government and state governments.

HISTORICAL THINKING

1. **CATEGORIZE** What makes the government of the United States a true federal system?
2. **DRAW CONCLUSIONS** Why do you think the term *federal government* has come to be a synonym for national government?

Other Systems of Government

When the Framers wrote the Constitution, they invented the principle of federalism. At the time they created the Constitution, they were familiar with two systems of government—unitary and confederate.

In a unitary system of government, the national government can assign some of its authority to subnational units. In 2000, Britain's Parliament created a municipal form of government for London, complete with an elected mayor. Sadiq Khan, meeting supporters at a rally, became the third directly elected mayor of London in 2016—and the first Muslim mayor of a Western capital city.

Federalism was a compromise, a way to combine these two systems.

UNITARY SYSTEM Most nations in the world today have a unitary system of government. In such a system, the constitution gives the national government all governing authority and decision-making powers. The national government can **delegate**, or assign authority for, some activities to states, provinces, or other subnational units. But it does not have to. In a unitary system, these subnational units are created by the national government, and the national government has power over them. Britain, France, Israel, the Philippines, and Japan are countries with a unitary system of government.

The Constitution of the United States does not mention local governments, such as cities and counties. For this reason, local governments are considered creations of state government. In legal terminology, they are "creatures of the state." That means that state governments can both give powers to and take powers away from local governments. In other words, the governments of the individual American states are unitary systems.

CONFEDERATE SYSTEM In a confederate system of government, the national government exists and operates only at the direction of the states or other subnational units. The first American constitution, the Articles of Confederation, established a confederate system. This system allowed the 13 states, when they agreed to do so, to act as one nation while maintaining their independence.

Few true confederate systems of government exist today. The closest might be the European Union (EU), a group of more than two dozen nations, each of which retains its sovereignty. Those nations, however, are guided by a set of common institutions with a level of executive authority similar to that found in a federal system. So the EU is really a mixed system.

HISTORICAL THINKING

3. **MAKE INFERENCES** Are local governments, such as cities or counties, unitary systems? Why or why not?

4. **COMPARE AND CONTRAST** Which system of government—federal, unitary, or confederate—do you think is most stable, or least subject to conflict between its levels of government? Explain your answer.

Advantages of Federalism

Federalism appealed to the Framers because it established a strong national government capable of handling common problems. At the same time, it allowed state governments to keep many of the powers they had under the Articles of Confederation. The federal system of government continues to offer many advantages.

EFFICIENCY The United States is a big country. Even when it consisted of only 13 states, its geographic area was larger than that of England or France. In those days, people and news traveled slowly, so Americans living outside cities were isolated. They might not learn of a major political decision for several weeks. Governing from a far-off capital (as in a national unitary system) would not have been an efficient way to run the country. The federal system allowed for far more efficient governance. Under federalism, states had substantial governing power. States could more easily extend some form of government even to remote areas.

Look at the table of units of government at different levels. As you can see, the practical business of governing takes place largely at the state and local levels. Indeed, the most common type of governmental unit in the United States is the **special district**, an independent unit of government that operates separately from other local governments such as counties, cities, and townships.

Most special districts carry out a single activity at the local level. They provide services such as waste disposal, fire protection, or park maintenance. To a great extent, they control their own finances and manage their district with little oversight from other governmental units.

EXPERIMENTATION Federalism allows subnational units of government to act on their own to solve problems. As a result, state and local governments often experiment with innovative public policies and programs. Many people, including former Supreme Court Justice Louis Brandeis, have seen the benefits of these types of experimental approaches. Brandeis said a state may, "if its citizens choose, serve as a laboratory; and try novel social and economic experiments" for the development of **public policy**—a plan of action taken by a government to achieve a stated goal. For example, state governments have a variety of policies on how or whether state employees can form labor unions. Recently, many states have raised the minimum wage above the national minimum wage. The results in these states over time could help resolve questions about whether a higher minimum wage hurts or helps the overall economy.

If a specific experiment proves successful in one state, other states may implement similar programs. The federal government might also adopt a policy that has been successful at the state level. For instance, California was a pioneer in air-pollution control in the 1960s, creating an Air Resources Board under then-governor Ronald Reagan. Many of that state's regulations were later adapted by other states and eventually by the federal government. More recently, California has launched costly programs to address

Governmental Units in the United States, 2012

GOVERNMENT UNIT	NUMBER
Federal government	1
State governments and District of Columbia	51
Local governments	
• Counties	3,031
• Municipalities	19,519
• Townships	16,360
• Special districts	38,266
• School districts	12,880
Local Government subtotal	90,056
Total	90,108

SOURCE: U.S. Census Bureau, Census of Governments, 2012

climate change. For example, California has set more stringent auto-emissions standards than the federal government, and more than a dozen other states have followed its lead. As California and other states seek to limit the use of petroleum and increase reliance on renewable energy, it remains to be seen whether the federal government will move in the same direction.

REGIONAL DIFFERENCES We have always been a nation marked by regional differences. The Pilgrims of New England had different values and perspectives from the settlers at Jamestown in Virginia. Both of these groups differed from those who began to settle the Dutch colony of New Amsterdam in present-day New York City. The earliest New Englanders had a religious focus, whereas Dutch settlers were more business oriented. People who settled in the South wanted to create an agricultural society. Landowners saw themselves as individual farmers inclined to act independently.

A federal system of government allows political, cultural, and other regional interests to be reflected in state laws. In 1869, for example, Wyoming—then still a territory—gave women the right to vote, long before Congress passed the women's suffrage amendment in 1919. By the time the 19th Amendment became law, 18 other states and territories had passed laws giving women full or partial voting rights. Most were in the West, whose newer, more open societies tended to give women greater scope for political activity.

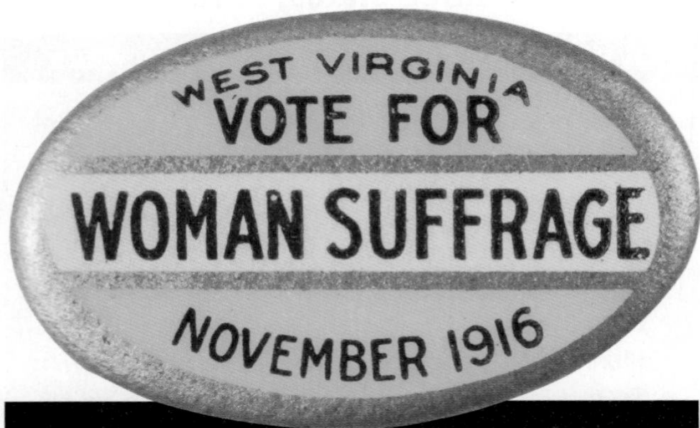

In 1916, West Virginia suffragists wore pins like this one to promote a referendum aimed at securing the vote for women. The all-male electorate voted against the referendum by a wide margin, but in 1920 the state legislature passed the proposed 19th Amendment to the Constitution, which secured the right to vote for women throughout the nation.

HISTORICAL THINKING

5. **IDENTIFY MAIN IDEAS AND DETAILS** How does federalism allow for more efficient governing of a large country like the United States?
6. **INTERPRET TABLES** Which type of government do you think Americans interact with most frequently? Explain your answer.

Disadvantages of Federalism

Federalism offers many advantages, but it also has some drawbacks. Scholars tend to agree that federalism promotes greater self-rule, or democracy. But they also point out that local self-rule may not always be in society's best interest. Historically, the most dramatic illustration of this sort of situation is slavery. Under federalism, states were free to permit or outlaw slavery. By 1804, all northern states had voted to abolish slavery within their borders, though in most of these states abolition was gradual. It took the Civil War to abolish slavery throughout the United States.

Another disadvantage of federalism is that state governments can impede the carrying out of national policies. For example, many politicians in southern states supported racial segregation, or the separation of different groups of people by racial ancestry or skin color. They continued to do so even after the Supreme Court ruled in 1954 that segregation in public schools was unconstitutional and must be eliminated "with all deliberate speed." Seven southern states continued to maintain segregated school systems, in defiance of federal law, until 1970.

A more recent example is the struggle over the health-care reforms adopted by Congress in 2010. These reforms sought to expand the number of low-income Americans eligible for health coverage under the Medicaid program. As of 2019, however, 14 states had not yet adopted this program, arguing that expansion of Medicaid in their states represented an unwarranted intrusion of national power into an area typically reserved for the states.

States have also fought against federal policies they believe can be harmful to citizens. In 2018, the attorneys general of 13 states joined with other state agencies to prevent the Environmental

Protection Agency (EPA) from implementing proposed federal rules that would restrict the EPA's ability to issue regulations to protect public health and the environment. Such state resistance to national policies and programs is not new. It is part of a long struggle over states' rights—the doctrine that states are sovereign and should retain all powers not explicitly assigned to the national government by the Constitution.

Federalism has other drawbacks. One of them is the difficulty of coordinating government policies at the national, state, and local levels. For example, each of these levels of government might have different rules related to businesses. Trying to deal with conflicting laws and regulations can be costly for companies doing business with more than one level of government.

HISTORICAL THINKING

7. **FORM AND SUPPORT OPINIONS** For two decades, starting in 1974, the national government pushed states to adopt a uniform highway speed limit of 55 miles per hour. Should states set highway speed limits, or should that be a federal responsibility? Explain your answer.

LESSON 4.2 The Constitutional Division of Powers

If you join a club at school, you might be given a list of rules and regulations that identify the club's mission and how responsibility for carrying out that mission is divided among the members. The Constitution is the rulebook for the United States. Among other things, it divides the powers and responsibilities for governing the country between the national government and the states. The Constitution spells out a number of those powers, but it leaves some open to interpretation. So, who gets what powers? The question is still not completely settled—and probably never will be.

The Powers of the National Government

As you have read, most nations have a unitary form of government. In a unitary system, it's clear who's in charge: all the sovereign powers are held by the central government. It may delegate some powers to subnational units, but it can take them back at any time.

In a federal system of government, however, as we have said, sovereign powers are divided, or allocated, between the national and state governments. Some powers can be exercised by the national government, and others are reserved for the states. Another way of saying this is that the national government has the major responsibility in some areas of government, and the state governments have the primary responsibility in other areas. For example, the national government is responsible for keeping the nation secure from foreign invasion, while state governments take responsibility for establishing public schools.

The Constitution does not systematically explain this division of powers, but it includes statements that identify what the national and state governments can do. The national government is accorded, or given, three types of powers. They are known as expressed powers, implied powers, and inherent powers. The Constitution also prohibits the national government from taking certain actions.

EXPRESSED POWERS As you have read, the Framers designed the Constitution in a way that would give the national government the powers needed to effectively govern the nation, but they did not want the national government to have too much power. So they enumerated, or listed, the national government's powers. The powers the Constitution specifically grants to the three branches of the national government in Articles I, II, and III are known as the enumerated powers or the expressed (clearly stated) powers.

Admitting New States

The standard process for gaining statehood calls for the people of a territory to submit a **petition**, or formal written request, to Congress asking for admission as a state. As a rule, Congress has required that a territory's population be large enough to support a state government and that the people are prepared for and capable of self-rule. If those conditions are met, Congress then has to pass an "enabling act" authorizing a constitutional convention in the territory. The territorial government then drafts a constitution. If the people of the territory vote to accept the proposed state constitution, it is submitted to Congress for approval. Congress then votes on an act of admission. Once the act passes and the president signs it, the territory officially joins the Union.

The admission process isn't always so straightforward. Take Maine, for example. Since the mid-1600s, Maine had been a part of Massachusetts. As Maine's population increased in the early 1800s, many in Maine complained about their limited representation in the Massachusetts legislature and demanded separation. But the Constitution prohibits the formation of any new state within the boundaries of another state unless the existing state and Congress approve. At first, Massachusetts resisted, but it finally gave in. In 1820, Congress allowed Maine to enter the Union as a free state while adding Missouri as a state that allowed slavery.

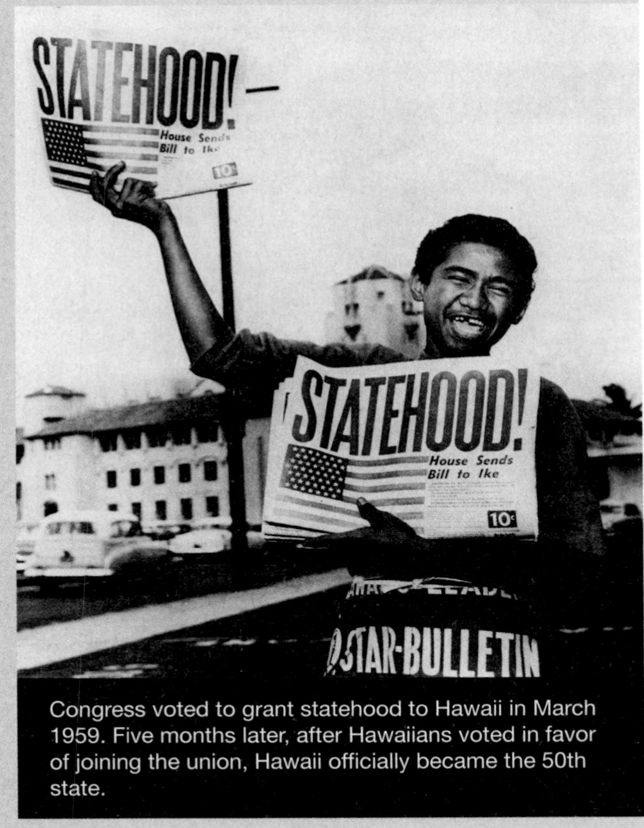

Congress voted to grant statehood to Hawaii in March 1959. Five months later, after Hawaiians voted in favor of joining the union, Hawaii officially became the 50th state.

Congress can also insist that specific conditions be met before it allows a grant of statehood to go forward. In 1819, Congress ruled that Missouri could not join the Union unless it was willing to allow free African Americans from other states to become residents with full constitutional privileges. Congress admitted Alaska in 1959 only after it agreed to end its claims to lands held by Native Americans.

The Framers understood the importance of the legislative branch to the government of a republic, so they sought to make clear what it could and couldn't do. Article I, Section 8, of the Constitution expressly lists 27 powers that Congress may exercise. These powers include the authority to "lay and collect Taxes," to "borrow Money," to "establish Post Offices," and to "declare War." The national government, through Congress, also has the right to regulate commerce not only with foreign nations and among the states but also "with the Indian Tribes." As a result, the national government is responsible for relations between Native American tribal governments and the rest of the country. A further consequence is that state governments face significant limits on their authority over Native American reservations within their borders.

This extensive list of powers reflects the desire of the Framers to give the national government a more robust set of powers than it possessed under the Articles of Confederation. Since 1789, constitutional amendments have laid out other expressed powers. For example, the 16th Amendment, added in 1913, gives Congress the power to impose a federal income tax.

The expressed powers of the other branches are not so extensive. Article II, Section 2, of the Constitution specifies the powers of the president, which include commanding the armed forces and making treaties. Article III, Section 2, spells out the powers of the Supreme Court. These include the authority to resolve disputes between states and between citizens of different states.

Although the Constitution assigned many powers, it left most of the practical details to be worked out by Congress. Article IV, Section 3, for example, gives Congress the power to admit states to the Union, but it doesn't describe the process. In this case, Congress looked to the example of a law passed under the Articles of Confederation, the Northwest Ordinance. It served as a model for all later laws governing the admission of new states.

IMPLIED POWERS Expressed powers are specifically stated in the Constitution, but implied powers are not. The constitutional basis for the implied powers of the national government is found in Clause 18 of Article I, Section 8. This clause, known as the necessary and proper clause, or the elastic clause, states that Congress has the power to make "all Laws which shall be necessary and proper for carrying into Execution the foregoing [expressed] Powers." The elastic clause states that Congress has additional, unspecified powers linked to the ones enumerated in the Constitution. Its inclusion in the Constitution reflects the Framers' pragmatic recognition that they couldn't foresee, much less spell out, all possible powers Congress might need.

Congress has used the elastic clause to extend its expressed powers over a variety of situations not specifically identified in the Constitution. One example of an implied power is the military draft. One of Congress's expressed powers allows it "to raise and support Armies." In this case, the link between the expressed and the implied power is clear. But what about another power that Congress has assumed—the power to establish national parks? That power

CRITICAL VIEWING Old Faithful is one of more than 500 active geysers in Yellowstone National Park. To create the park—and the national park system—Congress used the implied power found in the property clause of the Constitution (Article IV, Section 3). Based on the photo, what features of this land might have led Congress to agree to set it aside as a national park?

is implied in Article IV, Section 3, Clause 2. This section of the Constitution grants Congress the right to admit states, and it also states that Congress has the power to make "all needful Rules and Regulations respecting the Territory" of the United States. Congress also has set a federal minimum wage, although such a thing did not exist at the time of the Framers. Like many other implied powers, this one is based on the commerce clause, which you'll read more about later.

INHERENT POWERS Inherent powers are those powers that come with the job of governing a country. They are powers historically accepted as essential to enabling a national government to secure the country and deal with the outside world. For example, a national government must have the ability to make treaties, regulate immigration, acquire territory, wage war, and make peace. Some inherent powers, such as waging war and making treaties, are enumerated in the Constitution. Others aren't. For example, the Constitution does not speak of regulating immigration.

One inherent power is older than the Constitution itself—the power to own land. The United States won title to various western lands because of the Treaty of Paris of 1783 that ended the Revolutionary War. The Northwest Territory was organized during the ratification of the Constitution. Indeed, establishing the territory as the collective property of the entire Union was necessary to secure support for ratification in several states, including Maryland. The United States then sold land to new settlers—land sales were a major source of income for the national government throughout much of the 1800s. To this day, the national government owns most of the land in the western United States.

HISTORICAL THINKING

1. **MAKE PREDICTIONS** Do you think the Framers expected that the necessary and proper clause would ever be as "elastic" as it has become? Why or why not?
2. **MAKE CONNECTIONS** Why do you think many limits on the powers of the national government appear in the first eight amendments to the Constitution?

The Powers of the States

As you have read, the Tenth Amendment to the Constitution states that powers not delegated to the national government by the Constitution and not prohibited to the states "are reserved to the States respectively, or to the people." In a sense, the Tenth Amendment doesn't give the states any rights they didn't already possess. The Framers intended it as a general statement of principle that federal power is limited. But because the Tenth Amendment doesn't specify the powers reserved to the states, its exact meaning and even its relevance have varied over time.

In periods of widespread support for increased regulation by the national government, the Tenth Amendment has faded from the scene, virtually ignored by the Supreme Court. In periods during which states have sought to assert their rights and push back against the exercise of power by the federal government, the Tenth Amendment has taken on renewed importance. Since 1986, the Court has applied the Tenth Amendment in various rulings limiting the power of the federal government to regulate state governments. Whether they need to cite the Tenth Amendment in these decisions is unclear. Some scholars argue that by enumerating the national government's powers, the Constitution adequately limits the national government.

Regardless of how the Court rules on any particular case, supporters of states' rights who oppose what they believe is excessive federal power continue to draw on the Tenth Amendment. For example, in 2010, some members of Congress who believed the federal government had too great a role in Americans' lives formed a group aimed, they said, at defending "state sovereignty from increasingly overbearing federal encroachment." The group dubbed itself the Tenth Amendment Task Force, announcing in its very name how much the group valued the last amendment in the Bill of Rights.

POLICE POWERS The Tenth Amendment ensures that states retain police powers—the authority to enact and enforce whatever laws are necessary to maintain order and protect the health, safety, general welfare, and morals of a people—for their states. One of the police powers is the right to maintain a state militia, which generally consists of state National Guard units. But police powers do not simply apply to a state's various police forces. It is a much broader concept. Traditionally, the states' police powers include the right to regulate commerce within their borders. For example, states require businesses to obtain licenses and permits before they can operate. Police powers also cover the rights of states and local governments to establish public schools and regulate marriage and divorce, both of which serve to promote the general welfare.

During Hurricane Harvey in 2017, Texas National Guard troops rescued many Houston residents from flooded neighborhoods. Calling out the National Guard is one example of how state governments use their police powers to protect the health and safety of residents.

POWERS PROHIBITED TO THE STATES Article I, Section 10, of the Constitution denies certain powers to state governments. For example, unless they have "the Consent of the Congress," states cannot "lay any Imposts or Duties on Imports or Exports"—that is, they are prohibited from taxing goods transported across state lines. The same article declares, "No State shall enter into any Treaty, Alliance, or Confederation." Other prohibitions appear in various amendments.

FULL FAITH AND CREDIT CLAUSE Article IV, Section 1, of the Constitution contains what is, in effect, another kind of limit on the states. Known as the full faith and credit clause, it requires each state to respect and honor every other state's "public Acts, Records, and judicial Proceedings." Basically, that means a **judgment**, or court decision, in one state must be enforced in another. For example, if a state in one court orders a parent to pay child support, he or she cannot evade that responsibility by moving to another state.

This constitutional requirement posed a potential problem in the years 2004–2015, when same-sex marriage was legal in some states, but not all. According to the full faith and credit clause, if a couple was legally married in one state, all the other states would have to recognize the marriage. This applied to same-sex couples at a time when only a few states allowed them to marry. In 1996, Congress acted to prevent this possibility by passing the Defense of Marriage Act (DOMA). This act didn't ban same-sex marriages, but it allowed states the legal right to refuse to recognize those marriages.

Challenges to DOMA eventually made their way to the Supreme Court. In *United States* v. *Windsor* (2013), the Court ruled that by barring the national government from recognizing same-sex marriages, DOMA denied equal protection to same-sex couples. Nonetheless, the section of DOMA that allowed states not to recognize same-sex marriages made in other states remained in force. By 2015, 37 states and the District of Columbia permitted same-sex marriage. In June of that year, the Supreme Court overturned DOMA in *Obergefell* v. *Hodges*, a case you'll read more about later. With its decision in that case, the Supreme Court ruled that laws against same-sex marriage were unconstitutional throughout the entire country. This decision had the effect of overturning DOMA, but the Court never ruled on whether DOMA violated the full faith and credit clause.

HISTORICAL THINKING

3. **MAKE INFERENCES** Why do you think state laws aimed at regulating a state's affairs are called police powers?
4. **DRAW CONCLUSIONS** Why do you think the Supreme Court waited until 2015 to rule on the Defense of Marriage Act (DOMA)?

Concurrent Powers and the Supremacy Clause

Concurrent powers, also called shared powers, are powers that both state governments and the federal government have. They are called *concurrent* because they can be exercised by state governments and the federal government at the same time. For example, both state governments and the federal government can borrow money to fund their operations. Just because the federal government is borrowing money doesn't mean the state of Georgia can't. But a state can exercise a power it holds concurrently with the federal government only within its borders. Both state governments and federal governments can establish courts, for example, but Utah can't set up a court in Idaho. Moreover, by definition, concurrent powers do not include functions that the Constitution delegates exclusively to the national government. A state government might like to coin its own money, but the Constitution gives that power exclusively to the national government. Likewise, Alaska might like to work out an agreement on fishing rights with Canada, but it can't. Treaty-making power belongs only to the federal government.

The power to tax is perhaps the most familiar concurrent power. The states and the national government both have the power to impose income taxes and a variety of other taxes. States, however, are prohibited from imposing tariffs (taxes on imported goods), and as noted, the federal government may not tax articles exported by any state.

The Constitution makes it clear that the United States—that is, the federal government—holds ultimate power. As you read earlier, Article VI, Clause 2, known as the supremacy clause, declares that the Constitution and the laws of the United States "shall be the supreme Law of the Land." In other words, states cannot use their reserved or concurrent powers to counter national policies. Article VI goes on to say that all state or local officers, such as judges or sheriffs, "shall be bound by oath" to support the Constitution of the United States. National government power, as laid out by the Constitution, always takes precedence over any conflicting state action.

HISTORICAL THINKING

5. **CLASSIFY** Why shouldn't the coining (or printing) of money be a concurrent power?
6. **INTERPRET CHARTS** According to the chart, which powers are needed in order for government to be able to fund its operations? Explain your answer.
7. **DRAW CONCLUSIONS** Does it make sense in a federal system that the national government holds supreme power? Explain your answer.

NATIONAL *and* STATE POWERS UNDER FEDERALISM

NATIONAL *Powers*	SHARED *Powers*	STATE *Powers*
• Declaring war • Raising and maintaining the armed forces • Issuing money • Regulating interstate and international commerce • Running the postal system • Issuing copyrights and patents • Making all laws "necessary and proper" for carrying out these powers	• Making and enforcing laws • Operating a court system • Proposing constitutional amendments • Collecting taxes • Overseeing banks • Borrowing money	• Holding elections • Establishing local government • Ratifying constitutional amendments • Regulating commerce within the state • Making laws for marriage, divorce • Issuing licenses to professionals • Exercising powers not expressly granted to national government or denied to the states

LESSON

4.3 Federal–State Relationships

How can a political debate cause such deep divisions that it leads to violent conflict? When the debate is about power at the state and national levels, the stakes can be pretty high. From the time the Constitution was written, clauses related to federalism's division of powers set off arguments about states' rights versus national supremacy. Supreme Court decisions in the early 1800s came down largely on the side of the national government. When the national government seemed ready to use its supreme power to abolish slavery, however, the decades-old argument boiled over into civil war.

Supreme Court and Federalism

Much of the political and legal history of the United States has involved a clash of ideas—the supremacy of the national government versus the preservation of state sovereignty. It is a clash that is built into the nature of our federal system and into the Constitution itself. When disputes over the meaning of the Constitution arise, it is the responsibility of the Supreme Court to make the final judgment. In the early years of the nation, the Supreme Court under Chief Justice John Marshall made some key decisions that began to define the balance of power between the states and the federal government. In doing so, the Court helped define the contours of federalism in the United States.

As you have read, Marshall did much to establish the independence of the Court with his ruling in *Marbury* v. *Madison* (1803), in which he asserted the Court's power of judicial review. Marshall also did much to advance the power of the federal government in two other historic decisions the Court made in the early 19th century. *McCulloch* v. *Maryland* (1819) rested on the question of how to interpret the Constitution's necessary and proper clause. Thomas Jefferson and other advocates of states' rights argued for a narrow interpretation, which gave Congress only enough power as was absolutely necessary to carry out its expressed powers. Marshall was a Federalist who believed in a strong national government. He guided the Court to interpret the clause more broadly, laying the groundwork for the doctrine of implied powers.

CRITICAL VIEWING As chief justice of the United States from 1801 to 1835, John Marshall played a crucial role in making the Supreme Court an effective and independent institution. In the process, he enhanced the power of the national government within the federal system. What details in this 1880 portrait by Richard Norris Brooke suggest that Marshall was a scholar?

T

och

charter of the Second Bank of the United States lapsed in 1836, the institution limped along for a few mor
the Bank of the United States of Pennsylvania. It continued to issue banknotes such as this one from 184

March 6, 1819, 7–0

Chief Justice John Marshall wrote the
r the Court in favor of McCulloch.

concerned a tax imposed by the state of
on the Baltimore branch of the Second Bank
ed States. Congress had chartered the bank,
nents of the bank in various states passed
g its branches. The Baltimore branch, led
f cashier, James McCulloch, refused to pay
nd tax, believing it to be unconstitutional.
n continued to issue bank notes lacking
tax stamp, and Maryland courts ruled his
awful. McCulloch appealed the case to the
Court. The case rested on two questions: Did
ess have the power to charter a bank, even
e Constitution does not expressly grant that
nd if so, could a state tax a bank chartered by
l government?

ruled unanimously, 7–0, in favor of
n and the bank, striking down the Maryland
written opinion, Chief Justice Marshall
at Congress could charter a bank because
sary and proper clause gave it implied
at could be used to carry out its expressed
such as collecting taxes, borrowing, and

spending. Next, Marshall took up Maryland's
that it could tax the national bank. Marshall
that if a state had the right to tax the bank, i
other federal agencies, and if a state could a
power, the Constitution's claim to be the "su
law of the land" would be empty rhetoric. "T
Government of the Union, though limited in
is supreme within its sphere of action," Mars
"The States have no power, by taxation or c
to retard, impede, burthen [burden], or in an
control the operations of the constitutional la
enacted by Congress to carry into effect the
vested in the national Government."

In spite of the favorable ruling, the Second B
United States didn't survive the presidency
Jackson. In 1832, Jackson, a strong backe
rights, vetoed a bill to renew the bank's cha
license to operate, and *McCulloch* v. *Maryla*
from view. Still, since the ruling was never o
it remained a potentially powerful precedent
the 20th century, the Court's ruling in *McCu*
Maryland provided the constitutional basis f
federal government's use of implied powers
its involvement in the economy.

THINK ABOUT IT How did Marshall a
principle of judicial review in *McCulloch* v. *M*

In *Gibbons* v. *Ogden* (1824), the entire Court once again sided with the national government in a unanimous ruling. In this case, the Court cited the commerce clause in a case over whether the state of New York could control navigation between New York and New Jersey. As you have read, the commerce clause subsequently became an important tool that Congress used to regulate the economy.

HISTORICAL THINKING

1. **MAKE CONNECTIONS** Could the Supreme Court under Marshall have ruled as it did in the *McCulloch* and *Gibbons* cases without the *Marbury* decision? Why or why not?
2. **ASK AND ANSWER QUESTIONS** Why do you think Marshall sided with the national government in cases such as *McCulloch* v. *Maryland* and *Gibbons* v. *Ogden*?

A Bloody Conflict Over Slavery—and Supremacy

The great issue that provoked the Civil War was the future of slavery. People in different sections of the country had radically different views of slavery. Many White southerners believed states had the right to continue enslaving human beings. They defended slavery as essential to their states' agricultural economy. Many northerners had strong moral objections to slavery and wanted the United States to abolish it, even though many White northerners also benefited financially from products of slave labor. The slavery issue thus represented a dispute over states' rights versus the supremacy of the national government. The Civil War brought this dispute to a bloody climax.

NULLIFICATION CRISIS In 1824, the Supreme Court under John Marshall interpreted the commerce clause in a way that increased the power of the national government at the expense of state powers. By the late 1820s, however, the regulation of commerce became one of the major issues in federal–state relations. In 1828, Congress passed a law imposing tariffs (taxes) on goods imported into the United States. The tariff was designed to help manufacturers and factory owners in northern states. Southern states had few factories, and influential southern planters imported a lot of goods from Great Britain and France. They argued that they would end up paying the bulk of the tariff. They called the law the Tariff of Abominations and threatened to disobey it.

The dispute simmered for a few years. President Andrew Jackson refused to rescind, or repeal, the law. His own vice president, John C. Calhoun of South Carolina, led the opposition to it. Drawing on an idea first proposed by Thomas Jefferson, Calhoun said that states had the right to **nullify**, or cancel, any law that they believed to be unconstitutional. In 1832, Congress passed a new, lower tariff, but that didn't appease opponents.

South Carolina's legislature passed a law declaring the tariffs "null and void." It threatened that South Carolina would leave the Union if the federal government tried to enforce the law in the state. President Jackson issued a statement affirming the tariff, and Congress authorized the use of force against any state refusing to pay it. To defuse the crisis, Congress passed a new tariff in 1833 that would expire in 10 years. South Carolina accepted the new law, and the crisis passed—temporarily.

SLAVERY, STATES' RIGHTS, AND SECESSION Some three decades later, the dispute over states' rights versus the supremacy of the national government escalated. With the election of Abraham Lincoln as president, southerners feared that the national government would move to end slavery. In 1860 and 1861, 11 southern states opted for **secession**, or withdrawal from the Union. Together they formed the Confederate States of America.

The defense of slavery and the promotion of states' rights were both important to the South's decision to secede. Both concepts blended together in the minds of southern voters of that era. Which of these two was the more important cause of secession remains a matter of debate even today. Some modern defenders of state sovereignty view southern secession as entirely a matter of states' rights. Other people argue that slavery was the sole cause of the crisis. Although states' rights had a role, the formal declarations of secession issued by the southern states left little doubt that slavery was at the heart of the conflict.

Many African Americans under the protection of the Union Army during the Civil War were able to attend schools like this one in Richmond, Virginia, shown in an image taken by famed photographer Mathew Brady in 1865. These schools were forerunners of the schools established by the federal government after the war through the Freedmen's Bureau.

When the South was defeated in the war, the idea that a state has a right to secede from the Union was defeated as well. The defeat marked the end of a period of growing demand for states' rights. Instead of advancing states' rights, the Civil War had the opposite result—an increase in the political power of the national government. The so-called Civil War Amendments—the 13th, 14th, and 15th Amendments that followed the Union victory in the war—gave the national government the legal authority to enforce significant new rights. These included the power to

- abolish laws that allowed slavery,
- ensure that states would guarantee all persons due process of law and the equal protection of the laws, and
- require states to recognize the right of African Americans to vote.

DUAL FEDERALISM Scholars have devised various models to describe the relationship between the states and the national government at different times in our history. These models help us understand how federalism evolved after the Civil War.

The model of dual federalism assumes that the states and the national government are more or less equals, with each level of government having separate and distinct functions and responsibilities. The states exercise sovereign powers over certain matters, and the national government exercises sovereign powers over others. Starting around the time of Andrew Jackson, who was president from 1829 to 1837, this model of federalism prevailed in court decisions.

The Civil War brought a brief expansion of national authority. But in the years that followed, the balance characterized by dual federalism gradually returned. The Supreme Court once again relied on the dual federalism model in support of states' sovereignty in their own "spheres." As a result, the Court acted to strictly limit the powers of the federal government to regulate businesses under the commerce clause. For example, in 1918 the Supreme Court struck down a federal law that was designed to discourage the use of child labor by prohibiting products created using child labor from being distributed across state lines. The Court ruled the law unconstitutional because it attempted to regulate what the Court regarded as a local problem. The Supreme Court, and much of the rest of the nation, also turned a blind eye to **racial discrimination**, or unfair treatment based on ancestry or physical features such as skin color, allowing southern states to enact laws that restricted the rights of African Americans. This era of dual federalism only came to an end in the 1930s, in response to the greatest economic depression the United States had ever experienced.

HISTORICAL THINKING

3. **IDENTIFY MAIN IDEAS AND DETAILS** What are the two main explanations for why southern states seceded from the Union?
4. **MAKE INFERENCES** What do you think Chief Justice John Marshall would have thought about the dual federalism demonstrated in the Supreme Court's actions after the Civil War? Why?

Cooperative Federalism and the National Government

The Great Depression helped redefine the relationship between federal government and the states, and scholars have coined a term to describe the new relationship: cooperative federalism. In the model of cooperative federalism, all levels of government work together to solve problems, and the national and state governments are seen as complementary parts of a single governmental mechanism. For example, the Federal Bureau of Investigation (FBI) lends technical expertise to solve local crimes, and state agencies share information with federal agencies.

ROOSEVELT'S NEW DEAL The new model of federal–state relations emerged initially in fits and starts as a pragmatic, or practical, response to a pressing emergency: the Great Depression. In an attempt to jumpstart the nation's economic engine, President Franklin D. Roosevelt (1933–1945) launched his **New Deal**. This series of initiatives created jobs, public-assistance programs, and numerous government agencies to regulate parts of the economy—all of which required new levels of government spending and federal involvement in everyday life.

One problem that states and the federal government worked together to solve was the need for economic development in parts of the rural Southeast. In 1933, New Deal legislation created the Tennessee Valley Authority (TVA), whose mission was to provide flood control and electrical power to a region that included seven states. The project was overseen by a board of directors whose nine members included seven residents of the region.

Another example of cooperative federalism was the Agricultural Adjustment Act, a New Deal law from 1933 that established a program to bring relief to farmers by supporting, or raising, the prices they received for their crops. The national government funded nearly all of this program, but local officials administered it.

Roosevelt's New Deal faced opposition from the Supreme Court, which struck down many of the early New Deal laws as unconstitutional, including the Agricultural Adjustment Act. As mentioned earlier, well into the early part of the 20th century, the Court held a restrictive view of what the federal government could do under the commerce clause, and most of the New Deal legislation had relied on the commerce clause to justify federal action. Facing the prospect of continued setbacks at the hands of the Supreme Court, Roosevelt threatened to "pack" the Court in 1937 with up to six new members more open to new federal programs. Critics called Roosevelt's Court-packing scheme an assault on the Constitution, and Congress refused to support it. Later that year, however, Roosevelt had the opportunity—for the first time since taking office—to appoint a new member to the Supreme Court. Hugo Black, the new justice, tipped the balance on the Court. After 1937, the Court stopped trying to limit the scope of the commerce clause.

Once the Supreme Court began to cooperate, New Deal legislation again flowed from Congress. The era of cooperative federalism that began with the New Deal has more or less continued until the present day. So, too, despite efforts to reassert states' rights, has the era of national supremacy.

CRITICAL VIEWING Starting in the 1930s, the Tennessee Valley Authority (TVA)—a federal government corporation—undertook a program to build hydroelectric dams. One of its goals was to provide affordable electricity to seven rural southeastern states. The Fort Loudoun Dam in Tennessee, shown here during its construction, was completed in 1943. What does this photo suggest was an important benefit of TVA programs like this one?

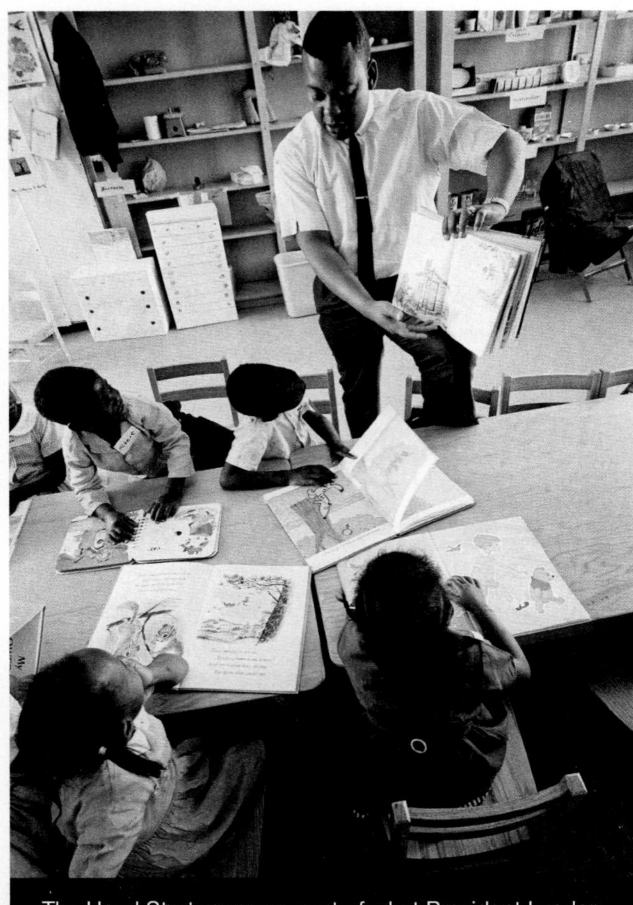

The Head Start program, part of what President Lyndon Johnson called his "war on poverty," is an example of cooperative federalism. Head Start classrooms such as this one provided early education to children from low-income families, many of whom were African American. This program resulted from cooperation between the federal government and the states.

JOHNSON'S "GREAT SOCIETY" The 1960s and 1970s saw an even greater expansion of the national government's role in domestic policy. The Great Society legislation of President Lyndon B. Johnson (1963–1969) created Medicaid, Medicare, the Job Corps, Head Start, and other programs. The Civil Rights Act of 1964 prohibited discrimination in public accommodations (hotels, restaurants), employment, and other areas on the basis of race, color, national origin, religion, or gender. In the 1970s, national laws protecting consumers, employees, and the environment imposed further regulations on the economy. Today, few activities are beyond the reach of the regulatory arm of the national government.

Nonetheless, the massive social programs undertaken in the 1960s and 1970s also resulted in greater involvement by state and local governments. The national government simply could not implement those programs alone. It needed the cooperation of the lower levels of government. Take as an example Head Start, a program that provides preschool services to children of low-income families. Head Start is funded by federal grants but is administered by local nonprofit organizations and school systems. Thus, it is a clear example of cooperative federalism.

CONGRESS AND THE COMMERCE CLAUSE The regulatory powers that the national government enjoys today rest on two Supreme Court decisions handed down two centuries ago. You have read about both—*McCulloch* v. *Maryland* and *Gibbons* v. *Ogden*. From 1937 on, based largely on these decisions, the Court consistently upheld Congress's power to regulate domestic policy under the commerce clause.

Recall that the commerce clause refers to interstate commerce. What about activities that occur entirely within a state? Even these have rarely been ruled outside the regulatory power of the national government. Consider a small farmer in Ohio who sold most of his wheat on the open market but grew some extra wheat intended wholly for consumption on his own farm. In 1942, the Court held that the farmer's extra wheat production was subject to federal regulation because the home consumption of wheat reduced the demand for wheat. That reduced demand could have an effect on interstate commerce.

In 1980, the Supreme Court acknowledged that the commerce clause had "long been interpreted to extend beyond activities actually in interstate commerce." Today, Congress can regulate almost any kind of economic activity, no matter where it occurs. In recent years, though, the Supreme Court has, for the first time since the 1930s, occasionally curbed Congress's regulatory powers under the commerce clause.

FEDERAL PREEMPTION The supremacy clause of the Constitution, fortified by the *McCulloch* decision, has also had significant consequences for federalism. One important effect is that when federal law and state law conflict, the federal law preempts, or supersedes, the state law. Federal preemption applied when Congress passed the Voting Rights Act of 1965. This act, aimed at ending

Ferries on the Hudson River serve a number of terminals in New York and New Jersey. The ferry service is an example of interstate commerce, which the federal government has the exclusive right to regulate according to the decision in *Gibbons* v. *Ogden* (1824).

SUPREME COURT

Gibbons v. *Ogden*, 1824

Decided: March 2, 1824, 6–0

Majority: Chief Justice John Marshall wrote the opinion of the Court in favor of Gibbons. Associate Justice William Johnson wrote a concurring opinion—one that offers a different reason for arriving at a decision.

Article I, Section 8, of the Constitution gives Congress the power to regulate commerce "among the several States," generally referred to as interstate commerce. But the Framers of the Constitution did not define the word *commerce*. At issue in *Gibbons* v. *Ogden* was how the commerce clause should be defined and whether the national government had the exclusive power to regulate commerce involving more than one state.

The New York legislature had given Robert Livingston and Robert Fulton the exclusive right to operate steamboats in New York waters. Livingston and Fulton then licensed Aaron Ogden to operate a ferry between New York and New Jersey. Thomas Gibbons, who had a license from the U.S. government to operate boats in interstate waters, decided to compete with Ogden, but he did so without New York's permission.

Ogden sued Gibbons in the New York state courts, which ruled in his favor. Gibbons appealed his case to the Supreme Court, which reversed the decision of the New York courts in a unanimous 6–0 decision. Chief Justice Marshall's opinion offered an expansive definition of *commerce*. He said it comprised all business dealings—including steamboat travel. Marshall also stated that the power to regulate interstate commerce was an exclusive national power. Furthermore, he wrote, this power had no limitations other than those specifically found in the Constitution. Since this 1824 decision, the national government has used the commerce clause repeatedly to justify its regulation of almost all areas of economic activity.

THINK ABOUT IT How did the Court's ruling in the *Gibbons* v. *Ogden* case add to the developing doctrine of the supremacy of the national government?

racial discrimination in voting, preempted state laws and regulations that were in conflict with the federal law. In such cases, the courts have held that a valid federal law or regulation takes precedence over a conflicting state or local law or regulation covering the same general activity.

HISTORICAL THINKING

5. **COMPARE AND CONTRAST** How is a cooperative federalist government like a complex machine?
6. **EVALUATE** Do you think cooperative federalism strengthened or undermined states' rights? Explain your answer.

LESSON

4.4 Federalism Today

Americans who suffered the hardships of the Great Depression were grateful for New Deal programs that created jobs and other forms of assistance. World War II brought new reasons to appreciate the power of the federal government to mobilize troops and weapons to defeat fascism. But by the 1970s, some Americans worried about the size of the national government, seeing it as a threat to the sovereignty of the states and the liberties of the people.

The New Federalism

Starting in the 1970s, several presidents worked to restore the doctrine of dual federalism. They renamed it the *new federalism*. The new federalism aimed to return to the states certain powers that had been exercised by the national government since the 1930s. The term **devolution**—the transfer of powers to political subunits—describes this process.

The new federalism was an outgrowth of conservativism. As you've read, conservatism is a political ideology that supports a limited role for government. At first, most of its supporters were Republicans. But its devolutionary goals appealed to some Democrats, such as President Bill Clinton. In 1996, Congress passed legislation reforming **welfare**, as government public-assistance programs that provide an economic safety net of benefits, including food, housing, and health care, are known. This legislation gained the backing of the president and other key officials of the executive branch because it furthered the goals of the new federalism by giving the states more authority. It also lowered costs to taxpayers by restricting benefits.

In the 1990s and early 2000s, the Supreme Court furthered the cause of states' rights. A variety of decisions either limited the power of the federal government or enhanced the power of the states. Two of them had to do with guns.

United States v. *Lopez* was a **landmark decision**, a historic Supreme Court ruling notable for changing or updating the law on a particular topic. In its 1995 ruling, the Supreme Court held, for the first time in 60 years, that Congress had exceeded its constitutional authority under the commerce clause. The case involved the Gun-Free School Zones Act of 1990. This legislation banned possession of a gun within 1,000 feet of any school. The Court ruled the act unconstitutional, because it attempted to regulate an activity that had, in the words of the Court, "nothing to do with commerce."

In a 1997 decision, the Court struck down portions of the Brady Handgun Violence Prevention Act of 1993. This act required state and local law enforcement officers to do background checks on persons seeking to buy handguns. Two county sheriffs, one in Montana and another in Arizona, objected to this part of the law. In a 5–4 decision, the Court agreed. It ruled that

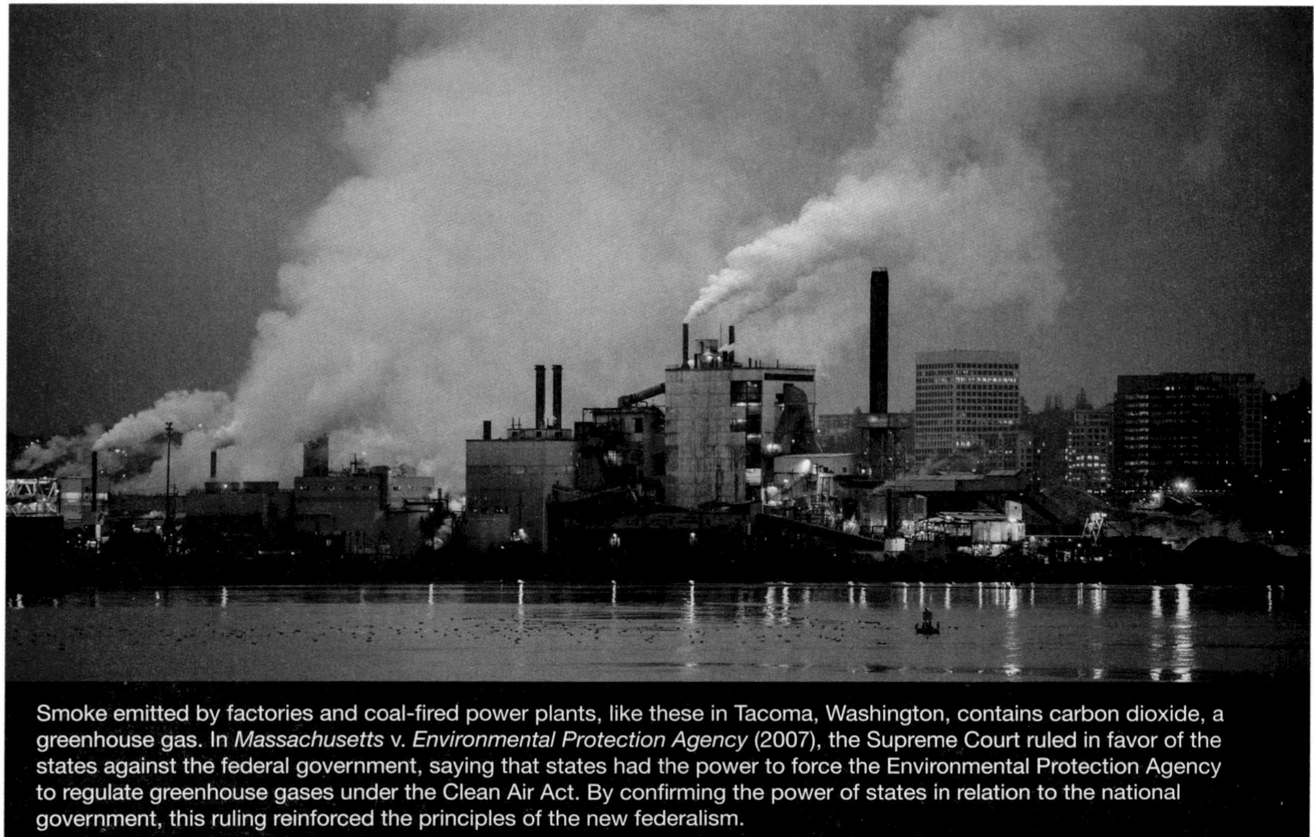

Smoke emitted by factories and coal-fired power plants, like these in Tacoma, Washington, contains carbon dioxide, a greenhouse gas. In *Massachusetts* v. *Environmental Protection Agency* (2007), the Supreme Court ruled in favor of the states against the federal government, saying that states had the power to force the Environmental Protection Agency to regulate greenhouse gases under the Clean Air Act. By confirming the power of states in relation to the national government, this ruling reinforced the principles of the new federalism.

Congress lacked the power to force state employees into federal service.

In 2000, the Court issued another ruling that limited Congress's use of the commerce clause. In *United States* v. *Morrison*, the Court invalidated a provision of the federal Violence Against Women Act of 1994 that allowed women who were victims of gender-motivated violence, such as rape, to sue in federal court. The Court ruled that the commerce clause did not justify national regulation of noneconomic, criminal conduct.

HISTORICAL THINKING

1. **IDENTIFY MAIN IDEAS AND DETAILS** What was new about the new federalism?
2. **MAKE PREDICTIONS** Do you think the national, or federal, government's powers based on a broad interpretation of the commerce clause will one day be completely eliminated? Why or why not?

Continuing Conflict over Federal and State Authority

Clearly, the boundary between federal and state authority has been shifting. Notably, issues relating to the federal structure of our government have in recent years been the subject of heated political debate among American citizens and political leaders. The federal government and the states seem to be in an ongoing tug-of-war over federal regulations, federal programs, and federal demands on the states.

THE POLITICS OF FEDERALISM The Republican Party is often viewed as the champion of states' rights. For example, when the Republicans took control of both chambers of Congress in 1995, they promised devolution. Power, they insisted, was about to shift from the national level to the states. Smaller central government and a state-centered federalism have long been regarded as the twin pillars of Republican ideology. In contrast, Democrats usually have sought greater centralization of power at the federal level. During the 2020 COVID-19 health crisis, however, many state governors, including many Democrats, pushed against efforts by the Trump administration to end state-imposed quarantines to get the national economy moving again.

Since the Democratic administration of Bill Clinton, however, there have been times when the tables seem to have turned. As you have read, Clinton backed welfare reform legislation, giving more responsibility to the states. Thus, a goal long pursued by the Republicans became a reality.

Conversely, Congress passed the No Child Left Behind Act of 2001 at the request of Republican president George W. Bush. This legislation gave the federal government a much greater role in education and educational funding than ever before. The Bush administration also made repeated attempts to block two state policies: California's medical-marijuana initiative and Oregon's physician-assisted suicide law.

MORE SUPREME COURT RULINGS In the last several years, the Supreme Court has again issued rulings that have affected the balance of power within the federal system. Sometimes, the Court's decisions have upheld the authority of the national government. For example, in *Arizona* v. *United States* (2012), the Supreme Court confirmed national authority over immigration by striking down three provisions of a tough Arizona immigration law. The first of the rejected provisions would have subjected undocumented immigrants to criminal penalties for activities such as seeking work. The second provision rejected by the Court made it a state crime for immigrants to fail to register with the federal government. Finally, the third rejected provision allowed police to arrest people without warrants if they had reason to believe the individuals could be deported.

The Court did allow Arizona to check the immigration status of individuals who had been lawfully arrested. But it reserved the right to rule against Arizona on that issue, too, if it could be shown that the state was considering race, color, or national origin in its arrests.

More often, however, the Court has extended the rights of the states, as it did in rulings on health-care reform and voting rights. In 2012, the Court considered the constitutionality of the Patient Protection and Affordable Care Act, the health-care reform law popularly known as Obamacare. In this case, *National Federation of Independent Business* v. *Sebelius*, the Court upheld most of the law. Two of the majority's arguments, however, seemed to set new limits on the powers of the national government.

Writing the majority opinion, Chief Justice John Roberts contended that the federal government could not, under the commerce clause of the Constitution, require individuals to purchase something—in this case, health-care insurance. The government, he wrote, can encourage such behavior through the tax code, which is what the Affordable Care Act did. Roberts also stated that the national government cannot force the states to expand Medicaid by threatening to take away Medicaid funds if they do not. Cutting the states off completely, he argued, would do too much damage to their budgets.

The Affordable Care Act survived the decision. But the case demonstrated that the Court was more willing to challenge the national government on its use of the commerce clause than at any time since 1937. Indeed, four of the nine justices advocated positions on the commerce clause that were, in terms of recent legal understanding, almost revolutionary.

The Voting Rights Act of 1965 was one of the most important pieces of civil rights legislation in American history. It included a variety of provisions to guarantee African Americans and others the right to vote. (Violations of this right, specified in the 15th Amendment, had been frequent in many southern states since 1870.)

One provision, known as preclearance, applied to state and local governments with a history of voting rights violations. Preclearance required any decision to change voting procedures or district boundaries to be cleared, or approved, by either the U.S. Attorney General or the U.S. District Court for the District of Columbia, before it could take effect in these jurisdictions.

In June 2013, in its *Shelby County* v. *Holder* decision, the Court held that Congress's 1965 determination of whether a state or local government should be subject to preclearance was outdated. Much of the preclearance system was therefore unconstitutional until Congress could agree on new methods for determining eligibility. Such legislation seemed unlikely to pass Congress anytime soon. The ruling was seen as a great victory for the rights of the affected states.

HISTORICAL THINKING

3. **COMPARE AND CONTRAST** Why is federalism such a hot political issue? Explain.
4. **DISTINGUISH FACT AND OPINION** Would you categorize the following statement as fact or opinion? "Replacement preclearance legislation seems unlikely to pass Congress anytime soon." Explain your answer.

The Fiscal Side of Federalism

Since the advent of cooperative federalism in the 1930s, the national government and the states have worked hand in hand to implement programs mandated, or ordered, by the national government. Whenever Congress passes a law that preempts a certain area of public policy or administration, the states are obligated to comply with the requirements of that law.

FEDERAL MANDATES A requirement that a state provide a service or undertake some activity to fulfill a federal law is called a federal mandate. Many federal mandates concern environmental protection or civil rights—the rights of every citizen to equal treatment under the law. Recent federal mandates require the states to

- provide persons with disabilities access to public buildings, sidewalks, and other areas,
- establish minimum standards of purity for water and air, and
- extend Medicaid coverage to all children with income below certain levels.

States have been critical of unfunded mandates—policies and programs required by the federal government that the states are expected to pay for on their own. To help states cover the costs of these mandates, the national government gives some of the tax dollars it collects back to the states. This money takes the form of **grants**, which are funds given for a specific purpose. As you will see, the states have come to depend on grants as an important source of revenue.

FISCAL FEDERALISM Taxes are often collected by one level of government (typically the national government) and spent by another level (typically state or local governments). This **fiscal**, or financial, relationship between levels of government is part of the process known as fiscal federalism. The origin of fiscal federalism goes back to the 1790s, when the national government assumed responsibility for the debts of the states. Later, during the Great Depression in the 1930s, numerous local governments could not cover their debts. The national government helped them by taking over some local functions and providing direct financial aid.

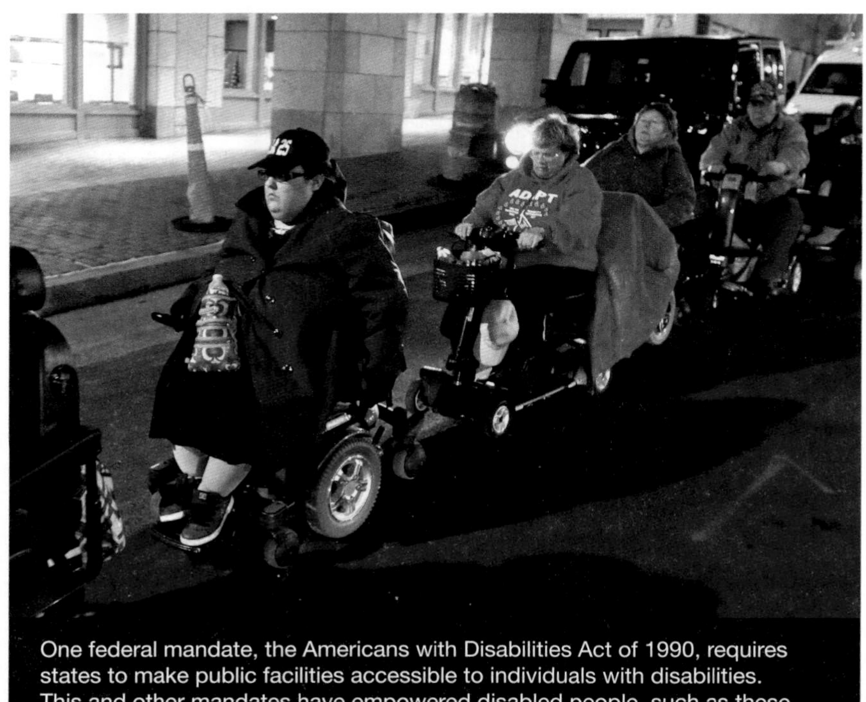

One federal mandate, the Americans with Disabilities Act of 1990, requires states to make public facilities accessible to individuals with disabilities. This and other mandates have empowered disabled people, such as these activists in Boston in 2016, to protest when they believe their rights have been violated.

FEDERAL GRANTS Even before the Constitution was adopted, the national government engaged in a form of fiscal federalism: It granted lands to the states to finance education. Using the proceeds from the sale of these lands, the

Sources of Revenue for State and Local Governments, 2015

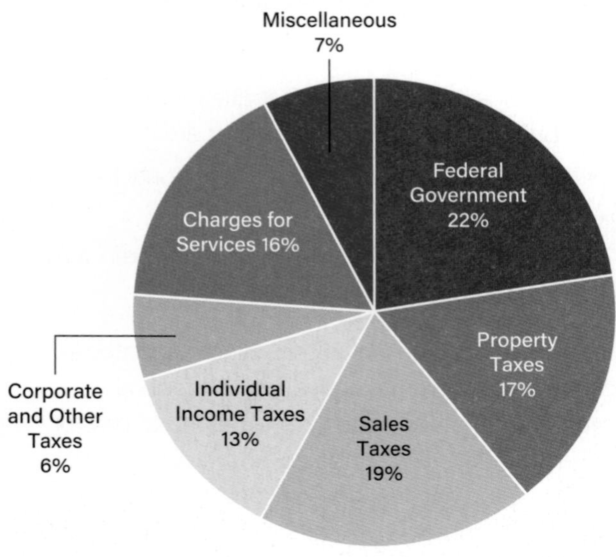

SOURCE: U.S. Census Bureau, *Annual Survey of State and Local Government Finances,* 2015

states were able to establish elementary schools and, later, land-grant colleges. In 1808, Congress started giving the states cash to pay for the state militias. Federal grants were also made available for other purposes, such as building roads and railroads.

Only in the 20th century, though, did federal grants become an essential source of funds to the states. The major growth began in the 1960s, when the dollar amount of grants quadrupled to help pay for the Great Society programs of the Johnson administration. Grants became available for education, pollution control, conservation, recreation, highway construction and maintenance, and other purposes. There are two basic types of federal grants: categorical grants and block grants.

A categorical grant is targeted at a particular category of spending, as defined by federal law. The federal government specifies hundreds of categories of state and local spending. Categorical grants give the national government control over how states use funds it provides by imposing certain conditions. For example, a categorical grant must be used for the defined purpose, such as repairing a highway or building an airport. It might also set conditions, like requiring that a project pay all workers at least the local prevailing wage.

A block grant is given for a broad area, such as job training, housing, or energy efficiency. The term *block grant* was coined in 1966 to describe a series of funding programs initiated by President Johnson. Block grants give the states more freedom and responsibility for deciding how the federal funds will be spent. Nonetheless, the federal government can exercise some control over how states use these grants by adding requirements that apply to all federal grants. Title VI of the 1964 Civil Rights Act, for example, bars racial discrimination in the use of all federal funds, regardless of their source.

FEDERAL GRANTS AND STATE BUDGETS Currently, about one-fifth of state and local revenue comes from the national government. In fiscal year 2017, the federal government transferred about $694 billion to state and local governments—more than half a trillion dollars. The largest single transfer by far was for Medicaid, the health-care program for the poor. It totaled $386 billion. The federal government also provided the states with about $59 billion for education, and highway grants ran to about $44 billion.

When the media discuss state and local budgets, they typically refer just to the general-fund budgets. General-fund budgets include spending that is supported by state and local taxes, but that is only about half of all state and local spending. Federal funds aren't listed in general-fund budgets. Also, more than one-third of state and local spending goes to fee-for-service operations, in which governments charge for the services they provide. Typically, these operations are also excluded from general-fund budgets. This fee-for-service category includes

- charges to customers for water supply, sewers, and other public utilities,
- fees charged by government-owned hospitals,
- fees for permits, licenses, and other documents,
- airport fees, and
- college tuition.

Unlike the federal government, most state governments are required by law to balance their budgets. A major **recession**, or economic downturn, can slash revenue and hike expenses, leaving states with severe budget problems. Because people in the

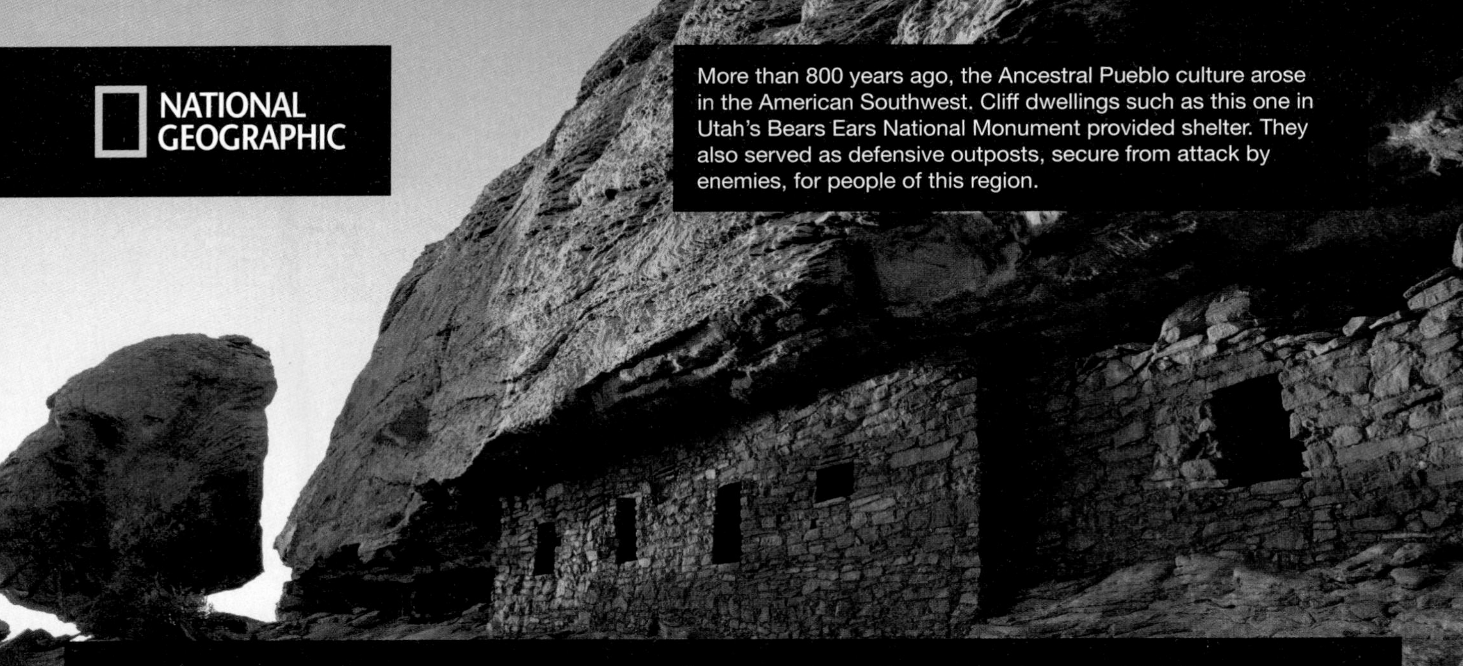

More than 800 years ago, the Ancestral Pueblo culture arose in the American Southwest. Cliff dwellings such as this one in Utah's Bears Ears National Monument provided shelter. They also served as defensive outposts, secure from attack by enemies, for people of this region.

Inside the New Battle for the American West

by Hannah Nordhaus ***National Geographic*** **Magazine, November 2018**

In December 2016, President Obama created Bears Ears National Monument, encompassing 1.35 million acres in southeastern Utah. The designation extended new levels of protection to the canyons, cliffs, and plant and animal life found in the area, as well as to the sites and artifacts reflecting at least 2,000 years of occupation by Native American cultures. It also opened a new chapter in the story of American federalism.

Bears Ears is public land, managed by the federal government. In her article "Inside the New Battle for the American West," Hannah Nordhaus examines a long-standing question: How should public lands be managed? Using Bears Ears as a starting point, Nordhaus examines the history of public lands in the West, from the time of conservation-minded President Theodore Roosevelt to development-oriented President Donald Trump.

The United States now has around 120 national monuments. Generally, they are managed as multiple-use areas. Visit one, and you might see cattle grazing and people hiking, camping, or fishing. Bears Ears and Grand Staircase-Escalante, like national monuments generally, prohibit mining within their boundaries. Such restrictions rankle some people in the West, who argue that states should have a greater say in how such lands are used.

In December 2017, as Nordhaus reports, Trump ordered the shrinking of Bears Ears by 85 percent and of Grand Staircase-Escalante by 46 percent. The areas removed from these national monuments are rich in mineral resources. While legal challenges have blocked mining in these areas for the time being, Nordhaus sees Trump's order and the legal reaction as skirmishes in an ongoing battle:

> *Drillers and miners, loggers and ranchers, face off against hikers and bikers, climbers and conservationists. It's the Old West versus the New; the people whose livelihoods depend on extracting resources from the land versus those who visit and the businesses that serve them—and at Bears Ears, the Native Americans who were there first.*

Access the full version of "Inside the New Battle for the American West" by Hannah Nordhaus through the Resources Menu in MindTap.

THINK ABOUT IT What are the advantages and disadvantages of federal control of large areas of public state are earning and spending less, state income and sales taxes fall. During a recession, state governments may be forced either to reduce spending and lay off staff—or raise taxes. Either choice may make the recession worse. State spending patterns tend to make economic booms more energetic and busts more painful.

The federal government can try to smooth over the effects of reduced state spending by increasing federal grants to the states, among other measures. Since the federal government is not legally bound to balance its budget, as long as Congress and the president agree, the federal government can increase spending or cut taxes to spur the economy during a recession. It makes up any reduced revenues and increased expenses by going further into debt.

CRITICAL VIEWING On 2018, after fierce competition among more than a dozen states, e-commerce giant Amazon chose sites in New York City and Virginia for its secondary corporate headquarters. Many New Yorkers protested the incentives of reduced taxes New York state and New York City offered Amazon, and those protests led Amazon to cancel its plan for a New York-based headquarters. Based on this cartoon, why do you think the New Yorkers were protesting?

To help stimulate an economy hit hard by the Great Recession of 2008–2009, legislation championed by President Obama in 2009 included federal grants as well as tax cuts. By the middle of 2010, however, the grants had largely dried up. With Congress and the presidency controlled by different parties, agreement on further spending measures proved elusive. From 2010 through 2012, with the economy slow to revive, states had to lay off a substantial number of employees to save money.

USING FEDERAL GRANTS TO CONTROL THE STATES Grants of funds to the states from the national government are one way the Tenth Amendment can be circumvented. Recall that the Tenth Amendment states that all powers not delegated to the national government are reserved to the states and to the people. You might well wonder, then, how the federal government has been able to exercise control over matters that traditionally have been under the authority of state governments. The answer involves the giving or withholding of federal grant dollars.

Setting the minimum drinking age, for example, is a state power. In 1984, the national government forced the states to raise their minimum drinking age to 21 by threatening to withhold federal highway funds from states that did not comply. Still, Supreme Court rulings have placed some limits on the ability of the federal government to coerce the states. As you have read, in the case *National Federation of Independent Business* v. *Sebelius*, the Court ruled unconstitutional a provision of the Affordable Care Act that would have cut Medicaid funding to states that failed to expand Medicaid benefits.

The education reforms embodied in the 2001 No Child Left Behind Act also relied on federal funding to pressure states to comply. States received block grants and, in return, had to meet federally imposed standards for testing and for accountability. But conservatives disliked the degree of national control imposed by the act. Teachers complained that too much class time was devoted to what they called "teaching to the test." Also, some of the national standards were impossibly strict. The Obama administration waived the harshest requirements and won wide acceptance for a new plan that returned power to the states, in part by letting them create their own tests and systems of accountability. In 2015, the Every Student Succeeds Act replaced the No Child Left Behind Act.

THE COST OF FEDERAL MANDATES In some areas, the federal government can order states to comply with federal authority outright. For example, the 14th Amendment requires states to grant all persons "the equal protection of the laws." In addition, when federal laws require states to implement certain programs, the states usually find that they must comply. But compliance with federal mandates can be expensive. The cost of compliance has been estimated at $29 billion annually, but some believe the true figure is much higher.

Congress passed legislation in 1995 to curb the use of unfunded federal mandates. But these costly mandates continue to put enormous stress on state budgets. Even when funding is provided for programs, it may be insufficient, resulting in an underfunded federal mandate. Critics argue that the national government should supply the states with enough funds to implement mandated programs properly. Others argue that complying with federal law is simply a basic cost of government.

COMPETITIVE FEDERALISM The debate over federalism is sometimes reduced to a debate over taxes. Which level of government will raise taxes to pay for government programs, and which will cut services to avoid raising taxes?

How states answer those questions gives citizens an option: They can move to a state with fewer services and lower taxes or to a state with more services but higher taxes. Political scientist Thomas R. Dye calls this model of federalism, in which state and local governments compete for businesses and citizens, competitive federalism. If the state of Ohio offers tax advantages for locating a factory there, for example, a business may be more likely to build its factory in Ohio. That could mean more jobs for local residents.

If Ohio has very strict environmental regulations, however, that same business may choose not to build there, no matter how beneficial the tax advantages, if it judges that complying with the regulations would be too costly. Although Ohio citizens may lose the opportunity for more jobs, they may enjoy better air and water quality than citizens of the state in which the new factory is ultimately built.

Some observers consider such competition an advantage: Americans have several variables to consider when they choose a state in which to live. Others consider it a disadvantage: A state that offers more social services or lower taxes may experience an increase in population as people "vote with their feet," or move to that state, to take advantage of its laws. Some fear that the resulting population increases could overwhelm the state's resources and force it to cut social services or raise taxes.

Regulations that make it easier to build new housing may also draw in new residents. Recent studies suggest that much of the differences in rates of population growth among states in recent decades may be due to differences in the cost of housing.

It appears likely, then, that the debate over how our federal system functions will continue. So will the battle for control between the states and the federal government. The Supreme Court, which has played umpire in this battle, will also likely continue to issue rulings that influence the balance of power.

HISTORICAL THINKING

5. **MAKE INFERENCES** Why should the federal government provide grants to the states? What are the benefits?
6. **COMPARE AND CONTRAST** Which form of federal grant do you think states prefer, a categorical grant or a block grant? Explain your answer.
7. **INTERPRET GRAPHS** What would state and local governments likely do to continue providing their services if the federal government significantly decreased the funds it sends them?
8. **ASK AND ANSWER QUESTIONS** If you received a job offer in another state, what would you want to learn about that state to decide whether the offer was a good one?

CHAPTER 4

FEDERALISM

Review

VOCABULARY

Match each of the following terms with its definition.

1. special district
2. public policy
3. petition
4. nullify
5. secession
6. administration
7. landmark decision
8. grant
9. fiscal
10. recession

a. federal money given to the states for a specific purpose
b. an independent unit of government
c. the president and other key officials of the executive branch
d. withdrawal from the Union
e. to cancel or overturn
f. a plan of action taken by a government to achieve a stated goal
g. a formal written request
h. a historic Supreme Court ruling changing the law
i. an economic downturn
j. financial

MAIN IDEAS

Answer the following questions. Support your answers with evidence from the chapter.

11. How does federalism limit the power of the national government? **LESSON 4.1**
12. Why did the Framers establish a federal system of government, as opposed to a unitary or confederate system? **LESSON 4.1**
13. What challenge does federalism create for businesses that want to operate nationwide? **LESSON 4.1**
14. How are the national government's implied powers related to the Constitution's necessary and proper clause? **LESSON 4.2**
15. How might the full faith and credit clause of the Constitution create problems for states? **LESSON 4.2**
16. What effect did the Supreme Court ruling in *McCulloch* v. *Maryland* have on states' rights and on the powers of the national government? **LESSON 4.3**
17. How did the nullification doctrine bring about a crisis in 1832? **LESSON 4.3**
18. What was the main goal of the new federalism? **LESSON 4.4**
19. In what way is a categorical grant an example of the process known as fiscal federalism? **LESSON 4.4**
20. How can the federal government help hard-hit state budgets during a recession? **LESSON 4.4**

HISTORICAL THINKING

Answer the following questions. Support your answers with evidence from the chapter.

21. **FORM AND SUPPORT OPINIONS** Do you think the United States would be better off with a unitary system of government? Why or why not?
22. **MAKE INFERENCES** How would the balance of power between the national government and the states be different if the national government had only the expressed and inherent powers?
23. **DRAW CONCLUSIONS** Why do you think the Framers decided not to allow states to establish their own post offices?
24. **ANALYZE CAUSE AND EFFECT** Do you think the commerce clause helped motivate those who sought to develop the new federalism? Explain your answer.
25. **MAKE INFERENCES** Why do you think the national government can get away with burdening the states with unfunded mandates?

INTERPRET VISUALS

Study the pie chart below. Then answer the questions.

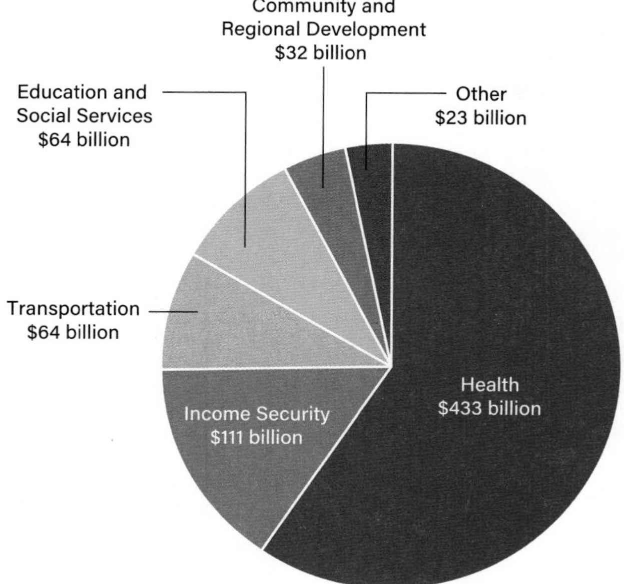

SOURCE: Congressional Research Service

26. Based on the pie chart, which program likely received the greater percentage of federal grant money in 2018, Medicaid or federal highways? Explain your answer.

27. If you were a community official seeking federal funds to improve bicycling infrastructure and safety training for cyclists and automobile drivers, which category of federal funds would you seek? Explain your answer.

ANALYZE SOURCES

In 1833, during the Nullification Crisis, John C. Calhoun of South Carolina spoke on the floor of the Senate against a bill that would have forced his state to obey tariff laws. Calhoun warned of potential conflict between what he referred to as the "sections" of the country—the South and the North.

> One section is the natural guardian of the delegated powers, and the other of the reserved; and the struggle on the side of the former will be to enlarge the powers, while that on the opposite side will be to restrain them within their constitutional limits. The contest will, in fact, be a contest between power and liberty, and such I consider the present—a contest in which the weaker section, with its peculiar labor, productions, and institutions, has at stake all that can be dear to freemen.

28. Which "section" of the country did Calhoun believe to be the "natural guardian of the delegated powers" that will struggle to "enlarge the powers"?

29. Based on this statement, do you think Calhoun favored states' rights or federal power?

CONNECT TO YOUR LIFE

30. **EXPLANATORY** Write a short essay explaining how the commerce clause expanded the power of the national government and how it affects your state today. Search for a news story about a federal law or program that requires participation by the states. Use it as an example of the commerce clause's continuing effect on states in general. Include information about the effect on your own state.

TIPS

- Review, in the chapter, what the Constitution says about interstate commerce, how the Supreme Court interpreted the commerce clause in an early decision, and the role of the commerce clause in the expansion of national power in the 20th century.
- In your introduction, respond to the essay prompt with a clearly written main idea statement and a brief overview of how the information in your essay will be organized.
- In the body of your essay, provide historical and recent examples of how the national government has applied the commerce clause.
- Describe the impact of the commerce clause on your own state, using one or more present-day examples.
- End with a conclusion that restates your thesis and summarizes the information you have presented.

UNIT 3

Civil Liberties and Civil Rights

UNIT 3 OVERVIEW

Chapter 5 Civil Liberties

Chapter 6 Citizenship and Civil Rights

CRITICAL VIEWING In 1963 around 250,000 people participated in the March on Washington, a protest highlighting continued unequal treatment of African Americans in employment and other sectors of American life. During this event, Martin Luther King, Jr., delivered his famous "I Have a Dream" speech. The march remains one of the largest, most significant peaceful protests in American history. What does this photo tell you about how some of the participants felt about the event?

"Our whole constitutional heritage rebels at the thought of giving government the power to control men's minds."

—Supreme Court Justice Thurgood Marshall, 1969

EQUALITY NOW
They Shall Not

CHAPTER 5

Civil Liberties

LESSONS

5.1 The Constitutional Basis of Our Civil Liberties

5.2 Freedom of Religion

***National Geographic* Magazine:**
Why Do Many Reasonable People Doubt Science?

5.3 Freedom of Expression

5.4 Freedom of Assembly and Petition

National Geographic Online:
How the Environment Has Changed Since the First Earth Day

5.5 Due Process Under the Law

5.6 The Right to Privacy

CRITICAL VIEWING Demonstrators marched in Minneapolis, Minnesota, days after the killing of George Floyd, an unarmed Black man, by a Minnesota police officer on May 25, 2020. The protest was just one of thousands that erupted around the nation following Floyd's death. These demonstrations called for police reform and an end to continued racial injustice in the United States. What messages are the demonstrators in this photo trying to communicate?

LESSON 5.1

The Constitutional Basis of Our Civil Liberties

In the United States, our Constitution allows us to express views that are as popular or unpopular as we wish. Our laws place few limits on how, when, and with whom we express our views. In fact, laws are meant to protect those who express unpopular views. But how much is too much? Can we say or do anything we want with no repercussions? It has often been up to the U.S. Supreme Court and its interpretations of the Bill of Rights to give us those answers.

What Are Civil Liberties?

Freedom of speech is an example of a **civil liberty**—a legal and constitutional right that protects citizens from government actions. The government typically cannot tell a person what he or she can and cannot say. Not surprisingly, the term *civil liberties* is often confused with civil rights, the rights of all Americans to equal treatment under the law. Scholars make a distinction that helps to keep the terms straight: Civil liberties limit government action, setting forth what the government cannot do. Civil rights, in contrast, specify what the government must do. The government must make sure that all individuals are treated equally under the law, regardless of their race or background, political beliefs, who they are, or what they do for a living.

In the United States, civil liberties and civil rights didn't receive federal protection until several years after the Constitution took effect, when the Bill of Rights was ratified. The Framers initially left responsibility for protecting civil liberties and civil rights to the states.

Perhaps the best way to understand what civil liberties are and why they are so important to Americans is to look at what might happen if we did not have them. For example, imagine the differences between the life of an American high school student and a high school student in China. Chinese students have to be much more careful in what they say and do than their American counterparts. The websites Chinese students use and the social media platforms they can access are behind The Great Firewall—a term that refers to the tight control the Chinese government keeps on online content. The government prohibits various kinds of speech, particularly any criticism of the role of the Communist Party. Anyone who criticizes the government in email messages or on a blog could be charged with breaking the law—and perhaps even go to prison.

In July 2016, members of Mothers of the Movement, a group formed by mothers of African Americans who were killed by police or in other instances of gun violence, spoke at the Democratic National Convention in Philadelphia, Pennsylvania. They exercised their right to freedom of speech to express their opposition to racism and violations of civil rights.

In the United States, people have not only freedom of speech (written and oral) but also a free press that can report what it chooses. Americans also can practice any, many, or no religions. These are just some of our civil liberties. It is safe to say that the United States would be a much different place if these freedoms were not recognized and closely guarded by both individuals and their government. Yet they weren't specifically protected in the country's infancy.

As you have read, the Framers initially believed that the constitutions of the individual states contained plenty of provisions to protect citizens from government actions. Therefore, they didn't think it necessary to include many explicit protections for individual civil liberties in the original document.

Nonetheless, the original Constitution did include some safeguards to protect citizens from an overly powerful government. Specifically, the Framers placed the following limits on the power of government:

- **Provision of the writ of *habeas corpus*:** Article I, Section 9, of the Constitution protects individuals against unlawful punishments by providing for the **writ of *habeas corpus*** (*habeas corpus* is a Latin phrase that roughly means "produce the body"), an order requiring that an official explain to a judge why a specified prisoner is being held. This protection applies to all residents of the United States—citizens and non-citizens alike—except in times of rebellion or national invasion. If the court finds that the imprisonment is unlawful, it can order the prisoner to be released. This constitutional provision prevents government from imprisoning people for no lawful reason, such as a political disagreement.
- **Prohibition of bills of attainder:** Article I also bans passage of a bill of attainder—a legislative act that directly punishes a specifically named individual (or a group or class of individuals) without a trial or any other involvement on the part of the judiciary. Over the centuries, Supreme Court rulings have upheld the principle that lawmakers cannot punish a person or group—such as former Confederate sympathizers—even if their actions might seem unpatriotic to many other Americans.
- **Prohibition of *ex post facto* laws:** Finally, Article I prohibits Congress and state legislatures from passing *ex post facto* laws, or laws that punish individuals for committing an act that was legal when it was committed. (The Latin term *ex post facto* roughly means "after the fact.")

HISTORICAL THINKING

1. **COMPARE AND CONTRAST** Explain how civil liberties differ from civil rights.
2. **DRAW CONCLUSIONS** Why are *ex post facto* laws perceived as such a threatening concept?

The Bill of Rights

As you have read, one of the contentious issues in the debate over ratification of the Constitution was its lack of specific protections of citizens from government actions. Although many state constitutions provided such protections, the antifederalists felt the Constitution needed to include explicit protections against actions by the national government. It took the promise of a bill of rights to ensure the ratification.

The Bill of Rights was ratified by the states and became part of the Constitution on December 15, 1791. As you have read, the first eight amendments grant the people specific rights and liberties:

- **First Amendment:** freedom of religion, speech, press, assembly, and petition
- **Second Amendment:** right to bear arms
- **Third Amendment:** freedom from quartering (housing) soldiers
- **Fourth Amendment:** freedom from unreasonable searches and seizures
- **Fifth Amendment:** right to grand jury hearing, protection against self-incrimination and double jeopardy, right to due process of law, right to fair compensation for land taken for public use by the government
- **Sixth Amendment:** right to a fair and public trial by jury in criminal cases, right to hear charges against the accused, right to confront witnesses against the accused, right to legal counsel, right to call witnesses in favor of the accused
- **Seventh Amendment:** right to trial by jury in civil cases

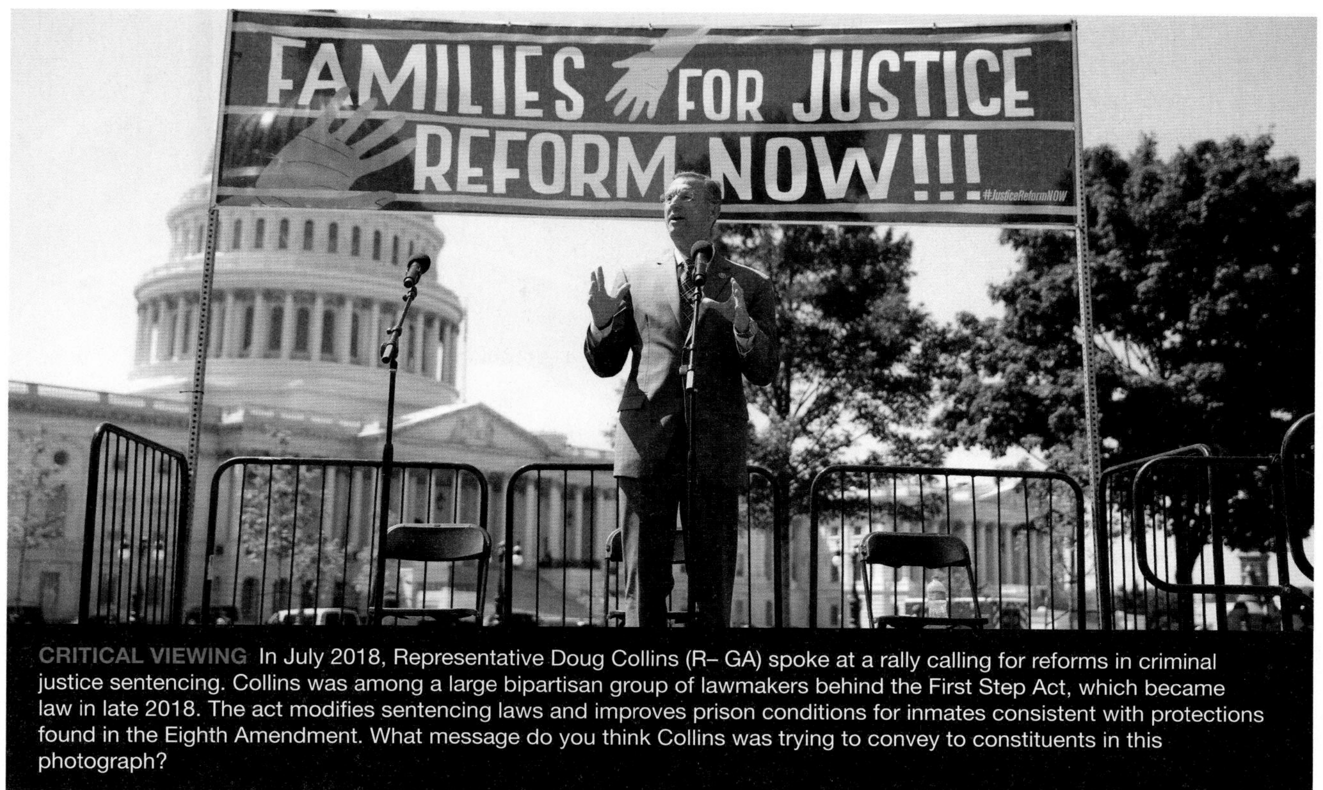

CRITICAL VIEWING In July 2018, Representative Doug Collins (R– GA) spoke at a rally calling for reforms in criminal justice sentencing. Collins was among a large bipartisan group of lawmakers behind the First Step Act, which became law in late 2018. The act modifies sentencing laws and improves prison conditions for inmates consistent with protections found in the Eighth Amendment. What message do you think Collins was trying to convey to constituents in this photograph?

- **Eighth Amendment:** protection from excessive bail and cruel and unusual punishment

The remaining two amendments of the Bill of Rights, the Ninth and Tenth, reserve certain rights and powers to the people and to the states.

- **Ninth Amendment:** protection against others taking away rights not mentioned in the Bill of Rights
- **Tenth Amendment:** right of states and the people to retain powers not given to the federal government

THE ROLE OF THE COURTS In a democracy, government policy tends to reflect the views of the majority. A key function of the Bill of Rights, therefore, is to protect the rights of those in the minority against the will of the majority. (Consider, for example, the free-speech rights of people who choose to make inflammatory comments after a national tragedy: They are legally allowed to make such statements, even if the vast majority of the country considers those comments reprehensible.) When there is disagreement over how to interpret the Bill of Rights, the courts step in.

The United States Supreme Court, as our nation's highest court, has the final say over the interpretation of the Constitution, including the Bill of Rights. The protection of American civil liberties has been shaped over time by Supreme Court decisions. It is the Supreme Court that determines where freedom of speech ends and the right of society to be protected from certain forms of speech begins.

THE DEBATE OVER THE SECOND AMENDMENT
The Supreme Court has also weighed in on the protections of the Second Amendment, which has been one of the most controversial parts of the Bill of Rights in recent decades. The amendment states that "[a] well regulated Militia, being necessary to the security of a free state, the right of the people to keep and bear Arms, shall not be infringed." Yet what the Framers actually meant and which "arms" these should be have been hotly debated by gun control advocates (those who want tighter restrictions on gun ownership), gun ownership lobbyists (including the National Rifle Association), and the courts. Supporters of fewer restrictions on gun ownership believe that the Constitution protects a person's right to own the type and number of guns he or she wants. They often claim that gun ownership is a

form of self-defense. Supporters of tighter gun control believe that Second Amendment protections were intended more for lawfully organized militias than for individuals and argue that gun ownership leads to increased violence.

Until the 1960s the few federal laws involving gun control mainly concerned gun manufacturers, importers, and dealers. The Gun Control Act of 1968 was the first major legislation to prohibit certain people from owning guns (including those under 21 years of age and the mentally ill) and to impose additional licensing and registration requirements. Later laws both tightened and then loosened regulations on gun sales.

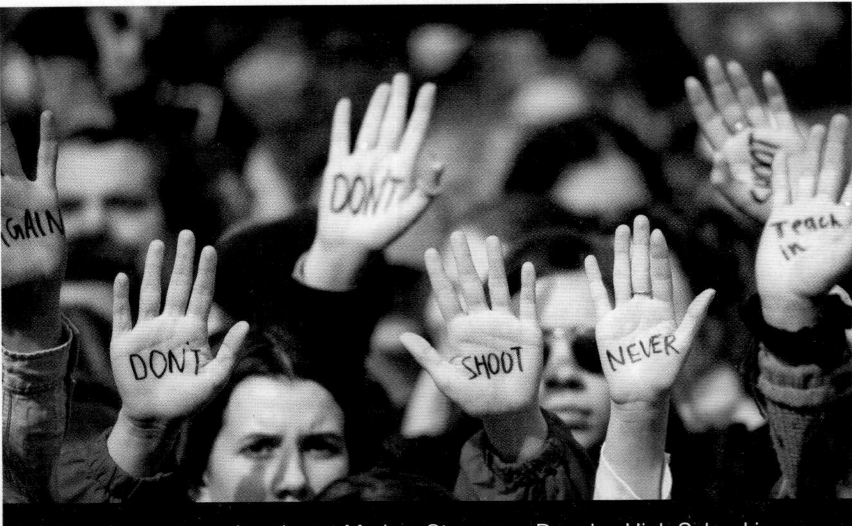

Soon after a mass shooting at Marjory Stoneman Douglas High School in Parkland, Florida, in February 2018—only one of many school shootings that have taken place in the United States over the past 20 years—hundreds of demonstrations calling for solutions to gun violence were held around the country. Many demonstrators were high school students who demanded that the government address their fear and anger.

In 2008 the case *District of Columbia* v. *Heller* brought modern gun control measures before the Supreme Court. For the first time, the Court specifically addressed an individual's right to own a gun. In a 5–4 decision, the justices ruled that the District of Columbia's prohibition on handguns (and relevant regulations on how already licensed guns had to be treated in a person's home) violated the Second Amendment.

Yet the *Heller* decision did not quiet the debate over gun control. An increase in mass shootings in the United States over the past 35 years has kept the Second Amendment at the forefront of American politics. In particular, the increase in school shootings (estimated by some news sources as more than 50 times as many as all those in other major industrialized countries) has led to large-scale efforts to change current gun control policies. In 2018 alone, there were more than 103 incidents involving gunfire on American schools and campuses. Sixty people died. The deadliest of these was the shooting at Marjory Stoneman Douglas High School in Parkland, Florida, where a 19-year-old former student brought an assault rifle to the school and opened fire, killing 17 students and faculty that February.

Grief-stricken and furious, several surviving students called for more action, using traditional and social media to organize protests and attempt to persuade legislators and gun manufacturers to make changes to protect people from continued gun violence. The Parkland students appealed in particular to young people to raise their voices (and use their voting power) for change. On March 24, 2018, hundreds of thousands of people gathered in Washington, D.C., to take part in the March for Our Lives to call for stricter gun control. Millions more gathered for the same reason in other U.S. cities and around the world.

HISTORICAL THINKING

3. **MAKE CONNECTIONS** Why are Supreme Court interpretations subject to change over time?
4. **EVALUATE** Americans often say that controversial social and political issues are ultimately "left to the courts." How might the actions of the students following the Parkland school shooting effect change without leaving the matter up to the courts? Explain.

The 14th Amendment

For more than 135 years after the ratification of the Bill of Rights, the courts assumed that the constitutional protections listed in the 10 amendments limited only the actions of the national government—not the actions of state or local governments. In other words, even if a state or local law was contrary to a basic freedom, such as the freedom of speech, the Bill of Rights did not come into play as far as the courts were concerned.

As you have read, the Framers believed that the states, being closer to the people, would be less likely to violate their own citizens' liberties. They were also aware that the states' own constitutions, most of which contain bills of rights, were designed to protect citizens against state government actions. The United States Supreme Court upheld this hands-off view when it decided in *Barron* v. *Baltimore* (1833) that the Bill of Rights did not apply to state laws.

THE LANGUAGE OF THE AMENDMENT The ratification of the 14th Amendment in 1868 laid the groundwork for a change in approach, but the change was long in coming. The amendment was passed in the wake of the Civil War to ensure that African Americans, including those who had previously been enslaved, would be recognized as citizens and that they would be afforded the same rights and liberties as other United States citizens throughout the country, including in those states that had once allowed slavery.

All persons born or naturalized in the United States, and subject to the jurisdiction thereof, are citizens of the United States and of the state wherein they reside. No state shall make or enforce any law which shall abridge the privileges or immunities of citizens of the United States; nor shall any state deprive any person of life, liberty, or property, without due process of law; nor deny to any person within its jurisdiction the equal protection of the laws.

The language of the amendment is notable for two reasons. First, it was written so as to apply to all Americans regardless of race. Second, it requires that states follow **due process** of law, or the right of all persons, not just citizens, to be treated fairly by the judicial system. A similar requirement, binding on the federal government, is found in the Fifth Amendment. Both provisions would become significant in later interpretations of the amendment.

For some time, however, the guarantees in the 14th Amendment were largely ignored. The Supreme Court determined that the basic civil rights and liberties remained under control of state laws. The 14th Amendment, the Court determined, didn't apply to or overturn its decision in *Barron* v. *Baltimore*. Moreover, the "privileges and immunities of citizens of the United States" referred to in the amendment were defined narrowly, such as the right to travel to and from the nation's capital. The result was the passage of a host of state laws that discriminated against African Americans.

Starting in 1925, however, the Supreme Court began to rule that the protections in the Bill of Rights are covered by the 14th Amendment's due process clause. Under this approach, states could not abridge a civil liberty that the national government had to protect. In other words, if a state passed a law denying someone a right guaranteed by the Bill of Rights, such an action would be unconstitutional. Through this process, most of the protections guaranteed by the Bill of Rights have been incorporated, or merged, into the 14th Amendment.

INCORPORATED RIGHTS The process of **incorporation**, or inclusion of rights into state and local law, reached its height during the 1960s. In a series of landmark cases, the Supreme Court

The American Civil Liberties Union

In 1920, in response to a number of warrantless searches and seizures of suspected communists, a group of civil liberties activists and lawyers formed the American Civil Liberties Union (ACLU). Now a national organization with more than 1.5 million members, the ACLU has become a fixture of the American legal system and appears in front of the Supreme Court more than any other group besides the U.S. Department of Justice. A stalwart defender of the Bill of Rights, the ACLU has been a vocal player in some of the biggest political and legal controversies of the past century, from its early condemnation of the internment of Japanese Americans during World War II to its ongoing efforts to defend the rights of those in the LGBTQ community. While many Americans consider the ACLU to be a liberal-leaning organization, it has in fact defended the civil liberties of groups with many different ideologies, including the Ku Klux Klan and other White supremacist groups.

Incorporation of the Bill of Rights

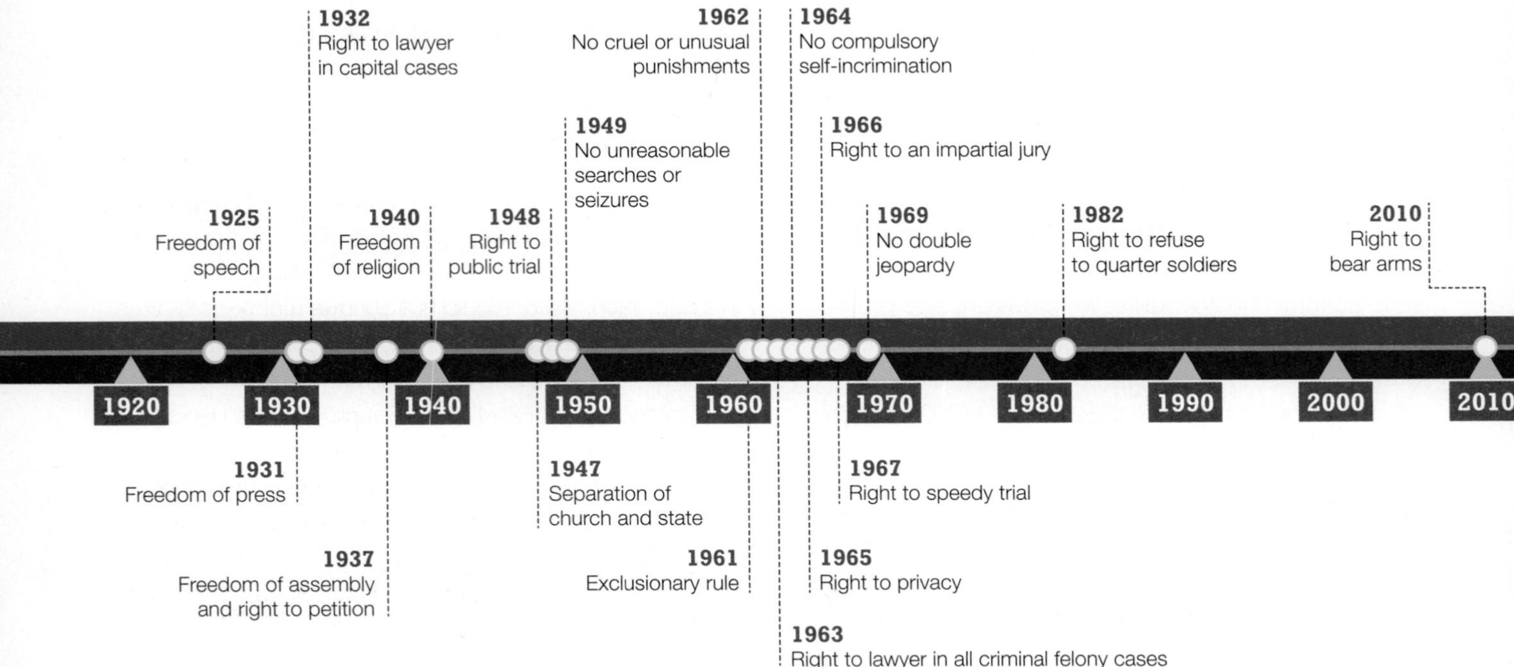

broadened its interpretation of the due process clause to ensure that states and localities could not infringe on most of the civil liberties protected by the Bill of Rights. Today, only a few federal protections of the Bill of Rights have not been incorporated, including the right to a grand jury specified within the Fifth Amendment. The right to bear arms of the Second Amendment was incorporated only in 2010, but not all of the justices involved in that Supreme Court case agreed that the right to bear arms is actually a fundamental right.

HISTORICAL THINKING

5. **ANALYZE CAUSE AND EFFECT** Explain the effect of the 14th Amendment on the protection of civil liberties.
6. **INTERPET TIME LINES** How would you characterize the timing of how individual rights have been incorporated? Note any patterns.

LESSON 5.2 Freedom of Religion

Signs of disagreement are everywhere in the United States today, from alarming newspaper headlines to people marching in the streets. Social media posts express extreme positions on both ends of the political spectrum. Congregations gather in churches, temples, or mosques with differing ideas about how to worship. Neighbors circulate petitions with demands for change—or to protest proposed changes. All these actions have one thing in common: they are all examples of activities that are protected by the First Amendment of the Bill of Rights.

Constitutional Protections of Religious Freedom

The First Amendment leads the list of amendments that make up the Bill of Rights in the U.S. Constitution. The text reads as follows:

> *Congress shall make no law respecting an establishment of religion, or prohibiting the free exercise thereof; or abridging the freedom of speech, or of the press; or the right of the people peaceably to assemble, and to petition the Government for a redress of grievances.*

This amendment protects some of Americans' most important civil liberties, guaranteeing the freedoms of religion, speech, the press, and assembly, as well as the right to petition the government. Landmark Supreme Court decisions have defined the meaning of these protections—and their limits.

A HISTORY OF RELIGIOUS INTOLERANCE The fact that freedom of religion was included in the Bill of Rights is not surprising, given American colonial history. Many colonists, including the Pilgrims who arrived on the *Mayflower*, came to America to escape religious persecution.

Even so, the English colonies did not necessarily promote tolerance. Religious requirements were often strict. For example, in 1610 the governor of the Jamestown colony enacted a law requiring attendance at religious services on Sunday "both in the morning and the afternoon." Missing Sunday service twice resulted in a public whipping. Missing it a third time was punishable by death. In Boston, newly arrived Quakers—members of a Christian sect known for pacifism and commitment to religious freedom—were beaten, imprisoned, and sometimes hanged by Massachusetts Puritans.

SEPARATION OF CHURCH AND STATE By 1787 the United States included people who practiced many different faiths. The First Amendment, therefore, says that "Congress shall make no law respecting an establishment of religion." This is known as the establishment clause, and it prohibits Congress from establishing an official national religion or national church. The free exercise clause states that Congress shall make no laws "prohibiting the free exercise" of religion.

In 1802, more than 10 years after the Bill of Rights was added to the Constitution, President Thomas Jefferson declared that the establishment clause should act as "a wall of separation between church and state." While the First Amendment provides a metaphorical wall between religion and the federal government, it says nothing about whether states can make laws respecting establishment of religion. As you will read, it has been left to the Supreme Court to determine the width and height of Jefferson's "wall."

The First Amendment allows people to worship and express their religion as they see fit, with no government interference. This freedom protects the right to wear religious attire, such as the hijab worn by this Muslim basketball player at a high school in Michigan.

CRITICAL VIEWING Throughout U.S. history, Americans have frequently debated the principle of separation of church and state. What is this political cartoon attempting to express about this separation?

HISTORICAL THINKING

1. **MAKE INFERENCES** What does the inclusion of the freedoms of religion, speech, press, assembly, and petition tell you about the purpose of the Bill of Rights?
2. **DRAW CONCLUSIONS** Why might the Framers have thought it necessary to include not only the establishment clause but also the free exercise clause in the First Amendment?

The Establishment Clause and Education

At first glance, the free exercise clause may appear straightforward: It protects a person's right to worship or to believe as he or she wishes without government interference. No law or act of government may violate this constitutional right. Yet this clause has also been at the center of some of the most sensitive and emotional legal debates of the 20th century.

What does separation of church and state, or the principle that government must remain neutral toward religion, mean in practice? The establishment clause, for instance, does not prohibit government from recognizing religious beliefs, and, in many cases, religion remains a part of public life. Most government officials take an oath of office in the name of God, and our coins and paper currency carry the motto "In God We Trust." In addition, many Americans maintain some kind of religious affiliation—attachment or identification—and have preferred political leaders to be people of faith.

Yet the Supreme Court has upheld Jefferson's "wall of separation" in multiple rulings, particularly in cases involving education. In 1947, for example, the Supreme Court upheld a New Jersey law that allowed the state to pay for bus transportation of students who attended **parochial**, or church-affiliated, schools. The Court determined that the payments didn't aid the church directly, but simply provided for the safety and benefit of the students. The ruling did two things at once. It affirmed the importance of separating church and state by stating that "No tax in any amount, large or small, can be levied to support any religious activities or institutions." In addition, it set an important precedent that not all forms of state and federal aid to church-related schools are forbidden under the Constitution. In later cases, justices addressed the constitutionality of prayer in schools, as well as aid to parochial schools and the teaching of evolutionary theory in public classrooms.

PRAYER IN SCHOOLS The Supreme Court has walked a fine line on the issue of prayer in public schools. In 1962 the Court ruled in *Engel* v. *Vitale* that the First Amendment makes encouraging prayer in public schools illegal. This case is also known as the Regents' Prayer Case. Since that ruling, the Supreme Court has continued to issue decisions on religious activities in public schools. For example, in 1980 the Court ruled that a Kentucky law requiring that the 10 Commandments be posted in all public schools violated the establishment clause. Many religious groups opposed this ruling.

The Court has also considered moments of silence in schools. In 1985 the Supreme Court ruled that an Alabama law authorizing a daily one-minute period for meditation and voluntary prayer was unconstitutional. The Court stated that the law endorsed prayer and therefore appeared to support religion in the classroom. In the years since, lower courts have generally allowed moments of silence if they serve a **secular** purpose (or one with no religious goal), but some legal scholars consider the issue unresolved.

In 2000 the Supreme Court addressed the issue of not just prayer on school property, but prayer using school property. In *Santa Fe Independent School District* v. *Doe*, the Court ruled that prayers before school sporting events on a school's public address

Students pray in a Texas classroom in June 1962, just days after the decision in *Engel* v. *Vitale* outlawed the use of prayer in public schools. Since that decision, the Court has also struck down school practices that endorse voluntary prayer or spiritual meditation.

SUPREME COURT

Engel v. *Vitale*, 1962

Decided: June 25, 1962, 6–1

Majority: Justice Hugo Black wrote the opinion in favor of Steven Engel. Justice William Douglas wrote a concurring opinion.

Dissent: Justice Potter Stewart wrote the dissenting opinion.

In the late 1950s the members of the State Board of Regents in New York (the state's general educational supervisory group) wrote and distributed a nondenominational prayer that they urged school districts to use at the beginning of each school day. The prayer read as follows: "Almighty God, we acknowledge our dependence upon Thee, and we beg Thy blessings upon us, our parents, our teachers, and our Country." Students were allowed to opt out of the prayer if they chose.

Those who supported the prayer claimed that its use promoted the free exercise clause. But Steven Engel and several other parents in Hyde Park, New York, sued the local school board president, William Vitale, in 1958 for violating the establishment clause of the First Amendment.

After the use of the prayer was upheld by the lower courts, the case (known as the Regents' Prayer Case) was heard by the Supreme Court in 1962. In a 6–1 decision, the Court ruled that it was unconstitutional for a state government to write a prayer and encourage its use in a government building, whether or not that prayer was affiliated with a particular religion or faith. Speaking for the majority, Justice Hugo Black wrote that the First Amendment must at least mean "that in this country it is no part of the business of government to compose official prayers for any group of the American people to recite as a part of a religious program carried on by government."

THINK ABOUT IT Did the Supreme Court's ruling in *Engel* v. *Vitale* infringe upon the free exercise clause while confirming the establishment clause? Explain your answer.

The courts have allowed government funding for some basic needs of religiously affiliated schools, including student transportation.

SUPREME COURT

Lemon v. *Kurtzman*, 1971

Decided: June 28, 1971, 8–0

Majority: Chief Justice Warren Burger wrote the unanimous opinion on the Pennsylvania statute ruling and the 8–1 majority on the Rhode Island statute, finding in favor of both citizen groups. Justices William O. Douglas, Hugo Black, Thurgood Marshall, and William Brennan wrote partial or entire concurring opinions.

Dissent: Justice Byron White concurred with the Pennsylvania statute ruling, but dissented from the Rhode Island statute ruling.

In 1971 the United States Supreme Court heard a case that combined decisions from lower courts in Pennsylvania and Rhode Island. In 1968 Pennsylvania passed a statute, or law, that allowed public funding of a portion of the salaries of teachers of secular subjects at non-public schools, as well as toward textbooks and other learning materials. A year later, Rhode Island passed a similar statute that allowed public funding to be applied to 15 percent of the salaries of teachers of non-public schools.

Citizens, taxpayers, and their representatives brought suits in each state for violation of the establishment clause of the First Amendment. A Pennsylvania lower court dismissed the case, but a Rhode Island court found in favor of those who had claimed a constitutional violation. It fell to the Supreme Court to reconcile the decisions. The justices established the *Lemon* test, and found nearly unanimously that the risk of "government entanglement with religion" (the third part of the *Lemon* test) put both statutes in violation of the establishment clause.

THINK ABOUT IT What aspect of public funding of private-school salaries and textbooks might the Supreme Court have believed would lead to "government entanglement with religion"?

system were unconstitutional. Yet the Supreme Court has not held that individuals cannot pray, when and as they choose, in schools or in any other place. In other words, cases that have upheld the establishment clause do not invalidate the free exercise clause.

AID TO PAROCHIAL SCHOOLS Over the years, the courts have often had to decide on whether specific types of aid do or do not violate the establishment clause. The courts have decided that transportation, equipment, and special educational services are owed to all students, including those at parochial schools. But public funds for teachers' salaries and field trips land squarely on the unconstitutional side.

To make these decisions, the courts usually turn to the *Lemon* test, a series of three requirements derived from the 1971 Supreme Court decision in *Lemon* v. *Kurtzman*. According to *Lemon*, a state's school aid must satisfy the following requirements: (1) The purpose of the financial aid must be clearly secular, (2) its primary effect must neither advance nor inhibit religion, and (3) it must avoid "excessive government entanglement with religion."

The Court has applied the *Lemon* test to school vouchers, or educational certificates provided by state governments that students can use at any school, public or private, religious or secular. Currently 15 states and the District of Columbia have voucher programs that use taxpayer dollars to help fund tuition at private schools for some students. In a 2002 decision, the Court concluded that a taxpayer-paid voucher program in Cleveland, Ohio, did not entangle church and state because the funds went to parents, not to the schools themselves.

TEACHING EVOLUTION IN SCHOOLS The Supreme Court has also had to decide whether public school districts can prohibit the teaching of evolution, or the scientific theory that humans evolved from other species. Certain religious groups have opposed teaching about evolution because they believe it contradicts biblical accounts. Representatives of those groups convinced some states to ban the teaching of evolution in public schools, but in 1968 the Court held that an Arkansas law prohibiting the teaching of evolution violated the establishment clause because it imposed religious beliefs on students. In 1987 the Court ruled that a Louisiana law requiring that the biblical story of creation be taught along with evolution was unconstitutional, primarily because the law promoted a specific religious belief.

In the search for a compromise, some activists have advocated teaching intelligent design. Intelligent design is the theory that an intelligent cause, rather than an undirected process such as natural selection, lies behind the creation and development of the universe and living things. Supporters claim that intelligent design is a scientific theory and does not violate the establishment clause. Opponents contend that "intelligent cause" is simply another way of referring to God.

HISTORICAL THINKING

3. **MAKE PREDICTIONS** What arguments might parents make for and against school voucher programs?
4. **FORM AND SUPPORT OPINIONS** Some Supreme Court cases involving possible violations of the establishment clause by public education systems have been initiated by atheist families. How would the views of atheists relate to the First Amendment's religious protections in schools?

The Free Exercise Clause

It is important to understand that the free exercise clause does not mean that individuals can act in any manner, based on their religious beliefs. There is an important distinction between belief and practice. The Supreme Court has ruled consistently that the right to hold any belief is absolute. The right to *practice* one's beliefs, however, may have limits. The issue of belief versus practice first appeared in front of the Supreme Court in 1878, in *Reynolds* v. *United States*. The Court ruled against George Reynolds, a member of the Church of Jesus Christ of Latter-day Saints (Mormon) who practiced **polygamy**, or the practice of having more than one spouse simultaneously. The justices allowed that Reynolds was free to *believe* that polygamy was acceptable, but that the practice itself would make religious doctrine superior to the law. In 1890 the Latter-day Saints prohibited new polygamous marriages.

RELIGIOUS PRACTICES IN THE WORKPLACE Title VII of the Civil Rights Act of 1964 requires employers to accommodate employees' religious practices unless such accommodation causes undue hardship. Thus, if an employee's religious beliefs prevent working on a particular day of the week, such as Saturday or

Scopes "Monkey Trial"

In early 1925 the Tennessee state legislature passed a law that banned the teaching of evolution in public schools because it "denies the story of the Divine Creation . . . and [teaches] instead that man has descended from a lower order of animals."

Shortly after the law passed, the American Civil Liberties Union (ACLU) began searching for teachers who would attempt to challenge the new law. Local business and public officials in Dayton, Tennessee, hoped to bring publicity and money to their town. They convinced a 24-year-old biology teacher named John Thomas Scopes to introduce the topic of evolution in his high school classroom. Scopes was soon charged with violating the new law. He pleaded not guilty.

The case pitted supporters of science against religious conservatives who viewed the Bible as the literal word of God. Media from around the country and from as far away as London, England, descended on the Dayton courthouse to cover the trial, which was soon dubbed the "Monkey Trial," in reference to the evolutionary theory being debated. Celebrity attorney Clarence Darrow represented Scopes, and three-time presidential candidate William Jennings Bryan represented the state of Tennessee.

At the end of a week, Scopes was charged a $100 fine. Even so, news reports mocked the opponents of evolution, draining away support for bans on teaching evolution. The ACLU claimed victory, and in 1925 the Tennessee Supreme Court acquitted Scopes. The actual law prohibiting the teaching of evolution was not repealed until 1967.

Famous attorneys and orators Clarence Darrow and William Jennings Bryan attracted national attention with their fiery arguments in a Tennessee courtroom during the *Scopes* trial. John Scopes (seated right of center, arms crossed, in a white shirt) was the only client Darrow (center) ever defended *pro bono*, or for no monetary payment.

Sunday, the employer must try to accommodate the employee's needs.

In 1999 two Muslim police officers in Newark, New Jersey, refused to shave their beards to comply with the police department's grooming policy, claiming that their faith required them to wear beards. The Third Circuit Court of Appeals ruled in the officers' favor, setting a precedent for Muslims and others to retain their customary dress or grooming. For example, in 2015 the Supreme Court ruled against the clothing store Abercrombie & Fitch, saying that its refusal to hire a woman who covered her head for religious reasons violated Title VII protections against discrimination in hiring. Title VII also protects employees from having religious practices forced upon them. In 2018 a federal jury awarded 10 employees of a New York discount medical plan company $5.1 million for being coerced into religious practices (including prayers and "spiritual cleansing") at their place of employment.

MEDICAL TREATMENT FOR CHILDREN Another issue that has cropped up under the free exercise clause is the right to refuse medical treatment on religious grounds. In most cases, adults have the right to refuse treatment for themselves. The right of parents to refuse treatment for their children, however, is much more limited. The courts have long held that a refusal by a parent to allow lifesaving treatments for a child on the grounds that it would violate religious beliefs can be considered a serious crime.

This principle also extends to vaccination. As a public health measure, states may require all children attending public schools to be vaccinated to prevent the spread of sometimes deadly diseases like meningitis. Typically, state law allows parents to opt out of vaccinations for religious or philosophical reasons. Such opt-outs are not required by the Constitution, however. California, Mississippi, and West Virginia do not allow an opt-out, unless a doctor says that a vaccination might be harmful to a child's health.

HEALTH INSURANCE COVERAGE FOR BIRTH CONTROL One free-exercise controversy has involved the question of whether businesses could be required to supply health-insurance coverage for birth control. Such coverage was required in health insurance plans that met the standards of the 2010 Affordable Care Act. Churches and other religious organizations that object to contraception on principle were exempt from the requirement.

In 2012, however, the government ruled that universities, hospitals, and similar organizations had to provide coverage for contraception even if they were affiliated with churches that opposed birth control. The result was a storm of opposition from organizations such as the Roman Catholic Church, which rejects contraception. These groups argued that they were being forced to support activities to which they were morally opposed and that such a requirement violated their free exercise rights. Yet some employees claimed churches were attempting to impose religious values on employees such as nurses or professors who were not directly involved in religious activities.

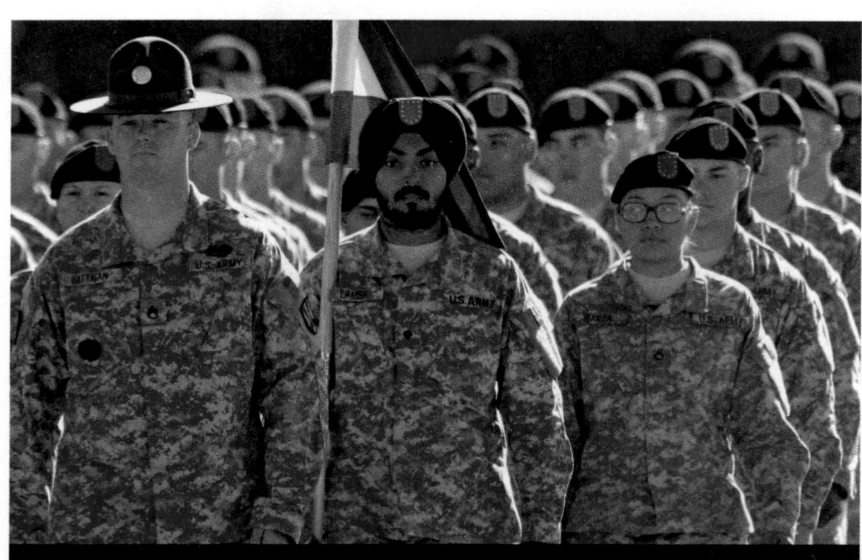
The U.S. military is one workplace in which religious accommodations have been made. In 2010, U.S. Army Specialist Simran Lamba was allowed to wear a beard, longer hair, and a turban in accordance with his Sikh faith, although all three are typically against military regulations.

President Barack Obama proposed a compromise under which church-affiliated hospitals and schools would not have to pay for the insurance coverage, but employees would still receive the benefit. This plan satisfied many schools and hospitals. It was not

For people who doubt the truth of certain scientific findings and events, the idea of humans landing on the moon might seem unlikely.

Why Do Many Reasonable People Doubt Science?

by Joel Achenbach *National Geographic* Magazine, March 2015

It has been more than 90 years since the *Scopes* trial and more than 50 years since laws banning the teaching of evolution have been struck down, but the battle over evolution lingers. In "Why Do Many Reasonable People Doubt Science," writer Joel Achenbach points out that the reluctance of some to accept the validity of evolution is just one instance of a broader trend—people refusing to accept widely held scientific findings that conflict with their own experiences and beliefs.

According to Achenbach, there are a multitude of reasons behind the reluctance to believe proven information. For one, people are apt to reject findings that contradict what they intuitively think should make sense, such as that a relatively tiny amount of carbon dioxide in Earth's atmosphere is hastening sea level rise. Further, people are simply more inclined to believe what they hear anecdotally—for example, that a friend's child was diagnosed with autism shortly after receiving a vaccine—than unfamiliar statistics. Achenbach also notes that scientific studies often seem to contradict each other, which can confuse people who are not scientists.

And then there is the internet. The internet can be a great resource for accurate scientific data, but it also contains much that is incomplete, misleading, or just plain wrong. More than ever before, people can communicate with like-minded others and find support for their beliefs, regardless of whether there is actual scientific data to back them up. Achenbach explains:

> *Meanwhile the Internet makes it easier than ever for climate skeptics and doubters of all kinds to find their own information and experts. Gone are the days when a small number of powerful institutions—elite universities, encyclopedias, major news organizations, even National Geographic—served as gatekeepers of scientific information. The Internet has democratized information, which is a good thing. But along with cable TV, it has made it possible to live in a "filter bubble" that lets in only the information with which you already agree.*

THINK ABOUT IT The right to believe in whatever one chooses is a basic principle of American government. What are the pros and cons of this freedom when it comes to new developments in science?

acceptable to the Catholic bishops, however, who filed a lawsuit aimed at overturning the requirement.

In 2014, in *Burwell* v. *Hobby Lobby Stores*, the Supreme Court held that a closely held for-profit corporation—here, interpreted as "persons" protected by the Religious Freedom Restoration Act of 1993 (RFRA)—could be exempt from the requirement to provide certain forms of birth control coverage if its owners object on religious grounds. The ruling was based on the RFRA, however, rather than the free exercise clause. It therefore left questions about future rulings unanswered.

After his election in 2016, President Donald Trump promised to expand religious exemptions for mandated birth control coverage. In 2017, the Trump administration issued new rules that achieved that goal. In addition, it added a new exemption for organizations that objected on moral grounds. Two states challenged the new rules. In July 2020, the Supreme Court upheld the administration's new rules expanding the number of entities that could claim exemptions.

HISTORICAL THINKING

5. **MAKE GENERALIZATIONS** How much freedom do employees have to exercise their religion in the workplace? Explain your answer.
6. **FORM AND SUPPORT OPINIONS** Considering public health concerns and First Amendment rights, who do you feel should have the final word on the vaccination of children—their parents or the government?

LESSON 5.3 Freedom of Expression

The true intention of the protections for free speech in the First Amendment isn't to protect people whose views are widely shared. The real challenge is to protect unpopular ideas. As Justice Oliver Wendell Holmes wrote, the First Amendment is "not free thought for those who agree with us but freedom for the thought that we hate." The First Amendment is designed to protect the freedom to express all ideas, including those many Americans may consider disgusting, unpatriotic, prejudiced, or bigoted.

Free Expression and Its Limits

Time and time again, the courts—and especially the U.S. Supreme Court—have interpreted the First Amendment to protect more than merely spoken words. They have viewed the First Amendment as protecting the actual expression of ideas, as with symbolic speech, or "speech" that involves actions and other nonverbal expressions. For example, wearing a black armband to protest a government policy is protected under what is loosely termed *freedom of expression*. Even burning the American

The 1969 landmark decision *Tinker* v. *Des Moines Independent Community School District* considered the question of whether an armband is protected by freedom of expression. The case originated with siblings Mary Beth and John Tinker, who were suspended from their high school in 1965 for wearing black armbands to support the call for a truce to end the Vietnam War.

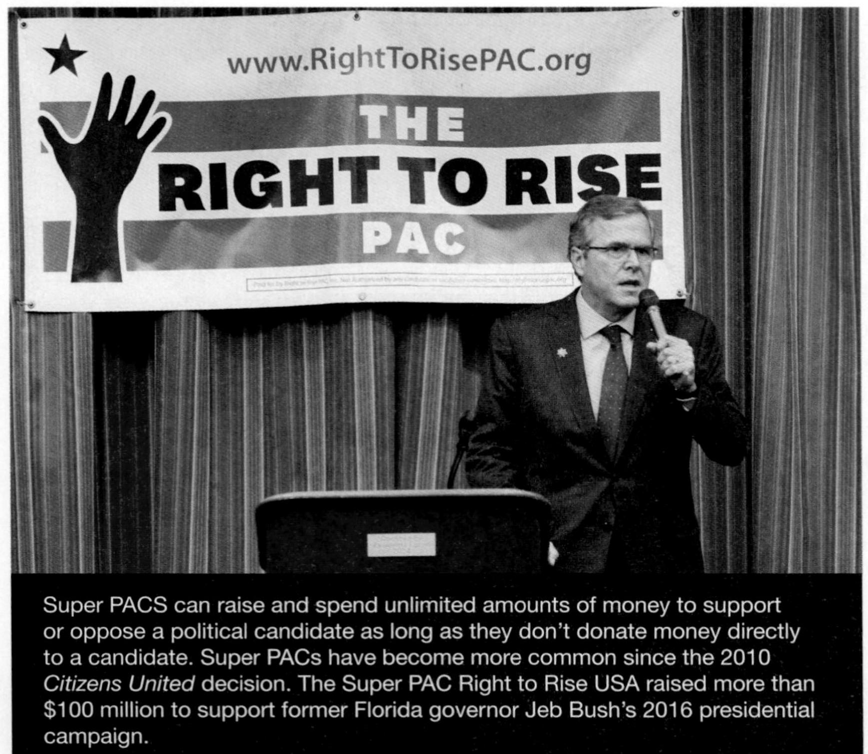

Super PACS can raise and spend unlimited amounts of money to support or oppose a political candidate as long as they don't donate money directly to a candidate. Super PACs have become more common since the 2010 *Citizens United* decision. The Super PAC Right to Rise USA raised more than $100 million to support former Florida governor Jeb Bush's 2016 presidential campaign.

flag as a gesture of protest is protected by the First Amendment.

Yet although the Supreme Court has zealously safeguarded the right to free speech, it has made clear that the right doesn't apply to *all* types of speech. Our constitutional rights and liberties aren't absolute, especially if they infringe on the rights of other Americans. The Court has imposed limits on speech for a variety of reasons, including to provide security against harm to one's person or reputation, or to protect the public order or the government.

LIBEL AND SLANDER Speech is not protected when the speech itself is part of a crime. An act of fraud, for example, can be carried out entirely through spoken words. Another type of speech that is unprotected is **defamation**, or the act of making false statements to hurt a person' s reputation. There are two types of defamation. The first form of defamation is **libel**, falsehood published with the intent of injuring someone's reputation or character. A publicly spoken statement that holds a person up for contempt, ridicule, or hatred is **slander**, the other form of defamation.

To prove libel or slander, certain criteria must be met. The statements made must (1) be untrue, (2) stem from an intent to do harm, and (3) result in actual harm. The Supreme Court has ruled that public figures (such as public officials or Hollywood celebrities) can't collect damages for remarks made about them unless they can prove the remarks were made with what the Court termed "reckless" disregard for accuracy. This exception has been made because, in general, public figures are in a better position to defend themselves against libelous or slanderous statements.

CAMPAIGN CONTRIBUTIONS AND FREE SPEECH Campaign contributions—either money or assistance given to candidates for public office to help them get elected—can be considered speech in some circumstances. Yet for many years, activists and even politicians tried to limit the amount of money that individuals and groups could contribute to political campaigns. They feared that without such limits, wealthy individuals, organizations, and businesses would have too much influence in Congress and state legislatures. The passage of the Bipartisan Campaign Reform Act (BCRA) of 2002 (an amendment to the Federal Election Campaign Act of 1971) put new limits on how much money an individual could donate to a candidate for federal office or to a national political committee. It also made it illegal for unions and corporations to donate money or sponsor certain types of targeted advertisements.

In its ruling in *Citizens United* v. *Federal Election Commission* (2010), however, the Supreme Court struck down key parts of BCRA. The case involved questions over the right of Citizens United, a conservative nonprofit corporation, to fund a film intended to portray future presidential candidate Senator Hillary Rodham Clinton as unfit for office. In a 5–4 decision, the Court ruled that unions and corporations, though they may be large, are still made up of individuals, and the BCRA violated the First Amendment rights of individuals making up those organizations. (The Court did uphold the BCRA's ban on direct contributions from corporations and unions to federal candidates, however.)

STUDENTS AND FREE SPEECH American students are in a unique position when it comes to free speech. Schools are places where students grapple with ideas, and debates are frequent, both in the classroom and out of it. In general, however, courts have ruled that speech that detracts from a school's primary mission can be justifiably limited. So, too, can speech that takes place as part of a school program. For example, the Court allows school officials to exercise some **censorship**, or the removal of objectionable images or ideas by a person in authority, over high school publications.

Free speech on American college campuses has had an eventful history since the 1960s. In the 1950s and early 1960s, the University of California, like many other colleges and universities, banned political activities on campus, including participating in or publicizing civil rights and anti-war activities. In 1964, Mario Savio, a civil rights activist and a student at the University of California at Berkeley, challenged the university's limits on student speech and political activities. Savio insisted that political speech and organizing were protected by the First Amendment. He inspired thousands of other students and faculty at the University of California at Berkeley to take part in what became known as the Free Speech Movement, a series of protests that eventually forced Berkeley administrators to lift restrictions on student activism. The movement spread to other campuses, where it met with similar success.

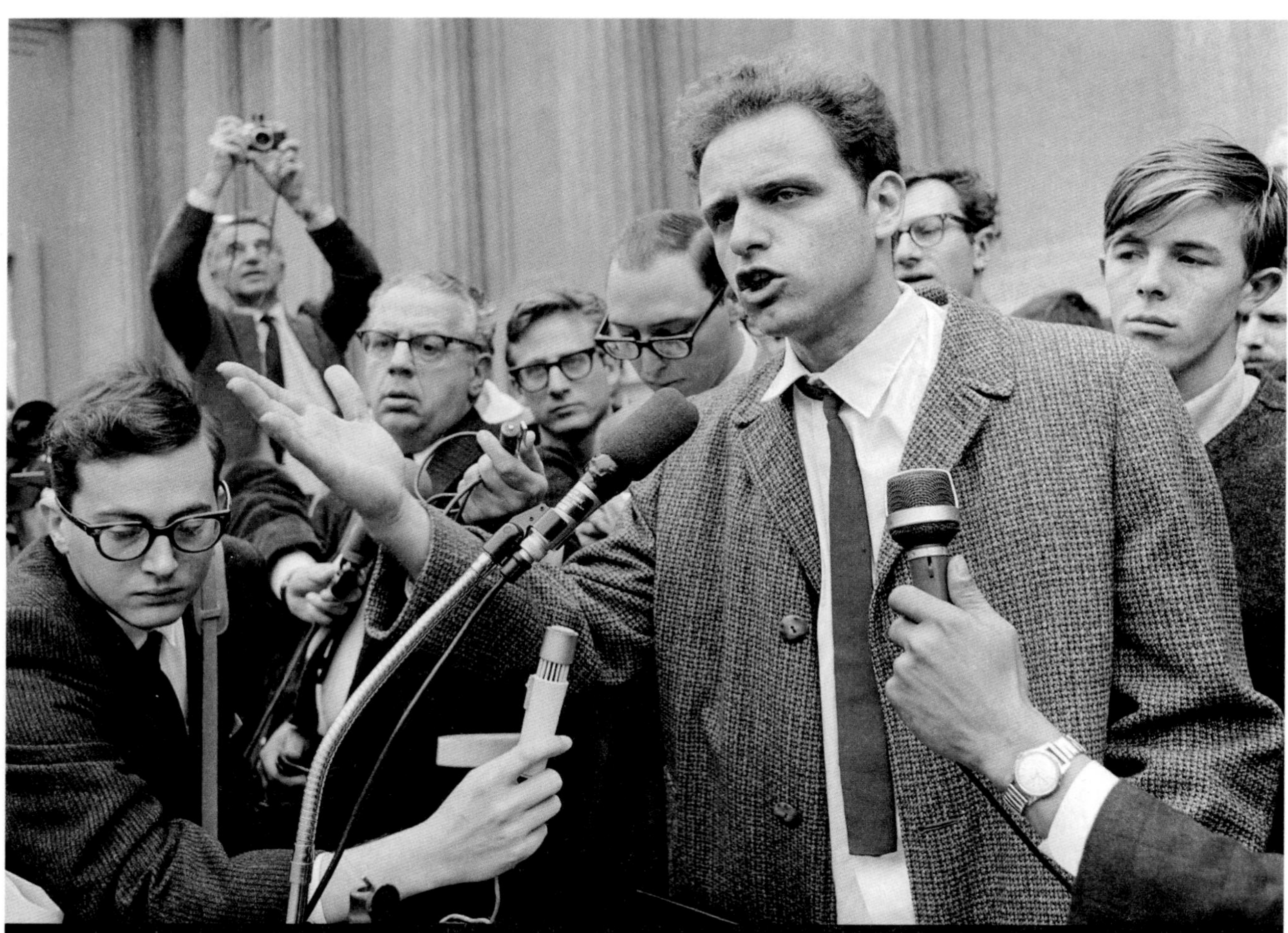

Mario Savio was considered a free-speech champion by many of his fellow students in the 1960s. He was suspended for his actions by the University of California at Berkeley and later finished his undergraduate and graduate education at San Francisco State University.

More recently, universities have tried to establish codes to ban hateful remarks about race, gender, or sexual orientation as well as speech that may incite violence. Violations can result in expulsion. The courts have viewed these efforts with skepticism, consistently striking down rules limiting speech on campuses receiving public funds as violations of free speech. Public colleges and universities can limit objectionable speech on campus on the grounds of public safety. Private colleges and universities that are not publicly funded don't have to abide by the Court's guidelines.

HISTORICAL THINKING

1. **COMPARE AND CONTRAST** Why has the Supreme Court ruled that well-known people should be treated differently from members of the general public in defamation lawsuits?
2. **FORM AND SUPPORT OPINIONS** Do you support the view that high school administrators should have the power to limit student speech when they deem it necessary? Explain your response.

Subversive Speech and Sedition

Ideas that challenge mainstream beliefs or the status quo—especially those that involve criticism of the government—have been part of American history ever since the colonists declared their independence in 1776. How the U.S. government has responded to its critics has varied over the centuries, however. When responding to individuals who oppose the U.S. form of government, who runs it, or how it is run, the government has drawn a line between legitimate criticism and the expression of harmful ideas. Obviously, the government may pass laws against violent acts. But things become murkier when determining whether subversive or **seditious** speech—speech that urges resistance to lawful authority or advocates overthrowing the government—is actually criminal or about to inspire violence.

As early as 1798, when it seemed like the United States was on the verge of going to war with France, Congress took steps to curb seditious speech. The Sedition Act made it a crime to utter "any false, scandalous, and malicious" criticism of the government. Several dozen individuals—many of them journalists—were prosecuted under the Sedition Act, and some were convicted. In 1801 President Thomas Jefferson pardoned those sentenced under the act, and it wasn't renewed after it expired.

During World War I, Congress passed the Espionage Act of 1917, which prohibited attempts to interfere with operations of the military forces, the war effort, or the process of recruitment. A 1918 amendment to the act was, like the 1798 legislation, also known as the Sedition Act. This amendment made it a crime to "willfully utter, print, write, or publish any disloyal . . . or abusive language about the government." Using the "bad tendency test," which held that speech could be restricted if it was likely to have harmful consequences, the Supreme Court

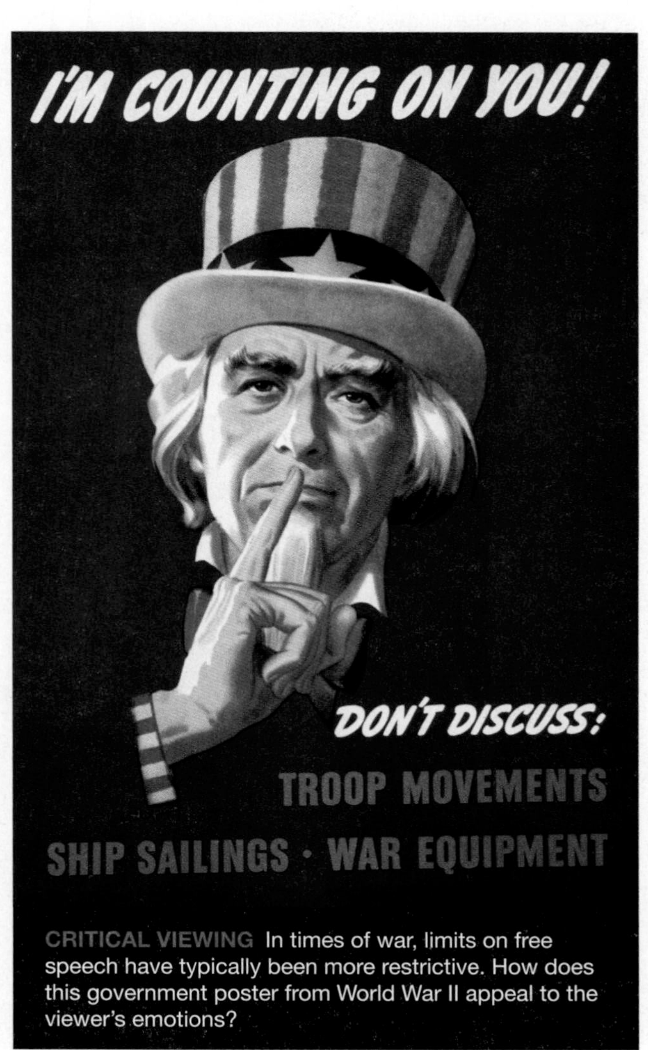
I'M COUNTING ON YOU!
DON'T DISCUSS:
TROOP MOVEMENTS
SHIP SAILINGS · WAR EQUIPMENT

CRITICAL VIEWING In times of war, limits on free speech have typically been more restrictive. How does this government poster from World War II appeal to the viewer's emotions?

SUPREME COURT

Schenck v. *United States*, 1919

Decided: March 3, 1919, 7–0

Majority: Justice Oliver Wendell Holmes wrote the majority opinion for the unanimous decision upholding the Espionage Act.

Shortly after Congress passed the Espionage Act of 1917, Charles Schenck, the general secretary of the U.S. Socialist Party, and an associate were arrested. They had printed and distributed about 15,000 leaflets urging American males to resist the draft or, if already drafted, to refuse to serve. Schenck believed the draft targeted men with less money and was unconstitutional. Schenck was tried, convicted, and sentenced to 30 years in prison.

Schenck appealed his conviction on the grounds that the Espionage Act violated his First Amendment right to free speech. In a unanimous decision, however, the Court upheld the constitutionality of the act, contending that courts needed to defer more heavily to government during times of war. In his majority opinion for the Court, Justice Oliver Wendell Holmes introduced a new "clear and present danger test" to be used when weighing First Amendment rights against possible sedition. He said, "Words which, ordinarily and in many places, would be within the freedom of speech protected by the First Amendment may become subject to prohibition when of such a nature and used in such circumstances as to create a clear and present danger that they will bring about the substantive evils which Congress has a right to prevent."

DON'T TALK
THE WEB IS SPUN FOR YOU WITH INVISIBLE THREADS
KEEP OUT OF IT
HELP TO DESTROY IT
STOP = THINK
ASK YOURSELF IF WHAT YOU WERE ABOUT TO SAY MIGHT HELP THE ENEMY
SPIES ARE LISTENING
INTELLIGENCE OFFICER NORTHEASTERN DEPT. U.S. ARMY

The "clear and present danger test" established by *Schenck* has long influenced how sedition cases are considered alongside freedom of speech protections, particularly during times of war. This poster implies that sharing too much information will help the German kaiser, the man at the center of the "invisible" web, and the leader of Germany, an enemy power in World War I.

In what became perhaps the most well-known part of the decision, Holmes also compared the distribution of leaflets that could affect the draft and overall war effort to inducing panic in a crowd: "The most stringent protection of free speech would not protect a man in falsely shouting fire in a theatre and causing a panic." Schenck was ordered to serve six months of jail time.

THINK ABOUT IT How might the Court's decision have been different if the case had been heard at a time when the United States was not at war?

SUPREME COURT

Texas v. *Johnson*, 1989

Decided: June 21, 1989, 5–4

Majority: Justice William Brennan wrote the majority opinion in favor of Gregory Lee Johnson. Justice Anthony Kennedy wrote a concurring opinion.

Dissent: Dissenting opinions were written by Chief Justice William Rehnquist and Justice John Paul Stevens.

In 1984, while the Republican National Convention was taking place in Dallas, Gregory Lee Johnson soaked an American flag in kerosene and burned it in front of Dallas City Hall to protest the policies of President Ronald Reagan's administration. Johnson was arrested for breaking a Texas law that prohibited desecration of the American flag. Johnson was tried, convicted, and sentenced to one year in jail. Upon a second appeal, his case was overturned by the Texas Court of Criminal Appeals, which ruled that the Texas law violated First Amendment rights.

The case was eventually heard by the U.S. Supreme Court, which would decide if flag burning qualified as symbolic speech protected under the First Amendment. In a controversial decision, the Court ruled 5–4 that Johnson's act was indeed protected. While acknowledging that flag burning angered many Americans, the justices in the majority declared that "The Government may not prohibit the expression of an idea simply because society finds the idea itself offensive or disagreeable." The majority also noted that it was unconstitutional for Texas to allow some actions, such as the respectful burial of a worn American flag, but not other actions.

THINK ABOUT IT What does the close ruling of the Court in this case indicate about the significance of Johnson's action?

upheld the Espionage Act's restrictions on speech in several cases. In the 1919 case of *Schenck* v. *United States*, the Court developed the "clear and present danger test," which stated that expression could be restricted if it would cause a dangerous situation. Parts of the Espionage Act of 1917 are still in effect. Edward Snowden, who in 2013 exposed the practices of the National Security Agency before seeking asylum in Russia, is one of several people charged with leaking classified national security information under the century-old legislation.

In 1940, while preparing for possible entry into World War II, Congress passed the Smith Act, or the Alien Registration Act. The act required that any alien, or foreign, resident of the United States complete a registration card with information about his or her political beliefs. Socialist and Communist leaders were prosecuted under the act, but later the Supreme Court ruled that it applied only to those who urged violent overthrow of the government.

The current standard for evaluating the legality of speech opposing the government uses a more stringent test than the "clear and present danger test." Known as the "the imminent lawless action test," it was established by the Supreme Court in 1969 and says that speech can be forbidden only when it is "directed to inciting [causing]. . . imminent [immediate] lawless action." As a result, subversive speech receives far more protection today than it did in the past, as evidenced by the 1989 decision in *Texas* v. *Johnson*, in which the Court ruled that a person could burn an American flag to protest government policies.

HISTORICAL THINKING

3. **COMPARE AND CONTRAST** What do the Sedition Act of 1798 and the Espionage Act of 1917 have in common?
4. **DRAW CONCLUSIONS** Why is it so diffcult for prosecutors to prove that speech is intended to cause "imminent lawless action"?

Freedom of the Press

As the Framers crafted the Constitution, the idea of a free press was very much on their minds. The Framers would have been familiar with the landmark trial of John Peter Zenger in 1735. Zenger was a German immigrant and printer who published the *New York Weekly Journal*, which had criticized the colonial governor of New York, William Cosby. Although Zenger himself hadn't written most of the articles, he was arrested in 1734 for libel, jailed, and tried about 10 months later. The jury acquitted Zenger, finding that the articles in question were based on fact. While this decision occurred well before the Bill of Rights or even independence, it was the first major step toward freedom of the press, or the right to publish without government censorship, in the American colonies.

Decades later, freedom of the press was included in the First Amendment, and in general, all the free speech protections in the First Amendment also apply to the press. The courts have placed certain restrictions on freedom of the press, however. Over the years, the Supreme Court has developed various guidelines to use in deciding whether freedom of speech and the press can be restrained.

One major guideline, called the preferred-position doctrine, states that certain freedoms—including freedom of speech and of the press—are so essential to a democracy that they hold a "preferred position." According to this doctrine, any law that limits these freedoms should be presumed unconstitutional unless the government can show that the law is absolutely necessary. The belief behind this doctrine is that spoken and printed words are the prime tools of the democratic process.

But limits do occur. For example, stopping an activity before it actually happens is known as prior restraint. With respect to freedom of the press, **prior restraint** means censorship, or removal of content by government officials before broadcast or publication. The Supreme Court has generally ruled

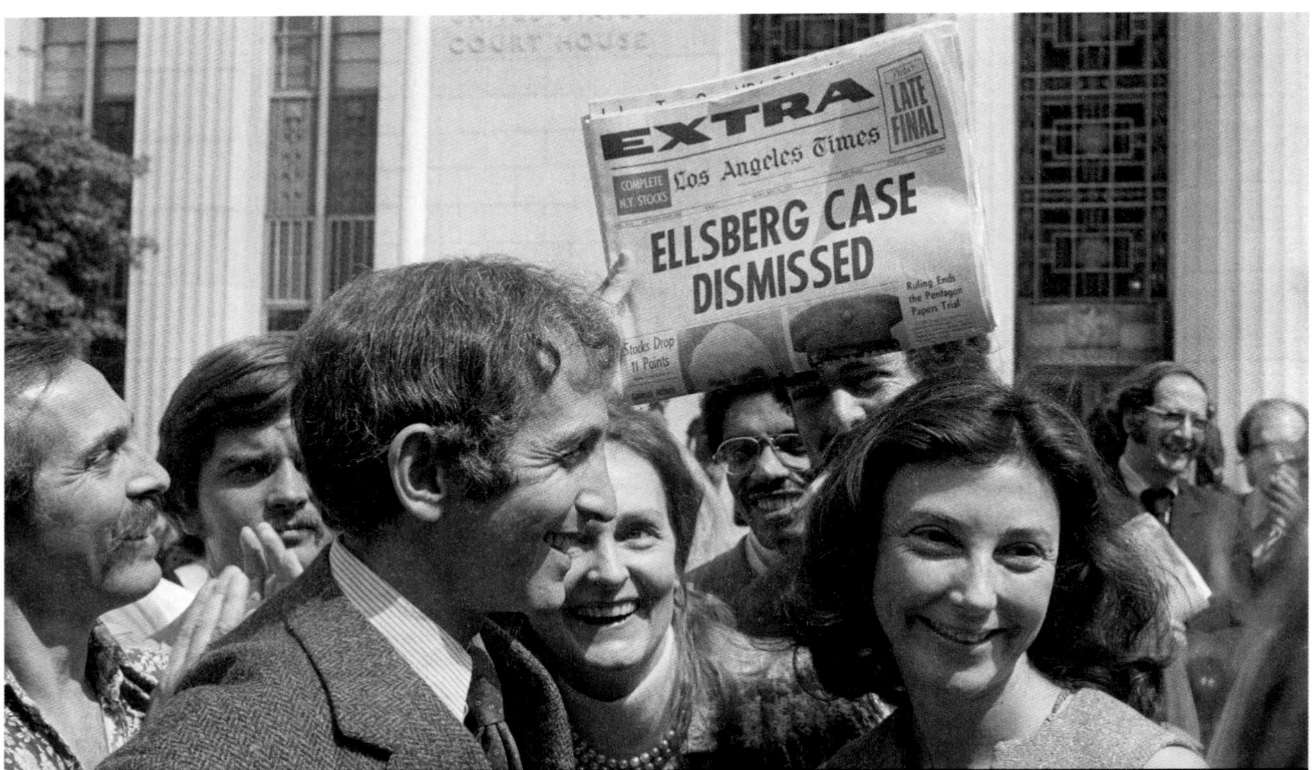

In 1971, military analyst Daniel Ellsberg leaked documents from a top secret U.S. Department of Defense study on the Vietnam War—known as the Pentagon Papers—to the *New York Times*, which then published a series of articles revealing information from the study. In the ensuing case *New York Times Co.* v. *United States*, the Supreme Court held that freedom of the press overcame the government's concerns about threats to national security. Charges against Ellsberg were later dismissed.

against prior restraint, arguing that the government can't curb ideas before they are expressed.

In certain circumstances, however, the Court has allowed prior restraint. For example, in a 1988 case a high school principal deleted two pages from the school newspaper just before it was printed. The pages contained stories on students' experiences with pregnancy as well as the impact of divorce. The Supreme Court, noting that students in school don't have exactly the same rights as adults in other settings, ruled that high school administrators can censor school publications. The Court said that school newspapers are part of the school curriculum, not a public forum.

JOURNALISM AND COMMERCIAL SPEECH
As anyone who has watched a thriller involving a journalist might guess, the statement "I won't reveal my sources" is a major element of a free press. This "reporter's privilege" isn't a constitutionally protected right, but 30 states and the District of Columbia have passed laws known as "shield laws" that protect a journalist from being forced to reveal confidential sources or share related, unpublished materials. In 1972, in the only U.S. Supreme Court case yet to deal with this issue, a divided Court ruled that journalists aren't granted immunity from grand jury subpoenas, and that such protection could only be possible through legislation.

For several years, attempts have been made to pass a federal shield law, yet none have been successful. Supporters of shield laws claim that possible sources for articles are less likely to speak with journalists if their confidentiality isn't guaranteed—a roadblock that could obstruct freedom of the press. These same supporters also say that forcing journalists to hand over their notes to the courts puts undue hardship on the editorial process and can violate freedom of speech. Opponents of shield laws argue that journalists often have inside knowledge that could impact how a crime is prosecuted. The issue of confidentiality in journalism therefore hasn't been resolved.

Advertising, or commercial speech, is also protected by the First Amendment, but not as robustly as regular speech. Generally, the Supreme Court has considered a restriction on commercial speech to be valid as long as the restriction (1) seeks to implement a substantial government interest, (2) directly advances that interest, and (3) goes no further than necessary to accomplish its objective.

Problems arise, though, when restrictions on commercial advertising achieve one substantial government interest but are contrary to the interest of protecting free speech and the right of consumers to be informed. In such cases, the courts have to decide which interest takes priority. State limits on liquor advertising to discourage liquor consumption illustrate this kind of conflict. Such limits have been ruled unconstitutional by the Supreme Court.

FREE SPEECH IN ENTERTAINMENT AND THE INTERNET American attitudes toward sexual expression have changed radically in the past 40 years. Once the internet became mainstream, U.S. officials no longer even tried to impose obscenity restrictions on printed or visual material (with the exception of child pornography, which is considered child abuse). Additionally, attempts by Congress in 1996 and 1998 to ban internet obscenity that might be seen by minors were ruled unconstitutional by the Supreme Court. Other attempts to censor the entertainment industry, such as proposals requiring video game retailers to ask for identification when selling violent games, have met with a similar lack of success.

The entertainment industry is still subject to some regulation, since the government retains the right to impose restrictions on activities that it subsidizes or media it controls, such as the broadcast spectrum. Thus, restrictions on radio and broadcast television remain in effect, which is why content such as nudity and profane language isn't allowed on broadcast television but can be seen on some subscription-based cable channels. Aware of the criticism leveled against it, especially when it comes to the increase in graphic violence in video games and movies, the entertainment industry has also instituted some self-censorship measures, such as a system of ratings for video games and TV shows.

The internet has also changed much of the landscape of free speech. **Cyberbullying**, or online harassment, has often crossed the line into criminal—and prosecutable—behavior. Much of this incendiary speech occurs on social media, giving offensive statements a potentially huge audience. Freedom of speech is a strongly protected right, and the courts have approached social media offenses carefully, including in cases involving student speech. Recently, district and state courts have ruled against students who have made bomb threats on Facebook, posted racist images on Instagram, and uploaded defamatory videos to YouTube—even when the content was posted outside of school property.

An influx of fake news stories with the purpose of influencing the 2016 and 2020 U.S. presidential elections has put legitimate news organizations under the microscope. Some of the online platforms via which fake news spreads, such as Facebook and Google, have begun to put protections in place to help users sort false content from the truth. Additionally, a recent spate of leaks of government information via online channels has raised questions about how far the First Amendment goes in protecting people who share classified data. WikiLeaks, an international organization that collects and publishes classified information anonymously on its website, has been front and center of this debate during the past 10 years. Throughout that time, the group has published more than half a million classified or sensitive U.S. government documents.

HISTORICAL THINKING

5. **MAKE CONNECTIONS** Given the fact that journalists and their colleagues are already protected by the First Amendment right to free speech, why do you think the Framers thought it necessary to specifically mention the freedom of the press?
6. **IDENTIFY MAIN IDEAS AND DETAILS** How has the government treatment of obscenity changed over the past 50 or so years?

LESSON 5.4 Freedom of Assembly and Petition

Americans today have more ways to voice their opinions than ever before. Some people gather in the streets to march or rally. Others sign online petitions to catch the attention of policymakers with tens or hundreds of thousands of signatures. Still others express their views on social media, or in text messages, emails, phone calls, or letters to their local, state, or national representatives. Yet while some of these actions rely on new forms of communication, all of them are protected by the First Amendment's guarantee of freedom of assembly and the right to petition.

The Right to Assemble and Petition

A phrase at the end of the First Amendment guarantees "the right of the people peaceably to assemble, and to petition the Government for a redress of grievances." These rights don't get as much attention as those that precede them in the First Amendment or those in the rest of the Bill of Rights. Many people think of the right to assemble or to petition for change as included in the right to freedom of expression.

Yet assembly implies a group. Assemblies come in many forms, such as community meetings, protest marches, rallies, sit-ins, and picket lines, and most of these require group preparation and cooperation. This group element of assembly has resulted in the now-recognized right to association.

The right to petition has been mostly absorbed by freedom of speech. Americans regularly petition government in person, in writing, online, or by phone, radio, or television. Whenever someone emails a congressional representative for help, he or she is petitioning the government. Yet, despite being lumped in with the other First Amendment rights, the specific right to petition the government is fundamental to our democracy. The Bill of Rights was written after Americans had spent decades sending lists of grievances to King George III. They wanted to be sure the officials they elected would hear their complaints

Supreme Court Justice Louis Brandeis once said that sometimes the best way to "avert the evil . . . is more speech, not enforced silence." Days after the violent clash between White supremacists and counterprotesters in Charlottesville, Virginia, in 2017, thousands of people held a candlelight vigil on the campus of the University of Virginia. They sang songs of inspiration and expressed their desire for peace.

and address them, so early American leaders included the right to petition in their list of protected rights. This right allows citizens to **lobby**, or seek to influence, members of Congress and other government officials, to sue the government, and to submit requests to the government without fear of punishment.

As with other First Amendment rights, freedom of assembly and the right to petition apply to state as well as federal laws. They were incorporated via the due process clause of the 14th Amendment through the Supreme Court's ruling in *DeJonge* v. *Oregon* (1937). The case involved Dirk DeJonge, who was convicted of violating Oregon's laws against **syndicates**, or organizations, that promoted the use of criminal violence as a means to achieve political change. DeJonge had attended a legal protest meeting in which no one suggested violence, even though some of those attending did belong to a political party that advocated violence to achieve political change. In his opinion, Chief Justice Charles Evans Hughes declared that "peaceable assembly for lawful discussion cannot be made a crime."

UNITE THE RIGHT PROTESTS The right of free assembly may be fundamental, but it is not absolute. It can be curtailed—reduced or restricted—in the interest of public safety. But determining when a situation poses a threat to public safety poses a challenge.

In August 2017 a group of White nationalists and supremacists planned a Unite the Right rally in Charlottesville, Virginia, in response to a plan to remove a statue of Confederate general Robert E. Lee from a city park. On the morning of August 12, violence erupted between Unite the Right rallygoers and counterprotesters in Charlottesville's Emancipation Park. Both sides had permits from public safety officials, but many White supremacists were armed with shields, clubs, and guns. Several counterprotesters also had sharp objects and shields.

Later that day, a Unite the Right supporter drove his car into a crowd of pedestrians, killing 32-year-old Heather Heyer and injuring 19 others. A few hours later, a state police helicopter monitoring the protest action crashed, killing two Virginia state troopers. Many Americans were dismayed that President Donald Trump appeared reluctant to condemn the White supremacists and seemed to blame both rallygoers and counterprotesters for the violence. Yet while the Bill of Rights protects the views of the minority (in this case, White supremacists) even if the majority finds them reprehensible, it does not protect the use of violence or weapons in protest actions.

CIVIL DISOBEDIENCE Throughout U.S. history, individuals have gathered to raise awareness of issues and try to effect change. Some have followed the letter of the law, while others have broken laws to get their points across. Acts of **civil disobedience**—public nonviolent refusal to follow a current law or laws—were used in the U.S. civil rights movement of the 1950s and 1960s. One of the most famous acts of civil disobedience was Rosa Parks's refusal to give up her bus seat to a White passenger as required by the law at that time in Montgomery, Alabama. When Parks was arrested, local African-American activists organized a city-wide bus boycott that ended only when the U.S. Supreme Court declared the Montgomery law unconstitutional.

During the Vietnam War era of the 1960s and 1970s, thousands of protesters turned out to march. Some protesters willingly faced arrest for burning draft cards, while others tried to stop vehicles transporting troops and armaments to U.S. ports for shipment to the war zone. Acts of civil disobedience such as these continued until the United States signed a peace agreement with North Vietnam at the beginning of 1973.

THE RIGHT OF ASSOCIATION The Constitution doesn't explicitly list the freedom of association, or the right to identify with or join a group for political or other purposes. But in a series of cases following World War II, the Supreme Court determined that the right to free association is clearly implied by, or derived from, the right of assembly. *NAACP* v. *Alabama* (1958) was pivotal in this regard. The National Association for the Advancement of Colored People (NAACP), a civil rights organization, had defied an Alabama law aimed at restricting it from operating in the state.

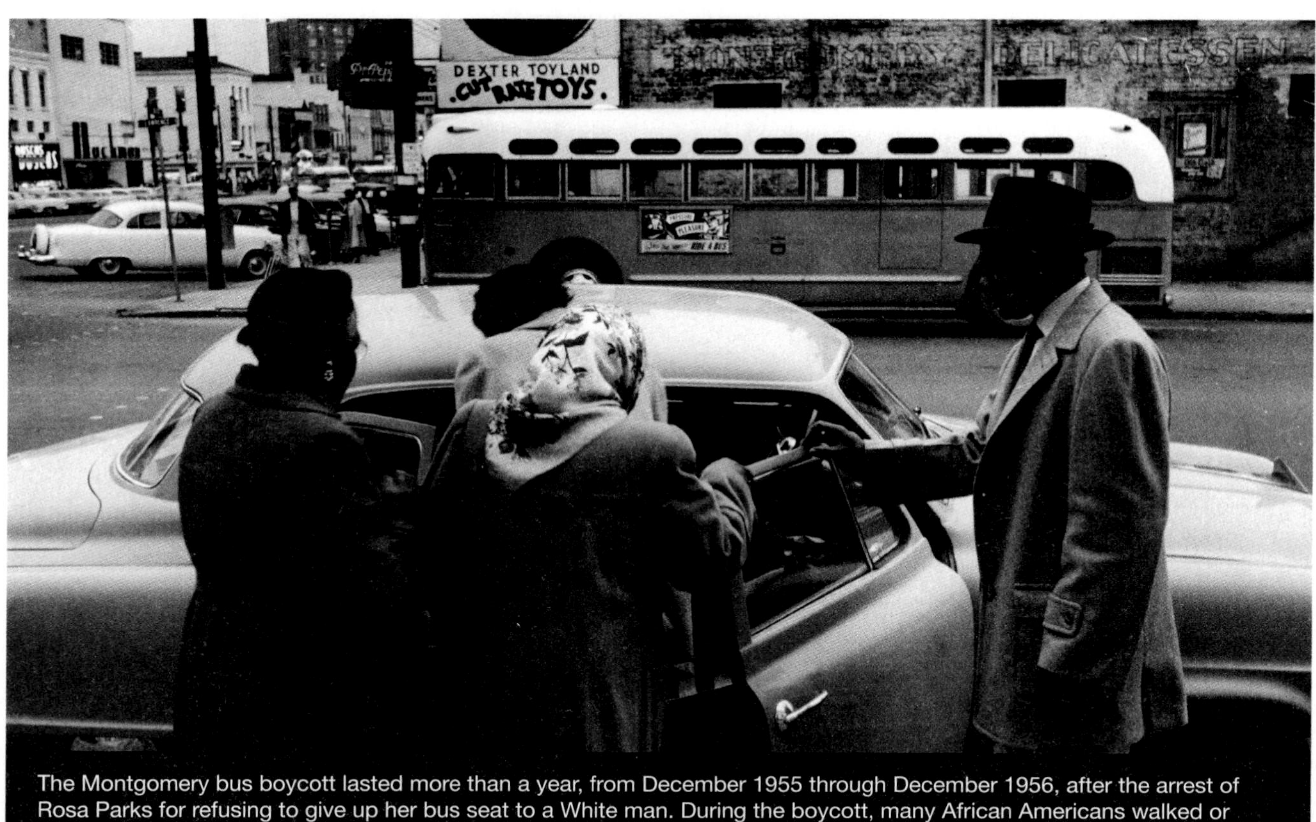

The Montgomery bus boycott lasted more than a year, from December 1955 through December 1956, after the arrest of Rosa Parks for refusing to give up her bus seat to a White man. During the boycott, many African Americans walked or carpooled, leaving city buses empty. Some boycotters were fired from their jobs. Others faced arrests, threats, and attack.

When an Alabama trial court requested access to the NAACP's state membership list, the organization argued that releasing the names of its members would expose them to harassment or worse. In a unanimous decision, the Supreme Court stated that asking to see membership lists infringed on the right "to pursue their lawful interests privately and to associate freely with others in doing so as to come within the protection of the 14th Amendment."

The relationship between an individual's right to associate has come into question over the years, particularly in cases in which the person is a union member or associates with political groups considered radical. The First Amendment rights of public-sector employees—those who work for the government—are clear: In most cases, they can't be fired because of their political views or how they choose to express them. Private-sector employers have more leeway to dismiss an employee if his or her actions reflect badly on the business or organization.

Today, people have more opportunities than ever to become members of or to identify with groups. The internet spreads petitions for change faster to larger, more diverse groups of people. Over only the past few years, online petitions have been important catalysts in the passage of certain legislation. Social media have also helped people feel a part of bigger movements by giving them quick, simple access to political and social platforms. For example, the Tea Party, a conservative populist political movement that began in 2009, attracted thousands of followers by publicizing events on social media. The Black Lives Matter movement has also expanded through social media platforms. The BlackLivesMatter hashtag was used an average of more than 17,000 times a day between July 2013 and May 2018.

HISTORICAL THINKING

1. **IDENTIFY MAIN IDEAS AND DETAILS** What is an act of civil disobedience, and why do some people knowingly engage in acts of civil disobedience?
2. **DRAW CONCLUSIONS** What does the increased use of social media to publicize calls for change tell you about how Americans rally together for a common cause?

Reasonable Rules

The Supreme Court has established a number of general rules for maintaining public safety while balancing the right of free assembly. Law enforcement officers can end a protest if violence breaks out. They can also act before violence breaks out, but only if conditions meet the "Clear and present danger test" established by the U.S. Supreme Court in *Schenck* v. *United States*. Law enforcement officials can also order protesters to disperse if officials believe protesters are inciting lawless action. One of the major criticisms of law enforcement during the 2017 Charlottesville events was that police waited until a number of fights had broken out before issuing a dispersal order.

Where one can assemble has also been addressed by the courts. In general, parks and many streets are considered safe enough and public enough for most assemblies. What is allowed on sidewalks, however, is not as clear. In the case *United States* v. *Grace* (1983), in which the appellants claimed they had a right to distribute leaflets and hold signs on sidewalks outside the U.S. Supreme Court building, the Court wrote that "public sidewalks forming the perimeter of the Supreme Court grounds, in our view, are public forums and should be treated as such for First Amendment purposes." In contrast, in 1990 the Supreme Court ruled that sidewalks outside U.S. post offices were not places where a group could promote its political beliefs. As the Court explained, "The location and purpose of a publicly owned sidewalk is critical to determining whether such a sidewalk constitutes a public forum." Post offices are used for sorting mail. The Supreme Court is used for deciding issues of constitutional importance.

In *Lloyd Corporation, Ltd.* v. *Tanner* (1972), the Supreme Court ruled that Vietnam War protester Donald Tanner and others could not hand out leaflets in the Lloyd Center Mall in Portland, Oregon. While the Court had ruled earlier that striking employees could picket on the property of their employer, it decided that Tanner and other protesters could have used public spaces—such as the sidewalks surrounding the mall—to distribute leaflets.

For assemblies to be peaceable, they must be safe for those assembling and for bystanders. Therefore, groups may be required to apply for and pay a

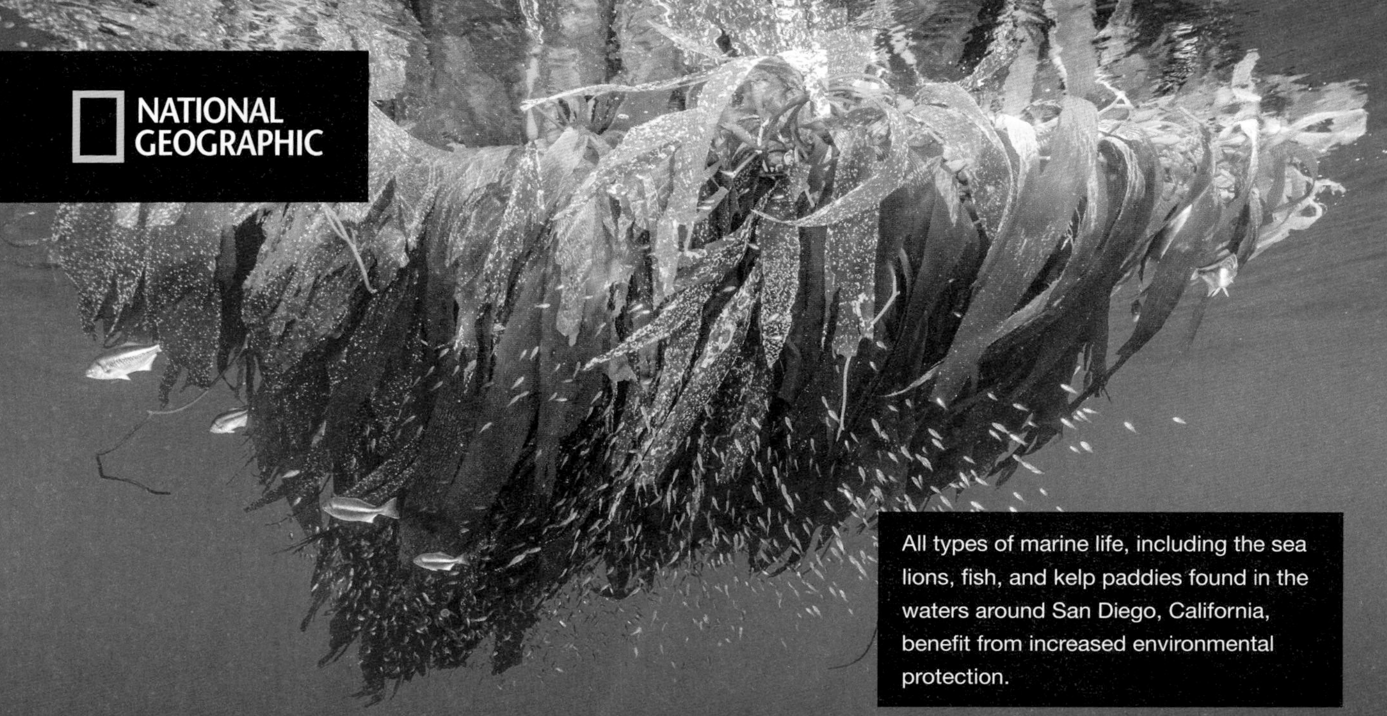

All types of marine life, including the sea lions, fish, and kelp paddies found in the waters around San Diego, California, benefit from increased environmental protection.

How the Environment Has Changed Since the First Earth Day

by Sarah Gibbens **National Geographic Online, April 21, 2018**

Environmental protection was not on the minds of most Americans 50 years ago. Air pollution levels were high, pesticide use often went unchecked, and certain animal species were becoming extinct. As Sarah Gibbens writes in "How the Environment Has Changed Since the First Earth Day," modern-day environmental awareness grew out of the exercise of some fundamental American rights—the right to assembly and the right to petition. On that first Earth Day, millions of Americans came together to celebrate the Earth and to petition their government to do more to protect the planet.

In the years leading up to the first Earth Day in 1970, various U.S. social movements had found strength in numbers. Americans from a variety of backgrounds had joined together during the 1960s to push for voting rights, civil rights, and women's rights. When U.S. senator Gaylord Nelson of Wisconsin announced his idea for Earth Day following a devastating oil spill in 1969, the momentum that built during the previous decade surged again. In April 1970, 20 million Americans exercised their right to assembly and joined demonstrations and projects across the country in support of paying more attention to humans' impact on the environment.

As Gibbens explains, this single, massive event had a domino effect on future government action and legislation to protect the environment:

> *It spurred a movement that pushed then president Nixon to create the Environmental Protection Agency. In the 48 years since the first Earth Day, there have been more than 48 major environmental wins. Protections have been put in place on everything from clean water to endangered species.*

Today, Earth Day is an international celebration—and day of service—for the planet. It continues to be recognized across the globe each year in April.

THINK ABOUT IT How were the first Earth Day and subsequent changes to environmental policy examples of the cooperative relationship between Americans and their government?

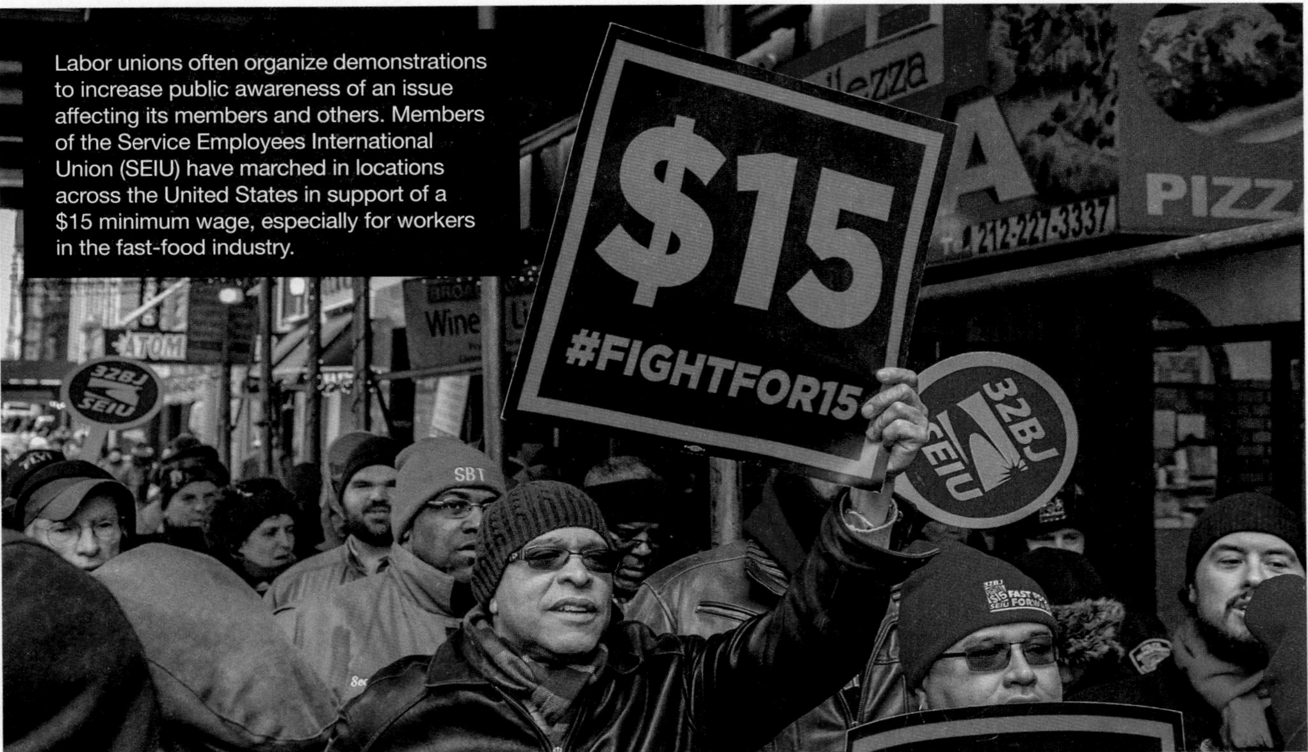

Labor unions often organize demonstrations to increase public awareness of an issue affecting its members and others. Members of the Service Employees International Union (SEIU) have marched in locations across the United States in support of a $15 minimum wage, especially for workers in the fast-food industry.

reasonable fee for permits. In general, officials enforce permit requirements to ensure public safety and traffic control. A march or rally may take place without a permit, especially in response to controversial legislation or confirmation of a contentious Supreme Court nominee. In the case of the Charlottesville Unite the Right events, permitting policies had been followed by both sides. The permits, however, didn't guarantee that the rallygoers wouldn't begin assembling until a certain time, or that they would adhere to the location information listed on the permits.

HISTORICAL THINKING

3. **SYNTHESIZE** Protesters are allowed to assemble outside the Supreme Court but not inside the building. Why is this?
4. **FORM AND SUPPORT OPINIONS** Do you think requiring permits for protests and other assemblies puts undue strain on protesters' freedom of assembly? Explain.

LESSON 5.5 Due Process Under the Law

Ever since the birth of the smartphone at the beginning of the 21st century, access to media and breaking news has made it nearly impossible not to know about the regularity of criminal activity throughout the United States. Burglaries, terrorist attacks, identity theft, financial fraud, homicide—the list goes on. It isn't surprising that many Americans have strong opinions about the rights of the accused. Some Americans complain that criminal defendants have too many rights. However, the protections for the rights of criminals protect the rights of law-abiding citizens as well.

What Is Due Process of Law?

The right to due process of law is very simple: Everyone has the right to be treated fairly under the legal system. That system and its officers must follow "rules of fair play" when they make decisions, when they determine guilt or innocence, and when they punish those who have been found guilty. Due process has two aspects—procedural and substantive.

PROCEDURAL DUE PROCESS Procedural due process focuses on procedure, or the process by which the government will equitably, or fairly and equally, apply laws that deprive a person of life, liberty, or property. The government must use "fair procedures" in determining whether a person will be punished with prison time or face some burden such as making a payment to a victim. Fair procedure has been interpreted as requiring that the person have at least an opportunity to object to a proposed action in front of an impartial, neutral decision maker (who isn't necessarily a judge).

SUBSTANTIVE DUE PROCESS Substantive due process focuses on the content, or substance, of legislation. If a law or other governmental action limits a fundamental right, it is considered to violate substantive due process unless it promotes a compelling state interest. All First Amendment rights plus the rights to interstate travel, privacy, and voting are considered fundamental. A compelling state interest might include the public's safety, for example. Defining state interests can be a thorny issue, however. Cases involving substantive due process, including those regarding a state's or territory's right to ban handguns in the home or deny the right of a married couple to receive counseling about birth control, have been some of the most controversial in U.S. legal history.

DUE PROCESS AND THE STATES The individual's due process rights are protected by two constitutional amendments. The Fifth Amendment requires the federal government to follow due process of law, and the 14th Amendment requires the states to do the same. As you have read, however, the states also have broad police powers to protect the general health,

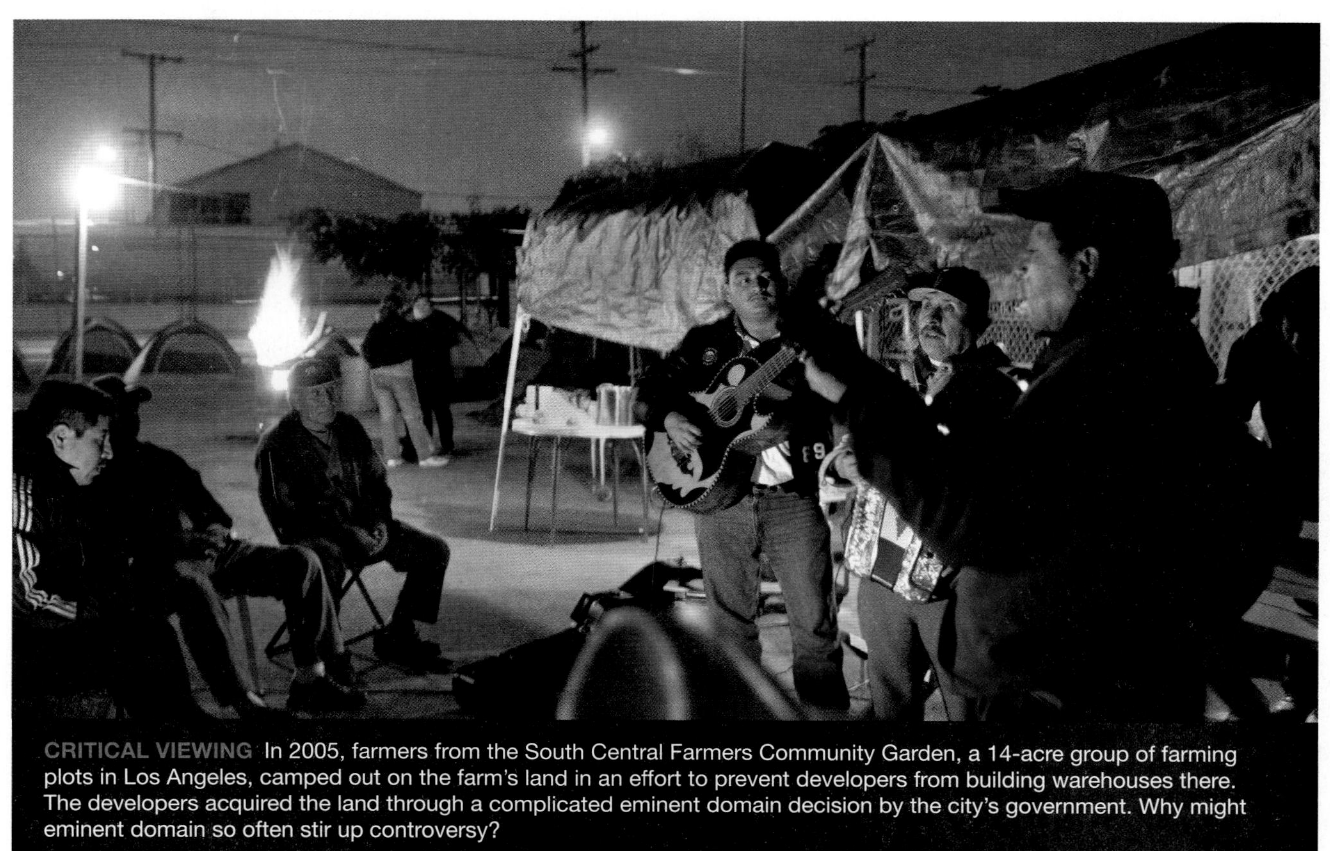

CRITICAL VIEWING In 2005, farmers from the South Central Farmers Community Garden, a 14-acre group of farming plots in Los Angeles, camped out on the farm's land in an effort to prevent developers from building warehouses there. The developers acquired the land through a complicated eminent domain decision by the city's government. Why might eminent domain so often stir up controversy?

SUPREME COURT

Mapp v. *Ohio,* 1961

Decided: June 19, 1961, 6–3

Majority: Justice Harry A. Blackmun wrote the opinion in favor of Mapp. Chief Justice Warren Burger and Associate Justices William O. Douglas and Potter Stewart wrote concurring opinions.

Dissent: Dissenting opinions were written by Associate Justices William H. Rehnquist and Byron White.

In 1957 police officers rang the doorbell of the Cleveland, Ohio, home of Dollree Mapp. Officers told Mapp that they wanted to search her house for a man connected to a recent bombing, as well as for evidence of illegal gambling. Mapp refused to let the police in, but they entered anyway. When she asked to see a search warrant, the police held up a piece of paper but wouldn't let Mapp see it. A search uncovered books and drawings Mapp said were left behind by a previous tenant. The police claimed the materials were obscene and therefore illegal under Ohio law at the time, and Mapp was arrested.

Mapp was tried, found guilty, and sentenced to one to eight years in prison, though no search warrant was produced during the trial. Mapp appealed her case to the Ohio Supreme Court, which affirmed the lower court's decision. Mapp appealed to the U.S. Supreme Court, which heard her case in 1961.

The justices all agreed that Ohio's obscenity law violated the First Amendment. But then they decided to look at the case in light of the Fourth Amendment, and ruled in Mapp's favor on that issue in a 6–3 decision, declaring that the search was illegal because officers did not have a search warrant. Mapp's conviction was therefore overturned, and the Court had confirmed Fourth Amendment protections in state courts.

THINK ABOUT IT Why do you think early American legislators approved and ratified the Fourth Amendment?

safety, morals, and welfare of their citizens. Sometimes, the exercise of these powers can result in conflict.

The landmark 2005 U.S. Supreme Court case *Kelo* v. *New London* was one such instance. The case involved **eminent domain**, or the power of government to take private land for public use. The Fifth Amendment allows the government to take private property for public use after following due process of law and in return for fair compensation. The courts have consistently acknowledged eminent domain as a legitimate use of police powers. In this case, however, the city of New London, Connecticut, took private land for use by private development, arguing that the development would create jobs and increase tax revenues for the city. When some of the original property owners sued, the Connecticut Supreme Court found in favor of the city. The U.S. Supreme Court upheld the decision, 5–4, ruling that public use doesn't just mean use of land by the public, but also use of land that will benefit the public. The decision has sparked controversy, and resistance to eminent domain actions has grown in recent years.

While states can't limit due process protections in the Constitution, they can afford protections that exceed those the Constitution requires. In 2018, for example, the Iowa Supreme Court ruled that police conducting a search without a **search warrant**—a document issued by a magistrate or judge—of a car infringed on the owner's rights under both the Iowa state constitution and the Fourth Amendment. The U.S. Supreme Court had ruled in several cases that warrantless inventory searches are legal, as long as they are reasonable according to local law enforcement. Through its ruling, the Iowa Supreme Court extended protections for citizens of Iowa against "unreasonable searches and seizures" as spelled out in the Fourth Amendment.

HISTORICAL THINKING

1. **COMPARE AND CONTRAST** What is the difference between procedural due process and substantive due process?
2. **FORM AND SUPPORT OPINIONS** Do you agree with the Supreme Court's broad definition of "public use" in *Kelo* v. *New London*? Explain your answer.

The Fourth, Fifth, Sixth, and Eighth Amendments all protect the rights of accused persons. Under the Sixth Amendment, even those accused of the most serious crimes are guaranteed the right to an attorney, as well as the right to a trial by jury. Casey Anthony, who was arrested for the murder of her daughter in 2008, was acquitted of a murder charge by a jury in 2011.

Rights of the Accused

Why do criminal suspects have rights? The answer is that all persons are entitled to the protections afforded by the Bill of Rights and are granted equal protection under the law, which includes a **presumption of innocence**, or an expectation that a defendant is innocent of a crime until proven guilty in a court of law. If criminal suspects were deprived of basic constitutional liberties, other people would eventually suffer the consequences, because there would be nothing to stop the government from accusing anyone of being a criminal. In a criminal case, a state official (such as the district attorney, or D.A.) prosecutes the defendant, and the state has immense resources that it can bring to bear against the accused person—especially compared to the resources the accused person might have. By protecting the rights of accused persons, the Constitution helps prevent the arbitrary use of power by the government.

SPECIFIC RIGHTS OF CRIMINAL DEFENDANTS The rights of the accused are described in the Fourth, Fifth, Sixth, and Eighth Amendments.

- **Fourth Amendment:** People are protected from unreasonable searches and seizures. To this end, warrants must be obtained to conduct a search or an arrest. A warrant should only

SUPREME COURT

Miranda v. *Arizona*, 1966

Decided: June 13, 1966, 5–4

Majority: Chief Justice Earl Warren wrote the opinion for the decision in favor of Miranda.

Dissent: Dissenting opinions were written by Associate Justices John Marshall Harlan and Byron White. Associate Justice Thomas Clark wrote an opinion in partial concurrence and partial dissent.

In 1963, Ernesto Miranda was charged with rape, kidnapping, and armed robbery. After his arrest Miranda was questioned by police, during which time he confessed to the crimes. He hadn't been informed of his legal rights and didn't have a lawyer present at the time of the questioning.

At his trial, Miranda was convicted of rape and kidnapping based on his confession. Miranda appealed, claiming that the questioning was conducted in an unconstitutional way. He hadn't been made aware of his Fifth Amendment right against self-incrimination or his Sixth Amendment right to an attorney.

Chief Justice Earl Warren issued the decision in favor of Miranda, stating that his confession was inadmissible in court because police hadn't informed him of his rights. As part of the decision, the Court created a statement of rights that police are required to read to any person they interrogate. Although the Court decided in favor of Miranda, he was retried without the confession, found guilty, and sentenced to 20 to 30 years in prison.

MIRANDA RIGHTS "You have the right to remain silent. Anything you say can and will be used against you in a court of law. You have the right to an attorney. If you cannot afford an attorney, one will be provided for you. Do you understand the rights I have just read to you? With these rights in mind, do you wish to speak to me?"

THINK ABOUT IT Who do you think the Miranda Rights help more: the person being interrogated or the person doing the interrogating? Explain your answer.

Gideon v. *Wainwright*, 1963

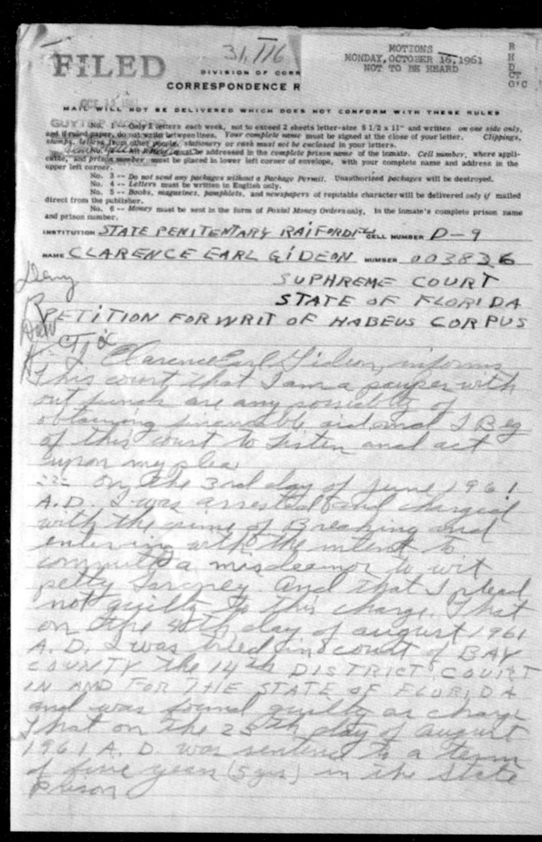

FILED 31,776

DIVISION OF CORR[...]

CORRESPONDENCE R[...]

MOTIONS
MONDAY, OCTOBER 16, 1961
NOT TO BE HEARD

MAIL WILL NOT BE DELIVERED WHICH DOES NOT CONFORM WITH THESE RULES

No. 1 -- Only 2 letters each week, not to exceed 2 sheets letter-size 8 1/2 x 11" and written on one side only, and if ruled paper, do not write between lines. Your complete name must be signed at the close of your letter. Clippings, stamps, letters from other people, stationery or cash must not be enclosed in your letters.

No. 2 -- All letters must be addressed in the complete prison name of the inmate. Cell number, where applicable, and prison number must be placed in lower left corner of envelope, with your complete name and address in the upper left corner.

No. 3 -- Do not send any packages without a Package Permit. Unauthorized packages will be destroyed.

No. 4 -- Letters must be written in English only.

No. 5 -- Books, magazines, pamphlets, and newspapers of reputable character will be delivered only if mailed direct from the publisher.

No. 6 -- Money must be sent in the form of Postal Money Orders only, in the inmate's complete prison name and prison number.

INSTITUTION STATE PENITENTARY RAIFORD FLA CELL NUMBER D-9

NAME CLARENCE EARL GIDEON NUMBER 003826

SUPHREME COURT
STATE OF FLORIDA

PETITION FOR WRIT OF HABEUS CORPUS

I, Clarence Earl Gideon, informs this court that I am a pauper with out funds or any possibility of obtaining Leagal aid and I Beg of this court to Listen and act upon my plea.

On the 3rd day of June 1961 A.D. I was arrested and charged with the crime of Breaking and entering with the intent to commit a misdemeanor to wit petty Larceny. And that I plead not guilty to this charge. That on the 4th day of August 1961 A.D. I was tried in a court of BAY COUNTY the 14th DISTRICT COURT IN AND FOR THE STATE OF FLORIDA and was found guilty as charge. That on the 25th day of August 1961 A.D. was sentenced to a term of five years (5 yrs) in the State prison.

Despite a long criminal history, Clarence Earl Gideon successfully challenged his conviction and imprisonment and left a lasting impact on how the Sixth Amendment is interpreted. His handwritten petition to the Supreme Court is now an important part of American legal history.

Decided: March 18, 1963, 9–0

Majority: Justice Hugo L. Black wrote the opinion for the unanimous ruling in favor of Gideon. Justices William O. Douglas, Thomas C. Clark, and John Marshall Harlan wrote concurring opinions.

In 1961 Florida resident Clarence Earl Gideon was arrested for breaking into and entering a pool hall. Under Florida law, such an offense was considered a felony, or a crime that typically involves violence and that can be punished by a year or more of imprisonment. When Gideon asked for an attorney to represent him at his trial, the judge denied the request, citing Florida law that allowed the appointment of an attorney only if a person too poor to afford one was charged with a capital crime (a crime punishable by death).

Gideon represented himself at trial and lost his case. While serving his five-year prison sentence, Gideon filed a petition for a writ of *habeas corpus*—a legal challenge to the validity of his imprisonment. Gideon claimed that the trial judge's refusal to appoint him an attorney violated his constitutional rights, and his case eventually went to the U.S. Supreme Court. In a unanimous decision, the Court ruled that the right to counsel specified in the Sixth Amendment of the Constitution applies to states through the due process clause of the 14th Amendment, overturning a 1942 decision that stated the opposite. Gideon was granted a new trial, during which he was acquitted of his original crime.

THINK ABOUT IT How did the Supreme Court's decision in *Gideon* reinforce protections within the Sixth Amendment?

be issued if there is **probable cause**, or a reasonable belief that there is a substantial likelihood that a person has committed or is about to commit a crime.

- **Fifth Amendment:** All people are entitled to due process in the legal system. A person can't be tried twice for the same criminal offense (known as double jeopardy) and can't be made to testify against him- or herself (known as the protection against self-incrimination and the right to remain silent).
- **Sixth Amendment:** People accused of a crime are entitled to a speedy and public trial and a trial by jury. A person has the right to confront witnesses. The case of *Gideon* v. *Wainwright* established that this amendment also gives an accused person the right to legal counsel, even if the accused can't afford an attorney.
- **Eighth Amendment:** People can't be subject to excessive bail and fines and are protected from cruel and unusual punishment.

Interpretations of these amendments have varied over the years. For example, a determination of what qualifies as "cruel and unusual punishment" has yet to be reached. The national debate over the death penalty and its uneven usage in the states is ongoing.

In contrast, the Third Amendment plays very little role in modern times. "No Soldier," it says, "shall, in time of peace be quartered in any house, without the consent of the Owner, nor in time of war, but in a manner to be prescribed by law." Americans deeply resented the British government's policy of housing, or quartering, soldiers in colonists' homes. But that practice, and the fear that it would resume, ended after independence. The Third Amendment has never been at the heart of any case heard by the Supreme Court.

THE EXCLUSIONARY RULE The Fourth Amendment spells out general rules for searches and seizures by law enforcement officials. Evidence obtained in violation of these constitutional rights isn't typically admissible at trial. This rule, which has been applied in the federal courts since at least 1914, is known as the exclusionary rule. The case of *Mapp* v. *Ohio* is an example of the effect of this rule. The exclusionary rule forces law enforcement officers to gather evidence properly. If they don't, they cannot introduce the evidence at trial. Recently, the Supreme Court has confirmed that the exclusionary rule also applies to the digital contents of mobile phones.

HISTORICAL THINKING

3. **MAKE CONNECTIONS** What did the ruling in *Gideon* v. *Wainwright* have in common with the ruling in *Mapp* v. *Ohio*?
4. **DRAW CONCLUSIONS** What is the danger in reducing the rights of persons accused of crimes?

LESSON 5.6 The Right to Privacy

A clearly stated right to privacy does not appear in the Bill of Rights. Yet, as far back as 1928, Supreme Court Justice Louis Brandeis wrote in a dissenting opinion that the right to privacy is "the most comprehensive of rights and the right most valued by civilized men." By the 1960s, Court opinion began to change in favor of privacy protections. Since then, expectations of privacy have been hashed out in a series of Supreme Court cases that have connected various situations to implications within the Constitution.

Right to Privacy in the Bill of Rights

In 1965, in the landmark case *Griswold* v. *Connecticut*, which questioned whether a Connecticut law unconstitutionally violated a married couple's right to use contraception, the Supreme Court held that a right to privacy is implied in the First, Third, Fourth, Fifth, and Ninth Amendments. For example, justices pointed to this statement in the Ninth Amendment:

"The enumeration [listing] in the Constitution, of certain rights, shall not be construed to deny or disparage [treat as being unimportant] others retained by the people." In other words, just because the Constitution and its amendments don't specifically mention the right to privacy doesn't mean that this right is denied to the people.

Although Congress and the courts have acknowledged a constitutional right to privacy, the nature and scope of this right aren't always clear. For example, Americans continue to debate whether the right to privacy includes the right to have an abortion. Questions arise constantly about the privacy of personal information on the internet and its treatment within the social media world. Additionally, ever since the terrorist attacks of September 11, 2001, another pressing privacy issue has been how the government can monitor potential threats without violating the privacy rights of all Americans.

HISTORICAL THINKING

1. **IDENTIFY** What is the constitutional basis for Americans' right to privacy?

The Abortion Controversy

One of the most divisive and emotionally charged issues debated in American society and politics today is abortion, or the medical termination of a pregnancy. Does a right to privacy, implied in the Bill of Rights and upheld by the Supreme Court, mean that a woman can choose to have an abortion? The landmark case *Roe* v. *Wade* offered an answer to this question in 1973, along with rules and exceptions regarding timing and other factors.

In the more than 40 years since that ruling, the Supreme Court hasn't overturned the *Roe* decision. Yet it has ruled in favor of state laws requiring counseling, waiting periods, notification of parents, and other actions. But the Court has also upheld laws, in 1997 and 2000, requiring buffer zones around abortion clinics. These buffer zones protect those entering the clinics from unwanted counseling or harassment by anti-abortion groups. (In 2014, however, the Court ruled that a 35-foot buffer zone established by Massachusetts was excessive.)

Abortion rights groups and anti-abortion activists have been at odds for decades over a rarely performed procedure known as a "partial-birth" abortion. This procedure is carried out during the second trimester, or three-month period, of a pregnancy. Abortion rights groups contend that the procedure is sometimes necessary to protect the health of the mother and that the government doesn't have the power to outlaw specific medical procedures. On the other side of the issue, anti-abortion activists claim that the procedure destroys the life of a developing human fetus that might be able to live outside the womb.

In 2000 the Supreme Court invalidated a Nebraska statute banning partial-birth abortions. Yet in 2003 President George W. Bush signed the Partial-Birth Abortion Ban Act. This legislation didn't include an exception for partial-birth abortions that might be necessary to protect the health of the mother. In a controversial 5–4 decision in 2007, the Supreme Court upheld the constitutionality of the 2003 act and ruled that the law didn't pose an undue burden on the right to an abortion decided in *Roe*.

Many were surprised at the Court's decision, given that the federal act banning this practice was quite similar to the Nebraska law that had been struck down by the Court just seven years earlier. But the Court had become more conservative after President George W. Bush appointed Justice Samuel Alito to replace Justice Sandra Day O'Connor in 2006. In her dissent from the majority opinion in the case, Justice Ruth Bader Ginsburg said that the ruling was an "alarming" departure from three decades of Supreme Court decisions on abortion.

HISTORICAL THINKING

2. **DESCRIBE** How has the Supreme Court approached issues having to do with abortion since *Roe* v. *Wade*?
3. **MAKE CONNECTIONS** Explain what abortion rights advocates might say about how the right to privacy relates to abortion.

Decided: January 22, 1973, 7–2

Majority: Justice Harry Blackmun wrote the opinion for the decision in favor of Roe. Chief Justice Warren Burger and Associate Justices William O. Douglas and Potter Stewart wrote concurring opinions.

Dissent: Dissenting opinions were written by Associate Justices William H. Rehnquist and Byron White.

In 1970 Norma McCorvey (recorded as "Jane Roe," to protect her identity) sued the district attorney of Dallas County, Texas, for the right to end a pregnancy with an abortion, a medical procedure that was almost always illegal in Texas. The case eventually landed in the U.S. Supreme Court, by which time McCorvey had given birth and put the baby up for adoption. McCorvey's lawyer argued that Texas's ban on abortions violated the right to privacy implied by the Constitution and protected by the due process clause of the 14th Amendment.

In a 7–2 decision, the Court invoked the right to privacy first identified in *Griswold* v. *Connecticut* to rule that a woman's right to an abortion was indeed constitutionally protected, holding that the "right of privacy . . . is broad enough to encompass a woman's decision whether or not to terminate her pregnancy." The justices didn't declare that right to be absolute throughout pregnancy, however. The Court declared that any state could impose certain regulations to safeguard the health of the mother after the first three months of pregnancy and, in the final stages of pregnancy, could act to protect potential life.

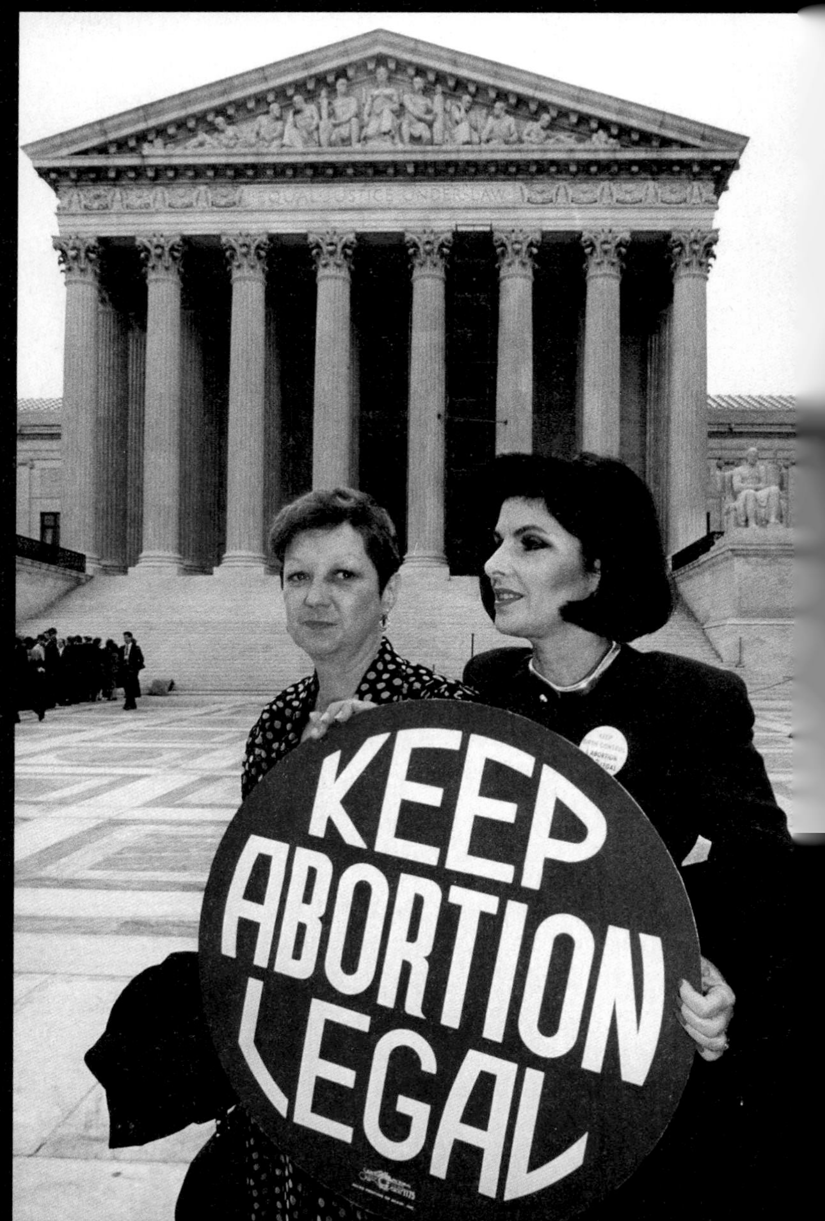

Norma McCorvey (left), better known to the American public as "Jane Roe," was the plaintiff in the first major abortion rights case heard by the U.S. Supreme Court. Since the Court's decision in 1973, justices have heard several challenges to the 7–2 ruling, yet the original *Roe* decision stands.

THINK ABOUT IT Given a recognized constitutional right to privacy, why do you think the Court put time constraints on when a woman can have an abortion with no state intervention?

Facebook founder and CEO Mark Zuckerberg testifies in front of the Senate Judiciary and Commerce Committees in 2018 amidst a public outcry over how the social networking site had managed users' personal data.

Privacy and Personal Information

Massive changes have come about with the expansion of information technology, or the use of computers to send, store, and retrieve information, in the past 20 years. These have resulted in a relatively new kind of national anxiety about privacy. Many Americans are now concerned that their personal information might be collected by individuals or organizations that will then use the data improperly or for criminal purposes.

Of course, some kinds of data have been collected and disseminated for far longer than the past two decades. For example, any economically active person has a **credit rating**, or a score that indicates ability to fulfill financial obligations. A poor credit rating can make it impossible to borrow money for a car or house. But now information technology has made it easier for businesses and other institutions to collect vast quantities of personal data. Retail websites may collect data on every purchase a person makes in an effort to more successfully sell that person more goods in the future. Search engines use cookies, or small text files created by a website and stored on a user's computer, to track browsing history that they sell to other companies. Even the skies are an area of concern, as some government agencies and businesses begin to consider how to use drones to collect visual intelligence.

PRIVACY LEGISLATION Beginning in the 1960s, Congress began passing legislation meant to protect the rights of individuals. Among the most important laws are the following:

- **Freedom of Information Act:** This 1966 legislation gives American citizens access to information maintained about them by government agencies.
- **Privacy Act of 1974:** Congress passed this law to restrict government disclosure of data to third parties.

- **Driver's Privacy Protection Act:** This 1994 legislation prevents states from disclosing or selling a driver's personal information without the driver's consent.
- **HIPAA Privacy Rule:** In 2000 the federal Department of Health and Human Services issued a regulation in compliance with the 1996 Health Insurance Portability and Accountability Act (HIPAA) to protect the privacy of medical information.

States also have their own privacy regulations, ranging from how privacy policies must be displayed on websites to how public employees are notified when their email is being monitored.

The vast amount of information available about individuals on the internet has led to additional attempts to safeguard privacy. In Europe, courts have come up with the "right to be forgotten," which allows individuals to require search engines to make personal information very difficult to locate. Most experts doubt that such a right could be extended to the United States because of our First Amendment guarantees of free speech. California, however, has adopted what is known as an eraser bill that allows persons under the age of 18 to remove material they have posted.

Social media sites have recently been under close scrutiny when it comes to privacy. Facebook, in particular, was in the international spotlight when it was discovered that third-party apps used with the social networking site had collected user data. Data analytics companies used that information to—among other things—attempt to influence the 2016 U.S. presidential election. Facebook executives have since pledged to tighten privacy and permissions when it comes to access of its users' personal information.

CYBERBULLYING The internet gives individuals a potent platform for communicating with and about other people, including highly damaging or very personal information and even outright lies. The resulting online harassment is called *cyberbullying*.

Cyberbullying is now taken so seriously that several cyberbullies have been charged with crimes. One example is a case involving a Rutgers University student who committed suicide after his roommate secretly recorded and posted online a sexual encounter he had with another man. The roommate was convicted of multiple computer-related crimes. All but one of the convictions, however, were overturned on appeal. Another example involved a woman who pretended online to be a boy so as to harass one of her daughter's classmates, who later committed suicide. The woman was found guilty, but her conviction was overturned on appeal, because the statute under which she was charged was inapplicable.

Both these cases raised troubling questions about whether verbal harassment can be protected by the First Amendment. While all states have laws against harassment, not all the laws are equally effective.

Some instances of internet harassment are perpetrated by individuals whose motives go beyond personal grievances. Online trolling, for example, is the posting of inflammatory online messages to provoke or upset other members of a community. Sometimes "trolls" cross the line to outright harassment. In 2014, women who had criticized the video game industry were targeted for harassment. The harassment campaign—which involved real-world as well as internet harassment—included threats of death, rape, and bombing and led some of the women involved to go into hiding. Another form of online harassment known as doxxing (a term that comes from *docs* and can refer to documents that reveal personal information) involves publicizing personal information to encourage harassment. Doxxing has been used to attack people with a range of perspectives, including feminists and LGBTQ persons as well as conservative conspiracy theorists.

HISTORICAL THINKING

4. **MAKE INFERENCES** What does the major privacy legislation passed in the past 50 or so years tell you about areas of concern when it comes to privacy?
5. **FORM AND SUPPORT OPINIONS** Do you think the benefits of social media outweigh the risks to your personal information? Explain.

Privacy and National Security

Since the terrorist attacks of September 11, 2001, the news media and Congress have frequently debated how the United States can strengthen national security while still protecting civil liberties, particularly the right to privacy. Attempts at finding this balance have proven tricky and, at times, controversial. Over the past two decades, Americans have discovered that their government has often been gathering more information about them than they previously realized.

Several laws and programs that infringe on Americans' privacy rights were created in the wake of the 9/11 terrorist attacks in an attempt to protect the nation's security. The USA Patriot Act of 2001 gave the government broad latitude to investigate people who are only vaguely associated with terrorists. Under this law, the government can access personal information to an extent never before allowed.

The Federal Bureau of Investigation (FBI) was also authorized to use national security letters. These are written requests to private companies such as banks and phone companies for personal information about individuals. These requests don't have to be approved by a judge. Moreover, the companies supplying the information aren't allowed to inform their customers about the requests. In one of the most controversial programs under the legislation, the National Security Agency (NSA) was authorized to monitor certain domestic phone calls without obtaining a warrant. When Americans learned of the NSA's actions in 2005, the ensuing public furor forced agencies in the Bush administration to obtain warrants for such activities.

In June 2013, materials released to the press by Edward Snowden, a national security contractor, revealed that **surveillance**, or monitoring actions, by the NSA had been more extensive than most people assumed. Snowden, aware that he could face serious legal trouble for leaking highly classified information, fled to Hong Kong and then Russia, where he was granted asylum.

Snowden revealed, for example, that under one program, the NSA had been collecting information about every landline phone call made in the entire United States—not the content of the call, but the time of the call, the number called, and the number making the call. Another NSA program, known as PRISM, was designed to collect vast quantities of data from the servers of corporations such as AOL, Apple, Facebook, Google, Skype, and others. The information included emails, chats, photos, and more, and was collected worldwide. In particular, the NSA considered itself free to access any data stored on a U.S. server by a foreign citizen. As a former NSA chief put it, "The Fourth Amendment is not an international treaty." This policy threatened the business prospects of American companies that provide remote servers for cloud computing services worldwide.

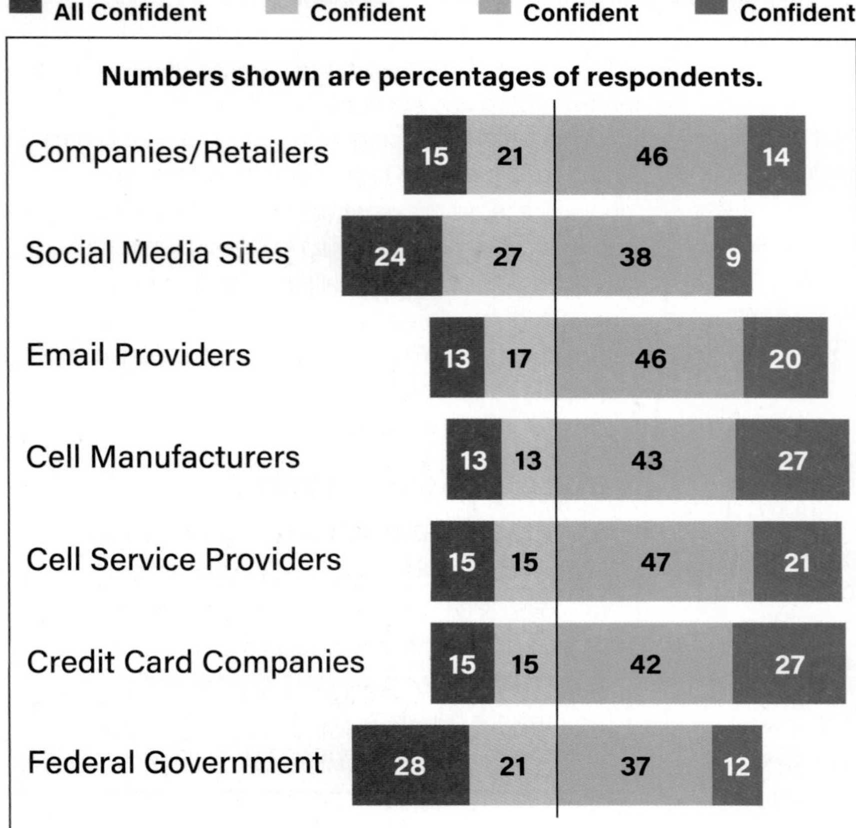

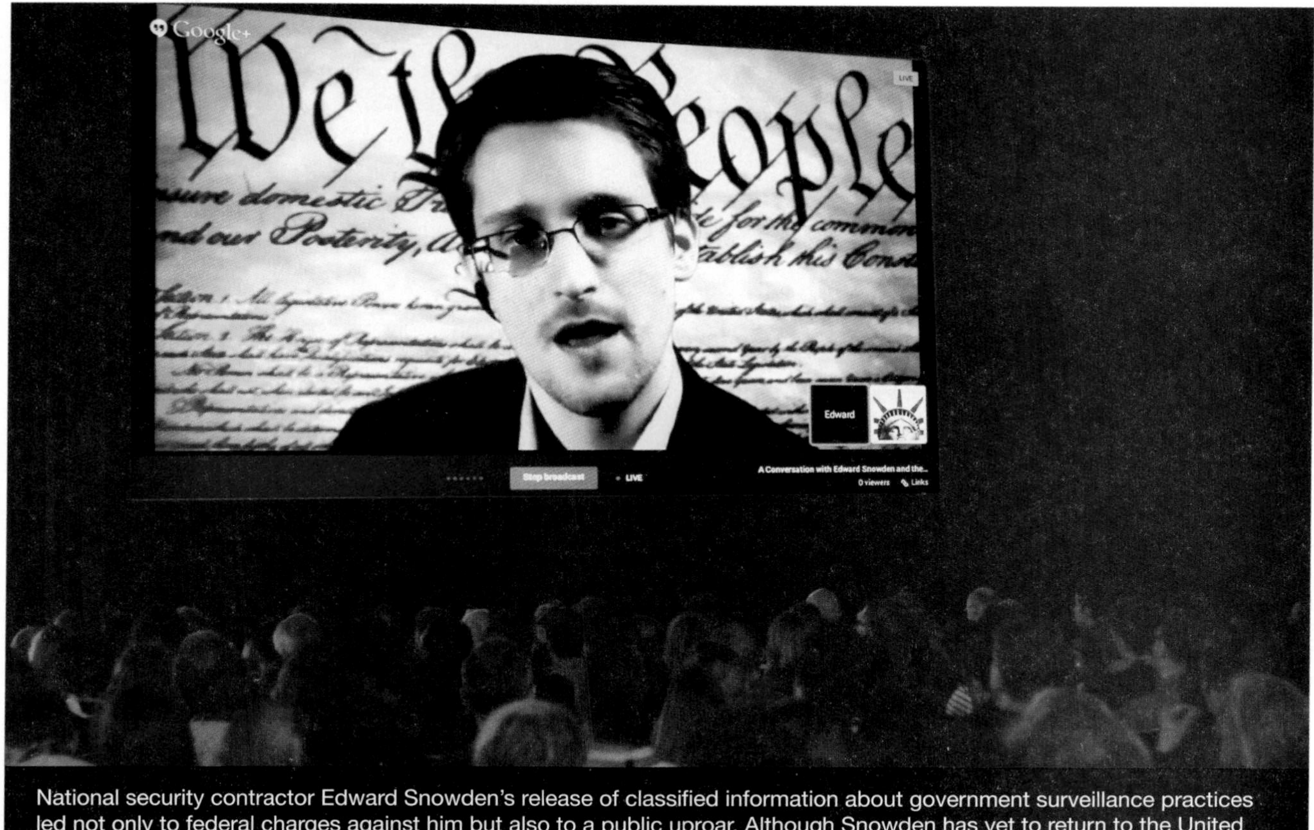

National security contractor Edward Snowden's release of classified information about government surveillance practices led not only to federal charges against him but also to a public uproar. Although Snowden has yet to return to the United States to face authorities, he sometimes speaks remotely in public forums, as he did in 2014 at the SXSW Music, Film + Interactive Festival in Austin, Texas.

It was also revealed that the NSA had collected massive amounts of data on foreign phone calls, including the telephones of dozens of foreign leaders such as German chancellor Angela Merkel and Brazil's president Dilma Rousseff. It also bugged the offices of European Union negotiators in advance of trade talks. These revelations created serious diplomatic problems for the U.S. government.

In June 2015 several key provisions of the USA Patriot Act expired. Debate in Congress on whether to renew the provisions was fierce. In an unusual coalition, Republican libertarians united with left-leaning Democrats in an attempt to place limits on the NSA's activities. The result was the USA Freedom Act.

The new act reauthorized most of the provisions of the USA Patriot Act. But it also sought to control the NSA's collection of data on domestic phone calls. Additionally, it attempted to shine some light on the Foreign Intelligence Surveillance Court (FISC). This secret court is responsible for authorizing searches by the NSA and other intelligence agencies. Upon its passage, civil liberties advocates argued that the new legislation would have little practical effect—massive data sweeps would continue under the authority of other laws. Tension about U.S. government surveillance and data collection remains a concern.

HISTORICAL THINKING

6. **MAKE INFERENCES** Why do you think Americans may have supported the USA Patriot Act in the years immediately following September 11, 2001, but not as much in recent years?
7. **EVALUATE** Do Americans have more privacy since Snowden's revelations and the passage of the USA Freedom Act? Explain.
8. **INTEGRATE VISUALS** How does the amount of trust that the American public puts in the federal government to protect their data compare to how much they trust other groups? What does this mean?

CHAPTER 5

CIVIL LIBERTIES

Review

VOCABULARY

Use each of the following vocabulary words in a sentence that shows an understanding of the term's meaning.

1. civil liberties
2. due process
3. parochial
4. defamation
5. civil disobedience
6. eminent domain
7. search warrant
8. probable cause
9. credit rating
10. surveillance

MAIN IDEAS

Answer the following questions. Support your answer with evidence from the chapter.

11. What sets the constitutional protection of writs of *habeas corpus* apart from other civil liberties? **LESSON 5.1**
12. Why has the free establishment clause been invoked so many times in cases involving the teaching of evolution in public schools? **LESSON 5.2**
13. What is symbolic speech, and how is it protected? **LESSON 5.3**
14. Why are examples of the government using prior restraint so rare? **LESSON 5.3**
15. Explain the arguments for and against shield laws for journalists. **LESSON 5.3**
16. Give an example of how Americans can use their First Amendment right to petition. **LESSON 5.4**
17. How has an increase in online media use affected the right to association? **LESSON 5.4**
18. Paraphrase the meaning of the 14th Amendment's due process clause. **LESSON 5.5**
19. Why is eminent domain such a controversial police power? **LESSON 5.5**
20. Explain why Edward Snowden's revealing of surveillance programs upset many Americans. **LESSON 5.6**

HISTORICAL THINKING

Answer the following questions. Support your answer with evidence from the chapter.

21. **MAKE CONNECTIONS** Explain the connection between the exclusionary rule, searches, and warrants.
22. **FORM AND SUPPORT OPINIONS** Explain whether you agree or disagree with the following statement: The government has been the biggest influence on the protection of civil liberties.
23. **DRAW CONCLUSIONS** Why did the Framers not specifically protect a right to privacy within the Constitution?
24. **SYNTHESIZE** What does the Supreme Court's role in defining the breadth of civil liberties tell us about the role of the judiciary in the U.S. government?

INTERPRET VISUALS

Study the map. Then answer the questions.

25. Based on the map, how would you describe the use of the death penalty in the United States?

26. The Eighth Amendment, which applies to state governments as well as the federal government, prohibits the government from imposing cruel and unusual punishment. What does this map tell you about how states interpret this amendment?

Death Penalty by State, 2018

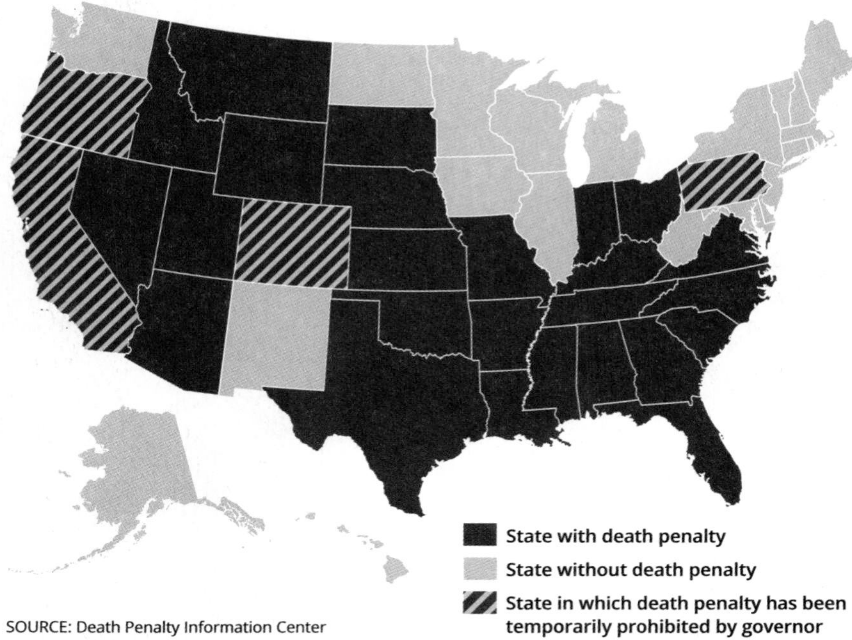

SOURCE: Death Penalty Information Center

ANALYZE SOURCES

In 1971 the Supreme Court heard the case *Cohen* v. *California*, which concerned whether or not a man should have been arrested for wearing a jacket decorated with an obscene, politically based slogan. Read the excerpt from the Court's majority opinion in favor of the man and answer the question that follows.

> For, while the particular four-letter word being litigated here is perhaps more distasteful than most others of its genre, it is nevertheless true that one man's vulgarity is another's lyric.
>
> —*Justice John Marshall Harlan*

27. According to the Court, what must be taken into consideration when protecting freedom of speech and expression?

CONNECT TO YOUR LIFE

28. **EXPLANATORY** Several landmark U.S. Supreme Court cases, such as *Tinker* v. *Des Moines*, *Hazelwood* v. *Kuhlmeier*, and *West Side Community Schools* v. *Mergen*, have involved teenagers' right to free speech and freedom of expression on school property. Research one of these cases, identifying the speech or form of expression in question. Then write a short essay summarizing the case, the constitutional issue in question, and the significance of the Court's decision. Conclude your essay with a description of how these types of cases impact freedom of expression in your own school or life.

TIPS

- Include a concise description of the case and the constitutional question involved in your introductory paragraph.
- Include well-researched details on the background of the case, the First Amendment issues raised, and the majority and any dissenting opinions of the Supreme Court in your essay.
- Your conclusion should indicate the impact that the Court's decision had on legal precedent surrounding similar First Amendment issues.
- Proofread your essay (by reading out loud, if necessary) to check for clear transitions and spelling and grammar errors.

CHAPTER 6

Citizenship and Civil Rights

LESSONS

6.1 Citizenship in the United States

6.2 Civil Rights and African Americans

National Geographic Magazine:
Why Do We See So Many Things as 'Us vs. Them'?

6.3 Women's Rights

National Geographic Magazine:
For These Girls, Danger Is a Way of Life

6.4 Extending Civil Rights

6.5 Beyond Equal Protection – Affirmative Action

CRITICAL VIEWING In 2016, San Francisco 49ers Eli Harold (58) and Eric Reid (black sweatsuit) joined teammate Colin Kaepernick (7) in kneeling during the playing of the national anthem before a football game. The players knelt to protest civil rights violations against Black citizens, an action that produced both support and opposition across the country. What details in the photograph show why the action had high visibility?

LESSON
6.1 Citizenship in the United States

The Framers spent a great deal of effort defining the structure and powers of national government, the distribution of power between the national government and the states, and the limits on government's power. The Framers talked about the people, but they did not say who was and who was not a citizen. Nor did they define the rights and responsibilities of citizens. Like so many other details, defining these terms has been left to the Americans who followed.

Defining Citizenship

In 1857 the Supreme Court heard the case *Dred Scott v. Sandford*, which addressed **citizenship**, the status of owing allegiance to a state and being entitled to its protection. Dred Scott, an enslaved man, argued that he became free after he was taken to a state where slavery was illegal. Chief Justice Robert Taney, who favored slavery, wrote the decision. He dismissed Dred Scott's suit on the grounds that Scott was not a citizen and as a result had no right to bring a lawsuit. Further, Taney wrote, African Americans "are not included . . . under the word 'citizens' in the Constitution."

Many abolitionists were shocked by the decision, since it implied that even if slavery ended, African Americans would not be recognized as citizens and would still have no rights. Anger over the *Dred Scott* decision was a key step along the path to the Civil War. After the defeat of the Confederacy in that war, disagreement with that decision led to passage of the 14th Amendment. That amendment states that "All persons born or naturalized in the United States, and subject to the jurisdiction thereof, are citizens of the United States and of the State wherein they reside."

The words "born or naturalized" indicate the two ways of becoming a citizen. Birthright citizenship is given

Women in traditional Chinese costumes celebrate the Lunar New Year, a holiday based on the traditional Chinese calendar, in New York City. The city is a port of entry for millions of immigrants, many of whom have become naturalized citizens.

SUPREME COURT

Dred Scott v. *Sandford* 1857

Decided: March 6, 1857, 7–2

Majority: Chief Justice Roger Taney wrote the opinion, which ruled in Sanford's favor.

Dissent: Justices John McLean and Benjamin Robbins Curtis filed dissenting opinions.

Dred Scott, an enslaved African American, traveled with his owner, Dr. John Emerson, to Illinois, a free state, and Wisconsin, a free territory, before settling in Missouri, a slave state. Scott sued for his freedom based on state court decisions holding that an enslaved person carried to free territory was free, but in 1852 the Missouri Supreme Court ruled against him.

When Scott lost a similar suit in federal court, he appealed to the U.S. Supreme Court. By this time, Emerson had died, leaving ownership of Scott to his brother-in-law John Sanford, whose name was misspelled as *Sandford* in the case name.

Seven justices denied Scott's claim to freedom. Taney said that the Framers of the Constitution did not consider African Americans as citizens. He claimed that meant Scott had no right to even bring the lawsuit. Taney went further, stating that slaves were property, and, since Congress cannot take away a person's property without due process, it had no authority to prohibit slavery from territories.

Justice Benjamin Curtis issued a stinging dissent. He pointed out that, when the Constitution was adopted, free African Americans in five states were recognized as citizens who had the right to vote if they met other qualifications.

Although the U.S. justice system denied Scott any rights, concern about publicity led the man who then enslaved him to release him from slavery in May 1857. Scott died after 17 months of living as a free man.

THINK ABOUT IT Taney's opinion in *Dred Scott* is often said to be the worst decision the Supreme Court has ever made. What grounds might there be for this assessment?

to everyone born in the United States, Puerto Rico, or any other U.S. territory, including overseas military bases, embassies, and territories. Immigrants can gain U.S. citizenship through naturalization. To be naturalized, a person must pay several hundred dollars in fees, file required paperwork, submit to an interview, and, in most cases, pass a civics and English test.

HISTORICAL THINKING

1. **IDENTIFY PROBLEMS AND SOLUTIONS** Explain the circumstances that led to passage of the 14th Amendment's citizenship clause.
2. **MAKE GENERALIZATIONS** How does the 14th Amendment illustrate the importance of the amendment process in a constitutional government?

U.S. Immigration Over Time

Both push factors and pull factors lead people to move from one country to another. Push factors are events or circumstances that encourage people to leave their homeland. About 2 million Irish people came to the United States from 1846 to 1851 due to a famine in Ireland. In the late 19th and early 20th centuries, a flood of eastern and southern Europeans left their countries because of a lack of farmland, poor education, religious persecution, and the threat of forced military service. An abundance of good farmland, a thriving economy, a promise of liberty, and generally open immigration and naturalization policies were pull factors that drew people to the United States.

CHANGING IMMIGRATION POLICY For nearly a century, the United States put no limits on immigration. That changed when Congress banned criminals from entering the country in 1875. The Chinese Exclusion Act of 1882 blocked entry by Chinese workers and barred Chinese immigrants from becoming citizens through naturalization. The Geary Act (1892) extended the ban on Chinese immigrants for another 10 years. In 1907, the government entered into what was called the "Gentlemen's Agreement" with Japan, in which the United States agreed not to ban Japanese immigrants while Japan agreed not to give its people travel documents to come to America.

Selected Immigration Legislation

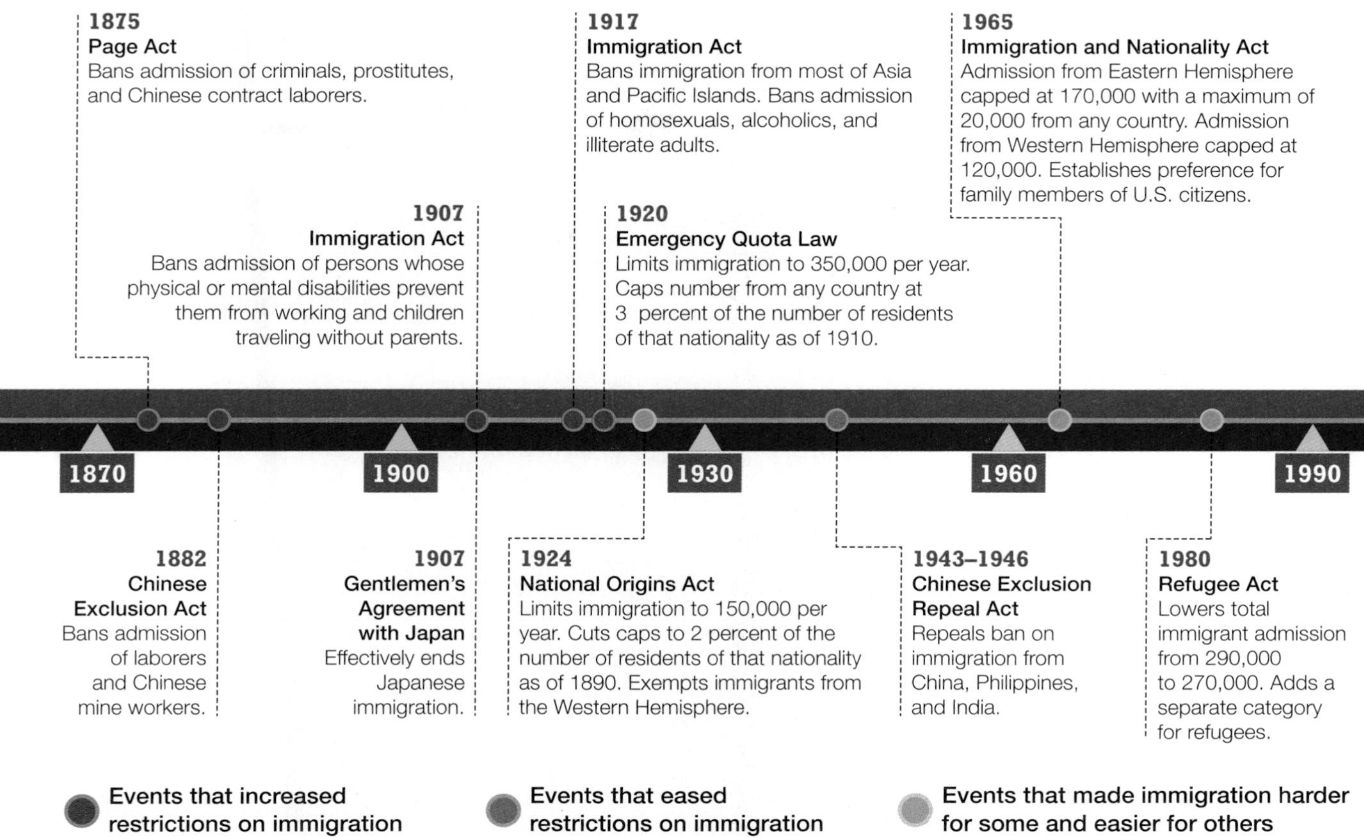

1875
Page Act
Bans admission of criminals, prostitutes, and Chinese contract laborers.
1907
Immigration Act
Bans admission of persons whose physical or mental disabilities prevent them from working and children traveling without parents.
1917
Immigration Act
Bans immigration from most of Asia and Pacific Islands. Bans admission of homosexuals, alcoholics, and illiterate adults.
1920
Emergency Quota Law
Limits immigration to 350,000 per year. Caps number from any country at 3 percent of the number of residents of that nationality as of 1910.
1965
Immigration and Nationality Act
Admission from Eastern Hemisphere capped at 170,000 with a maximum of 20,000 from any country. Admission from Western Hemisphere capped at 120,000. Establishes preference for family members of U.S. citizens.
1870
1900
1930
1960
1990
1882
Chinese Exclusion Act
Bans admission of laborers and Chinese mine workers.
1907
Gentlemen's Agreement with Japan
Effectively ends Japanese immigration.
1924
National Origins Act
Limits immigration to 150,000 per year. Cuts caps to 2 percent of the number of residents of that nationality as of 1890. Exempts immigrants from the Western Hemisphere.
1943–1946
Chinese Exclusion Repeal Act
Repeals ban on immigration from China, Philippines, and India.
1980
Refugee Act
Lowers total immigrant admission from 290,000 to 270,000. Adds a separate category for refugees.
Events that increased restrictions on immigration
Events that eased restrictions on immigration
Events that made immigration harder for some and easier for others

SOURCE: Beth Rowen, A Detailed Look at Immigration Legislation from the Colonial Period to the Present, Infoplease.

The arrival of millions of immigrants from eastern and southern Europe between 1880 and 1920 prompted more restrictions. Many Americans worried that these immigrants were changing the character of the nation and driving down wages. In response, Congress passed a law that capped the number of immigrants entering the country each year—the first time Congress put any limits on immigration from Europe. Just a few years later, the National Origins Act of 1924 set that cap at 150,000. That 1924 law also changed the makeup of immigration by reducing the number of southern and eastern Europeans who could enter the country and favoring immigrants from northern and western Europe.

Demands for labor during World War II led to the lifting of limits on immigration in the 1940s. The government launched the Bracero Program (*bracero* is from the Spanish word for *arm* and, in this case, is a figure of speech referring to a worker). This program, which lasted into the 1960s, allowed more than 4 million Mexicans to enter the United States on a temporary basis to work on farms.

A 1952 law ended all bans on immigration from Asia. The Immigration and Nationality Act of 1965 completely ended nationality-based quotas, replacing them with caps on immigration of 120,000 from the Western Hemisphere and 170,000 from the Eastern Hemisphere. The law also made it U.S. policy to attract skilled workers and reunite families. Family members did not count when considering the limits from a hemisphere.

Complicating the issue of immigration is the question of undocumented immigration. An **undocumented immigrant** is a person who lacks legal documents proving his or her right to live or work in the United States. Congress passed the Immigration Reform and Control Act of 1986 to address this issue. The law increased enforcement of border controls and imposed penalties on employers who hired undocumented immigrants. It also granted amnesty, or a pardon, to undocumented immigrants who had lived in the country continuously for five years. But some undocumented immigrants remained in the country

Immigrants from Asia and the Pacific, like these aboard their ship, were processed at Angel Island in San Francisco Bay. Applicants arriving at Angel Island between 1910 and 1940 underwent thorough and demeaning physical examinations. Many applicants were detained for weeks, months, or even years.

even without receiving the amnesty. In addition, enforcement of the employment provision was lax, and more undocumented immigrants arrived. By the 2010s, about 11 million undocumented immigrants were living in the United States.

ISSUES IN IMMIGRATION TODAY The issue of immigration—both legal and illegal—has become a focus of political debate. Questions about how many immigrants should be admitted each year, who should be given preference in immigration policy, and the best way to prevent illegal immigration, are extremely controversial. There is also the problem of what to do about undocumented immigrants who are already here. Any major reform to immigration law has been elusive because these are highly charged political issues.

President Donald J. Trump, who was elected in 2016, increased efforts to stop illegal immigration and to deport unauthorized immigrants. Some Americans opposed deportation of immigrants with no criminal offenses. They argued that many immigrants were seeking safety and economic security and that they stimulated the economy by providing needed labor and entrepreneurial activity. Others favored increased deportations, claiming that undocumented immigrants take jobs away from Americans.

In 2018, the Trump administration adopted a policy of separating undocumented children from their parents at the border. This measure was adopted to prevent parents from trying to enter the country. The outcry against the policy was so strong that the president ordered it stopped, although many children were still

Deferred Action for Childhood Arrivals (DACA)

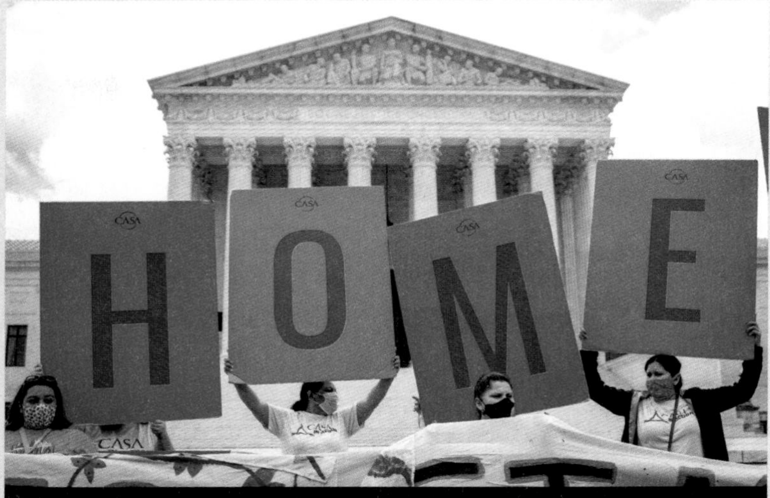

People wearing masks to protect against the coronavirus celebrate the June 2020 decision in *Department of Homeland Security* v. *Regents of the University of California*. The Supreme Court ruled that the administration had not provided adequate reasons for ending the DACA program in that case.

In 2012 President Barack Obama created a program called Deferred Action for Childhood Arrivals (DACA) to address the situation of undocumented immigrants who entered the country as children. A proposed program called the Development, Relief, and Education for Alien Minors (DREAM) Act was designed to offer these young people permanent residency. These young people became known as Dreamers, but the bill never passed Congress. Obama implemented DACA by issuing an executive order that allowed the so-called Dreamers to defer their deportation for two years if they met several criteria. They had to be of a certain age, had to have been brought to the United States when they were younger than 16, had to be in school or have a high school diploma or an honorable discharge from the military, and had to pass a criminal background check. After the two years, they could apply for an extension.

After taking office, President Trump began to wind down the program. He ended extensions and vowed to bring DACA to an end. But in June 2020, the Supreme Court ruled in a 5–4 decision that while the president had the authority to end DACA, his reasons for doing so were "arbitrary and capricious." The administration, according to the Court's majority opinion, did not address the fact that hundreds of thousands of people had pursued careers, bought houses, and started businesses and families based on their protected status. At the time of the decision, some 650,000 people were enrolled in the DACA program, and more than 250,000 American citizens had one or more parents who were DACA Dreamers. While the decision did not end all uncertainty for these immigrants and their families, it provided some relief for the short term.

held in government facilities apart from their parents years later. President Trump promised to build a wall along the U.S.–Mexico border in his campaign but met resistance to that plan once in office, and three years into his administration, only about 300 miles of the 2,000-mile-long border had a wall completed or under construction. Supporters said a wall would improve border security, while critics said it would be costly and ineffective.

HISTORICAL THINKING

3. **INTERPRET TIME LINES** Based on the time line of immigration legislation, what has been the overall thrust of immigration laws over time?
4. **MAKE GENERALIZATIONS** If the United States is, as many say, a nation of immigrants, why do many Americans support limits on immigration?

Responsibilities of Citizenship

The rights and privileges of citizenship come with responsibilities. Adults over the age of 18 have a duty to vote responsibly. A responsible voter is well informed about civic affairs to make a responsible, reasoned decision. To be able to vote in most states (North Dakota is the exception), citizens have to register. Deadlines for registering to vote vary from state to state. Today many states—and the District of Columbia—allow people to register online.

In most states, citizens may vote in person only at an officially designated polling place. While elections take place on specific days, most states offer early voting. In addition, every state allows absentee ballots, which can be obtained and completed by mail. A number of states require voters to show photo identification to obtain their ballot.

The duty to vote is part of citizens' more general duty to participate in the political process. There are other ways to participate. Citizens of any age can attend and contribute to public discussions of issues, such as at meetings of a town committee. They can communicate with representatives or other government officials. They can join or lead citizen movements to champion a certain policy, and they can take part in political campaigns.

Adult citizens also have a duty to serve on juries. The Sixth Amendment guarantees "the right to a speedy and public trial, by an impartial jury." Fulfilling this right requires ordinary citizens to make themselves available to sit on juries.

Paying taxes is a civic duty of citizens and noncitizens alike. Regardless of citizenship, persons of any age who earn money are required to pay income taxes. Obeying the law is also a duty of everyone in the United States, whether or not they are citizens.

Starting with the Civil War, the government instituted a military draft that required males of a certain age to register and serve in the army—though exceptions were always allowed for certain individuals. After the end of the Vietnam War, in 1973, the armed forces became an all-volunteer organization. Males still have to register with the Selective Service System within 60 days of their eighteenth birthday, however.

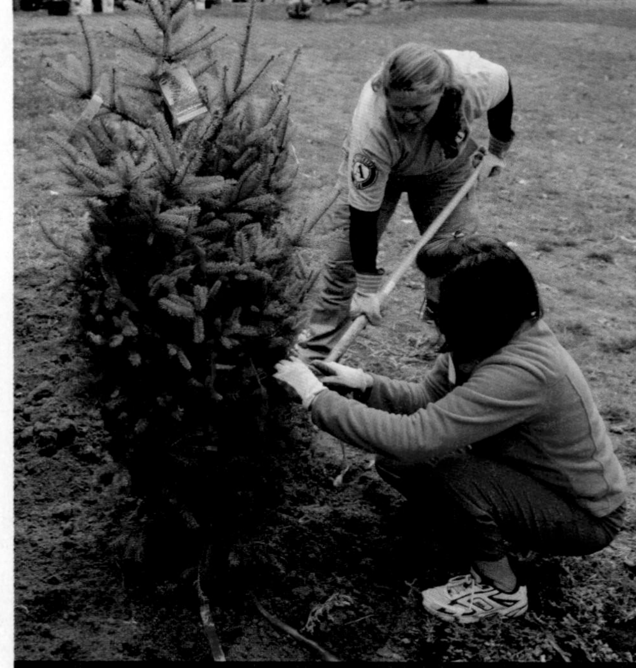

A local volunteer from the group Volunteers for Outdoor Colorado joins two members of AmeriCorps in planting a tree as part of an effort to restore a Colorado park. AmeriCorps, a national volunteer program formed by the federal government, began in the 1990s and has an arm that focuses on environmental projects.

Despite wide-spread opposition to the draft during the Vietnam War, today there are those who argue that universal military service would help bind Americans from different parts of the country or different groups together. They say that universal service would make political leaders more cautious about using the military to intervene in other countries' affairs. Further, they argue that when military service is voluntary, people with fewer school and job opportunities serve disproportionately. Therefore, some people favor one or two years of compulsory national service for all 18- or 19-year-olds.

HISTORICAL THINKING

5. **IDENTIFY PROBLEMS AND SOLUTIONS** Identify a significant issue currently in the news and the news sources you would use to become and remain well informed about it. How much time would this require of you each week?
6. **FORM AND SUPPORT OPINIONS** Do you think there should be a law requiring any form of national or community service of every citizen?

Equal Protection Under the Law

When the 14th Amendment was added to the Constitution, it included not only a definition of citizenship but also a guarantee of civil rights. **Civil rights** are the rights that enable Americans to participate as equals in public life. In a sense, the history of civil rights in the United States is a history of fighting unjust treatment, or discrimination, against various groups. The most basic civil right is the right to "equal protection of the laws," as provided by the 14th Amendment. Civil rights include equal rights to government services, such as police protection and basic education, and equal protection from unfair discrimination.

EQUAL PROTECTION The 14th Amendment is the basis of many civil rights. That amendment's equal protection clause states that "No State shall . . . deny to any person within its jurisdiction the equal protection of the laws." Section 5 of the 14th Amendment provides a legal basis for federal civil rights legislation by stating, "The Congress shall have power to enforce, by appropriate legislation, the provisions of this article." In effect, the government has the power to enforce equal protection if a state fails to provide it.

Equal protection may sound like a simple matter of treating everyone the same, but it's more complicated than that. People treat people differently all the time—it isn't reasonable to punish a 10-year-old for not behaving like an adult, for example. As the courts see it, the equal protection clause means that the government may not discriminate unreasonably against a particular group or class of individuals. It is acceptable to treat people differently if there is a fair reason to do so. For instance, if Dr. Martinez has a physician's license but Ms. Chavez does not, it is reasonable to allow only Dr. Martinez to practice medicine.

STANDARDS OF SCRUTINY Many other cases are less obvious, and the task of distinguishing between reasonable and unreasonable discrimination can be difficult. Over time, the U.S. Supreme Court has developed three tests, or standards, for determining whether discrimination is reasonable or unreasonable and whether the equal protection clause has been violated. These standards are strict scrutiny, intermediate scrutiny, and ordinary scrutiny, or the rational basis test.

If a law or action prevents an entire group of persons from exercising a fundamental right, such as a First Amendment right, it will be judged against the strict scrutiny standard. Under this standard, for a law or action to be allowed, it must be necessary to promote a compelling state interest and must be narrowly tailored to meet that interest. The courts also use strict scrutiny when they analyze any law based on a suspect classification, which refers to any group of people that has been unfairly subjected to discrimination over history. Race is a suspect classification.

Gender is not considered a suspect classification, so the courts needed a different standard to apply to laws treating men and women differently. The Supreme Court developed a different test—intermediate scrutiny. Under this standard, laws based on gender classifications are permissible if they are "substantially related to the achievement of an important governmental objective."

For example, in 1981 the Supreme Court upheld a law that required males to register for the military draft but not females. Since the 1970s, though, the Supreme Court has been skeptical of gender classifications and has declared many gender-based laws unconstitutional.

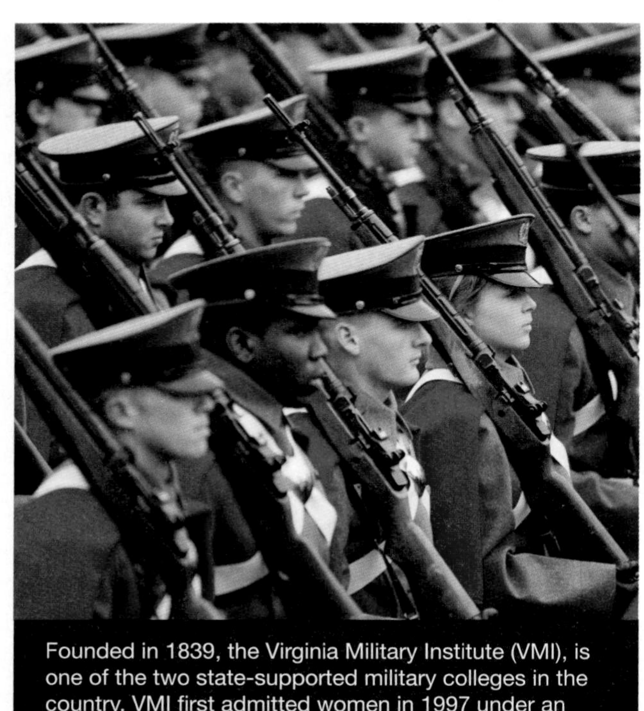

Founded in 1839, the Virginia Military Institute (VMI), is one of the two state-supported military colleges in the country. VMI first admitted women in 1997 under an order by the U.S. Supreme Court.

Many of these laws were based on narrow and rigid ideas of women's acceptable roles. For instance, in 1979 the Court used the equal protection clause to strike down a state law that allowed ex-wives but not ex-husbands to receive alimony, a payment made by one former spouse to the other after a divorce. In 1982 the Court declared that Mississippi's policy of excluding males from the School of Nursing at Mississippi University for Women was unconstitutional.

A third test to decide whether a law violates the equal protection clause is the rational basis test, also called the ordinary scrutiny standard. This test is used when none of the reasons to use the strict scrutiny or intermediate scrutiny standards apply. In those cases, courts consider these two questions:

- Does the law serve a legitimate government objective?
- Is the law a reasonable way to achieve that objective?

Few laws tested under the rational basis test are found invalid, because few laws are truly unreasonable or arbitrary. For instance, suppose a local law sets a curfew for teens and charges them with a crime if they are found on the street during the curfew period. If the city can prove it is protecting health and safety and the law promotes that end, the law will stand even if it is applied only to people of certain ages.

HISTORICAL THINKING

7. **MAKE CONNECTIONS** Why is ensuring equal protection of the laws necessary for maintaining the rule of law?
8. **COMPARE AND CONTRAST** Explain the differences between strict scrutiny and the rational basis test and identify why each is appropriate for the types of issues in which the courts use them.

LESSON 6.2 Civil Rights and African Americans

In 1962, Fannie Lou Hamer, an African-American woman living in Mississippi, tried to register to vote. The White farmer who employed her fired her and forced her and her family out of their home. When she tried to register the following year, she was severely beaten. Hamer persisted, and in 1964 she finally was able to register. The very first vote she cast was for herself—by then, she was running for office. She went on to help found the Mississippi Freedom Democratic Party. Hamer's story highlights the obstacles African Americans faced in securing their right to vote—and their courage in the struggle to secure that right.

Legacy of Slavery

As you read earlier, slavery existed when the Constitution was written, and the Constitution did not include any language limiting or hindering slavery. The Framers made that choice to ensure support for the Constitution by delegates from the southern states, where the economy depended on enslaved labor. Yet slavery stained the early republic. In addition to the fundamental injustice of slavery, enslaved people could be whipped or branded by enslavers if they were seen as disrespectful or disobedient. Enslaved people were subject to sexual assault. Even those spared these brutal treatments suffered from poor food, inadequate shelter, and little or no health care, as well as family separation when a spouse, parents, or children were sold.

Many African Americans resisted slavery. Some tried to escape, despite the danger of recapture and severe

The National Memorial for Peace and Justice opened in 2018 in Montgomery, Alabama. The centerpiece of this six-acre memorial to the more than 4,000 victims of lynching is a set of 800 monuments, one for each county in which a lynching took place. These counties are encouraged to confront their role in racial terror by claiming their monuments and installing them locally.

punishment. There were perhaps as many as 250 significant slave rebellions. Rebels, when caught, were usually harshly punished. Others resisted in less dramatic and risky ways, such as by breaking tools, claiming to misunderstand instructions, or deliberately working slowly.

A movement for **abolition**—or the ending of slavery—began in colonial times with Pennsylvania Mennonites and Quakers. Abolition won followers at the time of the American Revolution, when White Patriots began to see the fight for liberty as hypocritical if slavery was allowed to continue. By 1804, all of the northern states had laws ending slavery.

As the United States spread westward, the argument over slavery became a conflict over whether slavery would be extended to new territories. That struggle eventually led to the Civil War, which ended in the defeat of the 11 southern states that seceded to preserve slavery within their borders. In the period just after the war, the United States government made an effort to protect the rights of **freedmen**, formerly enslaved people who had been emancipated. Congress passed, and the states ratified, three amendments known as the Civil War amendments. The states of the defeated Confederacy had to accept these amendments. The 13th Amendment, ratified in 1865, abolished slavery. As you have read, the 14th Amendment, ratified in 1868, established birthright citizenship and asserted equal protection of the laws for all citizens. White southerners who had previously supported slavery quickly gained control of the new state governments formed after the war and tried to prevent African Americans from voting. That prompted ratification of the 15th Amendment in 1870, which said that the right to vote "shall not be denied or abridged . . . on account of race, color, or previous condition of servitude."

HISTORICAL THINKING

1. **IDENTIFY MAIN IDEAS AND DETAILS** Why are the 13th, 14th, and 15th Amendments called the Civil War amendments, and what do they have in common?
2. **ANALYZE CAUSE AND EFFECT** Why was the 15th Amendment necessary?

A Legacy of Discrimination

By the late 1880s, northern states had abandoned efforts to protect African Americans and former slaves. Southern legislatures began to pass **Jim Crow laws**, laws that required segregation, or separation, of the White and Black communities. The name *Jim Crow* came from a popular song and dance that caricatured African Americans. Some Jim Crow laws called for racial segregation in the use of public facilities, such as restaurants, hotels, theaters, restrooms, and public transportation.

SEPARATE BUT EQUAL DOCTRINE Jim Crow laws received the Supreme Court's blessing through its ruling in the case *Plessy* v. *Ferguson* in 1896. The Court majority endorsed the **separate-but-equal doctrine**, the idea that segregated facilities were legal as long as Blacks and Whites were provided separate but equal facilities. While this principle was used to justify racial segregation for more than 50 years, the separate facilities provided for Blacks were nearly always staggeringly inferior to those established for Whites.

Segregation was far from the only problem faced by African Americans. Violence and economic coercion were used to impose an elaborate code of conduct that severely limited their freedom. The Ku Klux Klan and other groups used force to intimidate Black citizens. The threat of violence kept African Americans from going out alone at night, walking on the same side of the street as a White person, or speaking as equals to Whites. This violence was not limited to southern states. Each year in the 1890s, nearly 200 African Americans were lynched, or hanged by mobs acting without the authority of law, including in states such as Illinois, Indiana, and Ohio that were far north of the former Confederacy.

VOTER SUPPRESSION White-controlled governments of southern states also moved to suppress voting rights. The 15th Amendment prohibited denial of the right to vote based on race, but in the 1880s and 1890s, southern leaders denied Blacks the vote by instituting laws and practices that did not mention race:

- **Literacy tests** required a would-be voter to read and interpret a passage of the Constitution. Since it was illegal to teach enslaved people to read, few African Americans could pass such a test. If an African-American man (women of all races were barred from voting) could read, White voting officials simply said his interpretation was wrong. Thus, African Americans were guaranteed to fail.
- **Poll taxes** required voters to pay for the opportunity to cast a ballot. Since African Americans were generally poor, they lacked the money to pay the tax.
- **Grandfather clauses** exempted a man from literacy tests or poll taxes if his grandfather could vote before the Civil War. Since the only people who could vote before the Civil War were White, these clauses simply prevented the other limitations from applying to White voters.
- **White primaries** excluded Black voters from voting in primary elections run by political parties. By not prohibiting African Americans from voting in actual elections, these laws evaded the ban imposed by the 15th Amendment. Since Democratic Party candidates invariably won the general election, blocking African Americans from voting in that party's primary effectively nullified any choice they might have had.

The effect of these laws was stunning. In Mississippi, for example, 90 percent of African-American men were registered to vote during **Reconstruction**—the period from 1865 to 1877 after the states that had seceded were readmitted to the Union. In 1892, after these barriers to voting were put in place, a mere 6 percent of African Americans were registered to vote.

HISTORICAL THINKING

3. **EVALUATE** To what extent were northerners responsible for the development of segregation in the South?
4. **DRAW CONCLUSIONS** How would literacy tests and grandfather clauses affect who stood for and held elected office in states with those laws?

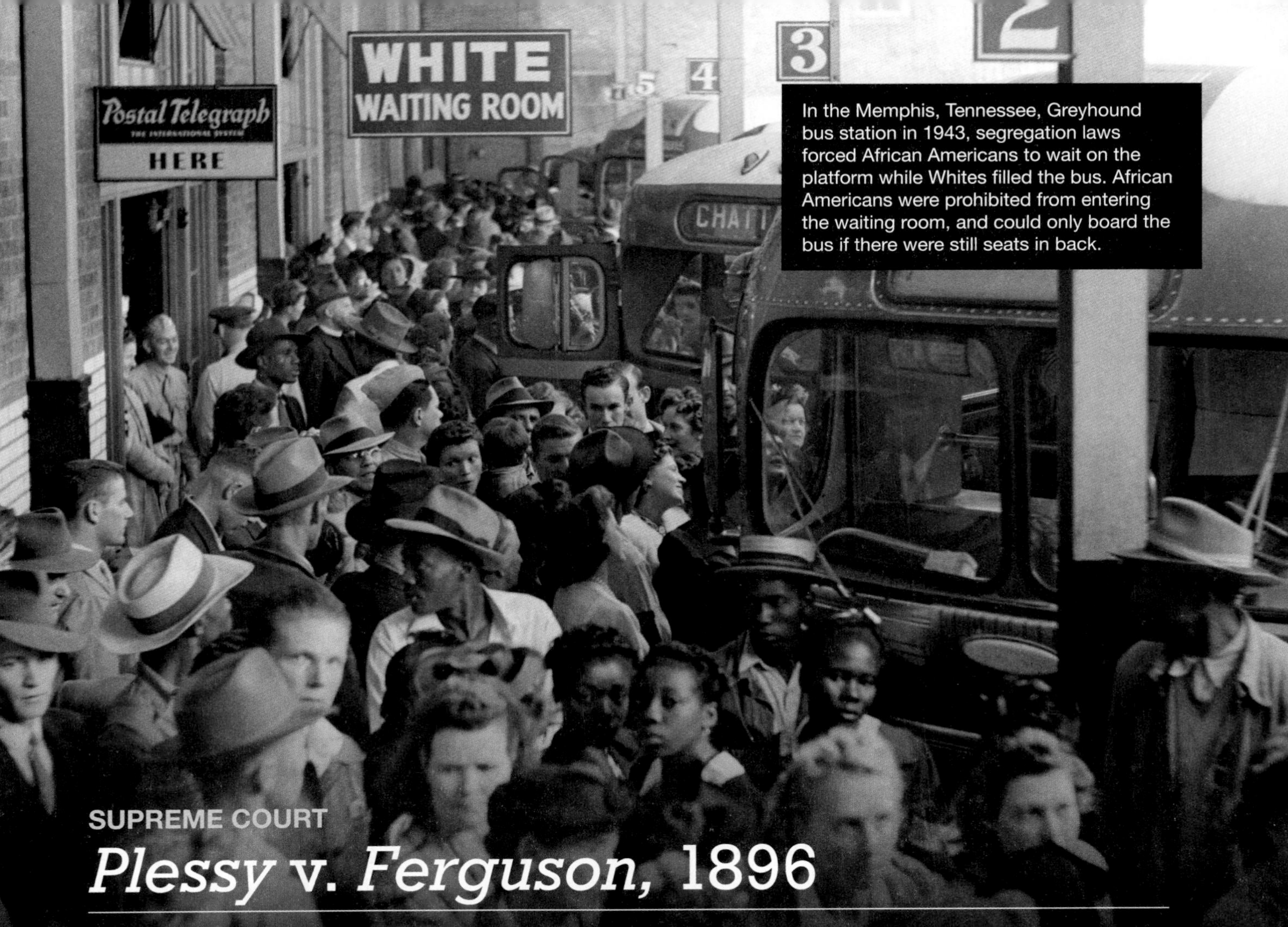

In the Memphis, Tennessee, Greyhound bus station in 1943, segregation laws forced African Americans to wait on the platform while Whites filled the bus. African Americans were prohibited from entering the waiting room, and could only board the bus if there were still seats in back.

SUPREME COURT

Plessy v. *Ferguson,* 1896

Decided: May 18, 1896, 7–1

Majority: Justice Henry Brown wrote the opinion of the Court, which ruled in favor of Ferguson and the parish of Orleans, Louisiana.

Dissent: Justice John Marshall Harlan filed a dissenting opinion.

A Louisiana law required passenger railways to provide "equal, but separate, accommodations for the white and colored races." A civil rights group in New Orleans recruited Homer Plessy, who was part African American, to challenge the law by buying a streetcar ticket. When he sat in a car reserved for Whites, he was arrested as planned, and then convicted and fined by Judge John Ferguson. Plessy's attorneys appealed the conviction to the Supreme Court. They argued that the Louisiana law was unconstitutional because it imposed a badge of servitude, in violation of the 13th Amendment, and denied the equal protection of the laws, in violation of

By a vote of 7–1, the Supreme Court rejected both arguments and made "separate but equal" the law of the land. Justice Henry Brown explained the majority's views by saying, first, the 13th Amendment was not relevant, since the issue did not reflect involuntary servitude. Further, Brown said that the 14th Amendment was meant "to enforce the absolute equality of the two races before the law, but . . . could not have been intended to abolish distinctions based upon color, or to enforce social . . . equality."

Today jurists, or legal experts, view the *Plessy* decision as not just unenlightened, but legally wrong. They agree with Justice John Marshall Harlan's dissent: "Our Constitution is color-blind, and neither knows nor tolerates classes among citizens. In respect of civil rights, all citizens are equal before the law," which has had a longer-lasting influence over present-day law.

THINK ABOUT IT What flaw can you see in

The Civil Rights Movement

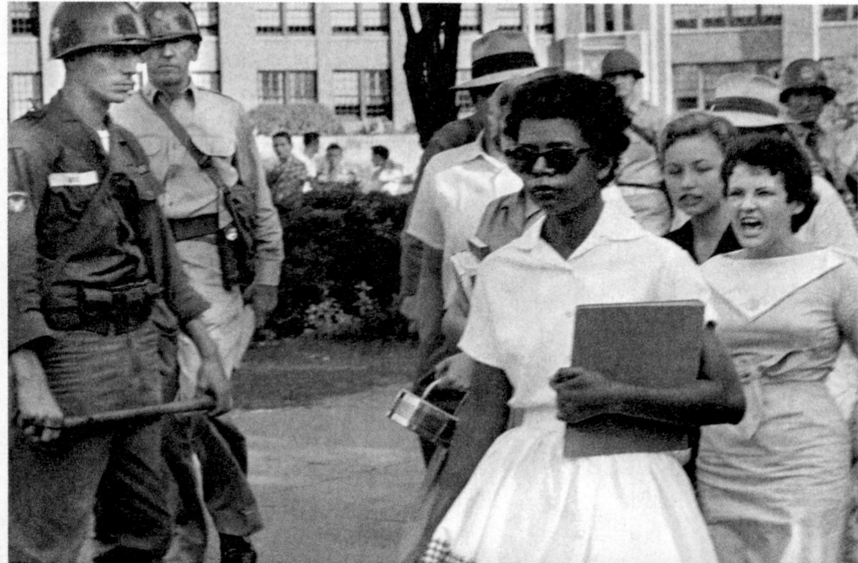

The Little Rock Nine—the first group of African-American students attempting to desegregate Central High School in Little Rock, Arkansas—intended to travel together for their first day, but 15-year-old Elizabeth Eckford ended up arriving at the school alone. After Arkansas National Guard troops barred her from entering the school, she walked through a hostile, racist mob and sat waiting for a city bus.

In the late 1930s and the 1940s, the United States Supreme Court gradually moved away from the separate-but-equal doctrine endorsed in the *Plessy* decision. Beginning in the 1930s, the National Association for the Advancement of Colored People (NAACP) Legal Defense and Education Fund won a series of court victories that overturned state segregation laws. They did this by proving that separate wasn't equal. Headed initially by Charles Houston and after 1938 by Thurgood Marshall, the Legal Defense and Education Fund achieved a crucial victory in 1950. In *Sweatt* v. *Painter*, the Supreme Court agreed that a Black law school could not provide an equal education because of the fact of segregation itself. The major breakthrough, however, didn't come until 1954, when the NAACP built on the *Sweatt* case to attack segregation in public education.

CHALLENGING SCHOOL SEGREGATION In the 1950s, public schools in many cities were segregated. African-American families in Topeka, Kansas, and four other cities sued to allow their children to attend all-White schools. The Supreme Court combined all the cases under the name *Brown* v. *Board of Education of Topeka*, the Kansas case. In 1954 the Supreme Court reversed *Plessy* v. *Ferguson* when it unanimously held that segregation by race in public education violated the 14th Amendment because it deprived African-American children of equal educational opportunity.

In 1955, in a second *Brown* v. *Board of Education* decision (sometimes called *Brown II)*, the Supreme Court ordered desegregation of public schools to begin "with all deliberate speed," an ambiguous phrase that recognized the significance of the 1954 ruling that required an end to school segregation. The *Brown II* ruling gave school districts time to implement the far-reaching change, but the language was so open-ended, that it could be—and was—interpreted in a variety of ways. School boards embraced the term "deliberate" rather than the injunction for "speed." White parents in many communities sent their children to newly established private schools, resulting in some formerly White-only public schools becoming 100 percent Black. In Arkansas, Governor Orval Faubus used the state's National Guard to block the desegregation of Little Rock's Central High School in 1957. Only after President Dwight D. Eisenhower federalized the Arkansas National Guard and sent in additional troops was Central High finally desegregated.

By 1970, **de jure segregation**—segregation established by law—had been abolished by school systems. But because nearly all neighborhoods were segregated in the 1960s, race-blind assignment to neighborhood schools still resulted in racially segregated schools. This situation created **de facto segregation** that was not imposed by law but was produced by social conventions, or customary practices.

To address de facto segregation, the Supreme Court endorsed busing students to schools outside their neighborhoods in a 1971 case involving the school system in Charlotte, North Carolina. Busing was unpopular with many groups, however, and by the mid-1970s, the courts had begun to retreat from their support for it. In 1974, in *Milliken* v. *Bradley*, the Supreme Court rejected busing children across school district lines when it struck down a plan to desegregate schools by busing students between the predominantly African-American city of Detroit and its predominantly White suburbs. De facto segregation in America's schools is still widespread.

THE MONTGOMERY BUS BOYCOTT The *Brown* decision was the first in a series of events that chipped away at de jure segregation. Earlier you read about the Montgomery Bus Boycott, so you may remember that in December of 1955, one and a half years after the first *Brown* decision, an African-American woman named Rosa Parks, a longtime activist in the NAACP, was arrested and fined for refusing to move to the rear of a segregated public bus in Montgomery, Alabama. Her arrest spurred the local African-American community to organize a year-long boycott of the entire Montgomery bus system. People walked, rode bicycles, or took part in carpools to get around town—but they stayed off the city buses.

During the year of protest, the Reverend Dr. Martin Luther King, Jr., a 27-year-old Baptist minister, emerged as a community leader. During the boycott, he was jailed, and his house was bombed. Yet, despite White hostility and what appeared to be overwhelming odds against them, the protesters triumphed in 1956, when a federal court prohibited the segregation of buses in Montgomery. The success launched the era of the **civil rights movement**, a mass movement by minorities and concerned Whites to end racial segregation and secure equal rights. The movement was led by a number of groups and individuals. Among the leaders were Bayard Rustin, the primary organizer of the famous March on Washington of 1963, and Martin Luther King, Jr., both of the Southern Christian Leadership Conference (SCLC). James Farmer of the Congress of Racial Equality (CORE), Roy Wilkins of the NAACP, and Ella Baker of the Student Nonviolent Coordinating Committee (SNCC) also played important roles.

CIVIL DISOBEDIENCE FOR CIVIL RIGHTS Civil rights protesters in the 1960s often used the tactic of civil disobedience—the deliberate and public refusal to obey laws considered unjust. On February 1, 1960, for example, four African-American students in Greensboro, North Carolina, sat at the "Whites only" lunch counter at a Woolworth's store and ordered food. The server refused to take their order, and the store closed early rather than allow them to eat. The next day more students returned to sit at the counter while supporters picketed the store out on the street. Day after day, students continued the sit-in, ignoring harassment from angry Whites. African Americans increased the pressure by staging sit-ins across the South and calling for a nationwide boycott of Woolworth's stores. In July, Woolworth's store officials began to desegregate their lunch counters across the country.

As the movement gained momentum and protests were met with violence, news photos and film footage showed nonviolent protesters being assaulted by police, sprayed with water from fire hoses, and attacked by dogs. These pictures shocked and angered Americans and led to nationwide demands for reform. The March on Washington for Jobs and Freedom, led by Martin Luther King, Jr., in 1963, demonstrated widespread public support for legislation to ban discrimination in all aspects of public life. More than 200,000 Americans from across the country, about a quarter of them White, marched peacefully in the nation's capital to show their support for an end to segregation. The march helped push Congress to act on a civil rights bill.

The movement also worked to restore voting rights to African Americans. In early 1965, activists planned a march from Selma, Alabama, to Montgomery, the state capital. On March 7, 1965, a day that became known as Bloody Sunday, police and state troopers attacked marchers with clubs and tear gas as they crossed the Edmund Pettus Bridge to leave Selma. President Lyndon B. Johnson decried the police action, and later that month, he submitted a voting rights bill to Congress. At a new march in support of the legislation, marchers were protected by the National Guard and the FBI.

THE BLACK POWER MOVEMENT Malcolm X, a speaker and organizer for the Nation of Islam (also called the Black Muslims), rejected the goals of integration and racial equality. He called instead for Black separatism and Black pride. Although he later moderated some of his views, his rhetorical style and

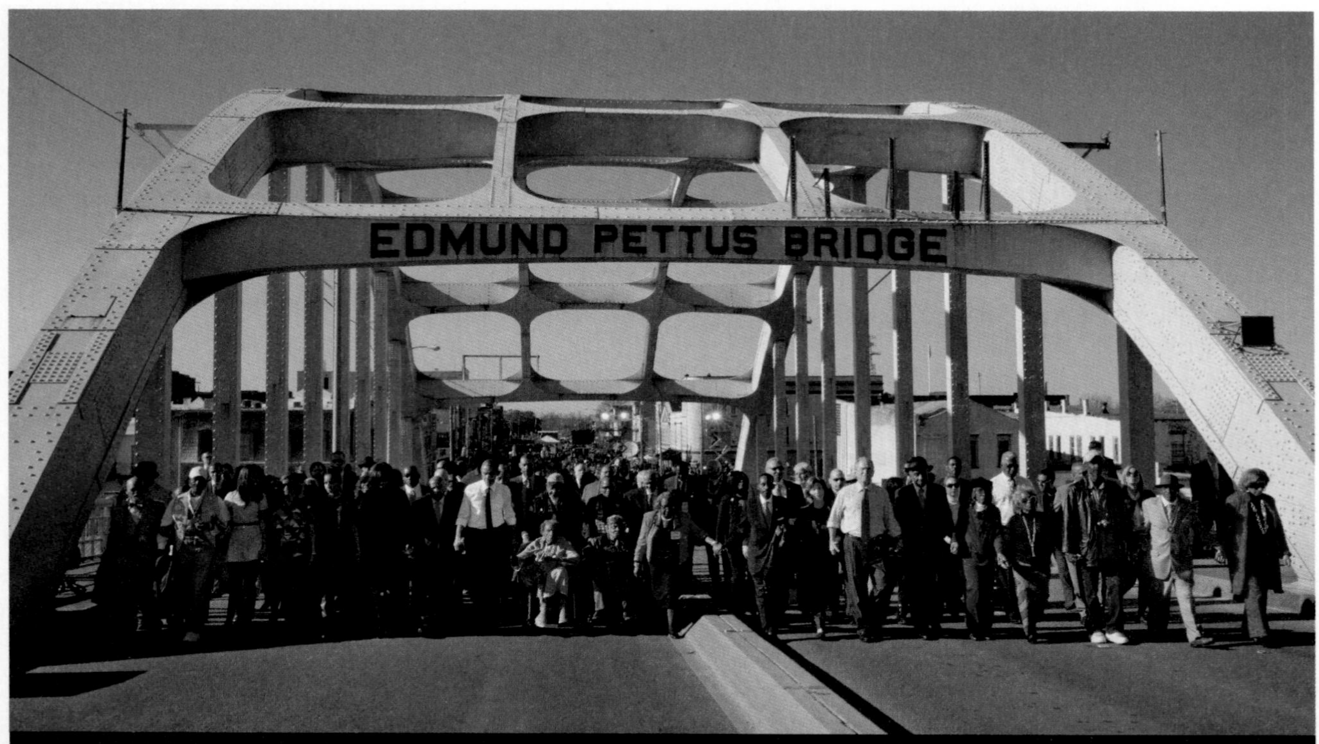

On March 7, 2015, President Barack Obama and former president George W. Bush joined an estimated 15,000 to 20,000 marchers honoring the 50th anniversary of Bloody Sunday by marching across the Edmund Pettus Bridge in Selma.

powerful message influenced many young African Americans. By the late 1960s, after the assassinations of Malcolm X in 1965 and of Martin Luther King, Jr., in 1968, the era of mass acts of civil disobedience in the name of civil rights came to an end.

HISTORICAL THINKING

5. **MAKE CONNECTIONS** Why would the NAACP lawyers see the Supreme Court's decision in *Sweatt* v. *Painter* as an opportunity to win the *Brown* case?
6. **DESCRIBE** Why was the Montgomery bus boycott so important?
7. **ANALYZE CAUSE AND EFFECT** Why did the civil rights movement adopt nonviolence? Why was that approach effective?

Legal Protections

As the civil rights movement demonstrated its strength, all three branches of the federal government moved to advance the cause of civil rights. Congress sought to address the issue of private businesses discriminating on the basis of race in the Civil Rights Act of 1964, the most comprehensive civil rights law since Reconstruction. This law made discrimination on the basis of race, color, religion, gender, and national origin in public places of accommodation, such as hotels, restaurants, movie theaters, public transportation, and employment illegal. The act also included these major provisions:

- It provided that federal funds could be withheld from any federal or state government project or facility that practiced discrimination.
- It outlawed arbitrary discrimination in voter registration.
- It authorized the federal government to sue to desegregate public schools and facilities.

The government took more action on voting rights. In 1964, the 24th Amendment was ratified. It declared that the right to vote in an election for any federal office "shall not be denied or abridged . . . by reason of failure to pay any poll tax." The following year,

Congress acted on the voting rights bill President Lyndon Johnson proposed after the Selma violence. The Voting Rights Act of 1965 made it illegal to interfere with anyone's right to vote in any election in this country. It also required states with a history of voting discrimination to obtain approval from federal authorities for any changes to their voting laws or practices.

In the late 1960s the courts and Congress addressed other types of discrimination. In 1967, in the case *Loving* v. *Virginia*, the Supreme Court declared that laws banning interracial marriage were unconstitutional. The next year, Congress passed the Civil Rights Act of 1968 prohibiting discrimination in housing.

African Americans Serving in Congress, 1999–2021

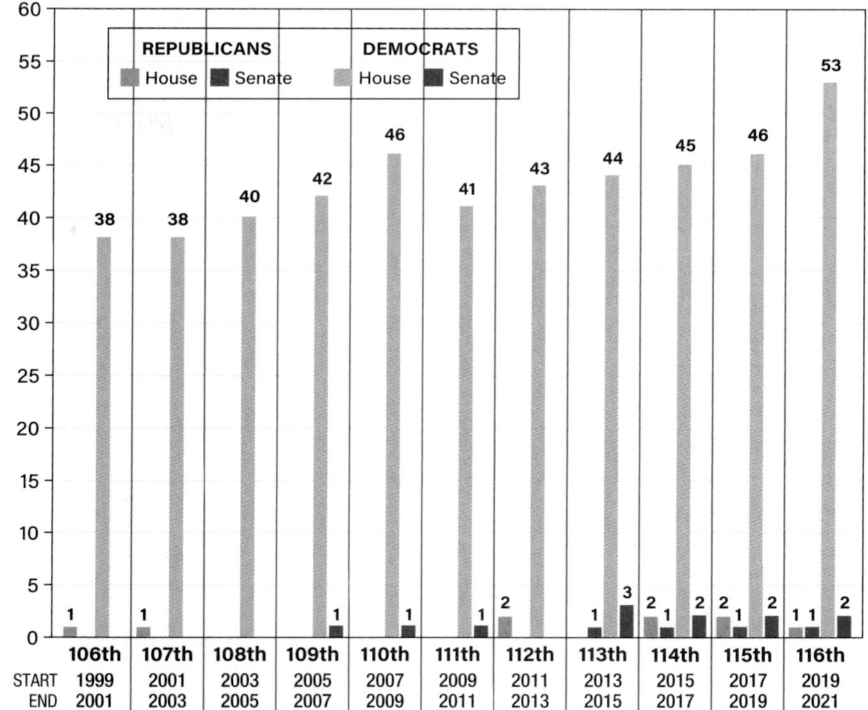

SOURCE: U.S. House of Representatives

HISTORICAL THINKING

8. **EVALUATE** Why is the Civil Rights Act of 1964 considered a landmark law?

9. **MAKE CONNECTIONS** How was the part of the Voting Rights Act that gave the government the right to review any changes in some states' voting laws a reflection of past experience?

Civil Rights Today

In the early 1960s, only 22 percent of African Americans of voting age in the South were registered to vote, compared with 63 percent of voting-age Whites. The Voting Rights Act of 1965 and the 24th Amendment ban on poll taxes had a dramatic effect. Today, the percentages of Blacks and Whites registered to vote are nearly equal. As a result of this dramatic change, political participation by African Americans has increased, as has the number of African-American elected officials.

More than 9,000 African Americans served in elective office in the United States in the 2010s. Following the 2018 elections, 57 African Americans were members of Congress. A number of African Americans have achieved high office in the executive branch, including Colin Powell, who served as President George W. Bush's first secretary of state, and Condoleezza Rice, his second secretary of state. Thurgood Marshall, the NAACP lawyer who led victories in the *Sweatt* and *Brown* cases, among others, became the first African American on the U.S. Supreme Court in 1967.

Famously, in 2008 Barack Obama, a U.S. senator from Illinois, won election as the first African-American president of the United States and went on to serve for two terms. As of 2018, only two African Americans had been elected to a state governorship, and only a few African Americans have been elected to the U.S. Senate since 1900. But the Democratic field for the 2020 election offered more diversity. Senator Cory Booker of New Jersey, an African-American man, and Senator Kamala Harris of California, a woman of mixed African-American and South Asian-American ancestry, met a number of criteria, including minimal polling results and numbers of donations, to make it onto the debate stage. Harris went on to secure nomination as the vice-presidential candidate on the Democratic ticket in 2020.

PROBLEMS WITH VOTING RIGHTS In June 2013 the Voting Rights Act received a significant setback at the hands of the U.S. Supreme Court. In *Shelby County v. Holder,* the Court ruled that Section 4 of the Voting Rights Act was unconstitutional. This section defined which state and local governments were subject to special federal oversight.

The governments identified by Section 4 had a history of voting rights violations. Under Section 4, these governments could not change voting procedures or district boundaries without preclearance, or prior approval from the federal government. In *Shelby County,* the Court ruled that this requirement was no longer needed since "the conditions that originally justified these measures no longer characterize voting in the covered jurisdictions." The Department of Justice can still challenge election procedures after they are implemented, but such lawsuits are less effective than the preclearance system.

Many feared that the *Shelby County* decision would result in new state laws that would make it difficult for many low-income people to vote. Their concerns were purportedly confirmed by laws in several states that placed limits on early voting or required photo identification, measures that seemed likely to reduce turnout among poor and minority voters. In several states, federal judges blocked the new laws in time for the 2016 elections. In North Carolina, a judge stated that the legislature had targeted Black voters with "surgical precision." Critics charged that failure to open enough polling places, or voting sites, in Black neighborhoods was also a major problem. In 2018, activists challenged laws in 18 states regarding such issues as removal of voters' names from registration lists, suspicious voter verification practices, and making early voting more difficult. Concerns about these laws prompted calls for federal legislation to ensure voting rights of minority voters.

PROBLEMS WITH LAW ENFORCEMENT Many African Americans live in neighborhoods that are struggling economically, and crime rates can be high in these areas. As a result, African Americans are disproportionately victimized by crime. They are also disproportionately arrested, no matter what neighborhood they are in.

Blacks are nearly four times as likely to be arrested for possession of marijuana as are Whites, even though studies show that the two groups use and sell the substance at similar rates. African Americans make up 12 percent of the total population of drug users but also constitute almost 40 percent of those arrested for drug offenses and 60 percent of those in state prison for drug offenses. Indeed, nearly 1 million of the 2.3 million persons in prison are African Americans. Add Hispanics, and these two groups make up 60 percent of all prisoners, twice their share of the U.S. population. Such data raise the suspicion that U.S. law enforcement is biased against minority group members.

In the years since 2015, police relations with people of color have become a major issue. One concern is that police regularly subject Black drivers and pedestrians, especially young men, to investigatory stops—stops made without evidence of a crime. African Americans charge that the stops represent the "crime of driving while Black." White people, including White males, almost never experience investigatory stops. In addition, critics have charged that some law enforcement officers have employed excessive force against African Americans—especially young men. Incidents in which unarmed Black men were killed during interactions with police have led to protests and riots in cities as varied as Ferguson, Missouri, and Baltimore, Maryland, and Charlotte, North Carolina.

The Black Lives Matter movement arose in response to violence against Black people. The name comes from the idea that Black lives are treated as if they don't matter. Yet statistics show that police are hardly ever charged with a crime for shooting unarmed Black people, and if they are charged, they are often acquitted. Black Lives Matter is a network of local chapters that views itself as "an affirmation of Black folks' humanity, [their] contributions to this society, and [their] resilience in the face of deadly oppression."

COLIN KAEPERNICK AND THE NATIONAL FOOTBALL LEAGUE In 2016 Colin Kaepernick, then a quarterback for the San Francisco 49ers of the National Football League (NFL), initiated another form of protest when he refused to stand during the pregame national anthem. Some critics viewed Kaepernick's protest as disrespectful of the anthem, the flag, the country, veterans, the military, or all of these. As the 2017 NFL season began, several players continued this protest (Kaepernick was no longer with the 49ers by then and had not been signed by any other team). The protests remained relatively small until President Donald Trump

Black Lives Matter marchers in Baltimore, Maryland, in 2015, expressed the outrage that was felt across the country after Freddie Gray, a 25-year-old African-American man arrested for possession of a switchblade knife, died while in police custody.

called for owners to punish protesting players and for fans to boycott the league. On the next game day, whether kneeling, sitting, or standing, the vast majority of players on every team—joined by many coaches, owners, and support staff—locked arms together to show their solidarity. In 2018, the league agreed with a players group to establish a multimillion dollar fund to support community efforts to address social inequality. Additional social justice initiatives have included the use of signage recognizing systemic racism and the playing of "Lift Every Voice and Sing," also known as the Black National Anthem, at NFL games.

CLASS VERSUS RACE IN EDUCATION The education gap between Blacks and Whites also persists, despite continuing efforts by educators—and by government—to reduce it. Recent studies show that, on average, African-American students in high school read and do math at the level of White students in junior high school. Also, while Black adults have narrowed the gap with White adults in earning high school diplomas, the disparity has widened for college degrees.

Some educators suggest that the real problem is economic. They point out that schools in poorer neighborhoods—where many African-American students live—generally have fewer educational resources, resulting in lower achievement levels for their students. Research shows that when students enrolled at a particular school come almost entirely from impoverished families, regardless of race, their performance is seriously depressed. When low-income students attend schools where the majority of the students are middle class, again regardless of race, their performance improves dramatically. These studies appear to provide evidence supporting the Supreme Court's ruling in *Brown* v. *Board of Education*—that schools separated by socioeconomic class are inherently unequal. Because of this research and recent Supreme Court rulings that have struck down some racial integration plans, several school systems have adopted policies that integrate students on the basis of socioeconomic class, not race.

HISTORICAL THINKING

10. **IDENTIFY PROBLEMS AND SOLUTIONS** How has the fact that voting is governed by state laws caused problems?
11. **INTERPRET GRAPHS** Based on the graph of African Americans in Congress, what can you conclude about the party alignment of African-American voters?
12. **COMPARE AND CONTRAST** What similarities do you see between the Black Lives Matter effort and the NFL anthem protests?

Why Do We See So Many Things as "Us vs. Them"?

by David Berreby *National Geographic* Magazine, April 2018

Borders are one way to reinforce group, specifically national, identity. This corrugated metal barrier, seen from the Mexican side, marks the border between the United States and Mexico, near San Diego. Behind the existing wall are four prototypes, or samples, of the enhanced border wall President Donald Trump proposed to build.

Though the United States was founded on the principle of human equality, through much of our history, African Americans and other racial and ethnic minorities have been deprived of their full rights. But a tendency to see what divides people over what unites us is not restricted to the United States. Nor are divisions always, or even often, based on race. Around the world, people see themselves as divided by heritage, culture, tribe, nation, religion, and sect as well as race.

The problem, writes David Berreby in "Why Do We See So Many Things as 'Us vs. Them'?" is that the tendency to divide people into various groups is instinctive.

It's a common misfortune around the world: People get along well enough for decades, even centuries, across lines of race or religion or culture. Then, suddenly, the neighbors aren't people you respect, invite to dinner, trade favors with, or marry. Those once familiar faces are now Them, the Enemy, the Other. And in that clash of groups, individuality vanishes and empathy dries up, as does trust. It can happen between herders and farmers in Nigeria or between native-born people and immigrants in France or the United States. The situations are very different, and the differences are important. But so is the shared root of their problems: People everywhere are "identity crazed," as the evolutionary psychologist John Tooby has put it. We can't help it: We're wired from birth to tell Us from Them. And we inevitably (and sometimes unconsciously) favor Us—especially when we feel threatened.

Now researchers are trying to understand the origins and dynamics of group identity to see if there are ways to overcome the damage it can do. One key insight that holds promise is that group identities themselves are fluid. People can shift their perceptions so that those who were once seen as "Them" can become "Us." Building on this insight, scientists are working to create training tools that can alert people to their own unconscious biases and alter behavior. For example, one study is examining the effectiveness of video simulation training for police officers, whose split-second decisions can have lethal consequences. "This kind of careful testing," Berreby writes, "may show that we've finally discovered a true science of human groupishness—one that can help us master these instincts, before they master us."

Access the full version of "Why Do We See So Many Things as 'Us vs. Them'?" by David Berreby through the Resources Menu in MindTap.

THINK ABOUT IT How might insights into group identity affect laws regarding racial discrimination?

LESSON 6.3 Women's Rights

In 1848, Elizabeth Cady Stanton, Lucretia Mott, and three other women organized the first women's rights convention in Seneca Falls, New York. One hundred women and men attended and endorsed a Declaration of Sentiments that proclaimed: "We hold these truths to be self-evident: that all men and women are created equal." The declaration listed "repeated injuries," including denial of the right to vote, denial of property rights, exclusion from educational opportunities and many professions and occupations, and unfairly low pay. Women's struggle for the right to vote took over 70 years to complete, but economic and political equality is an ongoing issue.

The Struggle for Voting Rights

Women have been treated as inferior and discriminated against since long before the nation's founding. Women's demand for suffrage—the right to vote—was an uphill battle in part because they were unable to vote to give themselves the right to vote. To gain the right to vote, they needed to persuade a majority of male voters to give it to them. Why would men do that? The answer of suffragists was simple and, they thought, obvious: because women were men's equals and thus were entitled to equal rights. But it took many years to convince a majority of men of this.

After the Civil War, two groups formed to press for women's suffrage. The American Woman Suffrage Association (AWSA), founded by Lucy Stone and others, worked toward amending state constitutions to give women the right to vote. The National Woman Suffrage Association (NWSA), founded by Susan B. Anthony and Elizabeth Cady Stanton, worked for a national constitutional amendment but also treated suffrage as only part of the struggle for full equality of social and political rights for women. The NWSA opposed the 15th Amendment, which gave Black men the right to vote but left White and Black women disenfranchised, and pushed for an amendment that would give women the vote.

In 1890 these two organizations joined to become the National American Woman Suffrage Association (NAWSA). While NAWSA was organizing parades, issuing printed materials, and lobbying legislators, radical splinter groups took to the streets and engaged in civil disobedience, including hunger strikes when they were jailed.

World War I (1914–1918) marked a turning point in the battle for women's rights. The war offered many opportunities for women. Several thousand women served in the U.S. Navy, and—with many men joining the military and leaving the workforce—about 1 million women took jobs in industry. However, when the war ended, soldiers and sailors returned to their former jobs, and women were forced out. They were told that the men needed the jobs because they had families to support, while women had responsibilities at home.

Meanwhile, women were making progress at the state level. Wyoming and Utah were admitted to the United States in 1890 and 1896 with equal voting rights for women. Colorado enfranchised women in 1893. Idaho allowed women to vote in 1896, Washington state enfranchised women in 1910, and California, in 1911. By 1918, 15 states allowed women the vote in state elections and declared that their congressional representatives had to be responsive to women's concerns as well as to men's. That year, Montana representative Jeannette Rankin—the first woman elected to Congress—began a debate on a national woman's suffrage amendment, which the House voted to approve.

President Woodrow Wilson offered little support to the movement when he first took office in 1913, but in 1918, after many protests on the part of suffrage activists, he finally called on senators to support women's suffrage. In 1919, the Senate approved the amendment: "The right of citizens of the United States to vote shall not be denied or abridged by the United States or by any State on account of sex." By the following summer, three-quarters of the state

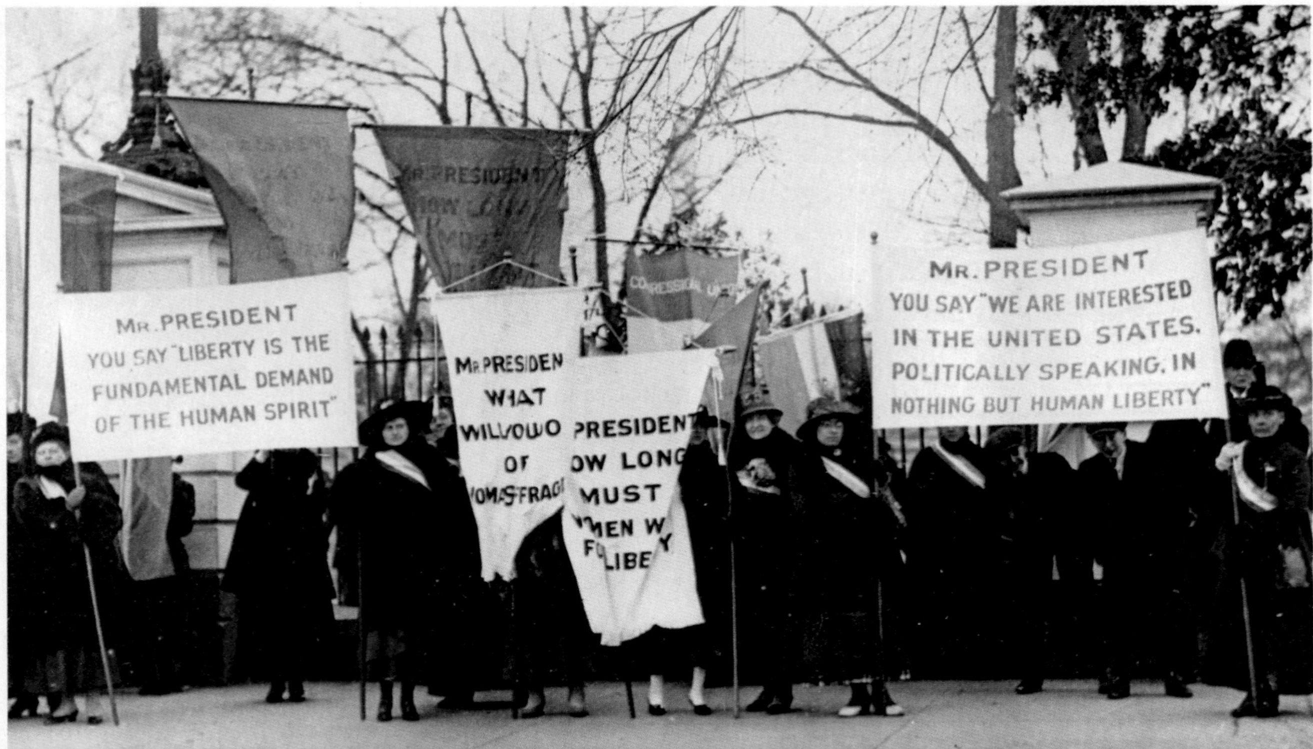

CRITICAL VIEWING In January 1917, just two months after President Wilson won re-election, suffragists began picketing nonstop at the White House demanding women's right to vote. How did these suffragists use Wilson's own words to help make their case for women's suffrage?

legislatures had ratified the 19th Amendment, and women had finally won the right to vote—more than 70 years after the Seneca Falls Convention had first proposed it.

HISTORICAL THINKING

1. **DESCRIBE** How did women affect public policy regarding the right of women to vote?
2. **MAKE INFERENCES** How do you think events during World War I changed the debate about woman suffrage?

The Women's Movement

For many years after winning the right to vote, women engaged in very little independent political activity. Their progress in professional fields, jobs in the construction trades, and higher education was slow. Even in fields where women were hired in large numbers, they faced disparities, or inequalities, in pay and professional advancement. In the 1960s, however, a new women's movement arose—the feminist movement. Women who faced discrimination in employment and other areas of life were inspired in part by the civil rights movement and the campaign against the war in Vietnam to push for equal rights.

WOMEN'S LIBERATION AND FEMINISM The National Organization for Women (NOW), founded in 1966, was the most visible new women's organization. But the feminist movement also consisted of thousands of small, independent groups on campuses and in neighborhoods throughout the nation. These groups focused on women's liberation, a movement to free women of limitations imposed by traditional gender roles. Some of these groups ran consciousness-raising exercises to help participants recognize subtle ways that they were being treated unequally. **Feminism**, the goal of the movement, meant full political, economic, and social equality for women.

During the 1970s, NOW and other organizations sought to win passage of the equal rights amendment (ERA) to the Constitution, which would have written gender equality into the heart of the nation's laws. First proposed in 1923, the amendment finally won congressional approval in 1972. While 30 states ratified it within a year, the push for ratification stalled as conservative groups claimed that the amendment would take privileges away from women. But efforts toward passage resumed in 2017, with ratification by Nevada, followed by ratification in Illinois in 2018. Adding the amendment to the Constitution, however, would require repealing or overruling the 1982 deadline imposed in 1972 and a determination on whether the five states that rescinded their ratification can legitimately do so.

Campaigns to change state and national laws affecting women were much more successful, as Congress and the various state legislatures enacted a range of measures meant to provide equal rights for women. The women's movement also enjoyed considerable success in legal action. Courts at all levels accepted the argument that gender discrimination violated the 14th Amendment's equal protection clause.

TITLE IX One important congressional action regarding women's rights was Title IX of the Education Amendments of 1972. This section stated that "no person in the United States shall, on the basis of sex, be excluded from participation in, be denied the benefits of, or be subjected to discrimination under any education program or activity receiving Federal financial assistance." In *Grove City* v. *Bell* (1984), the Supreme Court limited the scope of Title IX to apply only to specific programs that receive federal funds. This decision was overturned by the Civil Rights Restoration Act of 1988, which extended coverage of the act to any program or activity at an institution that receives federal funds.

The law has had an impact on secondary schools and on postsecondary institutions that receive federal money. Since the Title IX era began, opportunities for women in sports, the sciences, and extracurricular clubs have greatly increased, as have scholarships available to women. From the 1971–1972 school year to the 2017–2018 year, the proportion of high school athletes who were female increased from 7 percent to nearly 43 percent. The

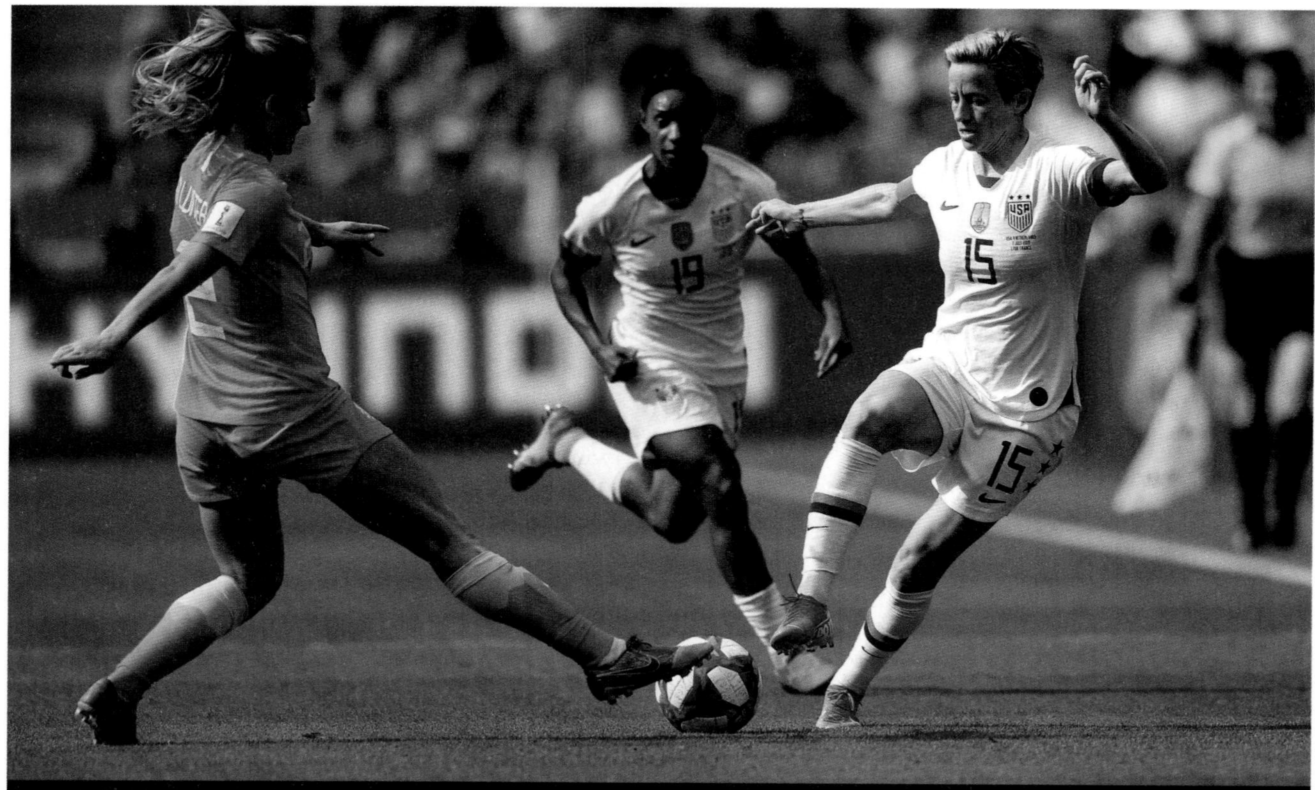

Megan Rapinoe (right) led the United States women's soccer team in the 2019 World Cup, winning the Golden Ball award as the tournament's best player. She has also been a vocal supporter of women's equality in the world of sports.

National Center for Educational Statistics estimates that in 2018, 56 percent of students enrolled in postsecondary education were women. The Association of American Medical Colleges found that in 2017, for the first time, more women than men entered medical school.

In addition to fighting gender discrimination, the feminist movement took up a number of other issues important to women. Some campaigns, such as the one to curb domestic violence, have been widely supported. Others have resulted in heated debate. Perhaps the most controversial issue, which you read about earlier, has been over the question of whether and when women have the right to terminate a pregnancy.

HISTORICAL THINKING

3. **MAKE INFERENCES** Why was consciousness-raising a priority for the women's movement?
4. **ANALYZE CAUSE AND EFFECT** How has Title IX affected women's economic potential?

Women's and Men's Experience of Workplace Discrimination

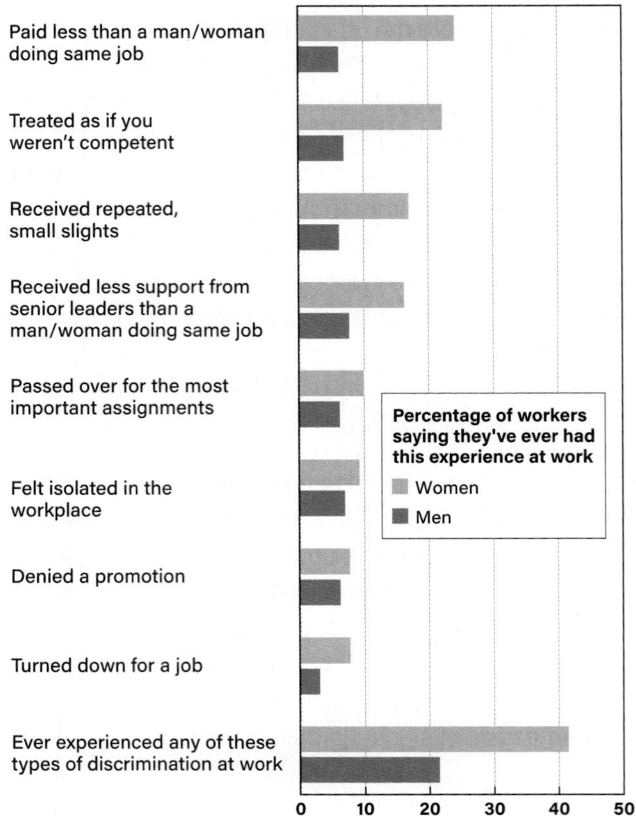

SOURCE: Data from Pew Research Center

Women in the Workplace

American women continue to face challenges in obtaining equal pay and equal opportunity in the workplace. In spite of federal legislation and programs to promote equal treatment of women in the workplace, gender discrimination continues. This unfair treatment takes several forms.

EQUAL PAY FOR EQUAL WORK LEGISLATION In 1963, Congress passed the Equal Pay Act, which requires employers to pay an equal wage for substantially equal work—males can't be paid more than females who perform essentially the same job. The following year, Congress passed the Civil Rights Act of 1964. Title VII of this act prohibits employment discrimination on the basis of race, color, national origin, gender, and religion. Despite this legislative action, women in many fields are still paid less than men.

A 2007 Supreme Court ruling weakened women's ability to seek redress for pay discrimination. In *Ledbetter* v. *Goodyear Tire and Rubber Co.*, the Court ruled that a company can't be sued for pay discrimination under Title VII if the complaint was made more than 180 days after the decision to discriminate took place. The plaintiff in this case was Lilly Ledbetter, who worked as a supervisor at a Goodyear tire plant for nearly 20 years before she learned that she was being paid less than three men with the same job. In 2009 President Barack Obama signed into law the Lilly Ledbetter Fair Pay Act, which resets the 180-day limit each time an employee receives a new paycheck that reflects discriminatory treatment.

The gap between men's and women's wages has narrowed significantly since 1963, but it remains a problem. As of 2017 it was estimated that for every dollar earned by men, women earn about 82 cents. The wage gap particularly harms women in management positions and older women. In addition, workers in occupations that are disproportionately female tend to be paid lower wages than those in other occupations requiring similar education and training.

Recent research suggests that wage inequality is concentrated in fields in which employees are expected to put in very long hours. Finance, where long hours are expected, may have the most unequal pay structure of any industry. Researchers believe this is because women still bear the brunt of child-care responsibilities that make it hard for them to work more than 40 hours a week.

Even though an increasing number of women now hold business and professional jobs once held only by men, relatively few women rise to the top of the career ladder due to the lingering bias against women in the workplace. This bias has been described as the **glass ceiling**—an invisible but real discriminatory barrier that prevents women and minorities from rising to top positions of power or responsibility. Today, even though women make up nearly 47 percent of the workforce, they hold less than one-sixth of the top executive positions in the largest American corporations.

The glass ceiling operates in politics as well. More than 170 years after the demand for equality at Seneca Falls, no woman has been elected president. Of 50 state governors serving in 2019, only 9 were women.

SEXUAL HARASSMENT Title VII's prohibition of gender discrimination also prohibits sexual harassment, which occurs when job opportunities, promotions, salary increases, or even the ability to retain a job depends on whether an employee complies with demands for sexual favors. Hostile environment harassment occurs when an employee is subjected to sexual conduct or comments in the workplace that interfere with his or her job

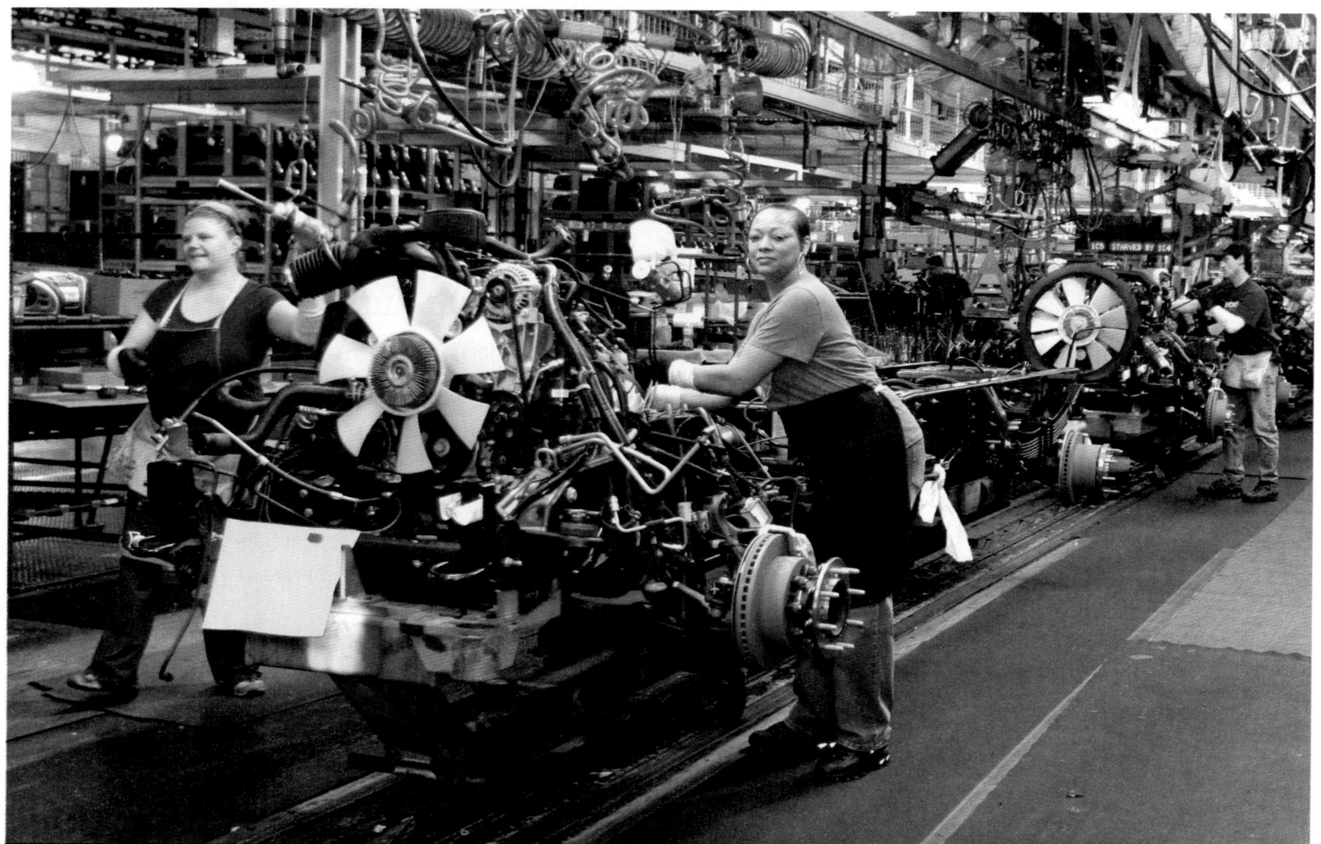

This female crew assembles pick-up trucks at Flint Assembly, the General Motors assembly plant in Flint, Michigan, where most employees are represented by the United Auto Workers. The Economic Policy Institute has found that women who are members of a labor union earn significantly more than nonunionized female workers and that the gender pay gap is much smaller among unionized workers.

performance or create an intimidating, hostile, or offensive environment. Sexual harassers and victims can be men or women, but those most likely to face harassment are women who are harassed by men.

The Civil Rights Act of 1991 greatly expanded the remedies available for victims of sexual harassment. Under the act, victims can seek damages as well as back pay, job reinstatement, and other compensation. But many victims of sexual harassment are reluctant to tell their stories. They may not want to relive their traumatic experiences. Many also fear being punished, humiliated, grilled, or shunned if they come forward to describe what happened.

In 1998 the Supreme Court made it clear that sexual harassment includes harassment by members of the same sex. In the same year, the Court held that employers are liable for the harassment of employees unless the employers can show that they exercised reasonable care in preventing such problems—which they can do, for example, by implementing policies and procedures designed to prevent harassment—and that employees failed to take advantage of any corrective opportunities provided by the employers.

Starting in October 2017, a large number of victims of sexual assault and harassment went public with their experiences, a trend that was called the MeToo movement. Most had kept silent for years or decades but were spurred to tell their stories in hopes that doing so would help other victims feel supported and galvanize public action. Some identified their harasser or assaulter. Dozens of women, including movie stars, directors, and producers, named Harvey Weinstein, perhaps the most successful film producer in Hollywood. More than 200 celebrities and prominent figures in the entertainment industry and in politics have also been publicly accused. Although many have lost their jobs, few have been arrested for their alleged criminal acts. One notable exception was Weinstein, who was convicted of a criminal sex act and third-degree rape in a court in New York in February of 2020, though he was also acquitted of two more serious charges of criminal sexual assault.

SEXUAL ASSAULT ON CAMPUS Title IX of the Education Amendments of 1972 prohibits gender-based discrimination in schools that receive federal money. Sexual assault, ranging from unwanted touching to acts of violence, is considered discrimination under Title IX, yet colleges' handling of sexual assault remains a serious problem. Use of alcohol is a major contributing factor. Under the broadest definition, about one in five college women has experienced sexual assault. As with workplace harassment, few women report assault to school authorities, and those who do often receive little help. In some cases, victims have actually been penalized for making complaints.

Beginning in 2011, the Obama administration began cracking down on the problem. By 2014, 55 colleges were under investigation for mishandling complaints. Twenty-five were under investigation for retaliating against persons reporting assault. Schools that failed to improve their procedures were at risk of losing federal funds. After Betsy DeVos took over as secretary of education under President Donald Trump, she rescinded Obama administration policies. New rules were aimed at protecting people from wrongful accusations and limiting the liability of colleges.

Today, many students are unwilling to accept policies or language that they consider discriminatory, whether the target is women or minority group members. Criticisms of language that is alleged to be discriminatory or hostile, however, have led to a reaction. Some observers reject what they see as attempts to police language.

HISTORICAL THINKING

5. **INTERPRET GRAPHS** Based on the graph about experiences of workplace discrimination, what single change in the workplace would help the greatest share of women workers?
6. **COMPARE AND CONTRAST** In what ways are the problems of sexual harassment in the workplace and sexual harassment in colleges similar?

Women in American Politics Today

More than 10,000 people have served in the U.S. House of Representatives since the First Congress was convened. Only 1 percent of them have been women, and women who serve continue to face a men's-club atmosphere. In 2002, however, a woman, Nancy Pelosi (D-CA), was elected minority leader of the House of

R. G. & G. R. Harris Funeral Homes, Inc. v. Equal Employment Opportunity Commission, 2020

Decided: June 15, 2020, 6–3

Majority: Justice Neil Gorsuch wrote the majority opinion in favor of the Equal Employment Opportunity Commission.

Dissent: Justice Samuel Alito and Justice Brett Kavanaugh wrote separate dissenting opinions.

It took six years from the time transgender activist Aimee Stephens was fired by her employer for her case to be heard by the U.S. Supreme Court on October 8, 2019.

n 2013, Anthony Stephens wrote an email to coworkers announcing an intention to appear at work as "my true self," Aimee Stephens. Stephens had worked at Harris Funeral Home in Garden City, Michigan, for six years and was considered a good employee. Nonetheless, two weeks after sending her letter, she was fired from her job. Her employer said the firing was because Stephens "was no longer going to represent himself as a man." Stephens filed a complaint with the Equal Employment Opportunity Commission, a federal agency that enforces civil rights laws against workplace discrimination. The EEOC filed a suit claiming that Harris had violated Title VII of the Civil Rights Act of 1964, which prohibits employment discrimination based on race, color, religion, sex, and national origin. The EEOC argued that as a transgender individual, Stephens was covered by the term sex in the Civil Rights Act language.

The original trial court sided with Harris, the employer, in 2016, but the appeals court sided with Stephens in 2018. As the case made its way to the U.S. Supreme Court, the EEOC switched sides. Though still the plaintiff of record, the commission, which was now run by Trump Administration appointees, supported Harris. n addition, the Court consolidated *Harris* v. *EEOC* with two related cases, *Bostock* v. *Clayton County, Georgia,* and *Zarda* v. *Altitude Express*. Both these cases hinged on the question of whether the term *sex* in Title VII covered workplace discrimination on the basis of sexual orientation.

n a 6–3 decision, the Court ruled in favor of Stephens and the other plaintiffs. In his majority opinion, Justice Neil Gorsuch argued that "an employer who fired an

that person for traits or actions it would not have questioned in members of a different sex. Sex plays a necessary and undisguisable role in the decision, exactly what Title VII forbids." In other words, Aimee Stephens would not have been fired for dressing as a woman had she not been transgender.

In his dissent, Justice Samuel Alito criticized the majority for, in his words, "attempting to pass off" its decision as the result of a textualist interpretation, or one that relies purely on the meaning of the words in a law rather than on the intent of those who made the law. In his view, the majority had revised Title VII to reflect society's current values.

Aimee Stephens did not live to see the Supreme Cour rule in her favor. She died in May, 2020, less than a month before the Court issued its decision.

THINK ABOUT IT Does Justice Samuel Alito support or criticize the idea that Supreme Court decisions should reflect society's current values?

Representatives. She was the first woman to hold this post. Pelosi again made history when, after the Democratic victories in the 2006 elections, she was elected Speaker of the House of Representatives, the first woman ever to lead the House. After Republicans took control of the House in 2011, Pelosi again became minority leader but resumed the speakership after Democrats regained a majority in the House in the 2018 midterms. In those midterm elections, women won a record number of seats in Congress, putting 25 women in the Senate and 102 in the House.

Franklin D. Roosevelt appointed the first woman to a cabinet post when he named Frances Perkins secretary of labor. She held this post from 1933 to 1945. All of the last three presidents prior to Donald Trump have appointed women to the most senior cabinet post—secretary of state. Bill Clinton named Madeleine Albright, George W. Bush picked Condoleezza Rice in his second term, and Barack Obama chose New York senator Hillary Clinton, his opponent in the Democratic primaries, to be secretary of state during his first term. Overall, however, women have been underrepresented in presidential appointments to federal offices.

President Ronald Reagan appointed the first woman to sit on the Supreme Court, Sandra Day O'Connor in 1981. President Bill Clinton appointed Ruth Bader Ginsburg, a former women's rights attorney, to the Court in 1993. President Obama selected Sonia Sotomayor in 2009—the first Hispanic justice on the Supreme Court—and Elena Kagan in 2010.

HISTORICAL THINKING

7. **IDENTIFY PROBLEMS AND SOLUTIONS** What do you think is the most pressing issue facing women in American politics today, and what can women do about it?

CRITICAL VIEWING *The Four Justices,* by Nelson Shanks, depicts the women who had served on the U.S. Supreme Court at the time the painting was completed in 2013. It depicts (standing, from left) Justice Sonia Sotomayor and Justice Elena Kagan, and (seated) Justice Sandra Day O'Connor, who retired in 2006, and Justice Ruth Bader Ginsburg. These four justices did not serve on the Court at the same time. Why do you think the artist portrays them as contemporaries?

AMERICAN GALLERY

Women in Politics

Alexandria Ocasio-Cortez Alexandria Ocasio-Cortez stormed onto the political scene in 2018 when she won a stunning Democratic primary victory over 20-year incumbent Joe Crowley in New York's 14th Congressional District, representing the Bronx and Queens. At the age of 29, Ocasio-Cortez became the youngest woman ever elected to Congress. A community organizer who has called for expanded health and education programs, Ocasio-Cortez is seen as the symbol of the most progressive elements of the Democratic Party. She was re-elected in 2020.

Kay Granger Kay Granger has represented Texas's 12th Congressional District in the U.S. House of Representatives for more than 20 years. The former mayor of Fort Worth and a staunch Republican, she has been recognized as one of the 25 most influential women in Congress. Granger serves as ranking member of the powerful House Appropriations Committee and is committed to a strong military as well as to supporting those who serve and their families.

Tammy Duckworth In 2010, before being elected to Congress, Tammy Duckworth was an assistant secretary in the Department of Veterans Affairs. She was born in Bangkok, Thailand, to a Thai mother and an American aid worker. She moved to the United States with her family at the age of 16. In 2004 she lost both her legs and won the Purple Heart medal while serving in the National Guard in Iraq. In 2012 she was elected to the House of Representatives, and in 2016 she was elected to the Senate by the state of Illinois.

Kamala Harris Then senator Kamala Harris questions nominees for executive branch positions in the intelligence community as part of her service on the Senate Intelligence Committee in 2017. Former California state attorney general Kamala Harris was elected to the U.S. Senate in 2016, when she became the first Indian American and second African-American woman to serve in the Senate. Known for her tough questioning and progressive politics, she was seen as a rising star of the Democratic Party when former vice president Joe Biden chose her as his running mate on the Democratic ticket in the 2020 election. Harris became the first female person of color to serve as vice president when the Biden-Harris ticket won the election in 2020.

Susan Collins Elected to the U.S. Senate from Maine in 1996, Susan Collins earned a reputation as a Republican moderate in more than 20 years of service to her state. She has been a leader in the Senate in issues related to homeland security and health care. Her willingness to vote outside her party occasionally in a sharply divided Senate has earned her visibility and a reputation as one of the most powerful women in Washington. Collins was re-elected in 2020. Here, she is shown answering questions from reporters following a Senate committee hearing on Russian election hacking in 2018.

NATIONAL GEOGRAPHIC

For These Girls, Danger Is a Way of Life

by Alexis Okeowo *National Geographic* **Magazine, January 2017**

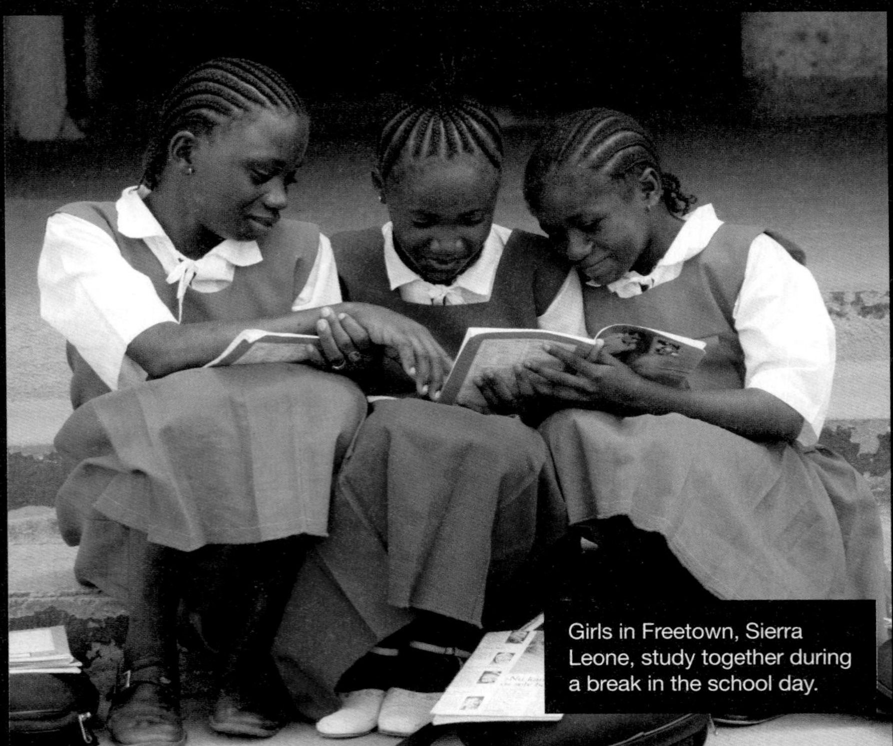

Girls in Freetown, Sierra Leone, study together during a break in the school day.

The United Nations and girls themselves see education as the best route for escaping sexual oppression and violence. During the Ebola crisis, the United Nations aid organization UNICEF sponsored schools for young girls. Though those centers were closed in 2016, the push for educational opportunity goes on. Okeowo tells the story of one young girl, Regina Mosetay, whose experience as a young mother returning to school speaks for others.

"I don't want my child to have the same experience that I had. I want a better future for her," Regina says. She lives with her boyfriend, who graduated with a business degree, and his mother and grandmother, who help care for [her daughter]. She hopes they can build a family together and knows that finishing her education is crucial. She wants to work for an organization that helps children, especially girls, have better lives. ... "When I'm educated, I'll be able to take care of my family; I will take care of myself," she says.

The struggle for equality is not limited to women in the United States. Around the world, women and girls must fight for educational opportunities and the right to make their own marital and reproductive choices. In "For These Girls, Danger Is a Way of Life," writer Alexis Okeowo looks at the struggle in one country, Sierra Leone. In that West African nation in 2013, more than 25 percent of girls ages 15 to 19 were pregnant or had children, one of the highest pregnancy rates in the world for that age group.

Sierra Leone bans pregnant girls from high school. As a result, pregnancy leads to less schooling and diminished work opportunities for females. In addition, some girls who become pregnant are shunned and kicked out by their own families, making them even more vulnerable. In addition, the country's history of civil war and an epidemic of the deadly virus Ebola contributed to the troubles girls and women face.

Access the full version of "For These Girls, Danger Is a Way of Life" by Alexis Okeowo through the Resources Menu in MindTap.

THINK ABOUT IT What obstacles facing pregnant girls in Sierra Leone are the result of laws, and which are the result of traditions? Which might be easier to change and why?

LESSON
6.4 Extending Civil Rights

In 1869, a great ceremony was held at Promontory Summit, Utah, where officials hammered the last spikes into a railroad track. The symbolic act completed the nation's first transcontinental railroad. Missing from official photographs of the event were any of the 12,000 or so Chinese immigrants who had built the rail line over difficult terrain from California to Utah. In 2014, 145 years after the ceremony, a group of Chinese Americans—some of them descendants of those intrepid workers—posed at the same spot, paying tribute to the unheralded builders.

The Struggle for Civil Rights for Hispanics

Inspired by the struggles of African Americans to claim their civil rights, other groups took up their own struggles. They used many of the same strategies African Americans had used. They employed techniques such as mass action, legal action, and awareness campaigns to advance their causes.

Hispanic people are those who have a Spanish or Spanish-speaking cultural ancestry. According to U.S. government terminology, Hispanic origin is not a race, and Hispanics can be of any race. While *Hispanic* is the official U.S. government term, some members of this group prefer *Latino* (for males) and *Latina* (for females). Most prefer to identify with the country of their ancestors and think of themselves as Mexican Americans, Honduran Americans, or Dominican Americans, for example.

As a group, however, Hispanics are the largest U.S. ethnic minority by far. Each year, the Latino population grows by more than 1 million people. By 2050 this group is expected to make up almost 30 percent of the U.S. population. Still, Latino immigration has declined since 2001, and while Latinos once made up more than half of all immigration to the United States, from 2012 to 2016 they were less than one-third of all immigrants.

The largest Hispanic group in the United States is Mexican Americans, who constitute 11.3 percent of the total U.S. population and 62.3 percent of Hispanics. Some 9.5 percent of all Hispanics are Puerto Ricans. The next three largest groups are Cuban Americans (3.9 percent), Salvadoran Americans (3.9 percent), and Dominican Americans (3.5 percent).

U.S. Minorities, 2000 and 2019

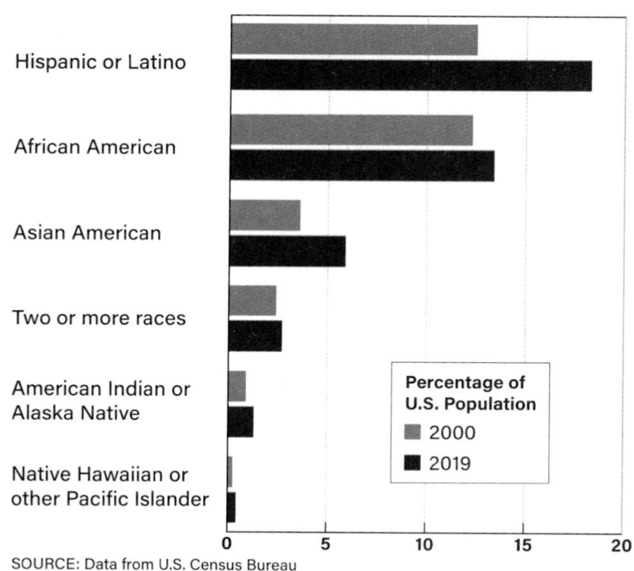

SOURCE: Data from U.S. Census Bureau

One lingering result of past discrimination can be low incomes and relatively high rates of poverty. Many Hispanic households are among the working poor, meaning that even though the adults in a household work full-time, the family income is below the official poverty line. Leaders of the Latino community tend to attribute low income levels to factors such as language problems, lack of job training, and continuing immigration.

FIGHTING DISCRIMINATION The history of discrimination against Latinos has involved segregation, denial of the right to vote, employment discrimination, violence, and public humiliation. After the United States won the Mexican-American War in 1848 and incorporated the huge area of land known as the Mexican Cession (present-day California,

Hispanic Origins, 2017

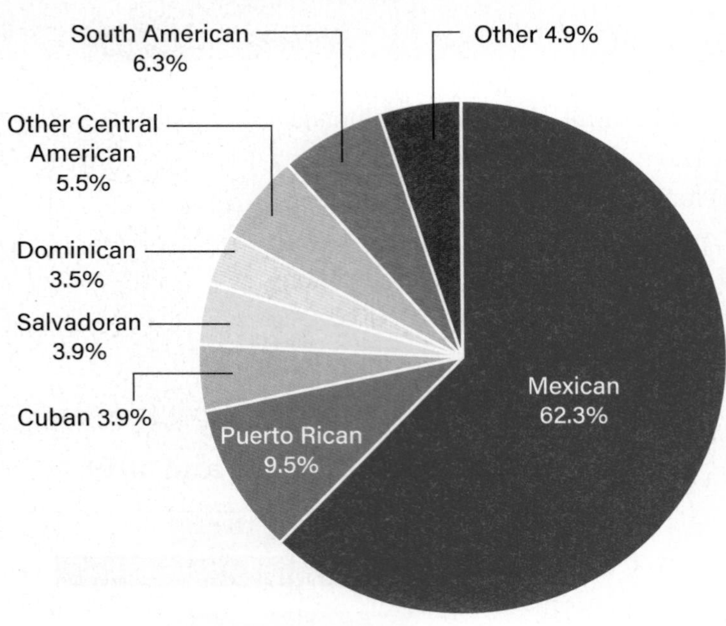

SOURCE: Data from U.S. Census Bureau

Nevada, Utah, and parts of Arizona, New Mexico, and Colorado), Mexican Americans were made full citizens, but many had their lands taken away. Within a short time, many Mexican Americans were living in poverty, had lost the right to vote, and were treated as foreigners in the land they had lived in for generations. Mexican-American children were placed in segregated schools, and public facilities, restaurants, and stores posted "No Mexicans" signs.

In 1929 a group of Mexican Americans in Texas formed a new group, the League of United Latin American Citizens (LULAC), to fight discrimination and improve Hispanics' economic conditions. While LULAC originated among Mexican Americans in Texas, it spread beyond Texas and embraced other Latino groups. In 1931 it began fighting segregated schools for Hispanics, an effort that gained success in California in the 1940s and in Texas in the 1950s. That same decade, LULAC lawyers filed a suit that resulted in the U.S. Supreme Court decision *Hernandez* v. *Texas* finding that Mexican Americans were wrongfully excluded from juries. The group also recruited and campaigned for Latino candidates for office.

In 1962 César Chávez and Dolores Huerta formed the National Farm Workers Association (NFWA), representing migrant farm workers, who were primarily Latinos. These workers commonly labored long hours, doing heavy physical work without access to toilets or running water. The NFWA's first major victory was winning federal Aid to Families with Dependent Children (AFDC) benefits and disability insurance for California farm workers. The group eventually became the United Farm Workers (UFW) union. When California farm owners refused to negotiate with the UFW, Chávez and Huerta organized a nationwide boycott of grapes and some other farm products. The boycott, which lasted five years, convinced the owners to recognize the union, and the union negotiated higher wages for the migrant workers.

Many Hispanic people lack the documents that allow them to legally live and work in the United States. Because undocumented immigrants may live in the United States undetected, some have been here for decades. Many have been working and paying taxes and participating in their communities as volunteers and neighbors. Some have become business owners who provide employment to others. They may have children who were born in the United States and are therefore citizens. When an undocumented parent is detained by authorities and deported, families may be split up or citizens forced into exile. Immigration reform has been and will continue to be an important issue for the Latino community.

HISPANICS IN AMERICAN POLITICS TODAY

Mexican Americans and Puerto Ricans have tended to support the Democratic Party, which has favored more government assistance and support programs for disadvantaged groups. Cuban Americans, in contrast, tend to identify with the Republican Party. Many Cubans fled to the United States during and after the communist revolution on that island. Their antipathy toward communism steered them to the more conservative Republicans. At the same time, U.S. tensions with communist Cuba meant that for many periods of time, most Cuban immigrants received preferential treatment in the form of a **green card**—a document that gave them permanent resident status that allows them to legally live and work in the United States—after just one year. Younger Cuban Americans are much more likely to vote for Democrats, but relations with Cuba continue to be a key political issue for these Hispanics.

Generally, Latinos have had a comparatively low level of political participation, in part because more than one-third of Latinos are too young to vote. In addition, more than a quarter can't vote because they aren't citizens. But voter turnout among Hispanics has been rising as more immigrants become naturalized or birthright citizens and as more Hispanics reach voting age. In the 2018 election, Latinos made up an estimated 11 percent of the electorate, which was the same as in 2016 but up from the presidential election years of 2012 (10 percent) and 2008 (9 percent). In four states, Latinos formed a significant bloc of eligible voters in 2018: 30 percent of voters in Texas, 23 percent in Arizona, 20 percent in Florida, and 19 percent in Nevada.

Latinos as a Share of State Population, 2018

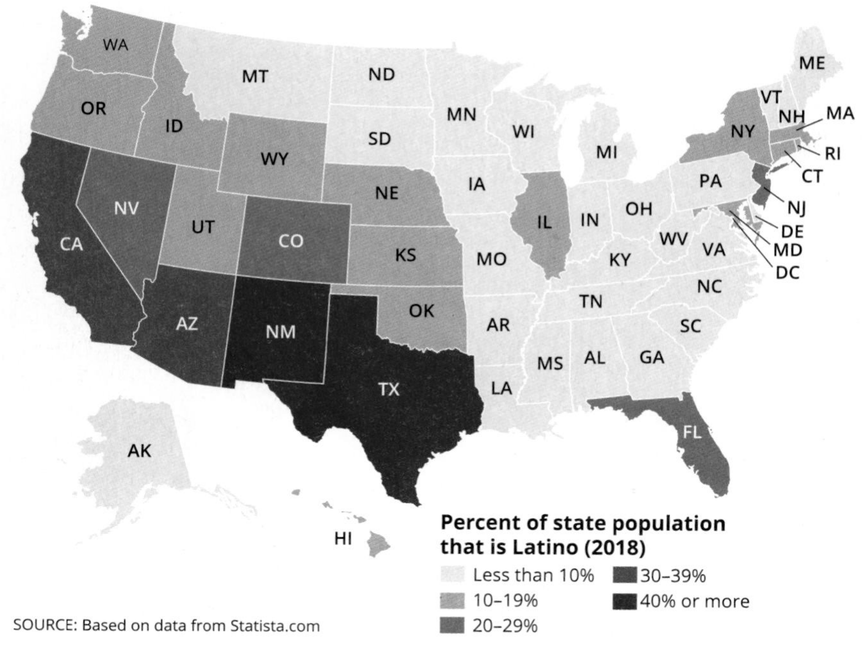

SOURCE: Based on data from Statista.com

Today, more than 5 percent of the state legislators in Arizona, California, Colorado, Florida, New Mexico, and Texas are Latinos. After the 2018 elections, Hispanic representation in Congress reached a record 42 members, with four in the Senate and the rest in the House. Cuban Americans have gained local political power, particularly in Miami-Dade County, Florida's most populous county. Two Cuban American senators—Ted Cruz of Texas and Marco Rubio of Florida—were candidates for the Republican nomination for president in 2016. In 2019, Julián Castro, former Secretary of Housing and Urban Development and former mayor of San Antonio, Texas, was among those who made it into the Democratic debates in his campaign for president.

HISTORICAL THINKING

1. **INTERPRET GRAPHS** Based on the graph of U.S. minority groups, which group grew the most between 2000 and 2019?
2. **MAKE GENERALIZATIONS** Viewing Hispanic Americans as an example, what advantages do you see of joining with others to work for changes in public policy?
3. **COMPARE AND CONTRAST** Identify similarities and differences between what you know about the experience of European immigrants in the early 1900s and the experience of Hispanic immigrants in the early 2000s.
4. **INTERPRET MAPS** Based on the map, which part of the country has the highest concentration of Hispanics?

Civil Rights of Asian Americans

About 20,000 Chinese immigrants came to the United States hoping to strike it rich after the discovery of gold in California in 1848. By 1870 Chinese Americans made up about a fifth of that state's workforce. Mostly single men, they did hard labor, building railroads, mining, and working in farms and factories for lower pay than men with families. As you have read, anti-Chinese prejudice resulted in pressure on Congress to pass the Chinese Exclusion Act of 1882, the first U.S. immigration law to ban an entire nationality from immigrating to the United States. After 1900, restrictions on Asian immigration expanded to include all Asian groups except Filipinos. First-generation Asian Americans were denied citizenship and the right to own land. All Asian Americans were subjected to prejudice and discrimination.

Decided: May 3, 1954, 9–0

Majority: Chief Justice Earl Warren wrote the unanimous opinion of the Court in favor of Pete Hernandez.

Pete Hernandez didn't dispute that he shot and killed a man. An all-White jury in Jackson County, Texas, convicted Hernandez of murder and sentenced him to life in prison. What Hernandez and his lawyer, Gus García, did dispute was the way the jury was selected. Hernandez appealed his case to the U.S. Supreme Court. He argued that he was denied equal protection of the laws as guaranteed by the 14th Amendment because the county carried out a systematic pattern of discrimination toward Mexican Americans in choosing juries. García pointed out that over 25 years not a single person with a Mexican- or Latin-American name had served on any jury in the county—a point that the state conceded. The state argued that this result was mere coincidence and that the 14th Amendment applied only to African Americans.

Gus García (left) and John Herrera (right), attorneys for Pete Hernandez (center), convinced the justices that the *Norris* rule should be extended to groups other than African Americans. The *Norris* rule, developed by the U.S. Supreme Court in 1935, was the determination that the absence of African Americans from juries was impermissible racial discrimination in jury selection.

In his decision, Chief Justice Earl Warren dismissed both state claims. "It taxes our credulity [ability to believe something]," he wrote, "to say that mere chance" resulted in the exclusion of Mexican Americans from juries for 25 years. In addition, he wrote, "The exclusion of otherwise eligible persons from jury service solely because of their ancestry or national origin is discrimination prohibited by the Fourteenth Amendment." The Court overturned the conviction as being unconstitutional, but in a new trial, with a jury that included Mexican Americans, Hernandez was again found guilty. The Supreme Court's decision regarding [illegible] numerous cases that allowed Mexican Americans to challenge discrimination in housing, employment, and voting rights.

THINK ABOUT IT Why do you think the Supreme Court agreed with Hernandez's view that it was important to include Mexican Americans on the jury

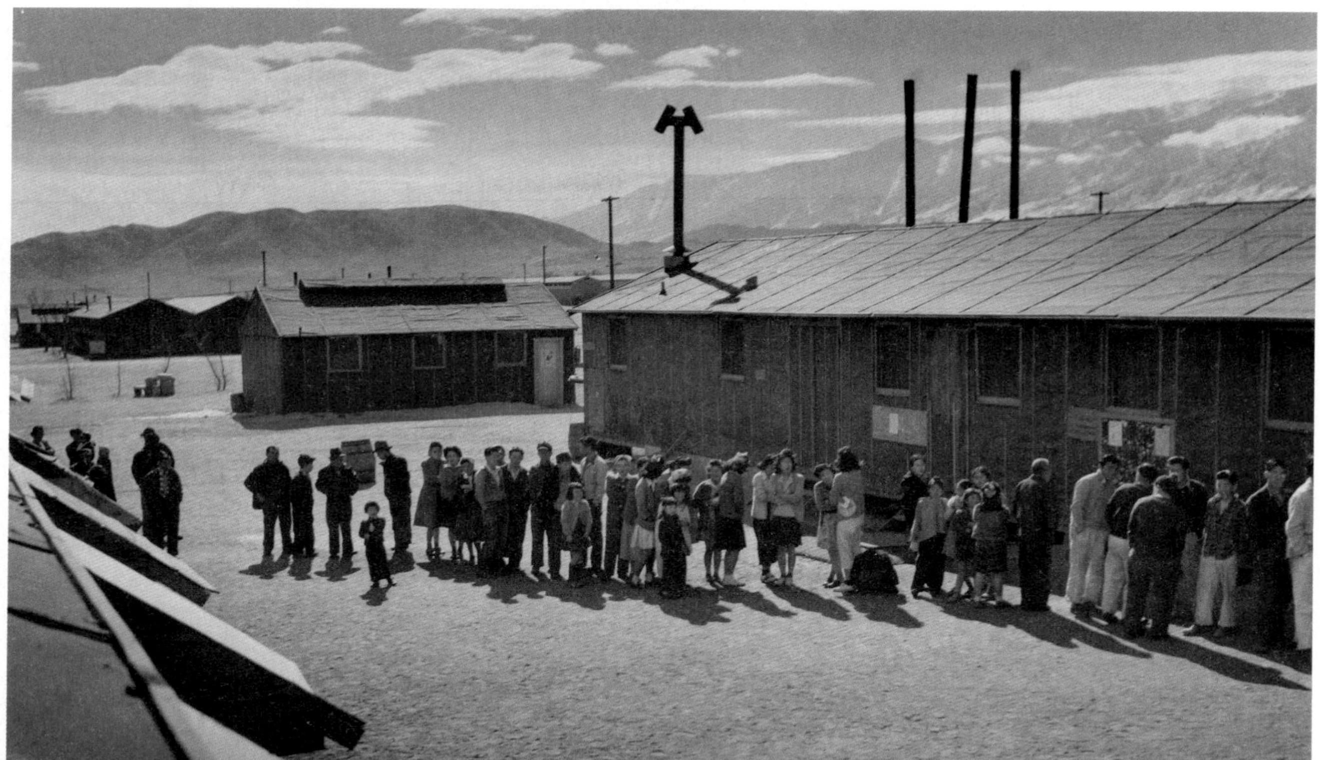

In 1943, photographer Ansel Adams created this image of internees at California's Manzanar Relocation Center waiting for lunch. Japanese Americans were held for up to three years at Manzanar and nine other camps with only the clothing and possessions they could carry. Eight people shared a 20-by-25-foot room with no furniture but beds.

JAPANESE INTERNMENT The Japanese bombing of the U.S. naval base at Pearl Harbor, Hawaii, in 1941, which provoked the entry of the United States into World War II, led to unabashed racism against Japanese Americans. Fear that they might be spies or traitors led President Franklin D. Roosevelt to issue Executive Order 9066, which allowed the military to exclude individuals from the West Coast. These fears were unfounded, as no Japanese Americans were found to have taken any action to support Japan at that point, and none did so during the course of the war. The executive order was applied only to Japanese Americans, as about 120,000 people—including many who were American citizens—lost their homes and businesses and were banished to internment camps, also called "relocation centers." Families lived in barracks in fenced areas patrolled by the military from 1942 until 1945, in most cases. In 1988 Congress provided $1.25 billion for approximately 80,000 people to partially **compensate**, or make amends for past ill treatment, former camp inhabitants for this unjust treatment.

The Supreme Court heard several cases that challenged the internment policy. In December 1944, the Court upheld the conviction of Fred Korematsu for refusing to cooperate with internment. On the same day, however, it ruled unanimously in favor of Mitsuye Endo, a young woman whom the Court found to be unquestionably loyal to the United States. The decision in the Endo case sent a signal to the executive branch, and in January 1945, the following month, the government began to release all interned Japanese Americans.

LIFTING THE BAN ON ASIAN IMMIGRATION The 1965 Immigration and Nationality Act lifted the long-standing ban on Asian immigration and allowed up to 20,000 immigrants per country, as was the case with other regions of the world. The law saw a burst of immigration from the region, and in recent years Asia has accounted for more than a third of annual immigration. About one million refugees from the war in Indochina, mostly from Vietnam, have come to the United States since the 1970s. India and China lead other countries as the main sources of immigrants today.

Sources of Asian Immigration, 2014

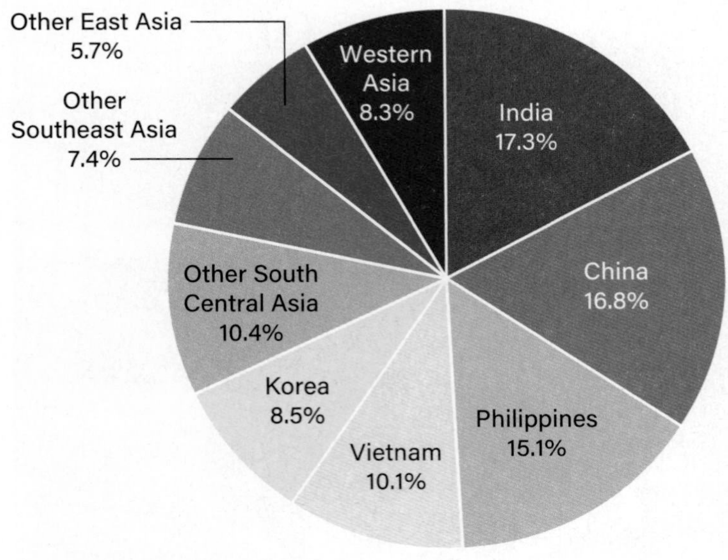

SOURCE: Data from Migration Policy Institute

Contenders for the 2020 Democratic nomination included three Asian Americans: Senator Kamala Harris of California, who became the vice-presidential nominee, entrepreneur Andrew Yang, and Representative Tulsi Gabbard of Hawaii. Today, Asian Americans lead other minority groups in median income and education. Just over half of Asian Americans over the age of 25 have college degrees. These stellar statistics have resulted in Asian Americans' being viewed as a "model minority," but there are great variations among different populations of Asian Americans, and many face challenges of poverty and discrimination.

HISTORICAL THINKING

5. **SEQUENCE** Briefly summarize the history of Asian immigration to the United States.
6. **FORM AND SUPPORT OPINIONS** Explain the reasoning for the assertion that the Japanese American internment program during World War II was unjust.
7. **INTERPRET GRAPHS** How is the data shown in the pie chart about Asian immigration similar to the data shown in the pie chart about Hispanic subgroups?

Native American Rights

We can't know exactly how many people lived in North America when Columbus arrived in 1492. Current estimates are anywhere from three million to eight million. What's clear, though, is that since the arrival of European explorers and settlers in the Americas, Native Americans have experienced one catastrophe after another. The greatest cause of death was diseases brought from Europe, to which North American peoples had no immunity. After a series of terrifying epidemics, the population of what are now the lower 48 states had dropped to perhaps 800,000 by 1600. When the Pilgrims arrived at Plymouth in 1620, they found a series of abandoned village sites.

In subsequent centuries, as the European American and African-American populations experienced explosive growth, the Native American population kept falling. It bottomed out in 1925 at about half a million. Today, the Native North American (including Alaska Natives) population has recovered to almost 3 million, or more than 5 million if we count those who are part Native American. These numbers do not tell the whole story, however.

EARLY POLICIES TOWARD NATIVE AMERICANS

The Northwest Ordinance, passed in 1787, stated that "the utmost good faith shall always be observed toward Native Americans; their lands and property shall never be taken from them without their consent." Over the next 100 years, these principles were violated far more often than they were observed—let alone remembered.

The Constitution gives Congress the power to "regulate Commerce with foreign Nations, . . . and with the Indian Tribes," essentially treating the native tribes as foreign nations. This power enabled the U.S. government to sign land and boundary treaties with them. But as members of foreign nations, Native Americans had no civil rights under U.S. laws. Even the 14th Amendment did not give Native Americans rights, as it applies to "All persons born or naturalized in the United States and subject to the jurisdiction thereof." Native Americans born on tribal lands weren't subject to the laws of the state or of

Korematsu v. *United States*, 1944

Decided: December 18, 1944, 6–3

Majority: Justice Hugo Black wrote the opinion of the Court in the decision in favor of the United States. Justice Felix Frankfurter wrote a concurring opinion.

Dissent: Justices Owen Roberts, Frank Murphy, and Robert H. Jackson filed dissenting opinions.

In 1998, President Bill Clinton honored Fred Korematsu for standing up to the United States government and challenging its illegal action. As of 2018, four states celebrate January 30 annually as Fred Korematsu Day of Civil Liberties and the Constitution, and several others have celebrated the day at least once.

Following an executive order by President Franklin Roosevelt in 1942, Japanese immigrants and Japanese Americans living in parts of California, Nevada, Oregon, and Washington, including those who immigrated to the United States and those who were born in the United States, were ordered to report to military facilities to face evacuation. Fred Korematsu, a U.S. citizen, was arrested for refusing to report. In court he argued that the order was not valid because there was no evidence Japanese Americans were disloyal or a threat, but he was convicted. His appeal made it to the Supreme Court.

Justice Hugo Black, in writing the decision, wrote a warning that "all legal restrictions which curtail the civil rights of a single racial group are immediately suspect [and] . . . courts must subject them to the most rigid scrutiny." He then ignored that caution, accepted the government's argument that Japanese Americans posed a danger, and denied Korematsu's appeal.

The three dissenting opinions strongly rejected the ruling. Justice Roberts declared flatly that "convicting a citizen as a punishment for not submitting to imprisonment in a concentration camp . . . solely because of his ancestry" violated Korematsu's constitutional rights. Justice Murphy denounced the evacuation order as "obvious racial discrimination" based on an "erroneous assumption of racial guilt." Justice Jackson said that the military order requiring Korematsu to report "has no place in law under the Constitution."

In 1983 Fred Korematsu's conviction was overturned. In 1998 President Bill Clinton awarded Korematsu the Medal of Freedom. *Korematsu* has long been viewed as a blot on the Supreme Court's record. In 2018 a Court majority, in ruling on another case, said "*Korematsu* was gravely wrong on the day it was decided and has been overruled in the court of history."

THINK ABOUT IT On what grounds could Korematsu's lawyers argue that Japanese Americans were "deprived of life, liberty, or property, without due process of law"?

the federal government. Instead, they were subject to the laws of their tribe or nation, so they didn't qualify for birthright citizenship. Over time Congress passed laws that conferred citizenship on some Native Americans, but not until it passed the Indian Citizenship Act of 1924 were all Native Americans granted citizenship. Still, Native Americans were not guaranteed the right to vote until the Voting Rights Act of 1965.

INDIAN REMOVAL AND ASSIMILATION Throughout the 1800s, the government policy toward Native Americans can be summed up as moving them out of areas White Americans wanted, fighting them if they resisted, and trying to make them adopt White culture. In 1830 Congress instructed the Bureau of Indian Affairs (BIA) to remove all tribes to reservations west of the Mississippi River in order to open up land east of the Mississippi for White settlement. The resettlement was a catastrophe for Native Americans in the eastern states. When tribes or bands refused removal—or left the reservation—the army fought them until it defeated them.

In the late 1800s, the U.S. government changed its policy. Instead of isolating Native Americans on reservations, the 1887 General Allotment Act adopted the goal of **assimilation**, or the absorption and integration of a minority group into the dominant society. Tribal lands were broken up into parcels and doled out to force people to ranch and farm like White Americans. The remaining acreage was sold to Whites, thus reducing the number of acres in reservation status from 140 million to about 47 million. Tribes that would not cooperate with this plan lost their reservations altogether.

The failure of this policy became evident in 1928, when a report into the living conditions of Native Americans shocked many in Congress. The Indian Reorganization Act of 1934 limited future land allotments and gave the tribes control of the lands that had been given to Whites. In addition, the tribes themselves were given more authority over their own affairs—a policy that continues to this day.

NATIVE AMERICANS TODAY Native Americans have the lowest employment rate of any racial or ethnic group in the United States, with unemployment soaring to 85 percent in some tribes. Job opportunities on tribal lands are limited because those lands have few resources that would allow economic development. Reservations were placed on land unsuited to farming, hunting, timber harvesting, and mining, far from population and transportation centers that could provide customers for businesses. Native Americans trail all other groups in high school graduation rates. Homes tend to be overcrowded, and a tenth of these homes lack access to clean water.

Since 1988 the Indian Gaming Regulatory Act has allowed Native Americans to run gambling operations on their reservations regardless of state laws prohibiting gambling. A few of these operations have been quite successful, creating the false idea that Indian tribes are wealthy. In reality, poverty and unemployment remain widespread on the reservations.

Native Americans have always found it difficult to obtain political power. In part, this is because the tribes are often small and scattered, diluting the influence that would come with greater unity. Decades without voting rights further suppressed political activity. Nonetheless, as of March 2020, a record four Native Americans—Tom Cole and Markwayne Mullin, both of Oklahoma, and Sharice Davids of Kansas and Deb Haaland of New Mexico—held seats in Congress.

Nonetheless, beginning in the 1960s, some Native Americans formed organizations to reclaim their heritage and to press their claims against the U.S. government, including for the return of their lands. For example, in 1973, supporters of the American Indian Movement took over Wounded Knee, South Dakota, where about 150 Sioux had been killed by the U.S. Army in 1890. Their goal was to protest government policies. More recently, the Standing Rock Sioux in North Dakota organized against the Dakota Access oil pipeline they believed would threaten the water supply of their reservation. President Barack Obama suspended work on the pipeline, but President Donald Trump reversed this action.

As more Americans became aware of the sufferings of Native Americans, pressure grew for Congress to bring change. In 1990 Congress passed the Native American Languages Act, which recognizes the important role of Native American languages in maintaining Native American culture and continuity. That same year, Congress passed the Native American Graves Protection and Repatriation Act (NAGPRA). NAGPRA also protects

The Standing Rock Sioux Nation occupies about 1 million acres between Pierre, South Dakota, and Bismarck, North Dakota, where several rivers merge into the Missouri River. In 2016, the tribe's efforts to prevent construction of an oil pipeline that would cross sacred burial grounds and threaten their water supply brought thousands of supporters to the reservation. A large sign directs people to different areas of the encampment they created.

Native American burial sites and gives native peoples control over objects of significance to their traditional culture, including human remains. The removal of their ancestors' remains from gravesites for display in museums has been insulting and painful to modern Native Americans. This legislation was the culmination of years of Native American activism aimed at getting researchers, museums, businesses, and governments to respect sacred sites and cultural artifacts.

Courts, too, have shown a greater willingness to recognize Native American treaty rights. For example, in 1985 the Supreme Court ruled that three tribes of Oneida could claim damages for the use of tribal land that had been unlawfully transferred in 1795. Other tribes have brought successful actions affirming old treaty rights to traditional hunting and fishing grounds. In addition, a 2020 Supreme Court decision, *McGirt v. Oklahoma*, found that lands in eastern Oklahoma that were reserved by treaty for the Muskogee (Creek) people retained a distinct political identity, at least for certain purposes. The State of Oklahoma had convicted Jimcy McGirt of crimes committed on those lands. On appeal, however, the U.S. Supreme Court overruled those convictions due to the state's lack of jurisdiction there, where treaties guaranteed Native Americans some degree of sovereignty.

HISTORICAL THINKING

8. **MAKE INFERENCES** Give examples of the issues that would have led Native Americans to push for the NAGPRA (Native American Graves Protection and Repatriation Act) legislation.
9. **PROBLEMS AND SOLUTIONS** How might living Native Americans be compensated for the harms done over the past 300 years to their ancestors and their traditional ways of life? Explain your opinion.

Rights of LGBTQ Persons

The broad movement in favor of sexual identity rights typically defends **LGBTQ persons**, that is, lesbians, gay men, bisexuals, transgender individuals, and queer or questioning individuals—persons whose sexuality is not easily categorized. In the past, most LGBTQ persons kept quiet about their sexual orientation because exposure might mean a loss of job opportunities as well as social ostracism, or rejection, and even physical harassment. Years ago, people could be arrested for having a romantic or sexual relationship with a person of the same sex.

THE STONEWALL RIOT In 1969, following a practice of raiding bars frequented by members of the LGBTQ community, police raided the Stonewall Inn in New York City. Instead of allowing themselves to be taken away and arrested, patrons responded by throwing beer cans and bottles at the police. The riot drew in

The Stonewall Inn, the site of the 1969 riots that launched the movement for LGBTQ rights, is still a business in New York's Greenwich Village. In 2016, the Stonewall National Monument was established by President Obama in this location as the first national monument focused on LGBTQ history.

others from the neighborhood, eventually including several thousand people. Six days of protests and demonstrations followed. By the end of the year, many LGBTQ persons throughout the United States had formed 50 organizations, including the Gay Activist Alliance and the Gay Liberation Front, to work for civil rights. The year after the Stonewall riot, the first Gay Pride March was held in New York City.

CHANGING ATTITUDES Today, the number of LGBTQ rights organizations in the United States has grown to several thousand. These groups have exerted significant political pressure on legislatures, the media, schools, and churches. As a result, 25 states and the District of Columbia have laws prohibiting discrimination in employment and housing based on sexual orientation, and 24 states plus the District of Columbia ban discrimination in public accommodations. About 250 cities and counties also have anti-discrimination laws. Social attitudes toward LGBTQ individuals have changed greatly since the 1960s. Since the first Pride March was held in New York City in 1970, pride events have been held throughout the country, and Pete Buttigieg, the former mayor of South Bend, Indiana, attracted significant support in his campaign for the 2020 Democratic presidential nomination.

In 2000, Vermont became the first state to allow same-sex domestic partnerships. A domestic partnership isn't a marriage, but it gave legal standing to same-sex couples and provided many of the benefits of marriage. Massachusetts became the first state to recognize same-sex marriage in 2003. In 2011, polling organizations reported that, for the first time, more than half of those questioned supported same-sex marriage. By 2015 same-sex marriage was legal in all but 13 midwestern and southern states.

Advocates for LGBTQ rights in those states argued that, while the right to legalize a domestic partnership was desirable, it was inadequate, because it didn't provide the full rights conferred by marriage. That point helped convince the Supreme Court to rule in *Obergefell* v. *Hodges* (2015) that the Constitution guarantees a right to same-sex marriage in every state.

For well over 200 years, LGBTQ persons were officially prohibited from serving in the armed forces. President Clinton wanted to end that prohibition, but he faced too much resistance from military and congressional leaders. In 1993 Clinton signed into law the "don't ask, don't tell" policy. This policy—while not making it legal for gays and lesbians to serve—prohibited commanding officers from questioning service members about their sexuality. In December 2010 Congress repealed the policy that banned their service. As a result, gay men and lesbians may now serve openly in the nation's armed forces. In 2016 the right to serve openly was extended to transgender individuals. That policy was opposed by President Trump, though his attempt to change the policy was challenged in federal courts.

A **transgender person** is someone who feels his or her sex or gender does not match his or her body—that is, a person with a male body feels she really is or should be a female, or a person with a female body feels he really is or should be a male. Many transgender persons undergo hormone therapy, which alters their secondary sex characteristics to reflect their gender identity. Some undergo sex or gender reassignment surgery (SRS). The term for a transgender person who has had or is undergoing SRS is **transsexual**. The full process requires several years and costs from $40,000 to $75,000, so not all transgender persons wish to undergo such invasive surgery. In 46 states, birth certificates can be altered to change a person's recorded sex, but in 28 states, such a change is possible only after SRS. In the wake of the gay and lesbian rights movement, transgender individuals also have come forward and demanded equal rights, but transgender people continue to face discrimination and even violence.

Some cultural conservatives have pushed back. A key tactic for repressing transgender persons, as exemplified by the state of North Carolina, has been to ban them from using public restrooms that do not accord with the sex listed on their birth certificates. North Carolina came under heavy criticism and was hit with boycotts for its bathroom law. The Obama administration announced that such bans in public schools would threaten federal funding, but the Trump administration reversed this policy. North Carolina later repealed the bathroom ban, but it retained other rules that many people perceive as discriminatory.

HISTORICAL THINKING

10. **ANALYZE CAUSE AND EFFECT** What was the outcome of the Supreme Court's ruling in *Obergefell* v. *Hodges*?

11. **MAKE PREDICTIONS** Given the changes in public attitudes toward same-sex marriage, do you think the social and legal situation for transgender people will improve or stay the same? Explain your answer.

Rights of Persons with Disabilities

Discrimination based on disability crosses the boundaries of race, ethnicity, gender, sexual orientation, and religion. Persons with a **disability**, a temporary or permanent condition that limits physical or mental abilities, face many forms of social bias. Attitudes toward persons with disabilities have changed considerably, but disabled people still face discrimination.

Persons with disabilities first became a political force in the 1970s, and in 1973 Congress passed the initial legislation protecting this group—the Rehabilitation Act. This act prohibited discrimination against persons with disabilities in programs receiving federal aid. The Individuals with Disabilities Education Act (IDEA) requires public schools to provide children who have disabilities with free, appropriate, and individualized education in the least restrictive environment appropriate to their needs. The Americans with Disabilities Act (ADA) of 1990, however, is by far the

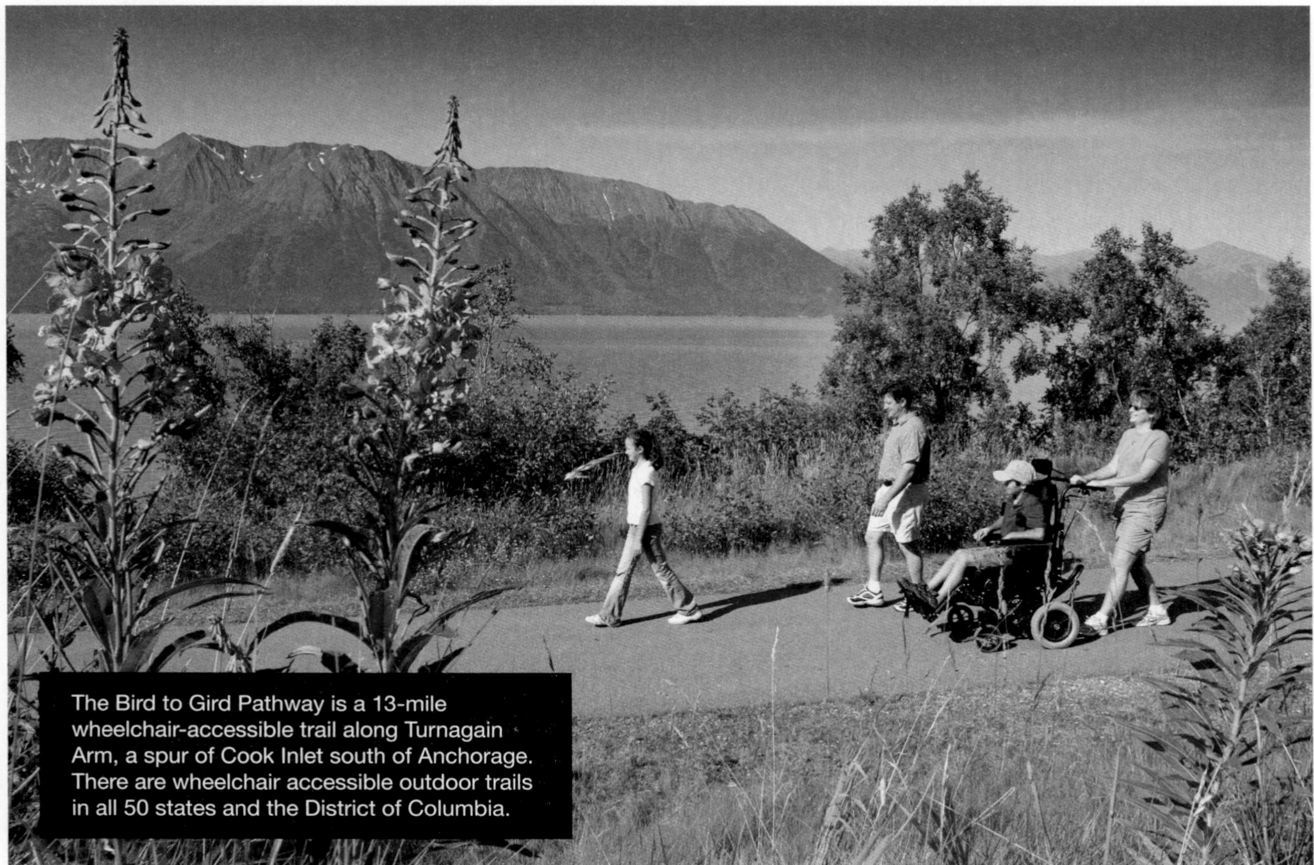

The Bird to Gird Pathway is a 13-mile wheelchair-accessible trail along Turnagain Arm, a spur of Cook Inlet south of Anchorage. There are wheelchair accessible outdoor trails in all 50 states and the District of Columbia.

most significant legislation protecting the rights of this group of Americans.

The ADA requires that all public buildings and public services be accessible to persons with disabilities. The act also mandates that employers make "reasonable accommodations" to meet the needs of workers and job applicants who are otherwise qualified for particular jobs unless doing so would cause the employer an "undue hardship." The ADA does not require employers to hire or retain workers who, because of their disabilities, pose a "direct threat to the health or safety" of their coworkers.

The ADA defines persons with disabilities as persons who have physical or mental impairments that "substantially limit" their everyday activities. Health conditions that have been considered disabilities under federal law include blindness, a history of alcoholism, heart disease, cancer, muscular dystrophy, cerebral palsy, paraplegia (partial or complete paralysis of the legs), diabetes, and acquired immune deficiency syndrome (AIDS).

From 1999 to 2002, the Supreme Court handed down a series of rulings that substantially limited the scope of the ADA. The Court found that any limitation that could be remedied by medication or by corrective devices, such as eyeglasses, did not qualify as a protected disability. According to the Court, even carpal tunnel syndrome was not a disability. In 2008, however, the ADA Amendments Act overturned most of these limits. Carpal tunnel syndrome and other ailments—though not the need for eyeglasses—could again qualify as disabilities.

HISTORICAL THINKING

12. **ANALYZE CAUSE AND EFFECT** What does the ADA require of employers?
13. **EVALUATE** How would the ADA affect the work of architects and contractors designing a public library?

LESSON
6.5 Beyond Equal Protection—Affirmative Action

Years of discrimination had resulted in underfunded schools for many students, particularly members of minority groups. Children whose parents made less money received fewer extracurricular lessons in music or art. They might need to spend their summers working for minimum wage rather than studying a foreign language. The federal government looked for other ways to equalize opportunities, especially for those who had had fewer opportunities in the past.

Affirmative Action

After the Civil Rights Act of 1964 prohibited discrimination in employment, the federal government began to legislate programs promoting equal employment opportunity. Because minorities often had fewer opportunities to obtain education and relevant work experience than did Whites, they were still excluded from many jobs. Even though discriminatory practices had been made illegal, the law did not make up for the results of years of discrimination.

Consequently, under President Lyndon B. Johnson, a new policy was developed. Called **affirmative action**, this policy required employers and educational institutions to take positive steps to

Leaders of the country's major civil rights organizations—(left to right) Roy Wilkins of the NAACP, James Farmer of CORE, Martin Luther King, Jr., of the SCLC, and Whitney Young of the National Urban League—met at the White House with President Lyndon Johnson on January 28, 1964.

Regents of the University of California v. *Bakke*, 1977

Decided: June 28, 1978, 8–1

Majority: Four decisions came out of this case. Justice Lewis Powell wrote the majority opinion of the Court for all four decisions, but Powell was the only justice who supported all four decisions. Each decision had a majority, but every other justice dissented from at least one of the four decisions.

Dissent: Justices William Brennan, Byron White, Thurgood Marshall, and Harry Blackmun filed an opinion in partial concurrence and partial dissent. Justices White, Marshall, and Blackmun also filed separate opinions. Justice John Paul Stevens filed an opinion in partial concurrence and partial dissent on which Chief Justice Warren Burger and justices William Rehnquist and Potter Stewart joined.

Allan Bakke attracted attention on his first day of medical school at the University of California, Davis, in the fall of 1978. Bakke's successful lawsuit was the first challenge that resulted in the need for organizations to refine affirmative action policies.

The University of California, Davis, medical school had two separate admissions programs—the open program, with 84 admissions spots, and the special program for minority applicants who were economically or educationally disadvantaged, with 16 spots. Allan Bakke, a White male, was rejected for the open seats. He filed a lawsuit claiming that he was excluded from the special admissions program solely on account of his race, in violation of the equal protection clause of the 14th Amendment.

On appeal, the U.S. Supreme Court ruled that the Constitution and the Civil Rights Act of 1964 do allow race to be used as a factor in making admissions decisions, but race cannot be the sole factor. Because access to the special admissions program was based solely on race, it was unconstitutional.

There were two parts to the Court's ruling.

- Justice Powell, along with justices Brennan, White, Marshall, and Blackmun, concluded that the medical school's quota system failed the strict scrutiny test and so violated the equal protection clause. Chief Justice Burger and justices Stevens, Stewart, and Rehnquist disagreed.
- Justice Powell, along with justices Burger, Stevens, Stewart, and Rehnquist, concluded that Bakke was rejected because of his race, in violation of Title VI of the Civil Rights Act of 1964, and must be admitted to the medical school. Justices Brennan, White, Marshall, and Blackmun disagreed.

So, Justice Powell was the only one who agreed with the entire decision.

Bakke entered the medical school that same year. He graduated in 1982 and became an anesthesiologist.

THINK ABOUT IT What does the fact that the decision was a divided one and that so many different opinions were written say about the issue of affirmative action?

remedy past discrimination. Affirmative action programs gave special consideration, in jobs and college admissions, to members of groups discriminated against in the past.

Following this policy, the University of California, Davis, medical school reserved 16 of its 100 admission slots for designated minority groups. Under these rules, a would-be medical student named Allan Bakke was ineligible for affirmative action admission because he was White. Bakke believed he was entitled to be admitted because his test scores were higher than those of many of the 16 students admitted under the affirmative action program. He sued the university, claiming that he was a victim of reverse discrimination—discrimination against Whites. In 1978, in *Regents of the University of California* v. *Bakke*, the Supreme Court decided that both the Constitution and the Civil Rights Act of 1964 allow race to be used as a factor in making admissions decisions but that race cannot be the sole factor. Because eligibility for the 16 special slots was based solely on race, it was unconstitutional.

In 1995 the Supreme Court issued a landmark decision on affirmative action in *Adarand Constructors* v. *Peña.* The Court held that any federal, state, or local affirmative action program that uses racial classifications as the basis for making decisions is subject to strict scrutiny by the courts. As discussed earlier in this chapter, this means that, to be constitutional, a law or action must be narrowly tailored to meet a compelling government interest.

The *Adarand* decision curtailed the scope of permissible affirmative action programs. Since *Adarand*, affirmative action programs can't make use of a **quota**—a fixed number or proportion—or preferences and can't be maintained simply to remedy past discrimination by society in general. They must be narrowly tailored to remedy specific, identifiable acts or patterns of discrimination. Further, once a program has succeeded in remedying that pattern of discrimination, it must be changed or dropped.

THE DIVERSITY ISSUE Following the *Adarand* decision, several lower courts heard cases concerning the constitutionality of affirmative action programs designed to achieve diversity on college campuses. In a 1996 case, *Hopwood* v. *State of Texas*, a federal appellate court challenged the Bakke decision by stating that any use of race in college admissions, even when diversity was a goal, violated the 14th Amendment. While this decision was appealed, the Supreme Court chose not to review it, leaving the lower court's decision to stand. But that decision applied only to Texas, Louisiana, and Mississippi—the area served by the Fifth Circuit Court, where the decision had been made.

In 2003 the United States Supreme Court reviewed two cases involving issues similar to those in the *Hopwood* case. Both cases involved admissions programs at the University of Michigan. In the two decisions, the Court tried to clarify when race could and couldn't be a factor in admissions.

In the first, *Gratz* v. *Bollinger,* two White applicants who were denied undergraduate admission to the university alleged reverse discrimination. The university's policy gave each applicant a score based on grade point average, standardized test scores, and personal achievements. The system automatically awarded every applicant from an underrepresented minority (African American, Hispanic, and Native American) one-fifth of the points needed to guarantee admission. The Court held that this policy violated the equal protection clause.

In contrast, in *Grutter* v. *Bollinger,* the Court held that the University of Michigan Law School's admissions policy did pass constitutional muster. The significant difference between the two admissions policies, in the Court's view, was that the law school's approach did not apply a mechanical formula giving points based on race or ethnicity. In short, the Court concluded that diversity on college campuses was a legitimate goal and that limited affirmative action programs could be used to attain this goal.

THE SUPREME COURT REVISITS THE ISSUE In 2007, another case involving affirmative action came before the Supreme Court. The case concerned the policies of two school districts—one in Louisville, Kentucky, and one in Seattle, Washington. Both school systems had policies aimed to achieve a more diversified student body within schools by giving preference to minority students if space was limited and a choice had to be made among applicants.

Decided: June 23, 2003, 5–4

Majority: Justice Sandra Day O'Connor wrote the opinion of the Court in favor of Bollinger and the University of Michigan Law School. Justice Ruth Bader Ginsburg wrote a concurring opinion that Justice Stephen Breyer joined.

Dissent: Justices Antonin Scalia and Clarence Thomas filed opinions in partial concurrence and partial dissent. Chief Justice William Rehnquist and Justice Anthony Kennedy filed dissenting opinions.

Barbara Grutter (left) met reporters outside the Supreme Court building following the oral arguments of her case in 2003. In a related case argued the same day, Jennifer Gratz (center) sued the University of Michigan for admission as an undergraduate, also on the grounds that the university's affirmative action admissions practices violated equal protection.

After *Regents of California v. Bakke*, the University of Michigan Law School—like many schools across the country—developed its admissions policy to accord with that ruling. It tried to achieve diversity through "a flexible assessment of [applicants'] talents, experiences, and potential," using not only grades and scores but also the enthusiasm expressed by those who wrote letters of recommendation, undergraduate course selection, and other factors. The policy relied on many factors while aiming for sufficient diversity to encourage "underrepresented minority students to participate in the classroom and not feel isolated."

Barbara Grutter, a White female, sued after being denied admission. Her petition alleged that the law school used race as a "predominant" factor and that there was no compelling interest to justify that choice.

Writing for the majority, Justice O'Connor applied the strict scrutiny test and held the following:

- The law school had "a compelling interest in obtaining the educational benefits that flow from a
- The law school's use of race as a factor in admissions decisions is narrowly tailored to further that interest.

Therefore, the Court held that the law school's affirmative action plan may stand and rejected Grutter's appeal. In dissent, Chief Justice Rehnquist, joined by justices Scalia, Kennedy, and Thomas, stated that the law school's failure to clearly explain its admissions policy plus its lack of a time limit for using the program were just a cover for "a naked effort to achieve racial balancing."

THINK ABOUT IT What do you think the Court means in citing "the educational benefits that flow from

Parents of White children who were turned away from schools because of these policies sued the school districts, claiming the policies violated the equal protection clause. The Supreme Court held in favor of the parents. The Court's decision did not overrule the 2003 *Grutter* case, however.

The Court's most recent ruling on affirmative action came in 2016 in *Fisher* v. *University of Texas*. In that decision, the Court found that diversity was a legitimate goal and that the university's policy of considering race as one factor among many in the admissions process could stand. The policy was acceptable because it was "narrowly tailored" to reach that goal—thus meeting the strict scrutiny standard. Still, challenges to affirmative action in higher education continue. In October of 2019, a federal judge ruled in favor of Harvard University in a case in which the university was charged with bias against Asian Americans in its efforts to achieve diversity through its admissions process. As of mid-2020, the case was being appealed.

HISTORICAL THINKING

1. **SYNTHESIZE** How does the idea that civil rights are rights of individuals help explain the Supreme Court rulings that racial or ethnic group preferences cannot be used to remedy past societal discrimination?
2. **IDENTIFY PROBLEMS AND SOLUTIONS** Given that reverse discrimination is illegal, what might be done to remedy the ongoing effects of past discrimination?

State Actions

Beginning in the mid-1990s, some states have taken actions to ban affirmative action programs or replace them with alternative policies. In 1996, by a ballot initiative, California amended its state constitution to prohibit any "preferential treatment to any individual or group on the basis of race, sex, color, ethnicity, or national origin in the operation of public employment, public education, or public contracting." Seven other states have also ended affirmative action.

In 2006 a ballot initiative in Michigan banned affirmative action in that state just three years after the *Gratz* and *Grutter* Supreme Court decisions. In 2012 a federal appeals court overturned the voter-approved ban. In 2014, however, the Supreme Court reversed the appeals court ruling, arguing that state voters had the right to eliminate affirmative action programs. This decision gave support to bans on affirmative action in other states.

In the meantime, many public universities have tried to find race-blind ways to attract and admit more minority students to their campuses. For example, in Texas the top students at every high school in the state are guaranteed admission to the University of Texas, Austin. Originally, the guarantee applied to students who were in the top 10 percent of their graduating class. Today the percentage varies from year to year. Beginning in 2005, the university reinstated an affirmative action plan, but it was limited to students who were not admitted as part of the top-student guarantee.

The guarantee ensures that the top students at minority-dominated inner-city schools can attend the state's leading public university. It also assures admission to the best White students from rural, often poor, communities. Previously, many of these students could not have hoped to attend the University of Texas. This policy may have a negative impact on students with high test scores but who are not the top students in their wealthier school districts.

HISTORICAL THINKING

3. **MAKE INFERENCES** Why might voters choose to eliminate affirmative action?
4. **EVALUATE** Do you think the University of Texas admissions program for the top 10 percent of high school graduates has a valid purpose and constitutes a reasonable means to achieve that purpose? Why or why not?

CHAPTER 6

CITIZENSHIP AND CIVIL RIGHTS

Review

VOCABULARY

For each pair of vocabulary words, write one sentence that explains the connection between the words.

1. citizenship; freedmen
2. undocumented immigrant; green card
3. feminism; glass ceiling
4. abolition; civil rights
5. Jim Crow laws; separate-but-equal doctrine
6. LGBTQ person; transgender person
7. Reconstruction; civil rights movement
8. affirmative action; quota

MAIN IDEAS

9. Who gains citizenship under the 14th Amendment? **LESSON 6.1**
10. Why is the idea of amnesty for undocumented immigrants controversial? **LESSON 6.1**
11. What is the strict scrutiny standard, and how is it used? **LESSON 6.2**
12. Why did White supremacists in the South in the late 19th century invent statutes like the grandfather clause? **LESSON 6.2**
13. When and why did the Supreme Court declare segregation in public schools illegal? **LESSON 6.2**
14. What forms of discrimination do women still face? **LESSON 6.3**
15. What are the legal protections against sexual harassment in the workplace? **LESSON 6.3**
16. How have policies toward Native Americans changed since 1900? **LESSON 6.4**
17. What rights does the ADA protect? **LESSON 6.4**
18. What was the purpose of affirmative action? **LESSON 6.5**

HISTORICAL THINKING

19. **SYNTHESIZE** Explain the significance of the 14th Amendment.
20. **EVALUATE** What do you think was the most important outcome of the civil rights movement? Explain.
21. **DETERMINE CHRONOLOGY** Place these events in the proper sequence: *Plessy* v. *Ferguson* decision, *Brown* v. *Board of Education* decision, Civil Rights Act, 14th Amendment, Civil War, *Bakke* decision.
22. **ANALYZE CAUSE AND EFFECT** How would you measure the wage gap?
23. **ANALYZE GRAPHS** Using the data in the circle graphs about the makeup of the Hispanic and Asian American communities, what can you conclude about the usefulness of the labels *Hispanic* and *Asian American*?
24. **COMPARE AND CONTRAST** Contrast the affirmative action programs evaluated in the *Bakke* and *Grutter* cases, and explain why one was rejected and the other was allowed to stand.

INTERPRET VISUALS

Study the photograph. Then answer the questions.

25. How would you characterize the postures and expressions of the people shown in this photograph? Suggest text for a thought bubble that might appear over one person's head in this image.
26. Based on what you have read, what episode in the fight for civil rights does this photograph represent?

ANALYZE SOURCES

On June 11, 1963, President John F. Kennedy made a speech to the entire nation over radio and television. He was responding to violence on the campus of

the University of Alabama following attempts to desegregate that campus. He reminded Americans of the founding principle of equality and discussed the effects of discrimination on international relations, pointing out that the United States cannot claim to stand for freedom while promoting inequality at home.

> We face . . . a moral crisis as a country and as a people. It cannot be met by repressive police action. It cannot be left to increased demonstrations in the streets. It cannot be quieted by token moves or talk. It is a time to act in the Congress, in your State and local legislative body and, above all, in all of our daily lives.
>
> —President John F. Kennedy, civil rights speech, June 11, 1963

27. What is the "moral crisis" that President Kennedy was talking about?

28. Why do you think he made the speech to the entire nation rather than to Congress or a small group within his party?

CONNECT TO YOUR LIFE

29. **EXPOSITORY** Think about one of the groups of people described in this chapter. Write a paragraph about the forms of discrimination a person from that group would likely have experienced in the United States at the end of the 19th century. Write a second paragraph to explain how the law has or has not changed to prohibit such discrimination and describe the actions and court cases that led to these changes.

TIPS

- Think about the discussions in the chapter of groups who have been denied civil rights.
- Describe the effects of being discriminated against and having one's civil rights denied.
- Describe the ways that people pushed for changes.
- Describe the impact of relevant legislation as well as judicial decisions since 1900.
- Use two or three key vocabulary terms from the chapter in your writing.

UNIT 4

The Legislative Branch

UNIT 4 OVERVIEW

Chapter 7 The Structure of Congress

Chapter 8 The Powers of Congress

Chapter 9 The Legislative Process

CRITICAL VIEWING The United States Capitol building in Washington, D.C., is home to the Senate and the House of Representatives. In this photo, the House chamber and offices are on the left, and the Senate chamber and offices are on the right. What makes this building stand out architecturally?

"Legislators represent people, not trees or acres."

—Chief Justice Earl Warren, *Reynolds* v. *Sims,* (1964)

CHAPTER 7

The Structure of Congress

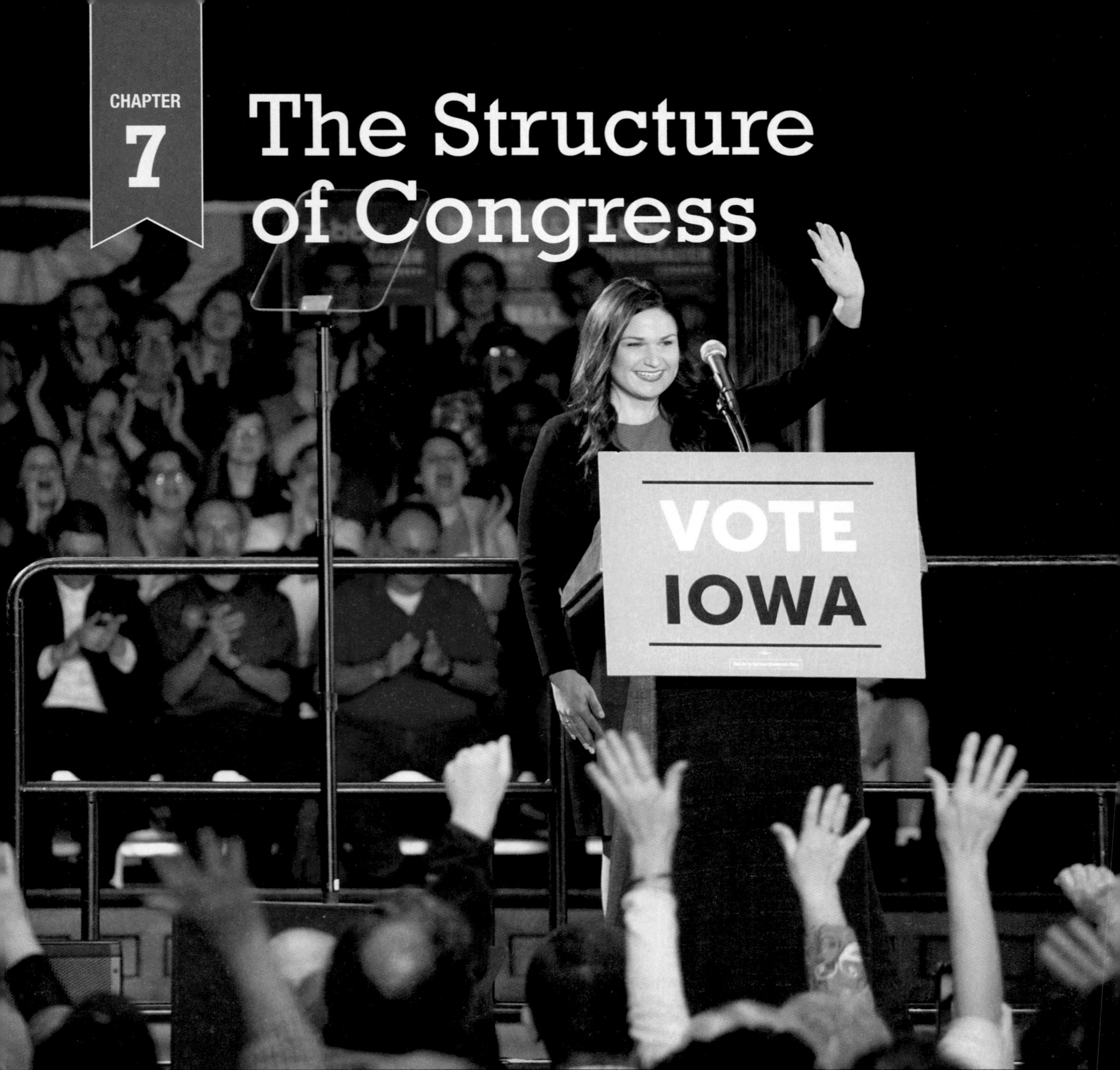

VOTE IOWA

LESSONS

7.1 A Bicameral Legislature

7.2 The House of Representatives

National Geographic Online:
Deb Haaland: "Why Not Me? Why Not Now?"

7.3 The Senate

7.4 Congressional Leadership and Committees

7.5 Congressional Elections

CRITICAL VIEWING Members of both houses of Congress are elected, and to win election, they must spend much of their time campaigning. Political campaigns can be exhausting. Why might a campaign rally help energize a candidate?

LESSON 7.1

A Bicameral Legislature

Congress is capable of exerting great power over the lives of Americans. For example, starting as early as the Civil War, Congress passed laws requiring young men to leave their homes for the battlefield. After World War II, all males age 18 to 26 had to sign up with their local draft board. During the 1960s, opponents of the Vietnam War pointed out that men between the ages of 18 and 20 could be sent to war. Yet they had no say in their government because the voting age at the time was 21. Chants such as "Old enough to fight, old enough to vote" led Congress to respond with the 26th Amendment, which lowered the voting age to 18, in 1971.

Two Houses of Congress

The Framers had a strong mistrust of powerful executive authority. They associated that authority with monarchs like King George, so they made Congress—not the executive branch, which is headed by the president—the central institution of American government. But while they agreed that the legislature should be, in James Madison's words, the "first branch of the government," they didn't immediately agree on how it should be organized. As you have read, after much wrangling between the larger states and the smaller states, the Great Compromise led to the creation of a bicameral legislature in which the two chambers, the House of Representatives and the Senate, would balance each other's power. The House was thought to represent the people, and membership in it would be apportioned, or distributed, on the basis of population. The Senate was meant to represent the states, and every state would have an equal number of senators.

The Framers laid out this bicameral structure in the very first section after the Preamble. Article I, Section 1, states: "All legislative Powers herein granted shall be vested in a Congress of the United States, which shall consist of a Senate and House of Representatives." The rest of Article I explains how the two chambers are to be organized.

New members of the 116th Congress (2019–2020) included Representative Deb Haaland (D-NM), one of the first Native American women to serve in Congress. On January 3, 2019, surrounded by family members, Haaland (center, right) took part in a ceremonial swearing-in administered by Speaker of the House Nancy Pelosi (center, left).

Article I also describes how members are to be elected, the length of their terms, the rules concerning how the Senate and the House are to operate, and the specific powers of Congress.

TERMS OF OFFICE Earlier, you read that the members of the House of Representatives serve two-year terms, and senators serve six-year terms. This means that House members are up for election every two years. Senate elections are staggered—only a third of the senators face election every two years.

Congressional elections are held in November of even-numbered years. The following January, a "new" Congress convenes. Actually, very few of the legislators are new to their office. Two-thirds of the senators didn't have to face re-election, and most current officeholders in both houses win re-election. Historically, 85 to 98 percent of the House is re-elected every two years. The 22nd Amendment states that the president can serve for no more than two four-year terms in office. But there is no limit on the number of terms a senator or representative can serve. For example, Robert Byrd (D-WV) served more than 52 years in the Senate, from 1959 until he died in 2010 at age 92.

Some Americans favor term limits for members of Congress, arguing that new members bring energy and fresh ideas. Opponents contend that Congress needs the judgment and experience that longer-serving members provide. The Supreme Court has ruled that state-level attempts to impose term limits on members of the U.S. House or Senate are unconstitutional. The process would likely call for a constitutional amendment, and several proposals have been made in recent years. In 2018, for example, a group of House members proposed an amendment that would limit representatives to six two-year terms and senators to two six-year terms.

TERMS AND SESSIONS OF CONGRESS The word *terms* applies not only to elected officials but also to Congress itself. A congressional **term**—the period of time during which a Congress that results from the most recent election meets—is two years long. Each term of Congress has been numbered consecutively, dating back to 1789. The Congress that convened in 2021 was the 117th.

A **session** is the period of time within a congressional term during which Congress meets. Most terms have two sessions, but it wasn't uncommon historically to have three. The first session of Congress lasted more than six months, running from March 4 to September 29, 1789. Until about 1940, Congress usually remained in session for six or seven months, unless the nation's business required members to stay in session longer. For example, the first session of the 77th Congress started on January 3, 1941, but it didn't adjourn until January 2, 1942. World War II was ongoing. Congress faced many crises that required decisions.

In recent years, the volume and complexity of legislation and the public's increased demand for services have required Congress to remain in session through most of each year. Both chambers schedule short recesses, or breaks, for holidays and vacations. The president may call a special session of Congress to deal with an emergency issue during a recess or after a regular session has ended. But because Congress now meets on nearly a year-round basis, such sessions are rare.

HISTORICAL THINKING

1. **MAKE CONNECTIONS** Why might the Framers, after agreeing to the Great Compromise, have thought of the House of Representatives as representing the people, and the Senate as representing the states?
2. **FORM AND SUPPORT OPINIONS** Do you think the argument favoring term limits for members of Congress makes sense? Why or why not?

Different Views of Representation

Of the three branches of government, the legislative branch has the closest ties to the American people. Members of Congress are expected to serve the interests and wishes of their **constituents**, or the voters a member of Congress represents. At the same time, they must also consider larger national issues, such as the economy and the environment.

Often, legislators find that the interests of their constituents are at odds with the demands of making national policy. For example, many people argue that limits on emissions of carbon dioxide would help reduce climate change and thus benefit not only all Americans but also the rest of the world's people. Yet some members of Congress come from states where most electricity is generated by coal-burning power plants. Coal-burning plants emit significant amounts of carbon dioxide, but reducing their use might hurt local economies or cause companies to lay off workers.

All members of Congress face difficult votes that set their home state's interests against national lawmaking realities. When faced with such a vote, how should they respond? Generally, legislators follow one of three different patterns of representation. They may choose to vote as trustees, as delegates, or as partisans.

THE TRUSTEE VIEW Legislators who vote as trustees vote in support of the broad interests of the entire nation as they see them. Legislators who vote as trustees will act according to their perceptions of national needs and tend to believe that what is good for the nation will, in the long term, be good for their home states. For example, a senator from North Carolina might support laws regulating cigarette sales, even though the state's tobacco-growing economy could be negatively affected in the short term. Trustees believe voters trust them to use their judgment, wisdom, and experience when making decisions.

THE DELEGATE VIEW Newly elected legislators, fresh from the campaign trail, often view themselves as delegates. Delegates believe members of Congress should mirror the views of their constituents, regardless of their own opinions. Following this approach, a senator from Iowa might strive to obtain subsidies, or government payments, for corn growers, and a representative from Michigan might seek to protect the state's automobile industry.

Legislators acting as delegates often resort to a special form of legislative amendment, or addition to a bill, known as an **earmark**, a spending provision that applies to only a small number of constituents. Earmarks often have nothing to do with the overall bill. Earmarks are categorized as *pork-barrel legislation*, a term that originated in the 1800s, when pork was something that brought farmers quick and easy cash. Legislators are said to "dip into the pork barrel" when they attach earmarks to bills to initiate spending that will benefit few people other than their own constituents.

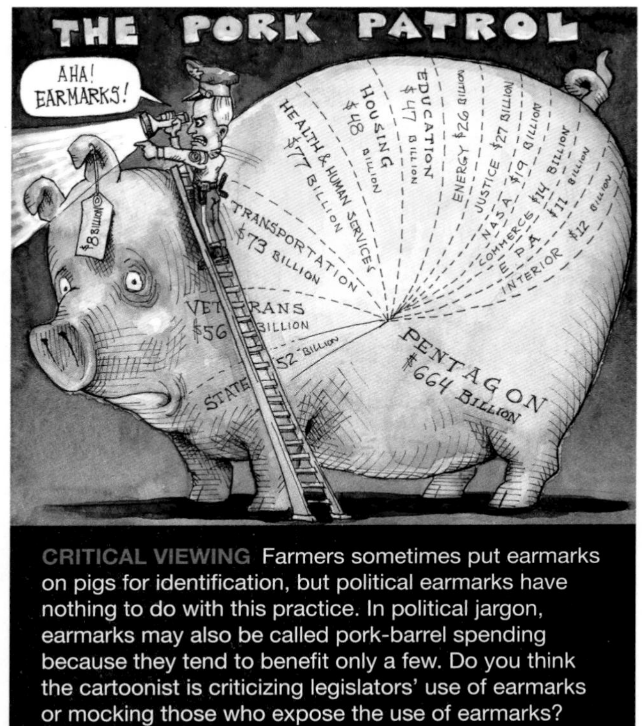

CRITICAL VIEWING Farmers sometimes put earmarks on pigs for identification, but political earmarks have nothing to do with this practice. In political jargon, earmarks may also be called pork-barrel spending because they tend to benefit only a few. Do you think the cartoonist is criticizing legislators' use of earmarks or mocking those who expose the use of earmarks?

THE PARTISAN VIEW One might say that rabid sports fans take a partisan view—they support their favorite team no matter what. Likewise, political partisans vote along party lines. The Democratic and Republican parties often take opposing positions on legislative issues. When it comes time to vote, partisans do what the party leaders tell them to do. The partisan view, taken to extremes, can result in gridlock—the inability to pass important, but controversial, legislation.

Legislators don't have to take the same approach all the time. In fact, experienced members of Congress typically combine these three approaches. They may take a trustee approach on some issues, adhere to the delegate view on other matters, and follow the party line on still others.

HISTORICAL THINKING

3. **MAKE GENERALIZATIONS** Why do you think newly elected members of Congress might take the delegate view of representation?
4. **DRAW CONCLUSIONS** Why might experienced members of Congress often combine all three approaches to representation in their voting behavior?

LESSON 7.2

The House of Representatives

Article I, Section 2, of the United States Constitution says that each state shall receive a member of Congress for every 30,000 people. As a result, the first House of Representatives consisted of 65 people. But the U.S. population kept growing after 1789—and so did the size of the House. Today, the House includes 435 representatives. The members with the smallest number of constituents represent more than 500,000 people. Some believe that no one person can effectively represent that many people.

Members of the House of Representatives

The two houses of Congress are quite different—in their size, how they are structured, and how they operate. Members of the two houses also differ in job qualifications and how they fulfill their roles in serving their constituents. The Framers of the Constitution expected members of the House of Representatives to view themselves as delegates who represent the interests of their constituents. Because House members are up for re-election every two years, they spend a lot of time on the campaign trail, listening to the concerns of people in their district and responding directly to their needs.

Members of the House may also represent fewer people than senators. Senators are elected by the voters of an entire state, but representatives are elected by the voters of a congressional district. Some congressional districts—in big, mostly rural states—cover a large geographic area. But the typical congressional district is small enough that a representative can travel around fairly easily to meet with constituents.

Members of the House are generally referred to as *representatives*. But they are also often referred to as *congresswomen* or *congressmen*—even though Congress also includes the Senate. The Constitution details only a few qualifications for serving in Congress. To be a member of the House, a person

- must have been a citizen of the United States for at least seven years before his or her election,
- must be a legal resident of the state from which he or she is to be elected, and
- must be at least 25 years of age.

The Supreme Court has ruled that neither Congress nor the states can add to these three qualifications.

Once elected to Congress, a representative receives an annual salary from the government. As of 2021, that was $174,000 for most House members. As Article I, Section 6, of the Constitution states, salaries are "paid out of the Treasury of the United States." Representatives also enjoy certain perks, or benefits and privileges beyond a salary, including an excellent subsidized health insurance program and generous retirement benefits.

HISTORICAL THINKING

1. **FORM AND SUPPORT OPINIONS** Which of the qualifications for House membership do you think is most important? Why?

The Size of House Membership

As you read earlier, Article I, Section 2, of the Constitution required that "the Number of Representatives shall not exceed one for every thirty Thousand." The process of distributing House seats among the states based on their respective populations is called **apportionment**. A member of the House represents a specific congressional district.

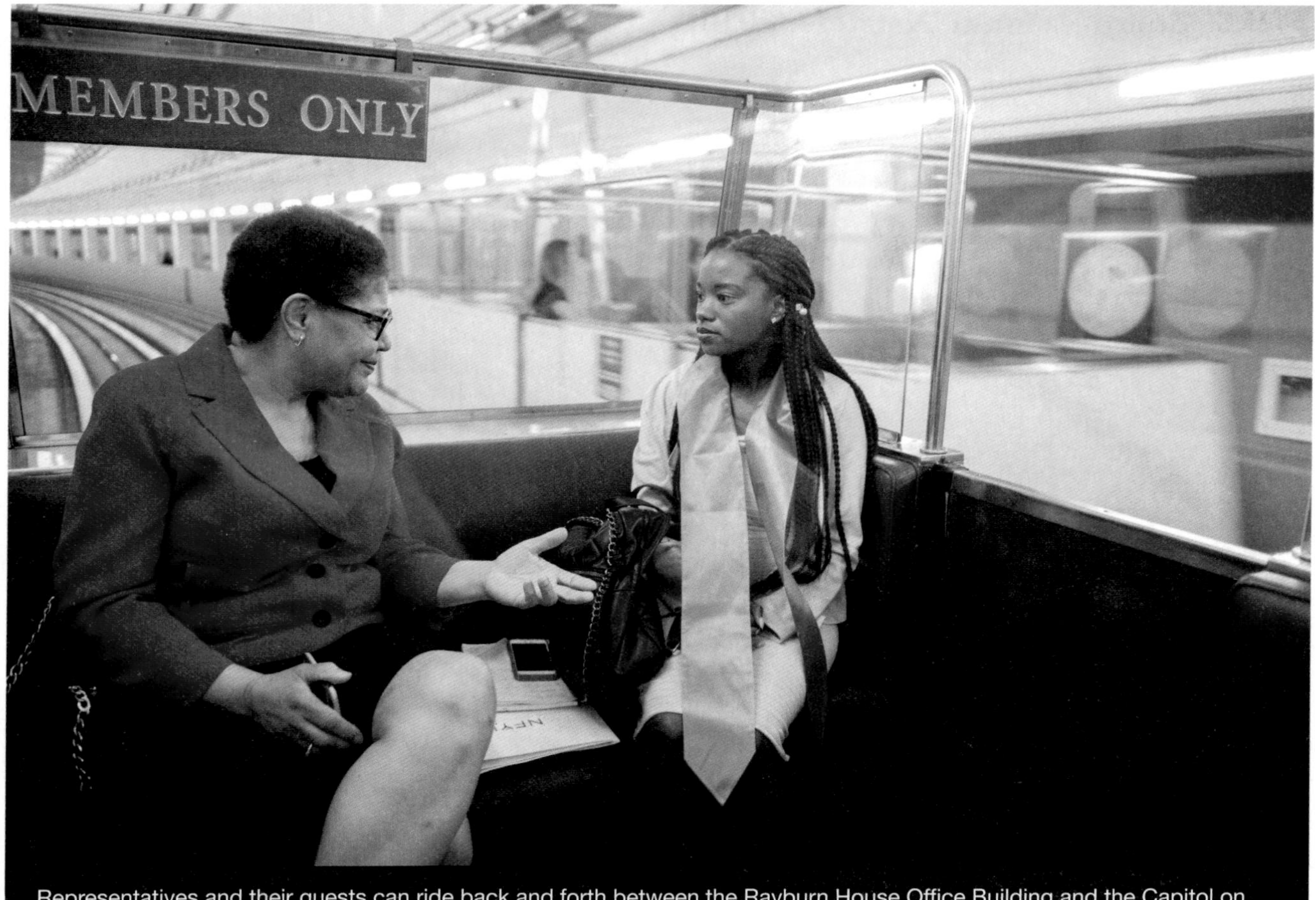

Representatives and their guests can ride back and forth between the Rayburn House Office Building and the Capitol on one of the three underground train lines serving members of Congress. Riding on the U.S. Capitol subway system is one of the perks of office that representatives and senators enjoy.

The Framers didn't establish provisions for congressional districts. Each state had the right to decide whether to have districts at all. Most states set up **single-member districts**, in which voters in each district elect one of the state's representatives. In some states, representatives were chosen by the state as a whole, but today, all members of Congress come from single-member districts.

For many years, the total number of House members increased as the nation's population expanded. But in 1929, Congress passed a law fixing House membership at 435. As a result, U.S. congressional districts on average now have huge populations—about 780,000 people each. Compare that with the figure of 30,000 people per district the Framers used in 1789. Critics today question how one member of the House can effectively represent so many people. They argue that Congress should significantly expand the membership of the House.

APPORTIONMENT OF HOUSE SEATS Every 10 years, House seats are reapportioned based on the outcome of the latest national census. States with fast-growing populations might add seats, while states that grow more slowly or lose population may have seats taken away. Texas, for example, gained four seats based on the 2010 Census, while Michigan lost a seat. The Constitution guarantees each state at least one House seat, however, no matter the size of a state's population. In addition, the District of Columbia, American Samoa, Guam, the Northern Mariana Islands, and the U.S. Virgin Islands all send nonvoting delegates to the House. Puerto Rico, a self-governing possession of the United States, is represented by a nonvoting resident commissioner.

DRAWING DISTRICT LINES Once House seats have been apportioned, states begin **redistricting**, the process of redrawing the boundaries of congressional districts. In drawing district lines, states must meet

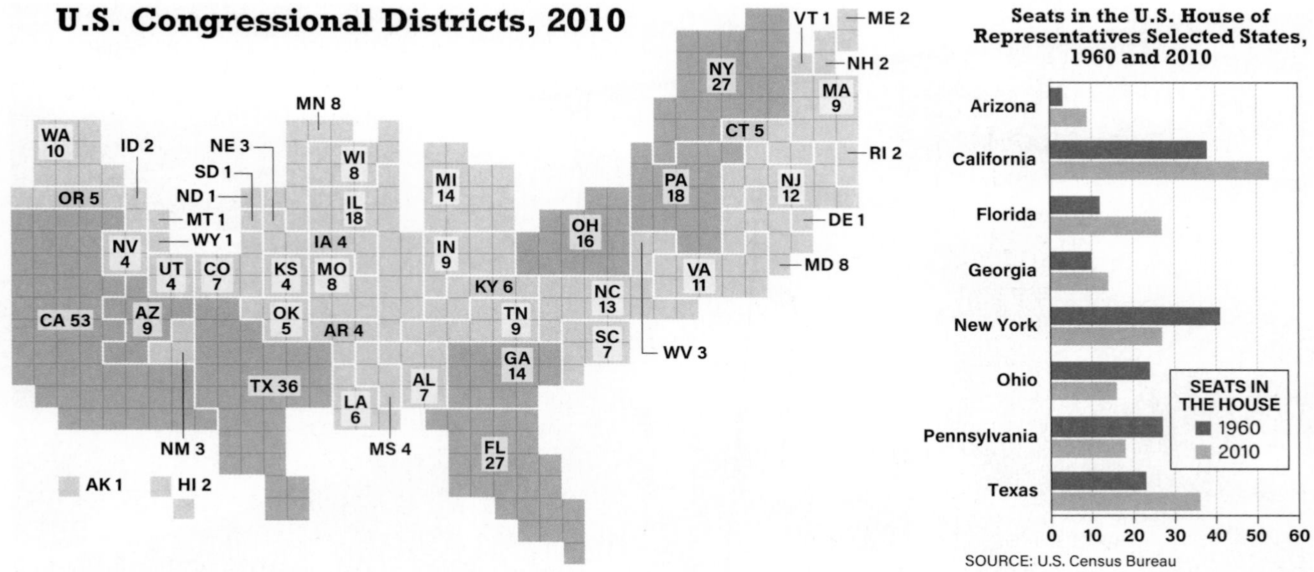

the following requirements. The first appears in the Constitution (Article I, Section 2), and the second, in the Voting Rights Act of 1965:

- Districts in a given state must contain, as nearly as possible, equal numbers of people to ensure equal representation in the legislature.
- State plans for drawing districts cannot discriminate on the basis of race.

Many states also follow certain traditional principles when drawing district lines, including:

- All parts of a district must be contiguous—connected to the rest of the district.
- Districts must be as geographically compact as possible, to ensure that a representative's constituents aren't spread out over a larger area than necessary.

In the past, state legislatures were under no legal obligation to redraw district boundaries to ensure districts had roughly equal populations. The result was that, as cities grew in population in the 20th century, sparsely populated rural districts retained influence far greater than their populations would warrant. At one point in the 1960s, this kind of antidemocratic apportionment was common. In fact, in many states the district with the largest population had twice the number of people as the smallest district. In effect, this meant that a person's vote in the largest district had only half the value of a person's vote in the smallest district. In 1962 the U.S. Supreme Court addressed this issue in the case of *Baker* v. *Carr*, in which the Court ruled that Tennessee's approach to apportionment of state legislative districts violated the constitutional requirement of equal protection under the law.

The *Baker* case determined that federal courts had **jurisdiction**, or the authority to interpret and apply the law, in apportionment disputes. It opened the floodgates to a wave of federal lawsuits seeking to solidify judicial support for equal representation. In 1964, two years after the *Baker* decision, the Supreme Court ruled on a similar case, *Wesberry* v. *Sanders.* But unlike the *Baker* case, which focused on state legislative districts, *Wesberry* was concerned with unequal congressional districts created by the Georgia state legislature.

In *Wesberry* the Court cited Article I, Section 2, of the Constitution, which requires members of the House to be chosen "by the People of the several States." The Court interpreted those words as meaning that congressional districts must have as roughly equal populations as possible. This principle has come to be known as the "one person, one vote" rule. In other words, one person's vote has to count as much as another's.

HISTORICAL THINKING

2. **INTERPRET MAPS** Why does Montana appear so small on the congressional districts map?
3. **INTERPRET GRAPHS** Why did some states gain House seats from 1960 to 2010, while others lost seats?
4. **MAKE INFERENCES** Why do you think all parts of a district must be connected with the rest of the district?

Gerrymandering

In the apportionment cases of the 1960s, the Supreme Court ruled that congressional districts must be equal in population. But the Court continued to be silent on a related issue—**gerrymandering**, or the shaping of congressional districts for political purposes. The term *gerrymandering* was originally used to describe the district lines drawn to favor the party of Governor Elbridge Gerry of Massachusetts, whose administration redrew state districts in 1812. This kind of partisan gerrymandering occurs when the **majority party**—the political party that has the majority of members in a legislative body—draws a district's boundaries to maximize the party's influence.

GERRYMANDERING AFTER THE 2010 CENSUS

In spite of a number of constitutional challenges to partisan gerrymandering, both parties continue the practice. Following the 2010 census, sophisticated computer programs were used to draw district lines to "pack" the opposing party's voters into the smallest number of districts, or "crack" the opposing party's voters into several different districts so they could not win a majority in any of them. Both practices decrease the number of representatives the party that was not in power is likely to win. Packing and cracking make congressional races less competitive by giving an advantage to the party in power.

Republicans won control of state legislatures across the country in the 2010 elections. These victories occurred just before the states were required to redraw the boundaries of congressional districts following the 2010 census and led to a large number of Republican gerrymanders. In the 2012 elections, Democratic candidates picked up only eight seats in the House even though they collected more total votes than Republican candidates.

Consider Pennsylvania, which President Barack Obama won by 5.4 percentage points in 2012. Pennsylvania voters cast 2.72 million votes for Democratic House candidates and 2.65 million votes for Republicans. These votes elected 5 Democratic representatives and 13 Republicans—even though more votes were cast for Democrats. In February 2018, the Pennsylvania Supreme Court ruled that the Republican-controlled state legislature had engaged in partisan gerrymandering and forced it to accept a new map of congressional districts with more objective boundaries.

Maryland's Third Congressional district, shown in the map, is an example of extreme partisan gerrymandering. It was the subject of a lawsuit brought by state Republican voters. A panel of federal judges upheld the Republican challenge, calling the district a "broken-winged pterodactyl." On appeal, the U.S. Supreme Court overruled the lower court decision in 2019, saying that the federal courts do not have the power to prevent legislators from drawing partisan districts.

RACIAL GERRYMANDERING Political gerrymandering has a long history, but racial gerrymandering—the shaping of congressional districts to empower minority groups—is a relatively new phenomenon. In the early 1990s the U.S. Department of Justice instructed state legislatures to draw district lines to maximize the voting power of minority groups. This has resulted in several minority-majority districts, in which a racial minority makes up the majority of voters. Many of these districts took on bizarre shapes. For example, North Carolina's newly drawn 12th Congressional District was 165 miles long—a narrow strip that, for the most part, followed Interstate 85.

The practice of racial gerrymandering has generated heated arguments on both sides of the issue. Some groups contend that minority-majority districts are necessary to ensure equal representation of minority groups, as mandated by the Voting Rights Act of

In the early 1960s, Nashville, the capital of Tennessee, had a growing population. But because the state had not reapportioned legislative seats since 1901, districts in Nashville and other urban areas had fewer seats in Tennessee's General Assembly than they should have. Citizens living in urban districts of the state filed the lawsuit that ended up in the Supreme Court.

SUPREME COURT

Baker v. *Carr*, 1962

Decided: March 26, 1962, 6–2

Majority: Associate Justice William Brennan wrote the opinion for the Court, which ruled in favor of Baker.

Dissent: Associate Justices John Marshall Harlan and Felix Frankfurter wrote dissenting opinions.

The issue in *Baker* v. *Carr* involved whether the federal courts had the authority to interpret and apply the law in cases involving apportionment of state legislative districts. These are districts from which representatives are elected to the state legislature, as opposed to Congress.

Charles W. Baker brought the case against the Tennessee secretary of state, Joe C. Carr. Baker had represented Tennessee citizens from several urban centers. Baker claimed that they were being denied the "equal protection of the laws" guaranteed by the 14th Amendment. Baker pointed out that, contrary to the Tennessee constitution, the state hadn't apportioned legislative seats since 1901 and that, even then, the apportionment failed to give city voters the appropriate number of seats in the General Assembly.

Beginning in 1901, Tennessee's cities and suburbs expanded greatly. But because the state had failed to apportion based on new census figures, people in urban areas were severely underrepresented in the legislature. In its 6–2 decision, the Court didn't rule on the merits, or actual legal rights or wrongs, of the case. But it did determine that the case involved a constitutional issue.

Brennan, writing for the majority, quoted Article III, Section 2, of the U.S. Constitution, which states: "The judicial Power shall extend to all Cases, in Law and Equity, arising under this Constitution, the Laws of the United States, and Treaties." Then Brennan continued, "It is clear," he wrote, "that the cause of action is one which 'arises under' the Federal Constitution." As such, he concluded, "the subject matter is within the federal judicial power defined in Article III, Section 2."

The Court's ruling in *Baker* v. *Carr* didn't immediately end attempts by states to limit the power of urban voters. Mainly, it affirmed that the federal judiciary system was legally allowed to review such cases. But it also put all state legislatures on notice that if their apportionment plans didn't create districts with equal populations, they could be charged with violating the equal protection clause of the Constitution.

THINK ABOUT IT Why was Article III, Section 2, of the Constitution so important to the Supreme Court's decision in *Baker* v. *Carr*?

Maryland's Third Congressional District

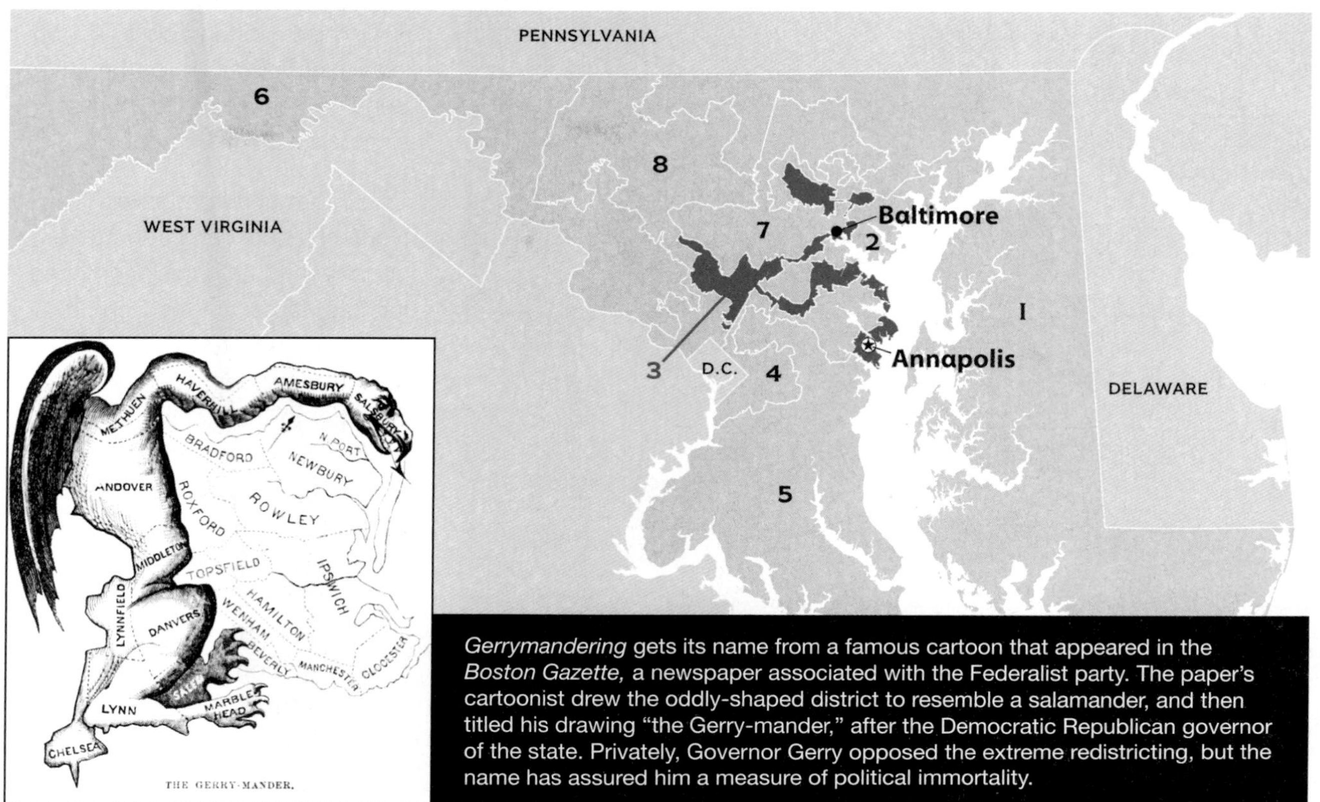

Gerrymandering gets its name from a famous cartoon that appeared in the *Boston Gazette,* a newspaper associated with the Federalist party. The paper's cartoonist drew the oddly-shaped district to resemble a salamander, and then titled his drawing "the Gerry-mander," after the Democratic Republican governor of the state. Privately, Governor Gerry opposed the extreme redistricting, but the name has assured him a measure of political immortality.

1965. They further contend that these districts have been instrumental in increasing the number of African Americans holding political office. Before 1990, redistricting plans in the South often created only White-majority districts.

Opponents of racial gerrymandering argue that such race-based districting is unconstitutional because it violates the equal protection clause. In a series of cases in the 1990s, the Supreme Court agreed and held that when race is the dominant factor in the drawing of congressional district lines, the districts are unconstitutional and must be redrawn.

In 1996, for example, the Supreme Court rejected North Carolina's 12th District as unconstitutional. In 2001 the Court backed off somewhat and accepted a redrawn version of the district. In 2017, however, the Court toughened its position and rejected both North Carolina's 12th District and its First District as well. But the Court clarified that it doesn't currently object to purely partisan gerrymanders.

HISTORICAL THINKING

5. **MAKE INFERENCES** Why do you think gerrymandering has survived for more than 200 years?
6. **MAKE CONNECTIONS** Why isn't gerrymandering an issue for the U.S. Senate?
7. **INTERPRET MAPS** Why might the Democratic Party, which drew the district shown in the map, have ensured inclusion of Baltimore and Annapolis in the district?

Rules in the House

With 435 voting members, the House can't operate in the same way as the Senate, which has only 100 members. With its larger size, the House needs both more rules and more formality. Without this increased structure, no work would ever get done.

The House Rules Committee also establishes a dress code for appropriate attire on the floor. Until recently, the rules banned head coverings of any type. With the swearing in of two Muslim women as members in 2019, the House voted to allow members to wear religious head coverings, such as the hijab, or headscarf, in the chamber.

Much of the work of the House is done by committees, groups of representatives with certain responsibilities. The committee assigned the task of overseeing the House's legislative business is the Rules Committee. This committee has existed since the opening days of the first Congress in 1789. Its earliest set of rules covered the duties and powers of the Speaker, the House's top leader, as well as how legislation would be processed. Some of the principles the first Rules Committee established still exist today, although as the size of the House increased, the rules changed as well.

Today the most obvious formal rules have to do with debate on the floor of the House chamber. In its early years, the House allowed unlimited debate, but lengthy speeches kept it from doing the people's business. In the 1840s, the House adopted a one-hour rule for debate. Today the House uses an elaborate system: The Rules Committee normally proposes time limits on debate for any bill. The rules are then accepted or modified by the full House. Despite its size, the House is often able to act on legislation more quickly than the Senate because of the House's stricter time limits on debate.

One informal rule adopted by House Republicans can prevent consideration of legislation even if it has passed in the Senate. That is the Hastert Rule, named after Dennis Hastert, Republican Speaker of the House from 1999 to 2007. Under the rule, when the Republicans have a majority in the House, the Speaker won't allow any measure to reach the floor unless it has the support of a majority of the Republican members of the House. Democratic Speakers also have the power to block legislation in this way, but they haven't turned this ability into an informal rule.

The Hastert Rule came under considerable pressure in late 2012 and 2013, when Republican Speaker John Boehner felt compelled to violate it several times. Legislation in December 2012 increased taxes for the wealthiest citizens in order to prevent more broadly distributed tax increases. This measure passed without the support of most Republicans. Boehner also ignored the rule in order to end a government shutdown that took place in October 2013. Divisions in the Republican ranks led Boehner to resign from the Speaker position in 2015.

HISTORICAL THINKING

8. **DRAW CONCLUSIONS** Why do you think rules and formality help the House operate more efficiently?
9. **FORM AND SUPPORT OPINIONS** Do you think most Republican members of Congress favor the Hastert Rule? Why or why not?

"Why Not Me? Why Not Now?"

by Rachel Jones **National Geographic Online, November 7, 2018**

National Geographic Explorer Daniella Zalcman captured this image of Congresswoman Deb Haaland hugging a supporter. This photograph is part of her ongoing work of capturing photographs and stories of indigenous communities throughout the United States.

When an interviewer asked Deb Haaland why she was running for Congress at this point in her life, she replied, "Why not me? Why not now?" Haaland had for years worked to give her people—not just the residents of the Pueblo of Laguna but also Native Americans throughout New Mexico—a voice in politics. Haaland began that quest by volunteering as a community organizer. She continued it by serving as her state's Democratic Party chair. Eventually, she decided it was time for her to make the move into national politics.

In her article "Deb Haaland: 'Why not me? Why not now?'" Rachel Jones tells how, in the midterm elections of 2018, Haaland and another indigenous woman—Sharice Davids of Kansas—won seats in the U.S. House of Representatives. Mark Trahant, editor of the *Indian Country Today* newspaper, and other observers credit a surge of Native American political activism to the Dakota Access Pipeline protests that began in 2016.

"Standing Rock was one of those moments that whether or not they were successful in blocking the

authority to do things was something that I think was infectious," Trahant says. It's estimated that several dozen candidates ran during the 2018 mid-term season, vying to join the only two Native Americans currently in Congress—Tom Cole, a Chickasaw, and Markwayne Mullin, a Cherokee. Both are Republicans from Oklahoma.

Deb Haaland prides herself on having relied on a grassroots effort to fund her winning campaign. She and a team of volunteers made thousands of phone calls and knocked on thousands of doors. When she took the oath of office in the House chamber on January 3, 2019, she understood that she was there to represent the people—her people—of New Mexico's first congressional district.

Access the full version of this article through the Resources Menu in MindTap.

THINK ABOUT IT What is the difference between the type of activism that organizes a protest and the type that organizes a political campaign? What are the

LESSON **7.3** # The Senate

The Framers of the Constitution envisioned individuals with admirable traits when they established the qualifications for serving as a U.S. senator. Senators, they decided, were to be older than representatives—and presumably wiser, more experienced, and perhaps even more dignified. The Framers wanted the Senate to be a check on the House, which they saw as being closer to the people and thus prone to the influence of popular passions and desires. James Madison characterized the Senate as the "anchor" of the government. It was designed to slow things down if needed and to keep the government from drifting too far off course.

The Senators

The first Senate, which convened in March 1789, had just 22 members. At that point, only 11 states had ratified the Constitution. Every state admitted to the Union since then has increased the number by two, bringing the total today to an even 100 senators. Senators have always served six-year terms. The Constitution originally called for their election by the state legislatures, whom the Framers assumed would select only the most qualified and dedicated individuals. In one of the Federalist Papers, John Jay characterized state legislators as "the most enlightened and respectable citizens."

The Framers believed that having state legislators choose U.S. senators reinforces the states' role as a counterbalance to the national government. Over time, however, powerful business interests and wealthy political leaders took control of some state legislatures. They chose senators who would do their bidding. During the early 20th century, people calling themselves **progressives**, reformers who sought to change government and make it more democratic, demanded change. Direct election of senators by voters, a proposal first introduced into the House in 1826, was added to the Constitution through the 17th Amendment, which was ratified in 1913.

To increase the Senate's stability and continuity, the Framers planned for the election of one-third of the Senate every two years, so that the whole membership wouldn't turn over at one time. To be elected senator, a person

- must have been a citizen for at least nine years before the election,
- must be a legal resident of the state from which she or he seeks election, and
- must be at least 30 years of age.

The minimum age for a representative, as you have read, is 25. In an essay in the Federalist Papers, Madison justified the age difference by saying that senators need a "greater extent of information and stability of character." Yet senators and representatives receive the same salary. Like representatives, senators must purchase health insurance, but the federal government pays nearly three-quarters of the cost. Like members of the House, senators receive perks such as funds to cover travel and office expenses.

HISTORICAL THINKING

1. **MAKE GENERALIZATIONS** Why do you think six-year terms might add to the Senate's stability and continuity?
2. **IDENTIFY PROBLEMS AND SOLUTIONS** What problem was the 17th Amendment proposed to solve?

How the Senate Operates

Like the House, the Senate has a Rules Committee that maintains rules for conducting the Senate's business. Senators are known for being courteous, even when outraged by the proposals or actions of another senator. The tradition of courtesy goes back to Thomas Jefferson, who compiled the *Manual of Parliamentary Practice,* which urged senators to avoid "reviling, nipping, or unmannerly words." It also instructed senators to avoid calling one another by name. Even today, senators commonly refer to another senator as "my distinguished colleague."

THE FILIBUSTER AND ITS LIMITS Besides its tradition of courtesy, the Senate is also known for its relatively slow legislative process. Unlike the House, the Senate normally permits unlimited debate on all issues. Senators are free to speak for as long as they want about any subject they choose on the floor of the Senate. This practice is known as the **filibuster**—the use of extended debate to delay or block legislation. In the 1930s, Senator Huey Long of Louisiana read recipes and recited Shakespeare during his filibusters of bills he claimed benefited the rich and ignored the poor. Senator J. Strom Thurmond of South Carolina set a record when he filibustered against the Civil Rights Act of 1957 for more than 24 hours.

The Senate does have a method for ending filibusters. Senators may file a motion, or official request, for **cloture**—a procedure for closing debate and forcing a vote. First, 16 senators must sign a petition requesting cloture. Then, after two days have elapsed, three-fifths of the entire membership must vote for cloture. Today, that's 60 senators.

Senate traditions and courtesy make it hard to persuade 60 senators to stop another senator's speech. One of the first times it succeeded was to end a filibuster of the Civil Rights Act of 1964. Recently, however, the number of successful cloture votes has risen from about a dozen per congressional term to sometimes more than 100. Once cloture is invoked, or implemented, each senator may speak on the matter at hand for no more than one hour before a vote is taken. Also, the Senate may limit consideration to 30 additional hours after the cloture process began.

Another limit on the filibuster is a Senate rule known as the reconciliation rule, which limits debates on revenue, or spending, bills that have been passed by the House and are then sent to the Senate. A reconciliation bill must meet three requirements:

- It must be limited to the topics of taxing and spending.
- It mustn't otherwise involve changes to regulations or laws.
- It must reduce the budget deficit at the end of a 10-year period.

A reconciliation bill can't be effectively filibustered. Congressional budget rules limit debate on reconciliation bills to 20 hours and also limit the types of amendments that can be added to the bills. After President Trump took office and Republicans had a majority in both houses, they used reconciliation rules to pass a major tax bill opposed by every Senate Democrat.

THE SENATORIAL HOLD Senators have another tool in addition to the filibuster that they can use to delay legislation. An individual senator may place a hold on a bill by informing the leader of his or her party of the hold. Senatorial holds are often anonymous, but cloture can be used to lift a hold. Senators often place holds on nominees for executive or judicial positions to win concessions from the executive branch. In 2010 Senator Richard Shelby placed holds on at least 70 of President Obama's nominations in an attempt to force the administration to support two military spending programs in Alabama.

CRITICAL VIEWING This cartoon, titled "Senatorial Courtesy," appeared on the cover of a popular humor magazine in October 1893. What elements of the cartoon express the idea that this senator has taken advantage of the rule that allows him to speak for as long as he wants?

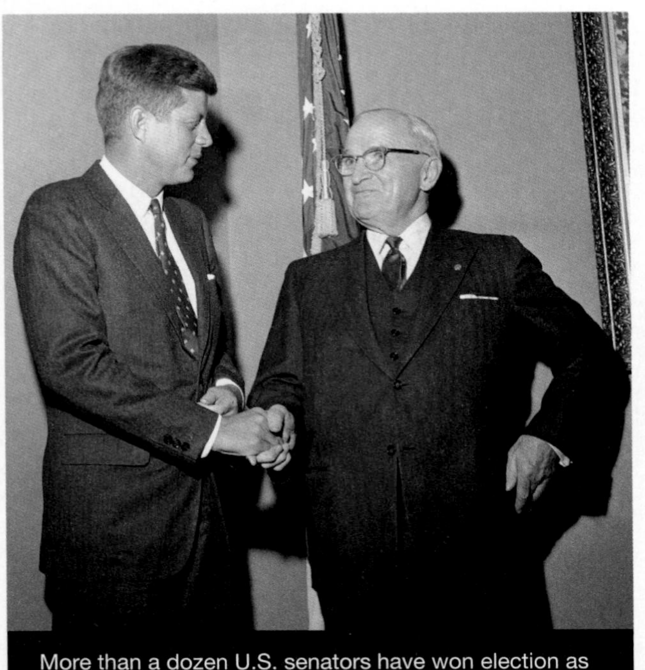

More than a dozen U.S. senators have won election as president, including Harry Truman (right), who served as president from 1945 to 1953, and John F. Kennedy, who was president from 1961 to 1963. Truman met with then senator John F. Kennedy (D-MA) in November 1959, a year before Kennedy won the presidency.

Because the House has so many more members than the Senate, few representatives gain the prestige a senator enjoys. When a controversial bill is pending, senators are often swarmed by TV reporters. The Senate's constitutional control over presidential appointments and treaties gives it considerable power. One consequence of this prestige and power is that the parties have often nominated senators as presidential candidates, and a number of senators have gone on to become president. In recent years, those senators have included Harry S. Truman, John F. Kennedy, Lyndon B. Johnson, Richard M. Nixon, and Barack Obama.

HISTORICAL THINKING

3. **DRAW CONCLUSIONS** Why do you think Jefferson urged senators not to speak the names of other members while engaged in debate?
4. **SYNTHESIZE** How does the filibuster support the idea that the Senate is a deliberative body that promotes discussion of issues?

LESSON 7.4 Congressional Leadership and Committees

Some people believe that leaders are born, not made. Others disagree. Leaders in the House and Senate may have certain personal qualities that help them lead, but effort and experience are required as well. The skills that effective leaders develop include the ability to plan, communicate, and persuade. Leaders also need to manage, motivate, gain the respect of, and even inspire those they lead. But leadership is also about being willing to delegate work to others. In both houses of Congress, committees take on the task of helping congressional leaders carry out the legislative agenda.

House Leadership

Leadership in the House of Representatives begins with the Speaker. The Constitution (in Article I, Section 2) states that the "House of Representatives shall choose their Speaker and other Officers," but it says nothing more about these positions. Today, important "other officers" include the party leaders on the floor of the House: the majority leader, the minority leader, and the whips.

SPEAKER OF THE HOUSE The Speaker is the most powerful leader in the House of Representatives. In fact, after the vice president, the Speaker of the House is next in line of succession should the president die in office. Traditionally, the Speaker is a member of the majority party who has risen in rank and influence through years of service in the House. In the nation's earliest years, the Speakers sought to serve all the members of the House, but over time, they became more partisan—and more powerful.

As the presiding officer of the House and the leader of the majority party, the Speaker has a great deal of power. The Speaker

- has substantial control over what bills are assigned to which committees,
- can recognize or ignore members who wish to speak,
- may interpret and apply House rules, put questions to a vote, and interpret the outcome of votes taken,
- plays a major role in making important committee member assignments, and
- schedules bills for action.

Under House rules, the only time the Speaker must vote is to break a tie. Otherwise, a tie automatically defeats a bill. On rare occasions, the Speaker may choose to vote and create a tie that defeats a bill.

OTHER LEADERS IN THE HOUSE The majority leader is elected by the members of the majority-party caucus, or group. The majority leader's job is to help plan the party's legislative program, organize other party members to support legislation, and make sure the chairs of the many committees finish work on bills that are important to the party.

The minority leader is the leader of the **minority party**, the party with fewer members in the legislative chamber. Although not as powerful as the majority leader, the minority leader has similar responsibilities. The primary duty of the minority leader is to maintain solidarity within the minority party.

The leadership of each party relies on an assistant floor leader known as a whip. Whips are named after the whippers-in, riders who keep the hounds together in a fox hunt. Assistant party leaders pressure party members to uphold the party's positions. The party whip finds out how each member plans to vote and then advises leaders on the strength of party support for an issue.

HISTORICAL THINKING

1. **MAKE INFERENCES** Why does the majority-party candidate for Speaker of the House nearly always win the position?
2. **ANALYZE CAUSE AND EFFECT** What might happen if the office of whip was eliminated?

Senate Leadership

Senate leaders have powers similar to those of House leaders. The vice president serves as president of the Senate. The vice president may call on members to speak and put questions to a vote. The vice president isn't an elected member of the Senate, however, and may not take part in Senate debates. The vice president may cast a vote in the Senate only in the event of a tie. Since vice presidents are not always available, senators choose a president *pro tempore,* or *pro tem* for short. This temporary presiding officer is elected by the whole Senate and is ordinarily the member of the majority party with the longest continuous term of service in the Senate.

The real power in the Senate lies with its floor leaders—the majority leader, the minority leader, and

Majority leader Mitch McConnell (R-KY, right) speaks with minority leader Charles Schumer (D-NY, left) as they head toward the Senate chamber in February 2018. The two leaders had just reached agreement on a bipartisan budget deal.

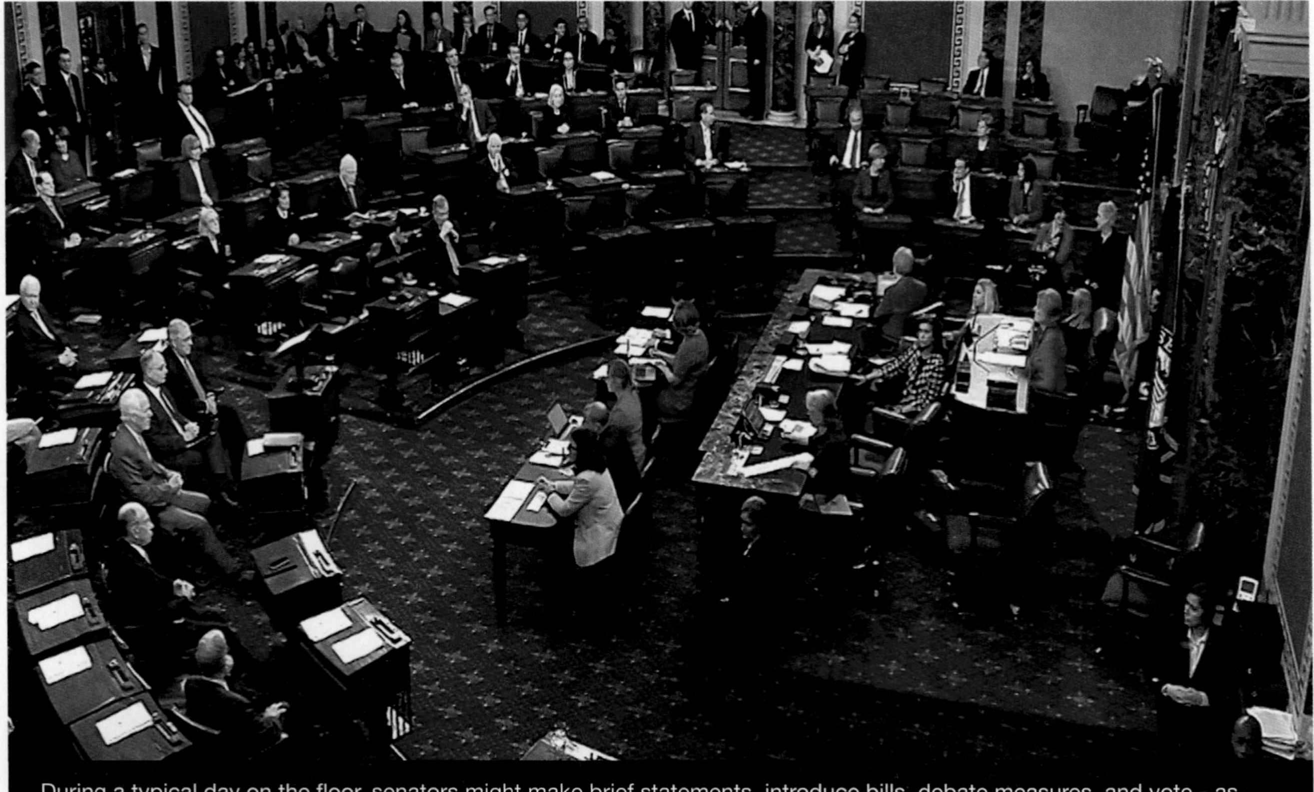

During a typical day on the floor, senators might make brief statements, introduce bills, debate measures, and vote—as they are doing here.

the whips. The majority leader is the most powerful individual in the Senate and chief spokesperson of the majority party. This leader's powers aren't as clearly or formally established as those of the Speaker of the House. As a result, the majority leader must have the leadership skills and personality required to fight for the passage of key bills or, when necessary, to compromise. The minority leader commands the minority party's opposition to the policies of the majority party. The minority leader is, in some ways, a majority-leader-in-waiting for the next time the minority party becomes the majority.

The task of whips in the Senate is much like that in the House. They serve as a link between the majority and minority leaders and the members and help maintain party unity on the issues. Some Senate whips have moved up the ladder to higher leadership positions. Senator Mitch McConnell served as a whip before becoming majority leader. President Lyndon Johnson had once been a whip, as had his vice president, Hubert Humphrey.

HISTORICAL THINKING

3. **COMPARE AND CONTRAST** Which official of the Senate is more involved in the details of legislation, the president of the Senate or the majority leader? Explain your answer.
4. **MAKE INFERENCES** On the Senate floor, the seats of the majority and minority leaders are close to each other. Why do you think that is so?

Congressional Committees

Thousands of bills are introduced during every session of Congress, and no single member can possibly be fully informed on all the issues that arise. The committee system is a division of the legislative labor. Committees concentrate on just one area—such as agriculture or transportation—and develop sufficient expertise to draft appropriate legislation. The flow of legislation through both the House and the Senate is determined largely by the speed with which these committees act on bills and resolutions.

Standing Committees in the 116th Congress, 2019–2020

House Committees	Senate Committees
Agriculture	Agriculture, Nutrition, and Forestry
Appropriations	Appropriations
Armed Services	Armed Services
Budget	Banking, Housing, and Urban Affairs
Education and Labor	Budget
Energy and Commerce	Commerce, Science, and Transportation
Ethics	Energy and Natural Resources
Financial Services	Environment and Public Works
Foreign Affairs	Finance
Homeland Security	Foreign Relations
House Administration	Health, Education, Labor, and Pensions
Judiciary	Homeland Security and Governmental Affairs
Natural Resources	Judiciary
Oversight and Reform	Rules and Administration
Rules	Small Business and Entrepreneurship
Science, Space, and Technology	Veterans' Affairs
Small Business	
Transportation and Infrastructure	
Veterans' Affairs	
Ways and Means	

SOURCE: U.S. House of Representatives; U.S. Senate

STANDING COMMITTEES Both the Senate and the House have **standing committees**. Standing committees are permanent—they stand, or continue, from one Congress to the next. Normally, a bill must be approved by the standing committee to which it was assigned before it comes before the entire House or Senate. In the 116th Congress, the House had 20 standing committees, and the Senate had 16. (See the table Standing Committees in the 116th Congress, 2019–2020.)

The chairperson of a standing committee is a member of the majority party, while the ranking member is the highest-ranking minority member. In both the House and the Senate, committee seniority—length of continuous service—plays a role in determining committee leadership positions. All members of Congress serve on one or more standing committees. Experienced members campaign for seats on the most powerful and prestigious committees. These include the money committees, such as Appropriations, which writes federal spending bills. Newly elected members try to join committees that best suit their area of expertise and that handle issues dear to their state and their constituents.

Most House and Senate committees are divided into **subcommittees**, smaller sets of the standing committees that examine a certain bill or handle certain tasks related to a bill. Standing committees typically send a bill to a particular subcommittee for study and analysis. When members of the subcommittee complete their work on a bill, they send recommendations to the full committee. Today, Congress has more than 200 subcommittees distributed among its 36 standing committees.

SELECT, JOINT, AND CONFERENCE COMMITTEES A select committee, also known as a special committee, studies a specific problem or issue. Once the committee finishes its work, it is usually disbanded, but not always. For example, in 1977 the Senate granted permanent status to its Special Committee on Aging.

Joint committees include members from each chamber of Congress. They are usually formed to conduct studies on a topic that concerns the whole Congress rather than to consider a bill. Some are permanent, and others are temporary.

The two chambers regularly pass legislative proposals in different forms. A conference committee, which includes members from both chambers, is formed to work out the exact wording of a bill. No bill can go to the White House to be signed into law until it passes both chambers in identical form. The leadership in either chamber can block legislation by refusing to appoint members to a conference committee. In 2013 the Republicans employed this technique on several bills.

HISTORICAL THINKING

5. **SEQUENCE EVENTS** What happens to a bill after it is introduced in the full House, before it can be put to a vote?

6. **IDENTIFY MAIN IDEAS AND DETAILS** Does most legislation have to pass through a select committee before it can be voted on in the full House?

7. **INTERPRET TABLES** What general statement can you make about the subject areas covered by House committees, compared with the subject areas covered by Senate committees?

LESSON

7.5 Congressional Elections

Though the Constitution lays out a few basic qualifications for members of Congress, the voters are the ultimate judges of who should serve in Congress. Candidates for the House of Representatives have to convince people in their congressional district to accept them as their representatives. Would-be senators have to persuade voters from their entire state to send them to Washington, D.C. Voters have the final say at the polls, but to get their names on the ballot, candidates for Congress must first pass a set of tests to win the confidence of their own party.

Candidates for Congressional Elections

In the 2018 elections, more than 2,600 Americans filed papers, or declared their intention to run, for congressional office. All these candidates had reasons for running. Some sincerely believed they could make a difference for the people of their congressional district or state. Others saw specific problems they wanted to fix. A few likely craved the public recognition that comes with being a member of the United States Congress. Whatever their reasons, those who wanted to win had to raise enormous amounts of money—millions of dollars, most likely—and put in long hours meeting with campaign workers and voters. A record 476 of those who ran in the House were women, and 234 of those women won their primaries to become their party's nominee. (In contrast, in 2016, 167 women were on the ballots for House races.)

Under Article I, Section 4, of the Constitution, state legislatures control the "Times, Places and Manner of holding Elections for Senators and Representatives." But Congress "may at any time by Law make or alter such Regulations." In other words, Congress can override state laws, and it has done so several times. For example, in 1869, Congress passed the 15th Amendment, which states that the right to vote cannot be denied "by any State on account of race, color, or previous condition of servitude." The amendment was ratified the following year.

Congress passed a law that required voting by congressional district in 1967. This was shortly after the Supreme Court ruled that congressional districts must have roughly equal populations in *Wesberry* v. *Sanders* in February 1964. As you have read, that case established the principle of "one person, one vote" for congressional districts. A related case, *Reynolds* v. *Sims,* decided a few months later, applied that principle of voter equality to state elections. As a result of this decision, state legislatures across the country had to redraw their legislative districts to ensure that one person's vote in a state election was worth as much as a vote cast by someone in another district in that state.

PRIMARY ELECTIONS One role of political parties is to take the large number of people who want to run for office and narrow the field. The **primary election** is a preliminary election to choose each party's final candidates. To represent their party in an

SUPREME COURT

Reynolds v. *Sims*, 1964

CRITICAL VIEWING These justices, who posed for this portrait in 1962, made up the Warren Court, named for Chief Justice Earl Warren (seated, center). Warren wrote the opinion for the majority in the *Reynolds* v. *Sims* case. John M. Harlan (seated, far right) was the lone dissenting voice in the case. How does this group of justices differ from the members of today's Supreme Court?

Decided: June 15, 1964, 8-1

Majority: Chief Justice Earl Warren wrote the opinion for the Court in favor of Sims.

Dissent: Justice John M. Harlan

The question facing the Supreme Court in *Reynolds* v. *Sims* was whether Alabama's apportionment of legislative districts violated the equal protection clause of the 14th Amendment. That clause reads, "No State shall... deny to any person within its jurisdiction the equal protection of the laws." A lower federal court decided that Alabama's apportionment did violate the 14th Amendment, so Alabama appealed to the Supreme Court.

In an earlier case, *Baker* v. *Carr*, the Court had ruled that federal courts had the authority to review cases related to legislative apportionment. A number of cases followed, including *Wesberry* v. *Sanders*, in which the Court determined that population differences in congressional districts violated the Constitution. In *Reynolds* v. *Sims*, the Court faced a similar issue related to state legislative districts.

M.O. Sims and other Alabama voters challenged Alabama's apportionment of the state legislature. They claimed that their district near the city of Birmingham had 41 times as many citizens eligible to vote than another district in the state. This population difference, they argued, meant that their votes in an election didn't have the same weight as the votes in the other district. The Supreme Court agreed, in an 8–1 decision, ruling that Alabama hadn't made an "honest and good faith" effort to equalize the populations of its legislative districts.

Writing for the Court, Chief Justice Warren pointed out that between 1901 and 1961, Alabama's population had grown from 1.8 million to 3.2 million, nearly all of the increase in urban areas. Yet the apportionment of legislative districts still reflected population data from the 1900 census. As a result, the distribution of seats in the state legislature heavily favored rural areas. The Court's ruling confirmed the "one person, one vote" principle. Warren wrote:

> A citizen, a qualified voter, is no more nor no less so because he lives in the city or on the farm. This is the clear and strong command of our Constitution's Equal Protection Clause. This is an essential part of the concept of a government of laws and not men.

THINK ABOUT IT How were the *Reynolds* v. *Sims* and *Wesberry* v. *Sanders* rulings similar and different?

election, individuals must seek their party's **nomination**—the naming of a candidate to run for elective office. This is usually done by direct primary, in which voters choose their candidate. Voter turnout for primaries is usually low. Those who cast ballots in a primary election are often strong supporters of their party.

In 2018, then U.S. representative Beto O'Rourke (D-TX) and incumbent U.S. senator Ted Cruz (R-TX) debated the issues in their battle to see who would represent Texas in the Senate. Together, the candidates raised more than $120 million.

GENERAL ELECTIONS

Candidates who win their party's nomination through a primary election compete in the **general election**, a regularly scheduled election in which voters choose who will represent them in a public office. To win, candidates have to expand their appeal to voters in the entire district, including members of the opposing party and independents. That takes a lot of effort—and a lot of money.

Campaigns for Congress have become more expensive in recent years. Candidates spend extensively on advertising, on travel around their district or state, and on staff and office expenses. The average cost of the winning race for the House in 2016 was more than $1.3 million. Winners in the Senate, on average, spent more than $10.4 million. The total cost of the 2018 congressional election exceeded $2 billion. Where do these huge amounts of money come from? There are a few main sources of campaign funds:

- **The candidates themselves**—wealthy candidates fund a significant portion of their campaigns.
- **Individuals**—candidates receive many small contributions, and also some large amounts from wealthy donors.
- **Organized groups**—much support comes from political action committees (PACs).

Political action committees are organizations formed to raise money to influence elections or legislation. In 1971, Congress passed a law restricting how much individuals, labor unions, and corporations could contribute to campaigns. PACs overcame the restrictions by expanding their fundraising to involve greater numbers of individuals, and campaign funding soared. In 2002 another campaign reform law, the McCain-Feingold Act, further limited campaign spending by political parties, corporations, and unions.

Then, in 2010, the Supreme Court's ruling in *Citizens United* v. *Federal Election Commission* invalidated parts of McCain-Feingold and a key section of the 1971 law. The decision led to so-called Super PACs, which could now raise unlimited amounts of money from corporations, unions, and individuals for use in promoting or opposing political candidates. President Barack Obama argued that the ruling would "open the floodgates for special interests . . . to spend without limit," but others applauded the decision as protection for free speech.

CONGRESSIONAL ELECTIONS AND THE PRESIDENT Congressional elections take place every two years, and presidential elections take place every four. House and Senate candidates who are running for Congress the same year as their party's presidential candidate can benefit from what is known as the coattail effect, a reference to coats with long flaps,

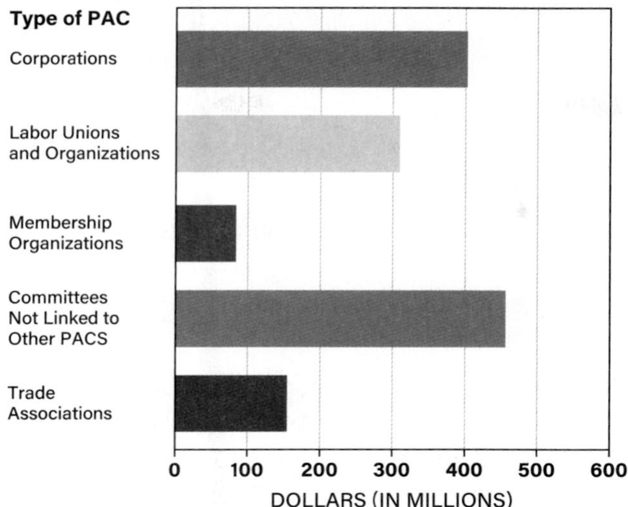

SOURCE: Federal Election Commission

or tails, at the back that men used to wear. The idea was that successful candidates could carry others to success on their coattails. Research suggests that candidates for Congress do get a boost on election day if their party's president wins. Presidents who are unpopular, however, have no coattails. In the 1966 congressional races, as Democratic president Lyndon B. Johnson faced growing criticism over the Vietnam War, Republican Richard Nixon declared, "There is a new fashion sweeping the country: skirts are shorter, pants are tighter, and the LBJ coattails are going out of style."

HISTORICAL THINKING

1. **MAKE PREDICTIONS** Candidates can run, even if they do not win a party primary. Why do so few candidates who don't win primaries continue to run?
2. **DRAW CONCLUSIONS** Why are PACs controversial?
3. **INTERPRET GRAPHS** What kind of economic policies would a candidate have to support to receive money from a labor PAC?

The Power of Incumbency

An **incumbent** is someone who already holds political office. Incumbent politicians enjoy several advantages. One is their fundraising ability. Incumbents usually have a much larger network of contacts, donors, and lobbyists than their opponents. Incumbents raise, on average, twice as much in campaign funds as their challengers. Other advantages that aid re-election include:

- **Professional staffs**—those who already hold office have large administrative staffs both in Washington, D.C., and in their home districts.
- **Lawmaking power**—members of Congress can back legislation that will funnel money and jobs into their states or districts and then campaign on that legislative record.
- **Access to the media**—elected officials have many opportunities to stage events for the press and attract free publicity.
- **Name recognition**—incumbents are usually far better known to the voters than are challengers.

Critics argue that the advantages enjoyed by incumbents reduce the competition necessary for a healthy democracy. Voters are less likely to turn out when an incumbent candidate is practically guaranteed re-election. As you have read, some people have called for the enactment of term limits to increase opportunities for a greater range of candidates. Others argue that government, especially Congress, needs the knowledge and expertise provided by experienced public officials.

HISTORICAL THINKING

4. **FORM AND SUPPORT OPINIONS** Which advantage of incumbency do you think helps an incumbent member of Congress the most? Why?
5. **MAKE GENERALIZATIONS** How do you think Congress would be affected if a large percentage of members were new to political office?

CHAPTER 7

THE STRUCTURE OF CONGRESS

Review

VOCABULARY

Use each of the following vocabulary words in a sentence that shows an understanding of the term's meaning.

1. term
2. session
3. constituents
4. apportionment
5. single-member district
6. jurisdiction
7. majority party
8. progressive
9. minority party
10. nomination
11. general election
12. incumbent

MAIN IDEAS

Answer the following questions. Support your answer with evidence from the chapter.

13. How does the arrangement of articles in the Constitution support the idea that the Framers saw Congress as the "first branch" of government? **LESSON 7.1**
14. Does a member of Congress who puts nation above party take a trustee view of representation or a delegate view? **LESSON 7.1**
15. What must be true about the population in every congressional district in a state? **LESSON 7.2**
16. What significance did the *Baker* v. *Carr* case regarding apportionment have? **LESSON 7.2**
17. Why would the majority party in a state legislature try to gerrymander congressional districts? **LESSON 7.2**
18. How does the filibuster contribute to the Senate's reputation for having a slower legislative process than the House? **LESSON 7.3**
19. How does the position of majority leader differ in power from the House to the Senate? **LESSON 7.4**
20. Which type of committee is a member of Congress more likely to serve on—a standing committee or a select committee? Explain your answer. **LESSON 7.4**
21. Did the Supreme Court ruling in *Citizens United* v. *Federal Election Commission* limit or expand the power of political action committees? Explain your answer. **LESSON 7.5**
22. Why do members of Congress from the president's party sometimes do poorly in a midterm election? **LESSON 7.5**

HISTORICAL THINKING

Answer the following questions. Support your answer with evidence from the chapter.

23. **EVALUATE** Would you support an amendment to the Constitution to make the terms of office for representatives four years instead of two? Why or why not?
24. **SYNTHESIZE** In a state with four congressional districts, under what circumstances could one of the districts be geographically huge but the others be geographically small?
25. **MAKE GENERALIZATIONS** How much political experience do you think newly elected senators typically have compared to new representatives? Explain your answer.
26. **DRAW CONCLUSIONS** Why do you think the Speaker of the House, rather than the majority leader of the Senate, is next in line after the vice president for presidential succession?
27. **FORM AND SUPPORT OPINIONS** Why do you think such a high percentage of people who seek a seat in Congress choose to run as a candidate of one of the major political parties?

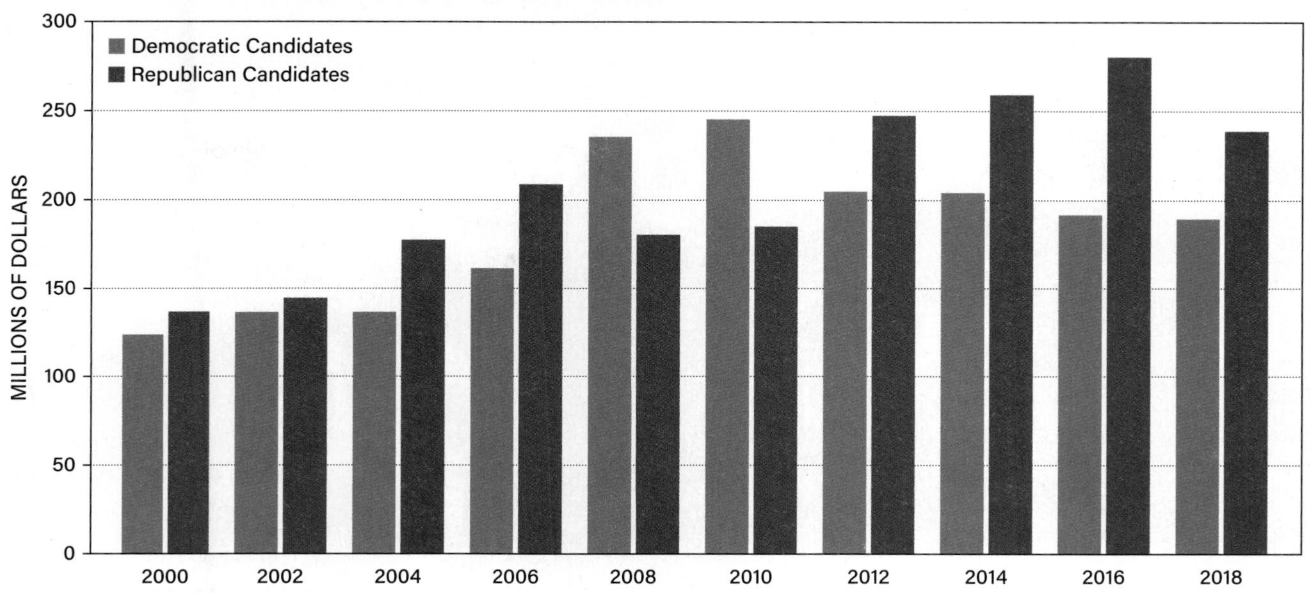

SOURCE: Center for Responsive Politics

INTERPRET VISUALS

Study the graph above. Then answer the questions.

28. In which years did Democrats receive more money from PACs than Republicans?

29. How would you summarize the change in total PAC contributions from 2000 to 2016?

ANALYZE SOURCES

Associate Justice Hugo Black wrote an opinion in the Supreme Court case *Wesberry* v. *Sanders*. His opinion included this statement concerning the importance of "the people" in the electoral process:

> We hold that ... the command of Article I, Section 2, that Representatives be chosen "by the People of the several States" means that, as nearly as is practicable, one man's vote in a congressional election is to be worth as much as another's.... To say that a vote is worth more in one district than in another would not only run counter to our fundamental ideas of democratic government, it would cast aside the principle of a House of Representatives elected "by the People," a principle tenaciously fought for and established at the Constitutional Convention.

30. Based on this statement, do you think Justice Black supported or opposed equal populations in a state's congressional districts? Explain your answer.

CONNECT TO YOUR LIFE

31. **INFORMATIVE** What are term limits, and how would they affect you if they were enacted? Find out more about your congressional representative and your senators—especially noting how long each one has been in Congress and their role in Congress. In three or more paragraphs, write a presentation that you might make to a local middle-school audience to answer these questions.

TIPS

- Review the discussions of term limits in the chapter. In your opening statement, describe what term limits are, and explain the present length of congressional terms of office.
- Do further research on the pros and cons of congressional term limits and the process needed to enact term limits.
- Look at the official website for each senator from your state and your Congressional representative. Describe any leadership roles in Congress and any committee memberships your representatives hold.
- Devote the end of your presentation to explaining the reasons for and reasons against enacting term limits.

8 The Powers of Congress

LESSONS

8.1 Enumerated Powers of Congress

8.2 Inherent and Implied Powers of Congress

8.3 Non-Legislative Powers of Congress

***National Geographic* Magazine:**
Scenes from the Japanese Internment Resonate Today

CRITICAL VIEWING Astronaut Edwin "Buzz" Aldrin, posing next to an American flag he and Neil Armstrong, the first humans to set foot on the moon, planted on the moon's surface in July 1969. The moon landing was the culmination of a major U.S. effort that began in 1961 when President John F. Kennedy delivered an address to a joint session of Congress. Why would Congress need to be involved in starting a space program?

LESSON
8.1 Enumerated Powers of Congress

Every time you hand over a dollar bill or some change, you are doing something that was made possible by the U.S. Congress. Congress is the government body that oversees the printing of dollars and creation of coins on behalf of the United States. If you pay for something with a debit card, Congress is involved because it oversees the banking system. If you pay with an app on your smartphone, Congress was directly involved. It makes laws affecting the company that made the phone, the one that designed the app, and the bank to which the app connects.

Taxing and Money Powers

Article I, Section 8, of the Constitution **enumerates**, or lists, 27 powers that Congress may exercise. The powers the Framers enumerate in the Constitution are the **expressed powers**, or the powers specifically assigned to the various branches of government. While the Framers listed these expressed powers, they provided very little detail on most of them. As a result, the way in which Congress has exercised some of those powers has been hotly debated.

THE POWER TO TAX As you have read, a major weakness of the Articles of Confederation was that the Confederation Congress could enact tax laws but not enforce them. The Framers took care of that problem in Article I. In Section 8, Clause 1, Congress is given the power to "lay and collect Taxes to pay the Debts and provide for the common Defence and general Welfare of the United States."

While the Framers granted Congress this important power, they didn't want Congress to have unlimited power to tax individuals. So they included restrictions on the taxing power. In Section 9, Clause 4, the Constitution states that any direct tax—that is, one paid directly by individuals—must be apportioned, or proportionally divided, among the states based on the census. Under this rule, the people in a state with one-tenth of the nation's population should bear one-tenth of the national tax burden. That limit was not placed on indirect taxes, which are levied on one person or entity and then passed on to someone else. For this reason, tariffs placed on imported goods—which are levied on businesses but passed on to consumers—are paid at the same rate from Florida to Alaska.

The 16th Amendment, ratified in 1913, changed the rules on direct taxes by throwing out the apportionment requirement in the case of income taxes. As the amendment states, "The Congress shall have the power to lay and collect taxes on incomes, from whatever sources derived, without apportionment among the several states, and without regard to any census or enumeration." Since then, income taxes have become the national government's biggest source of revenue.

OTHER MONEY POWERS Taxation is not the only money power that the Constitution enumerates for Congress. For example, Article I, Section 8, Clause 2, gives Congress the power to borrow money "on the credit of the United States." Congress uses this power when it faces a budget **deficit**, a situation that arises when government expenditures exceed revenues, by borrowing money to make up the shortfall. In fact, it uses this power regularly—since 1970, the federal government has faced a deficit every year except for the four years from 1998 to 2001. Each year that Congress borrows money, it adds to the public debt, also called the national debt. The net public debt is the total value of all outstanding federal government borrowing from the public. By 2021, that total was above $18 trillion.

Under Section 8, Clause 4, Congress also has the power to set the rules for **bankruptcy**, which is a legal declaration of the inability to pay all of one's debts. Under the rules set by Congress, bankruptcy cases are handled by some 90 bankruptcy courts where judges attempt to balance the individual or company's relief from debt with making sure that creditors—those who are owed money—are compensated as much as possible. These courts may order the liquidation, or sale, of the debtor's assets, such as real estate or financial accounts. The court may also order a new schedule of payments.

The Article also gives Congress the power "to coin money, [and] regulate the value thereof." The Mint Act of 1792 established the first U.S. coinage system, setting the dollar as the principal unit of American currency. Private banks circulated their own paper currency throughout the first half of the 19th century, and the government did not issue its own paper money until 1861. That year, Congress passed legislation to print and circulate financial instruments known as demand notes to help the government meet the costs of the Civil War. In a series of cases decided in the years following the war, the Supreme Court ruled that the power to coin included the power to print paper currency, or legal tender, on behalf of the national government. In 1913, Congress created the Federal Reserve System, through which 12 Federal Reserve Banks issue Federal Reserve notes, now the official paper currency of the United States.

Article I gives Congress the power to coin money, and since the 1860s, Congress has authorized the government to print paper money. The Federal Reserve estimates $1 trillion in U.S. paper money in circulation around the world, all of it printed at the U.S. Bureau of Engraving and Printing facilities in Washington, D.C., and Fort Worth, Texas.

HISTORICAL THINKING

1. **COMPARE AND CONTRAST** How are federal income taxes different from other direct taxes?
2. **ANALYZE CAUSE AND EFFECT** What would have to happen for the public debt to decrease dramatically?

Regulating Interstate Commerce

Article I, Section 8, Clause 3, is the **commerce clause**, which gives Congress the power to regulate commerce among the states, or interstate commerce. This has become the most controversial and wide-ranging power of Congress. The Constitution does not define interstate commerce, and over time, Congress has expanded the meaning of interstate commerce from the exchange of goods and services across state lines to a broader range of activities.

As you read in an earlier chapter, the landmark 1824 U.S. Supreme Court case *Gibbons* v. *Ogden* gave

Congress latitude to interpret its commerce power more broadly. This case defined commerce as not just the movement of goods but any kind of "commercial intercourse." Still, for many decades Congress did little to exercise the powers suggested by this expanded view. Then, in 1887, Congress created the Interstate Commerce Commission to regulate the railroad industry. This was the first of many federal regulatory agencies created to monitor how corporations acted and how commerce was conducted.

Unsurprisingly, the commerce clause has often been a point of contention between federal and state governments. The clause has been used to justify sweeping federal action, often at what is seen as the expense of state power. States retain the right to control economic activity within their own borders as long as the activity meets a three-pronged test established by the Supreme Court in *Southern Pacific Co.* v. *Arizona* (1945). According to this test, a state law is acceptable if it doesn't interfere with interstate commerce, doesn't supersede a larger federal interest, or doesn't affect commerce that requires regulation that should apply uniformly to all states.

In the 1960s, the commerce clause became a key tool in the civil rights movement. Bruce Boynton, an African-American law student, took a bus trip from Washington, D.C., to Alabama. At a rest stop in Richmond, Virginia, he was arrested for violating the state's segregation laws by sitting in the section of the restaurant set aside for White people only. Boynton challenged his conviction on the ground that the restaurant was involved in interstate commerce and thus could not discriminate on the basis of race under the Interstate Commerce Act. In *Boynton* v. *Virginia* (1960), the Supreme Court agreed with Boynton, banning segregation at bus terminals that served interstate passengers. Four years later, Congress passed the sweeping Civil Rights Act of 1964, invoking the commerce clause to prohibit racial discrimination in public accommodations involved in interstate commerce. The Supreme Court upheld the constitutionality of that law in *Heart of Atlanta Motel* v. *United States* later that year. In a unanimous decision, the Court ruled that the motel's policy of refusing rooms to Black guests violated the Civil Rights Act.

Congress's power under the commerce clause has not gone unchallenged, however. In 1990, Congress passed the Gun-Free School Zones Act, using the commerce clause to justify a ban on anyone possessing a handgun within 1,000 feet of a school. When that law was challenged in *United States* v. *Lopez* (1995), the Supreme Court struck it down.

In *Swift and Company* v. *United States*, a 1905 case that questioned the government's right to regulate a price-controlling beef trust formed by the biggest meatpacking companies in Chicago, the Supreme Court ruled in favor of the federal government. The Court said that the commerce clause gave it the power to regulate a "stream of commerce" that clearly crossed state lines.

HISTORICAL THINKING

3. **IDENTIFY MAIN IDEAS AND DETAILS** How does the language of the Constitution make a broad interpretation of Congress's power under the commerce clause possible?

4. **ANALYZE CAUSE AND EFFECT** How did the Supreme Court's decision in *Boynton* v. *Virginia* pave the way for the Civil Rights Act of 1964?

SUPREME COURT

United States v. *Lopez* 1995

Decided: April 26, 1995, 5–4

Majority: Chief Justice William Rehnquist wrote the opinion in favor of Lopez. Justices Anthony Kennedy and Clarence Thomas wrote concurring opinions.

Dissent: Justices John Paul Stevens, David Souter, and Stephen Breyer filed dissenting opinions. Stevens, Souter, and Justice Ruth Bader Ginsburg all joined Breyer's dissent.

In 1992 high school senior Alfonso Lopez, Jr., brought a handgun into his San Antonio, Texas, high school. Lopez was found guilty of illegal possession of a gun under the Gun-Free School Zones Act of 1990. He appealed his conviction to the Fifth Circuit Court of Appeals, which ruled in favor of his claim that Congress had exceeded its authority under the commerce clause when it passed the 1990 law. The government appealed that decision to the U.S. Supreme Court, arguing that the Gun-Free School Zones Act was within Congress's power to regulate interstate commerce for two reasons. First, guns in school could disrupt education and result in Americans' being less prepared to contribute to the economy. Second, guns in school can lead to gun violence, which would discourage interstate travel in the area of the school.

In a 5–4 decision, the Court ruled against the government. In the majority opinion, Justice Rehnquist called the law a "criminal statute that . . . has nothing to do with 'commerce' or any sort of economic enterprise, however broadly one might define those terms." Further, the Chief Justice wrote, "If we were to accept the Government's arguments, we are hard-pressed to posit any activity by an individual that Congress is without power to regulate." The Court's majority was unwilling to allow Congress such a broad definition of its power.

THINK ABOUT IT Why is the *Lopez* decision significant?

Additional Powers of Congress

Article I, Section 8, gives Congress several additional enumerated powers, and still more powers are enumerated in two other articles. For example, Section 8, Clause 4, states that Congress has the power to set the requirements for **naturalization**, or the process by which a person not born in the United States becomes a citizen. While early laws allowed only "free white" men to become naturalized citizens, current law rejects race-based prohibitions. Any immigrant who wishes to become a citizen must meet several requirements. For example, he or she must have lived legally in the country continuously for at least five years. Would-be citizens must also be able to communicate in spoken and written English and must have a basic understanding of U.S. history and government.

Congress has the power to establish a national postal service, including the power to make laws that govern postal routes, transportation of postal materials, and materials that can be sent through the postal system. Congress established the Post Office Department and placed it under the direction of the president in 1789. Further legislation passed in 1792 prohibited postal officials from opening letters. During the 20th century, the Post Office Department became the United States Postal Service (USPS). The USPS is a corporation owned by the government but which is largely self-funded. It has lost billions of dollars in recent years.

Congress also has the power to establish weights and measures. In 1866, Congress passed the Metric Act to allow for use of the internationally used metric system in order to promote international trade. In 1975 and 1988, Congress again passed legislation encouraging—but not mandating—the use of the metric system. Most Americans remained unconvinced, though, and the traditional system of weights and measures remains in use.

Section 8 also gives Congress the responsibility to "promote the progress of Science and useful Arts" by granting copyrights and patents. **Copyright** is the exclusive legal right to publish, sell, or distribute material such as music or writing, thereby protecting the right to benefit financially from artistic endeavors. Patents protect owners from having inventions used or sold without their permission for a specific period of time. Protecting these rights promotes innovation and

CRITICAL VIEWING Patents, regulated by Congress, inspire further innovation by guaranteeing inventors that their creations will be attributed to them and not infringed upon by others. Between 2001 and 2020, the number of patents granted for clean energy technology, such as the wind turbines shown above, more than doubled. What role do patents play in competition within a mixed economy like the United States?

new technology, which can stimulate employment and new industries.

In Article III, the Constitution calls for creation of the United States Supreme Court. It then gives Congress the power to establish the rest of the federal judicial system. As you have read, Congress began this task with the Judiciary Act of 1789. This law created the district courts and circuit courts under the Supreme Court. Later legislation changed the number of justices on the Supreme Court, reorganized judicial districts, expanded the jurisdiction of various courts, and established bankruptcy courts.

Under Article IV, Section 3, Congress regulates and governs public lands—such as national parks and forests—and U.S. territories, or lands controlled by the United States that are not states. In addition, Congress has the ultimate say regarding when an area or a territory can become a new state. Most of the states added since ratification of the Constitution have become such by first achieving territorial status, then meeting other requirements that often related to writing a territorial constitution and meeting a population requirement.

HISTORICAL THINKING

5. **MAKE CONNECTIONS** How do you think copyrights and patents promote the arts and innovation?
6. **IDENTIFY** Which branch of government has the power to determine whether an area or territory can become a state?

Congress and Foreign Policy

The Constitution enumerates specific powers that Congress can exercise regarding the nation's foreign policy. These include the powers to regulate commerce with foreign nations and for the Senate to approve any treaties made by the president with foreign nations as well as presidential diplomatic appointments. While the president is commander in chief, Congress is authorized to raise, provide for, and maintain an army and a navy and to set rules that the armed forces must follow. Finally, Congress has the power to declare war.

American troops, like these U.S. Marines in action in 2011, have been deployed in Afghanistan since late 2001. The September 11 terrorist attacks of that year and the subsequent joint resolution passed by Congress authorized the use of force to retaliate against those responsible for the attack, although a formal declaration of war was never made by Congress.

At times, Congress locks horns with the president in the exercise of these powers. After World War I, the Senate refused to ratify the Treaty of Versailles, thwarting President Woodrow Wilson's efforts to have the United States join the League of Nations. But no congressional approval is necessary for executive agreements, which are arrangements with foreign governments entered into by presidents as an exercise of their executive authority. These can address such issues as trade or formal recognition of a foreign government. The use of executive agreements has increased dramatically since World War II. In one analysis, researchers judged that over 90 percent of international agreements with foreign countries have been made via executive agreements. While congressional approval of executive agreements is not required, a 1972 law does mandate that Congress be given the text of all such agreements within 60 days of the day they were entered into.

Congress does hold some power over executive agreements—and additional power over treaties beyond the Senate's role in ratification. Some executive agreements and treaties can't be implemented without legislation. Congress thus can check the executive's freedom of action through its power to write that legislation.

War powers can be another point of contention between the legislative and executive branches. As commander in chief of the American armed forces, the president has the power to deploy the military abroad, but the power to declare war is reserved to Congress. Many military deployments initiated by the executive branch have not been accompanied by a declaration of war, which has led to tension between presidents and Congress. For example, U.S. military action in Vietnam in the late 1960s and early 1970s is commonly called the Vietnam War, yet Congress never issued a war declaration during those years. Partly in response to the U.S. commitment in Vietnam, Congress passed the War Powers Resolution in 1973, which put certain limits on executive actions, as you read earlier. Many presidents since have bristled at these limits, considering them obstacles to the exercise of their executive power.

HISTORICAL THINKING

7. **CATEGORIZE** What powers of Congress allow it to check the power of the president in matters of foreign policy?
8. **DRAW CONCLUSIONS** What did Congress hope to achieve by passing the War Powers Resolution?

Powers Prohibited to the National Government

In Article I, Section 9, Congress is specifically denied certain powers by the Constitution. As you read earlier, Congress cannot tax exports. This was originally included in the Constitution to settle economic differences between northern and southern states. At the time of the Constitutional Convention, the South's economy depended in large part on its exports of agricultural products. Southerners worried that a northern-dominated Congress might tax these exports, hurting its economy. The Framers reached a compromise by which the South agreed to allow congressional oversight of interstate commerce in return for a constitutional guarantee that no export taxes could be levied.

In addition, safeguards for civil liberties within the Constitution block Congress from passing certain laws. The legislature can't enact bills of attainder, which are laws aimed at a particular person or group. Nor can it pass ex post facto laws, which punish people for actions that are made illegal after people have taken them. The Bill of Rights puts other constraints on congressional power—for example, Congress cannot pass laws limiting speech or the practice of religion. In rare cases, particularly during times of war, there have been exceptions that have then been upheld by the Supreme Court. For example, Congress passed the Espionage Act of 1917, which was declared constitutional in *Schenck* v. *United States* (1919). In that case, the Supreme Court ruled that if an act of speech or symbolic speech presented a "clear and present danger" to public safety, it could be restrained.

HISTORICAL THINKING

9. **EXPLAIN** Why did the Supreme Court uphold the Espionage Act's restraints on freedom of speech in its ruling in *Schenck* v. *United States* in 1919?

LESSON 8.2 Inherent and Implied Powers of Congress

Congress exercises its powers by passing laws. In a recent year, it considered a host of bills, including bills addressing income tax rates and sanctions against certain foreign governments, and bills about health care for veterans and for miners. Congress also considered a bill about immigration and border security and another focused on broadband internet service. Clearly, the Framers couldn't have given Congress the express power to act on some of these issues—sanctions of other countries weren't part of foreign policy back in 1787, and broadband internet was far in the future. And yet the Constitution gives Congress the power to act on these questions through the ideas of inherent and implied powers.

Inherent Powers

Along with the many enumerated powers granted to Congress, the national government also enjoys certain **inherent powers**—the powers a national government must have by virtue of being a government. Any national government needs to be able to make treaties, regulate immigration, acquire territory, wage war, and make peace. If a government does not have the power to carry out these activities, the country is not going to function efficiently—or even remain in existence.

While some of the Constitution's enumerated powers are also inherent powers, such as the power to declare war, make treaties, and grant naturalization, others are not. For example, the Constitution doesn't say anything specific about what powers the government has to regulate immigration or what exactly to do with newly acquired territory.

Each branch of the U.S. government employs inherent powers. For example, Congress uses its inherent power to regulate immigration to pass laws about how many people can enter the United States legally each year and what rules immigrants must follow once they are here. President George W. Bush used inherent power when he ordered the formation of military commissions to try the cases of foreigners captured in the fight against international terrorists. Judges sometimes exercise the inherent power of the judiciary to recall a jury after it has rendered a verdict to ask jurors to re-examine that verdict.

Claims to inherent powers can be challenged. President Bush's military commissions were challenged by lawsuit, and in *Hamdan* v. *Rumsfeld* (2006), the Supreme Court ruled against the president. Justice John Paul Stevens, in writing the decision, stated that the military commission "lacks power to proceed because its structure and procedures violate both the UCMJ [Uniform Code of Military Justice, Sections 821 and 836] and the Geneva Conventions." (The Geneva Conventions are a series of international treaties regarding wartime behavior. The United States, along with more than 180 other nations, has signed one or more of these agreements.)

One inherent power is the power of the national government to own land. Through the Treaty of Paris that ended the American Revolution, the United States collectively acquired lands beyond the borders of the 13 original states. Under the Articles of Confederation, some of that land was organized as the Northwest Territory, which included what are now Illinois, Indiana, Michigan, Ohio, Wisconsin, and part of Minnesota. Once the Constitution was ratified and the new national government was operating, the United States sold parcels of Northwest Territory land to new settlers, a practice that continued with other publicly owned lands. Indeed, land sales were a major source of

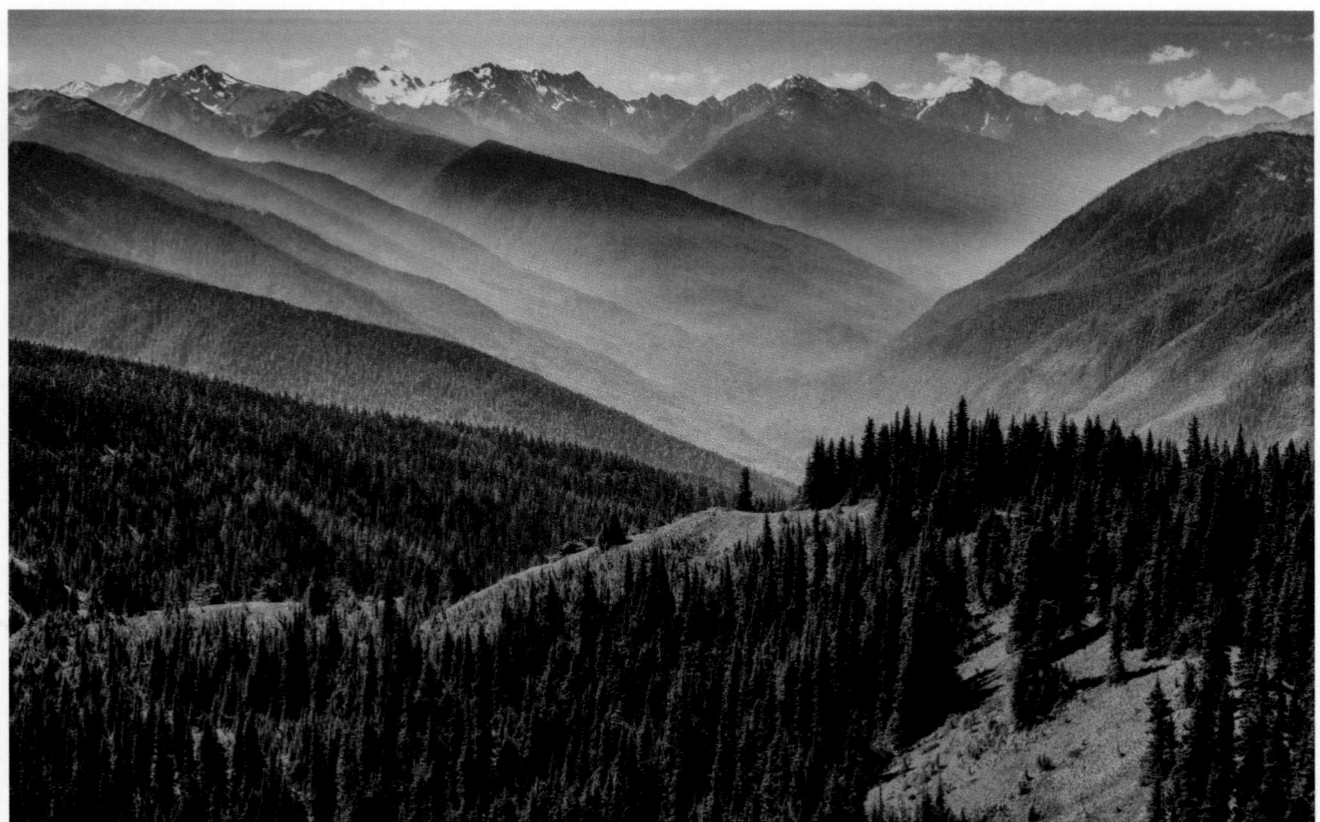

CRITICAL VIEWING The federal government has the inherent power to own and dispose of land. While federally owned land may be used to generate income, such as through grazing leases, the government also puts aside much of this land for recreation. This is especially true of the country's more than 415 national parks and other sites, including Olympic National Park in Washington, which includes both old-growth rainforests and glacier-topped mountains. Why do you think the federal government chooses to protect parks like Olympic from private ownership?

Share of Federal Land in Each State

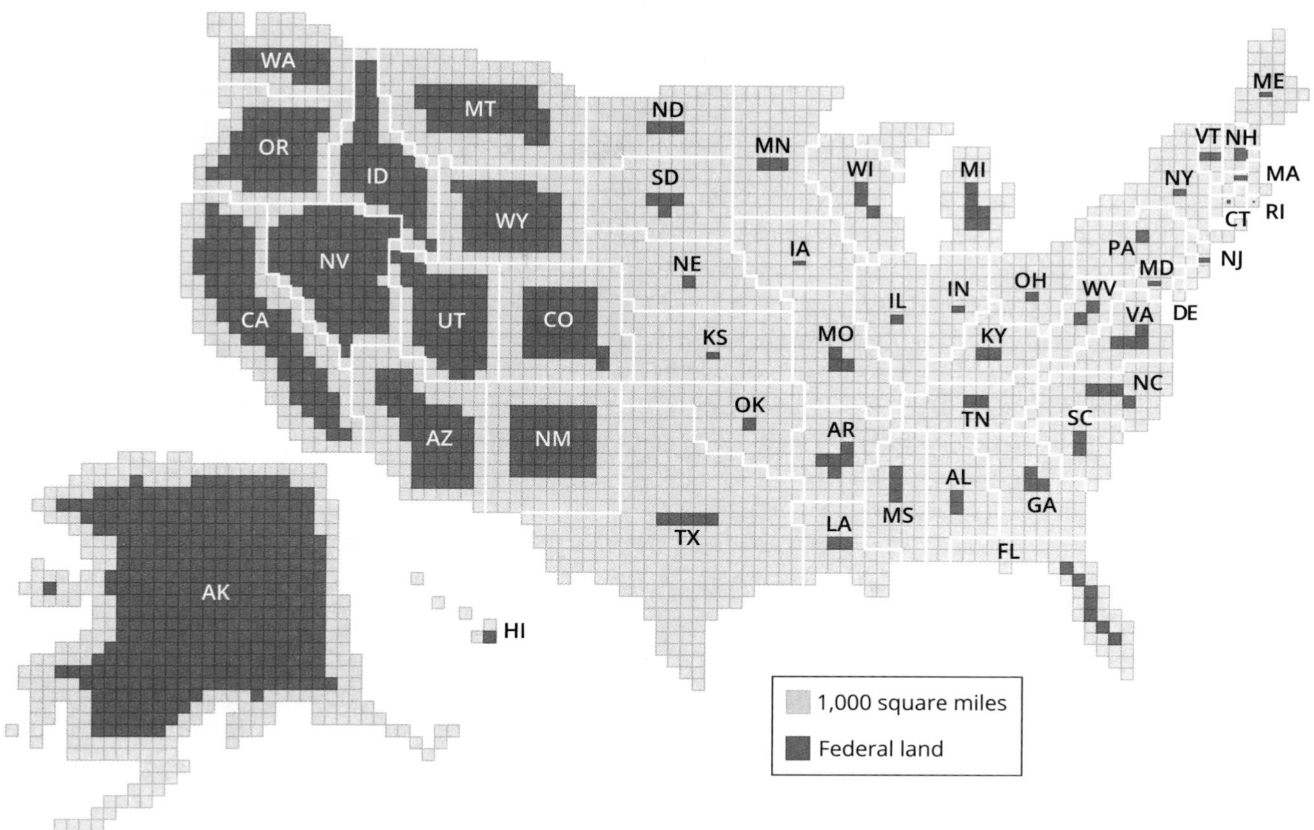

income to the national government throughout much of the 1800s. To this day, the national government owns most of the acreage in most far western states. One in every 10 acres of land in the United States remains under the control of the U.S. Bureau of Land Management (BLM). The BLM reserves this land for uses including general conservation and for certain economic activities, such as mining, energy production, and livestock grazing. Individuals and businesses must lease the land or get permits to use it for those economic activities.

HISTORICAL THINKING

1. **COMPARE AND CONTRAST** What is the difference between enumerated and inherent powers?
2. **INTERPRET MAPS** Why do you think it is important that the federal government owns public land in every one of the 50 states?

Implied Powers

Implied powers are those that are indirectly expressed, or implied, by the Constitution. For example, in Article III, Section 1, the Constitution says that Congress has the power to create "inferior Courts" as it deems necessary. That section says further that federal judges "shall, at stated Times, receive for their Services, a Compensation," which implicitly grants Congress the power to set the compensation of the federal judiciary.

IMPLIED POWERS AND THE ELASTIC CLAUSE
Earlier you read about the necessary and proper clause in Article I, Section 8, Clause 18, of the Constitution:

> *[Congress has the power to make] all Laws which shall be necessary and proper for carrying into Execution the foregoing [expressed] Powers, and all other Powers vested by this Constitution in the Government of the United States, or in any Department or Officer thereof.*

The necessary and proper clause is also known as the **elastic clause**, because it gives elasticity to our constitutional system. In *McCulloch* v. *Maryland* (1819), a case involving the power of Congress to charter a national bank, Chief Justice John Marshall of the Supreme Court issued an expansive definition of what qualifies as an implied power: "Let the end be legitimate, let it be within the scope of the constitution, and all means which are appropriate, which are plainly adapted to that end, which are not prohibited, but consist with the letter and spirit of the constitution, are constitutional."

Congress has taken a staggering number of legislative actions under the umbrella of the necessary and proper clause, from passing laws to set national economic policy to those that establish government departments. Yet, as the clause states, implied powers need to be based on expressed powers. For example, the Constitution says only that Congress has the power to coin money, presumably in the form of gold or silver coins. But Congress also has the expressed power to borrow, and on that basis it eventually issued paper currency that represented sums owed by the government to the person holding the paper currency. In the past, dollar bills could be exchanged for silver coins. Today, they can only be exchanged for other dollar bills. Another example is the establishment of federal financial aid for education, a program that provides more than $120 billion in grants, loans, and other funds to college and career-school students. The implied power to pass such legislation originates from Congress's enumerated power to tax and spend tax revenue for the general welfare.

IMPLIED POWERS AND THE COMMERCE CLAUSE As you know, Congress has frequently pointed to the commerce clause to justify its involvement in a variety of issues, ranging from the economy to communications to civil rights. During President Franklin D. Roosevelt's New Deal, a policy aimed at addressing the economic crisis caused by the Great Depression, the Supreme Court repeatedly upheld Congress's power under the commerce clause. Even activities that occurred entirely within a state were rarely viewed as outside the regulatory power of the national government. For example, in 1942 the Supreme Court held that the wheat a farmer grew for his own consumption was subject to federal regulation. The Court reasoned that the farmer's consumption of his own wheat reduced the

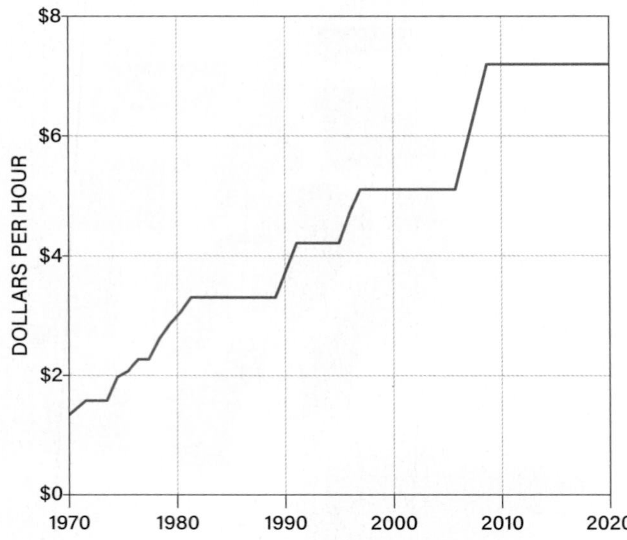

demand for wheat and therefore could have an effect on interstate commerce. In 1941, the Court ruled unanimously that a 1938 law establishing a minimum wage as well as other conditions in the workplace was constitutional. It reasoned that the use of substandard conditions in one or more states could give those states an economic advantage in interstate commerce.

In 1980 the Supreme Court acknowledged in *McLain* v. *Real Estate Board of New Orleans, Inc.,* that the commerce clause had "long been interpreted to extend beyond activities actually in interstate commerce to reach other activities that, while wholly local in nature, nevertheless substantially affect interstate commerce." Today, Congress can regulate almost any kind of economic activity, no matter where it occurs. In recent years, though, the Court has occasionally curbed Congress's expansive use of the commerce clause. A variety of decisions have either limited the power of the federal government or enhanced the power of the states.

As you read, the Supreme Court held in *United States* v. *Lopez* (1995) that Congress had exceeded its constitutional authority under the commerce clause when it proclaimed a gun-free zone around schools. Two years later, in another gun-related case, the Court struck down portions of the Brady Handgun Violence Prevention Act of 1993, which required state and local law enforcement officers to conduct background

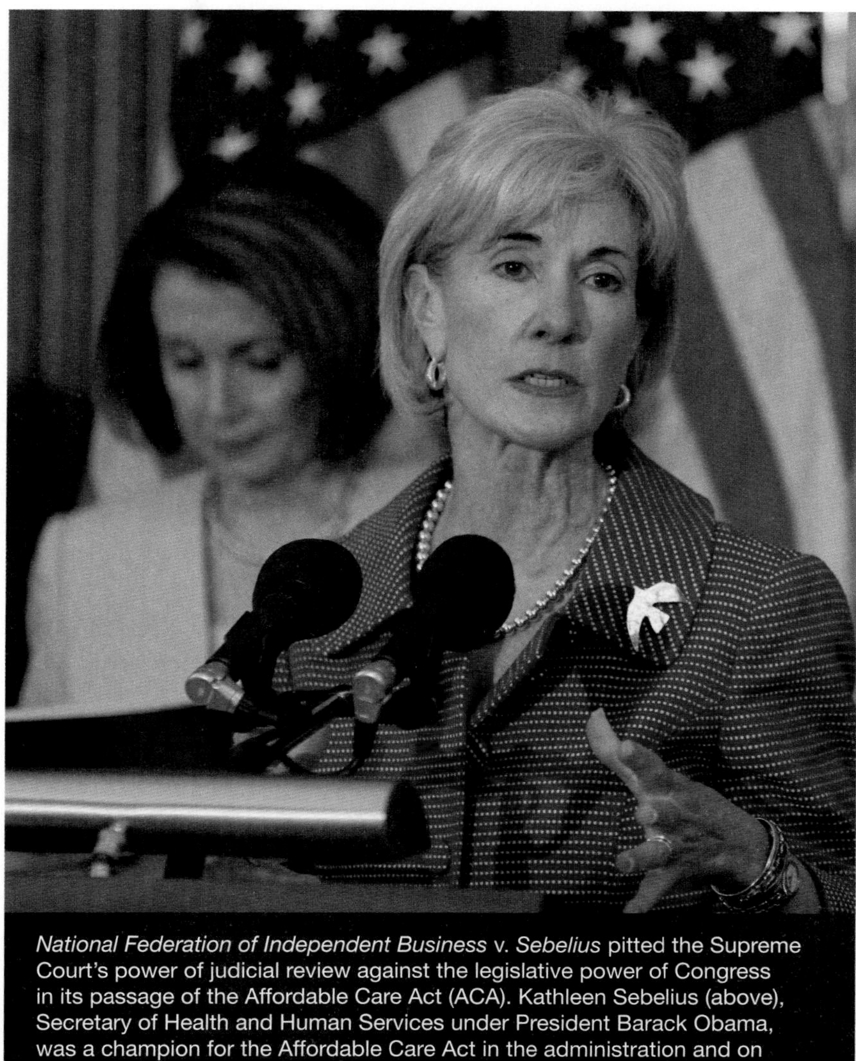

National Federation of Independent Business v. *Sebelius* pitted the Supreme Court's power of judicial review against the legislative power of Congress in its passage of the Affordable Care Act (ACA). Kathleen Sebelius (above), Secretary of Health and Human Services under President Barack Obama, was a champion for the Affordable Care Act in the administration and on Capitol Hill.

checks on prospective handgun buyers until a national instant-check system could be implemented. The Court stated that Congress lacked the power to force state employees into federal service in this way.

In 2000 the Supreme Court again drew attention to use of the commerce clause when it invalidated a key provision of the federal Violence Against Women Act of 1994. This legislation allowed women to sue in federal court when they were victims of gender-motivated violence, such as rape. But the Court upheld a federal appellate court's ruling that the commerce clause did not justify national regulation of noneconomic, criminal conduct.

Perhaps the biggest news regarding use of the commerce clause in recent years was the 2012 ruling in *National Federation of Independent Business* v. *Sebelius*, which concerned the constitutionality of the Affordable Care Act, popularly known as Obamacare. In this case, the Court upheld most of the legislation that Congress had passed. But two of Chief Justice John Roberts's arguments in the decision set limits on the powers of the national government. Roberts contended that the federal government cannot, under the commerce clause, require individuals to purchase something—in this case, health-care insurance. Yet, Roberts wrote, the government can encourage such behavior through the tax code, which is what the Affordable Care Act did. Roberts also stated that the national government cannot force the states to expand Medicaid by threatening to take away each state's share of federal Medicaid funds if they do not comply. This had been one of the most controversial parts of the original legislation. Roberts argued that cutting the states off completely would do too much damage to their budgets.

HISTORICAL THINKING

3. **SYNTHESIZE** What is necessary for an implied power to be constitutional?
4. **ANALYZE VISUALS** Based on the graph showing changes in the minimum wage, what generalization can you make about how often Congress raises the minimum wage?
5. **ASK AND ANSWER QUESTIONS** What questions do you think a judge might ask to determine whether Congress had the power to raise the minimum wage?

LESSON 8.3

Non-Legislative Powers of Congress

The Framers created a system of checks and balances to prevent abuse of power by any branch of government. Therefore, in addition to its legislative role, Congress also plays the role of watchdog, overseeing the executive branch and the many actions it takes. It is the first line of defense against the power of the executive. Furthermore, Congress provides the last line of defense against wrongdoing by officials in any of the three branches through its power to impeach. As you might imagine, these powers sometimes lead to tension between the legislative branch and the executive branch.

Investigation and Oversight

The executive bureaucracy is massive and wields tremendous power. Numerous congressional committees and subcommittees regularly hold hearings to investigate the actions of this bureaucracy and key executive branch officials, including the president. The committees and subcommittees can issue a **subpoena**, which is a legal order requiring someone to testify or to supply evidence regarding matters under investigation. After it completes an investigation, Congress can produce a report or pass bills or resolutions aimed at correcting or commenting on any executive branch actions it deems objectionable. Congress wields another important weapon—it can rein in executive power by choosing not to provide the money the bureaucracy needs to function.

CRITICAL VIEWING Two months after he was fired by President Richard Nixon, former White House counsel John Dean testified before the Senate Select Committee on Presidential Campaign Activities. His testimony was immediately explosive. Dean was eventually convicted of obstruction of justice for his involvement in the Watergate scandal and served four months in prison. How do details in this photograph reveal the heightened attention given to this example of congressional oversight?

Former FBI Director James Comey was one of several current and former government officials among the more than 200 witnesses called to testify before the Senate Intelligence Committee for its hearings on possible Russian involvement in the 2016 U.S. presidential election.

THE WATERGATE HEARINGS A classic example of congressional oversight is the Watergate hearings. In 1973, after a break-in at the Democratic National Committee office at the Watergate complex in Washington, D.C., the year before, the Senate formed a special committee. The purpose of this committee was to investigate the role of President Richard Nixon, a Republican, and White House staffers in the break-in. The committee also held hearings to investigate Nixon's use of his position to cover up the crime. Senators and committee attorneys who questioned many members of the Nixon administration and campaign staff learned of a host of questionable and illegal or perhaps illegal activities. Former White House lawyer John Dean stunned the committee—and the national television audience—by stating that the president had ordered an illegal cover-up of the break-in. While not all Americans accepted Dean's testimony, the revelation by another witness that the White House had a recording system in the Oval Office provided a way to verify Dean's charges.

Nixon claimed that executive privilege, a president's right to keep communications with advisors confidential and private in the interest of national security, protected him from having to release all the recordings to investigators. He argued that a president needs honest and frank conversation with his aides in order to receive the best advice and make the best decisions. In 1974 the Supreme Court ruled unanimously against Nixon, stating that executive privilege did not apply if the communications pertained to an actual criminal investigation.

Soon after the Supreme Court ruling, the House Judiciary Committee approved three articles of impeachment. Forced by the Court decision, Nixon released transcripts of the requested tapes that included clear evidence of his guilt in the cover-up. With support even from his own Republican party evaporating, Nixon resigned from office.

POLITICS AND OVERSIGHT The zeal with which Congress wields its oversight power varies, depending on which political party or parties control Congress and which controls the White House. Many people believe Congress goes overboard in investigations when the congressional majority and the White House are from different parties. Republicans made such accusations against Democrats who controlled Congress during Republican George W. Bush's administration. Democrats lodged the same complaint after Republicans took control of both chambers while Democrat Barack Obama was president. When the Democratically controlled House launched investigations into the actions of the Trump administration, President Trump made it a matter of administration policy to refuse to allow current and former executive branch officials to testify before Congress in investigations he labeled as political.

But when the same party controls both Congress and the White House, critics say Congress exercises far too little oversight. In the first two years of Donald Trump's presidency, there were allegations that members of the Trump campaign may have communicated improperly with the Russian government during the 2016 election. While both the Republican-dominated House and Senate intelligence committees launched investigations, the House committee split into partisan factions and produced no unified findings. The Senate Intelligence Committee remained more bipartisan, but the Republican Congress did little to investigate other issues involving the Republican president and his administration.

Even when only one chamber is controlled by the same party as the president, congressional oversight can be less effective. After winning control of the House in the 2018 midterm election, for example, Democrats vowed to wield the oversight power more vigorously. But the Senate remained in Republican hands after that election, and its leadership cast House oversight actions as politically motivated. During the first impeachment trial of President Trump, the Republican majority in the Senate voted against issuing subpoenas for witnesses and documents and moved quickly to acquit the president of all charges.

One way Congress has tried to oversee its own operations is by establishing separate oversight bodies. One such body is the Congressional Budget Office (CBO), charged with evaluating the impact of every piece of proposed legislation on the federal budget and the budget deficit. CBO reports are available to the public, and members of Congress often adjust details of bills to earn a better evaluation from the CBO.

IMPEACHMENT POWER Congress has the power to impeach and remove from office the president, vice president, and other civil officers, such as federal judges or members of Congress. The House of Representatives is vested with the power to impeach,

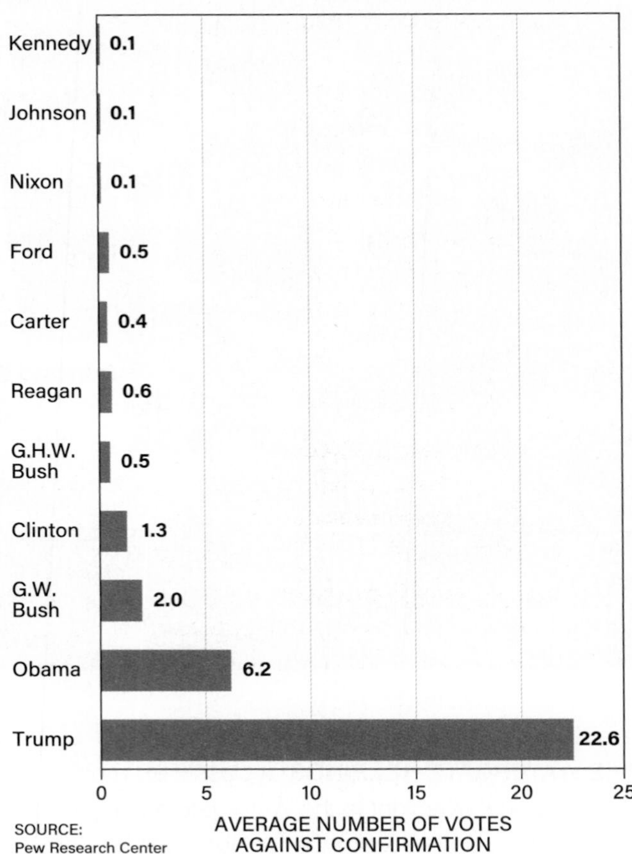

or charge a public official with improper conduct. Once impeached by the House, the accused official is tried in the Senate, where a two-thirds supermajority is needed to convict the accused official. A convicted official is removed from office and is disqualified from ever holding any "Office of honor, Trust or Profit under the United States," as stated in Article I, Section 3.

The House has impeached three presidents: Andrew Johnson in 1868, Bill Clinton in 1998, and Donald Trump in 2019 and 2021. Trump was the first U.S. president to be impeached twice and had the most members of his own party vote for his impeachment. All three presidents were acquitted by the Senate. (Editor's Note: President Trump was acquitted by the Senate for his 2019 impeachment, but his second impeachment trial had not yet taken place at the time this program was released.) As you have read, a vote to impeach President Richard Nixon was pending before the full House of Representatives in 1974 when Nixon became the only president to resign from office.

Although presidential impeachments get the most attention, Congress has impeached other officials. Only one United States Supreme Court justice—Samuel Chase, in 1804—has ever been impeached, but he was later acquitted by the Senate. In all, the House has voted to impeach 20 officials, the majority of whom have been judges. Of these 20 people, only 8 have been found guilty by the Senate, though several others resigned rather than face trial. In 2010, Judge Thomas Porteous, of a federal district court in Louisiana, was found guilty of bribery and perjury, or lying under oath, and removed from office.

HISTORICAL THINKING

1. **DRAW CONCLUSIONS** Why do you think Congress is more or less aggressive in its use of oversight power, depending on what party holds the White House?
2. **FORM AND SUPPORT OPINIONS** Why do you think evaluations from the Congressional Budget Office influence how members of Congress write legislation?
3. **SEQUENCE** What has to happen within Congress for a president or another official to be forced to leave office?

Senate Confirmation

Article II, Section 2, gives the Senate an additional tool for oversight. This section of the Constitution states that the president may appoint ambassadors, justices of the Supreme Court, and other officers of the United States "with the Advice and Consent of the Senate." The Constitution leaves the precise nature of how the Senate will give this advice and consent up to the lawmakers. Unsurprisingly, this constitutional leeway has resulted in some contentious moments in American political history.

THE CONFIRMATION PROCESS The Senate's role in the confirmation process is to confirm or deny a president's nominee for the cabinet, for the Supreme Court or other federal judgeship, or for other top executive branch offices. Nominees appear first before the appropriate Senate committee—for example, the Judiciary Committee for federal judges or the Foreign Relations Committee for the secretary of state. During the hearings, senators ask the nominee questions and hear from other witnesses who favor or oppose the nomination. If the individual committee approves the nominee, the full Senate then votes on the nomination.

Senate confirmation hearings have been very politicized at times. Judicial appointments often receive the most intense scrutiny, because federal judges serve for life. The president is typically given a freer hand in cabinet appointments, since the heads of executive departments are expected to be loyal to the president and these appointments generally end when a president leaves office. Nonetheless, Senate confirmation is an important check on the president's power.

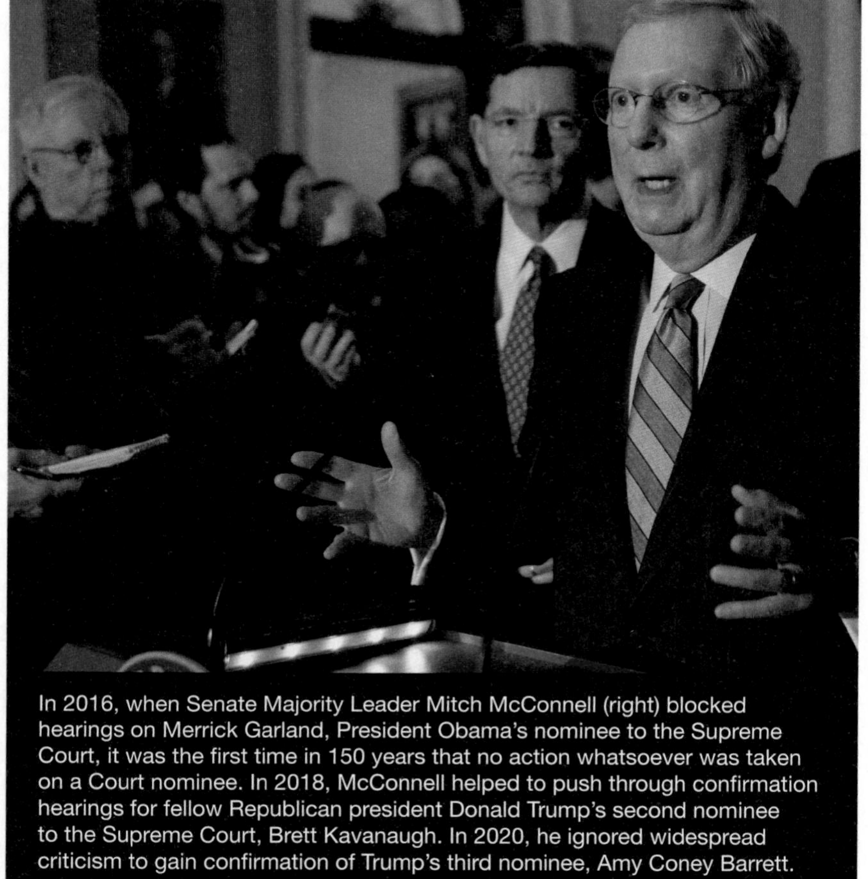

In 2016, when Senate Majority Leader Mitch McConnell (right) blocked hearings on Merrick Garland, President Obama's nominee to the Supreme Court, it was the first time in 150 years that no action whatsoever was taken on a Court nominee. In 2018, McConnell helped to push through confirmation hearings for fellow Republican president Donald Trump's second nominee to the Supreme Court, Brett Kavanaugh. In 2020, he ignored widespread criticism to gain confirmation of Trump's third nominee, Amy Coney Barrett.

Throughout history, the Senate has at times rejected presidential nominees for executive and judicial positions. In recent decades, however, it has become more common for senators from one party to delay nominations as part of an ideological struggle with a president from the other party. Senate rules make delaying tactics available to both the minority and majority parties.

FILIBUSTERS AND THE NUCLEAR OPTION The filibuster, which allows a senator or team of senators to postpone a vote by speaking without letup on the Senate floor, has often been used to delay nominations. This maneuver was first employed on a significant scale in the 1990s by Republicans who wanted to block judicial nominations by President Bill Clinton, a Democrat. Democrats then adopted it against Republican president George W. Bush. Under Obama, Republicans resumed the practice, but in 2013 the Democratic majority in the Senate curbed the practice by exercising what has been called the nuclear option.

The nuclear option is a workaround for the Senate rule that requires a supermajority vote to end a filibuster. While a supermajority is required to end a filibuster, a simple majority is all that is needed to change Senate rules. Prior to the early 21st century, such a rule change was considered unthinkable, much like nuclear war. Senators of both parties cherished the power of the filibuster, but intense partisanship changed the mood in the 2000s.

In 2005, after Senate Democrats filibustered many Bush nominees, Republicans threatened to use the nuclear option to move nominations forward. At the last minute, a bipartisan group engineered a compromise in which senators agreed to reserve the filibuster for extraordinary circumstances. In 2013, with Republicans blocking a large number of Obama nominees, Democrats claimed the Republicans had violated this agreement, and the Democratic majority voted to change the rules. They deployed the nuclear option and eliminated use of the filibuster against all executive and judicial nominees other than those to the Supreme Court.

When Republicans took control of the Senate after the 2014 midterm elections, they no longer needed the filibuster to block nominations. Following the death of conservative Supreme Court Justice Antonin Scalia in February 2016, Senate Majority Leader Mitch McConnell argued that the November presidential election, 10 months away, should be a referendum on what party the American people preferred to fill the vacancy. When President Obama nominated Merrick Garland, a respected moderate, to fill the late Justice Scalia's seat, the Republican majority in the Senate refused to hold a confirmation hearing.

In November 2016, Republican Donald Trump was elected president. McConnell's gamble that a Republican would win the election had paid off: Trump nominated Neil Gorsuch, a respected and very conservative jurist. Angry over the Republican treatment of the Garland nomination, Senate Democrats filibustered Gorsuch's nomination. The Republican majority quickly abolished use of the filibuster for Supreme Court nominations, and the Senate confirmed Gorsuch in April 2017. The rule change meant the Democrats could do little to block Trump's 2018 nomination of Brett Kavanaugh to replace retiring justice Anthony Kennedy. Kavanaugh, who faced allegations of sexual assault, was confirmed by the Senate in a 50–48 vote. (Two senators did not vote.)

One week following the death of Justice Ruth Bader Ginsburg in September 2020, President Trump nominated Amy Coney Barrett to fill her vacancy. Barrett's quick nomination sparked controversy, as did the timing of her confirmation—only eight days before the presidential election. Barrett was confirmed by a narrow Senate vote of 52–48, mostly along party lines.

HISTORICAL THINKING

4. **ANALYZE VISUALS** How does the graph showing the average number of *no* votes for federal judicial nominees connect with what you read about partisanship in recent years?
5. **ANALYZE CAUSE AND EFFECT** Explain the effect of the implementation of the so-called nuclear option in 2013.
6. **COMPARE AND CONTRAST** How does responsibility for the confirmation power of Congress differ from the responsibility for oversight power between the two chambers?

NATIONAL GEOGRAPHIC

Scenes from the Japanese Internment Resonate Today

by Ann Curry *National Geographic* Magazine, October 2018

Japanese-American Boy Scouts in Wyoming's Heart Mountain Relocation Center salute the flag of the United States in 1943.

Congress supported the internment of Japanese Americans during World War II, but decades later, it exercised non-legislative powers by appointing a commission to investigate and reveal the history of the camps. As Ann Curry writes in "Scenes from the Japanese Internment Resonate Today," that investigation provided insight into the profound suffering of the victims of this policy.

After Japan attacked the U.S. naval base in Pearl Harbor, Hawaii, on December 7, 1941, anti-Japanese sentiment skyrocketed in the United States. Following recommendations from American military leaders, President Franklin D. Roosevelt signed an executive order in February 1942 that allowed the military to identify and place U.S. residents of Japanese ancestry in internment camps. Congress quickly lent its support to the decision.

Between 1942 and 1946, more than 120,000 civilians of Japanese descent (two-thirds of whom were American citizens) living on the West Coast were forcibly relocated to internment camps in remote, desolate areas. People could bring only what they could carry and were forced to dispose of everything else they owned in a short time, suffering huge financial losses.

This forced relocation had a lifelong impact on detainees. Curry describes how many struggled for decades after the internment ended to understand how their own country could have treated them in such a way. One former detainee, Satsuki Ina, described this feeling to Curry:

> *The numbers placed on tags to identify detained families in the U.S. were so humiliating that many who were incarcerated are still wrestling with their emotions about it, Ina says, adding, "To become a number means to no longer be known. Many felt this loss of identity and meaning as America turned its back on us."*

In 1980, Congress created the Commission on Wartime Relocation and Internment of Civilians to research the internment. The commission's report revealed that the detainees had been held in deplorable conditions and that prejudice against people of Japanese ancestry—not any real security concern—prompted the action. In 1988, Congress exercised its legislative powers to pass a law authorizing payments to those detainees who were still living. The restitution came late, but it reflected the country's effort to atone for a terrible wrong.

Access the full version of "Scenes from the Japanese Internment Resonate Today" by Ann Curry through the Resources Menu in MindTap.

THINK ABOUT IT How did Congress approach the internment of civilians of Japanese descent during and

CHAPTER 8

THE POWERS OF CONGRESS

Review

VOCABULARY

Complete each sentence below with one of the vocabulary terms from this chapter.

1. The federal government borrows money when it faces a(n) _______ because expenditures outpace revenues.
2. Congress has invoked Article I, Section 8, Clause 3, known as the _______, to enact a variety of legislation that can be argued to affect economic activities.
3. An immigrant must go through many steps in the _______ process before he or she can become a citizen.
4. Through _______, writers and musicians can control the rights to the works that they produce.
5. All three branches possess certain _______ that are spelled out in the Constitution.
6. The implied powers of Congress are granted through the necessary and proper clause, also known as the _______.
7. To aid in their investigations, House and Senate committees can issue a _______, which legally orders people to appear before them to testify.

MAIN IDEAS

Answer the following questions. Support your answer with evidence from the chapter.

8. What event prompted the U.S. government to issue its own paper currency for the first time in 1861? **LESSON 8.1**
9. How is bankruptcy resolved so as to be fair to all parties involved? **LESSON 8.1**
10. How do treaties and executive agreements differ? **LESSON 8.1**
11. What is the difference between enumerated and implied powers? **LESSON 8.2**
12. Why is *elastic clause* an appropriate alternate name for the necessary and proper clause? **LESSON 8.2**
13. What check can be placed on Congress if it interprets its powers under the commerce clause too broadly? **LESSON 8.2**
14. In general, how have most impeachment efforts fared in Congress? **LESSON 8.3**
15. What is the role of the Congressional Budget Office? **LESSON 8.3**
16. Why is the Senate confirmation process for a federal judgeship typically more complicated than for a nominee for an executive branch position? **LESSON 8.3**

HISTORICAL THINKING

Answer the following questions. Support your answer with evidence from the chapter.

17. **MAKE CONNECTIONS** What American political value—the right to liberty, to equality, or to property—is represented in the constitutional requirement that all tariffs on imports "shall be uniform throughout the United States"? Explain your answer.
18. **IDENTIFY PROBLEMS AND SOLUTIONS** What do you think the experiences under the Articles of Confederation taught the Framers about the power to tax?
19. **MAKE INFERENCES** How do the characteristics of democratic republics help explain why the Framers gave Congress the degree of power it has?
20. **ANALYZE CAUSE AND EFFECT** Why does tension sometimes exist between the executive and legislative branches when it comes to foreign policy?
21. **EVALUATE** What do you think are the biggest advantages and disadvantages of the wording of the necessary and proper clause for Congress?

22. **MAKE GENERALIZATIONS** Explain why each word in the phrase *interstate commerce* has made the commerce clause so controversial over the years.

23. **MAKE CONNECTIONS** In what way are the laws Congress passed to create and empower the Internal Revenue Service—which collects taxes for the federal government—an exercise of implied powers?

24. **DRAW CONCLUSIONS** How do you think congressional oversight power is affected when the party that does not hold the White House holds a majority in at least one house of Congress? Why?

INTERPRET VISUALS

The table below shows the projected change in outlays (expenditures), revenues, and the annual budget deficit associated with the laws passed by Congress in 2015. (The projections were made before the 2015 budgetary impact could be known.) Study the table, then answer the questions.

Projected Budget Impact of Laws Enacted by Congress in 2015 (in billions of $USD)

Year	Total Outlays	Total Revenue	Net Increase on Deficit
2015	+ $9	– $1	+ $10
2016	+ $27	– $134	+ $161
2017	+ $24	– $90	+ $114
2018	+ $13	– $61	+ $74
2019	+ $29	– $47	+ $76
2020	+ $28	– $2	+ $30
2021	+ $29	+ $3	+ $26
2022	+ $31	– $6	+ $37
2023	+ $32	– $18	+ $50
2024	+ $29	– $28	+ $57
2025	– $8	– $35	+ $27

Source: Congressional Budget Office, 2017

25. What is the general impact of legislation enacted in the first session (2015) of the 114th Congress (2015–2016), according to the CBO?

26. What challenge does the CBO face in making estimates regarding the national budget over the course of many years?

ANALYZE SOURCES

Read the following excerpt from Federalist No. 51. Then answer the question that follows.

> In framing a government, which is to be administered by men over men, the great difficulty is this: You must first enable the government to control the governed; and in the next place, oblige it to control itself.

27. What point was the author of this quotation trying to convey about the power of a democratic legislature?

CONNECT TO YOUR LIFE

28. **EXPLANATORY** Conduct research to find an example of legislation that your district's member of the House of Representatives has recently proposed or supported. Use the representative's website or reliable news sources to determine the purpose and intended impact of the law and the representative's reasons for supporting it. Then write a paragraph or two describing the legislation and how it might affect your life. Explain whether you agree or disagree with your representative and why.

TIPS

- Visit the House of Representatives website and enter your zip code to find your representative.
- Visit your representative's congressional website to find a list of bills your representative has authored or supports.
- Find an issue that interests you, and read about your representative's views on a bill related to that issue.
- Summarize the legislation and its intended impact as concisely as possible.
- Identify the congressperson's reasons for supporting the legislation.
- Explain how you think the legislation will affect you and others, and state your opinion on the legislation.

CHAPTER 9

The Legislative Process

LESSONS

9.1 Introducing and Passing Laws

9.2 Conference Committees and Presidential Action

9.3 The Budgeting Process

CRITICAL VIEWING Speaker of the House Nancy Pelosi, surrounded by other members of the House of Representatives, signs the Coronavirus Aid, Relief, and Economic Security (CARES) Act on March 27, 2020. In the face of the coronavirus threat, Congress acted with unusual swiftness. How can you tell from the photo that the signing was a matter of importance?

LESSON
9.1 Introducing and Passing Laws

When some people hear the word *law*, they think of rules that define crimes and punishments. Laws are more than that, though. Federal laws direct the power of the national government toward purposes Congress chooses: Laws create government agencies and instruct them in what to do, enable the government to collect taxes, and control every penny the government spends. Laws created the National Weather Service, which warns people when hurricanes or tornadoes are about to slam into their communities. Laws also created the Federal Emergency Management Agency (FEMA), which helps communities recover after such storms hit. Because laws are so important, the procedures governing lawmaking are important, too.

Introducing a Bill

A **bill** is a proposed law. It is called a bill from the time it is introduced in the legislature until it is either enacted and becomes a law or statute (also called an act)—or rejected. A bill becomes law only if it is passed by both the House and the Senate and then signed by the president. If the president vetoes a bill, it can still become a law if a supermajority of each house passes the bill again to override the veto. While the process sounds simple, it is often long and involved and can include the input of many people. Every word and detail of a bill may be examined, discussed, and negotiated before the process is finished.

What do we get for the $17–18 billion spent annually by the Federal Aviation Administration (FAA)? The FAA monitors compliance of the safety systems, environmental programs, and finances of more than 19,000 U.S. airports. Nearly 46,000 FAA employees supervise more than 43,000 flights that carry more than 2.6 million passengers each day. It licenses aircraft and pilots and certifies training courses. The agency also coordinates with international carriers and airports to ensure safe and smooth international air travel.

While only members of Congress can formally introduce a bill, ideas for legislation may come from many sources, including congressional staff, individual citizens, individual businesses, and lobbying groups. Most bills, however, are proposed by the executive branch, and even the texts of many bills are developed and written by the White House or an executive agency. Then a senator or representative who supports the bill introduces it in Congress. A member who introduces a bill becomes its sponsor. Most bills have multiple sponsors, or co-sponsors.

While most bills can be introduced in either the House or the Senate, the Constitution has a special rule regarding laws that create taxes. The first clause of Article I, Section 7, is known as the origination clause. It states that "all Bills for raising Revenue shall originate in the House of Representatives." This language reflected the Framers' belief that the legislative chamber closest to the people should be the only one that can impose taxes. (Remember that when the Constitution was written, senators were chosen by state legislators, not elected by the people.)

By requiring that tax bills originate in the House, the Framers gave large-population states—which have more representatives—a stronger voice in tax rules. That was the theory behind the origination clause. Actually, it's a moot, or irrelevant, point. Since the Senate can amend the language of any tax bill, just as it can any other bill, the origination requirement is simply a formality.

TYPES OF LEGISLATION The most familiar type of bill is a public bill, which applies to the nation as a whole. Bills making possession of anti-tank missiles a crime or setting income tax rates are public bills—they apply to everyone. Private bills apply only to specific persons or places, and members of Congress generally introduce them to help constituents. For instance, a private bill may confer legal resident status on one or a few individuals named in the bill or exempt a specific business from a certain tax or regulation. Private bills generally come about after a personal appeal to a member of Congress.

In addition to bills, Congress also issues formal statements of its will or intent, known as **resolutions**. There are three types of resolution.

- A joint resolution has the force of law. It must be passed by both chambers of Congress in identical form, and it requires the president's signature. Joint resolutions are used to propose changes in law for temporary or unusual purposes and to propose amendments to the Constitution.
- Concurrent resolutions deal with matters that require joint action by both chambers. They don't have the force of law, and they don't require the president's signature. Typically, they are used to publicly express a position or to cover rules applying to both chambers, such as the date they will adjourn. The annual budget resolution is also a concurrent resolution.
- Simple resolutions deal with matters affecting only one chamber. Like concurrent resolutions, they do not have the force of law and they do not require the president's signature. Simple resolutions are typically used to change a chamber's rules or procedures.

LEGISLATIVE STRATEGIES It's easier for a bill to win passage if members think it has support. That's why a bill's sponsor typically informs other members about the measure before introducing it and invites them to sign on as co-sponsors. One reason a member might co-sponsor a bill is to demonstrate to constituents that he or she is working in their interests on a particular issue.

Members of Congress sometimes use tricks of the trade to turn policy initiatives into law without writing a bill. One trick is to add policy riders to appropriations

Admission is free to the Smithsonian National Museum of Natural History in Washington, D.C., as it is at most Smithsonian Institution museums and galleries and the National Zoo. The Smithsonian Institution was established by Congress in 1846 and receives a combination of federal and private funding. In early 2018, the Smithsonian Institution presented a 237-page document titled *Budget Justification to Congress* for its 2019 budget request of over $957 million.

bills. Appropriations bills are formal statements of how much money will be spent in a given year on a particular government activity. While appropriations bills are being considered, members of Congress can add a policy rider to the bill. Riders are additions to a bill that are unrelated to the rest of the bill's content. Policy riders are additions that make law in the guise of specifying—or prohibiting—spending in a certain way. These additions tend to be buried in a massive spending bill that Congress is under great pressure to pass in order to fund important programs. They can be useful ways to make policy because they are easily overlooked.

Earmarks are another technique that has been used to get funding for pet projects. An earmark is a spending rider to help a constituent or supporter. For instance, an earmark might award a large contract to a company in a representative's district. Earmarks were seen by many as the height of special interest politics and a subversion of democracy. The House stopped using earmarks in 2012. The Senate still allows earmarks, but in 2007 it began to require public disclosure of the name of the senator backing the earmark.

INTRODUCING A BILL When a bill is first introduced in the House, it is assigned a number. Numbering restarts with each congressional session, so the first bill introduced in the House in any session is assigned *H.R. 1*, and so on. Bills originating in the Senate begin with *S.* instead of *H.R.* and are also numbered in sequence.

Each bill receives a title describing its contents, and then the text of the bill is entered into the House *Journal*, which records each day's legislative actions, points of order, rulings of the chair, and so on. This record is required by Article I, Section 5, Clause 3, of the Constitution. The bill is also printed in the *Congressional Record*, which contains a complete transcript of each day's activities, debates, and background documents. (Of course, all such information is available online.)

By rule, each bill is supposed to be read three times in each chamber, with the third reading coming before the vote. An actual full reading of the text generally doesn't take place. Publication in the *Journal* and *Congressional Record* counts as a reading. A senator sponsoring a bill may speak briefly when a bill is introduced in the Senate to describe its purpose and main features, but even that does not occur with every bill.

HISTORICAL THINKING

1. **MAKE INFERENCES** What was the goal behind requiring the names of senators backing each earmark to be made public? Explain your answer.
2. **FORM AND SUPPORT OPINIONS** Do you see earmarks as a subversion of democracy or merely an example of good constituent service?

How Committees Work on Bills

Once a bill is formally introduced, it is sent to the appropriate standing committee. For example, a farm bill in the House would be sent to the Agriculture Committee. A clean water bill would be sent to the Natural Resources Committee. Complex bills that touch upon the expertise of more than one committee may be divided, with different parts sent to relevant committees. The speaker of the House and the presiding officer of the Senate make the committee assignments for their chambers.

The committee chairperson typically sends the bill to a subcommittee. For example, suppose the Senate Foreign Relations Committee is assigned a bill concerning **NATO**, the North Atlantic Treaty Organization, a mutual defense alliance that connects the United States with Canada and more than two dozen other nations, mostly in Europe. The committee chair may send that bill to the Subcommittee on Europe and Regional Security Cooperation. Alternatively, the chairperson may decide to put the bill aside and ignore it, an action called *pigeonholing*. Most bills that are pigeonholed receive no further action.

A pigeonholed bill that has been dormant can be forced out of committee through a discharge petition. If a discharge petition is signed by a simple majority of 218 House members, the committee is required to report the bill to the floor. The Senate has a similar mechanism called a discharge resolution.

If a bill is not pigeonholed, the subcommittee's staff begins studying it. The subcommittee may also hold public hearings, inviting executive agency officials, representatives of interest groups, and outside experts to explain their support for or opposition to the bill.

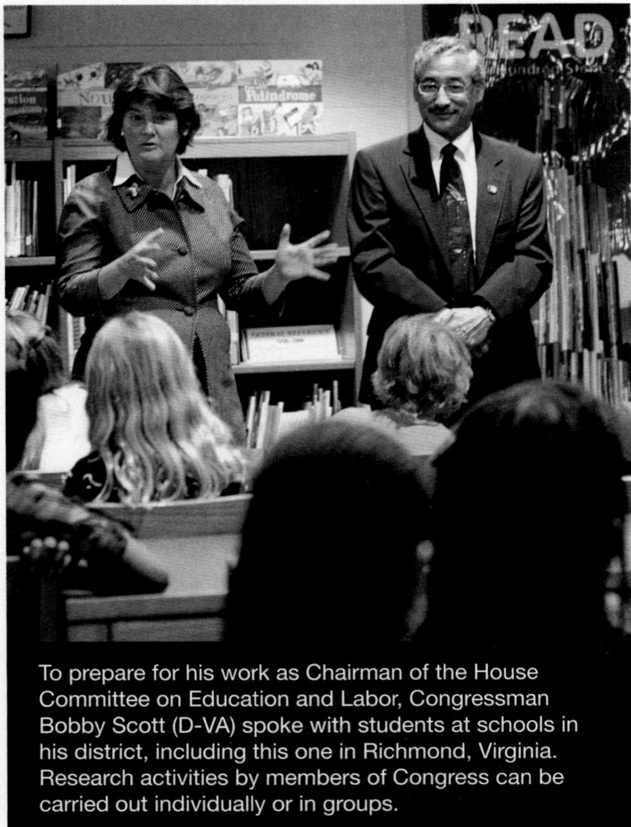

To prepare for his work as Chairman of the House Committee on Education and Labor, Congressman Bobby Scott (D-VA) spoke with students at schools in his district, including this one in Richmond, Virginia. Research activities by members of Congress can be carried out individually or in groups.

After any hearings and research are completed, the subcommittee meets in what is known as a markup session. In the markup session, the subcommittee can approve the bill as is, revise sections of the bill, add new amendments, or draft a new bill. It then votes on whether to move the bill to the full committee (the standing committee the subcommittee is part of). At that point the full committee has its own markup session. The full committee may hold more hearings, amend the subcommittee's version of the bill, or simply approve the subcommittee's recommendations.

Finally, the committee reports the bill back to the full chamber. It can report the bill favorably, report the bill with amendments, or report a substitute for the original bill. A committee may report a bill unfavorably, but usually such a bill would be pigeonholed. Along with the bill, the committee sends the full chamber a written report that explains the committee's actions, describes the bill, lists the major changes made by the committee, and gives opinions on the bill. The chair of the committee generally issues the report, but other members can add their own reports.

HISTORICAL THINKING

3. **ANALYZE VISUALS** Look at the diagram of how a bill becomes a law. Why do the yellow and teal arrows loop across and back up to the standing committee level after either the House or Senate votes?
4. **COMPARE AND CONTRAST** What is the main difference between the roles of a committee and a subcommittee?
5. **IDENTIFY** What can a committee do with a bill once the bill is assigned to it?

Floor Debate in the House

A bill can't be considered at all until it is put on a chamber's calendar. Typically, in the House, the Rules Committee plays a major role in the scheduling process. This committee, along with the House leaders, decides whether and under what conditions a bill will be considered. The Rules Committee, often known as the traffic cop of the House, can set conditions on debate, such as how much time is allowed, whether amendments can be made, and even which passages may or may not be amended. These rules are complex and extensive. The House rules of the 116th Congress filled 46 pages of small type. In practice, the House Rules Committee is largely controlled by the speaker. As you know, the speaker is chosen by the majority party.

It is rare that a floor debate changes a member's position on how to vote. The floor debate does matter, though. These debates give the full House the opportunity to consider amendments to the bill. In addition, the record of the floor debate informs the public of the issues that have been considered and gives the courts a complete legislative history of the bill if they are called on to interpret the bill.

FOLLOWING THE RULES To manage discussion among its 435 members, the House imposes limits on floor debate. Members may speak from the floor only after being recognized by the speaker, who has the power to cut off any member who strays from the subject. Additionally, at any time, any member may make a motion to end discussion and vote on the question at hand. If that motion passes, debate ends.

HOW A BILL BECOMES A LAW

Bills may be introduced in the House or the Senate or in both concurrently. Yellow and teal arrows indicate the typical paths a bill takes to passage. If both chambers pass identical bills, the proposed law is sent to the president.

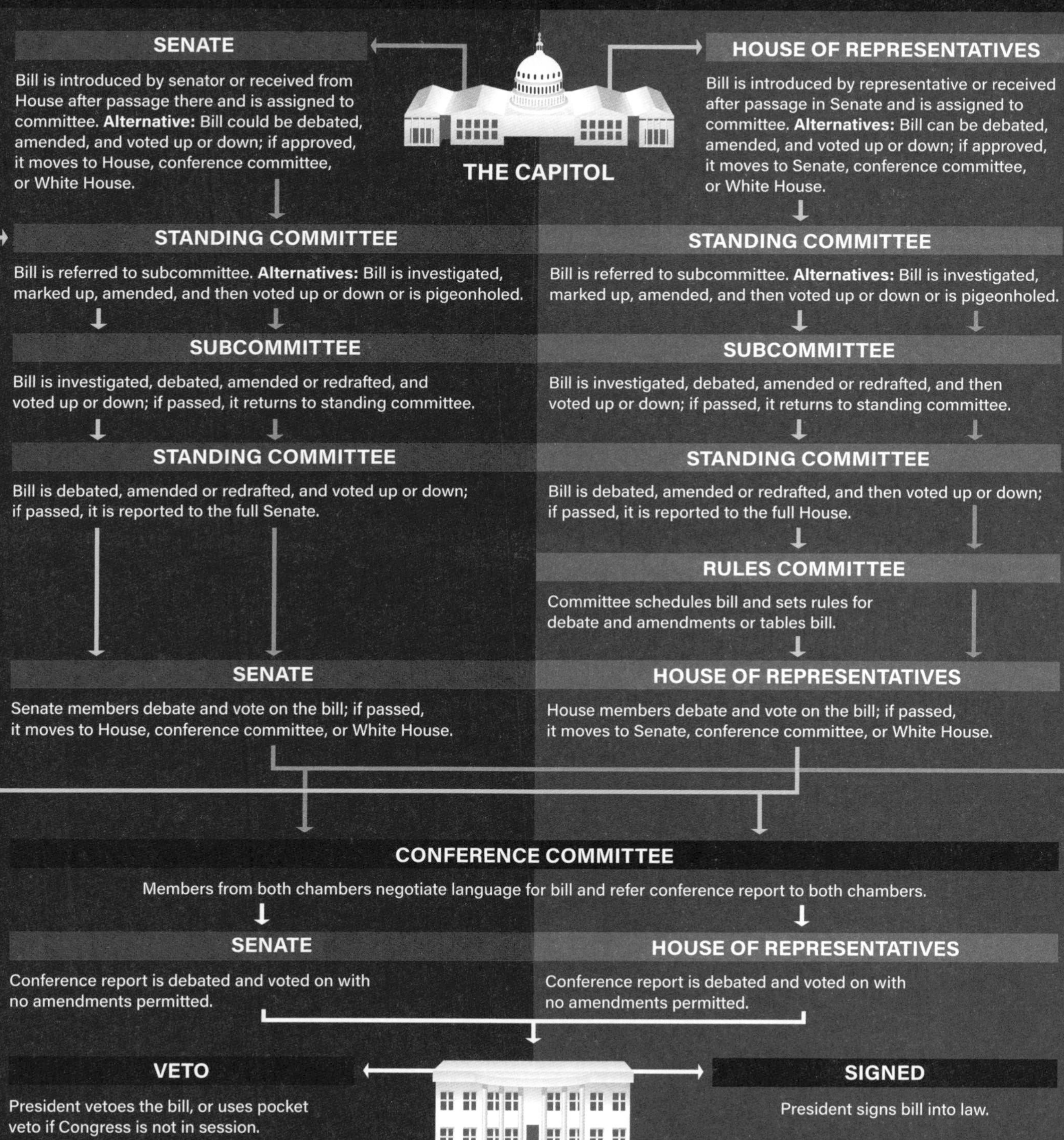

SENATE
Bill is introduced by senator or received from House after passage there and is assigned to committee. Alternative: Bill could be debated, amended, and voted up or down; if approved, it moves to House, conference committee, or White House.
THE CAPITOL
HOUSE OF REPRESENTATIVES
Bill is introduced by representative or received after passage in Senate and is assigned to committee. Alternatives: Bill can be debated, amended, and voted up or down; if approved, it moves to Senate, conference committee, or White House.
STANDING COMMITTEE
Bill is referred to subcommittee. Alternatives: Bill is investigated, marked up, amended, and then voted up or down or is pigeonholed.
STANDING COMMITTEE
Bill is referred to subcommittee. Alternatives: Bill is investigated, marked up, amended, and then voted up or down or is pigeonholed.
SUBCOMMITTEE
Bill is investigated, debated, amended or redrafted, and voted up or down; if passed, it returns to standing committee.
SUBCOMMITTEE
Bill is investigated, debated, amended or redrafted, and then voted up or down; if passed, it returns to standing committee.
STANDING COMMITTEE
Bill is debated, amended or redrafted, and voted up or down; if passed, it is reported to the full Senate.
STANDING COMMITTEE
Bill is debated, amended or redrafted, and then voted up or down; if passed, it is reported to the full House.
RULES COMMITTEE
Committee schedules bill and sets rules for debate and amendments or tables bill.
SENATE
Senate members debate and vote on the bill; if passed, it moves to House, conference committee, or White House.
HOUSE OF REPRESENTATIVES
House members debate and vote on the bill; if passed, it moves to Senate, conference committee, or White House.
CONFERENCE COMMITTEE
Members from both chambers negotiate language for bill and refer conference report to both chambers.
SENATE
Conference report is debated and voted on with no amendments permitted.
HOUSE OF REPRESENTATIVES
Conference report is debated and voted on with no amendments permitted.
VETO
President vetoes the bill, or uses pocket veto if Congress is not in session.
OVERRIDE
If two-thirds of each house of Congress votes to override veto, bill becomes law.
SIGNED
President signs bill into law.
WHITE HOUSE

When the floor debate ends, the House is ready to vote. For major legislation that is likely to be controversial, the House begins by voting to adopt the rules for the bill set by the Rules Committee. Rules can cover limits on amendments that can be added from the floor as well as which parts of the bill can be debated. The House then forms itself into a body called the Committee of the Whole, which includes all the members present in the House at the time it is formed. This body is presided over by someone other than the speaker of the House—usually the chair of the committee that reported the bill.

In the Committee of the Whole, members initially debate the entire bill until the time set by the Rules Committee has been exhausted. That time is equally divided between those for and those against the bill. After the opening debate, the bill receives its second reading—though the actual reading of the bill can be waived.

The Committee of the Whole then considers the bill section by section, with members proposing any amendments permissible under the rule—and germane, or relevant, to the content of the bill. After debate using special time limits that operate in the Committee of the Whole, each amendment is voted on. Votes may occur by voice vote, in which members as a group respond *yea* or *nay*, or by roll-call vote, in which each member present casts a vote that is recorded. Then the Committee of the Whole dissolves itself and the House resumes session, with the speaker presiding. The House then votes on whether to adopt the bill as revised. If a bill is approved, it is printed, or engrossed. The bill gets its third reading—which is generally just a reading of the title of the bill—before the House takes a final vote.

SUSPENDING THE RULES For some bills, the House may decide to suspend the rules. Debate on the motion to suspend the rules can only be 40 minutes (20 minutes each for supporters and opponents) and no amendments to the motion can be made. If the measure to suspend the rules passes, then the bill up for consideration must be approved by a two-thirds vote. Because of this higher bar for a bill's passage, rules are suspended only for relatively uncontroversial, widely popular measures.

HISTORICAL THINKING

6. **DRAW CONCLUSIONS** If the membership of the House Committee of the Whole and the House of Representatives are the same, why does the House switch between them?
7. **MAKE INFERENCES** Why would the House suspend the rules only for bills that are not controversial?

Floor Debate in the Senate

Rules governing floor debate in the Senate are quite different from those in the House. The Senate places no time limits on debate, nor does it require members to speak only to the measure before the chamber during debate. And the Senate's rules do not allow any member to cut off debate by introducing a motion to call for a vote. In short, a senator can talk about anything he or she wants to for about as long as he or she wants to.

The Senate generally begins debate by adopting a motion for unanimous consent. To achieve unanimous consent, the majority and minority leaders come to an agreement about the rules for debating a bill.

Cloture Motions Filed and Invoked, 1921–2018

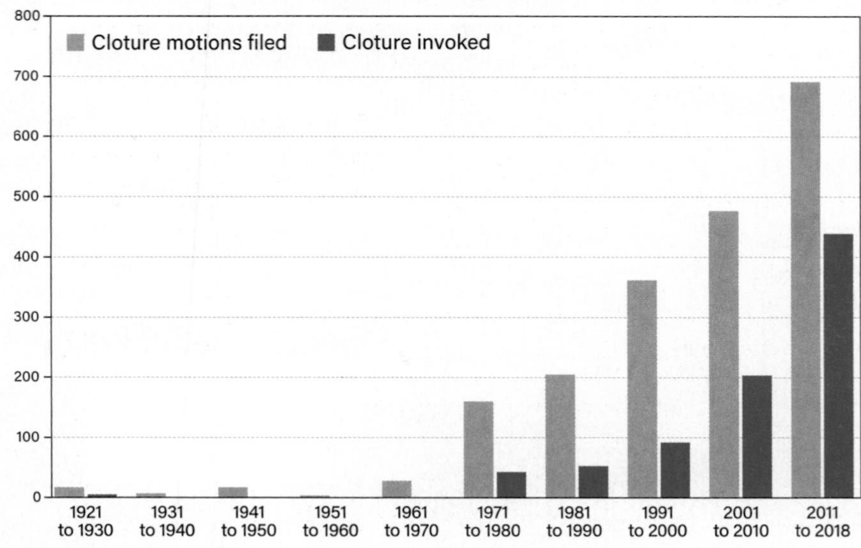

SOURCE: Data from the U.S. Senate

The Filibuster

In years past, filibustering senators would speak for hours to block a proposed bill—as dramatized in Frank Capra's 1939 film *Mr. Smith Goes to Washington*. There was no requirement to stay on topic, but if a senator sat down or stopped talking to eat something, that would end the filibuster. In recent decades, though, Senate rules have permitted filibusters in which actual continuous floor speeches are not required. Senators merely announce that they are filibustering.

The ability to threaten a filibuster means that important legislation needs the support of 60 senators to ensure a cloture vote if needed to end the filibuster. This makes the filibuster a check against the majority party's imposing its will on the minority. Viewed another way, it enables the minority to prevent the majority from carrying out its will. It has been rare for either party to hold 60 or more seats in the Senate. When they do, there may still be a wide range of positions within the party that make a unified vote difficult.

These agreements typically limit the amount of time a bill may be debated and the number and content of amendments that may be offered. The time limits can be broken by two senatorial privileges—filibuster and holds.

FILIBUSTERS AND CLOTURE As you have read, use of unlimited debate in the Senate to obstruct legislation is called *filibustering*. Under Senate Rule 22, filibusters may be ended by invoking cloture—a procedure for closing debate and bringing the matter under consideration to a vote. Sixteen senators must sign a petition requesting cloture. Then, after two days have elapsed, three-fifths of the entire membership must vote for cloture. Once cloture is invoked, debate is limited to one hour per senator, and a final vote must take place within 30 hours.

Another way Senate leaders may prevent a filibuster is through the reconciliation rule. A bill covered by this rule must be limited to the topics of taxing and spending and must not otherwise involve changes to regulations or laws. Debate is limited to 20 hours, and passage can be secured with a simple majority. In 2007, the Senate adopted the Conrad rule, named after Senator Kent Conrad (D-ND). The rule stated that any bill passed through the resolution process must reduce the budget deficit at the end of a 10-year period. For years, that last requirement was met through creative accounting. In 2015, the Senate repealed the Conrad rule, opening the way for budget-busting legislation.

The reconciliation rule was created by the Congressional Budget Act of 1974 to make it easier to resolve budget issues. Since the 1990s it has been used to enact measures that had substantial and intense partisan opposition, including welfare reform in 1996 and the tax cuts in 2001 and 2003. Both the Democrats' enactment of the Affordable Care Act in 2010 and the failed Republican attempts to dismantle it in 2017 used the reconciliation process.

SENATORIAL HOLDS Another tool senators can use to delay legislation is the senatorial hold. Any senator has the power to place a hold on a bill by simply informing the leader of his or her party of the hold. The senator can enforce a hold by withholding consent from the motion to suspend the rules, thus blocking any unanimous consent agreement. Senators often place holds on nominees for executive or judicial positions in an attempt to win concessions from the executive branch. Because party leaders do not announce who has placed a hold, holds are often anonymous. Rule changes designed to curb anonymous holds have been ineffective. As with a filibuster, however, cloture can be used to lift a hold.

HISTORICAL THINKING

8. **IDENTIFY MAIN IDEAS AND DETAILS** When the Senate adopts a unanimous consent agreement, what are the senators consenting to?
9. **FORM AND SUPPORT OPINIONS** Do you think the use of the reconciliation rule to pass legislation promotes bipartisan compromise in legislating?
10. **ANALYZE VISUALS** What might the increased frequency in the use of cloture indicate about the Senate?
11. **MAKE PREDICTIONS** Are holds more or less likely if a senator is from the minority party and the president is from the same party as the majority? Why?

LESSON 9.2

Conference Committees and Presidential Action

As you've learned, to become a law, a bill must be passed by both chambers and then signed by the president. If both the House and the Senate pass identical bills, the measure can go straight to the White House. That doesn't always happen, though. When the House and Senate pass bills meant to achieve the same goals but that use different wording, those differences must be resolved before the bill can go to the president.

Arriving at Common Language in a Bill

The two houses of Congress can reach agreement on the language of a bill in several ways. The most straightforward method is to have the bill pass through one chamber first and then be submitted to the other, which approves it without change. Often, though, both houses consider bills on the same subject at the same time. Even in these situations, they might end up with the same bill if one house waits for action by the other and then takes up the bill passed by that house.

But sometimes, the two houses of Congress pass differing versions of the same bill. In those cases, one or both versions must be changed to make the two identical before the bill can be signed into law by the president. There are two methods of resolving these differences. One is for the two chambers to amend their bills until they say the same thing in exactly the same way. The second is to send the two bills to a conference committee. In some cases, the two houses use a combination of approaches. They begin by making amendments and then move the bill to a conference committee. Alternatively, they may send the bill initially to a conference committee. If the conference committee members can't resolve all the differences, they send the bill back to the two chambers, where the amendment process is used to settle the outstanding issues.

THE AMENDMENT APPROACH Say the Senate has made amendments to a bill passed by the House. Those changes are sent back to the House for consideration. If the House approves the amendments, the disagreement in language is resolved, but the House can amend the amendments. In that case, the newly amended bill must go back to the Senate for it to approve the House changes. Rules permit only two levels of amendment on any point in the bill, which means the Senate cannot amend the House amendment to its amendment.

This situation has several possible outcomes. If the Senate approves the amended amendments, the bill is passed and moves to the White House. But the Senate might insist on its original amendment and refuse to pass the House version. In that case, the bill shifts back to the House, which must decide whether to accept the original Senate amendment. With the two houses at an impasse, there are two possibilities—either the bill dies or one chamber requests a conference committee.

The amendment approach is sometimes known as ping-ponging. The two chambers take turns adding amendments until disagreements are resolved. On occasion—particularly near the end of the legislative session, when there is a push to pass legislation quickly—bills can ping-pong back and forth between the House and the Senate on an hourly basis.

CONFERENCE COMMITTEES A conference committee's task is to develop a single bill that both houses will pass. Conference committees are temporary and ad hoc—that is, they are formed as needed. Each chamber appoints members to the conference committee, with the speaker of the House and the presiding officer of the Senate making the selections.

The chair and the ranking member—the member of the committee from the minority party who has the most seniority—of the relevant committees typically suggest conferees, or conference committee

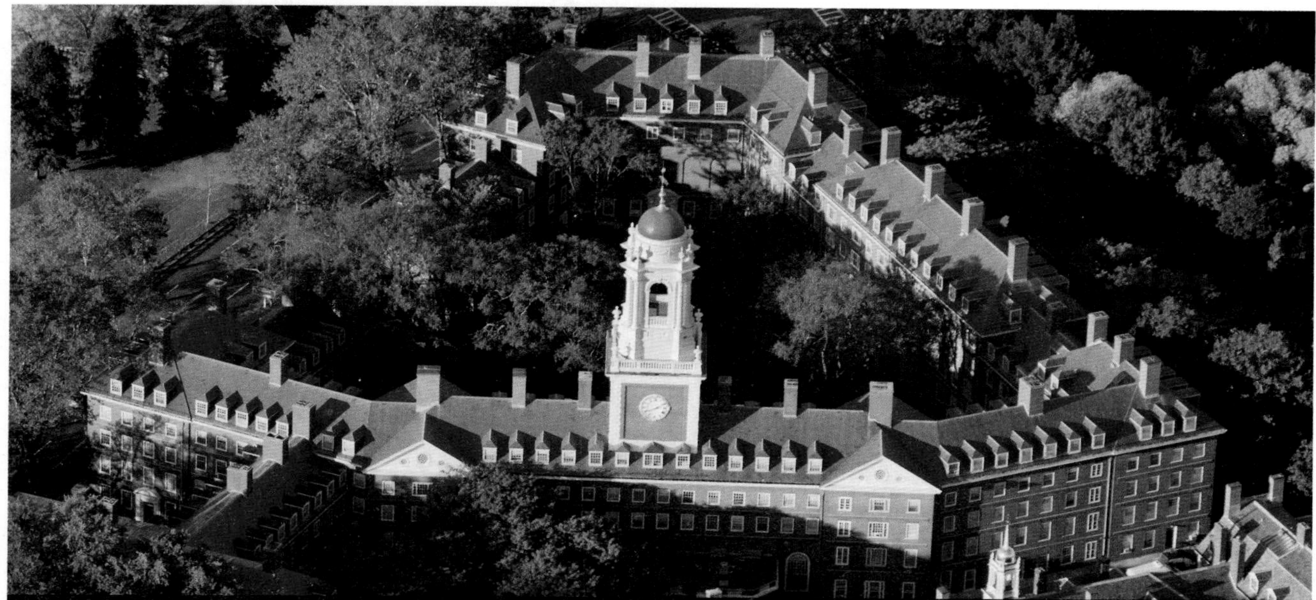

Harvard University, a private non-profit school on the Charles River in Cambridge, Massachusetts, earned nearly $4 billion on its endowment (investment holdings) of over $39 billion in 2018. More than half of that income was reinvested. Until a change in the tax law in 2017, university endowment income was untaxed. The final language of the tax provision that made some university endowments taxable was worked out in a conference committee.

members. Most conferees come from the standing committees that handled the bill in each chamber. The two houses do not necessarily name the same number of conferees—votes in conference are by chamber. That is, House conferees vote for the House, and Senate conferees vote for the Senate. Both chambers name an odd number of conferees to avoid a tie vote. In theory, a conference committee is authorized to consider only those points on which the two versions differed. No proposals are supposed to be added. In reality, though, a conference committee sometimes makes important changes or adds new provisions.

Once conference committee members agree on the final compromise bill, they submit a report to each chamber. Then each chamber votes the bill up or down. Members may debate the revised bill, but no further amendments are allowed. If the bill is approved by both chambers, it is ready for action by the president. If either house votes it down, the bill dies.

A majority in either chamber can effectively kill a bill before it gets to conference. If the leadership in either chamber believes an acceptable compromise with the other chamber is impossible, it can block the bill simply by refusing to appoint members to a conference committee. In 2013, Republicans employed this technique on several bills.

HISTORICAL THINKING

1. **COMPARE AND CONTRAST** Which method of resolving differences in bills—the amendment process or a conference committee—do you think is more likely to result in a final version? Why?
2. **MAKE INFERENCES** What might be the ideal qualifications for a member of a conference committee?

Presidential Action

If the president signs a bill passed by both houses, it becomes law. The president can also **veto** the bill, that is, reject it. In this case, the president must send the bill back to Congress within 10 congressional working days. If the president misses the 10-day deadline, the bill becomes law without his or her signature. But if Congress adjourns before the 10 days elapse and the president refuses to sign the bill, the bill dies in a procedure called a *pocket veto*.

Congress can still enact a bill into law after a presidential veto. By a two-thirds vote in each chamber, Congress can override the president's veto. Because an override requires a supermajority, however, the veto power is a significant check on the power of Congress. Congress can't override a pocket veto since it is no longer in session, though it can pass the bill again in the next session.

Presidents used the veto power sparingly until the administration of Andrew Johnson (1865–1869). Johnson—who became president after Abraham Lincoln was assassinated and opposed many of the post–Civil War plans of the Republican-controlled Congress—vetoed 21 bills and used pocket vetoes on 8 more. That Republican Congress exerted its will by voting to override 15 of Johnson's 21 vetoes. For example, President Johnson vetoed a bill extending the life of the Freedmen's Bureau. Congress then approved a new bill, which Johnson also vetoed. This time, however, the bill had enough support in both houses to override the veto and the extension became law.

Franklin D. Roosevelt (1933–1945) vetoed far more bills than any other president. He issued 372 regular vetoes, 9 of which were overridden by Congress, and 263 pocket vetoes. Of course, Roosevelt served longer than any other president, so he had far more opportunity to veto bills! The number of vetoes has declined significantly among recent presidents.

Congress attempted to give the president more power by passing the 1996 Line Item Veto Act. This law gave the president authority to give overall approval to a bill while vetoing or canceling individual spending items in the bill. The goal was to enable the executive to eliminate earmarks and wasteful spending that benefited only narrow special interests. But in *Clinton* v. *City of New York* (1998), the Supreme Court declared the law unconstitutional. The Court ruled that under Article I, Section 7, the president does not have the power to cancel, amend, or repeal a law or a section of a law, because the Constitution gives those powers exclusively to Congress. The president's only legal options are to sign bills or veto bills.

HISTORICAL THINKING

3. **MAKE INFERENCES** Why might a president choose to pocket veto a bill rather than veto it?
4. **MAKE CONNECTIONS** Which fundamental constitutional principle did the *Clinton* v. *City of New York* decision uphold? Explain how that principle was upheld.

Recent Changes in Legislative Procedures

The steps for a bill to become a law described so far represent the process that has been used throughout most of our nation's history, a process known as regular order. In recent decades, though, Congress has transformed the lawmaking process by adopting some new approaches. They include omnibus bills and generic bills.

Omnibus bills, proposed laws that include numerous unrelated issues loaded into the same legislation, have become much more common, particularly with appropriations bills. Authors of omnibus measures try to ensure passage by including so many different items that it is impossible for lawmakers to read the entire bill, and they may allow only a small window of time for passage. Omnibus spending bills often go to the floor just before the government runs out of authorized funds. These bills can be massive. The 2018 omnibus spending bill was some 2,200 pages long, included $1.3 trillion in government spending, and was made available to members of both chambers just 2 days before the vote.

Members are often under pressure to vote for an omnibus bill to prevent the government from shutting down. During a government shutdown, hundreds of thousands of federal workers are barred from coming

CRITICAL VIEWING The elephant and donkey have come to symbolize the Republican and Democratic parties, respectively. In this cartoon, both parties are shown taking improper advantage of omnibus bills. Why are the pigs in the cartoon labeled "pet projects," "earmarks," and "pork"?

In September of 2008, no one knew when or how the Great Recession would end. These demonstrators protested Congress's plan to spend $700 billion to bail out financial firms instead of bailing out individuals who were out of work and unable to pay their mortgages.

to work. While essential defense and security functions continue, many activities grind to a halt. This can inconvenience and anger constituents, who depend on government services. It can also cause hardship for the government workers and contractors who are not being paid in a timely manner.

Another recent and increasingly common innovation in lawmaking is for the two chambers to each pass a superficial, generic bill on the same topic. The details of the legislation are left to be filled in by the conference committee. Republicans tried that approach in 2017 to fulfill a frequent campaign promise to repeal and replace the Affordable Care Act. Senate Majority Leader Mitch McConnell (R-KY) offered what he called a skinny repeal bill that didn't match the language of a bill already passed by the House in hopes he could win just enough votes to move the process into a conference committee. In that case, the tactic failed. Three Republicans joined Senate Democrats to vote against the bill, and it was defeated.

These changes to the traditional lawmaking process can be traced to the fact that the two political parties have found less and less common ground in recent years. Because of the deep and wide partisan disagreements, the majority party has granted its leaders greater leeway to insert themselves more directly into key stages of the process. These efforts are meant to thwart the goals of the opposing party or overcome opposition resistance to its own goals. Both parties have used these unorthodox, or unusual, approaches to advance their initiatives in the modern Congress.

Occasionally, emergencies arise during which the legislature must act quickly. For instance, President Franklin Roosevelt pushed through a massive amount of legislation aimed at helping Americans suffering from the Great Depression. During his first 100 days in office, more than a dozen major bills went from introduction to presidential signature. The Emergency Banking Relief Act, for example, was introduced just five days after Roosevelt's inauguration. It was passed by both houses and signed into law that same day.

More recently, the Emergency Economic Stabilization Act of 2008 authorized the Treasury Department to purchase up to $700 billion worth of mortgage-backed securities and other assets. This measure was passed in response to the failures of a number of large banks and other financial institutions in a severe economic downturn called the Great Recession. It was feared that without fast action, more failures would lead to the collapse of the nation's financial system. The administration first discussed the bill in late September, but on September 29, the House rejected it. As the situation worsened, the Senate passed a revised measure that the House approved, and on October 3, President George W. Bush signed it into law.

In response to another emergency, the coronavirus (COVID-19) pandemic, Congress passed a series of unprecedented spending measures to prop up an economy thrown into paralysis by the social distancing measures required to blunt the spread of the disease. The largest of the measures, the CARES Act, passed after little more than a few weeks of legislative maneuvering in March of 2020. It funneled $2.1 trillion to individuals and groups in the form of direct payments and loans to businesses. Less than a month later, with the money for small businesses from the CARES Act exhausted, Congress passed another stimulus package totaling $484 billion.

HISTORICAL THINKING

5. **COMPARE AND CONTRAST** How does passage of omnibus or generic bills differ from the process used for regular bills?
6. **FORM AND SUPPORT OPINIONS** Do you think it was good or bad that Congress passed the CARES Act, at a cost of over $2 trillion, after just a few weeks of legislative maneuvering?

LESSON 9.3 The Budgeting Process

The Constitution makes it very clear that Congress has the power of the purse, and this power is significant. Only Congress can impose taxes and authorize expenditures. Congress creates an annual budget to plan its spending and to try to keep the country debt-free, or at least solvent. When you think of all the tasks the government undertakes, it's no surprise that the budget for the U.S. government is huge—for fiscal year 2020, the budget was over $4.7 trillion. As you might imagine, the process for deciding how that money is spent is not always easy.

Authorization and Appropriation

Congress's decisions about how that money is spent determine what policies will or will not be implemented. For example, the president might order executive agencies to undertake specific programs, but these orders are meaningless if there is no money to pay for their execution. Congress can nullify a president's ambitious plans simply by refusing to allocate money to the relevant executive agencies. Remember that all revenue bills, including tax bills, must originate in the House although the Senate can get around that rule by rewriting a House-passed revenue bill.

Congress's role in budgeting and spending is important not only to the operation of the government. Since 2008, federal spending has been near—and often more than—20 percent of the gross domestic product (GDP), meaning that it contributes mightily to U.S. performance. That spending includes the salaries of the more than 4 million employees who work for the federal government as well as the cost of all the goods and services the government purchases, from office supplies to an aircraft carrier.

Federal spending has a role in determining which sectors of the economy grow. For example, defense spending since World War II has stimulated the growth of private defense industries. It has also aided the development of numerous technologies used in artificial intelligence, network computing, mapping and GPS, imagery, weather prediction, clothing, adhesives, and plastics.

OVERVIEW OF THE BUDGET PROCESS While Congress is the keeper of the purse, the budgeting process begins with the executive branch. Executive agencies submit their requests to the Office of Management and Budget (OMB), and, under the direction of the president, the OMB outlines a proposed budget to submit to Congress. Congress has no obligation to approve the president's budget request, but it normally uses the president's proposal as a starting point for developing its own spending plan.

Congress performs three general steps in the budgeting process. First comes passing a budget resolution, which sets the spending plan for the coming fiscal year. A **fiscal year** is a 12-month period adopted for accounting purposes. The federal government's fiscal year runs from October 1 through the next September 30. Each chamber is supposed to pass a budget resolution describing revenue targets and spending levels for each of the major functional areas of the government. A function includes a set of programs that contribute to a shared purpose, such as education, health, or national defense. A function can include multiple executive agencies. For example, the transportation function includes programs administered by the Federal Aviation Administration, the Federal Highway Administration, the Coast Guard, and the Federal Transit Administration as well as other departments.

As with bills, a conference committee reconciles the House and Senate versions, and then the two chambers approve a concurrent resolution. This resolution serves as an agreement between the two houses to guide further decisions. But as a concurrent resolution, it does not have the force of law.

Budget Expenditures by Function, Fiscal Year 2019

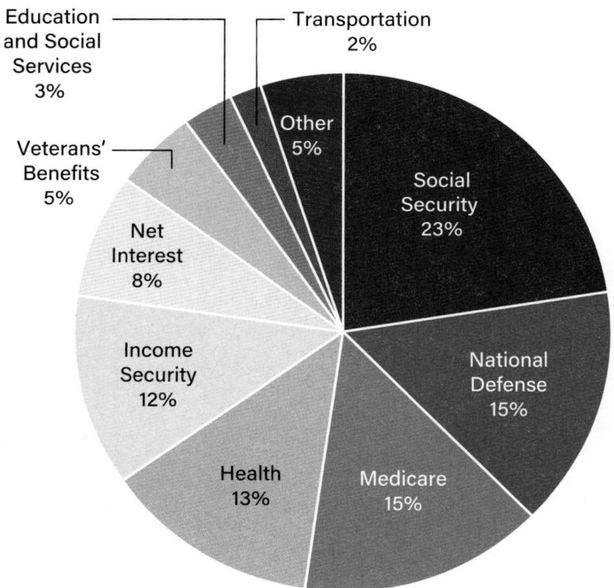

SOURCE: U.S. Department of the Treasury, Bureau of the Fiscal Service

The second step is **authorization**, which is the congressional action that involves specifying the legal basis for government spending. Congress must pass authorization bills outlining the rules governing the expenditure of funds. It may place limits on how much money can be spent and for what period of time. In authorization, Congress estimates the extent to which the budget has a shortfall of revenue—a federal deficit—or an excess of revenue—a federal surplus. (But the federal budget hasn't had a surplus since 2001.) In estimating the deficit, the congressional budget suggests how much the government intends to borrow for that fiscal year, which will add to the national debt.

The third step in budgeting undertaken by Congress is appropriation. **Appropriation** is the congressional action of determining how many dollars the government will actually spend in a given year on each particular government activity. The Congressional Budget and Impoundment Control Act of 1974 dictates there be 12 appropriations bills, each covering specified subjects of legislation. Appropriations must never exceed the authorized amounts, but they can be less.

Entitlement programs constitute exceptions to the regular budgeting process. **Entitlement programs**

Wildfires in California in November 2018 damaged 19,000 structures and generated over $3 billion in estimated cleanup costs. There are also the costs of fighting the fires, rescuing people, diverting traffic, health issues caused by smoke, and extensive damage to natural areas. Federal agencies like FEMA and the Small Business Administration help people and businesses rebuild after disasters like this one, but if the costs of disasters exceed FEMA funding, the agency has to ask Congress for a supplementary appropriation.

are government programs, such as Social Security, that require the government to provide specified benefits to persons who qualify. Many such programs operate under open-ended authorizations that, in effect, place no limits on how much can be spent. In addition to Social Security, major entitlements include Medicare, which helps cover the health-care costs of those 65 and older, and veterans' benefits. In the president's 2018 budget request, entitlement programs accounted for nearly 63 percent of all federal spending. Another important category of domestic spending is income security, which includes payments to disabled workers, aid to families living in poverty, and the federal food stamps program.

PREDICTING THE FUTURE Throughout the budgeting process, the Congressional Budget Office (CBO) informs Congress of its estimates of the consequences of various decisions and costs of implementing proposed legislation. Budgeting for future years requires predictions about the future state of the economy. The OMB and the CBO need to predict the state of the economy so they can predict the amount of tax revenue that will be raised based on current or proposed tax laws. Based on these predictions, both agencies try to calculate the effects of different spending plans.

Predicting future revenue and spending is necessarily very imprecise, or inexact. While one- and two-year predictions are often fairly realistic, long-term projections rarely come close to being accurate. One reason is that many items must be estimated based on predictions that are based on other predictions, and so on. Another contributing factor is wishful thinking: The administration wants predictions that will allow it to carry out its spending agenda. Finally, events are inherently unpredictable, and their effects on the economy even more so. The coronavirus pandemic that broke out in early 2020 triggered a sudden economic downturn that reduced expected revenues while requiring large, unanticipated spending. When the 2020 budget was passed, for example, the Congress Budget Office projected a deficit of $1.07 trillion for the year. By April of

2020, following the passage of virus relief packages, the CBO had upped its estimate to $3.8 trillion.

HISTORICAL THINKING

1. **DRAW CONCLUSIONS** Why is so much time and energy devoted to preparing the budget?
2. **INTERPRET GRAPHS** Based on the circle graph showing the budget for fiscal year 2019, how many budget categories represent spending on meeting the health and income needs of Americans, and what share of the federal budget do they make up?
3. **IDENTIFY MAIN IDEAS AND DETAILS** What is the difference between authorization and appropriation?
4. **MAKE INFERENCES** Why is it important for the CBO to be objective?

The Actual Budgeting Process

The budgeting process begins about a year and a half before the beginning of the fiscal year in which the budget will be used. For example, the budgeting process for the fiscal year beginning October 2020 began in the spring of 2019. The OMB and the president use about two-thirds of that time to prepare the executive budget proposal. Normally, the executive budget is close to final when the president delivers the State of the Union Address in late January.

The legislative budgeting process begins when Congress receives the president's proposed budget, eight to nine months before the start of the fiscal year. After Congress receives the executive budget, it begins working with the CBO on the congressional budget resolution, which is due by May 15. The deadline is almost always missed. In addition, amendments made by one chamber or the other after the conference report is issued create new discrepancies. When this happens, the budget resolution may be renegotiated, or the differences will remain to be resolved in the appropriations process.

The House is supposed to pass the 12 appropriations bills by June 30. To ensure funding is in place before the start of the subsequent fiscal year, the Budget Act strictly limits debate on these bills in the Senate. As with other budget deadlines, the appropriations deadline is usually missed.

If summer arrives before Congress has completed its budgeting process or appropriations are passed, the government is heading toward a crisis. The government faces a crucial deadline on September 30. That is the date on which the current fiscal year ends. That means that the prior year's appropriations no longer apply. Without a new authorization and appropriations, the government cannot spend any money for the new fiscal year that begins on October 1.

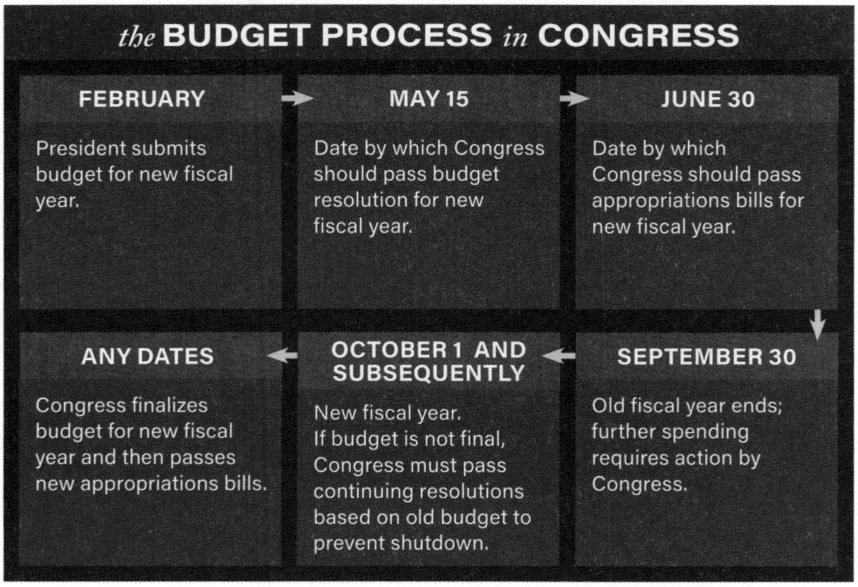

the BUDGET PROCESS *in* CONGRESS

FEBRUARY →	MAY 15 →	JUNE 30 ↓
President submits budget for new fiscal year.	Date by which Congress should pass budget resolution for new fiscal year.	Date by which Congress should pass appropriations bills for new fiscal year.
ANY DATES ←	**OCTOBER 1 AND SUBSEQUENTLY** ←	**SEPTEMBER 30**
Congress finalizes budget for new fiscal year and then passes new appropriations bills.	New fiscal year. If budget is not final, Congress must pass continuing resolutions based on old budget to prevent shutdown.	Old fiscal year ends; further spending requires action by Congress.

AVOIDING A SHUTDOWN When Congress is unable to pass a complete budget by September 30—which is very common—it usually passes short-term continuing resolutions. A short-term continuing resolution continues the funding for specified agencies at the same level of expenditures by which they operated in the previous fiscal year, for a specified amount of time. Continuing resolutions enable executive agencies to keep doing whatever they had been doing until an actual budget can be passed.

Congress hasn't always been able to pass continuing resolutions on time. Any agency that has not been funded for the new year has to shut down, which is a significant problem. When a shutdown happens, or when one appears likely, Republicans and Democrats in Congress and the president all try to pin the blame on someone else. Congress has used the threat of imminent shutdown to try to pressure the president to sign a budget that reflects Congress's rather than the president's priorities. Similarly, presidents have announced that they will not sign a continuing resolution unless it meets some specified criteria. Under President Obama, Republicans twice attempted to gain legislative advantage by refusing to pass such resolutions.

THE DEBT CEILING In any year in which the federal government spends more than it takes in, the resulting deficit adds to the national debt. U.S. law sets a ceiling on the size of the national debt. In order to borrow more, Congress must vote to raise the debt ceiling. Note that raising the debt ceiling does not authorize additional, future spending. It only gives the Treasury permission to borrow if it needs to in order to complete approved spending.

Just as the threat of a government shutdown can be used to apply pressure, the debt ceiling can be used as a bargaining chip. In 2011, Republicans in the House threatened to refuse to raise the debt ceiling unless the Obama administration made major spending concessions. If the debt ceiling was not raised, the government would not be able to pay out on already established obligations. Bankers and economists warned that such a default would result in disaster. In the end, the Republicans were at least partially successful, as the administration agreed to a variety of restraints on spending.

House Republicans attempted to repeat the tactic in 2013, with the added pressure of refusing to pass a continuing resolution to fund the government. Democrats, believing they had been taken advantage of in 2011, refused to budge. The House tactics were very unpopular, and Republicans were forced to abandon them. Despite that unpopularity, different groups of members of Congress, both Democrat and Republican, subsequently talked openly about the possibility of once again refusing to raise the debt ceiling or vote on continuing resolutions.

HISTORICAL THINKING

5. **MAKE INFERENCES** The budget resolution is not a law, so what is its value in the budgeting process?
6. **ANALYZE VISUALS** Based on the diagram of the budget process and the text, why is it reasonable to say that Congress doesn't really face any deadlines in the budget process?
7. **IDENTIFY PROBLEMS AND SOLUTIONS** What is the problem with relying on continuing resolutions to fund the government?

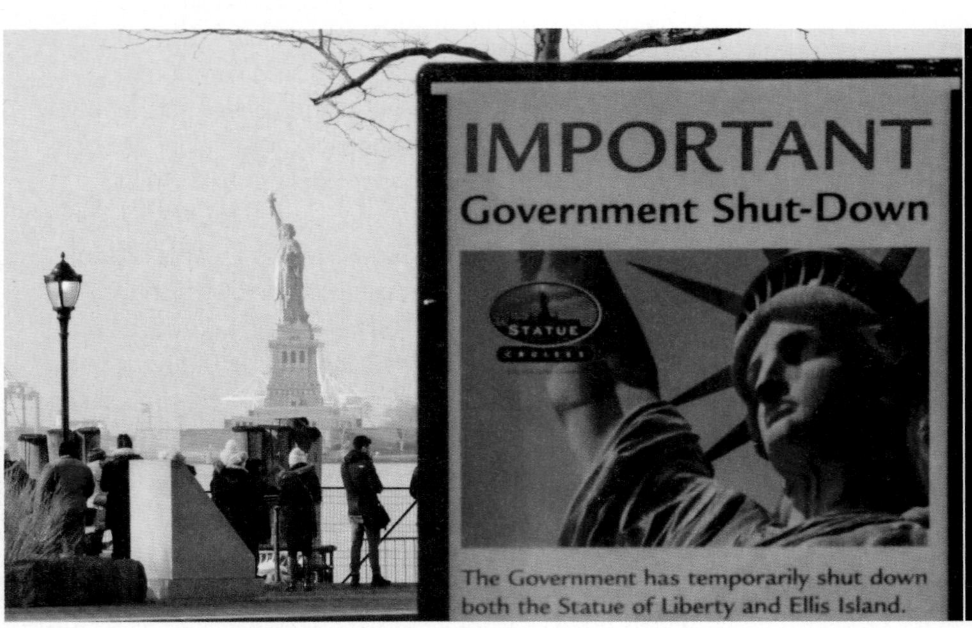

IMPORTANT
Government Shut-Down
STATUE
The Government has temporarily shut down both the Statue of Liberty and Ellis Island.

In January 2018, the government shutdown closed the Statue of Liberty and Ellis Island, among other national monuments and parks. A full shutdown also pauses investigations by regulatory agencies and stops the processing of applications for passports, gun permits, patents, Social Security benefits, and education loans. It also closes government advice and help lines. Services that are essential to protect lives and property continue, as do entitlement programs and government corporations, which are not funded by appropriations.

People in food-insecure households numbered 40 million in 2017. Soup kitchens like the one shown here are a reliable source of meals for families, but many only serve meals once a week. This location also serves as a food pantry, providing canned and dry goods—until they run out. Tragically, the healthiest foods—fresh meats and produce—are the hardest to obtain.

The New Face of Hunger

by Tracie McMillan ***National Geographic*** **Magazine, August 2014**

At $4.4 trillion, the federal budget is about one-fifth of the entire U.S. economy. Amid the months of congressional hearings, committee meetings, and presidential bargaining that produce the budget, it's easy to lose sight of the fact that decisions about how that money gets spent have real consequences for real people. In "The New Face of Hunger," writer Tracie McMillan looks at how budgetary decisions regarding food affect the nearly 17 percent of Americans who don't have enough to eat.

About 42 million Americans depend on the Supplemental Nutrition Assistance Program (SNAP), a government program that provides benefits of about $1.40 per person per meal to supplement family food budgets. A recent cut of $5 billion from the SNAP program—less than one-eighth of one percent of the federal budget—means that SNAP benefits don't last through the month, forcing needy recipients to turn to sources such as food banks or to buy cheaper food.

Unfortunately, cheaper food is often less healthy food. And once again, the federal budget plays a role. Federal crop subsidies originated to help small farmers survive fluctuating harvests. Today, billions of federal dollars go to large agricultural companies and cooperatives to subsidize a few staple crops, like corn and soy. Much of that subsidized production goes to create unhealthful foods.

The government spends much less to bolster the production of the fruits and vegetables its own nutrition guidelines say should make up half the food on our plates. In 2011 it spent only $1.6 billion to subsidize and insure "specialty crops"—the bureaucratic term for fruits and vegetables. . . Those priorities are reflected at the grocery store, where the price of fresh food has risen steadily while the cost of sugary treats like soda has dropped. Since the early 1980s the real cost of fruits and vegetables has increased by 24 percent. Meanwhile the cost of nonalcoholic beverages—primarily sodas, most sweetened with corn syrup—has dropped by 27 percent.

Access the full version of "The New Face of Hunger" by Tracie McMillan through the Resources Menu in MindTap.

THINK ABOUT IT What could the government do to promote healthier eating by people who rely on

CHAPTER 9

THE LEGISLATIVE PROCESS

Review

VOCABULARY

Match each vocabulary word with its definition by writing the letter of the correct definition in the space next to the term.

1. bill	**a.** a congressional action to set how much the government will spend on each government activity in a given year
2. resolution	**b.** a proposed law that includes numerous unrelated issues loaded into the same legislation
3. veto	**c.** a congressional action that involves specifying the legal basis for government spending
4. omnibus bill	**d.** a program, such as Social Security, that requires the government to provide specified benefits to those who qualify
5. fiscal year	**e.** a proposed law
6. authorization	**f.** a formal statement of the will or intent of Congress
7. appropriation	**g.** rejection of a bill by the president
8. entitlement program	**h.** a 12-month period used for accounting purposes

MAIN IDEAS

9. What role do standing committees play in turning a bill into a law? **LESSON 9.1**

10. What is the purpose of a discharge petition? **LESSON 9.1**

11. What is the difference between cloture and filibuster? **LESSON 9.1**

12. Why was reconciliation developed? **LESSON 9.1**

13. What is the role of a conference committee? **LESSON 9.2**

14. Why was the line-item veto declared unconstitutional? **LESSON 9.2**

15. Why are omnibus bills nearly certain to win passage? **LESSON 9.2**

16. When is the federal fiscal year? **LESSON 9.3**

17. Why must authorization precede appropriations? **LESSON 9.3**

18. What does a continuing resolution do? **LESSON 9.3**

HISTORICAL THINKING

19. **COMPARE AND CONTRAST** Explain what earmarks and holds are, and describe how they are similar.

20. **SEQUENCE** Suppose a bill is introduced in the House and wins passage in the House. What must happen next before it can be presented to the president for signing?

21. **MAKE CONNECTIONS** How does the legislative process, including the budget process, incorporate checks and balances?

22. **SYNTHESIZE** What is the purpose of having both the House of Representatives and the Senate debate the same bill?

23. **COMPARE AND CONTRAST** Who has more power, an individual member of the House or an individual senator? Why do you think so?

INTERPRET VISUALS

The graph shows the change in the number of people represented by each member of the House. Study the graph, and then answer the questions.

24. How has the number of persons represented by each representative changed since 1930, the first apportionment to occur after the number of representatives was capped at 435 in 1929?

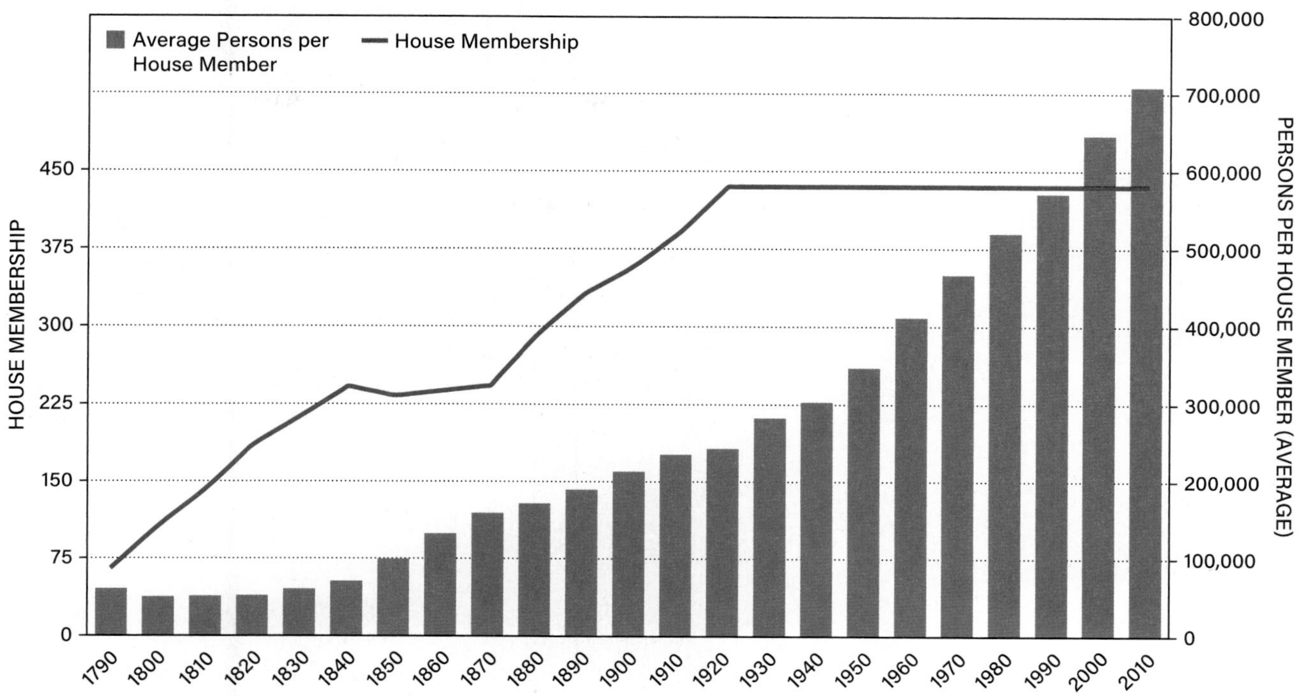

SOURCE: House of Representatives; Census Bureau

25. What would have to happen to the House for each member to represent fewer people?

ANALYZE SOURCES

Read the following excerpt. Then answer the questions that follow.

> If the earth be the gift of nature to the living their title can extend to the earth in its natural State only. The improvements made by the dead form a charge against the living who take the benefit of them. . . . Debts may be incurred for purposes which interest the unborn, as well as the living. . . . Debts may even be incurred principally for the benefit of posterity: such perhaps is the present debt [incurred to pay for the Revolutionary War].
>
> —Letter from James Madison to Thomas Jefferson, February 4, 1790

26. Why did Madison think it was fair that future generations be forced to pay off some of the debt incurred in fighting the Revolutionary War?

27. Based on this statement, how do you think Madison would view a law that required the government to have a balanced budget, in which it borrowed no money? Explain.

CONNECT TO YOUR LIFE

28. **NARRATIVE** In this chapter you have learned about the complicated process through which a bill becomes a law. It's a lot to learn. How did you learn it? Did you memorize a diagram? Did you make careful notes? Write a two- to four-paragraph narrative telling how you learned this process. Be sure to identify the steps as you explain them.

TIPS

- Think about what kind of learning works best for you: Do you learn better from words or pictures such as diagrams or charts?
- Describe the activities you used to learn the steps of the legislative process.
- Identify the steps you learned most easily and those you had to work on more.
- Describe how you assessed or tested yourself to see how much you had learned and what you needed to study more.

UNIT 5

The Executive Branch

UNIT 5 OVERVIEW

Chapter 10 The Presidency

Chapter 11 The Bureaucracy

CRITICAL VIEWING The central building of the White House has function rooms such as the State Dining Room on lower levels and the president's residence on the second floor. To the right is the West Wing, which includes the Oval Office, the Press Briefing Room, and other staff offices. To the left is the East Wing, which includes the First Lady's Office. What do these various rooms tell you about the purposes of the White House?

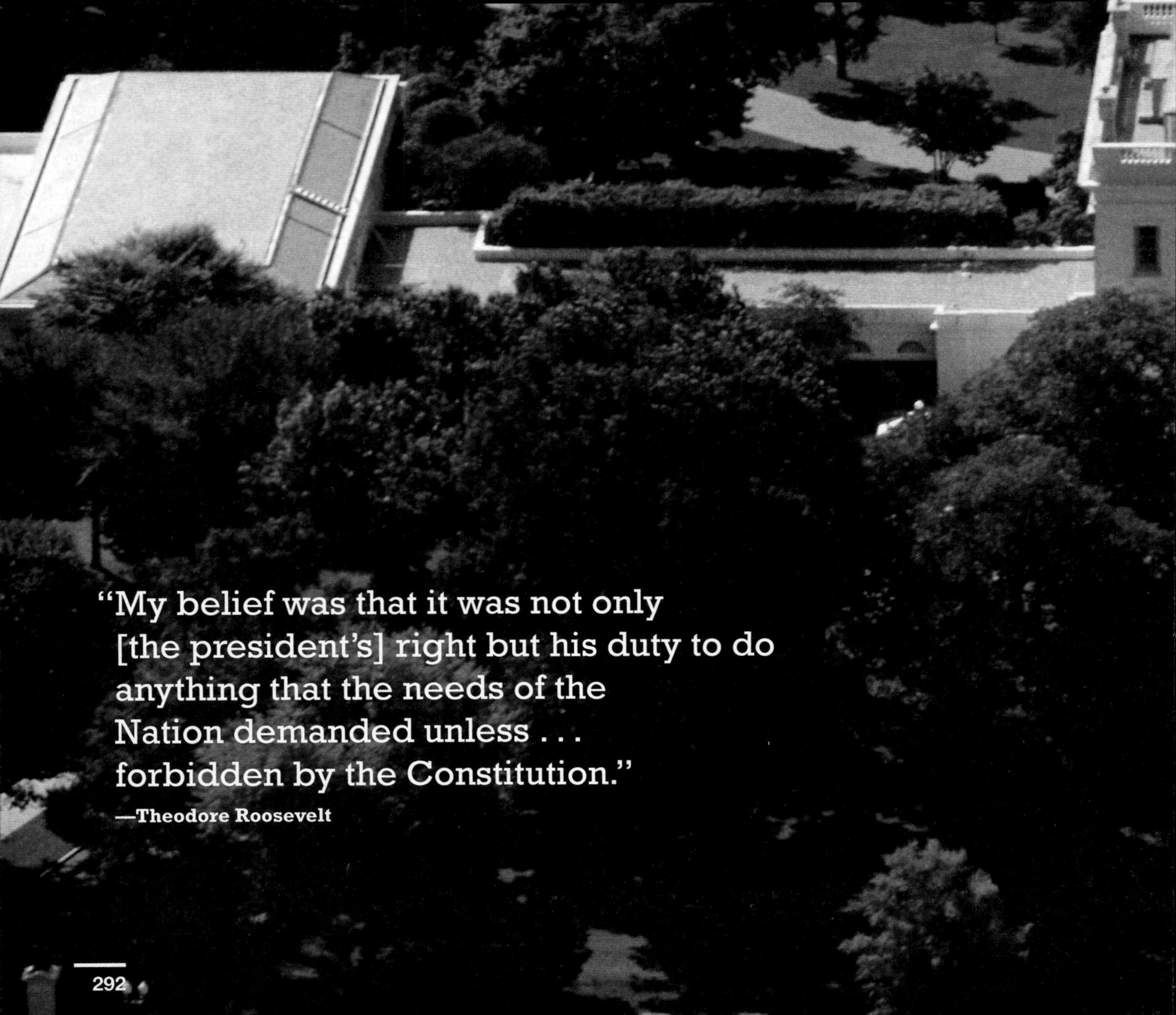

"My belief was that it was not only [the president's] right but his duty to do anything that the needs of the Nation demanded unless . . . forbidden by the Constitution."

—Theodore Roosevelt

CHAPTER 10

The Presidency

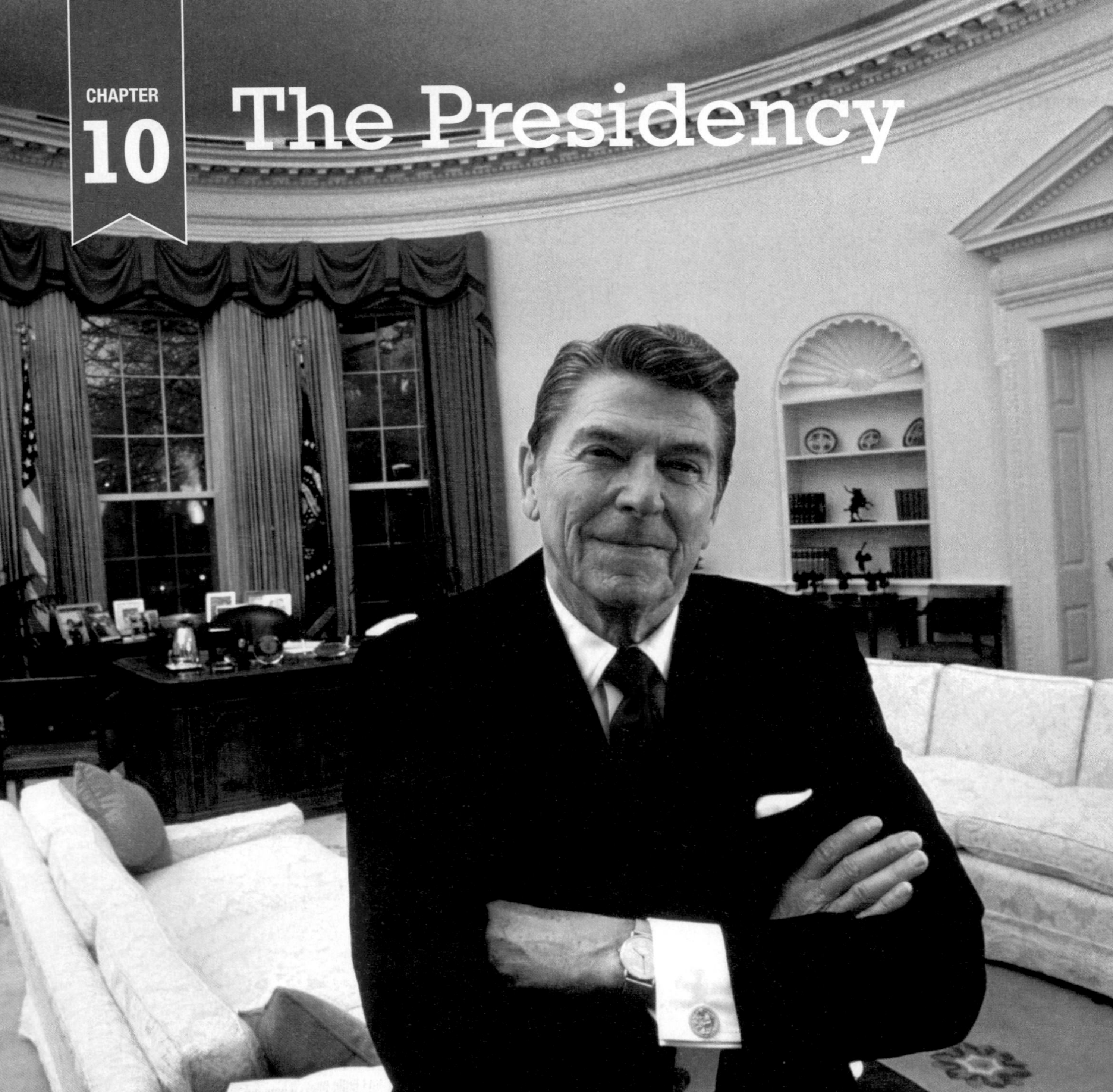

CRITICAL VIEWING President Ronald Reagan poses in the Oval Office late in his first year in office. The Oval Office—the key workspace for the president—was added by President Howard Taft after the West Wing was constructed by President Theodore Roosevelt. Before that, most presidents worked out of the room now known as the Lincoln Bedroom in the central building. Why do you think a president might prefer to work out of a corner of the West Wing instead of in the central building?

LESSONS

10.1 The Roles of the President

National Geographic Magazine:
50 Years of Wilderness

10.2 Presidential Powers

10.3 The President and Congress

10.4 Organization of the Executive Branch

LESSON 10.1 The Roles of the President

Few jobs in the world have the perks that come with being president of the United States. On the one hand, there are the plusses—living in the White House, flying anywhere in a jet full of gadgets, hearing "Hail to the Chief" played when entering a room, and receiving the accolades of people around the world. On the other hand, the presidency is full of work and effort. Martin Van Buren, president from 1837 to 1841, may have captured that aspect of being president best. "The two happiest days of my life," Van Buren said, "were those of my entrance upon the office [of president] and my surrender [leaving] of it."

Requirements, Demands, and Perks of the Office

Despite the burdens of the office, presidents have more power to reach their political objectives than any other individual in the American political system. Given this, it is not surprising that so many Americans—politicians and nonpoliticians alike—aspire to attain this office. The notion that anybody can grow up to be president has always been part of the American mythology. This is largely because Article II, Section 1, of the Constitution lists few requirements for the job:

> *No Person except a natural born Citizen, or a Citizen of the United States, at the time of the Adoption of this Constitution, shall be eligible to the Office of President; neither shall any Person be eligible to that Office who shall not have attained to the Age of thirty-five Years, and been fourteen Years a Resident within the United States.*

The Framers of the Constitution—many of them under the age of 35 themselves—chose the age requirement of 35 years in part because they believed it signaled maturity and better judgment. George Mason of Virginia, at the Constitutional Convention, said that "his political opinions at the age of 21 were too crude and erroneous to merit an influence on public measures." But there was another reason. Life expectancy was lower in the 18th century than today, and James Madison saw the age requirement as a way to prevent dynasties within the presidency. He reasoned that "in the course of nature very few fathers leave a son who has arrived to that age." In other words, he thought it was unlikely that a living ex-president would have a son old enough to hold the office. Despite Madison's intention, two sets of fathers and sons have served as president. John Adams served from 1797 to 1801. His son John Quincy Adams took office in 1825, while his father, who died the following year, was still alive. George H. W. Bush, who served from 1989 to 1993, lived through both terms of his son George W. Bush's presidency from 2001 to 2009.

The other two requirements for the presidency are fairly straightforward, though not without their share of controversy: The president must be a "natural born Citizen of the United States" and have lived in the country for at least 14 years. Therefore, it is impossible for a naturalized citizen to become president, even if that person came to this country as an infant. The requirement stemmed from a fear that foreigners would become U.S. citizens in hopes of becoming president with plans to use the office to help strengthen their country of birth.

The native birth requirement gained prominence in the 21st century when conspiracy theorists known as "birthers" claimed that President Barack Obama—whose mother was American but whose father was from Kenya—was not actually born in the United States. These people claimed that Obama's birth certificate from Hawaii was forged, and they were undeterred by the fact that Obama's birth was also announced in two Honolulu newspapers decades before his political career or his presidential campaign. Some critics of President Donald Trump claim he rose to political prominence by promoting this false claim.

While the requirements to attain the presidency are few, the responsibilities of the office are seemingly endless. In his autobiography, President Lyndon

B. Johnson wrote: "Of all the 1,886 nights I was President, there were not many when I got to sleep before 1 or 2 a.m., and there were few mornings when I didn't wake up by 6 or 6:30." President Harry Truman once observed that no one can really understand what it is like to be president, as there is no end to "the chain of responsibility that binds him," and he is "never allowed to forget that he is president." The duties and demands of the office are relentless. Unlike Congress, the president can never adjourn.

Yet these demands are accompanied by some very special perks. The president enjoys, among other things, the use of the White House (so named by President Theodore Roosevelt in 1901), where the president and the president's spouse and family members have a staff of more than 80 people, including chefs, gardeners, maids, butlers, and a personal tailor. Additionally, the president can call on a fleet of automobiles, helicopters, and jets (including Air Force One, which costs about $230,000 an hour to run) for transportation. For relaxation, the presidential family can go to Camp David, a resort hideaway in the Catoctin Mountains of Maryland. In addition, nearly any celebrity a president might like to meet, whether from the United States or another country, is likely to accept an invitation or a phone call from the president.

A three-level jet with 4,000 square feet of working and living space is always ready for the president's use. Air Force One is a traveling office, as well as a mobile command center in the case of an attack on the United States. On September 11, 2001, President George W. Bush (left) and his staff, including Chief of Staff Andrew Card (right), spent eight hours in the air.

HISTORICAL THINKING

1. **MAKE GENERALIZATIONS** What were the Framers trying to prevent by setting a specifc age and citizenship requirement for presidents?
2. **FORM AND SUPPORT OPINIONS** If you were helping to write the Constitution today, what requirements for the presidency would you want to see? Why?

The Varied Backgrounds of Presidents

The United States has been led by more than 40 presidents since George Washington first took office. While these individuals have often shared some characteristics—for instance, all have been men so far—they have differed starkly from each other as well. Modern presidents have included men who followed a traditional political career path. For example, Franklin D. Roosevelt and Bill Clinton pursued public service directly out of law school and became state governors before being elected president. Dwight Eisenhower entered politics after a distinguished military career. But they have also included people with more varied backgrounds. President Harry Truman began his career in retail before being elected to the Senate. President Lyndon Johnson was a high school teacher before entering politics. President Jimmy Carter managed his family's peanut farm before he was elected to Georgia's state senate and then governor of Georgia. President Ronald Reagan was first a sportscaster, later an actor, and then president of the Screen Actors Guild, a labor union, before being elected governor of California.

In contrast, Donald Trump was a business executive and reality television star who never held public office before being elected president. The most common previous occupation of U.S. presidents has been the legal profession—26 of 46 presidents have been lawyers. Many presidents have also been wealthy. Three presidents—Herbert Hoover, John F. Kennedy, and Donald Trump—were so wealthy that they donated their presidential salaries to charitable organizations or other causes.

The ages of presidents have also covered a wide spectrum. Despite the minimum age requirement of only 35 years, the average age of a president at inauguration has been 55 years old. The youngest person to be elected president was John F. Kennedy, who assumed the presidency at the age of 43. Theodore Roosevelt, however, was only 42 when he became president in 1901 after the assassination of William McKinley. Ronald Reagan was nearly 74 when he was inaugurated for his second term. The oldest president at the time of taking office was Joe Biden, who was 78 years old when he was inaugurated in 2021.

In terms of race, gender, and religious background, presidential candidates up until the early 20th century—even those of minor parties—were White and male, with a Protestant religious background. In 1928 Democrat Al Smith became the first Roman Catholic to run for president on a major party ticket, and in 1960 Democrat John Kennedy was the first Catholic to be elected president. Among more recent unsuccessful Democratic presidential candidates, Michael Dukakis was Greek Orthodox and Mitt Romney was Mormon. Vice-presidential candidates have included former senator Joe Lieberman, who is Jewish and who ran in 2000 on the Democratic ticket with Al Gore; and Congresswoman Geraldine Ferraro (D-NY), the first woman and first Italian American on a major party ticket when she ran with presidential candidate Walter Mondale in 1984.

More recently, the pool of presidential candidates has become more diversified. In 2008, Democrats chose between a White woman, Hillary Clinton, and an African-American man, Barack Obama. By that time, about 90 percent of Americans told pollsters they would be willing to support an African American or a woman for president. Although the majority of the candidates in the 2016 primaries were Protestant, including Democrat Hillary Clinton and Republicans Jeb Bush, John Kasich, and Donald Trump, their competition included a Roman Catholic (Republican Marco Rubio) and a Jewish candidate (Democrat Bernie Sanders).

The 2020 Democratic presidential primaries saw the most diverse field of candidates yet. Several women announced their candidacy, and both male and female candidates of a variety of racial and religious backgrounds vied for voter attention. Pete Buttigieg, the first openly gay presidential candidate, won significant support in the lead-up to the nomination. Joe Biden, a White Roman Catholic man, received the Democratic nomination and chose Kamala Harris, a woman of mixed South Asian and Jamaican descent with an upbringing that included both Hindu and Christian traditions, as his running mate. When the Biden-Harris ticket won the 2020 election, Harris became the first woman to win the vice-presidency in U.S. history.

HISTORICAL THINKING

3. **COMPARE AND CONTRAST** In what ways were the backgrounds of Donald Trump, Barack Obama, and John F. Kennedy each different from those of other presidents?
4. **FORM AND SUPPORT OPINIONS** How might a younger president lead the country differently than an older president? Explain.

The President as Chief Executive

The president of the United States has the authority to exercise a variety of powers. As you will read in the next lesson, some of these are explicitly granted by the Constitution. Many others have simply been assumed by past presidents, thereby setting precedents for subsequent presidents. In the course of exercising these powers, the president performs a variety of roles, including the role of head of the executive branch. A president's success in these different roles depends on what is happening domestically and internationally as well as on the president's personality, abilities, and experience.

Some presidents, such as Bill Clinton, have shown more interest in domestic policy than in foreign policy. Others, such as George H. W. Bush, were more interested in foreign affairs than in domestic issues. Still others have concentrated on one major area and promoted policy changes stemming from that area. For example, early in his presidency, Donald Trump focused on the economy, pursuing policies he believed would promote economic growth, including renegotiating foreign trade agreements and pushing for tax cuts.

The executive branch is unique among the three branches of government because it is headed by a single individual, versus a group of presiding officers. When the Framers established the office of the president, they created a uniquely American institution. No other country in the world at that time had a democratically chosen chief executive.

Yet the Framers never intended for the president to have as much power as the chief executive has today. The constitution preceding the current U.S. Constitution—the Articles of Confederation—did not even include an executive branch. Although the Framers saw the need for an individual to lead the executive branch, they didn't spend much time debating the powers of the office. Instead, they spent many days arguing over the length of the president's term and how a president would be elected.

In American government, the president is the chief executive, or the head of the executive branch of the federal government. In that role, the president has the responsibility to see that the laws are executed and to direct all the departments, agencies, bureaus, and offices in the executive branch. Article II details aspects of this presidential role in different sections:

Constitutional Duties of the President of the United States

Section 1, Clause 1	The executive Power shall be vested in a President of the United States of America
Section 2, Clause 1	[H]e may require the Opinion, in writing, of the principal Officer in each of the executive Departments, upon any Subject relating to the Duties of their respective Offices
Section 2, Clause 2	[H]e shall nominate, and by and with the Advice and Consent of the Senate, shall appoint . . . Officers of the United States
Section 3, Clause 1	[H]e shall take Care that the Laws be faithfully executed

The degree to which presidents succeed in the chief executive role is closely tied to how well they communicate with Americans. From the beginning of his first of four consecutive terms as president, Franklin D. Roosevelt delivered radio addresses to the country on everything from drought and New Deal policies to entry into and the progress of World War II. During these 30 or so addresses, Roosevelt spoke much like a person chatting comfortably with a friend, and his broadcasts became known as fireside chats.

HISTORICAL THINKING

5. **DESCRIBE** How have presidential powers evolved over time?
6. **ANALYZE VISUALS** Which clauses in Article II suggest that the Framers envisioned that the executive branch would consist of more than the president and vice president? Explain.

Commander in Chief, Head of State, and Chief Diplomat

The Constitution states that the president "shall be Commander in Chief of the Army and Navy of the United States, and of the Militia of the several States, when called into the actual Service of the United States." For many Americans, the president's role as commander in chief, or commander of the nation's armed forces, springs to mind first. This is far from surprising, given that U.S. military action almost always receives a large amount of press attention and a strong emotional response.

As the person with the power to **deploy**, or order into action, troops whose lives may be on the line, the president is under close scrutiny when acting as commander in chief. While Congress has the power to declare war and to raise and maintain the country's armed forces, the president, as commander in chief, determines where, when, and how the armed forces are used. The president can send troops into combat for up to 90 days without a declaration of war.

The president is also very much in the public eye in the role of head of state—the country's representative to the rest of the world. Traditionally, a country's monarch has performed the function of head of state. Because the United States has no king or queen, the president fulfills this role and performs symbolic or ceremonial roles ranging in seriousness, from throwing out the first pitch of the baseball season to decorating war heroes. Some people claim that ceremonial duties clutter the president's schedule and distract from the real work of leading the country. Yet most presidents have found the role of head of state to be politically useful—and an excellent way to connect with the people of the United States.

As head of state, the president is also fulfilling the role of chief diplomat, or the most senior person representing the United States to representatives of another country. The Constitution did not explicitly reserve this role to the president, but since the beginning, presidents have assumed it, based on their explicit constitutional powers to "receive [foreign] Ambassadors" and, with the advice and consent of the Senate, to appoint U.S. ambassadors and make treaties. As chief diplomat, the president directs the foreign policy of the United States and is our nation's most important diplomatic representative.

HISTORICAL THINKING

7. **IDENTIFY MAIN IDEAS AND DETAILS** What war powers does the Constitution grant to the president?

8. **SYNTHESIZE** What is the constitutional basis for the president's role as chief diplomat?

Chief Legislator

Nowhere in the Constitution do the words *chief legislator* appear. The Constitution, however, does require that the president "from time to time give to the Congress Information of the State of the Union, and recommend to their Consideration such Measures as he shall judge necessary and expedient." In addition, the president has the power to sign or veto legislation passed by Congress, thus holding a central role in lawmaking.

Most 19th-century presidents let Congress lead the way in proposing and implementing policy. Andrew Jackson's use of veto power and Abraham Lincoln's wielding of presidential war powers were exceptions. But Theodore Roosevelt's presidency, beginning in 1901, ushered in the era of presidential activism, or the assertive use of presidential power to promote certain policies and legislation. After his presidency was over, Theodore Roosevelt stated his expansive view of presidential power in his autobiography:

> *I declined to adopt the view that what was imperatively necessary for the Nation could not be done by the President unless he could find some specific authorization to do it. My belief was that it was not only his right but his duty to do anything that the needs of the Nation demanded unless such action was forbidden by the Constitution or by the laws.*

Roosevelt vigorously pursued a range of policies, from protecting natural resources to regulating corporations.

Many subsequent presidents have adopted Teddy Roosevelt's activist approach. His cousin Franklin Roosevelt greatly increased presidential power by persuading Congress to pass scores of New Deal laws with the aim of ending the Great Depression. Lyndon B. Johnson flexed his presidential muscle to expand the country's social welfare programs and bolster the civil rights movement. In the 1980s, Ronald Reagan convinced a Democratically controlled Congress to pass laws that cut taxes and slashed government regulation in an effort to stimulate the economy. Two decades later, George W. Bush responded to the terrorist attacks of September 11, 2001, in part by pressuring Congress to pass legislation that enhanced the government's ability to search for and constrain suspected terrorists.

It is now a foregone conclusion that presidents develop a legislative program and that Congress looks to the White House when shaping legislative language. Of course, one person's vigorous leader is someone else's hard-hearted tyrant. Conservatives railed against the legislative programs of the two Roosevelts and Johnson. Liberals decried Reagan's cuts to social programs and warned that George W. Bush's monitoring of communications to find potential terrorists violated rights to privacy and the First Amendment.

In addition, the president in the role of chief legislator also comes into conflict with how members of Congress see their own power. Different presidents have approached this tension in different ways. President Bill Clinton's administration, for example, drew up a health-care reform package in 1993 and presented it to Congress on an almost take-it-or-leave-it basis—and Congress left it. In contrast, President Barack Obama let Congress determine much of the content of the Affordable Care Act, the health-care reform bill that came to be called Obamacare. Yet President Obama's deference to Congress had several negative consequences. These included an unusually large number of earmarks, a protracted and unpopular legislative process, and opportunities for conservatives to mobilize against the reforms. But in the end, Obama succeeded where Clinton had failed.

Few presidents were as masterful a chief legislator as Lyndon B. Johnson, shown here meeting with civil rights leader Martin Luther King, Jr., in 1966. At the time of the meeting, Congress was considering a bill that would end discrimination in housing. Johnson, who had served six terms in the House and a decade in the Senate, knew the ins and outs of getting legislation through Congress.

HISTORICAL THINKING

9. **MAKE GENERALIZATIONS** How has the presidential role in legislation changed over time?
10. **MAKE CONNECTIONS** How can presidential activism affect the direction of legislation?

Political Party Leader

In today's party-driven political system, presidents are the de facto leaders of their political parties. The president, in effect, chooses the chairperson of the party's national committee. The president can also exert political power within the party through presidential powers of appointing people to and removing them from office.

As party leader, a president typically appoints the party's national chairperson and other leading officers. In addition, a president can use the appointive powers of the office to cement the loyalty of party members, rewarding supporters with government jobs. This is known as **patronage**—the practice of appointing individuals to government or public jobs to reward those who helped victorious candidates win election. Patronage has the added advantage of stocking an administration with people pledged to carry out the party's policies. Presidents may also campaign for party members running for office. In the 2018 midterm elections, President Trump campaigned vigorously for candidates he saw as like-minded Republicans. His support was seen as decisive in the victories of some candidates for Senate and governorships, but his message and rhetoric may have cost Republicans their majority in the House of Representatives.

The president may also reward party members with fund-raising assistance. Presidents are, in a sense, fund-raiser in chief for their parties. Recent presidents, including Bill Clinton, George W. Bush, and Barack Obama, have been prodigious fund-raisers. Donald Trump, who filed for re-election the day he was sworn in as president, raised over $135 million between his inauguration and the weeks leading up to the 2018 midterm elections. Much of the money raised went toward Trump's own re-election fund, but contributions made to the Republican National Committee and state Republican committees could support other candidates.

HISTORICAL THINKING

11. **MAKE PREDICTIONS** If an independent candidate were elected president, what effect might that have on patronage and political fund-raising?

12. **INTERPRET TABLES** Which presidential role was not foreseen by the Framers when outlining the president's duties in the Constitution? Explain.

The Roles and Activities of the President of the United States

PRESIDENT'S ROLES	RELEVANT ACTIVITIES
Chief Executive: enforces laws and federal court decisions, along with treaties approved by the United States	• Appoints, with Senate approval, and removes high-ranking officers of the federal government • Grants reprieves, pardons, and amnesties • Handles peacetime national emergencies such as riots or natural disasters
Commander in Chief: leads the nation's armed forces	• Can commit troops for up to 90 days in response to a military threat (War Powers Resolution) • Can make secret agreements with other countries • Can set up military governments in occupied nations • Can end fighting by calling a cease-fire (armistice)
Head of State: performs ceremonial activities as a personal symbol of the nation	• Decorates war heroes and noteworthy civilians • Dedicates parks and museums • Lights national Christmas tree and pardons national Thanksgiving turkey • Receives foreign heads of state
Chief Diplomat: directs U.S. foreign policy and is the nation's most important representative in dealing with foreign countries	• Negotiates and signs treaties with other nations, which go into effect with Senate approval • Makes pacts (executive agreements) with other heads of state, without Senate approval • Can accept the legitimacy of another country's government (power of recognition)
Chief Legislator: informs Congress about the condition of the country and recommends legislative measures	• Proposes legislative program to Congress in traditional State of the Union address • Suggests budget to Congress and submits annual economic report • Can veto a bill passed by Congress • Can call special sessions of Congress
Political Party Leader: heads political party	• Chooses a vice president • Makes several thousand top government appointments, often to party faithful (patronage) • Tries to execute the party's platform • Attends party fund-raisers • May campaign for party members running for office as mayors, governors, or members of Congress

Dawn breaks over the Front Range of the Rocky Mountains in Montana. The Front Range is where the Great Plains (right) reach the mountains. In 2014, President Barack Obama signed a bill into law that protected more than 275,000 acres of the Front Range, part of which was added to an existing wilderness area.

50 Years of Wilderness

by Elizabeth Kolbert *National Geographic* Magazine, September 2014

In 1964, President Lyndon B. Johnson signed the Wilderness Act into law, thereby protecting millions of acres of public land from commercial development. In "50 Years of Wilderness," journalist Elizabeth Kolbert examines the long-term impact of the law on the American landscape.

Kolbert begins her account by looking at the genesis of the act 30 years before its passage. During the Great Depression, New Deal programs created jobs for unemployed Americans in national parks and forests. Workers cleared trails throughout dense woods and built roads leading to and within the parks. The number of visitors coming to previously inaccessible areas soon increased—and so did the anxiety of conservationists who worried that additional human activity would further harm the various ecosystems.

These conservationists petitioned federal officials to create a new class of public lands—wilderness areas off-limits to commercial use and to tourists using motorized vehicles. It took many years and 60 drafts to arrive at the legislation that finally became law in 1964. The law immediately designated this new level of protection for 54 areas, with the promise that they would remain "untrammeled [untouched] by man, where man himself is a visitor who does not remain."

In the more than 50 years since the Act was signed into law, over 5 percent of the total U.S. land area has been designated for protection in more than 750 official wilderness areas. Few, if any, are truly "untrammeled." But Kolbert explains that restricting how Americans can interact with wilderness has had important consequences. She goes on to highlight the larger implications of land protection, especially as nature adjusts to the impact of global warming:

Today even the most remote wilderness areas, like the Bering Sea Wilderness off Alaska or the Innoko Wilderness in the state's interior, are being dramatically altered by the grand geophysical experiment that humans are conducting. Sea ice is disappearing, permafrost is thawing, and woody plants are invading the tundra, all thanks to global warming. The impossibility of escaping human influence, even in those few parts of the globe that people have never inhabited, has led some scientists to propose that we are living in a new geologic epoch, the Anthropocene.

In the age of man the Wilderness Act may seem futile—but it has arguably become more important. Designating land as wilderness represents an act of humility. It acknowledges that the world still transcends our comprehension, and its value, the use we can make of it.

Access the full version of "50 Years of Wilderness" by Elizabeth Kolbert through the Resources Menu in MindTap.

THINK ABOUT IT How does protective legislation like the Wilderness Act highlight the government's role

LESSON
10.2 Presidential Powers

Whenever the president arrives at a formal occasion, a military band strikes up "Hail to the Chief." Yet like so much connected to the presidency, nothing in the Constitution requires this music to be played. First Lady Sarah Polk requested that the song, originally written for a popular musical about the chief of a Scottish clan, be played whenever her husband, President James K. Polk, arrived at a formal event. Apparently, Polk was not a commanding figure, and people often overlooked his presence. Use of the music became a tradition that was observed on and off, but in 1954, the Department of Defense established the piece as the official musical tribute to the U.S. president.

The President's Constitutional Powers

It's unlikely that anyone worried that George Washington would be overlooked when he entered the room. Tall and dignified, he was viewed as bringing prestige to the newly created office of president. He was the natural choice for the first president, but the Framers knew he would not be president forever, and they wanted to define this new office in the Constitution.

The Framers might have held different views of what the president could do, but they identified some specific constitutional powers. Article I, Section 7, gives the president the power to veto bills passed by Congress. Most presidential powers, though, are spelled out in Sections 2 and 3 of Article II. These powers parallel the roles of the president discussed in the previous section:

- to serve as commander in chief of the armed forces and the state militias when they are called into service
- to appoint, with the Senate's consent, the heads of the executive departments, ambassadors, justices of the Supreme Court, and other top officials
- to make treaties, with the advice and consent of the Senate
- to grant reprieves and pardons, except in cases of impeachment
- to inform Congress of the State of the Union and to recommend "such Measures as he shall judge necessary and expedient"
- to call either or both houses of Congress into special sessions
- to receive ambassadors and other representatives from foreign countries
- to commission all officers of the United States
- to ensure that laws passed by Congress are "faithfully executed"

THE TREATY POWER While the Constitution gives the president the sole power to negotiate and sign treaties with other countries, the Senate must approve a treaty

Nearly every U.S. president since Woodrow Wilson has made State of the Union speeches before both houses of Congress, as George H.W. Bush does here in 1990. Traditionally, the president of the Senate, who is also the vice president (here Dan Quayle, seated left), and the speaker of the House (here Tom Foley, seated right) sit behind the president during this speech.

by a two-thirds vote before it becomes effective. Once a treaty is approved by the Senate and signed by the president, it becomes law. That process might seem fairly straightforward in concept, but it is not always so in reality. Presidents have not always succeeded in winning the Senate's approval for treaties. In 1999, for example, Bill Clinton was unable to persuade the Senate to approve the Comprehensive Test Ban Treaty, which would have prohibited all signers from testing nuclear weapons. The Senate did not buy his argument that the ban meant little to the United States but was an important step in limiting the spread of nuclear weapons.

In contrast, Barack Obama convinced the Senate to approve the New Strategic Arms Reduction Treaty (New START) with Russia in December 2010. The treaty reduced by half the number of nuclear missiles in both countries and provided for inspections of nuclear facilities. New START was supported by all the Democrats in the Senate and by many Republicans.

TRADE AGREEMENTS Presidents also sign trade agreements with other nations. Like treaties, they are negotiated by the president. Congress, however, has the power "to regulate commerce with foreign nations." Therefore, trade agreements must be submitted to Congress for approval. That approval takes the form of legislation implementing the provisions of the agreement. Unlike treaties, trade agreements require approval from both houses of Congress, but only by a simple majority vote, not the two-thirds vote required in the Senate for treaty approval. Because trade agreements are complex and may involve many nations, presidents may ask Congress to grant them what is called fast-track authority. This requires Congress to vote the entire deal up or down without amendments and with limited debate.

In 2015, President Obama won congressional support to negotiate the Trans-Pacific Partnership (TPP), a proposed agreement between the United States and 11 other nations on the Pacific Rim. But details were not finalized until 2016, in the middle of that year's presidential campaign. When both Republican Donald Trump and Democrat Hillary Clinton came out against the deal, failure was inevitable. Once in office, Trump announced that the United States was withdrawing from the TPP, and he began focusing on restructuring NAFTA, the North American Free Trade Agreement. After months of negotiation, Trump and the leaders of Mexico and Canada finalized the United States-Mexico-Canada Agreement, or USMCA, in late 2018. As of May 2020, legislatures in all three nations had approved the agreement, but full implementation awaited completion of steps on the part of all three nations required to ensure compliance with the agreement's many provisions.

THE PARDON POWER The president's power to pardon serves as a check on judicial power. It is granted through Article II, Section 2, Clause 1, of the Constitution, which allows the president what is known as clemency power, or the "Power to grant Reprieves and Pardons for Offenses against the United States." A **pardon** is a release from punishment or the legal consequences of a crime that restores the full rights and privileges of citizenship to a person. In 1925, the Supreme Court upheld an expansive interpretation of the president's pardon power, saying that it covers all offenses "either before trial, during trial, or after trial, by individuals, or by classes, conditionally or absolutely . . . without modification or regulation by Congress." The president can grant a pardon for any federal offense, except in cases of impeachment. The same is true for the commutation, or shortening, of a sentence. The difference is that with a commutation, the original conviction stands. Any civil disabilities, or penalties, such as a loss of voting rights or the right to run for public office, still apply. A pardon removes all civil disabilities.

While many pardons and commutations go largely unnoticed by the American public, others attract more attention. For example, a series of pardons and commutations granted by President Trump in late 2019 and early 2020 catapulted the clemency process into the national spotlight. Trump pardoned and commuted sentences of several individuals charged or convicted of fraud, conspiracy, and other serious federal crimes. Critics pointed out that some of those receiving pardons and commutations were personal friends or political supporters of the president.

Sometimes pardons are given to an entire class of individuals, an action known as granting **amnesty**. For example, in 1977, President Jimmy Carter granted amnesty to tens of thousands of men who had resisted the draft during the Vietnam War, either by refusing to register for the draft or by moving to another country. Carter's amnesty plan expanded on an earlier conditional amnesty offered by President Gerald Ford.

THE VETO POWER The president can veto legislation in two ways:

- In a regular veto, the president sends the bill back to the chamber in which it originated, usually with a message explaining the reason for the veto. Congress can override the veto with a two-thirds vote by the members present in each chamber. The bill then becomes law, against the wishes of the president.
- The president can employ a **pocket veto** by refusing to sign a bill within 10 working days of a congressional adjournment. Once Congress adjourns, the unsigned bill is killed for that session of Congress.

The frequency of vetoes can be affected by whether Congress is controlled by the president's party or the opposition. With a Congress led by his own party during the first two years of his presidency, President Obama exercised the veto power only twice. Surprisingly, Obama issued no vetoes during the next four years, even though the Republicans were in control of the House. Apparently, no measure Obama would have opposed was able to make its way through the Democratic-controlled Senate. In his last two years, however, with Republicans in control of both chambers, Obama issued 10 vetoes, one of which was overridden by Congress. President Trump—who enjoyed Republican majorities in both houses of Congress in his first two years in office—did not veto a single bill in that time. By May 2020, however, with the Democrats in control of the House of Representatives, Trump had vetoed seven bills. Congress was unable to muster the votes to overturn any of those vetoes.

HISTORICAL THINKING

1. **COMPARE AND CONTRAST** How are the processes for negotiating and approving treaties and trade agreements similar, and how are they different?
2. **ANALYZE CAUSE AND EFFECT** How do party politics affect the way a president is likely to use constitutional powers?

Expansion of the President's Inherent Powers

Like Congress, the president has inherent powers—powers that are necessary to carry out expressed powers. How those inherent powers are wielded depends largely on the personality of the chief executive. Some powers seen today as belonging to the president are the result of strong presidents who assumed inherent powers that their successors continued to exercise. President Woodrow Wilson clearly described this interplay between presidential personality and power:

> *The President is at liberty, both in law and conscience, to be as big a man as he can. His capacity will set the limit; and if Congress be overborne [overwhelmed] by him, it will be no fault of the makers of the Constitution—it will be from no lack of constitutional powers on his part, but only because the President has the nation behind him, and Congress has not.*

Even the Framers were uncertain about how the president would perform the various functions. As the first president, George Washington set many of the precedents that have defined presidential power. For example, he removed officials from office, interpreting the constitutional power to appoint officials as implying the inherent power to remove them as well. Washington established the practice of meeting regularly with the heads of the executive departments and of turning to them for political advice. He set a precedent for the president to act as chief legislator by submitting proposed legislation to Congress.

Subsequent presidents expanded the scope of the office through their exercise of inherent powers. Thomas Jefferson purchased the vast Louisiana Territory from France despite being unsure of any constitutional justification for the purchase. Andrew Jackson pulled federal funds from the Second Bank of the United States so he could destroy the bank, which had been created by Congress. Abraham Lincoln, confronting the problems of the Civil War, took several major actions while Congress was not in session. He suspended certain constitutional liberties (including the writ of *habeas corpus*), spent funds that Congress had not appropriated, blockaded southern ports, and

CRITICAL VIEWING President Theodore Roosevelt considered the presidency a "bully pulpit"—his term for an excellent position from which to try to persuade Americans of the need for various policies. Roosevelt traveled around the country, arguing for his policies in a variety of public speeches, including this 1902 appearance in New York. What might be the benefits and disadvantages of frequent in-person presidential addresses, such as those Roosevelt delivered?

banned what he labeled "treasonable correspondence" from the U.S. mail. Lincoln carried out all of these actions in the name of his power as commander in chief and his constitutional responsibility to "take Care that the Laws be faithfully executed." Other presidents, including both Roosevelts, Woodrow Wilson, Lyndon Johnson, and George W. Bush, also greatly expanded the powers of the president.

HISTORICAL THINKING

3. **EVALUATE** What did President Wilson mean when he said that the president can "be as big a man as he can" because he "has the nation behind him" while Congress has not?

Growth of the President's Legislative Powers

The expansion of presidential legislative powers is perhaps best exemplified in the presidency of Franklin Roosevelt. Facing crippling unemployment, failing farms and banks, and collapsed industrial output due to the Great Depression, Roosevelt pushed Congress to pass a host of laws during his first 100 days in office. Congress, as hungry for an economic turnaround as Roosevelt, quickly enacted the president's many New Deal programs, appropriating money for farm subsidies, public works, short-term relief payments, and much, much more. Roosevelt's unprecedented legislative action broadened the president's inherent powers as chief legislator.

Congress has come to expect the president to develop a legislative program. The president calls on Congress to enact laws the president thinks are necessary. The president may work closely with members of Congress to shape legislation. The president writes, calls, and meets with congressional leaders to discuss pending bills. The president also sends aides to lobby on Capitol Hill. And presidents use political favors—a campaign rally, support for a pet project—to persuade wavering legislators to vote for administration measures. Using every means available, a president can set the policy agenda like no other single actor in the political system.

The president's political skills and ability to persuade others play a large role in determining the administration's success in getting legislation enacted. Persuasive powers are particularly important when a president from one political party faces a Congress dominated by the other party. Typically, a president's success record is very high upon first taking office. That's when Congress is most likely to work with the president, but over time, the president's influence over Congress declines. Lyndon Johnson, a master at persuading and pressuring members of Congress to act, explained this decline this way: "Every day I'm in office and every day I push my program, I'll be losing part of my ability to be influential, because that's in the nature of what the president does. He uses up [political] capital."

One way presidents try to advance their legislative agenda is by going public—that is, using press conferences, public appearances, social media, and televised events to build public support for the administration's legislative program. Presidents hope the public will then pressure legislators to support the administration's bills. A president who has the support of the public can wield significant persuasive power over Congress. Soon after first taking office, Ronald Reagan addressed a joint session of Congress in February 1981 to urge Congress—with a Democratic majority in the House and a Republican-controlled Senate—to adopt his plan for large tax cuts and lower federal spending. The nationally televised address won popular support for Reagan's program, and by August, Congress enacted it into law. Yet in periods of severe political polarization, going public can be counterproductive. If a president endorses a proposal that might have had bipartisan support, the issue may become linked to the president's party and those of the opposing party may refuse their support. Without support from at least some members of both parties, the proposal might fail.

HISTORICAL THINKING

4. **IDENTIFY MAIN IDEAS AND DETAILS** What tools can a president use to convince members of Congress to support legislation?
5. **MAKE INFERENCES** What do you think Lyndon Johnson meant when he said that the president "uses up [political] capital"?

Executive Orders and Signing Statements

Presidents have also expanded their role through the use of two other tools—executive orders and signing statements. **Executive orders** are presidential orders to carry out policies described in laws. Executive orders have the force of law and have been issued for everything from restructuring the White House bureaucracy to rationing consumer goods under emergency conditions. Over the years, executive orders have been a very powerful tool for presidents.

One of President John F. Kennedy's priorities was the development of a well-funded U.S. space program. Here he is viewing an early one-person space capsule with astronaut John Glenn. His support for the space program led Congress to provide the needed funding, and thus the United States achieved Kennedy's goal of landing astronauts on the moon before the end of the 1960s.

In recent times, the use of executive orders has aroused great controversy. While President Obama issued relatively few executive orders, Republicans argued that several of them exceeded the president's constitutional authority, particularly those that suspended deportation of over 600,000 undocumented immigrants who had been brought to the country as small children and who were not otherwise in trouble with the law. These Dreamers (named for an acronym referring to a failed piece of legislation) were also allowed to obtain work permits. In 2014, Obama attempted to expand this program, largely to cover the parents of these young people. Federal courts blocked some of these suspensions to deportations, however, and in 2017 President Trump revoked them altogether. In June 2020, however, the Supreme Court ruled that the Trump administration had not followed proper procedure in revoking President Obama's actions. That ruling placed a hold on further action until the administration completed a review of its policy.

Almost all of President Trump's actions in the opening months of his administration took the form of executive orders. Among these were highly controversial orders that blocked admission into the United States of persons from several Muslim-majority nations. Federal courts blocked the first order on the grounds that it violated the rights of lawful holders of travel visas and legal permanent residents. The second order—issued to replace the first—was blocked on the grounds that it discriminated on the basis of religion. But in 2018 the Supreme Court upheld the travel ban. Chief Justice John Roberts, writing for the 5–4 majority, stated that because the order said nothing about religion and affected only 8 percent of the world's Muslim population, it was not discriminatory.

The **signing statement**, a written statement issued by a president at the time of signing a bill into law, is another technique presidents use to exert influence. Before the presidency of Ronald Reagan, only 75 signing statements were issued, mostly to praise legislation or to criticize those who had voted against it. On occasion, however, the statements noted constitutional problems with one or more clauses of a bill or provided details as to how the executive branch would interpret legislative language.

Reagan broke precedent by issuing a flurry of nearly 250 signing statements. Many of these signing statements questioned the constitutionality of legislation. George W. Bush issued 161 statements that challenged more than 1,100 clauses of federal law—more legal provisions than were challenged by all previous presidents put together. Obama dramatically reduced the number of such statements, but later presidents may well resume the practice.

HISTORICAL THINKING

6. **MAKE INFERENCES** What role does executive interpretation play in executive orders and signing statements?
7. **DRAW CONCLUSIONS** Why might presidents find issuing executive orders more appealing than trying to get legislation passed?
8. **MAKE INFERENCES** How do federal courts and the Supreme Court serve as a check against executive orders?

Evolving Presidential Power in Foreign Affairs

While the president is commander in chief and chief diplomat, only Congress has the power to formally declare war, and the Senate must ratify any treaty that the president has negotiated with other nations. Nevertheless, from the beginning of government under the Constitution, presidents have taken the lead in foreign affairs. George Washington laid the groundwork for this role. For example, when war broke out between Britain and France in 1793, Washington chose to disregard the country's existing treaty of alliance with France and pursue a course of strict neutrality, refusing to take sides in the conflict. Since that time, presidents have often taken military action and made foreign policy without consulting Congress.

In foreign affairs, presidential power is enhanced by the ability to make executive agreements. Earlier you read about these pacts between the president and other heads of state. They do not require Senate approval, yet they have the same legal status as treaties. Because executive agreements remove the obstacle of treaty approval, presidents have used them for everything from promises of assistance to other countries to matters of great importance, such as the exchange of military equipment for access to international military bases. To prevent presidents from abusing the power of these agreements, Congress passed a law in 1972 that requires the president to inform Congress of any executive agreement within 60 days of making it. But the law did nothing to limit the president's power to actually make executive agreements, and presidents continue to use them far more than treaties in making foreign policy.

For example, in 2015, the United States and six other world powers approved a deal to limit Iran's ability to obtain nuclear weapons. President Obama treated the pact as an executive agreement rather than a treaty, in part because he knew there would not be enough votes in the Senate to pass it as a treaty. Unsurprisingly, Republicans (and a few Democrats) strongly opposed this agreement. In May 2018, President Trump announced that the United States would withdraw from the deal.

HISTORICAL THINKING

9. **MAKE GENERALIZATIONS** How did the 1972 legislation concerning executive agreements affect how presidents use them?

Presidents and Military Actions

Though the United States has engaged in more than 200 actions involving the armed services, only five of those actions were wars declared by Congress. The rest were the result of unilateral action on the part of various presidents acting in their role as commander in chief. Some of those actions have been short-lived. Under President Reagan, for example, the United States took just four days to oust the socialist government from the Caribbean nation of Grenada. Other military interventions have been long and costly. President Truman, for instance, sent U.S. armed forces to Korea in 1950 without a declaration of war. U.S. troops remain on the Korean peninsula to this day. The undeclared war in Vietnam, which began with the commitment of just a few military advisors in 1955, dragged on well into the 1970s with troop levels at times as high as 500,000.

The American experience in Vietnam inspired Congress to pass (over President Nixon's veto) the War Powers Resolution of 1973, which requires the president to notify Congress within 48 hours of deploying troops. That resolution also prevents the president from keeping troops abroad for more than 60 days (or 90 days, if more time is needed for a successful withdrawal) without congressional authorization. These limits have not prevented subsequent presidents from pursuing military action when they believed it to be in America's national interest.

TWENTY-FIRST CENTURY MILITARY ACTIONS The war against terrorism that began on September 11, 2001, was approached differently than other military engagements. Congress passed a joint resolution authorizing President George W. Bush to use "all necessary and appropriate force against those nations, organizations, or persons he determines planned, authorized, committed, or aided the terrorist attacks that occurred on September 11, 2001." The broad wording of "nations, organizations, or persons" made possible military action against non-state actors like terrorist groups. This resolution became the basis for America's involvement in Afghanistan, where the government allowed the terrorist group al Qaeda—the planners of the September 11 attacks—to operate. In October 2002, Congress passed another joint resolution to authorize the use of U.S. armed forces against Iraq.

President Obama hoped to bring the conflicts in Afghanistan and Iraq to an end and avoid other involvement in Southwest Asia or North Africa. In 2011, however, Obama used air power in Libya without congressional authorization. Then, in 2013, with clear reluctance, Obama asked for authority to bomb the forces of dictator Bashar al-Assad in Syria. Assad later agreed to turn over chemical weapons for destruction, making congressional approval for military action unnecessary. When Obama did not request authority to attack the terrorist group ISIS in Iraq and Syria in 2014, some critics claimed that Obama was only willing to seek authority from Congress for military actions he was not eager to take.

In 2017, it became clear that Assad had used poison gas on civilians, counter to his earlier promise of having yielded all such weapons. Hundreds died, including children. One day later, with no congressional approval, President Trump ordered the bombing of an airfield used to undertake the chemical attack.

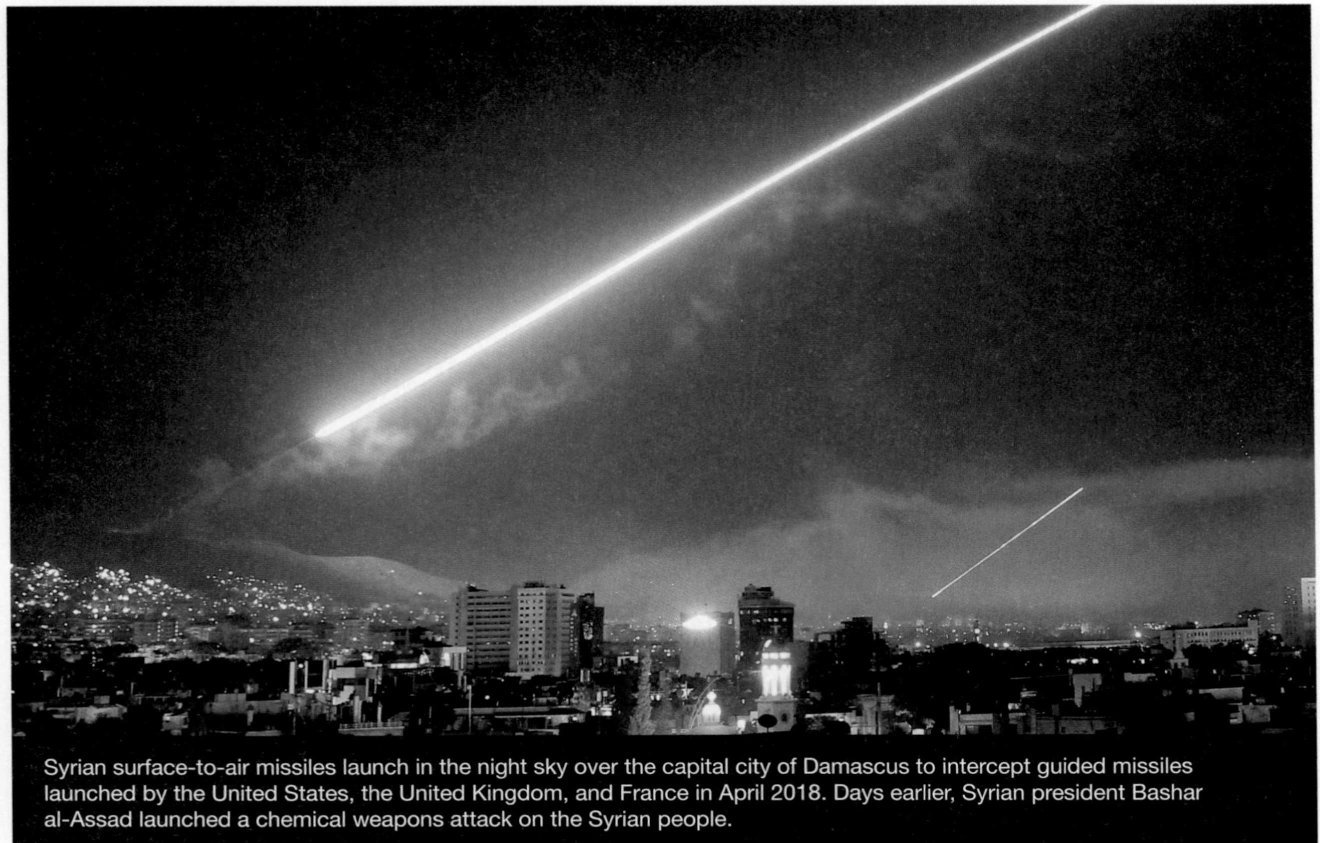
Syrian surface-to-air missiles launch in the night sky over the capital city of Damascus to intercept guided missiles launched by the United States, the United Kingdom, and France in April 2018. Days earlier, Syrian president Bashar al-Assad launched a chemical weapons attack on the Syrian people.

The following year, Trump ordered missile strikes (in conjunction with French and British strikes) as retaliation for further chemical attacks. But in October 2019, the Trump administration withdrew U.S. forces from war-torn northern Syria. This decision surprised U.S. allies among the Kurdish population of the region, who had fought alongside U.S. troops.

President Trump later increased U.S. troops in the region following an escalation of tensions with Iran that culminated in a U.S. airstrike killing Qassem Soleimani, leader of Iran Revolutionary Guards, in January, 2020. U.S. officials had long contended that Soleimani orchestrated terrorist attacks aimed at U.S. interests and allies. Iranian officials reacted to the attack by firing missiles at a U.S. airbase in Iraq. Fearing an outbreak of war, Congress quickly passed a war powers resolution seeking to prevent the president from further use of military action against Iran without congressional approval. President Trump vetoed the resolution, and Congress failed to override the veto.

USE OF NUCLEAR WEAPONS Since 1945, the president, as commander in chief, has been responsible for the most difficult of all military decisions: whether and when to use nuclear weapons. In 1945, President Truman made the decision to drop atomic bombs on the Japanese cities of Hiroshima and Nagasaki. Today, the president travels at all times with an aide who carries the so-called nuclear football—a briefcase containing the codes to launch a nuclear attack. Should any president ever authorize a nuclear attack, there is no legal recourse for stopping the action.

HISTORICAL THINKING

10. **MAKE INFERENCES** Why do you think Congress has accepted so many presidentially directed military actions without declarations of war?
11. **DRAW CONCLUSIONS** What does the fact that the president is never without the so-called nuclear football tell you about both the presidency and national security?

LESSON **10.3**

The President and Congress

Six weeks before George Washington was inaugurated as the first president of the United States, Thomas Jefferson wrote the following to James Madison: "The tyranny of the legislature is really the danger most to be feared, and will continue to be so for many years to come. . . . The tyranny of the executive power will come in its turn, but at a more distant period." As the power of the president has grown dramatically over the past century, some Americans—among them, members of Congress—have questioned whether Jefferson's longer-term prediction about the tyranny of the executive branch has come true.

How Congress Limits the President's Power

Despite the immense powers of the presidency, in the constitutional system of checks and balances, a president must still share power with the legislative and judicial branches. The Framers hoped this system of shared power would lessen the likelihood of the tyranny Jefferson feared on the part of either branch. Over the years, the president's power has also been checked by the media, public opinion, and voters. Recall Wilson's statement about the ability of the president to wield more power than Congress. He rested that assumption of power on the basis of the president having the support of the people. When that support shrinks or disappears, a president's scope of action is severely limited, and the initiative passes over to Congress.

ULTIMATE LAWMAKING AUTHORITY When it comes to making laws, Congress has a built-in advantage: It is the lawmaking branch of government. Presidents go to great lengths to overcome this basic fact of constitutional life. Each year, the president's staff spends months generating ideas, crunching numbers, and honing legislative language. Legislative and budgetary plans are rolled out with elaborate fanfare. The president courts public opinion, tries to boost approval ratings, and meets with the press—all with an eye to gaining leverage with Congress. But unless a member of Congress decides to take up a president's proposal and introduce it as a bill in Congress, all that presidential effort is wasted. Congress retains ultimate lawmaking authority.

What's more, only Congress can appropriate money. If Congress doesn't agree with a presidential policy, it can cut off the funding for that policy. If Congress wants to fund a program the president doesn't like, it can put funding in an appropriations bill. The most the president can do constitutionally is veto an entire bill if it contains something the president does not like. The president then risks both the political fallout, or negative consequences, of cutting off funding for other programs in the same bill and the possibility that Congress will override the veto, leaving the president to take a political hit for nothing.

CRITICAL VIEWING In 2015, President Barack Obama used his veto power to reject a bill approving the construction of the Keystone XL oil pipeline that would run from Canada to Nebraska. Obama stated that his veto was due to the fact that State Department research on the national impact of the pipeline had yet to be completed. What does this political cartoon convey about the power of presidential vetoes?

As you have read, presidents—particularly recent ones—have used signing statements to try to nullify parts of laws they object to. Congress has considered—but has not passed—legislation that would ban courts from using signing statements as the basis for any ruling on the constitutionality of a law. So far, at least, courts have shown no inclination to use signing statements in this way.

Indeed, courts have gone out of their way to ignore presidential signing statements or to question their pertinence. President Franklin Roosevelt signed a 1943 appropriations bill into law with a signing statement in which he expressed his misgivings over the constitutionality of one section. In 1946, when a challenge to the law reached the Supreme Court, the majority sided with the late president and his reasoning when it voided the provision. The Court did not use the signing statement as an authority for its decision, however. In 1972, a federal district court, taking on a challenge to another law that had been subject to a signing statement by President Richard Nixon, declared that no statement by a president that denies the legal force of any part of a bill "could have either validity or effect."

DIVIDED GOVERNMENT AND INTERESTS When government is divided—with at least one house of Congress controlled by a different party than the White House—the president can have difficulty even getting a legislative agenda to the floor of the legislature. President Barack Obama faced such a problem in 2011, when Republicans had a majority in the House of Representatives. During his first two years as president, Obama had worked with a very cooperative Democrat-led Congress. After Republicans became the majority party in the House, however, divided government existed again. Partisan hostilities seemed unusually intense, which set the stage for a particularly partisan 2016 presidential election that ended with Republican control of both chambers of Congress and the presidency. Yet even this was no guarantee for cooperation. In 2017, the Republican House and Senate failed to pass their promised replacement for the Affordable Care Act (Obamacare). After the 2018 midterm elections, the House had once again come under the control of Democrats, and President Donald Trump faced the prospect of divided government for the first time.

Apart from their partisan leanings, members of Congress and the president have different constituencies, which also influences their relationship. Members of Congress have a regional focus. They want legislative successes to bring home to their constituents—military bases that remain open, public-works projects that create local jobs, or trade rules that benefit a big local employer or industry. The focus of the president, in contrast, should be on the nation as a whole. At times, this difference in scope can put the president at odds even with members of the president's own party in Congress. A major factor in the defeat of the Republican plan to repeal Obamacare was that senators Susan Collins (R-ME) and Lisa Murkowski (R-AK) voted against the bill because they were concerned it would mean cuts in health care they thought would hurt the people of their states.

Furthermore, members of Congress and the president face different election cycles (every two years in the House, every six years in the Senate, and every four years for the president), and the president is limited to two terms in office, whereas members of Congress face no limits. Consequently, the president and Congress sometimes feel a different sense of urgency about implementing legislation. For example, members of Congress feel little pressure from a president in the last two years of a second term in office—even if the president is from the same party. One way or another, the president will be gone in two years or less, but the member of Congress has to worry about his or her own electoral future.

HISTORICAL THINKING

1. **MAKE INFERENCES** Why are members of Congress more likely to get provisions they favor included in bills the president supports?
2. **FORM AND SUPPORT OPINIONS** Who do you think has the advantage of time when in office: the president or a senator? Explain.

How the President Limits the Power of Congress

Though Congress plays a key role in lawmaking and in oversight of the executive branch, the president has the advantage over Congress in setting foreign policy and in influencing public opinion. There is another time when the president's power becomes very obvious: In times of crisis, the president can act quickly, speak with one voice on behalf of the government, and represent the nation to the world. Americans tend to turn to their president for leadership during uncertain times.

Some presidential scholars have argued that recent presidents have abused the powers of the presidency by taking advantage of crises. Others contend that there is what they call an unwritten doctrine of necessity under which presidential powers can and should be expanded during a crisis. Most of the time, Congress has retaken some control when the crisis was over, in a natural process of institutional give-and-take. Following the terrorist attacks of September 11, 2001, however, the institutional balance of power tipped toward the president, and Congress has been slow to reassert itself. The administration of George W. Bush launched a war on terrorism, an international military campaign. At the time, it was not clear when the crisis of terrorism would end and the nation could return to normal government relations. Nor was it clear when the civil liberties that had been limited would be restored. In fact, the Obama administration, which took office in January 2009, kept most of Bush's policies in place. In this case, the extension of presidential power remained a fact years after the initial crisis itself.

A president is generally in a much stronger bargaining position after winning a **landslide election**, or an election in which one candidate receives a notably high majority of the vote. Presidents elected in landslides include Lyndon Johnson in 1964 (61 percent of the vote), Ronald Reagan in 1984 (59 percent) and Richard Nixon in 1972 (61 percent). Winners of landslide margins often proclaim their victory is a mandate from the people to pursue their policy agenda. In reality, however, no president has ever received the votes of a majority of all eligible adults due to low voter turnout in the United States. Johnson came closest, but even he won the votes of fewer than 40 percent of the electorate. Note, though, that presidents and their running mates are the only officials voted for by the entire country. That counts for something.

The role of the president as the country's leader is rarely more obvious than during times of national crisis. When the U.S. space shuttle *Challenger* exploded shortly after liftoff on January 28, 1986, President Ronald Reagan canceled his State of the Union address and, instead, delivered an emotional speech to mourn with and comfort the American people.

Presidents have another advantage over Congress in terms of their influence. They have the upper hand when it comes to appointing people to top administration posts. Generally speaking, the Senate defers to presidential choices for the Cabinet and such high-level positions as national security advisor and the director of national intelligence. The thinking is that the president has a right to have trusted allies in these roles. Court nominations, however, have become more of a partisan battleground because these lifetime appointments are likely to far outlive the administration of any president.

In 1950, Senator Joseph McCarthy (R-WI) began a multi-year campaign that used lies and false charges to claim that communists had infiltrated the American government. In 1954, he launched hearings to investigate many of these false charges, prompting President Dwight D. Eisenhower to coin the term "executive privilege" and invoke its use to prevent members of his administration from being questioned by McCarthy.

Executive privilege, or the confidentiality of presidential decision-making, gives the president further advantages. While Congress has oversight authority, both Congress and the public accept that a certain degree of secrecy within the executive branch is necessary for national security. Executive privilege has been invoked by presidents from the time of George Washington to the present. Such claims may be controversial, but whether Congress will challenge them often has to do with the party affiliation of the congressional majority and the president. Richard Nixon invoked executive privilege to avoid releasing taped White House conversations to Congress during the Watergate scandal. The Supreme Court ruled against the president, however, declaring that since the tapes provided evidence in a criminal case, they had to be turned over.

More recently, Donald Trump has invoked executive privilege to block congressional access to various White House documents, such as reports pertaining to Russian meddling in the 2016 presidential election. He has also claimed privilege when attempting to block the testimony of former advisors during his impeachment trial in the Senate in 2020.

In July 2020, the Supreme Court issued two decisions concerning President Trump's efforts to shield his tax returns and other financial information from scrutiny on the grounds of presidential immunity. The Court ruled that Trump didn't have to comply with wide-ranging congressional subpoenas of his financial information because such wide-ranging requests would place too heavy a burden on a president's ability to perform the duties of the office. In a parallel ruling, however, the Court found that executive privilege did not protect Trump from a subpoena by a New York state prosecutor investigating possible criminal acts.

HISTORICAL THINKING

3. **MAKE INFERENCES** Why do you think Americans turn to the chief executive during a national crisis?
4. **FORM AND SUPPORT OPINIONS** Explain the possible advantages and disadvantages of executive privilege.

LESSON
10.4 Organization of the Executive Branch

When George Washington was president, he had five top advisors. Today's White House is much larger—President Donald Trump's White House staff neared 400 people (a decline from President Barack Obama's staff). That figure doesn't include the numerous advisors in the executive departments and other executive agencies. One thing hasn't changed from Washington's time, however. No matter how much presidents seek the opinions of their advisors, in the end the decisions remain theirs alone. After a Cabinet meeting in which all seven Cabinet members voted ***no*** on an issue the president supported, President Lincoln reportedly said, "Seven nays and one aye; the ayes have it." Or, as President George W. Bush put it, "I'm the decider."

The President's Cabinet

As with so many other details of government, the Constitution does not specify who should assist and advise the president. It states only that the president "may require the Opinion, in writing, of the principal Officer in each of the executive Departments." The First Congress established four executive departments—state, treasury, war, and the post office, plus the office of the attorney general—and under Washington these five officials formed the original presidential Cabinet. Over time, other departments have been added as

The 15 Executive Departments

DEPARTMENT	YEAR ESTABLISHED	DEPARTMENT	YEAR ESTABLISHED
Department of State	1789	Department of Health and Human Services[4]	1953
Department of the Treasury	1789	Department of Housing and Urban Development	1965
Department of Defense[1]	1789	Department of Transportation	1967
Department of Justice[2]	1789	Department of Energy	1977
Department of the Interior	1849	Department of Education	1979
Department of Agriculture	1889	Department of Veterans Affairs	1989
Department of Commerce[3]	1903	Department of Homeland Security	2002
Department of Labor[3]	1903		

[1]Established in 1947 as the National Military Establishment by merging the Department of War, created in 1789, and the Department of the Navy, created in 1798; renamed the Department of Defense in 1949.
[2]Formerly the Office of the Attorney General; renamed and reorganized in 1870.
[3]Formed in 1913 by splitting the Department of Commerce and Labor, which was created in 1903.
[4]Formerly the Department of Health, Education, and Welfare; renamed when a separate Department of Education was created in 1979.

the federal government has become more involved in other aspects of national life and different issues became priorities. Some executive departments have been reconfigured, and the Postal Service office was reformed as an independent entity. Today, there are 15 executive departments. A department secretary heads 14 of these, with the Department of Justice led by the attorney general. Some departments were originally created under other names or exist today as the result of mergers or splits.

Because there is no actual constitutional requirement that a president consult or even have a Cabinet, the makeup and use of this body of advisors are purely discretionary and may change in the course of a president's administration. In addition to the heads of the executive departments, the vice president is a member of the Cabinet, but presidents may wish to include other high officials as well, to signal a policy priority. President George W. Bush added five officials to the Cabinet, and President Barack Obama added eight. In addition to the vice president, recent Cabinets have included officials such as the following:

- administrator of the Environmental Protection Agency
- administrator of the Small Business Administration
- director of the Central Intelligence Agency
- director of National Intelligence
- director of the Office of Management and Budget
- United States representative to the United Nations
- United States trade representative
- White House chief of staff

Presidents also vary greatly in how they use their Cabinet. Some presidents rely on their Cabinet for counsel and advice. Other presidents rely principally on one or two members of the Cabinet and meet with the full assembly irregularly. In general, presidents recognize that department heads are often more responsive to the wishes of their own staffs, to their own political ambitions, or to obtaining resources for their departments than they are to the presidents they serve.

Team of Rivals

When Abraham Lincoln was elected president in November 1860, he surprised many people by appointing to key Cabinet posts three men who competed with him for the Republican nomination. Edward Bates became attorney general, Salmon P. Chase became secretary of the treasury, and William H. Seward became secretary of state. Lincoln knew that the country was on the brink of a civil war, and he hoped to unify the Republican Party before the war began. The president was also keen to hear a variety of opinions and viewpoints to weigh against his own as he adjusted to the power of the presidency. In addition, he cleverly realized that if these former rivals were in his administration, they would be less likely to criticize it. More recently, President Barack Obama's appointment of former Democratic rival Hillary Clinton to a key Cabinet position—secretary of state—stands as a modern example of a team of rivals.

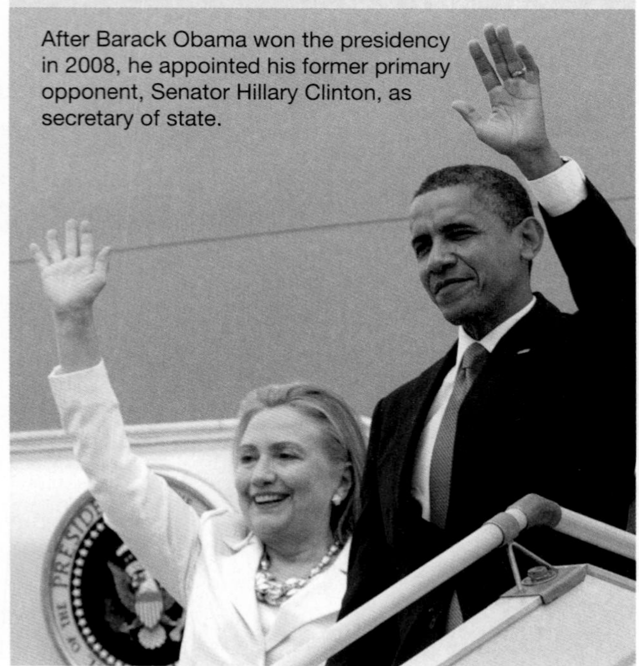
After Barack Obama won the presidency in 2008, he appointed his former primary opponent, Senator Hillary Clinton, as secretary of state.

A president's initial appointments to Cabinet posts receive a great deal of media attention, in part because these appointments provide an early glimpse into the direction a new administration will take. Those first picks do not necessarily serve a president's full term in office—

especially if he or she wins re-election to a second term. President Trump's Cabinet experienced an especially high rate of turnover in his first three years in office, with 10 members leaving their positions.

Many presidents rely on a so-called kitchen cabinet, an informal group of unofficial advisors. The term originated during the presidency of Andrew Jackson, who sought advice from a group of close friends who were said to meet with him in the White House kitchen. Trump has sought much of his most important advice from White House staff members, a kitchen cabinet in all but name.

Trump's closest advisors included traditional Republicans and former military leaders. But family members, including his daughter Ivanka Trump and her husband, Jared Kushner, played a significant role in the Trump administration as well. Trump also relied on **ideologues**, or extremely partisan advocates. One prominent ideologue was Stephen Miller, whose anti-immigration positions and assertions of expansive presidential power won him a major role as speechwriter and policymaker in the Trump administration.

HISTORICAL THINKING

1. **EVALUATE** Does the presence of a large number of advisors weaken or strengthen the role of president as chief executive? Explain.
2. **MAKE GENERALIZATIONS** Given the enormous demands of the presidency, why do you think it is that some presidents listen more closely to their kitchen cabinet than their official Cabinet?
3. **ANALYZE VISUALS** What does the increase in the number of executive departments over time suggest about the nature of the federal government's role in American life? Explain.

The Executive Office of the President

While the executive department heads and other Cabinet members advise the president, they usually spend much of their time managing their agencies. Presidents rely on a group of specialized staffers whose one job is to formulate policy alternatives for the president. These staffers are part of the Executive Office of the President (EOP). As part of his New Deal, Franklin Roosevelt established the EOP in 1939 to help him manage the increased responsibilities of the executive branch as it tackled the Great Depression. Since then, the EOP has grown significantly. The EOP includes the top advisors and assistants who help the president carry out major duties and has become an increasingly influential part of the executive branch. Like the Cabinet, its makeup also tends to change according to the needs and leadership style of each president. In 2018, the EOP included eight divisions:

- Office of the President
- Office of the Vice President
- Council of Economic Advisers
- Council on Environmental Quality
- National Security Council
- Office of Management and Budget
- Office of National Drug Control Policy
- Office of Science and Technology Policy

The EOP is overseen by the White House chief of staff, who advises the president on important matters and directs the operations of the rest of the presidential staff. A number of other top officials, assistants, and special assistants to the president work in such areas as national security, the economy, and political affairs. One of the most public of these officials is the White House press secretary, who regularly meets with reporters and makes public statements for the president. The Office of the White House Counsel provides legal advice to the president and the EOP on matters touching on the president and the White House.

Many, many other staffers work behind the scenes, including speechwriters, researchers, the president's physician, and a correspondence secretary. Some staffers investigate and analyze problems that require the president's attention. Specialists in areas such as diplomatic relations or foreign trade gather information for the president and suggest actions. Other staffers screen questions, issues, and problems presented to the president and delegate them to officials who can answer them. Additionally, the staff provides public relations support with both the press and Congress. Several staff members work directly with members of Congress to advance legislation the administration wants and to monitor the progress of bills through Congress.

OFFICE OF MANAGEMENT AND BUDGET One of the most important and influential units within the

The White House press secretary is one of the most public roles within the Executive Office of the President. As the primary spokesperson for the president, this individual expresses the administration's views to national and international media. Here Dana Perino, who served as press secretary under President George W. Bush from 2007 to 2009, gives a daily briefing in the White House in 2008.

Office of the President is the Office of Management and Budget (OMB). The OMB is responsible for helping the president draw up a budget to submit to Congress each year. The federal budget lists the revenues and expenditures expected for the coming year, including which programs the federal government will pay for and how much they will cost. In other words, the budget is an annual statement of the president's view of government policies translated into dollars and cents. Making changes in the budget is a key way for presidents to influence the direction and policies of the federal government.

The Senate must confirm the president's appointment for the director of the OMB. This person oversees the OMB's work, argues the administration's positions before Congress, and lobbies members of Congress to support the president's budget or to accept key features of it. Once the budget is approved by Congress, the OMB has the responsibility of putting it into practice. In an overseer role, the OMB checks that federal agencies are using funds efficiently and that any new bills prepared by the executive branch work within budgetary constraints. The OMB also keeps an eye on legislative matters to ensure that they agree with the president's own positions.

NATIONAL SECURITY COUNCIL The National Security Council (NSC) was established in 1947 to coordinate the flow of information and advice to the president on matters of national security. By statute, its members are the president (who acts as chair), the vice president, and the secretaries of state and defense. It also includes the chairperson of the Joint Chiefs of Staff, who represents the armed forces, and the director of national intelligence, who coordinates the country's intelligence agencies. More recently, as a measure of the importance of the economy to the national security, the secretary of the treasury and the director of the Council of Economic Advisers have joined the council. The president's assistant for national security affairs, an official commonly called the **national security advisor**, heads the NSC staff and serves as the president's chief in-house advisor on national security.

OFFICE OF THE FIRST LADY The Office of the First Lady is made up of the staff of the president's spouse. Staffers coordinate the first lady's schedule, plan foreign trips, and assist the first lady in working on her agenda. First ladies have at times taken important roles within the White House. Franklin Roosevelt's wife, Eleanor, took a much more public role than most first ladies before her, advocating strenuously for the rights of women, workers, and African Americans. Since then, many first ladies have also concentrated on specific issues while in office. Laura Bush—wife of George W. Bush—worked to promote childhood literacy, Hillary Clinton concentrated on health-care reform, and Michelle Obama targeted childhood obesity by actively promoting fitness and healthful eating. First Lady Melania Trump was an advocate for teaching children the responsible use of social media.

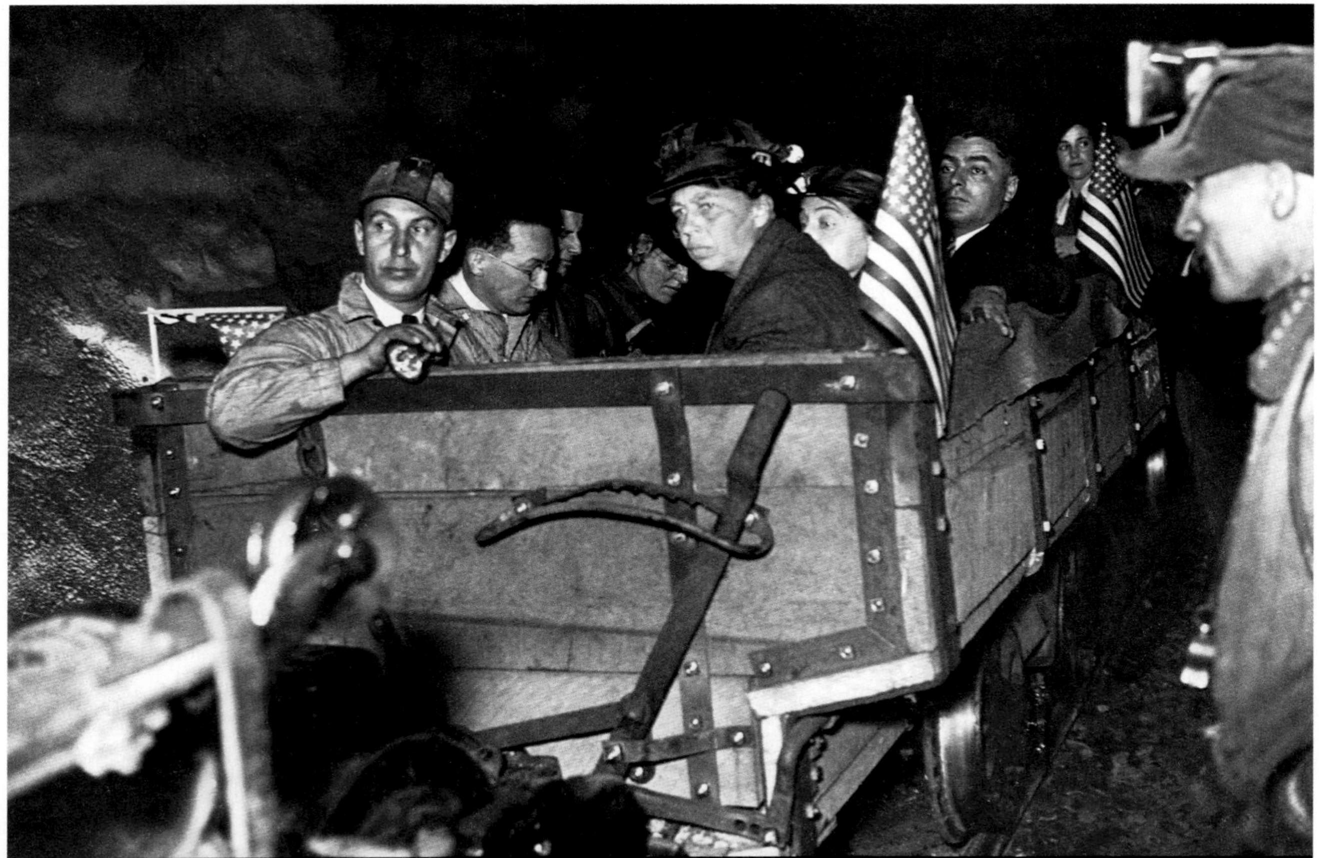

Eleanor Roosevelt (center), wife of President Franklin Roosevelt, was the first presidential spouse to take a visible stance on various policy issues. She became well-known for her support for increased civil rights for women and African Americans and was also an advocate for American workers, particularly when it came to improving working conditions. In 1935, she drew national attention to the dangers and difficulties faced by mine workers when she traveled underground to visit a coal mine in Neffs, Ohio.

HISTORICAL THINKING

4. **MAKE INFERENCES** What can you learn about the president's highest priorities by looking at the offices that make up the EOP?

5. **ANALYZE CAUSE AND EFFECT** Do you think the OMB makes the executive branch more or less accountable to Congress? Explain.

The Vice Presidency and Presidential Succession

Presidential candidates choose their running mates carefully, knowing that a vice presidential candidate can balance the ticket in areas where the presidential nominee might look weak, inexperienced, or out of touch. For example, in 2008, nominee Barack Obama, still only in the middle of his first term as a senator, picked Delaware senator Joe Biden, who had 35 years of experience in Congress. Obama wished to counter detractors who claimed he was too inexperienced. Running mates are also frequently chosen to appease vocal party factions. In 2012, Republican presidential candidate Mitt Romney, a moderate, chose Representative Paul Ryan of Wisconsin to join his ticket in hopes of appealing to the party's conservative wing, which held Ryan in high regard.

The vice presidential choices in 2016 demonstrated similar strategic thinking. Donald Trump named Indiana governor Mike Pence as his running mate. Pence—a thoroughly conventional Republican—was clearly meant to balance the very unconventional Trump. One week later, Hillary Clinton named Virginia senator and former governor Tim Kaine to complete her ticket. Fluent in Spanish, Kaine began his legal career by representing African Americans in housing discrimination cases. Clinton's campaign hoped to appeal to a more diverse group of Democratic voters by choosing Kaine.

Until fairly recently, the role of vice president entailed very few actual responsibilities. John Adams, the first vice president, called the position "the most insignificant office that ever the invention of man contrived or his imagination conceived." Yet the position is vital and extremely important, considering that the vice president becomes the nation's chief executive should the president die, be impeached and convicted, or resign. Nine vice presidents have become president—eight due to the death of a president and one due to a presidential resignation.

ROLE OF THE VICE PRESIDENT In recent years, the responsibilities of the vice president have grown substantially, and the vice president has become one of the most important of the president's advisors. The first modern vice president to play such a role was Walter Mondale, who was President Carter's vice president from 1977 to 1981. Later, President Bill Clinton relied heavily on Vice President Al Gore, who shared many of Clinton's values and beliefs. In the opinion of many historians, however, the most powerful vice president in American history was Dick Cheney, who served under George W. Bush. The unprecedented delegation of power that Cheney enjoyed would not have been possible without the president's agreement. Joe Biden and Mike Pence were important advisors as vice presidents, and Pence assumed an important public role during the COVID-19 pandemic in 2020, when President Trump named him as the leader of the federal government's response to the virus. But neither Biden nor Pence held as much power as Cheney.

PRESIDENTIAL SUCCESSION AND THE 25TH AMENDMENT Despite living in an era of frequent, untreatable illnesses, the Framers of the Constitution never addressed what the vice president should do if the president becomes incapable of carrying out necessary duties while in office. It remained a largely unanswered question until John F. Kennedy was

CRITICAL VIEWING Vice President Dick Cheney wielded considerable influence in the administration of President George W. Bush. In the aftermath of the September 11, 2001, terrorist attacks, Cheney (seated at right) was involved in the nation's response to the attacks from the safety of the Emergency Operations Center. What role can actively involved vice presidents play in an administration, and why do you think vice presidents do not always play this role?

assassinated in 1963 and the medical history of his successor, Lyndon B. Johnson, came under closer scrutiny. The 25th Amendment to the Constitution, ratified in 1967, addressed the issue. The amendment states that when the president believes that he or she is incapable of performing the duties of the office, he or she must inform Congress in writing of this fact. When the president is unable to communicate, a majority of the Cabinet, including the vice president, can declare that fact to Congress. In either case, the vice president then serves as acting president until the president is able to resume normal duties. If a dispute arises over the president's ability to resume the duties of office, a two-thirds vote of both chambers of Congress can keep the vice president in the role of acting president.

The U.S. secretary of state is fourth in line in order of presidential succession, but only if he or she meets the constitutional qualifications. Madeleine Albright, who served as secretary of state under President Bill Clinton from 1997 to 2001, could never have succeeded to the presidency, because she was born in the former Czechoslovakia (now the Czech Republic) and was a naturalized—rather than native-born—U.S. citizen.

The 25th Amendment also addresses the question of how the president should fill a vacant vice presidency. Section 2 states, "Whenever there is a vacancy in the office of the Vice President, the President shall nominate a Vice President who shall take office upon confirmation by a majority vote of both Houses of Congress." In 1973, Gerald Ford became the first appointed vice president of the United States after Spiro Agnew, Richard Nixon's vice president, was forced to resign. One year later, President Richard Nixon resigned, and Ford advanced to the office of president. President Ford named Nelson Rockefeller as his vice president, meaning that for the first time in U.S. history, neither the president nor the vice president had been elected to that position.

It is an act of Congress, and not a constitutional amendment, that deals with the question of what should be done if both the president and the vice president die, resign, or become disabled. The Presidential Succession Act of 1947—legislation encouraged by Harry Truman after succeeding to the presidency upon the death of President Franklin D. Roosevelt—dictates that the Speaker of the House of Representatives fills the void, after resigning from Congress and the role of Speaker. The president pro tempore of the Senate is next in line. Should that individual be unable to take the office, he or she is followed by the heads of the 15 executive departments in the order of the creation of their departments.

HISTORICAL THINKING

6. **DRAW CONCLUSIONS** Why do you think presidential succession moves to the leaders of the legislative branch first, before the heads of the executive departments?
7. **FORM AND SUPPORT OPINIONS** Do you think the Framers would have provided for presidential succession if they had been familiar with the fierce partisanship that characterizes modern-day federal government? Explain.

CHAPTER 10

THE PRESIDENCY

Review

VOCABULARY

Match each of the following vocabulary words with its definition.

1. deploy
2. patronage
3. pardon
4. amnesty
5. pocket veto
6. signing statement
7. landslide election
8. ideologue
9. national security advisor

a. a pardon bestowed on an entire class of people

b. the person a president might consult on domestic terrorism threats

c. a president's official comment on a bill signed into law

d. appointing individuals to government or public jobs to reward those who helped victorious candidates

e. extremely partisan advocate

f. to order troops into action

g. a release from punishment or the legal consequences of a crime that restores the full rights and privileges of citizenship to a person

h. a presidential refusal to sign a bill before Congress adjourns

i. outcome in which one candidate receives a significant majority

MAIN IDEAS

Answer the following questions. Support your answer with evidence from the chapter.

10. What are the only three requirements for presidents listed in the U.S. Constitution? **LESSON 10.1**

11. Explain the relationship between presidential activism and the president's roles. **LESSON 10.1**

12. Name three powers the Constitution gives the president, and explain how each one is balanced by the powers of Congress. **LESSON 10.2**

13. How is the president's power to issue executive orders balanced by the power of another branch of government? **LESSON 10.2**

14. How is the War Powers Resolution representative of the ongoing relationship between the president and Congress? **LESSON 10.2**

15. How are executive orders, executive agreements, and executive privilege similar and different? **LESSON 10.3**

16. What is the difference between a president's official Cabinet and the kitchen cabinet? **LESSON 10.4**

17. President Woodrow Wilson suffered a stroke during his second term in office and was incapacitated for part of that time. How does the 25th Amendment address this kind of situation? **LESSON 10.4**

HISTORICAL THINKING

Answer the following questions. Support your answer with evidence from the chapter.

18. **FORM AND SUPPORT OPINIONS** How has the country benefited from the presidency slowly becoming more diverse?

19. **EVALUATE** Which role of the president do you think American government could best do without? Explain your answer.

20. **MAKE CONNECTIONS** How can the personality of a president affect the way the powers of the office are exercised? Give an example.

21. **SYNTHESIZE** How have various presidents used the vagueness of constitutional language regarding the roles and powers of the presidency to their advantage?

22. **COMPARE AND CONTRAST** How is the office of the president, and public perception of that office, different from the office of a member of Congress?

23. **ANALYZE CAUSE AND EFFECT** How is the nature of the war on terrorism a different kind of national crisis from other types of wars, especially in terms of presidential involvement?

24. **DRAW CONCLUSIONS** How can a landslide election help a president when government is divided?

25. **MAKE GENERALIZATIONS** How has the increased role of the federal government affected the perception and reality of the presidency?

INTERPRET VISUALS

The bar graph below shows the number of times presidents Bill Clinton and George W. Bush exercised their veto power in each session of Congress. Study the graphs, and then answer the questions.

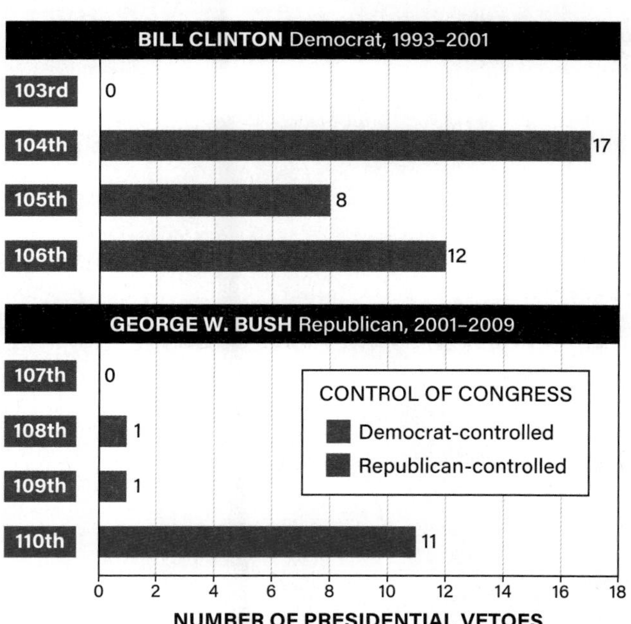

SOURCE: The American Presidency Project, Presidency Research Group

26. How did divided government affect the use of the veto power during each president's time in office?

27. What can you infer about Clinton's relationship with Congress by examining his veto usage?

ANALYZE SOURCES

Read the following quotation from Ronald Reagan, the 40th president of the United States. Then answer the question that follows:

> The greatest leader is not necessarily the one who does the greatest things. He is the one who gets the people to do the greatest things.
>
> —President Ronald Reagan, 1975

28. What role(s) of the president is President Reagan describing here? Explain.

CONNECT TO YOUR LIFE

29. **EXPLANATORY** Read a print or digital copy of a recent national newspaper or watch or listen to a recent national news broadcast covering presidential policies. Alternatively, you can seek out coverage of the president's most recent State of the Union address. Identify key items on the president's current agenda, such as economic or social policies. Then write a letter to the president in which you offer your perspective on how some aspect of presidential policy aligns—or does not align—with your understanding of how the president's actions to promote those items reflect presidential roles and powers.

TIPS

- Summarize the president's agendas succinctly, clarifying any pertinent issues being promoted and explaining how they are being promoted.
- Evaluate the president's actions against your own opinion on those issues.
- Connect the president's actions and advocacy to the expressed, implied, and inherent powers and roles of a president.

CHAPTER 11

The Bureaucracy

LESSONS

11.1 The Nature of Bureaucracy

11.2 The Structure of the Federal Bureaucracy

11.3 The Growth of the Federal Bureaucracy

National Geographic Online:
What Trump's Shrinking of National Monuments Actually Means

CRITICAL VIEWING The Internal Revenue Service (IRS) collects the taxes that fund the federal government. The IRS forms just a small part of the federal bureaucracy. What does this 1965 photo of an IRS regional office suggest about the overall bureaucracy?

LESSON
11.1 The Nature of Bureaucracy

In August 2005, Hurricane Katrina crashed into the Gulf Coast, causing a staggering amount of death and destruction in Mississippi and Louisiana. Rising floodwaters forced thousands of New Orleans residents to seek refuge in the Louisiana Superdome. More than 1 million people fled the region. The federal government's blueprint for dealing with such a disaster—the National Response Plan—failed miserably. People went without medical supplies, food, water, and shelter for far too long and more than 1,800 people died. Disaster relief agencies at the local, state, and federal levels nearly all fell down on the job. It was a classic bureaucratic nightmare.

Characteristics of Bureaucracy

Much of the blame for the bungled response to Katrina fell on the Federal Emergency Management Agency (FEMA), the arm of the federal government responsible for disaster response. FEMA is just one of the numerous departments, agencies, bureaus, commissions, and administrations whose 2 million or so employees carry on the work of the federal government. Together they comprise the federal **bureaucracy**, a complex administrative organization with a hierarchical structure. The people who work within a bureaucracy are known as bureaucrats. Government bureaucrats are professionals with responsibility to carry out the policies of elected government officials.

Nearly every large organization has a bureaucratic structure: Workers report to supervisors, supervisors report to managers, and managers report to executives. The chief executive of the U.S. government, the president of the United States, is the head of the federal bureaucracy.

Bureaucracies have some typical characteristics. One key aspect of any bureaucracy is that the power to act resides in the position rather than in the person. Another is that bureaucracies generally use a **merit system**, a system in which people are hired and promoted on the basis of demonstrated skills and achievements, not on political affiliations, family connections, wealth, or demonstrations of loyalty. Also, bureaucracies are governed by standard operating procedures that describe practices to be followed in specific circumstances. FEMA officials had a plan for dealing with a major disaster like Hurricane Katrina. They just didn't carry it out effectively.

The federal government bureaucracy exists because Congress, over time, has delegated certain tasks to specialists. Congress creates and delegates authority to **agencies**, organizational units that provide a particular service or are concerned with a particular category of functions. Government under the rule of law means that even the president is only permitted to use bureaucratic organizations within the range of activities approved by Congress. It is important that bureaucrats have appropriate technical expertise. They are not political appointees, because their goal is not to act politically. Their job is to support Congress in achieving its goals.

The word *bureaucracy* often evokes a negative reaction. It conjures up visions of faceless robots performing their tasks without sensitivity toward the needs of those they serve. When things go wrong, the bureaucracy seems to make what should be simple tasks, like applying for a professional license or receiving disaster relief, complex and time-consuming. In spite of these negative views of bureaucracy, it can be an efficient form of organization. It allows employees to concentrate on their areas of knowledge and expertise, and, because the agencies do the day-to-day work of governing and providing services, Congress and agency heads can focus on policy.

HISTORICAL THINKING

1. **FORM AND SUPPORT OPINIONS** Do you think voters have any control over government bureaucrats? Why or why not?
2. **MAKE GENERALIZATIONS** How do you think the merit system benefits a bureaucracy?

Creating the Bureaucracy

Congress is responsible for creating all agencies and bureaus within the federal government. To create a new agency, Congress must pass enabling legislation, which specifies the name, purpose, composition, and powers of the organization being created. The enabling legislation also authorizes the new agency to undertake actions delegated to it by Congress.

For example, Congress created the Federal Trade Commission (FTC) to protect consumers and promote competition. The enabling legislation for the FTC was titled the Federal Trade Commission Act. This act created the FTC, described its basic structure, and authorized it to hire and pay employees. The act also gave the new agency the power to enforce specified laws, make rules to prohibit unfair or deceptive acts or practices, and investigate businesses suspected of wrongdoing. The agency can also hold trial-like hearings and issue orders requiring offenders to take corrective action. Finally, the legislation restricted the commission's actions by describing procedures the FTC must follow for charging persons or organizations with violations of the act, specifying punishments the FTC may impose, and providing for judicial review of any of the agency's orders, or legal judgments.

Today, the FTC is run by a group of five commissioners who are nominated by the president and confirmed by the Senate. They establish agency policy and make key decisions. Various FTC offices and bureaus that provide consumer information and handle complaints about deceptive and unfair trade practices carry out these policies. Employees in these offices include investigators, lawyers, and information technology experts.

Enabling legislation not only creates agencies it also gives them their specific, but limited, powers. For example, the Securities Exchange Act of 1934 established the Securities and Exchange Commission (SEC) to oversee practices related to the buying and selling of stocks and bonds. The SEC imposes **regulations**, or detailed rules issued by the government, regarding disclosures that companies must make to those who purchase newly issued stock. Under its enforcement authority, the SEC also investigates and prosecutes alleged violations of these regulations. Finally, the SEC judges whether regulations have been violated and, if so, determines the punishment for the offender. The SEC isn't all-powerful, however. As is true for other agencies, a judgment handed down by the SEC may be appealed to a federal court. If the court doesn't overturn it, the order becomes final.

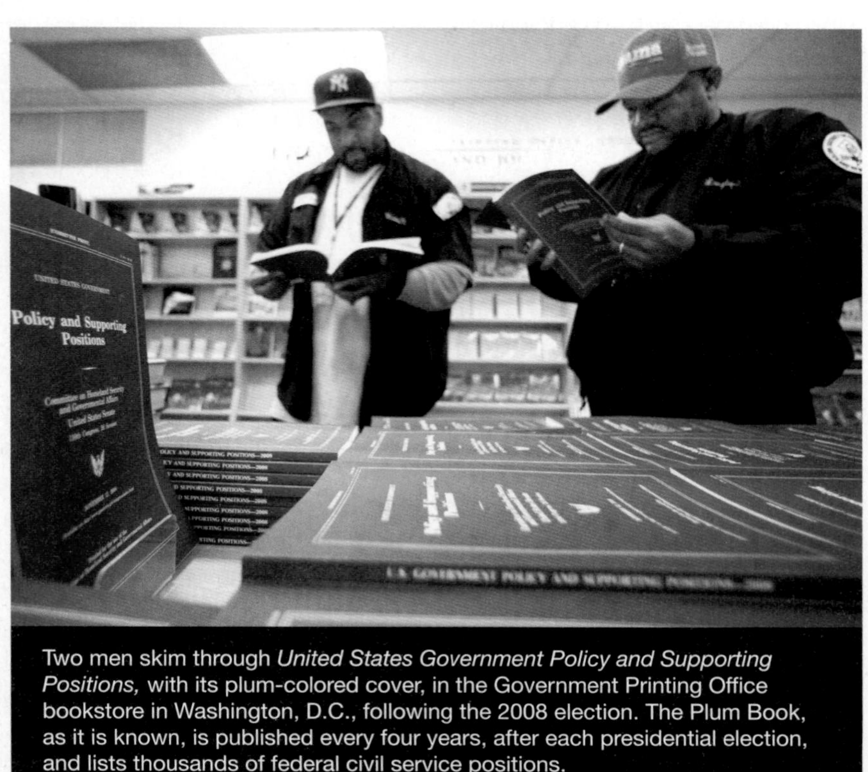

Two men skim through *United States Government Policy and Supporting Positions,* with its plum-colored cover, in the Government Printing Office bookstore in Washington, D.C., following the 2008 election. The Plum Book, as it is known, is published every four years, after each presidential election, and lists thousands of federal civil service positions.

HISTORICAL THINKING

3. **EVALUATE** How does enabling legislation allow Congress to limit the actions of an agency?
4. **CATEGORIZE** Why do you think Congress decided to create the SEC to regulate practices related to the selling of stocks?

How Bureaucrats Get Their Jobs

While the vast majority of bureaucrats are hired on the basis of their qualifications for a position and remain in their roles through many changes of presidential administrations, top-level officials are presidential appointees. These positions include department and agency heads, their deputy secretaries, undersecretaries, assistant secretaries, and others. Following their nominations by the president, the Senate must confirm them. These political appointees guide the agency they lead in accord with the president's policy directives. The list of positions filled by appointment is published in *United States Government Policy and Supporting Positions,* more commonly known as the Plum Book, because the jobs it lists are viewed as political plums, or rewards. Normally, these jobs—which numbered more than 9,000 after the 2016 election—go to those who supported the winning presidential candidate.

THE CIVIL SERVICE While 9,000 people may sound like a lot, only a small portion of government employees are political appointees. The rank-and-file bureaucrats—the rest of the 2 million or so people in the federal bureaucracy—are part of the **civil service**, or the nonmilitary employees of the government. The civil service system developed largely in response to abuses common in the federal appointment and hiring system that was in place for most of the 19th century. New administrations of that era tended to fill nearly all federal offices with individuals whose only qualification was their political loyalty. This method became widely known as the spoils system. Spoils are loot or plunder taken from a defeated enemy.

The spoils system remained in place until after the Civil War, when Americans began to demand an end to the incompetence and corruption it bred in the federal government. In 1883, Congress passed the Pendleton Civil Service Act, which established the principle of government employment on the basis of merit through open, competitive examinations. The Pendleton Act also set up a Civil Service Commission to oversee the application of the new law. Initially, only about 10 percent of federal employees were covered by the merit system, but that figure gradually rose.

Andrew Jackson believed that "The duties of all public officers are, or at least admit of being made, so plain and simple that men of intelligence may readily qualify themselves for their performance." In other words, Jackson argued, any public office can be filled by any reasonably intelligent person. Even if that were true in Jackson's time, it is not true today. More than 90 percent of federal civil service employees are specialists who obtain their jobs through the Office of Personnel Management (OPM), an agency established by the Civil Service Reform Act of 1978. The OPM supervises the creation of highly

The OPM Hacking Scandal

In June 2015, federal cybersecurity experts discovered that hackers had downloaded personal information on millions of Americans from computers at the OPM. The database in question, EPIC, contains information from government background checks undertaken for security clearances, including past addresses and jobs, friends and relatives, and foreign contacts. EPIC also holds Social Security numbers and information about problems with drugs, drinking, gambling, and mental health, and any history of criminal records, debts or bankruptcies. EPIC even contains fingerprint data on millions of people.

The total number of Americans affected by the data breaches in the OPM hacking scandal was estimated at 21.5 million, most of them current or former federal workers. In August 2017, the FBI arrested a citizen of China whom they linked to the malware used to access the OPM database. U.S. officials fear the Chinese government could use the hacked database for recruiting Americans as spies.

detailed job descriptions. It also recruits, interviews, and tests potential government workers. Finally, it makes recommendations to individual agencies as to which persons meet relevant standards for each position. The Civil Service Reform Act also created the Merit Systems Protection Board (MSPB) to oversee promotions, workers' rights, and other employment matters. The MSPB has the authority to evaluate charges of wrongdoing, hear employee appeals of agency decisions, and order corrective action against agencies and employees.

HISTORICAL THINKING

5. **CATEGORIZE** Are political plums good or bad for the country? Explain your answer.
6. **MAKE INFERENCES** Did the Pendleton Civil Service Act eliminate the spoils system in 1883? Explain your answer.

Rulemaking

A major function of many government agencies is legislative rulemaking. An agency's rulemaking power is conferred on it by Congress through the agency's enabling legislation. For example, the Occupational Safety and Health Administration (OSHA) was authorized by the Occupational Safety and Health Act of 1970. This legislation enabled OSHA to develop and issue rules governing workplace safety. Under this authority, OSHA has issued various health and safety standards that employers and employees must follow in order to prevent injuries and the spread of diseases in the workplace. For example, the rules specify standards for how health-care workers must handle needles contaminated with the AIDS virus. They also state what equipment and materials must be provided to health-care workers. Many of OSHA's other safety standards apply to factories and construction sites.

COSTS AND BENEFITS By protecting workers and the public at large, agency-imposed rules provide enormous benefits. But the expense of dealing with not only these regulations but also extensive record-keeping and reporting requirements adds to the cost of doing business and can make the difference between whether or not a project is profitable. Therefore, rulemaking must involve a process that takes both costs and benefits into consideration.

To make a rule, agencies must follow procedural requirements, particularly those set forth in the Administrative Procedure Act of 1946. These include notifying the public of proposed rules and considering comments. Agencies must also make sure their rules are based on substantial evidence and are neither arbitrary (based on personal preference) nor capricious (based on whim). Therefore, before proposing a new rule, an agency normally engages in extensive investigation to obtain data on the problem to be addressed by the rule. Based on this information, the agency will conduct a **cost-benefit analysis**, a process in which the costs and the benefits of an action are calculated and then compared. If the analysis finds that the benefits of the new rule outweigh the costs of implementing it, the rule can go ahead.

As an example of cost-benefit analysis in rulemaking, consider the Clean Air Fine Particle Implementation Rule, issued by the Environmental Protection Agency (EPA) in 2007. The EPA estimated the costs of this regulation at $6.9 billion per year. This estimate reflected the expense of designing and implementing

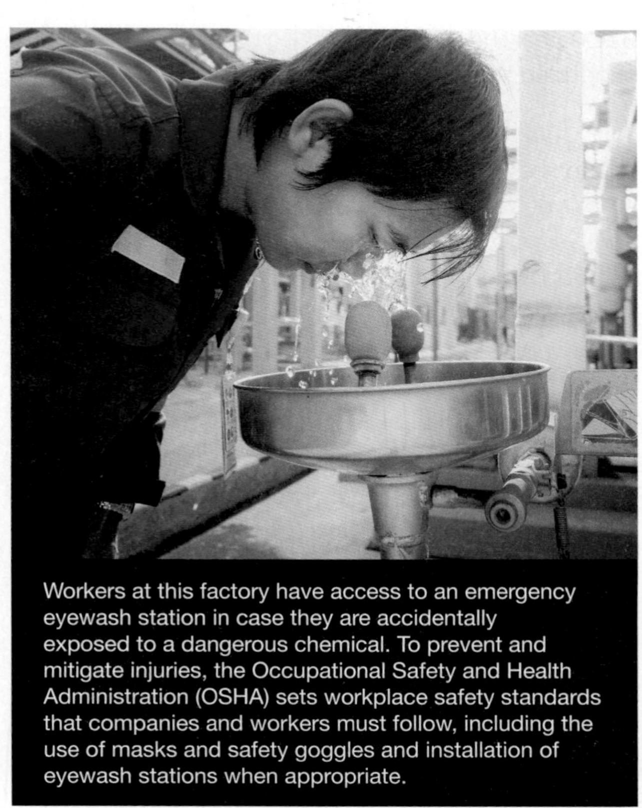

Workers at this factory have access to an emergency eyewash station in case they are accidentally exposed to a dangerous chemical. To prevent and mitigate injuries, the Occupational Safety and Health Administration (OSHA) sets workplace safety standards that companies and workers must follow, including the use of masks and safety goggles and installation of eyewash stations when appropriate.

systems to reduce vehicle emissions and other sources of air pollution. The EPA also estimated benefits ranging from $43 billion to $97 billion per year, largely due to savings from reduced needs for health care and lower rates of premature deaths. Thus, this rule was expected to save the country no less than $36.1 billion per year and possibly close to $90.1 billion. As the range of benefit figures suggests, such calculations can be highly uncertain, and subsequent analysis indicated that the range of benefits was far lower and the costs far higher than these projections.

OPPOSITION TO REGULATION Political conservatives believe that the United States suffers from excessive government regulation. Conservatives argue that regulations are inordinately expensive to implement and interfere with the ability of businesses to operate profitably. Estimates of the total cost of regulation vary dramatically. According to the Office of Management and Budget (OMB), the annual cost of all federal regulations lies between $59 billion and $88 billion, while the value of total benefits is between $287 billion and $911 billion. Critics argue that the OMB's estimates don't cover all the costs. One study quoted by some conservatives puts the total cost of regulations at $2.03 trillion per year. Opponents of this view do not find this figure credible—it puts the total cost of regulations at 11 percent of the entire economy.

One way in which opponents of regulation may overestimate its costs is by treating one-time expenses as if they were ongoing. For instance, to meet EPA regulations, many coal-fired electrical power plants have installed expensive scrubbers that remove pollutants from emissions. Installation of a scrubber is a one-time expense. Eliminating this regulation would not make it cheaper to use coal in power plants, because most of the scrubbers are already installed. The scrubbers cost relatively little to run once they are installed, and they would be expensive to remove.

The Trump administration and congressional Republicans were active in dismantling regulations they viewed as placing undue burdens on individuals and businesses. They relaxed or eliminated rules restricting the release of mercury, methane gas, and air pollutants by power plants, landfills, and mines, among other industrial facilities. In an effort to speed construction of federal infrastructure projects, the Trump administration reduced the period and scope of public review. The Trump administration also reduced the threshold at which employees can be categorized as salaried workers and therefore ineligible for overtime pay to a level below that proposed by the Obama administration. The Trump administration also attempted to reverse Obama-era auto emission and gas mileage standards for new cars.

HISTORICAL THINKING

7. **MAKE INFERENCES** Which regulatory agency do you think has made the hard hat a required part of many workers' uniforms? Explain your answer.
8. **MAKE GENERALIZATIONS** Why do you think it's so difficult to calculate an exact figure for the benefits of regulating air pollution?

Policymaking

Bureaucrats in federal agencies are expected to exhibit neutral competence, which means they are supposed to apply their skills to their jobs in an objective way. This applies to policymaking as well. In principle, an official's role in implementing or helping to make policy decisions should not be influenced by the person's political allegiances or beliefs, much less by the thought of personal or political gain. In reality, each department and agency is interested in its own survival and growth. Top-level officials in the bureaucracy wish to retain or expand their functions and staffs. To do this, they must gain the goodwill of Congress, which controls their funding.

Departments and agencies of the federal government are prohibited from directly lobbying Congress. Nevertheless, they have developed strategies to gain congressional support. The most important one might be establishing a congressional information office, quickly supplying legislators with any information they request and helping to solve their constituents' problems. For example, if a member of the House of Representatives receives a complaint from a constituent whose Social Security payments are not arriving on time, that representative may contact the Social Security Administration and ask that something be done. Typically, such requests receive immediate attention. Interactions like these build relationships that

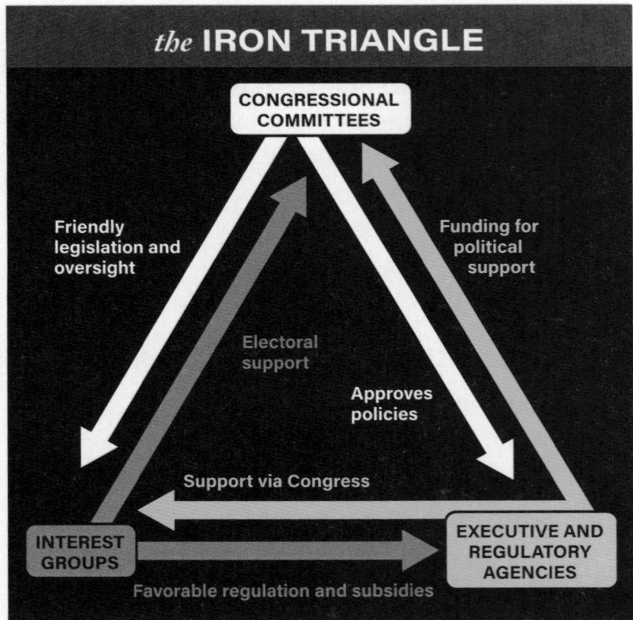

help agencies achieve their funding goals and at the same time give bureaucrats some say in congressional policymaking.

IRON TRIANGLES Analysts have determined that one way to understand the bureaucracy's role in policymaking is to examine relationships among bureaucrats, members of Congress, and interest groups. In particular, a three-way alliance known as an iron triangle often forms among these three factions, as shown in the diagram. Presumably, the laws that are passed and the policies that are established benefit the interests of all three corners of this triangle.

Iron triangles are well established in almost every part of the federal bureaucracy. But they do not always result in the best legislation for the country as a whole. Congressional committees have a duty to serve as watchdogs over agencies with which they work on policy matters. Being too comfortable with those agencies can interfere with this duty. The same goes for a committee's relationship with interest groups, which can encourage overspending on pet projects. Likewise, too close a relationship between an industry interest group and a regulatory agency that oversees that industry can lead to watered-down regulations that protect that industry rather than the public.

THE IRON TRIANGLE AND AGRICULTURE Consider the iron triangle involved in the making of agricultural policy. The Department of Agriculture (USDA) consists of almost 90,000 individuals working directly for the federal government and thousands of other individuals who work indirectly for the department as contractors, subcontractors, and consultants. Now think about the various interest groups that are concerned with how agricultural policies affect them. These groups include the American Farm Bureau Federation, the National Milk Producers Federation, the U.S. Lumber Coalition, regional growers' associations and cooperatives, gigantic corporations such as Cargill and ConAgra, and many others. Finally, two major congressional committees are devoted to agricultural matters: the House Committee on Agriculture and the Senate Committee on Agriculture, Nutrition, and Forestry.

The USDA's mission is to provide "leadership on food, agriculture, natural resources, rural development, nutrition, and related issues based on sound public policy, scientific evidence, and efficient management." That vague mission statement gives the department bureaucrats, interest groups, and legislators who make up this iron triangle great leeway to create mutually beneficial regulations and legislation. In part because of the connections between agricultural interest groups and policymakers within the government, the agricultural industry has benefited greatly over the years from significant farm subsidies. In 2018 the USDA spent about $140 billion on programs to benefit various groups with agricultural interests or ties.

Congress plays an important role in the functioning of the Department of Agriculture. The department is headed by the secretary of agriculture, who is nominated by the president (and confirmed by the Senate). But that secretary can't even buy a desk lamp if Congress doesn't approve the appropriations for the department's budget. Within Congress, the responsibility for considering Agriculture's request for funding belongs first to the House and Senate appropriations committees and then to the agriculture subcommittees of the appropriations committees. The members of those committees, most of whom represent agricultural states, have been around a long time and have their own ideas about how big the Agriculture Department's budget should be. As

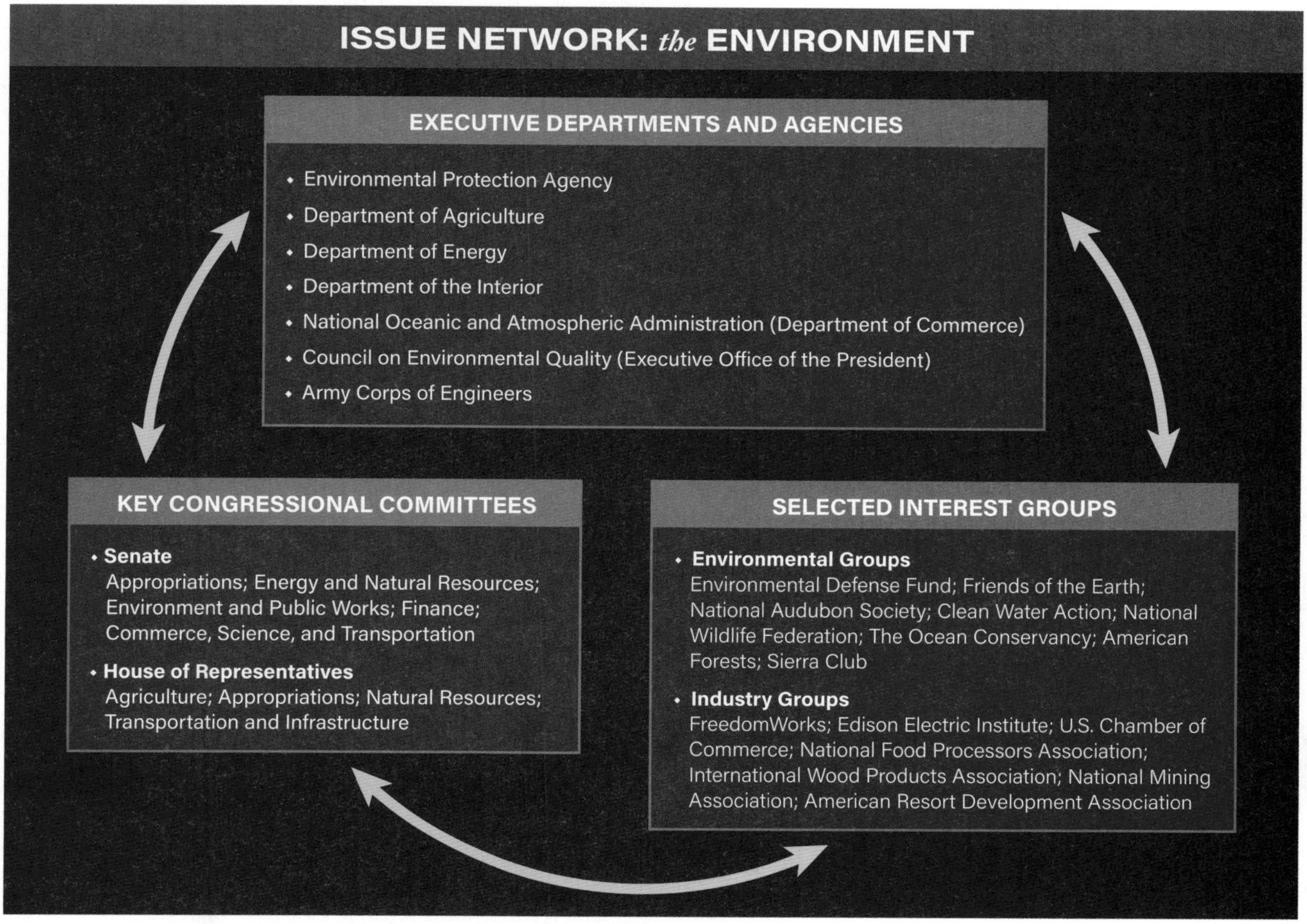

ISSUE NETWORK: *the* ENVIRONMENT

EXECUTIVE DEPARTMENTS AND AGENCIES

- Environmental Protection Agency
- Department of Agriculture
- Department of Energy
- Department of the Interior
- National Oceanic and Atmospheric Administration (Department of Commerce)
- Council on Environmental Quality (Executive Office of the President)
- Army Corps of Engineers

KEY CONGRESSIONAL COMMITTEES

- **Senate**
  Appropriations; Energy and Natural Resources; Environment and Public Works; Finance; Commerce, Science, and Transportation
- **House of Representatives**
  Agriculture; Appropriations; Natural Resources; Transportation and Infrastructure

SELECTED INTEREST GROUPS

- **Environmental Groups**
  Environmental Defense Fund; Friends of the Earth; National Audubon Society; Clean Water Action; National Wildlife Federation; The Ocean Conservancy; American Forests; Sierra Club
- **Industry Groups**
  FreedomWorks; Edison Electric Institute; U.S. Chamber of Commerce; National Food Processors Association; International Wood Products Association; National Mining Association; American Resort Development Association

well, the House Committee on Agriculture and the Senate Committee on Agriculture, Nutrition, and Forestry exercise oversight over the department and control legislation pertaining to agriculture and agricultural interests. These committees are also made up of legislators representing states with powerful agricultural interests.

Interest groups—including producers of farm chemicals and farm machinery, biotechnology companies, agricultural cooperatives, grain dealers, exporters, and conservation and environmental advocates—also exert a strong influence on the Department of Agriculture. They have vested interests in what the department does and in what Congress lets the department do. Those interests are well represented by the lobbyists whom they hire to work the halls of Congress. Many lobbyists have been working for agricultural interest groups for decades. They know the congressional committee members and Agriculture Department staff very well and meet with them routinely.

ISSUE NETWORKS The iron triangle relationship does not apply to all policy domains. When making policy decisions on environmental and welfare issues, for example, many members of congressional committees and heads of departments and agencies rely heavily on outside experts for information. They also tend to depend on their staff members—in-house experts—for specialized knowledge of rules, regulations, and legislation.

Congressional staff members haven't necessarily always worked in the public sector. Many have also served as interest-group lobbyists and consultants. They might move back and forth between the public and private sectors several times in their career, which has come to be known as the revolving door phenomenon. Staff experts often use their specialized knowledge of a policy area, as well as their lobbying experience, to persuade legislators and bureaucratic officials to take a particular policy position on an issue.

The relationship among committee staff, department or agency staff, and lobbyists is often referred to as an issue network. Issue networks and iron triangles both consist of people with similar policy concerns. Issue networks aren't as structured, interdependent, or unified as iron triangles, however, and often include more players.

Another characteristic of issue networks is that there can be more than one of them in a given policy area. To take the example of the environment, one issue network might advocate greater environmental regulation to better conserve resources, while another network might oppose such regulations as undue burdens on businesses and landowners. In other words, competing interests often form rival issue networks that tend to limit each other's power.

HISTORICAL THINKING

9. **IDENTIFY** Why is neutral competence the correct standard by which to judge the work of bureaucrats?
10. **DRAW CONCLUSIONS** If a congressional committee wanted to undercut an executive department or regulatory agency, what action could it take?
11. **INTERPRET CHARTS** Which of the industry groups shown in the Issue Network chart do you think might lobby Congress for weaker environmental regulations? Explain your answer.
12. **IDENTIFY PROBLEMS AND SOLUTIONS** How is the reliance on experts by legislators and bureaucrats a necessary but potentially problematic situation?

LESSON 11.2 The Structure of the Federal Bureaucracy

Normally, the first step in organizing a large number of items—whether of shoes in a shoe store or books in a library—is to identify and group the items according to their shared characteristics. This may be relatively easy with shoes. You only have to count the number of shoes and then group them so customers can find what they're looking for—sneakers on one set of shelves, work shoes in yet another spot—but the federal bureaucracy is a different story. For one thing, it's not even clear how many agencies are in the bureaucracy. Official sources vary, with some listing a little over 60 and others identifying more than 400. Counting agencies housed within larger agencies raises the figure to around 2,000.

The Executive Departments

An organization chart showing every entity in the government would cover an entire wall. The chart "Organization of the Federal Government" is a simplified version, believe it or not. Notice that the legislative and judicial branches are directly responsible for just a few agencies. The government consists primarily of the federal bureaucracy, nearly all of which is within the executive branch. The executive branch, the main home of the federal bureaucracy, has four major types of structures: executive departments, independent executive agencies, independent regulatory agencies, and government corporations.

The **executive departments** are the main organizations within the executive branch. These departments are also called cabinet departments, because the heads of these departments are part of the president's cabinet. The 15 executive departments are shown in the center of the chart. Each executive department has many, many bureaus, agencies, and offices within it.

The 15 cabinet departments are the major service organizations of the federal government and are directly accountable to the president. They perform functions such as training troops (Department of Defense), printing currency (Department of the Treasury), and setting

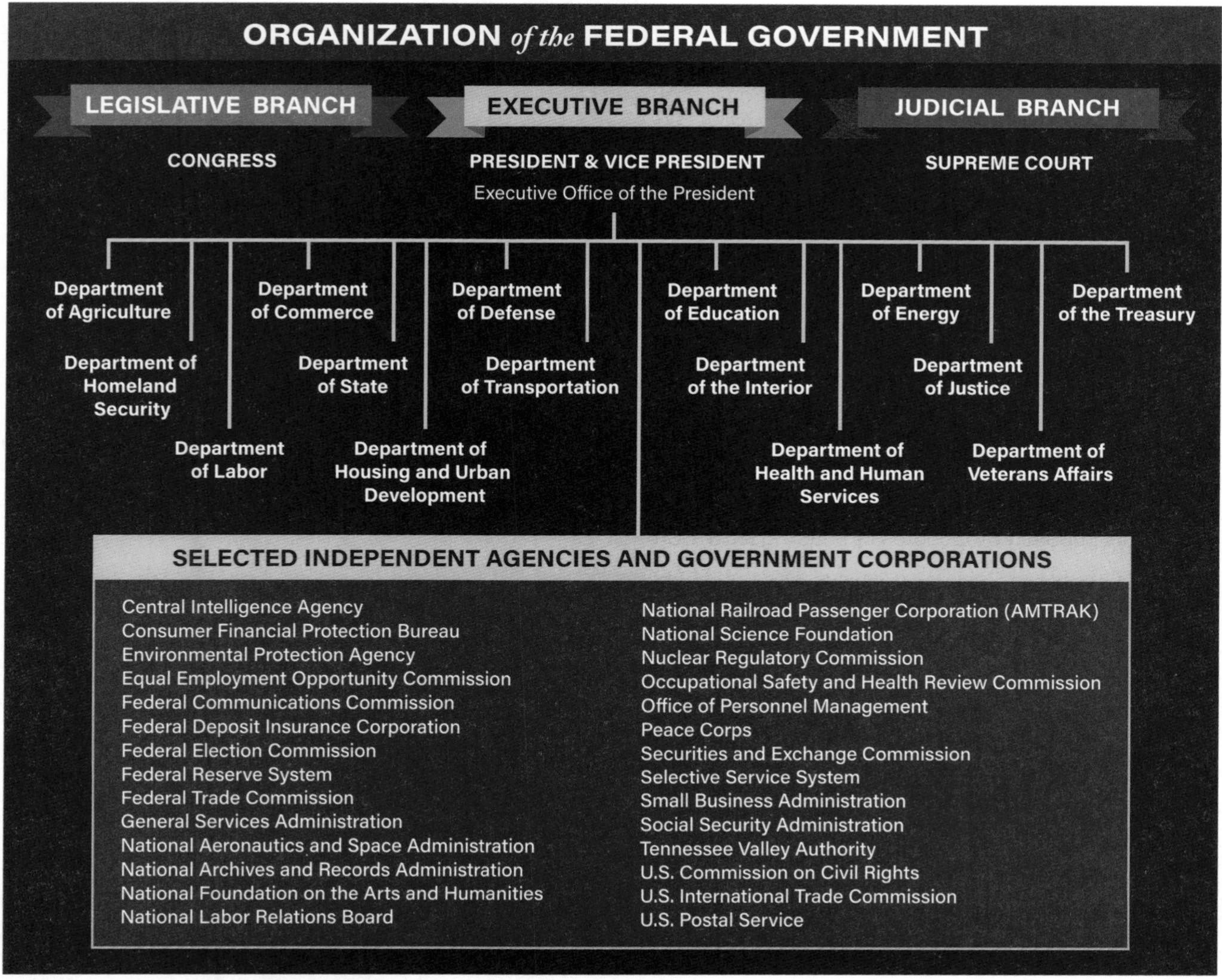

SOURCE: United States Government Manual 2018

safety and health standards for workers (Department of Labor). For an overview of each of the departments within the executive branch, examine the table titled "Organization of the Federal Government." This table lists a few of the many activities undertaken by each department.

Congress has created new executive departments as the need has arisen, giving each one broad responsibility for a particular area of public policy. In 2002, for example, after the September 2001 terrorist attacks on the World Trade Center and the Pentagon, Congress created the Department of Homeland Security. This department carries out laws and policies related to terrorism and other threats—including natural disasters. FEMA is a subagency of the Department of Homeland Security.

Each executive department has many subagencies, only a few of which are shown in the table. Subagencies handle specific aspects of their department's responsibilities. For example, the National Park Service, which manages the 60 national parks as well as over 350 federally held areas such as national monuments, national battlefields, national seashores, and national recreation areas, is a subagency within the Department of the Interior. This department is responsible for public lands, natural resources, and environmental conservation. The Drug Enforcement Administration (DEA) is a subagency within the Department of Justice, which enforces federal laws. The Centers for Disease Control (CDC), a subagency within the Department of Health and Human Services, works to protect the United States from health and safety threats. The CDC played a leading role in combating the deadly coronavirus that first appeared in the United States in early 2020.

The head of each cabinet department, except for the Department of Justice, is known as the secretary of that department. The Department of Justice is headed by the attorney general. The secretaries meet regularly with the president to provide information and advice. The president appoints the secretaries, who must be confirmed by the Senate. The same process applies to the other top administrators in the cabinet departments—the deputy secretary and one or more undersecretaries or assistant secretaries. Once confirmed, all these officials are expected to help carry out the president's policy objectives within the constraints imposed by Congress's enabling legislation.

Although the departments are not all organized in the same way, they follow a similar hierarchical structure, in which each person is accountable to someone at a higher level. For example, the secretary of agriculture is assisted by a deputy secretary and several undersecretaries and assistant secretaries. Each of these officials manages a particular area within the department and oversees a group of staff members, including supervisors who oversee other employees.

HISTORICAL THINKING

1. **MAKE INFERENCES** Why do you think communication is important within the executive departments?
2. **INTERPRET CHARTS** Which agency or government corporation do you think has the greatest effect on your life? Explain your answer.
3. **ANALYZE VISUALS** Identify two executive departments whose functions or responsibilities overlap, and give an example of an issue on which they must work together.

Independent Agencies

In addition to the executive departments, the federal bureaucracy includes a number of independent agencies. Unlike executive departments, each of which manages a broad policy area, independent agencies

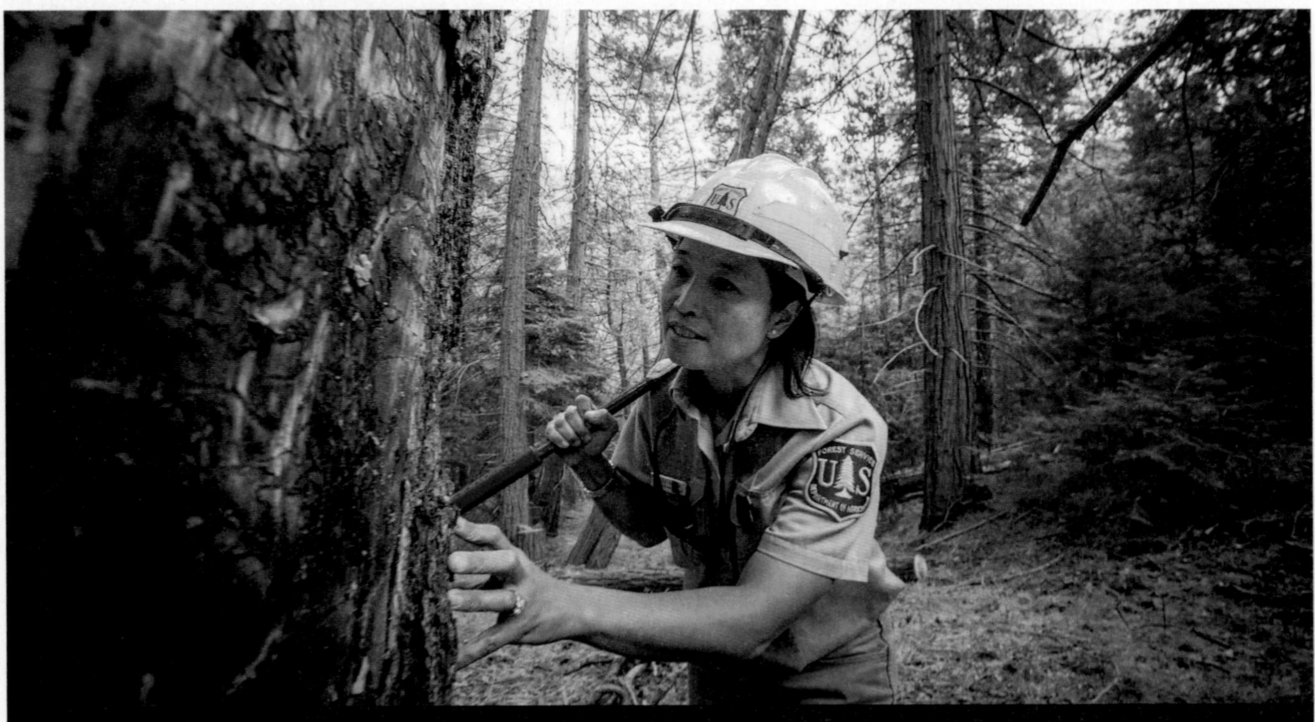

The Department of Agriculture, an executive department, includes the Forest Service, which is responsible for protecting America's national forests. This Forest Service scientist is examining a dead Ponderosa pine in California's Sequoia National Forest, which has been plagued by destructive pine bark beetles.

Selected Independent Executive Agencies

AGENCY	DATE FORMED	PRINCIPAL DUTIES
Central Intelligence Agency (CIA)	1947	Gathers and analyzes political and military information about foreign countries; conducts covert operations outside the United States
General Services Administration (GSA)	1949	Purchases and manages federal government property; oversees and audits federal government spending
Small Business Administration (SBA)	1953	Promotes the interests of small businesses; provides low-cost loans to small businesses
National Aeronautics and Space Administration (NASA)	1958	Runs the U.S. space program, including building, testing, and operating space vehicles
Environmental Protection Agency (EPA)	1970	Undertakes programs aimed at reducing air and water pollution; works with state and local agencies to fight environmental hazards
Social Security Administration (SSA)[1]	1994	Manages the Social Security programs, including Retirement and Survivors Insurance, Disability Insurance, and Supplemental Security Income (SSI)

[1]Originated in 1935 as the Social Security Board; renamed the Social Security Administration in 1946; separated from the Department of Health and Human Services and made independent in 1994.

are created to manage limited areas of responsibility. They are independent in the sense that they are not located within 1 of the 15 cabinet departments. Congress established the first independent agency in 1887, when it created the Interstate Commerce Commission to regulate the railroads. Since then, Congress has created over 200 independent agencies. There are two main types of independent agencies.

INDEPENDENT EXECUTIVE AGENCIES Independent executive agencies are within the executive branch but not controlled by the president. Each is responsible for administering laws and regulations within a specified area. For example, the General Services Administration (GSA) monitors federal spending, and the Central Intelligence Agency (CIA) is responsible for gathering information on foreign powers. Some agencies stand out either because of the mission they were established to accomplish or because of their large size. A few of them are listed in the table titled "Selected Independent Executive Agencies."

Making an agency independent is one way for Congress to protect it from partisan politics. The CIA, which was formed in 1947, is a good example. Both Congress and the president know that the intelligence activities of the CIA could be abused if the agency were not independent. Independence also helps the GSA, created in 1949, to carry out its key responsibilities of providing services and office space for most federal agencies and auditing agency spending. To serve all parts of the government well, the GSA has to be independent.

Some independent executive agencies have a single head, nominated by the president and confirmed by the Senate, who answers to the president and can be removed from office by the president. The CIA, the GSA, and the EPA (Environmental Protection Agency) each have a single head. Other agencies are led by a board or commission. The U.S. Commission on Civil Rights, created in 1957, is a case in point. Congress wanted to protect the work of the commission from not only the influences of Congress's own political interests but also those of the president. Its enabling legislation requires that half its members be appointed by the president and half by Congress.

INDEPENDENT REGULATORY AGENCIES You have learned about the system of checks and balances among the three branches of the U.S. government—executive, legislative, and judicial. Some say it may be time to regard the independent regulatory agencies as a fourth branch of the government. Although the U.S. Constitution does not mention regulatory agencies, they can and do make legislative rules that are as legally binding as laws passed by Congress. Regulatory agencies thus have an influence that rivals that of the president, Congress, and the courts.

Each regulatory agency is entrusted with protecting the public interest by overseeing a particular sector of the economy. They do this primarily by writing and enforcing regulations. These agencies thus have both legislative and judicial powers. The rules they put in place are, essentially, laws. Private enterprises must obey them. If they don't, the agency can hold them accountable through fines or by denying the company permission to operate. An agency's punishments can be appealed, but appeals are heard outside of the regular court system.

An example is the Nuclear Regulatory Commission (NRC). The NRC ensures the safety and security of nuclear reactors by requiring energy companies to obtain a license for permission to operate a reactor, and it monitors plants to ensure they continue to meet NRC requirements. The NRC also governs the production, use, and storage of nuclear materials, including nuclear waste. It also develops emergency preparedness policies and guidelines and maintains an emergency response program.

Like independent executive agencies, independent regulatory agencies operate independently of any executive department. Typically, they are headed by a board of commissioners whose members are nominated by the president and confirmed by the Senate. Commissioners serve fixed terms that are staggered in such a way as to make it unlikely that a president can appoint all of a board's members. Regulatory agencies are staffed by highly trained individuals with specialized knowledge appropriate to the areas of the economy their agencies regulate. For example, the NRC is staffed by nuclear physicists

The responsibilities of one independent executive agency carry it beyond the bounds of Earth. The National Aeronautics and Space Administration (NASA) launched the United States into the space age with a number of successful missions, including the first moon landing in 1969. NASA continues to carry on scientific research. In 2018, the uncrewed lander *InSight* brought cheers and applause from NASA engineers at the Jet Propulsion Laboratory in Pasadena, California, when it touched down on Mars.

Selected Independent Regulatory Agencies

AGENCY	DATE FORMED	PRINCIPAL DUTIES
Federal Reserve System (Fed)	1913	Determines policies to control interest rates, credit availability, and the money supply
Federal Trade Commission (FTC)	1914	Polices unfair trade practices and prohibits monopolies
Securities and Exchange Commission (SEC)	1934	Regulates stock and bond exchanges; oversees financial disclosure by public companies
Federal Communications Commission (FCC)	1934	Regulates interstate and international communications by radio, television, wire, satellite, and cable
National Labor Relations Board (NLRB)	1935	Protects employees' rights to join unions and to bargain collectively with employers; polices unfair practices by both employers and unions
Equal Employment Opportunity Commission (EEOC)	1964	Works to eliminate discrimination in hiring and employment based on religion, sex (including gender identity and sexual orientation), race, color, national origin, age, or disability; examines claims of discrimination

and engineers, while the Securities and Exchange Commission (SEC), which regulates stock and option trading, employs economists and experts in accounting and stock trading. By delegating authority to a regulatory agency, Congress can place the detailed crafting and enforcement of legislation in the hands of specialists who understand it best.

The first independent regulatory agency was the Interstate Commerce Commission (ICC), established in 1887. Congress created this agency to regulate railroads, which often operated as **monopolies**—businesses that are the sole source of a good or service in a certain area. The ICC also acted to rein in oil firms and, later, trucking companies.

Since forming the ICC, Congress has created a series of agencies designed to regulate diverse segments of the economy. These regulatory agencies ensure the safety of medicines (Food and Drug Administration, 1927), establish and preserve radio service nationwide (Federal Communications Commission, 1934), and prevent corporate fraud and manipulation of stock prices (Securities and Exchange Commission, 1934). The ICC was abolished in 1996, but the others still exist, as you can see in the table titled "Selected Independent Regulatory Agencies."

The 1960s and 1970s saw a proliferation of regulatory agencies. At the time, Congress was enacting a great number of laws aimed at controlling pollution and addressing social problems. It chose to delegate much of the actual process of making sure all these new laws were properly administered to regulatory agencies. These included the Equal Employment Opportunity Commission (EEOC), the Environmental Protection Agency (EPA), and the Consumer Product Safety Commission (CPSC), all still pursuing their missions.

HISTORICAL THINKING

4. **MAKE CONNECTIONS** What clause in the Constitution gave Congress the authority to establish the first regulatory commission?
5. **INTEGRATE VISUALS** Based on the table listing independent executive agencies, what special expertise do you think employees of the General Services Administration (GSA) might have? Why?
6. **ANALYZE VISUALS** Look at the table listing independent regulatory agencies to determine which of them works to keep inflation under control. Explain your answer.

Selected Government Corporations

CORPORATION	DATE FORMED	PRINCIPAL DUTIES
Tennessee Valley Authority (TVA)	1933	Controls flooding and erosion on Tennessee River watershed; promotes the navigability of the Tennessee River and generates power for a seven-state region
Federal Deposit Insurance Corporation (FDIC)	1933	Insures individuals' bank deposits up to $250,000 and oversees the business activities of banks
National Railroad Passenger Corporation (AMTRAK)	1970	Provides a national and intercity passenger rail service network; controls more than 21,000 miles of track with about 505 stations
U.S. Postal Service (USPS)[1]	1971	Delivers mail throughout the United States and its territories; the largest government corporation

[1]Originated in 1775; designated the Post Office Department in 1792; reorganized as the U.S. Postal Service in 1971.

Government Corporations

Government corporations are businesses established by Congress to provide goods or services in support of some public purpose. They are owned or controlled by the government. Government corporations exist within the executive branch and are accountable to the president. But as corporations, they have more independence and flexibility than the other types of federal agencies. Government corporations are expected to support themselves financially, and they often do, which makes members of Congress happy—Congress doesn't have to sink public funds into profitable corporations. Depending on how strictly or broadly they are defined, government corporations may number fewer than two dozen or more than 100. The table titled "Selected Government Corporations" describes a few of the better-known ones.

The history of U.S. government corporations goes back at least to 1903. That year, as part of its preparations to build the Panama Canal, the federal government bought the Panama Railroad Company, a private corporation that had been owned by a group of American investors. The railroad was independently run, but President Theodore Roosevelt appointed its board of directors, and Congress oversaw its finances.

Government corporations are similar to private corporations in many ways. They provide goods and services that could be handled by the private sector. The way they differ is that they offer their goods and services more widely and extensively than a private corporation might. They may also charge less than private corporations would for similar products.

THE U.S. POSTAL SERVICE One of the best-known government corporations, the United States Postal Service (USPS), does not sell shares. Neither does it make a profit, although it keeps trying. The Postal Service lost money each year from 2006 to 2017 and seemed destined to continue reporting annual financial losses. As Americans have increasingly relied on the internet for communications, the volume of first-class mail has dropped sharply. Parcel deliveries have increased, mainly because of online shopping, but not enough to make the USPS profitable. Although the USPS has cut costs dramatically, it lost $5.6 billion in 2016 and $2.7 billion in 2017.

If the USPS were a regular business operating solely to make a profit, it might raise prices on some services, leaving some Americans unable to afford postal rates, and drop unprofitable services. For instance, it might close post offices in very small towns and provide less frequent pickups and deliveries in rural areas. Unlike private delivery services, the Postal Service is required to provide equal services and charge equal rates.

Some inside the USPS claim the corporation's real problem is that Congress, in 2006, passed legislation forcing the USPS to fund, in advance, 75 years' worth of retiree health benefits. USPS officials argue that no other private business or government agency faces a similar requirement. The union covering postal workers, the National Association of Letter Carriers, points out that the USPS was profitable until 2006, when this legislation passed.

To stop losing money, the USPS has proposed to lay off additional employees, close rural post offices, reduce retiree benefits, increase stamp prices, and even end Saturday delivery. Some of these steps require congressional approval, which has not been forthcoming. As a self-supporting government corporation, the USPS receives no tax dollars to cover its operating expenses—yet. Some see direct federal subsidies as the only way to keep the USPS functioning.

INTERMEDIATE FORMS OF ORGANIZATION Many organizations don't exactly fit the definitions of either a government corporation or a private corporation. They're somewhere in between. But these agencies are often called government corporations because the government controls them. Various circumstances allow this to happen. In some cases, the government can take control of a private corporation. When a company goes bankrupt, for example, it is subject to the supervision of a federal judge until it exits from bankruptcy or completely shuts down. Until one of those things happens, the federal government maintains lawful authority over the company.

The government can also purchase stock in a private corporation. During the financial crisis that began in 2007, the government used this technique to funnel funds into major banks that were on the verge of failing. The Treasury Department deemed these banks too big to fail, meaning that if they collapsed, the entire economy would suffer. These stock purchases were,

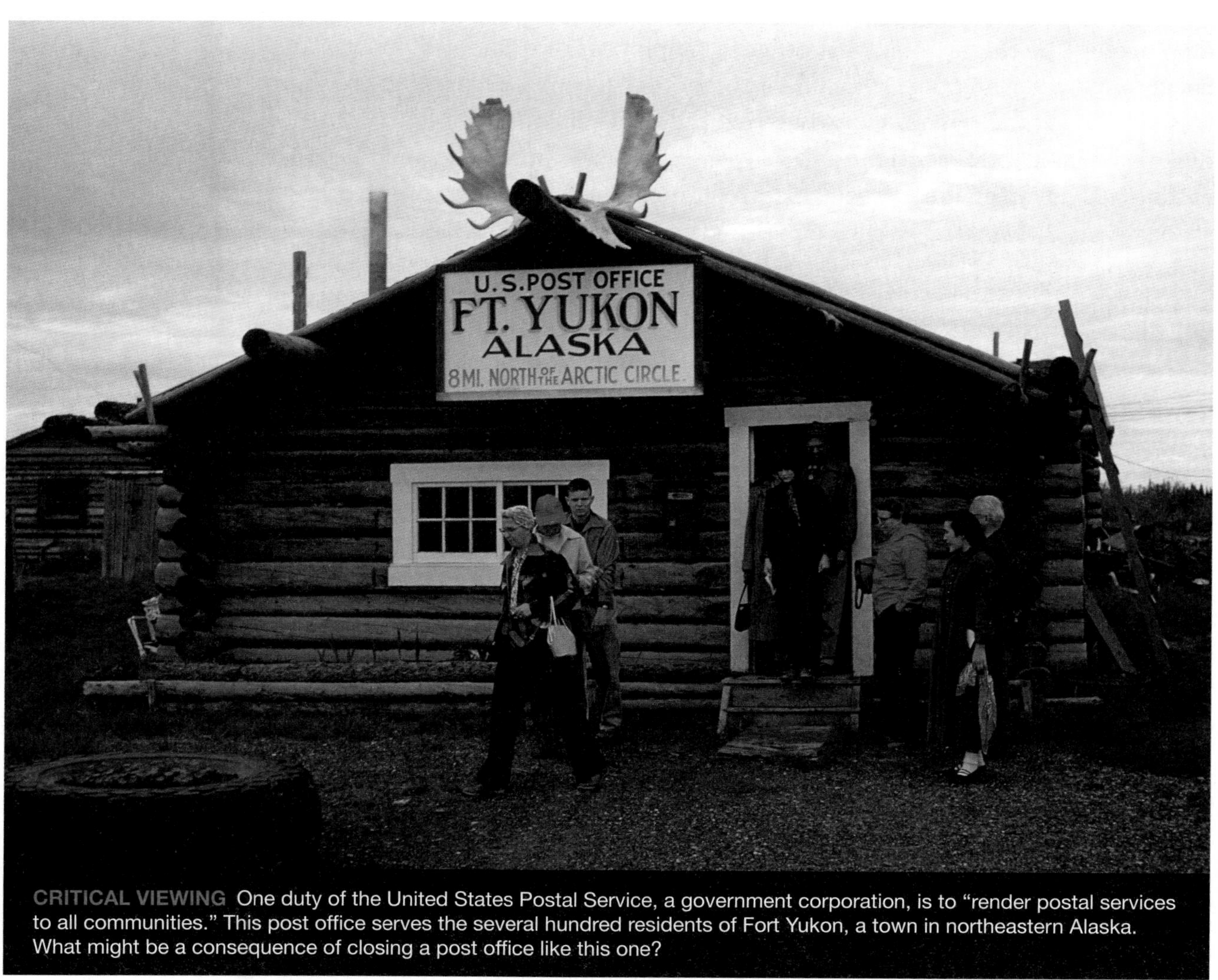

CRITICAL VIEWING One duty of the United States Postal Service, a government corporation, is to "render postal services to all communities." This post office serves the several hundred residents of Fort Yukon, a town in northeastern Alaska. What might be a consequence of closing a post office like this one?

in effect, loans. Once the economy recovered and the banks' financial position stabilized, the Treasury sold its shares and recovered its investments. It even made a profit.

The government can also set up a public corporation that sells stock. The Federal National Mortgage Association (Fannie Mae) and the Federal Home Loan Mortgage Corporation (Freddie Mac) are examples of stockholder-owned, government-sponsored enterprises. Fannie Mae and Freddie Mac buy, resell, and guarantee home mortgages. During the 2007–2008 financial crisis, the two businesses were about to collapse when the federal government bailed them out. The government also took an 80 percent share of the stock of each firm. Today, Fannie Mae and Freddie Mac are making money again, and most of their profits go into the U.S. Treasury.

HISTORICAL THINKING

7. **CATEGORIZE** A government corporation must have what feature?
8. **FORM AND SUPPORT OPINIONS** Do you think the federal government should continue to own an 80 percent share in the stock of Fannie Mae and Freddie Mac? Explain your answer.

LESSON 11.3 The Growth of the Federal Bureaucracy

The federal bureaucracy of 1789 had three departments, each with a handful of employees. The Department of State had 9 employees, the Department of War had 2 employees, and the Department of the Treasury had 39 employees. There was also an attorney general to advise the president on legal matters. By 1798, nine years later, the federal bureaucracy was still quite small. The secretary of state had seven clerks. His total expenditures on stationery and printing amounted to $500, or about $10,500 in 2018 dollars. In 2019, the Department of State had some 69,000 employees. Its budget for fiscal year 2019 was $54.22 billion.

The Size of the Federal Bureaucracy

The government grew slowly during the nation's first century. The Democratic Party of Thomas Jefferson and, later, of Andrew Jackson dominated the government until the Civil War. This party was committed to a vision of limited government in which most power was exercised at the state rather than national level. Its opponents were focused on the overall economy of the nation. They called for a program of internal improvements such as canals, roads, and lighthouses—infrastructure intended to benefit the country as a whole—but they rarely exercised enough power to implement these plans.

GROWTH OF THE GOVERNMENT TO WORLD WAR I
Though the federal government remained relatively small in its first 70 years or so, important groundwork was being laid for future expansion. In cases such as *Fletcher* v. *Peck* (1810), *McCulloch* v. *Maryland* (1819), *Gibbons* v. *Ogden* (1824), and *Ableman* v. *Booth* (1859), the Supreme Court helped consolidate federal authority by protecting the supremacy of the federal government over the states. In 1849, the first new executive department, the Department of the Interior, was established to consolidate functions assigned to other departments but also to manage territories acquired as a result of the Mexican-American War (1846–1848).

In the second half of the 19th century, the federal government expanded. The Civil War required a large military force. Congress set up a national bank system in 1863 partly to fund this expansion. Following the war, as industrialization and the spread of railroads transformed the economy, Congress expanded

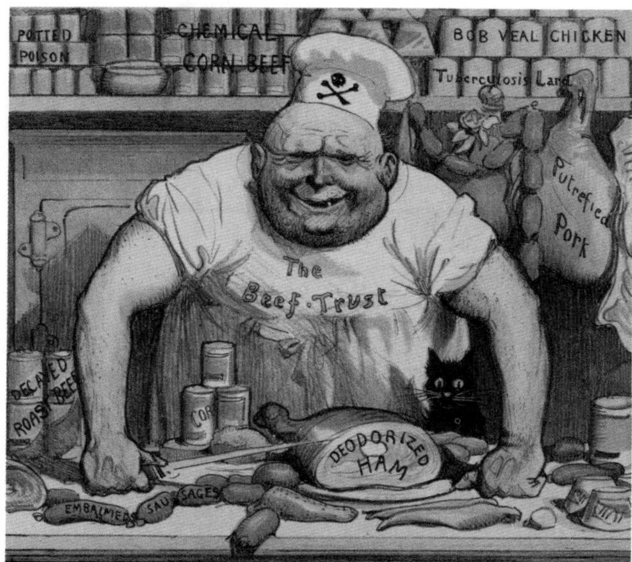

CRITICAL VIEWING In the early 1900s, progressive reformers called for more government regulation of big business. This 1906 cartoon targets a group of large meat-packing companies. The cartoonist accuses them of selling tainted, even poisonous, meats. In that same year, Congress sought to improve food safety by passing the Pure Food and Drug Act. Do you think a cartoon as provocative as this one is an effective way to make a point? Why or why not?

the federal government's functions by creating the Interstate Commerce Commission (1887). This was the first regulatory agency established in the United States. The progressives of the early 20th century worked to make government more responsive to the needs of the broader population. For instance, they supported enforcement of the Pure Food and Drug Act and creation of the Federal Trade Commission to protect consumers from unfair business practices. But the Progressive Era faded as the country dealt with the First World War.

THE FEDERAL BUREAUCRACY SINCE THE NEW DEAL Starting with President Roosevelt's New Deal of the1930s, government has grown relatively consistently. The New Deal was a series of emergency measures aimed at all aspects of the economy. But many of the new agencies and programs created during the New Deal have stayed and continued to have broad approval, including Social Security, the Securities and Exchange Commission, the Federal Deposit Insurance Corporation, the Tennessee Valley Authority, and the Federal Communications Commission. After World War II, the government rapidly decreased the number of federal employees, but even at its smallest it had twice as many employees as before the war.

President Johnson's Great Society of the 1960s expanded the use of the federal government to protect civil rights and voting rights, to combat poverty and hunger, and to widen access to health care. Like the New Deal, the Great Society reflected a consensus about the need for a larger role of government in everyday life.

Look at the graph showing executive branch employment since 1940. It shows that from 1950 to the present, on average, the number of workers employed by civilian agencies has increased by about one percent a year. The total number of nonmilitary federal government employees has stayed around 2 million.

That is the broad picture. Looking more closely, one can see sharp declines in 1981–1982 and 1985–1986, the first years of President Ronald Reagan's first and second terms, respectively. Shrinking the government was high on President Reagan's stated conservative agenda. The graph also shows sharp increases in federal government employment from 2000 to 2003 as the George W. Bush administration reacted to the 9/11 terrorist attacks and from 2007 to 2009 as first President Bush and then President Obama, coming into office in January 2009, faced a dire recession.

Another perspective on the growth of the bureaucracy comes from comparing changes in federal employment relative to overall employment. Since the early 1950s, the portion of all employed people who were civilian employees of the federal government decreased from about 4.5 to 2 percent.

OTHER FACTORS IN BUREAUCRATIC SPREAD The numbers presented so far do not reflect the number of private contractors and contracting firms working for the government. These are people hired on a per-job or term-limited contract. Although they work for and are paid by the government, they are not government employees. They do not receive government employee benefits, and they are not subject to government employment regulations. Estimates of the number of such workers vary. As you will read in the next lesson, much of the increased use of outside contractors has

Civilian Employment in Executive Branch Since 1940*

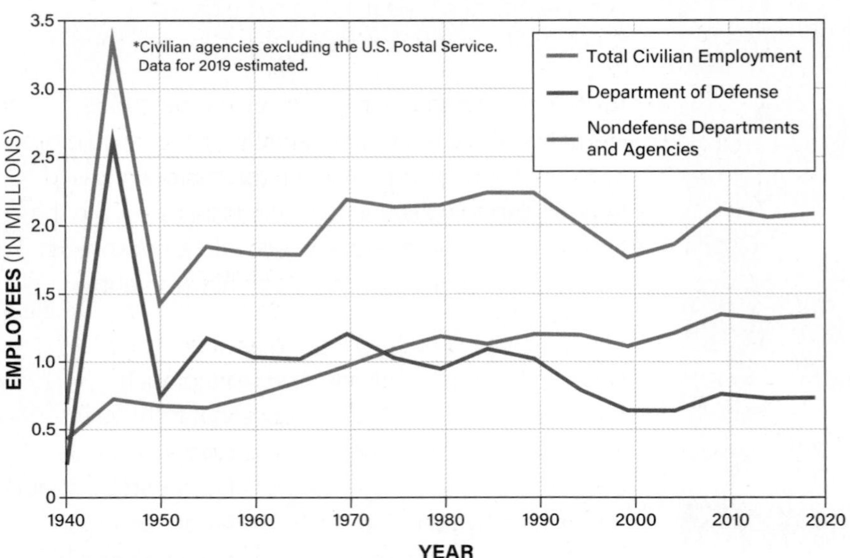

SOURCE: Office of Personnel Management; the White House

been due to pressure from critics who argue that private companies guided by the profit motive are more efficient than government agencies.

While the federal bureaucracy may not have grown as much as many think, the situation appears different when we examine the growth of government at all levels. State and local government have grown much more than the federal government. From 1959 to 1980, while the number of federal employees grew by about 20 percent, the number of government workers at all levels nearly doubled. All in all, the three levels of government employ more than 15 percent of the civilian labor force. Put another way, more Americans are employed by government at all three levels than by the entire manufacturing sector of the U.S. economy. Similarly, spending for all levels of government has also increased. In 1929, government at all levels accounted for about 11 percent of the U.S. **gross domestic product (GDP)**—the total value of all goods and services produced by the United States economy in a year. Today, that figure is about 36 percent.

Some of the growth of state and local government stems from a need to address **federal mandates**—expenses imposed by the federal government on state or local governments as well as on businesses. An example would be the requirement that public buildings be accessible to people in wheelchairs because of the Americans with Disabilities Act (ADA). Many of these mandates are conditions for receiving federal grants. For example, to be eligible for federal funding, educational institutions—including public schools—must fully comply with Title IX of the Education Amendments Act of 1972, which states that "no person in the United States shall, on the basis of sex, be excluded from participation in, be denied the benefits of, or be subjected to discrimination under any education program or activity receiving Federal financial assistance." Some commentators believe that measurements of the true size of the federal government should include the cost of addressing federal mandates at the state and local levels.

Recently, government employment has once again dropped, in absolute as well as relative terms. President Obama's 2009 stimulus program, aimed at pulling the economy out of recession, transferred large sums to local governments. This helped stabilize government employment through 2010. By 2017, however, almost 750,000 fewer people worked for the various levels of government. Most of those who lost their jobs had worked at the local level. It is also notable that the U.S. Postal Service shed more than 200,000 jobs between 2006 and 2017.

HISTORICAL THINKING

1. **ANALYZE CAUSE AND EFFECT** Why do you think the bureaucracy grew so much more in the 20th century than it did in the 19th?
2. **INTERPRET GRAPHS** In the graph that shows levels of employment in the executive branch since 1940, what explains the one very sharp increase in the Defense Department's civilian employment?

Paying for the Federal Government

In 2018, the individual income tax and taxes collected along with it made up 37 percent of the federal government's revenues. The corporate income tax added another 5 percent. Income from Social Security and Medicare taxes contributed about 26 percent. All other taxes and revenue sources came to 12 percent. That left 19 percent of the budget to be funded by borrowing—down considerably from the depths of the recession of 2007–2009, but still high by historical standards.

Citizens and residents support federal, state, and local government spending by paying income taxes, sales taxes, property taxes, and many other types of taxes and fees. Businesses, small and large, pay income taxes and various other taxes as well. Taxes represent significant costs for both individuals and businesses, but they pay for important services that benefit citizens and enable businesses to function, such as schools, roads, flood control, and law enforcement. Taxes also pay for the maintenance of the government itself: upkeep of offices, computers, telephone service, and salaries for census takers and prison guards—and even tax collectors! Government may be costly, but cutting back on government spending means reducing services, which could mean longer waits for disaster relief and longer delays before unsafe bridges are repaired and innovative medicines are approved. While any of us could probably name several categories of government expenditures we would be glad to eliminate, another person would find those same programs or services indispensable. The trade-off between government spending and demand for services has been central to American politics throughout our history.

HISTORICAL THINKING

3. **DRAW CONCLUSIONS** The various taxes and fees paid by Americans in 2018 did not equal the expenses of the federal government. How did the government make up the difference?
4. **ASK AND ANSWER QUESTIONS** What question might you ask someone who complains about high taxes? Your question should reflect the trade-off between government spending and services.

Where Does All the Money Go?

Americans answer this question in various ways, depending on their point of view. Some argue that the government spends too much on welfare benefits to low-income people. Others insist that it spends too much on the military. It is worth examining how the federal government actually spends its money.

SOCIAL SPENDING Social spending refers to the federal expenditures that provide benefits to individuals and households in need as well as Americans in general. As you can see in the graph showing the major components of federal government spending for 2018, over half the federal budget consists of various social programs.

Some of these programs, such as Social Security and Medicare, are funded by **payroll taxes**. Payroll taxes are paid roughly equally by employers and employees, based on the amount of the employee's pay. The employer withholds the employee's portion from the employee's pay and sends it directly to the Internal Revenue Service (IRS), so payroll taxes are often called withholding taxes.

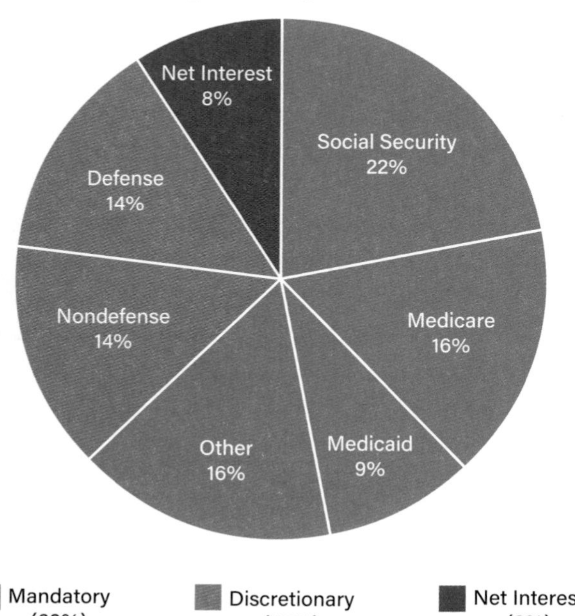

**Does not include $283M listed as "Offsetting receipts."

SOURCE: CBO 10-year Budget Projections Jan 2019 Table 3-1

Defense spending to maintain military readiness includes the ongoing training of troops. Highly trained and physically fit Navy SEALs, members of an elite group within the Department of Defense, undertake special military operations across the globe in support of U.S. foreign-policy goals. (SEAL stands for Sea Air Land, signifying that SEAL teams are prepared to carry out almost any type of mission.)

As you may know, Social Security and Medicare are paid out to all who qualify, regardless of need or income. Together, these two programs make up almost 40 percent of the federal budget. Other programs are available only to persons or families whose income falls below specified levels. Such programs include the health-care program Medicaid, the Children's Health Insurance Program (CHIP), and Supplemental Security Income (SSI), which helps aged, blind, and disabled people meet basic needs for food, clothing, and shelter. Medicaid and CHIP, together with the Supplemental Nutrition Assistance Program (SNAP) and miscellaneous other low-income and disability support programs, account for 25 percent of spending.

DEFENSE SPENDING One of the key reasons people establish governments is for security. Defense spending encompasses federal expenditures used to defend the United States—to keep it secure from foreign attack. Defending the country has always been a high priority, and it has always been costly. In the 1790s, the Department of War spent, on average, around $1.4 million each year on national defense, or $29.4 million in 2018 dollars. With the extension of the defense mission across the globe, and as warfare technology has developed, the price of security has gone way up. The budget of today's Department of Defense is in the hundreds of billions of dollars.

A large chunk of the budget for national defense goes toward supporting U.S. foreign policy. As long as the United States is determined to be a global power, national defense will also involve international operations to support U.S. allies and protect U.S. interests abroad. For instance, in 2002, in response to the September 11, 2001, al Qaeda terrorist attacks, President George W. Bush ordered a military operation to remove the Afghan Taliban government that was protecting al Qaeda in Afghanistan. U.S. forces have remained in the country since that time, attempting to maintain or impose peace while some Afghans work to build a stable society and others work to undermine U.S. efforts and restore the Taliban to power. As of 2019 the United States was conducting active military operations in Iraq and Syria as well as in Afghanistan. One estimate of the cost of such operations under President Obama was $170 billion a year, or 4.6 percent of the total federal budget. That does not include the human costs of the war to Americans and the Afghan people or the costs of physical and mental health benefits to returning veterans. Nor does it include the costs of military readiness exercises and naval and air patrols at strategic locations all over the world.

In the past, former commander of U.S. Central Command James Mattis has urged increased emphasis on diplomacy over military action, saying: "If you don't fund the State Department fully then I need to buy more ammunition." But a competing theory holds that increased military spending makes diplomacy more effective because potential enemies take threats more seriously.

EVERYTHING ELSE At 14 percent of the total, nondefense discretionary spending includes a vast range of programs. One example is military and economic foreign aid. At $46 billion, it's a substantial sum, but it amounts to about one percent of total federal spending, less than many people imagine it to be.

One item that bears watching is the interest on the **national debt**, which is the total amount of money the federal government has borrowed over the years. The federal government has to borrow money in any year in which its spending exceeds its revenue. In 2020, for example, the unpredicted spending needed to meet the many challenges posed by the coronavirus pandemic forced the government to borrow a huge amount of money—estimated at several trillion dollars—which greatly expanded the national debt. The interest currently paid on the national debt is about $385 billion per year. Annual federal budget deficits are expected to cause this figure to grow.

HISTORICAL THINKING

5. **IDENTIFY MAIN IDEAS AND DETAILS** What do Americans get in return for all they pay in various taxes and fees?
6. **INTERPRET GRAPHS** In the graph showing major components of federal government spending in 2018, which spending category reflects the cost of federal government borrowing?

LESSON 11.4 Curbing Waste and Improving Efficiency

The more than $700 billion that the federal government spends yearly on Medicare has tempted some people to try to siphon off a bit for themselves. Robert McCaslin, an employee at the Houston Hospital District, discovered that the district was billing Medicare for patients who weren't covered. He reported this illegal practice to his superiors, but was told that's how things were done there. He helped the Justice Department build a case against the hospital district. The district paid $15 million back to the federal government—and McCaslin got a $3 million reward. Not everyone who reports illegal actions by an employer is rewarded, however.

Whistleblowers

The federal bureaucracy is costly, and at times it can be wasteful and inefficient. The government has made many attempts to reduce waste, inefficiency, and wrongdoing. For example, federal and state governments have passed laws requiring more openness in government. Other laws encourage employees to become a **whistleblower**, someone who blows the whistle on, or reports, waste or gross inefficiency, illegal activities, and other wrongdoing.

Employees who act responsibly and report wrongdoing to higher-ups are often brushed off, as Robert McCaslin was. If they persist or report supervisors or managers to outside authorities, they risk being reassigned to dead-end tasks or obscure locations, publicly smeared, and even fired. While such retaliation still occurs, Congress has passed laws to protect whistleblowers in order to encourage federal employees to speak up about such issues. The Whistleblower Protection Act of 1989 authorizes the Office of Special Counsel, an independent agency, to investigate complaints of reprisals against whistleblowers. Many federal agencies also have toll-free hotlines that employees can use to anonymously report bureaucratic waste and inappropriate behavior.

Tourists, campers, hikers, and bicyclists bring economic benefits to businesses near national monuments. But they can also clog local roads and damage cultural treasures within the monuments.

What Trump's Shrinking of National Monuments Actually Means

by Hannah Nordhaus **National Geographic Online, February 2, 2018**

In December 2017, President Donald Trump ordered a dramatic reduction in the size of two national monuments, Bears Ears and Grand Staircase Escalante, both in Utah. Writer Hannah Nordhaus considers what Trump's order might signify for the future of these two national monuments and of public lands in general.

The reductions are the culmination of a wide-ranging Interior Department review of recent monument designations and a highly symbolic salvo in a larger campaign to reverse Obama-era public land policies. The Trump administration's recent edicts—opening new mineral and oil and gas leasing opportunities in protected lands, easing drilling regulations, and rolling back habitat protections for endangered species—have met with furious opposition from conservation groups, outdoor tourism advocates, and Democratic lawmakers.

As Nordhaus notes, "The 1906 Antiquities Act gives presidents broad discretion to protect 'historic landmarks . . . and other objects of historic or scientific interest,' without any input from Congress." Yet Congress has the responsibility to direct federal agencies in protecting such landmarks. National monuments are managed by the Bureau of Land Management (BLM), an agency within the Interior Department.

The BLM manages land and natural resources for recreational use, for use by energy and mining companies, for cultural preservation, and for environmental conservation. These goals frequently conflict. For instance, Nordhaus tells of how recreational visitors have already caused damage in Bears Ears: "tourists pocketing potsherds [pottery fragments]; campers using century-old Navajo hogans [dwellings] for firewood; graffiti on ancient rock panels; all-terrain vehicles blasting through ancestral burial grounds."

While some argue for the potential economic benefits of jobs extracting the natural resources of these lands, some local business owners counter that the monuments are good for the economy as well. Will tourists continue to visit, if there are drilling rigs in the foreground and mining plumes in the background?

A coalition of five Indian nations as well as conservation groups have filed suit to block Trump's downsizing of the two national monuments.

Access the full version of "What Trump's Shrinking of National Monuments Actually Means" by Hannah Nordhaus through the Resources Menu in MindTap.

THINK ABOUT IT How might the Bureau of Land Management's policies be affected if the agency were headed by someone who formerly worked for an environmental organization?

REWARDS The government also encourages reporting by making cash rewards to whistleblowers. The earliest such program was the False Claims Act, signed into law by Abraham Lincoln in 1863. The two most recent pieces of federal legislation to encourage reporting, passed in 2010, cover violations of the law related to stock trades.

Many reward cases involve illegal activities by corporations and individuals rather than wrongdoing by the government. In September 2012, the government paid out the largest such reward ever—$104 million. The money went to a banker who blew the whistle on a Swiss bank that was helping U.S. citizens defraud the Internal Revenue Service. The whistleblower, however, was sentenced to 40 months in prison for his part in the fraud.

RETALIATION In spite of these laws, protection from retaliation against whistleblowers remains inadequate. The Government Accountability Office (GAO) studied whistleblowers who turned to the Office of Special Counsel for protection and found that 41 percent were no longer employed by the agencies on which they blew the whistle. Given how difficult it is to fire a federal employee under normal circumstances, it is amazing how quickly whistleblowers are shown the door. Many federal employees who have blown the whistle say that they would not do so again because it was so difficult to get help from their superiors. Even when they did get help, the process of reporting was highly stressful.

Barack Obama's supporters expected that, as president, he would protect whistleblowers. Many of them were disappointed when the Obama administration took an unusually harsh line regarding information disclosures. Indeed, some say Obama's record on whistleblowers was less supportive than any prior administration's.

President Trump also took a hard line against whistleblowers. He insisted that the identity of a whistleblower who anonymously reported a questionable phone call made by the president be revealed. The whistleblower alleged that Trump appeared to encourage Ukrainian President Volodymyr Zelensky to investigate former vice president Joe Biden for actions taken against a Ukrainian prosecutor. Any such investigation might have undermined Biden's campaign for president. While the form the whistleblower completed to file the complaint stated that whistleblowers must have firsthand knowledge of the allegations, and the whistleblower was not on the July 2019 call with Zelensky, current law does not require this of whistleblowers. The Inspector General of the Intelligence Community determined that the whistleblower had credible information and followed the law in filing an urgent concern complaint. This whistleblower's report led to the impeachment of Trump by the U.S. House of Representatives. The Senate acquitted Trump, and the anonymity of the whistleblower was preserved.

LEAKERS Some whistleblowers leak their findings to the press if their superiors fail to act on their information. During the Obama administration, eight such individuals faced charges of violating the Espionage Act of 1917, legislation aimed at stopping spying during the First World War. In the 90 years before Obama took office, only three persons had ever been charged under that act for talking to the press. Some of the people charged may have endangered national security by leaking **classified** documents, or materials designated as containing government secrets. In other cases, the leaker's sole offense would appear to have been embarrassing the government.

Leaking can be controversial. In 2013, Edward Snowden, a computer security expert employed by a federal contractor, released classified documents concerning the National Security Agency (NSA) to newspapers. The documents revealed that the NSA had been secretly collecting and storing information on many domestic and international phone calls, text messages, and internet communications and had the capacity to eavesdrop on virtually every American. The documents also revealed that the agency had been spying on foreign leaders, which created serious diplomatic problems for the U.S. government.

Judges had secretly issued court orders approving this data collection, but no attorney was ever permitted to oppose the government in these secret hearings. The NSA asserts that it needs all these data in order to protect Americans from terrorism. Snowden felt he had to expose the programs because "This is something that's not our place to decide. The public needs to decide whether these programs and policies are right or wrong."

The United States government and the Obama administration accused Snowden of disloyalty and charged him with espionage and revoked his passport. For now, he is living in Russia, the only country willing to defy demands to turn him over to U.S. officials. Although he is certain Russian authorities are spying on him, he refuses to return to the United States to stand trial as long as he is prohibited from arguing in court that his disclosures were made in the public interest and not for any sort of personal gain.

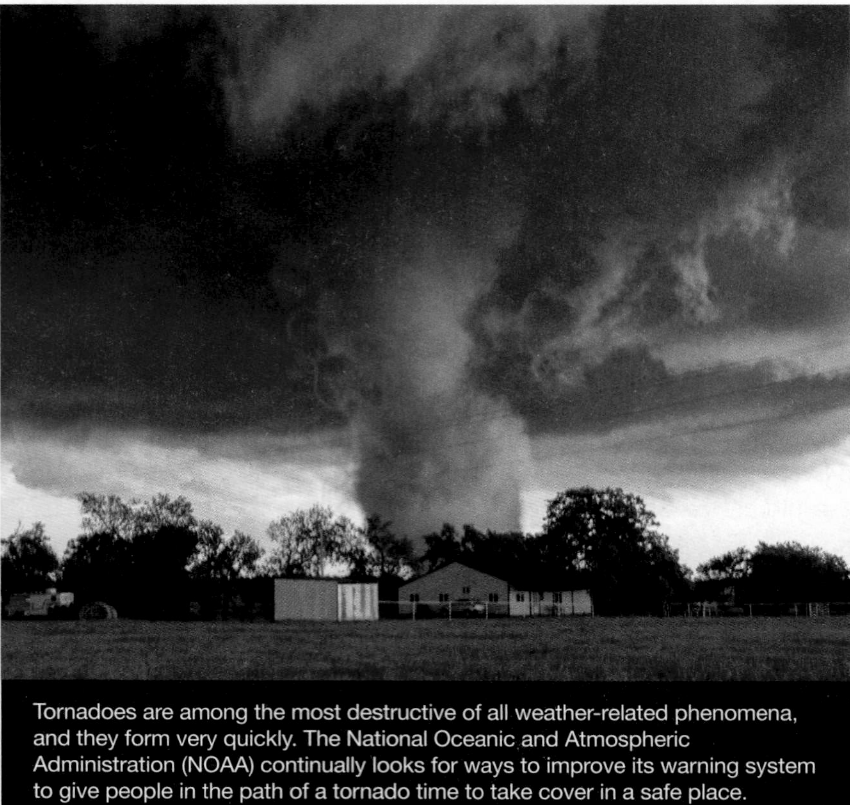

Tornadoes are among the most destructive of all weather-related phenomena, and they form very quickly. The National Oceanic and Atmospheric Administration (NOAA) continually looks for ways to improve its warning system to give people in the path of a tornado time to take cover in a safe place.

Like President Obama, President Trump supported the use of the Espionage Act of 1917 against people who leaked government secrets to the press. In May 2017, during Trump's first year in office, an NSA translator named Reality Winner released a smuggled report that described Russian hacking of computerized voter registration databases. Unlike Snowden, Winner was arrested soon afterward, and in August 2018, she was sentenced under the Espionage Act to more than five years in prison.

HISTORICAL THINKING

1. **MAKE GENERALIZATIONS** Why do you think some government agencies supply a toll-free hotline to encourage whistleblowers to act?
2. **COMPARE AND CONTRAST** Under what circumstances might a leaker also be considered a whistleblower?

Improving Efficiency and Getting Results

Congress and the president have increasingly looked for ways to make government more efficient. They have passed laws that seek to reduce paperwork and red tape and to increase accountability. They have begun to require that government agencies adopt some of the methods used by private businesses.

EFFECTIVENESS PROGRAMS AND INCENTIVES
The Government Performance and Results Act, which went into effect in 1993, has forced the federal government to change the way it does business. Since 1997, almost every agency (except the intelligence agencies) has had to describe its goals and identify methods for evaluating how well those goals are met. A goal can be as broad as lowering the number of highway traffic deaths or as narrow as reducing the number of times an agency's phone rings before it is answered.

As one example, consider the National Oceanic and Atmospheric Administration (NOAA). One of its goals was to improve the effectiveness of its short-term forecasting services, particularly concerning tornadoes. NOAA tries to issue warnings as far in advance of a tornado as possible. The more warning people have, the more chance they have to protect themselves and their property. The agency has succeeded in increasing its warning time from 7 minutes to 15 minutes before a tornado strikes an area. These additional minutes can be critical for those in the path of a tornado.

In the late 1990s, the government looked at other ways to improve government efficiency and productivity, too. At the time, pay-for-performance plans were already common in the private sector, such as team-based pay, skill-based pay, profit-sharing plans, or individual bonuses. Some federal agencies began experimenting with similar alternatives. The U.S. Postal Service, for example, implemented the Economic Value Added Variable Pay Program, which tied bonuses to performance. The Air Force also began testing a new results-based pay system for 3,000 scientists working in Air Force laboratories. And in 2018, the OMB proposed replacing automatic pay raises with a pay-for-performance plan that would make a total of $1 billion available to "reward and retain high performers."

PRIVATIZATION Another idea for increasing the efficiency of the federal bureaucracy is **privatization**, or turning over certain types of government work to the private sector. The aim of privatization is to eliminate inefficiencies, something private enterprises are adept at doing. However, private enterprises also seek to make a profit. For privatization to work, the savings from eliminating inefficiencies must be more than the amount extracted as profit, while the enterprise and its staff remain focused on the public interest as their overriding goal.

State and local governments have been experimenting with privatization for some time. Almost all the states have privatized at least a few of their services, and some states, including California, Colorado, and Florida, have privatized more than 100 activities formerly undertaken by government. States have also engaged in public–private partnerships in which a government agency and a private enterprise cooperate in financing, building, and operating hospitals, airports, wastewater facilities, sports stadiums, and other projects.

Some of the savings gained through privatization have been achieved because workers in the private sector do not always have the same protections that government workers have. By using contract and part-time workers instead of regular full-time employees, employers can legally deny workers benefits that are standard for regular government employees, such as overtime pay, health insurance, retirement plans, and paid vacation.

HISTORICAL THINKING

3. **MAKE PREDICTIONS** How might Americans respond if they saw a headline such as "Postal Service Loses Billions While Top Officials Receive Bonuses"?
4. **EVALUATE** Would you prefer to receive an automatic pay raise every year or additional pay based on your performance? Why?

Government in the Sunshine

The latter part of the 20th century saw a trend toward more openness in government. During the Cold War, successive administrations laid greater and greater emphasis on secrecy in the interests of national security. Congress eventually responded by pushing for more transparency. A historic step came in 1966, when Congress passed the **Freedom of Information Act (FOIA)**. This act requires federal agencies to disclose any information in agency files, with some exceptions, to any persons requesting it. In 1976, Congress passed the Government in the Sunshine Act, which required government meetings to be open to the public. Since the 1970s, sunshine laws have been enacted at all levels of American government.

With openness comes criticism, and in the 1970s and 1980s, more and more Americans criticized the government for wasteful spending, neglectful oversight, and increasing taxes. Critics demanded more information about government operations, claiming they had a right to know exactly how the government is spending their tax dollars.

The trend toward greater openness in government came to an abrupt halt after the terrorist attacks on the World Trade Center and the Pentagon on September 11, 2001. Expressing concern for public safety, the government tightened its grip on information that might be useful to terrorists. Officials removed hundreds of thousands of documents from government websites, fearing they could compromise national security. No longer can the public access layouts of nuclear power plants, descriptions of airline security violations, or maps of pipeline routes. Agencies were instructed to be more cautious about information in their files and were given new guidelines on what should be considered public information.

Nonetheless, the FOIA and sunshine laws remain on the books. Today, private individuals, businesses, and law firms are the main FOIA users, but requests made by news media may have the greatest public impact. Journalists regularly make use of FOIA requests to keep government accountable to the people. In 2018, for example, journalists used FOIA requests to write news stories that exposed the misuse of government resources by Environmental Protection Agency (EPA) head Scott Pruitt. As a result, Pruitt resigned.

HISTORICAL THINKING

5. **MAKE INFERENCES** How easy or difficult do you think it is to successfully access a bureaucratic agency's records through a Freedom of Information request? Explain your answer.
6. **CATEGORIZE** Why do you think sunshine laws are so named?

Government Online

Increasingly, government agencies have attempted to improve their effectiveness and efficiency by making use of the internet. They have, for example, made a wide range of information available to the public online. Americans can now go online to obtain tax forms and filing instructions, analyze census and immigration data, view regulations, get help finding affordable housing, learn about student financial aid programs, and much more.

Some government agencies enable citizens to file forms and apply for services online. For example, the federal government distributes payments for Medicare, tax refunds, SNAP benefits, and a variety of other programs automatically and electronically. States' and localities' websites enable people to renew a driver's license or car registration, find and apply for a job, and apply for and receive unemployment benefits without visiting an unemployment office.

One danger of automatic payments is the possibility of electronic fraud, or e-fraud, in which online deception is used for illegal gain. This problem is not new. Criminals have long attempted to defraud the government—and the taxpayer—by filing false income tax forms or by making improper claims following natural disasters. Use of electronic processing and payments has made it possible for wrongdoers to game the system without being examined by an actual person. The potential for fraud posed by automatic payment systems demonstrates that human beings still have an important role in the bureaucracy, even in the high-tech era.

How to Make an FOIA Request

1. **Do a preliminary search.** Much information is already publicly available on agency websites. Before making an FOIA request, search the relevant website, or go to the FOIA website to conduct a search across all government websites at once.
2. **Prepare the request.** If the documents you seek are not publicly available, prepare your request in writing. No form is required. Write a letter to the agency describing the documents you want. Include as much detail as you can. Include your full name, address, and phone number. If you want the documents emailed to you, you must also include your email address. The first 100 pages and the first two hours of search time are free, but more extensive requests may incur a fee.
3. **Submit the request.** Most federal agencies accept FOIA requests electronically, including by email, fax, or web form.

Agencies usually respond to a simple FOIA request within a month. For more information on a specific agency's process, do a web search using the agency's name and FOIA—for example, search "*Federal Communications Commission FOIA.*"

Another kind of criminal in the digital age poses a threat to democracy itself. As you have read, in 2017 an NSA employee leaked a report about Russians hacking into computerized voter registration databases. That hacking took place during the 2016 presidential elections. Government spokespeople told the public that no voter registrations were altered or erased. Other investigations have demonstrated that many of the estimated 350,000 voting machines used across the United States are vulnerable to hackers, although again, officials have consistently reported that no actual votes have ever been tampered with. Yet experts believe that internet criminals might be able to access voting machines or the systems used to program them and alter the results of an election.

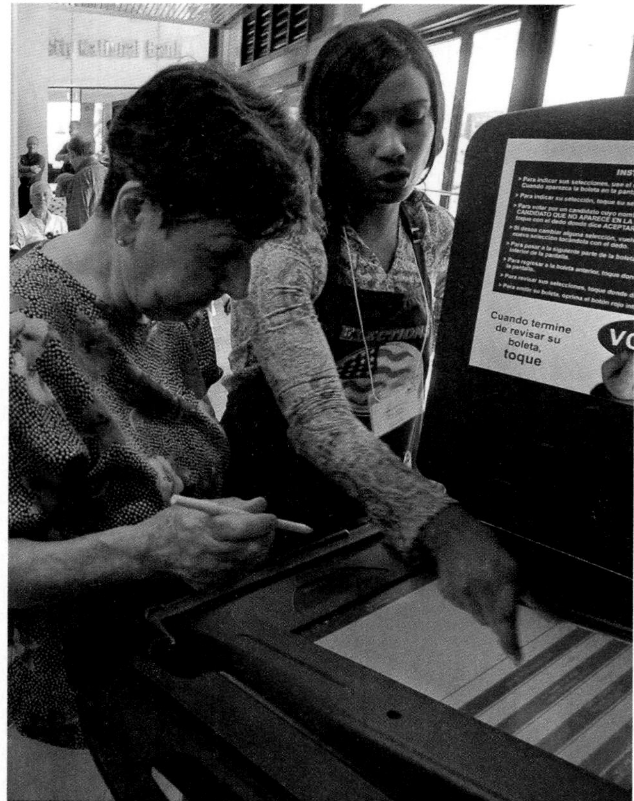

Many voters cast votes using electronic voting machines rather than paper ballots. Critics of electronic voting fear that unless the machines are protected by a strong security system, they can be vulnerable to hacking. So far, there have been no documented cases in the United States of hackers altering the results of an election.

The digital age has also given rise to concerns about privacy. Cell phone and search engine companies collect vast amounts of data about their customers. Law enforcement agencies such as the Federal Bureau of Investigation (FBI) want the widest possible access to that information in order to help prevent crimes or identify criminals. Internet service providers and technology companies could provide this information. But should the government be allowed to require such cooperation? Such powers run the risk of infringing on privacy and due process rights.

Do we have an expectation of privacy when it comes to the digital devices we use? For example, what if a person's cell phone is suspected of containing evidence of a crime? May the police examine it without first obtaining a search warrant? In 2014, the U.S. Supreme Court considered this question in light of the Fourth Amendment, which protects people against unreasonable searches and seizures. The Court ruled unanimously that law enforcement personnel can't search cell phones without a search warrant.

It remains an open question, moreover, what kinds of demands law enforcement agencies can make if they do have a search warrant. In one major incident, following a terrorist attack in San Bernardino, California, in 2015, the FBI recovered an Apple iPhone that had been used by one of the perpetrators. The FBI wasn't immediately able to access the information stored on the phone because the data were encrypted. The FBI therefore demanded that Apple write a new operating system that would bypass the phone's security features. Apple refused, citing security risks that such a backdoor would pose for its customers. The FBI then obtained a court order requiring Apple to cooperate. Shortly thereafter, however, the FBI announced that it had found a way to crack the phone without Apple's help. The court order was lifted, but the underlying issue remains.

HISTORICAL THINKING

7. **ANALYZE CAUSE AND EFFECT** How does use of the internet improve the efficiency of government agencies?
8. **FORM AND SUPPORT OPINIONS** Do you think police should be able to search a cell phone without a warrant if it might prevent an innocent person from being injured? Explain your answer.

Whistleblowers Time Line

In 1777, 10 crew members aboard a Continental Navy warship wrote a petition to Congress accusing their commander, Esek Hopkins, of torturing British prisoners of war "in the most inhuman and barbarous manner." Congress suspended Hopkins and a year later passed the country's first whistleblower protection law, stating that it is the duty of all Americans to report "any misconduct, frauds, or misdemeanors committed by any officers or persons in the service of these states."

Today, courageous Americans are still stepping forward to report misconduct and fraud by government officials and firms dealing with the government. As this time line shows, whistleblowers have helped expose abuses of power in many government agencies. Their actions haven't always been rewarded.

1971 Pentagon Papers
Daniel Ellsberg leaked a top-secret Defense Department report, later known as the Pentagon Papers, that revealed that the federal government had lied to the public about U.S. prospects in the Vietnam War. Ellsberg was charged under the Espionage Act and could have faced more than 100 years in prison, but all charges against him were dismissed after a trial lasting 4 months.

1972 Tuskegee Syphilis Study
In 1966, **Peter Buxtun** learned that his employer, the U.S. Public Health Service, had used nearly 400 African-American men with syphilis as research subjects without their consent for some 40 years. The men were examined, but they never received treatment that would have cured the disease.
In 1972, after officials ignored his concerns, Buxtun took his story to the press. Eventually, the government paid a $10 million settlement and provided lifetime medical and burial services to all survivors, spouses, widows, and offspring. At a White House ceremony in 1997, President Bill Clinton offered a formal apology to the 8 living survivors, including 94-year-old Herman Shaw, shown here, who introduced the president to the gathering.

1972 Watergate Break-In
Mark Felt, while deputy director of the FBI, secretly gave *Washington Post* reporter Bob Woodward details about the Watergate break-in and White House attempts to cover it up, which led to President Richard Nixon's resignation in 1974. Felt kept his identity secret until 2005.

1974 Nuclear Safety Violations
Karen Silkwood was a technician and union activist at a plant that produced fuel for nuclear reactors. Her employers deemed her a troublemaker, and she was routinely harassed at work. After she reported safety violations to the Atomic Energy Commission in 1974, she died in a car crash under questionable circumstances on her way to deliver evidence to a journalist. The plant was shut down in 1976, and the owners eventually provided $1.38 million to Silkwood's estate.

2000 Protection for Whistleblowers
As an EPA liaison to South Africa, **Marsha Coleman-Adebayo** sought investigations into health problems among South African miners working for an American company. Her supervisors told her to keep quiet, and she received rape threats and death threats. In 2000, Coleman-Adebayo won a lawsuit claiming a hostile work environment and discrimination on the basis of race, sex, and color. Her testimony to Congress led to passage of the No FEAR Act to prohibit retaliation against whistleblowers. President George W. Bush signed the No FEAR Act into law in 2002.

2004 Abuse and Torture of Military Prisoners
Joseph Darby, an army sergeant at the U.S.

military prison in Abu Ghraib, Iraq, provided photographic evidence of the appalling abuse and torture of detainees by guards, which led to criminal charges against 11 American soldiers.

2009 Racial Profiling in Airports
Cathy Harris, a senior inspector for the U.S. Customs Service, reported racial profiling and race-based humiliation by agents at the international airport in Atlanta. Her action resulted in federal legislation to ban these discriminatory practices.

2010 Civilian Airstrikes
U.S. Army intelligence analyst **Chelsea Manning** leaked hundreds of thousands of top secret documents in the hope of informing the public of what she termed "the true nature of 21st-century warfare." Among the documents was a video of a U.S. airstrike on a group of civilians, including news reporters. Manning was arrested in 2010, and three years later a military court convicted her of espionage, theft, and other charges and sentenced her to 35 years in prison. President Barack Obama commuted Manning's sentence, freeing her from prison after she had served seven years.

2013 Mass Surveillance
Edward Snowden, a security contractor for the NSA, disclosed mass surveillance programs collecting Americans' cell phone, email, text, and internet communications. Snowden was charged with theft of government property, unauthorized communication of national defense information, and willful communication of classified communications intelligence by the United States government. He fled to Russia, where he received asylum, in 2013.

2015 Flint Water Crisis
In 2014, to save money, Michigan officials changed the source of drinking water for the city of Flint. People immediately began complaining of foul tap water. City and state officials conducted no tests but insisted that the water was safe. Pediatrician **Dr. Mona Hanna-Attisha** conducted a study that showed high levels of lead in Flint children's blood. After she publicized her results at a press conference, national pressure finally led government officials to address the problem.

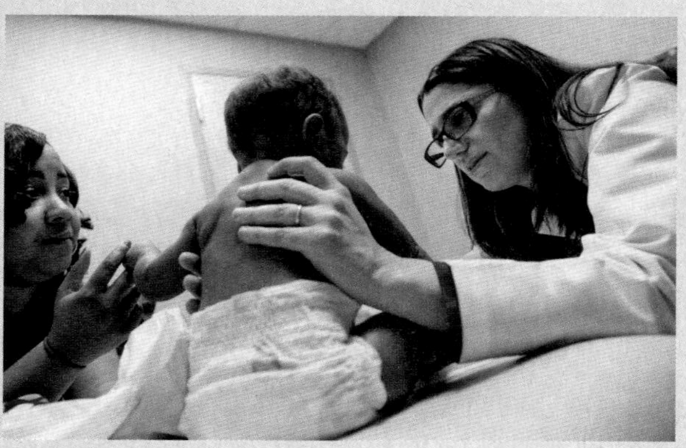

2017 Climate Change
Soon after Donald Trump took office, dozens of environmental experts at the Interior Department were assigned to new positions. **Joel Clement**, a climate expert whose new position did not involve any work on climate, published a letter in the *Washington Post* in which he characterized the reassignments as a way to silence the scientists' demands to base environmental policy on scientific fact. Clement later resigned.

2018 Family Separation and Detainment of Children
Dr. Pamela McPherson and **Dr. Scott Allen**, experts in medical and mental health hired by the Department of Homeland Security, reported that the Trump administration's policy of forcible separation of children from their families and confinement in detention centers was "an act of state-sponsored child abuse." Many media outlets reported on their exposé, and the practice drew widespread public opposition. Although the policy was officially ended in June 2018, reports indicated that thousands of children remained in detention many months later.

CHAPTER 11 THE BUREAUCRACY Review

VOCABULARY

For each of the following vocabulary words, write a sentence that shows an understanding of the term's meaning.

1. bureaucracy
2. merit system
3. regulations
4. civil service
5. executive department
6. monopoly
7. federal mandate
8. payroll tax
9. whistleblower
10. classified

MAIN IDEAS

Answer the following questions. Support your answers with evidence from the chapter.

11. Why do many people have a negative feeling about bureaucrats? **LESSON 11.1**
12. Under what circumstances does Congress pass enabling legislation? **LESSON 11.1**
13. What three interests tend to form what is known as an iron triangle within the U.S. government? **LESSON 11.1**
14. Do you think regulatory agencies need to be as independent as they are? Why or why not? **LESSON 11.2**
15. What key power differentiates independent regulatory agencies from independent executive agencies? **LESSON 11.2**
16. Name two characteristics that make the U.S. Postal Service a government corporation. **LESSON 11.2**
17. Who benefits from the federal government's social spending? **LESSON 11.3**
18. What category of federal expenditures covers foreign wars? **LESSON 11.3**
19. What has the federal government done to protect whistleblowers? **LESSON 11.4**
20. How might a government leak endanger national security? **LESSON 11.4**
21. How has the internet made e-fraud not only possible but more and more common? **LESSON 11.4**

HISTORICAL THINKING

Answer the following questions. Support your answers with evidence from the chapter.

22. **EVALUATE** In the federal bureaucracy, the power to act resides in the position rather than the person. What problem might occur if the reverse were true?
23. **MAKE INFERENCES** Why do you think an interest group might be eager to hire an expert who formerly worked for a federal regulatory agency?
24. **SYNTHESIZE** Why do you think the Bureau of Economic Analysis is located in the Commerce Department?
25. **MAKE GENERALIZATIONS** Why do you think many taxpayers call for decreasing government spending?
26. **FORM AND SUPPORT OPINIONS** Do you think whistleblowers should receive money as a reward? Why or why not?

INTERPRET VISUALS

Study the graph, which provides data on the proportion of the total U.S. population (including children, retired people, and others not employed) who are government employees. Then answer the questions.

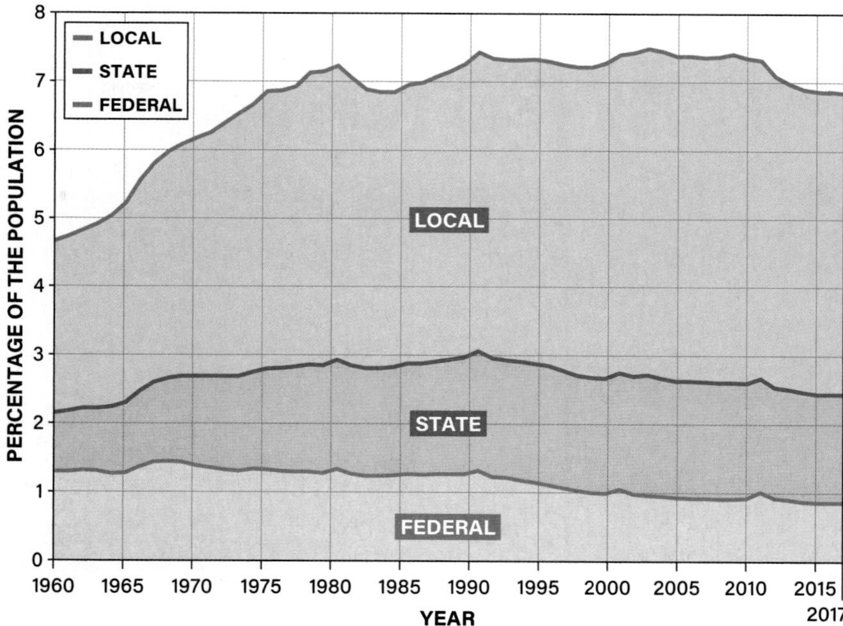

27. How did the percentage of the population employed by the federal government in 1965 compare with the percentage of the population working for local governments?

28. What trend has federal government employment exhibited since 1980? What might this trend signify?

ANALYZE SOURCES

Sociologist Paul du Gay has written that bureaucracies should be respected for their

> important achievements that those of us who are lucky enough to live in pacified societies [societies in which conflicts are typically resolved through government structures rather than violence] should not take so readily for granted.

29. Choose one essential feature of bureaucracy, and write a few sentences explaining how that feature contributes to the "important achievement" du Gay identifies.

CONNECT TO YOUR LIFE

30. **ARGUMENT** Think about the local, state, and national government services you and members of your household use or receive. Include things that are available to everyone in your community, such as consumer and financial protections, food safety regulations, occupational safety and employment rules, roads, schools, libraries, and so forth, as well as any veterans, medical, or social benefits.

Write a couple of paragraphs to make an argument for expanding or cutting back on one or more of these services. Include an explanation of how doing so would affect your life and the lives of people around you.

TIPS

- To help you prepare, list all the government services you can think of that affect your life. This is for your use only.
- Choose one or more services that you think should be cut or expanded.
- Write a few sentences to explain how these changes would affect people, either positively or negatively.
- Consider the implications of the action you are recommending. If the service is to be expanded, would taxes increase? If you think the service should be cut, would private businesses fill the gap—and would they charge more or less than the government? Or is the service unnecessary?
- Describe how the increase or loss in the service would affect you and others.

UNIT 6

The Judicial Branch

UNIT 6 OVERVIEW

Chapter 12 The American Court System

Chapter 13 The Supreme Court

CRITICAL VIEWING The U.S. Supreme Court is the highest court in the judicial branch of government. Opened in 1935, the U.S. Supreme Court building recalls a classical Roman temple in design. Though designed by architect Cass Gilbert, it is largely the result of the efforts of Chief Justice William Howard Taft, who began advocating for the Court to get its own building of "dignity and importance" as soon as he took office. Prior to 1935, the Court was housed for most of its life in the U.S. Capitol building. Why would the "dignity and importance" of the Court be enhanced by having its own building?

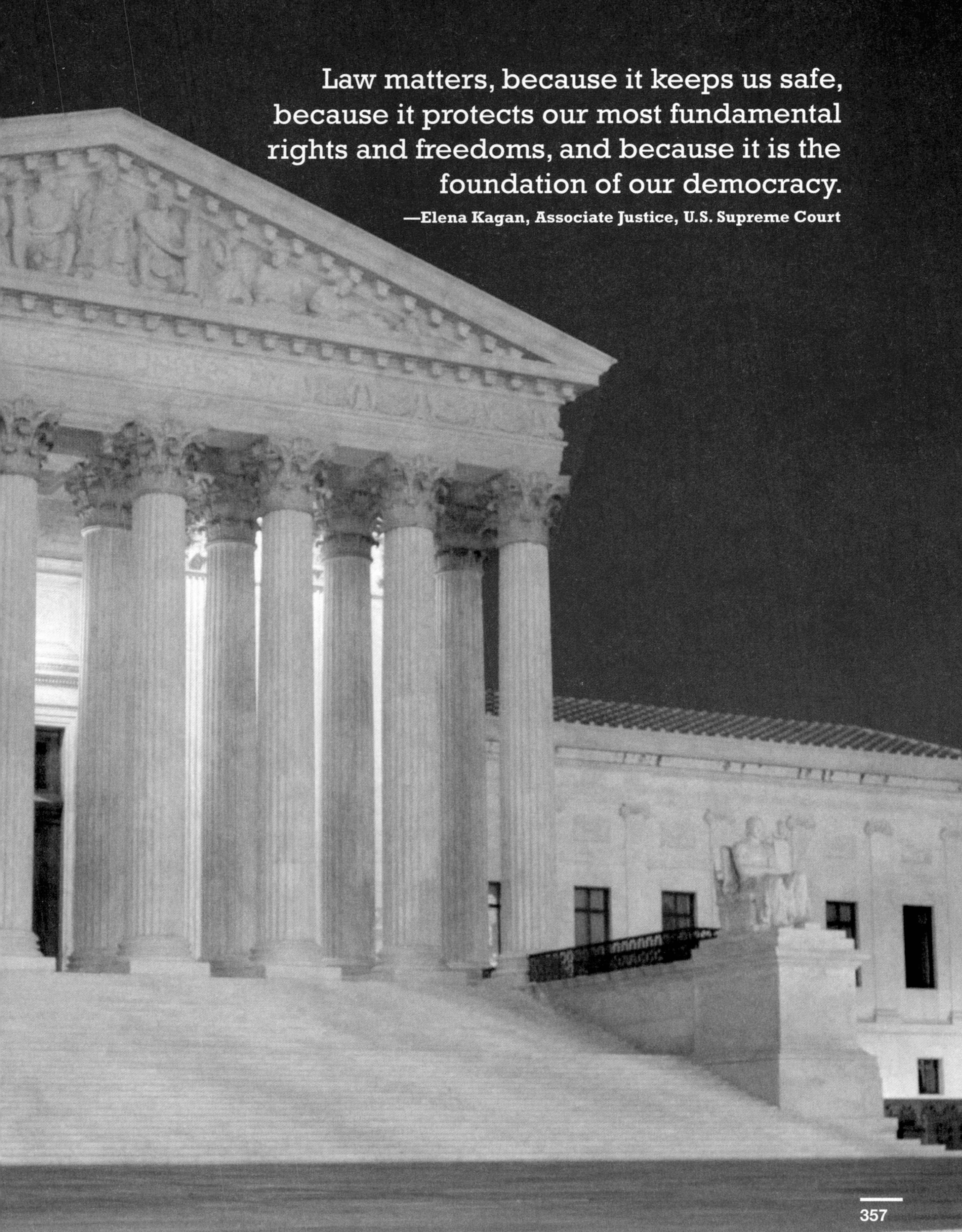

Law matters, because it keeps us safe, because it protects our most fundamental rights and freedoms, and because it is the foundation of our democracy.

—Elena Kagan, Associate Justice, U.S. Supreme Court

CHAPTER 12

The American Court System

LESSONS

12.1 Origins and Sources of American Law

12.2 The Federal Court System

12.3 Other Trial Courts

***National Geographic* Magazine:**
They Are Watching You—and Everything Else on the Planet

CRITICAL VIEWING Protesters unfurl a banner with words from the Preamble of the U.S. Constitution. The action was part of a larger demonstration against a 2010 Supreme Court decision striking down sections of the McCain-Feingold campaign finance law as an unconstitutional restriction of the First Amendment's guarantee of free speech. Why would

LESSON 12.1

Origins and Sources of American Law

Maybe you know someone who plans to go to law school or who has recently completed a law degree. If so, you probably know that a full-time law student will spend at least three difficult years studying, and at the end of that time, he or she will likely know only a fraction of the laws of the United States and any particular state. There are laws that apply to the kinds of crimes you see on TV dramas and in movies, but there are also laws that apply to government operations, businesses, international relations, and technical and scientific innovations. This complex system of laws has evolved over centuries—and new laws are constantly being added.

The Common Law Tradition

The origins of American law can be traced back to English law. Prior to 1066, the English lived under Anglo-Saxon law, a patchwork of mostly local or tribal rules that were enforced by the people in the community. Some laws were also imposed by kings. Laws were more likely to be issued by kings in the 10th century, when England was united into a single kingdom. Still, the laws were piecemeal and varied depending on the community.

Then, in 1066, the Normans, led by William the Conqueror, invaded England from France. William became King William I of England, and he and his successors began the process of unifying the country under their rule. One of the methods they used was the establishment of the "king's courts." The law developed by the king's courts applied to the country as a whole. In other words, these courts created a body of **common law**, laws that were applied in common to every county in England rather than leaving laws up to local customs. This helped to unify and standardize English legal practices.

PRECEDENTS Judges in the early English courts tried to be consistent, and whenever possible, they based their decisions on the principles applied in earlier cases dealing with similar issues. When new kinds of cases were brought before them, judges knew their decisions would make new law. Each decision they made would become part of the law on a subject, serving as a legal precedent, or a model for later cases involving similar legal issues.

The practice of deciding new cases with reference to precedents is a cornerstone of the English and American legal traditions. It is often referred to by the Latin phrase *stare decisis*, in other words, "to let the decision stand." Under the doctrine of *stare decisis*, judges are obligated to follow the precedents established in their jurisdictions, which are areas in which they have authority. For example, if the Supreme Court of Georgia holds that a state law requiring candidates for state office undergo and pass drug tests is unconstitutional, that decision will control the outcome of future cases on that issue brought before state courts in Georgia. Similarly, a decision on a given issue by the United States Supreme Court, which is the nation's highest court, is binding on all inferior, or lower, courts. For example, the Georgia case on drug testing might be appealed to the United States Supreme Court. If the Court agrees that the Georgia law is unconstitutional, the high court's ruling will be binding on all courts in the United States. In other words, similar drug-testing laws in other states will be invalid and unenforceable.

Common law wasn't the invention of the Normans. This tradition goes back thousands of years. For example, according to Christian and Jewish tradition, the biblical leader Moses presented the Ten Commandments, a list of religious rules believed to have come from God, to the Hebrews. But these rules required interpretation. Tradition holds that Moses appointed judges who interpreted these rules in specific cases arising among the people. These decisions formed the precedents for future cases, thus imposing a predictable system on the laws.

In England, hundreds of years of legal decisions, even when those decisions were based on precedents, produced a somewhat messy legal system. In the 18th century, Sir William Blackstone (1723–1780), an English legal expert, organized these decisions to create a uniform legal system when he published *Commentaries on the Laws of England*. This four-volume work, published in 1765–1769, is a comprehensive overview of English law up to that time. It gives particular emphasis to the role of common law in the English legal system. The work helped provide structure to legal thought and the application of law not just in Britain but also in the United States for many decades.

By the 1300s, the main sources of justice in England were the common-law courts, where cases were decided based on tradition and earlier court decisions. Other courts, including the Court of Chancery, were developed later to deal with issues such as property and business disputes that could not be resolved using common law and written statutes alone. This image shows a session of the Court of Chancery in the early 1700s.

At the heart of the U.S. legal system is the promise that all people have the right to the "due process of law." This right is guaranteed by the U.S. Constitution in the Fifth and 14th amendments. By applying and interpreting common law, courts ensure that no one can be deprived "of life, liberty, or property without due process of law." In other words, there must be a legal reason, founded on precedents, for the government to take someone's life, freedom, or property.

DEPARTURES FROM PRECEDENTS While precedents are central to the American legal system, courts do not follow precedent blindly. If the facts of the case point away from precedent, if changing social norms and values call for a fresh interpretation of a law, or if the courts determine that prior decisions run afoul of fundamental constitutional principles, courts will depart from precedent. At times, the changing composition of the Court can lead to interpretations that depart from precedent as well. Such decisions often spark controversy.

An example is the 1954 *Brown* v. *Board of Education of Topeka* decision by the U.S. Supreme Court. In earlier cases, separate educational facilities for African Americans had been upheld as constitutional under the "separate-but-equal" doctrine. In *Brown*, the Court considered new evidence about the negative effects of racial segregation and concluded that such separation was inherently unequal and violated the equal protection clause of the Constitution. The Supreme Court's departure from precedent in *Brown* triggered enormous controversy and protest, especially in the South, where the decision disrupted

Brown v. *Board of Education of Topeka*, 1954

Decided: May 17, 1954, 9–0

Majority: Chief Justice Earl Warren wrote the opinion of the Court in favor of Brown.

Oliver and Leola Brown of Topeka, Kansas, wanted their seven-year-old daughter, Linda, to attend a school near their home. But because the school was for Whites only, she was refused admission and forced to attend an all-Black school much farther away. The National Association for the Advancement of Colored People (NAACP) helped the Browns sue the Topeka Board of Education in order to end segregation in public schools. NAACP lawyer Thurgood Marshall argued that segregated schools were fundamentally unequal and therefore violated the 14th Amendment. A U.S. district court ruled against Brown, who appealed the case to the Supreme Court, where this case was consolidated with similar cases against four other school systems in South Carolina, Delaware, Virginia, and the District of Columbia.

Linda Brown (left) and her sister Terry Lynn walk to the bus that will take them to Monroe Elementary School, an all-Black school far from their home in Topeka, Kansas. Linda Brown was refused admission to the White elementary school near her home because of segregation laws.

After hearing arguments in 1952, a majority of the Court was ready to overturn *Plessy* v. *Ferguson*. This 1896 decision established the precedent that separate facilities for Blacks and Whites were legal as long as the facilities were about equal in quality. The justices disagreed on crucial points, however. They decided to hear new arguments in December 1953. But before the case came forward, Chief Justice Fred Vinson died.

The new chief justice, Earl Warren, was determined to build agreement among the justices. On May 17, 1954, Warren announced the unanimous opinion of the Court: Racially segregated schools were illegal because they violated equal protection of the laws as required by the 14th Amendment.

Warren wrote, "In the field of public education, the doctrine of 'separate but equal' has no place. Separate educational facilities are inherently unequal."

THINK ABOUT IT Why was Chief Justice Earl Warren intent on getting the Supreme Court to make *Brown* a unanimous decision?

long-settled patterns of racial discrimination. Yet today, few Americans, and even fewer constitutional scholars, would object to that decision.

More recently, the Supreme Court departed from precedent in its 2010 ruling in *Citizens United* v. *Federal Election Commission*. In a 5–4 decision, the Court overturned two precedents that had upheld restrictions on corporate spending in election campaigns. In those earlier decisions, the Court had determined that the government's legitimate interest in protecting the election process from possible corruption outweighed minimal and narrowly tailored restrictions on free speech.

In deciding *Citizens United*, however, the Court found that such restrictions contradicted the fundamental principle of freedom of speech as guaranteed in the First Amendment. As long as corporations did not coordinate their expenditures with individual candidates, they were free to spend as much as they liked to advocate for their positions or to support, or oppose, a candidate. "There is no such thing," the majority declared, "as too much free speech." The decision, which covers labor unions and nonprofit groups as well as corporations, remains highly controversial. Critics charge that it is unnecessarily broad, addressing concerns that were not at issue in the case, and that it opened a floodgate of campaign donations that have corrupted the election process.

CRITICAL VIEWING In January 2010 the U.S. Supreme Court ruling in *Citizens United* v. *Federal Election Commission* overturned earlier rulings restricting corporate spending in election campaigns. The Court held that banning corporate funding of independent political broadcasts was a violation of the First Amendment right to freedom of speech. What is the cartoonist's opinion of this ruling? How do you know?

HISTORICAL THINKING

1. **DRAW CONCLUSIONS** How did Sir William Blackstone influence the American legal system?
2. **ANALYZE CAUSE AND EFFECT** Are Supreme Court justices who hold to the doctrine of *stare decisis* more or less likely to vote to overturn a decision made by the Court before they became justices?

Foundations of American Law

In the United States, the courts interpret and apply several sources of law when deciding cases. When these laws come into conflict, the courts apply them according to priority. The U.S. Constitution is the basis of all law in the United States. In other words, laws must comply with the Constitution to be valid, or have legal force. Any law that violates the Constitution is invalid and unenforceable. State constitutions are supreme within the borders of their respective states unless they conflict with the U.S. Constitution or a federal law. Constitutional law consists of the rights and duties outlined in the federal and state constitutions.

Statutory laws, or laws enacted by legislatures, are another source of law. Federal, state, or local legislative bodies can all create statutory law. Statutory law overrides common law, but it is often based on common law. Statutory laws can therefore be thought of as common law that has been formalized and written down. Federal statutes—laws enacted by the U.S. Congress—apply to all of the states. State statutes—laws enacted by state legislatures—apply only within the state that enacted the laws. Any state statute that conflicts with the U.S. Constitution, with federal laws enacted by Congress, or with the state's constitution will be deemed invalid if challenged in court and won't be enforced.

Statutory law also includes the ordinances, or local laws, passed by cities and counties, such as local zoning or housing construction laws. None of these can violate the U.S. Constitution, the relevant state constitution, or any existing federal or state laws.

Another important source of American law is administrative law—the rules, regulations, orders, and decisions of administrative agencies. At the federal level, Congress creates executive agencies, such as the Food and Drug Administration and the Environmental Protection Agency, to perform specific duties. Typically, when Congress establishes an agency, it authorizes the agency to create rules that enable it to do its work. These rules have the force of law. The agency can enforce those rules by bringing legal action against violators.

Rules issued by various government agencies now affect nearly every aspect of our lives. For example, almost all of a business's operations are subject to government regulation. These include hiring and firing practices, the safety of the work environment, relations with employees and unions, the way it manufactures and markets its products, and any practices it might have regarding credit and lending.

Government agencies exist at the state and local levels as well. States commonly create agencies that parallel federal agencies. Just as federal statutes take precedence over conflicting state statutes, federal agency regulations take precedence over conflicting state regulations, unless federal law has explicitly permitted more stringent state regulations.

As you read earlier, another basic source of American law is common law, also known as case law, which are rules of law resulting from court decisions. Sometimes referred to as "judge-made laws," these rules of law encompass interpretations of constitutional provisions, statutes enacted by legislatures, and regulations issued by administrative agencies. Thus, even though a legislature passes a law to govern certain practices, how that law is interpreted and applied may depend on the courts if the law is challenged. The importance of case law is one of the distinguishing characteristics of the common-law tradition.

HISTORICAL THINKING

3. **COMPARE AND CONTRAST** How are statutory laws different from common law?
4. **ANALYZE CAUSE AND EFFECT** Why is it necessary for courts to interpret constitutional law?

Civil Law and Criminal Law

All law can be divided into two categories. **Civil law** spells out the duties individuals owe to others or to their governments. It is largely concerned with disputes involving private parties. **Criminal law** covers crimes and wrongful actions committed against the public as a whole.

Typically, civil law comes into play when an individual, business, organization, or other private party files a **lawsuit**, a legal claim against another party that is brought to court for a ruling. The purpose of such a lawsuit, also known simply as a suit, is to gain relief (in the form of payment) or to resolve some complaint or alleged wrongdoing. The government can also sue a party for a civil law violation. The object of a civil lawsuit is to make the defendant—the person being sued—comply with a legal duty. For example, someone might sue a company for not abiding by the terms of a contract. Other examples might include a suit brought by a spouse who wants a divorce, or by homeowners who want a neighbor whose tree fell on their house to pay the costs of repairs and inconvenience. Defendants who lose civil cases cannot be sentenced to jail time.

Criminal law is a more serious breach of law. It includes cases such as burglary, murder, or sexual assault. Criminal acts are prohibited by local, state, and federal government statutes. Public officials, such as a district attorney (DA), prosecute criminal defendants on behalf of the government. In a criminal case, the government seeks to impose a penalty (usually a fine and/or imprisonment, and in certain cases death) on a person who has violated a criminal law. For example, when someone robs a convenience store, that person has committed a crime and, if caught and proved guilty, will usually spend time in prison.

There are two kinds of crimes. **Misdemeanors** are relatively minor crimes such as petty theft, disturbing the peace, and traffic violations. Punishment includes fines or imprisonment in a county jail for up to a year. **Felonies** are serious crimes usually involving violence that can be punished by more than a year of imprisonment. Felonies include crimes such as rape, arson, robbery, and kidnapping. A **capital crime** is a felony punishable by death.

CRIMINAL *and* CIVIL LAW

CRIMINAL LAW	CIVIL LAW
An offense against the public	An injury to a private party
Imposes penalty for serious violation of law	Compels defendant to comply with legal duty
Government prosecutes defendant	Plaintiff files lawsuit against defendant
Public represented by district attorney; defendant hires attorney or is provided one by the government	Parties represented by own lawyers
Burden of proof: beyond reasonable doubt	Burden of proof: preponderance of evidence
Penalty: possible fine or prison time	Penalty: usually financial payment to plaintiff; no loss of liberty

Unlike defendants in civil cases, criminal defendants can be sentenced to jail time if they are found guilty. Such a loss of personal liberty is a serious matter. Therefore, the burden of proof in criminal cases is higher than in civil cases. Criminal cases must be proved beyond a reasonable doubt, while civil cases require only a preponderance of evidence, or enough evidence to indicate guilt or innocence.

HISTORICAL THINKING

5. **DRAW CONCLUSIONS** Why does a district attorney, rather than a private attorney, prosecute someone accused of a criminal offense?
6. **INTERPRET CHARTS** Given the different burden of proof in a civil case, why might a private party file a lawsuit against someone who was accused of a felony but declared innocent?

Basic Judicial Requirements

Before a court can hear and decide a case, specific requirements must be met. These requirements act as restraints on the judiciary because they limit the types of cases that courts can hear and decide. Courts also have procedural requirements that judges must follow.

First, courts must have jurisdiction, which literally means the power "to speak the law." In other words, jurisdiction gives a particular court the right to hear and speak about the law, or make decisions, on specific types of cases. Jurisdiction applies to the geographic area in which a court has the right and power to decide cases. It also applies to the right and power of a court to decide matters concerning certain persons, types of property, or subjects. A court is said to have original jurisdiction when a case can be brought directly to that court for a first hearing.

TYPES OF JURISDICTION A state trial court usually has jurisdiction over the residents of a particular area of the state, such as a county or district. A state's highest court, which is often called the state supreme court, has jurisdiction over all residents within the state. In some cases, if an individual who resides in another state has committed an offense, such as injuring someone in an automobile accident, the state court where the offense occurred can exercise jurisdiction. State courts can also exercise jurisdiction over those who reside outside a state but do business within the state. A New York company that distributes products in California, for example, usually can be sued by a California resident in a California state court.

Federal courts have jurisdiction concerning any matters over which the federal government has authority. These include issues arising under the U.S. Constitution, the laws of the United States, treaties with foreign governments, federal taxes, and interstate

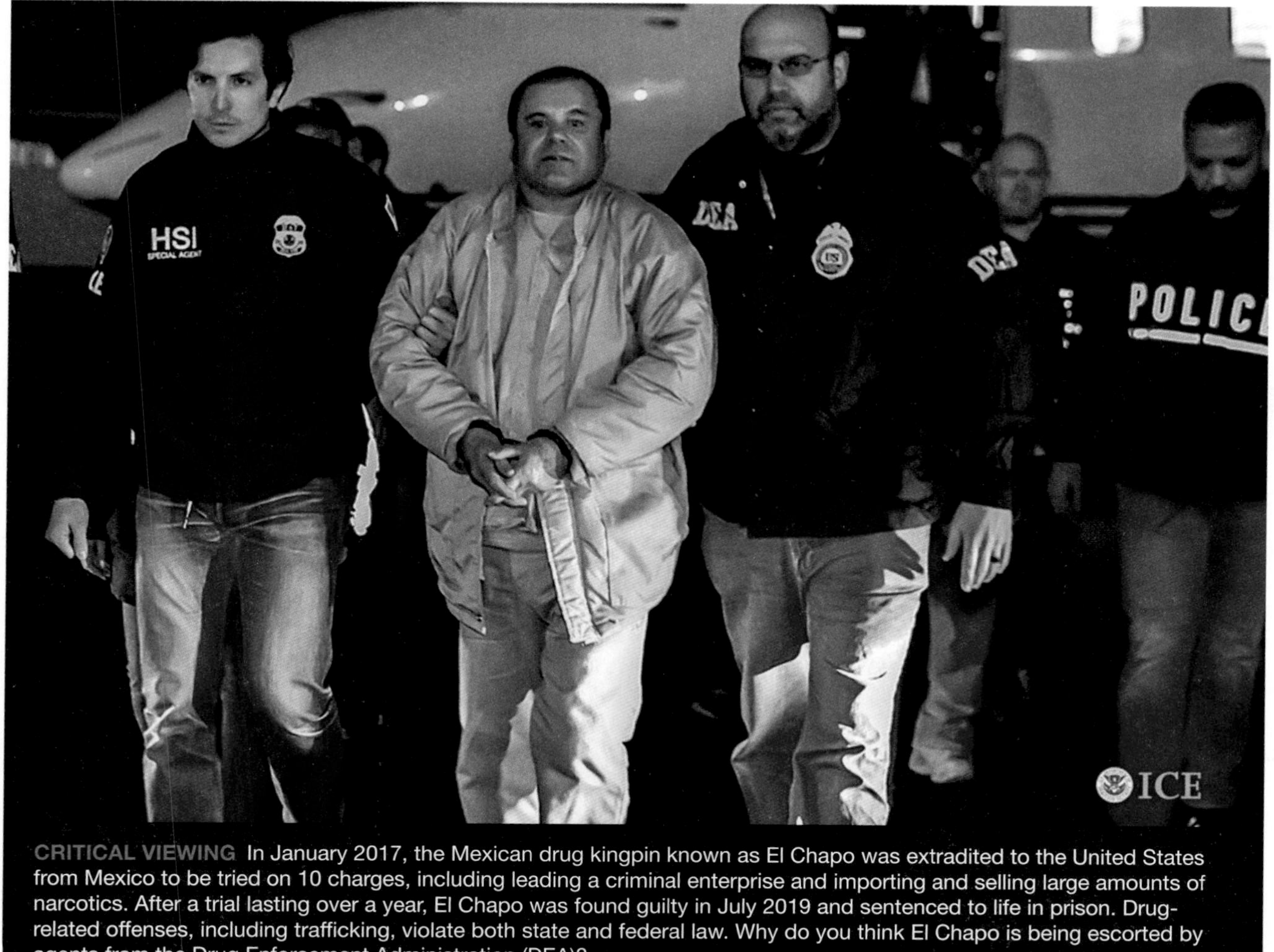

CRITICAL VIEWING In January 2017, the Mexican drug kingpin known as El Chapo was extradited to the United States from Mexico to be tried on 10 charges, including leading a criminal enterprise and importing and selling large amounts of narcotics. After a trial lasting over a year, El Chapo was found guilty in July 2019 and sentenced to life in prison. Drug-related offenses, including trafficking, violate both state and federal law. Why do you think El Chapo is being escorted by agents from the Drug Enforcement Administration (DEA)?

commerce, for example. Any lawsuit involving a federal question can originate in a federal court.

Federal courts can also have jurisdiction over cases involving diversity of citizenship, a situation in which parties to a lawsuit live in different states or when one of the parties is a foreign government or citizen. A federal court can take jurisdiction in a diversity case only if the amount in controversy is more than $75,000.

BRINGING A CASE BEFORE THE COURTS To bring a lawsuit before a court, a person must have standing to sue, or a sufficient stake in the matter to justify bringing a suit. Thus, the party bringing the suit must have suffered a harm or been threatened with a harm by the action. Someone who suffers injury as a result of someone else's actions has a standing to sue. A bystander who wasn't involved in the action likely doesn't have standing.

Moreover, the issue must be justiciable, that is something that can be tried on legal principles in court. A justiciable controversy is one that is real and substantial. A case involving food poisoning at a restaurant may be justiciable. A complaint based on some hypothetical event that might happen isn't.

The requirement of standing to sue clearly limits the issues that can be decided by the courts. Furthermore, both state and federal governments can specify by law when an individual or a group has standing to sue. For example, the federal government won't allow a taxpayer to sue a federal agency for spending tax dollars wastefully.

Both the federal and the state courts have established court procedures, or rules that must be followed in every case a court hears. These procedures help protect the rights and interests of the parties and ensure that court proceedings occur in a fair and orderly manner. They also help identify the issues that must be decided by the court—thus saving court time and costs. Different procedural rules apply in criminal and civil cases. Generally, criminal procedural rules attempt to ensure that defendants aren't deprived of their constitutional rights.

Parties involved in civil or criminal cases must comply with court procedural rules. If they fail to, they may be held in **contempt of court**, a ruling by a judge that a person has disobeyed a court order or shown disrespect to the court. If found in contempt, the party can be fined, taken into custody, or both. A court must take care to ensure that the parties—and the court itself—comply with procedural requirements. Procedural errors often serve as grounds for a **mistrial**—a ruling that a trial has no legal effect due to some error or mistake in judicial proceedings—or it may be the basis for appealing the court's decision to a higher court.

ATTORNEYS AND JURIES Besides the judge in a state or federal court, cases typically involve attorneys and juries. In criminal cases, a government official, such as a district attorney, prosecutes, or brings the case against, the defendant. A defense attorney defends the accused. In civil cases, both the person who filed the lawsuit and the defendant, or the person being charged or sued, are represented by attorneys. In criminal cases, the defendants always have the right to an attorney, even if the defendant can't afford to pay for one. The government, in that case, will provide an attorney at the government's expense. In some cases, defendants may choose to waive the right to an attorney and defend themselves.

Juries often play a prominent role in court cases. There are two types of juries: a grand jury and a trial or petit jury. A grand jury is called for criminal cases to consider whether the government has sufficient reason and evidence to bring a case to trial. The grand jury doesn't make a decision about guilt or innocence. A trial jury hears the case, considers the evidence, and returns a verdict.

In a trial by jury, the judge oversees the case and makes rulings on any issues regarding the law. The jury then considers the facts presented and delivers a verdict. In some cases, the party or parties may choose to forgo a jury and have the case decided by the judge alone. These are called bench trials, because the judge (who sits on the bench) determines both points of law and the validity of the evidence presented.

THE ABA The American Bar Association (ABA) is a professional organization for members of the legal profession, including lawyers and judges. Established in 1878, the ABA has more than 400,000 members, making it one of the largest voluntary professional organizations in the world. As the national voice of the legal profession in the United States, the ABA works to improve the administration of justice in a variety of ways. For example, the association ensures law schools meet certain educational standards for students seeking a career in law. Today, there are more than 200 ABA-accredited law schools in the United States. The ABA provides continuing education to lawyers and judges. It also recommends model rules of professional conduct for lawyers, judges, and paralegals in the United States.

Another function of the ABA is to provide the U.S. Senate, the president, and the public with evaluations of nominees for federal judgeships, including people nominated to the U.S. Supreme Court. A committee of the ABA assesses each nominee and considers qualities such as professional competence, integrity, and temperament. It then issues a rating of "well-qualified," "qualified," or "not qualified."

In the United States and around the world, the ABA works to build public understanding about rule of law and the importance of law in society. To achieve these goals, the ABA's Division for Public Education produces educational materials about important topics, including how courts work, the work of lawyers and judges, important trials and cases, understanding legal concepts and documents, and civic education.

It also offers and promotes numerous programs for students, teachers, and the general public, including:

- National Civics & Law Academy, which brings 20 high school students from across the country to Washington, D.C., for a week to meet with government leaders to learn how the federal government works.
- Summer Institute for Teachers: Federal Trials and Great Debates in United States History, which is run in collaboration with the Federal Judicial Center and brings together scholars, judges,

and 20 teachers from across the country to study key federal cases.

- Law Day programs, held every year on May 1 to raise awareness about the rule of law, which engage hundreds of public audiences with activities as varied as lectures, art contests, naturalization ceremonies, and essay competitions on the annual Law Day theme. These programs are often led locally by courts, law firms, bar associations, community groups, and schools.

Outside of the United States, the ABA's Rule of Law Initiative (ROLI) "promotes justice, economic opportunity, and dignity through the rule of law." ROLI staffers collaborate with lawyers, judges, or leaders in other countries to help establish new court systems, write new constitutions, ensure free and fair elections, and implement civic education programs.

An ABA member serves as president of the association each year. Notable ABA presidents have included former U.S. President and U.S. Supreme Court Chief Justice William Howard Taft (1913); U.S. Supreme Court Justice Lewis Franklin Powell, Jr. (1965); Watergate Special Prosecutor Leon Jaworski (1972); Roberta Cooper Ramo, the first woman to serve as ABA president (1996); and Dennis W. Archer, former mayor of Detroit and the first African-American ABA president (2004).

HISTORICAL THINKING

7. **MAKE INFERENCES** Why would Congress refuse to give standing to sue to citizens who believe a government agency is misspending tax dollars?
8. **FORM AND SUPPORT OPINIONS** What purpose do you think a grand jury serves in protecting the rights of Americans?

LESSON 12.2 The Federal Court System

The Constitution established the federal judiciary, but it specifically mentions only one federal court—the Supreme Court. The Constitution gave Congress the power to create the other federal courts on an as-needed basis. This congressional power to create courts is actually mentioned in two places—Articles I and III. The courts that were created under Article III, known as constitutional courts, are said to exercise the "judicial Power of the United States." Article III courts include the Supreme Court, the U.S. district courts, and the U.S. courts of appeals. Article I courts are more specialized. Each type of court, whether created under Article I or Article III, has specific responsibilities for ensuring laws are applied correctly.

U.S. District Courts

The U.S. district courts have **original jurisdiction**—the power of a court to hear a case for the first time—over both criminal and civil cases involving federal law. The cases in these courts are decided by a judge or by a jury. There is at least one federal district court in every state, and there is one in the District of Columbia. In addition, four territories of the United States have their own district courts. The territories are Puerto Rico, the Virgin Islands, Guam, and the Northern Mariana Islands.

The number of judicial districts has varied historically, but no new district has been created since 1966. Currently, there are 94 judicial districts and 678 district court judgeships. The number of judges per district varies, from 2 in North Dakota to 28 in the Southern District of New York. Certain districts require more judges simply because more cases are brought before the courts there, and so more judges are needed to handle the workload.

To help manage the number of cases assigned to each district judge, district court judges appoint federal magistrate judges. These judges don't have the full authority of federal district judges, but they perform specific roles, such as issuing search and arrest warrants, conducting the initial hearings for cases, setting bail, hearing certain misdemeanor cases, and so forth. Magistrate judges serve terms of four to eight years. They can be reappointed after their terms expire.

District courts are **trial courts**, meaning they hear cases for the first time, rather than on appeal. A trial judge may consider whether certain kinds of evidence are admissible in court or whether a particular law applies to a case. In a criminal case, a judge or jury determines if the evidence of guilt presented by the prosecution is compelling and legitimate. The court listens to witnesses and decides if they are truthful and if the information given is credible and relevant to the case. Then the court makes a determination of the guilt or innocence of the accused based on the merits of the evidence and testimony. In most cases, it is a jury that makes the decision. But, as you read earlier, in cases where the accused chooses a trial by judge, it is the judge who makes the decision.

Federal appeals courts, which you'll read about later, are organized into 13 circuits. There are 13 federal courts of appeals in the United States. The courts of appeals for 12 of the circuits, including the Court of Appeals for the D.C. Circuit, hear appeals from the U.S. district courts located within their respective judicial circuits. If, for example, a case originating with a district court in New Mexico is appealed, it will be heard by the U.S. Court of Appeals for the Tenth Circuit, which is located in Denver, Colorado.

HISTORICAL THINKING

1. **COMPARE AND CONTRAST** How does the role of a magistrate judge differ from that of a district court judge?
2. **MAKE INFERENCES** Why might a person accused of a crime choose to have his or her case decided by a judge, rather than by a jury?
3. **INTERPRET MAPS** How does clustering federal courts according to geographic area benefit people involved in federal trials?

U.S. Courts of Appeals

In the middle tier of the federal court system are the U.S. courts of appeals, which are federal courts that hear appeals of decisions made by U.S. district courts. Courts of appeals don't hear or make decisions based on evidence or testimony. Rather, they are appellate courts, or courts whose responsibility is to review the records of the trial court's proceedings, other records relating to the case, and determine whether attorneys' arguments as to why the trial court's decision should or shouldn't stand are valid. The task of the appellate court is to determine whether the trial court erred in applying the law to the facts and issues involved in a particular case. In contrast to a trial court, where normally a single judge presides, an appellate court consists of a panel of three or more judges.

In addition to hearing appeals from the U.S. district courts, the U.S. appellate courts also take a few other kinds of cases. They can review cases from state courts based on claims that local or state laws violate federal statutes or the U.S. Constitution. Among the most common of these cases are those involving *habeas corpus*, which is a court order requiring that a jailed person accused of a crime be brought before a court in order to determine if the prisoner is legally jailed. The purpose of this constitutional procedure is to protect against imprisonment of the innocent.

Appellate courts also hear cases involving federal agencies, such as the Social Security Administration, National Labor Relations Board, and Federal Trade Commission. In all, the U.S. courts of appeal may hear more than 50,000 cases a year. Of these, about 5,000 may be appealed from the courts of appeals to the Supreme Court, which will review fewer than 100.

The decisions of the federal appellate courts may be appealed to the Supreme Court. If a decision isn't appealed, or if the high court declines to review the case, the appellate court's decision is final.

SELECTION OF JUDGES The U.S. Constitution imposes no qualifications for becoming a federal judge. Judges for both the district and appeals courts are nominated by the president and must be confirmed by the U.S. Senate before they are appointed. When judges are nominated to a vacancy in the district courts (and, to a lesser extent, the U.S. courts of

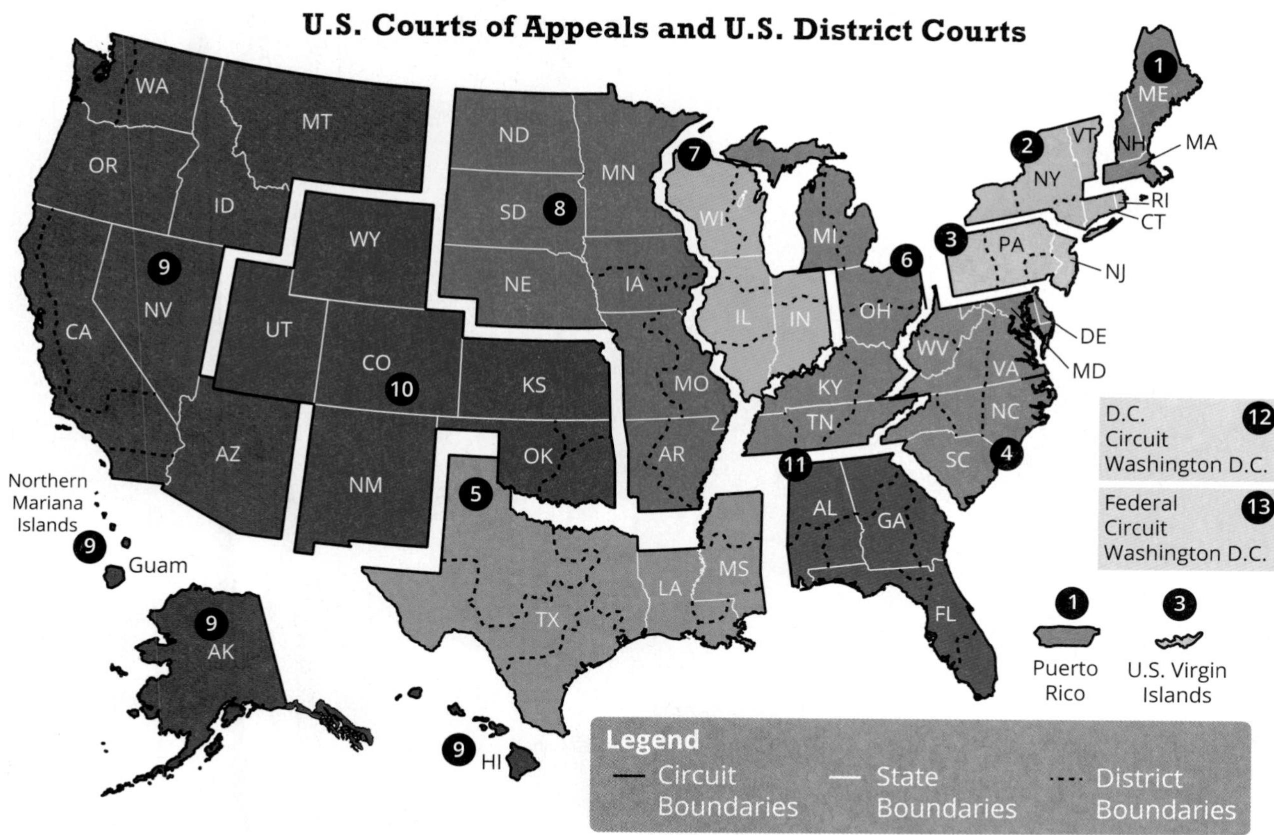

appeals), a senator of the president's political party from the state where the district court is located has traditionally been given **senatorial courtesy**, which means the senator is allowed to veto the president's choice. At times, senatorial courtesy has even been extended to senators from the opposing party. In 2018, however, Republicans in the Senate dispensed with many traditions in the nominating process, including that of senatorial courtesy. The result was a flurry of confirmations of conservative judges appointed by the Trump administration, because Republicans controlled the Senate.

ORGANIZATION *of the* FEDERAL COURT SYSTEM

SUPREME COURT

12 Courts of Appeals

Court of Appeals for the Federal Circuit

Independent Regulatory Agencies

94 District Courts

Specialized Courts (Court of Federal Claims, Court of International Trade, and Court of Appeals for Veterans' Claims)

It should come as no surprise that partisanship plays a significant role in the selection of nominees to the federal bench. In recent history, the minority party in the Senate has tried to block the president's judicial appointments through use of the filibuster. In the 1990s, Republicans filibustered many of President Clinton's nominees, and in the early 2000s, the Democrats responded by filibustering many of President George W. Bush's nominees. In 2013, frustrated by Republican efforts to derail

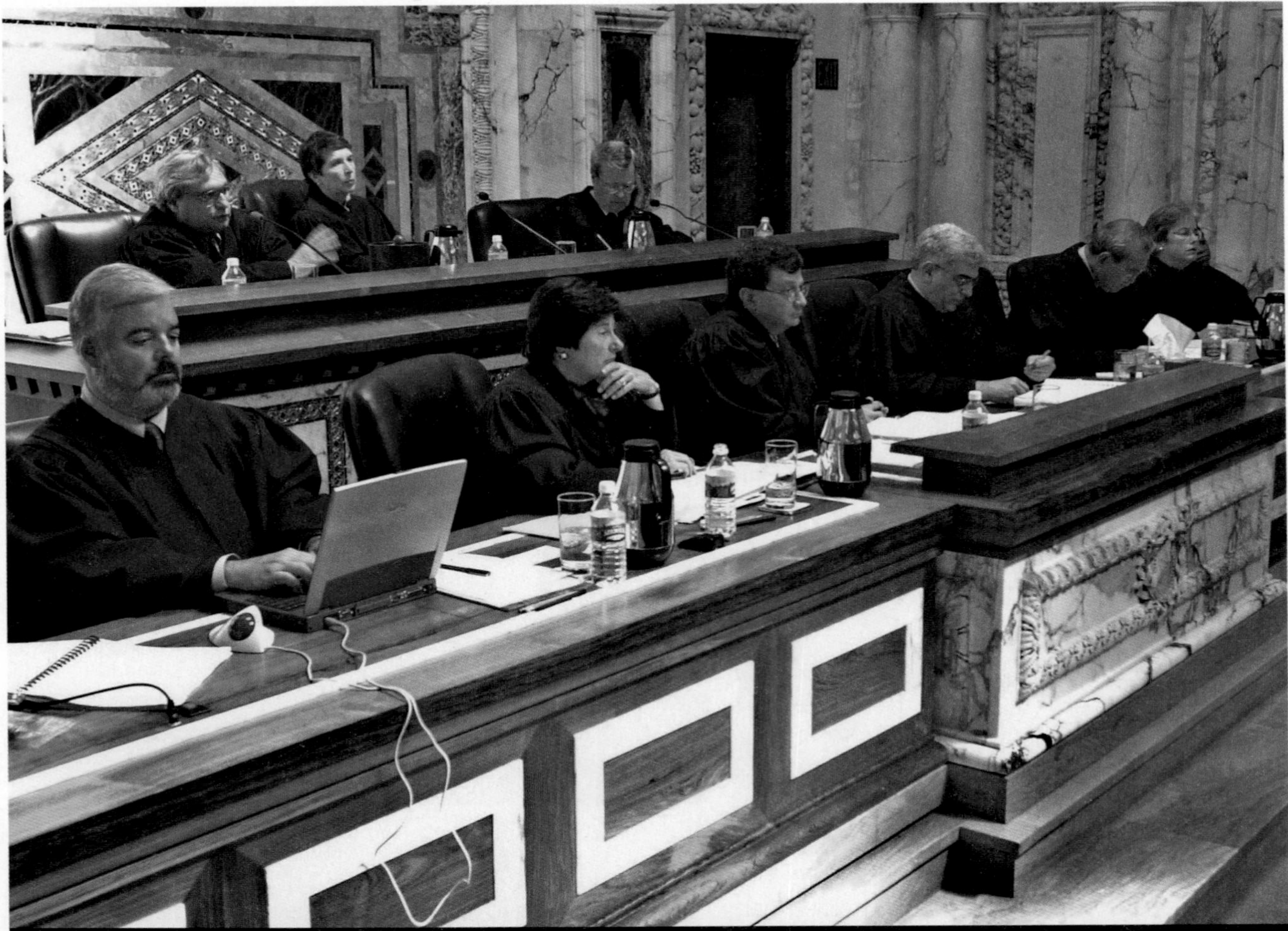

Judges of the 9th U.S. Circuit Court of Appeals listen to oral arguments in San Francisco, California, in 2003. Future U.S. Supreme Court Justice Elena Kagan sits second from left in the front. U.S. courts of appeals review the procedures and decisions of trial courts in order to ensure that laws were applied correctly and that the decisions made were fair.

President Obama's judicial appointments, Senate Democrats eliminated the filibuster for all nominees except those to the Supreme Court.

Thus when Republicans took control of both the White House and the Senate in 2017, Democrats had no way to influence, let alone block or delay, nominations to the federal bench. By May 2020, President Trump had appointed nearly 28 percent of all judges on federal courts of appeals, far more than his recent predecessors had by the same point in their administrations. In addition, the average age of Trump's appointees was younger than that of his five predecessors' nominees.

One reason that this is notable, and that nomination fights have grown so heated, is because once confirmed, federal judges "hold their offices during good behavior," according to Article III. In other words, these are lifetime appointments so long as a judge does nothing unethical or illegal.

HISTORICAL THINKING

4. **DRAW CONCLUSIONS** Why might the U.S. courts of appeals decline to review witness testimony and evidence?
5. **ANALYZE CAUSE AND EFFECT** The U.S. Constitution doesn't require federal judges to meet certain qualifications. How does the nomination and confirmation process ensure that trained, qualified judges serve on federal courts?

LESSON
12.3 Other Trial Courts

In addition to the three levels of federal courts discussed in the previous lesson, there are other federal courts that lie outside the tiered structure of the federal judiciary. They can be divided into two types. Article III courts, in the words of that section of the Constitution, exercise the "judicial power of the United States." The second type, Article I courts, are those created under the provision of that section of the Constitution. These are courts with jurisdiction confined to a narrowly defined set of concerns, such as military law, disputes in the U.S. territories, and taxes. What these courts have in common is that all have been created by Congress to rule on particular areas of law.

Courts with Certain Jurisdictions

Article III of the Constitution establishes the Supreme Court and empowers Congress to create "such inferior courts" as it thinks necessary for the exercise of the "judicial power of the United States." Using this power, Congress has created the federal courts of appeals and the district courts. From time to time, it has also created courts to rule on certain types of cases. For example, the Special Railroad Court was established to hear cases dealing with the reorganization and consolidation of financially struggling railroad companies in the 1970s. It was eliminated when it was no longer needed. Judges in Article III courts are nominated by the president, are confirmed by the Senate, and have lifetime appointments. Currently, there are two Article III courts with carefully defined areas of jurisdiction—the Court of International Trade and the Foreign Intelligence Surveillance Court.

THE COURT OF INTERNATIONAL TRADE This court has nationwide jurisdiction over disputes arising from U.S. customs and international trade laws. The current court was established by the Customs Courts Act of 1980. The court is made up of nine judges appointed for life by the president and confirmed by the Senate. Most

A Chinese cargo ship docks at the Port of Long Beach in California. The U.S. Court of International Trade handles civil actions involving trade with foreign countries, including China. The court was established under Article III of the Constitution.

court sessions are overseen by a single judge. Decisions may be appealed to the U.S. Court of Appeals.

The Court of International Trade hears cases involving private parties and federal agencies. Lawsuits arising from any type of trade dispute can be brought before the court. Those coming before the court may include both foreign and domestic manufacturers, individuals, trade associations, labor unions, and consumer groups. The court hears cases involving disputes over decisions made by the U.S. International Trade Commission and the Department of Commerce's International Trade Administration. It may, for example, deal with questions of duties, or taxes, charged on imported goods, or with charges of unfair competition from foreign companies.

CRITICAL VIEWING The USA Patriot Act of 2001 gave the National Security Agency (NSA) the ability to collect intelligence on a wide range of subjects and targets. How does the cartoonist view the NSA's role in providing security to the American people?

FOREIGN INTELLIGENCE SURVEILLANCE COURT
The Foreign Intelligence Surveillance Court (FISC) was initially created by Congress in 1978 through the Foreign Intelligence Surveillance Act (FISA) and has recently received exceptional scrutiny. FISA was passed in response to a report by a Senate committee that the executive branch was overstepping its authority to conduct intelligence-gathering operations in the United States for national security purposes.

FISA requires intelligence agencies to obtain a warrant from the FISC in order to conduct electronic surveillance, searches of property, and other types of investigations for foreign intelligence purposes. The warrant is similar to that required for domestic criminal investigations. When FISA was first passed, it required agencies to prove that they were targeting a foreign power or its agents in their surveillance or searches. In addition, they were limited in the kinds of information they could collect. The USA Patriot Act of 2001, passed in response to the September 11, 2001, terrorist attacks on the United States, removed some of these restrictions. That law made it possible for agencies to gather many kinds of information, and on other types of targets, as long as a foreign target was included in the search. The FISC almost never rejects a warrant request. It meets in secret and releases no information on individual cases.

In 2013, revelations of large-scale surveillance by the National Security Agency (NSA) raised questions about the FISC's practices. (The NSA's actions must be approved by the FISC.) Some legal experts doubted that the FISC's decisions could be squared with the Fourth Amendment to the U.S. Constitution, which bars unreasonable searches. The USA Freedom Act of 2015 tightened some rules governing the FISC's authority. The law reduced the government's ability to collect vast stores of phone records to search for intelligence. For example, the court can no longer authorize collection of all phone data within an entire area code. Instead, searches are limited to phone numbers in direct contact with a suspect.

HISTORICAL THINKING

1. **IDENTIFY** If a U.S. company's products were being pirated and sold on the internet by a firm based in another country, what court might it approach for relief?
2. **ANALYZE CAUSE AND EFFECT** Why do you think the September 11, 2001, attacks resulted in fewer restrictions on agencies conducting international surveillance?

Specialized Courts

Under Article I of the Constitution, Congress has the power to create "tribunals inferior to the Supreme Court." Congress has used this power to create courts with jurisdiction over specialized subject matter. Article I judges are nominated by the president and, with the exception of the territorial courts, require approval by the Senate. Unlike Article III judges, however, Article I judges don't have lifetime appointments, serving terms of 10 to 15 years, depending on the court.

THE COURT OF FEDERAL CLAIMS This court was created in 1982 to handle cases in which private parties sue the federal government over alleged damages they suffered as a result of laws of the United States. Many of these are complex issues involving tax laws. Others have to do with environmental and natural resource statutes, contracts with the federal government for construction and supplies, and payment for property the government has taken. The court usually has exclusive jurisdiction over these types of claims when the suit is for more than $10,000. It has concurrent jurisdiction with U.S. district courts in cases that involve less than this amount. There are 16 judges, who serve terms of 15 years.

DISTRICT COURTS FOR U.S. TERRITORIES The United States currently holds three territories: Guam, the Northern Mariana Islands, and the Virgin Islands. Congress has created courts for these territories that function like district and local courts in the United States. The district court in the Virgin Islands is part of the Third Judicial District, and the courts in Guam and the Northern Mariana Islands are part of the Ninth Judicial District. Judges in these courts are appointed by the president and serve 10-year terms. Puerto Rico, a self-governing commonwealth within the U.S. federal system, was originally set up with a territorial court, but this changed in 1966. Puerto Rico now has a U.S. District Court and judges with lifetime appointments.

TAX DISPUTES The United States Tax Court was established in 1969 to oversee disputes over taxes and tax laws. Cases may involve income, estate, and gift taxes, as well as underpayment of taxes. The court operates independently of the Internal Revenue Service (IRS). If a taxpayer is deemed by the IRS to have underpaid taxes, a complaint can be lodged with the tax court. A single judge hears the case and renders a decision. Case decisions can be appealed to the U.S. Court of Appeals. In cases involving taxes of less than $50,000, a taxpayer can request that the case be handled following a small tax case procedure. These decisions are more streamlined, but the cases can't be appealed.

HISTORICAL THINKING

3. **CATEGORIZE** A small manufacturer feels she has been financially hurt by a federal law requiring her to comply with what she believes are expensive and unnecessary regulations to control pollution. To which of the specialized courts could she appeal? Explain.
4. **DRAW CONCLUSIONS** Why is it important to have a tax court that operates independently from the IRS?

Military Courts

Along with the power to create courts, Article I of the Constitution gives Congress the authority "to make rules for the government and regulation of the land and naval forces." Acting on this power, Congress created **courts-martial**, or military courts that enforce military discipline and rule on accusations against service members. In 1950, Congress modified the military justice system under the Uniform Code of Military Justice. This new code standardized military justice, defining its crimes, procedures, and penalties.

Military courts are a component of the command structure of the military and, as such, don't operate in the same way as civilian courts or provide the same safeguards to defendants. So, for example, when a service member is thought to have committed a crime, the matter is first reviewed by the commanding officer. This officer may decide whether or not to have the service member charged and face a court-martial.

There are different kinds of courts-martial, but in general, they are supervised by a commissioned military officer who serves as judge. A lawyer usually represents the accused, and a prosecuting attorney presents the case. Sometimes there is a panel, or jury, made up of at least three service members. The panel decides guilt or innocence. If there is no panel, the presiding officer makes that decision. Penalties for conviction in a court-martial can include imprisonment, dishonorable discharge, reduction in rank, and fines.

COURT OF MILITARY APPEALS One important result of the Uniform Code of Military Justice was the creation of the Court of Military Appeals. This court provides an avenue for those convicted in courts-martial to appeal

U.S. Army Staff Sergeant Robert Bales (shown seated at the right in this courtroom illustration) was tried by court-martial after he was accused of murdering 16 civilians in two villages in Kandahar Province in Afghanistan in March 2012. Bales pleaded guilty and was sentenced to life in prison without parole. He later appealed his sentence to the U.S. Army Court of Criminal Appeals, but his appeal was denied.

their sentences. As such, the Court of Military Appeals parallels the U.S. court of appeals.

The Court of Military Appeals is set up with three judges. These are civilians rather than members of the military and are appointed by the president and confirmed by the Senate. They serve 15-year terms. Rulings by the military appeals court can be further appealed to the U.S. Supreme Court.

COURT OF APPEALS FOR VETERANS CLAIMS The Court of Appeals for Veterans Claims hears appeals of decisions made by the Board of Veterans Appeals. If a military veteran makes a claim for benefits and is turned down by the Department of Veterans Affairs, he or she can appeal the decision to the Board of Veterans Appeals.

MILITARY COMMISSIONS Military commissions have been created from time to time in areas where U.S. armed forces have established military government or martial law. The most recent commissions were formed by President George W. Bush following the September 11, 2001, terrorist attacks on the United States. Bush issued a military order creating military commissions to try cases concerning non-U.S. citizens who were considered terrorists.

Hundreds of the suspected terrorists were housed at the U.S. detention camp at Guantanamo Bay, Cuba. When President Barack Obama took office, he attempted to close Guantanamo, as the camp is known. His effort was blocked by Congress, but the number of people imprisoned there fell from 242 to 55 by the time he left office. In December 2019, President Donald Trump signed a bill that promised to keep the detention camp open indefinitely by barring the use of funds for any attempt to close it.

HISTORICAL THINKING

5. **IDENTIFY PROBLEMS AND SOLUTIONS** Why is it important for the military to maintain its own system of courts with their own procedures separate from civilian courts?

6. **EVALUATE** The Court of Military Appeals has civilian judges. Is it appropriate to ask civilian judges to hear appeals from courts-martial that have been decided by military officers?

Operators in a London, England, control room monitor images from 180 surveillance cameras. The city has about 420,000 closed-circuit surveillance cameras, or roughly one for every 48 people. All told, the United Kingdom has more surveillance cameras per capita than any country except China.

They Are Watching You—and Everything Else on the Planet

by Robert Draper *National Geographic* **Magazine, February 2018**

The Federal Intelligence Surveillance Court (FISC) was created to deal with matters of foreign intelligence, but electronic surveillance is a growing issue in the lives of ordinary people, not just foreign agents. In this article, Robert Draper looks at the debate over the loss of privacy that has resulted from this surveillance.

Draper explains that cameras are everywhere and are constantly recording people's lives. In addition, social media accounts, the internet, and location services on smartphones open windows into our lives that we may not even be aware of. Draper points out that the topic of surveillance has long been subject to debate. In 1949, George Orwell published the novel *1984*, which described a world in which cameras watched people constantly. "If you want a picture of the future . . . ," Orwell warned, "imagine a boot stamping on a human face—forever."

Draper says that Orwell's prediction of a world under surveillance has proved extraordinarily insightful:

> *We may well be photographed at unsettlingly close range perhaps dozens of times daily, from lenses we may never see, our image stored in databases for purposes we may never learn. Our smartphones, our Internet searches, and our social media accounts are giving away our secrets. Gus Hosein, the executive director of Privacy International, notes that "if the police wanted to know what was in your head in the 1800s, they would have to torture you. Now they can just find it out from your devices."*

Most people, Draper continues, recoil from the prospect of losing their privacy. Draper also suggests, however, that in some cases, a loss of privacy can be useful as well. For example, rangers in Kenya's Masai Mara National Reserve use thermal imaging to guard wildlife against poachers. Satellite cameras locate refugees in need of help in the deserts of Iraq. Police officers wear body cameras to limit abuses against and by law enforcement officers. The outcome of the debate, Draper suggests, is far from clear.

Access the full version of "They Are Watching You—and Everything Else on the Planet" by Robert Draper through the Resources Menu in MindTap.

THINK ABOUT IT The U.S. government uses aerial cameras to carry out bombings in Yemen, spot people crossing the border from Mexico, fight forest fires in California, and catch cattle thieves in North Dakota. Could or should limits be placed on these forms of surveillance? Explain your answer.

CHAPTER 12

THE AMERICAN COURT SYSTEM

Review

VOCABULARY

Complete each sentence below with one of the vocabulary words.

1. _______ is law that is written and enacted by a legislative body.
2. A _______ is a law that defines the duties that people in society owe to other people or to the government.
3. _______ describes wrongful actions that harm people or society and for which society demands punishment.
4. When someone files an official complaint in court about a business, the person who filed the complaint has brought a _______ against the business.
5. A _______ is not as serious as a felony, but it can still be punished by a fine or a short stay in a county jail.
6. When someone in court shows disrespect for a judge or disobeys the judge, that person may be held in _______.
7. When an accused person appears in a court in which evidence and the testimony of witnesses are presented, the accused is probably appearing in a _______.
8. _______ are military courts where service members who disobey superior officers or commit crimes will be forced to appear.

MAIN IDEAS

Answer the following questions. Support your answers with evidence from the chapter.

9. Why is English common law so important to the American legal system? **LESSON 12.1**
10. What is the hierarchy, or order, of laws that a court uses when deciding among conflicting laws? **LESSON 12.1**
11. What is original jurisdiction, and how is it different from appellate jurisdiction? **LESSON 12.1**
12. What are three conditions that must exist before a particular court can hear and decide a civil case? **LESSON 12.1**
13. What is the difference between a grand jury and a trial jury? **LESSON 12.1**
14. How do the proceedings of judicial review of the U.S. courts of appeals differ from those of a U.S. district court to determine the guilt or innocence of someone accused in a criminal trial? **LESSON 12.2**
15. How is the Court of Appeals for the Federal Circuit—the 13th court of appeals—different from the other 12 courts of appeals? **LESSON 12.2**
16. What is typically the process for making an appeal in a federal court of appeals? **LESSON 12.2**
17. What is the role of the Foreign Intelligence Surveillance Court? **LESSON 12.3**
18. How are specialized Article I courts different from the other federal courts? **LESSON 12.3**

HISTORICAL THINKING

Answer the following questions. Support your answer with evidence from the chapter.

19. **ANALYZE CAUSE AND EFFECT** How does the doctrine of *stare decisis* influence American law today?
20. **FORM AND SUPPORT OPINIONS** The American legal system is built upon precedent. What should judges consider before making a ruling that departs from precedent? Explain.
21. **COMPARE AND CONTRAST** What role do defense attorneys typically play when they take cases to the court of appeals?
22. **EVALUATE** The Foreign Intelligence Surveillance Court meets in secret and almost never rejects a warrant request. It also never releases information about requests, so the court's actions cannot be reviewed by the public. Do you think this secrecy serves the interests of the public? Explain your answer.

INTERPRET VISUALS

Study the graph. Then answer the questions.

23. During which decades did the growth in criminal cases outpace the growth in civil cases?

24. How would you summarize the historic trends in cases involving criminal cases and civil cases in the trial courts?

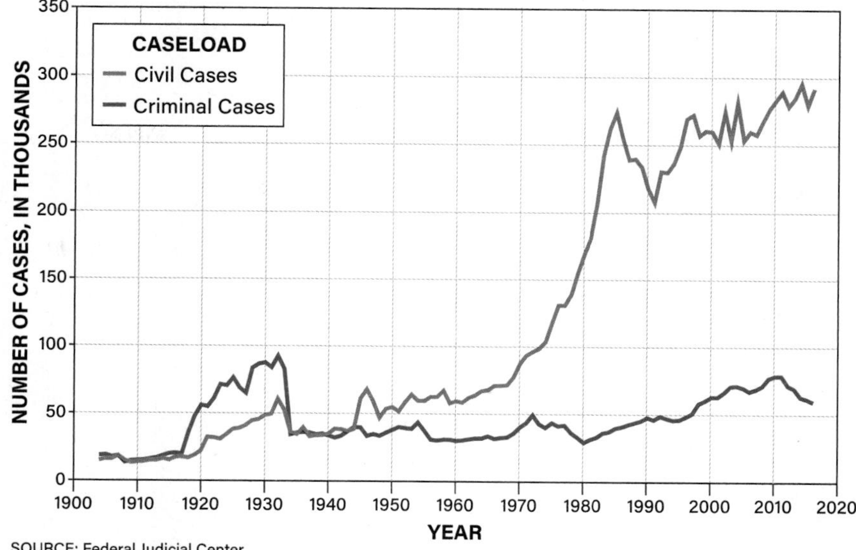

ANALYZE SOURCES

Read the following excerpt from an interview with Associate Justice Sonia Sotomayor of the Supreme Court. Then answer the question that follows.

> I'm a common law judge. I believe in deciding every case on its facts, not on a legal philosophy. And I believe in deciding each case in the most limited way possible, because common law judges have a firm belief that the best development of the law is the one that lets society show you the next step, and that next step is in the new facts that each case presents.
>
> —Sonia Sotomayor, Associate Justice, U.S. Supreme Court

25. Based on this excerpt, what does Sotomayor believe about precedent and common law?

CONNECT TO YOUR LIFE

26. **ARGUMENT** How much weight should judges give to precedents in applying the law? In cases like *Citizens United* v. *FEC*, the justices broke with precedent and made new law. Think about this precedent-breaking case, or choose another that you've studied. Consider how the decision might affect your life. Do you think the justices were correct in making this radical change in the law? Should they have followed precedent? Take a position and then write a short essay stating your position and giving valid reasons for your point of view. Cite evidence from the text.

TIPS

- Review the discussion of precedents in the chapter and especially the section on departures from precedent.
- Consider the implications for society resulting from the Supreme Court case cited.
- In your opening paragraph, explain why precedent is important and then state your point of view on the issue.
- In the rest of your essay, give reasons for your opinion. Also, be sure to address arguments someone who takes the opposite point of view would give, and tell why you disagree.

CHAPTER 13

The Supreme Court

LESSONS

13.1 Jurisdiction of the Supreme Court

13.2 Federal Judicial Appointments

13.3 The Courts as Policymakers

***National Geographic* Magazine:** The Many Colors of Matrimony

13.4 The Role of Federal Courts

CRITICAL VIEWING This photograph of the courtroom in the Supreme Court building does not have any people in it because the Supreme Court does not allow photography or video cameras during judicial proceedings. Numerous bills to allow video recording or broadcasting have been introduced in Congress, but none have become law. Some judges in the federal system argue that any law passed by Congress to allow cameras in the courtroom would violate the separation of powers. The public does have access to Supreme Court proceedings through audio recordings available on the Court's website. How might video recordings and broadcasts affect the Court?

LESSON
13.1 Jurisdiction of the Supreme Court

The U.S. Supreme Court is a rather exclusive institution. It is made up of a small number of justices who serve on the Court for life. The Court hears very few cases, especially compared with the other, lower federal courts. But as you will read in this chapter, those very few cases can have a great impact on Americans' everyday lives. Supreme Court decisions have affected the way Americans conduct business, changed the way police treat people they arrest, prohibited school prayer, upheld violations of civil rights in wartime, ended legal school segregation, legalized same-sex marriage, ruled that corporations have the same free-speech rights as individuals, and preserved expanded health-care coverage.

Overview of the Supreme Court

As you read in an earlier chapter, the federal court system is multitiered. The bottom layer (the U.S. district courts and the specialized trial courts) is the largest layer, and the middle layer (the U.S. Courts of Appeals) is somewhat smaller. The top layer is the U.S. Supreme Court, the one federal court whose creation the Constitution actually mandates. Congress is empowered to create additional inferior, or lower-level, courts as it deems necessary, which is how the district, appeals, and specialized courts have come to be.

Compared with the lower tiers of the federal court system, which include nearly 900 judges, the Supreme Court is surprisingly small. It has only nine justices: eight associate justices and one Chief Justice. The Chief Justice shares the same powers as the other eight justices but also presides over the Court during public sessions and when the justices hold private conferences on cases. The Chief Justice also traditionally administers the oath of office during presidential inaugurations. Like the associate justices, the Chief Justice is nominated by the president and confirmed by the Senate. A Chief Justice doesn't need to have first served as an associate justice, although 5 of the 17 U.S. Chief Justices have done so.

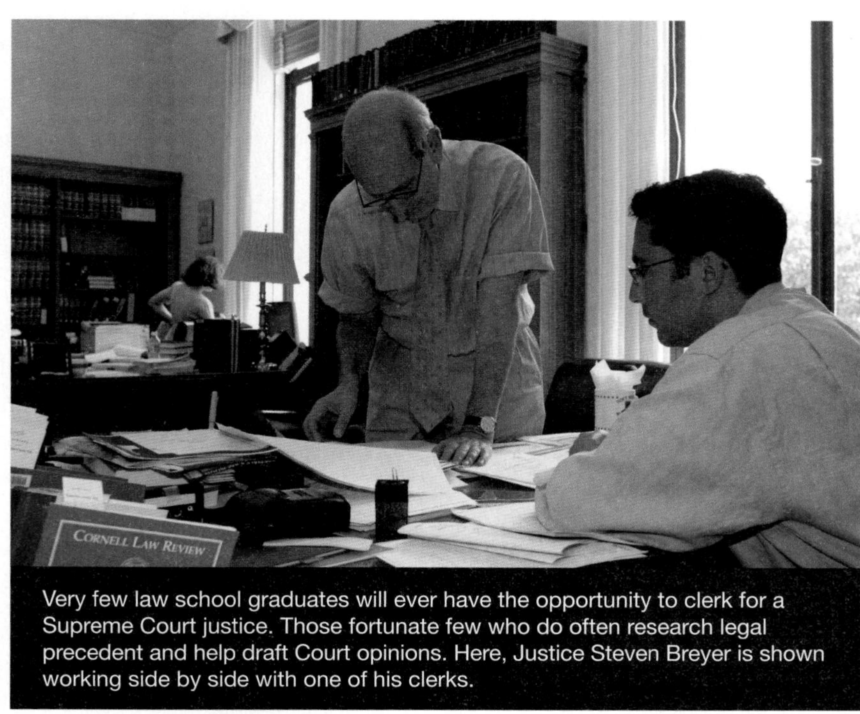

Very few law school graduates will ever have the opportunity to clerk for a Supreme Court justice. Those fortunate few who do often research legal precedent and help draft Court opinions. Here, Justice Steven Breyer is shown working side by side with one of his clerks.

The Supreme Court has original jurisdiction, or trial jurisdiction, only in certain circumstances that were initially set forth in Article III, Section 2—namely, lawsuits involving two or more states, or cases concerning ambassadors and certain other federal officials. In other words, only rarely does a case originate at the Supreme Court level. The vast majority of the Court's work is as an appellate court. The Supreme Court has appellate authority over cases

Supreme Court Opinions, 1955 to 2020

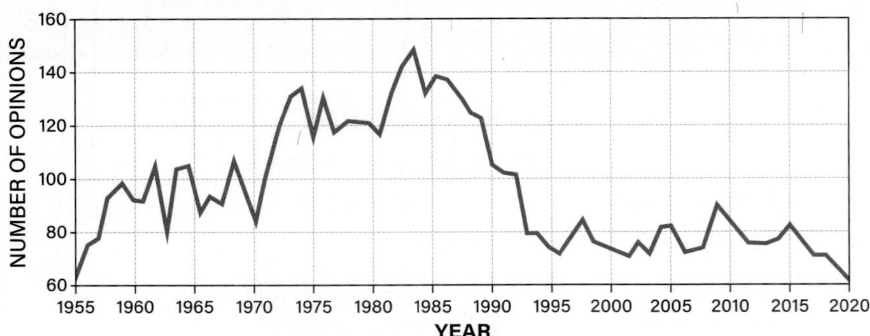

already decided by the U.S. courts of appeals, as well as over some cases decided in the state courts but involving federal questions.

As you might imagine, a great many people want to appeal decisions to the highest court in the land. To do this, a party in a case officially requests that the Court issue a writ of *certorari* or cert (from a Latin word that means "to be informed or made more certain"). When the Supreme Court issues a writ, it requests the record of a case from the lower court that has already decided the case. This order must be approved by at least four of the nine justices.

Any party may petition the Supreme Court to issue a writ of *certiorari*, yet the decision to do so is entirely up to the Court—there is no constitutionally mandated instance in which the Court must issue a writ. In fact, most petitions for writs of *certiorari* are denied. It is important to remember that such a denial isn't a decision on the merits of a case, nor does it indicate that the Court agrees with a lower court's opinion. The denial of a writ has absolutely no value as a legal precedent. It simply means that the decision of the lower court remains the law within that court's jurisdiction.

HISTORICAL THINKING

1. **IDENTIFY MAIN IDEAS AND DETAILS** What cases fall under the original jurisdiction of the Supreme Court?
2. **DRAW CONCLUSIONS** What happens if the Supreme Court denies a petition for a writ of *certiorari*?

Which Cases Reach the Supreme Court?

Thousands of cases are filed with the Supreme Court each year. On average, however, the Court hears fewer than 100. The Court heard only 72 cases in the 2018–2019 term. As shown in the graph, the number of cases heard by the Court each year has declined significantly since the 1980s. For the most part, this is because the Court has raised its standards for accepting cases. Typically, the Court now hears cases that raise important policy issues that need to be addressed. In the 21st century, this has included thorny social and legislative constitutional questions, including the First Amendment protections given to video games and the constitutionality of requirements under the Affordable Care Act (or Obamacare), which you read about previously.

Below are examples of cases the Court decided from 2016 to 2020:

- **Issue:** Can a state remove individuals from its voter registration lists if they don't vote or respond to voter notifications after four years? **Decision:** The Court said yes, under existing voter change-of-residence legislation passed by Congress, in *Husted* v. *A. Philip Randolph Institute*, 2018.
- **Issue:** Can a public school prevent a girl with severe cerebral palsy from bringing her service dog to school? **Decision:** The Court determined that the school's refusal violated federal law and could result in a denial of federal funds in *Fry* v. *Napoleon Community Schools*, 2017.
- **Issue:** Can Muslim residents (who are not citizens of the United States) who were subjected to illegal detainment by federal officials in the months following the September 11, 2001, terrorist attacks sue those officials for monetary damages? **Decision:** The Court found that no law existed that would allow such a penalty in *Ziglar* v. *Abbasi*, 2017.
- **Issue:** Can police without a warrant use historical data from cell-phone towers to track a person's past movements and locations?

Decision: The Court held that a warrant is necessary, except perhaps in times of national or international crises in *Carpenter* v. *United States*, 2018.

- **Issue:** Can a state prosecute a member of a tribal nation for a crime committed on land that is historically considered tribal land, even if it is not formally called a reservation? **Decision:** The Court found that land put aside for Indian nations through treaties and federal statutes remains tribal land in *McGirt* v. *Oklahoma*, 2020. As such, state and local governments do not have jurisdiction to prosecute.

If the lower courts have rendered conflicting opinions on an important issue, the Supreme Court often reviews one or more cases involving that issue to define the law on the matter. For example, in 2014, four different appellate courts ruled that same-sex couples had a constitutional right to marry. The Sixth Circuit Court, however, issued an opinion that denied that right. These conflicting judgments forced a somewhat reluctant Supreme Court to take up the issue. The result was the landmark case *Obergefell* v. *Hodges* (2015), which established a nationwide right to same-sex marriage via the 14th Amendment.

HISTORICAL THINKING

3. **ANALYZE CAUSE AND EFFECT** How do you think the decline in the number of cases the Court hears each year affects the public's awareness of Court decisions?
4. **SYNTHESIZE** Why do you think Supreme Court justices were reluctant to hear a case involving same-sex marriage?
5. **INTERPRET GRAPHS** Describe how the number of opinions issued by the Supreme Court has changed over the past 60 years.

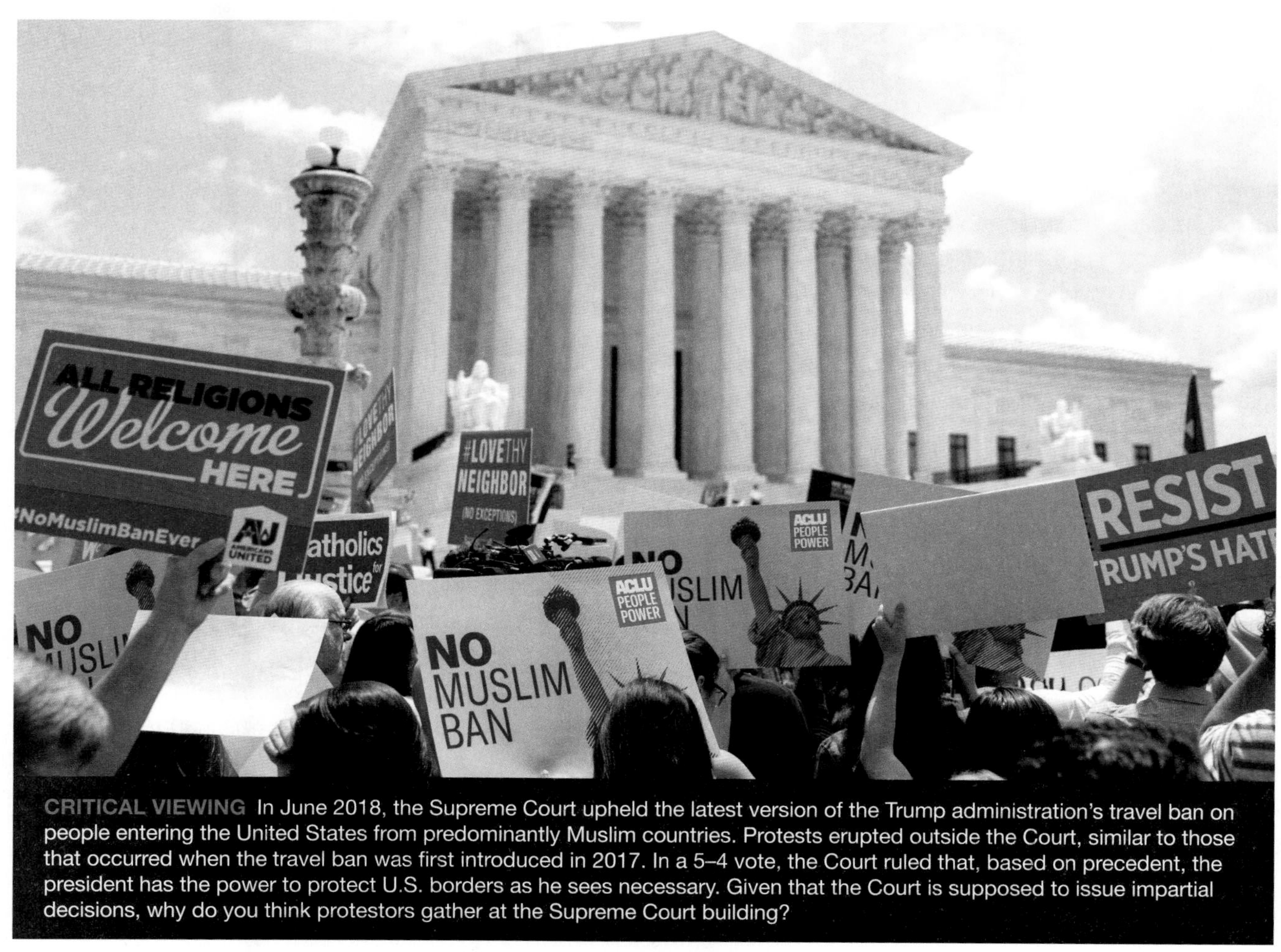

CRITICAL VIEWING In June 2018, the Supreme Court upheld the latest version of the Trump administration's travel ban on people entering the United States from predominantly Muslim countries. Protests erupted outside the Court, similar to those that occurred when the travel ban was first introduced in 2017. In a 5–4 vote, the Court ruled that, based on precedent, the president has the power to protect U.S. borders as he sees necessary. Given that the Court is supposed to issue impartial decisions, why do you think protestors gather at the Supreme Court building?

Supreme Court Opinions

As you learned earlier, appellate courts don't usually hear evidence—that is the job of the lower trial courts. The Supreme Court works no differently, except in rare original jurisdiction cases in which the Court orders the collection of evidence. In general, the Court's decision in a particular case is based on the written record of the case forwarded from the lower courts and the **written arguments**, or legal summaries, that the attorneys submit. In addition to the written arguments, the attorneys present 30-minute **oral arguments**—arguments presented in person rather than on paper—to the Court, which hears an average of two oral arguments, three days a week, two weeks a month, between October and April. Oral arguments often consist mainly of answering questions that have come up during the justices' review of written arguments. Some people believe oral arguments should be recorded and televised. The Court doesn't agree, however, and cameras are banned from the courtroom.

After hearing all the information from each party, the justices consider a case individually or with their legal clerks, and then in conference, usually during the same week as the case was argued. The conference is strictly private—only the justices are allowed in the room. Each justice is allowed a chance to speak about the case, according to seniority—the length of time he or she has served on the Court—and then a vote is taken, also in order of seniority. When the Court reaches a decision, the chief justice, if part of the majority, either writes the opinion or assigns the task of writing it to one of the associate justices. An opinion that commands the support of more than half the justices is called a majority opinion. When the Chief Justice isn't in the majority, the most senior justice voting with the majority assigns the writing of the Court's opinion. The opinion outlines the reasons for the Court's decision, the rules of law that apply, and the judgment.

HISTORICAL THINKING

6. **DRAW CONCLUSIONS** What does the fact that the Court rarely hears evidence tell you about its role in the federal judiciary?

Although dissenting opinions don't affect the outcome of the case in which they are issued, they can influence the deliberation of later, related cases. In *Olmstead* v. *United States* (1928), Justice Louis D. Brandeis, shown here, famously dissented against a 5–4 majority opinion that allowed for federal wiretapping without judicial approval. Brandeis's dissent, which described a "right to be let alone," would influence the overturning of *Olmstead* by *Katz* v. *United States* in 1967.

Concurring and Dissenting Opinions

Many times, one or more justices included in a majority opinion agree with the Court's decision for reasons other than those that are outlined within the majority opinion. These justices might choose to write what are called concurring opinions, an explanation of their own legal reasoning on the issue. The justices who don't vote with the majority opinion also often write their own opinions, called dissenting opinions—explanations of why they believe the majority was incorrect in its decision.

Although they don't affect the outcome of the case at hand, dissenting opinions can have a great impact on future cases. In later cases concerning the same legal question or a version of it, a judge or an attorney may use the reasoning in the dissenting opinion as the basis for an argument to reverse the previous decision and establish a new precedent. Dissenting opinions can also resurface in later cases with different versions of the same issue. For example, Associate Justice John Marshall Harlan's lone dissenting opinion in *Plessy* v. *Ferguson* figured into the opinion of the landmark civil rights case *Brown* v. *Board of Education*.

There is yet another category of opinion as well: the plurality opinion, or an opinion with the support of the largest number of justices that still doesn't command a majority of the Court. A plurality opinion can only become the Court's opinion if it is supported by enough concurring opinions to form a majority. Likewise, a plurality opinion can become a dissent if enough alternative opinions are in agreement. This is a rare circumstance, however.

Another unusual but still plausible scenario is a tie vote—a possibility if a seat on the Court is vacant or if a justice recuses (excuses) him- or herself for a possible conflict of interest. In the case of a tie vote, the earlier decision of the lower court stands.

HISTORICAL THINKING

7. **COMPARE AND CONTRAST** What is the difference between a concurring opinion and a dissenting opinion?
8. **MAKE INFERENCES** Consider the number of justices on the Supreme Court. Why do you think vacancies are such a concern when the Court is in session?

LESSON 13.2 Federal Judicial Appointments

When deciding which candidate to vote for in a presidential election, many Americans consider how the federal courts might be affected by their vote. One of the most important powers of the president is to appoint federal judges to office. Over the past few decades, the country has become more divided along party lines, and thus the judicial appointment process has also become more controversial and partisan. Appointees to most federal courts serve for life, so changes to the composition of the court can have a long-term legal impact that extends far beyond a president's term in office.

Nominating Candidates to the Court

As you read in an earlier chapter, federal judges, including Supreme Court justices, are appointed by the president and serve for life. Of course, the impeachment clause of the Constitution also applies to federal judges, so a lifetime appointment isn't an ironclad promise to judges who behave badly. But impeachment of a judge is extremely rare and has only been undertaken if the judge in question engaged in blatantly illegal conduct, such as bribery. Since the federal court system was established, only 15 federal judges have been impeached. Of those 15 judges, 8 were found guilty by the Senate and removed from office. Only one of the judges who has been impeached by the House was a Supreme Court justice, Samuel Chase—and he was acquitted by the Senate.

CHOOSING A SUPREME COURT CANDIDATE

A good deal of effort goes into the selection of a presidential nominee to the Supreme Court, not the least of which is ensuring that a nominee is the right kind of person for the Court. A number of factors figure into who is selected, ranging from the person's professional record to his or her personal qualities. Although the Constitution sets no specific qualifications for those who serve on the Court, all

CRITICAL VIEWING During his two terms, President Barack Obama nominated three justices: Sonia Sotomayor (pictured here with Obama), Elena Kagan, and Merrick B. Garland. While Garland's nomination never came to a confirmation vote in the Senate, Sotomayor and Kagan were confirmed in 2009 and 2010, respectively. What do the expressions on the faces of the other justices in the room tell you about their attitude toward the addition of a new justice?

of those who have done so have been trained in the law. (Many early justices did not actually attend law school, however. These justices were often self-taught with little formal training in the law.) Other characteristics these justices have held in common reflect the country's history more than they do the qualifications a justice needs to be effective: Of the 114 Supreme Court justices who have served or currently serve on the Court, 84 have been Protestant, 110 have been male, and 111 have been White and non-Hispanic.

Several recent presidents have made efforts to diversify the Court, in terms of gender, race, and ethnicity, to better reflect the demographics of the country. In 1981, President Ronald Reagan appointed the Court's first female justice, Sandra Day O'Connor, who served until her retirement in 2006. Since then, three more women have sat on the Court: Ruth Bader Ginsburg (nominated by President Bill Clinton), Sonia Sotomayor (nominated by President Barack Obama), and Elena Kagan (also nominated by Obama).

Justice Sotomayor's nomination was historic for another reason as well: The daughter of native Puerto Ricans, she is the first Hispanic and the first Latina ever to sit on the Court. President Lyndon Johnson nominated Thurgood Marshall, the first African-American Supreme Court Justice, in 1961. Following Marshall's retirement in 1991, President George H.W. Bush nominated the second African-American Supreme Court justice, Clarence Thomas. These fairly recent appointments reflect some modern presidents' desire for a Court that better reflects the U.S. population as a whole. Nonetheless, all the justices now on the Court attended law school at exclusive Ivy League universities on the East Coast; eight of them graduated from either Harvard or Yale. Some critics argue that there are many excellent law schools around the country and that justices from a wider range of institutions would better reflect the American population as a whole.

One thing that has remained consistent about Supreme Court nominations is their partisanship. Despite the fact that the Framers intended for the judiciary to be the least partisan of the three branches, presidents generally appoint judges whose judicial history reflects the political or philosophical views of the president's own party. The Supreme Court is an enormously powerful part of the federal government, and its decisions can have far-reaching ramifications for American social, economic, and political policy.

Associate Justice Clarence Thomas
Nominated by George H.W. Bush in 1991

Associate Justice Stephen Breyer
Nominated by Bill Clinton in 1994

Chief Justice John Roberts, Jr.
Nominated by George W. Bush in 2005

Associate Justice Samuel Alito
Nominated by George W. Bush in 2006

Associate Justice Sonia Sotomayor
Nominated by Barack Obama in 2009

Associate Justice Elena Kagan
Nominated by Barack Obama in 2010

Associate Justice Neil Gorsuch
Nominated by Donald Trump in 2017

Associate Justice Brett Kavanaugh
Nominated by Donald Trump in 2018

Associate Justice Amy Coney Barrett
Nominated by Donald Trump in 2020

In the history of the Supreme Court, fewer than 13 percent of the justices nominated by a president have been affiliated with an opposing political party. Of course, party affiliation isn't a guarantee that judges will adhere to party doctrine. Presidents have sometimes been surprised when justices they appointed took very different positions than the presidents expected. President Dwight D. Eisenhower, for example, appointed Chief Justice Earl Warren, never anticipating that Warren would rule against the system of racial segregation in the United States.

HISTORICAL THINKING

1. **SYNTHESIZE** Supreme Court justices typically serve for a much longer time than the presidents who appoint them. How does the appointment of a justice affect a president's legacy?
2. **DRAW CONCLUSIONS** Knowing what you do about the Supreme Court, why do you think the Framers chose to make seats on the Court lifelong appointments?

Confirmation or Rejection by the Senate

As with other federal court nominees, the president submits a nominee for a Supreme Court seat to the Senate for approval. From 1893 until 1987, most nominations to the high court sailed through the Senate with little trouble; the Senate rejected only five Court nominees. Since 1987, however, the process of nominating and confirming federal judges, especially Supreme Court justices, has involved increased political debate and controversy, and confirmation is no longer a sure thing.

In 1987, two nominations by Republican president Ronald Reagan failed. The most significant of these nominees was Robert Bork, who faced hostile questioning about his strongly conservative views during the confirmation hearings in the Senate, which was controlled by the Democrats. One of President George H.W. Bush's nominees to the Supreme Court—Clarence Thomas—was also the subject of considerable controversy. In a televised hearing, Anita Hill, a former legal adviser to Thomas, leveled charges of sexual harassment by the nominee. Thomas was confirmed by the Senate in spite of the fact that it was controlled by Democrats.

The confirmation of Thomas in 1991 was the last time a Supreme Court nominee was approved by a Senate that wasn't controlled by the president's own party. Given the rising partisanship of the past two decades, it is likely that a president will have an extremely difficult time getting a Senate controlled by the opposing party to confirm a Supreme Court nominee. Even when the Senate is controlled by the president's own party, a nominee may face extreme opposition from the minority. To limit this possibility, in 2018, Senate Republicans employed the so-called nuclear option, which you read about earlier, to prevent Senate Democrats from filibustering a vote to confirm Supreme Court nominee Neil Gorsuch. Gorsuch had been nominated by Trump to fill the Court seat left empty by the death of Justice Antonin Scalia.

The months prior to the Gorsuch appointment were some of the most antagonistic months ever in Congress. Senate Republicans had blocked consideration of President Obama's nominee for Scalia's seat, Merrick Garland. The seat remained empty for a year, until President Trump took office and nominated Gorsuch.

While the confirmation of Gorsuch was otherwise uneventful, hearings for Brett Kavanaugh, President Trump's second nominee (to replace retiring Justice Anthony Kennedy) were extremely controversial. Several women who attended high school or college with Kavanaugh accused him of sexual assault when he was a student. The Senate extended the confirmation process to allow time for the FBI to conduct a second, brief investigation into the charges against Kavanaugh. Following that investigation, Kavanaugh was confirmed by a 50–48 vote, with only one Democrat voting to confirm.

HISTORICAL THINKING

3. **IDENTIFY MAIN IDEAS AND DETAILS** How have Supreme Court confirmation hearings changed over the past three decades?
4. **MAKE INFERENCES** Why might a confirmation for a federal appellate judge be less contentious than that of a Supreme Court nominee, even though both are life appointments?

Justice Ruth Bader Ginsburg, Advocate for Equality

Supreme Court Justice Ruth Bader Ginsburg, who died in September, 2020, brought the issue of gender equality to the forefront in her majority opinions as well as in her dissents. Ginsburg, the second woman to sit on the Court, was appointed by President Bill Clinton in 1993. Praised by some as "the Thurgood Marshall of women's rights," she built her argument for the recognition of equal treatment of women over many years of carefully chosen cases, sometimes arguing that men faced unfair discrimination to make her point that discrimination on the basis of sex, whether directed at men or women, violated the 14th Amendment. Her most famous majority opinion was in the 1996 case *United States* v. *Virginia*, in which she stated that Virginia's creation of a separate military academy for women did not meet the criteria for equal protection.

In the last years of her life, Ginsburg became a beloved figure in popular culture. First dubbed the Notorious R.B.G. (a riff on the name of well-known 1990s rapper Notorious B.I.G.) in 2013 by a New York University law student blogging about the justice's achievements, Ginsburg developed a following that expanded into mainstream culture. Her determination to maintain her strength with renowned gym sessions through the end of her life, and her use of different lace and beaded collars to symbolize her dissent or concurrence with a majority opinion, won admiration from both sides of the political aisle. Strikingly, the notably liberal Ginsburg shared her love of theater and opera with Justice Antonin Scalia, one of the Court's leading conservatives. The two were devoted friends though they rarely shared the same views on the legal cases.

Ginsburg's dissents were distinctive for their fire and passion, especially as the Court grew more conservative in the final two decades of her service. She was the subject of a book using her Notorious nickname, a widely released documentary, a Hollywood biopic, and numerous *Saturday Night Live* skits. Her likeness and nickname were found on everything from T-shirts to Halloween costumes, as well as many internet memes, most of which highlighted her toughness and dedication to her principles and causes.

Following her death, Ginsburg became the first woman and the first Jewish American to lie in state with her coffin on view in Statuary Hall in the Capitol of the United States.

LESSON 13.3 The Courts as Policymakers

If you were asked to describe the purpose of the federal courts, you might say they apply the law in court cases, or that they ensure that the principles of justice are applied equally to all Americans. You might not mention policymaking, however. Many Americans forget this role of the Court, but when a landmark case comes along, the Supreme Court's decision can have a strong impact on lawmaking. This ability of the Court to affect legislation tends to draw quite a bit of attention when it involves an issue that affects many Americans, or about which many people feel strongly. Often, these types of decisions prompt people to take another look at just how the justices arrive at their conclusions.

The Issue of Broad Language

It falls to the federal courts to interpret the constitutionality of the laws and actions of the other two branches of government. Often, this is a difficult, multilayered task that makes people on one side of a court decision unhappy. Because the law doesn't always provide clear answers to the many questions that come before the courts, the courts must sometimes wade into areas where their interpretations have the effect of lawmaking. For instance, when the Constitution addresses an issue only in broad terms (or not at all), the courts must apply interpretations of constitutional provisions to a specific set of circumstances.

There are plenty of examples of the Supreme Court taking the role of policymaker. Privacy rights are a good example. As you read in an earlier chapter, nothing in the Constitution or its amendments guarantees Americans a right to privacy. Yet a series of Supreme Court rulings have established a right of personal privacy by declaring that certain constitutional amendments implicitly guarantee a right to privacy. The Court has even held that the right to privacy encompasses other actions and rights, such as the right to have an abortion.

The Constitution isn't the only document or law that sometimes requires interpretation by the courts. Legislation, statutory provisions, and other legally binding rules tend to be expressed in very general terms, and the federal courts must decide how this unspecific wording applies to specific cases. For example, the Americans with Disabilities Act of 1990 mandates that employers reasonably accommodate the needs of employees with disabilities. But the legislation doesn't detail what these accommodations must be, or how far they should go. The courts have had to decide, on a case-by-case basis, what qualifies as reasonably accommodating—or not accommodating—a disabled person.

Another area lacking in constitutional or legislative precedent is modern communications technology.

CRITICAL VIEWING When a Supreme Court decision is interpreted by some Americans as "making law," controversy can erupt. In the 2013 case *Arizona* v. *Inter Tribal Council of Arizona*, the Court declared an Arizona law requiring voters to present proof of citizenship before registering to vote and before voting unconstitutional. In the 7–2 decision, the Court said the requirement would overstep the federal registration requirements of the National Voter Registration Act of 1993. What does this cartoon imply about the strength and reach of the Supreme Court?

Because the Framers and past legislators could never have anticipated the enormous changes in American society resulting from the internet and all its permutations (such as smartphones and data sharing), the Supreme Court has frequently found itself in the role of policymaker through its rulings on technology cases. This has been true of cases involving everything from the use of cell-phone location data by law enforcement agencies to how sales tax should be collected for online purchases.

HISTORICAL THINKING

1. **IDENTIFY MAIN IDEAS AND DETAILS** How does the broad language of the Constitution give the federal courts added responsibility?
2. **MAKE CONNECTIONS** How might Supreme Court decisions affect future legislation?

The Power of Judicial Review

As you have read, each branch of government has the ability to check the powers of the other two branches to ensure a balance of power. The courts' role as chief interpreter of the constitutionality of laws and actions of the other two branches serves as one of these. The power of judicial review, or the courts' power to interpret the constitutionality of the other two branches' actions, wasn't always assumed to be a responsibility of the courts, however.

There is no mention of judicial review in the Constitution. In fact, it was the Supreme Court itself that declared the existence of this power, slightly more than a decade into the Court's existence. As you read in an earlier chapter, in the 1803 case *Marbury* v. *Madison*, Chief Justice John Marshall held that a provision of a 1789 law affecting the Supreme Court's jurisdiction violated the Constitution and was thus void. In his written opinion, Marshall declared that "It is emphatically the province and duty of the judicial department [the courts] to say what the law is. . . . If two laws conflict with each other, the courts must decide on the operation of each. . . . [I]f a law be in opposition to the constitution . . . the court must determine which of these conflicting rules governs the case. This is the very essence of judicial duty." In other words, the Court has the ultimate authority to not only review a law against the Constitution but also to interpret its constitutionality, from issues ranging from the appropriateness of Congress's use of the power to regulate interstate commerce to the correct use of executive privilege.

Most constitutional scholars believe the Framers meant for the federal courts to have this power of judicial review, even if they didn't include that exact wording in the Constitution. For example, in Federalist No. 78, Alexander Hamilton stressed the importance of the complete independence of federal judges and their special duty to invalidate all acts contrary to the manifest tenor of the Constitution. Hamilton pointed out that if there is no judicial review by impartial courts, nothing will prevent the other branches of government from overstepping their own constitutional limits when exercising their powers, and all the reservations of particular rights or privileges would amount to nothing.

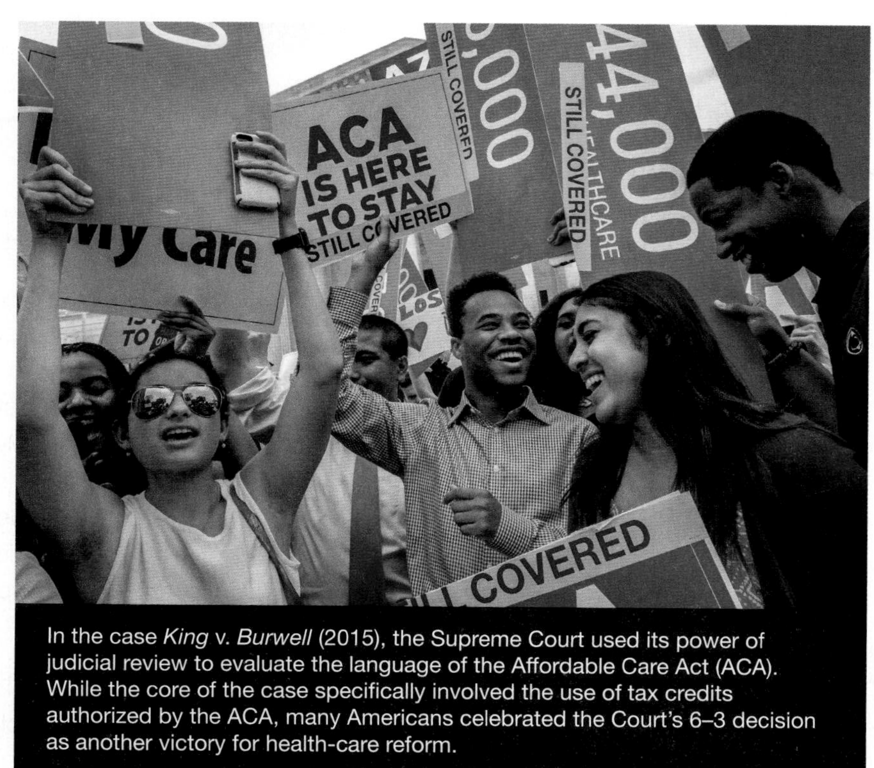

In the case *King* v. *Burwell* (2015), the Supreme Court used its power of judicial review to evaluate the language of the Affordable Care Act (ACA). While the core of the case specifically involved the use of tax credits authorized by the ACA, many Americans celebrated the Court's 6–3 decision as another victory for health-care reform.

HISTORICAL THINKING

3. **MAKE INFERENCES** Explain the natural connection between the broad language of the Constitution and the power of judicial review.

Judicial Activism Versus Judicial Restraint

As you have just read, the role of the Supreme Court as official interpreter of the law, in conjunction with the often very general language of the Constitution, makes it impossible for the Court not to influence or even establish policy at times. If the Supreme Court upholds or invalidates a state or federal **statute**, or law, the effects on the nation can be profound.

But judges differ in how they use the power of judicial review. The decisions of some judges may reflect the philosophy of **judicial activism**, or the belief that the courts should be willing to rule on constitutional issues and to check actions of the legislative and executive branches. Others may practice **judicial restraint**, the idea that the courts should limit the use of their own powers to strike down laws or otherwise oppose actions of the other two branches. Supporters of the latter concept view judicial restraint as part of a natural democratic hierarchy—members of Congress and the president are elected by the people, whereas federal judges aren't. In other words, the courts shouldn't strike down a law unless that law is unmistakably unconstitutional.

Earl Warren was Chief Justice of the Supreme Court from 1953 to 1969. Many of the highly significant legal decisions made during his tenure involved race relations and criminal justice, giving the Warren Court a reputation as an activist court. "It is the spirit and not the form of law that keeps justice alive," Warren once said.

Under the leadership of Chief Justice Earl Warren from 1953 to 1969, the Supreme Court embraced judicial activism. The Warren Court propelled the civil rights movement forward by ruling that laws upholding racial segregation violated the equal protection clause. The Warren era also brought about landmark decisions on the rights of the accused and freedom of the press. The activist approach of the Warren Court led to the association of the term *judicial activism* with liberalism. Today, a conservative judge isn't typically considered an activist judge. Yet neither judicial activism nor judicial restraint is necessarily linked to a particular political ideology. In fact, many observers claim that a majority of justices on today's Supreme Court exercise judicial activism on behalf of a conservative agenda—something you will read about shortly.

HISTORICAL THINKING

4. **MAKE GENERALIZATIONS** Is a justice known for judicial activism more or less likely to issue a decision that nullifies existing legislation? Explain.
5. **DRAW CONCLUSIONS** *Judicial activism* is a term that is often used critically. Why do you think this is?

Approaches to Legal Interpretation

Though Supreme Court justices are often viewed as tied to the political ideology of the president who appointed them, or to their own personal judicial history, it's a mistake to identify any particular judicial philosophy solely as conservative or liberal. Scholars often point to other factors that can influence the way justices reach decisions, ranging from attitudes toward legal interpretation itself to the way they personally perceive the Supreme Court's role in the federal judiciary.

STRICT CONSTRUCTION AND TEXTUALISM The judicial philosophy called *strict construction* reflects the idea that the Constitution should be interpreted

Decided: June 12, 1967, 9–0

Majority: Chief Justice Earl Warren wrote the unanimous opinion in favor of the Lovings.

The *Loving* case negated a number of state laws that banned interracial marriage, including those of Virginia, where Mildred and Richard Loving lived and raised their three children.

In 1958, Virginia residents Mildred Jeter, a Black woman, and Richard Loving, a White man, were married in Washington, D.C. A few weeks after the couple returned home to Virginia, police entered their bedroom in the middle of the night and arrested them for breaking Virginia's law against interracial marriage. The penalty for breaking that law was one to five years in state prison for both individuals involved. The Lovings pled guilty and were sentenced to a year in prison, which a judge later suspended with the caveat that the couple leave Virginia and not return for at least 25 years.

After relocating to Washington, D.C., the Lovings filed a suit to overturn their conviction. Their appeal was based on the argument that Virginia's ban on interracial marriage was unconstitutional under the 14th Amendment. When a state court rejected the case, the Lovings appealed the decision to the state appeals court, which upheld the conviction because the punishment was applied equally to people of all races. The appeals court did, however, void the Lovings' sentence.

The Lovings then petitioned the U.S. Supreme Court to review their case, which it did in April 1967. Two months later, the Warren Court reached a unanimous decision in favor of the Lovings, holding that the Virginia law violated the equal protection clause of the 14th Amendment and that there was no legitimate overriding purpose independent of racial discrimination behind the law. Furthermore, Chief Justice Warren wrote, "Under our Constitution, the freedom to marry, or not marry, a person of another race resides with the individual, and cannot be infringed by the State."

THINK ABOUT IT Was the *Loving* decision an example of judicial activism on the part of the Warren Court? Explain your answer.

ORIGINALISM *and* MODERNISM: A CASE STUDY

ORIGINALISM
4 justices

The Constitution does not address same-sex marriage. There is no precedent for forcing a state to alter its definition of marriage. The issue falls to the states, their legislatures, and their electorate to decide. It is not the role of the Court to legislate, which is what defining a right does.

***Obergefell* v. *Hodges*, 2015**

Does the 14th Amendment require states to issue marriage licenses to same-sex couples, as well as recognize the marriage of a same-sex couple who were legally married in another state?

MODERNISM
5 justices

The right to marry is an individual liberty. Thus it is protected by the due process clause of the 14th Amendment. Therefore the Court is entitled to expand on the original intent of existing law to protect same-sex marriage under the equal protection clause of the 14th Amendment.

strictly as it is written, and as giving little power to the federal government beyond what is explicitly stated in the Constitution. This term is widely used in the press and by politicians, particularly Republican presidential candidates, who routinely promise to appoint justices who will closely follow the wording of the Constitution, instead of using court decisions to make new policy. (The terms *broad construction* and *loose construction* are also used and mean the opposite of *strict construction*. These terms reflect the idea that judges who interpret the language of the Constitution loosely or broadly give more power to the federal government.) Advocates of strict construction often contend that the government shouldn't do anything that isn't specifically mentioned in the Constitution, which makes for a very limited government. In 1803, for example, some strict constructionists argued that the national government had no power to double the size of the country by purchasing the Louisiana Territory.

Although the concept of strict constructionism remains popular among many conservatives, conservative members of the current Supreme Court resist labeling themselves as such. Justice Kavanaugh, for example, says he supports the philosophy of **textualism**, or the idea that the plain meaning of the text of a law is all that should be used to review and interpret that law. Textualists specifically refuse to consider other factors related to the law, such as any legislative debates that took place when a law was first passed, or even the nature of the problem that the legislation was intended to address. The late Justice Scalia, who is often noted as one of the purest examples of a strict constructionist on the Court, preferred to call himself a textualist. Scalia wrote, "I am not a strict constructionist, and no one ought to be. . . . A text should not be construed strictly, and it should not be construed leniently; it should be construed reasonably, to contain all that it fairly means."

ORIGINALISM A second conservative philosophy is called originalism, the idea that, to determine the meaning of a particular constitutional phrase, the Court should look to **original intent**, or the basic intentions of the Framers of the Constitution. In other words, what did the Framers mean when they included a particular phrase in the document? To discern the intent of the Framers, justices such as Clarence Thomas, well known as an advocate of originalism, might look to sources that shed light on the Framers' views. These sources could include writings by the Framers, newspaper articles from the period, the Federalist Papers, and notes taken during the Constitutional Convention. Supporters of originalism claim it protects the objective ideas of the

NATIONAL GEOGRAPHIC

The Many Colors of Matrimony

by Patricia Edmonds *National Geographic* Magazine, April 2018

It has been more than 50 years since the U.S. Supreme Court ruled that state laws banning interracial marriage were unconstitutional. In the decades that have followed, interracial marriage has become much more common. Many marriages today are made up of couples who are of different races or ethnicities.

Some landmark Supreme Court decisions reshape American society in fundamental and visible ways. The 1967 case *Loving* v. *Virginia* was one such decision. In the article "The Many Colors of Matrimony," writer Patricia Edmonds examines how American marriages have changed during the more than 50 years since the Supreme Court's ruling on *Loving* struck down state laws against interracial marriage.

Since that ruling, Edmonds reports, there has been a fivefold increase in marriages between people of different races or ethnicities. In the late 1960s, only 1 out of every 33 marriages was interracial. Today, that ratio is 1 in 10. And as the article's photographs demonstrate, those marriages encompass many combinations of race, ethnicity, age, and gender.

Edmonds says that this shift in marriage reflects a transformation in American society as a whole. Though the *Loving* decision changed the law in 17 states, it didn't "necessarily do anything to change people's minds," says Syracuse University law professor Kevin Noble Maillard. The broader increase in intermarriage, argues Maillard, is tied to greater open-mindedness about race and ethnicity.

Syracuse University law professor Kevin Noble Maillard suggests that the growing acceptance of interracial marriage in the past 50 years—and of same-sex marriage in the past dozen years—has been influenced by shifting social norms and by public and media validation. Partners of different races or ethnicities are nothing new, he notes: "But it's very different when there's public recognition of these relationships and when they become representations of regular families—when they're the people in the Cheerios commercial."

Access the full version of "The Many Colors of Matrimony" by Patricia Edmonds through the Resources Menu in MindTap.

THINK ABOUT IT Do you think acceptance of interracial marriage would have increased if the Court had

Constitution from subjective interpretation. Opponents (among them, textualists) argue that the Framers couldn't possibly have anticipated the changes that have taken place in the United States over more than two centuries, many of which have required judicial involvement to protect democracy.

Originalism can be contrasted with modernism, or the idea that judges should examine the Constitution in the context of today's society. For an example of how to compare originalism and modernism, consider *Lawrence* v. *Texas*, a 1993 case in which the Court abolished laws against homosexual acts. In the majority opinion, Justice Anthony Kennedy wrote that laws that criminalize same-sex intimate relations are unconstitutional under the 14th Amendment. Justices Scalia and Thomas, both originalists, opposed the ruling on the grounds that the legislators who adopted the amendment probably never intended for it to apply to gays and lesbians. In contrast, modernists might argue that discrimination against LGBTQ individuals is exactly the type of infringement on individual freedom that the amendment sought to prevent, even if such an application didn't occur to those who wrote it. A similar breakdown can be seen in the 2015 landmark decision in *Obergefell* v. *Hodges*, which legalized same-sex marriage in a 5–4 vote. The opinions in that case are summarized in the graphic "Originalism and Modernism: A Case Study."

HISTORICAL THINKING

6. **COMPARE AND CONTRAST** How are textualism and originalism alike and how are they different?
7. **MAKE CONNECTIONS** Would judicially activist judges be more or less likely to follow an approach of textualism? Explain.
8. **ANALYZE VISUALS** Paraphrase both the originalism and modernism interpretations of the *Obergefell* case in one sentence each.

LESSON 13.4 The Role of Federal Courts

Judicial decision-making, particularly at the Supreme Court level, can be mind-bogglingly complex. When deciding a case, judges often must consider many sources of law, including state constitutions and the U.S. Constitution, statutes, and administrative agency regulations, as well as earlier cases that interpret relevant portions of those sources. Demographic data, public opinion, foreign laws, and other factors can also be thrown into the mix. Even if it isn't intentional, it is only natural that a judge's life experiences, personal biases, intellectual abilities, and predispositions will influence the reasoning process for determining how much weight to give to each of these sources and factors. Reasoning of any kind, including judicial reasoning, doesn't take place in a vacuum.

Ideology and the Courts

As you read earlier, there are several influences on how federal judges approach judicial interpretation. While political ideology is far from a judge's sole motivator, history has shown that ideology, along with personal policy preferences, can affect the direction of a judge's decisions. Scholars of the U.S. Supreme Court often study the relationship between political ideology and judicial decision-making. They point out that as new justices replace old ones and new ideological alignments form, the Court's decisions are affected. While it isn't the role of a justice to start the review of a Supreme Court case with a personally motivated conclusion (for example, that Congress should have passed a specific law) and then look for legal sources to support that conclusion, some critics claim that justices behave in exactly this fashion. Whether or not the justices are conscious of what they are doing, they appear to sometimes begin with a conclusion and then engage in motivated reasoning to justify their beliefs.

HISTORICAL THINKING

1. **IDENTIFY MAIN IDEAS AND DETAILS** What factors can affect the way a Supreme Court justice arrives at a decision?
2. **FORM AND SUPPORT OPINIONS** How do you think the life tenure of a Supreme Court justice might affect his or her personal ideology?

Ideology and Today's Supreme Court

In contrast to the liberal, judicially activist Warren Court of the 1950s and 1960s, the Court generally has been more conservative over the past 40 years. The Court began its rightward shift after President Ronald Reagan appointed conservative William Rehnquist as Chief Justice in 1986, and it moved further to the right as Reagan and President George H.W. Bush made additional conservative appointments. After President George W. Bush named Chief Justice John Roberts and Associate Justice Samuel Alito to the Court in 2006, the drift to the right was solidified. Alito, a staunch conservative, replaced retiring justice Sandra Day O'Connor, who was often the Court's **swing vote**, a member whose decisions might be said to swing between liberal and conservative rulings when others are equally divided in taking consistent positions. O'Connor didn't vote according to a set ideology but rather with one side or the other, depending on the details of the case at hand.

The five conservative justices on the bench voted together and cast deciding votes in numerous cases during the Roberts Court's first several terms. The remaining justices, who held liberal to moderate views, often formed an opposing bloc. President Obama's choice of justices Sotomayor and Kagan in 2009 and 2010 didn't change the Court's ideological balance: While both women joined the liberal bloc, the men they replaced had been fairly liberal as well. Likewise, President Donald Trump's appointment of Neil Gorsuch in 2017 involved no long-term change to the Court's ideological balance, because Trump replaced one conservative justice—Scalia—with another.

From February 2016 until April 2017, the time between the death of Justice Scalia and the confirmation of Justice Gorsuch, the eight-person Court was somewhat more liberal because it was short one conservative justice. This changed after Justice Anthony Kennedy retired at the end of July 2018. Widely considered the swing vote on the Roberts Court after O'Connor's departure—though generally more conservative than O'Connor—Kennedy often determined the outcome of a case. From October 2010 through June 2016, Kennedy

Public Opinion of the Supreme Court, 1991–2018

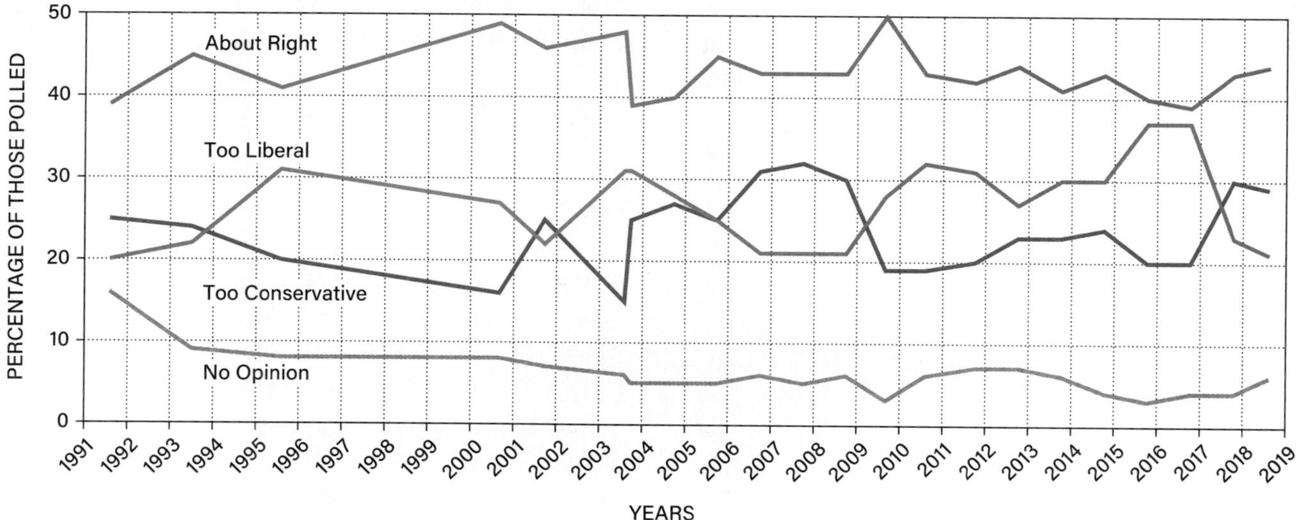

SOURCE: Gallup

was in the majority in 84 percent of the cases decided by a narrow 5–4 vote. No other justice came close to this percentage. The conservative leaning of the Court was further solidified by the confirmation of Amy Coney Barrett in October 2020.

CRITICAL VIEWING Justice Anthony Kennedy (second from the left), who retired from the Supreme Court in 2018, often sided with conservative justices. But he was also seen as an occasional swing vote. Kennedy [shown here with Representative Ralph Regula (R-OH) (far left), Justice Clarence Thomas (center), and Representative Jose Serrano (D-NY)] would sometimes confer with members of Congress on both sides of the aisle. What kind of relationship should Supreme Court justices have with members of Congress?

THE COURT'S CONSERVATISM
In recent years, the nature of the Court's conservatism has come into sharper focus. As mentioned earlier, it is a mistake to equate the ideology of the Court's majority with the conservatism of Republicans in Congress, or with the specific ideology of the conservative movement. While there are members of the Court who are unmistakably conservative—such as Justice Thomas, for example, whose opinions lean farther to the right than those of any other justice on the Court—Chief Justice Roberts has surprised some observers.

Chief Justice Roberts's 2015 ruling on the Affordable Care Act (also known as Obamacare) took many political observers aback. In the case *King* v. *Burwell*, the justices were faced with the issue of how to interpret one clause in a very long bill. The clause referred to subsidies granted to low-income individuals who used state exchanges to buy health-care insurance. But the federal exchange for insurance wasn't mentioned. Opponents of Obamacare argued that subsidies for the federal exchange were contrary to the plain text of the legislation. In a 6–3 majority opinion, Chief Justice Roberts found that it was clear from the language of the bill taken as a whole that Congress meant to grant federal exchange subsidies. The ruling angered many conservatives, including then-presidential candidate Donald Trump.

Another area in which Court conservatives have parted from the conservative movement is that of rights for those in the LGBTQ community. As you read in the last lesson, while Justice Kennedy decided with conservatives in most cases, he argued in *Lawrence* v. *Texas* (1993) that criminalizing homosexual behavior violated the due process clause of the 14th Amendment. Kennedy's vote was also decisive in later cases regarding rights for LGBTQ individuals, including *Obergefell* v. *Hodges* (2015). Progressives celebrated *Obergefell* and a number of other cases considered liberal victories during that same term. Some Court watchers explained the liberal trend by noting that in 2014–2015, conservatives had sponsored a large number of cases in an attempt to push the law to the right. Often, the Court resisted that effort.

In June 2015, however, the Court announced that it would take up several questions on which it had a conservative record. In February 2016, conservatives on the Court **stayed**, or blocked, implementation of Environmental Protection Agency (EPA) regulations on carbon dioxide emissions from power plants by a 5–4 vote. Four days later, Justice Scalia died. His eventual replacement on the Court, Gorsuch, helped bring about several decisions with a clear conservative majority in the 2017–2018 term, including a decision to uphold a later version of President Trump's 2017 travel ban on people arriving from several Muslim-majority countries. Those who wanted a more moderate or liberal Court saw the appointments of Kavanaugh and Barrett as barriers to that goal. Associate Justice Stephen Breyer is more than 80 years old. When he dies or retires the current president will appoint a replacement.

In November 2018, in a rare instance of a public comment from the Court, Chief Justice Roberts responded to a criticism of a federal judge by President Trump. The president had objected to a decision by a judge on the U.S. Ninth Circuit Court of Appeals, referring to the judge as "an Obama judge" because he had been appointed by President Obama. Roberts, in response, issued a statement in which he said, "We do not have Obama judges or Trump judges, Bush judges or Clinton judges. What we have is an extraordinary group of dedicated judges doing their level best to do equal right to those appearing before them. That independent judiciary is something we should all be thankful for." Many found this a surprising remark by a generally conservative justice about a conservative president.

HISTORICAL THINKING

3. **SEQUENCE** Explain the trend regarding liberal and conservative perspectives in Supreme Court appointments over the past 30 years.
4. **SYNTHESIZE** What unpredictable circumstances determine whether a president has the opportunity to appoint a Supreme Court justice?
5. **INTERPRET GRAPHS** According to the graph, how has public opinion of the ideology of the Supreme Court changed over the past 10 years?

Criticism of the Court

Federal courts have made many landmark decisions since their creation more than 200 years ago. Some of these decisions have changed American society and left a permanent imprint on the nation's history. Decisions involving racial segregation, abortion, and LGBTQ rights established new national policy, and these decisions were made by judges and justices in the federal court system who were appointed, not elected. Given this, it isn't surprising that some Americans, including many conservatives, contend that judicial policymaking and activism has upset the balance of powers envisioned by the Framers of the Constitution. These critics cite Thomas Jefferson, who once said, "To consider the judges as the ultimate arbiters of all constitutional questions [is] a very dangerous doctrine indeed, and one which would place us under the despotism of an oligarchy."

But supporters of the federal courts stress the mediator and watchdog role of the federal judiciary in an otherwise very political context and have sharply criticized congressional efforts to interfere with the courts' authority. They claim that such efforts violate the Constitution's separation of powers. Additionally, American government, per the Constitution, doesn't include an alternative to judicial review: Only the judiciary—and ultimately, the Supreme Court—can determine whether or not something is constitutional. As Chief Justice Roberts said during his confirmation hearings, "Judges are like umpires. Umpires don't make the rules; they apply them."

HISTORICAL THINKING

6. **SUMMARIZE** Briefly describe the arguments by critics of the courts as policy makers and by supporters of the courts as mediators.

Checks on the Courts

Even though the federal courts enjoy a great deal of legal power, there are several checks on this power. Judicial restraint is one such check. For example, the Court doesn't choose which cases to hear simply to have the opportunity to rule on a specific issue; a case must have legal merit (through either original or appellate jurisdiction) to be heard. Justices also sometimes admit to restraining themselves on an individual level, making decisions that fly in the face of their personal values and policy preferences, simply because they feel obligated to do so in view of existing law. Certain judicial traditions also reinforce this restraint, including the doctrine of *stare decisis*, by which the courts are obligated to follow precedent. Finally, the judges often narrow their rulings to focus on just one aspect of an issue, even though there may be nothing to stop them from broadening their focus and thus widening the impact of their decisions.

Another check on judicial power is simple: money. A federal court may rule that a current law or practice is unconstitutional, but the funding for changes needed to rectify the situation (improving conditions in prisons, for example) must come from the federal or state legislatures. The appropriations process, which must be handled by the legislature, is therefore a built-in check on the judiciary.

Additionally, legislatures can revise old laws or pass new ones in an attempt to negate a court's ruling. This may happen when a court interprets a statute in a way that Congress didn't intend. Congress may also propose amendments to the Constitution to reverse Supreme Court rulings, and Congress has the authority to limit or otherwise alter the jurisdiction of all federal courts besides the Supreme Court. Finally, although it is most unlikely, Congress could even change the number of justices on the Supreme Court, in an attempt to change the ideological balance on the Court. (President Franklin D. Roosevelt proposed such a plan in 1937, in an effort to muster judicial support for his economic proposals.)

The debate over how much power should remain with the Supreme Court and the other federal courts is sure to be an ongoing one. Yet hovering above it is one important fact: Americans consistently hold the Supreme Court and the rest of the federal judiciary in high regard. The Court continues to be respected as a fair arbiter of conflicting interests and the protector of constitutional rights and liberties. For example, following the very close 2000 presidential election, the Court halted the manual recount of votes in Florida. This decision allowed George W. Bush to win Florida by a margin of 537 votes and claim the presidency with an electoral college victory. Though many Americans disagreed with the Court's decision, the nation as a whole and members of the opposition party respected the Court's decision-making authority. Polls continue to show that Americans have much more trust and confidence in the Supreme Court than they do in Congress.

HISTORICAL THINKING

7. **MAKE GENERALIZATIONS** Identify three checks on the Supreme Court and lower federal courts.
8. **FORM AND SUPPORT OPINIONS** Do you think partisanship has influenced public opinion of the Supreme Court? Explain.
9. **INTERPRET GRAPHS** Use the graphs to compare the trust the American people have in Congress and in the Supreme Court.

Levels of Confidence, 2018

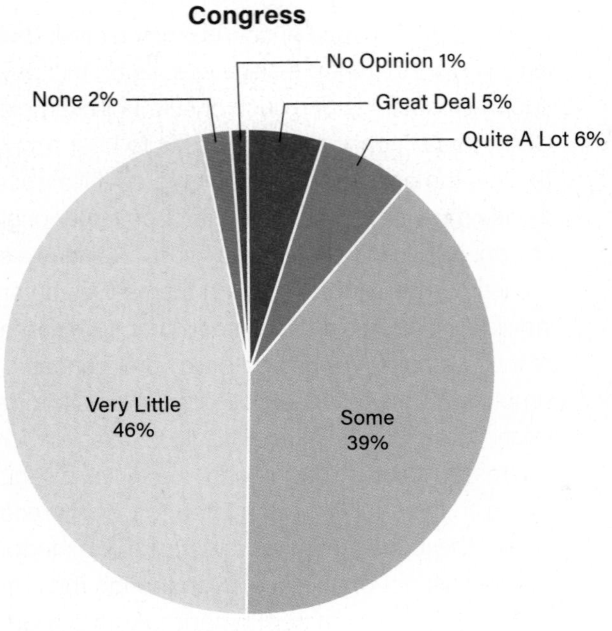

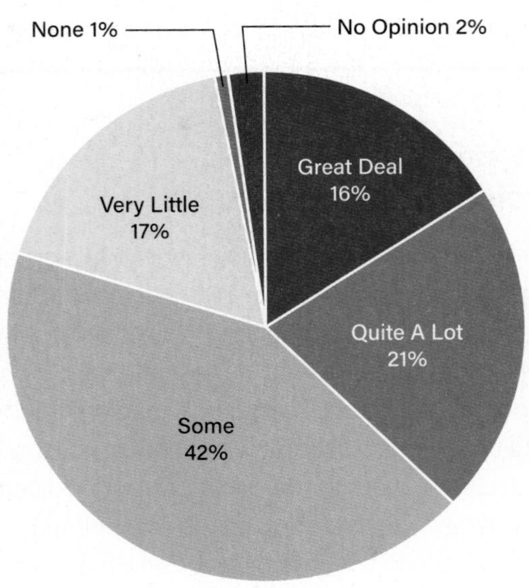

SOURCE: Gallup

SUPREME COURT

Masterpiece Cakeshop, Ltd. v. Colorado Civil Rights Commission, 2018

Decided: June 4, 2018, 7–2

Majority: Justice Anthony Kennedy wrote the opinion in favor of Masterpiece Cakeshop. Justices Elena Kagan (joined by Justice Stephen Breyer), Neil Gorsuch (joined by Justice Samuel Alito), and Clarence Thomas (joined by Gorsuch) wrote concurring opinions.

Dissent: Justice Ruth Bader Ginsburg wrote a dissenting opinion, in which she was joined by Justice Sonia Sotomayor.

Colorado baker Jack Phillips's refusal to make a cake to celebrate the marriage of a same-sex couple sparked a national debate that pitted the ideas of discrimination and First Amendment rights against each other.

In 2012, same-sex marriage was legal in only a handful of states and was being actively debated in the courts and legislatures. It had been banned in Colorado, but a gay couple in Colorado who had been married in a state where same-sex marriage was legal asked Jack Phillips, the owner of Masterpiece Cakeshop, to create a cake for a wedding celebration. Phillips declined, explaining that while he would sell the couple other baked goods, his religious beliefs prevented him from making a cake to celebrate a same-sex wedding. The couple filed a complaint with the Colorado Civil Rights Commission for discrimination on the basis of sexual orientation in a place of public accommodation—a violation of Colorado's anti-discrimination law. The commission recommended the case for a bench trial. When the judge found in favor of the couple, Phillips appealed to the Colorado Court of Appeals, claiming that the commission's charge against him violated both the free speech and the free exercise of religion clauses of the First Amendment. The appeals court didn't reverse the charge, and Phillips petitioned the Supreme Court to review his case.

In 2017, in a 7–2 ruling, the Court reversed the earlier court decisions. Although many Americans perceived the case as either supporting or undermining same-sex marriage (which had been legalized two years earlier in the Court's *Obergefell* decision), the justices decided the case on the basis of how the Colorado Civil Rights Commission applied the state's anti-discrimination law. Because the commission hadn't charged earlier bakers who had refused to bake cakes with anti-gay messages, the Court found that the commission had treated Phillips and his religious views with bias. The majority opinion also recognized that, for Phillips, the creation of a cake was a form of artistic expression and a reflection of his religious beliefs; therefore, forcing Phillips to bake the cake violated his First Amendment rights.

THINK ABOUT IT How might the *Masterpiece* case have been different if Phillips had owned a limousine that the couple wanted to rent for their wedding celebration?

CHAPTER 13

THE SUPREME COURT

Review

VOCABULARY

Use each of the following vocabulary words in a sentence that shows an understanding of the term's meaning.

1. written argument
2. oral argument
3. statute
4. judicial activism
5. judicial restraint
6. textualism
7. original intent
8. swing vote

MAIN IDEAS

Answer the following questions. Support your answer with evidence from the chapter.

9. Explain the jurisdiction of the Supreme Court. **LESSON 13.1**
10. What types of decisions can individual Supreme Court justices issue? **LESSON 13.1**
11. What do most presidents look for when choosing nominees for the Supreme Court? **LESSON 13.2**
12. How might a possible Supreme Court nominee's judicial philosophy make him or her more attractive to a president? **LESSON 13.2**
13. Can the judicial philosophies of originalism and modernism ever lead to the same opinion in a case? Explain. **LESSON 13.3**
14. How do judicially activist judges and judicially restrained judges differ in their attitudes toward laws made by Congress? **LESSON 13.3**
15. Explain what you would expect of a Supreme Court justice who claims a judicial philosophy of broad construction. **LESSON 13.3**
16. In general terms, compare the Warren Court and the Roberts Court. **LESSON 13.4**
17. Do the changing demographics of the Court correlate to a change in the Court's direction? Explain. **LESSON 13.4**
18. How can the Court show judicial restraint when issuing a ruling? **LESSON 13.4**

HISTORICAL THINKING

Answer the following questions. Support your answer with evidence from the chapter.

19. **FORM AND SUPPORT OPINIONS** What factors might contribute to the increased contentiousness of recent Senate judicial confirmation hearings?
20. **MAKE CONNECTIONS** Why are some judges considered conservative and some liberal? Give examples.
21. **SYNTHESIZE** What are the advantages and disadvantages of strict construction?
22. **MAKE INFERENCES** During his administration, President Franklin D. Roosevelt proposed an unsuccessful "court-packing" plan to appoint one new Supreme Court justice for every justice on the Court over 70 years old who had already served at least 10 years. Why do you think this proposal, which would have resulted in six new justices on the Court, was so controversial?
23. **DRAW CONCLUSIONS** Hypothesize as to why public opinion of the Supreme Court is consistently high or fairly high, especially in relation to Congress.

INTERPRET VISUALS

When Supreme Court Justice Antonin Scalia died in 2016, the Republican-controlled Senate refused to hold hearings on Court nominees named by President Barack Obama, stating it would wait until a new president was elected that November. Examine the line graph that compares Scalia's judicial ideology with that of his fellow justices. Then answer the questions that follow.

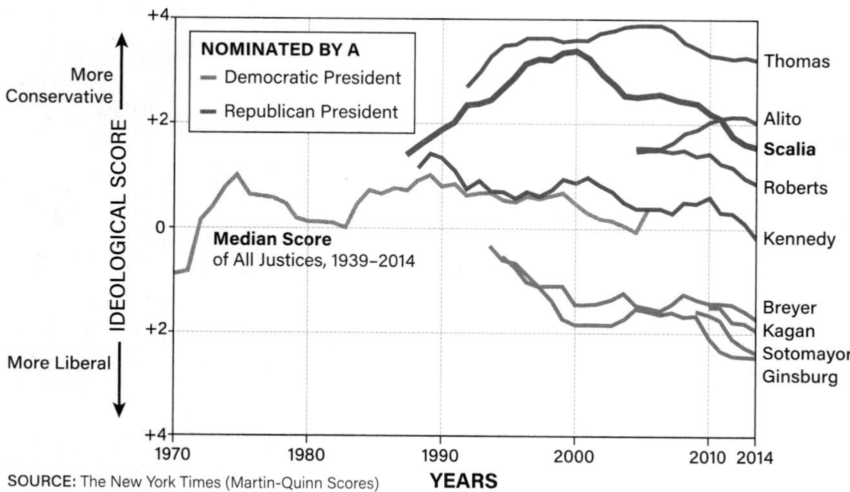

24. How did Scalia's judicial ideology compare with that of justices who served with him, and with the median justice score?

25. Given Scalia's ideological history, why do you think Republicans wanted to wait until after the 2016 presidential election to confirm his replacement? How did this plan work out for them?

ANALYZE SOURCES

Read the following quotation from Supreme Court Justice Elena Kagan. Then answer the question that follows:

> The Supreme Court, of course, has the responsibility of ensuring that our government never oversteps its proper bounds or violates the rights of individuals. But the Court must also recognize the limits on itself and respect the choices made by the American people.

26. How does Justice Kagan's statement connect to the idea of judicial review, as well as the debate between judicial activism and judicial restraint?

CONNECT TO YOUR LIFE

27. **EXPOSITORY** Choose one of the nine current Supreme Court justices, and research the justice's early life: childhood, education, and initial career path. Identify when and how this justice decided to pursue a career in the law, and connect those decisions to his or her eventual appointment to the Supreme Court. Use your research findings to write a one-page essay, looking for parallels to your own life and your career or personal aspirations. In what way is this person a role model for you? Given your own circumstances and aspirations, what lessons can you draw from this person's life?

TIPS

- Clearly identify the justice in your introduction, and preview the background you will describe.
- Give an overview of the justice's life, highlighting any events or experiences that may have influenced a decision to pursue a career in law.
- Explain the judicial philosophy of the justice and the influence of this philosophy.
- In your concluding paragraph, discuss the parallels between your own life and aspirations and those of the justice you researched. Describe the lessons you can draw from the justice's life and career.
- Use two or three key vocabulary terms from the chapter in your essay.

UNIT 7

The Politics of Democracy

UNIT 7 OVERVIEW

Chapter 14 Political Parties and Interest Groups

Chapter 15 The Electoral Process

Chapter 16 Voting and Voting Rights

CRITICAL VIEWING Balloons fall over the delegates at the Republican National Convention in Cleveland, Ohio, on July 21, 2016, following Donald J. Trump's speech accepting his party's nomination for president. In recent years, with the nomination already decided by the primary contests, the conventions have become well-choreographed television spectaculars. In 2020, the national conventions for both parties were held virtually, with only a few people on site as tens of millions watched on television and untold numbers streamed them on mobile devices. If the nominations are already decided, why do political parties still consider nominating conventions important?

"Both of our political parties . . . agree conscientiously in the same object: the public good; but they differ essentially in what they deem the means of promoting that good."

—**Thomas Jefferson (1804)**

CHAPTER 14

Political Parties and Interest Groups

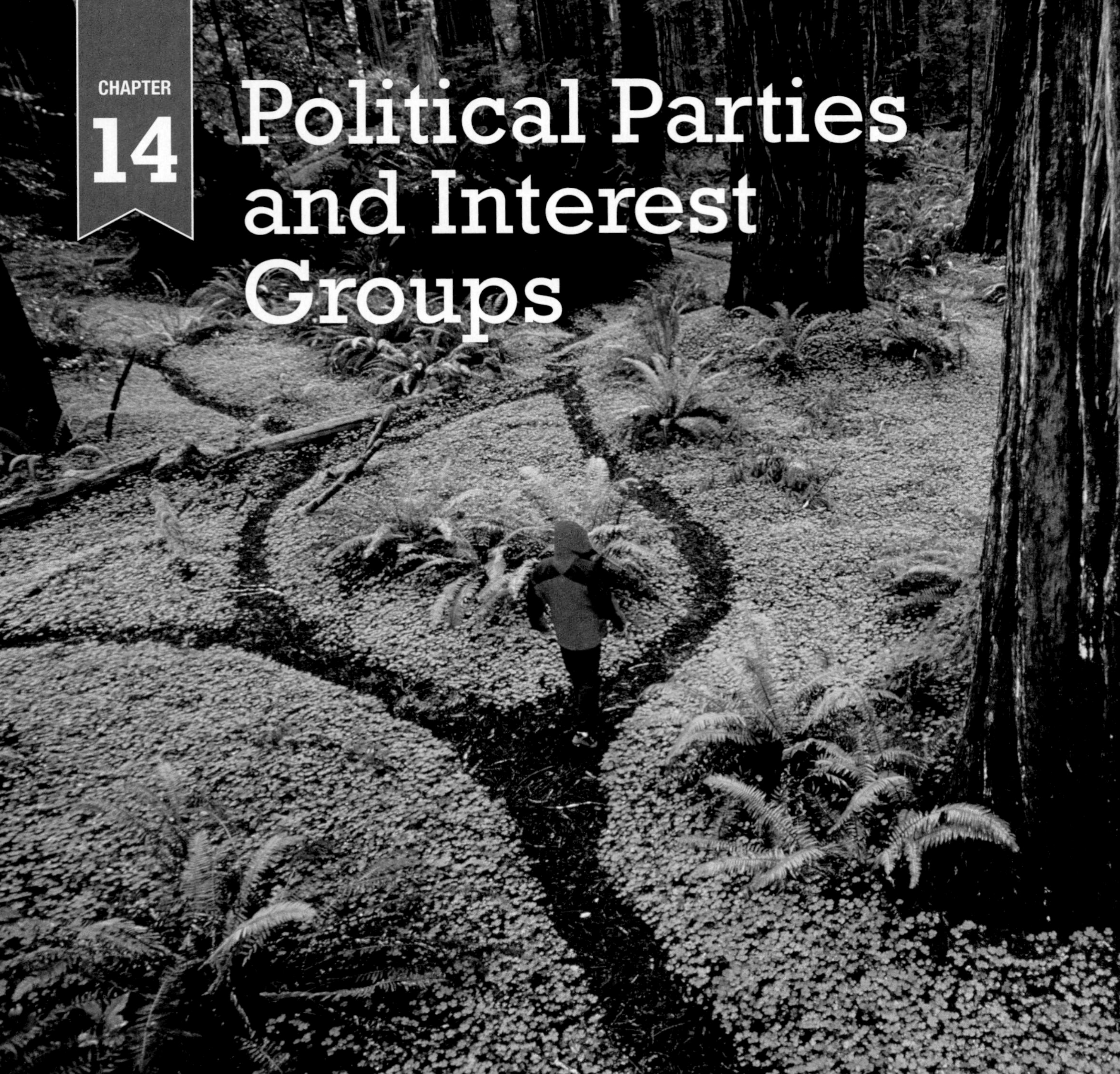

LESSONS

14.1 Political Parties, Then and Now

National Geographic Magazine: How Latinos Are Shaping America's Future

14.2 Our Two-Party System

14.3 Third Parties in American Politics

14.4 What Are Interest Groups?

14.5 What Interest Groups Do

CRITICAL VIEWING Interest groups saved the magnificent redwood trees in Redwood National Park in California. In the early 1900s, the Save-the-Redwoods League convinced the state of California to preserve some stands of trees as state parks. In the 1960s, under pressure from the Sierra Club and the National Geographic Society, Congress passed a law to create the national park. Why would an interest group like the Save-the-Redwoods League or the Sierra Club have better luck getting legislation passed than an individual?

LESSON
14.1 Political Parties, Then and Now

The Framers defined the Congress and the presidency in the Constitution, but they said nothing about political parties. In fact, they condemned factions and parties. But political parties are part of every system in countries in which leaders and representatives are chosen by voters. Parties organize political campaigns and mobilize supporters for the party's candidates. Despite their initial misgivings, early national leaders soon realized some type of party organization was needed. Several even helped establish the first political parties.

The First Political Parties

The Framers saw parties as disruptive and subject to self-interest. As George Washington said when he left the presidency after two terms, the "spirit of party . . . agitates the community with ill-founded jealousies and false alarms, kindles the animosity of one part against another, foments [stirs up] occasionally riot and insurrection." The Framers even feared that a party leader might seize power as a dictator.

In spite of these fears, two major political factions—federalists and antifederalists—formed even before the Constitution was ratified. Those factions continued, in somewhat altered form, after the Constitution was ratified. Alexander Hamilton, the first secretary of the Treasury, became the leader of the Federalist Party, which Vice President John Adams also joined. The Federalists supported a strong central government that would encourage the development of commerce and manufacturing.

Opponents of the Federalist Party and Hamilton's policies referred to themselves as Republicans. Today, they are often called Jeffersonian Republicans or Democratic Republicans (names not used at the time), to distinguish them from today's Republican Party, which was established later. Jefferson's Republicans favored a limited role for government and preferred vesting more power in the states rather than in the central government. They thought Congress, not the executive branch, should dominate the government, and they supported government policies that served the interests of small farmers and enslavers, such as those who owned plantations, rather than promoting commerce and manufacturing.

The tensions between state and federal power that motivated the federalists and antifederalists continue today. One example of this tension is the debate over

Despite federal laws making the possession and sale of marijuana illegal, a growing number of states have legalized medical and recreational marijuana within their borders. Businesses like the company that operates this Ohio plant-growing facility produce and market the product.

the manufacture and sale of marijuana. The federal government classifies marijuana as a controlled substance and makes possession a crime. In response to research findings that the plant has properties that may be useful to some people as a medication, most states and the District of Columbia have either passed laws allowing use of medical marijuana or decriminalized use of the drug. A number of states have also legalized recreational uses of marijuana.

HISTORICAL THINKING

1. **COMPARE AND CONTRAST** What was the main point of dispute between members of the Federalist Party and their opponents after ratification of the Constitution?

Parties From 1796 to 1860

The nation's first two parties clashed openly in the election of 1796, when George Washington was no longer a candidate. That year, Federalist John Adams defeated Jefferson. Over the next four years, Jefferson and James Madison worked to extend the influence of their Republican Party. In the presidential elections of 1800 and 1804, Jefferson won the presidency, and his party also won control of Congress. The transition of political power from the Federalists to Jefferson's party in those elections is the first example in American history of what political scientists call a **realignment**, a shift in the relative strength of political parties as a substantial number of voters change their political allegiance.

Jeffersonian Republicans dominated American politics for the next 20 years, as the Federalist Party essentially vanished. In the mid-1820s, Jefferson's party split into two groups, marking the second political realignment. This type of realignment, a **rolling realignment**, is a political realignment that occurs over several years as large numbers of legislators as well as voters gradually shift their party loyalties. One of the groups that resulted from this split were the supporters of Andrew Jackson, who was elected president in 1828. These people called themselves Democrats. The Jacksonian Democrats appealed to small farmers and the growing class of urban workers. They tended to oppose strong central government—although Jackson, once he was elected, was more than willing to exercise strong presidential power.

The other party that resulted from the split was the National Republican Party. This party later became the Whig Party. It was led by John Quincy Adams, Henry Clay, and Daniel Webster. The National Republicans wanted a strong national government but with power concentrated in Congress instead of in the executive branch. They campaigned for a program of high tariffs on imported goods. The tariffs would stimulate the growth of domestic manufacturers and fund an ambitious scheme of road and canal building. The National Republicans drew support from bankers, business owners, and many southern planters.

As Whigs and Democrats competed for the White House from 1835 to 1854, the two-party system as we know it today emerged. Both parties were large, with well-known leaders and supporters across the nation. Both had grassroots organizations of party workers committed to winning as many political offices as possible at all levels of government for their party.

By 1856, however, the Whig Party had fallen apart, destroyed by a combination of bad luck—both presidents elected as Whigs had died in office, leaving the party without a strong leader—and the growing sectional dispute over slavery. Most northern Whigs were absorbed into a newly formed party, the Republican Party. This is the Republican Party that exists today. The Republicans embraced some ideas from the Whigs, such as support for small business and for government efforts to improve transportation by building canals and railroads. They also opposed the extension of slavery into new territories. Campaigning on this platform in 1860, Abraham Lincoln became the first president elected under the banner of the Republican Party.

HISTORICAL THINKING

2. **ANALYZE CAUSE AND EFFECT** How did the first political realignment, in the early 1800s, affect American politics?
3. **COMPARE AND CONTRAST** How were the National Republicans and the Jacksonian Democrats alike and different?

From the Civil War to the Great Depression

When the former Confederate states rejoined the Union after the Civil War, the Republicans and Democrats were roughly equal in strength. Republicans, though, were more successful in presidential contests. From 1860 to 1896, Democrats won only two presidential elections—both with Grover Cleveland. During these years, the Republicans picked up the nickname GOP, for "grand old party."

In the 1890s, party alignments shifted again. In that decade, the Democrats allied themselves with the Populist movement, which consisted largely of indebted farmers in the west and south. The Populists—also called the People's Party—advocated inflation as a way of lessening their debts. When inflation is high, money borrowed in earlier years, when the dollar was worth more, can be repaid with dollars worth less in the present. In effect, inflation would give farmers more dollars to repay those old debts. A bushel of corn that might have cost $5 in an earlier year might be worth $7.50 after some years of inflation.

Not everyone favored inflation, however. Paychecks do not necessarily increase to keep up with inflation, so wages lose value as prices for food and other necessities increase. Urban workers in the Midwest and the East, who depended on paychecks rather than on selling crops, strongly opposed high inflation. In the 1896 election, these urban workers—long supporters of the Democrats—shifted to the Republican Party. Many Americans saw the Republican Party as the party that could manage the nation's economy. Republicans went on to win the four presidential elections from 1896 to 1908.

In 1912, however, the Republicans underwent a temporary split between Republican regulars—led by sitting president William Howard Taft—and more progressive Republicans—led by former president Theodore Roosevelt. When the Republicans nominated Taft for president, Roosevelt and his supporters bolted from the party. This Republican split allowed Democrat Woodrow Wilson to win the

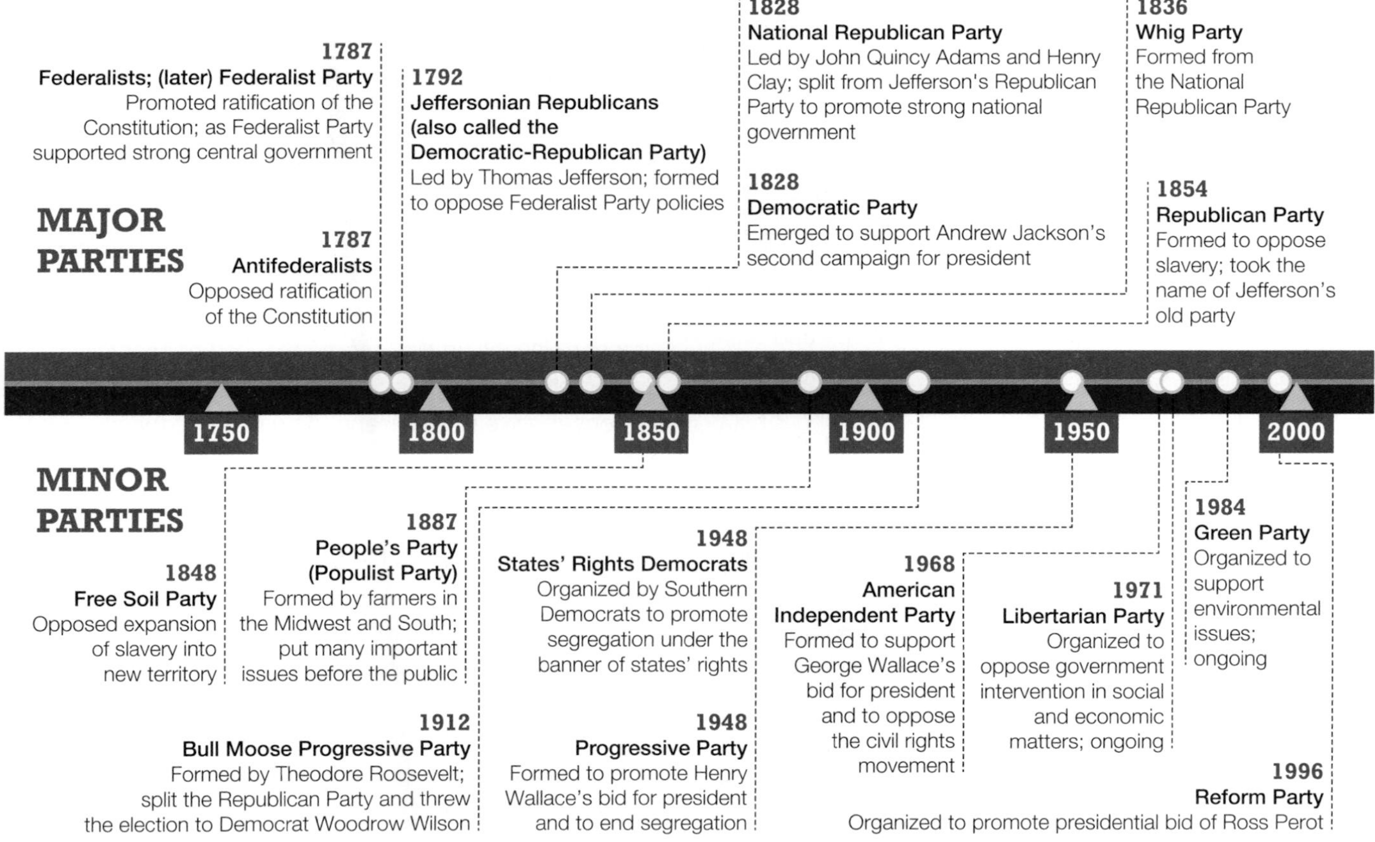
U.S. Political Parties Running Presidential Candidates
MAJOR PARTIES
1787
Federalists; (later) Federalist Party
Promoted ratification of the Constitution; as Federalist Party supported strong central government
1787
Antifederalists
Opposed ratification of the Constitution
1792
Jeffersonian Republicans (also called the Democratic-Republican Party)
Led by Thomas Jefferson; formed to oppose Federalist Party policies
1828
National Republican Party
Led by John Quincy Adams and Henry Clay; split from Jefferson's Republican Party to promote strong national government
1828
Democratic Party
Emerged to support Andrew Jackson's second campaign for president
1836
Whig Party
Formed from the National Republican Party
1854
Republican Party
Formed to oppose slavery; took the name of Jefferson's old party
1750
1800
1850
1900
1950
2000
MINOR PARTIES
1848
Free Soil Party
Opposed expansion of slavery into new territory
1887
People's Party (Populist Party)
Formed by farmers in the Midwest and South; put many important issues before the public
1912
Bull Moose Progressive Party
Formed by Theodore Roosevelt; split the Republican Party and threw the election to Democrat Woodrow Wilson
1948
States' Rights Democrats
Organized by Southern Democrats to promote segregation under the banner of states' rights
1948
Progressive Party
Formed to promote Henry Wallace's bid for president and to end segregation
1968
American Independent Party
Formed to support George Wallace's bid for president and to oppose the civil rights movement
1971
Libertarian Party
Organized to oppose government intervention in social and economic matters; ongoing
1984
Green Party
Organized to support environmental issues; ongoing
1996
Reform Party
Organized to promote presidential bid of Ross Perot

presidential election in 1912, and he was re-elected in 1916. In 1920 and the next two elections, however, Republicans once again won the presidency with candidates Warren G. Harding, Calvin Coolidge, and Herbert Hoover. Thus, they dominated national politics until the onset of the Great Depression.

HISTORICAL THINKING

4. **DRAW CONCLUSIONS** Why did the issue of inflation undermine the Democrats in the 1890s?
5. **ANALYZE CAUSE AND EFFECT** How did Theodore Roosevelt's behavior lead to a victory for the Democrats in the presidential election of 1912?
6. **INTERPRET TIME LINES** Based on the time line, how many political parties were formed to support or oppose slavery, segregation, or civil rights and what were they called?

The Great Depression and Political Parties

The **Great Depression**, the worldwide economic downturn that struck in 1929, contributed to another realignment. The financial collapse began less than a year after Republican Herbert Hoover became president, and deepened throughout his tenure, destroying the perception that the GOP was the party that was better at managing the economy. The election of 1932 brought Franklin D. Roosevelt, a Democrat, to the presidency and gave the Democrats large majorities in Congress.

The coalition that put Roosevelt into power—and led to continued support for the Democrats into the 1970s—included unionized workers, city dwellers, small farmers, and African Americans. The shift of this last group to the Democrats was a major change; African Americans had long supported the Republicans, viewed as the party of Lincoln. Franklin Roosevelt won the support of African Americans because, thanks to the influence of First Lady Eleanor Roosevelt and administration officials such as Frances Perkins and Harold Ickes, New Deal programs were open to people of all races. Roosevelt appointed a number of African Americans, such as Mary McLeod Bethune, to influential positions in the federal government. While the New Deal did not eliminate racial segregation or discrimination, it paved the way for later advances, and the Democrats built upon this new constituency in 1948. That year, for the first time, Democrats adopted a call for civil rights for African Americans as part of its **party platform**, the document drawn up as a statement of a political party's positions and principles. A number of White southern Democrats revolted against this position and ran a separate candidate, Strom Thurmond, for president.

In 1964, the Democrats, under President Lyndon Johnson, won a landslide victory and a majority in Congress. During the 1960s, the Democratic Party came to be dominated by more liberal ideas, endorsing civil rights and an expansion of government's role in combating poverty and inequality. Conservative Democrats, particularly in the South, did not like the direction in which their party was headed. Under President Richard Nixon, the Republican Party welcomed these conservative Democrats. Over a period of years, most of them became GOP voters in another rolling realignment. As a result of this particular shift, what had long been the solidly Democratic South became increasingly Republican. Republican President Ronald Reagan helped cement the new Republican coalition and won every southern state but one in 1980. The lone holdout, Georgia, was the home state of Reagan's opponent, President Jimmy Carter.

The Democrats continued to hold majorities in the House and Senate until 1994, but during the 1970s and 1980s, a large bloc of Democrats in Congress, mostly from the South, sided with the Republicans on almost all issues. In time, some of these conservative Democrats changed parties, and others were replaced by conservative Republicans. As a result of these changes, the Democrats became a minority party in the South.

The result of this rolling realignment was that the two major parties were once again fairly evenly matched. The elections of 2000 were a striking demonstration of how evenly the **electorate**, or group of people eligible to vote, was now divided. Republican George W. Bush won the presidency that year by carrying Florida by just 537 votes. In addition, the Congress that formed in 2001 had 50 Republicans and 50

Democrats in the Senate and a razor-thin GOP majority of just 7 Republican seats out of a total of 435 in the House.

HISTORICAL THINKING

7. **ANALYZE CAUSE AND EFFECT** How did the Great Depression undermine confidence in the Republican Party?
8. **MAKE INFERENCES** Why did African Americans vote overwhelmingly for Republican candidates until the Great Depression?
9. **IDENTIFY MAIN IDEAS AND DETAILS** How did Democrats become a minority party in the South in the 1970s and 1980s?

Red States, Blue States, Purple States

Historically, political parties draw together people with similar economic interests, policy preferences, and values. Today, too, individuals with similar characteristics tend to align themselves more often with one or the other major party. Factors such as race, age, income, education, marital status, and geography all influence party identification.

Geography exerts a strong influence on party identification, as shown in a map of the 2020 presidential elections. Like other Republicans in recent decades, Donald Trump did well in the South, the Great Plains, and the Rocky Mountain states. He also carried most of the Midwest in 2016, a traditional stronghold for Democrats. But in 2020, the electoral votes of some states that had supported Trump in 2016 went to Democrat Joe Biden, along with the votes from states in the Northeast, on the West Coast, and in other midwestern states—like Illinois and Minnesota—that had supported Democrat Hillary Clinton in 2016. Arizona and Georgia, two states that had not supported a Democratic presidential candidate since Bill Clinton, also tipped for Biden.

Beginning with the presidential election of 2000, the press has made much of the supposed cultural differences between the blue states that vote Democratic and the red states that vote Republican. In reality, though, many states could better be described as purple—a mixture of red and blue, with voters shifting in their support of Democrats and Republicans. These states may give their electoral votes to either party in any given election.

A deep dive into the 2020 presidential vote in Minnesota reveals a pattern found in many purple states. Trump carried the great majority of the counties in the state, but Biden carried Minnesota by 7.2 percentage points. On this map, Minnesota looks red, or Republican, because Trump carried so many of the state's large, rural counties. The counties Biden won were fewer and covered less of the state's area, but they included cities, so they had larger populations. As a result, more of Minnesota's voters chose Biden, and he won the state. This voting pattern was seen all over the country: The more urban the county, the more likely it was to vote Democratic.

But other factors influence voting patterns as well, including national and world events. During 2005, the seemingly endless wars in Afghanistan and Iraq began to cut into support for the Republicans. In 2006, the Democrats regained control of the House and Senate. In 2008, in the shadow of a global financial crisis called the Great Recession, which began when Republican George W. Bush was president, Americans elected Democrat Barack Obama as president.

By the next election, however, the Democratic advantage had vanished. Continued high rates of unemployment were one major reason. Also, a sharp increase in government activity during Obama's first two years in office bothered many voters. In November 2010, Americans handed the House to the Republicans, though Democrats maintained control of the Senate. Republican successes in 2010 were backed up by the growth in new conservative movements such as the Tea Party. By 2012, some analysts wondered whether the strong conservatism of the newly elected Republicans might be alienating independent voters. In fact, in the 2012 elections, Democrat Obama won re-election as president by almost 4 percentage points.

In 2014, however, Republicans won enough seats to have a majority in the U.S. Senate, giving them control of both houses of Congress. The Republicans also did well in state-level races. At least one cause of the Republican success is that America has recently had

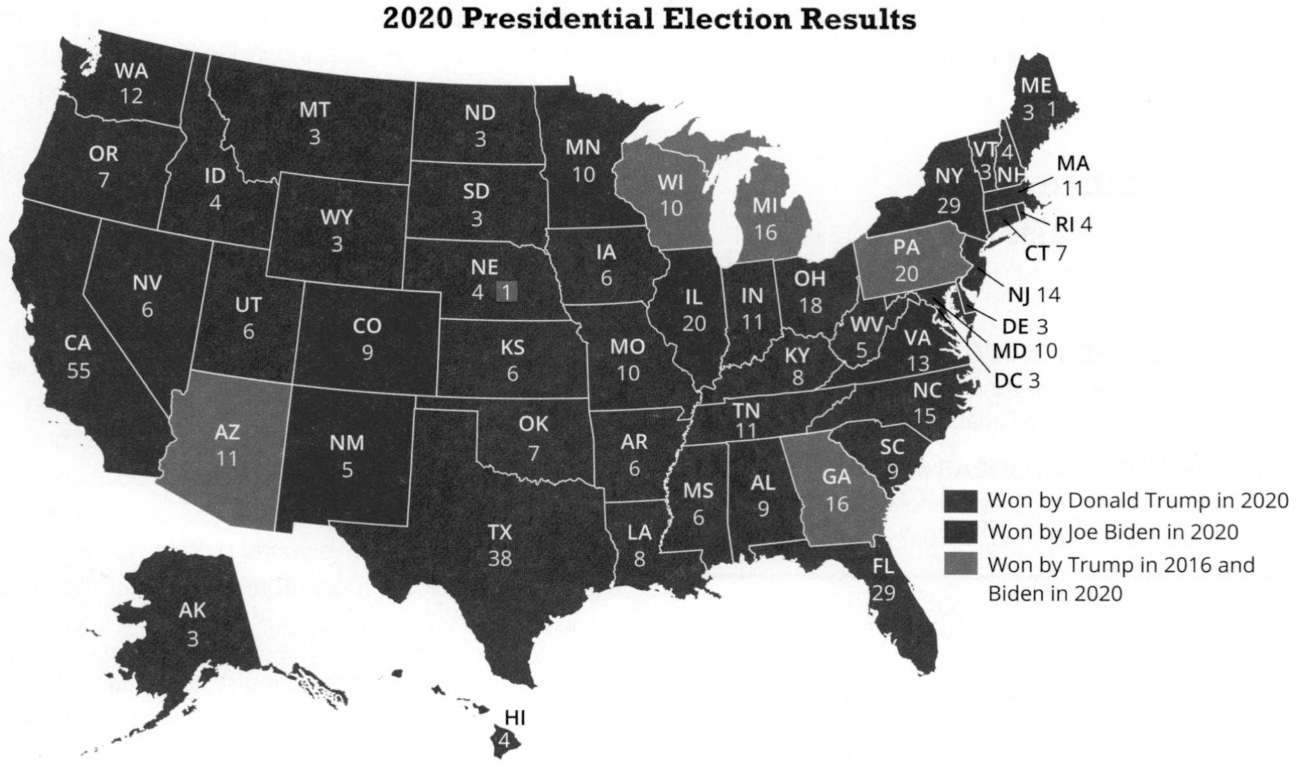

two very different electorates, one for the midterms and one when presidential candidates are on the ballot. The midterm electorate was significantly more Republican than the electorate for the presidential race. In recent years, younger voters have become more Democratic, even as older people have moved toward the Republicans. Voter turnout has declined across the board in the midterms, but the falloff among younger voters (and minority group members) was especially large. This helps to explain why, between 2008 and 2016, Republicans did much better in midterm elections than they did in years with a presidential race.

Despite the higher voter turnout among young voters in a presidential election year, larger trends worked in favor of Donald Trump in the 2016 election. This election revealed a continuing shift in sources of support for the two major political parties. By narrow margins, Trump picked up a swath of states in the industrial heartland—Iowa, Wisconsin, Michigan, Ohio, and Pennsylvania—that had not voted Republican in 12 years or more. These states have above-average numbers of less-well-educated, White, working-class voters, precisely the demographic group most drawn to Trump. College-educated voters in those states chose Clinton, but only by narrow margins.

These developments tended to move the country away from the red–blue map. The Democrats were becoming a coalition of minority groups plus northern White progressives of all socioeconomic classes. The Republicans were continuing to shed minority voters as they became more and more the party of White voters, particularly White evangelical Christians and White working-class men.

The 2018 midterm elections continued the Democratic advantage in more urbanized areas, with suburbs playing a key role. That year, Democrats gained more than 40 seats in the House, giving them the majority in that chamber. Nearly all of those victories were the result of gains that Democratic candidates made in suburban counties. This trend was nationwide, from areas around Philadelphia and New York in the East to Chicago and Minneapolis in the Midwest, Atlanta and Houston in the South, and Denver and Los Angeles in the West. Meanwhile, Republicans continued to win in rural House districts.

The 2018 midterms broke sharply with one trend. Turnout in midterms had long been on the decline

2020 Presidential Election Results in Minnesota

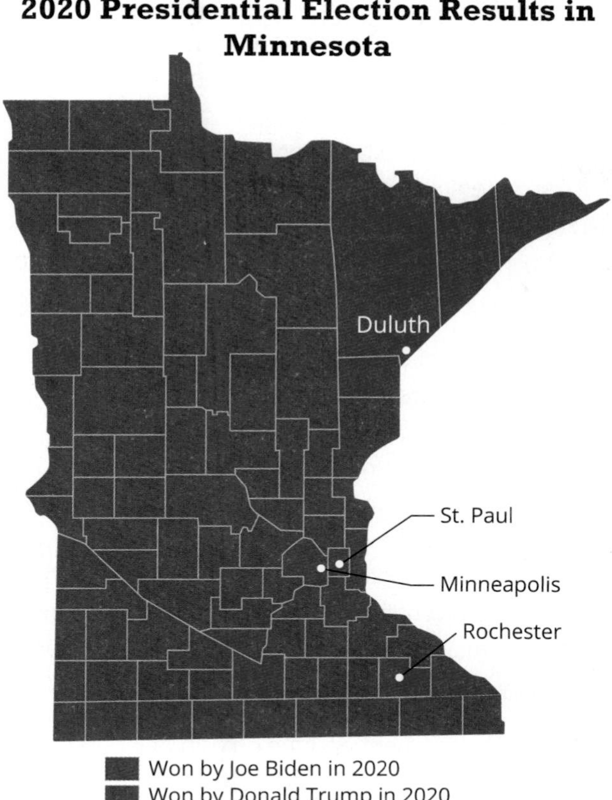

and hit a record low of only about a third of eligible voters in 2014. In 2018, however, just under half of all eligible voters cast ballots—the highest percentage of voters in a midterm since 1914. Democrats gained a strong majority in the House in 2018, only to see that majority eroded by the results of the 2020 election. In 2020, Black women and suburban women of all races were seen as crucial to the Biden victory, even though a slight majority of all women voted for Trump. White working-class rural women, like their male counterparts, favored Republicans in 2020.

Like the 2018 midterms, the 2020 general election saw an enormous increase in voter turnout. More than 66 percent of eligible voters cast ballots, either by mail or by going to polling places and voting in person. This was the highest rate of voting by Americans since 1900. Voter turnout also played a major role in the 2021 Senate runoff in Georgia, the results of which gave the Democrats control of the U.S. Senate. Far more voters from both parties turned out than usual in a runoff, a second election required by state law when no candidate wins 50 percent of the vote in the November elections. But the Democratic turnout was stronger, primarily because of Black voters. Candidates Jon Ossoff and Raphael Warnock prevailed and flipped the Senate, with voter turnout reaching 93 percent of 2020 election levels in Georgia precincts where Black voters made up at least 80 percent of the electorate.

HISTORICAL THINKING

10. **IDENTIFY** Give an example of how domestic and global events affect elections.
11. **INTERPRET MAPS** Based on the presidential election map for 2020 and what you have read about the election, what can you conclude about Biden's source of strength in the election?
12. **INTERPRET MAPS** Based on the map of the 2020 election results in Minnesota, how can you explain Biden's victory in that state?

Radical Partisanship, Dealignment, and Tipping

A key characteristic of recent politics has been extreme partisanship, or a strong inclination or bias in favor of one party over others. Until the 1960s, party coalitions included a variety of factions with a range of political positions. The rolling realignment that began in the election of 1968 initiated a process that has resulted in parties that are much more homogeneous, or uniform, in ideological makeup. Political scientists have concluded that by 2009, the most conservative Democrat in the House was to the left of the most moderate Republican. In other words, the Democratic Party had become mainly liberal and the Republican Party predominantly conservative.

Strong partisanship has made it easier for the parties to maintain discipline in Congress. Personal friendships across party lines, once common in Congress, have become rare. Increasingly, compromise with the other party is seen as a form of betrayal. According to this view, members of the minority party should not cooperate with the majority on any legislation. Instead, they should oppose majority-party measures in an effort to block any action and make the majority appear ineffective. The Republican Party employed such tactics after President Obama's inauguration. The Democrats likewise adopted them when President Donald Trump took office.

THE TEA PARTY Political polarization grew even more severe after the 2010 elections. Many of the new Republican members of Congress were pledged to the Tea Party philosophy of no-compromise conservatism. In later years, the Freedom Caucus in the House largely displaced the Tea Party as a home for that chamber's most conservative members. Tea Party—and later, Freedom Caucus—members of Congress insisted on small-government conservatism.

Tea Party advocates were not necessarily opposed to government benefits as such. Rather, they opposed benefits that, in their opinion, went to undeserving recipients. Undocumented immigrants were one group they believed were undeserving. In contrast, most Social Security and Medicare recipients were seen as deserving. The belief by Tea Party activists that the government supports the undeserving was combined with the sense that they were losing control to what they saw as new groups that were culturally, morally, and politically alien. These beliefs matched Donald Trump's campaign rhetoric and the beliefs of many of his supporters. In this way, the Tea Party movement can be seen as a precursor to the movement that put Trump in the White House.

Reasons Independents Don't Join a Major Party, 2016

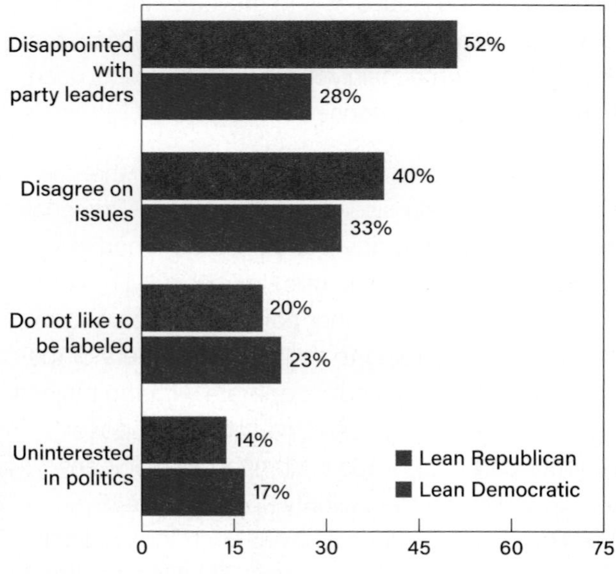

SOURCE: Pew Research Center

THE RISE OF INDEPENDENTS While party members are growing more partisan and less willing to compromise, the number of independent voters is growing. By the 2016 elections, 42 percent of the electorate claimed to be independent. True, many of these voters admitted to leaning toward the Republicans or the Democrats. Still, anyone claiming to be an independent has a weakened attachment to the parties.

Some political scientists argue that with so many independent voters, the concept of realignment becomes irrelevant. Rather, they say, we are witnessing a **dealignment**, with large numbers of people leaving the two major parties. In such an environment, politics would be unusually volatile, because independents could swing from one party to another. The dramatic changes in fortune experienced by the two major parties in recent years help support this theory.

TIPPING Realignment and the growth of independent voters are not the only processes that can alter the political landscape. What if the various types of voters maintain their political identifications, but one type of voter becomes substantially more numerous? This can happen due to migration between states or between nations, or due to changes in education levels and occupations. The result could tip a state from one party to another.

It appears likely that in the future, a growing number of Latinos and young urban professionals might give the Democratic Party an edge. Beginning in 2008, a growing number of Mexican-American voters won several western states for the Democrats in presidential races. Also, new citizens and urban professionals moving into Virginia from the North have turned that formerly Republican state into a swing state.

But as these groups of voters increased support for the Democrats, older White, working-class voters have thrown their support to the Republicans, counteracting the growth in the Democratic immigrant and urban professional votes. Still, the Republicans face a potential problem. Population growth among Whites lags behind that of other racial and ethnic groups, and members of minority groups are expected to outnumber Whites by 2045. Republicans, then, face a long-term danger of running out of newly conservative

Members of the Palmer Society, a campus women's organization, celebrate their graduation from Whittier College in California. The school ranks among the most diverse colleges in the United States. The city of Whittier is predominantly Latino and increasingly affluent.

How Latinos Are Shaping America's Future

by Héctor Tobar ***National Geographic*** **Magazine, July 2018**

By 2050, the United States will be a minority-majority country, meaning that no single racial or ethnic group will make up 50 percent or more of the population. No minority group is likely to have as great an impact as Latinos, but as Héctor Tobar writes in the *National Geographic* magazine article "How Latinos Are Shaping America's Future," Latinos are a diverse group. According to Tobar, Latinos can be "African, Mesoamerican, Asian, or White. They are evangelical, Roman Catholic, and Jewish."

What "Latino" means, more than anything, is that you are part of a story that links you to other people with roots in a southern place: Ecuador or El Salvador, for example. Or maybe an old Southwestern town founded by Spaniards, such as Española, New Mexico. More than likely this story involves the journey a migrant made in search of work and opportunity.

Tobar details the growing presence of Latino and Latina people in America. Many have lived here for generations, while others are more recent arrivals. Some are undocumented and face deportation, in spite of decades of living and working in the United States. Many are winning elections, like Alicia Almazan, the Latina mayor of Wilder, Idaho, a small farming community that also has an all-Latino city council.

Even so, the growing Latino population has raised fears among some Americans about job competition and cultural changes. These fears helped fuel the victory of Republican President Donald Trump, who promised to curb illegal immigration in the 2016 presidential election. At the same time, Latino voters have made California a stronghold of the Democratic Party.

Access the full version of "How Latinos Are Shaping America's Future" by Héctor Tobar through the Resources Menu in MindTap.

THINK ABOUT IT How do you think Latino and Latina voters will affect the outcome of future elections in

Whites before the Democrats run out of new minority and progressive White voters.

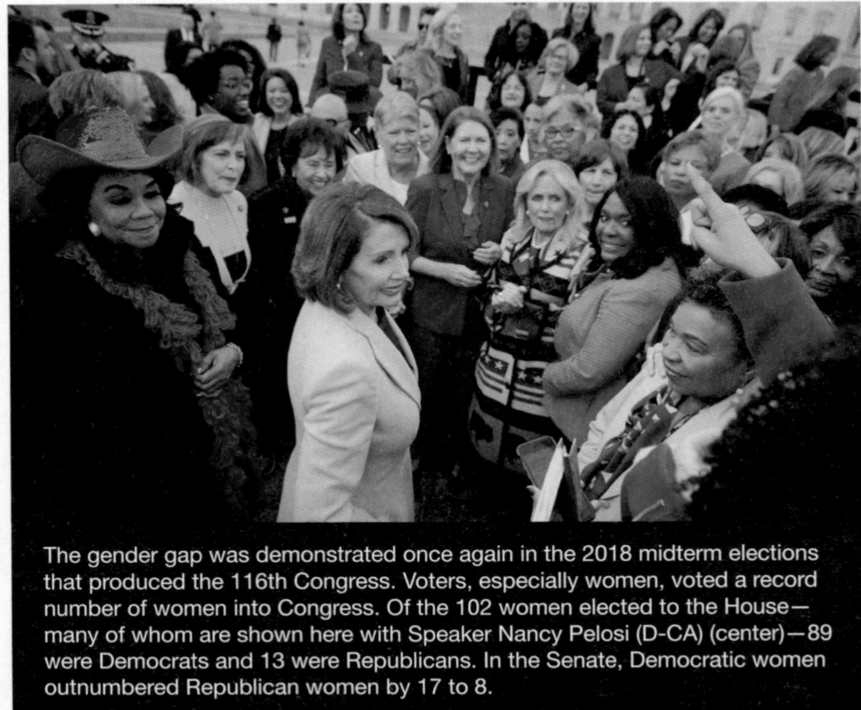

The gender gap was demonstrated once again in the 2018 midterm elections that produced the 116th Congress. Voters, especially women, voted a record number of women into Congress. Of the 102 women elected to the House—many of whom are shown here with Speaker Nancy Pelosi (D-CA) (center)—89 were Democrats and 13 were Republicans. In the Senate, Democratic women outnumbered Republican women by 17 to 8.

Another troubling trend for the GOP is the gender gap. Historically, a majority of women have tended to vote Democratic, while a majority of men have usually voted Republican. That difference has intensified in recent years. In the 1994 House congressional elections, women voted for Democratic candidates by a margin of 6 percentage points while men favored Republican candidates by 16 points. In the 2016 congressional election for the House, women voted Democratic by a margin of 10 percentage points. Men, on the other hand, voted Republican by a margin of 12 points. The 2018 congressional races in both the House and Senate saw the trend among women deepen and male support for Republican candidates fall. According to exit polls, women favored Democrats by a whopping 19 points, while the Republican margin for men was down to 4 points. Combined with other trends tipping the scales toward Democrats, the gender gap may prove disastrous for the GOP.

HISTORICAL THINKING

13. **EVALUATE** Is partisanship an effective political strategy? Why or why not?
14. **INTERPRET GRAPHS** What does the graph reveal about why many independents don't align themselves with a party?

LESSON 14.2 Our Two-Party System

As you have read, political parties have played a vital role in our democratic system almost from the beginning. Their main purpose has been to link members' policy preferences to actual government policies. Political parties also perform many other functions. Among the most important of these is to recruit and nominate candidates for political office. Many candidates from the same party may seek the same office, but the party sorts through them, narrowing the field and making clear to the public what the chosen candidate stands for. This function simplifies voting choices.

What Do Political Parties Do?

In the past, candidates were typically chosen by party leaders who identified individuals they thought were suited to an office or who merited a reward for loyal party service. Today, parties often choose candidates by holding a primary election. This candidate then runs against the opposing party's candidate in the general election.

Voter turnout for primaries is lower than it is for general elections. The voters who do vote in primaries are often the strongest supporters of their party. Indeed, in many states, voters registered as independents cannot participate in primary elections, even if they lean toward one or the other of the two major parties. As a result, the Republican primary electorate is very conservative, and Democratic primary voters are quite liberal, causing primary candidates to run to the political right or left in order to win the primary. Many candidates then move to the center during the general election campaign to capture the votes of independents. In recent years, this pivot to the center has been less common as congressional districts and whole states have become more solidly partisan. In 2020, for example, Democratic presidential nominee Joseph Biden embraced progressive issues like a national $15 per hour minimum wage during the primaries. Once he secured the nomination, he threw his support behind other progressive stances such as the Green New Deal and the expansion of tuition-free college education in hope of uniting his party.

Once candidates are chosen, parties coordinate campaigns through their national, state, and local organizations. Political parties take care of a large number of minor and routine tasks that are essential to the electoral process. For example, they work to get party members registered to vote and to recruit new voters.

Political parties also help educate the public about important political issues. In recent years, major issues have included tax policy, ways to stimulate the economy, health care, education, environmental policies, criminal justice, and immigration. Each party presents its views on these issues through television commercials, social media, newspaper ads, web pages, campaign speeches, and debates. These activities help citizens learn about the issues, form opinions, and consider proposed solutions.

In the complex government of the United States, political parties are essential for coordinating policy among the various parts of the government. Parties act as the glue of the federal structure by connecting members of the various levels of government—local, state, and national—with a common bond. Within the states and in the federal government, parties are usually the major institution through which the executive and legislative branches cooperate with each other. Each president, cabinet head, and member of Congress is normally a member of one of the two major parties. The president works through

Sometimes the party members who choose candidates for office are the rank-and-file, or ordinary voters, and not party leaders. Ayanna Pressley, talking to reporters outside a Boston middle school in the 2018 Democratic primary, challenged 10-term incumbent Michael Capuano for a seat in Congress. Most party leaders backed Capuano in the primary, but after Pressley's surprise 59–41 percent victory in the primary, she won the support of the party and became the first African-American woman from Massachusetts to serve in the U.S. House.

party leaders in Congress to promote a legislative program. Ideally, parties work together to fashion compromises—legislation that is acceptable to both parties and that serves the national interest. Recent years have seen little bipartisan compromise in Congress, however.

Parties even play important roles when they are in the minority in the legislature and out of the executive branch. The minority party does what it can to influence the majority party and its policies and to serve as a check on actions it opposes. For example, depending on how evenly Congress is divided, the minority party may be able to attract some members of the majority party to pass or defeat certain legislation. The minority party also informs voters of what it believes to be the shortcomings of the majority party's agenda.

PARTIES AS COALITIONS A political party is essentially a **coalition**—an alliance of individuals and groups with a variety of interests and opinions. What binds them is support for the party's platform, or at least parts of it. Each party includes a number of groups with different views on such issues as health care, national security, and the economy. The role of party leaders is to adopt a broad enough view on these issues that no group will be alienated. In this way, different groups can hold their individual views and still come together under the umbrella of the party.

The coalitions making up each of the two major parties differ. The Democrats might be characterized as a coalition of social groups seeking government action on particular issues. Republicans generally share an ideology of small-government conservatism. In many ways, this echoes the arguments of the early antifederalists, who advocated for a weak central government with more power retained by the state governments. However, Republicans also generally support government policies that allow businesses to operate with more freedom and less regulation—more akin to the position of the early Federalist Party.

HOW AMERICAN POLITICAL PARTIES ARE STRUCTURED Each of the two major American political parties consists of three components: the party in the electorate, the party organization, and the party in government. The party in the electorate—the largest component—consists of all of those people who describe themselves as Democrats or Republicans. In most states, a voter can register as a Democrat or a Republican, but voters can change registration at will.

Each major party has a nationwide organization with national, state, and local offices. Party organizations include groups of people who maintain the party's strength between elections, make its rules, raise money, organize conventions, help with elections, and recruit candidates. The party in government consists of all of the party's candidates who have won elections and hold public office.

HISTORICAL THINKING

1. **IDENTIFY** How are political parties helpful to voters?
2. **COMPARE AND CONTRAST** How are the Democratic and Republican parties alike and different?
3. **DESCRIBE** Can members of the party in government also be members of the party organization and the party in the electorate? Explain.

The Party in the Electorate

In many European countries, being a party member means a person actually joins a political party. The person gets a membership card, pays dues, and votes to select local and national party leaders. In the United States, party membership is less formal.

In most states, voters may declare a party preference when they register to vote. This declaration allows them to participate in party primaries. Some states do not register party preferences, however. In short, to be a member of a political party, an American citizen simply has to think of herself or himself as a Democrat or a Republican—or a member of a third party, such as the Green Party. Members of parties do not have to work for the party or attend party meetings, nor must they support the party platform.

Generally, the party at the electorate level consists of two types of people: party identifiers, people who identify themselves as members of the party, and party activists, people who work or volunteer for the party and may even become candidates for office. To survive, political parties need year-round support from party activists. During election campaigns, candidates depend on these activists to answer phones, canvass for votes by going door to door, organize speeches and appearances, and, of course, donate money. Between elections, parties need activists to plan upcoming elections, organize fundraisers, and stay in touch with activists in other communities to keep the party strong. Party activists are vital to the functioning of American political parties.

Most members of the party in the electorate are ordinary citizens. Yet the party in the electorate is also made up of elites of various kinds—opinion leaders, media personalities, and prominent persons in all walks of life. The party in the electorate also includes financial contributors, former politicians, and nationally known political operatives. Consider talk radio personality the late Rush Limbaugh and deep-pocket campaign contributors Charles and his brother, the late David Koch. These people had no official position in government or in the Republican Party. While they were merely members of the party in the electorate, their influence on the GOP was considerable. Likewise, television commentator Rachel Maddow of MSNBC and financier George Soros are influential among Democrats.

Various interest groups are also part of the party coalitions. Labor unions are almost always seen as a base of support for the Democrats. Business groups such as the U.S. Chamber of Commerce are generally key Republican players. Leaders and members of these interest groups can help the party, particularly during election campaigns.

People join political parties for many reasons. Generally, it is because they agree with many of the party's goals and positions on certain issues and because they support many of its candidates. Their reasons for choosing a party may include three types of incentives, or motivating factors:

- **solidarity incentives** Some people join a particular party to express their solidarity, or mutual agreement, with the views of like-minded people. People also join parties because they enjoy the excitement of engaging in politics with others who share their views.
- **material incentives** Many people believe that by joining a party, they will benefit through better employment or personal career advancement. The traditional institution of patronage—rewarding the party faithful with government jobs or contracts—lives on, even though it has been limited to prevent abuses.
- **purposive incentives** Finally, some people join political parties because they wish to actively promote a set of ideals and principles that they feel are important. As a rule, people join political parties because of their overall agreement with what a particular party stands for.

HISTORICAL THINKING

4. **MAKE INFERENCES** Why are party activists important to political parties?
5. **DRAW CONCLUSIONS** Why is solidarity an incentive for joining a party?

Candidates for office rely on the enthusiasm and hard work of party activists. These volunteers work a phone bank urging voters to cast their ballots on election day 2018 for Young Kim, a Republican candidate for the U.S. House in California. Get-out-the-vote efforts mark the final push in any campaign.

The Party Organization

In theory, each of the major American political parties has a pyramid-shaped organization. This structure is much like that of a large company, with the bosses or owners at the top and employees at lower levels. In reality, however, neither major party is closely knit or highly organized. Instead, they are fragmented and decentralized. State party organizations, moreover, are all very different and are only loosely tied to the party's national structure. Local party organizations are often quite independent of the state organization. In short, no single individual or group directs all party members. Instead, a number of persons, often at odds with one another, form loosely identifiable leadership groups.

In general, the state party organization is built around a state committee and a chairperson. The committee raises funds, recruits new party members, maintains a strong party organization, and helps candidates who are running for state offices. The state chairperson is usually a powerful party member chosen by the committee. In some instances, the chairperson is selected by a prominent elected member of the party, such as the governor or a senator from that state.

Local party organizations differ greatly, but generally there is a party unit for each district in which elective offices are to be filled. These districts include congressional and state legislative districts, counties, cities and towns, wards, and precincts. A **ward** is a political division or district within a city. A **precinct** is a political district where a polling place is located, either within a city, such as a block or a neighborhood, or in a rural portion of a county. The local, grassroots foundations of politics are formed within precincts.

On the national level, the party's presidential candidate or the current president is considered to be the political leader of the party. Influential members of Congress may also be viewed as national party leaders. The structure of each party includes four other major elements: the national convention, the national committee, the national chairperson, and two congressional campaign committees.

THE NATIONAL CONVENTION The parties hold a national convention every four years during the summer before the presidential election. Each party presents its nominee for president at these events, though the name of the nominee is generally known before the convention. The news media always cover the conventions, and as a result, these gatherings have become quite extravagant. Big business and interest groups provide millions of dollars to the parties to stage these events in the hope of influencing policy.

The conventions inspire and mobilize party members throughout the nation. They provide voters with an opportunity to see and hear the candidates directly, rather than through a media filter or characterizations provided by supporters and opponents. Candidates' speeches at conventions draw huge audiences. For example, in 2016, more than 30 million people watched the acceptance speeches of Donald Trump and Hillary Clinton after each was formally presented at the Republican and Democratic conventions.

CRITICAL VIEWING George W. Bush, then governor of Texas, and his wife Laura celebrate his nomination for the presidency at the Republican National Convention in 2000. In the past, party leaders often chose a nominee after much political in-fighting and closed-door deal-making at their conventions. Today, the nominee is generally known in advance and the convention is designed to boost the nominee's support with the public. What impression did convention planners hope to create with this photograph?

The national conventions are attended by delegates chosen by the state party organizations. The delegates' most important job is to nominate the party's presidential and vice-presidential candidates, who together make up the party ticket. A select group of key delegates also writes the party platform, which sets forth the party's positions on national issues—and which is heavily influenced by the candidate's policy preferences. Through its platform, the party promises to initiate certain policies if its candidate wins the presidency. Despite the widespread perception that candidates can and do ignore these promises once they are in office, the reality is that many of the winning party's promises become law.

In 2020, the COVID-19 pandemic disrupted the nominating conventions. Party delegates are typically awarded to the winners of primary and caucus contests. But with many of those contests postponed, that process was delayed. Fearing that large gatherings posed a health risk, Democrats rescheduled their Milwaukee, Wisconsin, convention from mid-July to August 17–20 in the hope that infection rates would have fallen by then. The Republican convention, scheduled for August 24, was held in Charlotte, North Carolina. Both party conventions held only a few events in their host cities and without delegates and large audiences. Programming included prerecorded segments and live speeches by party figures and ordinary citizens from various remote locations around the country. Democratic nominees Joseph Biden and Kamala Harris delivered their acceptance speeches from a convention center in Wilmington, Delaware, Biden's home town. Vice President Mike Pence spoke from Fort McHenry in Baltimore, Maryland. President Trump delivered an address to the party convention in Charlotte after it formally nominated him. He accepted his party's nomination from the South Lawn of the White House on the last night of the convention.

THE NATIONAL COMMITTEE Each state elects a number of delegates to the national party committee. The Republican National Committee (RNC) and the Democratic National Committee (DNC) direct the business of their respective parties during the four years between national conventions. The committees' most important duties, however, are to organize the next national convention and to plan how to support the party's candidate in the next presidential election.

Each party's national committee elects a national chairperson to serve as administrative head of the national party. The main duty of the national chairperson is to direct the work of the national committee from party headquarters in Washington, D.C. The chairperson is involved in raising funds, providing for publicity, promoting party unity, encouraging the development of state and local organizations, recruiting new voters and candidates, and other activities. In presidential election years, the chairperson's attention is focused on the national convention and the presidential campaign. In the years between presidential elections, the chairperson works to strengthen the party. The chairperson of the party that does not hold the presidency can offer his or her party's vision for the country in opposition to the president's policies.

Each party has both Senate and House campaign committees. Members are chosen by their colleagues and serve two-year terms. These committees work to help elect party members to Congress.

HISTORICAL THINKING

6. **FORM AND SUPPORT OPINIONS** What are some advantages of the loose party structure typical of American political parties?
7. **MAKE INFERENCES** Why are national conventions important to the election success of the parties?

The Party in Government

Even though most candidates run for office as either Democrats or Republicans, members of a given party do not always agree with one another on government policy. The party in government helps to organize the government's agenda by coaxing and convincing party members in office to vote for its policies. If the party is to translate its platform promises into public policies, the job must be done by the party in government.

Disagreement on how to accomplish the party platform can create trouble for a party. Consider the Republican approach to health-care insurance after they gained control of the national government in the 2016 elections. As soon as the Affordable Care

Act (Obamacare) was adopted in 2010, Republicans united in calling for its repeal. Over time, Republicans came to think that a complete repeal was ill-advised, and so their slogan became "repeal and replace." Still, at the time they assumed power in 2016, the Republicans had yet to come to an agreement on what the replacement ought to look like.

House Speaker Paul Ryan (R-WI) sought to rally the party around a replacement bill titled the American Health Care Act. The bill maintained much of the structure of Obamacare but substantially reduced subsidies to low-income persons and made large cuts to Medicaid benefits. Freedom Caucus Republicans opposed the legislation because it was too similar to Obamacare. More moderate Republicans opposed the cuts in the plan. Ryan modified the bill enough to satisfy both conservatives and moderates and won passage in the House. In the Senate, however, Senate Majority Leader Mitch McConnell (R-KY) was unable to find the necessary votes, and a few Republicans joined the Democratic minority to vote down all repeal proposals.

HISTORICAL THINKING

8. **MAKE INFERENCES** Why might it be difficult for party members to agree on a party platform?
9. **DRAW CONCLUSIONS** How does the issue of the Affordable Care Act illustrate the difficulty in organizing a party to act on a single issue?

The Dominance of the Two-Party System

Since the 1830s, the United States has had a two-party system. This means that two major parties—now the Democrats and Republicans—dominate national politics. One of the major reasons for the perpetuation of the two-party system is simply that there is no alternative. Parties other than these two major parties, called **third parties**, even at times when there might be two or three of them, have found it extremely difficult to compete with the major parties for votes.

When young people or new immigrants learn about U.S. politics, they tend to absorb the political views of those who are providing them with information. Parents pass their political beliefs on to their children, often without even trying. Those beliefs frequently involve support for one of the two major parties, which helps perpetuate the parties' dominance.

Even so, about two-fifths of voters today regard themselves as independents (although they may lean toward one party or another). These voters often believe that neither major party fully represents their views. Such attitudes, however, do not mean that independents are looking for a third party. Typically, true independents are content to swing between the Democrats and the Republicans from one election to another. On the other hand, some poll results show that Americans in general support the idea of having a third party compete with the Republicans and Democrats.

The two parties also dominate politics because American election laws tend to favor them. In many states, for example, the established major parties need relatively few signatures to place their candidates on the ballot, whereas a third party must get many more signatures. The number of signatures required is often based on the total party vote in the last election, which penalizes a new party that is competing for the first time. The rules governing campaign financing also favor the major parties.

One of the major institutional barriers to third parties is the election, by the people, of governors and (through the electoral college) the president. Voting for governors and members of the electoral college takes place on a statewide, winner-take-all basis. (Maine and Nebraska are exceptions—they can split their electoral votes.) Third-party candidates find it hard to win when they must campaign statewide instead of appealing to voters in a smaller district, which might be more receptive to their political positions and more prone to support candidates for their personal qualities.

The popular election of executive officers like governors and the president contrasts with the parliamentary system. In that system, parliament, which is the legislature, chooses the nation's executive officers rather than the people. Third-party voters therefore have a greater chance of affecting the outcome by electing a few members to parliament. Even if the party's delegation is small, it may be able to participate in a coalition government with other parties.

Another institutional barrier to a multiparty system is the single-member district. Today, all federal and most state legislative districts are single-member districts. That is, voters elect one member from their district to the House of Representatives and to the houses of their state legislature. In some countries, by contrast, districts are drawn as multimember districts. Each district may be represented by multiple elected officials from different parties, according to the proportion of the vote each party received.

In many democracies that use single-member districts to choose members of parliament, additional members are chosen from statewide or nationwide party lists. The number of additional members elected from the party lists is calculated to guarantee that the election results are proportional. Under a proportional election system, each party obtains a share of seats in the national parliament that reflects its percentage of the overall vote. If one party receives 40 percent of the total national vote, another party wins 35 percent, and a third party takes 25 percent, the number of seats they each have in the national parliament would be similar to those proportions.

While third parties are rarely successful in the United States, the two major parties do not compete in all elections. Some state offices and many local offices are filled by nonpartisan elections. In these elections, party identification never appears on the ballot.

HISTORICAL THINKING

10. **FORM AND SUPPORT OPINIONS** Should American election laws be changed to give third parties a better chance to participate in elections?
11. **COMPARE AND CONTRAST** How is the parliamentary system similar to and different from America's system?
12. **DRAW CONCLUSIONS** With two-fifths of voters today regarding themselves as independents, what trend does that suggest about voter preference for a third party compared to the two-party system?

LESSON 14.3 Third Parties in American Politics

Despite the obstacles they face, third parties have often played an important role in American politics. These parties are as varied as the causes they represent, but all have one thing in common: Their members and leaders want to challenge the major parties because they believe those parties are not addressing certain needs or values. Some third parties have tried to appeal to the entire nation. Others have focused on particular regions, states, or local areas. Whatever the cause or geographical focus, most are spearheaded by a small but dedicated group of activists who are convinced they can make a difference.

Types of Third Parties

Every third party is different. Each has its own issues to promote and a particular constituency. These parties, however, can be roughly divided into categories based on their goals and organizing principles.

An issue-oriented third party is formed to promote a particular cause or timely issue. For example, the Free Soil Party was organized in 1848 to oppose the expansion of slavery into the western territories. The Prohibition Party was formed in 1869 to advocate banning the manufacture and use of alcoholic beverages.

Most issue-oriented parties fade into history as the issue that brought them into existence loses the public's interest, is taken up by a major party, or is resolved. Some issue-oriented parties endure, however, when they expand their focus beyond a single area of concern. For example, the Green Party was founded in 1972 to raise awareness of environmental issues, but it is no longer a single-issue party. Today, the Green Party campaigns against what it sees as corporate greed and the major parties' indifference to such issues as poverty, problems caused by globalization, and the failure of the war on drugs.

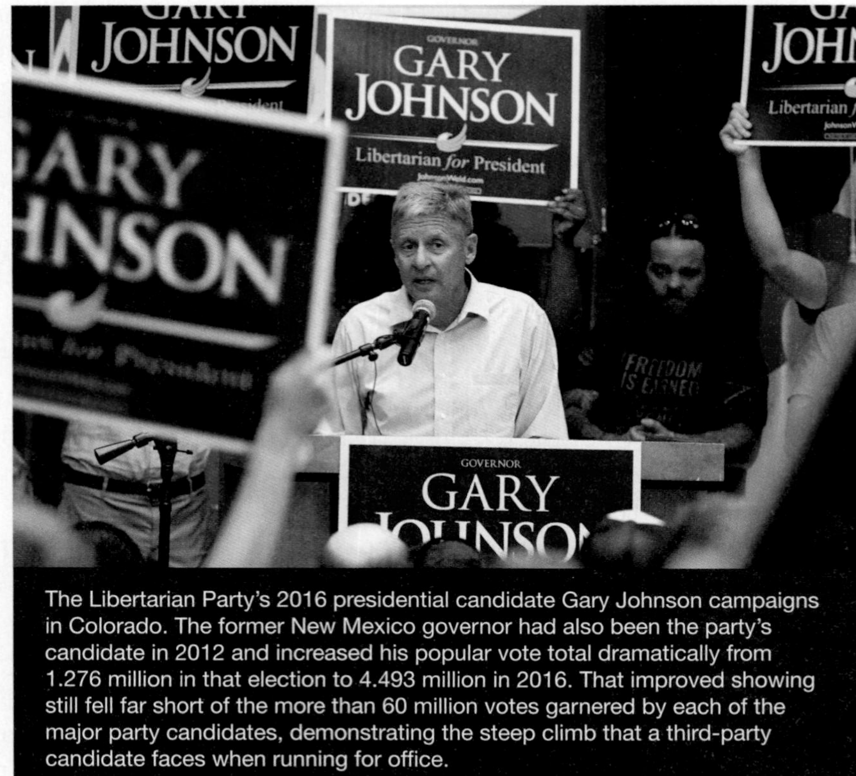

The Libertarian Party's 2016 presidential candidate Gary Johnson campaigns in Colorado. The former New Mexico governor had also been the party's candidate in 2012 and increased his popular vote total dramatically from 1.276 million in that election to 4.493 million in 2016. That improved showing still fell far short of the more than 60 million votes garnered by each of the major party candidates, demonstrating the steep climb that a third-party candidate faces when running for office.

As you have read, a political ideology is a system of political ideas rooted in beliefs about human nature, society, economics, and government. An ideological party supports a particular political doctrine or a set of beliefs. For example, the Party for Socialism and Liberation, a communist party centered in California, advocates a "socialist transformation of society." It wishes to abolish the existing political system and replace it with a "new government of working people." In contrast, the Libertarian Party opposes almost all forms of government interference with personal liberties and private enterprise. One of the longer-lasting third parties, the Libertarian Party was founded in 1971 and won 3 percent of the popular vote in the presidential election of 2016.

A splinter party develops out of a split within a major party. This split may be part of an attempt to elect a specific person. For example, when Theodore Roosevelt did not receive the GOP nomination for president in 1912, he created the Bull Moose Party (also called the Progressive Party) to promote his candidacy. Splinter parties can also be ideological in origin. Two splinter parties formed from the Democratic Party in 1948—the leftist Progressive Party, which supported Henry Wallace, and the segregationist States' Rights (Dixiecrat) Party, which backed Senator Strom Thurmond (D-SC). In 1968, the American Independent Party was formed to support the presidential campaign of former Democrat George Wallace, one of the nation's most visible opponents of racial integration in public schools. His party won almost 10 million popular votes—13.5 percent of the total national vote—and 46 electoral votes.

Most splinter parties form around a leader with a strong personality, which is why they are sometimes called personality parties. When that person steps aside, the party usually collapses. That was the case with the Bull Moose, Progressive, States' Rights, and American Independent parties, all of which attracted support through just a single election cycle, like musicians who become known for a single song known as a one-hit wonder.

HISTORICAL THINKING

1. **SYNTHESIZE** Why are issue parties and splinter parties generally short-lived?
2. **MAKE INFERENCES** Why might people not vote for a third party even if they supported its core issue, ideology, or candidate?

The Effects of Third Parties

Although most Americans do not support third parties or vote for their candidates, third parties have influenced American politics in several ways. They introduce important issues, sometimes with lasting impact. They can have a significant effect on elections. Third parties also give Americans who feel alienated from the major parties a voice in politics.

INTRODUCING ISSUES One of the most valuable services provided by third parties is to bring political issues to the public's attention. They have highlighted significant issues that major parties seemed to ignore. Third parties are in a position to take bold stands on issues that major parties avoid because third parties are not trying to be all things to all people. Some people have argued that third parties are the unsung heroes of American politics, often bringing new issues to the forefront of public debate.

The Populist Party was an especially successful third party. It not only put important ideas before the public but also saw them acted on. The party sprang up after midwestern and southern farmers who had been suffering from low farm prices rebelled. Blaming government and business for many of their problems, they formed their own party in 1892. They went on to win several governorships and congressional seats, and many local and regional positions. More importantly, the Populists pushed for several policies that were later taken up by other parties. Among these were adoption of an income tax and the direct election of senators. Both measures became law in 1913 with the ratification of the 16th and 17th amendments.

Most third parties have not been as successful as the Populist Party, but many have raised awareness of issues of national and regional importance. Many of the ideas proposed by third parties were never accepted, but others were taken up by the major parties as those ideas became increasingly popular. Progressive social reforms such as the minimum wage, women's right to vote, railroad and banking legislation, and old-age pensions were first proposed by third parties. The Free Soil Party (1848–1854) was the first true antislavery party.

AFFECTING ELECTORAL OUTCOMES Third parties can also influence the results of elections. On occasion, they have taken victory from one major party and given it to another, thus playing the spoiler role. For example, in 1912, former president Theodore Roosevelt, backed by his Progressive (or Bull Moose) Party, and incumbent president William Howard Taft split the Republican vote. As an offshoot of the Republican Party, the Progressive Party took votes away from Taft and spoiled his chances for victory. The Democrat, Woodrow Wilson, won the election, but without Roosevelt's third party, Taft might have won.

Third parties have continued to cause problems for major parties in more recent times. The presidential election of 2000 pitted Vice President Al Gore, a Democrat, against Texas governor George W. Bush, a Republican. Entering the contest as a third-party candidate, Ralph Nader represented the Green Party. While Gore and Bush ran neck and neck and garnered most of the votes, Nader won a mere 3 percent. Nevertheless, many experts believe his participation in the contest threw the election to Bush. Nader was a liberal, so most of his votes came from voters who would likely otherwise have voted for Democrat Gore, the more liberal major party candidate. In an incredibly close election, Nader's votes in Florida and other close states probably kept Gore from getting the votes he needed to win. While winning the popular vote, Gore fell three electoral votes short of victory.

Similarly, some commentators contended that third parties may have helped determine the results of the 2016 presidential election. The third-party vote was unusually large that year, with Libertarians winning more than 3 percent of the vote and the Green Party winning more than 1 percent. Given how close the

CRITICAL VIEWING Candidates seen as principled, independent-minded crusaders by their third-party supporters are viewed differently by major party members who fear the third-party candidate will take votes vital to defeating an opponent. In 2004, Democrats hoping to defeat George W. Bush's re-election and elect John Kerry viewed Green Party presidential candidate Ralph Nader as just such a threat. Who is the actual target of this cartoonist's satire?

results were in the key states of Wisconsin, Michigan, and Pennsylvania, Hillary Clinton might have won if the Green Party had not attracted so many votes. The assumption is that Green voters would have turned out to vote anyway and would have been much more likely to vote for Clinton than for Donald Trump.

A VOICE FOR DISSATISFIED AMERICANS Third parties provide a voice for voters who are frustrated with and alienated from the two major parties. Third parties give these Americans an opportunity to participate in American politics through party vehicles that reflect their opinions on political issues. For example, many first-time Minnesota voters turned out during the 1998 elections to vote for Jesse Ventura, a former actor and professional wrestler who became the Reform Party candidate for governor in that state. In a three-way battle against the Republican and Democratic candidates, Ventura won.

Ultimately, third parties find it difficult to break through in the electoral system in national elections. Because third parties normally do not win national elections, Americans tend not to vote for them or to contribute to their campaigns, so they continue not to win. At the state and local levels, however, third parties and independent candidates may be gaining traction. In 2018, for example, Libertarians won four local races in Indiana, three in Minnesota, and seven in Florida, as well as individual races in eight other states. In Vermont and Maine, both of which have senators who are independents and members of neither major party, independents and third-party candidates won many local races. Yet another trend may offer insight into the future. As of the fall of 2018, more than 47 percent of California 16- and 17-year-olds who pre-registered to vote under a 2016 law said they had "no party preference."

HISTORICAL THINKING

3. **FORM AND SUPPORT OPINIONS** Some people have argued that, given the polarization of the two major parties, Americans should organize a new party based on moderate politics. Why might such an initiative fail—or succeed?
4. **EVALUATE** Because a vote for a third-party candidate can swing an election from one major party candidate to another, is a vote for a third-party candidate a wasted vote?
5. **DRAW CONCLUSIONS** Do you think that third-party candidates cost Hillary Clinton the election? Explain.

LESSON 14.4 What Are Interest Groups?

All of us have interests we would like to have better represented and promoted. Labor unionists would like rules that guarantee better working conditions. Young people want good, affordable educational opportunities. Business owners want economic policies that encourage growth and put limits on government regulation. Environmentalists want cleaner air and water. So how do we make our ideas heard and put the pressure on government to take those desired actions? In America, people form interest groups to try to convince—or force—the government to act. These interest groups significantly influence American government and politics.

Interest Groups and American Government

An **interest group** is an organized group of people sharing common objectives who attempt to influence government policymakers through direct and indirect methods. Interest groups pursue their goals on every level and in every branch of government. On any given day, national interest groups are at work in Washington, D.C., urging government officials to support their positions on agriculture, voting rights, civil rights, oil and gas exploration, international trade, conservation and the environment, and much more. Many interest groups maintain headquarters in Washington, including those of the National Rifle Association (NRA), AARP (formerly the American Association of Retired Persons), and the National Wildlife Federation.

The right to form interest groups and ask government officials to act in a certain way is protected by the Bill of Rights. The First Amendment guarantees the right of the people "to petition the Government for a redress of grievances." The right to petition the government allows individual citizens and groups of citizens to lobby members of Congress and other government officials. To **lobby** is to engage in activities meant to influence the actions of the government. The term *lobbying* arose because, traditionally, individuals and groups interested in influencing government policy would gather in the lobby of the legislature to corner legislators and express their concerns. In addition to the right to lobby, interest groups have the right to sue the government if they believe laws or executive actions are wrongfully made or violate constitutional principles.

WHY INTEREST GROUPS FORM The United States includes many regions, scores of ethnic and economic groups, and a huge variety of businesses and occupations. The number of potential interests that can be represented is therefore enormous. It is worth remembering that not all groups that include people with a shared concern are considered interest groups. A group becomes an interest group when it is organized and actively seeks to affect the policies or practices of the government. Many groups do not meet this standard.

Sometimes a group founded with little or no desire to influence the government can become an interest group if its members decide that the government's policies are important to them. Alternatively, lobbying the government may initially be only one of several activities pursued by a group. Over time, lobbying may become the group's primary purpose.

The NRA provides an example of this process. From its establishment in 1871 until the 1930s, the group took little part in politics. As late as the 1970s, a large share of the NRA's members joined the organization for reasons that had nothing to do with politics. Many joined solely to participate in firearms training programs or to win certification for marksmanship. The NRA continues to provide training and certification programs today, but it is now so heavily politicized that any new member is likely to broadly agree with the NRA's political positions.

Interest groups may form—and existing groups may become more politically active—when the government expands its scope of activities. More government, in other words, means more interest groups. Prior to the 1970s, for example, the various levels of government were not nearly as active in attempting to regulate the use of firearms as they would be after that point. This change in government activity provides one explanation of why the NRA became more politically active.

Interest groups also may come into existence in response to a perceived threat to a group's interests. For example, the National Right to Life Committee, which opposes abortion, formed in response to *Roe v. Wade*, the Supreme Court's 1973 decision that legalized abortion. Interest groups can also form in

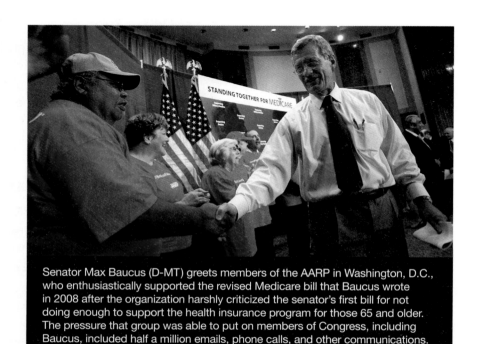

Senator Max Baucus (D-MT) greets members of the AARP in Washington, D.C., who enthusiastically supported the revised Medicare bill that Baucus wrote in 2008 after the organization harshly criticized the senator's first bill for not doing enough to support the health insurance program for those 65 and older. The pressure that group was able to put on members of Congress, including Baucus, included half a million emails, phone calls, and other communications.

reaction to the creation of other interest groups, thus pitting two groups against each other.

Some interest groups are established and thrive due to the importance and vitality of their leaders. AARP is an example of a group with a committed founder—Dr. Ethel Percy Andrus, a retired high school principal. Andrus organized the group in 1958 to enable older Americans to purchase health insurance collectively. Like the NRA, AARP did not develop into a lobbying powerhouse until years after it was founded.

Political scientists have looked into why people join interest groups. They are similar to the incentives you read about regarding the reasons people join political parties.

- Some people enjoy the sense of belonging that comes from associating with other people who share their interests. That enjoyment can be called a solidarity incentive.
- Some groups offer members material incentives for joining, such as discounts on products, subscriptions, or group insurance. These are material incentives.
- If a group stands for something that people believe is very important, they can gain satisfaction in taking action from within that group. Such satisfaction is a purposive incentive.

THE FREE RIDER PROBLEM Most of the goods and services that people use are private goods. These are goods that someone purchases for the purpose of consuming them. When that individual consumes them, no one else can do so. If someone eats a sandwich, no one else can have it.

Public goods are goods shared by everyone. One person's use of a public good does not diminish its use by someone else. National defense is an example. If this country is protected through its national defense system, one person's protection from enemy invasion does not reduce any other person's protection. Some people, nonetheless, benefit from some public goods but never pay for them or contribute their share. The existence of persons who benefit from the actions of a group but do not contribute to the group is known as the **free rider problem**.

Lobbying, collective bargaining by labor unions, and other forms of representation by interest groups

Political scientist Elinor Ostrom of Indiana University discusses her work at a press appearance at the university after winning the Nobel Prize in Economics in 2009. Ostrom argued that members of local communities often solve the free rider problem through collective management of natural resources.

can also be public goods. As a result, the free rider problem affects these groups as well. If an interest group is successful in lobbying for laws to improve air quality, for example, everyone who breathes that air will benefit, whether they paid for the lobbying effort or not. In some instances, the free rider problem can be overcome. For example, social pressure may persuade some people to join or donate to a group out of guilt. This motivation is more likely to be effective for small, localized groups than for large, widely dispersed groups like AARP, however.

The government can also ensure that the burden of lobbying for the public good is shared by all. When the government classifies interest groups as nonprofit organizations, it gives them tax-exempt status. The groups' operating costs are reduced because they do not have to pay taxes. The government's lost revenue is absorbed by all taxpayers.

HISTORICAL THINKING

1. **ANALYZE CAUSE AND EFFECT** Why do more interest groups arise or become more active when government expands its role or activities?
2. **SYNTHESIZE** Identify a public good other than national defense that is associated with a significant free rider problem, and explain why that problem arises.

How Interest Groups Function in American Politics

Though millions of Americans belong to interest groups, interest groups in general do not have a sterling reputation. People see them as having undue influence on political leaders, who are seen as overly susceptible to the demands of interest groups that contribute to their campaigns. To be more specific, people see the interest groups they don't belong to as having an undue influence, but they exempt the groups they belong to from this criticism. Despite this bad image, interest groups do serve several purposes in American politics:

- Interest groups help bridge the gap between citizens and government and enable citizens to explain their views on policies or issues to public officials.
- Interest groups help raise public awareness and inspire action on issues.
- Interest groups often provide public officials with specialized information that might be difficult to obtain otherwise. Public officials may draw on this information in making policy choices.
- Interest groups serve as another check on public officials to make sure they are carrying out their duties responsibly.

The American system of government invites the participation of interest groups by offering them many ways to influence policy as it is being considered and even once it is implemented. Consider the possibilities at just the federal level. An interest group can lobby members of Congress to act in the interests of the group. If the House of Representatives passes a bill opposed by the group, the group's lobbying efforts can shift to the Senate. If the Senate passes the bill and the president signs it, the group can try to influence the new law's application by lobbying the executive agency responsible for implementing the law. The group

CRITICAL VIEWING Lobbying is not always done by well-financed lobbyists in tailored suits who meet quietly with lawmakers behind closed doors. In late 2018, around 200 members of the Sunrise Movement staged a sit-in at the Capitol Hill office of House Minority Leader Nancy Pelosi (D-CA) to urge her to support a package of environmental actions called the Green New Deal. Why might this kind of lobbying be effective in persuading lawmakers to support a particular action? How might it backfire?

might even challenge the law—or the executive agency's implementation—in court.

THEORIES OF INTEREST GROUP INFLUENCE Political scientists analyze interest groups and their influence on government from several points of view. A traditional view of American democracy called **majoritarianism** is based on the idea that public policy should be set in accordance with the opinions of a majority of the people. Many Americans hold this view, but political scientists find it a poor description of how politics actually works. Many political scientists instead favor one of two other perspectives—pluralism and elite theory.

According to the **pluralist theory**, politics is a contest among various interest groups trying to gain benefits for their members. Pluralists maintain that the influence of interest groups on government is not undemocratic because individuals' interests are indirectly represented in the policymaking process through these groups. Although not every American belongs to an interest group, inevitably some group will represent at least some of the interests of each individual. Thus, each interest is satisfied to some extent through the compromises made in settling conflicts among competing interest groups.

Amount Spent on Lobbying, 1998–2018

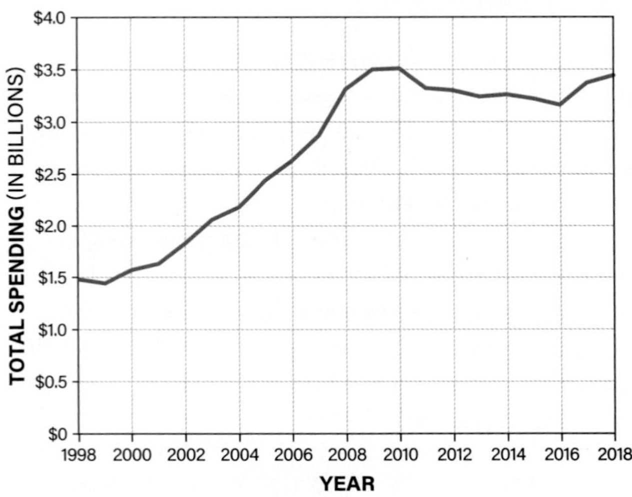

SOURCE: Data from Center for Responsive Politics

Pluralists also contend that because of the extensive number of interest groups vying for political benefits, no one group can dominate the political process. Additionally, because most people have more than one interest, conflicts among groups do not divide the nation into hostile camps. Not all scholars agree that this is how American democracy functions, however.

In contrast to the pluralist theory, **elite theory** is the view of democracy that sees the government as controlled by one or more elite groups, typically drawn from the wealthiest members of society. One version of elite theory posits that multiple elites compete for power. Although these two theories may seem to be at odds, it is worth noting that many interest groups are largely funded—or even controlled—by wealthy individuals, so pluralism and elite theory may overlap.

Many political scientists have long believed that both pluralism and elite theory contain elements of truth and reflect how groups influence government policy. Majoritarianism, in contrast, is only an ideal. Political scientists point out that the influence of average citizens, when separated from the impact of interest groups or elites, is effectively zero. It follows that ordinary citizens have a good reason to join interest groups. Only by doing so will they be heard.

Top Lobbying Groups, 2018

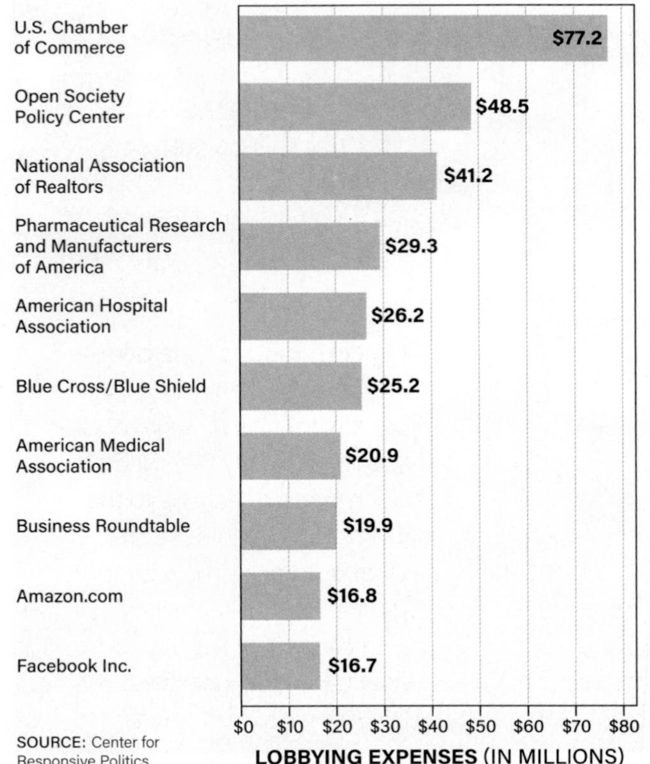

SOURCE: Center for Responsive Politics

INTEREST GROUPS VERSUS PARTIES Although both interest groups and political parties are groups of people who join together for political purposes, they differ in several important ways. A political party is organized to win elections, operate the government, and determine policy. Interest groups try to influence policy, but they don't necessarily attempt to win elections or operate the government. They also differ from political parties in these other ways:

- Political parties are broad-based organizations that must attract the support of many opposing groups and consider a large number of issues. Interest groups, in contrast, may promote only a handful of key policies, and their issues of concern tend to be clustered in one or two areas of public policy. An environmental group, for example, will not be as concerned about immigration policy as it is about combating pollution.
- Interest groups are usually more tightly organized than political parties. They are often financed through contributions or dues-paying memberships. Organizers of interest groups communicate with members and potential members through conferences, mailings, newsletters, and electronic formats such as email, Facebook, and Twitter. Parties do not usually reach out to all registered party members except during election campaigns.
- A political party's main sphere of influence is the electoral system. Parties run candidates for political office. Interest groups may try to influence the outcome of elections, but unlike parties, they do not compete for public office. Although a candidate for office may be sympathetic to—or even be a member of—a certain group, he or she does not run for election as a candidate of that group.

HISTORICAL THINKING

3. **ANALYZE CAUSE AND EFFECT** What would happen if interest groups were no longer permitted to lobby Congress?
4. **FORM AND SUPPORT OPINIONS** Which of the three theories describing American democracy do you find most convincing or reasonable? Why?
5. **INTERPRET GRAPHS** Based on the line graph of total spending on lobbying, how can you describe the trend in lobbying spending from 1998 to 2018?

Different Types of Interest Groups

American democracy embraces almost every conceivable type of interest group, and the number is increasing rapidly. Some interest groups have large memberships. AARP, for example, has more than 38 million members. Others, such as the Colorado Auctioneers Association, have fewer than 100 members. Some, such as the U.S. Chamber of Commerce, are household names and have been in existence for many years, while others crop up overnight. Some are highly structured and have full-time professional staffs, while others are loosely structured and informal.

BUSINESS GROUPS The most common interest groups are those that promote private business interests. These groups seek public policies that benefit the economic interests of their members and work against policies that threaten those interests. Business has long been well organized for effective action. Hundreds of business groups operate in Washington, D.C., in the 50 state capitals, and at the local level across the country.

There are also hundreds of trade organizations that represent a particular industry or segment of business. They are far less visible than some business organizations, such as the Chamber of Commerce, which broadly represents business interests, but trade organizations are an important resource for members. For example, the American Petroleum Institute (API), the primary trade organization of the U.S. oil and gas industries, has a mission "to influence public policy in support of a strong, viable U.S. oil and natural gas industry." Other business groups work for policies that favor the development of coal, solar power, or nuclear energy.

Traditionally, business interest groups have been staunch supporters of the Republican Party. This is because Republicans are seen as more likely to promote government policies friendly toward business. Since 2000, however, corporate donations to the Democratic National Committee have more than doubled. One reason that businesses now support both parties is that in some industries, business leaders are more likely to be Democrats than in the past. In others, some business leaders simply have positions that align more closely with that

Corn isn't just grown for human and animal feed—it's used in processing plants like this one to make ethanol, which is mixed with gasoline to run cars and trucks. In 2018, the Renewable Fuels Association—an energy industry interest group with ties to agricultural businesses—spent more than $1 million lobbying the Environmental Protection Agency to write new rules that would require that fuel contain up to 15 percent ethanol year-round—a change that would boost corn producers' sales and profits.

party. Financial industry leaders were once almost entirely Republican. Today some of them support the Democrats. Information technology, a relatively new industry, contains both Republicans and Democrats as well.

An additional reason many business interests support both parties is to ensure that they will have some influence regardless of who wins elections. There is another possible motivation: Campaign contributions may be made not to gain political favors but rather to avoid political disfavor that could damage the interests of business.

In our capitalist society, farms clearly are businesses. They are a particular kind of business, however, and receive special attention. Producers of specific farm commodities, such as dairy products, soybeans, grain, corn, and sugar beets, have formed their own organizations to promote their interests. In addition, many groups work for general agricultural interests.

Three broad-based agricultural groups represent millions of American farmers, from peanut farmers to dairy producers to tobacco growers. They are the American Farm Bureau Federation (Farm Bureau), the National Grange, and the National Farmers Union.

Interest groups representing farmers have succeeded in winning **agricultural subsidies**, financial assistance from the federal government to farmers and ranchers. The government can also restrict imports of a specific commodity, such as sugar. The restrictions raise the price of sugar, which benefits sugar beet growers at the expense of consumers.

LABOR INTEREST GROUPS Interest groups representing labor have been some of the most influential groups in our country's history. The largest and most powerful labor interest group today is the AFL-CIO (the American Federation of Labor–Congress of Industrial Organizations), a confederation of 55 unions representing 12.5 million organized workers.

Some unions not affiliated with the AFL-CIO also represent millions of members. For example, the Change to Win federation consists of four unions—the Teamsters, Service Employees International, the United Farm Workers, and the Communication Workers of America—that include 5.5 million workers. Dozens of other unions are independent.

States with Right-to-Work Laws, 2020

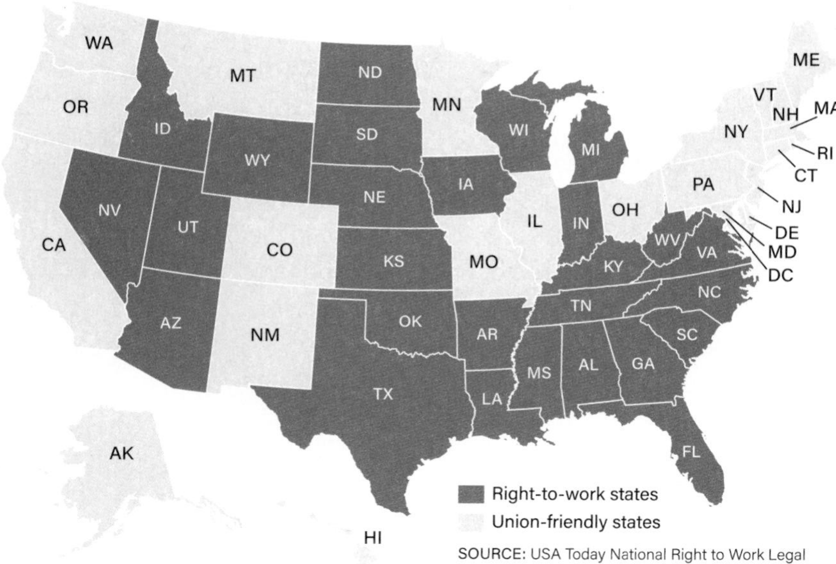

American labor unions press for policies to improve working conditions and ensure better pay for their members. Unions may compete with one another for new members. In many states, for example, the National Education Association and the AFL-CIO's American Federation of Teachers compete fiercely for members.

The goals of unions, however, are not necessarily limited to measures that directly benefit their own members. An example is the national campaign for a $15 minimum wage, which has received heavy union support. Very few of those who would benefit from a higher minimum wage are union members or likely to join in the future. Still, labor leaders push for the change, reasoning that a higher minimum wage would tend to push up wages generally, which would benefit all workers, including union members.

Another major issue for the labor movement is foreign trade. Unions have traditionally been hostile to trade agreements. Such agreements, in the view of many unions, cost American jobs. But unions split over their support for the United States-Mexico-Canada Agreement (USMCA), which the Trump administration negotiated in 2018 to replace the North American Free Trade Agreement (NAFTA). The AFL-CIO, one of the largest federations of labor unions in the United States, approved the Trump administration's tough stand on the trade practices of China. At the same time, the labor organization sharply criticized the administration's tariff policy, especially tariffs imposed on allies like Canada.

Although unions were highly influential in the 1930s, 1940s, and 1950s, their strength and political power have waned in the last several decades. One reason for the decline is the continuing fall in the proportion of the nation's workforce employed in blue-collar jobs—a term that refers to jobs that require protective clothing such as helmets, work boots, or safety goggles—in manufacturing and transportation. These sectors have always been among the most heavily unionized. Another factor in labor's decline is the general political environment. Forming and maintaining unions is more difficult in the United States and is not encouraged by U.S. laws the way it is in most other industrial nations. Many business owners in the United States oppose unions and try to ensure that their own businesses remain nonunionized.

The impact of the political environment on labor's organizing ability can be easily seen by comparing rates of unionization in various states. These rates are especially low in conservative southern states. Georgia and South Carolina are both major manufacturing states, but unions represent only 3.9 percent of those employed in Georgia and only 1.6 percent in South Carolina. Compare these figures with rates in more liberal states, such as California, where unions represent 15.9 percent of the workforce, and in New York, in which 23.6 percent of the workforce is in unions. One factor that depresses, or lowers, unionization rates is that many states in the South and West have a **right-to-work law**, a law that keeps unions from requiring dues or other fees from nonunion members. Under right-to-work laws, workers who benefit from union-negotiated wages and working conditions are not required to pay dues to the union, thus weakening the union. Twenty-eight states have right-to-work laws.

While organized labor has suffered from declining numbers and a resulting loss in lobbying power, labor has held the line in one industry—government. In the 1960s and 1970s, public-sector unions enjoyed rapid growth. The percentage of government workers who are union members then leveled off, but it remains high. More than one-third of all public-sector workers are union members today.

In contrast to unions in the private sector, public-sector unions do not have the right to strike over wages and working conditions. Still, they are influential. Unlike workers in private industry, public-sector employees—in their role as citizens—have the right to vote for their own bosses. As a result, elected officials are often reluctant to antagonize public-sector unions. One consequence of the influence of these unions is that government workers typically enjoy pension benefits that are substantially more generous than those received by private-sector workers.

Since the 2010 elections, several Republican governors in the Midwest have attempted to curtail the bargaining rights of state and local government employee unions. These governors argue that pension benefits and other perks won by the unions threaten the financial stability of state and local governments. The role and status of public-sector unions, therefore, have become important political issues.

Public unions endure one additional problem, one determined by the Supreme Court decision of *Janus v. AFSCME* in 2018. Similar in effect to right-to-work laws, this decision declared that public-sector unions cannot charge fees to public employees who do not join the union. Although these employees may benefit from union activities, they cannot be required to pay dues to the union.

PROFESSIONAL INTEREST GROUPS Most professions that require advanced education or specialized training have organizations to protect and promote their interests. These groups are concerned mainly with the standards of their professions, but they also work to influence government policy. Major professional groups include the American Medical Association (AMA), representing physicians; the American Bar Association (ABA), representing lawyers; and the American Association for Justice, representing trial lawyers. There are dozens of other less well-known and less politically active professional groups.

HISTORICAL THINKING

6. **MAKE INFERENCES** What interest groups might differ with labor unions over trade agreements with other countries? Why?
7. **COMPARE AND CONTRAST** How are professional interest groups different from labor interest groups?
8. **MAKE INFERENCES** With union membership over 25 percent of its workforce, do you think it is likely that New York state would pass a right-to-work law? Explain.

Public Interest and Other Types of Groups

Some interest groups have aims other than benefiting narrow economic interests of their members. These include so-called **public-interest groups**, groups formed with the broader goal of working for the public good. The American Civil Liberties Union (ACLU) and Common Cause are examples. Of course, there is no such thing as a single clear public interest in a nation of more than 325 million diverse people. While the ACLU works to protect the civil liberties of all Americans and Common Cause is a nonpartisan group that works to promote open and honest government throughout the nation, only a small portion of the population belongs to these groups.

CONSUMER INTEREST GROUPS In the 1960s and 1970s, a number of groups organized to protect consumer rights, and some are still active today. One well-known group is Consumers Union, a nonprofit organization started in 1936. In addition to publishing *Consumer Reports* magazine, Consumers Union monitors and criticizes government agencies when they appear to act against consumer interests. Consumer groups are active in many cities. They deal with such problems as substandard housing, discrimination against minorities and women, discrimination in the granting of credit, and business inaction on consumer complaints.

IDENTITY INTEREST GROUPS Americans who share the same race, ethnicity, gender, or other characteristics often have important common interests. African Americans, for example, have a powerful interest in combating racism and racial discrimination. Numerous groups have formed to promote civil rights, including the National Association for the Advancement of Colored People (NAACP), founded in 1909, and the National Urban League, created in 1910. During the civil rights movement of the 1950s and 1960s, African Americans organized a number of new groups, including the Southern Christian Leadership Conference (SCLC), founded in 1957, which remains active today. Among the most recent interest groups formed to address the concerns of African Americans is Color of Change, an online racial justice organization, and the loosely organized Black Lives Matter movement. While its mission varies widely in different locations, at its core Black Lives Matter seeks to publicize and end alleged police violence toward African Americans and other minority group members.

The campaigns for dignity and equality of Native Americans, Latinos, women, the LGBTQ community, Americans with disabilities, and other groups have all resulted in important interest groups. Older American citizens are numerous, are politically active, and have a great deal at stake in debates over certain programs, such as Social Security and Medicare. As a result, groups representing them, such as AARP, can be a potent political force.

IDEOLOGICAL INTEREST GROUPS Some interest groups are organized to promote not an economic

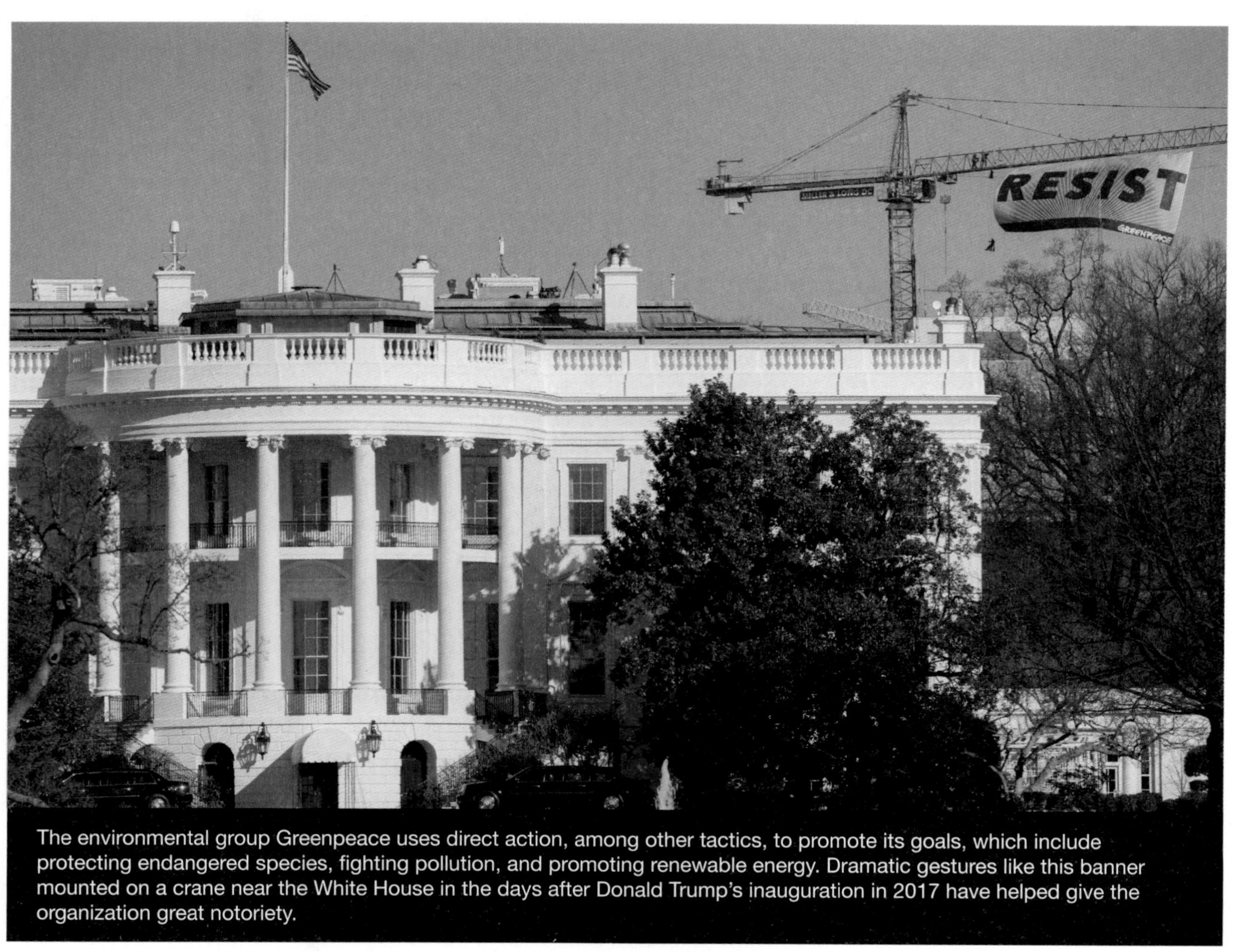

The environmental group Greenpeace uses direct action, among other tactics, to promote its goals, which include protecting endangered species, fighting pollution, and promoting renewable energy. Dramatic gestures like this banner mounted on a crane near the White House in the days after Donald Trump's inauguration in 2017 have helped give the organization great notoriety.

interest or a collective identity but a shared political perspective or ideology. Examples include MoveOn, an Internet-oriented liberal group, and the Club for Growth, a conservative organization that favors lower taxes. The Tea Party movement, which sprang into life in 2009, has been described as an ideological interest group, but political scientists don't see it that way. Because some Tea Party groups have attempted to gain control of local Republican Party organizations, they see the Tea Party as a political party faction rather than an interest group.

Environmental groups have supported water pollution controls, wilderness protection, and clean-air legislation. They have opposed strip mining, nuclear power plants, logging activities, chemical waste dumps, using fracking to extract oil and natural gas, and many other potential environmental hazards. Environmental interest groups range from traditional organizations that focus on education and lobbying, such as the National Wildlife Federation with more than 4 million members and the Sierra Club with 3 million members, to smaller groups that focus on activism, such as Greenpeace USA with a membership of 250,000.

In the past, environmental groups have been characterized as single-interest groups, not ideological organizations. Issues such as climate change, however, have led many present-day environmental groups to advocate sweeping changes to the entire economy. Groups with such broad agendas could be considered a type of ideological interest group.

RELIGIOUS GROUPS Religious organizations are another type of group that could be included in the ideological category. Many religious groups work on behalf of conservative social causes. Others advocate for policies they believe will further the well-being of those suffering from poverty and discrimination, including immigrants. Catholic organizations, Lutherans, the National Council of Churches, Jewish organizations, Unitarians, and Quakers are among the many religious groups who try to influence such policies. The U.S. Council of Muslim Organizations lobbies for measures that promote the welfare of American Muslims and U.S. support for human rights for Muslims worldwide.

OTHER INTEREST GROUPS Numerous interest groups focus on a single issue. For example, Mothers Against Drunk Driving (MADD) lobbies for stiffer penalties for driving while intoxicated. The abortion debate has created various single-issue groups, such as the National Right to Life organization (which opposes abortion) and NARAL Pro-Choice America (which favors abortion rights). Other examples of single-issue groups are the NRA; Everytown for Gun Safety, which lobbies for stronger gun control laws; and the American Israel Public Affairs Committee (AIPAC), a pro-Israel group.

Efforts by state and local governments to lobby the federal government have escalated in recent years. The federal government has sometimes lobbied in individual states, too. Until 2009, for example, the U.S. Attorney General's office lobbied against medical marijuana use in states that were considering ballot measures on the issue.

People living in poverty have not formed their own interest group, but they have been aided by the activities of liberal and religious interest groups. Due to lobbying by these groups, low-income taxpayers are largely exempt from income taxes. They pay only payroll taxes, and in many cases, they can get rebates on these. In addition, the government has many programs that provide those in poverty with subsidized housing, assistance in purchasing food, and health-care coverage through Medicaid. The Brookings Institution has estimated that all federal low-income programs together cost more than $800 billion a year. If there were no federal programs aimed at low-income persons, as many as 25 percent of U.S. families would have incomes below the official poverty line. If all benefits that low-income families receive are taken into account, that number drops to about 10 percent.

HISTORICAL THINKING

9. **MAKE GENERALIZATIONS** What goal do public-interest groups have in common?
10. **ANALYZE VISUALS** Is hanging a banner behind the White House, as Greenpeace did after Trump's inauguration, more typical of a single-interest group or an ideological interest group? Explain.

LESSON
14.5 What Interest Groups Do

Interest groups operate at all levels of government and use a variety of strategies to steer policies in ways beneficial to their interests. They can attempt to influence policymakers directly by meeting with them and supporting their election campaigns with donations. They may try to exert indirect influence on policymakers by shaping public opinion. The extent and nature of a group's activities depend on its goals and its resources. Success may bring intense scrutiny to the strategies used to influence legislators, agencies, and other public officials—and sometimes raises ethical questions.

How Interest Groups Shape Policy

As you have read, lobbying refers to the methods used by organizations or individuals to influence the passage, defeat, or contents of legislation or to influence the administrative decisions of government. A lobbyist is someone who handles a particular interest group's lobbying efforts. Most of the larger interest groups have lobbyists in Washington, D.C.

DIRECT LOBBYING TECHNIQUES Lobbying can be directed at the legislative branch of government, at administrative agencies, and even at the courts. Many lobbyists also work at state and local levels.

Interest groups often become directly involved in the election process. Many group members join and work with political parties to influence party platforms and the nomination of candidates. Interest groups provide campaign support for legislators who favor their policies and sometimes encourage their own members to try to win posts in party organizations. Most importantly, interest groups urge their members to vote

PAC and Super PAC Contributions to Federal Candidates, 1980–2018

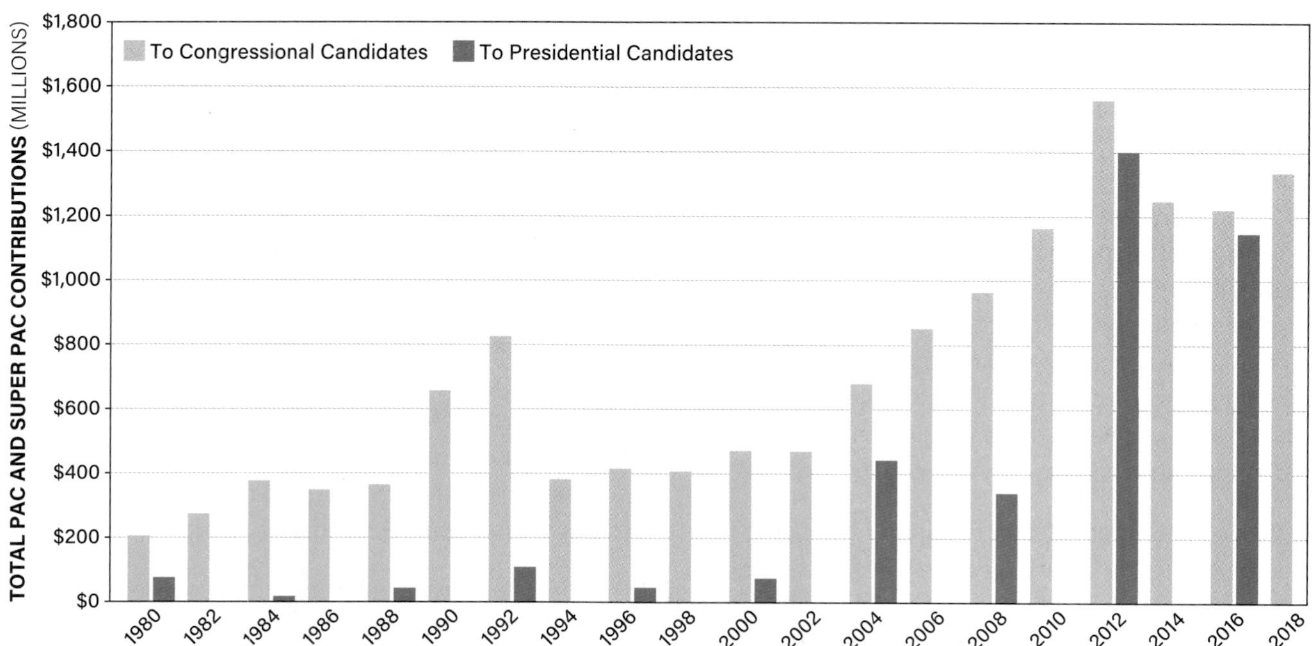

SOURCE: Bipartisan Policy Center, Center for Responsive Politics

Direct Lobbying Techniques

TECHNIQUE	DESCRIPTION
Personal contact	A lobbyist's personal contacts with key legislators or other government officials—in their offices, in the halls of Congress, or on social occasions such as dinners, boating expeditions, and the like—are one of the most effective direct lobbying techniques.
Providing expertise and research results	Lobbyists often have knowledge and expertise that are useful in drafting legislation, and these can be major strengths for an interest group. Harried members of Congress cannot possibly be experts on everything they vote on and therefore eagerly seek information to help them make up their minds.
Testifying before congressional committees	When testifying before a congressional committee on pending legislation, lobbyists offer as much evidence as possible to support their group's position.
Providing legal advice	Many lobbyists assist legislators in drafting legislation. Lobbyists are a source of ideas and sometimes offer legal advice on specific details.
Following up on legislation	Because executive agencies responsible for carrying out legislation can often change the scope of the new law, lobbyists may also try to influence the bureaucrats who implement the policy.

for candidates who support the group's views. They can also threaten legislators with the withdrawal of votes and with the prospect of contributing money and lending support to challengers when those lawmakers run for re-election. The larger the group, the more important its support.

Since the 1970s, federal laws governing campaign financing have allowed corporations, labor unions, and special interest groups to raise funds and make campaign contributions through political action committees (PACs). Both the number of PACs and the amount of money PACs spend on elections have grown significantly. There were about 1,000 PACs in 1976. Today, there are more than 4,500 PACs. In 1973, total spending by PACs amounted to $19 million. In the 2015–2016 election cycle, contributions to federal candidates by PACs totaled about $450 million. Of course, campaign contributions do not guarantee that officials will vote the way the groups wish, but they usually ensure the groups will have the ear of the public officials they helped elect.

In 2010, the Supreme Court upended campaign finance in *Citizens United* v. *Federal Election Commission*. The Court ruled that PACs could accept unlimited contributions from individuals, unions, and corporations as long as they were used for independent expenditures—that is, spending that is not coordinated with a candidate's campaign or a political party. This ruling led to the creation of organizations called Super PACs, which channeled almost $1.8 billion into election spending in the 2016 election cycle and more than $1.5 billion in the 2018 midterm elections.

INDIRECT LOBBYING TECHNIQUES Interest groups also try to influence public policy indirectly through the general public. Such indirect techniques may appear to be spontaneous, but they are generally as well planned as direct lobbying techniques. Indirect techniques can be particularly effective because public officials are often more impressed by contacts from voters than from lobbyists.

Public opinion weighs significantly in the policymaking process. If public opinion favors a certain group's interests, officials will be more ready to listen to that group. Groups can cultivate public opinion through social media and email, television publicity, advertisements, and mass mailings. Whatever the group and whatever the method of presenting the message, the goal is to influence public opinion.

Some interest groups also try to influence legislators by publishing rating systems that evaluate each lawmaker according to his or her support for the particular group's goals. After selecting legislative issues that align with its goals, a group rates legislators according to how often they voted favorably on those issues. For example, a score of 90 percent on the Americans for Democratic Action (ADA) rating scale means a legislator supported that liberal group's position to a high degree. The group can publicize these ratings when the lawmaker is up for re-election, highlighting for its members the candidate's fidelity—or opposition—to the group's positions.

One of the most powerful indirect techniques used by interest groups is the issue ad, such as a television commercial taking a position on an issue. The Supreme Court has ruled that the First Amendment's guarantee of free speech protects any interest group's right to promote its position on issues. It must, however, fund such activities through independent expenditures that are not coordinated with a candidate's campaign or a political party. Nevertheless, issue ads are controversial, or divisive, because the funds spent to air issue ads have had a clear effect on the outcome of elections. Both political parties have benefited from such interest group spending.

The Bipartisan Campaign Reform Act of 2002 banned unlimited donations to campaigns and political parties, known as soft money. Since then, interest groups that had previously given soft money to parties set up new groups called 527s, named after the provision of the tax code that covers these groups. The 527s engaged in such practices as voter registration, but they also began making large expenditures on issue ads. These were determined to be legal so long as the 527s did not coordinate their activities with candidates' campaigns. In the 2008 presidential elections, campaign finance lawyers created a new type of group, the 501(c)4 organization, also named after a section of the tax code. Interest groups such as the Sierra Club and Citizens Against Government Waste have set up special 501(c)4 organizations.

Lawyers have argued that a 501(c)4 group could spend some of its funds on direct campaign contributions as long as most of the group's spending was on issue advocacy. Further, these attorneys claimed, a 501(c)4 group had the right to conceal the identity of its contributors. Federal agencies and the courts have not yet determined the legality of these claims.

Interest groups sometimes urge members to contact government officials—by email, social media, text message, or telephone—to show their support for or opposition to a policy. Such efforts are known as grassroots organizing. Large interest groups

One approach taken by interest groups is the pursuit of their goals through the courts, a major tactic employed by the NAACP through its Legal Defense Fund (LDF). Founded by Thurgood Marshall, shown here working on a 1949 case, the LDF pursues equal rights by bringing legal action to prevent discrimination in such areas as voting rights, education, criminal justice, and economic rights.

can convince members to generate hundreds of thousands of letters, emails, texts, tweets, and phone calls. Interest groups often provide form messages for constituents to use. The NRA used this tactic to block strict federal gun control legislation by delivering half a million letters to Congress within a few weeks. Policymakers recognize that these types of communications are initiated by interest groups. The volume of communications has to be very large to impress them.

The legal system offers another avenue for interest groups to influence the political process. Throughout the 20th century, civil rights groups paved the way for interest group **litigation**, or the act of bringing a lawsuit against another party, winning major victories in cases concerning equal housing, school desegregation, and employment discrimination. Environmental groups, such as the Sierra Club, have also used litigation to press their concerns. For example, an environmental group might challenge in court an activity that threatens to pollute the environment. The legal challenge forces those engaging in the activity to defend their actions and may delay or derail the project.

An interest group can also attempt to influence the outcome of litigation without being an actual party to a lawsuit. It does so by filing a statement in court called an *amicus curiae*, or simply amicus brief. *Amicus curiae* means "friend of the court." (The phrase is pronounced ah-MEE-kus KURE-ee-eye.) The brief states the group's legal argument in support of its desired outcome in a case.

For example, the case *Arizona v. United States*, heard by the Supreme Court in 2012, turned on whether a state government could enact immigration laws tougher than those of the federal government. Dozens of organizations filed amicus briefs. Conservative groups supported the state, as did Arizona elected officials, including the state legislature. Those backing the federal government, which had challenged the Arizona law, included the organization of Catholic bishops, labor unions, the American Bar Association, and a variety of civil liberties groups. In such briefs, interest groups often cite statistics and research that support their position on a certain issue in addition to making legal arguments. This research can have considerable influence on the judges deciding the case. In this case, the Court upheld the federal government's contention that Arizona could not enact state immigration laws more stringent than the immigration laws of the federal government.

Some interest groups stage protests to dramatize an issue. The Boston Tea Party of 1773, in which American colonists disguised as Native Americans threw tea into Boston Harbor to protest British taxes, shows how long this tactic has been around. Over the years, many groups have organized protest marches and rallies to support or oppose legalized abortion, LGBTQ rights, the treatment of Native Americans, the killing of Black men by police officers, protests by students against school shootings, military actions, and many more issues.

Protest marches were a major tactic of the civil rights movement of the 1950s and 1960s, and they continue

Labor activist César Chávez (center) leads migrant workers of the National Farm Workers Association—the labor group he co-founded—in picketing outside a California farm in 1966. The year before, Chávez launched a strike against grape growers to win recognition of his labor organization. Chávez used picketing to promote the farmworkers' cause, which forced growers of grapes, lettuce, and other products to recognize the workers' union.

to be prominent today. In January 2017, for example, about 4.2 million people across the country joined women's marches against President Trump's policies. These women's marches—also attended by many men—may have been the largest demonstrations in U.S. history.

Not all demonstrations are peaceful. Anti-abortion rights groups have bombed abortion clinics, and members of the Animal Liberation Front have broken into laboratories and freed animals being used for experimentation. Such tactics tend to backfire, however. Violent demonstrations can hurt the cause of those who use them by calling their motives into question and angering the public.

HISTORICAL THINKING

1. **MAKE INFERENCES** Why might some lawmakers pay more attention to contacts by ordinary people than those from lobbyists?
2. **INTERPRET TABLES** Based on the table listing direct lobbying techniques, how might lobbyists claim they provide a valuable service to legislators and the public through their work?

Lobbyists and Government

Interest groups and their lobbyists have become a permanent fixture of American government. All the major interest groups have headquarters in Washington, D.C., where lobbyists and staff members move freely between their groups' headquarters, congressional offices and committee rooms, and the offices of executive branch agencies and bureaus. Interest group representatives are routinely consulted when Congress drafts new legislation and are frequently asked to testify before congressional committees on the potential effect of legislation or regulations. As a result, lobbying has developed into a profession. A professional lobbyist is a valuable ally to any interest group seeking to influence government.

In recent years, it has become increasingly common for those who leave positions with the federal government to become lobbyists or consultants for the private-interest groups they once helped regulate. In fact, lobbying is a popular job choice among retiring members of Congress. The practice is controversial, however. Ex-government officials can parlay valuable connections and expertise into huge salaries. Sometimes these retired officials return to government to work in the agencies or departments that oversee the industry for which they once lobbied. Many people question whether former lobbyists can remain objective in government careers. Legislation and regulations have been designed to reduce this revolving door, but it still functions quite well.

HISTORICAL THINKING

3. **FORM AND SUPPORT OPINIONS** Should former members of Congress be prohibited from becoming lobbyists? Explain your response.
4. **EVALUATE** Do lobbyists have too much access to members of Congress and other government officials? Why do you agree or disagree?

Why Do Interest Groups Get Bad Press?

Despite their importance to democratic government, interest groups are often criticized by both the public and the press. Every so often, political cartoons appear in the media depicting lobbyists standing in the hallways of Congress with briefcases stuffed with money. These cartoons are not entirely factual, but they are not entirely fictitious either.

Consider an example that illustrates the influence of money on government decisions—in this instance, a court case. In 2004, the chief executive officer of a coal company donated $3 million to the election campaign of Brent Benjamin, a candidate for the West Virginia Supreme Court, who won the election. At that time, the coal company was appealing a decision against it that imposed $50 million in damages on the company. The state supreme court ruled 3–2 in favor of the coal company, with Benjamin voting with the majority. Hugh Caperton, who had won the original suit against the company, appealed the decision to the U.S. Supreme Court, on the grounds that Benjamin should not have been involved in the decision. In 2009, in *Caperton* v. *Massey Coal Co.*, the U.S. Supreme Court agreed with Caperton that the judge should have refrained from participating in the case because of the appearance of bias and reversed the state supreme court decision.

In 2015 and 2016, Republicans alleged that foreign interests had benefited from donations they made to the Clinton Foundation, a charitable fund organized by former secretary of state Hillary Clinton and her husband, former president Bill Clinton. Republicans charged that donors received access to Hillary Clinton when she was secretary of state and that she recommended government actions favorable to donors' interests as a result of this access. Critics were unable to establish any clear connection between the donations to the foundation and the secretary of state's actions, however.

A major complaint by critics of interest groups is that the benefits these groups obtain are not in the general public interest. Critics say there is an enthusiasm gap between supporters and opponents of any given issue. Sugar producers, for example, benefit greatly from restrictions on sugar imports and thus work to ensure that these restrictions continue. Yet for sugar consumers—everyone else—the price of sugar is a trivial matter. Candy-makers and soft drink manufacturers aside, those who consume sugar have little incentive to organize. This enthusiasm gap is referred to as the problem of concentrated benefits and dispersed costs, meaning that a few people benefit in a major way, while many people are disadvantaged in a small way.

People tend to think that lobbyists representing business interests target federal regulation. Many of the restrictions that can hobble economic activity, however, are imposed at the state and local levels. For example, California requires an individual to obtain a license to work as a manicurist in the beauty industry. To qualify for the license, an individual must train for 400 hours. A license must be renewed every five years at a cost of up to $100. Established businesses often pressure state governments to enact such requirements, which limit competition.

HISTORICAL THINKING

5. **FORM AND SUPPORT OPINIONS** Why should voters be concerned about restrictions on sugar imports when the cost to them is trivial?

The Regulation of Lobbyists

In an attempt to control lobbying, Congress passed the Federal Regulation of Lobbying Act in 1946. The major provisions of the act are as follows:

- Any person or organization that receives money to influence legislation must register with the clerk of the House and the secretary of the Senate.
- Any groups or persons registering must identify their employer, salary, amount and purpose of expenses, and duration of employment.
- Every registered lobbyist must make quarterly reports on his or her activities.
- Anyone violating this act can be fined up to $10,000 and be imprisoned for up to five years.

The act did not significantly limit lobbying, however. For one thing, the Supreme Court restricted the application of the law to only those lobbyists who sought to influence federal legislation directly. Any lobbyist seeking to influence legislation indirectly through public opinion did not fall within the scope of the law. Second, only persons or organizations whose principal purpose was to influence legislation were required to register. Many groups avoided registration by claiming that their principal function was something else. Third, the act did not cover those whose lobbying was directed at agencies in the executive branch or lobbyists who testified before congressional committees. Fourth, the public was almost totally unaware of the information in the quarterly reports filed by lobbyists. Not until 1995 did Congress finally address those loopholes by enacting new legislation.

In 1995, Congress passed the Lobbying Disclosure Act that reformed the 1946 act in the following ways:

- Strict definitions now apply to determine who must register with the clerk of the House and the secretary of the Senate as a lobbyist. A lobbyist is anyone who either spends at least 20 percent of his or her time lobbying members of Congress, their staffs, or executive-branch officials or is paid more than $5,000 in a six-month period for such work. Any organization that spends more than $20,000 in a six-month period conducting such lobbying activity must also register. These amounts have since been adjusted to $2,500 and $10,000 per quarter, respectively.

- Lobbyists must report the names of their clients, the issues on which they lobbied, and the agency or chamber of Congress they contacted, although they do not need to disclose the names of those they contacted.

Tax-exempt organizations, such as religious groups, were exempted from these provisions, as were organizations that engage in grassroots lobbying, such as a media campaign that asks people to write or call their congressional representative. Nonetheless, the number of registered lobbyists nearly doubled in the first few years after the new legislation took effect simply because the rules for disclosure were more tightly written.

In 2005, a number of lobbying scandals in Washington, D.C., came to light. As a result, following the midterm elections of 2006, the new Democratic majority in the Senate and House undertook lobbying reform. Congress made changes to the rules that the two chambers impose on their members. Bundled campaign contributions, in which a lobbyist arranges for contributions from a variety of sources, would have to be reported. Expenditures on the sometimes lavish parties to benefit candidates with contributions from party guests would have to be reported as well.

In 2007, President George W. Bush signed the Honest Leadership and Open Government Act. This law increased lobbying disclosure requirements and further restricted members of Congress from receiving gifts and travel paid for by lobbyists. The act included provisions requiring the disclosure of lawmakers' requests for earmarks, which are special provisions that benefit a lawmaker's constituents added to other legislation. Earmarks often support projects in the congressperson's district or state.

In March 2010, the Republican-led House Appropriations Committee banned earmarks that benefit profit-making corporations. Thousands of such earmarks had been authorized in the previous year, to the value of roughly $20 billion. The ban was renewed in 2012. The Senate did not ban earmarks, but it did require public disclosure of the names of the senators who support the earmarks.

HISTORICAL THINKING

6. **ANALYZE CAUSE AND EFFECT** The right to lobby is protected by the Constitution. If that weren't so, would it be a good idea to ban lobbying? Why or why not?
7. **DRAW CONCLUSIONS** What is wrong with earmarks if they benefit a lawmaker's constituents?

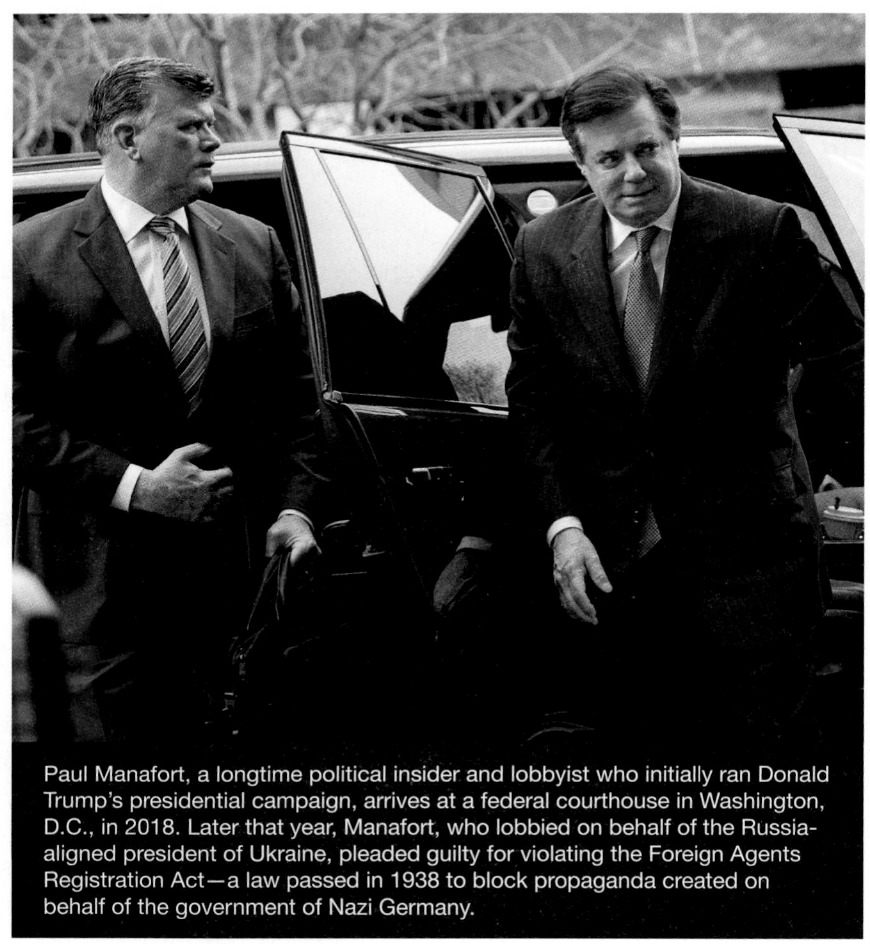

Paul Manafort, a longtime political insider and lobbyist who initially ran Donald Trump's presidential campaign, arrives at a federal courthouse in Washington, D.C., in 2018. Later that year, Manafort, who lobbied on behalf of the Russia-aligned president of Ukraine, pleaded guilty for violating the Foreign Agents Registration Act—a law passed in 1938 to block propaganda created on behalf of the government of Nazi Germany.

CHAPTER 14

POLITICAL PARTIES AND INTEREST GROUPS

Review

VOCABULARY

For each pair of vocabulary words, write one sentence that explains the connection between the words.

1. realignment; electorate
2. party platform; interest group
3. coalition; third party
4. ward; precinct
5. lobby; litigation
6. free rider problem; right-to-work laws
7. majoritarianism; pluralist theory

MAIN IDEAS

Answer the following questions. Support your answer with evidence from the chapter.

8. How did the first political parties arise? **LESSON 14.1**
9. Why is a party platform so important? **LESSON 14.1**
10. What are the advantages and disadvantages of partisanship in today's political environment? **LESSON 14.1**
11. How has dealignment affected politics today? **LESSON 14.1**
12. What purposes do political parties serve in our democratic system? **LESSON 14.2**
13. Why do people join political parties? **LESSON 14.2**
14. How do the three types of third parties differ? **LESSON 14.3**
15. Explain the difference between the pluralism and elite theories used to describe the influence of interest groups on government. **LESSON 14.4**
16. What was the significance of the *Janus* v. *AFSCME* decision, in which the Supreme Court ruled that non-union members cannot be forced to pay union dues, even if they benefit from union protections? **LESSON 14.4**
17. How do public interest and consumer interest groups serve the public? **LESSON 14.4**
18. What is the difference between direct and indirect lobbying techniques? **LESSON 14.5**
19. What is the enthusiasm gap, and how can it affect policy on an issue? **LESSON 14.5**

HISTORICAL THINKING

Answer the following questions. Support your answer with evidence from the chapter.

20. **FORM AND SUPPORT OPINIONS** Washington said that "spirit of party . . . agitates the community with ill-founded jealousies and false alarms." Is this an accurate description of how parties operate? Explain.
21. **IDENTIFY MAIN IDEAS AND DETAILS** How did the Republican Party win over African-American voters in the 1860s? How did it lose them in the 1930s?
22. **DRAW CONCLUSIONS** Demographers expect that minority group members will form a majority of the U.S. population by 2050. How might this affect the two major parties?
23. **IDENTIFY PROBLEMS AND SOLUTIONS** Do third parties make an important contribution to American politics? Explain.
24. **FORM AND SUPPORT OPINIONS** Do interest groups improve the democratic process or obstruct it?
25. **MAKE CONNECTIONS** If you are a member of an interest group, why did you join? If you are not, would you join one? Why or why not?
26. **MAKE INFERENCES** Why has Congress passed various laws aimed at forcing lobbyists to make public their activities?

INTERPRET VISUALS

The graph below shows how people voted during the 2018 election for members of the House of Representatives based on their age and level of education.

27. Which age group voted most heavily Democratic?

28. How did college education affect the party that voters supported?

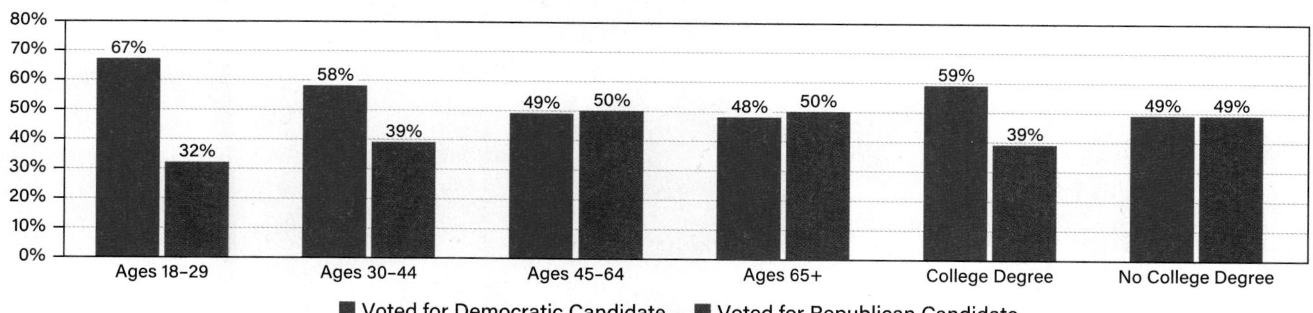

SOURCE: Data from National Election Pool exit polls

ANALYZE SOURCES

Read the following excerpt from a fireside chat delivered by President Franklin Roosevelt in 1938.

> An election cannot give a country a firm sense of direction if it has two or more national parties which merely have different names but are as alike in their principles and aims as peas in the same pod.
>
> —President Franklin D. Roosevelt, June 24, 1938

29. Based on this quotation, what does Roosevelt see as the role of parties in the American political system?

CONNECT TO YOUR LIFE

30. **ARGUMENT** Political action committees (PACs) are highly controversial. The Supreme Court in *Citizens United* v. *Federal Election Commission* ruled that these organizations can channel almost unlimited funds toward elections as long as they are not coordinated with a particular candidate's campaign or with a political party. What is your point of view? Do research to learn what people think about the right of PACs to operate and what their arguments are. Then write an essay presenting your views, giving reasons and examples to support your position.

TIPS

- Review the discussion of PACs in the chapter, and do research as necessary to learn about the arguments for and against their campaign activities.
- Consider the implications for society resulting from the Supreme Court ruling. Consider the ways your own life has been affected as you develop your analysis.
- In your opening paragraph, briefly explain how PACs work and then clearly state your point of view on the question of whether PACs should have unlimited rights to be involved in campaigns. Include a brief description of how your life has been affected.
- In the rest of your essay, give strong reasons, data, or examples to support your opinion.
- Be sure to address arguments someone who takes the opposite point of view would give, and tell why you disagree with that position.

CHAPTER

15

The Electoral Process

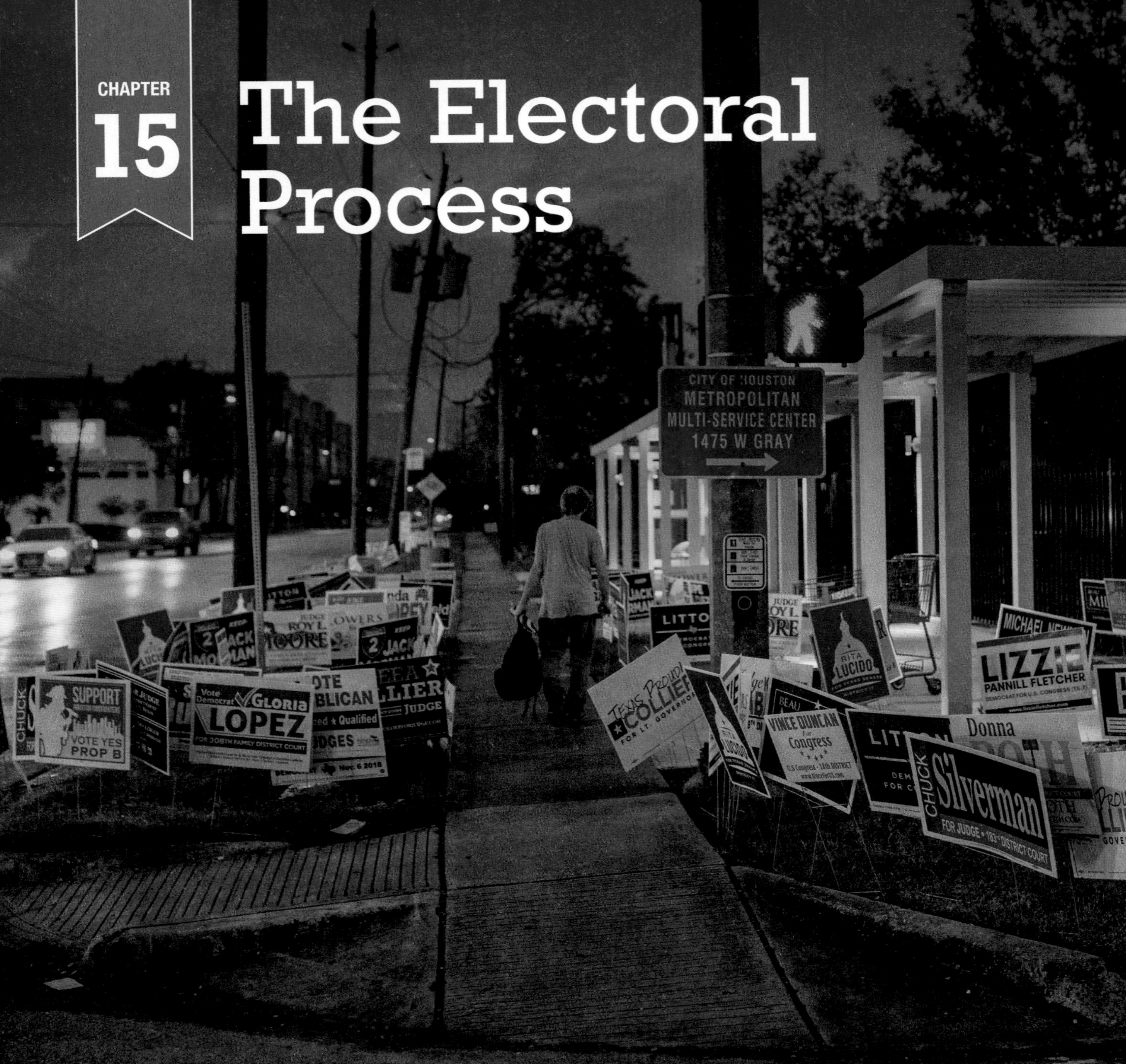

LESSONS

15.1 How We Nominate Candidates

15.2 Nominating Presidential Candidates

15.3 How We Elect Candidates

National Geographic Online:
Election Maps Can Be Misleading—Here's a Solution

15.4 The Modern Political Campaign

15.5 Financing Political Campaigns

CRITICAL VIEWING The process of getting elected to public office can be lengthy, costly, and complex. During election campaigns, candidates work hard to connect with voters and publicize their positions on important issues. Do you think campaign signs like these in Houston, Texas, on election day in 2018 play a critical role in the electoral process? Why or why not?

LESSON
15.1 How We Nominate Candidates

Many Americans groan when they see a political ad or a fundraising appeal from a campaign, yet campaigns are a vital part of the election process, and elections are an essential feature of American democracy. It is through campaigns—advertisements as well as personal appearances, speeches, debates, opinion polls, news coverage, and commentary—that citizens learn about the candidates and decide how they will cast their votes. Campaigning for elective office is a long and expensive undertaking that starts with the decision to seek nomination.

The Role of Parties in Nominations

As you have read, a key role of political parties is to narrow the field of candidates for state and federal elective office through the nomination process. The nomination process at the local level is different, however; political parties generally don't participate directly in local elections.

NOMINATIONS FOR LOCAL, STATE, AND FEDERAL OFFICES In elections at the local government level, self-nomination is the most common way to become a candidate. A self-proclaimed candidate usually files a petition to be listed on the **ballot**—a list of candidates that voters mark to indicate their choices in an election. State laws specify how many signatures on a petition qualify a candidate to appear on the ballot. Such requirements eliminate candidates who cannot get a minimal amount of public backing.

Most candidates for state or national office are nominated by a political party and receive considerable support from their party throughout their campaigns. Once nominated, the candidates from each party, along with any qualified independent candidates, run against one another in what's called a general election.

An alternative to self-nomination or nomination by a political party is to run for office as a write-in candidate. Write-in candidates lack the advantage of having their names listed on the ballot. These candidates must urge voters to add their name to the ballot on election day. Winning election as a write-in candidate is far more feasible at the local level, where it may be possible to meet most voters in person, than at the state or national level.

GROWTH OF THE PARTY SYSTEM The methods used by political parties to nominate candidates have changed during the course of American history. Broadly speaking, the process has grown more open over the years, with the involvement of ever-greater numbers of local leaders and ordinary citizens. Today, any voter can participate in choosing party candidates. This was not true as recently as 1968, however, and was certainly not possible during the first years of the republic.

George Washington was essentially unopposed in the first U.S. presidential election of 1788–1789. No other candidate was seriously considered in any state. As

CRITICAL VIEWING Third parties have occasionally exerted a strong influence on national elections. This was the case during the 1916 campaign for president, when Democrat Woodrow Wilson (left) faced off against Republican Charles Evans Hughes (right). At the time, former president Theodore Roosevelt, leader of the Bull Moose Party (officially the Progressive Party), was enormously popular among voters. What do you think is the main idea of this cartoon?

you have read, however, by the end of Washington's eight years in office, political divisions among the nation's leaders had solidified into two political parties—the Federalists and Thomas Jefferson's Republicans. The Federalist Party favored a strong centralized government, while the Republicans favored increased power for the states. Ever since then, except for a period between the elections of 1816 and 1828, the United States has had two major parties. Other parties are referred to as third parties, even though there may be four or many more.

CAUCUSES The two parties were organized by influential people, often meeting in secret. Their meetings came to be called caucuses. Beginning in 1800, members of Congress who belonged to either of the two parties held caucuses to nominate candidates for president and vice president. Through its caucus, the renamed Democratic Republicans chose Jefferson in 1800, as expected, and the Federalist caucus nominated the incumbent president, John Adams. By 1816, the Federalist Party had ceased to exist, and the Democratic Republican caucus had complete control of selecting the president of the United States.

The caucus system was widely seen as undemocratic—opponents derided it as "King Caucus"—and by 1824 it was in decline. The candidate nominated by the poorly attended Democratic Republican caucus came in third, losing to two self-nominated candidates. Altogether, four candidates split the electoral vote, and none won a majority. As the 12th Amendment directs: "if no person have [a] majority, then from the persons having the highest numbers . . . the House of Representatives shall choose immediately, by ballot, the President." The House chose John Quincy Adams, even though Andrew Jackson had won more popular and more electoral votes.

The caucus did not die out completely, but today's caucuses are much more democratic than those of the early 19th century. In a number of states today, citizens from each party gather to discuss the candidates' positions and vote on which they prefer. Anyone registered with the party is welcome to take part.

THE CONVENTION SYSTEM In the run-up to the 1828 elections, two new parties emerged around the two major candidates. Supporters of John Quincy Adams called themselves the National Republicans, later known as the Whigs. Andrew Jackson's supporters organized as the Democratic Party, which won the presidential election. By 1832, both parties had largely replaced the caucus system with another method of nominating candidates for president and vice president. They held a **nominating convention**, an official meeting of a political party in which party members vote to select its candidates.

Under the convention system, the people of an electoral district, such as a state or precinct, select delegates to represent them at a convention. A county convention might choose delegates to attend a state convention. The state convention, in turn, might select delegates to the national convention. A majority vote of convention delegates is required to win the party's nomination as its candidate for office.

The convention system drew in a much broader range of leaders than had the caucus, but like the caucus, it was not a particularly democratic institution. Party officials at each level, often referred to as bosses, found ways to manipulate the process of selecting convention delegates. Most party bosses were wealthy businesspeople who used their economic power to gain political power, doling out jobs, housing, or other favors in exchange for loyalty. Not until 1972 did ordinary voters in all states gain the right to select delegates to the national presidential nominating conventions.

PRIMARY ELECTIONS AND LOSS OF PARTY CONTROL Through much of the 1800s, bosses and other party leaders working behind the scenes, rather than the delegates on the floor, made most key decisions at national nominating conventions. The corruption that pervaded this system led reformers to call for a new way to choose candidates. They turned to the primary election, in which ordinary party members go to the **polls**—places where votes are cast, also called polling places—to select nominees. In a primary election, two or more candidates compete for a party's nomination. The winner competes against candidates from other parties in the general election.

In 1842, Democrats in Crawford County, Pennsylvania, may have held the first direct primary election. They developed a system designed to give voters control over the party's choice of nominees. The editor of the local paper wrote that "every man's vote will act directly on the result—there will be no intermediate channels through which bargain and trickery can flow to prevent the will of the people from being honestly carried out." The system was not widely used, however, until the end of the 19th century and the beginning of the 20th, when progressive reformers brought social and political change to many areas of American life.

HISTORICAL THINKING

1. **IDENTIFY MAIN IDEAS AND DETAILS** Why was the caucus system considered undemocratic?
2. **COMPARE AND CONTRAST** Was the convention system significantly more democratic than the caucus system? Explain your answer.

The Modern Primary System

Despite the growing popularity of the primary system in the 20th century, many states continued to choose delegates to the national party conventions in ways that froze out ordinary voters. Even in states that conducted presidential primaries, these elections were often held just for show. Primary results were nonbinding, and no actual delegates were chosen. Party bosses continued to select the delegates.

In 1968, however, this system failed the Democrats. In that year, incumbent Democratic President Lyndon B. Johnson announced that he would not seek re-election. His championing of the Vietnam War, then at its height, had severely eroded his popularity. Vice President Hubert H. Humphrey became the candidate of the **establishment**, an elite and powerful group of political and social leaders. Although Humphrey had earlier opposed U.S. involvement in Vietnam, he had spent the last four years defending the war and Johnson's policies. Primary results indicated that Democratic voters opposed continuing the war, but Humphrey avoided running in any primaries; he had the party rulers behind him, along with the delegates they controlled.

The 1968 Democratic National Convention was scheduled to be held in Chicago. Anti-war protesters poured into the city as the convention got underway. Outside the convention hall, police and National Guard troops attacked demonstrators with tear gas and clubs. Inside the convention hall, delegates clashed over the statement of the party's principles and goals as listed in the party platform. Chicago police forcibly ejected delegates who opposed the party platform's support for the Vietnam War. As expected, Humphrey won the nomination, but he lost the general election to his Republican opponent Richard Nixon, who campaigned on a promise of law and order.

Subsequently, the Democratic National Committee (DNC) appointed a special commission to reform the nomination process. At the heart of the reforms was a requirement, beginning in 1972, that convention delegates be chosen through more democratic processes. New rules fostered the participation of minorities and women, and party leaders and elected officials were stripped of special privileges. State conventions were allowed as an alternative to primary elections, but only if the nominating system used in those conventions was based on the choices of ordinary voters.

In 1984, the DNC created a new class of superdelegates in order to restore some power to party leaders and elected officials. Superdelegates were unpledged, meaning that, unlike delegates chosen through primaries and caucuses, they could vote for any candidate they wanted. The Republican Party adopted similar reforms, including limited participation by superdelegates.

DIRECT AND INDIRECT PRIMARIES The reforms undertaken by both parties after 1968 strengthened the primary system. Still, rules for conducting primary elections vary greatly from state to state, and several different types of primaries exist. One major distinction is between a direct and an indirect primary. In a direct primary, voters cast their ballots directly for candidates. Nearly all elections to nominate candidates for Congress and for state or local offices are direct primaries.

In an indirect primary, voters elect delegates, who in turn elect the candidates. Most delegates are pledged to support a particular candidate, but some delegates run as unpledged. The major parties use indirect primaries to elect delegates to the national nominating conventions, who then choose the party's candidates for president and vice president.

THE ROLE OF THE STATES Normally, state governments conduct primary elections, setting the date and providing polling places, election officials, and registration lists. After the polls close, they count the votes. By sponsoring the primaries, state governments have obtained considerable influence over the rules by which the primaries are conducted. The power of the states is limited, however, by the parties' First Amendment right to freedom of association, a right that has been repeatedly affirmed by the United States Supreme Court. For example, the Court has ruled that a political party has the right to invite independent voters to take part in its primaries.

On occasion, parties that objected to the rules imposed by state governments have opted out of the state-sponsored primary system. The major parties—the Republicans and the Democrats—rarely opt out of state elections, however, because the financial and political costs of going it alone are high. Third parties typically do not participate in state-sponsored primaries but hold nominating conventions instead.

PRIMARY VOTERS AND CANDIDATES' STRATEGIES Voter turnout for primaries is lower than it is for general elections. The voters who do go to the polls are often strong supporters of their party. Indeed, in states with so-called closed primaries, independents cannot participate in primary elections even if they lean toward one of the two major parties. As a result, the Republican primary electorate is more conservative than the party as a whole, and the Democratic primary electorate is similarly more liberal. Candidates often find that they must run well to the political right (conservative) or left (liberal) during the primary campaign. After winning the nomination, they usually moderate their positions, moving closer to the center to attract a broader range of voters during the run-up to the general election.

The most important result of the primary system has been to reduce dramatically the power of elected and party officials over the nominating process. Ever since primary elections were first held, campaigns by political **insurgents**—party members who run against the party establishment—have been a common occurrence. Many candidates at the local, state, and national levels, including Donald Trump, won nominations by emphasizing the ways they differed from the party leadership.

Occasionally, an insurgent who becomes a party's candidate has strikingly different principles and objectives from those of the party as a whole. His or her politics might even be abhorrent to the rest of the party—for example, an insurgent might make an outright appeal to racism. In spite of this, the party has no way to deny the party label to the insurgent in the general election.

HISTORICAL THINKING

3. **IDENTIFY** What is the difference between a direct and an indirect primary?
4. **FORM AND SUPPORT OPINIONS** Why do you think running against the party establishment can be an effective political strategy?

Types of Primaries

As you have read, states are responsible for conducting primary elections, which includes establishing dates and providing polling places. Both parties' primaries take place at the same time and at the same polling places. For example, on a primary election day, a neighborhood polling place—such as a school gymnasium—is where both Republicans and Democrats (and in some cases independents) would go to vote.

CLOSED OR OPEN PRIMARY States can establish primaries that are either closed, open, or something in between; these categories reflect who is permitted to vote in the primary. In a closed primary, only members of the party can vote; for instance, only registered Democrats can vote in the Democratic primary, and only registered Republicans can vote in the Republican primary. Regular party workers favor the closed primary because it promotes party loyalty. Independent voters usually oppose it because it forces them to join a party if they wish to participate in the nominating process. Voters usually establish party membership when registering to vote. Some states have a semi-closed primary, which allows voters to register with a party or change their party affiliation on election day.

In an open primary, any voter may participate, regardless of whether they belong to the party. In most open primaries, all voters receive both a Republican ballot and a Democratic ballot. Voters then choose either the Democratic or the Republican ballot in the privacy of the voting booth. In a semi-open primary, voters request the ballot for the party of their choice.

The 50 states have developed variations on the open and closed primary. In some states, primaries are closed only to persons registered to another party, and independents can vote in either primary. In several states, an independent who votes in a party primary is automatically enrolled in that party. In other states, the voter remains independent. The two major parties often have different rules. For example, in five states, Democrats allow independent voters to participate in their primaries or caucuses, but Republicans do not. In one state, Alabama, the reverse is the case. Also, a state's rules for presidential primaries often differ from those for its local, state, and congressional primaries.

BLANKET PRIMARY Until 1998, California and a few other states employed a blanket primary, a type of open primary in which voters could choose the candidates from any party. A voter might participate in choosing the Republican candidate for governor, for example, and at the same time vote for one of the Democratic candidates for the U.S. Senate. In 1998, however, the Supreme Court ruled (in *California Democratic Party* v. *Jones*) that the blanket primary violated the parties' First Amendment right to freedom of association. Similar primary systems in Washington and Alaska were struck down in later cases.

LOUISIANA AND THE TOP-TWO PRIMARY
Beginning in 1977, Louisiana had a unique system, nicknamed the jungle primary, in which all candidates participated in the same primary, regardless of party. That is, all candidates were listed on the same ballot. The two candidates receiving the most votes then proceeded on to the general election. In 2008, Louisiana abandoned this system for the U.S. House and Senate but kept it for state and local offices. The state restored it for all offices after 2010.

Even as Louisiana was questioning its system, other states began picking it up. Washington was challenged

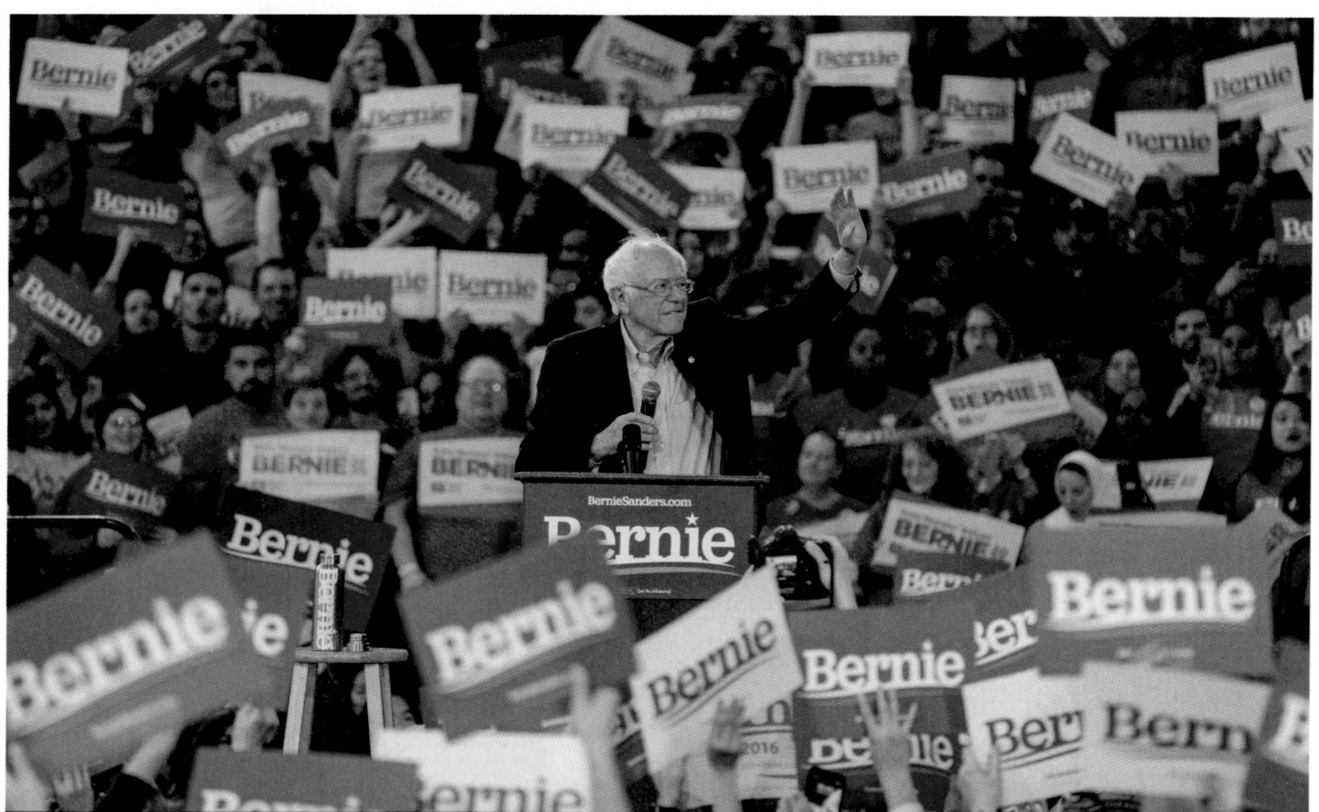

Although he was a political independent, Senator Bernie Sanders sought the Democratic nomination for president in 2016 and again in 2020. His progressive ideas—single-payer, government-run health insurance and tuition-free universities, for example—made him an insurgent candidate in 2016, when he finished a strong second to Hillary Clinton. He ran again in 2020, and though he once again came in second, many of his ideas had been adopted by other Democratic office seekers.

in court after adopting the Louisiana system in 2004, but in 2008 the Supreme Court ruled that it was constitutional. In June 2010, California voters adopted a system known as the top-two primary that was patterned on the one in Washington. In both states, as in Louisiana, all candidates appear on the same ballot. After California's 2014 primaries, seven U.S. House contests featured two members of the same party facing off against each other in the general election. The 2016 elections featured seven such races for the House and one for the Senate.

When states use a top-two primary like Louisiana's, the parties continue to have the right to designate preferred candidates, using conventions or other means, but their endorsements do not appear on the ballot. An insurgent Republican and an establishment Republican, for example, would both be labeled simply *Republican*.

RANKED-CHOICE VOTING In the typical primary, votes are split among several candidates, sometimes up to 20 or more, and achieving a majority is quite difficult. This issue has been addressed in a few different ways. Commonly, whoever receives a **plurality**, or the greatest number of votes, even if it is not more than half of the votes, wins the party nomination. This means that a candidate can be nominated with far less than a majority of the votes. Another solution is to hold a runoff election between the two candidates who receive the most votes.

Starting in 2018, Maine voters opted for a new system intended to ensure that each party would choose one candidate by a majority without any runoff. In this ranked-choice voting system, also known as an instant runoff, voters rank their party's candidates—first choice, second choice, and so forth. After the first-place votes are counted, the candidate who received the fewest first-place votes is eliminated. Any ballot that listed that person first is then recounted, using the second choice. Ranked-choice voting was also used in Maine's general election for some offices.

HISTORICAL THINKING

5. **COMPARE AND CONTRAST** What is the main difference between an open primary and a closed primary?
6. **MAKE CONNECTIONS** Why do you think the Supreme Court ruled that the blanket primary violated the parties' right to freedom of association?

LESSON 15.2 Nominating Presidential Candidates

Few people have heard of John W. Davis. He was a former advisor to President Woodrow Wilson and ambassador to Great Britain who gained a small measure of fame in 1924, when the Democratic National Convention nominated him for president. Unlike most of today's national party conventions, in which the winner has been determined long in advance, the 1924 convention was a raucous affair. Davis emerged as the compromise candidate after 16 days and 103 ballots, as well as backroom dealing and the occasional fistfight. He soon sank back into obscurity after winning just 29 percent of the popular vote in the general election, which was won by Republican Calvin Coolidge.

Presidential Primaries and Caucuses

In some respects, being nominated for president is more difficult than being elected. The nominating process, carried out through primaries and caucuses, must often narrow a very large number of hopefuls down to a single candidate from each party. The process can vary from state to state, but the goal is the same—to choose a presidential candidate who can win the election on behalf of the party.

THE PRIMARY SEASON The official primary and caucus season begins in the year of the election. Well before that, however, candidates for president are busy garnering as much support as possible. In recent years, unofficial presidential campaigns have often begun as much as three years before election day; President Trump filed for re-election in the 2020 race on the day of his inauguration in 2017.

Before the primaries begin, candidates attempt to enhance their public image and increase their name recognition. They also try to gain the support of their party's insiders—a network of elected officials, fund-raisers, and other leaders. This effort has been called the invisible primary, and it can have a major impact on the outcome of the presidential primaries and caucuses.

The 2016 primary season, however, proved to be dramatically different, at least on the Republican side. Many Republican voters that year were in open revolt against the party's leaders. Establishment support for former Florida governor John E. (Jeb) Bush, the initial front-runner, appeared to hurt rather than help him. Businessman and reality TV star Donald Trump, the eventual Republican nominee, openly expressed his contempt for party leaders. U.S. Senator Ted Cruz (R-TX), who finished second to Trump, gloried in his unpopularity among his Senate colleagues.

Most states hold presidential primaries beginning early in the election year. A good showing in the early primaries results in plenty of media attention for a candidate, as television and newspaper reporters play up the results. Subsequent primaries tend to eliminate candidates who are unlikely to be successful.

State presidential primaries do not necessarily follow the same rules states use for nominating candidates for the U.S. Congress or for state and local offices. Presidential primaries are often held on a different date from the other primaries. Many states have pushed the date of their presidential primary earlier in the election year, hoping to exercise greater influence on voters in other states.

HOW A CAUCUS WORKS Presidential caucuses are an alternative to primary elections. Unlike the caucuses of two centuries ago, which were limited to political party bosses, modern caucuses are open to all party members. It is not hard to join a party. At the famous Iowa caucuses, anyone who attends a local caucus becomes a party member. Taking part in a caucus, however, is not like voting in a primary. A caucus is a time-consuming event that can last a few hours. It takes place in the evening, so people who have jobs that require them to work at night or family responsibilities may not be able to attend. For this reason, caucuses generally attract a lower percentage of party members than primaries.

The caucuses, run by the major parties and not the states, begin with preliminary conventions at the local level. Each locality is charged to select a specific number of delegates, often based on turnout in the last election, who will represent it at the next level of caucus. The number of people attending the caucus divided by the number of delegates to be chosen yields the minimum number of people needed to elect each delegate. For example, suppose 200 people attend a caucus that needs to choose 20 delegates; then 10 participants are needed to elect each delegate.

Caucuses commonly begin with each candidate or a surrogate giving a speech explaining the candidate's strengths and intentions. Then participants physically separate themselves into groups according to which candidate they support. The number of each group is counted to reach a preliminary delegate count. Continuing with the example, suppose 35 of the 200 people in attendance are in the group supporting candidate Han. That gives Han enough support to win three delegates, but not enough support for four. To win a fourth delegate, Han's supporters need to convince five more people to join them. If Han's supporters are persuasive, they might even get more than one more delegate. In contrast, some other candidate's supporters may convince some of Han's supporters to defect to their candidate.

The process continues until nobody is willing to change groups. Then each group selects from among themselves the number of delegates it is entitled to. As you might imagine, when each group selects its delegates, a candidate's most articulate, knowledgeable, and persuasive advocates are usually chosen. Those delegates will attend a

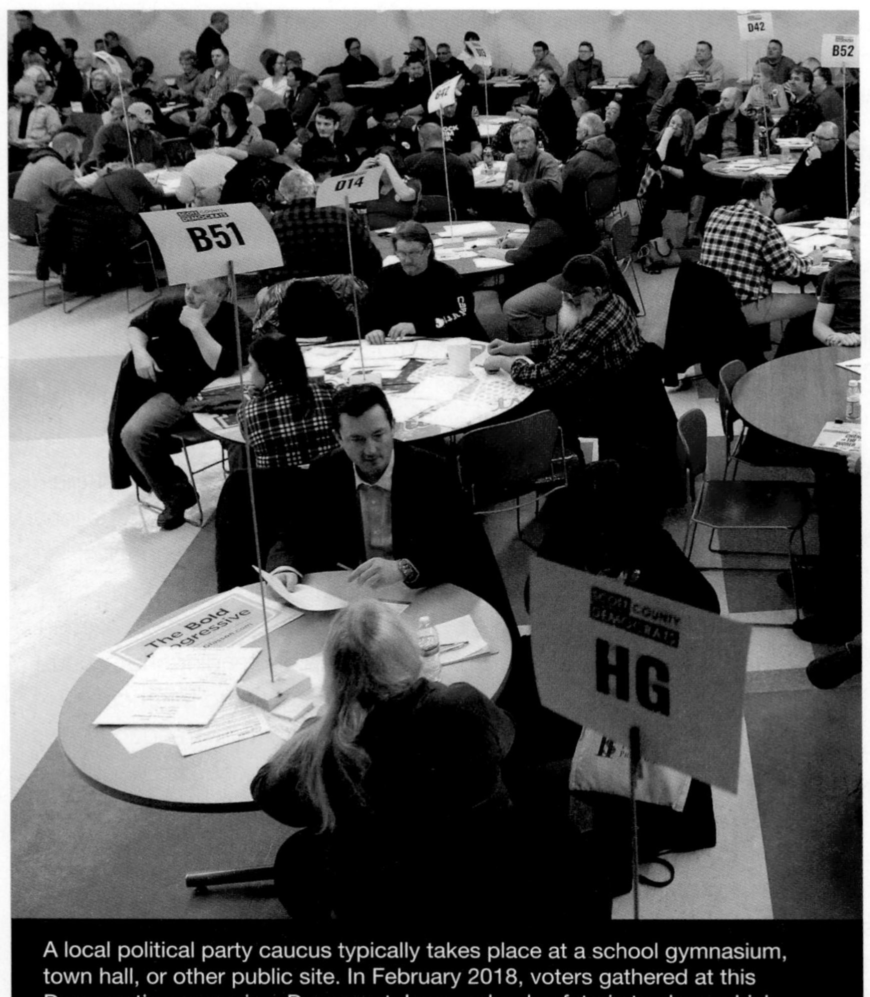

A local political party caucus typically takes place at a school gymnasium, town hall, or other public site. In February 2018, voters gathered at this Democratic caucus in a Davenport, Iowa, school cafeteria to show which candidates they support for governor and Congress and which issues they want their party to pursue.

as several states, concerned about low participation in their caucuses, decided to switch to the primary system for the 2020 elections.

Iowa stayed with the caucus in 2020, but what happened there only added to concerns about the future of the caucus system. The state, for the first time, relied on a new and largely untested smartphone app that allowed each of its caucuses to report its results to the state party headquarters. Numerous caucus chairpersons had trouble downloading and installing the app. Once it was working, they often could not successfully transmit the data. Many chairs frantically called headquarters to submit their results only to be put on hold, sometimes for hours, by officials overwhelmed by the flood of phone calls. The chaotic events in Iowa cast doubt on the caucus system and left many Americans wondering whether they could trust the American electoral system to accurately count their votes.

mid-level convention in which delegates to the next level will be chosen, and so on, until finally the state convention selects delegates to the national party convention. There they join with delegates from other states to select the party's nominees for president and vice president. Some states with presidential caucuses, such as Iowa, also rely on caucuses to nominate candidates for state and local positions. However, most states with presidential caucuses nominate candidates for other offices through primaries.

In 2016, Republican and Democratic Party members in more than a dozen states used caucuses to choose delegates to their state conventions. In one state, Idaho, only the Democrats used this system. The caucus, however, seems to be on the decline,

THE RUSH TO BE FIRST Traditionally, states have held their presidential primaries and caucuses at various times over the first six months of a presidential election year. Several states, however, in order to gain greater media coverage of their primary or caucus and give it more influence in the political process, moved the date of their primary or caucus to earlier in the year—a practice known as front-loading. In 1988, a large group of mainly southern states created a Super Tuesday by holding their primaries on the same day in early March. Then other states moved their primary or caucus to an earlier date, too.

The practice of front-loading primaries and caucuses gained momentum during the first decade of the 21st century. The states with later primary dates worried that nominations would be decided before they even had a chance to vote, and even more states moved up their contests. By 2008, around 40 states had moved the date of their primary or caucus to January or February. Observers noted that, with a shortened primary season, long-shot candidates would no longer be able to propel themselves into serious contention by doing well in small, early-voting states, such as New Hampshire and Iowa.

As it turned out, the practice of front-loading had reached its limits. In most Republican primaries, the winner gets all the state's delegates. But in the Democratic primaries, each candidate is awarded a number of delegates proportional to his or her percentage of the vote. Therefore, Democratic candidates cannot ensure victory by winning the early contests; they need to win lots of states—especially big states. In 2008, the Democrats went into June with no candidate having yet won a majority of the delegates. As a result, the primaries held late in the season became decisive. States that had moved their primaries to January or February discovered they were lost in the crowd of early contests. Front-loading, in other words, had become counterproductive.

In 2012, the Republican National Committee attempted to reduce front-loading by dictating that only four traditionally early states—Iowa, New Hampshire, South Carolina, and Nevada—could choose delegates in February. The committee further directed that in 2016, states other than these four could not vote until March 1. Super Tuesday was moved to March 1, and 11 states, mostly in the South, selected delegates on that date. Additionally, states choosing delegates before March 15 had to allocate them proportionally; from March 15 on, delegates could be selected on a winner-take-all basis. The Democratic Party generally fell in line with these rules, although it did not allow winner-take-all primaries.

HISTORICAL THINKING

1. **MAKE INFERENCES** Why do you think most states hold primaries rather than caucuses?
2. **ANALYZE CAUSE AND EFFECT** Why does winner-take-all voting during primary season tend to lead to a winner earlier than proportional voting?

The National Nominating Convention

At one time, national nominating conventions were often giant free-for-alls. It wasn't always clear who the winning presidential and vice presidential candidates would be until the delegates actually voted. As you have read, the 1924 Democratic National Convention needed 103 ballots to determine its presidential nominee, and chaos consumed the convention floor. As more states opted to hold presidential primaries, however, the drama of national conventions diminished.

Today's national nominating conventions have been described as massive pep rallies. Nonetheless, each convention's task remains a serious one. On the first day of the convention, delegates hear the reports of the credentials committee, which inspects each prospective delegate's claim to be seated as a legitimate representative of her or his state. When the eligibility of delegates is in question, the credentials committee decides who will be seated. Then a keynote speaker whips up enthusiasm among the delegates. Later, the convention deals with other committees' reports and any debates concerning the party platform.

Balloting takes place with an alphabetical roll call of states and territories as each delegation's chair, one by one, announces the delegation's choice of nominee for president. Usually the nominee has already selected his or her vice presidential running mate. The nomination for vice president takes place later in the process. Acceptance speeches by the presidential and vice presidential candidates are timed to take place during prime-time television hours.

As you have read, the COVID-19 pandemic required the parties to adopt some new approaches for their 2020 national nominating conventions. Most speeches were delivered to small crowds, or even to empty rooms, and intended mainly for television and streaming audiences. But many of the traditional elements of national conventions remained in place. Keynote addresses set out each party's visions. A roll call of states tallied the nominees' ballots. Nominees delivered acceptance speeches and pledged to lead their parties to victory. In lieu of the traditional balloon drop, Democrats closed their convention with a lengthy fireworks display. Republicans used the White House itself as a backdrop for Donald Trump's acceptance speech.

ROAD *to the* PRESIDENCY

Many people want to be president, but only one will generate enough support to make it all the way to the White House.

1 PRIMARY AND CAUCUS SEASON

Primary and caucus season begins early in the presidential election year. Candidates campaign throughout the country, seeking to gain their party's nomination.

Using either the caucus system or the primary system, each state party chooses delegates to the national party conventions. To win the nomination, a candidate needs a majority of delegates at the national convention.

CAUCUS STATES

In caucuses, or local party conventions, party members discuss candidates and select delegates to the state party convention. At the state convention, supporters of each candidate select delegates to the national convention.

PRIMARY STATES

In a state primary, voters cast ballots for the candidate they favor. Their votes determine which candidate's supporters attend the national convention as delegates.

2 NATIONAL CONVENTIONS

At each party's national convention, delegates choose their party's nominee for president by majority vote. The nominee of each party announces his or her running mate for the office of vice president.

3 GENERAL ELECTION

Voters in every state cast ballots for president and vice president on Election Day. They are actually voting for electors—party members from the state who represent the pair of candidates.

4 ELECTORAL COLLEGE

In the electoral college system, each state has as many electors as it has U.S. senators and representatives. After the general election, the electors meet in their state capitals to vote for president and vice president.

Each elector has one vote for president and one vote for vice president. To gain the presidency, a candidate must win a majority of electoral votes.

5 INAUGURATION

In January, the newly elected president and vice president take an oath of office and are inaugurated.

HISTORICAL THINKING

3. **COMPARE AND CONTRAST** Why aren't national nominating conventions today the giant free-for-alls they once were?
4. **FORM AND SUPPORT OPINIONS** What aspect of a typical national nominating convention do you think would be most exciting or enjoyable for a delegate? Why?

Recent Nomination Contests

A series of more or less formal televised debates has become a staple of both parties' nomination process. The most striking feature of the Republican contest to determine a nominee for president in 2016 was the huge number of contenders. The field vastly exceeded the number that could reasonably participate in a group debate. The broadcast and cable networks that sponsored the debates had to establish new rules as to who could participate. Invitations were limited to the top 8 to 10 candidates, as shown by opinion polls. In 2020, the Democratic Party also produced a large field of candidates seeking the nomination for president. The Democratic National Committee required candidates to meet certain polling as well as fund-raising levels to qualify for its debates.

The main debates during the 2016 campaign season enjoyed enormous audiences. Twenty-four million viewers watched the first Republican debate, sponsored by Fox News in August 2015. It was the most-watched live broadcast of a non-sporting event in the history of cable television.

WINNING THE 2016 REPUBLICAN NOMINATION Early in 2015, former Florida governor Jeb Bush led the field as the establishment favorite. Jeb is a brother of President George W. Bush and a son of President George H.W. Bush. In June 2015, however, Donald J.

CRITICAL VIEWING In August 2015, Republicans vying to represent their party in the 2016 presidential election took part in the first Republican primary debate. So many Republicans sought the nomination that the debate sponsor, Fox News, limited participation to the 10 leading candidates, based on opinion polls. If you were writing a political blog, how would you describe this pre-debate lineup of candidates in one summary sentence?

Trump, a businessman and television personality with no political experience, entered the race. Trump was such an unusual candidate that most political experts did not believe he could ultimately prevail. But by July, Trump had risen to first in the polls. Bush's support quickly eroded, while Trump's following grew from week to week.

In February 2016, Donald Trump won the New Hampshire primary, confirming his front-runner status. Most other candidates, including Bush, soon dropped out of the race. By late February, the Republicans were down to five major contenders. Only three were realistic possibilities: U.S. senator for Texas Ted Cruz, U.S. senator for Florida Marco Rubio, and Trump.

In principle, there were enough Republican anti-Trump votes to defeat him, but those votes were ineffective in winner-take-all primaries because they were split among multiple candidates. No single traditional small-government conservative had the support needed to stop Trump. Even after Super Tuesday, March 1, the anti-Trump field was still split between Cruz, Rubio, and Ohio governor John Kasich. Trump continued to win delegates in large, winner-take-all states, and frantic efforts by party leaders to derail his candidacy failed. In May, Trump crossed the finish line: He accumulated enough delegates for nomination at the Republican National Convention. Most Republicans, though not all, rallied behind their nominee.

WINNING THE 2016 DEMOCRATIC NOMINATION

Democrat Hillary Clinton, who had barely lost the nomination to Barack Obama in 2008, sought to win enough early support to dissuade other candidates from running against her. As a former senator and secretary of state, as well as a former first lady, she was viewed as highly qualified. Clinton's effort to pull ahead in the primaries was relatively successful, but Clinton still faced one major opponent: Bernie Sanders, an independent U.S. senator from Vermont. Although he was an independent, Sanders was seeking the nomination of the Democratic Party, and he ran on what he called a democratic socialist or progressive platform.

Sanders won strong support from younger voters and, to an extent, from older liberals and hard-pressed White, working-class Democrats. Sanders championed liberal causes that included a universal health-care insurance program run by the government, as found in Canada and most European countries, and free tuition at state colleges and universities. To pay for such programs, he called for more **progressive taxes**, a system of higher rates of taxation on higher taxable amounts. Sanders vowed to increase taxes for the wealthiest, especially those known as the one percent, the multimillionaires and billionaires who make up the wealthiest one percent of individuals in the United States.

In contrast, Clinton emphasized her political experience. Clinton's supporters argued that her depth of knowledge and policy expertise would translate into greater progress toward liberal goals than Sanders's ideological passion.

Although Sanders did relatively well among White voters, he lost the African-American vote by large margins. For example, Clinton beat Sanders 84 percent to 16 percent among Black voters in South Carolina. African Americans recognized Clinton as a politician who had been their friend for decades. In June, Clinton wrapped up enough delegates to win the nomination.

Many of Sanders's supporters rallied around the slogan "Bernie or Bust." This implied that they would never back Clinton. In July, however, on the eve of the Democratic National Convention, Sanders **endorsed**, or recommended support for, Clinton, and proceeded to back her presidential campaign. Most of his followers joined him.

SUPERDELEGATES In 2016, almost 15 percent of the more than 4,700 delegates to the Democratic National Convention were superdelegates. They included Democratic federal and state officeholders, such as senators and governors, and state and local party officers. As superdelegates, they were seated automatically and were free to support any candidate; the great majority backed Clinton. Sanders and many of his supporters therefore claimed that the convention was rigged against him. Clinton also won a majority of the regular delegates, however, so Sanders's claim lost some of its punch.

Still, the Democratic National Committee, at its 2018 summer meetings, altered its rules to limit the power of superdelegates. In the future, superdelegates would continue to be able to back any presidential candidate, but they would not be allowed to vote on the first ballot. In the case of a contested convention, in which multiple ballots are needed to choose the nominee, their votes could prove decisive.

Republicans had superdelegates at their 2016 national nominating convention, too. However, they comprised only about 7 percent of the 2,500 or so delegates—far fewer in number than their Democratic counterparts. Republican superdelegates were already bound to vote for their state's winner, so they were viewed as having less of an impact.

2020 NOMINATION SEASON Prior to the outbreak of COVID-19, the 2020 primary season had resembled previous seasons. The Iowa caucuses and New Hampshire primary gave the candidates a forum to hone their messages in intimate settings with modest-sized crowds. Candidates hoped to use those early contests to generate momentum and money to carry them through the pivotal Super Tuesday showdowns, in which 14 states would cast their ballots and, on the Democratic side, about one-third of the delegates would be awarded. Unlike in years past, California, the biggest prize, was at stake on Super Tuesday. The state's leaders had moved their primary forward in the calendar so that the state would play a bigger role in the nominating process.

As a sitting president, Donald Trump faced only token opposition for the Republican nomination. But Democrats fielded a large number and diverse slate of candidates vying for their party's nomination. The field was noted for its diversity, featuring six women candidates, four African Americans, two Asian Americans, and one Hispanic American. The 2016 runner-up Senator Bernie Sanders garnered significant support, and newcomer Pete Buttigieg, former mayor of South Bend, Indiana, made a surprisingly strong showing in the Iowa caucuses. The party held 11 debates, gradually narrowing the field based on criteria such as a candidate's polling numbers. Eventually, two contenders were left—Senator Sanders and former vice president Joseph Biden, who emerged as the front-runner, as one by one his moderate competitors dropped out and endorsed him. Senator Sanders made a strong showing, capturing California on Super Tuesday. But by early March, Biden had amassed a nearly insurmountable lead in the delegate count. Senator Sanders dropped out of the race in early April.

By the time Sanders dropped out, some states had already moved into lockdown to address the COVID-19 pandemic conditions. In addition, the pandemic scrambled the carefully laid plans of the major political parties, not to mention their primary calendars. With in-person voting a potential hazard, states ramped up mail-in and early voting. At least 16 states postponed their primaries. Connecticut held its primary just days before the start of the Democratic National Convention, which had itself been postponed by more than a month.

HISTORICAL THINKING

5. **MAKE INFERENCES** Why do you think Republican Party leaders made frantic efforts to derail Donald Trump's candidacy?
6. **EVALUATE** Is it a problem that many candidates were excluded from the televised debates during the Republican primaries in 2016? Explain your thinking.

LESSON
15.3 How We Elect Candidates

Since 1845, nearly all general elections in the United States have been scheduled for the first Tuesday following the first Monday in November. (In other words, if November 1 is a Monday, the election takes place the following Tuesday, November 2.) It is a practice rooted in a time when the United States was largely an agricultural country. By early November, the crops had been harvested and winter had not yet set in. In the mid-1800s, travel was still by horse and buggy. Many people had to set out for distant polling places the day before. For many Americans, traveling on Sunday was forbidden for religious reasons, so Monday was out. Wednesday was commonly market day, so that was out, too. Tuesday seemed to work, so Congress said elections would be held on Tuesdays.

Conducting Elections and Counting the Votes

As you know, the president and vice president are elected every four years. Members of the House of Representatives are elected every two years, and senators are elected every six years on a rotating schedule (in other words, one-third of the Senate is up for election every two years). People cast their votes for members of the House of Representatives, the Senate, and the president and vice president in the biannual general election. Prior to 1845, each state scheduled its election on a day of its choosing. But as communication among the states improved, there was concern that the outcome in early-voting states would influence the election in other states. Thus, Congress passed a law to set the general election "on the Tuesday next after the first Monday in November."

CRITICAL VIEWING Through much of U.S. history, the typical polling place collected ballots in a wooden box like this one, which was used in a Chicago election in 1912. Voters marked a paper ballot and slid it into the box through a slot or handed it to an election official for depositing. What features of this ballot box helped ensure secrecy and security?

The United States is unusual among industrial democracies for holding its general election on a weekday; most other industrialized democracies hold elections on a weekend or declare election day a national holiday. As of 2020, however, 38 of the 50 states and the District of Columbia allowed early voting. Three additional states used mail-in voting systems that eliminated the need for early voting. Depending on the state, early voting allows people to cast their votes as much as 45 days before an election.

States usually hold their general elections for state officials at the same time as those for national offices. If needed, a state or local government can hold a special election on some other date. Reasons for special elections include the need for voters to decide an issue before the next general election or to fill a vacancy when an elected official resigns or dies.

THE BALLOT In the early years of the nation's history, Americans voted by signing their names on a sheet of paper posted in a public place. This allowed for rampant fraud. For example, a person could vote multiple times for the same candidate by writing other people's names on the sheet. Later, each political party would print paper ballots, called tickets, listing its candidates. Each voter took a ticket from one party or another and inserted it into the ballot box. But voting was still not private, since it was clear to anyone watching which party a voter supported.

Today, all states in the United States use a secret ballot, also known as the Australian ballot. The ballots list all the certified candidates with their party affiliation and are prepared, distributed, and counted by government officials at public expense. As its name implies, this type of ballot was first used in an election in Australia, in 1856. Britain adopted it in 1872, and it quickly caught on in the United States after the 1884 election. Voting by secret ballot takes place privately, often in a voting booth.

The modern ballot can take several forms. Most common in the United States is the paper ballot, a sheet of paper with each elective office identified and a list of candidates for each office. Voters mark their ballots with a pen, filling in bubbles or boxes or completing arrows to indicate their choices. In many jurisdictions, these marked ballots are fed into optical scanners that count votes electronically, but in some areas, they are counted by hand. Less common are electronic voting machines, which enable voters to simply press a button or touch a computer screen to cast their vote. Punch cards used to be popular, allowing voters to make their selection by punching a hole next to the candidate's name. Lever-voting machines were also widely used for a time; people cast their votes by flipping a small lever that corresponded to the candidate's name. State polling places no longer use punch cards or lever-voting machines.

Today, many people submit their ballots by mail. Perhaps they are unable to travel to the polling place or will be out of town on election day. At least 22 states hold some elections completely by mail, and as stated earlier, three of these states—Oregon, Washington, and Colorado—conduct all elections by mail. By federal law, members of the armed forces and their families stationed outside of their legal voting residence must be allowed to vote by mail, as well as U.S. citizens living overseas.

POLLING PLACES For the purposes of conducting elections, local units of government, such as cities, are divided into smaller voting districts called precincts. An election board supervises the polling place and the voting process in each precinct. The board sets hours for the polls to be open according to the laws of the state, sees that ballots or voting machines are available, and recruits volunteers to run the polling stations. In most states, the board provides the list of registered voters and a system for ensuring that only qualified voters cast ballots. When the polls close, staff members count the votes and report the results, usually to the county clerk or the board of elections.

As you have read, paper ballots might be hand-counted or read by an optical scanning machine—similar to the way answer sheets for standardized tests are read. Electronic voting machines automatically record and store the votes. To avoid the possibility of hacking, or the gaining of unauthorized access to electronic data, these machines are never directly connected to the internet. But computer security experts warn that election results are still susceptible to a skilled hacker; results are often transmitted to county election offices using a phone line and modem, and often via the internet. Hackers can also gain access to computerized voter lists. State and federal authorities are working on ways to keep all voter and election data secure.

Political parties and campaign organizations may send poll watchers to polling places on election day. These volunteers monitor the voting process, from the handing out of ballots to the counting of the votes. Their job is to make sure the election is run fairly, that nobody is intimidated, and that there is no voter fraud.

HISTORICAL THINKING

1. **MAKE GENERALIZATIONS** Why might a voter prefer to fill out a ballot in the privacy of a voting booth rather than publicly?
2. **COMPARE AND CONTRAST** Which method of voting—going to a polling place or sending the ballot by mail—do you think results in a higher number of votes cast? Why?

Presidential Elections and the Electoral College

Many people are surprised to learn that their vote for president and vice president is not actually a vote for the candidates. It is a vote for a slate, or group, of electors who belong to the candidates' political party and support that candidate. Each pair of candidates for president and vice president has a slate of electors representing them in each state. These electors are selected during each presidential election year, generally by the states' parties and often at the state party convention, subject to the laws of the state.

The selection of electors is a key part of the Constitution's presidential election system, known as the electoral college. As you read earlier, the Framers designed the electoral college as a kind of compromise. They did not want Congress or the courts to choose the president because that would violate the principle of separation of powers. They did not want the people to choose the president directly, by popular vote, because they feared that, in Madison's words, "an interested and overbearing majority" might "sacrifice to its ruling passion or interest both the public good and the rights of other citizens" (Federalist No. 10).

Article II, Section 1, of the Constitution requires that "Each State shall appoint . . . a Number of Electors, equal to the whole Number of Senators and Representatives to which the State may be entitled in the Congress." The 23rd Amendment to the Constitution dictates that the District of Columbia, even though it is not a state, is also allowed three electors: The "number of electors of President and Vice President equal to the whole number of Senators and Representatives in Congress to which the District would be entitled if it were a State, but in no event more than the least populous State." Thus, the electoral college includes 538 electoral votes. This total represents the sum of 435 members of the House, 100 members of the Senate, and 3 electors from the District of Columbia. In December, following the November general election, each group of state electors meets in their state capital to vote for the

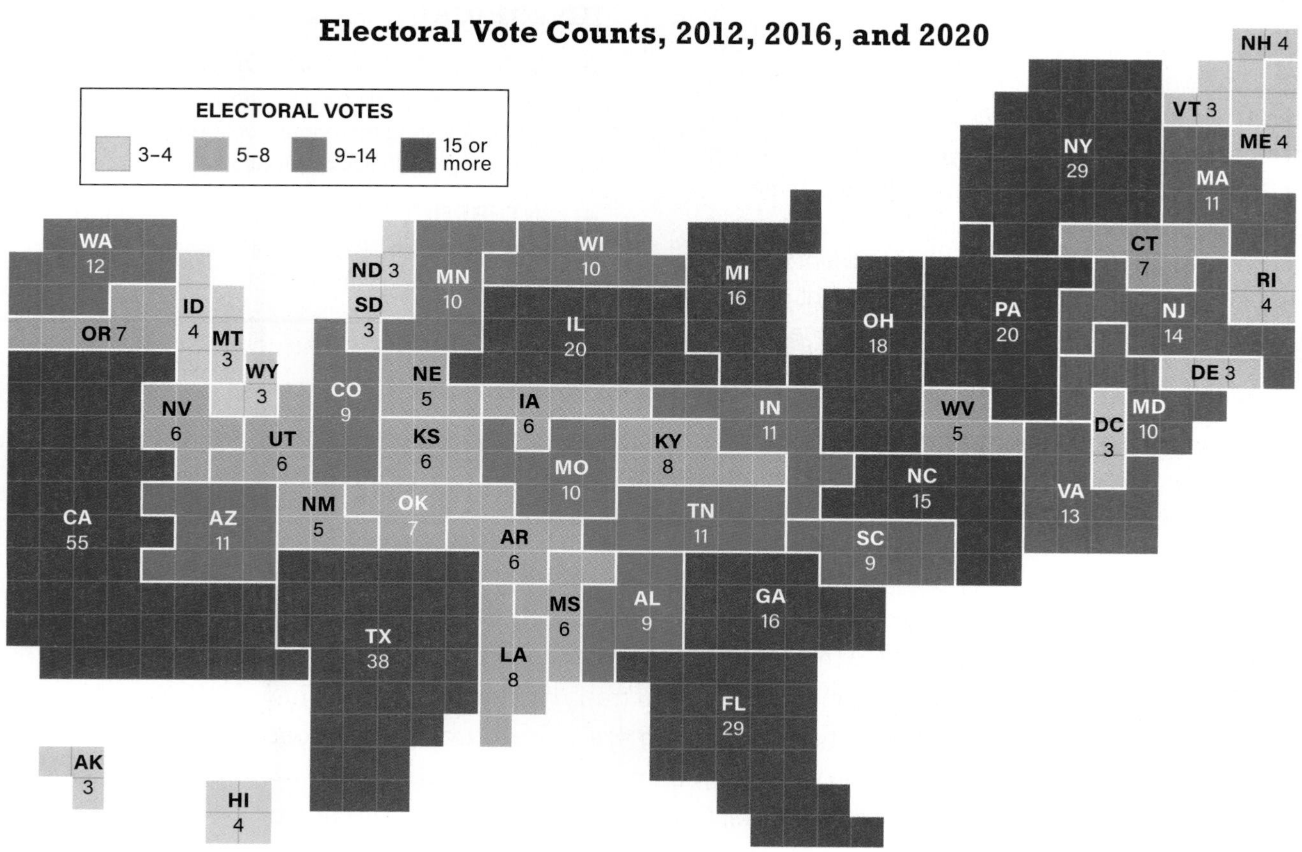

president and vice president. Electors for the District of Columbia meet in the district.

As you know, the electoral college is primarily a winner-take-all system. In most states, the candidate receiving the most popular votes in a state is credited with all that state's electoral votes. The only exceptions are Maine and Nebraska, where the winner of the popular vote in each congressional district gets one electoral vote, and the remaining two votes (linked to the states' number of senators) go to the statewide winner.

When the Constitution was drafted, the Framers intended that the electors would use their discretion in deciding who would make the best president. Beginning as early as 1796, however, electors have, with few exceptions, voted for the candidates to whom they are pledged. In July 2020, the Supreme Court ruled that states could punish electors who voted for a candidate other than the one they had pledged to support.

After each state's electors vote, their ballots are sent to the U.S. Senate, which counts and certifies them before a joint session of Congress in early January. The candidates who receive a majority of the total 538 electoral votes—at least 270—are officially declared president and vice president. If no presidential candidate gets an electoral college majority (which has happened twice—in 1800 and 1824), the House of Representatives chooses among the top three candidates, with each state delegation casting only a single vote. If no candidate for vice president gets a majority of electoral votes, the vice president is chosen by the Senate, with each senator casting one vote.

The electoral college system has many critics who argue that it gives too much power to rural states and that the popular vote better reflects the will of the people. They point to four elections in U.S. history—1876, 1888, 2000, and 2016—in which the winner of the electoral vote did not win the nationwide popular vote. In 2016, for example, Hillary Clinton won the popular vote by nearly 3 million votes, or 2 percent of the total vote. But because she won only 19 states in the electoral college, she lost the electoral college vote to Donald Trump, 232 to 306, and with it the election.

The 2000 election was even closer. With all but Florida's electoral votes determined, Vice President Al Gore led Republican George W. Bush by around 500,000 votes nationwide. But Gore was behind in the electoral vote and trailed Bush by just a few hundred votes in Florida. Gore demanded a manual recount, which Bush sought to delay and to block in court. In a controversial decision, *Bush* v. *Gore*, the Supreme Court shut down the recount. Bush thereby won Florida's 25 electoral votes—and the presidency.

HISTORICAL THINKING

3. **FORM AND SUPPORT OPINIONS** Do you think the electoral college system still makes sense today, or should the popular vote determine who wins the presidential election? Explain your answer.
4. **INTERPRET MAPS** What advantage do you think this type of electoral vote map has over a geographically correct map?

LESSON 15.4 The Modern Political Campaign

Candidates for elective office must mount an effective campaign just to get nominated by their political party, but the work doesn't end there. They don't spend a lot of time celebrating after they win the nomination, because the election is not far off. They need to get right back on the campaign trail. The term *campaign* has military roots. Generals mounted campaigns, using scarce resources—weapons, vehicles, soldiers—to achieve military objectives. In a political campaign, candidates also use scarce resources—time, funds, volunteers—in an attempt to defeat their adversaries in the battle for votes.

Decided: December 12, 2000, 5–4

Majority: Chief Justice William H. Rehnquist wrote ne opinion for the Court in favor of Bush.

Dissent: David H. Souter wrote the dissenting pinion.

On election night 2000, it appeared that Texas overnor George W. Bush had won the presidency vith 271 electoral votes versus 266 for Vice President l Gore. But the popular vote in Florida, where 25 lectoral votes were at stake, was extremely close. lorida law requires a machine recount of the ballots the margin of victory is less than 0.5 percent; ush's margin of victory in Florida was estimated at .01 percent.

fter Florida's machine recount was completed, Bush d by just 327 votes out of the 6 million cast. Gore equested a hand recount in four Florida counties, ting problems with punch-card ballots—many of hich had incompletely punched holes (so-called anging chads) or punches that failed to pierce e card. Bush sued to block Gore's request. On ovember 14, seven days after the election, the orida Supreme Court ruled in favor of Gore and dered the hand recounts.

s election workers moved ahead with the hand counts, Bush backers filed dozens of lawsuits stop them. On December 8, 30 days after the ection, the Florida Supreme Court again ruled at the recounts should continue. The next day, ush petitioned the U.S. Supreme Court to end the counts, and the Court put the recounts on hold nding its final decision.

n December 12, the U.S. Supreme Court reversed e Florida Supreme Court's ruling and ended the anual recounts. It held that the recounts ordered the Florida court violated equal protection d due process because Florida had no clear, tablished standard for deciding whether a hole had en punched. Further, the Court said, it was now cember 12, Florida's legal deadline for finalizing the te, and it was not possible for Florida to establish a procedure for a recount and conduct the recount

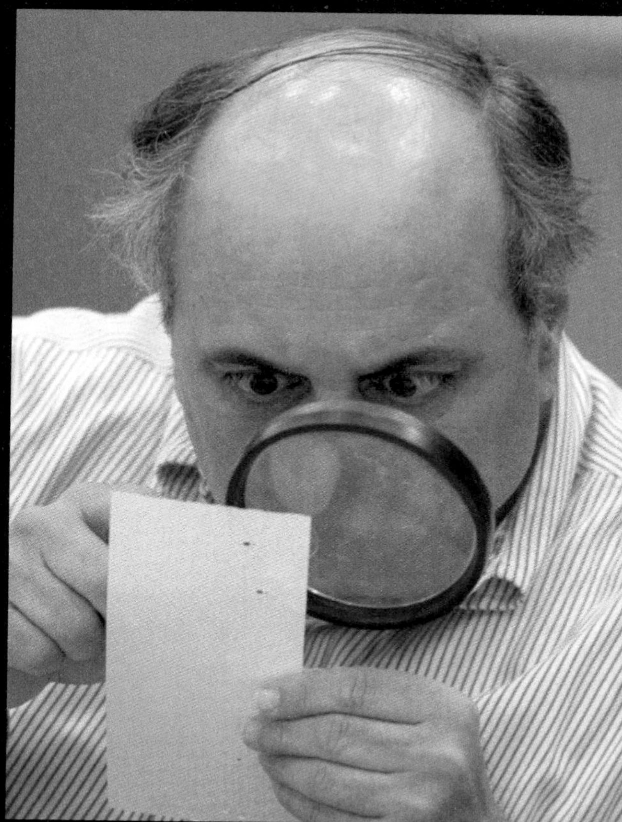

CRITICAL VIEWING In the 2000 presidential election between George W. Bush (R) and Al Gore (D), the vote in Florida was so close—even after a machine recount of the punch-card ballots—that officials undertook a manual recount. After 30 days, however, the U.S. Supreme Court ended the manual recount. What does this photo suggest about why the manual recount was taking so long to complete?

Following the U.S. Supreme Court's 5–4 decision, Florida's 25 electoral votes—and, therefore, the election itself—were awarded to Bush. On December 13, Gore officially conceded the election to Bush, saying, "While I strongly disagree with the Court's decision, I accept it."

THINK ABOUT IT Why do you think the *Bush* v.

Election Maps Can Be Misleading—Here's a Solutio

by Greg Miller **National Geographic Online, October 5, 2016**

Greg Miller, a science and technology journalist and amateur cartographer, or mapmaker, believes the traditional map of election results is "deeply flawed."

Miller offers as an example the traditional map of the 2012 presidential election. The "vast sea of red in the middle of the country" might lead a viewer to believe that Republican Mitt Romney won that election. "But land masses don't decide elections," Miller explains; "the electoral college does." Although red states take up more space on the 2012 election map, the blue states along the coasts and the Great Lakes represent more people and more electoral votes.

Cartographers have been experimenting with ways to better illustrate election results and polling data. One representation that seems to be getting traction . . . is the cartogram, which distorts the shapes of the states so their size corresponds to the number of electoral votes they have. In the cartogram version of the 2012 election map . . . , you can see more clearly how coastal states and states in the upper Midwest carried the election for Obama.

. . . Cartograms have drawbacks, though. They mess with geography and make the states look bloated, blocky, or pixelated, depending on the method used. Some people think they're downright ugly. And for most people they're not as familiar and intuitive as an old-fashioned map. At least not yet.

Miller would like to see wider use of cartograms—maps that use area to represent another statistic. For example, in an election cartogram, each state is shown in its proper place, but its size reflects its electoral votes rather than its land area.

Access the full version of "Election Maps Can Be Misleading—Here's a Solution" by Greg Miller through the Resources Menu in MindTap.

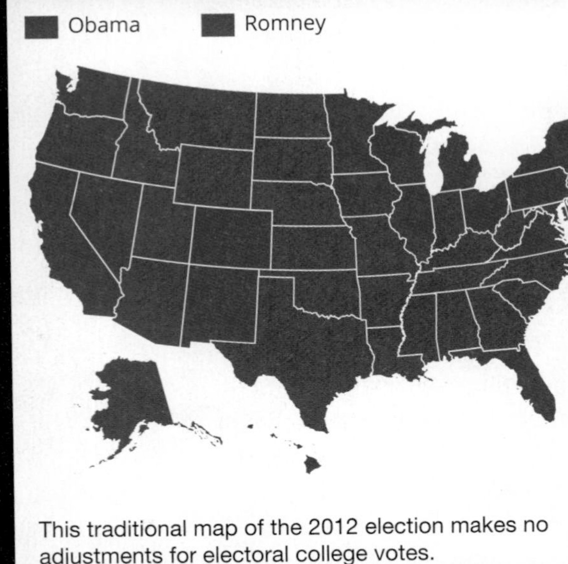

This traditional map of the 2012 election makes no adjustments for electoral college votes.

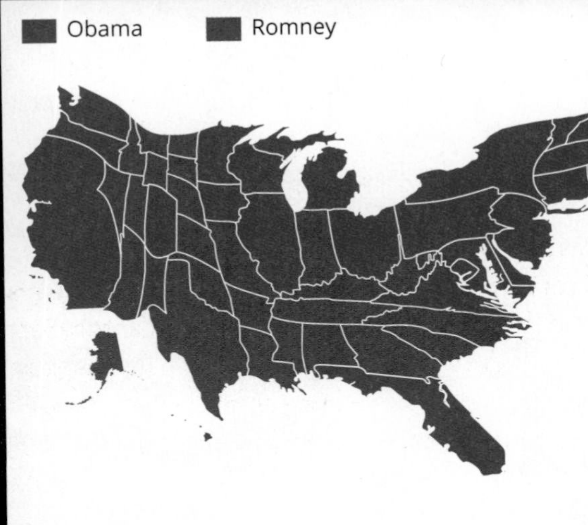

This map shows the same results as the one above, but with adjustments for electoral college votes. Barac Obama won the states in blue, and the election.

THINK ABOUT IT Do you think election maps or cartograms are more useful sources of information? Explain your answer.

The Professional Campaign Organization

To run a successful campaign, a candidate's staff must handle a multitude of complex tasks. It must raise funds, attract media coverage, and produce and pay for political ads. It must schedule the candidate's time effectively with constituent groups, potential supporters, and the media. The campaign must also publicize the candidate's positions on the issues, conduct research on the opposing candidate, and persuade voters to go to the polls. It's not an easy job.

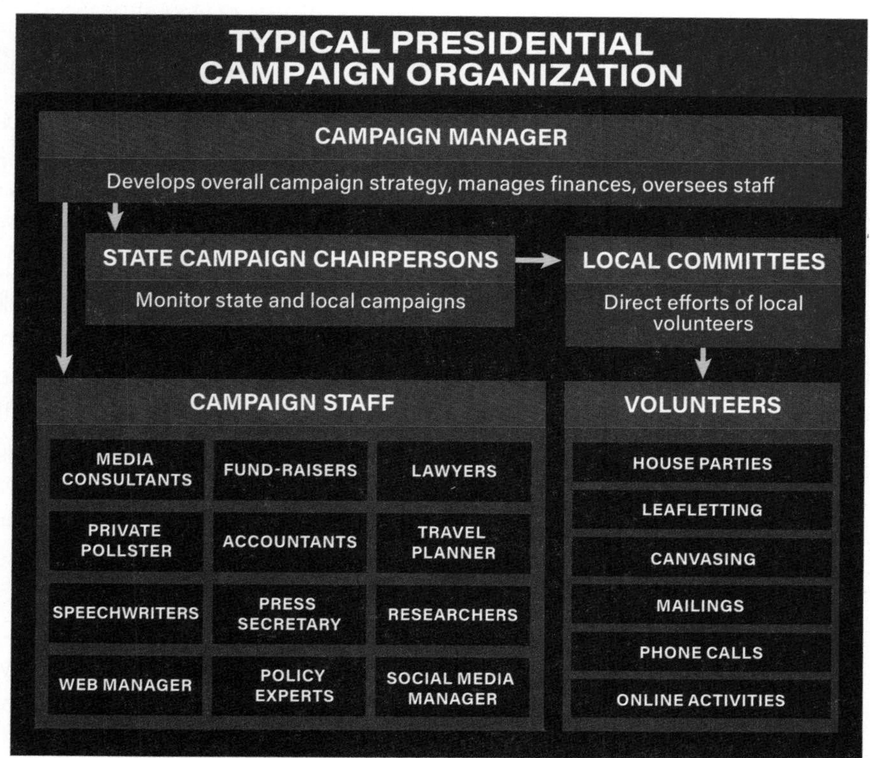

At the state level, chairpersons must coordinate activities across a state and locally as well. Some volunteers will focus on reaching voters in a particular precinct. Others will work on efforts to reach voters throughout a state.

A DIMINISHED ROLE FOR PARTIES Years ago, a strong party organization on the local, state, or national level could furnish most of the services and expertise a candidate needed. Today, instead of relying so extensively on political parties, candidates often turn to professionals to manage their campaigns. The role of political parties in managing campaigns may have declined, but the parties continue to be important in recruiting volunteers and getting out the vote. This means that political parties still have a strong impact on campaigns. Parties establish clear policies that candidates tend to adhere to—especially in the atmosphere of intense political **polarization**, or division into opposing camps, that has developed in recent times. Today, a national politician's party label is a strong indicator of how that person will vote on almost any issue. Many voters understand this fact of political life and use it to help decide for whom to vote.

THE ROLE OF POLITICAL CONSULTANTS Professional political consultants, experts hired to give advice or provide specialized services, now manage nearly all aspects of a presidential candidate's campaign. Most candidates for governor, the House, and the Senate also rely on a professional campaign staff to handle the many tasks associated with running for elective office. The consultants generally specialize in a particular area of the campaign, such as researching the opposition, conducting polls, developing campaign advertising, or writing speeches. Most candidates also hire an experienced campaign manager to coordinate the efforts of the staff and handle finances, including complying with campaign finance regulations. Campaign managers also take responsibility for developing an effective campaign strategy—a comprehensive plan for winning an election.

Media consultants are pivotal members of the campaign staff. A major development in modern-day American politics is the focus on reaching voters through effective use of the media, particularly television. In campaigning for the 2018 midterm elections, outside groups and candidates for governor and Congress aired 4 million television ads. At least half of the budget for a major political campaign is consumed by television advertising. Digital advertising and direct mail are also significant expenses.

Political advertising is sometimes referred to as the air game—a reference to the use of over-the-air broadcasting media, whether television or radio. Today, the air game also includes digital advertising as well as a constantly active social media presence.

HISTORICAL THINKING

1. **MAKE GENERALIZATIONS** Why do you think political parties are better at attracting volunteers than professional consultants are?
2. **INTERPRET CHARTS** Which members of a presidential candidate's campaign staff likely have the most interaction with news reporters?

Opposition Research

Negative campaigning has long been a part of American politics. Rather than presenting a candidate's own proposals or opinions on issues, negative ads attack an opponent's opinions, past behavior, or personality. The more money a campaign raises, the more people it can hire to research and publicize negative information about opposing candidates. Publicity is often free, to the extent that journalists rely on the candidates' opposition research for their stories. What follows are two stories of opposition research from the 2016 presidential campaigns.

RESEARCHING HILLARY CLINTON Democratic presidential candidate Hillary Clinton had long been a target of criticism—based primarily, her supporters said, on sexism. As the likely Democratic nominee, Clinton was the target of intense opposition research well before 2016. Republicans recognized that any claims of improper behavior during Clinton's time as first lady (1993–2001) or as a U.S. senator from New York (2001–2009) would be old news. Their hope was to find something damaging that took place when she was secretary of state (2009–2013).

Opposition research and Republican attacks focused on three areas where they thought Clinton was most vulnerable. One was her handling of the September 2012 attack on the U.S. diplomatic mission in Benghazi, Libya. The attackers burned consulate buildings and killed several staffers, including U.S. Ambassador Christopher Stevens. Clinton was faulted for the lack of security at the embassy. A second was the accusation that Clinton had mishandled classified material by using her private email server for official government email. A yearlong FBI investigation did not lead to criminal charges against Clinton, however. Third, some researchers examined donations from foreign officials and governments to the Clinton Foundation, a Clinton family charity. Clinton's adversaries saw potential there for a conflict of interest, claiming that donations could be used to influence the secretary of state.

No one ever found clear proof of wrongdoing, but even the most reputable news sources reported all the accusations, and the constant drumbeat of accusations served its purpose. People began

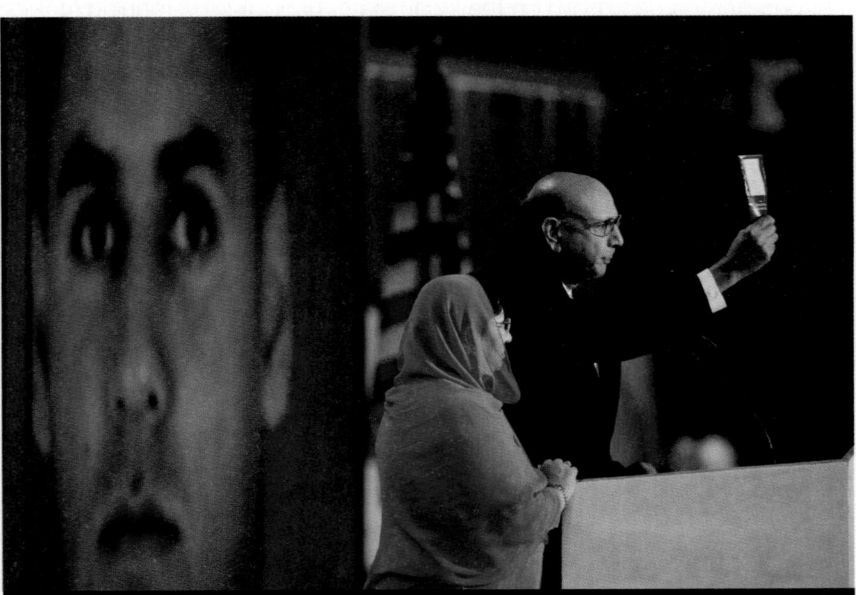

At the Democratic National Convention in 2016, Khizr Khan, with his wife, Ghazala Khan, at his side, held up a copy of the U.S. Constitution and challenged Republican nominee Donald Trump by asking whether he had even read it. The Khans, whose son, U.S. Army Capt. Humayun Khan (shown at the left) was awarded the Bronze Star and died in Iraq, criticized Trump's call for banning the entry of Muslims into the United States.

to believe the Republican claim that Clinton was fundamentally dishonest. On the campaign trail, Donald Trump contributed to this characterization by continually referring to Clinton as "crooked Hillary." He repeatedly stated that Clinton shouldn't be allowed to run for president and even led his audiences in chants of "Lock her up." In the end, the attempt to demolish Clinton's reputation effectively persuaded many voters that she was an unsuitable candidate for high office.

RESEARCHING DONALD TRUMP Donald Trump, the Republican candidate for president, seemed to be vulnerable to opposition research. He claimed to be a brilliant real-estate tycoon, yet he had engineered four corporate bankruptcies, freezing out hundreds of creditors, many of them small businesses. During the presidential campaign, a for-profit real estate school Trump had founded, Trump University, faced lawsuits by former students who claimed it was a scam to squeeze money out of them. Trump called all the accusations "fake news," and his supporters believed that any criticism of Trump in the **mainstream media**—the major, legitimate television networks, newspapers, and news websites—was a lie. Trump was also the first presidential candidate in 40 years to refuse to release his personal income tax return, thereby preventing anyone from fact-checking his claims about his business success and blocking efforts to investigate his financial connections and conflicts of interest. Trump had established himself as someone who could act in ways that formerly would have spelled the end of a politician's career. Making offensive remarks was part of the Trump brand, and any new instance simply confirmed what everyone already believed about him.

A few incidents during the general election seemed to cut into Trump's support, but not by enough to keep him from ultimately winning the presidency. Trump caused many of his backers to flinch in 2015 when he insulted Senator John McCain (R-AZ), a former navy pilot who was captured during the Vietnam War and tortured. "He's not a war hero," Trump said. "He was a war hero because he was captured. I like people who weren't captured." Trump also lost support when he insulted ordinary citizens such as Khizr and Ghazala Khan, a Pakistani American couple whose son was a U.S. Army war hero killed in Iraq. After Khizr Khan spoke at the Democratic National Convention expressing his grief for his son and criticizing Trump, Trump responded with belittling remarks about the Khans and their religion.

Trump made these and other remarks openly. Democrats did not need to conduct research to uncover them. Opposition research, however, was responsible for locating a videotape in which Trump bragged that his star power allowed him to physically molest women. Even that statement, however, had only a limited effect on his support. Following the election, it was revealed that Trump's Republican opponents, and later, the Clinton campaign, had hired a former British spy to compile information on possible ties between the Trump campaign and the Russian government and to investigate damaging information that the Russians might be using to blackmail him. The report was obtained by the FBI and members of Congress and leaked to the public, but Trump's supporters dismissed it.

HISTORICAL THINKING

3. **FORM AND SUPPORT OPINIONS** Do you think opposition research is a fair and objective way to assess an opponent's strengths and weaknesses? Why or why not?
4. **MAKE PREDICTIONS** How might opposition research be used to create a negative television advertisement?

The Internet Campaign

Over the years, political leaders have benefited from understanding and using new communications technologies. In the 1930s, command of a new medium—radio—gave President Franklin D. Roosevelt an edge. His fireside chats calmed a jittery public during the Great Depression. In 1960, Democratic presidential candidate John F. Kennedy's understanding of the visual impact of television gave him an advantage over Republican Richard Nixon in the first televised debate. Kennedy was the picture of health and vitality, wearing make-up and a dark suit to look better in front of a camera, while Nixon, in a light suit and no make-up, looked pale and weak.

Today, candidates must have the ability to make effective use of the internet, especially social media. Websites and apps such as Facebook, Instagram, and Twitter allow users to share information or communicate ideas constantly to huge audiences. In the 2008 presidential election, Barack Obama gained an edge on his rivals in part because of his superior use of the new technologies. His team relied on the internet for raising funds, targeting potential supporters, and creating local political organizations. His 2012 campaign was even more sophisticated. By 2016, every major presidential candidate understood the need for an effective online operation.

FUND-RAISING Online fund-raising grew out of an earlier technique: the direct-mail campaign. In direct mailings, campaigns send advertising and solicitations to large numbers of likely prospects, typically seeking contributions. Developing good lists of prospects is central to an effective direct-mail operation, because postage, printing, and the rental of address lists make the cost of each mailing high. Yet the number of people who respond with a donation is low; a 1 or 2 percent response rate is considered a success. From the 1970s on, conservative organizations became especially adept at managing direct-mail campaigns. They learned which voters to target, how to shape and polish their message, and how to cut costs. For a time, this expertise gave conservative causes and candidates an advantage over liberals.

To understand the old system is to recognize the superiority of the new one. The cost of emailing is very low. Lists of prospects need not be prepared as carefully, because email sent to unlikely prospects costs virtually nothing. Email fund-raising did face one problem when it was new: Many people were not yet online. Today, the extent of online participation is no longer a concern.

The new technology changed the groups that benefited most from it. Conservatives were no longer the most effective fund-raisers. Instead, liberal and libertarian political organizations enjoyed some of the greatest successes. As noted, Barack Obama took internet fund-raising to a new level. One of the defining characteristics of his fund-raising was its decentralization. The Obama campaign attempted to recruit as many supporters as possible to act as fund-raisers. Instead of seeking money from strangers, they solicited contributions from their friends and neighbors. In 2015 and 2016, Hillary Clinton sought to emulate Obama's online success. But her chief opponent in the Democratic primaries, Senator Bernie Sanders (I-VT), also had a strong internet presence. His popularity among the most active users of social media allowed Sanders to raise more money in small donations than Clinton.

In 2007, a year before he won the presidency, candidate Barack Obama reached out to potential donors through an effective internet fund-raising campaign. By the time of the 2008 election, he had raised nearly $750 million.

One Republican candidate for president used the internet with great success in 2008, however. Representative Ron Paul (R-TX) espoused a Libertarian philosophy that appealed to many high-tech enthusiasts. The Libertarian Party opposes almost all government regulation of the economy and any actions by the government that redistribute wealth. Libertarians believe "that government's only responsibility, if any, should be protecting people from force and fraud." Paul pioneered the online money-bomb technique, described by the San Jose *Mercury News* as "a one-day fund-raising frenzy." Despite Paul's fund-raising prowess, his politics were sufficiently far from the conservative Republican mainstream that he was able to win only a handful of national convention delegates. Later Republican presidential candidates, such as 2012 nominee Mitt Romney, had more limited internet operations.

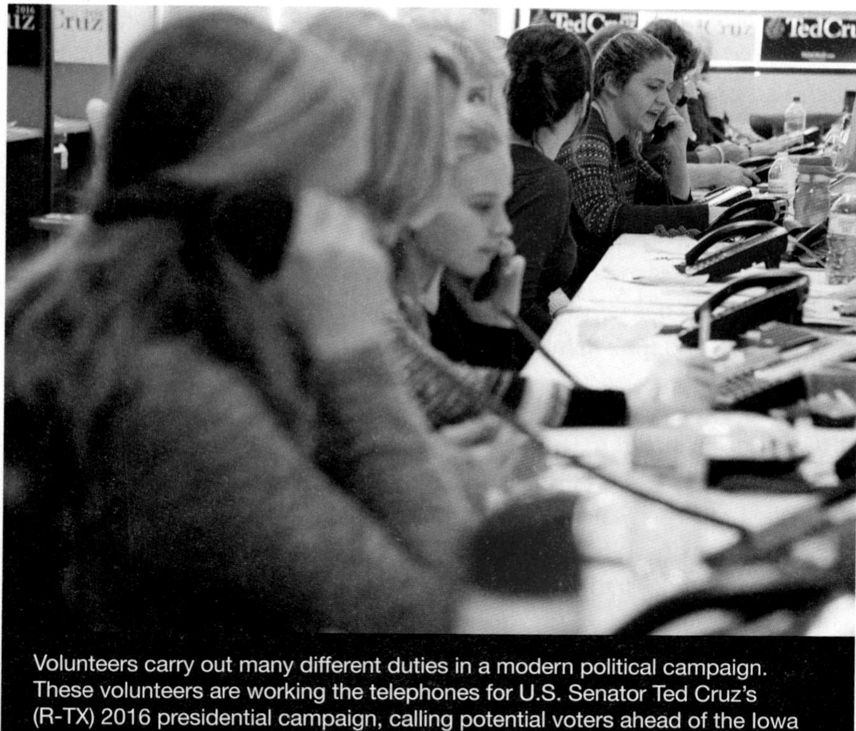

Volunteers carry out many different duties in a modern political campaign. These volunteers are working the telephones for U.S. Senator Ted Cruz's (R-TX) 2016 presidential campaign, calling potential voters ahead of the Iowa caucuses.

Donald Trump's fund-raising organization was neither large scale nor particularly innovative. Indeed, Trump raised less money for his 2016 campaign than any major-party presidential candidate in years. Trump did make great use of the internet in rallying his supporters, however, as you will read shortly.

For the 2020 campaign, Trump made sure to beef up his fund-raising operation. In fact, he established his re-election committee the same day as his inauguration in 2016, and it immediately began fund-raising for 2020. From January 2019 to July 2020, his campaign and party had raised more than $1.1 billion. Despite this success, when he emerged from his nominating convention, Trump's fund-raising hadn't managed to outstrip that of his Democratic rival Joe Biden.

MICROTARGETING In 2004, President George W. Bush's chief political adviser, Karl Rove, pioneered a new national campaign technique known as microtargeting. The process involves collecting as much information as possible about voters in a gigantic electronic database, sorting them into various groups based on shared characteristics, and tailoring different messages to specific groups.

Through microtargeting, the Bush campaign was able to identify Republican prospects living in heavily Democratic neighborhoods. The campaign might otherwise have neglected these potential supporters, because the neighborhood as a whole seemed so unpromising. In 2004, the Democrats had nothing to match Republican efforts. In 2012, however, Obama's microtargeting operation vastly outperformed Romney's. Both major candidates in 2016 made effective use of the technique, though Clinton's operation was better funded.

Google, Twitter, and Facebook have all helped politicians target their ads to specific groups of voters, based on users' online profiles and other information they have shared online. Critics argue that such targeting violates social media users' privacy. Facebook, especially, came under fire after the 2016 presidential election when it was discovered that a data science firm, Cambridge Analytica, had collected personal data from millions of Facebook users with Facebook's assistance. Applying psychological marketing techniques, the firm created political messages aimed at influencing those users' political decisions. Investigators also learned that in the run-up to the 2016 election, a Russian company, funded by the Russian government, had created thousands of fake Facebook and Twitter accounts to spread false and inflammatory stories. The program's goal was to undermine Hillary Clinton's presidential campaign and in the process undermine Americans' confidence in democracy.

In 2020, with in-person campaigning radically scaled back due to the COVID-19 pandemic, the internet played an even greater role. For months, Joe Biden campaigned mainly by live-streaming talks and interviews from his own home. President Trump, meanwhile, cut back on the rallies that had been a feature of his presidency from the start and preferred to communicate with and encourage his political base via Twitter. Both campaigns spent heavily to place targeted ads and fund-raising appeals on social media platforms.

ORGANIZING SUPPORTERS Perhaps the most effective use of the internet has been as an organizing tool. One of the earliest internet techniques was to use a scheduling website to organize real-world meetings. In this way, a candidate's professional campaign staff was able to gather supporters without relying on the existing party and activist infrastructure.

A modern campaign collects as much data as it can to identify the people whose votes it wants to capture and to direct volunteers toward the voters they most need to reach. Such get-out-the-vote drives have been called the ground game—as opposed to advertising, the air game. An important aspect of the ground game is sending volunteers, often young people, to knock on doors so they can talk about the candidate face to face with potential voters in their communities. Volunteers also make telephone calls to voters, especially on election day.

By 2012, President Obama's team had had years to perfect its ground game, and it showed. The Obama re-election campaign was able to create active local support groups in towns and counties across the country—many in areas that had traditionally supported Republicans. By comparison, Romney's ground game sometimes looked like a comedy of errors.

In 2016, Bernie Sanders's ground game enjoyed relative success in caucus states, where turnout is lower than in primary states. That spoke well for the enthusiasm of his supporters, but it was not enough to overcome Clinton's advantages. In 2020, Senator Sanders had an even more impressive campaign infrastructure. But again, it was not enough to convince enough voters to support him. On the Republican side in 2016, political novice Donald Trump was slow in setting up his ground game. He wound up relying largely on the Republican National Committee (RNC) for local organizing. Fortunately for Trump, the RNC was able to launch a major ground-game effort on his behalf.

HISTORICAL THINKING

5. **SYNTHESIZE** Suggest three different messages that a candidate who opposes universal, government-funded health care could use to microtarget three different groups of voters—wealthy people, health-care workers, and people without health insurance.
6. **FORM AND SUPPORT OPINIONS** Which method of contacting potential voters would you think is more effective, email or a personal visit? Why?

LESSON 15.5 Financing Political Campaigns

In the race for president in 1860, Stephen Douglas spent $50,000—$1.5 million in 2018 dollars. Abraham Lincoln, who beat Douglas, spent twice as much. This contest may have been the origin of the notion that money wins elections. The amounts spent by winners and losers went up and down through the years that followed, but the trend was ever higher. George W. Bush set a record for spending in the 2004 campaign—$345 million. In 2012, Barack Obama broke that record and spent $775 million, and outside spending added another $211 million to his campaign. People wondered where it would end.

Regulating Campaign Financing

A presidential campaign is significantly more expensive than a congressional campaign. In the 2015–2016 presidential election cycle, spending on behalf of the major-party candidates was almost $1.5 billion. Compared with that, $175 million for a Senate race in Pennsylvania almost seems paltry. In today's campaign-finance environment, the sums spent by the candidates themselves and by the parties are only part of the story. Independent expenditures by outside groups nominally unconnected with the campaigns have become as important as spending by the candidates themselves.

The high cost of campaigns gives rise to the fear that wealthy campaign contributors and special interest groups will try to buy favored treatment from those they help elect to office, and that candidates and elected officials will use their votes and their influence to help donors get richer rather than working for the majority of their constituents. To prevent these abuses, the government has tried to regulate campaign financing.

THE FEDERAL ELECTION CAMPAIGN ACT The first reform that actually had teeth was the Federal Election Campaign Act (FECA), enacted in 1971 and amended in 1974. This law imposed many regulations and created a Federal Election Commission (FEC) to administer and enforce its provisions.

The FECA's restrictions are aimed more at funding than spending, although the act did restrict the amount that a campaign could spend on mass media advertising. The FECA limited how much individuals and groups could contribute to a candidate and even limited the amount that candidates could contribute to their own campaigns. To further inhibit bribery by means of campaign donations, the FECA tried to eliminate secret donations by requiring disclosure of all contributions and expenditures of more than $100.

The act restricted the role of corporations and labor unions in elections by prohibiting them from participating directly in political campaigns. However, it did allow groups to set up political action committees (PACs) to raise money for candidates. Each PAC can contribute up to $5,000 per candidate in each election, but there is no limit on the total amount candidates can receive from PACs.

In addition, the FECA provided public financing for presidential primaries and general elections. It was thought that if candidates received enough public funds, they would not need private funds, and so they would not be beholden to large donors. From 1976 through 2000, presidential campaigns were partially

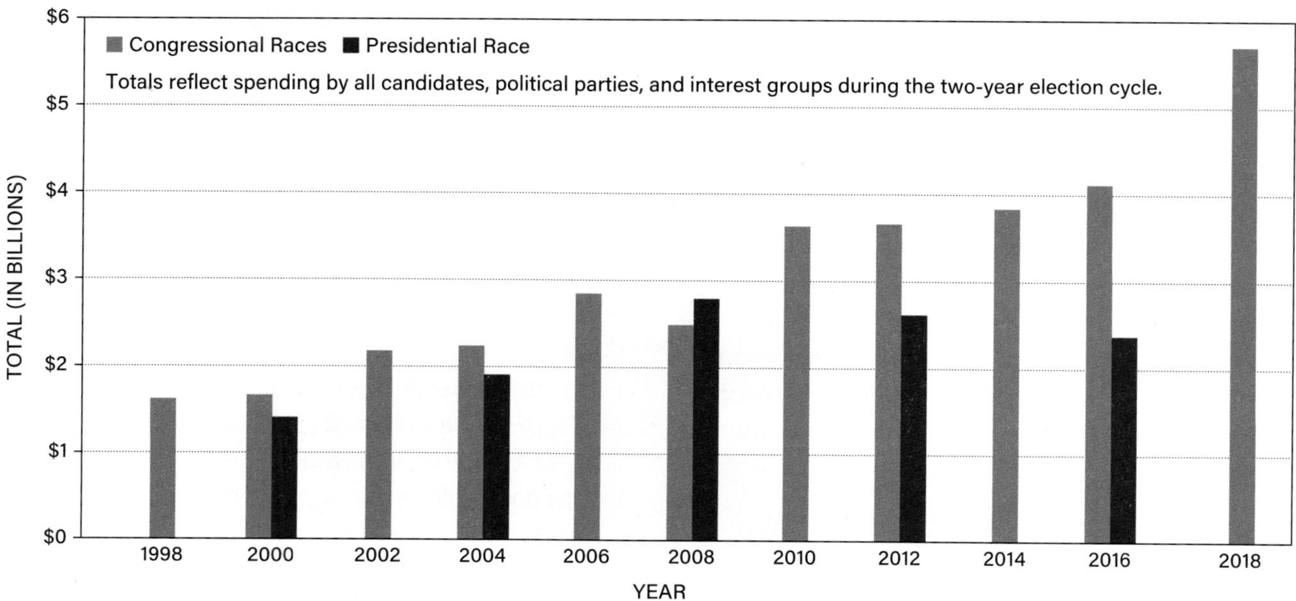

SOURCE: Center for Responsive Politics

funded by the public purse, in the form of matching grants to the candidates. Beginning in 2004, however, leading candidates were refusing public funding for the primaries because they could raise much more money without it. By 2012, the public financing of presidential campaigns had effectively ended.

In 1976, the U.S. Supreme Court declared unconstitutional the provision in the 1971 act that limited the amount an individual could spend on his or her own campaign. The Court held that a "candidate, no less than any other person, has a First Amendment right to engage in the discussion of public issues and vigorously and tirelessly to advocate his own election."

THE RISE OF THE PAC AND SOFT MONEY The FECA was designed to regulate funds given to the campaign organizations of candidates for office. There are ways, however, to influence the political process without giving money directly to a candidate's campaign.

Because there were limits on how much each PAC could contribute but no limits on how much could be contributed to PACs, the number of PACs grew significantly for several decades, as did their campaign contributions. In the 2004 election cycle, about 36 percent of campaign funds spent on House races came from PACs. Since 2004, however, other methods of raising campaign funds that do not have these limitations have reduced the relative importance of the standard PACs.

The FECA and its amendments also allowed individuals and corporations to contribute to political parties to cover the costs of registering voters, printing flyers, producing and airing radio and television advertising, developing campaigns to get out the vote, and holding fundraising events. Donations to political parties were called **soft money** because they can be spent with far fewer restrictions than donations made directly to campaigns. By 2000, the parties were raising nearly $463 million per election season through soft-money contributions. Soft money soon became the main source of campaign funds in the presidential race.

INDEPENDENT EXPENDITURES The FECA also permitted corporations, labor unions, and special interest groups to make independent expenditures on campaigns. As the term *independent* implies, these expenditures and the activities they fund may not be coordinated with those of a candidate or a political party. This prohibition is difficult to enforce.

Decisions by the courts have distinguished two types of independent expenditures. In the first, a contributor backs a particular issue without mentioning any candidates. An issue campaign might, however, publish voter guides informing voters of candidates' positions. The courts have repeatedly upheld the right of groups to spend money in this way.

In the second type, a group might explicitly campaign for a candidate. The Supreme Court has held that an issue-oriented group has a First Amendment right to advocate for the election of its preferred candidate as long as it acts independently of the candidate's campaign. In 1996, the Court held that this right applies to expenditures by political parties as well.

HISTORICAL THINKING

1. **INTERPRET GRAPHS** Comparing the cost of congressional versus presidential elections, which year's totals surprise you the most? Why?
2. **FORM AND SUPPORT OPINIONS** Which of the Federal Election Campaign Act (FECA) provisions do you think did the most to limit money spent on campaigns? Why?
3. **MAKE INFERENCES** How did independent expenditures skirt campaign-finance rules?

The McCain–Feingold Act

The increasing use of soft money and independent expenditures led to a demand for further campaign-finance reform. In 2002, Congress passed, and President George W. Bush signed, the Bipartisan Campaign Reform Act, also known as the McCain–Feingold Act after its chief sponsors, Senators John McCain (R-AZ) and Russell Feingold (D-WI). The new law—which further amended the FECA—banned soft-money contributions to national party committees. It also regulated issue-based campaign ads paid for by interest groups, prohibiting any such ads within 30 days of a primary election or 60 days of a general election.

The McCain–Feingold Act set the amount that an individual could contribute to a federal candidate at $2,000 and the amount that an individual could give to all federal candidates over a two-year election cycle at $95,000. Individuals could still contribute to state and local parties, so long as the contributions did not exceed $10,000 per year per individual. The new law went into effect the day after the 2002 general elections.

SHIFTING SUPREME COURT DECISIONS Several interest groups immediately filed lawsuits challenging the constitutionality of the new law. Supporters of the law's restrictions on campaign ads argued that the large amounts of money spent on these ads could corrupt the democratic political process by allowing interest groups to buy elections. An attorney for one group, the National Rifle Association (NRA), disputed that conclusion. He argued that because the NRA represents "millions of Americans speaking in unison . . . [it] is not a corruption of the democratic political process; it is the democratic political process." In December 2003, the Supreme Court upheld nearly all of the clauses of McCain–Feingold in *McConnell* v. *Federal Election Commission*.

Between 2003 and 2007, however, President George W. Bush appointed two conservatives to the Supreme Court—Chief Justice John Roberts and Associate Justice Samuel Alito—and the Court began to chip away at the limits on independent expenditures. In a 5–4 decision in *Federal Election Commission* v. *Wisconsin Right to Life, Inc.* (2007), the Court held that issue ads could not be prohibited in the time period preceding elections unless they were "susceptible of no reasonable interpretation other than as an appeal to vote for or against a specific candidate." The Court asserted that restricting all television ads in the weeks before an election amounted to censorship of political speech.

OPENING THE CAMPAIGN-FINANCE FLOODGATES A January 2010 Supreme Court ruling helped establish the current wide-open campaign-finance system. In *Citizens United* v. *Federal Election Commission*, the Court went further than it had in the *Wisconsin Right to Life* case to allow ads that attack or praise specific candidates, including ads that urge viewers to vote for particular candidates. Two months later, in *SpeechNOW* v. *Federal Election Commission*, a

SUPREME COURT

Citizens United v. *Federal Election Commission*, 2010

Decided: January 21, 2010, 5–4

Majority: Justice Anthony M. Kennedy wrote the opinion for the Court in favor of Citizens United.

Dissent: Justice John Paul Stevens wrote a dissenting opinion.

In 2008, a nonprofit corporation called Citizens United released a documentary film critical of Hillary Clinton. At the time, Clinton was seeking the Democratic nomination for president. Citizens United wanted to distribute and advertise the film on television just before the Democratic primary election. But it was then illegal for a corporation to use its own funds in an ad for or against a particular candidate for federal office in the 30-day period before a primary. A federal district court ruled that Citizens United could not air its TV ads.

The case reached the U.S. Supreme Court in 2009. The Court had earlier recognized that the First Amendment could apply to corporations and their political speech. Now a sharply divided Court, in a 5–4 decision, ruled that corporations such as Citizens United may not be prevented from funding political ads. Justice Kennedy summarized the Court's findings when he wrote that "no sufficient governmental interest justifies limits on the political speech of nonprofit or for-profit corporations."

THINK ABOUT IT Why might Justice Stevens have believed that corporations should not be allowed to fund ads like the ones produced by Citizens United?

SUPREME COURT

McCutcheon v. *Federal Election Commission*, 2014

Decided: April 2, 2014, 5–4

Majority: Chief Justice John G. Roberts wrote the majority opinion in favor of McCutcheon.

Dissent: Justice Stephen G. Breyer wrote a dissent.

The 1971 Federal Elections Campaign Act (FECA), as amended, placed limits on the amounts of money an individual could contribute to national party committees, candidates for federal office, and political action committees during a two-year election cycle and also established an aggregate limit for these contributions. The aim of the overall limit was to avoid "the reality and appearance of corruption."

In a lawsuit filed in federal district court in 2012, businessman Shaun McCutcheon, backed by the Republican National Committee, maintained that Congress did not have a right to impose limits on the total amount of an individual's political contributions. He stated that he had reached his total limit, but he wanted to contribute to more candidates and PACs. He argued that existing overall limits were unnecessary, because the base limits made it very hard for anyone to funnel a huge amount of money to any one candidate. McCutcheon lost his case in federal district court, but in 2013, the U.S. Supreme Court decided to hear his appeal.

In a 5–4 ruling, the Court agreed with McCutcheon that provisions of the FECA limiting the total political contributions by an individual undermined his First Amendment rights. Writing for the majority, Chief Justice John Roberts reasoned that aggregate limits are unnecessary, that the base limits go far enough toward preventing corruption or the appearance of corruption.

THINK ABOUT IT Why do you think it is important to avoid not only corruption but the appearance of corruption in the election system?

federal court of appeals held that Congress may not limit contributions to independent-expenditure groups based on the size or source of the contribution.

As a result of these decisions, there is now no limit on the ability of corporations, unions, nonprofit groups, or individuals to fund advertising, provided that they do not contribute directly to a candidate's campaign. Republican leaders applauded the *Citizens United* ruling as a victory for free speech, but most Democratic leaders expressed alarm. They feared that the ruling would result in a massive tilting of the political landscape toward corporate wealth.

In April 2014, the Supreme Court handed down yet another ruling that freed up campaign financing. In *McCutcheon* v. *Federal Election Commission*, the Court struck down a decades-old cap on the total amount that any individual can contribute to federal candidates in a two-year election cycle. (By 2014, that total amount had risen to $123,000.) As a result of this ruling, to give one example, a wealthy individual could now make the maximum legal contribution to every single House candidate of a particular party.

HISTORICAL THINKING

4. **IDENTIFY PROBLEMS AND SOLUTIONS** Why do you think Congress tried to ban soft money?
5. **MAKE GENERALIZATIONS** How could the Court's ruling in the *Citizens United* case be considered a victory for free speech?

The Current Campaign-Finance Environment

Citizens United and related decisions changed the campaign-finance environment. Individuals and PACs still face limits on what they can contribute directly to candidates' campaigns and to the parties. Despite these limits, campaigns and political parties are still able to raise huge sums.

INDEPENDENT ORGANIZATIONS A new type of organization, the independent expenditure-only committee, came into existence to take advantage of the new rules. Soon dubbed **Super PACs**, these

Groups Making Independent Campaign Expenditures, 2017–2018 Election Cycle

Organization	Affiliation	Total Expenditures, 2018 Election Cycle	Type	Disclosure of Contributors
Congressional Leadership Fund	Republican	$137,501,727	Super PAC	partial
Senate Majority PAC	Democratic	$112,847,349	Super PAC	full
Senate Leadership Fund	conservative	$95,054,956	Super PAC	partial
Democratic Congressional Campaign Committee	Democratic	$84,491,681	Party committee	full
National Republican Congressional Committee	Republican	$74,348,828	Party committee	full
House Majority PAC	Democratic	$71,623,390	Super PAC	full
Majority Forward	liberal	$45,862,781	501c	full
Independence USA PAC	liberal	$37,506,875	Super PAC	none
National Republican Senatorial Committee	Republican	$35,222,531	Party committee	full
America First	conservative	$31,474,416	Super PAC, 501c	partial

SOURCE: Center for Responsive Politics

organizations had no limits on the amount of money they could raise, although they were not allowed to contribute to or work directly with a party or candidate. They ended up, however, collaborating indirectly. Super PACs could run negative ads to damage a candidate's opponents, while the candidate committee—the committee entirely under the candidate's own control—could focus on the positive about the candidate. Super PACs are also allowed to give unlimited donations to other Super PACs.

In addition to Super PACs, another type of independent committee is the 527 committee, named after the provision of the tax code that covers it. A 527 is allowed to "advocate positions" but not to "expressly advocate" voting for specific candidates. In the 2004 election cycle, 527s spent about $612 million, but their role was soon replaced by Super PACs, which are allowed to campaign for and against candidates.

Another reason for the decline of the 527 committee was the creation of a new kind of organization, known as the 501c. According to some lawyers, a 501c could make limited contributions directly to campaigns and, perhaps more importantly, conceal the identities of its donors. Republicans argued that donors needed the right to remain anonymous so they would not have to fear retribution. Democrats contended that anonymous contributions were simply a further corruption of the political process.

INDIVIDUAL DONORS The *Citizens United* decision resulted in more corporate (and union) spending, but far less than anticipated. What caught everyone by surprise was the huge sums poured into Super PACs by individuals, notably individuals of great wealth. For example, in the 2018 election cycle, casino magnate Sheldon Adelson and his wife made total donations of more than $123 million to Republican candidates, parties, and PACs. Tom Steyer, a California hedge fund billionaire and environmentalist, donated nearly $71 million to Democrats during the same period. Some individuals who can afford to donate only $5 or $10 find these figures discouraging.

HISTORICAL THINKING

6. **IDENTIFY MAIN IDEAS AND DETAILS** How did Super PACs skirt campaign-finance rules related to directly aiding a candidate?
7. **ANALYZE VISUALS** Based on the campaign spending table, do you think conservative groups or liberal groups tend to spend more to get congressional candidates elected? Explain your answer.

CHAPTER 15

THE ELECTORAL PROCESS

Review

VOCABULARY

Match each of the following vocabulary words with its definition.

1. ballot
2. nominating convention
3. polls
4. plurality
5. progressive tax
6. endorse
7. polarization
8. mainstream media

a. recommend
b. a meeting of party members to choose candidates
c. a system in which those with greater assets pay the government at higher rates
d. major, legitimate television networks, newspapers, and news websites
e. the greatest number of votes received
f. list for indicating one's choices in an election
g. places where voters cast votes
h. division into opposing camps

MAIN IDEAS

Answer the following questions. Support your answers with evidence from the chapter.

9. Why do you think critics referred to the congressional caucus system as King Caucus in the 1800s? **LESSON 15.1**
10. How did the development of the primary election affect political party bosses? **LESSON 15.1**
11. What are two reasons party officials might support closed primaries? **LESSON 15.1**
12. Why do you think a presidential candidate's seeking of support from party insiders and fund-raisers has been called the invisible primary? **LESSON 15.2**
13. How was the creation of Super Tuesday an example of front-loading? **LESSON 15.2**
14. How did the Australian ballot improve the U.S. election process? **LESSON 15.3**
15. What determines how many electoral votes each state has? **LESSON 15.3**
16. Why are political consultants vital to a campaign for president? **LESSON 15.4**
17. What is the main purpose of opposition research? **LESSON 15.4**
18. Why is a Super PAC categorized as an independent organization? **LESSON 15.5**

HISTORICAL THINKING

Answer the following questions. Support your answers with evidence from the chapter.

19. **MAKE CONNECTIONS** Why might the growing number of independent voters lead to fewer closed primaries?
20. **EVALUATE** What practical purpose do you think the modern national nominating convention serves?
21. **DRAW CONCLUSIONS** What roles does the popular vote play in the electoral college system at the state level and at the national level?
22. **COMPARE AND CONTRAST** How was direct-mail campaigning similar to and different from a modern email campaign?
23. **MAKE INFERENCES** How has the Supreme Court's interpretation of the First Amendment affected limits set by political campaign financing laws?

INTERPRET VISUALS

Study the table below. Then answer the questions.

24. According to the table, what is the maximum a single-candidate PAC could contribute to a presidential candidate in one election cycle?

25. How do you know that neither of the two PAC categories listed in the table represents Super PACs?

Campaign Contribution Limits for 2020[1]

	To each candidate or candidate committee per election	To each PAC per year	To the national party committee per year	To additional national party committee accounts, per account per year
Individual	$2,800	$5,000	$35,500	$106,500
PAC (multicandidate[2])	$5,000	$5,000	$15,000	$45,000
PAC (not multicandidate)	$2,800	$5,000	$35,500	$106,500

[1]Limits not shown for contributions made by and to state, district, and local party committees.
[2]Multicandidate PACs are those that receive contributions from at least 51 persons and contribute to at least 5 candidates.
SOURCE: Federal Election Commission

ANALYZE SOURCES

In 1999, Senator John McCain issued a press release expressing his hope that

> Congress, at long last, may accede to . . . the wishes of the vast majority of the people we represent, by repairing a campaign finance system that has become a national embarrassment and assails the integrity of the office we are privileged to hold.

26. Based on this statement, what can you infer was McCain's main criticism of the U.S. campaign finance system?

CONNECT TO YOUR LIFE

27. **EXPLANATORY** The nomination of candidates for president is a key part of the election process. But voter participation in primaries is low, and in caucuses even lower. One way to help motivate people to vote is to demonstrate how easy voting is. Write a letter to the editor of a local newspaper urging people to vote in the upcoming primary election or caucuses by explaining the voting process in your state.

TIPS

- Familiarize yourself with the presidential nomination process in general by reviewing the lessons on nominating candidates, and research your state government to find out what kind of system your state has. (For instance, does your state have primaries or caucuses? If primaries, are they closed, open, or some mix?)
- In your letter, describe the process of voting in your state's primary or caucus.
- Consider your audience's possible reasons for not participating, and suggest how obstacles to participating can be overcome.
- You might end your letter with an appeal to civic responsibility, love of country, and support for democracy, or the importance of selecting effective government officials.
- Use two or three key vocabulary terms from the chapter in your letter.

CHAPTER 16

Voting and Voting Rights

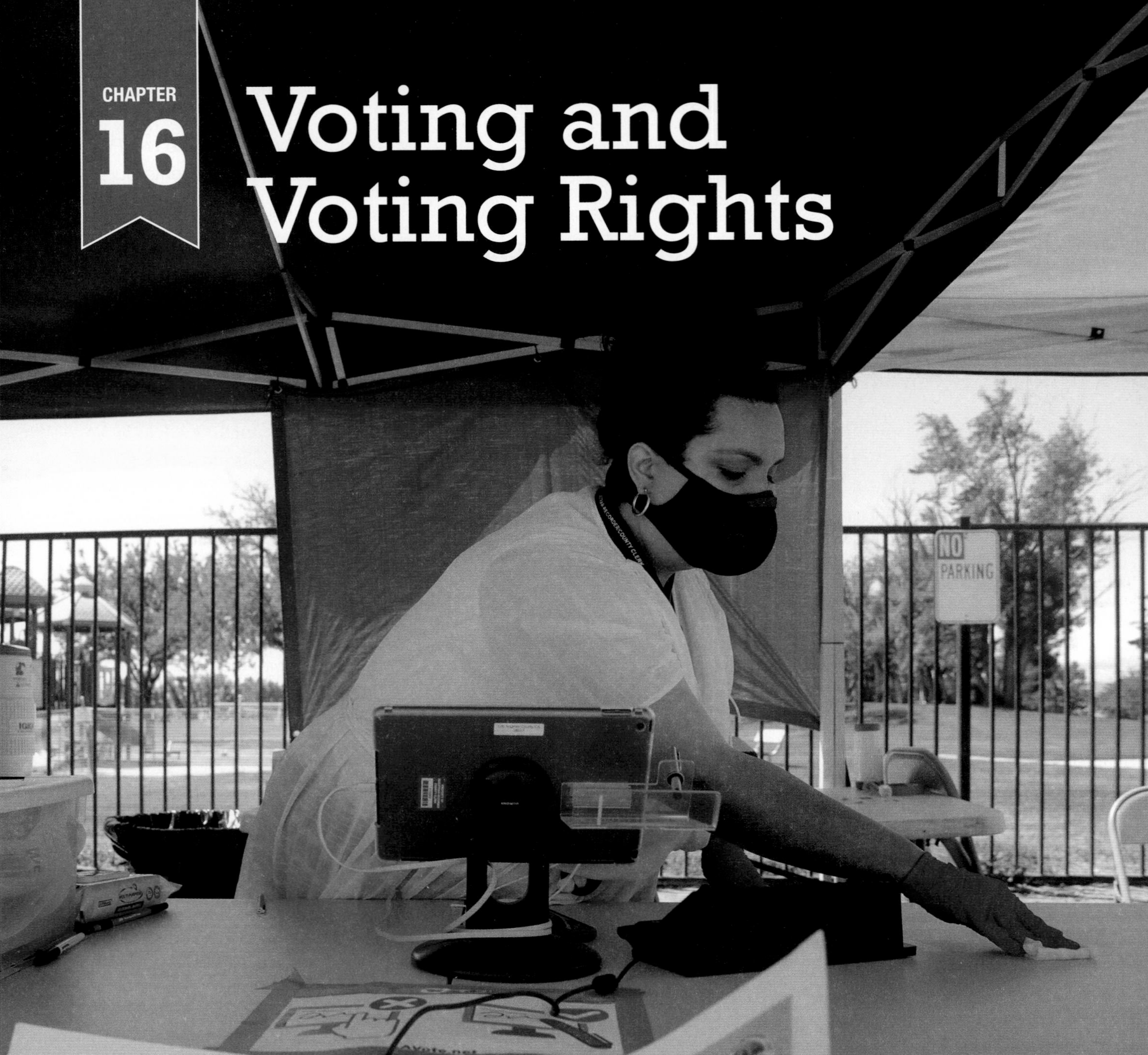

LESSONS

16.1 Who Gets to Vote?

16.2 The Struggle for Voting Rights

***National Geographic* Magazine:**
A Century After Women's Suffrage, the Fight for Equality Isn't Over

16.3 The Process of Voting

16.4 Understanding Voter Behavior

16.5 Public Opinion Polls

CRITICAL VIEWING Voting is a key to citizen participation in modern democracies, and people must have accessible, secure, and private procedures for voting. During a special election in California held amid the COVID-19 pandemic in 2020, voting precincts were set up out of doors and election workers regularly applied disinfectant to make the voting stations safer. Why are voting rights important? Why does the process matter so much?

LESSON 16.1

Who Gets to Vote?

Voting is arguably the most important way in which citizens participate in the political process. Americans vote to elect politicians to represent their interests and values. Politicians who are unresponsive or who work against their constituents' interests can be voted out of office. In some circumstances, such as with referendums or bond issues, voters decide directly on public policy. Elections can affect everything from whether the country goes to war to the purity of drinking water, from the cost of health insurance to legal access to marijuana. Elections determine what the government does and what it does not do.

Qualifying to Vote

Despite the importance of elections, voter turnout in the United States is lower than in many other democratic republics around the world. In most of the rest of the world, voting is considered a civic responsibility, a duty that all eligible voters owe to their society. A Pew Research Center survey revealed that 40 percent of Americans do not see voting this way. Many of these citizens feel their vote does not make a difference, and, in one sense, they are correct: Mathematically, no individual vote is likely to be the deciding vote. The smaller the percentage of people voting, however, the less an election can be said to express the will of the people. In this sense, every vote does count, for every vote contributes to the legitimacy of the electoral process and the government.

Even people who rarely or never vote value the right to vote—they would not choose to live under a dictator. Yet neither the original U.S. Constitution nor the Bill of Rights guaranteed anyone the right to vote. The Constitutional Convention left voting to the states, and the issue was not addressed at the federal level until ratification of the 15th Amendment in 1870.

Although the 15th Amendment was written to give African-American men the right to vote and the 19th Amendment to give all women the right to vote, states limited African Americans' access to the ballot box for many years. The Voting Rights Act of 1965 was a big step in resolving that issue, restoring the vote to many people who had been **disenfranchised**, or deprived of the right to vote.

Every state except North Dakota requires voters to register with the appropriate state or local officials before voting. Registering to vote puts voters on a list that shows they are qualified to vote. In order to register, voters must meet three qualifications: citizenship, residency, and age. U.S. citizenship is required for a person to vote in any federal or state election held anywhere in the United States. This was not always the case. Until the early 20th century, several states allowed noncitizens to cast ballots. But most states do not permit prison inmates, people with mental illness, or election-law violators to vote.

Traditionally, residency requirements have been imposed for voting. Residency requirements prevent anyone from bringing in large numbers of people to steal an election. They also help ensure that new residents have had a chance to become familiar with the community before voting. In the past, these requirements could be for extended periods of time. Through the 1960s, Tennessee, for instance, required one year of residency in the state and three months residency in the county where a voter intended to cast a ballot. James Blumstein learned of this requirement when he moved to Nashville, Tennessee, after graduating from law school in 1970. Blumstein sued when he was not allowed to register to vote in an election scheduled about a month later because he didn't meet residency requirements. *Dunn* v. *Blumstein* reached the U.S. Supreme Court, which ruled in 1972 that Tennessee's residence requirement unreasonably discriminated against new residents and so violated

The final step in the naturalization process is a public swearing-in ceremony. Once naturalized, an immigrant who is 18 or older is eligible to vote in all local, state, and federal elections. This ceremony was conducted on July 3, 2018, at the New York Public Library.

equal protection. That ruling has meant that no state can impose a residency requirement of more than 30 days.

Today, 26 states still have residency requirements ranging from 10 to 30 days. The other states do not have such requirements. They only require proof that the person has established residency and is not just visiting or traveling through. Even if no minimum residency period is defined, some states impose a cutoff date for registering to vote before an election, although 21 states and the District of Columbia allow voters to register and vote the same day.

From before the Civil War, most states had set the voting age at 21. No state had a voting age lower than 21 until Georgia lowered its voting age to 18 during World War II. By 1971, only 3 other states had a voting age less than 21, so nearly every state was affected when the 26th Amendment, which forbade any jurisdiction from setting a minimum voting age greater than 18, was ratified that year. Further, a 17-year-old who will turn 18 before the general election is entitled to vote in a primary for that election.

HISTORICAL THINKING

1. **FORM AND SUPPORT OPINIONS** What might be an argument for allowing legal residents who do not have U.S. citizenship to vote in local elections?
2. **MAKE INFERENCES** What is an argument in favor of residency requirements for voting registration?

Registering to Vote

Registering is one of the key steps required of almost all people who choose to vote in the United States. Registering voters is a state function, and every state has different guidelines for registration. As you have read, North Dakota is the one state that does not require registration at all.

In 2016, the U.S. Census Bureau reported that there were about 245.5 million Americans of voting age. Of these, fewer than 158 million were registered to vote—about 64 percent of those eligible. Many people wonder why so few Americans have an interest in voting, but failing to register may not always reflect a lack of interest. Millions of Americans of voting age are not eligible to vote. For instance, in many states, felons do not have the right to vote even after they have served their time in prison, and the millions of legal immigrants who have not become citizens are also ineligible to vote.

Many critics cite technical registration requirements as a cause of poor voter turnout. The 2018 election in Georgia provides one striking example. Georgia placed more than 53,000 voter registrations on hold because the applications didn't exactly match the information on state driving records. It might have been because the voter moved and neglected to update the address with either the board of elections or the motor vehicles office. In some cases, the denial was as simple as a clerk's typing an extra space or omitting a hyphen in the voter's name or street address.

Many states have recently passed laws to make registering more convenient. The National Voter Registration Act (the Motor Voter Law) of 1993 simplified the voter-registration process. The act requires states to provide anyone eligible with the opportunity to register to vote when they apply for or renew a driver's license. It also requires states to allow mail-in registration and to provide mail-in forms at public-assistance agencies. The law, which took effect in 1995, has facilitated millions of registrations. As of July 2020, some 80 percent of the states and the District of Columbia offered online registration.

Sixteen states and the District of Columbia automatically register all citizens age 18 or above who have a driver's license or state ID card. Colorado and other states also allow preregistration of 16- and 17-year-olds when they apply for a driver's license. In at least seven states, adults applying for or receiving social services are also automatically registered. Alaska automatically registers anyone who applies for a Permanent Fund Dividend, an annual payment drawn from Alaska's state oil and gas revenue.

Some people may find it difficult to register to vote. They might have problems getting to the place where they need to register. They may not have a residence or proof of residence, like a utility bill, if they are homeless or living with other people. Work, childcare, and other responsibilities can make it hard to get to a voter registration site. People who find it difficult to register to vote tend to be people of color, the elderly, and people of low income. These groups usually favor Democratic Party candidates. Many, for example, are African Americans, a reliably Democratic voting bloc. As a result, Republicans often oppose efforts to make registration easier and have even enacted laws designed to make registration and voting more difficult.

The courts have recently begun to agree that such laws go too far. In July 2016, a U.S. appeals court struck down a series of voting restrictions in Texas on the grounds that they amounted to racial discrimination. In North Carolina, a federal appeals court blocked a new voting law that it said was aimed "with almost surgical precision" at preventing African Americans from voting. Nonetheless, in the 2018 election, voter turnout for all groups of voters, including African Americans and Hispanics, reached the highest levels for a midterm election since 1900.

HISTORICAL THINKING

3. **EVALUATE** Do you approve of Georgia's 2018 effort to remove people from the voter list? Why or why not?
4. **DRAW CONCLUSIONS** Why do Democrats, in particular, want to make it easier for citizens to register to vote?

LESSON
16.2 The Struggle for Voting Rights

Restrictions on suffrage, the legal right to vote, have existed since the founding of our nation. Hamilton and Madison, among others, held the opinion that only land-owning males should be able to vote because they believed people who did not own property could be controlled by their employers or others on whom their livelihood depended. In most cases women, who generally could not own property and were also assumed to be uninformed on political questions, were barred from voting. In many states, African Americans did not have citizenship or were blocked from voting. Asian Americans, Native Americans, and Mexican Americans all faced barriers to voting. The expansion of suffrage to greater numbers of Americans is one of the most important stories in the growth of democracy in the United States.

Voting Rights to 1900

Those who drafted the Constitution left it to the individual states to set voting qualifications. As you just read, most states limited suffrage to adult White males who owned a specified amount of land. These property restrictions were challenged early in the history of the republic. By 1828, property ownership and tax-payment requirements for voting began to disappear.

Although the Constitution prohibited religious requirements for officeholders, voters did not have similar protection. Religious restrictions on voting continued in some states until 1828, when Maryland permitted Jews to vote. By 1850, White males of any religion were allowed to vote, but restrictions based on race and gender continued.

The 15th Amendment, ratified in 1870, guaranteed suffrage to African-American men. Yet, for many decades, African Americans in the former slave states were effectively denied the ability to exercise their voting rights by means of mob violence, threats, economic pressure, and legal trickery. Some states required African-American citizens to pass literacy tests with complicated questions about government and history before they could register to vote. In the mid- to late 1800s, 40 to 60 percent of African Americans were illiterate, due to the lasting effects of laws against teaching enslaved persons to read. But regardless of anyone's actual abilities, registrars made sure that nearly all African Americans failed these tests. Another device used to discourage African Americans, as well as poor Whites, from voting was the poll tax, which you read about earlier. This tax represented a sizable burden for anyone with little money, which included nearly all formerly enslaved people and their families.

ORIGINAL
POLL TAX RECEIPT
STATE OF TEXAS
COUNTY OF BEXAR
No 45073
PRECINCT 11 PAGE ____ LINE ____
San Antonio, Texas, 1-28 193_
1931
RECEIVED OF Mrs. Carrie Turk
the sum of One and 50/100 Dollars in payment of Poll Tax for the year 1931
ADDRESS 2154 ...
AGE 40 | LENGTH OF RESIDENCE State 20 County 20 City 20
Native Born / Naturalized | Citizen of United States and was born in Texas
Occupation ... Where Issued ...
Race - White - Colored Sex - Male - Female
The said Tax Payer being duly sworn by me says that the above is correct. All of which I Certify.
By ... Deputy. ... Tax Collector, Bexar County, Texas.

Two years into the Great Depression, Mrs. Carrie Turk of San Antonio, Texas, a White woman, paid a $1.50 poll tax—the equivalent of about $25 in 2019—to secure her right to vote. In some places, everyone had to pay a tax to vote, but since African Americans were only allowed to work at the lowest paying jobs and had the highest rates of unemployment, they were the least likely to be able to pay the tax. Poll taxes were finally banned in 1964 with ratification of the 24th Amendment.

Seven southern states carved out exemptions from any poll tax and literacy test for anyone who had a father or grandfather who had voted prior to 1866 or 1867. Known as grandfather clauses, these laws enabled many impoverished and illiterate Whites to vote. The grandfathers of African Americans, whether enslaved or free, had been denied the right to vote prior to the Civil War, so grandfather clauses did not help them. The United States Supreme Court struck down the use of grandfather clauses in 1915, by which time most White voters could no longer take advantage of them in any case.

African Americans were also blocked from voting in Democratic primary elections in many states. The Supreme Court initially upheld these so-called White primaries on the grounds that, while the 15th Amendment protected the right to vote in elections, primaries were separate from the general election. They were conducted by political parties, rather than by the states, and the parties could do as they wished.

The disenfranchisement of felons represents one more obstacle to voting imposed after Reconstruction. Many former Confederate states passed new criminal laws aimed at Black men. For example, in the years after the Civil War, unemployed freedmen could be arrested for the vaguely defined crime of vagrancy—in other words, the crime of being unemployed. Additionally, these states made lifetime disenfranchisement part of the penalty for those convicted of felonies. Traditionally, only those convicted of particularly heinous crimes or crimes involving elections were denied suffrage. These new laws used convictions of minor crimes as an excuse to keep African Americans from voting. In the decades that followed and continuing up to the present, the disenfranchisement of persons convicted of a felony, even after serving their sentence, has limited voting rights for a considerable portion of the African-American population.

Gerrymandering, in which voting districts are redrawn for the purpose of limiting the voting power of specific groups, was another strategy used to limit the electoral power of African Americans. In one case, the Alabama state legislature redrew the boundaries of the city of Tuskegee to remove virtually every registered Black voter from the city limits. The new district was a 28-sided figure.

HISTORICAL THINKING

1. **SYNTHESIZE** How did southern states get around the 15th Amendment guarantee of voting rights for African-American men?
2. **DRAW CONCLUSIONS** How did the so-called White primary limit the power of Black voters who did manage to vote in an election?

Voting Rights in the 20th Century

As you have read, while some progress was made in expanding voting rights for White men in the 1800s, African Americans were effectively kept from voting, despite the 15th Amendment. In the 20th century, the movement to extend the vote to White women finally saw success, while the fight for suffrage for African-American men and women continued at a frustratingly slow pace.

WOMAN SUFFRAGE Early in the republic's existence, certain women had been able to vote in some states. New Jersey, for example, allowed women who met property and residency requirements to vote under its 1776 state constitution. (In 1807, the New Jersey legislature passed laws that limited voting to White men who paid taxes.) These early voting rights were never universal among the states, however, and not recognized at the national level.

The women's suffrage movement was successful at the state level well before the passage of the 19th Amendment in 1919. Wyoming became the first territory (1869) and the first state (1890) to grant women the **franchise**. Fifteen states, all in the West, granted women the right to vote before 1917. Wyoming was the first state to recognize women's right to vote after the Civil War. Even before it became a state, Wyoming granted women the right to vote in territorial elections in 1869, and it kept that provision when it became a state in 1890. Women won protection for their right to vote in 15 states, all in the West, before 1917. Finally, in 1920, ratification of the 19th Amendment fully enfranchised women. While the amendment gave African-American women the legal right to vote, they faced the same barriers to voting as African-American men. Asian-American, Hispanic, and Native American women and men likewise continued

Extending the Right to Vote

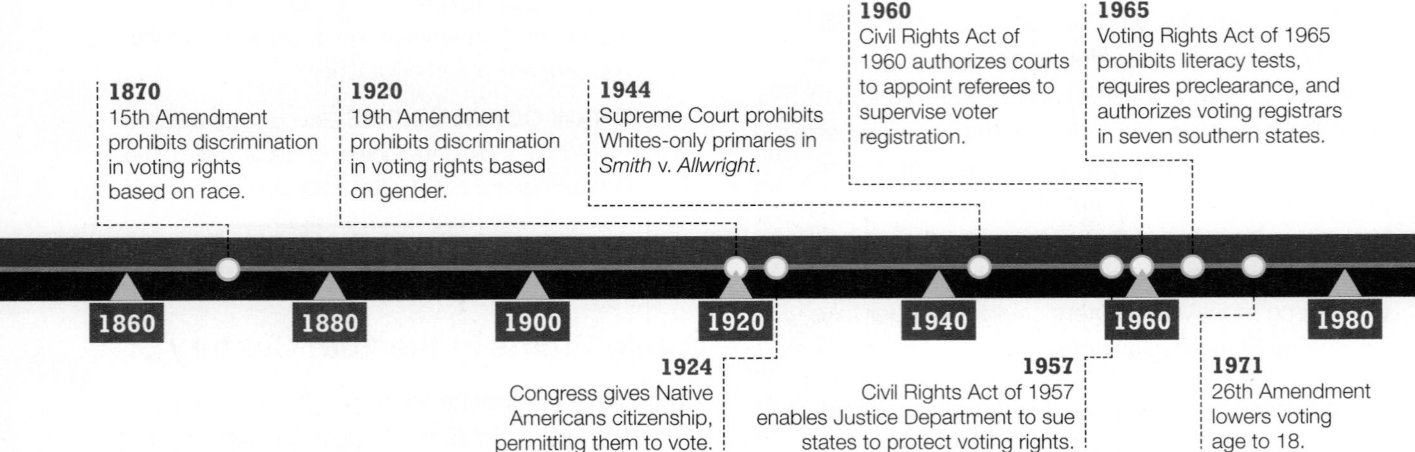

to face denial of their right to vote in the years that followed.

1870
15th Amendment prohibits discrimination in voting rights based on race.
1920
19th Amendment prohibits discrimination in voting rights based on gender.
1944
Supreme Court prohibits Whites-only primaries in Smith v. Allwright.
1960
Civil Rights Act of 1960 authorizes courts to appoint referees to supervise voter registration.
1965
Voting Rights Act of 1965 prohibits literacy tests, requires preclearance, and authorizes voting registrars in seven southern states.
1860
1880
1900
1920
1940
1960
1980
1924
Congress gives Native Americans citizenship, permitting them to vote.
1957
Civil Rights Act of 1957 enables Justice Department to sue states to protect voting rights.
1971
26th Amendment lowers voting age to 18.

AFRICAN-AMERICAN SUFFRAGE In the 20th century, laws and practices stripping African Americans of their constitutional right to vote began to fall one by one. Although the Supreme Court ruled that the use of grandfather clauses was unconstitutional in 1915, it did not outlaw literacy tests or poll taxes which were used in the North to bar immigrants from voting. Nor did the Court issue a clear ruling on barring African Americans from voting in primaries. But in 1940, Lonnie Smith, a Black dentist, brought a suit against a Texas election judge, S. E. Allwright, claiming the White primary was unconstitutional. In 1944, future Supreme Court Justice Thurgood Marshall argued on behalf of Smith in *Smith* v. *Allwright*. The Supreme Court decided 8–1 in favor of Smith, overturning a precedent from the Jim Crow era.

In 1960, the Supreme Court, in *Gomillion* v. *Lightfoot*, ruled that gerrymandering by race violated the 15th Amendment. The 1964 Supreme Court decision in *Reynolds* v. *Sims* and *Wesberry* v. *Sanders,* which you read about earlier, affirmed the principle of "one person, one vote" as it concerned U.S. House voting districts and state elections, respectively.

While these legal cases were expanding recognition of African-American voting rights, the civil rights movement was producing legislative results. The Civil Rights Act of 1957 provided important protections for voting rights. It created the Civil Rights Division of the Justice Department, empowered to prosecute people or institutions that attempted to deny or limit any citizen's right to vote, and the U.S. Civil Rights Commission, an independent agency charged with investigating complaints about the infringement of voter rights.

A few years later, the Civil Rights Act of 1960 permitted federal courts to appoint voting referees to conduct voter registration in southern states and established penalties for attempting to infringe on anyone's right to register or to vote. The law also renewed the Civil Rights Commission, which had been scheduled to expire after two years. Another Civil Rights Act, in 1964, outlawed discrimination on the basis of race, color, religion, gender, and national origin and forbade arbitrary discrimination in voter registration.

The Voting Rights Act of 1965 was one of the most important pieces of civil rights legislation in American history. It included a variety of provisions to guarantee African Americans and others the right to vote. One provision of the act, known as preclearance, required state and local governments with a history of voting rights violations to obtain prior approval before changing any laws on voting procedures or district boundaries. Approval could be granted only by the U.S. Attorney General or the U.S. District Court for the District of Columbia. The Voting Rights Act also made it illegal to interfere with anyone's right to vote in any election held in this country. The Voting Rights Act of 1965 was authorized by Congress for five years. It has since been extended in 1970, 1975, 1982, and 2006.

At age 75, Representative John Lewis (D-GA) spoke at a ceremony held in Washington, D.C., in commemoration of the 50th anniversary of the Voting Rights Act of 1965. Lewis was a Freedom Rider who helped plan the 1963 March on Washington for Jobs and Freedom, led voter registration drives in Mississippi Freedom Summer, and was a leader of the Selma march. When he died in 2020, his body lay in state in the U.S. Capitol.

The last extension was for 25 years, so the law is now in effect until 2031. Some elements of the law have been successfully challenged in the courts, however, as you will read later in this lesson.

OTHER CHANGES TO VOTING RIGHTS The youth movement of the 1960s and the anti-war movement also led to an expansion of voting rights. The average age of U.S. soldiers serving in the Vietnam War was 19. The vast majority were draftees, ordered by law to serve in the military. At the time, the 14th Amendment guaranteed voting rights for those 21 and older, although some states enfranchised younger people. Many people were troubled that the young men who were compelled to risk their lives in a war were considered too immature or irresponsible to vote for the leaders who were sending them to war. In 1970, Congress lowered the voting age to 18, but the Supreme Court ruled that Congress had no authority to lower the age for voting in state and local elections. In 1971, Congress passed and the states ratified the 26th Amendment, lowering the voting age to 18 for all elections.

HISTORICAL THINKING

3. **SYNTHESIZE** What was the impact of using constitutional amendments rather than statutes to expand voting rights?
4. **INTERPRET TIME LINES** How much time passed between the ratification of the 15th Amendment and Congress giving the Justice Department the power to sue states and enforce the amendment?

Voting Rights Today

The 21st century has witnessed additional developments in voting rights. Most changes have represented progress in expanding and protecting those rights. Some developments demonstrate a continued need for vigilance in the safeguarding of voting rights, however.

EXTENDING VOTING RIGHTS One significant development in the expansion of voting rights is the Americans with Disabilities Act (ADA), a 1990 civil rights law that ensures that people with disabilities have the same rights as anyone else, including an equal opportunity to vote. Currently, approximately 35 million people with disabilities are qualified to vote in the United States. The ADA requires that disabled persons be enabled to register to vote and have access to polling places. There is a checklist for election officials that indicates necessary features a polling place must provide, such as accessible parking, appropriate drop-off facilities, ramps, door openings wide enough for wheelchairs, and so on.

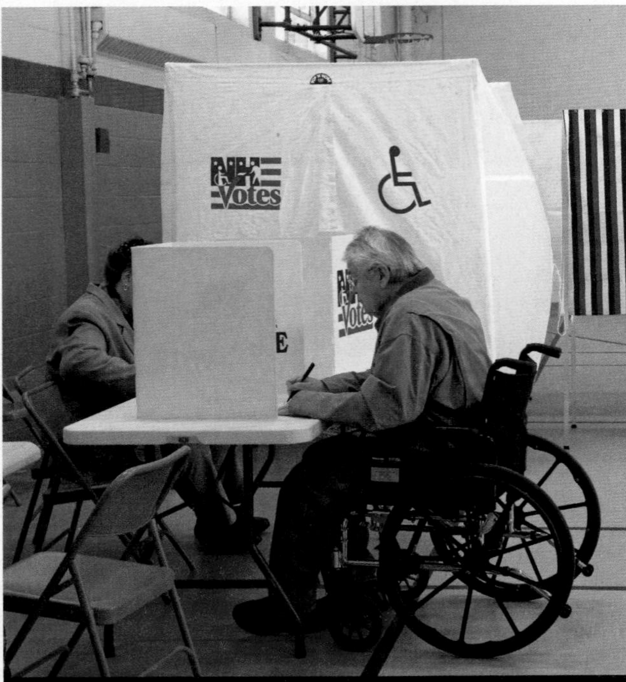

A Government Accountability Office (GAO) study found 60 percent of polling places in 2016 did not provide equal access to a secret ballot. Despite nationwide efforts to educate and make voting easier for people with disabilities, their turnout rate in 2016 was about 6 percent less than that of people without disabilities—little changed from 2012.

Voting rights have also been expanded by early voting and **absentee voting**, which is a ballot submitted by a voter who cannot be present at the polling place on election day. Depending on state law, absentee ballots may be submitted by mail or dropped off at a municipal office. Absentee voting began during the Civil War and has expanded ever since. The Uniformed and Overseas Citizens Absentee Voting Act (UOCAVA) of 1986 requires states to accept mail-in registration and absentee ballots from members of the U.S. Armed Forces and other citizens living overseas. With the absentee ballot as a precedent, early voting made its appearance and today is a common feature of U.S. elections. Online voting is beginning to receive serious consideration as well, though experts urge caution. Given computer and internet vulnerability to hacking and the Russian election meddling of 2016, it will no doubt be some time before mobile voting proves secure enough for wide use.

MOVES TO ABRIDGE VOTING RIGHTS As you read earlier, the practice of disenfranchising felons was a technique adopted to prevent African Americans from voting. Unlike poll taxes and literacy tests, this policy continues today in many parts of the United States. In some states, felons do not regain the right to vote after they have served their time in prison. Many people are affected by this practice, because the United States puts a larger share of its people behind bars than almost any other nation. As of 2018, felon disenfranchisement affected about 6 million Americans. Because African-American men face greater levels of prosecution and punishment than others, the percentage of African Americans convicted of felonies is much higher than their share of the total population. At least 13 percent of African-American men are disenfranchised. Furthermore, regardless of race, those who are convicted of felonies are disproportionately poor.

Opponents of felon disenfranchisement say that excluding many low-income people and minority group members leads to bias in the vote and denies a fundamental right. Supporters contend that felons should not be choosing leaders. Currently, 12 states ban some or all felons from voting after their release from prison. In most of these states, felons must appeal to have their rights restored. In states such as Florida, however, the appeals process was so restrictive that few felons were able to use it. That changed in 2018, when Florida voters approved a law

Activists attend a Voting Rights Amendment Act rally on Capitol Hill, June 25, 2014. The rally marked the one-year anniversary of the Supreme Court decision in *Shelby County* v. *Holder*, which ended preclearance requirements except for those specifically imposed by a court after a finding of intentional discrimination.

SUPREME COURT

Shelby County v. *Holder*, 2013

Decided: June 25, 2013, 5–4

Majority: Chief Justice John Roberts wrote the opinion of the Court in favor of Shelby County, Alabama.

Dissent: Justice Ginsburg wrote a dissenting opinion.

A key element of the Voting Rights Act of 1965 was the provision that, before making any changes to voting laws, states and local jurisdictions with a history of discrimination must submit all proposed changes to the Federal District Court for Washington, D.C., or to the U.S. Department of Justice for approval. This policy is called preclearance. Shelby County argued that preclearance was unconstitutional because it was beyond the scope of Congress's authority and was no longer needed because of progress in racial equality and justice. U.S. Attorney General Eric Holder defended the law.

The Court was split. Chief Justice John Roberts, writing for the majority, argued that the country had changed in the almost 50 years since the Voting Rights Act was passed. "While any racial discrimination in voting is too much," he wrote, "Congress must ensure that the legislation it passes to remedy that problem speaks to current conditions." As a result of the ruling, the nine states and other jurisdictions that were originally subject to preclearance can now change their election laws at will. Consequently, any complaint about a new voting law must be framed as a lawsuit by an affected group and brought before the courts.

Texas wasted no time in taking advantage of the ruling. It immediately implemented a voter ID law it had proposed, but which had been prevented from taking effect under preclearance, and a redistricting plan that dispersed the effectiveness of minority voters. Numerous other states, some previously subject to preclearance, have enacted or tightened voter ID laws and have also purged, or eliminated, registered voters from their voter rolls. Although there are legitimate reasons for purging—voters do move or die—many of the purges have been inaccurate and excessive. In 2017, Georgia, formerly subject to preclearance, purged more than 500,000 voters from its lists.

THINK ABOUT IT Do events since 2013 reinforce or undercut Chief Justice Roberts's written opinion in *Shelby County* v. *Holder*? Explain.

Voting Restrictions Enacted, 2011–2018

	2011	2012	2013	2014	2015	2016	2017	2018
Restricts voter registration	TN, WI					KS		GA, NH
Limits voter registration drives	FL, IL	TX						IA
Implements defective voter-registration purging process			GA				IN	
Makes it more difficult for formerly incarcerated to regain voting rights		FL, IA, SD						
Increases burdens or restrictions on absentee/early voting	FL, GA, WI, WV	TN		OH, WI		AZ, NE, OH		IA, MT, NC, WI
Requires (with exceptions) photo ID at polls	AL, MS, RI, SC, TN, TX, WI	KS, NH, WI	TN		NH	AL, IN, MO, MS, ND, TX, VA, WI	AR	IA, NC

SOURCE: Brennan Center for Justice

ending disenfranchisement for most felons once they have served their sentence.

A setback in voting rights took place in June 2013 when the Supreme Court ruled, in the case of *Shelby County* v. *Holder*, that most preclearance requirements, a principal element of the landmark Voting Rights Act of 1965, were no longer necessary. This opened the door to a wide range of state and local laws that some claim are intended to reduce voter turnout. Among them are restrictive voter ID laws, removal of registered voters from voting rolls, reduction of early voting periods, and increased limits on voter registration.

As of 2018, 16 states accept minimal voter identification at the polls, which may involve nothing more than saying one's name to a clerk. In 34 states, however, some form of identification is required. Some require a photo identification card, such as a driver's license, military ID card, or passport. Other states accept non-photo identification, such as a birth certificate or Social Security card. Many states also require an exact match between the information on the ID and the information on the voter registration list. A mismatch may mean the voter can submit only a provisional ballot, which is a ballot issued to persons who want to vote but whose eligibility is questioned at the voting station. Such a ballot's legitimacy is decided later by election officials.

These stringent voter ID laws are controversial. Supporters argue that strict laws are necessary to prevent fraudulent voting. They also claim the laws foster public confidence in voting systems and that photo ID requirements do not restrict anyone's rights. Moreover, in 2008 the U.S. Supreme Court upheld an Indiana law requiring a photo ID for voting.

Those opposed to voter ID laws argue that the evidence shows that voter fraud is very rare. The real intent of these laws, opponents claim, is to make it more difficult for certain segments of the population to vote—people who are poor, elderly, or disabled, and people of color. These people may lack the specified IDs and may find it more difficult to obtain them. Texas, for example, offers free voter IDs, but these can be obtained from a limited number of state offices that are open only during normal business hours. Getting to these offices places a burden on the working poor, who may be fired or lose pay for taking time off from work and who may lack access to transportation.

With the COVID-19 pandemic threatening to disrupt in-person voting for some time to come, universal voting by mail has become a new battleground. Opponents see increased chances for voter fraud, despite safeguards election officials can put in place. Supporters point out that absentee voting, which is conducted by mail, doesn't have high incidence of voter fraud. They also point out that voting by mail provides a safe way to ensure a basic democratic right during times when in-person voting may be unsafe.

NATIONAL GEOGRAPHIC

A Century After Women's Suffrage, the Fight for Equality Isn't Over

by Rachel Hartigan *National Geographic* Magazine, August 2020

August 2020 marked the 100th anniversary of the 19th Amendment. Traditionally seen as guaranteeing American women the right to vote, the amendment is justly celebrated. But as Rachel Hartigan explains in her article, the amendment's ratification was just one moment in the long, politically complicated, and ongoing story of women's political empowerment.

As Hartigan relates, the first stirrings of a national movement for suffrage began in 1848 at the hastily convened Seneca Falls Convention. The delegates, led by Elizabeth Cady Stanton, called for an expansion of women's rights, including the right to vote. Abolitionists and suffragists joined forces, identifying a common desire for enfranchisement.

After the Civil War, the suffrage movement splintered over tactics and goals. One of the biggest divides was over race. Leading suffragists like Susan B. Anthony, for example, refused to support the 15th Amendment because, as Hartigan explains, "it removed race but not sex as a barrier to voting." Some activists pursued a remedy in the courts, arguing that suffrage was a right of citizenship. After Missouri suffrage activist Virginia Minor was barred from registering to vote, her case went to the Supreme Court. But the Court's ruling in *Minor v. Happersett* proved a devastating setback. The "Constitution," the Justices decreed, "does not confer the right of suffrage upon anyone."

In the second decade of the 20th century, large-scale marches and silent protests in front of the White House publicized the fight for the vote. The brutal treatment of jailed suffragists softened opposition to suffrage. Soon both Congress and President Woodrow Wilson began to express a willingness to consider a constitutional amendment. By the summer of 1920, the 19th Amendment had become the law of the land. Yet it was, in Hartigan's words, "at best, a qualified victory."

Women had worked for more than 70 years to gain access to the ballot, and now they finally had it. But Black women still faced nearly insurmountable hurdles to voting in the south. Native Americans—men and women—weren't even citizens until 1924; Chinese Americans had to wait until 1943. The real watershed moment for many minority women would be Congress's passage of the Voting Rights Act of 1965.

In January 1917 suffragists began standing outside the White House six days a week, with only their banners declaring their cause. Known as the Silent Sentinels, the protesters were determined to shame President Woodrow Wilson into supporting a federal suffrage amendment.

In addition, as Hartigan points out, women were initially slow to push for greater representation in political office. When they did, they faced severe obstacles. Even in 2020, though women make up a little more than half of the population and vote in far greater numbers than men, they make up only about 25 percent of the members of Congress.

But Hartigan sees new stirrings of a broad political awakening among America's women today, citing the Women's March in Washington, D.C., in 2017 following President Trump's inauguration. "It seems," she writes, "that each generation of women finds ways to exercise its collective voice."

Access the full version of "A Century After Women's Suffrage, the Fight for Equality Isn't Over" by Rachel Hartigan through the Resources Menu in MindTap.

THINK ABOUT IT How do you think women's suffrage has changed American politics?

These opposing positions played out during the Wisconsin primary election of 2020. Unlike several other states, Wisconsin decided to hold primary elections early in April, in the midst of the COVID-19 pandemic, despite concerns related to in-person voting and the spread of the disease. The Democratic governor, Tony Evers, pressed for expanded absentee voting. Yet an executive order he signed to accomplish this was challenged by opponents and overturned by the Wisconsin Supreme Court the same day. This ruling was later supported by a United States Supreme Court decision. In the end, the primary was held with in-person voting and no expansion of previously accepted absentee voting. But disagreements over issues surrounding voters' rights, potential fraud, and the rules that guide voting procedures remain.

HISTORICAL THINKING

5. **DRAW CONCLUSIONS** How does disenfranchisement of persons with disabilities and those who have served time as felons affect democracy?
6. **EVALUATE** What do you think is the most significant development in voting rights since the 1980s? Explain your thinking.
7. **ANALYZE VISUALS** Based on the table showing enactment of voting restrictions, do you think the 2013 decision in *Shelby County* v. *Holder* led to an increase in more stringent voter ID laws? Explain your answer.

LESSON 16.3 The Process of Voting

Elections are the people's business, and what a big business it is! In the United States, there are more than 90,000 government units, including 50 state governments, over 3,000 county governments, approximately 12,800 school districts, and numerous others at the town and city level. Each of these state and local units of government has elected officials—hundreds of thousands in all—and each goes through an election process. Running these elections is a complex and time-consuming task but a vital part of our political process. It is through elections that citizens decide how they will be governed.

Organizing Elections

The U.S. Constitution doesn't say much about the election process. Article 1, Section 4, is known as the election clause. It says that state legislatures shall set the time, place, and manner of holding elections for members of the House and Senate, but that Congress can alter these regulations. In Article 2, Section 1, the Constitution gives Congress the power to decide when voters cast ballots for presidential electors and when members of the electoral college cast their ballots for president.

Congress has gone beyond these simple guidelines. It has established the first Tuesday after the first Monday of November during even years as the official election date for congressional elections. Every fourth year, the presidential election is held on this day.

States and local jurisdictions have their own laws and policies for when, where, and how to conduct elections for local officials. In general, local and state elections are set to align with federal elections. **Special elections**—which are local or sometimes state elections held when an issue must be decided before the next general election—are an exception. Special elections are also called when a death or resignation creates a vacancy in an elected office.

Back in the 19th century, state and local jurisdictions deliberately chose different dates for elections, chiefly because hand counting made it difficult to deal with long ballots. Separate, shorter ballots for elections held on different dates made more sense. Now that machine counting has eliminated that concern, only Kentucky, Louisiana, Mississippi, New Jersey, and Virginia hold statewide elections in odd-numbered years when there are no congressional or presidential elections. These states deliberately separate local elections from federal elections that might influence the results.

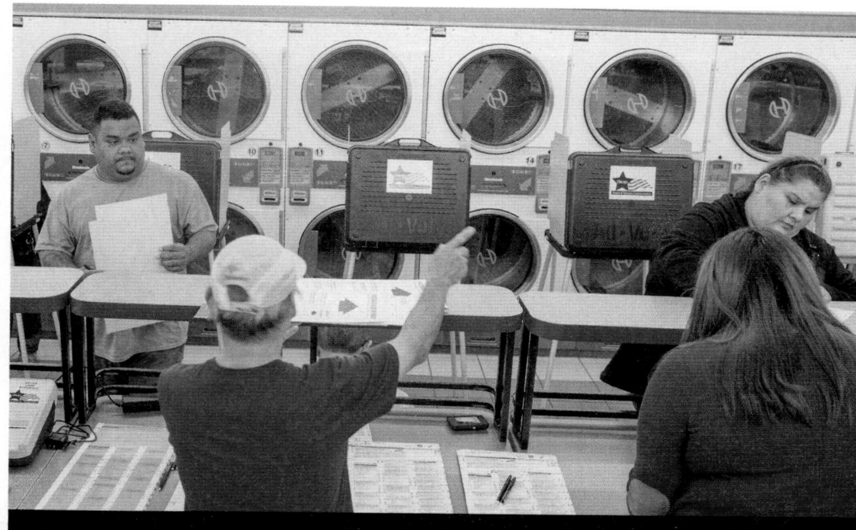

Most states position polling places where they are easy for potential voters to get to. Some polling locations, such as this one in a Chicago laundromat, are in places that have nothing to do with government. State laws govern voting locations and hours, ballots, and vote counting.

Prior to elections, governments publish information to help the electorate prepare for voting. The information varies widely by jurisdiction but always includes where and when citizens may vote. Some states and municipalities provide sample ballots; some provide extensive voter pamphlets with statements by candidates and professional analyses of ballot measures as well as position statements by proponents and opponents.

HISTORICAL THINKING

1. **EVALUATE** Is it a good idea to hold state and local elections at the same time that national elections are taking place, or is it better to hold them at separate times? Explain.
2. **DRAW CONCLUSIONS** Why is it useful for the government to provide some voter information, such as where and when to vote, rather than political parties or private sources?

Polling Places

Local units of government, such as cities, are divided into precincts, or small voting districts. Precinct boundaries are usually drawn by the county or city clerk or by the county board of elections. Within each precinct, voters cast their ballots at a **polling place**, which is a location designated for voting—often a school, library, community center, city or county government building, or church. The election board usually chooses the location of the polling places, and typically they are located within or near the precinct.

An election board supervises the polling place and the voting process in each precinct. The board sets hours for the polls to be open according to the laws of the state and sees that ballots and voting machines are available. In most states, the board provides the list of registered voters and makes certain that only qualified voters cast ballots. When the polls close, staff members count the votes and report the results, usually to the county clerk or the board of elections. Representatives from each party, called poll watchers, are allowed at each polling place. Their job is to make sure the election is run fairly and that fraud doesn't occur.

THE BALLOT After signing in at the polling place, each voter is given a ballot listing the candidates for office and any measures to be voted on, such as ordinances or bond issues. The word *ballot* itself indicates the many forms the ballot has taken throughout history. The word comes from the Italian word *ballotta,* which means *ball.* In Venice, Italy, during the Renaissance, people voted by tossing one or another colored or marked ball into a container. Each color indicated a vote for a particular candidate.

During colonial days, qualified voters called out their choice of candidates. It was a very public performance. In the early days of the republic, voting was usually

CRITICAL VIEWING George Caleb Bingham completed his painting *The County Election* in 1852. The blue banner on a pole reads "The Will of the People The Supreme Law," and the diversity of attire and social class shows that every vote counts equally. Note, however, the activities of the men in the foreground, many of whom appear drunk, and the apparent campaigning and dealing. There is only one African-American man in the painting, who probably was not allowed to vote. He is at far left, farther from the polls than anyone else in the painting, pouring a drink for a man who looks inebriated. Do you think Bingham meant to praise or criticize American democracy?

done on paper, but for a long time that remained a public affair, too. Voters might simply write their names on a list under the name of the candidate they preferred. Counting was easy, and the signature helped guarantee authenticity, but there was no secrecy.

As time passed and the size of government increased, printed ballots appeared. Until 1859, they were usually printed by the parties or published in newspapers and often carried the symbol or other identification of the party that printed them. Voters would take the ballot they preferred to the polling station and deliver it to the election judge. This was not a secret ballot, either, because anyone watching could tell who the voter was voting for. Election intimidation was common. Would-be voters were threatened or even attacked, and their ballots stolen.

THE SECRET BALLOT As more groups of people were brought into the voting process, the problems became more serious until the introduction of the **Australian ballot**, a secret ballot that is prepared, distributed, and counted by government officials at public expense. As its name implies, this ballot was first developed in Australia. It was first used in the United States in a municipal election in Louisville, Kentucky, in 1888. Later that year, Massachusetts became the first state to pass a law requiring use of the Australian ballot. By 1896, 39 of the 45 states then in the Union had adopted the Australian ballot. It soon became a crucial element of the democratic process.

Another occasional problem for voters is known as the bedsheet ballot. This is a very long ballot found most frequently in local elections in which numerous candidates run for a lengthy list of offices such as county clerk, council member, register of probate, and so on. In 2018, voters in Valley Park, Missouri, were faced with decisions on 52 candidates and issues. The ballot in Seminole County, Florida, in 2018 measured 56 inches long.

Many people argue that a long list of elected positions proves that the people are represented in all parts of government. Others dispute this, arguing that there is no good reason to require elections for positions that have no authority to create policy but simply provide skilled services, such as surveyor or coroner. They reason that it would be better to simply hire the person who is more qualified. Moreover, opponents point out that with so many candidates, voters have a difficult time informing themselves and making meaningful decisions.

Another issue with bedsheet ballots is known as ballot fatigue. When there are too many names and issues on a ballot, many voters feel overwhelmed and stop voting after a while. When voters do continue to the end of the ballot, studies suggest, the quality of their decision-making deteriorates. This raises issues such as the effects of position on the ballot. Research has shown that candidates stand a better chance of getting elected if their names appear at the top of a long ballot rather than farther down the list.

HISTORICAL THINKING

3. **IDENTIFY PROBLEMS AND SOLUTIONS** What are some reasons that elections should be conducted by secret ballot?
4. **EVALUATE** Should voters elect minor local officials, such as the county surveyor or coroner, or should these be appointed positions?

How Votes Are Cast and Counted

For much of the 20th century, many polling places used lever-operated voting machines in which the voter pulled a handle to select a candidate or party. Lever-operated machines made the vote faster and more reliable than ever before, but the machines are expensive. They also require significant maintenance for their many moving parts—up to 20,000.

Lever-operated machines have been gradually replaced over the last few decades by other machines. At one time, many states used punch-card voting systems—testimony to the growing importance of electronic computers, which were originally programmed using punch cards. Voters using punch cards receive a paper ballot card with perforated blocks, a foam backing, a clipboard-like device to hold them, and a stylus. Voters use the stylus to punch out perforated blocks, leaving small, rectangular holes in the card indicating their choices. Votes are tabulated either manually by election workers or scanned by a computer. In principle, punch-card technology is simple and reliable. In reality, it can cause serious problems, as it did in the 2000 presidential election.

When a voter punches the card, a small, pre-perforated piece of the card, called a chad, is pushed out of the card into the foam backing. The chad should completely detach from the card and be caught in the foam backing. But that doesn't always happen. In Florida in 2000, the presidential vote was extremely close, so every ballot was examined very carefully. Many issues were raised for which Florida law had no answer, such as how to count hanging chads (those that were only partially punched out), how to count a chad that was punched but not detached at all, and how to count a ballot that had two or three hanging chads for the same office. The legal wrangling lasted for weeks before the vote was settled.

ELECTRONIC VOTING In 2002, partly in response to Florida's voting problems, the federal Help America Vote Act provided funds to help states purchase new electronic voting equipment. Concerns about the possibility of hacking into electronic voting machines then replaced the worries over inaccurate vote counts. Some states now use optical scanners, such as those used for standardized tests. Voters use a marker to fill in circles or ovals on a ballot that is scanned and read electronically.

Direct-response electronic voting machines allow voters to indicate their choices by touching a computer screen or pushing buttons. But many electronic voting machines do not create a paper record of a voter's choices, so in tight or contested elections that require recounts, there is no valid way to assess the results. Plus, whenever computers are involved, there is the threat of hacking.

In the 2006 elections, about half the states that were using new electronic voting systems reported problems. As a result, fewer polling places used electronic systems in 2008 and 2010. More than half of all votes cast in these years used old-fashioned paper ballots, and vote counting was predictably slow.

The development of voter-verified paper audit trail (VVPAT) printers enabled digital voting machines to produce receipts for each vote, which led many states to return to using electronic machines in 2012. In 17 states, however, some or all precincts used electronic devices that produced no paper record. A full quarter of all votes were cast using these questionable systems. The trend toward the reintroduction of electronic systems continued with the 2014 and 2016 elections. Still, five states—Delaware, Georgia, Louisiana, New Jersey, and South Carolina—did not back up any votes with a paper trail in 2016. In 10 states, at least some votes had no supporting paper trail.

Despite all these efforts to ensure fair and accurate elections, issues remain. In 2018, the North Carolina State Board of Elections and Ethics refused to certify a U.S. House race. At issue were allegations of election fraud regarding absentee ballots. State law required that ballots be returned by the voter or a close relative. Instead, some North Carolina canvassers engaged in ballot harvesting, collecting large numbers of absentee ballots. Ballot harvesting is illegal because it can easily be used to manipulate the vote—for instance, by discarding the collected ballots instead of turning them in to be counted, or by collecting blank ballots and voting in bulk. Ballot harvesting and other forms of election tampering, such as computer hacking and meddling with voting machines, remain a considerable threat. While mail-in ballots are slightly more susceptible to fraud than in-person voting, states have multiple tools, including identity verification on the ballot envelope and ballot tracking with bar codes, to prevent and detect fraud.

EARLY AND ABSENTEE VOTING

Election law continues to evolve as many governments try to improve access and voter turnout. In the past, for example, voters had to appear at a polling place during set hours on election day. Since at least the Civil War, some voters have been allowed to submit absentee ballots if they were unable to visit their polling place on election day, perhaps due to military service, travel, or ill health. Usually, an absentee ballot is mailed to the voter, who then completes it and either returns it by mail or in person to the election office. Today most states allow any eligible voter to submit an absentee ballot. An excuse is needed to vote by absentee ballot in 19 states, but 28 states and the District of Columbia permit absentee voting with no excuse required.

In 1998, Oregon voters approved a ballot initiative requiring that all elections in that state, including presidential elections, be conducted exclusively by mail. Washington State required all counties to use postal ballots beginning with the 2012 elections, and Colorado began using postal ballots exclusively in 2014. Ballots are mailed out well before the election, and voters have a set amount of time to complete and return the ballot. Voter turnout in these states is now well above the national average, especially in midterm elections, when it has been commonplace for many voters to stay home. As of 2020, at least 22 states permit voting entirely by mail in certain elections, and most other states had expanded their vote-by-mail programs in response to the COVID-19 health crisis.

Thirty-nine states plus the District of Columbia allow early voting. Some states allow voting up to 45 days before election day. Others may begin the Friday before the election. Typically, voters will go to an election official's office or a satellite polling place to cast their votes. No excuse is needed to participate. As you read earlier, some states have started to consider the use of online voting. For the 2018 midterm election, West Virginia became the first state to embrace this form of voting by allowing overseas members of the military, merchant

Federal Elections: Percent Voting Absentee, by Mail, and Early, 2004–2020

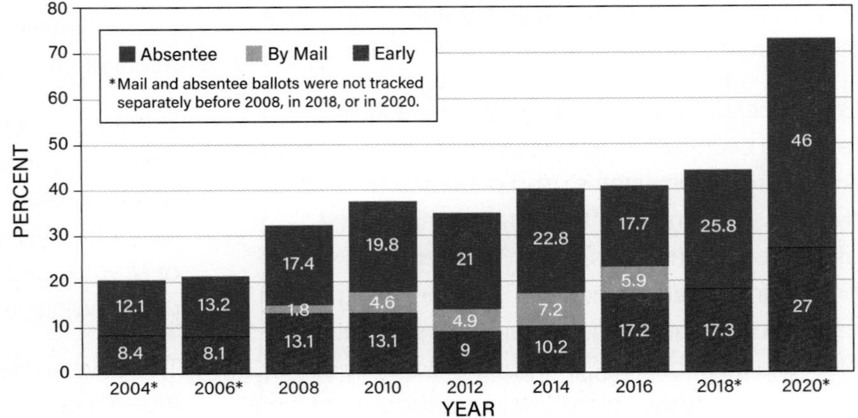

SOURCE: U.S. Election Assistance Commission for 2004–2018 data; 2020 data from Pew Research

marine, and other overseas citizens to vote using a smartphone app.

Because of the COVID-19 pandemic, many states moved to increase early and absentee ballot access in the 2020 election. As states expand absentee or mail-in voting, opposition has grown. Those opponents, including former president Trump, cite the fear that mail-in voting will open the door to voter fraud. Despite increasing incidents of such fraud, supporters of absentee voting deny any widespread abuse of the practice and affirm its safe use given proper safeguards.

As discussed previously, some states have enacted laws that make it more difficult to vote. Besides imposing photo ID requirements, some states have reduced early voting, and some have been reducing the number of polling places. Wisconsin, for example, reduced the early voting period to two weeks—it had been as much as seven weeks in some parts of the state. In North Carolina, where African-American church members had adopted the practice of marching as a group to polling places at the conclusion of Sunday services, Sunday early voting was eliminated. These changes have the biggest effect on minority groups and the poor, groups who are also more likely to vote for Democratic candidates and policies.

HISTORICAL THINKING

5. **INTERPRET GRAPHS** Based on the graph of absentee, mail, and early voting, what can you conclude about voter attitudes toward these forms of voting? Explain.
6. **IDENTIFY** Why are paper trails needed if voters use electronic voting?

LESSON 16.4 Understanding Voter Behavior

For a democracy to be effective, members of the public must educate themselves on issues, form opinions, and then express their ideas to their elected officials. Only when Americans communicate their opinions can those opinions form the basis of government action. The ultimate way that citizens communicate their views is by casting ballots for their preferred candidates. But citizens communicate with elected officials in many ways, including tweets, email, texts, telephone calls, and attendance at meetings and protests. As you'll see, many factors affect the political beliefs that motivate voters.

How Do People Form Political Opinions?

Your political opinions are your views about issues facing the communities of which you are a part. You may have opinions about what your town or city government should do, what your state should do, and what the federal government should do. You may have opinions about which of the officials who represent you are doing a good job and about which candidates you want for governor or Congress. You may have opinions about the minimum wage, college tuition, gun control, police violence, immigration, and climate change. When asked, most Americans are willing to express their opinions on such issues.

No one is born with such opinions, however. The social process of acquiring political attitudes, opinions, and beliefs is called **political socialization**. It is an aspect of **socialization** in general, which is the process of acquiring group characteristics, including norms, or standards for conduct, and the ability to communicate. Socialization, including political socialization, begins early and continues throughout life. But note that in mature adults, political socialization is quite different from political education, which involves adopting beliefs based on relevant evidence and is more under the control of the individual.

FAMILY Political socialization begins during early childhood, when the primary influence on a child is the family. Children first see the political world through the eyes of their family, which tends to be the most important force in political socialization. Children learn by hearing the conversations around them about politicians and issues and by observing their parents' actions and reactions.

The family's influence is strongest when children can clearly perceive their parents' attitudes, and most can. In one study, more high school students could identify their parents' political party affiliation than their parents' other attitudes or beliefs. The political party of the parents often becomes the political party of the children, particularly if both parents support the same party.

SCHOOL AND RELIGION From their earliest days in school, children learn about the American political system. They say the Pledge of Allegiance and sing patriotic songs. They celebrate national holidays and learn the history and symbols associated with them. In the upper grades, students acquire more knowledge about government and democratic procedures through civics and history classes and through participation in student government and various clubs. They learn citizenship skills through school rules. Generally, those with more education know more about politics and policy than do those with less education. A person's level of education also influences that person's political values.

A majority of Americans hold strong religious beliefs, and these attitudes can also contribute significantly to political socialization. For example, if a family's religion emphasizes a collective obligation to care for the needy, the children in that family may be influenced in a liberal direction. If a family or church instead depicts the government as a threat to morality, children will receive a conservative message.

THE MEDIA The media—newspapers, magazines, television, radio, social media, and the internet—have an impact on political socialization. The most influential of these media is still television, which continues to be a leading source of political information, especially for older voters, who vote at significantly higher rates than younger people. The internet and various social media are extremely important sources of information for younger citizens. Social media are also important for politicians. In 2020, years after President Obama left office, his Twitter account had well over 100 million followers, more than any other account in the world.

Some contend that the media's role in shaping public opinion has increased to the point that the media are as influential as the family, particularly among high school students. In one study, high school students mentioned the internet and social media as the main sources of information on which they base their attitudes far more than they mentioned their families, friends, and teachers. Other studies have shown that the media's influence may not be as great as some have thought. Generally, the media tend to wield the most influence over the views of persons who have not yet formed opinions about various issues or candidates. Typically, however, people already have opinions, sometimes strong

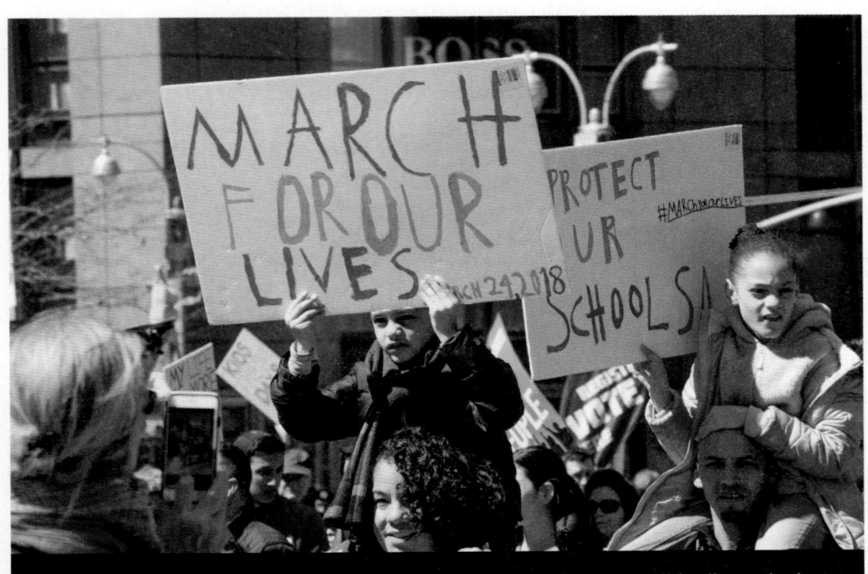

Children learn largely from their parents how to participate politically and what issues are important. They also tend to share their parents' political opinions and party affiliation.

opinions, on issues before they go online, watch television, or view social media. These preconceived ideas act as a kind of perceptual screen that blocks information that challenges them. Psychologists refer to this and similar phenomena as **confirmation bias**, the human tendency to interpret experience and information in ways that support what one already believes.

These young people spend Martin Luther King, Jr., Day of Service volunteering at a local food bank. At the same time, they help encourage each other's sense of community and shared responsibility. The Martin Luther King, Jr., Day of Service is one way people honor King on the Martin Luther King, Jr., holiday. The Day of Service aims to "move us closer to Dr. King's vision of a 'Beloved Community'" by encouraging people to spend a "day on, not a day off."

OPINION LEADERS Every city or community has **opinion leaders**, well-known citizens who influence the opinions of others. These people may be public officials, religious leaders, teachers, activists, writers, entertainers, YouTubers, or other celebrities. They are the people to whom others listen and from whom others draw ideas and opinions about issues of public concern. These opinion leaders play a significant role in the formation of political opinion.

Opinion leaders often include politicians and former politicians but are not limited to political figures. In different ways, both Beyoncé Knowles and former president Jimmy Carter are opinion leaders. Media figures such as Chance The Rapper and pastor Rick Warren are opinion leaders as well. Yet not every member of the public follows the lead of any opinion leader. Opinion leaders may have a group of followers, but they exert only limited influence on most of the public.

PEER GROUPS Once children enter school, the views of friends begin to influence their attitudes and beliefs. Starting in junior high or middle school, the peer group—friends, classmates, co-workers, club members, or religious group members—becomes a significant factor in the political socialization process. For adolescents, peer groups are one of the strongest influences. The greatest political socialization effects of peer groups occur when the group is involved with political activities or other causes. For example, advocating for transgender rights or campaigning for a favorite candidate will tend to strongly influence members.

OTHER INFLUENCES The political attitudes of an entire generation of Americans may be influenced by a major event. For example, the generation that lived through World War II (1939–1945) tends to believe that American intervention in foreign affairs is good. In contrast, the generation that came of age during the Vietnam War (1965–1975) is more skeptical of American interventionism. The recent Great Recession and the financial crisis that struck in September 2008 will probably affect attitudes about the economy for years to come.

Economic status may influence people's political views, but the connection is not always straightforward. For example, poorer people are more likely to favor government assistance programs. That is a case of favoring a policy that is simply in the group's interests. On an issue such as abortion, polls have found that lower-income people are more likely to oppose abortion rights than are higher-income groups. In this case, it is unclear if or how attitudes toward the policy may reflect economic interests.

Where people work can have a strong effect on their opinions. Co-workers who spend much time working together tend to influence one another. For example, labor union members working together may have similar political opinions, at least on issues of government involvement in the economy. Individuals working for a nonprofit agency that depends on government funds will tend to support government spending in that area.

Those who create political ads and commercials, telephone canvassers, organizers of political rallies, and speechwriters who create talking points try to take advantage of these factors and loyalties in their efforts to persuade. Political operatives invest heavily to understand which issues influence voters. Then they use their understanding of voters and their influences to benefit their candidates and their issues.

HISTORICAL THINKING

1. **MAKE CONNECTIONS** What sources of political socialization are most important to you? How have they influenced your beliefs?
2. **MAKE INFERENCES** Why might social media and the internet have such a strong influence on political socialization?

Why People Vote as They Do

Researchers have collected more information on voting than on any other form of political participation in the United States to better understand why people vote for particular candidates and favor one political party over another. Many voters are motivated by party identification, or a commitment to a political party, although the proportion of the population with strong party identification has fallen in recent decades. For established voters, party identification is one of the most important and lasting predictors of how a person will vote. Party identification is an emotional attachment that is influenced by family, age, peer groups, and other factors in the political socialization process. Many voters call themselves independents, but many independents actually lean, sometimes strongly, toward one of the major parties.

Political ideology, a system of political ideas rooted in religious or philosophical beliefs about human nature, society, and government, is another indicator of voting behavior and is closely linked with party identification. Recent polls indicate that 37 percent of Americans consider themselves conservatives, 24 percent consider themselves liberals, and 35 percent identify themselves as moderates. Typically, liberals and some moderates vote for Democrats, and conservatives vote for Republicans. The large numbers of Americans who fall in the political center do not adhere strictly to a liberal or conservative ideology.

It is important to note that party ideologies change over time. One hundred years ago, Democrats were seen as less likely than Republicans to support government intervention in the economy. The Democrats were also the party that opposed civil rights. Today, the Democrats are often regarded as the party that supports big government and programs promoting civil rights. Thus, the ideologies of the two major parties have actually undergone a reversal.

PERCEPTION OF THE CANDIDATES Voters often vote for candidates based on their perception of the candidates' personalities rather than on their qualifications or policy positions. Such perceptions were important in 2010 and 2012. Following each of those elections, many political analysts concluded that the Republican Party had forfeited two to three U.S. Senate races by nominating Tea Party–supported candidates who were regarded by many as too extreme. This perception was, to a large extent, based not on the political positions taken by the candidates, but on the attitudes the candidates projected. In 2014, Republican leaders worked to ensure that the party's candidates were not the kinds of people who would be seen as unacceptable. By and large, the party succeeded.

The kind of candidate vetting that Republicans engaged in during 2014 works only if voters are willing to listen to the party elders. If major segments of a party are willing to rebel against the leadership, the dynamic changes, and primary candidates who are perceived as rebellious may win that vote. In 2016, Donald Trump benefited from just such circumstances. When members of the Republican establishment attacked Trump, his supporters saw the attacks as a validation of his candidacy.

POLICY CHOICES People engage in policy voting when they vote for candidates who share their positions on particular issues—for example, voters may vote for a candidate who opposes gun control laws for that reason alone. Historically, economic issues have had the strongest influence on voters' choices. When the economy is doing well, it is difficult for a challenger, particularly a presidential candidate, to defeat the incumbent. In contrast, when the economy is in a downturn, the incumbent may be at a disadvantage.

One factor that limits the impact of issues on voting decisions is that party identification can define policy choices for voters. For example, someone who believes global warming is a serious problem is unlikely to vote for a candidate from a party that rejects that view. People with strong party loyalty may alter their positions on issues to match those of their party rather than vote for a candidate from a different party, however.

Senator John McCain (R-AZ) and Senator Barack Obama (D-IL) met for three debates in the weeks leading up to the 2008 general election. Since 1987 the Commission on Presidential Debates (CPD), a private nonprofit corporation, has negotiated with the leading presidential candidates to arrange "high quality, educational debates." According to the CPD, 80 percent of the public watched at least some of the 2008 debates. Complete transcripts and videos of nearly all the presidential debates since 1988 are available to the public.

EDUCATION, OCCUPATION, AND INCOME Social and economic characteristics that describe individuals and groups are referred to as **socioeconomic factors**. They can be powerful influences. Socioeconomic factors include educational attainment, occupation and income, age, gender, religion, geographic location, ethnicity, and race. Many socioeconomic factors have to do with the circumstances into which individuals are born. Others have to do with personal choices and experiences.

One powerful socioeconomic factor is education. Traditionally, people with more education were more likely to vote Republican. In part, this tendency was due to the fact that educational attainment is linked to income level, and people with higher incomes have long preferred Republicans. In recent years, however, well-educated people have moved away from the Republican Party. For the last seven presidential elections, the Democratic candidate won the largest number of votes from those with post-graduate degrees. Republicans retained an increasingly narrow lead among college graduates without a post-graduate degree—until 2016. That year, Democrat Hillary Clinton carried the college-educated vote.

At the same time, Republicans have made inroads on the Democrats' hold on the less well-educated. While Democrats still managed to retain a majority of people with no more than a high school diploma in most presidential election cycles, in 2014 and 2016 Republican candidates won a majority of such voters. In 2016, Donald Trump won that group of voters, scoring a decisive majority among those who had no college experience at all. College-educated people now tend to be Democrats, while those with less education tend to be Republicans.

Two other socioeconomic factors that influence how people vote are occupation and income. Business owners have for years tended to vote Republican, reflecting the pro-business stand traditionally adopted by that party. Recently, professionals such as attorneys, professors, and physicians have been more likely to vote Democratic. For the most part, labor union members remain loyal to the Democratic Party, which historically has been pro-labor.

Given that income and education are correlated and that less-well-educated persons now lean Republican, we might assume that today the wealthy tend to be Democrats, and the poor, Republicans. In 2016, however, Hillary Clinton carried the votes of families with incomes below $50,000, while Trump won among voters with higher incomes. Still, the correlation of high incomes with Republicanism is far weaker today than in the past. It follows from these statistics that those with less formal education who earn a good income are likely to vote Republican. A successful plumber with only a high school diploma, for example, might have favored Trump. Likewise, well-educated people with lower incomes—for example, teachers, ministers, and social workers, all of whom may have master's degrees—tend to be drawn to the Democrats.

AGE AND GENDER Conventional wisdom holds that the young are liberal and the old are conservative. This has held true recently: Younger voters heavily supported Barack Obama in the 2008 and 2012 elections, and they supported Hillary Clinton in 2016. In earlier decades, however, age bore little relation to support for either party.

People's attitudes are often shaped by the events that unfolded as they grew up. As we observed earlier, many voters who came of age during Franklin Roosevelt's New Deal continued to prefer Democrats. Voters who were young when Ronald Reagan was president tend to prefer Republicans. Younger voters today are more liberal on the rights of minorities, women, and LGBTQ individuals.

In the 1960s and 1970s, women and men tended to vote for the different presidential candidates in roughly equal numbers. Some political analysts believe a gender gap became a major factor for voters in the 1980 presidential election. That year, Ronald Reagan outdrew Jimmy Carter by 16 percentage points among male voters. But women gave about equal support to each candidate.

Since then, the gender gap has grown. For example, in 2016, Clinton carried the women's vote by 54 to 41 percentage points, while losing among men by a 41- to 53-point margin. That result appears consistent with Clinton's being the first female presidential candidate nominated by a major party and Trump's notoriety for his alleged disrespect of women.

The 2018 midterm elections and the 2020 presidential election did not show a big change in the gender gap. In both races, women voted for Democrats by roughly 8 to 10 percentage points more than men, and the votes of suburban women of all races were seen as critical to the Biden-Harris victory in 2020. But another group who played a crucial role in that victory were men. While only 41 percent of all men voted for Hillary Clinton in 2016, 46 percent of all men voted for Biden in 2020. That was still a minority of men, but the increase in the number of men who voted for a Democrat, combined with the larger majority of women who did so, was enough to change the outcome of the 2020 election.

RACE, ETHNICITY, AND RELIGION The combination of gender and race can be especially potent. Black women provided more support to the Democratic presidential ticket in 2020 than any other group—93 percent of black women voted for Biden. Such patterns can change over time, however. Historically, White Catholic voters in the cities of the Northeast and Midwest were likely to be Democrats, and White Protestant voters were generally Republicans. There are a few places around the country where this pattern continues, but for the most part, non-Hispanic White Catholics are now almost as likely as their Protestant neighbors to support Republicans.

In recent years, a different religious variable has become important. Among White Christians, regardless of denomination, those who say they attend church regularly favor Republicans by substantial margins, whereas those who say they attend church rarely or who find religion less important are more likely to vote Democratic. Although some Christian churches promote liberal ideals, the number of churches that promote conservative values is much larger.

Muslim Americans are an interesting example of changing preferences. In 2000, a majority of Muslims of Middle Eastern background voted for Republican presidential candidate George W. Bush because he promoted the culturally conservative views shared by many Muslims. Today, Muslims are the most Democratic religious group in the nation. Anti-Muslim campaigns attributed to certain conservative groups appear to be a major cause of this transformation.

A shared racial or ethnic identity can be one of the strongest socioeconomic factors influencing voting behavior. Most African Americans, for example,

VOTING BY GROUPS *in the* 2016 PRESIDENTIAL ELECTION

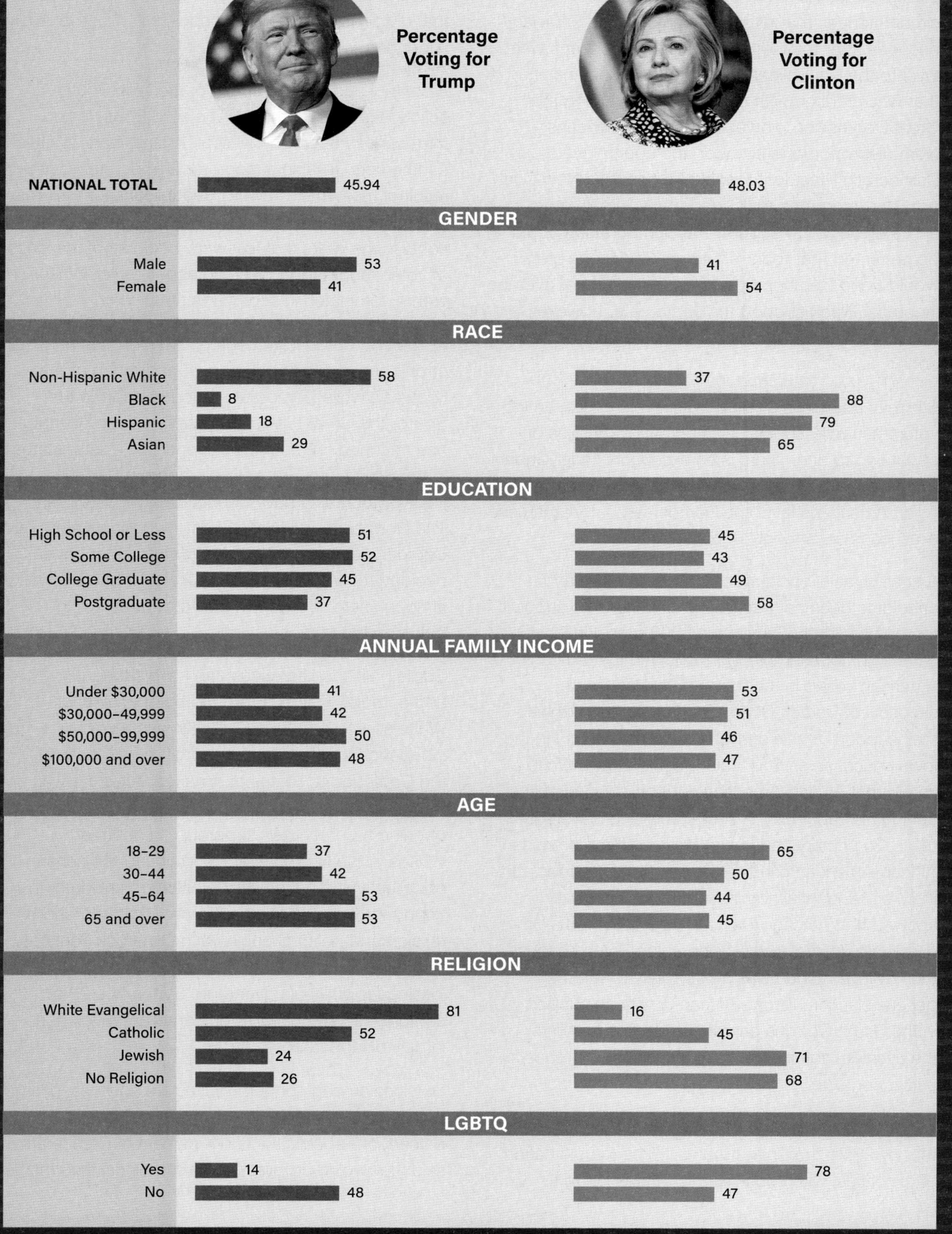

Sources: National Election Poll; Latino Decisions Election Eve Poll; Dave Leip's Atlas of U.S. Presidential Elections are Protestants, but African-Americans are one of the most solidly Democratic constituencies in the United States. This is a complete reversal of the circumstances that existed a century ago. For many decades after the Civil War, African-Americans were loyal to the Republican Party, the party of Lincoln that was credited with ending slavery. During the Great Depression, however, African-Americans were disproportionately poor and unemployed. Democratic President Franklin Roosevelt's New Deal provided programs that aided many Black voters, and they began to support the Democrats. It could be predicted that today's African-American voters would trend Democratic based on their lower average incomes. Black support for Democrats, however, far exceeds the levels that could be expected from economics alone.

Ethnicity also plays a role in voter preferences. Latino voters generally support Democrats by margins of about two to one. There is an exception: Older Cuban Americans are strongly Republican. Likewise, most Asian Americans favor the Democrats, but Vietnamese Americans are strongly Republican.

A shared racial background between voters and a candidate does not necessarily translate into support for the candidate. Early in the 2008 presidential campaign, for example, polls showed that African-American voters in the Democratic Party were skeptical of Barack Obama's chances and withheld their support. It was only after Obama's victory in the Iowa caucuses proved that he could attract White voters that African-American support swung firmly behind his candidacy. A similar scenario played out in the 2020 primary campaign, in which three prominent African-American candidates vied for the Democratic Party's presidential nomination. Polls continually showed that African-American voters favored a White candidate, former vice president Joe Biden because they believed Biden was mostly likely to win the general election. Strong African-American support in the South Carolina primary catapulted Biden to the eventual nomination despite lackluster finishes in earlier contests.

DIVISIONS AMONG WHITE VOTERS It is projected that by 2050, the United States will become a nation of minorities, with non-Hispanic Whites falling to 49.7 percent of the population. Even then, however, non-Hispanic Whites will remain the largest racial or ethnic group by a wide margin. What this means is that divisions among White people will still be crucially important.

A century ago, people spoke of the solid South—solidly Democratic, that is. The solid South lasted for a century after the Civil War. In large part, White southerners' reliable support for Democrats was the result of resentment toward Republicans for their role in the Civil War and their support of African-American rights in the years that followed. Because of the kinds of voter suppression you read about earlier, White voters dominated in southern states.

At the end of the 19th century, Republicans had strong support in the Northeast and much of the Midwest, while Democrats found support in the South, the Great Plains, and the far West. All that has changed. In recent presidential contests, states in the South, the Great Plains, and parts of the Rocky Mountains have been strongly Republican. The Northeast, the West Coast, and Illinois are firmly Democratic. Many of the swing states that have decided recent elections are located in the Midwest, although several Rocky Mountain states swing between the parties as well.

Some political differences can have a long and complex history. From the point of view of White southerners, the Civil War was a war of independence, fought to establish a new nation—the Confederate States of America. After the war, Reconstruction solidified the southern White sense of being a persecuted subgroup. In contrast, Whites in the North never experienced the sense of collective identity felt by Whites in the South. In important ways, White northerners were divided by religion and national origin, with old-stock Yankees, Irish Catholics, Germans, Italians, Jews, and others jostling for political advantage. By the late 20th century, such ethnic divisions among Whites had largely disappeared.

Divisions among northern Whites are now based largely on cultural and ideological differences. In 1960, only 5 percent of Republicans and 4 percent of Democrats said they would be upset if one of their children married a supporter of the other party. Today, 49 percent of Republicans and 33 percent of Democrats express concern over interparty marriage. Psychologists believe that bias based on partisanship is today substantially more powerful than bias based on race.

HISTORICAL THINKING

3. **MAKE INFERENCES** Explain why divisions among White people are important to understanding politics in the coming years.
4. **INTERPRET GRAPHS** What data in the graph that shows voting by groups surprise you most? Why?

Who Actually Votes

Just because an individual is eligible to vote does not necessarily mean that the person will cast a ballot. Voter turnout rarely rises above 40 percent in the midterm elections—those national elections that fall between presidential elections. Presidential elections draw a bigger turnout, but even then, the average in recent elections has been just 50 to 60 percent. In 2018, voter turnout reached a near-record for a midterm election as over 47 percent of eligible voters went to the polls.

Education appears to be the most important factor affecting turnout: The more education people have, the more likely they are to be regular voters. People who graduated from high school vote more regularly than those who dropped out, and college graduates vote more often than high school graduates. Differences in income also correlate to differences in voter turnout. Wealthy people tend to be regular voters. Generally, older voters vote more regularly than younger voters do, although participation tends to decline among the very old.

Racial and ethnic minorities traditionally have poor voter turnout. In several recent elections, however, participation by these groups, particularly African Americans and Hispanics, has increased. In part because the number of Latino citizens has grown rapidly, the increase in the Hispanic vote has been even larger than the increase in the Black vote.

Voter turnout in the United States has been affected in recent decades by high rates of immigration: Many people of voting age are not eligible to vote because they are not citizens. As you read earlier, millions more are affected by high rates of incarceration and cannot vote because they are felons. Additionally, the voting-age population only counts those residing in the country and excludes Americans abroad, who can cast absentee ballots. Whereas in the past voter turnout was commonly expressed as a percentage of the total voting-age population, today political scientists calculate the vote-eligible population, the number of people who are actually entitled to vote in American elections. All told, the vote-eligible population may be 20 million fewer than the voting-age population. Therefore, voter turnout is actually greater than the percentages sometimes cited.

The reasons people fail to vote are many. As you read earlier, difficulties with the voter registration process or voter ID requirements may hinder some from voting. Others may feel they don't know enough about the candidates or the issues. Some think the government is run by an elite group of people who don't understand them or care about them. Some, for a variety of reasons, lack a sense of civic responsibility. Democracy depends on the involvement of its citizens, and these arguments are precisely why more voters should go to the polls: Citizens need to express their views in order for government to be responsive to them.

As you have read, many steps have been taken to try to increase voter participation. These have included adoption of early voting, increased absentee balloting, and voting by mail. Some other proposals to improve voter participation include requiring people to vote, making election day a national holiday, and finding a reliable way to implement online voting.

HISTORICAL THINKING

5. **IDENTIFY** Why don't more young people vote? What can be done to encourage them to do so?
6. **MAKE CONNECTIONS** Do you favor requiring people to vote? Why or why not?

LESSON 16.5

Public Opinion Polls

You may hear a news report stating that a significant number of Americans feel this or that way about an issue. For example, you may hear or read that "*x* percent of Americans surveyed approve of the president's job performance." Such reports most often come from polls of public opinion. A public opinion poll is a survey of people's views on a certain topic at a particular moment. This lesson will discuss how politicians try to find out what the public thinks and why we all should take poll results with a grain of salt.

How Polling Has Developed

Elections are probably the most important way that voters communicate their opinions. As you read earlier, however, it is also important for citizens to communicate with their representatives through social media, by writing letters, texting, phoning, signing petitions, or by attending town hall meetings, marches, and rallies to express their views on specific issues. But only some voters bother to contact their representatives, and elected officials cannot wait until the next election to understand what their constituents—the voters in their district—want because by then it may be too late. This is where public opinion polls come in. They attempt to answer the most pressing question a political leader can ask: What is important to voters?

No poll can survey the entire U.S. population of over 325 million, or even the well over 200 million adults who are eligible to vote. Modern opinion pollsters have devised scientific techniques for selecting their **survey sample**, the set of survey respondents, with the goal of interviewing a small population that is representative of the general population. But scientific polling is a relatively recent innovation.

EARLY POLLING Since the 1800s, magazines and newspapers have often spiced up their articles by conducting **straw polls** of readers' opinions. A straw poll is a nonscientific poll in which there is no way to ensure that the opinions expressed are representative of the larger population. Straw polls simply ask a large number of people the same question. The problem with straw polls is that the opinions expressed represent an atypical subgroup of the population—what is called a biased sample. A survey of those who read *Teen Vogue* will produce different results than a survey of those who read *Sports Illustrated*, for example. Likewise, a survey offered to a website's visitors will only collect the opinions of people who both (a) happen upon the website and (b) believe it is worth their while to respond to a nonscientific survey.

Scientific polling began to develop in the 1930s. George Gallup and Elmo Roper, both of whom started out using polls as tools for market research, pioneered today's political polling methodology. Both won acclaim when they independently predicted President Franklin Roosevelt's 1936 landslide re-election, contrary to the expectations of many opinion leaders. Today, polling is used extensively by political candidates and policymakers. Polls can be quite accurate when they are conducted properly. In the 20 presidential elections in which Gallup has participated, its polls conducted in late October correctly predicted the winner in 16 of the races. Even polls taken several months in advance have been able to predict the eventual winner.

TELEPHONE AND INTERNET POLLING In the earliest days of scientific polling, interviewers typically went door to door locating respondents. Such in-person surveys were essential in the days when many homes did not have telephones. Eventually, polling organizations began sampling voters through telephone interviews. In recent years, poll takers have instituted computer dialing and even replaced human interviewers with prerecorded, interactive messages that solicit, record, and tally responses. Automated polling enables companies to poll many people at little

Telephone Survey* Response Rates, 1997–2017

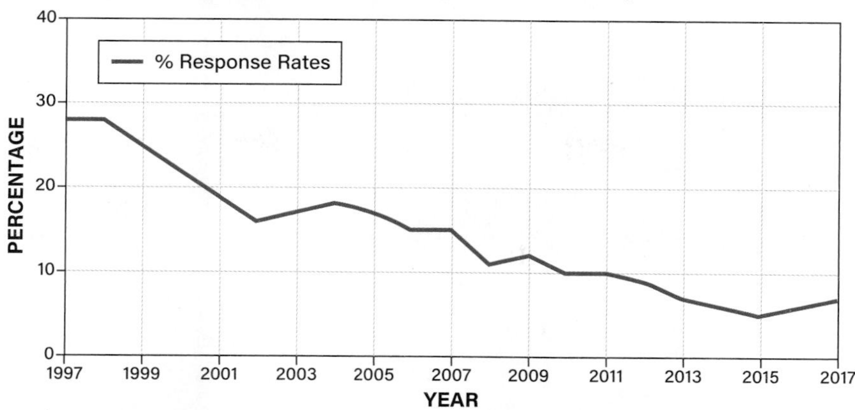

*Gallup Poll Social Series surveys of "adults' views on numerous social, economic, and political topics."
SOURCE: Gallup

cost, but because it may produce biased samples, many consider it less accurate than polling conducted by live interviewers.

Further complications include the increase in the use of cell phones. Cell phones are not listed in public directories, so it's difficult to obtain a sample that includes an appropriate mix of respondents of different ages or even to know in which state or district the respondents live. Therefore, some pollsters do not call cell numbers. An additional problem is the growing use of VoIP (Voice over Internet Protocol), apps such as Skype and FaceTime, and other internet-based, real-time communication systems rather than traditional phone lines. Poll takers have not determined how to integrate users of such technologies into their polls. Finally, a growing number of people simply refuse to participate in telephone surveys.

The internet survey has become increasingly popular. The Harris Poll now specializes in this type of research. As when telephone interviews were introduced, however, people question whether the samples obtained by internet polling firms can be representative. Internet usage has become extremely widespread, but it is still not close to universal.

SAMPLING ISSUES A sample is random if each person among the entire population being polled has an equal chance of being sampled. If the sample is large enough and is truly random, the chance that it will be representative of the total population is very high. If a poll is trying to measure how women feel about increasing the minimum wage, for example, a properly drawn random sample would include numbers of women of particular ages, races, ethnicities, education levels, geography, income levels, employment status, religious affiliations, and other categories in proportion to the percentage of that group among the total population.

It is important to bear in mind that scientific polling results are probabilities. News reporting that treats poll results as definitive gives a misleading picture of what polling can actually tell us. Consider that today's most reputable polls sample between 1,000 and 1,500 people. That may not seem like much in a country of over 325 million, but if the sample is chosen well, that number will produce results that are better than 95 percent likely to be accurate within 3 percentage points. In this example, 3 percent is the confidence interval, or margin of error, and 95 percent is referred to as the confidence level. Suppose a national poll finds 48 percent in favor; what that really means is there is, at best, a 95 percent chance that the actual percentage in favor is between 48 – 3 (45) and 48 + 3 (51). Therefore, while a margin of error of 3 percent might sound small, it can make the difference between losing and winning for a given candidate. Any flaws in the polling decrease the confidence level and increase the confidence interval.

But it is extremely difficult to select a truly random sample. To take a simple example, suppose you were to conduct a telephone poll over three days using randomly selected phone numbers that you call between 7 p.m. and 8:30 p.m. First of all, notice that you are not starting with a randomly selected group; the sample selection is biased toward people who have more than one phone number. Further, the likelihood of your interviewing people who work in the evening, people who are unable to pay their phone bills, people who don't answer their phones because your number is hidden or unfamiliar, people who are

CRITICAL VIEWING When the fortune-teller calls the pollster an amateur, she means that he is incompetent, whereas she is an expert. Why is it humorous for a fortune-teller to compare herself favorably to a pollster?

attending evening meetings of community groups, people who are at a movie or concert, and people who feel polls invade their privacy is much lower than average. If the percent of your sample in any of these groups is less than their percent in the total population, your sample is biased: You have sampling errors. A sampling error is the difference between what the poll shows and what the results would have been if everyone in the relevant population had been interviewed.

Pollsters determine what confidence level and confidence interval they want to achieve and then calculate the sample size needed. The 95 percent confidence level is an industry standard. That means that out of the thousands of polls released every year, we expect at least 5 percent to yield results that are outside their margin of error. Increasing the margin of error increases the confidence level; if the target is bigger, it is easier to hit. But hitting a target that is too big is meaningless.

HISTORICAL THINKING

1. **INTERPRET GRAPHS** Describe the trend shown on the graph of telephone survey response rates. How might you explain this trend?
2. **ANALYZE DATA** Why is it important to know the margin of sampling error in a particular poll? Give an example.

Factors Affecting Polling Accuracy

Many factors can interfere with the validity of a poll. As was just discussed, a perennial source of error is that it is almost impossible to obtain a body of respondents that truly reflects the population at large. Many people refuse to be interviewed. Some groups of people are hard to reach. Women answer their phones more frequently than do men. And because so many people now rely solely on cell phones, poll takers must find a way to access these numbers, a task that is much more difficult than obtaining landline numbers.

WEIGHTING Polling firms respond to such difficulties by weighting the responses of various groups. For instance, a poll taker will use publicly available data to model the general population, estimating the percent that are in any relevant group. Suppose that, after conducting the polling, the poll taker finds that the survey did not collect enough responses from evangelical Christians aged 30–50: The percent in the sample is lower than the (estimated) percent in the general population. The poll taker will then use a multiplier to give more weight to the responses of the evangelicals aged 30–50 who were interviewed. If the statistical model the poll taker uses to weight the responses is flawed, however, the poll results will be off as well.

Estimates of simple demographic variables are fairly accurate, but weighting for these variables does not resolve the most serious modeling problems. More problematic are attempts to adjust for the number of Republicans, Democrats, and independents, numbers that are less certain and less stable. Perhaps the greatest difficulty is determining who is likely to vote. Each major polling firm has its own model for weighting groups of respondents and determining who is a likely voter. Most of these models are trade secrets. Thus, there is substantial variation in the results from the various polling companies.

Because of their differing models, some polling firms consistently publish results more favorable to one or the other of the two major parties. When a pollster's results consistently favor one of the parties, polling experts refer to the phenomenon as a house effect. Not surprisingly, firms that exhibited house effects in 2016 frequently had ties to the political party favored by their results. The connection was not consistent, however. Some partisan firms did not exhibit a house effect, and some pollsters who were well known for nonpartisanship did have one. Also, a firm with a house effect is not always wrong; it may be noticing something that its competitors have missed.

BIAS IN FRAMING QUESTIONS How a question is phrased can significantly affect how people answer it. To obtain accurate results, poll takers must ensure that there is no bias in their questions. The ways in which survey questions can be poorly worded are vast. One problem is loaded terms, as in the question: "How would you rate the career of basketball legend LeBron James?" To call James a legend biases the question in his favor. Another issue is combining two or more queries that ought to be separate, as in "Which of the following companies provides the fastest and most economical internet service?" The most economical service may or may not be the fastest.

Polling questions sometimes reduce complex issues to questions that call for a simple yes or no answer, creating a false dilemma. For example, a question might ask whether respondents favor giving aid to foreign countries. A respondent's opinion might vary, depending on the country or on the purpose of the aid. The poll nonetheless forces the respondent to give a yes or no answer that does not fully reflect his or her opinion.

Poll respondents are not obligated to be consistent in their opinions. For instance, poll takers nearly always find that a majority of Americans favor cuts to federal spending, but when asked if they favor cutting the budgets of particular programs, the answer is almost always no. The question then is whether politicians should—or even can—respond to such survey results.

Respondents are not universally reliable, either. It is well known that respondents sometimes answer that they don't know or don't have enough information to answer, even when the poll does not offer such options, but the issue is much more complex. One study included two alternate versions of a question. Some respondents were asked whether they favored or opposed school vouchers. About 4 percent

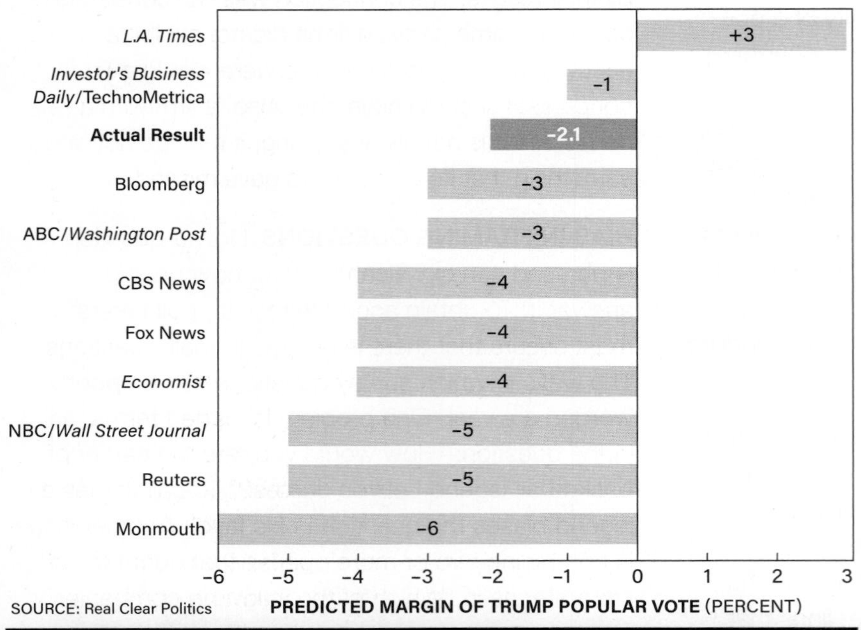

The graph presents the final projections by various polling organizations (shown on the left) of the outcome of the 2016 presidential contest between Republican Donald Trump and Democrat Hillary Clinton. Actual popular vote results appear in orange. Of course, the election of the president depends on the results of the electoral college, not on the national popular vote.

volunteered the answer that they didn't know how they felt. In the other version of the survey, respondents were offered a third option: They could say that they hadn't read enough to answer. About 30 percent chose that answer. Perhaps people in the first poll gave a definite answer even when they didn't have a definite opinion; or perhaps people in the second poll who did have a definite opinion answered that they didn't. Clearly, the way the question is phrased affects how people respond to it, but also clear is that interpreting polling data is not simple.

In addition to potential bias in framing questions, poll takers must also be concerned with related issues that affect the reliability of their polls. For example, respondents may be influenced by the interviewer's personality or tone of voice, and some respondents may give the answer that they think will please the interviewer.

TIMING OF POLLS Opinion polls cannot reflect rapid shifts in public opinion unless they are taken frequently. Consider what occurred during the 1980 presidential election in which Republican Ronald Reagan challenged incumbent Democratic president Jimmy Carter. Almost to the end of the campaign, polls showed Carter in the lead. Only the most capable analysts noted that the very large number of undecided voters meant the outcome was still very much in doubt. The week before the election, these voters broke sharply for Reagan. Few polls were conducted late enough to detect this development.

POLLING PROBLEMS IN RECENT ELECTIONS In the 2012 and 2014 elections, public opinion polls faced significant problems in predicting how many voters would actually cast ballots. In 2012, several major poll takers overestimated turnout among Republican voters and underestimated turnout among Democrats. Several firms predicted that Republican presidential candidate Mitt Romney would win. In the end, President Obama was re-elected with a margin of almost 4 percentage points. Likewise, in the 2014 midterm elections, the biggest problem pollsters faced was the very low voter turnout. Because many citizens who did not vote leaned Democratic, a majority of the polls overestimated the Democratic vote.

In 2016, Donald Trump's victory came as a surprise to almost everyone except his own supporters. Most poll takers thought Hillary Clinton had an edge in the popular vote of 3 or 4 percentage points. These results were not that far off—when all the votes were counted, Clinton's popular vote margin was about 2 percent. This margin did not keep Donald Trump from winning a majority in the electoral college and, therefore, the presidency, however. Only a composite of state-level opinion polls can predict electoral college results; a nationwide poll is limited to predicting the overall popular vote.

That said, Trump's strong position in key swing states that secured his victory—most notably Wisconsin, Michigan, and Pennsylvania—should have shown up in state-level polls taken in those states. In fact, those state-level polls were relatively inaccurate. Clearly, Trump mobilized people in those states who had not previously voted and therefore were not considered in polling. Failure to account for this mobilization probably accounts for why many pollsters had Clinton with 1 to 2 more percentage points than the actual results. Hispanic voters, mobilized by a fear of Trump, also seemed to have turned out in record numbers, but these voters were concentrated in strongly partisan states such as California and Texas, where strong Latino turnout did not affect the results.

The polls in 2020 were misleading as well. While polls predicted a Biden win in the electoral college, the predicted margin of victory far exceeded the reality. Final polls predicted an 8 point victory for Biden nationally, but the reality was under 5 percent. Democrats were expected to win the states of Florida and North Carolina, both of which went for Trump. Pollsters also expected Democrats to win a significant majority in the Senate and to expand their majority in the House. Neither of these events took place.

People frequently complain that, instead of measuring public opinion, polls end up creating it. For example, a candidate might claim that all the polls show that he or she is ahead in a race. People who want to support a winner may back this candidate despite their true feelings. This is often called the bandwagon effect. Presidential approval ratings lend themselves to the bandwagon effect. Misleading polls can affect campaigns as well. Constituents make decisions about campaign donations based on polls. In 2020, both the Trump and Biden campaigns made decisions about where to spend money and candidate time based on polling. In many cases, this meant they wasted resources in areas they had no chance of winning—and neglected to focus efforts in places they might have won.

The media also sometimes misuse polls. Many journalists take the easy route during campaigns and base their political coverage almost exclusively on poll findings. Media companies often report only the polls conducted by their affiliated pollsters, announcing the results as indisputable regardless of whether the results are typical or differ significantly from polls taken by other organizations. Indeed, it is because of the diversity of results among different polling organizations that savvy political analysts look at as many polls as they can. Experts often average the results of polls that ask a particular question. Some even calculate weighted averages based on how reliable they believe each poll to be.

THE PROBLEM OF PUSH POLLS One tactic some political campaigns use is the **push poll**, which asks fake polling questions designed to push voters toward one candidate or another. The National Council on Public Polls describes push polls as outright political manipulation—the spreading of rumors and lies by one candidate about another. Push pollsters usually do not give their name or identify the poll's sponsor, and their interviews typically last less than a minute, whereas legitimate pollsters normally interview a respondent for 5 to 30 minutes.

Some researchers argue that identifying a push poll is not always straightforward. Political analyst Charlie Cook points out that "there are legitimate polls that can ask push questions, which test potential arguments against a rival to ascertain how effective those arguments might be in future advertising." Distinguishing between push polls and push questions can be challenging, though, and that is exactly what push pollsters want. A candidate does not want to be accused of conducting a push poll, because the public views a push poll as a dirty trick and may turn against the candidate.

HISTORICAL THINKING

3. **ANALYZE CAUSE AND EFFECT** Suppose you learned that a reputable pollster had weighted the responses of a certain group by counting them double. What can you conclude?
4. **INTERPRET GRAPHS** Which two polls gave the most accurate prediction for the outcome of the 2016 presidential election?

CHAPTER 16

VOTING AND VOTING RIGHTS

Review

VOCABULARY

Match each of the following vocabulary words with its definition.

1. disenfranchise
2. absentee voting
3. special election
4. polling place
5. political socialization
6. confirmation bias
7. opinion leader
8. socioeconomic factors
9. straw poll
10. push poll

a. survey conducted with no attempt to select a representive sample
b. deprive of the right to vote
c. tendency to interpret information in a way that supports current beliefs
d. campaign tactic that uses questioning to present false or misleading information
e. social and economic characteristics that describe individuals and groups in society
f. location designated for voting
g. submission of a ballot in advance of an election, often by mail
h. a well-known person able to influence others
i. occurs when an issue must be decided before the next general election
j. the learning process through which people acquire their early political attitudes, opinions, beliefs, and knowledge

MAIN IDEAS

Answer the following questions. Support your answers with evidence from the chapter.

11. What are the three qualifications voters must fulfill before they can register to vote in national or state elections? **LESSON 16.1**

12. Why do some people criticize technical voter registration requirements? **LESSON 16.1**

13. How were laws used to limit voting rights for African Americans prior to the 1960s? **LESSON 16.2**

14. How did the Voting Rights Act of 1965 affect rights guaranteed by the 15th Amendment? **LESSON 16.2**

15. What impact did the *Shelby County* v. *Holder* Supreme Court decision have on voting rights? **LESSON 16.2**

16. How did the Australian ballot change American elections? **LESSON 16.3**

17. How has voting by mail affected voting? Why? **LESSON 16.3**

18. Why is party identification such a strong predictor of voting behavior? **LESSON 16.4**

19. How has the correlation between education and party affiliation shifted over time? **LESSON 16.4**

20. Why do pollsters use weighting? What can happen if a pollster uses a flawed model to apply the weighting? **LESSON 16.5**

21. Why is the timing of polls important to predicting the outcome of elections? **LESSON 16.5**

HISTORICAL THINKING

Answer the following questions. Support your answers with evidence from the chapter.

22. **FORM AND SUPPORT OPINIONS** Should states have authority to establish laws governing voter eligibility and procedures for registering and voting, or should these matters be set by the federal government? Explain.

23. **CATEGORIZE** Why is preclearance an important protector of voter rights? What argument can be made to support the Supreme Court's decision to restrict it?

24. **ANALYZE CAUSE AND EFFECT** What are the advantages of absentee voting and voting by mail?

25. **IDENTIFY PROBLEMS AND SOLUTIONS** Why do you think economic issues have a stronger influence on voters' choices than other issues, such as gun control laws or education?

26. **DRAW CONCLUSIONS** Do you think the media are as important as family in shaping political opinion? Why or why not?

27. **FORM AND SUPPORT OPINIONS** Do public opinion polls provide an important service, or do they interfere with the democratic process? Explain.

INTERPRET VISUALS

28. How did the views of White respondents on the necessity for the Voting Rights Act of 1965 change between 1965 and 2015?

29. What can you conclude about how African Americans felt about their voting rights in 2015 versus what they believed in 1965?

Opinions on the Voting Rights Act, 1965 and 2015

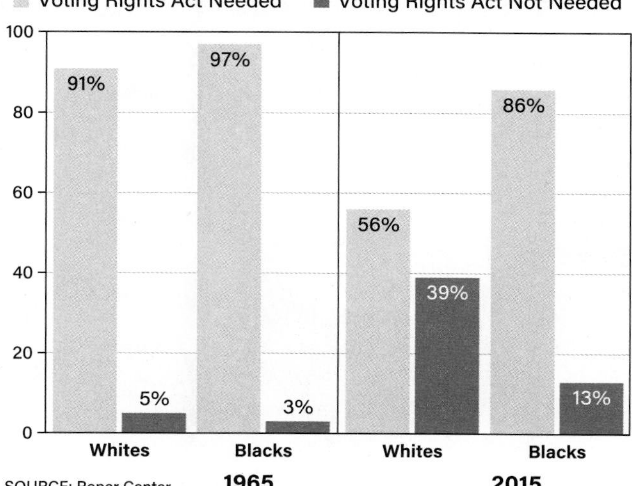

SOURCE: Roper Center

ANALYZE SOURCES

Read the following excerpt from a speech delivered by President John F. Kennedy in May 1963.

> The educated citizen knows how much more there is to know. He knows that "knowledge is power," more so today than ever before. He knows that only an educated and informed people will be a free people, that the ignorance of one voter in a democracy impairs the security of all.
>
> —John F. Kennedy, 35th President of the United States

30. What quality does President Kennedy say is essential to a democracy? Do you agree? Why or why not?

CONNECT TO YOUR LIFE

31. **EXPLANATORY** As you know, states set many of their own laws and policies governing elections. Investigate the laws for your state. Does your state have early voting, and if so, when does voting begin and where do people vote? Look into rules for filing absentee ballots. Does the state use voting by mail? Find out if there have been problems with recent elections in your state and what they were. Now consider how the voting process can be improved. Write a short essay explaining one way that you would improve your state's election procedures.

TIPS

- Summarize the aspect of your state's voting procedures that you think can be improved. Tell why they don't work as well as they could.
- Explain your plan for improving voting.
- Discuss any potential problems with your proposals and how they can be overcome.

8 Government in Action: Public Policy

UNIT 8 OVERVIEW

Chapter 17 Government and Domestic Policy

Chapter 18 Government and Foreign Policy

Chapter 19 Government, Politics, and the Media

CRITICAL VIEWING Sean Spicer served as President Donald Trump's press secretary during Trump's first six months in office. Like the press secretaries of every administration, Spicer was often criticized by White House reporters and other members of the news media. What point do you think the photographer was making by choosing to shoot this photo from behind a television camera?

Civility does not require us to stifle our disagreements. We still can and should vigorously debate issues and even tell unpleasant truths."

—Senator Susan Collins (R–ME)

CHAPTER 17

Government and Domestic Policy

LESSONS

17.1 The Policymaking Process

17.2 Economic Policy, Budgeting, and Taxes

17.3 Health-Care Policy

17.4 Energy and the Environment

***National Geographic* Magazine:**
This Refuge May Be the Most Contested Land in the U.S.

CRITICAL VIEWING Domestic policies deal with issues of critical importance to the American people, such as health care. In March 2010, President Barack Obama signed the Affordable Care Act (ACA) into law in a ceremony at the White House. The law was the end product of a health-care policy that he and Democratic leaders in Congress had fought hard to enact. Who do you think attended this signing ceremony?

LESSON
17.1 The Policymaking Process

Politicians seeking election or re-election must communicate to voters not only their general ideas about governing but also specific public policies, or plans of action, they support. Their goals might include issues such as campaign finance reform or expanded treatment for drug addicts. As you have read, political parties create party platforms stating their policy goals on many issues, ranging from health care and taxation to immigration and energy development. Once in office, party officials attempt to enact their platforms through laws that will put these policies into action. Laws that affect the nation's internal issues are the way politicians enact domestic policies.

A Multistep Process

A new law doesn't appear out of the blue. It's written and passed to solve a particular problem, or what at least some people perceive as a problem. Before a law can be passed, however, the problem it is meant to solve must be identified as one that requires government action. The problem must become part of the political agenda before proposed solutions are created and adopted.

Identifying issues, setting agendas, formulating policy, and adopting new policy are all steps in how policy is made. The policymaking process doesn't end there, however. Once a law is passed, it has to be implemented, or carried out. Then its results must be evaluated. You can see the entire series of policymaking steps in the chart titled "The Policymaking Process."

Individuals and groups work together at each phase of the policymaking process. The president and members of Congress are key participants in the process, but interest groups and federal agencies also play an important role. Groups that may be hurt by a new policy will try to convince Congress or a federal agency not to adopt the policy. Groups that will benefit from the policy will argue in favor of implementation. Congressional committees and subcommittees may investigate the issue the policy is meant to address. Federal agencies may invite comments in their efforts to gain input from groups or industries that might be affected by the policy.

The participants in policymaking and the nature of the debates depend on which policy is being proposed, formed, and implemented. Whatever the policy, however, debate over its pros and cons occurs during each stage of the policymaking process. Policy decisions typically involve **trade-offs**, or compromises in which policymakers sacrifice one goal to achieve another because of budget limitations and other factors.

HISTORICAL THINKING

1. **EVALUATE** Why might the policymaking process sometimes fail to resolve an issue of national importance?
2. **INTERPRET CHARTS** What do you think might happen if the evaluation process determines that a law is a failure?

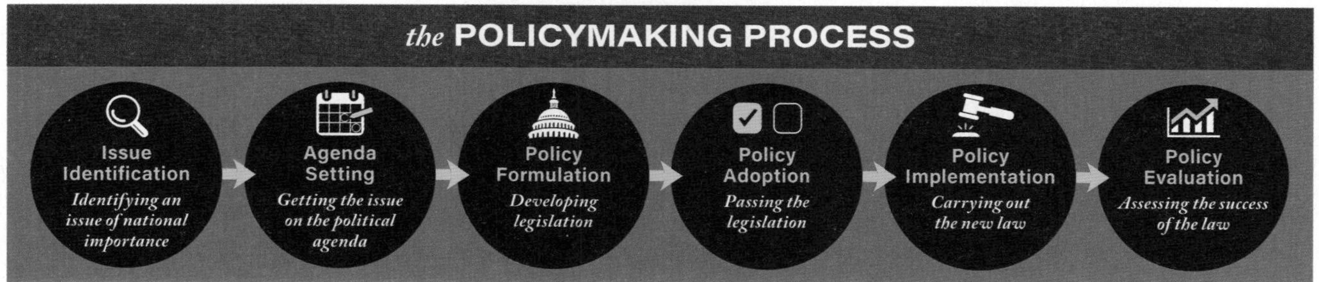

Policymaking: From Identification to Evaluation

The making of public policy is a complex process. It involves many different people and groups, in and out of government, who often have conflicting ideas about how to deal with a pressing problem. The step-by-step nature of the process, however, helps move the nation forward in resolving problems of great national importance.

FIRST STEPS IN MAKING POLICY If no one recognizes something as a problem, then, politically speaking, it doesn't really exist, no matter how important it may be. Thus, issue identification is part of the first stage of the policymaking process. Some group—whether it's the media, the public, or politicians—must identify a problem that can be solved through the political process.

The second part of the policymaking process involves getting the issue on the political agenda. This is called agenda setting, or agenda building. As you have read, presidents develop a legislative program based on issues they believe need to be addressed. Members of Congress, too, can work to bring an issue to the public's notice and, by introducing legislation or holding hearings, place that issue on the political agenda. Ultimately, it is Congress that makes the laws.

The American people, interest groups, and the media often play a key role in agenda setting. Issues typically become part of the political agenda when an event or series of events leads to public calls for action. For example, the failure of a major bank in 2008 led economists to conclude that the financial industry was in trouble and that the government should act to rectify the problem. More recently, rates of addiction and death from opioid drugs have dramatically increased. As a result, American citizens, the media, and others have insisted that the opioid epidemic should be on the domestic political agenda.

FORMULATION AND ADOPTION After an issue becomes part of the political agenda, the policymaking process enters a new stage. This stage involves making and adopting specific plans for achieving a particular goal. The president, members of Congress, administrative agencies, and interest group leaders typically are the key participants in the formulation and adoption of public policy. They develop proposed legislation and then work to get it passed. Iron triangles and issue networks—individuals and groups both inside and outside the federal government who support one another's interests—try to develop mutually beneficial policies. The courts can also revise public policies when they interpret statutes passed by legislative bodies. To a certain extent, the courts can actually establish policies if they make decisions concerning conflicts not yet addressed by any law, such as disputes involving new technology.

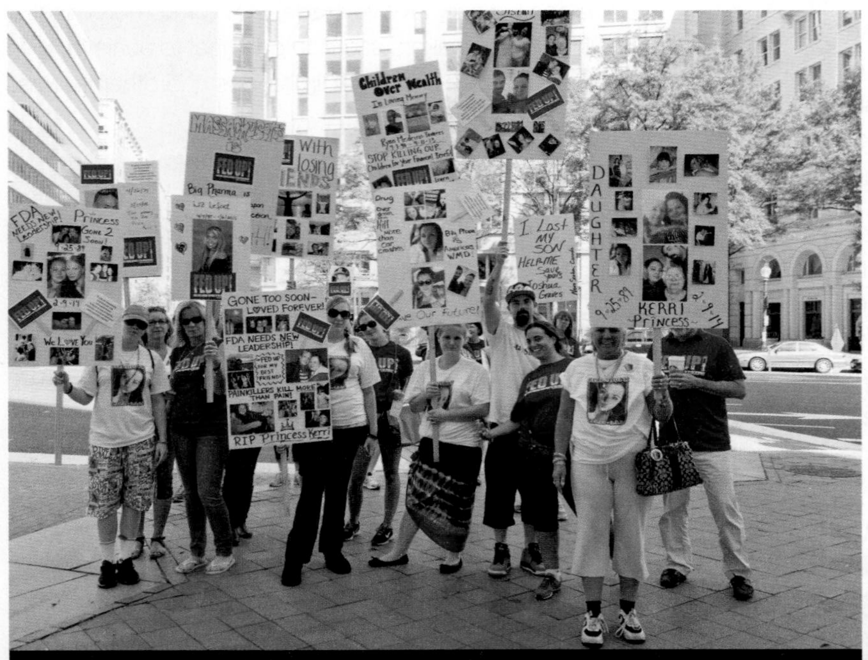

CRITICAL VIEWING Many Americans have issues they think belong near the top of the president's and Congress's political agenda. These demonstrators are calling attention to one of them, the opioid crisis—the growing overuse and abuse of powerful, addictive prescription pain relievers and illegal drugs. Do you think public demonstrations are an effective way to get an issue onto the political agenda? Why or why not?

Note that sometimes the push to deal with an issue may lose steam well before this point in the policymaking process. The issue may become a part of the political agenda but never proceed beyond that stage. Usually, this happens when it's impossible to achieve a consensus on how to formulate policy or what policy should be adopted.

IMPLEMENTATION Once a policy is adopted through legislation, it must be implemented. As you read earlier, one or more agencies within the executive branch ensure that new policies are enforced, often by issuing rules or regulations. Law enforcement officials at the federal, state, and local levels are also often involved in carrying out public policy. The courts, too, have a role in implementation, because the legislation and administrative regulations detailing the new policy must be interpreted and applied to specific situations by the courts.

In the U.S. federal system, the carrying out of national policies works most smoothly when there is cooperation among the national government and the state and local governments. That doesn't always happen. For example, the Patient Protection and Affordable Care Act (ACA), also known as Obamacare, assumed that the states would set up their own marketplaces where individuals could buy health-care insurance. Most state governments, however, refused to participate. In 2018, 39 states relied either completely or partially on the federal government to set up a marketplace. This example shows that in the federal system, cooperation isn't assured. But it also shows that the federal government can act without the states if it must.

For a policy to be successfully implemented, it must be clearly communicated to the relevant government agencies charged with carrying it out. Successful implementation also usually requires the support of groups outside the government. For example, the state health-care insurance marketplaces established under Obamacare were effective only because of the participation of commercial insurance companies.

EVALUATION The final stage of policymaking involves evaluating the success of a policy. This assessment takes place during and after the policy's implementation. Groups both inside and outside the government participate in the evaluation process.

Congress may hold hearings to obtain feedback from different groups on how a statute or regulation has affected them. Scholars and scientists may conduct studies to determine whether a particular law, such as an environmental law designed to reduce air pollution, has achieved the desired result—less air pollution. Sometimes, feedback obtained in these or other ways indicates that a policy has failed in whole or in part, and a new policymaking process may be undertaken to modify the policy or create a more effective one.

HISTORICAL THINKING

3. **MAKE GENERALIZATIONS** What role do you think funding plays in the implementation stage of the policymaking process?
4. **MAKE INFERENCES** Which step in the policymaking process can members of the public participate in? What form might that participation take?

Policymaking and Special Interests

The steps in policymaking may seem straightforward, but they aren't. The formulation and adoption step can be particularly problematic. Every bill that passes through Congress requires compromise to become law. Every bill that passes through Congress also presents an opportunity for individual members of Congress to help their constituents, including special interest groups that contributed financially to the members' re-election campaigns.

Consider the Agricultural Act of 2014, commonly known as the 2014 Farm Bill. The act authorizes the spending of about $95 billion per year for 5 years. About $75 billion of that amount actually supports the Supplemental Nutrition Assistance Program (SNAP), or food stamps. Combining SNAP authorization with agricultural subsidies—financial assistance to farmers—has been a way to encourage representatives from urban areas to vote for farm bills. Liberal members of Congress who balk at federal support for large-scale, industrial farms will generally agree to back social programs such as SNAP. But farmers benefit from the program as well. Money spent by SNAP recipients to buy food may boost farm production and the number of farm jobs.

The centerpiece of the 2014 Farm Bill was the ending of direct payments from the federal government to farmers for certain crops. The U.S. Department of Agriculture had been making these fixed annual payments regardless of whether the recipient actually planted the crops in question. Direct payments were seen as income support for the struggling agricultural community. In the early 2000s, many farmers found it difficult to make a living.

Most of the funds saved by ending these payments were transferred to a much-enlarged crop insurance program. This program helped farmers pay for insurance against crop loss due to natural causes, such as drought and crop diseases, as well as low yields or falling market prices. A federal agency oversaw and regulated the program. Supporters claimed that the new bill would reduce federal expenditures at a time of increasing budget deficits. Critics, pointing to falling prices for corn, soybeans, and wheat, argued that it would in fact increase government spending.

Congress was divided along party lines, which meant that the Farm Bill would be hard to pass. Special provisions, not requested by the Department of Agriculture but added to the bill by members of Congress, helped the bill along. A pilot program for industrial hemp production helped secure the support of members from Kentucky. Profit-margin insurance for catfish farmers helped sew up the Mississippi delegation. The bill included livestock disaster relief and funds to combat a disease called citrus greening in Florida. Products newly insured under the bill included biofuels, lamb, peanuts, poultry, sesame, sushi rice, and swine. Various GMO (genetically modified organism) crops also received special insurance treatment. These various special provisions helped secure the votes the bill needed to pass.

HISTORICAL THINKING

5. **FORM AND SUPPORT OPINIONS** Should the SNAP program be part of the Farm Bill? Why or why not?
6. **DRAW CONCLUSIONS** How do the special provisions of the 2014 Farm Bill reflect the general need to compromise in order to pass legislation?

LESSON 17.2 Economic Policy, Budgeting, and Taxes

The 2008 recession hit the auto industry hard, and auto manufacturers General Motors (GM) and Chrysler faced bankruptcy. The failure of this industry could put 3 million jobs at risk, according to analysts. President George W. Bush and his economic advisers devised a government rescue plan offering billions in loans to U.S. auto manufacturers. Under President Obama, the federal government provided additional help. All told, federal help to the auto industry had amounted to about $80 billion. The industry survived. By 2011, GM once again led the world in the manufacture of motor vehicles. The federal government, however, failed to recover billions of dollars from its investment.

The Goals of Economic Policy

When the economy is in trouble, policies that affect the economy are often seen as the most important activities of the U.S. government. The term *economic policy* refers to all the actions taken by government to address the ups and downs of the nation's business activity. National economic policy is determined solely by the national government, not the states.

Since the very beginning of U.S. history, the national economy has passed through periods of boom and bust. Economists refer to the alternating periods of strong economic growth and weak or no growth as the **business cycle**. This cyclical rhythm is part of all economies, even those in which the government plays a stronger role.

Economists refer to boom periods in the business cycle as expansions. A bust period, in which the economy stops expanding and undergoes a contraction, or decline, is called a recession. As you read earlier, in 2008 the United States experienced a major economic downturn that many economists refer to as the Great Recession. It began in December 2007 and officially ended in June 2009. We say "officially" because even though economic growth resumed in 2009, the nation's economy was still operating below its potential.

The most important sign of an economic downturn, or a period when businesses are shrinking or closing, is a high rate of unemployment. People are said to be unemployed if they don't have a job and are actively looking for one. Unemployment rates of 8 or 9 percent are clear signs of economic and social distress. At the end of the Great Recession, in June 2009, the jobless rate reached 9.5 percent, and a few months later it peaked at 10 percent. During the COVID-19 public health crisis, unemployment was even higher, as many businesses were forced to close to limit rates of infection. Reducing high levels of unemployment can be a major policy objective.

Another economic problem is associated with economic booms, or periods of rapid growth and business expansion. That problem is inflation, a sustained rise in average prices. A rise in prices is equivalent to a decline in the value of the dollar because as overall prices rise, a dollar buys less. High rates of inflation were a serious problem in the 1970s. Even though the rate of inflation is currently low, many people fear the return of high rates in the future.

HISTORICAL THINKING

1. **IDENTIFY MAIN IDEAS AND DETAILS** Why does the government need to address both the ups and downs of the economy?
2. **MAKE INFERENCES** Why would high inflation hurt consumers?

Monetary Policy

The U.S. government uses two main tools to smooth the business cycle and reduce unemployment and inflation. One of these is **monetary policy**, which involves changing the amount of money in circulation to affect interest rates, credit markets, the rate of inflation, the rate of economic growth, and the rate of unemployment. The Federal Reserve System (the Fed), an independent regulatory agency, sets monetary policy. Congress established the Fed as the nation's central banking system in 1913. It consists of 12 regional Federal Reserve Banks located in major cities across the country, along with a Board of Governors that oversees the Fed. The U.S. president nominates the seven members of the Board of Governors and nominates a chairperson and vice chairperson from among them. The chairperson has significant influence over Fed policy. The Senate must approve all Fed nominations. Members of the board serve 14-year terms.

In addition to controlling the money supply, the Fed has a number of responsibilities for supervising and regulating the banking system. The Fed makes decisions about monetary policy several times a year through its Federal Open Market Committee (FOMC). The FOMC is composed of the 7 members of the Board of Governors and 5 of the 12 presidents of the Federal Reserve Banks. The president of the New York bank is a permanent member of the FOMC.

EASY MONEY, TIGHT MONEY In theory, monetary policy is relatively straightforward. In periods of recession and high unemployment, the Fed pursues an easy-money policy—expanding the rate of growth of the money supply to stimulate the economy. An easy-money policy theoretically will lead to lower interest rates, making borrowing more attractive. This will induce consumers to spend more and producers to invest more.

In periods of rising inflation, the Fed does the reverse. It reduces the rate of growth in the amount of money in circulation. This is called a tight-money policy. This policy should cause interest rates to rise, making borrowing less attractive and thus inducing consumers to spend less and businesses to invest less.

ADJUSTMENTS TO EASY-MONEY POLICY Although an easy-money policy may sound simple, the reality is not simple at all. To create money in the marketplace, the Fed typically purchases **government bonds**, or debt issued by the government to raise funds needed to meet expenses. (You will learn more about these later in the lesson.) The Fed deposits the payment used to purchase those bonds into the accounts of the sellers, including banks. Those deposits become a source of investment funds for banks, who hold the deposits in reserve and use them to make loans. To encourage borrowers to take on loans, the banks lower the interest rates they charge. Lower interest rates normally encourage people and businesses to borrow—to buy a car, for example, or expand a factory. Borrowing helps the economy grow.

After 2008, however, the rate of borrowing fell. The Great Recession left many people wary of borrowing, even though the Fed kept the interest rate almost at zero. They did not want to take out loans and then find themselves without a job that would allow them to repay the loan. Instead of percolating into the economy, much of the new money created by the Fed remained in the banks.

The Fed responded to the failure of its easy-money policy by adopting some unorthodox tactics. As described earlier, the Fed ordinarily expands the money supply by purchasing short-term federal government bonds, or debt issued by the government to raise funds needed to meet expenses. (You will learn more about these later in the lesson.) After 2010, the Fed began buying long-term U.S. government bonds and other types of debt obligations, to try to stimulate the economy.

Beginning in 2013, with the unemployment rate declining and the economy growing steadily, the Fed began reversing some of these unusual policies. In December 2015, for the first time since the Great Recession, the Fed raised its key interest rate by 0.25 percent to 0.5 percent. It raised the rate eight more times until, in December 2018, the rate reached 2.5 percent. Some economists argued that the Fed was moving too fast. They recommended hiking interest rates only after the economy was clearly overheating—that is, when the rate of inflation was steadily rising. However, when the COVID-19 pandemic hit in 2020, the Fed quickly reversed course and cut the key interest rate to zero.

CRITICISMS OF FED POLICY Some critics expressed alarm at the Fed's expansion of the money supply during and after the Great Recession. They noted that the extra money the Fed created sat in banks as excess reserves—in digital form, not actual bills, but still available for banks to loan out. They feared a sudden upsurge in borrowing that would pour money into the economy with explosive speed and significantly increase inflation.

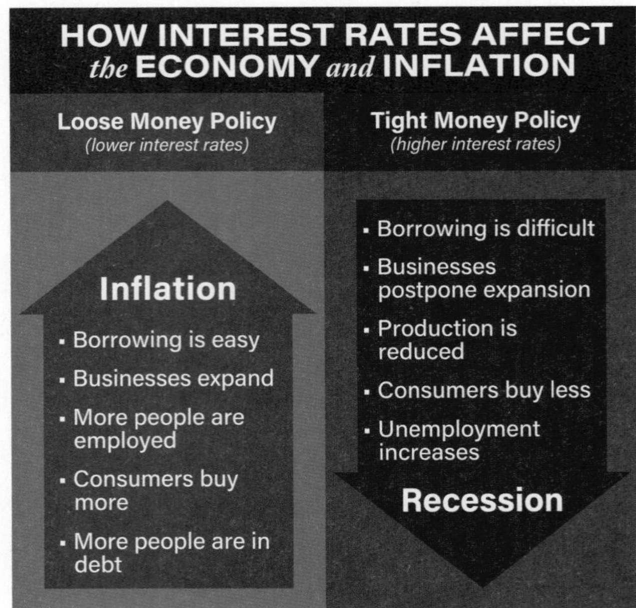

HOW INTEREST RATES AFFECT the ECONOMY and INFLATION
Loose Money Policy
(lower interest rates)
Tight Money Policy
(higher interest rates)
Inflation
• Borrowing is easy
• Businesses expand
• More people are employed
• Consumers buy more
• More people are in debt
• Borrowing is difficult
• Businesses postpone expansion
• Production is reduced
• Consumers buy less
• Unemployment increases
Recession

A second response to the Fed's expansionist policies has been a growth in the hard-money philosophy among more radical conservatives. Hard-money advocates believe that the government should tie the value of the dollar to an actual concrete and valuable item, such as gold. Mainstream economists believe that returning to a hard-money policy today would lead to a dramatic contraction in the money supply and a recession of unprecedented severity.

HISTORICAL THINKING

3. **MAKE GENERALIZATIONS** Would a factory owner seeking to expand prefer that the Fed establish an easy-money policy or a tight-money policy? Explain your answer.
4. **ANALYZE CAUSE AND EFFECT** Why do you think the Fed raised interest rates from 2013 through 2018?
5. **INTERPRET CHARTS** Under what circumstances would the Fed likely raise interest rates?

Fiscal Policy

Before the onset of the Great Recession, most economists agreed on one point: Under ordinary circumstances, monetary policy would be sufficient to steer the economy. But what if monetary policy proved inadequate to deal with a severe economic downturn? In that case, many economists recommended the use of **fiscal policy**—adjusting government spending and taxation to influence the economy.

The principle underlying fiscal policy, like the one that underlies monetary policy, is relatively simple: When unemployment is rising and the economy is entering a recession, fiscal policy should stimulate economic activity by decreasing taxes, increasing government spending, or both. When unemployment is decreasing and prices are rising (that is, when we have inflation), fiscal policy should curb economic activity by reducing government spending, increasing taxes, or both.

KEYNES AND THE GREAT DEPRESSION U.S. fiscal policy grew out of economic theories advanced by the British economist John Maynard Keynes (1883–1946). According to those theories, which came to be known as Keynesian economics, a nation cannot automatically recover from an economic disaster such as the Great Depression or the Great Recession. Such an economic crisis is so frightening that consumers and businesses reduce their borrowing and spending. Unfortunately, if everyone in the economy cuts spending at the same time, demand for goods and services drops sharply. That, in turn, reduces the income of everyone selling goods and services. They cut back on hiring, and unemployment increases. People become even more reluctant to borrow and spend. The cycle feeds on itself.

The Keynesian solution to this type of impasse is for the government to undertake a huge, if temporary, spending program to be paid for through borrowing, not taxes. The government, in other words, starts borrowing when the private sector stops borrowing. During the Great Depression of the 1930s, President Franklin D. Roosevelt applied Keynes's theories in an effort to stem rising unemployment and revive a stagnant economy. Before the Great Depression, the federal government had tried to maintain a balanced budget and severely limited its involvement in the economy. Roosevelt's administration borrowed money to expand government spending and replaced balanced budgets with budget deficits. The goal was to add jobs and stimulate the economy. This New Deal fiscal policy helped to an extent. But some economists believe that it was the greatly increased spending needed to fund the U.S. effort in World War II (1939–1945) that actually broke the back of the Great Depression.

After World War II, fiscal policy usually consisted of raising or lowering rates of taxation. Such changes could be accomplished quickly and didn't trigger disputes about government spending and budget deficits. The severity of the Great Recession, however, led some economists to recommend increases in government spending as well.

CRITICAL VIEWING During the COVID-19 pandemic in 2020, the federal government contracted with various manufacturers, including Ford Motor Company, to produce badly needed supplies and equipment. Workers at this Ford plant near Detroit switched from assembling automobile components to assembling ventilators—life-saving devices that help critically ill COVID-19 patients breathe. Why do you think government officials chose an auto assembly plant like this one for the production of ventilators?

KEYNESIAN POLICY AND THE GREAT RECESSION Until recently, support for Keynesian economics was relatively bipartisan. Even President Richard Nixon, a Republican, was said to have once described himself as "now a Keynesian in economics." From the end of World War II until the first years of the 21st century, it was fairly easy to be a Keynesian. After all, Keynesian solutions could be implemented through relatively small changes to rates of taxation. The administration of President George W. Bush sponsored just such a tax-based stimulus in early 2008, when the Great Recession had already begun but was not yet a major disaster. Bush justified his tax cuts with Keynesian rhetoric.

By February 2009, at the start of Barack Obama's presidency, the full scope of the recession had become evident. Initially, Obama followed a Keynesian approach to the problem. He proposed, and Congress passed, the American Recovery and Reinvestment Act. This stimulus package, made up mostly of spending rather than tax cuts, injected roughly $800 billion into the economy. The money, aimed at growing the economy and decreasing unemployment, funded infrastructure projects, health-care expansion, education, and more.

Republicans in Congress had begun to reject the Keynesian approach, however. Many simply objected to the use of budget deficits as a recession-fighting tool. Some argued that stimulus spending would have to be three times the $800 billion already committed. That type of program was politically impossible. They argued that few Americans would accept new government spending programs amounting to trillions of dollars.

Economists disagree about the effects of the stimulus package, but five months after it passed Congress, in June 2009, the recession officially ended. The economy was no longer in decline. By 2011, the economy had begun to recover, and the unemployment rate was decreasing. The government continued to run trillion-dollar budget deficits through 2012, however, as it took longer for tax revenues to recover. The size of these deficits became a major political issue, and after much wrangling, Congressional Republicans and President Obama agreed to measures to curtail spending. By 2013, the deficit had begun to decline noticeably.

KEYNESIAN POLICY AND THE COVID-19 PANDEMIC Restrictions on spending were abruptly lifted in spring 2020, when the COVID-19 pandemic hobbled the U.S. economy. Federal and state governments took strong measures to combat the virus and the disease it causes, COVID-19. All but a handful of states acted to limit the spread of the disease by ordering people to stay home and by shutting down all nonessential businesses. Many Americans found themselves out of a job—and unable to pay their bills or even buy enough food. The economy seemed headed for a major recession. Saving lives and rescuing the U.S. economy took precedence over fears of expanding the deficit.

Congress responded to the economic and public-health crisis in late March by passing the $2.2 trillion CARES Act, a stimulus package aimed at shoring up businesses, unemployed workers, and others. It included funds to help small businesses keep workers on the payroll and provided payments to state, local, and tribal governments to help cover the extraordinary costs of trying to keep COVID-19 in check. The CARES Act also expanded unemployment benefits, for which more than 40 million Americans had applied by June. In addition, many American taxpayers received an "economic impact payment" of up to $1,200. Still, millions of Americans continued to suffer financially, and even as more and more states chose to reopen to some extent by June, Congress continued working on additional stimulus measures.

HISTORICAL THINKING

6. **DESCRIBE** What does Keynesian economics propose as the solution to a severe economic downturn?

7. **EVALUATE** Why did some economists and members of Congress oppose Keynesian economics as a response to the Great Recession?

The Federal Tax System

The federal government raises money to pay its expenses in two ways. One is through taxes levied on business and personal income. The American income tax system is progressive—meaning that those

Federal Income Tax Rates for Unmarried Persons, Tax Year 2020

TAXABLE INCOME	TAX DUE
$0–$9,875	10% of taxable income
$9,876–$40,125	$987.50 *plus* 12% of the amount over $9,875
$40,126–$85,525	$4,617.50 *plus* 22% of the amount over $40,125
$85,526–$163,300	$14,605.50 *plus* 24% of the amount over $85,525
$163,301–$207,350	$33,271.50 *plus* 32% of the amount over $163,300
$207,351–$518,400	$47,367.50 *plus* 35% of the amount over $207,350
$518,401 or more	$156,235 *plus* 37% of the amount over $518,400

SOURCE: Forbes

who earn more income pay a higher tax rate than those who earn less.

Income tax rates for individuals are shown in the table listing income tax rates for 2020. The highest rate, 37 percent, applies only to income in excess of $518,401. More than 40 percent of American households earn so little that they have no income tax liability at all, thanks in part to various tax deductions and credits. Deductions can reduce overall taxable income. Taxpayers can list, or itemize, them or take the standard deduction set by the government. Credits are amounts that can be subtracted from taxes owed for certain types of spending.

TAX LOOPHOLES Generally, taxpayers subject to the highest tax rates are most likely to complain about those rates. Their reasoning often includes the argument that high taxes will limit the amount of money they can use to produce or consume goods and services, which would mean less of their money going into the marketplace. Individuals and corporations facing high tax rates have, in the past, tried to get Congress to add various loopholes, or exceptions, to the tax laws that will allow them to reduce their taxable incomes.

THE TAX CUTS AND JOBS ACT In 2017, Congress passed the Tax Cuts and Jobs Act, with the goal of reducing taxes and simplifying the tax code. One result of this act was to nearly double the standard deduction for individuals from $6,350 to $12,000. This will allow many more taxpayers to take the standard deduction, rather than the more time-consuming itemized deductions. For many, this will simplify the filing process. Another result of this act was to reduce the maximum corporate income tax rate from 35 percent to 21 percent.

The Tax Cuts and Jobs Act of 2017 was the first substantial revision of the tax code since 1986, when Congress passed the Tax Reform Act. This law, too, was intended to lower taxes and simplify the tax code—and it did just that for most taxpayers. A few years later, however, large federal budget deficits forced Congress to choose between cutting spending and raising taxes, and Congress opted to do the latter. Tax increases occurred under the administrations of both George H.W. Bush (1989–1993) and Bill Clinton (1993–2001). To appease wealthy Americans, however, Congress legislated special exceptions and loopholes that made the tax code even more complicated than before. Time will tell whether the simplifications of the 2017 act will last.

HISTORICAL THINKING

8. **EVALUATE** Do you think a progressive tax system is a fair or unfair way of assessing taxes for different income levels? Explain your answer.
9. **DRAW CONCLUSIONS** Why do you think Congress substantially decreased the corporate income tax in the Tax Cuts and Jobs Act of 2017?
10. **ANALYZE VISUALS** How much personal income tax would an unmarried person have to pay on a taxable income of $8,400?

The Public Debt

When the government spends more than it receives, it has to finance the shortfall. The U.S. Treasury sells IOUs on behalf of the U.S. government. They are called U.S. Treasury bills, notes, or bonds, depending

Net Public Debt as a Percentage of the Gross Domestic Product (GDP), 1970–2020

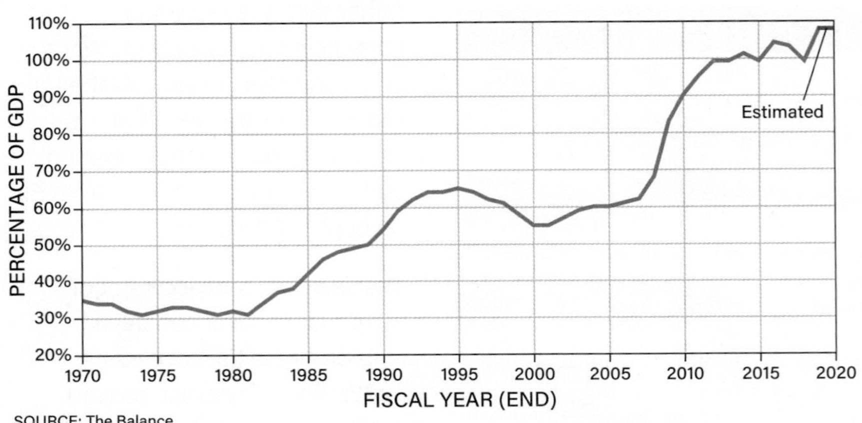

SOURCE: The Balance

on the length of time for which the funds are borrowed. Collectively, these debts are referred to as Treasury securities or **Treasuries**. The sale of these debt obligations to corporations, private individuals, pension plans, foreign governments, foreign companies, and foreign individuals is big business. Federal government expenditures typically exceed federal government revenues, and the amount the government borrows each year can be huge.

Every time there is a federal government deficit, there is an increase in the total accumulated public debt (also called the national debt), which is the total amount of money the federal government owes to investors. The table titled "Net Public Debt as a Percentage of the Gross Domestic Product (GDP)" shows the net public debt over time, compared with the overall size of the economy. (The net public debt doesn't count sums the government owes to itself, although it does include funds held by the Fed.)

THE BURDEN OF THE PUBLIC DEBT Politicians and economists often talk about the burden of the public debt. Some even maintain that the government, if it continues piling up debt, will eventually go bankrupt. As long as the government can collect taxes to pay interest on its public debt, however, that will never happen. What happens instead is that when Treasuries come due, they are simply "rolled over," or refinanced. That is, if a $1 million Treasury bond comes due today, the U.S. Treasury pays it off by selling another $1 million bond. The government uses federal tax revenue to pay the interest on Treasuries. Even though much of the interest is being paid by American citizens, the government ends up borrowing to cover some of this interest. The more the federal government borrows to meet these payments, the greater the percentage of its budget is committed to paying interest. This reduces the government's ability to cover the cost of other needs, such as transportation, education, housing, and the military.

THE DEFICIT AFTER THE GREAT RECESSION AND TODAY As discussed earlier, the federal government initially responded to the Great Recession by increasing spending. At the same time, the economy was shrinking, so tax revenues were shrinking, too. Between increased spending and decreased revenues, the federal budget deficit shot up. The deficit for 2011 was $1.3 trillion. That was about 8.3 percent of the entire economy. Looking at all levels of government spending together, for every $5 spent, $3 were backed up by tax receipts. The other two were borrowed.

By 2015, the federal budget deficit was down to $438 billion. Then it began to rise. The Tax Cuts and Jobs Act contributed to this increase in the years after its passage in 2017. Then, in 2020, the spending needed to deal with the effects of the COVID-19 pandemic was projected to boost that year's budget deficit to at least $3.5 trillion. Even if this stimulus spending had not been needed, the budget deficit—unless major policy changes were made—was still expected to exceed $1 trillion and continue to grow steadily. Some economists contend, however, that as long as the net public debt does not grow faster than the economy as a whole, the U.S. economy will continue to function normally.

HISTORICAL THINKING

11. **MAKE INFERENCES** Why do you think the national debt is commonly called the public debt?
12. **IDENTIFY** How does the government pay the interest on the public debt?
13. **INTERPRET GRAPHS** In what year shown on the graph was net public debt at its lowest in relation to GDP?

Government and Private Enterprise

The principle of limited U.S. government involvement in private enterprise does not mean that the government has no role in advancing the interests of businesses. One reason for the success of the American economy has been the support offered by the federal and state governments. This support includes not only laws and regulations that help stimulate the development of certain types of industries but also financial incentives to help support their growth.

PATENTS AND COPYRIGHTS In Article I, Section 8, Clause 8, the Constitution grants Congress the power "To promote the Progress of Science and useful Arts, by securing for limited Times to Authors and Inventors the exclusive Right to their respective Writings and Discoveries." Congress carries out this responsibility in part by granting and regulating patents and copyrights. A **patent** is a license that, for a limited time, excludes anyone but the inventor from making, selling, or using his or her invention. A copyright gives the creators of original works the right to publish, produce, sell, or perform their creations, such as books, art, music, and software.

Inventions and other creative works are considered intellectual property. The U.S. Commerce Department's Patent and Trademark Office protects intellectual property. (As mentioned earlier, Article I of the Constitution establishes the power of the federal government to issue patents and copyrights.) Providing this protection promotes **entrepreneurship**, or the willingness to assume the risks of a business or enterprise. Inventors holding a patent, for example, are assured of being able to receive any money earned from their creation. Of course, someone might come along with a slightly different, somewhat better creation, which the government would also protect. In this way, the government also promotes competition that benefits the whole society.

GOVERNMENT SUPPORT FOR RESEARCH The government supports private enterprise in other ways as well. An important example is the research behind technological innovation. Overall, the government funds around 60 percent of the basic research carried out in the United States. This includes medical advances such as new cancer therapies and vaccines. It also includes improvements to the computer and communications technologies that Americans have come to rely on. The internet, for example, began in the late 1960s as a computer network within the U.S. Department of Defense. Today the internet serves as a research archive, a marketplace for goods, and a means of making business deals. It has also made possible the various social media that serve to connect people with one another in an electronic community.

HISTORICAL THINKING

14. **MAKE INFERENCES** How do you think the government protects patent holders?
15. **MAKE CONNECTIONS** How do domestic policies supporting basic scientific and technological research reflect a key purpose of government, as stated in the Preamble to the Constitution: to "promote the general Welfare"?

LESSON 17.3 Health-Care Policy

When President Barack Obama took office in 2009, the government covered about half of the nation's health-care costs through various programs that benefited more than 100 million Americans. Covering the cost of health care for a large number of Americans was a major federal responsibility, and questions about how the government should carry out that function in the future had to be answered. Obama put forward one answer, and in March 2010, urged on by the president, Congress passed the Affordable Care Act (ACA), now known as Obamacare. The ACA, a series of health-care reforms, was one of the most consequential government initiatives in many years. Yet it didn't solve all the problems of the nation's health-care system.

Health Status of Selected Developed Countries, 2016

Health Indicator	Germany	Japan	New Zealand	Norway	Turkey	United States
Life Expectancy in Years: Women/Men	83.5/78.6	87.1/81	83.4/80	84.2/80.7	80.7/75.3	81.1/76.1
Perceived Health Status						
→ Good/Very Good	65.2%	35.5%	87.8%	77.1%	69.4%	88.0%
→ Fair	26.5%	49.2%	9.8%	15.2%	21.3%	9.1%
→ Bad/Very Bad	8.3%	14.1%	2.5%	7.7%	9.3%	2.5%
Covered by Health Insurance	100%	100%	100%	100%	98.2%	91.2%
GDP Spent on Health Care	11.1%	10.8%	9.2%	10.5%	4.3%	17.1%

SOURCE: Organisation for Economic Co-Operation and Development

Problems with U.S. Health Care

Critics of the U.S. health-care system cite two major problems. One is that health care in the United States is expensive. As of 2017, almost 18 percent of the gross domestic product (GDP) in the United States went to health care, compared with 11 percent in France, 10 percent in Canada, and 8.5 percent in Britain.

A second problem has been a lack of insurance to cover health-care costs. About 18 percent of the population had no health insurance as of 2013, before the ACA was fully implemented. Lack of coverage can have several consequences. People may put off seeing a physician until it is too late for effective treatment. They may resort to going to a hospital emergency room for treatment. Or, unable to pay large medical bills, they may be forced into bankruptcy. All of these consequences are costly for society, and the governments of most large economies, including Australia, Canada, France, Germany, Singapore, Switzerland, and the United Kingdom, have a system of providing health care coverage to prevent them. Studies have estimated that before 2013, more than 20,000 people per year may have died prematurely in the United States because they lacked health insurance. Still, many conservatives in the United States believe that the government has no business providing health insurance.

HISTORICAL THINKING

1. **EVALUATE** What does the comparison of U.S. health-care costs with those of other developed nations imply about the U.S. system?
2. **IDENTIFY MAIN IDEAS** Why do you think Congress accepted the need to pass a comprehensive health-care insurance program in 2010?
3. **INTERPRET TABLES** How does the health status of the U.S. population compare with that of the other countries in the table, considering how much it spends on health care?

Medicare and Medicaid

Before passage of the ACA, several government-funded health-care programs were already in place. Like many major employers, the federal government buys health insurance for its employees. Members of the armed forces, military veterans, and Native Americans receive medical services provided directly by the government. Most federal spending on health care, however, is for Medicare and Medicaid.

MEDICARE The federal government provides a health-care program for persons 65 and older. It is known as Medicare, and it is now the government's second-largest domestic spending program, after Social Security. Medicare currently accounts for more than 3 percent of the GDP, and costs are expected to

CRITICAL VIEWING More than half of the federal budget is spent on entitlement programs, including Medicare, Medicaid, and Social Security. What opinion does this cartoonist seem to have about entitlement spending, and how does the cartoon express that opinion?

rise as millions of baby boomers retire over the next two decades. By 2030, the 65-and-older population is expected to double. Furthermore, advances in medical science are driving medical costs up every year. New medications and medical devices keep people alive longer—and Americans naturally want to take advantage of them.

MEDICAID Medicaid offers health-care subsidies to people with low incomes. The federal government provides more than 60 percent of the $560 billion Medicaid budget, and the states provide the rest. About 70 million people are in the program. Many Medicaid recipients are elderly residents of nursing homes—the Medicare program doesn't pay for nursing home expenses.

Although recent cost-containment measures have slowed the growth of Medicaid spending, the cost of Medicaid has doubled in the last decade. Fortunately for state budgets, the ACA has increased the share of Medicaid spending assumed by the federal government. Medicaid now amounts to an average of about 16 percent of state budgets. Another program, the Children's Health Insurance Program (CHIP), covers children in families who cannot afford health-care coverage but have incomes that are too high to qualify for Medicaid. By fiscal year 2018, the total cost of Medicaid and CHIP for all levels of government was $646 billion.

ENTITLEMENT PROGRAMS

Medicare and Medicaid are examples of government entitlement programs. An entitlement program is one in which people who meet certain requirements are entitled to receive the program's funds. The government issues Social Security payments based on a recipient's age at retirement and the taxes the recipient has paid into the program during working years. Unemployment compensation is another entitlement program. People who have lost their jobs due to business decisions on the part of their employers receive payments meant to help them weather unemployment while they search for a new job. These payments are covered by unemployment insurance taxes paid by employers and collected by the state and federal government.

A special characteristic of entitlement programs is that they continue from year to year, regardless of whether Congress passes an annual funding measure. An entitlement exists until the government explicitly adopts a new law to change the benefits or otherwise alter the program. Furthermore, Congress has no direct control over how much an entitlement program will cost in any particular year. It is usually possible to estimate the cost, but the actual amount of spending depends on how many eligible persons sign up for the benefits.

Entitlement spending, therefore, continues from year to year without congressional action. The same isn't true for **discretionary spending**, which must be supported each year by an appropriation, or allotment of money through the federal budget. In a discretionary program, Congress establishes a binding annual budget for a government agency that the agency can't exceed.

HISTORICAL THINKING

4. **DRAW CONCLUSIONS** Why do you think Medicare covers only people aged 65 or older?
5. **EVALUATE** What do you think the main criticism of entitlement programs is?

Universal Health-Insurance Coverage

For a long time, the United States was the only economically advanced nation that didn't provide health-insurance coverage to all of its citizens. Democratic president Bill Clinton (1993–2001) and First Lady Hillary Clinton tried to create a universal coverage plan during President Clinton's first term. Congress failed to pass the plan.

CONGRESS ADDRESSES THE ISSUE The Affordable Care Act that passed in 2010 didn't provide for universal coverage, but it came closer than any previous program. The ACA assumed that employer-provided health insurance would continue to be a major part of the system. Medicaid would be expanded to cover people with incomes up to 133 percent of the federal poverty level. (In 2018, the poverty level for a family of four was $25,100.)

The ACA set up a new Health Insurance Marketplace consisting of state and federal health exchanges, where individuals, families, and small employers could shop for ACA-approved health-insurance plans. Most individuals would be required to obtain coverage or pay an income tax penalty. This requirement is known as the individual mandate. The ACA wouldn't allow insurance companies to deny coverage to anyone or to charge more if a person had a preexisting condition, such as cancer or heart disease, two practices that were common before the ACA.

The ACA was to be implemented over a period of several years. One immediate change was that young adults could remain on their parents' insurance until they turned 26. (Previously, they had to be full-time students or live with their parents to avoid losing coverage at the age of 19.) Also, the ACA made subsidies available right away to small employers that obtained insurance plans for their employees. The most important provisions, however, didn't take effect until January 1, 2014, when subsidies became available to help citizens with low to middle incomes purchase health insurance if they weren't covered by Medicare, Medicaid, or an employer's plan. These subsidies would be phased out for those earning more than four times the federal poverty level.

THE CONSERVATIVE REACTION In 2010, the Democrats were able to win the support of groups that had opposed universal health-care plans in the past. These included the American Medical Association, hospitals, insurance companies, and pharmaceutical firms. Nevertheless, opposition to the ACA was widespread and strong. Many states, for example, refused to take part in the Medicaid expansion linked to Obamacare. To some extent, this was a political move by Republican-dominated state governments. But these states also feared that the cost of adding substantially more people to their Medicaid rolls would overwhelm their budgets in coming years.

In the eyes of conservatives, the ACA was a big government takeover of health care and a threat to freedom. The individual mandate stirred up the greatest opposition because it pressured people to do something they might not otherwise do. But supporters of the ACA pointed out that the individual mandate was a key to the success of the health-care reform plan. The only way to hold down the cost of health insurance, they argued, was if everyone, healthy or unhealthy, bought insurance.

Critics of the individual mandate called it—and the federal government's threat to withhold all Medicaid funding from states that refused to expand coverage—unconstitutional. In 2012, a case challenging the ACA, *National Federation of Independent Business* v. *Sebelius*, reached the U.S. Supreme Court. In the Court's majority opinion, Chief Justice John Roberts exercised judicial restraint when he argued that the Court shouldn't strike down an act of Congress unless Congress lacked "constitutional authority to pass [the] act in question." The Court thus upheld the individual mandate and the ACA itself, although it did allow state governments to opt out of expanding their Medicaid program.

IMPLEMENTATION After the Supreme Court's ruling in June 2012, repeated attempts by Republicans in the House to repeal or delay the ACA failed. The House alone couldn't abolish Obamacare. Republicans would need to control both chambers of Congress and the presidency. In November 2012, however, Obama won re-election and the Democrats retained control of the Senate.

On October 1, 2013, Americans who were eligible to buy health-care insurance through a state or federal exchange had their first chance to do so. It was expected, though not required, that most of the signups would take place online. Problems arose immediately. Most of the state online exchanges performed as

National Federation of Independent Business v. *Sebelius*, 2012

Decided: June 28, 2012, 5–4

Majority: Chief Justice John Roberts wrote the opinion for the decision in favor of Sebelius.

Dissent: Associate Justices Antonin Scalia, Clarence Thomas, Samuel Alito, and Anthony Kennedy jointly wrote a dissenting opinion.

In March 2010, surrounded by fellow Democrats and guests, President Barack Obama signed the Affordable Care Act (ACA). House Speaker Nancy Pelosi (standing behind President Obama) compared the importance of the ACA to that of Social Security and Medicare. "But," she cautioned, "our fight is not over yet." A key victory in that fight came two years later, when the Supreme Court, in *National Federation of Independent Business* v. *Sebelius*, upheld the individual mandate provision of the ACA.

In March 2010, 26 states, 2 individuals, and the National Federation of Independent Business filed a lawsuit against President Obama's secretary of health and human services, Kathleen Sebelius, on the heels of Congress's passage of the Affordable Care Act (ACA). In the U.S. District Court for the Northern District of Florida, these petitioners claimed that the ACA was unconstitutional for two main reasons. The first related to the individual mandate's income tax penalty. Congress, they argued, didn't have the authority through its power to tax or through the commerce clause to require Americans to buy health insurance or pay a penalty. The petitioners also contended that Congress couldn't compel states to expand Medicaid by threatening to withhold federal Medicaid funding.

The district court decided that neither Congress's right to tax nor its right to regulate commerce justified the ACA's individual mandate. Because the individual mandate was inextricably bound up with other provisions, the court ruled that the entire ACA was invalid. But the court decided in favor of the federal government's provisions regarding Medicaid expansion.

The case reached the Supreme Court in March 2012. the ACA. It ruled that the individual mandate was constitutional under Congress's authority to collect taxes. The Court also held that Medicaid expansion was constitutional—as long as the federal government didn't withdraw Medicaid funding from states that decided against expanding.

THINK ABOUT IT Was the decision in *National Federation of Independent Business* v. *Sebelius* a complete victory for backers of the ACA? Explain expected, but a few never worked properly. Many people had to sign up offline. The federal website turned out to be almost completely nonfunctional. It wasn't fully operational until the end of the year. Obamacare's troubled rollout was a political blow to the Democrats.

By the end of the signup period in April 2014, however, 8 million Americans had obtained insurance policies through the state and federal exchanges. This was 2 million more than predicted by the Congressional Budget Office. In 2018, the number enrolled reached 11.8 million.

HISTORICAL THINKING

6. **FORM AND SUPPORT OPINIONS** Do you think conservatives had a valid point when they challenged the ACA's individual mandate? Explain your answer.
7. **ANALYZE CAUSE AND EFFECT** Why do you think many Americans signed up for Obamacare within a few months of its introduction?

Evaluation and Potential Replacements

The ACA was a complex piece of legislation, with many moving parts. Inevitably, some didn't work as well as intended. Normally, Congress would revisit such a program and make various fixes to it. That proved impossible with the ACA, because Republicans in Congress were interested only in repealing the legislation. By 2017, when President Trump took office at the head of a unified Republican government, a greater consensus had developed over the key problems with Obamacare.

CRITICISMS OF THE ACA In addition to the individual mandate, another criticism of the ACA was that policies bought through the exchanges didn't cover enough of the costs incurred by those who needed health care. Copays, the consumer's share of the cost of an office visit or medication, were too high. Deductibles, the sums a consumer had to pay before insurance kicked in, were too high as well. Also, while subsidies kept premiums—what consumers paid for the policies—reasonable for low-income persons, those with incomes just high enough to receive no subsidies found their premiums to be uncomfortably large. These criticisms were leveled by Democrats as well as Republicans, including Senate majority leader Mitch McConnell and President Trump.

"REPEAL AND REPLACE" Nearly everyone agreed that Obamacare had its issues, but repealing it altogether posed a problem for Republicans. Too many Americans had come to rely on the program. "Repeal and replace" became the Republican slogan. In 2017, the party put forth several ideas for replacement programs but didn't attempt to win Democratic support for any of them. Both chambers bypassed the normal committee process—Republican leaders drafted the bills in private.

The House was the first to report a new health-care bill. Under this legislation, low-income people, especially those who were elderly, would have had to pay premiums that were more than half of their total income. Effectively, they would be uninsurable. The bill also sought to phase out the expansion of Medicaid in states that had adopted it and, in time, cut Medicaid benefits below what they were before Obamacare was even

Republican opponents of Obamacare characterized it as a takeover of health care by big government, but their repeated repeal efforts failed to gain the necessary majorities in Congress.

adopted. According to the Congressional Budget Office (CBO), 24 million people would eventually lose their insurance. In spite of these negatives, the Republican-controlled House passed the bill by a single vote. Republicans in the Senate tried to remake the bill, but in the end, the legislation failed to pass.

In short, Republicans found Obamacare remarkably hard to kill, though they kept trying. From the beginning, Democrats had hoped that once it was actually in effect, the ACA would become popular. That didn't happen right away, but by 2017, polls showed that the majority of Americans supported the ACA. Only 17 percent of the public supported the reworked Senate bill. In December 2017, however, the Republican-led Congress made a dent in Obamacare. As part of the Tax Cuts and Jobs Act, Congress eliminated the individual mandate's tax penalty, beginning in 2019 (although some states considered establishing their own penalty). Enrollment in the ACA was expected to drop as a result.

Republican efforts and legal challenges to undermine the ACA continued through 2018 and into 2019. The people who President Trump appointed to carry out the program were opposed to its very existence. The Trump administration issued various rules that weakened some ACA programs. It reduced the federal role in administering other programs, turning more of that responsibility over to the states. It also cut back funding aimed at educating the public about the ACA and encouraging more people to enroll. These actions didn't destroy the ACA, but they made it less stable. Faced with uncertainty about whether the ACA could survive, several insurance companies withdrew from the exchanges.

In 2020, health-care policy became a hot topic among Democrats seeking their party's nomination for president. Bernie Sanders and Elizabeth Warren proposed "Medicare for All," a single-payer plan in which the federal government would cover the cost of all medically necessary health-care services for all Americans. Other candidates, including the eventual nominee, Joe Biden, took a more moderate position on health care. They focused on improving the ACA while also offering Americans a public option—that is, access to a Medicare-like program instead of private insurance.

HISTORICAL THINKING

8. **ANALYZE CAUSE AND EFFECT** What effect do you think the popularity of Obamacare had on Republicans' efforts to repeal it?
9. **IDENTIFY PROBLEMS AND SOLUTIONS** Why do you think Republicans had such a difficult time trying to come up with a replacement for the ACA?

LESSON 17.4 Energy and the Environment

Like health-care policy, energy policy is a major issue at the national level. The U.S. reliance on foreign oil has long posed diplomatic and economic problems for U.S. policymakers. Foreign producers can raise prices or cut production as it suits them. In addition, oil is a finite resource. At some point, scientists warn, it will run out—and maybe sooner than we expect. As ominous as this sounds, in recent years the issue of importing oil from other countries has shrunk in importance. What has grown is concern over environmental damage related to the production and use of fossil fuels. Energy policy and environmental policy are now intertwined concerns.

The Problem of Imported Oil

In 2017, net imports of petroleum amounted to an estimated 25 percent of total U.S. consumption. This figure represents a substantial decrease from earlier years. In 2005, for example, imports made up more than 60 percent of consumption. Still, oil imports are a potential problem largely because many of the nations that export oil aren't particularly friendly to

A Canadian Pacific Railway locomotive pulls tanker cars full of crude oil and other petroleum products across the prairie of southern Alberta. Canada supplies the United States with about 50 percent of its imported oil. The vast majority of it flows through pipelines, but about 200,000 barrels per day, or 6 percent of the total, are transported to the United States by rail.

the United States. Some, such as Iran, are outright adversaries. Other oil exporters that could pose difficulties include Iraq, Libya, Nigeria, Russia, and Venezuela. Many of America's European and Asian allies, however, depend on imports from questionable regimes.

Fortunately for the United States, the sources of imported oil are diversified, and the country isn't excessively dependent on unfriendly nations. Canada, a friendly neighbor, supplies around 50 percent of the oil imported by the United States. Historically, the United States has had a good relationship with Saudi Arabia, the second-largest supplier of oil to the United States. The brutal murder of *Washington Post* journalist Jamal Khashoggi, in the fall of 2018—apparently on the order of the Saudi regime—has strained that relationship, however.

The price of oil has seen ups and downs. It spiked to higher than $120 a barrel in the 1970s, before the trend headed downward. In 1998, the price per barrel fell below $20. At that point, the U.S. government felt little pressure to address the nation's dependence on imports. In June 2008, however, the price of oil spiked again, to higher than $160 a barrel, forcing U.S. gasoline prices above $4 per gallon.

Recent history indicates that oil prices may have stabilized. In June 2014, the price of oil, then at about $110 per barrel, began to fall. By March 2015, the price was down to nearly $50 per barrel. After bottoming out at under $40 the next year, it stabilized in the $50–$70 range. What happened? The answer is that the high prices of the preceding years persuaded the U.S. oil industry to make substantial—and successful—efforts to increase the oil supply.

By increasing supply, however, U.S. oil companies contributed to a glut of oil on world markets that limited their profits. Then, in 2020, the COVID-19 pandemic swept across the world. People stopped driving. Factories and businesses shut down. The price of oil took a drastic nosedive, one benchmark grade of crude oil falling from around $60 per barrel at the start of the year to just $18 in April. The best that oil companies could hope for was a quick return to price stability—even with lower profits—when the U.S. economy reopened.

HISTORICAL THINKING

1. **ANALYZE CAUSE AND EFFECT** How does a spike in oil prices affect the U.S. economy, and why does it have that effect?

Climate Change

The increased availability of oil may be good for consumers in the short run but not so good for the environment or long-term economy. Observations collected by federal agencies such as the National Aeronautics and Space Administration (NASA) suggest that during the last half century, average global temperatures increased by about 0.85°C (1.53°F). Climate scientists believe that this change in climate is the result of human activities, especially the release of greenhouse gases such as carbon dioxide (CO_2) into the atmosphere. The burning of oil (and other fossil fuels) is a major source of greenhouse gases. These gases form a barrier in the atmosphere that, like a greenhouse, holds in heat from the sun.

At a conference sponsored by the UN in Paris in 2015, representatives of 195 countries endorsed an agreement aimed at avoiding the most severe economic and social effects of climate change. While the United States was among the countries that signed on to the agreement, President Donald Trump pledged to withdraw from the agreement and began the formal process for doing so in November 2019.

EFFECTS OF CLIMATE CHANGE The predicted consequences of climate change vary, depending on the climate models on which they are based. As the oceans grow warmer, seawater expands and polar ice melts. These developments cause sea levels to rise, flooding many coastal areas. Rainfall patterns are expected to change, turning some areas into deserts but allowing agriculture to expand elsewhere. Habitats for both plants and animals have been lost due to these changes. Other likely effects include increases in the frequency and severity of extreme weather events.

THE CLIMATE CHANGE DEBATE Although the vast majority of active climate scientists believe that the warming climate is most likely the result of human activity, many Americans believe that observed warming is due to natural causes and may not continue. A 2019 poll, for example, revealed that 20 percent of Americans believe that global warming is not caused by human activity.

Attitudes toward climate change have become highly politicized. Some Americans on the political right believe global warming is a liberal hoax designed to clear the way for increased government control of the economy and society. At the same time, many on the political left believe that the refusal to accept the existence of climate change threatens the very future of the human race.

OBAMA AND TRUMP ON CLIMATE CHANGE In the early 2000s, political deadlock in Washington, D.C., meant that Congress would take no action on CO_2 emissions. The Obama administration therefore sought to act on its own. In 2015, the Environmental Protection Agency (EPA) issued the Clean Power

CRITICAL VIEWING Warmer ocean waters—one result of climate change—increase the heat energy available to hurricanes, making them more destructive. In September 2018, Hurricane Florence achieved sustained winds of 125 miles per hour before making landfall in the Carolinas, where it dumped up to 20 inches of rain. Before the hurricane hit, state officials ordered the evacuation of more than 1 million people. Why might seeing a satellite image like this one encourage coastal residents to obey evacuation orders?

Plan (CPP), a program to reduce CO_2 emissions from existing power plants, most of them fueled by coal. Twenty-nine states sued to stop the CPP. In 2016, the Supreme Court blocked the plan pending a Court ruling. Then Donald Trump was elected president. Immediately after taking office in January 2017, Trump halted support for the CPP, and a few months later he promised to withdraw the United States from the Paris Convention on climate change. He formally notified the UN of the withdrawal on November 4, 2019, which started a one-year process that would culminate the day after the 2020 presidential election.

THE GREEN NEW DEAL Democrats seeking the nomination for president in 2020 criticized Trump for planning to withdraw from the Paris Convention and for ignoring the warnings of climate scientists. All the leading candidates supported a proposed joint resolution of Congress called the Green New Deal, and a few of them co-sponsored it. First introduced by Representative Alexandria Ocasio-Cortez (D-NY) and Senator Edward J. Markey (D-MA), portions of the resolution call for steadily decreasing the use of fossil fuels to reduce greenhouse gas emissions. It also calls for overhauling the nation's infrastructure to focus on clean energy, including wind and solar power.

HISTORICAL THINKING

2. **MAKE CONNECTIONS** Why do you think climate scientists use the preindustrial era as a starting point when measuring the rise in global temperatures?
3. **MAKE PREDICTIONS** What business or sector of the economy do you think will be most affected by a full-fledged effort to counteract climate change? Why?

New Energy Sources

The issues of U.S. energy security and climate change raise the question of whether we can develop new sources of energy. Establishing energy security—ensuring that we have access to the energy we need—can best be achieved by relying on energy sources produced either in this country or by friendly neighbors such as Canada. A reduction in global warming may require using energy sources that don't release greenhouse gases into the atmosphere. New energy sources, however, sometimes come with their own problems.

EXPANDED SUPPLIES OF OIL AND NATURAL GAS By 2012, many Americans had begun to realize that they were entering a new era of energy expansion. U.S. oil production, which declined rapidly after 1985, began to grow again in 2009. Technological improvements, along with higher prices for petroleum, contributed to this development. For example, the costly extraction of petroleum from oil sands in Alberta, Canada, wasn't economical when prices were low. With gasoline selling for nearly $4 per gallon, however, the process became profitable.

Oil companies also set their sights on Alaska—again. Since 1977, they have been extracting oil from the region known as the North Slope, in far northern Alaska. Just to the east of this region lies the Arctic National Wildlife Refuge, a wilderness area thought to have enormous petroleum deposits. This area is federal land that has been off-limits to drilling in the past. In 2020, in spite of potential environmental consequences, the Trump administration moved ahead with plans to lease drilling rights in the refuge to oil companies.

Even more dramatic than the expansion of oil production was the increase in supplies of natural gas. Only a few years ago, experts believed that the United States would soon need to import natural gas. Because gas can't be transported by ship efficiently unless it is converted to liquefied natural gas (LNG), imports would be costly.

By 2012, however, gas producers were extracting so much natural gas that the nation was running out of facilities to store it. Instead of importing LNG, U.S. producers were planning to export it. Low natural gas prices plus new EPA air-pollution regulations made coal uncompetitive as a source of electricity. As a result, about 130 coal-based power plants were closed or scheduled for retirement, and construction of new coal-fired generators nearly came to a standstill. Coal-producing regions such as eastern Kentucky and West Virginia faced serious economic difficulties.

An unexpected consequence of the boom in natural gas production was its environmental impact. Burning natural gas does release some CO_2 into the atmosphere, but less than half as much as coal. By 2009, U.S. emissions of CO_2 were falling. They leveled

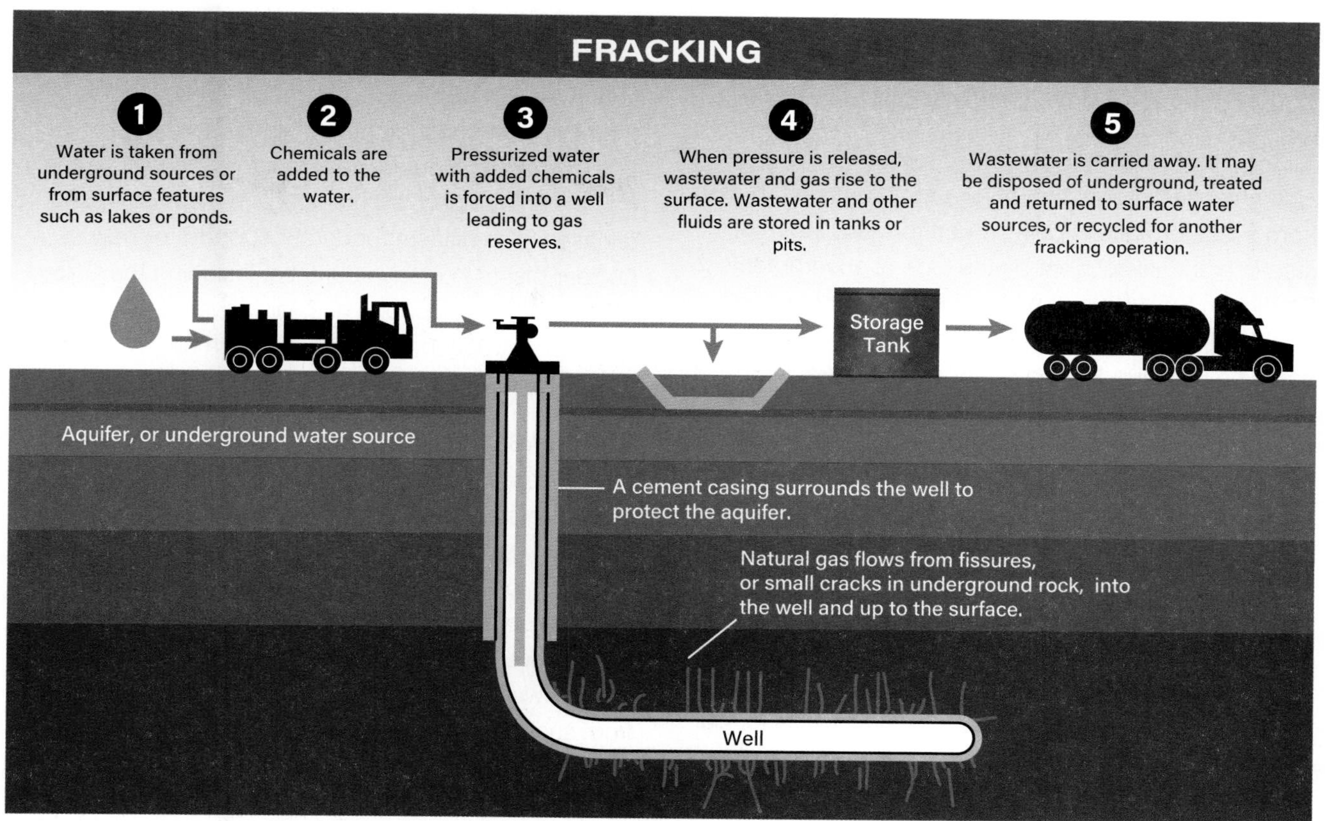
FRACKING
1
Water is taken from underground sources or from surface features such as lakes or ponds.
2
Chemicals are added to the water.
3
Pressurized water with added chemicals is forced into a well leading to gas reserves.
4
When pressure is released, wastewater and gas rise to the surface. Wastewater and other fluids are stored in tanks or pits.
5
Wastewater is carried away. It may be disposed of underground, treated and returned to surface water sources, or recycled for another fracking operation.
Storage Tank
Aquifer, or underground water source
A cement casing surrounds the well to protect the aquifer.
Natural gas flows from fissures, or small cracks in underground rock, into the well and up to the surface.
Well

off after 2012. More fuel-efficient vehicles on the road added to the reduction.

Why has it been possible for the United States to ramp up oil and natural gas production during the last several years? The answer is what some experts view as an improved (but controversial) extraction technique. Known as hydraulic fracturing, or **fracking**, it involves pumping a high-pressure mixture of water, sand, and chemicals into oil- or gas-bearing underground rock, usually shale. Fracturing the rock releases the oil or gas trapped within it. In the past, the expense of fracking limited its use. Higher prices for oil and gas, combined with improvements in the process, however, have made fracking cost-effective. New oil fields in Texas and North Dakota are based on fracking, as are natural gas fields in Pennsylvania, West Virginia, and other states.

Some Americans, including scientists, object to fracking because of its risks. One major concern is that the technology could lead to the contamination of underground water sources. By-products of fracking have been linked to asthma in people who live near fracking sites and have also been seen to cause problems for pregnant women and developing fetuses.

Another concern is that fracking causes underground shifts that lead to earthquakes. This can happen, although scientists have found that the vast majority of earthquakes near oil fields have been caused by "wastewater disposal," the standard industry practice of injecting fluid waste from oil and gas production far below groundwater or drinking water aquifers. Various state governments are developing regulations aimed at preventing these problems.

By 2014, the United States had become the number-one oil producer in the world. As you read earlier, increased supplies of petroleum had by then caused the price of oil to fall dramatically. In the past, Saudi Arabia would have cut its production in an attempt to keep prices up. In 2014, however, Saudi Arabia maintained production in the hopes of driving high-cost U.S. fracking companies out of business. The Saudi move did reduce the number of new wells developed by U.S. oil firms. Vigorous cost-cutting measures by the U.S. industry, however, meant that the United States was able to maintain oil production despite lower prices. The long-term impact of COVID-19 on the U.S. oil industry is yet to be determined. Oil production dipped with the initial lockdowns and then rebounded as the economy reopened. But analysts feared that U.S. oil producers would continue to face uncertainty until the virus was brought under control.

The increased production of oil and natural gas from shale formations owes much to many years of research and investment by the federal government. Starting in the 1970s, the U.S. Department of Energy (DOE) helped drill the first wells to extract shale gas. The DOE funded the development of fracking technologies that have increased U.S. oil and gas production. The federal government has also taken the lead in finding ways to curb the environmental risks associated with fracking. Some critics point out, however, that improved technology and production methods only perpetuate a national—and global—reliance on fossil fuels.

NUCLEAR ENERGY One energy source that doesn't contribute to global warming is nuclear power. Nuclear reactors don't release greenhouse gases. Still, owing to concerns over possible dangers and difficulties of storing spent nuclear fuel, no new nuclear power plants have been built in the United States in more than 30 years. The key obstacle to the construction of nuclear plants is cost. Nuclear power plants must compete on price with natural gas plants. Currently, nuclear energy simply can't compete. Despite the costs of construction, two new reactors that have been under construction since 2012 will be on line in Georgia starting in 2021 and 2022.

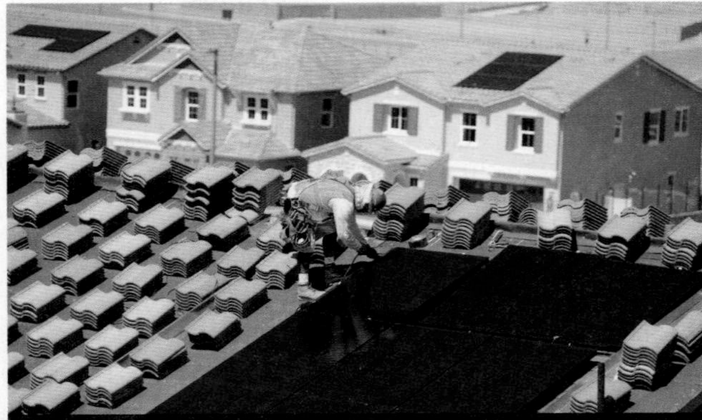

California has played a leading role in the movement toward renewable energy. In 2018, the state revised its energy policy to require nearly all newly built homes in California to have a solar-powered electrical system. Builders will meet this requirement mainly through the installation of rooftop solar panels.

Nuclear power also suffered a severe blow in 2011 as a result of a major disaster. A tsunami—a huge tidal wave set off by an earthquake—devastated the northeast coast of Japan, killing more than 20,000 people. Four nuclear reactors located on the coast were flooded, and radioactive material was released. The disaster undercut support for new nuclear plants in many countries, including the United States. In 2018, just one nuclear power plant was under construction, although a few smaller nuclear generators were in the planning stages.

RENEWABLE ENERGY Not all methods of supplying energy come with potentially hazardous by-products, such as greenhouse gases or radioactive waste. For example, hydroelectric energy, generated by water flowing through dams, is a widely used technology that employs no coal, natural gas, oil, or other fossil fuels. Solar power—energy captured from the sun's rays—and wind power are similarly clean sources of energy. Energy from such technologies is referred to as renewable energy, because it doesn't rely on extracting resources that can run out, such as fossil fuels and uranium ore.

Until recently, most existing renewable technologies, such as solar power cells, were expensive. But the cost of solar power and wind energy has been falling fast. In some locations, wind power now competes with natural gas in price. As a result, the number of solar- and wind-power installations has grown rapidly. Of course, the wind doesn't always blow, and the sun doesn't always shine, so until we see significant improvements in battery technology that can store energy generated by renewable sources, there are practical limits to how much of our electricity can be provided by these technologies.

HISTORICAL THINKING

4. **IDENTIFY MAIN IDEAS AND DETAILS** What are the key environmental advantages of solar and wind power and, to a lesser extent, natural gas?
5. **MAKE PREDICTIONS** How do you think the United States will meet its energy needs in the next 10–20 years?
6. **INTERPRET CHARTS** How might fracking contaminate the aquifer shown in the diagram?

Among the wildlife roaming the Arctic National Wildlife Refuge (ANWR) are polar bears, caribou, and musk oxen like the two shown here. The animals and landscape might be endangered if oil drilling were allowed in the refuge.

This Refuge May Be the Most Contested Land in the U.S.

by Joel K. Bourne, Jr. ***National Geographic*** **Magazine, June 2018**

The U.S. Congress has long debated how federal energy policy should apply to the 19.3-million-acre Arctic National Wildlife Refuge (ANWR) in Alaska. For thousands of years, ANWR has been a hunting ground for native Alaskans and home to a variety of animals, including polar bears and caribou. In the last few decades, its coastal plain has also been the target of oil companies eager to extract the oil lying beneath this vast wilderness landscape.

In his article "This Refuge May Be the Most Contested Land in the U.S.," Joel K. Bourne, Jr., interviews stakeholders—both for and against drilling in the refuge—and ponders the region's future.

The oil and gas industry funds 90 percent of the state budget—plus an annual dividend of over $1,000 to each Alaskan—mostly through a tax on North Slope oil flowing through the Trans-Alaska Pipeline System (TAPS). Since oil prices plummeted in 2014, the state has suffered multibillion-dollar budget deficits. More ominously, in spite of a recent uptick, the amount of oil oozing through the pipeline has fallen steadily since 1988.

On the other hand, Alaska needs its wilderness. Bourne describes the thrill of flying over a migrating herd of caribou, tens of thousands strong. The caribou are flourishing, he writes, but polar bears aren't.

The southern Beaufort Sea [polar bear] population fell 40 percent in the first decade of this century. The bears are less healthy, they're having fewer cubs, and more cubs are dying. As sea ice thins in the warming Arctic, more bears will need to den on land in winter. ANWR's coastal plain has the best denning habitat in Alaska.

In 2017, Congress passed the Tax Cuts and Jobs Act, which contained a provision opening ANWR to drilling. Experts assure Bourne that no drilling will start until completion of a thorough environmental impact study, which will take many years. By that time, Bourne writes, just a trickle of oil may be flowing from North Slope. Alaska's need for income and jobs may outweigh concerns for wildlife.

Access the full version of "This Refuge May Be the Most Contested Land in the U.S." by Joel K. Bourne, Jr., through the Resources Menu in MindTap.

THINK ABOUT IT Do you think it is a positive or a negative that an environmental impact study, requiring many years, has to be completed before drilling could begin in ANWR? Explain your answer.

CHAPTER 17

GOVERNMENT AND DOMESTIC POLICY

Review

VOCABULARY

Use each of the following vocabulary words in a sentence that shows an understanding of the term's meaning.

1. trade-off
2. business cycle
3. monetary policy
4. fiscal policy
5. Treasuries
6. patent
7. copyright
8. entrepreneurship
9. discretionary spending
10. fracking

MAIN IDEAS

Answer the following questions. Support your answer with evidence from the chapter.

11. Why is compromise a key part of making domestic policy? **LESSON 17.1**
12. What role can interest groups and the media play in getting an issue on the administration's agenda? **LESSON 17.1**
13. Why is evaluation, the final stage of domestic policymaking, important? **LESSON 17.1**
14. How are interest rates linked to the inflation rate? **LESSON 17.2**
15. What are the two fiscal policy options, and which of those options is more controversial? Explain your answer. **LESSON 17.2**
16. Why does each increase in the public debt lead to a decrease in budgeted funds available for federal programs? **LESSON 17.2**
17. Which program—Medicare, Medicaid, or the Affordable Care Act—is aimed mainly at low-income Americans? **LESSON 17.3**
18. Why was the individual mandate provision of the Affordable Care Act controversial? **LESSON 17.3**
19. Why are Americans today less concerned about imported oil than they once were? **LESSON 17.4**
20. According to climate scientists, what role does carbon dioxide (CO_2) play in climate change? **LESSON 17.4**

HISTORICAL THINKING

Answer the following questions. Support your answer with evidence from the chapter.

21. **MAKE INFERENCES** Why do you think members of Congress spend so much time and effort debating the pros and cons of a proposed public policy and gaining input from groups who might be affected by it?
22. **MAKE GENERALIZATIONS** Why do you think a high rate of unemployment is a key indicator of an economic downturn?
23. **MAKE CONNECTIONS** How is the U.S. government's federal structure reflected in the Medicaid program?
24. **CATEGORIZE** How is the goal of repealing and replacing the Affordable Care Act a prime example of the partisan political divide?
25. **ANALYZE CAUSE AND EFFECT** What public policy do you think nearly all climate scientists would support related to the burning of fossil fuels?

INTERPRET MAPS

Study the map. Then answer the questions.

26. This map shows the areas covered by each of the 12 districts of the Federal Reserve System. Explain why the Federal Reserve System is a centralized bank even though it consists of 12 districts.

27. At the time the 12 districts were created by Congress in 1913, the districts were roughly equal in population. More than 100 years later, the San Francisco district is by far the largest, with roughly 7 times the population of the least populous district, Minneapolis. But the law that created the bank did not provide for redistricting. Do you think the varying populations of the Fed regions affect the ability of the bank to do its job? Why or why not?

Federal Reserve System

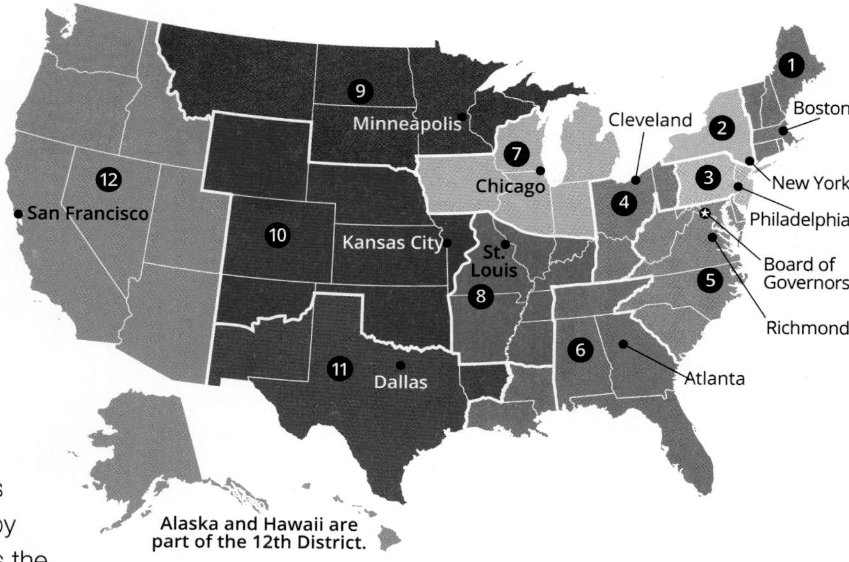

ANALYZE SOURCES

House speaker Nancy Pelosi played a key role in getting Congress to pass the Affordable Care Act (ACA). Speaking to a legislative conference on March 9, 2010, two weeks before the ACA became law, she described the bill:

> Imagine an economy where people could follow their aspirations, where they could be entrepreneurial, where they could take risks professionally because personally their family's health-care needs are being met. Where they could be self-employed or start a business, not be job-locked in a job because they have health care there, and if they went out on their own it would be unaffordable to them, but especially true, if someone has a child with a pre-existing condition. So when we pass our bill, never again will people be denied coverage because they have a pre-existing condition.

28. Based on this statement, what do you think Pelosi believed to be the most important benefit of the ACA? Explain your answer.

CONNECT TO YOUR LIFE

29. **ARGUMENT** What direction do you think U.S. energy policy should take in the future, and how might this affect you or your state? Write a blog post arguing in support of an energy policy that you believe would make the most sense for people of your state.

TIPS

- Review the lesson on energy and the environment and take notes on the pros and cons of each source of energy.
- Research further to find out more about how energy policy can affect jobs, the cost of electricity, forms of transportation, and other aspects of American life, and life in your state.
- Write a clear thesis statement to respond to the essay prompt.
- Conclude your blog with a restatement of your thesis and a brief summary of how you supported it.

CHAPTER 18

Government and Foreign Policy

LESSONS

18.1 Who Makes Foreign Policy?

18.2 A Short History of American Foreign Policy

18.3 Global Challenges

National Geographic Magazine:
A Thawing Arctic Is Heating Up a New Cold War

18.4 Diplomacy and International Economics

CRITICAL VIEWING After hurricanes devastated parts of Haiti in 2008, the international community organized various relief efforts to provide much-needed supplies to the island nation's residents. U.S. contributions to the humanitarian mission were coordinated by the United States Agency for International Development (USAID), which promotes social and economic development in foreign countries. Why do you think the U.S. federal government sent the supplies shown here?

LESSON

18.1 Who Makes Foreign Policy?

You might think of foreign policy as something that's, well, foreign to you. But foreign policy is not always so remote. It's not only world leaders shaking hands or the president giving a speech at the United Nations. If you travel to another country—even one that borders the United States, such as Canada or Mexico—your ability to enter that country is determined by agreements made by the foreign policy teams of the United States and the other country. You can use a smartphone made in another country because of trade agreements. Whether Americans are deployed to other countries and whether U.S. firms can open factories or offices in other countries are also affected by foreign policy decisions.

The Importance of Foreign Policy

As you know, domestic policy comes from decisions the United States government makes about the economy, education, health care, crime, and similar issues. The federal, state, and local governments are all involved in making these policies. Foreign policy, in contrast, is strictly a federal concern. In general, **foreign policy** is a systematic plan that guides a country's attitudes and actions toward other countries and international issues. It includes all of the ways the country interacts economically, diplomatically, and militarily with other countries. Of course, the way these interactions take place is always changing, as new leaders take office and situations in other countries shift and change.

Since the founding of the United States, American foreign policy has been shaped by two principles. The first principle is **moral idealism**, the belief that the goal of foreign policy is to promote the ideals and values of the United States. Moral idealists think nations should relate to each other as part of a rule-based community. Policy decisions based on moral idealism attempt to advance ideals such as freedom, justice, and equal rights.

The second, contrasting principle of foreign policy is **political realism**, the belief that nations are inevitably self-centered. In this view, foreign governments act to assert and protect their interests. Therefore, foreign policy must always be crafted with an eye to protecting the national security and interests of the United States—regardless of moral arguments. At some points in American history, this view has dominated foreign policy. At other times, moral idealism has prevailed. Generally, however, U.S. foreign policy has been a mixture of both.

Foreign policy requires fostering and maintaining careful relationships with other countries, especially those who share common global policy interests. In 2006, U.S. Secretary of State Condoleezza Rice (right) met with German Chancellor Angela Merkel to discuss the approach their two allied countries would take to address Iran's nuclear program.

HISTORICAL THINKING

1. **MAKE GENERALIZATIONS** How is it possible for U.S. foreign policy to reflect both moral idealism and political realism?
2. **MAKE PREDICTIONS** Identify a time in American history when a foreign policy of political realism may have dominated.

The President's Role

The Framers of the Constitution envisioned foreign policy as the shared responsibility of the executive and the legislative branches. The president and Congress are to work together to develop American foreign policy. How this cooperation would actually work was not spelled out in detail, however. Over time, through history and tradition, the president has become the chief decision-maker regarding foreign policy. The president's role as commander in chief, the official who oversees the military and guides the armed forces, provides much of the justification for this power. As you have read, presidents have interpreted this role broadly, at times sending American troops, ships, and weapons to trouble spots around the world even without a congressional declaration of war. As commander in chief, the president also has ultimate control over the use of nuclear weapons.

President John F. Kennedy spoke for American values of freedom and democracy when he traveled to West Berlin in June, 1963. The city, an island of democracy in what was then Soviet-controlled East Berlin, had been recently isolated by the construction of the Berlin Wall. Kennedy delivered a speech, thrilling about 400,000 listeners by proclaiming "Ich bin ein Berliner!" ("I am a Berliner!").

Of course, foreign policy is much more than initiating and carrying out military action. In fact, much of foreign policy involves negotiating with leaders of other countries—another area in which the president is the lead actor. The Constitution authorizes the president to make treaties, though they must be approved by two-thirds of the Senate. In addition, the president is empowered to form executive agreements, which are pacts between the president and the heads of other nations. These agreements do not require Senate approval.

Finally, the president influences foreign policymaking as head of state. As the symbolic head of our government, the president represents the United States to the rest of the world. When a serious foreign policy issue or international question arises, the nation expects the president to stand for the country's interests and values.

DEPARTMENT OF STATE The president is far from alone in making foreign policy decisions. Many cabinet members are concerned with international issues and oversee staff that carries out research into them. As the role of the United States as a world power has grown over the past century and as economic factors have become increasingly important, even departments like Agriculture, Commerce, and Energy are involved in foreign policy decisions. But the secretary of state and the secretary of defense focus on foreign policy and national security on a full-time basis.

The State Department is the cabinet department most directly involved in foreign policy. The department is responsible for diplomatic relations with the nearly 200 independent nations around the globe, as well as with the United Nations and other international agencies, such as the Organization of American States. In addition to the secretary of state, State Department

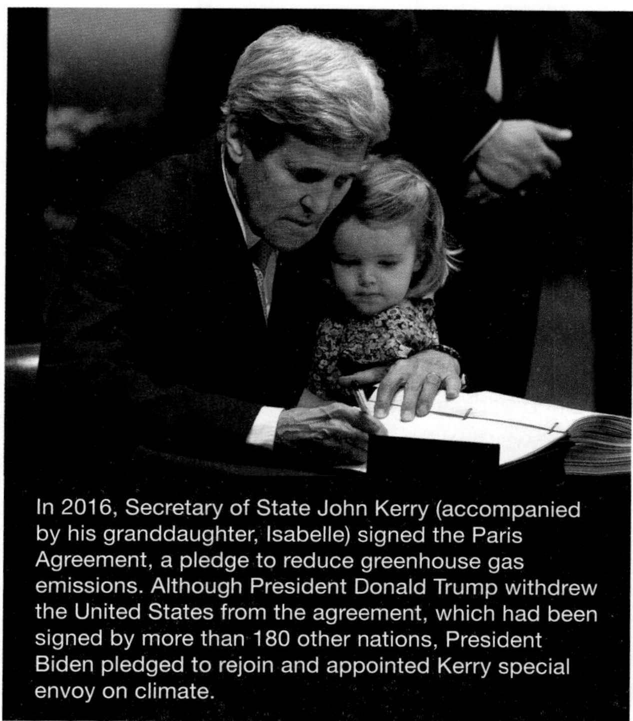
In 2016, Secretary of State John Kerry (accompanied by his granddaughter, Isabelle) signed the Paris Agreement, a pledge to reduce greenhouse gas emissions. Although President Donald Trump withdrew the United States from the agreement, which had been signed by more than 180 other nations, President Biden pledged to rejoin and appointed Kerry special envoy on climate.

officials include ambassadors who represent the United States to the governments of other countries. As the head of the State Department, the secretary of state has traditionally had significant responsibilities in foreign policymaking, and many presidents have relied heavily on the advice of their secretaries of state. In the Obama administration, secretaries of state Hillary Clinton and John Kerry played leading roles in foreign policy issues.

Since the end of World War II, however, many presidents have sought guidance in foreign policy from the national security advisor. You'll read more about this position later in this lesson. Under President Donald Trump, the State Department initially receded into the background, but Trump's second secretary of state, Mike Pompeo, held a more prominent role.

DEPARTMENT OF DEFENSE The president also seeks advice in matters of foreign policy from the Department of Defense, particularly the secretary of defense and the Joint Chiefs of Staff. The Department of Defense establishes and carries out defense policy and protects U.S. national security. The secretary of defense advises the president on all aspects of U.S. military and defense policy, supervises all the military activities of the U.S. government, and works to see that the decisions of the president as commander in chief are carried out.

The secretary of defense is also the president's liaison with all the branches of the military. As such, the secretary works closely with U.S. military leaders, especially the Joint Chiefs of Staff (JCS). The JCS includes the chair and vice chair of the JCS; the military service chiefs of the Army, Navy, Air Force, and Marines; and the chief of the National Guard. All are appointed by the president and confirmed by the Senate. The joint chiefs serve as the key military advisors to the president, the secretary of defense, and the National Security Council. They are responsible for preparing strategic plans, recommending military actions, and handing down the president's orders to the nation's military units. They also propose military budgets, new weapons systems, and military regulations. Their recommendations are considered in many major foreign policy decisions.

HISTORICAL THINKING

3. **DRAW CONCLUSIONS** Why do you think the issue of presidential candidates' military service often comes up in presidential campaigns, even though many candidates with no military background have been elected?
4. **FORM AND SUPPORT OPINIONS** In what kind of situation might the secretary of state and secretary of defense make different recommendations to the president?

Influence of Other Agencies and Congress

Certain bodies outside the Cabinet also have important roles in foreign policy. Key among these are the National Security Council and the Central Intelligence Agency. Additionally, Congress is involved in examining how—and when—foreign policy decisions are made, and in exerting indirect influence over some decisions.

THE NATIONAL SECURITY COUNCIL In 1947, the National Security Act of 1947 was enacted to reorganize the many federal bodies involved in foreign and military policy. As part of this restructuring, the

National Security Council (NSC) was established. The formal members of the NSC include the president, the vice president, the secretary of state, and the secretary of defense. Meetings are often attended by the chair of the Joint Chiefs of Staff, the director of the Central Intelligence Agency, and representatives from other departments. The national security advisor, who is a member of the president's White House staff, is the director of the NSC. The advisor informs the president, coordinates advice and information on foreign policy, and serves as a liaison with other officials.

The NSC and its members can be as important and powerful as the president wants them to be. Some presidents have made frequent use of the NSC, whereas others have convened it infrequently. Similarly, the importance of the role played by the national security advisor in shaping foreign policy can vary significantly, depending on the administration and the advisor's identity and relationship with the president. The national security advisor does not have to be confirmed by the Senate.

THE CENTRAL INTELLIGENCE AGENCY Also established by the National Security Act of 1947, the Central Intelligence Agency (CIA) was created to coordinate non-military American intelligence activities abroad. (The Defense Department has its own intelligence-gathering unit, the Defense Intelligence Agency.) The CIA provides the president and the president's advisors with up-to-date information about the political, military, and economic activities of foreign governments. The CIA gathers much of its intelligence from overt, or public, sources, such as foreign radio broadcasts and newspapers, people who travel abroad, the internet, and satellite photographs. Other information is gathered from covert, or undercover, activities, such as secret CIA investigations into the economic or political affairs of other nations. Covert operations may involve secretly supplying weapons to a rebel force fighting an unfriendly government or seizing suspected terrorists and holding them for questioning.

The CIA has tended to operate autonomously, and the details of its work, methods, and operating funds have been kept confidential, giving it a legendary mystique. But after a review of how intelligence groups communicated—and failed to communicate—before the terrorist attacks of September 11, 2001, Congress passed legislation in 2004 that made the CIA report to a new official, the national intelligence director. This individual is responsible for ensuring collaboration among all the agencies of the federal government that gather and analyze intelligence.

AUTHORITY OF CONGRESS Although the executive branch takes the lead in foreign policy matters, Congress also has some power in this area. As explained earlier, Congress alone has the power to declare war, and the 1973 War Powers Resolution limits the president's use of troops in military action without congressional approval. But presidents have often interpreted the resolution much more loosely than Congress intended. Additionally, Congress has the power to appropriate funds to build new weapons systems, equip the U.S. armed forces, and provide foreign aid. In addition, the Senate can check the power of the president with its power to approve or reject treaties and the appointment of ambassadors.

A few congressional committees are directly concerned with foreign affairs. The most important committees in the House are the Armed Services Committee and the Foreign Affairs Committee. In the Senate, the Committee on Armed Services and the Committee on Foreign Relations are most concerned with foreign policy. Other congressional committees deal with matters that indirectly influence foreign policy, such as oil, agriculture, and imports. These committees have oversight authority that empowers them to review the foreign policy actions of the executive branch. They also are the primary congressional vehicle for researching foreign policy issues and writing legislation that can affect the direction and shape of foreign policy.

HISTORICAL THINKING

5. **FORM AND SUPPORT OPINIONS** Considering its membership, is the National Security Council redundant? Explain your reasoning.

6. **MAKE INFERENCES** The position of national intelligence director has been described as one of the most difficult positions in national government. Why do you think this is?

LESSON 18.2 A Short History of American Foreign Policy

Over the years, the United States has attempted to preserve its national security, or its independence and safety, in many different ways. This variety of strategies is the natural result of a system in which a number of groups are involved in making foreign policy for a country with a changing position in a changing world. Political parties, a vocal voting public, interest groups, Congress, and the president and relevant agencies of the executive branch—all of these entities influence foreign policy, as they do domestic policy. Over time, millions of Americans have also played a vital role in foreign policy. They have volunteered or been drafted to carry out aspects of that foreign policy through service in the armed forces.

Isolationism

For a long time after the founding of the United States, the country followed a policy of **isolationism**, avoiding involvement in international affairs. The nation's founders and early presidents believed this approach was the best way to protect American interests. Not strong enough to influence developments in other parts of the world, the United States generally attempted to avoid conflicts and political engagements elsewhere during the 1700s and 1800s. In 1823, President James Monroe made the foreign policy of the United States explicit when he issued what became known as the **Monroe Doctrine**. He said that the United States would not tolerate foreign intervention in the Western Hemisphere, but it would also stay out of European affairs. This policy remained in place for several decades.

HISTORICAL THINKING

1. **FORM AND SUPPORT OPINIONS** How do you think European leaders initially reacted to the Monroe Doctrine?

Interventionism and the World Wars

At the end of the 19th century, isolationism gradually gave way to **interventionism**, or a policy of direct involvement in foreign affairs. The first major step in this direction occurred when the United States intervened in Cuba's war for independence from Spain in 1898. The government's decision to enter the Spanish-American War stemmed from American economic interests on the island and sympathy for Cubans who were suffering and dying due to lack of food, medical care, or shelter. The United States won the war, which lasted only a few months, and Spain ceded, or yielded, control of several possessions, including Puerto Rico, and its Pacific holdings of Guam and the Philippines, to the United States. The United States emerged from the war with a colonial empire and was acknowledged as a world power. That empire expanded in 1900, after American business leaders with land in Hawaii convinced President William McKinley and Congress to annex those islands. Initially a U.S. territory, Hawaii would become a state in 1959.

The growth of the United States as an industrial economy solidified its position internationally. In the early 1900s, President Theodore Roosevelt proposed that the United States could intervene in Latin American countries when it was necessary to guarantee political or economic stability. In 1903, his administration helped Panamanians achieve independence from Gran Colombia, which included Panama as well as present-day Colombia, Venezuela, and Ecuador. The United States quickly recognized Panama as independent, negotiated with the new government to gain control of a strip of land across the Panamanian isthmus, and built the Panama Canal. President Roosevelt became the first president to leave the country while in office when he visited Panama to observe construction of the canal in 1906. This waterway drastically cut the shipping time between the Atlantic and Pacific oceans because it was no longer

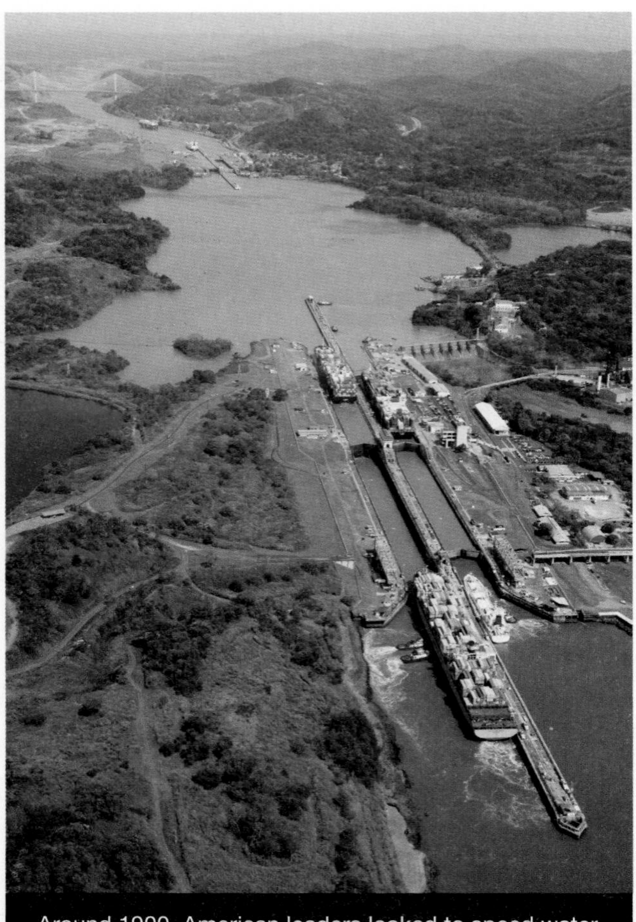

Around 1900, American leaders looked to speed water transport between the Atlantic and Pacific oceans both for commercial and military reasons. The result was construction of the Panama Canal, completed in 1914. The 40-mile-long canal cut about 8,000 nautical miles of travel for ships sailing between the east and west coasts of the United States.

necessary for ships to sail around South America. The canal remained under American control until 1999, when Panama took possession.

When World War I broke out in Europe in 1914, President Woodrow Wilson initially proclaimed a policy of **neutrality**, or not taking sides in a conflict. After German submarines sank several American merchant ships carrying goods to Britain, Wilson asked Congress to declare war on Germany. Wilson saw U.S. entry into the war in 1917 as a way to "make the world safe for democracy," basing his policy on moral idealism.

At the peace conference that ended World War I in 1918, President Wilson supported formation of a League of Nations that would have mechanisms to end international conflicts without war. But the Senate voted not to join the League of Nations, returning the United States to a policy of isolationism following the war. In the 1920s, the nation focused on a process of **disarmament**, which is reducing a nation's supply of weapons or the size of its armed forces. This policy focused on reducing the size of the navy, as the country negotiated with four other nations to reduce the number of war ships each could possess.

The policy of isolationism ended a little over 20 years later, when Japan attacked the U.S. Navy base at Pearl Harbor, Hawaii, in 1941. Now involved in World War II, the United States joined the Allied Forces, consisting of Australia, Britain, Canada, China, France, and the Soviet Union against the Axis nations of Germany, Italy, and Japan. When the Allies finally gained victory in 1945, the United States and the Soviet Union emerged as the two major world powers.

HISTORICAL THINKING

2. **IDENTIFY MAIN IDEAS AND DETAILS** What was the driving force behind the U.S. departure from isolationism in the Spanish-American War?
3. **SYNTHESIZE** How might the international community have regarded the United States differently at the beginning of World War II than at the beginning of World War I?

The Cold War

Relations between the Soviet Union and the United States deteriorated quickly following the end of World War II. The communist ideology of the Soviet Union was seen as a menace to America's political and economic systems, especially as eastern European nations such as Bulgaria, Czechoslovakia, East Germany, Hungary, Poland, and Romania fell under Soviet domination. American leaders saw the spread of what was called the Soviet bloc as a threat to both democracy and world peace.

CONTAINMENT AND THE MARSHALL PLAN

American apprehension over the spread of communism increased in 1947, when it appeared that local Communist parties, backed by the Soviets, would take over Greece and Turkey. President Harry Truman convinced Congress to appropriate $400 million ($4.6 billion in 2018 dollars) in aid for those countries to stem the spread of communism. The president also proclaimed what became known as the **Truman Doctrine**. It was, Truman said, "the policy of the United States to support free peoples who are resisting attempted subjugation by armed minorities or by outside pressures."

The Truman administration took further steps to prevent the spread of communism. In 1948, Congress passed the Economic Cooperation Act, dubbed the **Marshall Plan** after Secretary of State George Marshall, who announced it. The Marshall Plan instituted a policy of giving economic aid to war-torn Europe to prevent the countries from turning to communism in an effort to improve their economies. By 1952, the nations of Western Europe, with U.S. help, had largely recovered and were again prospering.

The Truman Doctrine and the Marshall Plan marked the beginning of a policy of **containment**, an effort to contain and prevent the spread of communism by offering U.S. military and economic aid to threatened nations. To put teeth in this policy, the United States formed mutual defense alliances with other nations. In 1949, the United States, Canada, and 10 European nations formed a military alliance—the North Atlantic Treaty Organization (NATO). Member countries agreed that an attack on any one member would be considered an attack against all members.

CRITICAL VIEWING By helping European countries rebuild from the destruction caused by World War II, the Marshall Plan provided economic and political assistance that blunted the appeal of communist parties. Over four years, U.S. economic aid was funneled to almost 20 countries, helping boost industrial production, agriculture, and urban reconstruction. Which type of project is shown in the photograph?

THE COLD WAR BEGINS In 1949, communism expanded again. Communist leader Mao Zedong won a civil war in China, and the Communists took control of that vast nation. By 1949, the United States found itself leader of a bloc of democratic nations in North America, Europe, and the Pacific. The constant tensions between the Soviet Union and the United States became known as the **Cold War**. This war of competing ideologies and political influence lasted from the late 1940s to 1991.

Although the Cold War was mainly a war of words and belief systems, actual military conflicts erupted at times. In 1950, the Communist government of North Korea invaded South Korea, a U.S. ally. The United States and United Nations allies fought on the side of South Korea, while the Soviet Union and China aided North Korea. Fighting ended in 1953 after more than 2 million deaths, including more than 35,000 Americans, with Korea still divided.

In the 1960s, the United States sent troops to another divided Asian nation, Vietnam, in hopes of stopping the spread of communism there. Over nine years, more than 58,000 American soldiers died in that effort, with estimates of total casualties on both sides ranging from 1.3 million to nearly 4 million. Ultimately, North Vietnam defeated South Vietnam.

As Cold War anxiety grew, both the United States and the Soviet Union competed to build more and more powerful weapons, particularly nuclear weapons. This arms race reflected a U.S. policy of **deterrence**, or an effort to make the United States and its allies so strong militarily that other countries would be discouraged from attacking. Out of deterrence came the theory of what was known as mutually assured destruction, or MAD. In this theory, if the two superpowers were capable of destroying each other with nuclear weapons, neither nation would take a chance on war.

The theory was tested in 1962. That year, the United States learned that the Soviet Union had placed nuclear weapons in the territory of its ally, Cuba, 90 miles from Florida. The result was the Cuban missile crisis, a tense confrontation that raised the specter of nuclear war. A U.S. naval blockade of Cuba convinced the Soviet Union to remove the missiles. The United States also agreed to remove some of its missiles from Turkey, near the Soviet border.

A SHIFT TO DÉTENTE In 1969, Cold War tensions abated somewhat when the United States and the Soviet Union began negotiations on a treaty to limit nuclear weapons. The talks included both offensive missiles and antiballistic missiles (ABMs)—that is, missiles meant to shoot down offensive missiles. In 1972, both sides signed the first Strategic Arms Limitation Treaty (SALT I) that placed limits on both types of missiles. This historic event marked the beginning of a period of **détente**, French for "relaxation of tensions," which was a policy of improved relations with the Soviet Union.

In 1983, President Ronald Reagan proposed a space-based missile defense system called the strategic defense initiative (SDI), which was also referred to as Star Wars by detractors. Fears of the high cost of trying to compete in a new arms race prompted Soviet leader Mikhail Gorbachev to agree to new talks on arms limitations. Those talks resulted in a new arms control treaty signed in 1991.

THE END OF THE COLD WAR Meanwhile, the communist world was crumbling. The Soviet economy could not meet the needs of its citizens for basic goods like food and clothing, and many Soviet people were pushing for more freedom. Gorbachev launched an effort to democratize the Soviet political system and decentralize the economy. These reforms quickly spread through eastern Europe. Popular nonviolent uprisings led to the overthrow in 1989 of communist rule in Poland, Hungary, East Germany, Czechoslovakia, Bulgaria, and Romania. The following year, East Germany and West Germany—an ally of the United States—were reunited.

In August 1991, a number of disgruntled Communist Party leaders who wanted to reverse Gorbachev's reforms briefly seized control of the Soviet government. Russian citizens rose up in defiance. The attempted coup collapsed after three days, and the Communist Party in the Soviet Union lost almost all of its power. The 15 republics constituting the Soviet Union—including the Russian republic—declared their independence in the months that followed. By the end of the year, the Soviet Union no longer existed.

During the 1990s, Russia posed little or no threat to world peace. But Vladimir Putin, who served at different times as either president or prime minister of Russia from 1999 to the present, has pursued a more aggressive foreign policy. Beginning in 2011, Russia provided support, including Russian troops, to Syrian leader Bashar al-Assad, who used brutal tactics to defeat pro-democracy rebels and other civilians. In 2015, Russia seized the region of Crimea from its neighbor Ukraine. In addition, Russia has been accused of using social media to interfere in elections in other countries, including the 2016 U.S. presidential election and the 2018 midterms.

Under President Donald Trump, U.S. policy toward Russia sent mixed signals. The president came into office hoping to craft better relations with Russia, but that country's apparent interference with the 2016 election precluded that. Strong majorities in both houses of Congress—both under the control of Trump's Republican Party—insisted on new sanctions on Russia to punish it for the interference. Trump signed the bill reluctantly and was unwilling to publicly chastise Putin for the election meddling. The mixed signals continued. On the one hand, the Trump administration provided

The fall of communism in many eastern European countries was generally peaceful, especially in Berlin. After the fall of East Germany's communist government, the new leaders opened the Berlin Wall on November 9, 1989, removing the symbol of the east–west division and prompting celebrations throughout the city.

Ukraine with more weapons to defend itself from Russia, and it imposed new rounds of sanctions on Russia for "blatant disregard of international norms . . . [and] attempts to interfere in the 2016 U.S. election." On the other hand, the president came under criticism for a lackluster response to continued Russian aggression in Crimea. These positions worried American allies, as did Trump's frequent criticisms of NATO.

HISTORICAL THINKING

4. **ANALYZE CAUSE AND EFFECT** Explain the connection between the enactment of the Marshall Plan and the U.S. policy toward communism.
5. **MAKE CONNECTIONS** What does the move to détente tell you about the effectiveness of the theory of mutually assured destruction?

Post–Cold War Foreign Policy

With the fall of the Soviet Union, American policymakers had to rethink foreign policy. During the Cold War, the United States had acted as defender and protector of what it termed the free world—countries with democratic governments and market economies. With that conflict ended, policymakers struggled to identify the role of the United States in international conflicts. During the 1990s, the question was answered on a case-by-case basis. Troops were sent on peacekeeping missions in response to civil or ethnic conflicts in Bosnia and Rwanda and to provide humanitarian aid, such as in a famine that ravaged Sudan. Yet no overriding framework drove U.S. foreign policy until the terrorist attacks of September 11, 2001. As you will read, the primary goal of foreign policy since then has been to prevent future terrorist attacks against Americans.

HISTORICAL THINKING

6. **FORM AND SUPPORT OPINIONS** As the world's sole superpower, does the United States have a responsibility to provide humanitarian aid whenever possible to the rest of the world? Explain your opinion.

LESSON 18.3 Global Challenges

Your generation is unique for many reasons, and one of those reasons has to do with the global challenges that the United States has faced in your lifetimes. Indeed, for your entire life, the United States has been involved in fighting what is called the war on terrorism. This war has been waged both domestically and internationally. You may know people who have served in Afghanistan, Iraq, Syria, or other regions of the world. For many Americans, the war on terror has reshaped expectations about safety and surveillance, and the degree to which the United States should seek to assert its values around the world. Your generation is unique in another respect. It has been marked by a once-in-a-century event, the COVID-19 pandemic. For many, that event closed schools and isolated people from friends. Ironically, those are experiences you had in common with people your age around the world.

The Problem of Terrorism

The main foreign policy problems that confront the United States can be sorted into two categories: those that can be dealt with primarily through diplomacy and those that are handled with the use of force. When a problem requiring the use of force takes place in the United States itself, it is often handled by U.S. law enforcement agencies such as the FBI. When the need for force arises in a foreign country, that means a deployment of the U.S. armed forces.

A major foreign problem that has troubled the United States—and other countries around the world—for decades is how to control **terrorism**, or the use of planned violence, often against civilians, to achieve political goals. For the United States, terrorism became a central security issue on September 11, 2001, when the most devastating terrorist attack in U.S. history was carried out. The attackers were extremists who employed a militant interpretation of Islam to justify acts of violence. Four groups of radicals hijacked airliners that morning. Three teams used them as missiles to crash into the two World Trade Center towers in New York City and the Pentagon building—home of the Department of Defense—near Washington, D.C. A fourth plane crashed in a Pennsylvania field after passengers fought the hijackers and diverted the aircraft from another Washington, D.C., target. In all, almost 3,000 civilians were killed that day.

The September 11 attacks were not the last terrorist assault on the United States—nor do they represent the only kind of terrorist action. Foreign policy and national security experts try to understand the root causes of terrorism and the tactics of terrorists so they can stop or apprehend terrorists before they carry out their attacks. They identify three types of terrorism: nationalist terrorism, domestic terrorism, and terrorism orchestrated by foreign networks.

Nationalist terrorism consists of acts committed by extremists who are determined to obtain freedom from a country or government that they see as an oppressor. For example, Palestinian extremists have carried out numerous suicide bombings and other attacks against Israel. Nationalist terrorism has also been used by extremists involved in separatist movements in Ireland and Spain. For example, a group known as ETA, an abbreviation for words that mean Basque Homeland and Freedom, used terrorist attacks in an unsuccessful effort to win independence for the Basque region of Spain. ETA operatives carried out a series of bombings, kidnappings, and assassinations that led to the deaths of more than 800 people over a period of 50 years. ETA disbanded in 2018 after issuing an apology to their victims and their families.

Domestic terrorism is any act of terror committed within a country by citizens of that country. This type of terrorism has a long history, including in the

On September 11, 2001, terrorists hijacked four commercial jets, crashing two of them into the twin towers of Manhattan's World Trade Center. The buildings collapsed within two hours, leaving a pile of rubble and approximately 2,750 people dead. This vast number of casualties included more than 400 police officers and fire fighters who had rushed to the scene.

United States. It was widely used to prevent African Americans from voting from the late 19th century until the 1960s and less extensively used by a small number of antiwar radicals during the Vietnam War era. In the 1990s, domestic terrorism by right-wing extremists became an issue. The bombing of a federal office building in 1995 in Oklahoma City, which killed 168 people, was the act of American right-wing extremists who claimed to fear an oppressive federal government. Incidents of right-wing domestic terrorism have been on the rise for a decade or longer. Members of the so-called alt-right have committed dozens of shootings, bombings, and other forms of attack motivated by racist, anti-Muslim, antigovernment, and other right-wing ideologies. In October 2018, for example, a man shouting anti-Semitic slurs opened fire in a Pittsburgh synagogue during a worship service and killed 11 people.

Since September 11, 2001, many Americans have worried about attacks by domestic Islamists who have been radicalized through the internet. These types of attacks constitute about 25 percent of all acts of terrorism in the United States. While these individuals may communicate with foreign terrorist groups, they are not controlled by those groups. They carry out attacks independently. This was the case with the two brothers who set off bombs at the Boston Marathon in 2013. Three people died in this incident, and many more suffered serious wounds. The 2015 terrorist attack in San Bernardino, California, that killed 14 people was another example, as was the 2016 attack that killed 49 people and injured 53 in an Orlando, Florida, nightclub popular among members of the LGBTQ community.

The third type of terrorism that causes concern for many Americans is exemplified by the work of foreign terrorist networks such as al Qaeda, led by Saudi dissident Osama bin Laden until his death in 2011. Throughout the 1990s, al Qaeda had training camps in the mountains of Afghanistan, which was ruled by an ultraconservative Islamic faction known as the Taliban. The U.S. government determined that al Qaeda was responsible for terrorist attacks on two U.S. embassies in Africa in 1998. Additionally, al Qaeda was behind the bombing of the U.S.S. *Cole* in 2000 as it prepared to enter a harbor on the coast of Yemen for refueling. In 1998, President Bill Clinton ordered the bombing of al Qaeda training camps in

Afghanistan in retaliation for the embassy bombings, but with little effect. Al Qaeda cells continued to operate largely unimpeded until the terrorist attacks of September 11. Al Qaeda became a target of the U.S. government soon after those attacks.

HISTORICAL THINKING

1. **CATEGORIZE** Give an example of an act of domestic terrorism in the United States and of an act of foreign terrorism against the United States.
2. **MAKE GENERALIZATIONS** Identify two reasons why terrorism has been so difficult for U.S. government officials to stop.

The U.S. Response to Terrorism in Afghanistan and Iraq

The U.S. government undertook retaliatory action soon after the attacks of September 11, 2001. Within a week, Congress passed a joint resolution authorizing President George W. Bush to use "necessary and appropriate force" against nations, organizations, and individuals that the president determined had "planned, authorized, committed, or aided the terrorist attacks." By the next month, supported by a coalition of other countries, the U.S. military attacked al Qaeda camps in Afghanistan as well as the forces of the Taliban regime that harbored them.

Once the Taliban had been ousted, the United States helped establish a new government in Afghanistan that did not support terrorism. Instead of continuing the hunt for al Qaeda members in Afghanistan, however, the Bush administration turned its attention west, to Iraq. Increasingly, it viewed Iraq as a major threat to U.S. security, citing the country's potential for developing nuclear weapons.

A SHIFT TO IRAQ The roots of the Bush administration's concentration on Iraq lay in an earlier conflict. In 1990, Saddam Hussein, Iraq's dictator, had seized Kuwait, a small neighboring country. President George H.W. Bush (George W. Bush's father) organized an international coalition to free Kuwait, an effort that became known as the Persian Gulf War, or simply the Gulf War. Once Iraqi forces were expelled from Kuwait, the coalition forces halted operations, leaving Hussein still in control of Iraq.

The cease-fire that ended that first Gulf War required Iraq to agree to inspections for chemical, biological, and nuclear weapons—collectively called weapons of mass destruction. In 1998, however, Hussein ceased to cooperate with these inspections. The George W. Bush administration believed that Hussein was developing an atomic bomb and that the Iraqi regime was in some way responsible for the 9/11 terrorist attacks, beliefs later shown to be incorrect. Bush sought United Nations support for the use of military force against Iraq, but China, France, and Russia blocked the move.

Undeterred, Bush told Hussein to leave Iraq or face war. Hussein was defiant. On March 19, 2003, President Bush announced that military operations against Iraq had begun. As U.S. and British-led forces moved into the country with massive force,

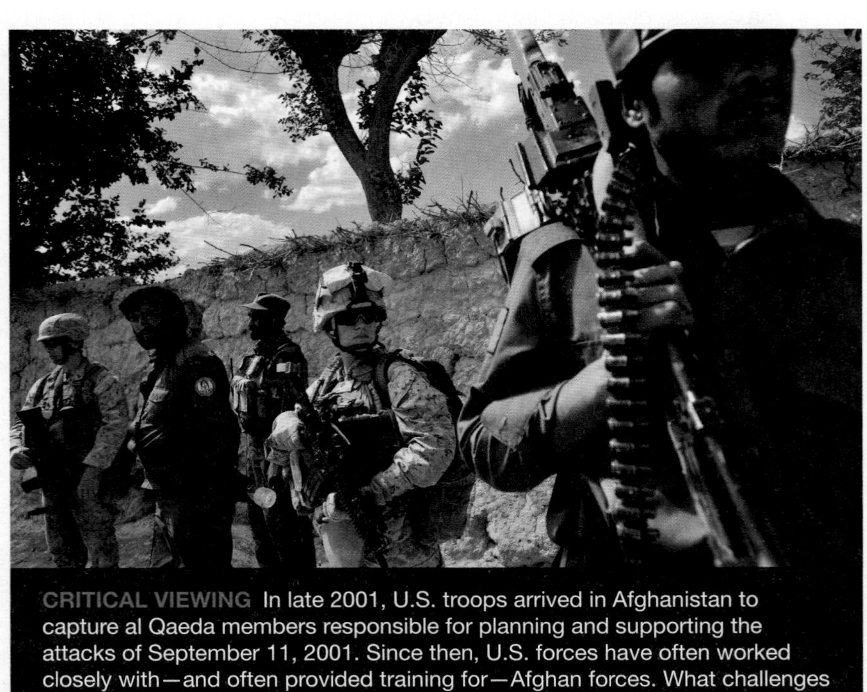

CRITICAL VIEWING In late 2001, U.S. troops arrived in Afghanistan to capture al Qaeda members responsible for planning and supporting the attacks of September 11, 2001. Since then, U.S. forces have often worked closely with—and often provided training for—Afghan forces. What challenges might U.S. and Afghan troops face in working together?

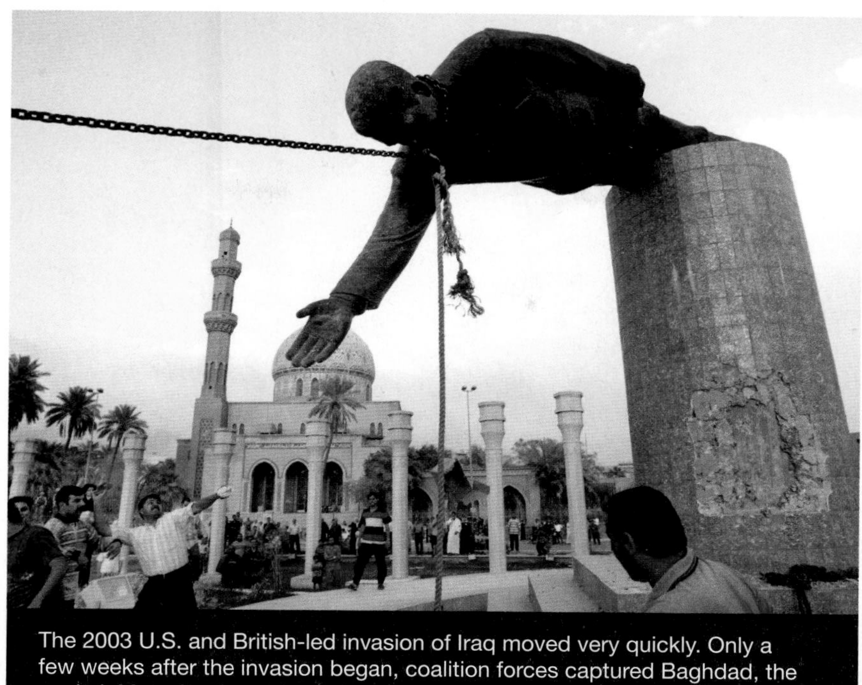
The 2003 U.S. and British-led invasion of Iraq moved very quickly. Only a few weeks after the invasion began, coalition forces captured Baghdad, the capital. Many Iraqis celebrated by toppling a large statue of dictator Saddam Hussein in the city's Firdos Square.

Iraqi military units crumbled quickly. Saddam Hussein, Iraq's dictator, was captured in December 2003 and executed after a trial in an Iraqi court in 2006. Yet what was now known as the Second Gulf War would keep U.S. military forces in the country for years to come.

THE RISE AND FALL OF THE INSURGENCY IN IRAQ The fall of Saddam Hussein did not end the violence in Iraq. Iraq is a country divided into three main groups: Arabs of the Sunni branch of Islam, Arabs of the Shiite branch of Islam, and ethnic Kurds who are predominantly Sunni Muslims. The Kurds live in the north. Arab Sunni Muslims live mostly in west-central Iraq and held power under Hussein's rule. Shiite Muslims, who live mostly in the south, make up the majority of the population, but under Hussein, they were persecuted by the Sunnis.

After the overthrow of Hussein's government, Sunni rebels launched an insurrection. The insurgents, including a newly formed group that called itself al Qaeda in Iraq, attacked not only U.S. and Iraqi government forces but also Shiite civilians. Shiite radicals responded with attacks on Sunnis, and Iraq appeared to be drifting toward an ethnic civil war. The Bush administration responded to the growing chaos by increasing troop levels in 2007 and undertaking new operations.

This surge, as it was called, was successful. Many Sunnis who, along with Shiites, had been terrorized by al Qaeda, turned against the insurgency and allied themselves with the Americans. With the insurgency fatally undermined, the United States planned its withdrawal. Barack Obama—elected president in 2008 on a vow to end the fighting in Iraq—announced that U.S. combat forces would leave Iraq by the end of August 2010, and the rest of the troops would be out by the end of 2011.

BACK TO AFGHANISTAN
President Obama believed that the United States still needed to continue fighting in Afghanistan, which remained torn by conflict. By 2006, the Taliban had regrouped. The United States and its allies found themselves the new government's principal military defenders. In 2009, during his first year in office, President Obama increased the number of U.S. troops in Afghanistan by 47,000.

Hampering the allied effort in Afghanistan was the ability of Taliban forces to hide over the border in Pakistan, in a region largely free from control of Pakistan's government. Under the George W. Bush administration, the CIA used Predator drones to launch small missiles that killed a number of Taliban and al Qaeda leaders in Pakistan. President Obama ramped up the Predator program significantly, increasing tensions with Pakistan.

The relationship between the United States and Pakistan became more complicated in 2011. In the winter of 2010–2011, U.S. intelligence agencies learned that Osama bin Laden was hiding in Pakistan. In the early morning hours of May 2, 2011, U.S. Navy SEALs entered a residential compound in Pakistan and killed him. While many Americans felt relief and satisfaction, many Pakistanis considered the incident a violation of their country's sovereignty.

On May 1, 2011, Vice President Joe Biden (left), President Barack Obama (second from left), and key members of the administration's national security team watched intently from the White House Situtation Room as Navy SEAL teams moved on the compound housing al Qaeda leader Osama bin Laden, who was located and killed in Pakistan.

At the same time, Obama's stated intention to withdraw some U.S. forces from Afghanistan as early as 2011 faced challenges. Eventually, though, troops were withdrawn, and by 2016, the American presence was down to about 10,000 troops who provided close air support to Afghan forces. In May 2017, President Trump approved a request by U.S. military leaders for additional soldiers, many of whom would train members of the Afghan army. In 2018 he reversed course, directing the Pentagon to withdraw about half of the 14,000 U.S. troops in Afghanistan.

HISTORICAL THINKING

3. **COMPARE AND CONTRAST** What did the insurgencies in Afghanistan and Iraq have in common?
4. **FORM AND SUPPORT OPINIONS** Was the U.S. war on Iraq a preventive or reactive foreign policy decision? Explain.

Civil War in Syria and the Growth of ISIS

Despite the troop withdrawals from Iraq under President Obama, U.S. forces continued to be involved in the region. New trouble spots arose from a wave of protests against autocratic rulers that swept across the Arab world beginning in December 2010. This pro-democracy movement—called the Arab Spring—failed to gain success except in Tunisia. In Syria, the Arab Spring had lasting, and devastating, consequences.

Protests in Syria developed into a civil war, as rebels attempted to forcibly overthrow the regime of Bashar al-Assad. Hundreds of thousands of Syrians were killed, and more than 11 million people—nearly half the country's population—were forced from their homes. Of these, more than 6 million were displaced within Syria. Another 5 million were driven out of the country, more than half of whom ended up in Turkey.

The stories of the refugees and what they had lost or left behind were heartbreaking. People around the world called for Western intervention to assist the rebels, but aid remained limited. One problem was that only a minority of the rebels fighting Assad and his government actually wanted democracy. Many others were Islamists of varying levels of radicalism, making the United States and other countries wary of them. The most radical faction in Syria was called ISIS, short for the Islamic State in Iraq and Greater Syria.

As the name indicates, ISIS was active in both Syria and Iraq, where it enjoyed considerable success. In June 2014, ISIS swept through northern Iraq, almost to Baghdad. Even though they outnumbered ISIS forces, Iraqi soldiers fled their posts. ISIS then set up a government in Mosul and changed its name to simply the Islamic State. When Islamic State forces next threatened to overrun the autonomous Kurdish region in northern Iraq, President Obama provided air support to the Kurds. In September 2014, the air forces of the United States and five Arab states began a campaign of bombing ISIS areas in Iraq and Syria.

The success of ISIS in Iraq was helped by the hostility that many Iraqi Sunnis felt toward the Shiite-dominated government of Iraq, which had not treated them well. As a result, the Obama administration provided limited support for the Iraqi government. After that government was reorganized in an attempt to conciliate the Sunnis, however, the United States furnished air support. By late 2016, ISIS was losing territory in Iraq and Syria. The group initiated a new strategy—terrorist attacks on nations such as France and Belgium.

By 2017, Iraqi forces had retaken Mosul and were fighting to regain the rest of ISIS-controlled areas. American allies pushed ISIS into just a tiny part of the area it once dominated in Syria. Late in 2018, President Donald Trump—determined to reduce U.S. involvement in the volatile region—ordered withdrawal of 2,000 or so U.S. troops in Syria, claiming that ISIS had been defeated. But in early 2019, U.S. intelligence officials warned that ISIS, while weakened, remained a significant threat. The group still had thousands of

ISIS Control in Syria and Iraq, 2015 and 2018

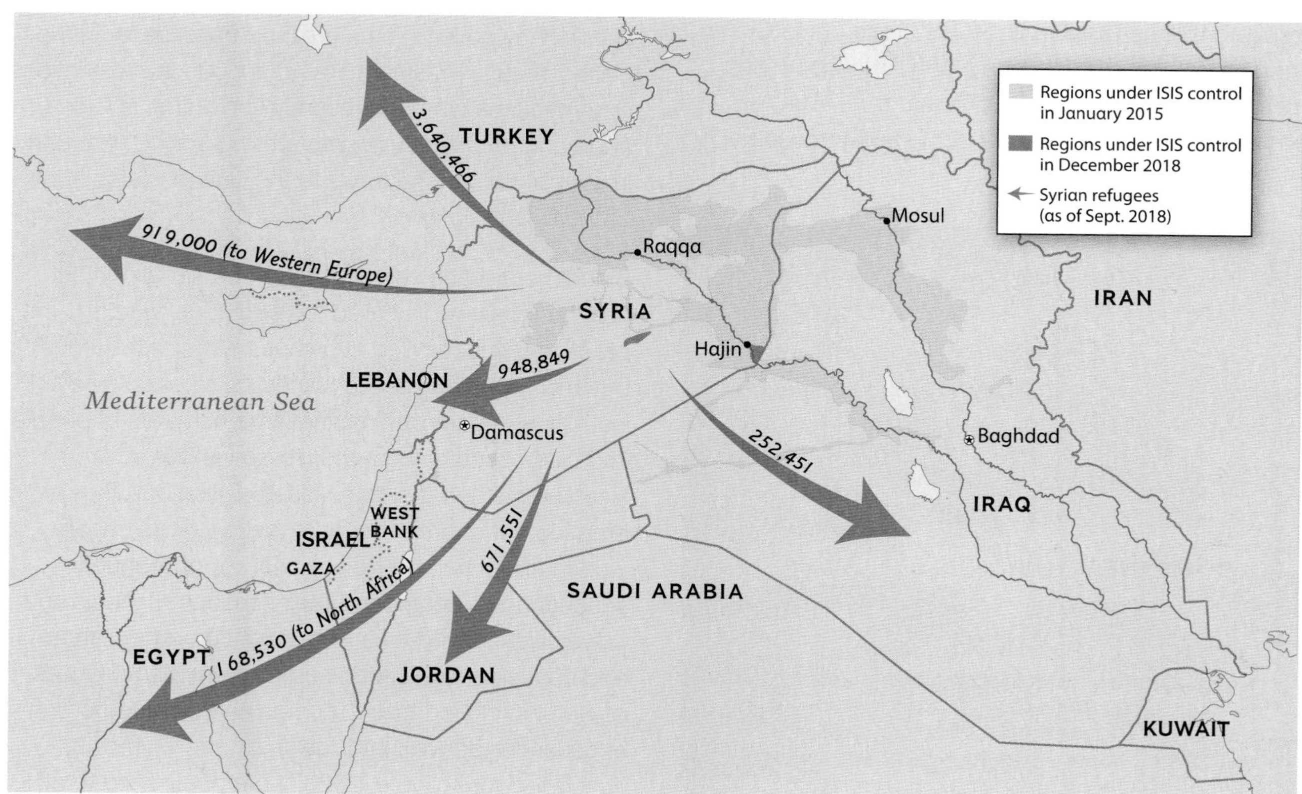

fighters in the region and might also return to terrorist attacks on targets outside the region.

HISTORICAL THINKING

5. **IDENTIFY MAIN IDEAS AND DETAILS** Explain how U.S. involvement in Iraq the second time during the 21st century was different than the first time.
6. **INTERPRET MAPS** Based on the map of ISIS and what you know of the region, why do you think most refugees have fled to Turkey?
7. **DESCRIBE** Why did U.S. intelligence officials warn that ISIS remained a significant threat, even though it controlled only a tiny part of the area it once dominated?

The Global COVID-19 Pandemic

In today's globalized world, with people and goods moving constantly between continents, infectious diseases pose a major new challenge. If they reach pandemic proportions, infectious diseases can destroy countless lives, undermine national economies, and threaten the bonds between nations. In 2003, a deadly respiratory illness known as SARS broke out in China and spread through Asia and North America. Seven years later, in 2009, a new influenza virus, H1N1, was declared a global pandemic. In 2014, the lethal Ebola virus spread through West Africa. Rapid action by national and international health organizations contained these outbreaks. In 2020, a new acute respiratory illness known as COVID-19 spread rapidly around the world. Its effects far outweighed those of earlier disease outbreaks in the century, demonstrating just how big a challenge such diseases present.

On January 30, 2020, the World Health Organization (WHO) led by Director-General Tedros Adhanom Ghebreyesus, shown here, declared the COVID-19 outbreak a "public health emergency of international concern." By March 11, the WHO announced that COVID-19 officially qualified as a pandemic.

COVID-19 first appeared in Wuhan, China, at the end of 2019. By January 11, 2020, the disease claimed its first known fatality in China. In the following weeks, Chinese officials downplayed the outbreak and were slow to share information with the World Health Organization (WHO) and other nations. On January 23, however, the Chinese imposed a **quarantine** on the population of Wuhan, restricting movement in and out of the city of 11 million. Yet millions of Chinese residents had traveled in the weeks before then, thousands outside of the country, unknowingly spreading the virus to areas around the world, including Europe and the United States. By February, COVID-19 cases were already spiking in Italy, Spain, Iran, and elsewhere. By March, with the spread of the disease largely unchecked, the WHO declared the disease a global pandemic.

UNITED STATES RESPONSE Nations around the world took various measures to slow the spread of the virus. Many governments enacted travel bans. In the United States, President Trump announced restrictions on Americans who had recently spent time in China, and banned foreign travelers arriving from China. Early in March, he banned travel to the United States from 26 European nations.

Since the disease spread through personal contact, health professionals called for **social distancing**, the practice of maintaining substantial physical distance between people in public places. Businesses and institutions reliant on bringing large numbers of people into close contact were the first to feel the impact. Restaurants and theaters closed. Office buildings emptied out and a majority of their workers began working from home. Professional sports leagues suspended or postponed their seasons. Schools and universities moved their instruction to online platforms and cancelled graduation ceremonies. Many houses of worship closed their buildings and provided online experiences as well. Internationally, the Olympics, scheduled for Tokyo in 2020, were postponed to at least 2021.

In the United States, the response to the COVID-19 pandemic was complicated by its federal structure of national, state, and local governments. Creating a coherent set of policies proved difficult. At the national level, the government provided a flow of information from the Centers for Disease Control and Prevention (CDC), a federal agency tasked with researching and preventing just such threats as COVID-19. The disease was new and not even public health experts fully understood how it spread. Many of the statements issued by the CDC were contradictory. At first, people were told that face coverings were not necessary. Later, they were urged to wear masks.

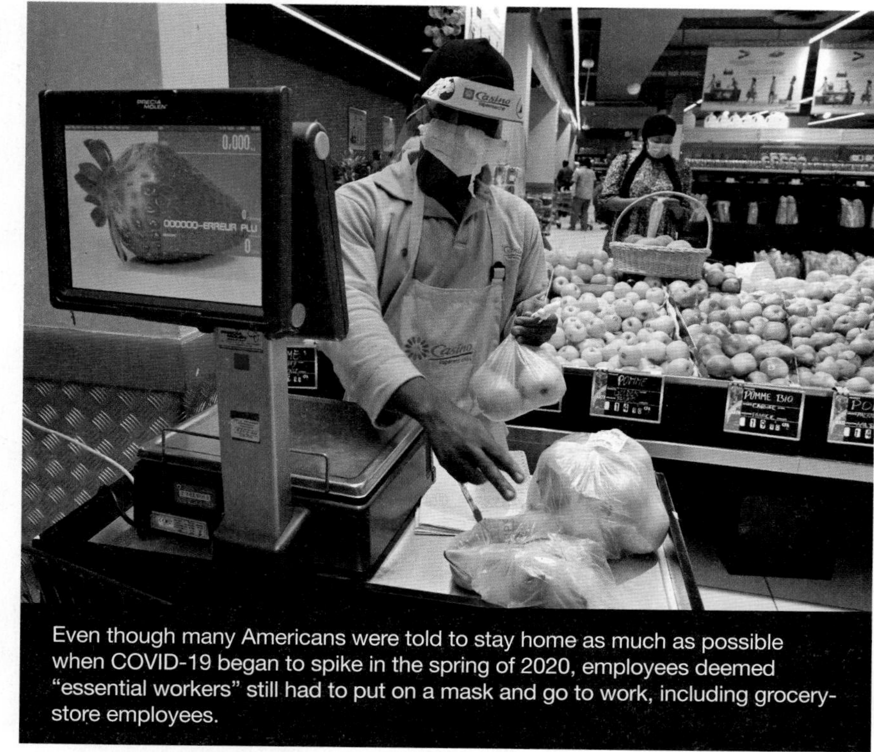
Even though many Americans were told to stay home as much as possible when COVID-19 began to spike in the spring of 2020, employees deemed "essential workers" still had to put on a mask and go to work, including grocery-store employees.

State governors used executive orders to impose restrictions on businesses, institutions, and residents of their states. These restrictions were often described as "lockdowns" or "shutdowns," and generally involved restricting public gatherings deemed non-essential. Those who did interact with people outside their homes often wore masks, either voluntarily or because they were required to do so.

Some governors, especially those in states with large cities, acted earlier and were more aggressive in their shutdown policies. Within states, more densely populated urban areas imposed more severe shutdown orders, while rural areas sought to maintain more of a semblance of normal life. States also differed in how quickly they moved to re-open their economies. Georgia, for example, lifted many closures well before other states.

ECONOMIC AND SOCIAL COSTS With many businesses forced to close and others—like airlines, theme parks, and hotels—unable to attract customers, the impact on the economy was immediate and startling. Stock prices plunged, and unemployment spiked to levels not seen since the Great Depression and with a speed never before experienced. To stimulate the faltering economy, the federal government passed the CARES (The Coronavirus Aid, Relief, and Economic Security) Act. The Small Business Administration (SBA) instituted a Payroll Protection Program (PPP) designed to assist small businesses that kept employees on their payroll even while they were closed.

Nonetheless, by mid-May of 2020, over 38 million Americans had filed claims for unemployment insurance. The combined expense of paying for unemployment compensation along with these other policies sent the United States budget deficit soaring to an estimated $3.7 trillion for 2020. The Congressional Budget Office estimated that over 10 years the pandemic would cost the U.S economy up to $16 trillion in reduced output.

This massive disruption of daily life carried social costs as well. Psychologists warned that social distancing could have mental health effects ranging from growing domestic violence, to more drug and alcohol abuse, to increased rates of suicide. With schools closed, millions of American school children and their families who had relied on school nutrition programs faced severe food shortages and hunger. Food banks were overwhelmed by those needing food assistance in the face of massive unemployment.

COVID-19 disproportionately affected people of color, many of whom performed essential jobs requiring them to interact with potential disease carriers.

The attack submarine U.S.S. *Connecticut* protrudes through an ice floe in the Beaufort Sea (northeast of Alaska). For decades the U.S. and Russian navies have jockeyed for position in the Arctic. Now China is ready to enter the fray, investing in icebreakers and other technology as melting opens new, potentially lucrative shipping lanes.

A Thawing Arctic Is Heating Up a New Cold War

by Neil Shea ***National Geographic* Magazine, September 2019**

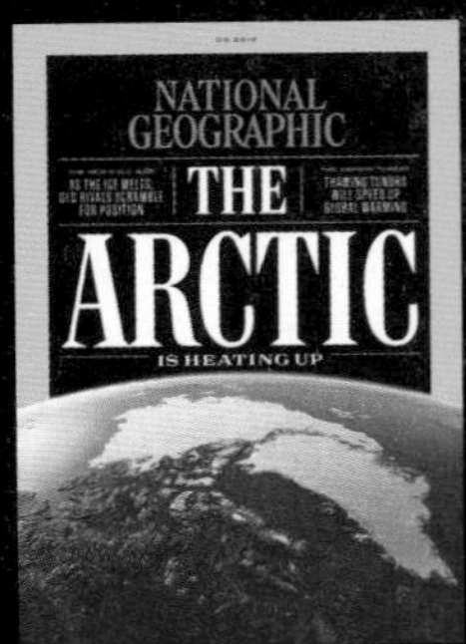

A handful of nations border the Arctic. They include the United States and Russia, which have both started to pursue greater access to the vast region and its resources. So has China, which describes itself as a "near-Arctic state." In his *National Geographic* magazine article, Neil Shea writes that competition for the Arctic's resources may someday lead to conflict.

The extreme Arctic cold and ice covering the Arctic Ocean have kept the area's resources from being fully exploited. But those natural barriers are disappearing. The Arctic is warming faster than any other region on Earth, leading climate experts to predict that the Arctic Ocean could be "ice free in summer before 2050." The expansion of shipping would surely follow, as would development of the Arctic's petroleum, natural gas, and mineral resources.

Today, Russia—with dozens of icebreakers and military bases in the Arctic—is the dominant power in the region. The United States, however, plans to expand its involvement, as Shea reports:

In early May, U.S. Secretary of State Mike Pompeo ° [delivered] a speech to the Arctic Council, a group made up of the eight nations that border the Arctic, plus representatives of the region's indigenous peoples. For about 20 years the council has encouraged collegial debate, cooperation, and a progressive perspective on climate change. Pompeo's appearance, as the emissary of an administration that is opposed to that approach, made for an awkward moment.

"This is America's moment to stand up as an Arctic nation and for the Arctic's future," Pompeo declared at an event the night before the official meeting. "Because far from the barren backcountry that many thought it to be . . . the Arctic is at the forefront of opportunity and abundance."

Pompeo's speech, in Shea's opinion, signaled the rebranding of the Arctic—once considered a frozen wasteland but now routinely described as an emerging frontier. The Arctic, in other words, is open for business.

Access the full version of "A Thawing Arctic Is Heating Up a New Cold War" by Neil Shea through the Resources Menu in MindTap.

THINK ABOUT IT While Russia has nearly 70 icebreakers either in operation or under development, the other seven Arctic Council nations combined have a little over 50. What foreign policy do you think the United

In addition, underlying health conditions such as diabetes and respiratory ailments, both of which occur at higher rates among Black and Hispanic people, as well as inadequate access to health care, magnified the rates of infection and mortality among immigrants and people of color.

After early bipartisan action on legislation such as the CARES Act, later responses to the disease were often viewed through partisan lenses. Some claimed that public health lockdowns represented an infringement on basic rights. The president and his supporters argued that the overall economic damage was more severe than the threat of the disease itself. In late May of 2020, in the midst of the pandemic, a horrifying video portraying the death of George Floyd at the hands of a Minneapolis police officer began to circulate. Widespread protests erupted across the country and around the world. They continued even as four Minneapolis police were charged with murder or with aiding and abetting the crime.

While the majority of the rallies and vigils were nonviolent, there were riots and property damage in many cities as well. The combined pressures of the effects of the pandemic and outrage over the death of Floyd and of numerous other deaths and dramatic incidents of police misconduct aimed at unarmed African Americans led to challenges to policing behavior and institutional racism throughout the nation.

By the end of 2020, the Trump administration's Operation Warp Speed, a partnership between government, private industry, and educational research institutions, made medical history when a number of major pharmaceutical firms announced the development of an effective COVID-19 vaccine in record time. Several nations, including the United Kingdom, Canada, and the United States, began inoculating health-care workers and the most vulnerable populations. The process of vaccinating the general population would take many months or longer. Throughout the world, institutions and industries struggled over the question of when and how to resume their operations. Many of the changes triggered by the COVID-19 may continue to affect the fabric of life in the United States and across the globe for years to come.

HISTORICAL THINKING

8. **ANALYZE CAUSE AND EFFECT** How did social distancing help to slow the spread of disease but also contribute to an economic slowdown?
9. **MAKE PREDICTIONS** How might the experience of millions of people having to work and learn online change business and education in the future?

LESSON 18.4 Diplomacy and International Economics

Diplomacy is negotiating between two or more parties, each of which has particular interests, to reach agreement on a common course of action. Presidents, members of the State Department, and other top U.S. officials engage in diplomacy around the world. They hold talks and attend meetings for many purposes—to forge alliances, seek common goals, solve international problems, make trade agreements, and settle disputes. They meet with allies and rivals for power. The successes or failures of these negotiations can affect the price of ordinary goods, the health of the world's oceans, or the prospects for peace in large regions of the world.

Tools of Diplomacy

Countries use different tools to carry out diplomacy. Some are non-coercive, meaning they are designed to persuade another country to join in agreements or work toward a common goal. Non-coercive tactics include providing economic aid, such as helping with construction projects or assistance to needy populations, to gain a country's gratitude or goodwill. One country can gain the support of another by agreeing to back that country in a dispute with a third country. A country can make friends by allowing another nation to buy armaments or by sharing new technology. Countries that have conflicting claims to an area or to resources can agree to mediation by a third party or an international organization.

Some forms of diplomacy are more coercive, using force or threats to try to compel another country to act in a certain way. An **economic sanction** is a penalty aimed at hurting a country's economy in an effort to get that country to agree to meet certain conditions. In the past, sanctions were used to pressure South Africa to drop its policy of apartheid, or racial separation. Sanctions have also been imposed on Russian companies to protest hostile actions against Ukraine. Of course, the ultimate coercive form of foreign policy is a declaration of war.

HISTORICAL THINKING

1. **MAKE INFERENCES** When might a country use coercive forms of diplomacy instead of non-coercive forms?

The Israeli-Palestinian Conflict

Over the past several decades, American presidents and diplomats have devoted a great deal of effort to address the intractable, or difficult to resolve, conflict between Israel and the Palestinian people. This long-running conflict has poisoned the atmosphere in the Middle East for more than half a century. While an agreement has seemed possible at times, lasting peace in the region remains elusive.

THE HISTORY OF THE CONFLICT For decades before World War II, many people campaigned for the creation of a Jewish nation in Palestine, an area of the eastern Mediterranean long considered by Jews to be their traditional homeland. After the atrocities of the Holocaust before and during World War II—when the Nazi government of Germany deliberately killed more than 6 million European Jews—there was new support for creation of a Jewish state. As a result, in 1947, the United Nations declared that Palestine would be divided into two states: one Jewish and one Arab. Palestinians—Arab peoples who lived in the region—and nearby Arab states objected to what they saw as the unfair displacement of Palestinians from their homeland.

In 1948, Jews in Palestine declared the existence of the new state of Israel, which the United States and other countries quickly recognized. Conflict erupted immediately and continued for decades. Wars between Israel and its Arab neighbors raged in 1948, 1956, 1967, and 1973. As a result of these wars, a huge number of Palestinians were forced into exile. Many went to live in the Gaza Strip. Others went to a region called the West Bank. Israel gained control of these areas in the 1967 war. Some Palestinians fled to other lands. Over time, some Palestinians formed a group named the Palestine Liberation Organization (PLO). It campaigned in the region and around the world for support for the Palestinian cause. The PLO also launched terrorist attacks against Israelis in Israel and elsewhere.

Efforts to bring peace to the region saw some success. In 1979, partly due to the efforts of President Jimmy Carter, Egypt and Israel signed a peace treaty that marked the end of an era of major wars between Israel and its neighbors. In 1994, Israel and Jordan signed a peace treaty. But Israel and Syria have not agreed on a treaty, and the conflict between Israel and the Palestinians continues.

UNDERSTANDING BOTH SIDES Both Israelis and Palestinians see the region as their homeland, making any resolution extremely difficult. Violence between the two sides has hampered the possibility of reaching an agreement. On the one hand, many Israelis are bitter over the deaths caused by Palestinian terrorist attacks over the years. Many Palestinians, on the other hand, see themselves as an oppressed people subjugated by an unjust occupying power.

Poverty is widespread in the Palestinian territories. Unemployment was at approximately 25 percent in 2020. For young adults, it has been as high as 41 percent. Accordingly, some 80 percent of the Palestinian population relies on humanitarian aid. Many Palestinians want compensation for the homes they lost when Israel took control of the land years ago. Other Palestinians want the descendants of

In 2002, Israel began building a more than 440-mile wall separating its land from the Palestinian-inhabited West Bank. The construction of this wall is said to prevent terrorist attacks, but some view it as an impediment to peace negotiations and an obstacle to movement of people.

those who were exiled to be allowed to return. Israeli Jews object to this proposal because it would leave them outnumbered by Palestinians. Many Israelis insist that Israelis who have built settlements in the West Bank—generally seen as one part of a future Palestinian state—should be allowed to remain, another sticking point.

NEGOTIATIONS For decades, U.S. presidents and other world leaders have worked toward a two-state solution that would grant Palestinians autonomy to rule some of the land in return for their recognition of Israel's right to exist and mutual promises of security and safety by both sides. In 1993, an apparent breakthrough occurred in Oslo, Norway, when representatives of Israel and the PLO met officially for the first time. The resulting Oslo Accords were signed in Washington, D.C. They established a governing body called the Palestinian Authority to oversee the West Bank and the Gaza Strip. Although militant Islamic groups, such as Hamās, were opposed to the agreement made in Oslo, elections within the Palestinian Authority took place in 1996.

The Oslo breakthrough did not lead to a final settlement, however. In 2000, talks between Israel and the Palestinian Authority ended in acrimony. An uprising by Palestinian militants followed. Before long, the Israeli military was back in the West Bank. In 2002, Israel began building an enormous security fence between Israel and the West Bank. The fence came under strong international criticism because it incorporated parts of the West Bank into Israel.

Meanwhile, the Palestinian areas became divided, with Hamās gaining control of the Gaza Strip while the Palestinian Authority remained in charge of the West Bank. Attempts by the United States to restart talks between the Israelis and the Palestinians collapsed in 2014. In 2017, President Trump announced his intention to reopen peace talks. In early 2020, the Trump administration unveiled a new peace plan, yet the tense situation in the region remained unresolved. In August of the same year, Israel and the United Arab Emirates agreed to normalize relations between their two countries. As part of the historic deal, which President Trump helped broker, Israel suspended its plans to annex a part of the West Bank important to Palestinians.

HISTORICAL THINKING

2. **IDENTIFY MAIN IDEAS AND DETAILS** Explain the role of other countries in the Israeli-Palestinian conflict.
3. **DESCRIBE** Explain the goals of the two-state solution advocated by U.S. presidents and other world leaders.

Weapons of Mass Destruction

Although the Cold War ended in 1991 with the collapse of the Soviet Union, the threat of nuclear warfare remains a major focus of U.S. foreign policy. As you have read, since September 11, 2001, the United States has remained on high alert for any sign of terrorist groups gaining control of these or other weapons of mass destruction. In addition, the United States and other countries have monitored the ongoing efforts of North Korea and Iran to develop nuclear weapons. These countries are led by governments hostile to their neighbors and to the United States. Iran also has ties to terrorist groups.

NORTH KOREA'S NUCLEAR PROGRAM North Korea signed the Treaty on the Non-Proliferation of Nuclear Weapons in 1985 and submitted to weapons inspections by the International Atomic Energy Agency (IAEA) in 1992. As the time line demonstrates, however, this attempt to constrain North Korea's behavior has not succeeded. After yet another missile test in 2013, China imposed economic sanctions on that country. This was significant because China is a major supplier of economic aid to North Korea that helps keep its economy afloat.

Tensions over North Korea's nuclear plans increased early in Donald Trump's presidency. In July 2017, North Korea engaged in a new series of tests involving nuclear weapons and long-range missiles. Once the technology was perfected, experts warned, missiles of this type could potentially reach Alaska. That August, North Korea threatened to fire ballistic missiles close to Guam, a U.S. territory. In response, President Trump used a combination of fiery rhetoric, diplomatic

North Korea Weapons Negotiations, 1985–2019

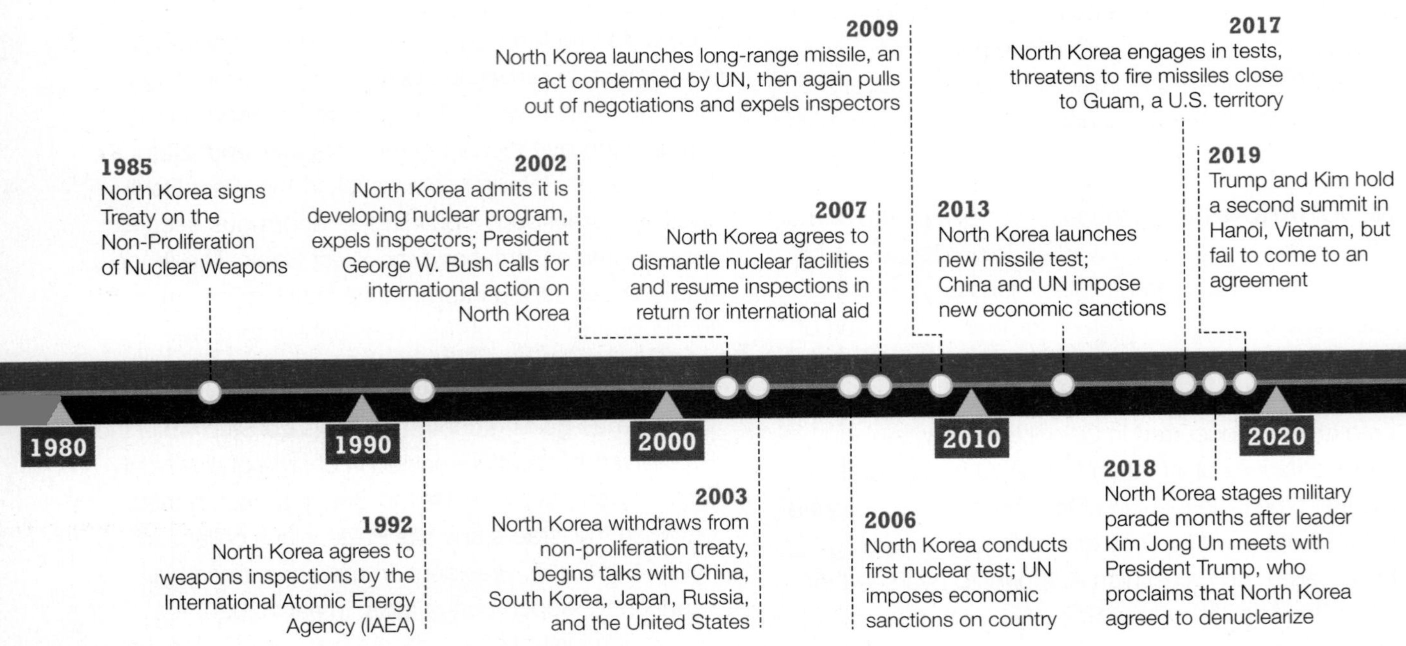

1985
North Korea signs Treaty on the Non-Proliferation of Nuclear Weapons
1992
North Korea agrees to weapons inspections by the International Atomic Energy Agency (IAEA)
2002
North Korea admits it is developing nuclear program, expels inspectors; President George W. Bush calls for international action on North Korea
2003
North Korea withdraws from non-proliferation treaty, begins talks with China, South Korea, Japan, Russia, and the United States
2006
North Korea conducts first nuclear test; UN imposes economic sanctions on country
2007
North Korea agrees to dismantle nuclear facilities and resume inspections in return for international aid
2009
North Korea launches long-range missile, an act condemned by UN, then again pulls out of negotiations and expels inspectors
2013
North Korea launches new missile test; China and UN impose new economic sanctions
2017
North Korea engages in tests, threatens to fire missiles close to Guam, a U.S. territory
2018
North Korea stages military parade months after leader Kim Jong Un meets with President Trump, who proclaims that North Korea agreed to denuclearize
2019
Trump and Kim hold a second summit in Hanoi, Vietnam, but fail to come to an agreement
1980
1990
2000
2010
2020

pressure, and offers of talks to try to defuse the situation. Trump enlisted the aid of China, which has substantial economic leverage over North Korea, and Chinese leaders applied pressure on North Korean leader Kim Jong Un.

Meanwhile, North Korea's leader Kim Jong Un and South Korean president Moon Jae In made history when they met in April 2018. Their meeting was the first time a North Korean leader had ever entered South Korea. Two months later, in another historic first, Kim met Trump, the first time a North Korean leader had met with a U.S. president. Kim and Trump discussed the termination of North Korea's nuclear program. According to Trump, Kim committed to denuclearization, though subsequent events showed little progress toward that end. In early 2019, Director of National Intelligence Dan Coats told Congress that the intelligence community believed that North Korea would not denuclearize. In February 2019, a second summit between Trump and Kim ended in a stalemate with no agreement on nuclear disarmament.

IRAN'S NUCLEAR PROGRAM Iran came under the control of Shiite Muslim religious leaders in 1979 after a revolution overthrew the ruling monarch, an ally of the United States. Since then, Iran and the United States have had testy relations. The United States placed economic sanctions on Iran, citing the country's sponsorship of terrorism, its opposition to a resolution to the Israeli-Palestinian conflict, and its efforts in developing nuclear weapons.

Concern heightened when investigators for the IAEA reported that Iran was enriching uranium that could be used to make a nuclear bomb. When efforts to negotiate with Iran appeared to be going nowhere, the United States and its allies turned to coercive measures. Sanctions were imposed by the United States, the European Union, and the United Nations. The United States persuaded most nations not to buy Iran's oil and to cut Iran off from the international banking system. This step made it extremely difficult for Iran to finance trade. By 2013, the Iranian economy was in serious trouble.

That same year, the country's new president, Hassan Rouhani, began working to resume negotiations. Two years later, Iran reached an agreement with the United States, Britain, China, France, Germany, and Russia. The 2015 agreement required Iran to hold only about half the uranium needed to make one bomb and reduce its number of centrifuges—devices needed to enrich uranium. International representatives would have the right to demand inspections of Iranian nuclear facilities. In return, all sanctions tied to Iran's nuclear program would be lifted, although certain other U.S. sanctions would remain in effect.

Critics charged that the plan was inadequate. One of the sharpest critics was presidential candidate Donald Trump. In 2018, after he became president, he withdrew from the agreement. The United States reinstated its own original sanctions against Iran, as well as imposing new sanctions. The other signatories, including Iran, announced that they would honor the agreement, and in 2019, U.S. intelligence assessed that the country had not resumed efforts to develop any nuclear capability.

HISTORICAL THINKING

4. **IDENTIFY MAIN IDEAS AND DETAILS** Why is China an important partner in negotiations between the United States and North Korea?
5. **INTERPRET TIME LINES** Based on the time line, summarize North Korean nuclear negotiations over the past 30 years.
6. **COMPARE AND CONTRAST** How did the situations in both North Korea and Iran change after Donald Trump was elected president?

China: The Next Superpower?

For the United States, China is a partner in some contexts—as during negotiations with North Korea—and a foreign policy challenge in others. Enormous economic growth—an average of almost 10 percent a year for more than 30 years in a row—has made China one of the world's economic superpowers. It also remains an important military power in Asia and the Pacific. Thus, U.S.-Chinese relations are extremely important.

U.S.-CHINESE TRADE RELATIONSHIP Relations between the United States and China have recently

CRITICAL VIEWING Since China's leaders adopted market reforms in 1978, the country's economy has grown at an astounding average of almost 10 percent a year, lifting more than 850 million people out of poverty. What details in this photograph of Shanghai show the results of this growth?

grown tense, largely due to the success of China's powerful manufacturing export sector. China's gross domestic product (GDP)—the total value of all goods and services produced and consumed in an economy during one year—is 200 times what it was in 1978, when China began economic reforms to promote growth. Never in the history of the world have so many people—850 million of them—been lifted out of poverty so quickly.

The export sector that fueled this growth has also impacted the United States. American consumers regularly buy toys, electronics, hardware, clothing, and many other items that are made in China more cheaply than they can be in the United States. While low prices benefit consumers, American workers who used to make such products have lost their jobs. This job loss became a major issue in the 2016 presidential race. Donald Trump in particular demanded a tougher line on trade with China.

Another contentious trade issue is widespread theft of U.S. **intellectual property**—patented, trademarked, and copyrighted inventions and other creations used in commerce—by Chinese companies. In June 2018, frustrated by the inability to forge a new trade deal with China, President Trump imposed 25 percent tariffs on $50 billion worth of imports from China. China quickly countered with sizable tariffs on U.S. products. Later that year, Trump announced another round of tariffs on yet more goods. While talks in the fall of 2018 suggested that the two sides could be nearing an agreement, it took until January 2020 for the first part of a trade deal to be signed. Among other stipulations, China agreed to better protect U.S. intellectual property, ease tariffs, and purchase $200 billion more American goods and services. In response, the United States agreed to reduce tariffs on Chinese products by half. That same month, the outbreak of COVID-19 in China that rapidly spread across the world added new complications to U.S.-China trade relations. President Trump repeatedly expressed dissatisfaction with China's efforts to stop the spread of the virus, declaring the need for future economic consequences.

CHINA AND THE PANDEMIC The COVID-19 pandemic that swept the world in 2020 threatened to set back China's position on the world stage. The disease originated in December 2019 in the city of Wuhan, in the Chinese province of Hubei. While Chinese health officials declared that measures had been put into place to stop the spread of what they reported was a pneumonia-like virus, Chinese President Xi Jinping failed to share crucial information. Residents of Wuhan were able to fly to northern Italy, San Francisco, and New York.

The international reaction to China's response to the disease soon known as COVID-19 was mixed. Some world leaders, among them President Trump, claimed that China had been too slow to contain the virus and too secretive about its true breadth. Soon after, the Trump administration announced that it would halt its funding to the World Health Organization (WHO) because it claimed that the agency had "failed to call out China's lack of transparency." Australia and countries in Europe also called for an investigation by the WHO. In response, China criticized what it labeled as the failings of Western government in confronting the disease. At the same time, it pledged to increase its support of the WHO. China also engaged in some high-profile efforts to mend fences by delivering shipments of needed medical equipment to countries hit hard by the pandemic. In May 2020, the WHO announced that it would conduct an inquiry into the global response to the pandemic.

THE ISSUE OF TAIWAN AND NATIONALISM Another source of tension is China's rather expansive definition of its territory. For example, China considers Taiwan, a former Chinese province, to be a legal part of China. In practice, however, the island has functioned as an independent nation since 1949. The United States has historically supported a free and separate Taiwan and maintained that any reunion of China and Taiwan must come about by peaceful means. While China has not initiated any military action against Taiwan, it has not ruled out the use of force to achieve reunification.

China has also alarmed some of its neighbors with other claims. China is engaged in a territorial dispute with Japan over uninhabited islands in the East China Sea. China has also claimed almost all of the uninhabited islands in the South China Sea, resulting in military confrontations with the Philippines and Vietnam. The United States has supported the rival claims, putting it in opposition to China.

HISTORICAL THINKING

7. **SYNTHESIZE** Why is the U.S.-Chinese trade relationship so complicated?

8. **MAKE INFERENCES** What can you infer about U.S. foreign policy from the manner in which American officials pay close attention to issues like Chinese nationalism?

Globalization and World Trade

Another aspect of foreign policy focuses on world trade. Various institutions of the federal government, such as the U.S. Export-Import Bank and the International Trade Administration, have been created to promote the flow of American goods and services abroad. In 2018 alone, the United States exported about $1.7 trillion worth of goods and $910 billion worth of services and imported about $2.6 trillion worth of goods and $600 billion worth of services from other countries.

THE BOOMING POSTWAR MARKET After the end of World War II, the United States promoted **free trade**—meaning international commerce with few barriers to trade, like tariffs. At war's end, the United States was in an excellent position to export more goods. The economies of many countries of Europe were devastated by the war, meaning they could not produce all the goods the people in those countries wanted. In addition, U.S. factories were eager to turn from producing planes, tanks, and weapons needed for war to making consumer goods. U.S. allies needed to import American goods to rebuild their own economies. International trade was about to take off like never before.

The postwar trade boom boosted **globalization**, or the development of an integrated, interdependent global exchange of goods, culture, and politics. Globalization is nothing new. Silk Road trade routes connected ancient China and the Roman Empire 2,000 years ago. But the decades after World War II saw the advent of new communications, manufacturing, and transportation technologies that suddenly made it much easier for people to share ideas. Governments, including that of the United States, began to negotiate agreements promoting free trade.

CRITICAL VIEWING One major effect of globalization has been the increased reach of multinational companies, giving consumers around the world access to goods originally made far from where they live. What familiar brands can you identify in this Tokyo shopping district?

In 1947, the United States and 22 other countries signed the General Agreement on Tariffs and Trade (GATT), which detailed tariff and quota agreements and opened trade equally among the member countries. Lacking the support of Congress for all of GATT's provisions, President Harry Truman joined the agreement through executive order. After several updates, GATT was replaced in 1995 by formation of the World Trade Organization (WTO). Today, the WTO has more than 160 member countries and is the main international body for negotiating new and current open trade policies, as well as for resolving trade disputes. It also aims to help developing countries as they navigate the world market.

FREE-TRADE AGREEMENTS Some countries have sought to boost their economies by entering into free-trade agreements with their neighbors. In these agreements, the participating countries eliminate all tariffs and other barriers to trade among the participating countries. They may also impose agreed-upon tariff rates on non-member countries, creating a trading bloc that aims to build the regional economy. The largest such agreement is the European Union (EU), a 27-country organization that includes most of Europe. The EU has provisions that take it beyond a simple trade agreement by allowing for the free movement of people (labor), services, and capital across member country boundaries. In the 2010s, though, dissent arose over the EU's influence over member states' autonomy. In 2016, in a surprising result, a majority of people in the United Kingdom voted to withdraw from the EU. This action—dubbed Brexit—was completed in 2021.

The United States is part of another major free-trade agreement, this one with its neighbors, Canada and Mexico. The original deal was the North American Free Trade Agreement (NAFTA), which went into effect in 1994. It progressively eliminated tariffs and other trade-related fees among the three countries. In his campaign for the presidency, Donald Trump often criticized NAFTA, which he complained was unfair to the United States. He threatened to withdraw from the agreement to force Mexico and Canada to negotiate a revised deal. A new deal with Mexico and Canada was reached in the fall of 2018, when the three North American countries announced they had a new agreement called the United States-Mexico-Canada Trade Agreement (USMCA). The new agreement, which updated the original pact, went into effect in 2021.

The United States has also joined with countries to the south in the Dominican Republic-Central American Free Trade Agreement. As you read in an earlier chapter, under President Obama, the United States helped negotiate the Trans-Pacific Partnership (TPP) agreement with 11 other Pacific Rim countries. But the agreement was never ratified, and on his first day in office in 2017, President Trump announced that the United States would pull out of that agreement.

THE PROS AND CONS OF GLOBALIZATION Trump did not believe that free-trade agreements always work in the best interest of the U.S. economy. He shocked many longtime trading partners in 2018 by imposing tariffs on imported steel and aluminum. Designed to protect those industries in the United States, the tariffs were even placed on imports from such close partners as Canada, Mexico, and the EU, which caused some dismay among longtime American allies.

Supporters of globalization argue that the resulting global economy creates jobs, inspires competition that results in lower prices for consumers, and offers new opportunities for developing countries to build their economies. They also argue that economic growth leads countries to have more democratic governments.

Critics see globalization as causing severe problems in both richer and poorer nations. They argue that an open market for labor and manufacturing has resulted in job losses in rich countries. They say that this market allows companies to resort to **outsourcing**, shifting production of goods or services to countries with lower labor costs, where many manufacturers exploit workers by paying low wages and offering few or no benefits and inadequate worker safety protections. Critics of globalization also argue that foreign operations often cause damage to the environment.

Despite the ongoing debate over the pros and cons of globalization, the U.S. economy remains closely linked to the world economy and continues to be an economic powerhouse. As of 2018, GDP was on the increase at a faster rate than in previous years. Inflation—the average rate at which prices are increasing—remained low, which means that consumers' purchasing power remained strong. In addition, unemployment was at record low levels.

That situation changed dramatically as a result of the COVID-19 pandemic. By the end of only the first quarter of 2020, U.S. GDP dropped for the first time since 2014. Unemployment numbers rose into the tens of millions. The pandemic also renewed debate about the downsides of globalization. Critics pointed out that the constant flow of people and goods between nations helped the disease spread rapidly. Moreover, a global supply chain that depended on China to produce a large share of the world's manufactured goods, either wholly or in part, proved vulnerable to disruption. Factories in the United States and other Western nations had to quickly retool to produce life-saving medical equipment when shipments from China slowed down or proved unable to meet demand. Finally, as country after country went into some form of lockdown, a global recession set in. A June 2020 report by the International Monetary Fund, an international organization that supports development projects, estimated that global GDP would plummet by almost 5 percent due to the pandemic.

The long-term economic effects of the pandemic remain to be seen. Economists hoped that the U.S. economy would eventually continue to grow at a steady rate, and predicted that the U.S. dollar would remain an extremely strong currency, inspiring foreign investments in the United States. History has shown that as long as the United States remains an economic force to be reckoned with, it will continue to have a strong influence on the global community.

HISTORICAL THINKING

9. **MAKE GENERALIZATIONS** What are the main goals of free-trade agreements?
10. **FORM AND SUPPORT OPINIONS** Do you think globalization has more advantages or disadvantages? Explain your answer.

CHAPTER 18 GOVERNMENT AND FOREIGN POLICY

Review

VOCABULARY

Complete each sentence below with key vocabulary.

1. As chief diplomat and commander in chief, the president plays the main role in the country's _______ and its relations with other countries.
2. For the country's first century, its foreign policy was marked by _______ that kept it uninvolved in world affairs.
3. The Spanish-American War marked a shift in U.S. foreign policy to ______.
4. The Truman Doctrine stated the U.S. policy of _______ of communism.
5. The build-up of the American nuclear arsenal was a direct result of the foreign policy of _______ to prevent nuclear war.
6. President Richard Nixon began a policy of _______ with the Soviet Union that led to a reduction in nuclear weapons.
7. Since the attacks of September 11, 2001, fighting _______ has been a major focus of U.S. foreign policy.
8. The _______ levied on Iran in recent years have taken a toll on how, when, and with whom the country can trade or do business.
9. The size of a country's economy is measured by its _______, which measures all the goods and services produced.
10. Counterfeit consumer goods, such as phones and designer handbags, are examples of _______ theft.

MAIN IDEAS

Answer the following questions. Support your answer with evidence from the chapter.

11. Give three examples of non-military foreign policy, and explain who typically creates and administers these policy actions. **LESSON 18.1**
12. What is the main difference between the foreign policy approaches of moral idealism and political realism? **LESSON 18.1**
13. What do the foreign policy actions of the United States right after World War I tell you about Americans' reaction to that war? **LESSON 18.2**
14. Explain the Truman Doctrine and its relationship to the Cold War. **LESSON 18.2**
15. Why did it take time for the United States and its allies to become militarily involved in Syria, and how was this delay related to ISIS? **LESSON 18.3**
16. What does the sometimes-strained relationship between the United States and Pakistan tell you about how some Muslim nations regard U.S. military actions in Iraq and Afghanistan? **LESSON 18.3**
17. Identify various types of alliances that the United States has entered into as part of its foreign policy. **LESSONS 18.3 and 18.4**
18. Name two main issues at the heart of the Israeli-Palestinian conflict. **LESSON 18.4**
19. Why are weapons of mass destruction a global, not just a regional, concern? **LESSON 18.4**

HISTORICAL THINKING

Answer the following questions. Support your answer with evidence from the chapter.

20. **ANALYZE CAUSE AND EFFECT** How might increased globalization have affected U.S. foreign policy geared toward moral idealism?
21. **COMPARE AND CONTRAST** How has terrorism changed the focus of U.S. foreign policy over the past 20 years?
22. **EVALUATE** What characteristics of the Cold War made it such an all-encompassing part of U.S. foreign policy?
23. **SYNTHESIZE** When the United States attacks another country, such as Iraq, what factors beyond military success need to be considered?

24. **FORM AND SUPPORT OPINIONS** Has a more open global market been a good or bad thing for Americans and the U.S. economy? Explain.

INTERPRET VISUALS

The graphs below indicate Americans' feelings about the role the United States should play in international affairs one month into the first terms of President George W. Bush (2001) and President Barack Obama (2009), and President Donald Trump (2017). Examine the graphs and then answer the questions that follow.

25. How have Americans' attitudes toward the role the United States should play in international affairs changed over the past 20 years or so?

26. Use what you know of major events between when George W. Bush took office and when Barack Obama took office to hypothesize why some Americans may have changed how they felt about involvement in foreign affairs.

ANALYZE SOURCES

Read the following quotation. Then answer the question that follows:

> *The purpose of foreign policy is not to provide an outlet for our own sentiments of hope or indignation; it is to shape real events in a real world.*
>
> —President John F. Kennedy, 1963

27. To what extent does President Kennedy's approach to foreign policy seem to lean more toward moral idealism or more toward political realism? Explain.

CONNECT TO YOUR LIFE

28. **EXPLANATORY** Research how globalization has affected your state's economy by searching phrases such as "how does outsourcing affect [name of your state]." Read at least three articles from reputable sources about the effects of outsourcing on local jobs and industries. Summarize your findings in a short essay.

TIPS

- Your introduction should clearly state whether outsourcing has or has not affected your state and preview at least three different areas where the effect is obvious.
- The body of your essay should explain the affected areas you listed in your introduction. Support these explanations with statistics and other data available in your source materials.
- Clearly attribute any data you use, citing authors, publishers, and publication dates.
- Your conclusion should reinforce the explanations and connections you have made in the body of the essay.

Opinions on Role U.S. Should Play in World Affairs

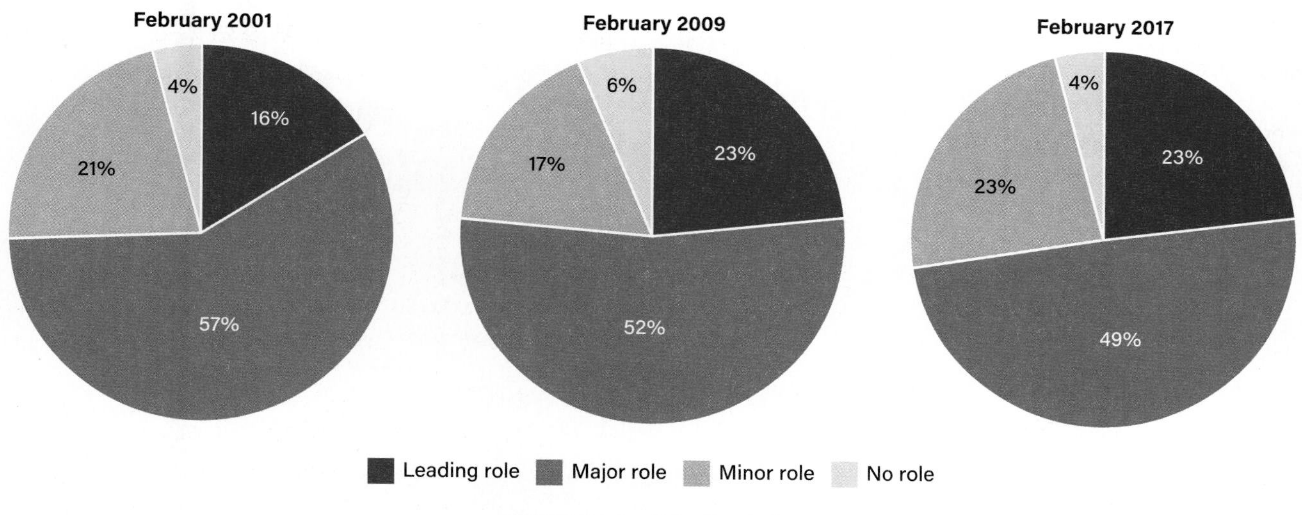

SOURCE: Data from Gallup Organization

CHAPTER 19

Government, Politics, and the Media

LESSONS

19.1 Media in a Democracy

19.2 Politics, Television, and Radio

19.3 The Power of the Internet and Social Media

National Geographic Online:
The Internet Is Drowning

CRITICAL VIEWING Newspapers, television, and radio are important sources of news about government and politics, but digital media play an increasingly significant role in keeping Americans informed. Why is it important in a democracy that citizens have access to a variety of news media?

LESSON
19.1 Media in a Democracy

In 1735, New York's colonial governor, William Cosby, had John Peter Zenger arrested on a charge of seditious libel, the crime of publishing false statements that encourage rebellious opposition to the government. Cosby was angered because Zenger's newspaper regularly lambasted him for his arrogant use of power. But Zenger's attorney convinced the jury that Zenger's articles were not libelous because they were not false. They were based on fact. Zenger's trial was the first legal victory in the colonies for the right to freedom of the press, including the right to criticize the government. These rights recognize the special role of journalism in a free society.

Mass Media

A newspaper is a medium, a means for communicating or transmitting something. So is a TV show, so is a podcast, and so is a streaming video series. The plural form of the word *medium* is *media*. When people talk about *the media*, they are referring to **mass media**, means of communication designed to reach a mass, or large-scale, audience. All mass media, whether print (newspapers, magazines, and books) or electronic (radio, television, and the internet), transmit information to the public.

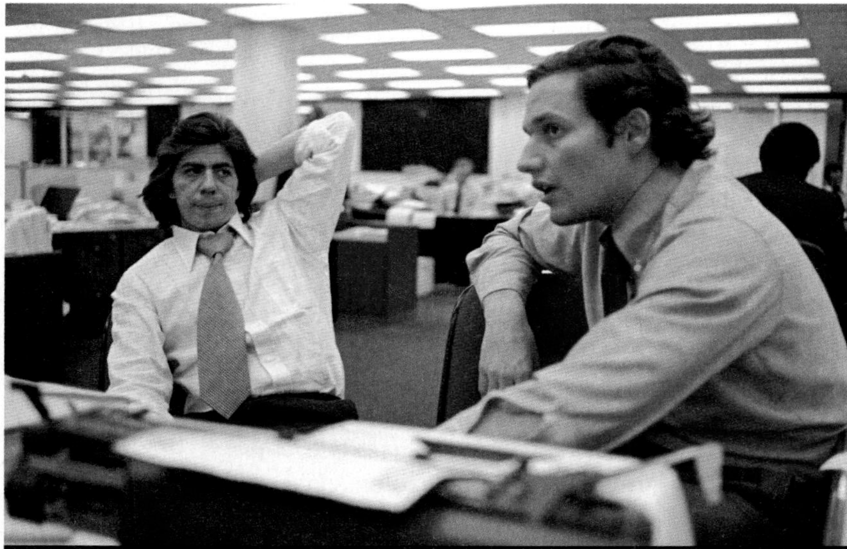

A free press is a vital source of information that helps citizens assess the conduct of their elected officials, especially when the government attempts to hide information. The investigation into the 1972 Watergate break-in conducted by two journalists for the *Washington Post*, Carl Bernstein (left) and Bob Woodward (right), exposed wrongdoing by President Richard Nixon and ultimately led to his resignation in 1974.

The media are a dominant presence in our lives largely because they provide information and entertainment. Americans today enjoy more leisure than at any time in history, and we use a lot of it on social media, reading on screens and print, and watching videos, movies, and TV. The media play a vital role in our political lives as well, particularly during campaigns and elections. Politicians and political candidates have learned—often the hard way—that positive media exposure and news coverage are normally essential to winning votes.

THE ROLE OF THE PRESS Among the mass media, the press—or news media—has a special role. The information that news media communicates and how it communicates it influences what Americans think about political issues. The news media also *reflect* what Americans think about those issues.

Like free speech, a free press is vital to the success of the democratic process. If people are to cast informed votes, they must have access to a forum in which they can discuss public affairs fully and assess the conduct and competency of their officials. The news media provide such a forum. Also, as mentioned earlier, citizens need information that is produced and distributed independently of the government, and news media serve as independent sources of information.

Government censorship of the press is common in many nations. China, for example, has more internet users than any other country on Earth. But China's government heavily censors the World Wide Web, the system most widely used on the internet. The government also controls China's two news agencies, which feed news stories to the media that serve the public.

THE MEDIA: NEW AND OLD From the founding of the nation through the early years of the 20th century, all mass media were print media. Beginning in the 20th century, radio and motion pictures, or movies, became important additions to print media. Machines that projected moving images were developed in the 1890s, and systems for adding sound to movies were introduced in the 1920s.

At around the same time, in the 1920s, radios brought the first broadcast media into people's homes. The term **broadcast** refers to the electronic transmission of information or entertainment to multiple recipients, simultaneously, over a wide area. Radio stations transmit using radio waves, which are received and transformed into sounds by radios in cars, homes, and other locations. Early radio brought sports events, news and politics, music, comedy, and drama into the homes of millions of listeners. Transmittals came from local stations, but much of the programming came from national networks such as the National Broadcasting Company (NBC), the American Broadcasting Company (ABC), and the Columbia Broadcasting System (CBS).

After the end of World War II in the 1940s, a number of large radio networks—NBC, ABC, and CBS—began to transmit moving images along with sound to create programming for a newer invention, the television. Antennas, often on a building's roof, received radio waves and carried them through a wire to a TV set. Access to this programming was free to anyone who owned a television set—the cost of programming was covered by advertising revenue, just as it had been for radio programming. The three major networks shared control of U.S. TV audiences through the 1970s, when cable TV—television programming carried through metal or fiber-optic cables connected directly to individual television sets—entered the market. But viewers had to pay a monthly fee to get cable programming, and it wasn't until the 1980s that most households felt the programming offered by cable stations was worth the cost. By the end of the 1980s, American viewers who once had access to only 3 major TV networks could choose from 50 or more cable channels.

The internet, including email and the World Wide Web, came into widespread use by the general public in the 1990s. Most internet data travels through fiber-optic cables, including through cables laid along the ocean floor. Individual homes and businesses exchange data with an internet service provider over fiber-optic cables, metal cables, or telephone wires. The internet has made a greater variety of programming—including sports, entertainment, and news—available than ever before. It has also allowed an explosion of creativity. Musicians, artists, animators, inventors, writers, crafters, and creators of all stripes do not need to rely on network executives to broadcast their creative endeavors over a limited number of channels.

THE DECLINE OF THE OLD MEDIA Although some early radio stations were owned by the same companies that owned newspapers, the ability of radio to provide late-breaking news reports threatened

Decline of the Daily Newspaper, 1957–2017

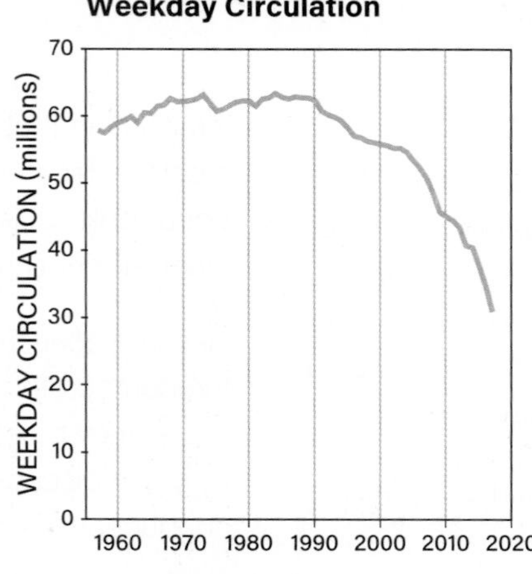

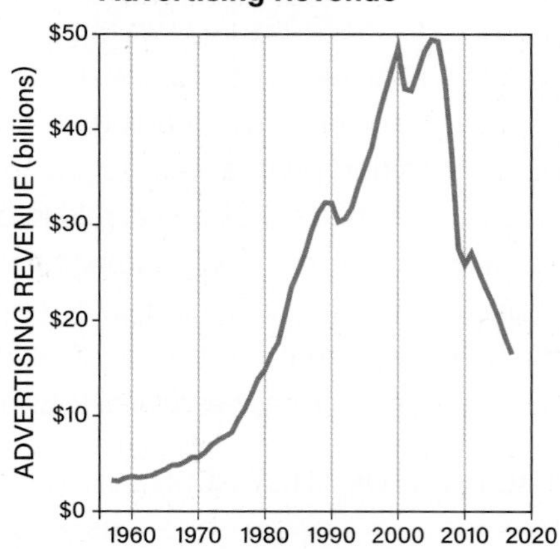

SOURCE: Pew Research Center

the power of print media and its advertising revenue. Television had an even greater impact. Beginning about 1950, more and more people turned to television for their news. The percentage of adults reading a daily paper began to decline, although circulation remained steady as a result of population growth. The internet proved more devastating to newspapers. Newspaper circulation fell modestly in the 1990s. In 2006, however, circulation began to collapse, declining more than 5 percent each year. You will read more about these changes later in the chapter.

CRITICAL VIEWING The First Amendment protects the press from undue government interference. But market forces can also exert pressure on the press. Read this cartoon from left to right. It shows a newspaper editor allowing leaders of various religions (Islam, Catholicism, Judaism, and Wiccan) to censor any news they do not like. What do you think is the cartoonist's underlying message about a free press?

YOUTH AND THE NEW MEDIA
Today, millions of Americans have unprecedented habits of media consumption. New consumers, especially the young, rarely read newspapers, and while young people still watch a variety of television programs, they view such shows online, as streaming video. Many younger viewers and other early adopters have abandoned both broadcast and cable TV service in favor of online streaming services such as Netflix and Hulu. These cord cutters, as people who do not subscribe to cable services are known, may pay little or no attention to the television news anchors and radio talk-show hosts their parents and grandparents rely on.

NEW MEDIA AND OLDER VOTERS Older Americans largely rely on 20th-century media—radio, television, and print—so the impact of these media shouldn't be underestimated. Many young people may have considered radio host the late Rush Limbaugh irrelevant because his audience was composed largely of middle-aged White men. But Limbaugh was not irrelevant to American politics. He had millions of listeners who voted, and his conservative opinion could sway enough of his large audience to affect the outcome of Republican presidential primaries.

Older media remain particularly important to American politics and government partly because older voters outnumber younger ones. As of 2018, approximately 116 million Americans were 50 or older. That was more than double the number of Americans aged 18 through 29. Older citizens are much more likely to vote than younger people, and some of the most enthusiastic adopters of new media aren't yet 18 and couldn't vote if they wanted to. Thus, considering the electorate as a whole, radio and television remain key media in terms of political influence.

HISTORICAL THINKING

1. **CATEGORIZE** Why are movies considered a mass medium but not a broadcast medium?
2. **INTERPRET GRAPHS** Based on the graph showing the decline of the daily newspaper, do you think newspaper advertising revenue is directly related to daily circulation? Why or why not?

The Media and the First Amendment

It's clear that freedom of the press is essential to the democratic process. The concept of freedom of the press—which is closely linked to freedom of speech—has been applied to print media since before the adoption of the Bill of Rights, but these freedoms were not immediately extended to other types of media as they came into existence.

Film was one of the first types of nonprint media to be considered under the First Amendment. In 1915, the United States Supreme Court ruled that, "as a matter of common sense," freedom of the press did not apply to the movies. The Court finally extended First Amendment protections to the cinema in 1952—not to protect freedom of the press, but to protect freedom of expression, or the right to create a work of art. But in 1977, a federal court ruled that the First Amendment right to freedom of the press extended to documentary filmmakers.

The same does not apply to broadcast media—radio and television. Although the Supreme Court has stated that the First Amendment is relevant to broadcast media, it has not granted these media complete freedom of speech nor complete freedom of the press. That's because the air waves are considered a public resource. They are managed by the Federal Communications Commission (FCC) in the public interest. In exchange for the privilege of exclusive use of a radio wave frequency in a specified geographic area (which prevents radio and TV stations from interfering with one another's transmissions), the FCC imposes various conditions on broadcasters. In 1949, the FCC established the **fairness doctrine**, a rule that required television and radio broadcasters to air opposing views on issues of public interest, to reserve time for discussion of "controversial issues of public importance," and to make their studios available for "the expression of contrasting viewpoints." The fairness doctrine sought to ensure that Americans had access to more than one opinion on key political issues. As cable television grew, broadcasters argued that the fairness doctrine had become obsolete because the increased programming had brought many more viewpoints into the public space. In 1987, the government repealed the doctrine.

While television and radio depend on radio wave frequencies managed by a central government authority, the internet does not. Most of the cables the internet relies on are privately owned. Due to this difference, the Court extended First Amendment protections to the internet in 1997. It struck down—as an abridgment of free speech—two provisions of the Communications Decency Act, which restricted obscene or indecent content on the internet. First Amendment protections now clearly prohibit the U.S. government from restricting speech on the internet. Nonetheless, some social media platforms have voluntarily removed posts or accounts they felt were spreading disinformation. Some lawmakers have accused these companies of practicing censorship in such situations.

HISTORICAL THINKING

3. **MAKE CONNECTIONS** How does First Amendment freedom of the press help protect Americans against the rise of a tyrannical leader?
4. **EVALUATE** Do you agree that the internet should have broader First Amendment protections than broadcast media? Explain your answer.

The Media and Agenda Setting

One of the criticisms often leveled against the media is that they play too large a role in determining the issues, events, and personalities that are in the public eye. When taking in the day's top news stories, do you assume that these stories cover the most important issues facing the nation? In actuality, it is the news media that assign labels like "top stories" and "old news" and make choices about what to publicize, what to investigate, how to characterize people and events, and what to ignore. In doing so, they make judgments about which events will turn out to be most significant and which stories will attract the biggest audience.

By helping determine what people are aware of and concerned about, the news media play a large role in what is known as **agenda setting**, focusing public attention on particular issues or problems and the solutions to be considered in addressing them. Agenda setting is a key part of the policymaking process that you read about earlier. American political scientist Bernard Cohen offered the classic statement on the media and public opinion when he wrote: "The press may not be successful much of the time in telling people what to think, but it is stunningly successful in telling its readers what to think about."

For example, television played a significant role in shaping public opinion about the Vietnam War (1965–1975), the war that has been called the first television war. Public opposition to the war in the late 1960s grew as television news increased coverage of

Walter Cronkite's calm and professional reporting earned the CBS television news anchor the trust of his viewers, who relied on him to report the facts objectively. In 1968, after traveling to war-torn Vietnam, Cronkite uncharacteristically offered viewers his opinion that the war would end not with a U.S. victory but in stalemate. Cronkite's on-air pronouncement helped solidify public opposition to the conflict.

the war's horrors. In February 1968, when CBS news anchor Walter Cronkite, trusted and respected by his many viewers, told America that the war was "mired in stalemate," public opinion turned against the war.

One key concept related to agenda setting is known as priming. In everyday usage, *priming* means "preparing something for use." In political sociology, *priming* refers to preparing people to adopt certain opinions. Priming influences the standards people use to evaluate policies, government actions, and officials.

For example, consider a policy proposal to tax the top 10 percent of incomes at a much higher rate than the tax rate for lower-income people. Suppose one news source reports that the general rate of taxation in the United States is lower than it has been at any time since the 1950s. This report primes listeners to be more receptive to a tax rate hike. Another source may report that the United States collects a much larger share of its tax revenue from the upper income brackets than other wealthy nations. This report primes listeners to oppose tax rate increases on the wealthiest Americans.

Framing is another concept related to agenda setting. If agenda setting tells people what to think about, framing shows them how to think about it. Frames, also known as frameworks or interpretive schemas, are essentially stories that give people a way to understand actions, events, or policies. For instance, a news station might frame a newly proposed spending program with a story about Darla Doe, who left school to support her ailing mother and younger siblings, quit a job in a restaurant to escape sexual harassment, was injured on her next job as a home health aide, and could no longer work. Another station might frame the spending program with the story of Ron Roe, who was kicked out of high school because he was disruptive, abandoned his girlfriend when she became pregnant, and then refused to work because he didn't want his pay garnished for child support. People who think the spending program will help people like Darla Doe are more likely to approve of it than are people who think it will help people like Ron Roe.

HISTORICAL THINKING

5. **COMPARE AND CONTRAST** How are priming and framing similar?
6. **FORM AND SUPPORT OPINIONS** Do you think it's wrong for the news media to try to influence public opinion about important political issues? Why or why not?

How the Medium Affects the Message

Television still has a great impact on many Americans, especially older ones. Today, Americans watch more television than ever, and it is the primary news source for well over half the citizenry. Television reaches almost every home in the United States, as well as airports, shopping malls, golf clubhouses, restaurants, and waiting areas in hospitals and dental clinics. People can watch television whenever and wherever

Television has helped blur the line between celebrity and politics. In this episode of NBC's news discussion program "Meet the Press," host David Gregory (right) speaks with Pennsylvania Governor Ed Rendell (left). Next to Gregory is billionaire businessman Michael Bloomberg, who served as mayor of New York City from 2002 to 2013 and ran unsuccessfully for the Democratic nomination for president in 2020. Next to Bloomberg is Arnold Schwarzenegger, a bodybuilder and movie star who served as governor of California from 2003 to 2011.

they want on their computers, their tablets, and their phones. Let's look at how television itself affects political messages.

TIME CONSTRAINTS The medium of television can impose constraints on how political issues are presented. Time is limited on the 30-minute evening news broadcasts on the major networks. Each news story must be reported in only a few minutes.

In contrast, the print media, particularly leading newspapers such as the *New York Times*, the *Los Angeles Times*, or the *Chicago Tribune*, often deal with an important issue in much more detail than broadcast television does. In addition to news stories based on reporters' research, papers offer editorials taking positions on the issue and arguments supporting those positions.

A similar comparison can be made between broadcast networks and the major cable news networks—Fox News, CNN, and MSNBC. These networks cover the news all day and all night and can devote a significant amount of time to an important news story. Broadcast news reports, in contrast, sometimes offer little more than a sound bite, a recorded comment of just a few seconds that seems to sum up a thought or perspective, but may be quite misleading.

Experienced politicians understand the concept of the sound bite. To suit the time constraints of news broadcasts, they learn to craft public statements that express a sharp opinion in a brief but memorable way. Sound bites aren't just a broadcast news phenomenon, and they are nothing new. President Franklin D. Roosevelt's "The only thing we have to fear is fear itself" is a famous sound bite. So is President Ronald Reagan's often-repeated statement: "Government is not the solution to our problem; government is the problem."

A VISUAL MEDIUM The visual aspect of television contributes to its power, but it also creates potential biases. For instance, television news producers may seek images that are more exciting or controversial than they are informative. Viewers may tend to discount messages and opinions delivered by people they perceive as unattractive. And those watching television news don't know what portions of a video have been deleted, or whether other records of the event exist.

THE BIG BUSINESS OF TELEVISION To make profits, or even to stay in business, TV stations need viewers. TV networks compete to be first to air a breaking story and to produce interesting programs that attract viewers. Such competition has had an effect on how television news is presented. To attract viewers, the news industry has turned to so-called infotainment—programs that inform and entertain at the same time. Slick sets, attractive reporters, and animated graphics or visual and sound effects that create a sense of excitement are commonplace on most news programs, particularly on the cable news channels.

TV networks also compete for advertising income. While the media in the United States are among the freest in the world in terms of government interference, their programming remains vulnerable to the influence of advertising sponsors. Advertisers have been known to drop programs or stations that present the news in ways that put their business in a bad light.

HISTORICAL THINKING

7. **DRAW CONCLUSIONS** How does knowing that news broadcasters compete for audience and advertising affect how you watch the news? Explain your answer.
8. **EVALUATE** Name one strength and one weakness of sound bites.

Ownership of the Media

The question of influence also pertains to the concentrated ownership of media. Many media outlets are owned by giant corporations, such as Comcast, News Corporation, and Disney Media Networks. Many analysts express concern that these powerful corporations will try to shape news coverage to benefit their economic or political interests. Even though newsrooms aim to remain objective and unbiased, they are answerable to their owners. Comments like this one from a 1997 interview with the CEO of Westinghouse Electric, then the owner of CBS—"We are here to serve advertisers. That's our *raison d'être* [reason for existence]."—suggest that corporate leaders would use their news operations to serve their own rather than the public interest. Similarly, the CEO of Walt Disney Co., the company that owns ABC, said in a 1981 memo, "We have no obligation to make history. We have no obligation to make art. We have no obligation to make a statement. To make money is our only objective."

To maintain the trust of its viewers, however, a news enterprise must be seen as independent of outside influence. A possible exception to the claim that major corporations don't influence reporting is the News Corporation, owned by Rupert Murdoch. Murdoch has supported conservative causes and politicians throughout his career, first in his native Australia, later in the United Kingdom, and later still in the United States, where he is now a citizen. His media properties, which include the *New York Post*, a newspaper with one of the largest readerships in the country, and Fox News, reflect his conservative perspective. A 2014 study by the Pew Research Center, for instance, placed Fox News furthest to the right of all the major broadcast networks. Moreover, Murdoch has consistently hired figures with ties to the Republican Party to staff Fox News. These have included Fox News founder Roger Ailes, who was a former media consultant to Republican presidents Richard Nixon, Ronald Reagan, and George H.W. Bush. More recently Murdoch hired former Republican House Speaker Newt Gingrich and former vice presidential candidate Sarah Palin.

The success of Fox News indicates that there are many Americans who embrace its outlook, but it is only one voice among many in America. Rival networks MSNBC and CNN have also hired commentators and anchors who are explicitly opposed to the conservative agenda, and their combined prime time viewership far exceeds that of Fox News.

THE ROLE OF THE FCC As you have learned, one part of the FCC's mission is to allocate bandwidth in the public interest. Historically, the FCC has limited the ability of media companies to dominate or monopolize the media outlets in any one region on the grounds that the public interest is best served by access to the widest variety of opinions. In 2017, however, the FCC eliminated a set of regulations, put in place in the 1970s, that aimed to make sure different news programs offered a variety of opinions from diverse sources. As a result of this deregulation, companies are no longer prevented from owning multiple newspapers, television stations, and radio stations serving the same community or region.

LOCAL MONOPOLIES Concentrated ownership may be a more serious problem at the local level than at the national level. If only one or two companies own a city's newspaper and its major radio and TV stations, these outlets are unlikely to air information that could be damaging either to their advertisers or to themselves, or even to publicize views that they disagree with politically. For example, TV networks have refused to run antiwar commercials created by religious groups. Even if station owners do not intentionally engage in agenda setting, monopolistic control of broadcasting in a region is not likely to provide access to a diversity of opinion. Large media conglomerates have argued that concern about concentrated ownership of traditional outlets is misguided now that the internet makes available to every community a massively diversified set of information sources.

HISTORICAL THINKING

9. **MAKE INFERENCES** How might the Federal Communications Commission's 2017 ruling limit the variety of opinions presented on important issues?

LESSON

19.2 Politics, Television, and Radio

If you have lived in the United States during an election year, you have almost certainly been exposed to negative campaign ads. You've probably seen these dire warnings, supplemented with dramatic music, charging that this candidate is a racist or that candidate is a socialist. Personal attacks on the character of an opposing candidate are a tradition going back to at least 1800. That's when an article in the *Federalist Gazette of the United States* described Thomas Jefferson as having a "weakness of nerves, want of fortitude, and total imbecility of character." But campaigns today use all the lighting, sound effects, and digital tools of the modern age to increase the impact that television and radio have had on politics in recent years.

The Candidates and Television

When political advertising first appeared on television during the 1952 presidential campaign, about a third of American households had access to television. In 2018, that figure was 96 percent. Today, televised political advertising consumes about half the total budget for a major political campaign. During the 2018 midterm election cycle, candidates and outside groups spent more than $8 billion on advertising, including $3.5 billion for broadcast television ads and $1.1 billion for ads on cable television.

Given the TV-saturated environment in which we live, it should come as no surprise that candidates spend a great deal of time and money cultivating a TV presence through political ads, debates, and general news coverage. Candidates and their campaign managers know television has a strong impact on the way people see the candidates, understand the issues, and cast their votes.

NEGATIVE ADVERTISING Personal attacks on political opponents have become so familiar and yet so ferocious that they make old-fashioned name-calling almost quaint. Indeed, negative political advertising has come to dominate our impressions of campaigning. Consider the 2004 campaign against John Kerry, the Democratic presidential candidate, by Swift Boat Veterans for Truth. The group accused Kerry, a decorated Vietnam War veteran who became a leader in the antiwar movement, of lying to obtain his

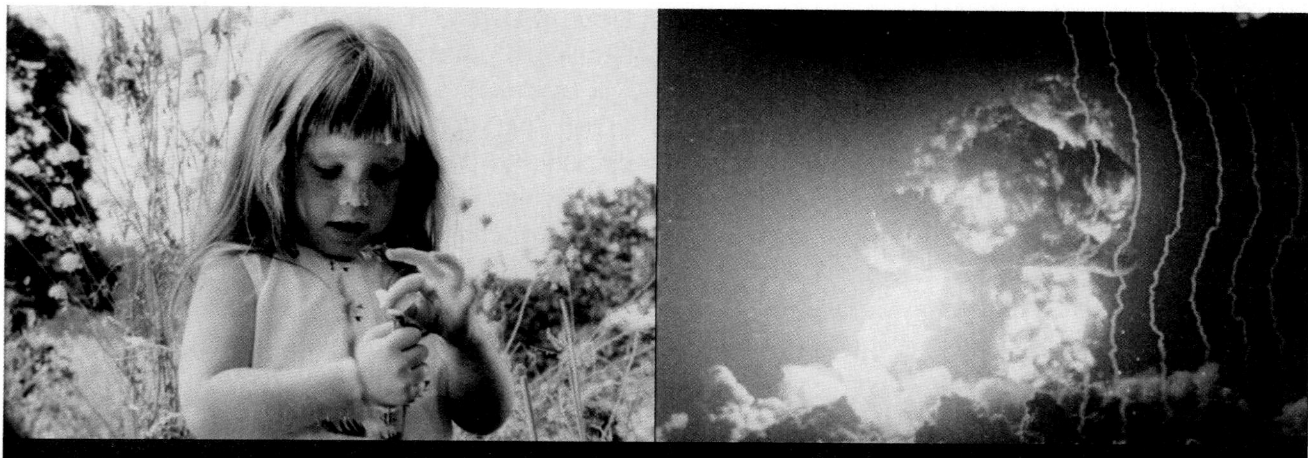

CRITICAL VIEWING During the Cold War, many Americans feared the country would be drawn into nuclear war with the Soviet Union. In 1964, Lyndon Johnson's presidential election campaign used a television advertisement suggesting that Johnson's rival, Barry Goldwater, was overly eager to use nuclear weapons. Why do you think these two scenes in particular strongly affected viewers?

medals. The story was completely fabricated, yet Kerry felt forced to defend himself, and the false accusation brought attention to the group's other personal attacks on him.

In 2016, Hillary Clinton's ads highlighted Donald Trump's contemptuous and lewd statements about women. For his part, Trump called Clinton a criminal and a traitor because she used a private, nongovernmental email server while secretary of state. While Clinton may have used poor judgment regarding security and the FBI found evidence of potential violations regarding the handling of classified information, then-FBI director James Comey said, "no reasonable prosecutor would bring such a case." Yet Trump's attacks were effective. Media Matters, a liberal nonprofit research organization, reported that, in 2016, major networks gave the Clinton emails story almost seven times as much coverage as all other policy issues put together.

Issue ads can be even more devastating than personal attacks, as Barry Goldwater learned in 1964, when his opponent in the presidential race, President Lyndon Johnson, aired the "daisy girl" ad. A marked departure from the usual negative advertising, this ad began with a little girl counting to herself as she pulled the petals off a daisy, one by one. Suddenly, a deep male voice began a missile launch countdown: "10, 9, 8, ..." When the countdown hit zero, an image of a mushroom cloud from a nuclear bomb explosion filled the screen. Then President Johnson's voice said, "These are the stakes: to make a world in which all of God's children can live, or to go into the dark. We must either love each other or we must die." The ad clearly implied that Goldwater, if elected, would lead the country into a nuclear war. The Goldwater campaign was furious, and the Johnson campaign ran the ad only once. But the ad stirred up so much controversy that network news programs ran the ad repeatedly to explain the source of the outrage.

The debate over the effect of negative advertising on our political system is ongoing. Some observers argue that negative ads can backfire, creating sympathy for the candidate being attacked or anger at the attacker, particularly when the attacks are not credible. Others argue that negative advertising sharpens public debate, thereby enriching the democratic process. But more people fear that attack ads and dirty tricks used by both parties during a campaign may stoke partisan division, stifle debate, and alienate citizens from the political process.

Yet candidates and their campaign managers typically assert that they use negative advertising simply because it works. Negative TV ads are more likely than positive ads to grab attention and make a lasting impression. Also, according to media expert Shanto Iyengar, "the more negative the ad, the more likely it is to get free media coverage. So there's a big incentive to go to extremes." The free coverage comes when an ad is so controversial or outrageous that it becomes newsworthy.

TELEVISION DEBATES Televised debates provide an opportunity for voters to find out how candidates differ on issues as well as how well they handle themselves in a high-pressure situation. They also give candidates a chance to improve their image or point out the failings of their opponents. The first televised presidential debate, held in 1960 between Republican Richard M. Nixon and Democrat John F. Kennedy, demonstrated that television was truly a game-changer. Many people who heard the debate on the radio thought Nixon had performed better than Kennedy, but people watching the debate on television believed Kennedy had won.

There is some doubt, however, as to whether debates do affect the outcome of elections. Evidence on this question is mixed. Voter surveys conducted by Gallup Polls suggest that, in 1960, the debates helped Kennedy to victory. In 1980, Republican Ronald Reagan did well in a final debate with Democratic incumbent Jimmy Carter. Reagan impressed many voters with his sunny temperament, which helped dispel fears that he was a right-wing radical. But according to Gallup's analysis, Reagan would have won the election even without the debate.

Evidence of the effects of more recent presidential debates supports the view that debates do not greatly influence election outcomes. In the first 2012 debate, Democrat Barack Obama turned in a surprisingly poor performance compared with Republican Mitt Romney, but Obama still won re-election easily. In 2016, Hillary Clinton was generally regarded as the debate winner, and she ultimately won the popular vote. Clinton was disciplined and focused, while Trump, who refused to prepare, was at times almost incoherent. After the three debates, Clinton surged from a narrow lead in the polls to a 7-percentage-point advantage. Yet this lead soon evaporated. Several pollsters suggested that, despite appearances, the debates did not actually change anyone's vote. They speculate that Trump's poor performance embarrassed his supporters and made them unwilling to talk to pollsters, whereas Clinton's supporters were energized and eager to participate. In this view, the changes in the polls were due solely to sampling error.

The 1992 debates, which featured Republican George H.W. Bush and Democrat Bill Clinton, also included a third-party candidate, H. Ross Perot. Since 1996, however, the Commission on Presidential Debates, which organizes the events, has allowed only candidates who already have substantial support to participate in the debates. This policy effectively precludes third-party candidates and independents from gaining enough support to run a significant nationwide campaign.

HISTORICAL THINKING

1. **COMPARE AND CONTRAST** What is the difference between personal attack ads and negative issue ads? Explain your answer.
2. **FORM AND SUPPORT OPINIONS** What value to the voters, if any, do you think televised presidential debates have?

News Coverage

Political ads are expensive, but coverage by the news media is free. For this reason, candidates try to take advantage of the media's interest in campaigns to increase the quantity and quality of news coverage. This isn't always easy. It can be difficult for candidates to get their messages out if the media devote the lion's share of their coverage to explaining who is ahead in the race.

MANAGED NEWS COVERAGE In recent years, candidates' campaigns have shown increasing sophistication in creating newsworthy events for journalists and TV camera crews to cover. This effort is commonly referred to as managed news coverage. Typically, one job of a campaign manager is to create newsworthy events that demonstrate the candidate's strengths and that attract positive media coverage. For example, candidates might visit a school to show their concern for education or an army base to show their support for a robust defense.

In the run-up to the 2016 presidential election, one candidate was such a master at winning press attention that he hardly needed the services of a campaign manager. That candidate was Donald Trump, who had spent many years as host of a TV reality show. Outrageous comments gained Trump more free news coverage from the top three TV networks in 2015 than any other story except the

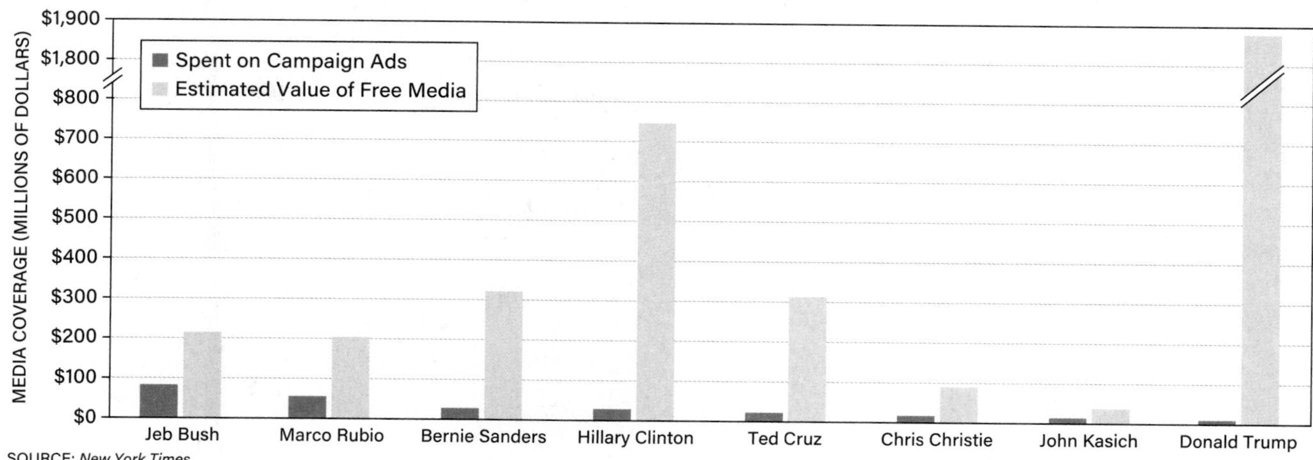

weather, as you can see from the bar graph comparing free and paid media coverage of all the 2016 presidential candidates.

SPINNING THE STORY Many aspects of a campaign focus on potential news coverage. Political consultants plan political events to attract the press, but they also know that journalists and political reporters compete for headlines and that they can be manipulated. A reporter might be granted an exclusive personal interview with the candidate, with conditions imposed by the campaign. For instance, the reporter might be directed to avoid a certain topic that could cause the candidate embarrassment. Each candidate also has advisers whose job is to **spin**, or manipulate the coverage and context of, stories and events.

POLITICS IN NON-NEWS TV PROGRAMS Television dramas and situation comedies aren't normally regarded as forums for political debate. But a number of them pursue political themes. For example, the popular Netflix drama *House of Cards* depicts the successes of a ruthless and corrupt politician, and the satirical HBO series *Veep* follows the political career of a fictional vice president.

For some years now, many viewers have tuned in to politically oriented late-night satire for an amusing, often outrageous take on the day's news. Among the most famous of these is *The Daily Show* on Comedy Central, which presents itself as a fake news program. *The Daily Show* gained a large following by using real news footage and actual quotations from public figures to mock politicians and political events. Other late-night programming has expanded on this concept.

HISTORICAL THINKING

3. **MAKE PREDICTIONS** What event might a campaign manager arrange to show that a candidate cares about farmers?
4. **IDENTIFY MAIN IDEAS AND DETAILS** Why do you think managing spin has become such a key part of many candidates' campaigns?
5. **INTERPRET GRAPHS** Based on the graph and what you know of the 2016 campaign, what type of candidate is most likely to benefit from free media coverage?

Talk Radio—The Wild West of the Media

The power of radio was proven by President Franklin D. Roosevelt's first fireside chat in March 1933. To prevent a financial crisis from turning to a full-fledged panic, Roosevelt halted all banking operations in the entire country on March 6—only two days after his inauguration. In the following week, Roosevelt, his Cabinet, and Congress worked on new legislation and prepared to reopen the banks. On March 12, Roosevelt delivered a brief talk over the radio to 60 million listeners—close to half the population of the country—to calm the public and explain the banking crisis. When the first banks were allowed to reopen the next day, instead of depositors withdrawing their money in a panic, people stood in line waiting to redeposit their money to help their president rescue the country.

From radio's earliest years, the medium has been a favorite outlet for the political right. One of the nation's most successful radio personalities in the 1930s was Father Charles Coughlin, a Roman Catholic priest based in Michigan. Coughlin's audience numbered more than 40 million listeners—and remember that the nation had only 123 million inhabitants in 1930. Coughlin started out as a Roosevelt supporter, but he soon moved to the extreme right, not only attacking the New Deal but also advocating anti-Semitism and expressing sympathy for Adolf Hitler. Coughlin's fascist connections eventually destroyed his popularity.

Modern talk radio took off in the United States during the 1990s. In 1988, there were 200 talk-show radio stations. Today, there are more than 1,200. The growth of talk radio was made possible by the FCC's repeal of the fairness doctrine in 1987. As you have read, the fairness doctrine required broadcasters to present both sides on controversial issues of public importance. *Talkers* magazine, which provides annual ratings of talk radio shows based on impact, ratings, revenue, and other characteristics, chose six politically conservative talk shows among those they named in the top 10 for 2018. Of the others in the top 10, one is an apolitical (nonpolitical) financial advice show, another provides light entertainment, and only two offer liberal and progressive perspectives.

AUDIENCES AND HOSTS The Pew Research Center for the People and the Press reports that 17 percent of the public regularly listen to talk radio. This audience is predominantly male and middle aged. Some 45 percent consider themselves conservatives. Political talk-show hosts don't attempt to hide their biases. If anything, they exaggerate them for effect. Leading talk show personalities such as Rush Limbaugh, Sean Hannity, and Michael Savage espouse a brand of conservatism that is robust, even radical. Talk radio is sometimes characterized as the Wild West of the media. Hosts disdain journalistic conventions and regularly characterize opponents in aggressively negative terms.

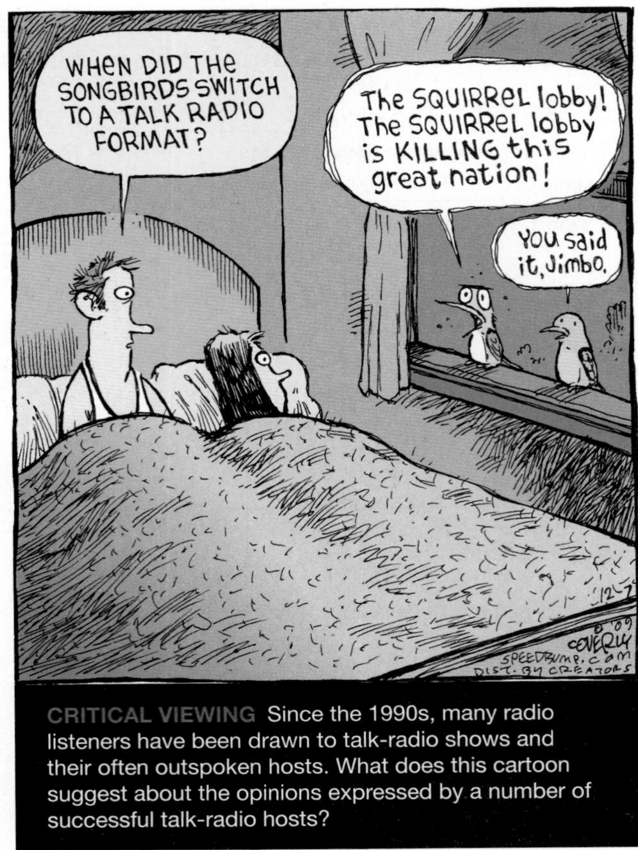

CRITICAL VIEWING Since the 1990s, many radio listeners have been drawn to talk-radio shows and their often outspoken hosts. What does this cartoon suggest about the opinions expressed by a number of successful talk-radio hosts?

Talk-show hosts sometimes appear to care more about the entertainment value of their statements than whether or not they are true. Hosts have often publicized false or hateful beliefs, such as the contention that President Barack Obama wasn't really born in the United States. The government of Britain barred talk-show host Michael Savage from entry into that country, based on his remarks about Muslims. Conspiracy theorist Alex Jones, who has profited from false stories that school shootings were staged and that the September 11, 2001, attacks were orchestrated by the U.S. government, has effectively been removed from the airwaves as well as from major social media platforms. He faces a number of lawsuits for defamation, including from the parents of murdered children.

THE IMPACT OF TALK RADIO Some supporters of entertaining, if biased, radio talk shows argue that they are simply a response to consumer demand. Others say talk shows that encourage listeners to call in to express their opinions provide a valuable forum for the exchange of ideas. Critics fear that talk shows empower **fringe groups**—small groups of people who share an uncommon or extreme opinion outside the mainstream of society—by magnifying their rage and seeming to give their views credibility by airing them. As yet, no one has proposed a rule to reign in talk-show hosts. This is consistent with the rights to freedom of expression, freedom of the press, and due process.

In a 1969 ruling, the Supreme Court upheld the fairness doctrine. The FCC repealed it in 1987, but it's possible the FCC might one day choose to reinstate the doctrine. In 2009, after Democratic victories in the 2008 elections, a few liberals advocated doing just that. President Obama and the Democratic leadership in Congress quickly put a stop to this notion. Americans have come to accept talk radio as part of the political environment. Any attempt to curtail it would be seen as infringing on First Amendment rights and could prove highly unpopular.

HISTORICAL THINKING

6. **MAKE GENERALIZATIONS** Why have there been few serious attempts to put limits on talk radio or its hosts?

The Question of Media Bias

Strong conservative voices dominate talk radio. Supporters say the dominance of conservatives on talk radio counters what they perceive as liberal bias in the mainstream print and TV news media. The question of media bias is important in any democracy. After all, for our political system to work, citizens must be well informed. And they can be well informed only if the news media, the source of much of their information, do not slant the news.

Today, however, relatively few Americans believe the news media are unbiased in their reporting. Accompanying this perception is a notable decline in the public's confidence in the news media in recent years. In a 2017 Gallup poll measuring the public's confidence in various institutions, only 27 percent of the respondents stated that they had "a great deal" or "quite a lot" of confidence in newspapers. Fewer of them, 24 percent, had the same degree of confidence in television news. Still fewer, only 16 percent, reported that level of confidence in internet news sources. Because of these low percentages, some analysts believe that the media are facing a crisis of confidence.

Despite these low figures, the public does believe that the press is successful in fulfilling its role as a government watchdog. In a recent poll by the Pew Research Center, 68 percent of respondents agreed that "press criticism of political leaders keeps them from doing things that should not be done." Republicans, Democrats, and independents were equally likely to agree with this statement.

PARTISAN BIAS For years, conservatives have argued that there is a liberal bias in the news media, and liberals have complained that the news media reflect a conservative bias. The majority of Americans think that the media reflect a bias in one direction or the other. According to a 2016 Gallup poll, 40 percent of the respondents believed that the news media favored the Democrats, whereas only 14 percent thought that the news media favored the Republicans.

Surveys and analyses of the attitudes and voting habits of reporters have suggested that most journalists do indeed hold liberal views. One organization calculated that from 1999 to 2016, campaign contributors who listed their occupation as journalist or reporter gave 73 percent of their donations to Democrats. Only 14 percent of the donations went to Republicans. Many journalists themselves perceive the *New York Times* as liberal—which might be expected given that the population of New York City is more liberal than much of the rest of the country. Still, members of the press are likely to view themselves as moderates. In a recent study, the Pew Research Center found that 64 percent of reporters in both national and local media applied the term *moderate* to themselves.

BALANCE AND FACT-CHECKING Perhaps the most important protection against bias in reporting is a commitment to professionalism on the part of most journalists. Professional ethics dictate a commitment to objectivity and truthfulness. Reporters may sometimes violate this code, but it does have an impact.

Unlike reporters, who do their best to be unbiased and hide their political views, many television and radio **pundits**—people whose opinions are treated as authoritative—make their names as representatives of a certain political persuasion or point of view. A common technique of broadcast news programs that aim to be neutral is to have two pundits, one allegedly liberal and the other allegedly conservative, state their views. One drawback of this practice is that it fails whenever there are more than two plausible perspectives on an issue. Another problem with trying to be neutral by simply presenting both sides is that it sets up what is often termed a "false equivalency" by giving the false impression that each of the two views presented is equally reasonable and supported by the facts.

A recent, helpful development is the growing number of political fact-checking operations by such organizations as the Poynter Institute and the Annenberg Public Policy Center. Both claim to be independent, nonpartisan, nonprofit, and dedicated to the truth. Services such as these enable journalists to be more objective in identifying and cracking down on political lies and deception.

Media fact-checkers had to work overtime to keep up with President Trump's regular use of the social media platform Twitter to communicate his ideas. The *Washington Post* fact-checker counted over 8,000 false or misleading statements in Trump's first two years in office. Several were repeated over 100 times each. In response, Trump attacked the media in especially harsh terms, often calling their reports "fake news." His venomous attacks on the media were unprecedented in presidential history.

A BIAS AGAINST LOSERS Research suggests that rather than having a partisan bias, the news media may have a bias against losers. A candidate who falls behind in a race is called the loser. This makes it more difficult for the candidate to regain favor in the voters' eyes. The media use the framework of winners and losers to describe events throughout the election cycle. Even a presidential debate is regarded as a sporting match that results in a winner and a loser. Even a candidate who is popular with voters may lose momentum after being branded as the loser in a debate.

In the days leading up to the 2016 debates, reporters focused on what each candidate had to do to win the debate. When each debate was over, reporters immediately speculated about who had won as they waited for post-debate polls to answer that question. Debates serve as an important source of political information for voters, but this function can be undercut by the media's focus on winning and losing.

A CHANGING NEWS CULTURE News organizations are redefining their purpose and increasingly looking for special niches in which to build their audiences. For some, the niche is personal commentary, revolving around highly politicized TV figures such as Sean Hannity (conservative) and Rachel Maddow (liberal). In a sense, news organizations have begun to base their appeal more on how they cover the news and less on what they cover. Traditional journalism—fact-based reporting—is becoming less important. Expressions of opinion and punditry, or the use of mass media for commentary by self-proclaimed or recognized experts, now plays a larger role.

For others, the niche is narrowcasting, or aiming at a narrowly defined area or audience. This can take the form of hyperlocalism—that is, focusing news coverage on events in the local community. Narrowcasting can also involve covering only highly specific subject matter that appeals strongly to a limited number of viewers. Magazines have always done this: Consider the many magazine titles on topics such as model railroading, crocheting, or life in a particular city. With the large number of cable and streaming channels, narrowcasting has become important on television as well. Cable networks now appeal to members of particular racial and ethnic groups, hobbyists, or history buffs, while streaming services offer channels with programming for people with a special interest in the NASA space programs, classic cartoons, or British comedies.

Online streaming services also provide niche programming. True, users who rely only on streaming video may have trouble accessing the most up-to-the-minute network television news shows. Overall, however, there is no shortage of late-breaking news sources online.

HISTORICAL THINKING

7. **FORM AND SUPPORT OPINIONS** Do you think a journalist who consistently votes for candidates from one party can objectively write a news story about the other party? Explain your answer.

8. **MAKE GENERALIZATIONS** Why might a newspaper with a hyperlocal approach be successful in terms of readers and profits?

LESSON
19.3 The Power of the Internet and Social Media

In the late 1960s, the Advanced Research Projects Agency (ARPA), a unit within the U.S. Defense Department, created the first computer network. ARPA soon extended its network, called ARPANET, to university researchers. By 1983, when the network became known as the internet, it was open to the public at large. Its creators believed censorship of the internet was impossible. "The internet interprets censorship as damage," one early engineer exulted, "and routes around it." In other words, the internet would carry information on new paths to skirt around any censorship blocks. In time, the internet became an international—not just an American—institution. Every nation with a modern economy has embraced the internet. Many developing nations have done so as well.

News on the Internet

Today, computers connect and communicate across the globe. This online world of computer networks, known as cyberspace, is getting bigger every day. More than 4.6 billion people were using the internet in 2020—some 60 percent of the world's inhabitants. About half of all users live in Asia. In the United States, about 88 percent of the population use the internet. More than two-thirds of American households access the internet using mobile devices, including smartphones. In addition, popular social media sites have enormous numbers of personalized pages. **Social media** are online platforms for communication in which users form communities with whom to share information and opinions. Two of the largest social media are Twitter, with about 335 million active accounts, and Facebook, with more than 2.2 billion.

Not surprisingly, the internet is an important source of information. All the major newspapers are online, as are transcripts of the most-watched television news programs. About two-thirds of internet users consider the internet to be an important source of news. In addition, having an internet strategy has become an integral part of political campaigning.

NEWS ORGANIZATIONS ONLINE Almost every major American news organization, both print and broadcast, delivers news through the World Wide Web, a part of the internet. Indeed, an online presence is required to effectively compete for revenues with other traditional news companies. The online share of newspaper company revenues has increased over the years. Still, only about a quarter of U.S. newspaper revenues come from online sources.

Some newspaper sites simply post articles from their print versions. Major newspapers, however, offer a different array of coverage and options on their websites because they can be constantly updated with breaking news, while their print editions can be revised only once or twice a day, at a high cost. Websites can also link readers to more extensive reports on particular topics and may include videos, podcasts, and other multimedia features.

Newspapers and TV news organizations also use the World Wide Web to expand the reach of the content they produce beyond their own websites. They publish stories—some newly written, some copied from their website—to platforms such as Facebook Instant Articles, Apple News, and Google AMP (Accelerated Mobile Pages). Online news sites invite readers to subscribe to the organization's LinkedIn, Facebook, Twitter, Instagram, and Pinterest accounts and email feeds. Readers who receive online content from news sites may also transmit lots of personal information—in particular, their digital address and their internet usage history—which enables the site to deliver narrowly targeted advertising.

Still, news organizations haven't yet mastered the online world. The people who read newspapers online are typically the same people who read the print edition. The same is true for online TV news programs: Viewers are typically those who also watch news programs on their television sets. Therefore, investing heavily in online news delivery may not be a solution for news organizations seeking to increase revenues by adding readers or viewers.

THE ECONOMICS OF ONLINE NEWS Newspapers rely heavily on advertising revenue. By 2012, however, the advertising industry was spending more on the internet than it spent on all print newspapers and magazines put together. Furthermore, the additional revenues that newspapers have gained from their online editions don't come close to making up for the massive losses in advertising revenue suffered by their print editions. Even worse, in many instances, publications haven't sold enough advertising in their online editions to cover the expense of publishing on the web.

The issue isn't that there's an absolute shortage of online advertising revenue. The real issue is that content providers—such as newspaper sites that employ journalists to create new material—receive just a small share of the online advertising revenue. Most of the revenue goes to **aggregators**—mass or social media that collect and retransmit news or opinion from other sources. News aggregation websites develop little new content but mostly direct users elsewhere. Google's parent company Alphabet, by far the largest of these aggregators, collects one-third of all online ad revenues. By 2016, at $25 billion, Google's U.S. ad revenues exceeded the revenues of the entire U.S. newspaper industry.

HISTORICAL THINKING

1. **ANALYZE CAUSE AND EFFECT** Why don't the newspapers that employ journalists to create content receive all the revenue from advertisers?
2. **INTERPRET GRAPHS** Which top media company had the greatest percentage increase in revenue during the period 2012–2018? Explain your answer.

Blogs and Podcasts

As mentioned earlier, the news culture is changing. Blogs (short for weblogs: logs or diaries on the web) lie at the heart of this change. A blog is a regularly updated website on which individuals with little technical expertise can post what they write. Blogs are responsible for much of the innovation in news delivery today, and recent years have seen a veritable explosion of them. Mainstream news organizations seek to make their websites more appealing, in part to compete with blogs run by private citizens and those not in the news business. As a result, they have been adding blogs to their own websites.

CITIZEN JOURNALISM Anyone can create a blog and post news or opinions, including photos and videos, to share with others: independent journalists, scholars, political activists, candidates, local officials, or community organizers. Taken as a whole, the collection, analysis, and dissemination of information online by the citizenry can be called citizen journalism. Other terms that have been used to collectively describe news blogs or bloggers include *people journalism* and *participatory journalism*. The term *community journalism* applies to blogs that focus on news and developments in a specific community.

Selected Top Media Companies (by Total Revenue), 2012–2018

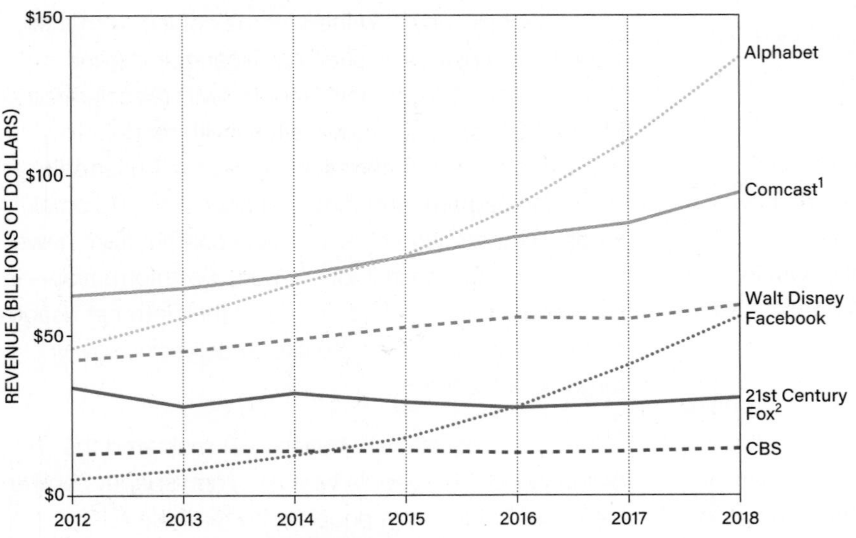

[1]Comcast 2018 figure includes revenue from Sky, acquired 2018.
[2]In 2018, Disney began acquiring the entertainment assets of 21st Century Fox.
SOURCE: Securities and Exchange Commission (SEC)

The increase in news blogs and do-it-yourself journalism on the web is a threat to mainstream news sources. Compared with the operational costs faced by a major news organization, the costs of creating and maintaining blogs is trivial. Moreover, the most successful blogs are able to sell advertising. Because of their low costs, it doesn't take much advertising to keep such sites in business.

Podcasting is a growing method of delivering news and information. Talk Art, a popular audio podcast hosted by gallery director Robert Diament (left) and actor Russell Tovey (right), consists of lively conversations with a wide variety of individuals from the art world. Here, the hosts interview Salman Toor, a Pakistani American artist.

Blogging and citizen journalism have generated other concerns. Unlike professional news organizations, which do their best to verify the facts in their stories, many independent bloggers do not adequately fact-check material on their websites. Major news sources struggle to pay the professionals needed to meet their traditional standards and still compete with reporting and opinions generated by unpaid amateurs, who may not understand the protocols and methods used by professionals to confirm and document the accuracy of their stories.

PODCASTS Another nontraditional form of news distribution is the podcast—an audio or video file that can be downloaded to a computer or mobile device, such as a smartphone. Though still a relatively small portion of the overall news-delivery system, podcasts are becoming increasingly popular. They can take a variety of forms, from interviews and panel discussions to commentaries. Like blogging, podcasting is inexpensive and requires little skill. People with a variety of interests and areas of expertise produce podcasts. More and more, political candidates make both blogging and podcasting part of their campaign strategies.

HISTORICAL THINKING

3. **EVALUATE** What advantage do bloggers and podcasters have over traditional media?
4. **MAKE CONNECTIONS** Do you think citizen journalism supports a free press and a healthy democracy? Why or why not?

Cyberspace and Political Campaigns

Today's political parties and candidates understand the benefits of using the internet to conduct online campaigns and raise funds. Voters also are increasingly using the web to access information about parties and candidates, promote political goals, and obtain political news. Generally, the use of the internet is an inexpensive way for candidates to contact, recruit, and mobilize supporters, as well as to disseminate information about their positions on issues and to raise money. In effect, the internet can replace brochures, letters, and position papers. Individual voters or political party supporters can use the internet to avoid having to go to special meetings or to a campaign site to do volunteer work or learn about a candidate's positions.

A 2016 study by the Pew Research Center showed that the internet is now a viable medium for communicating political information and ideas to voters. According to the study, 50 percent of young adults—those in the 18-to-29 age group—turned to the internet for news often. Of all the adults surveyed, 81 percent obtained news from online sources at least some of the time, and 38 percent often got their news online. The Pew study also found that, in contrast, 20 percent of adults often got news from print newspapers, down from 27 percent in 2013.

One reason for these numbers is that most people who prefer to read the news now do so online. Most of those who prefer to watch or listen to the news rather than read it continue to rely on television and radio. Since 2013, the percent of adults who obtained some of their news through a mobile device, such as a smartphone, increased from 54 to 72.

INTERNET CAMPAIGN STRATEGIES Internet campaigning has become a necessary part of running for office. Candidates typically hire a web manager or web strategist to create a well-designed, informative, and user-friendly campaign website to attract viewers, hold their attention, manage their emails, and track their contributions. Fund-raising on the internet by presidential candidates increased significantly after a decision by the Federal Election Commission (FEC) in June 1999. The FEC ruled that the federal government could distribute matching funds to presidential primary election candidates for credit-card donations received through the internet. Gone are the days of mass-mailing letters to prospective donors through the post office. Email cuts the cost to near zero.

As you read earlier, web managers employ microtargeting to increase the efficiency of their internet campaigns. This involves collecting and storing an enormous amount of personal information about existing and potential voters. Political scientists have long known that information such as age, marital status, and place of residence offer clues to a person's political leanings. But microtargeting adds other characteristics to the mix, such as what magazines a person reads, what products and brands they shop for, what shows they watch and music they listen to, who their friends are—personal information that can often be learned from social media. With these facts in hand, technicians can engage in **data mining**, the use of sophisticated analytical methods on large amounts of data to identify patterns. Data mining enables campaigns to identify likely supporters and then narrowly craft messages relating to each person's interests and views. It can also single out the people most likely to contribute money to the campaign.

Web managers also have other ways of contacting voters and generating interest in a campaign. They hire bloggers to promote their candidate's views, they arrange for podcasting of campaign information, and they post frequently to the campaign Facebook pages and Twitter and other feeds to maintain contact with supporters and potential supporters. Managers also hire staff to monitor the web for news about the candidates and repost it.

Campaign staffers also track the online publications of netroots groups. Netroots activists are online supporters who back the candidate but aren't controlled by the candidate's organization. (The term is a portmanteau, or mash-up, of *internet* and *grassroots*.) One of the challenges facing candidates today is delivering a consistent campaign message, and netroots groups can make this task more difficult. Such a group might publish online promotional ads or other materials that don't accurately represent a candidate's position. They might also attack the candidate's opponent in ways that the candidate doesn't approve. Yet no campaign manager wants to alienate these groups, because they can raise significant sums of money and garner votes for the candidate.

CONSTANT EXPOSURE Just as citizen journalism has altered the news culture, citizen videos have changed the traditional campaign. Candidates never know when a comment they make may be caught on camera by someone with a cell phone and published on the internet for all to see. A candidate's opponents might post a compilation of video clips showing inconsistent comments on a controversial or complex topic, such as abortion or health-care reform legislation. The effect can be very damaging, because it opens candidates to charges of flip-flopping, or inconsistency in their positions.

Political scientists have argued over the importance of political gaffes. Awkward comments by Mitt Romney and Barack Obama in 2012 didn't seem to have much effect on their standing in the polls. In 2016, Donald Trump continually made statements that crossed long-established lines of decency and dignity. Based on past assumptions about what the public would allow, these should have been fatal to his campaign. In reality, nothing that Trump said about politicians, journalists, Latinos and African Americans, or, for that matter, policy issues seemed to disturb his supporters.

Trump's opponent in 2016, Hillary Clinton, was a disciplined candidate, and her list of misstatements was relatively short. She made a few serious gaffes, however. For example, she described half of Trump's supporters as a "basket of deplorables." An even more damaging quote was "Because we're going to put a lot of coal miners and coal companies out of business, right? And we're going to make it clear that we don't want to forget those people." Clinton seemed to be taking personal responsibility for the projected future loss of coal jobs, when in fact almost all of them would be lost to automation and competition from other energy sources, such as natural gas, and she was expressing the need to find new opportunities for them.

According to some pundits, Clinton's real problem was that she disliked reporters, and they disliked her. Her attitude was shaped by her opponents' decades-long efforts to pin a scandal on her. Most of these scandals were bogus, according to her supporters. Clinton's supporters also argued that issues such as the security risk of her private email server had been blown out of proportion. Still, the constant barrage of bad press damaged her reputation. Some feminists perceived the attacks on Clinton, and the major news media's reporting of these attacks, as expressions of sexism. They argued that, while the seriousness of the charges and criticisms against Trump and the evidence supporting them were far more damning, Clinton was treated more harshly by the press.

DIGITAL DIRTY TRICKS Public opinion polls in the run-up to the 2016 presidential election predicted that Clinton would beat Trump, and much of the news media accepted this conclusion. But social media told a different story. "The only place that we're hearing that Donald Trump honestly is losing is in the media or these polls," a conservative political commentator pointed out. "You're not seeing it with the crowd rallies, you're not seeing it on social media—where Donald Trump is two to three times more popular than Hillary Clinton on every social media platform."

As it turned out, much of the polling was suspect. Supporters of both campaigns used bots—software that performs an automated task—to inflate the poll numbers favoring their candidate, often by repeatedly submitting votes to an online poll. Bots (short for *robots*) may have distorted social media statistics on the popularity of the candidates as well. For

CRITICAL VIEWING Groups linked to the Russian government interfered with the 2016 presidential election by posting fake news stories and political advertisements on social media. For example, Russians impersonating a Muslim organization, United Muslims of America, posted the fake news story shown at the lower right. What do you think was the goal of this fake story?

example, especially during the 2016 debate season, bots generated posts on Twitter that were forwarded thousands of times, distorting the candidates' levels of support on social media.

The 2016 political season was marred by both misinformation—incorrect information—as well as **disinformation**—false information or propaganda dispersed to deceive or mislead. One example of the former is a Fox News report, just before Election Day, that foreign intelligence agencies had hacked Clinton's computer and presumably gained access to classified material. The story was incorrect, and the reporter later retracted it. That misinformation may or may not have been distributed maliciously.

An example of disinformation is the deliberate posting on Facebook of false news reports by the Internet Research Agency (IRA), a hacking and disinformation organization of the Russian government. In the lead-up to the 2016 election, Russians created thousands of fake social media accounts, many of them purporting to be Americans. The IRA created bots to post comments on discussion boards, not only on news outlets but also on sites as diverse as *Pokémon Go* and Tumbler. When they managed to get their fake news stories published on American news sites, they touted these as evidence backing up their initial claim. They also recruited Americans, including some legitimate campaign workers, to do favors or tasks for them.

The IRA's goals were to disrupt reasoned discussion, create partisan hostility, and erode trust in the government and the democratic process. One means for doing this was to promote the candidacies of insurgent candidates Donald Trump and Bernie Sanders and to insult and criticize Hillary Clinton. In 2018, the special counsel investigating the 2016 Trump campaign's ties to Russian agents indicted the IRA and a number of other Russians for engaging in a criminal conspiracy to defraud the United States by their interference with the election process.

Facebook and Twitter were harshly criticized for allowing the creation of fake accounts without any oversight, allowing false and defamatory stories to be reposted by their users, and accepting payment for thousands of advertisements promoting hoaxes related to polarizing political issues. Google also came under severe criticism for allowing malicious users to manipulate their search algorithms to promote their disinformation in search results. As a result of this experience, it is clear that social media users must learn to recognize misinformation and disinformation and avoid spreading it.

By the summer of 2020, a coalition of civil rights groups, including the NAACP and the Anti-Defamation League (ADL), an organization founded to combat anti-Semitism, had called for an advertiser boycott of Facebook. Their concerns had expanded beyond the spread of disinformation to outrage over the spread of hate speech on Facebook. Numerous advertisers joined the campaign. Other large companies, such as Coca-Cola, Ford, Honda, Microsoft, Starbucks, and Verizon announced plans to halt advertising on Facebook and other social media platforms. Meanwhile, social networking site Reddit removed a thread that included more than 790,000 people, many of whom were supporters of President Trump, for using hate speech to target and harass others. While these efforts seem to have had little long-term effect on social media's advertising revenue, they have raised awareness of the issue of hate speech on these platforms.

In late summer of 2020, Twitter and Facebook pledged to step up their efforts to police their platforms for misinformation. Both began removing posts that spread misleading information about the coronavirus. Facebook created a special hub where users can access accurate information about voting rules and resources in their areas. Twitter tightened its rules regarding the spread of misleading information on voting by its users. After a mob of Trump supporters stormed the U.S. Capitol on January 6, 2021, Facebook, Twitter, and Instagram temporarily suspended the accounts of the president of the United States, stating concerns that his posts—many of which had previously been flagged as inaccurate—would inflame more rioting. Days later, Twitter permanently suspended his account.

HISTORICAL THINKING

5. **MAKE PREDICTIONS** What does it mean for the future of print newspapers that half of the young adults surveyed in 2016 often got their news online?
6. **EVALUATE** What concerns do you think critics might have about microtargeting?

This photo of Seven Mile Bridge provides a visual idea of what the coastline of Florida and other states might look like 100 years from now if the sea level rises according to current climate change models. Rising seas could disable critical components of the nation's internet infrastructure, much of which is located along the coast.

The Internet Is Drowning

by Alejandra Borunda **National Geographic Online, July 16, 2018**

Nearly every aspect of modern life, from banking to manufacturing to medical services to transportation, depends at least partly on internet communications. In her *National Geographic* article "The Internet Is Drowning," Alejandra Borunda explores an impending and formidable threat to the internet: climate change. As Borunda reports, the inertia in the climate system means there's nothing humans can do to stop climate change from melting the polar ice caps within 15 years. Here's what the resulting sea level rise will mean for the internet:

Scientists mapped out the threads and knots of Internet infrastructure in the U.S. and layered that on top of maps showing future sea level rise. What they found was ominous: Within 15 years, thousands of miles of fiber optic cable—and hundreds of pieces of other key infrastructure—are likely to be swamped by the encroaching ocean. And while some of that infrastructure may be water resistant, little of it was designed to live fully underwater. . . .

"Considering how interconnected everything is these days, protecting the Internet is crucial," says Mikhail Chester, the director of the Resilient Infrastructure Laboratory at the University of Arizona. Even minor hits, like when storms knock out Internet connectivity for a few days, can affect things we take for granted, from traffic lights to flight patterns. . . .

"We live in a world designed for an environment that no longer exists," says Rich Sorkin, the co-founder of Jupiter Intelligence, a company that models climate-induced risk. Accepting the reality of what the future will look like, he says, is key to planning for it—and studies like this, he says, highlight just how quickly we'll all have to adapt.

Access the full version of "The Internet Is Drowning" by Alejandra Borunda through the Resources Menu in MindTap.

THINK ABOUT IT What role do you think government should play in responding to the threat that rising sea levels pose to the infrastructure of the internet?

CHAPTER 19

GOVERNMENT, POLITICS, AND THE MEDIA

Review

VOCABULARY

For each of the following vocabulary terms, write a sentence that shows an understanding of the term's meaning.

1. mass media
2. agenda setting
3. spin
4. pundit
5. fairness doctrine
6. fringe group
7. aggregator
8. social media
9. disinformation
10. data mining

MAIN IDEAS

Answer the following questions. Support your answers with evidence from the chapter.

11. What are the two roles of the news media regarding what Americans think about political issues? **LESSON 19.1**
12. How did the creation of radio depend on new technology? **LESSON 19.1**
13. If you hear a podcast citing the efficiency of wind power and statistics about its success in Europe, and you then vote to install wind turbines in your county, would you say the podcast employed priming or framing to convince you? Why? **LESSON 19.1**
14. Why do you think political campaigns, in spite of sharp criticism, continue to broadcast personal attack ads against opponents? **LESSON 19.2**
15. Why do candidates take part in televised debates? **LESSON 19.2**
16. Trump spent little on campaign ads, so how did he get his messages out? **LESSON 19.2**
17. Why do you think the press has come to rely more and more on political fact-checkers? **LESSON 19.2**
18. What is one factor that gives internet news sites an advantage over print news? **LESSON 19.3**
19. How does citizen journalism, such as blogging, reflect democratic ideals? **LESSON 19.3**
20. How does the use of bots by political campaigns distort the accuracy of polls? **LESSON 19.3**

HISTORICAL THINKING

Answer the following questions. Support your answers with evidence from the chapter.

21. **FORM AND SUPPORT OPINIONS** Do you think politicians should avoid expressing hostility toward the press for criticizing them? Explain your answer.
22. **EVALUATE** Why do you think Lyndon Johnson's "daisy girl" ad was so effective?
23. **MAKE INFERENCES** If the fairness doctrine were still in effect, how might talk radio be different?
24. **MAKE CONNECTIONS** Why do you think only a handful of print newspapers do more than simply copy articles from their print version to their website?
25. **MAKE GENERALIZATIONS** Why would campaign web managers want up-to-the-minute news about their candidate, and how does the web help provide that?

INTERPRET VISUALS

Study the time line. Then answer the questions.

26. Why did internet use begin to soar in the 1990s?

The Internet and New Media

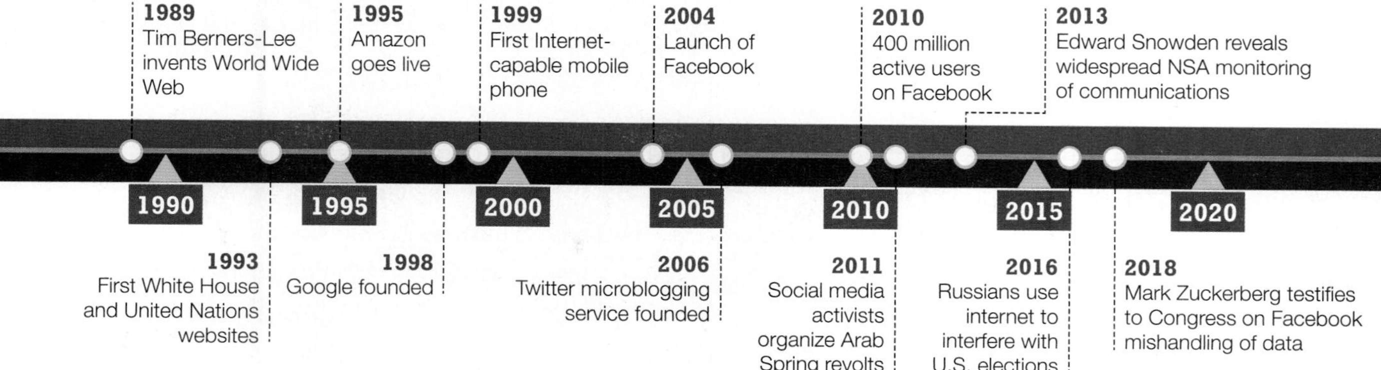
1989
Tim Berners-Lee invents World Wide Web
1995
Amazon goes live
1999
First Internet-capable mobile phone
2004
Launch of Facebook
2010
400 million active users on Facebook
2013
Edward Snowden reveals widespread NSA monitoring of communications
1990
1995
2000
2005
2010
2015
2020
1993
First White House and United Nations websites
1998
Google founded
2006
Twitter microblogging service founded
2011
Social media activists organize Arab Spring revolts
2016
Russians use internet to interfere with U.S. elections
2018
Mark Zuckerberg testifies to Congress on Facebook mishandling of data

27. Based on the time line, how would you explain why Barack Obama's election in 2008 was the first presidential election to be profoundly affected by the internet?

ANALYZE SOURCES

In April 2018, Mark Zuckerberg, the chief executive officer of Facebook, testified before the House Energy and Commerce Committee about Russia's misuse of Facebook to interfere in the 2016 U.S. election. He explained what happened this way:

> What we found was that bad actors had used coordinated networks of fake accounts to interfere in the election: promoting or attacking specific candidates and causes, creating distrust in political institutions, or simply spreading confusion. . . . We also learned about a disinformation campaign run by the Internet Research Agency (IRA)—a Russian agency that has repeatedly acted deceptively and tried to manipulate people in the U.S., Europe, and Russia. We found about 470 accounts and pages linked to the IRA, which generated around 80,000 Facebook posts over about a two-year period. Our best estimate is that approximately 126 million people may have been served content from a Facebook page associated with the IRA at some point during that period.

28. What in Zuckerberg's statement indicates that Russian interference in the 2016 election was skillfully carried out and effective?

29. Do you think Facebook could or should have prevented the activities described in Zuckerberg's testimony? Why or why not?

CONNECT TO YOUR LIFE

30. **EXPOSITORY** Has the shift from old to new media made it easier or more difficult to understand political issues? Talk with older family members or other adults you know about how they used to access the news when they were your age and how they get their news today. Invite their opinions on how the news media have changed over time. Write a couple of paragraphs describing what you learned from your interviews.

TIPS

- Prepare for your interviews by making a list of the various ways of accessing news and information, both old and new.
- Use the list to prompt responses from the adults you interview.
- Summarize the information you gathered from the adults about the shift from old to new media, and compare their opinions with your own.
- Draw a conclusion based on what you learned.

9 State and Local Government

UNIT 9 OVERVIEW

Chapter 20 State Governments

Chapter 21 Local Governments

CRITICAL VIEWING Spectators ring the rotunda of the Texas Capitol during a special session of the state legislature in 2013. The state lawmakers were locked in a bitter dispute over a bill that would redefine the state's laws regarding abortions. What does the photograph indicate about people's involvement with state government?

"Our challenges can only be solved
if we face them together."
—Chicago Mayor Lori Lightfoot

CHAPTER 20

State Governments

LESSONS

20.1 State Constitutions

20.2 State Legislative Branches

National Geographic Online:
How Geography Shaped American History, Law, and Politics

20.3 State Executive Branches

CRITICAL VIEWING Danica Roem (D-Prince William), left, becomes the first openly transgender member of the Virginia House of Delegates as she takes the oath of office in January 2018. The Virginia House of Delegates traces its roots to the House of Burgesses—the first legislative assembly formed in what is now the United States. Why are government officials required to take an

LESSON
20.1 State Constitutions

Though some Americans may think that the power of state governments is dwarfed by that of the national government in Washington, D.C., the states actually have a great deal of power. As U.S. Supreme Court Justice Louis Brandeis wrote in 1932, "a single courageous state may . . . serve as a laboratory; and try novel social and economic experiments without risk to the rest of the country." As laboratories of democracy, state governments try to identify workable solutions to their own problems. Sometimes, these novel experiments are adopted by other states, or even nationally. For example, many of the provisions of the 2010 Affordable Care Act originated with health-care reform efforts passed in 2006 in the state of Massachusetts.

Principles of State Constitutions

State governments have a profound impact on many areas of people's daily lives. Take driving. The curriculum of your driver's education classes is set by the state. After you pass the state-mandated driving test, you receive your license from the state. Once you are licensed to drive, your insurance coverage must comply with state law. As you drive on state roads, you must obey state traffic laws.

States are involved in many other areas of life as well. In early 2019, two outgoing governors—John Hickenlooper (D–CO) and Bill Haslam (R–TN)—wrote an open letter to the newly elected governors taking office that month. They described what they called "the bread and butter issues" on which state governments focus. "Citizens care about the roads they drive to work, the schools they trust with their children, the health care available when they get sick, the safety of the communities they call home and the opportunity available to themselves and those they love," they wrote. In other words, states have the power to make laws on issues like transportation, education, health care, and public safety. This is due to the way powers are distributed under the U.S. Constitution.

STATE POWERS WITHIN THE FEDERAL SYSTEM

According to the U.S. Constitution, the federal government has certain expressed and implied powers that remain under its sole authority. But the Tenth Amendment says that "the powers not delegated to the United States by the Constitution, nor prohibited by it to the States, are reserved to the States respectively, or to the people." These reserved powers allow states to make laws regarding such things as licensing teachers and setting school curricula.

Of course, the states' authority isn't absolute. As you know, Article VI, Clause 2, of the Constitution establishes the laws of the federal government as the supreme laws of the land. That means that they supersede, or overrule, state laws if the two are in conflict, and all state laws must comply with federal law.

Originally, however, the protections of the Bill of Rights applied only to the federal government and to federal court cases. Therefore, while the U.S. Congress was prohibited from passing laws that infringed on the freedom of speech or the press, state governments weren't similarly bound. As you read earlier, court decisions extended Bill of Rights protections to the states through what is known as the doctrine of incorporation. An example of how this affected state law is that states are now required to provide a lawyer to any person accused of a crime who can't afford to pay for legal counsel, a protection provided by the Sixth Amendment.

Finally, under Article I, Section 10, certain powers are prohibited to the states. While states can pass laws regarding commerce within their territory, they cannot regulate interstate commerce. This is a federal power. The states also are prohibited from printing or coining their own money or from entering into treaties with

A worker stocks shelves in a California sporting goods store. California is one of many states that has passed laws setting a higher minimum wage than the national minimum wage set by the U.S. Congress. Setting minimum wage laws is one example of powers shared by the federal and state governments.

foreign governments. Those, too, are the province of the federal government.

The federal and state governments also share certain powers, such as the power to set up courts. Both levels of government also have some powers to provide for public safety. Congress passes laws related to federal crimes, which are enforced by such bodies as the Federal Bureau of Investigation or the Drug Enforcement Agency. Each state passes laws regarding other crimes that are enforced by state or local police.

PRINCIPLES OF STATE GOVERNMENT All states have their own constitutions, and these constitutions incorporate many of the same principles as the U.S. Constitution. State constitutions also stipulate, or specify, which state offices are filled through elections and how elections are run. Each state has a republican form of government, as required by the U.S. Constitution in Article IV, Section 4. State governments also reflect the principle of popular sovereignty—the idea that the people are the ultimate source of the government's power.

Like the federal government, state governments have their powers separated among state legislative, executive, and judicial branches. These branches are able to check and balance the powers of the other branches, much like the branches of the federal government. Like the U.S. president, state governors have the power to veto laws. All state legislatures except Oregon's have the power to impeach governors and remove them from office. Each state's supreme court has the power of judicial review and can overturn laws that violate the state constitution.

Finally, state governments reflect the principle of limited government. Limited government is ensured in part by the systems of separation of powers and checks and balances, which together prevent any one branch of government from having too much power. Limited government is also guaranteed by the state constitutions, including state bills of rights. In fact, bills of rights were included in state constitutions even before they were added to the U.S. Constitution. Recall that one argument Federalists initially gave for not including a federal bill of rights was that such protections were already present in the state constitutions.

Some rights enumerated in state bills of rights are similar to those found in the U.S. Constitution. For instance, the constitution of New York protects freedom of religion, freedoms of speech and of the press, and the right to a trial by jury. State constitutions often go even further in guaranteeing certain rights to their citizens. The New York constitution, for example, says that divorce can take place only with proper judicial proceedings, allows for lotto and bingo games under certain conditions, and affirms the right of workers to organize into labor unions.

Two other examples of rights specified in state constitutions that are absent from the U.S. Constitution are environmental rights and the right to privacy. Pennsylvania guarantees its citizens the right to a clean environment: "The people have a right to clean air, pure water, and to the preservation of the natural, scenic, historic and aesthetic values of the environment." A few other states also have similar statements regarding their citizens' right to a clean environment. While the U.S. Supreme Court has interpreted the U.S. Constitution to include the right to privacy, it isn't stated explicitly in that document. Several states, however, have straightforward statements protecting this right. Alaska's constitution, for example, says "the right of the people to privacy is recognized and shall not be infringed."

These provisions work to extend individual freedom. While state governments can't make laws that violate protections in the U.S. Constitution, state constitutions can give citizens of a state more rights than are recognized by federal courts. For instance, the First Amendment to the U.S. Constitution says "Congress shall make no law respecting an establishment of religion." The Illinois constitution goes further: "No person shall be required to attend or support any ministry or place of worship against his consent, nor shall any preference be given by law to any religious denomination or mode of worship."

HISTORICAL THINKING

1. **CATEGORIZE** What are examples of a power reserved to the states and of a power shared by both the federal and state governments?
2. **MAKE INFERENCES** Why might a resident of Pennsylvania take a lawsuit against a company dumping waste in a nearby stream to a state court rather than a federal court?

Structure of State Government

As noted earlier, each state constitution specifies the structure of state government, which generally parallels the structure of the federal government. All states divide the government into three separate branches, each of which has certain responsibilities. The legislative branch, like the U.S. Congress, makes laws. The executive branch, headed by the governor, executes state laws. The judicial branch—the state court system—evaluates the laws and ensures that justice is carried out.

This temple in Wilmette, Illinois, is one of only nine Baha'i temples in the world. The constitution of Illinois protects the free exercise of religion by members of the Baha'i faith and of other faiths.

State constitutions specify the powers of each branch of government and often include rules on how those powers can be exercised. For instance, they establish which state offices are filled through gubernatorial appointments. They also say whether a branch of the legislature has to approve those appointments. The constitutions also stipulate the qualifications an individual must meet to hold office, such as age and residency requirements. Some states establish **term limits**—a maximum number of times a person can hold the same office. For example, several states set limits on the number of terms a person can serve as governor. Fifteen states

States that Limit Terms for State Legislators, 2020

State	Maximum Number of Years for State House Members	Maximum Number of Years for State Senate Members
Arizona	8	8
Arkansas	16	16
California	12	12
Colorado	8	8
Florida	8	8
Louisiana	12	12
Maine	8	8
Michigan	6	8
Missouri	8	8
Montana	8	8
Nebraska	n/a	8
Nevada	12	12
Ohio	8	8
Oklahoma	12	12
South Dakota	8	8

SOURCE: National Council of State Legislatures

have term limits of varying durations for members of the state legislature. Of those, 14 have term limits written directly into their state constitutions.

State constitutions also address another important state power—the power to organize local governments. There are four types of local governments:

- Counties are the major subdivisions of a state and are generally responsible for enforcing state laws within their boundaries. (In Louisiana, the equivalent of a county is a parish. In Alaska, counties are called boroughs.) The county sheriff's office handles law enforcement, while the county courts carry out trials. County officials register voters, issue marriage licenses, oversee roads, and collect taxes.
- In many states, counties are divided into townships, which have their own governments. The state constitution spells out what officials each township has and their responsibilities.
- Another level of local government is municipal, which includes cities and towns. These entities exist only if recognized by the state government. About 80 percent of Americans now live in some kind of municipality and thus are subject to municipal government.

Members of the Fire Department of New York (FDNY) fight a fire in Brooklyn. Fire protection and public safety are two major activities of city and town government.

- The fourth type of local government is the **special district**. This is a unit created for a specific purpose. School districts are often special districts, as are those formed for purposes such as fire protection and park management.

HISTORICAL THINKING

3. **FORM AND SUPPORT OPINIONS** Do you think it is a good idea to place term limits on state legislators? Why or why not?
4. **ANALYZE VISUALS** Why do you think relatively few states have term limits for their legislators?
5. **COMPARE AND CONTRAST** How is the relationship of county government to state government similar to the relationship of state government to the federal government?

Changing State Constitutions

State constitutions differ from the U.S. Constitution in several ways. First, they undergo more changes. Thirty states have had at least 2 constitutions, and nearly 20 of the states have had at least 4. Massachusetts has the oldest constitution—it was written in 1780. Rhode Island has the newest—it adopted its second constitution in 1986.

COMPARING THE FEDERAL AND STATE CONSTITUTIONS State constitutions generally have more amendments than the U.S. Constitution as well. The U.S. Constitution has had only 27 amendments. Only Illinois has had fewer amendments. That state's current constitution, which is its fourth, was adopted in a special election in 1970 and has been amended only 15 times as of summer 2020. Alaska, with a constitution that went into effect with statehood in 1959, has the next lowest number of amendments, at 29. Alabama's state constitution, adopted in 1901, has had an astounding 926 amendments.

Partly because they have been amended so many times, state constitutions are much longer than the U.S. Constitution. The U.S. Constitution, including all of its amendments, has fewer than 8,000 words. No state constitution is that short—though Utah's, at 8,565 words, is close. The average length of state constitutions is 39,000 words, and the longest—Alabama's—is nearly 400,000 words.

Another reason state constitutions are longer than the U.S. Constitution is that they are far more specific than the U.S. Constitution. The federal constitution uses 16 words to state its protection for freedom of religion. The New York state constitution devotes 77 words to protecting that freedom in its constitution. The Fifth Amendment to the U.S. Constitution states in 12 words that private property can't be taken from individuals without fair compensation. The New York constitution devotes more than 160 words to the subject, with specific language on compensation for road construction and the taking of farmlands.

State constitutions are also longer than the federal constitution because of how they address areas of government beyond protected rights. The U.S. Constitution gives Congress broadly defined powers such as the power to regulate interstate commerce. State constitutions often include language that's extremely specific. The Illinois constitution has nearly 400 words establishing rules on the ability of the state government to incur debts, and another 500 on funding for roads and highways. State constitutions also define some matters very narrowly. California's constitution details exactly what organizations and property are exempt from taxation. It specifies, for example, that tax-exempt property in that state includes fruit and nut trees less than four years old. That's because trees can't produce income for their owners before they reach this stage of maturity.

AMENDING STATE CONSTITUTIONS The states have established several ways to amend their constitutions. In every state, the state legislature can propose an amendment to the state constitution. In 36 states, after the legislature approves an amendment, the voters must approve it as well. In 11 states, the legislature must approve the amendment twice and there must be an election after the first approval and before the second vote. This effectively puts the amendment to the voters, as they can vote for or against members of the legislature based on their position on the proposed amendment. In three states—Connecticut, Hawaii, and New Jersey—the legislature has two ways to propose an amendment: Vote for it twice by majority vote or approve it once by a supermajority. The number required for a supermajority in each of the three states varies, ranging from 60 percent to 75 percent. In Delaware, a two-thirds vote by the legislature in two different sessions amends the state constitution. The people don't vote on the matter.

Forty-four states allow the legislature to call a special constitutional convention to consider amendments. Some require that such a convention be approved by the state's voters. In others, the state constitution actually requires that the people vote on the question of calling a convention every 10 or 20 years without the state legislature voting on the matter. Florida's constitution creates a commission that meets every 20 years to discuss and propose any amendments its members deem appropriate. In 1996, New Mexico adopted a similar plan.

In 18 states, the power of the people to place initiatives on the ballot can be used to bring constitutional amendments to the voters. While this may seem that it gives citizens considerable power, these provisions aren't always straightforward. Eight of these states make it quite difficult for the people to actually place a proposed amendment on the ballot. Nevada, for instance, requires voters to approve an amendment in two separate elections. The Massachusetts constitution bans any amendments that would affect provisions of the state's bill of rights. That state also allows the legislature to place an alternative amendment on the ballot to compete with any amendment proposed by the people.

HISTORICAL THINKING

6. **IDENTIFY MAIN IDEAS AND DETAILS** Why are state constitutions longer than the U.S. Constitution?

7. **COMPARE AND CONTRAST** In nearly every state, voters have the power to approve or reject amendments to their state constitutions. How is this different from the role of voters in changing the U.S. Constitution?

LESSON 20.2 State Legislative Branches

As you read earlier, certain powers are reserved to the states under the Tenth Amendment. Police power—the power of a government to place reasonable controls over its people to ensure their health, safety, and welfare—is one such power. The chief way that states exercise police power is by making laws through their legislatures. Each year, those state legislatures introduce tens of thousands of laws. These laws address topics as diverse as education policy, environmental protection, consumer safety, civil and criminal justice, and numerous other topics that affect the health, safety, and prosperity of the people of their state. It takes many people to exercise these powers. Nearly 7,400 Americans serve in state legislatures across the nation.

Structure of State Legislatures

Only a handful of states have full-time legislatures. In most states, legislators spend from around two-thirds of their time to as little as a couple of months a year on their legislative duties. These part-time legislators are citizen-lawmakers who typically have other jobs but devote some of their time to public service.

State lawmaking bodies go by a variety of names. Most are called the state legislature, but 14—most of them east of the Mississippi River—are known as the general assembly. Two states—Massachusetts and New Hampshire—call their legislatures the general court.

NUMBER OF CHAMBERS All but one of the state legislatures are bicameral, like the U.S. Congress, which

Then-governor Deval Patrick (D) of Massachusetts enters the State Senate chamber in 2011 to swear in members of the state legislature. The Massachusetts State House was completed in 1798, making it one of the oldest state capitol buildings in the country.

means they are made up of two houses. The exception is Nebraska, which has a unicameral, or single-house, legislature. The state adopted this form in 1934. Popular state politician George Norris championed the cause, arguing that "there is no sense or reason in having the same thing done twice, especially if it is to be done by two bodies . . . elected in the same way and having the same jurisdiction." Nebraska's legislative elections are also nonpartisan. That is, candidates aren't listed with a party affiliation on the ballot. The two candidates who come in first and second in the primary election run against each other in the general election, even if they are from the same party.

In the other 49 states, the house with fewer members, or the upper house, is called the senate. The larger, or lower, house is generally called the house of representatives, but eight states use other names. California, Nevada, New York, and Wisconsin call this chamber the state assembly, while New Jersey uses the name general assembly. Maryland, Virginia, and West Virginia call it the house of delegates.

The size of these houses varies. Nebraska's one-chamber legislature—the 49-member state senate—is the smallest. Of the bicameral legislatures, Alaska's is the smallest, with a 20-member senate and 40-member state house. While you might think that the states with the largest populations would have the largest legislatures, that isn't the case. California, Texas, and Florida have from 120 to 181 members, not far off the average of about 148. The largest state legislature belongs to tiny New Hampshire, which has a 400-member state house.

DRAWING LEGISLATIVE DISTRICTS As with districts for the U.S. House of Representatives, state legislative districts for both legislative bodies have to be redrawn periodically. In most states, the legislature draws district lines, but that isn't always the case. Reformers in many states have pushed for the adoption of

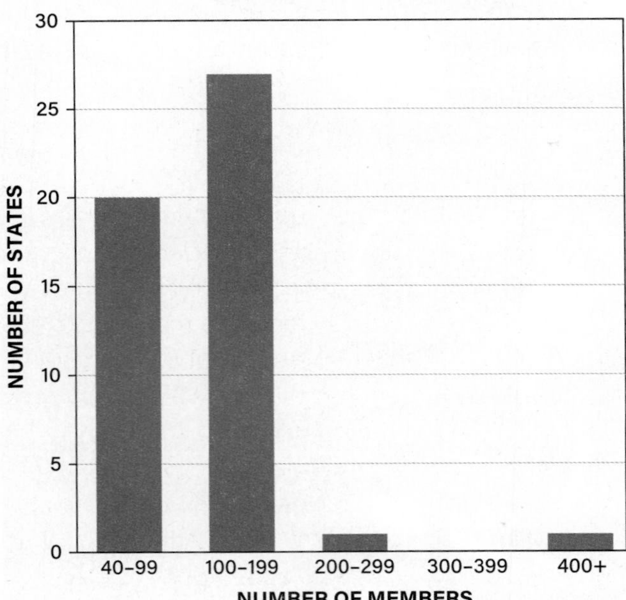

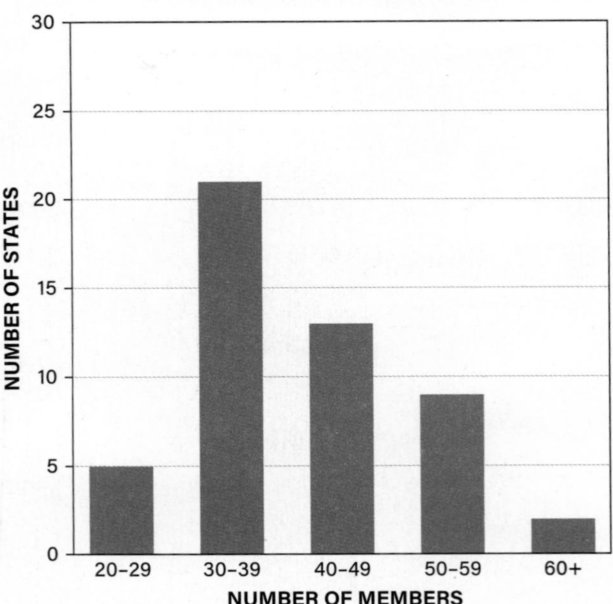

nonpartisan commissions to draw the lines for these districts. They believe that such groups are less likely to be influenced by special interests as they carry out the task of redistricting, or updating districts to reflect changes in population.

When new district lines are drawn, they must comply with U.S. Supreme Court decisions regarding the equal protection clause of the 14th Amendment. In *Gray* v. *Sanders* (1963), the Court established the one person–one vote principle for state legislative districts, which ensures that a state's districts are relatively equal in size based on the population they represent. In *Reynolds* v. *Sims* (1964), the Court held that districts in both chambers of a two-house legislature should be based on population. In addition, the Court said that districts should be redrawn regularly, preferably at a minimum of every 10 years, based on the most recent census results.

These rulings set the standards for fair apportionment, or determining representation in a legislative body. In addition, federal law sets certain rules for fairness based on race in establishing legislative districts. The 1965 Voting Rights Act aimed to undo decades of discrimination that prevented African Americans from voting. When some new districts were drawn to make African Americans the majority of voters in a district—thus giving them a greater ability to elect a candidate who would represent their interests—the district lines were challenged. The Supreme Court upheld such districts—called majority-minority districts—in *Thornburg* v. *Gingles* (1986).

Later Court rulings, however, placed limits on the use of such districts. In *Shaw* v. *Reno* (1993), the Court ruled against a majority-minority district. Plaintiffs complained that the shape of the district was bizarre and reflected **racial gerrymandering**, or favoring one racial group over another through the drawing of district lines. Recall that gerrymandering is the practice of deliberately drawing legislative districts to favor one group or party over another. The Court further refined the definition of racial gerrymandering in two other cases. In *Miller* v. *Johnson* (1995), the Court decided that district lines were unconstitutional if race was the predominant factor in creating them. In *Bush* v. *Vera* (1996), the Court said the best way to avoid racial gerrymandering would be to create relatively compact rather than strangely shaped districts. Federal courts have generally not acted on challenges to districts based on charges of **partisan gerrymandering**—when one party draws district lines in its own favor. In 2018, the Supreme Court received appeals on four such cases but gave no definitive ruling.

CHOOSING WHO WILL SERVE Each state holds elections to choose members of the legislature.

Authority for Drawing District Lines

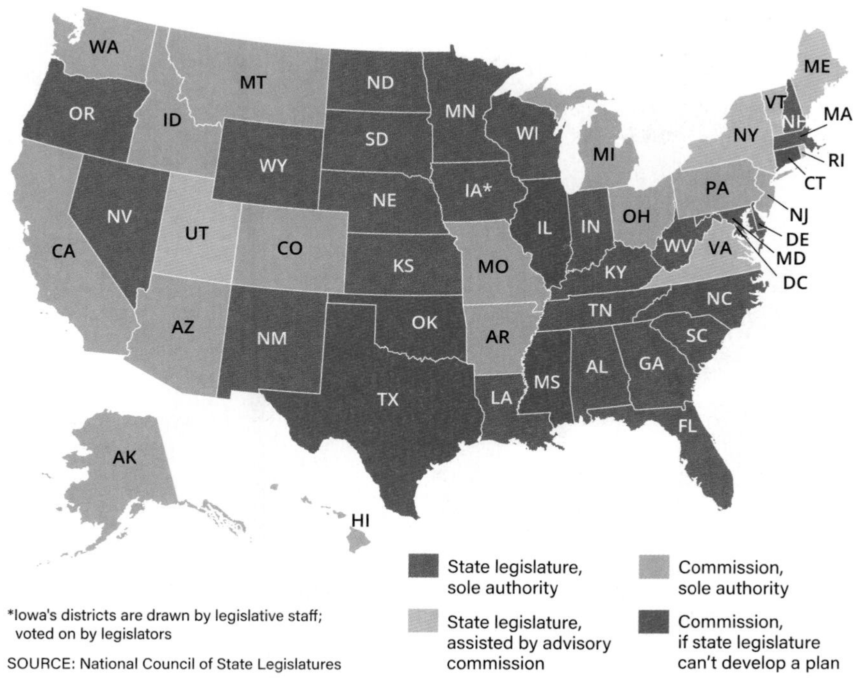

Primary elections take place early in the election year, and general elections are in the fall. Nine states have closed primaries, meaning that only party members can vote in their party's primary. Fifteen states have open primaries, meaning that any registered voter—even members of another party—can vote in a party's primary. Most of the other states have a mixed system that allows some voters to cast ballots in a party primary even if they aren't registered as members of the party. In some cases, only independents may do so. In other cases, voting in another party's primary changes the voter's registration. Two states have primaries in which the first- and second-place winners go on to the general election, even if they are from the same party.

In almost all states, members of the state house serve for two years. The five exceptions, which have four-year terms, are Alabama, Louisiana, Maryland, Mississippi, and North Dakota. Most state senate terms are 4 years long, but in 12 states senators serve two-year terms.

Republicans have dominated many state governments in recent decades. The 2018 vote left Republicans with majorities in both chambers in 30 states. Democrats controlled both chambers in 18 states. One state—Minnesota—was split, with each party having a majority in one chamber. Because Nebraska's unicameral legislature is nonpartisan, it does not allow for party control.

About 2,110 women served in state legislatures as of 2019, making up 28.5 percent of the total—the most ever. Nevada was the only state in which women formed a majority of state lawmakers. About 82 percent of state legislators are non-Hispanic White. African Americans are about 9 percent of lawmakers, with Hispanics or Latinos about 5 percent. Asian Americans make up about 1 percent, with other groups—Native Americans, Native Hawaiians, and people of more than one race—about 3 percent total.

COMPENSATION The way state legislators are compensated varies widely as well. States generally give lawmakers either a salary, a per diem allowance, or both. **Per diems** are payments made by the day. Lawmakers paid this way are paid for each day that the legislature is in session. New Hampshire legislators receive just $100 per year with no per diem allowance. New Mexico pays no salary but gives lawmakers a $161 per diem. Salaries in states with full-time legislatures like California, New York, and Pennsylvania tend to be higher, but the average salary for state legislators is less than $36,000, which is comparable to the salary for an entry-level position in many professions. State legislators are assisted by more than 31,000 staffers. Most staff members work in the state capital. Only about a quarter of the states provide funds for offices in lawmakers' home districts.

REGULAR AND SPECIAL SESSIONS Forty-six of the 50 legislatures meet in regular session every year. Four—Montana, Nevada, North Dakota, and Texas—have regular sessions every other year. The trend over time has moved toward having annual sessions—in the early 1960s, only 19 state legislatures met annually. The legislatures of eight states—Illinois, Massachusetts, Michigan, New Jersey,

New York, Ohio, Pennsylvania, and Wisconsin—meet throughout the year. For the rest, the regular session lasts only one to six months.

Legislatures can also meet in special sessions—a meeting called to address a specific issue or set of issues. For example, a special session can be called to address a court decision, a new federal law that affects the state government, a natural disaster, or another crisis. In 2018, the Arizona legislature met in a special session to address the opioid crisis. In 15 states, only the governor can call a special session. In the others, either the governor or the legislature can call a special session.

Party Control of State Government, 2019

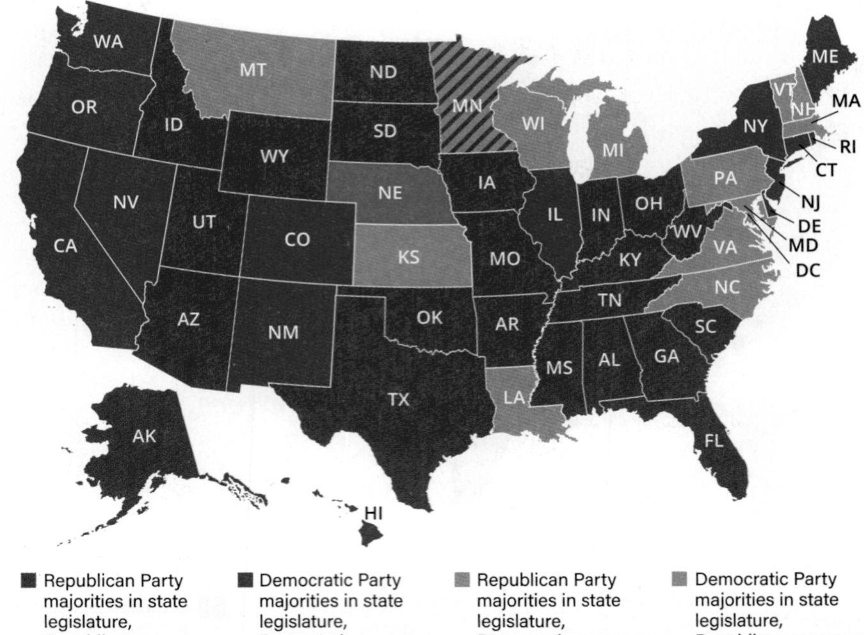

- Republican Party majorities in state legislature, Republican governor
- Democratic Party majorities in state legislature, Democratic governor
- Republican Party majorities in state legislature, Democratic governor
- Democratic Party majorities in state legislature, Republican governor
- Split legislature, Democratic governor
- Nonpartisan legislature, Republican governor

SOURCE: National Council of State Legislatures

HISTORICAL THINKING

1. **INTERPRET GRAPHS** Based on the graphs, what generalization can you make about the size of state senates compared to the size of the lower houses of the states?
2. **INTERPRET MAPS** Which party dominated state governments in 2019? Provide details to support your answer.
3. **EVALUATE** What are the pros and cons of low pay for state legislators?

Legislative Powers

State legislatures have three key roles: to make laws, to review and approve gubernatorial appointments, and to provide oversight of the executive and judicial branches. Leaders in each chamber guide these activities. As in the U.S. Congress, much legislative and oversight work is done in committees.

LEADERSHIP AND SUPPORT Almost every state legislature has a president to lead the senate and a speaker who leads the other chamber. The two exceptions are Nebraska and Iowa. Nebraska's unicameral legislature has both a president and a speaker. Iowa has a speaker leading the state house but has two leaders—one Democratic and one Republican—in the state senate. In about half the states, the lieutenant governor serves as president of the senate. In other states, the president is a state senator chosen by the body. The speakers are all elected by the membership.

The president and the speaker preside over legislative activities and maintain order in their respective chambers. Most states have other leadership positions, including *pro tempore* (or temporary) presidents and speakers, and majority leaders, minority leaders, and whips in each chamber. The *pro tem* leaders preside over sessions in the absence of the president or speaker. Majority and minority leaders play roles in setting the legislative agenda. As they do in the U.S. Congress, whips work to maintain party discipline when matters come up for a vote.

THE LEGISLATIVE PROCESS The process for passing laws in the states is similar to that in the U.S. Congress. The process begins when someone—a legislator, a staff member, a citizen, a citizen group, or an interest group—drafts a bill. If the bill isn't written by a legislator, the author or authors must convince a lawmaker to introduce it.

After lawmakers introduce a bill, it is referred to committee. After it is debated and revised, it is reported out of committee and debated, amended, and approved in each chamber. If the two chambers approve a bill on the same subject with different language, those differences must be reconciled and approved with common language. The bill then goes to the state governor for signature or veto. All state legislatures have the power to override a veto. In 44 states, the legislators need a supermajority of two-thirds or three-quarters to override a veto. In six states—Alabama, Arkansas, Indiana, Kentucky, Tennessee, and West Virginia—only simple majorities are required.

In most states, the legislatures have very short sessions, so lawmakers must get laws passed quickly. States have introduced various practices to expedite, or speed up, the legislative process. One approach is to place limits on the number of bills that can be introduced in a session. Another is to set deadlines to keep a bill moving through the legislative process and prevent a logjam of pending bills at the end of a session. Another approach is to allow lawmakers to pre-file a bill, submitting it before the legislative session begins. This makes it possible for staff to quickly complete the necessary paperwork to get the bill into the system.

POWER OVER APPOINTMENTS State governors, like the U.S. president, have the power to name people to various executive and judicial offices. State legislatures have the power to approve many of those appointments. Sometimes only one chamber has this power. For example, in Hawaii, New Jersey, and Wyoming, only the senate approves the governor's nominee for state attorney general. In other situations, both chambers must approve nominees. That is the case for attorney general nominees in Alaska.

OVERSIGHT POWER State legislatures, like Congress, have oversight power, meaning they can review the actions of executive branch officials and agencies. They also have certain oversight powers over the judicial branches of their states. These powers reflect the principle of checks and balances at the core of American constitutional government.

The most common way that state legislatures exercise the oversight function is through committees that can determine that the executive branch is carrying out the law appropriately by reviewing records and calling on officials to testify. In 41 states, the legislature has some kind of power to review administrative rules made by the executive branch, and in more than half of those states, the legislature has the power to veto the rules. That power has been challenged in courts in at least 11 states, however, and courts have ruled against the legislature in 9 of those states.

Nearly all state legislatures also have the power to impeach state officials and remove them from office. This power has been exercised very rarely. When a state judge was impeached in Pennsylvania in 1994, it was the first time the state legislature had taken such action in more than 180 years. The legislature of New Hampshire—one of the original 13 states—held its first impeachment proceeding in more than 200 years in 2000. In 2018, the West Virginia state house impeached all four of its state supreme court justices (the fifth seat was vacant). The move resulted in a flurry of lawsuits and two resignations. In the end, a panel of lower state court judges ruled that one of the impeachments was unconstitutional, but the justices who resigned were replaced.

HISTORICAL THINKING

4. **IDENTIFY MAIN IDEAS AND DETAILS** What are the three main powers of state legislatures?
5. **ANALYZE CAUSE AND EFFECT** Why do many state legislatures have to expedite lawmaking?

The Initiative, Referendum, and Recall

State legislatures are not the only body that can make state laws. In some states, the people can vote to approve initiatives, which are ballot questions that allow citizens to vote measures into law or recommend measures to the legislature. In some states, voters can pass a referendum, which is a ballot question asking the electorate to approve a new law or remove an existing law from the books. Citizens don't have the power to vote on these kinds of questions at the federal level.

To get either type of question—initiative or referendum—on the ballot, a required number of people must sign a petition requesting that the matter be put on the ballot. In some states, an initiative can be used to amend the state constitution. In others, citizens can approve an initiative to enact a law, a situation called direct initiative. In still others, the request for a new law goes first to the state legislature, which then can act to pass the law or not. If the legislature doesn't pass the law—or changes it—the proposed law then goes on the ballot. This arrangement is called the indirect initiative.

Nineteen states also give voters the power of **recall**—the right to remove a public official from office. Voters have the power to recall members of the state legislature and the executive branch. They can also recall elected judges. Like ballot measures such as initiatives and referendums, a significant number of people must sign a petition to bring a recall to a vote. In Kansas, for example, as many as 40 percent of registered voters must sign. There is typically a limit on the length of time in which signatures can be gathered. In six recall states—Arizona, California, Colorado, Nevada, North Dakota, and Wisconsin—the recall vote and the vote for a replacement official happen in the same election. If the recall vote fails to gain a majority, the vote for the replacement is ignored. In eight states—Georgia, Louisiana, Michigan, Minnesota, Montana, New Jersey, Rhode Island, and Illinois—a successful recall forces an official to leave office and triggers a special election for a replacement. In five states—Alaska, Idaho, Kansas, Oregon, and Washington—someone is appointed to fill a vacancy created by a recall vote. From 1913 to the most recent recall in 2013, 21 state legislators were recalled, and 17 survived recall. In 2011, Wisconsin held recall votes on eight state senators. Six of them survived recall, and two were removed from office.

HISTORICAL THINKING

6. **MAKE INFERENCES** Why are initiatives, referendum questions, and recall votes examples of popular sovereignty?

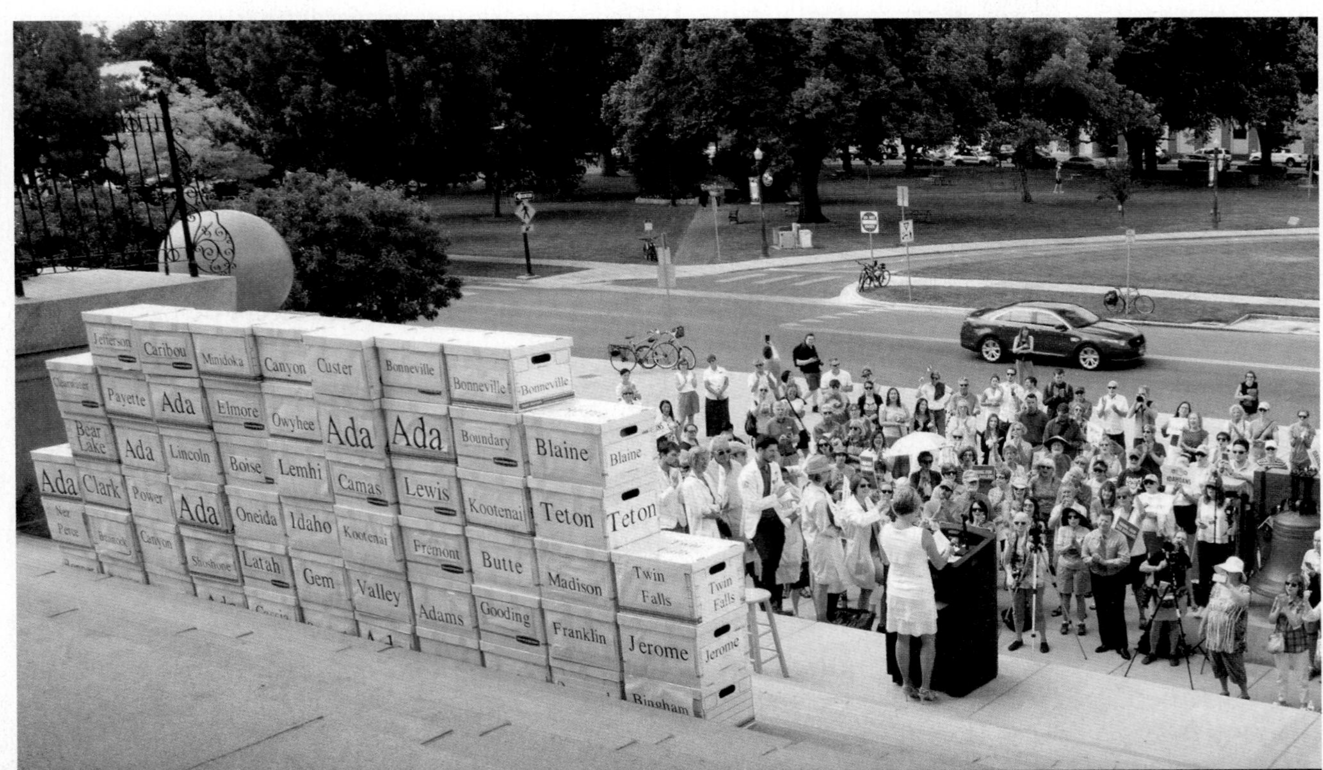

CRITICAL VIEWING Activists gathered on the steps of the state capitol building in Boise, Idaho, in July 2018 to present boxes full of petitions with thousands of signatures requesting that a referendum to expand Medicaid be placed on the state ballot. What detail in the photo shows wide popular support for the referendum?

Visitors view the *Battle of Gettysburg Cyclorama,* a 377-foot-long, 12.5-ton painting that depicts the last day of fighting in that pivotal battle of the Civil War. The painting, which was created in 1884 by Paul Philippoteaux, was purchased by the National Park Service in the 1940s and is on display at Gettysburg National Military Park.

How Geography Shaped American History, Law, and Politics

by Nick Romeo **National Geographic Online, May 3, 2015**

The geography of different states has an impact on their laws and politics, and the laws and politics of individual states affect the nation as a whole. In a National Geographic Book Talk, writer Nick Romeo interviewed political scientist Akhil Reed Amar about his book *The Law of the Land: A Grand Tour of Our Constitutional Republic*. In the interview, Amar explains how geography affected laws and politics in the past and how it continues to do so today.

Amar reflects on the parallels between two presidents from Illinois—Abraham Lincoln and Barack Obama. "Isn't it interesting," he says, "that Barack Obama, a tall skinny lawyer from Illinois, basically won all the states that Lincoln won and lost all the states Lincoln lost?" Amar explores the question further:

We are still living through the after effects of the Civil War. The different climate and geography of the North and the South made them differentially susceptible to first tobacco and later cotton production, a huge driver of the southern economy that was profitable due to slavery. Lincoln didn't want that system spreading because he thought it was an evil system.

Before 1850, the vast majority of winners of presidential elections won a popular majority in both the North and the South. Lincoln is different; he sweeps the North, winning every northern state except New Jersey, and he wins nothing in the South.

In the last six presidential elections, the South every time has voted for a different presidential candidate than the North. We're reverting in some ways to the cleavages and polarizations that have defined much of American history.

According to Amar, political scientists call the current polarization the result of "the Big Sort." He explains how this sorting of the population is taking place: "People are increasingly voting with their feet to move alongside like-minded folk. States are increasingly red or blue, and within states there's a sharp difference between cities and the hinterlands [rural areas]."

Access the full version of "How Geography Shaped American History, Law, and Politics" by Nick Romeo through the Resources Menu in MindTap.

THINK ABOUT IT Have you observed the effects of "the Big Sort" in your own state or region? Explain

LESSON 20.3 State Executive Branches

If your state has been stricken by a natural disaster—a major hurricane, flooding, or wildfires—you've probably seen news coverage of the response. First responders rescue people stranded in homes or on state highways. Relief workers provide food, water, and medical assistance. Amid all the activity, one figure tends to stand out, and that's the governor of the state. The governor talks to rescuers and relief workers to learn about the extent of the disaster and people's needs. The governor directs efforts to move supplies and personnel and requests further assistance if needed. He or she reassures people that help is on the way. During difficult times, the people of a state look to their governor to guide them through the crisis.

Chief Executive of the State

The qualifications and roles of the U.S. president are spelled out in a single document—the U.S. Constitution. A single legislative body—the U.S. Congress—supports or blocks the president's agenda. In contrast, the 50 U.S. states all have different constitutions and legislatures. This means that the qualifications for the office of governor—and the characteristics of those who have filled it—vary significantly from state to state.

QUALIFICATIONS AND BACKGROUNDS All but three states require that anyone serving as governor meet a minimum age requirement. In most cases, that age is 30. Six states set the limit at 25, and another 6 allow anyone 18 or over to run for governor. Most states require that the governor be a resident of the state. The shortest residency requirement is Rhode Island's 30 days. Missouri and Oklahoma have the longest residency requirements with 10 years. Most states also require that the governor be a citizen of the United States. Nine states require from 10 to 20 years of citizenship.

People who have served as governor come from diverse backgrounds. Many have held prior elected office, including as lieutenant governor of their state. Several people have moved from the business world to the governor's office. California, home of Hollywood, has had two former actors as governor—Ronald Reagan (1967–1975) and Arnold Schwarzenegger (2003–2011). In 1998, Minnesotans elected former professional wrestler Jesse Ventura as governor. Woodrow Wilson was the president of Princeton University before being elected governor of New Jersey,

Governors Who Later Served as President, 1900–Present

NAME	STATE	GOVERNOR	PRESIDENT
Theodore Roosevelt	New York	1899–1900	1901–1909
Woodrow Wilson	New Jersey	1911–1913	1913–1921
Calvin Coolidge	Massachusetts	1919–1920	1923–1929
Franklin Roosevelt	New York	1929–1932	1933–1945
Jimmy Carter	Georgia	1971–1974	1977–1981
Ronald Reagan	California	1967–1974	1981–1989
Bill Clinton	Arkansas	1979–1980, 1983–1993	1993–2001
George W. Bush	Texas	1995–2000	2001–2009

SOURCE: Rutgers University Center on the American Governor

the state where that university is located. Reagan and Wilson were two of many state governors who went on to become president of the United States.

Some governors have had family connections to the office. Since World War II, three sets of fathers and sons have served as governor of the same state. Pat Brown (1959–1967) and Jerry Brown (1975–1983 and 2011–2019) were governors of California. Mario Cuomo (1983–1994) and Andrew Cuomo (first elected in 2011) were governors of New York. And Jim Folsom, Sr. (1947–1951 and 1955–1959), and Jim Folsom, Jr. (1993–1994), were governors of Alabama. Three wives have followed their husbands as governor, beginning with Nellie Tayloe Ross—the country's first female governor. She was elected as governor of Wyoming after her husband's death in 1924.

Hawaii governor David Ige (D) presides over a 2016 awards ceremony in Honolulu. Ige became the nation's first governor of Okinawan descent when he was elected in 2014 after spending more than 20 years in the state legislature.

In all, 44 women have been governor, and 9 held the office in mid-2020—the highest number to serve at one time in U.S. history. Arizona has had four female governors, the most of any one state. Four African Americans have served as governor. The first—Pinckney Pinchback, Louisiana's lieutenant governor—became governor to serve out the remaining 35 days of the term of the impeached governor. The first African American to be elected governor was Douglas Wilder of Virginia, who served from 1990 to 1994. David Paterson and Deval Patrick led New York and Massachusetts in the 2000s.

There have been six Asian American governors, including three from Hawaii—George Ariyoshi was the first (1974–1986)—and one each from Washington, Louisiana, and South Carolina. The first Hispanic governor was Romualdo Pacheco of California. He served briefly in 1875, taking office after the previous governor resigned. Nine other Latinos have subsequently served as governor, six of them in New Mexico. In 2019, the nation's first Native American governor, Republican Kevin Stitt, a citizen of the Cherokee Nation, took office after being elected in Oklahoma.

TERM LIMITS AND COMPENSATION Most states place a limit on the number of terms a person can serve as governor. In 23 states, governors cannot serve more than two consecutive terms. A handful of states make the limit two terms total. Virginia prevents a governor from seeking immediate re-election, but a former governor can run for the office again after being out of office for at least one term.

Governors' salaries range from a low of $70,000 in Maine to a high of more than $195,000 in California. In 21 states, the salary is between $130,000 and $160,000. Four states join Maine in paying the governor less than $100,000. Most governors are entitled to live in an official state residence, although some governors use the official residence for ceremonial functions only. All governors can make use of an official state car. A majority can also use a state airplane, and some have access to a state helicopter.

REMOVAL FROM OFFICE Governors, like members of the state legislature, are subject to recall. The first-ever gubernatorial recall effort—in North Dakota in 1921—forced Governor Lynn J. Frazier from office. California voters have launched more than 30 efforts to recall one of their governors, but only one campaign met the high threshold of signatures to actually produce a recall election. In that 2003 vote, Governor Gray Davis was removed from office. In 2012, Wisconsin also mounted a recall effort, but Governor Scott Walker survived that recall vote.

In 49 states (Oregon is the exception), governors can be removed through impeachment. In most states, the state's house of representatives or general assembly votes to impeach, and the state senate tries the case and decides whether or not to convict and remove the governor from office. Five states have a different process. Nebraska's unicameral legislature handles all steps of the process. California's state senate handles the entire process, even though it has a two-chamber legislature. In Alaska, the roles of the two legislative chambers are reversed—the senate votes to impeach and the house determines whether to convict. In Oklahoma, both chambers sit in judgment of governors once they are impeached. In Missouri, the state senate chooses a panel of seven judges to handle the trial and vote to convict or acquit.

Over the years, 16 governors have been subject to impeachment votes, with 8 convicted and permanently removed from office of governor and 2 resigning before the full process was complete. The most recent impeachments were successful. Evan Mecham was removed from office in Arizona in 1988, and Rod Blagojevich was removed from the governorship of Illinois in 2009. (Mecham was also subject to a recall petition but was ousted by the impeachment process before the election could be held.)

Governors sometimes resign from office. Some have stepped down in the face of scandal or ethical questions. Such was the case with the resignations of Robert Bentley of Alabama in 2017 and of Eric Greitens of Missouri in 2018. Others have left to take another office, as when George W. Bush resigned as governor of Texas in 2000 to become president.

HISTORICAL THINKING

1. **FORM AND SUPPORT OPINIONS** Do you think candidates for governor should face a residency requirement for office? If so, for how long? Explain your answer.
2. **DRAW CONCLUSIONS** Why are the powers of impeachment and recall important, and why are the processes difficult?

The Powers of Governors

The governor is the chief executive of a state, a position analogous, or comparable, to that of the president. The two positions differ in some ways, however. In state governments, officials such as the secretary of state and the attorney general also have executive powers. In many states, these positions are elected separately and thus have powers independent of the governor. In the federal government, these officials are appointed and directed by the president. In addition, governors, unlike presidents, have no foreign policy role, though many meet with foreign leaders and business executives to strengthen their state's economy.

EVOLUTION OF GOVERNORS' POWERS Modern governors have a substantial amount of power, but that wasn't always the case. The first state constitutions were written during the American Revolution. They were crafted by state leaders who had seen colonial governors abuse their power. Seeing governors as potential tyrants, revolutionary leaders limited their powers. Only two states—Massachusetts and New York—gave governors the veto power. Some state constitutions made the governor's term only one year. Some even had the legislature choose the governor, which limited the independence of the executive branch.

Over time, many states changed their constitutions to allow election of the governor by the people, which gave governors more political power. Many state constitutions also gave the governor the veto power. In the late 19th century, some states gave governors more power to try to curb corporate power and rein in corruption on the part of political parties. With these changes, governors took on a more influential legislative role.

Later in the 20th century, most of the states that still had two-year gubernatorial terms expanded them to four years, and many governors were given the power of the line-item veto. This allows governors to sign a spending bill into law but to strike out individual lines that list budget items they disagree with. Governors also gained the power to propose and approve the state budget.

ROLES OF THE GOVERNOR Today, governors fulfill several roles in addition to chief executive.

While executive agencies have some discretion in implementing laws passed by the state legislature, governors try to shape how that discretion is exercised. As head of the executive branch, they also have the power to appoint other officials, usually with the consent of one or both houses of the state legislature. Forty-six governors also have the power to name someone to fill a U.S Senate seat left vacant through death, resignation, or removal from office until an election can be held for that seat.

Most governors have the power to issue executive orders under certain circumstances. The ways in which governors can use this power vary across the states. Most states allow governors to declare states of emergency in the face of natural disasters or civil defense crises. Most also let governors reorganize the executive branch to some degree by way of an executive order. Alaska, Washington, and Wyoming severely constrain this type of gubernatorial power, however. Wyoming's governor has virtually no authority to issue executive orders.

When the 2020 COVID-19 pandemic struck, many governors used executive orders to respond rapidly to the challenge. Because executive orders do not need to be passed through usual legislative channels, they can be enacted much more quickly than ordinary state laws. For example, Illinois governor J. B. Pritzker set important state policies, such as the order for Illinois residents to stay at home during the worst of the pandemic, and for social distancing when people had to go out in public. In a coordinated effort, Mayor Lori E. Lightfoot of Chicago issued a public health order detailing how the lockdown would affect the city, including its parks, beaches and more.

Governors set their state's legislative agenda, proposing laws and working with lawmakers to craft legislative language. Governors often lay out their policy goals for the year in the annual state of the state message. Like presidents, governors can try to influence lawmakers by campaigning for popular support of their policies. They also have the power to summon legislators for special sessions and, in many cases, set the agenda for those sessions.

Governors' role in the budgeting process also gives them some legislative power. Governors initiate this process by proposing the state budget for the coming fiscal year. The plan they propose reflects their policy preferences. Of course, state lawmakers have the power to remake that budget, and, if the governor and legislature are in the hands of different parties, the two branches can clash during the legislature's debate and vote on the final plan. Governors can wield the power of the veto—or the threat of a veto—to influence lawmakers. The 35 governors who have the power to issue line-item vetoes can also undo specific appropriations they dislike.

CRITICAL VIEWING Ohio governor Mike DeWine (R) addresses members of the press to give an update on the state's response to the COVID-19 pandemic. During the pandemic, governors enacted many of the key policies designed to combat the spread of the disease. What elements in the photo tell you that Governor DeWine is speaking in an official capacity?

Governors play an important role as the chief liaison between the state and federal governments. They can lobby the president—especially if they come from the same party—to try to win provisions that favor the state. They also work with the state's congressional delegation and, through the National Governors Association, with the governors of all the states to have a voice in pending federal legislation.

As commander of the state's National Guard units, a governor is a state's military leader. Governors sometimes call out National Guard units in times of natural disaster. They may also activate these troops when requested by the president.

Like presidents, governors have the power to pardon those convicted of crimes. They also oversee decisions about granting **parole**, or conditional release from prison, to state prisoners. Governors are also their state's chief of state, the symbol of the state's people, and represent the state in ceremonies and symbolic functions. Finally, governors serve as party leader at the state level for the political party to which they belong.

LEADING THE EXECUTIVE BRANCH Just as in the federal government, the executive branches of states carry out laws. Some executive branch employees work directly for the governor, whose staff ranges in size from 14 in Vermont to 277 in Texas. State governments, like the federal government, have shifted from the spoils system, in which government jobs were handed out to repay political debts or reward supporters, to a professional civil service that hires on the basis of qualifications and experience. The push for government reform that began in the late 19th century put more government agencies and boards in the states under the governor's control to promote strong management. Another reform shifted more state offices from being elected to being subject to appointment by the governor.

State bureaucracies work in many different areas. The oldest state agencies address such matters as corrections, education, transportation, tax collection, unemployment insurance, and parks. In the 1960s, in part due to the encouragement of—and flow of money from—the federal government, states began to add agencies to address environmental issues and economic development. The 1970s saw the addition of agencies active in the issues of civil rights, alcohol and drug abuse, and mass transit.

HISTORICAL THINKING

3. **CATEGORIZE** State governors have a role that is similar to which federal position? Explain the similarity.
4. **MAKE INFERENCES** Why is the power of the line-item veto significant?

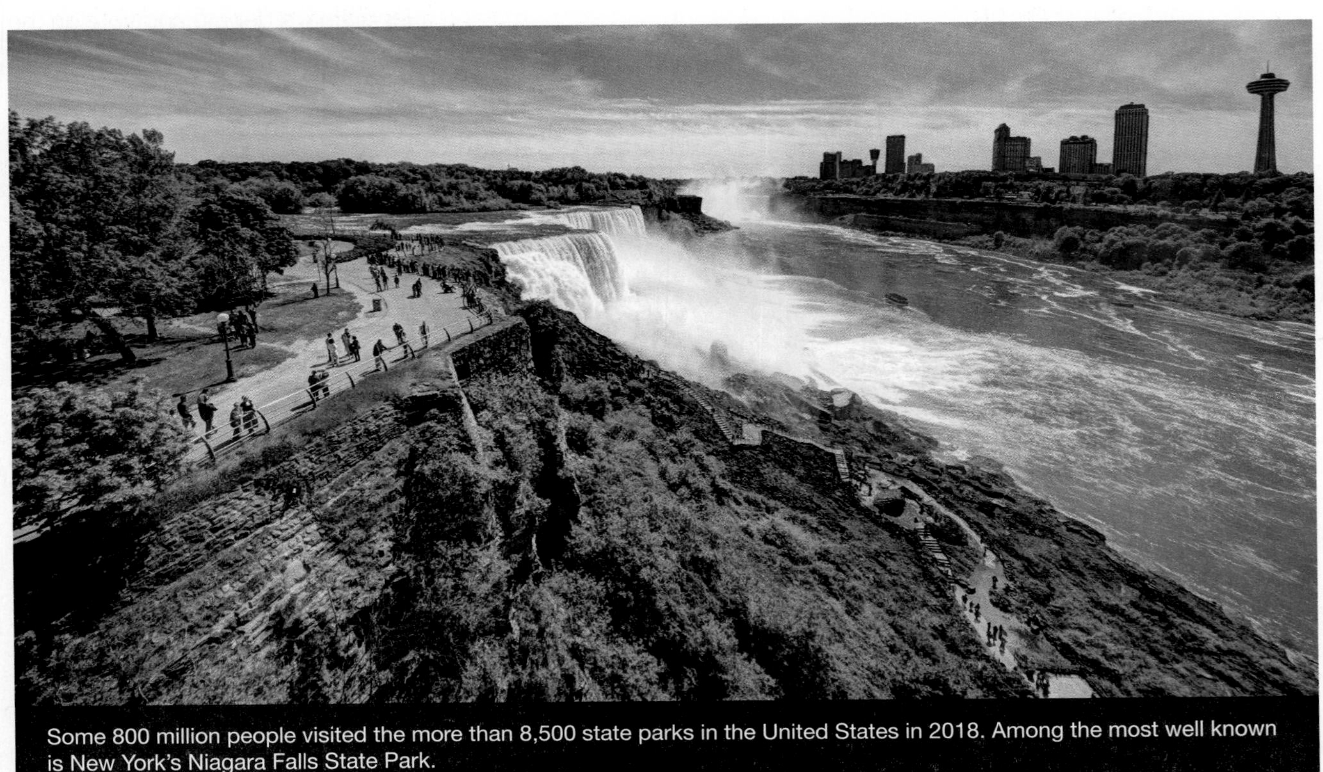

Some 800 million people visited the more than 8,500 state parks in the United States in 2018. Among the most well known is New York's Niagara Falls State Park.

Other Executive Officers

The exact lineup of other executive offices varies from state to state and can include such officials as an auditor general, insurance commissioner, and head of the state board of education. The powers and responsibilities of these officials vary, as does the manner of their selection. Among all the state executive positions, the most significant offices are those of lieutenant governor, secretary of state, state treasurer, and attorney general.

LIEUTENANT GOVERNOR Forty-five states have a lieutenant governor. Arizona, Maine, New Hampshire, Oregon, and Wyoming are the five that do not. In three states, the lieutenant governor serves other functions. In Hawaii, the lieutenant governor is also the secretary of state. In Tennessee and West Virginia, the president of the state senate is also the lieutenant governor.

In 26 of the 45 states with a lieutenant governor, that official is elected on the same ticket as the governor, just as the president and vice president are elected. In 17 states, they are elected separately, which means that the two officials can come from different parties. In Tennessee and West Virginia, the state senate elects its president, and that person is lieutenant governor.

Lieutenant governors generally have limited roles. Their chief duty is to assume the office of governor in the event of that official's death, resignation, or removal from office. In 29 states, the lieutenant governor can serve as acting governor when the governor is away from the state. In 27 states, the lieutenant governor is the presiding officer of the state senate, and in 24 of those states, he or she can cast a deciding vote on legislation in the event of a tie. In Texas, the lieutenant governor has substantial power through the ability to control committee assignments and the movement of bills through the state senate. The Texas lieutenant governor also sits on several state boards or commissions, and thus has influence on those bodies.

SECRETARY OF STATE Despite the similarity in name, a secretary of state at the state level is quite different from the federal secretary of state. Secretaries of state for the nation concern themselves only with foreign policy. At the state level, the secretary of state is, essentially, the official state record keeper. While duties vary across the states, secretaries of state typically have such responsibilities as making the official record of state government documents and registering businesses. In many states, the secretary of state has the responsibility of keeping official records of voters, overseeing elections, and recording official election results. Forty-seven states have a secretary of state. In Hawaii, the lieutenant governor doubles by filling this office. Alaska and Utah have no provision for this office. The secretary of state is elected in 35 states and appointed by the governor in 12.

STATE TREASURER The state treasurer oversees the state's finances, including revenue collection and making disbursements, or payments. Treasurers handle the state government payroll and oversee the state pension system. In many states, they are responsible for ensuring that funds allocated by the legislature are spent appropriately. In others, that task is the domain of a different official, the state auditor. All states have the equivalent of a treasurer, though in New York and Texas the official carrying out this role is the controller. Thirty-six states elect the state treasurer. In eight states, the governor appoints this official. In the other four, the state legislature makes this appointment.

ATTORNEY GENERAL The state attorney general, like the attorney general of the United States, is the government's chief legal officer. He or she oversees the state attorneys—who handle prosecutions of state criminal cases—and heads the office that represents the state in any legal matters. The attorney general also advises other state officials on legal matters. As the head of the team of state prosecutors, the attorney general has a substantial influence on law enforcement priorities and policies in the state. Attorneys general are elected by voters in 43 states. The governor appoints this official in five states (Alaska, Hawaii, New Hampshire, New Jersey, and Wyoming). Attorneys general are also appointed in Maine and Tennessee—in Maine by the state legislature and in Tennessee by the state supreme court.

HISTORICAL THINKING

5. **EVALUATE** What might be some advantages and disadvantages of having governors and lieutenant governors elected separately, rather than on the same ticket?

6. **IDENTIFY MAIN IDEAS AND DETAILS** Name a key responsibility for each of these state government offices: secretary of state, treasurer, and attorney general.

LESSON
20.4 State Judicial Systems

The foundational principle of the American judicial system, "Equal Justice Under Law," is engraved on the front of the U.S. Supreme Court building in Washington, D.C. Ensuring equal justice isn't a goal of just the federal court system, however. Ensuring due process of law—the right of all persons to be treated fairly by the judicial system—is the purpose of the entire system of American justice, including state judicial systems.

Foundations of State Law

State laws are based on several sources. The most fundamental source is constitutional law, the set of rules, rights, and principles established in the U.S. Constitution and a state's constitution. Because the federal and state constitutions are foundational—that is, they form the foundation, or basic structure, of the government and legal systems of the nation and the states—they deal with very basic questions. These include the relationship among the three branches of government, the relationship between the federal and state governments, and the fundamental rights of all Americans.

All other laws are subordinate to these constitutions. Any law found in violation of the federal or a state constitution is invalid. Decisions on constitutionality are

State legislatures pass statutory law to authorize the construction of roadways such as these in Houston, Texas, and also to address general safety concerns. Executive agencies issue administrative regulations to detail the rules for construction to implement those statutes.

made in the highest courts. The U.S. Supreme Court rules on constitutionality for the federal government, and the supreme courts of the individual states rule on questions regarding their state constitutions.

SOURCES AND TYPES OF LAWS In addition to constitutional law, there are statutory laws and administrative laws. Statutory law is any law enacted by a legislative body with the authority to make law. Laws passed by a state legislature to set the penalties for speeding on the state highway or the minimum number of days in a public school year are examples of statutory laws. **Ordinances**, as laws passed by city, town, or county governments are called, are also statutory laws.

Administrative law is the rules, regulations, orders, and decisions of administrative agencies in the state's executive branch. A state legislature may pass a statute that requires all drivers to have certain minimum levels of auto insurance. The office of the state insurance commission then sets the rules for what businesses are legally authorized to operate as insurers.

Case law is made by the courts through their decisions. You may remember that, in the United States, case law was originally based on an English legal tradition called the common law that began in the Middle Ages. Common law comes from custom and from judicial decisions on particular points of law. Precedent—prior judicial decisions—is very important to common law. Judges review records of cases similar to the one they are deciding, to be guided by those earlier decisions. Following precedent remains an important practice for judges in courts of appeals. While the common law tradition remains strong in the United States, statutory law came to predominate during the 20th century as legislatures became more active.

AREAS OF LAW Laws can be classified into two categories, criminal law and civil law. Criminal law addresses crimes. Civil law involves disputes between individuals or entities.

A crime is any action prohibited by law or any failure to carry out an action required by law. Theft of another person's property is a crime. Failure by a teacher or doctor to report evidence that a child has been abused is also a crime. There are three types of crime, which differ in seriousness and severity of punishment.

- Infractions are minor violations like traffic tickets. They rarely go to trial, and offenders are usually punished through payment of a fine.
- Misdemeanors are more serious crimes, like shoplifting, that can be punished by time in jail, a fine, or both. Some states have different classes of misdemeanors, ranging from petty—punished by something like six months in a city or county jail and a $500 fine—to high—punished by as much as a year in jail and a $1,000 fine. A misdemeanor conviction can affect a person's ability to get a scholarship or a job.
- Felonies—the most serious crimes—include acts such as murder, armed robbery, and certain cases of fraud. They result in more serious punishments, including up to life in state prison, substantial fines, or even death. A person found guilty of a felony three times may be given a very severe sentence, a policy aimed at trying to reduce repeat offenses. In many states, those convicted of felonies lose their right to vote. Illegal immigrants who are found guilty of a felony may be deported.

In criminal matters, the district attorney usually represents the state government to prosecute the person accused of the crime. For the defendant to be found guilty, the prosecutor must prove the case beyond a reasonable doubt. That is, the person or persons rendering the verdict must have absolutely no question of the defendant's guilt. If there is any doubt, those rendering the verdict must vote to acquit the defendant.

Civil law involves a lawsuit between two or more parties, which could be individuals, groups of individuals, or entities like a company or government agency. In a lawsuit, one party—the plaintiff—asks a court to settle a dispute or to force the other party—the defendant—to perform some action. Examples of disputes include those regarding child custody cases, claims that a party did not fulfill a contract, or claims that a plaintiff was injured by a defendant's actions. An injury could be a matter of physical, mental, or emotional harm—as when a person sues someone for injuries suffered in an auto accident caused by the defendant. It can also mean a loss of rights, as when a former tenant sues a landlord to have a security deposit returned.

In a civil case, the plaintiff has the burden of proof, which means the plaintiff must establish a claim with a preponderance, or large amount, of evidence, a less stringent standard than beyond a reasonable doubt. By this standard, the person or persons deciding the case must conclude that there is a greater than 50 percent chance that the plaintiff's claim is justifiable. If so, the plaintiff wins the case. If not, the defendant prevails.

HISTORICAL THINKING

1. **CATEGORIZE** What two categories can be used to classify laws?
2. **MAKE INFERENCES** Why is the burden of proof greater in criminal rather than in civil trials?

The Trial System

American law is based on the adversarial system. Under this system, two parties in a dispute have the right to present their side of the dispute before an impartial third party. That third party—a judge or jury—assesses the evidence provided by both parties, tries to find the truth in the dispute, and renders a decision.

In the pre-trial period, lawyers for the two sides share evidence in a process called **discovery**. Discovery is much more thorough in civil cases, in which both parties must provide all relevant and unprivileged evidence, or evidence not protected by attorney–client privilege, requested by the other side. The purpose is to ensure that both sides are working with the same facts. In criminal cases, different rules apply. On the one hand, the defendant, who is protected by the constitutional right to avoid self-incrimination, can withhold any evidence that could support a guilty verdict. The prosecution, on the other hand, is required to provide all evidence it possesses, including anything that could be favorable to the defendant.

TYPES OF JURIES The jury system is the heart of the American system of justice. As Supreme Court Justice Byron White wrote in 1968, "the jury trial provisions in the Federal and State Constitutions reflect . . . a reluctance to entrust . . . powers over the life and liberty of the citizen to one judge or to a group of

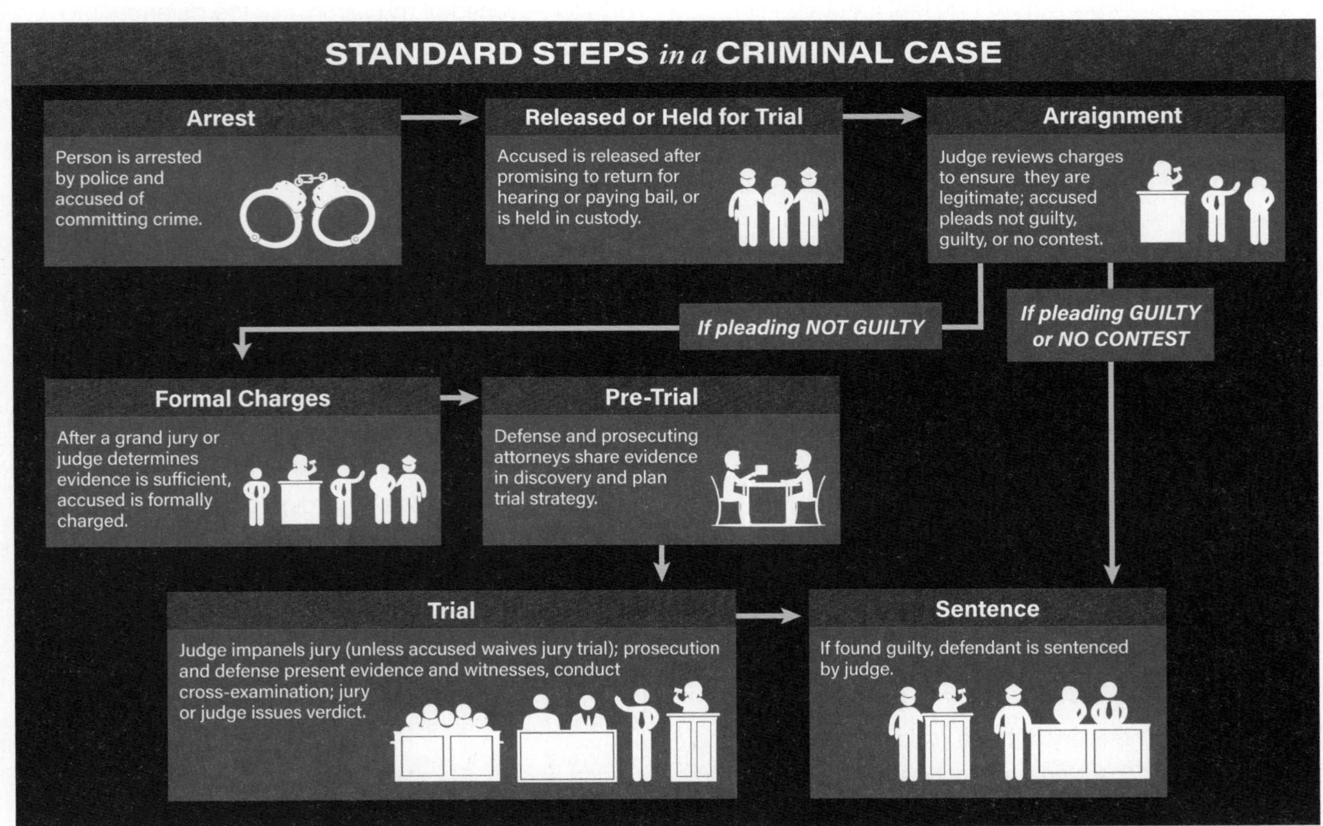

STANDARD STEPS in a CRIMINAL CASE
Arrest
Person is arrested by police and accused of committing crime.
Released or Held for Trial
Accused is released after promising to return for hearing or paying bail, or is held in custody.
Arraignment
Judge reviews charges to ensure they are legitimate; accused pleads not guilty, guilty, or no contest.
If pleading NOT GUILTY
If pleading GUILTY or NO CONTEST
Formal Charges
After a grand jury or judge determines evidence is sufficient, accused is formally charged.
Pre-Trial
Defense and prosecuting attorneys share evidence in discovery and plan trial strategy.
Trial
Judge impanels jury (unless accused waives jury trial); prosecution and defense present evidence and witnesses, conduct cross-examination; jury or judge issues verdict.
Sentence
If found guilty, defendant is sentenced by judge.

judges." One of the duties of citizenship is to serve on a jury when summoned. This service is one of the fundamental ways that Americans can participate in their democracy.

There are two kinds of juries. A grand jury is a panel of between 12 and 23 citizens that help prosecutors determine if they have sufficient evidence to charge someone with a crime. The members of the grand jury can meet for several months, though they do not always meet every day. Grand juries are involved in criminal cases only, not civil ones. Grand jury decisions are required in federal criminal cases. They are less common in state criminal trials, where a judge usually decides that sufficient evidence exists to bring charges. Grand juries hear only from prosecutors, though members of the jury have the right to question anyone they think is relevant to the case.

A trial jury, also called a petit jury, is smaller, consisting of from 6 to 12 people. Once a person is impaneled—or chosen—for a jury, he or she must sit for the duration of the trial, which might take a single afternoon or several days or weeks. Those who serve on a jury are generally exempt from being summoned again by the same type of court for a period of some years.

Potential jurors are chosen at random. Generally, they receive a summons that includes a questionnaire to establish eligibility. Only citizens are eligible for jury duty, and courts generally require jurors to speak and understand English sufficiently to follow their proceedings. People who are younger than 18 are not eligible, and those older than a certain age—for example, 70 in Massachusetts—can choose not to serve. There are a few other grounds to deny eligibility, including having been convicted of a felony. All those who are summoned and are eligible become the jury pool.

Members of the jury pool must appear at the courthouse on a particular day. In many states, they only need to appear for possible jury selection on one day. If chosen for a trial, they must serve for the duration of that trial. If not chosen for a trial, they are excused from jury duty in that year, though they may receive another summons in following years.

Once a group is randomly selected as potential jurors, they are asked a series of questions about their experiences and attitudes. The responses of some individuals might result in their being excused. The attorneys or judge might ask individuals additional questions, and their answers might lead to their removal. Once the jury is selected, members are instructed not to discuss the case with anyone.

Not all cases are heard by a jury. The defendant in a case—either criminal or civil—has the right to waive a jury trial. In that case, a judge listens to the evidence and decides the case.

THE TRIAL The trial begins with opening arguments in which the lawyers for each side lay out the outlines of their case. Throughout the trial, the prosecutor—in a criminal case—and the plaintiff—in a civil case—present first. After opening arguments, the prosecution or plaintiff offers evidence, which can consist of documents or other physical evidence, or witnesses. Each witness is subject to the cross-examination of the attorney for the defendant.

After the prosecution or plaintiff presents its case, the defense has the opportunity to present evidence and witnesses. Again, these witnesses are subject to cross-examination. After the defense concludes its presentation, the two sides make closing arguments. The judge then gives instructions to the jury.

Jurors meet privately to discuss the evidence and their understanding of the applicable law. They vote to determine guilt or innocence in the case of a criminal trial, or in the case of a civil trial, on which side prevails or wins. Juries in every state must reach a unanimous verdict to find a defendant guilty of a serious crime. About a third of the states allow a simple majority of jurors to reach a verdict in civil cases.

If the jury finds the defendant guilty, the judge issues a sentence, sometimes after a separate hearing in which the two sides present arguments for what sentence they think is appropriate. Sometimes juries will recommend sentences as well. In a civil case, the jury might decide on a fine or other action for the defendant if it found in the plaintiff's favor. If a jury cannot reach a decision, the result is a hung jury. The case might be tried again, if the prosecutor or plaintiff chooses to do so.

RESOLUTION WITHOUT A TRIAL Criminal and civil cases do not necessarily go to trial. Criminal charges against someone might be dropped if prosecutors determine that a person originally accused of a

CRITICAL VIEWING Some 8 to 10 million American citizens report for jury service in state and federal courts each year, though not all are chosen to serve on a jury. How important do you think it is to have a diverse jury?

crime was not involved in the crime or that there is insufficient evidence. The accused person can also plead guilty. A no contest plea means the accused accepts conviction but doesn't plead guilty. An accused person can also accept a **plea bargain**, which is a plea of guilty, often to a less serious charge than the original charge. In a criminal case, a plea of guilty or no contest or a plea bargain all move a case to sentencing. In a civil case, the plaintiff can drop the suit, or the two parties can reach a **settlement**, which is a mutual agreement to end a legal dispute. This step puts an end to proceedings.

HISTORICAL THINKING

3. **FORM AND SUPPORT OPINIONS** Why is it important for citizens to serve on juries?
4. **MAKE INFERENCES** How does the way a trial is conducted reflect the adversarial system that is the foundation of American law?
5. **INTERPRET DIAGRAMS** Why are there two possible outcomes after arraignment, the third step in a standard criminal trial?

Organization of State Courts

State court systems are organized much like the federal court system. Each state typically has a group of lower trial courts, a group of intermediate appellate courts that operate as the first court for appeals, and a state supreme court, which acts as the court of last resort for the state. State trial courts handle both criminal and civil matters and are called courts of general jurisdiction. Appellate courts and the state supreme court also hear appeals on both categories of cases.

Trial courts go by different names. In some states, they are called circuit courts. In others, they are called superior courts, district courts, or courts of common pleas. Some states have only one level of trial court, while others have more than one. Tennessee, for instance, has criminal trial courts, which handle criminal matters, and two types of civil trial courts, the chancery courts and circuit courts.

The federal court system has additional courts to handle specialized cases—such as the Court of International Trade—and states also have courts outside the basic system. These courts are said to have limited jurisdiction, meaning they have the authority to address only certain types of legal matters.

- Municipal courts or town courts hear minor violations of state law and/or cases arising from local ordinances. These courts may not have jury trials but leave decisions exclusively to judges.
- Family courts address such matters as child custody and child support. They generally do not have jurisdiction over divorce, which is taken up in the general jurisdiction trial courts.
- Traffic courts are for traffic violations like speeding and parking illegally. Cases involving auto accidents are usually heard in courts of general jurisdiction.
- Probate courts handle questions related to the estates of the deceased.
- Housing or landlord–tenant courts hear disputes between owners of buildings and their renters.
- Small-claims courts are the venue for minor disputes between two parties in which the value of the matter in dispute is small. While limits vary from state to state, they generally do not exceed $7,500.
- Juvenile courts hear cases involving juveniles, which states define variously as up to 16 or 18 years of age. Records of proceedings in juvenile courts—unlike those in adult courts—are sealed. Keeping these cases out of the public record protects young people from suffering lifelong consequences from a youthful mistake.

Most states have only one layer of appellate courts, where parties can appeal procedures from trial courts. Alabama and Tennessee have separate appeals courts for civil and criminal cases. In some states, the lower-level trial courts of general jurisdiction serve as appeals courts for the courts of limited jurisdiction. In Tennessee, for example, decisions in juvenile court can be appealed to a circuit court.

As in the federal system, appeals are usually made on the basis of the law, not the facts. That is, these courts do not typically evaluate the evidence or testimony of witnesses. They hear arguments from the party appealing the lower court ruling in order to determine whether proper procedures were followed in the trial or

A team of lawyers approaches a St. Louis courthouse prior to a session in the 2018 trial of Missouri's sitting governor, Eric Greitens. Criminal prosecutions of public officials bear out the principle that no person in the United States is above the law.

STRUCTURE *of* STATE COURTS

State Supreme Court	• Court of last resort • No juries
Courts of Appeals	• Appellate courts • No juries
Circuit Courts or Superior Courts	• Courts of general jurisdiction • Civil and criminal trial courts • Jury trials • Appeals court for municipal courts
Municipal Courts, Juvenile Courts, Family Courts	• Courts of limited jurisdiction • Trial courts • No juries

if the law was applied correctly. Generally, appeals are heard by a panel of judges who evaluate the arguments, discuss the matter, and vote on whether to accept or reject the arguments of the party making the appeal.

Decisions in the intermediate courts of appeals can be appealed to the state supreme court. As the courts of last resort for the state, their word on the application of state law is final and binding on all other courts in the state—except the state supreme court itself. While justices are guided by precedent, they can reject a decision in an earlier case and rule differently on a matter if they conclude that the earlier decision was mistaken. Decisions of the state supreme court can be appealed to the U.S. Supreme Court if federal constitutional rights are involved.

HISTORICAL THINKING

6. **COMPARE AND CONTRAST** What is the difference between a general jurisdiction court and a limited jurisdiction court?
7. **MAKE CONNECTIONS** How does the appeals process support the principle of due process?

Selecting Judges

About 340 people sit on state supreme courts, and about 1,000 more serve on the states' intermediate appeals courts. More than 9,000 judges oversee the general jurisdiction trial courts across the states. While most federal judges are appointed for life, that isn't the case with most state judges. In 40 states, justices on the highest courts serve for terms of 6 to 10 years. Only Rhode Island appoints these officials for life. Three states—Massachusetts, New Hampshire, and New Jersey—allow justices to sit on the court until age 70. Terms for trial court and intermediate appellate court judges are similar to those for supreme court justices in each state, and the same states are the exceptions in granting longer terms.

States follow different methods for selecting judges to fill these seats. In just under half the states, judges are elected. The election of judges is often nonpartisan, in an effort to reinforce the idea that judges should be independent. But in some cases, the candidates for general elections are chosen in party primaries.

In the rest of the states, justices are appointed by the governor, in some cases with confirmation by another body, such as the state legislature or an executive council. In some cases, the governors make their appointments from a list of recommendations by a nonpartisan commission of legal experts. That approach aims to ensure that highly knowledgeable and impartial judges are chosen. In around half of the states with gubernatorial appointments, after their first term, justices must stand for election in order to retain their seats. In South Carolina and Virginia, the legislature chooses all judges. Generally, within a state, the same methods are used to choose judges for all levels of the courts.

Supporters say the practice of electing judges gives the people the right to select individuals who, through their judicial decisions, have an enormous impact on their lives. One legal scholar who studied the history of judicial selection found that the move to elect judges arose from the 19th century as a reform. Reformers

Cheri Beasley (center) took office in 2019 as chief justice of the North Carolina Supreme Court—the first African-American woman to serve on the state's highest court. Beasley's position demonstrates the complex manner in which judges are selected in some states. She was named as chief justice by the state's governor, but she had to win election in 2020 to hold the office. Beasley lost the chief justice race to her Republican opponent.

of the time saw that appointed judges were beholden to party leaders and thus were not objective. They wanted judges to be elected, so that they would be free of partisan influence.

Critics of judicial elections say that voters lack the knowledge to fairly estimate the background, experience, and legal knowledge of judicial candidates. Some argue that candidates cannot campaign by making promises about how they will rule in cases, as doing so is inconsistent with judicial impartiality. Critics also worry that the increased influence of money in modern elections could result in massive spending by interest groups for or against certain candidates. Such spending could skew the election toward candidates with strong biases.

HISTORICAL THINKING

8. **FORM AND SUPPORT OPINIONS** What do you think is the best method for selecting state supreme court justices? Why?

CHAPTER 20

STATE GOVERNMENTS

Review

VOCABULARY

Match each of the following vocabulary words with its definition.

1. term limit	**a.** drawing legislative district lines to favor one racial group over another
2. special district	**b.** a plea of guilty to a less serious charge than the original charge
3. racial gerrymandering	**c.** a maximum number of times a person can hold the same office
4. partisan gerrymandering	**d.** the period before a trial during which the lawyers for the two sides share evidence
5. per diem	**e.** a mutual agreement to end a legal dispute
6. recall	**f.** payment made to a lawmaker each day that the legislature is in session
7. parole	**g.** a unit of local government created through state action for a specific purpose
8. ordinance	**h.** legislative district lines drawn to favor one political party over another
9. discovery	**i.** a conditional release from prison
10. plea bargain	**j.** citizens' right to remove a public official from office and replace him or her with a new officeholder
11. settlement	**k.** a law passed by a city council or state government

MAIN IDEAS

Answer the following questions. Support your answer with evidence from the chapter.

12. What is an example of checks and balances in state government? **LESSON 20.1**

13. What are the four types of local government established by state governments? **LESSON 20.1**

14. Most state legislatures do not meet throughout the year. What does this mean for the lawmakers who serve in them? **LESSON 20.2**

15. Describe two kinds of work done in legislative committees. **LESSON 20.2**

16. What are four ways in which a governor might be forced to leave office? **LESSON 20.3**

17. Name at least five roles of a state governor. **LESSON 20.3**

18. What are the three levels of crime, and how do they differ in terms of punishment? **LESSON 20.4**

HISTORICAL THINKING

Answer the following questions. Support your answer with evidence from the chapter.

19. **DRAW CONCLUSIONS** Based on what you have read about state constitutions, would you conclude that the amendment process for state constitutions is more or less difficult than that for the U.S. Constitution? Explain your answer.

20. **FORM AND SUPPORT OPINIONS** Do you agree with George Norris's statement justifying Nebraska's unicameral legislature: "there is no sense or reason in having the same thing done twice, especially if it is to be done by two bodies . . . elected in the same way and having the same jurisdiction"? Why or why not?

21. **MAKE CONNECTIONS** What two principles of American government are exemplified by the recall process? Explain your answer.

22. **COMPARE AND CONTRAST** In Maine and New Jersey, the governor is the only elected executive official and has the power to appoint people to the other positions. How does this make the office of governor in these states relatively stronger than that of other states?

23. **MAKE CONNECTIONS** What role does the attorney general, an executive branch official, play in the judicial branch?

24. **MAKE GENERALIZATIONS** How are plea bargains and settlements similar?

25. **COMPARE AND CONTRAST** What are some ways that state supreme court justices are different from U.S. Supreme Court justices?

INTERPRET VISUALS

The graph below shows how people responded to a poll in September 2018 asking them how much trust and confidence they had in different government bodies. Study the results and then answer the questions.

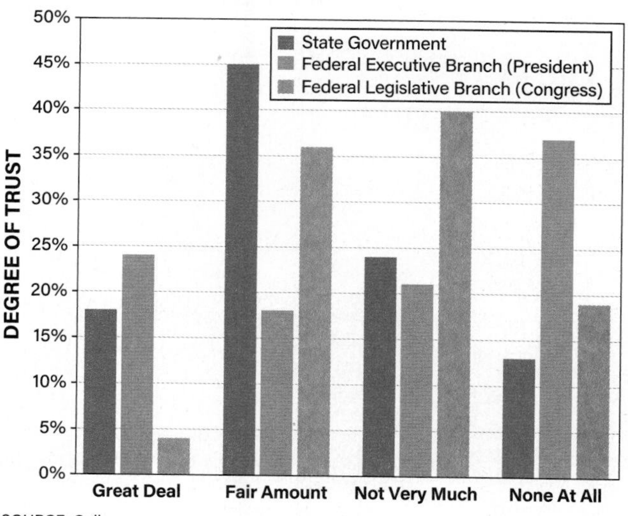

SOURCE: Gallup

26. How did trust in state government compare to trust in the president and Congress, according to these 2018 poll results?

27. What do you think explains these results?

ANALYZE SOURCES

Read the following excerpts from the Texas state constitution and the U.S. Constitution, and then answer the question.

> "Equality under the law shall not be denied or abridged because of sex, race, color, creed, or national origin."
>
> —Texas constitution, Article I, Section 3a
>
> "No state shall . . . deny to any person within its jurisdiction the equal protection of the laws."
>
> —U.S Constitution, 14th Amendment, Section 1

28. Which guarantee do you think is a stronger protection of equal rights? Why do you think so?

CONNECT TO YOUR LIFE

29. **ARGUMENT** Think about your regular activities in a week—going to school, working in a job, playing a sport, traveling on streets or roads, shopping, or any other common activity you engage in. Then think about how the laws or rules of state government affect you in those activities. What new law or rule do you think would make your life better? Write a letter that you might send to your state's governor and the state legislators who represent you to explain the change you want and why it is important.

TIPS

- Focus on a policy change that has broad applicability to other students or workers like you.
- Do some research online to find out what issues the governor and lawmakers are interested in. Try to connect your proposed change to their policy goals.
- Find a model for a formal letter to a public official, and craft your letter following that model.
- Make sure your letter uses persuasive language.

CHAPTER 21

Local Governments

LESSONS

21.1 Municipal Governments

***National Geographic* Magazine:**
Cities, Businesses, and Citizens Can Save the Planet

National Geographic Online:
Tough, Cheap, and Real, Detroit Is Cool Again

21.2 County, Township, and Tribal Governments

***National Geographic* Magazine:**
Native Lands

21.3 State and Local Government Finances

CRITICAL VIEWING Citizens watch a 2014 meeting of the Los Angeles City Council. The council voted unanimously at this meeting for a resolution requiring a large company that grows fruit for the city to recognize a union contract for its workers. How does this scene exemplify politics at a grassroots level?

LESSON
21.1 Municipal Governments

Have you ever wondered how that crack in the sidewalk you used to trip over was fixed, or how to recycle an old refrigerator? If you needed to, would you know where to go to get a copy of your birth certificate or confirm that the water you drink is safe? Most of these questions can be answered the same way: your local government. While the federal and state governments tend to get a lot more attention, your local government is also constantly at work, having more of an impact on your daily life than you might realize.

The Foundation of Local Government

Although it plays an enormous role in everyday life, local government is not mentioned anywhere in the U.S. Constitution. The Tenth Amendment reserves those powers not expressly given to the federal government—or denied to the states—to the states. It is up to those states to delegate and approve the power of their own local governments. Because each state's constitution is different, the way in which local governments within each state are set up varies across the country. If you think 50 different state governments offer a great variety of rules and practices, imagine the variety you'll find in the nearly 90,000 units of local government in the United States.

New York's City Hall, completed in 1812, is the oldest city hall still used for its original function. The David N. Dinkins Municipal Building, completed in 1914 and renamed in 2015 for the city's first Black mayor, stands behind city hall. These are just two of the numerous buildings in which the nearly 300,000 employees of the municipality of New York City work.

There are four main types of local government. The principal subdivision is counties, units of government that are also called *parishes* in Louisiana and *boroughs* in Alaska. Counties are generally responsible for enforcing state laws within their boundaries. Many states divide counties into townships, the second type of local government. Millions of Americans live in the third type, a **municipality**, a political subdivision that is incorporated, or officially recognized as an individual part of the state. These units—which include cities or towns—have the authority to govern themselves to a certain extent. The fourth type of local government, the special district, includes school districts and other governing units created to serve a specific purpose in a particular part of the state.

In the 1700s and 1800s, local governments had very little autonomy, or independent authority. In general, state and local governments followed a principle that later became known as Dillon's Rule, named after Iowa judge John Dillon, who ruled in two cases that local government could only undertake actions expressly granted by its state's government. The Supreme Court upheld Dillon's Rule in 1907 and then again in 1923.

In the 20th century, states found that keeping a tight rein on growing local governments was time-consuming and inefficient. At the same time, local governments were bogged down by having to make requests to the state before they could perform basic and necessary services. In response, many states began adding home-rule provisions to their constitutions. **Home rule** is a grant of authority to a local government over certain functions, although the state government still retains overarching authority. A local government with home rule often adopts a **charter**. This is a set of laws that describes its functions, its organization, and the powers of various officials. In some states, residents of an area create and approve the charter. In other states, the state government grants the charter.

Currently, 31 states allow for home-rule charters for some or all counties, and 44 allow home-rule charters for municipalities. Some states limit the charters to certain units of local government. In Arizona and Missouri, counties must have a minimum population to obtain a charter, and many states have population

What's in a Name?

The terminology for communities can be confusing. When does a village become a town and a town become a city? Is it a matter of incorporation? Are towns and cities incorporated, and villages not? Well, no. Vermont, New York, and more than a dozen other states have incorporated villages. Is it a function of size? Are villages small, towns of medium size, and cities large? Again, the answer is no. The village of Addison, Illinois, had more than 36,000 people in 2018—far more than the 3,000 or so living in the city of Abingdon, Illinois. The town of Cicero, south of Chicago, had just over 80,000 people, which was more than the approximately 75,000 in the city of Evanston to the north.

And here's one more wrinkle. New Jersey and Pennsylvania have municipal units called boroughs—the same name Alaska uses for its county equivalent—as well as cities, towns, townships, and villages in New Jersey and cities and townships in Pennsylvania. Given all of these complications, the best answer to "What's in a name?" is to find out what a place calls itself and just accept it.

Different states have different specifications for what qualifies as a city, town, township, or village. The popular tourist spot of Ketchikan, Alaska, is a city, but it has a population that is just slightly above 8,000 people. Hempstead, New York, officially a town, has over 750,000 residents.

minimums for municipal charters. In states that do not allow home-rule charters, local governments are what are called general law counties or municipalities. A general law local government has only the authority granted it by the state constitution and other state laws concerning local government in general. Local governments created under general law typically have less autonomy than those formed by a charter.

HISTORICAL THINKING

1. **IDENTIFY MAIN IDEAS AND DETAILS** What are four types of local government in the United States?
2. **EVALUATE** What do you think are two advantages of giving local governments a substantial amount of autonomy?

Municipal Governments

Municipal governments come in many shapes and sizes. U.S. towns and cities typically use one of five forms of municipal government. They are the mayor-council plan, the mayor-council-administrator plan, the council-manager plan, the commission plan, and the town meeting.

- **Mayor-council:** In this government structure, the mayor—the chief executive—is elected (and often paid a full-time salary), as is a council—the lawmaking body. This form of government is common in large U.S. cities. Such mayors are often referred to as strong mayors because they hold quite a bit of decision-making power, including veto power. In some mayor-council cities, however, the mayor has limited power.
- **Mayor-council-administrator:** In a variation on the mayor-council form, this form also includes a city administrator appointed by the mayor to help run various city departments.
- **Council-manager:** The most common form of municipal government today, the council-manager form gives both legislative and administrative power to an elected council, which chooses a mayor from among themselves. This so-called weak mayor is more of a figurehead, with few or no specific powers separate from those he or she already holds as a council member. A city manager is appointed to carry out everyday administration.
- **Commission:** Found in only a small percentage of U.S. municipalities, the commission form of government typically consists of five or seven elected commissioners. Each commissioner has responsibility for a specific area of government, such as education or public works, and the commission as a whole holds legislative power. Although one commissioner might be named chairperson or mayor, that person holds no more power than his or her fellow commissioners but runs the commissioner meetings.
- **Town meeting:** Also rare, the town meeting form leaves decisions regarding policy and laws to voters in the municipality. Voters also choose officials to administer the policies they choose.

Municipalities in different regions of the country tend to have the form of government typical of their region. For example, most large cities in Texas follow the

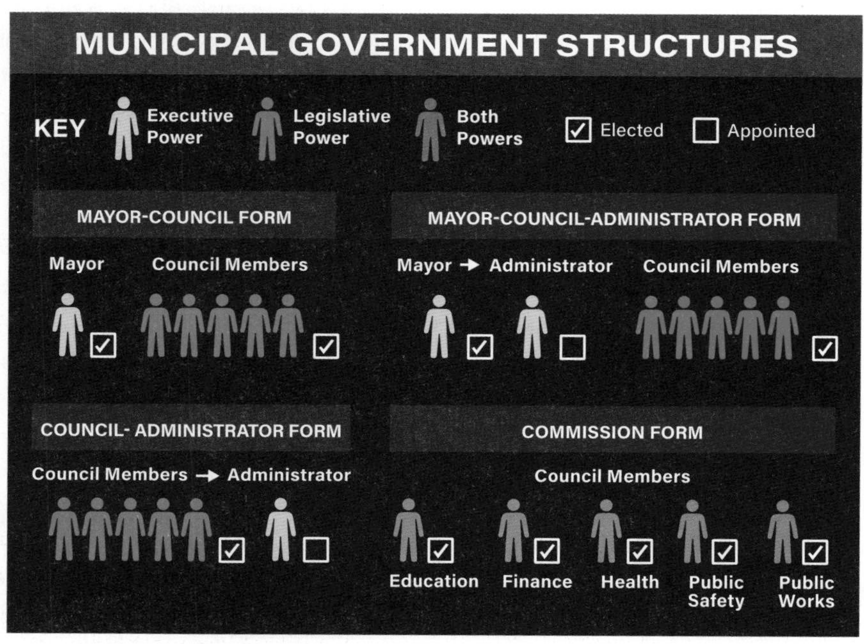

CRITICAL VIEWING Political machines dominated 19th and early 20th-century city governments. The corrupt leadership committee of New York City's Democratic Party, known as Tammany Hall, is thought to have stolen anywhere from $30 million to $200 million of public funds (about $616 million to $4.12 billion in 2020 dollars). At its height, the city's political machine operated under the leadership of William "Boss" Tweed, shown in the orange vest in this colorized version of an 1871 cartoon by Thomas Nast. What does the cartoon indicate about the nature of machine corruption?

council-manager form of government, while mayor-council structures are dominant in many major cities in the Northeast and Midwest. The town meeting form is found mainly in New England.

The way in which council members are elected can also vary among municipalities. In some cases, they are chosen through at-large elections, which means all are elected by and will serve all voters in the municipality. In other cities, council members are elected to represent a ward or district. About 20 percent of cities with councils have a mix of members elected from wards and at-large members.

HISTORICAL THINKING

3. **COMPARE AND CONTRAST** Explain how forms of government with a strong mayor differ from those with a weak mayor.
4. **SYNTHESIZE** Do you think a commission form of government would work better in a large or small municipality? Explain.
5. **INTERPRET VISUALS** In which forms of local government do voters elect all officials?

Reforming City Governments

Municipal governments did not always use the structures described in the previous section. Cities grew and urban populations skyrocketed in the second half of the 19th century due to immigration and industrialization. Municipal governments were often little more than a network of unscrupulous power brokers, often with one chief—the political boss. Bosses led political party operations known as political machines because they worked like well-oiled mechanisms. Supporters who helped get out the vote were often rewarded with government jobs, whether or not they were qualified. Voting fraud and voter intimidation were common. City contracts were regularly given to party supporters, with those receiving the contracts often paying kickbacks or bribes to the boss and his top aides.

By the beginning of the 20th century, reformers of the Progressive Era had begun to fight machine politicians. Journalists exposed the corrupt operations of the machines in different cities, particularly New York City and Chicago. Longtime political bosses began to face competition at the polls. Reforms put an end to patronage—or the awarding of most civil service jobs to political allies—in the federal government. Reformers pushed for similar changes in local government.

HISTORICAL THINKING

6. **IDENTIFY MAIN IDEAS AND DETAILS** Explain how journalists' exposure of machine politicians might have led to reform movements.

Managing Cities

At the time the nation was founded, the vast majority of Americans lived in rural areas. Between 1880 and

1900, about 15 million people arrived in or moved to U.S. cities. By 1920, the percentages of people in rural and urban areas were equal. The rapid growth of cities from the late 19th century to the early 20th century led to a host of problems.

THE ADVENT OF ZONING As more and more people poured into American cities, residential and commercial areas were hastily thrown together to deal with the sudden surge in population and industrial growth. Housing tenements, built quickly and cheaply to meet the urgent demand for housing, were not always safe. Rapid population growth strained public services from sanitation to mass transit systems.

In 1916, New York City became the first major U.S. city to pursue a policy of **zoning**, or the legal process of dividing land into specific zones to regulate development and use. Today, zoning is a regular responsibility of local government. Local officials regulate where new construction can take place and what kinds of construction—residential or commercial—are allowed in different parts of the city. Local officials also use zoning to decide how close commercial properties can be to residential areas or schools. Public safety and health are also at the heart of many zoning decisions. For example, how and where a city's waste is collected and transported can be subject to zoning restrictions.

PROS AND CONS OF ZONING Supporters of zoning see it as a way of managing growth and safety. Zoning ordinances can ensure that a factory that produces pollution is a safe distance from homes and schools. Officials review plans for new shopping areas or office buildings to evaluate the impact on traffic. Other regulations make sure that sidewalks are placed correctly and uniformly to protect pedestrians.

Critics argue that zoning can be taken too far. Property owners bristle at being told by local officials that they cannot alter their property as they wish. Strict laws on how and where commercial developers can build can dissuade businesses from locating within a municipality, which costs that community potential tax revenue. Similarly, if a business does build in a municipality but is restricted on how much it can build, that can have adverse, or negative, effects. For example, limits on the number of units a real-estate developer can put in a new apartment building might convince the company to increase rents on the units it can build. As a result, zoning leads to inequality by pricing low-income residents out of an area. And critics such as author Jane Jacobs argue that organic development of mixed-use spaces makes cities safer and more vibrant.

CRITICAL VIEWING The effects of city planning can be seen clearly when comparing the layout of an older American city, like Boston (top), which was first settled in 1630, with a newer city, like Denver (bottom), founded more than 220 years later. What signs of planning—or lack of planning—can you see in these photographs?

Over the years, zoning laws have been challenged in courts. In 1917, the U.S. Supreme Court declared zoning laws designed to segregate neighborhoods by race a violation of the 14th Amendment. A 1926 Supreme Court decision, however, found that local governments had the authority to make zoning rules.

OTHER CITY SERVICES Zoning is hardly a city's only responsibility. Local governments run public schools, build and maintain local roads, manage public transit systems, and provide for public safety—including police, fire, and other first-responder services. In addition, the city government has to find and budget the resources to pay for these vital services.

In some municipalities, the control of certain government functions is held by bodies separate from the main municipal government. For example, many cities and towns have separate school boards to oversee public education. Often, these boards are made up of elected members, and they may have the power to operate independently of the city government.

MANAGING CRISES Municipal leaders are sometimes faced with unexpected crises. Some crises, such as a major fire, are local events. Others are big enough that they require a city to coordinate its response with other levels of government. In 2020, the coronavirus pandemic put pressure on all levels of government. State and local governments were suddenly faced with major, potentially life-or-death decisions on how and when to close and then reopen schools, businesses, and other major areas of operation. The novelty of the virus, and lack of information about how it operated, created uncertainty about levels of COVID-19 infections. This lack of certainty sometimes led to disagreements between local and state officials, who often had varying perspectives on the level of risk the virus posed to the people they served. In Georgia, for example, Atlanta mayor Keisha Lance Bottoms strongly expressed her disagreement when the state's governor, Brian Kemp, chose to reopen some of the state earlier than federal guidelines recommended. While Kemp emphasized the need to protect Georgia's economy by allowing businesses to operate, Bottoms argued that the high rate of infection in Fulton County (where most of Atlanta is located) and other regions indicated that reopening was premature and dangerous.

HISTORICAL THINKING

7. **MAKE PREDICTIONS** Name three ways that zoning can protect public safety.
8. **DRAW CONCLUSIONS** In what way is a local public school system complicated enough to require its own governing body? Use your own experience as a student to answer.

Suburban and Metropolitan Governments

Today, much of local government is found in the suburbs, or in communities clustered around a larger city. In fact, the vast majority of Americans—175 million of them—live in counties made up of suburbs, while 98 million live in urban counties and 46 million live in rural ones. Yet few suburbs even existed 100 years ago. It took the invention and mass production of the automobile to entice people to leave the cities that had lured them decades earlier. By 1930, more than 50 percent of American families owned a car, making it possible for workers to live farther from their jobs.

When Congress passed the G.I. Bill, or the Servicemen's Readjustment Act, near the end of World War II, veterans of that war were able to obtain low-interest home mortgages. Many veterans purchased new homes outside cities, and suburbs grew. New roads were built and new communities attracted stores and added parks, schools, and other facilities. But federal housing regulations at the time did not allow mortgage loans to Black veterans and therefore encouraged greater racial segregation of residential communities.

As new suburban municipalities were incorporated, local governments formed. Residents paid property taxes to fund local government. Suburbs—and their governments—eventually became parts of larger metropolitan areas, which are made up of a major city, its suburbs, and any other regions connected to the core city economically and socially. As population shifted to the suburbs, many of these central cities suffered greatly. Cities that had developed around a specific industry were further affected when that industry either left or decreased production. For example, Detroit declined when its auto industry—which peaked in

Volunteers take part painting a New York City roof white in October 2010 as part of a global effort called the 10/10/10 Global Work Party. The white paint will reflect about 80 percent of sunlight, reducing energy costs for the building by cutting down on the need for air conditioning.

Cities, Businesses, and Citizens Can Save the Planet

***National Geographic* Magazine, February 2018**

While climate change is a worldwide problem that needs to be addressed by multinational efforts, municipal governments can enact important initiatives. That's the message of former New York City mayor and presidential candidate Michael Bloomberg in an interview with *National Geographic* editor in chief Susan Goldberg. In "Cities, Businesses, and Citizens Can Save the Planet," Bloomberg tells Goldberg about many of the latest innovations in environmental protection happening at the local level.

Estimates indicate that 66 percent of the world's people will be living in cities by the year 2050. As Bloomberg says, while urban life might not be for everyone, cities offer many benefits, from a faster pace of life to a rich variety of cultural experiences. They also offer, according to Bloomberg, opportunities to tackle environmental issues, like energy overuse. Employers within cities know that both their workers and investors are carefully watching how responsibly a company treats the local environment.

Bloomberg says that the place to watch for real change in environmental policy is at the grassroots level and not necessarily the national stage:

> *All this progress is not made by the federal government—not the last [Obama] administration, certainly not this [Trump] administration—and not made by the state governments. There are a handful that do a little bit; [California governor] Jerry Brown has tried to do some real things. But it's the local governments, the local companies, and the local nonprofits—that's where the progress is made.*

Access the full version of "Cities, Businesses, and Citizens Can Save the Planet" by Michael Bloomberg with Susan Goldberg through the Resources Menu in MindTap.

THINK ABOUT IT What advantages and disadvantages do local governments have when it comes to putting environmental action policies in place?

Tough, Cheap, and Real, Detroit Is Cool Again

by Susan Ager **National Geographic Online, July 15, 2013**

Detroit contains many crumbling properties and abandoned, overgrown lots. Yet its people are working to bring the city back to its full potential, from clearing abandoned lots for urban farming to putting Detroit-based art in the national spotlight.

Detroit is a prime example of how much, and how fast, cities can change—both for the worse and for the better. As Susan Ager recounts in "Tough, Cheap, and Real, Detroit Is Cool Again," the city once dubbed "the Paris of the Midwest" fell on hard times in the late 20th century. More than half its residents left for the suburbs or elsewhere, and the industries—especially the unionized auto industry—that created the city's prosperity collapsed. Today, Detroit is the poorest of large American cities. But, as Ager details, hope in Detroit is slowly growing, along with the city's economy.

Enthusiastic city officials, foundations, and investors have helped pull the city out of massive debt, and the city's residents have given it new optimism. Many small businesses, from vegan cafés to neighborhood barber shops, have opened. Both Detroit natives and those who have been lured by the city's up-and-coming reputation have bought land to build new homes, start urban agricultural projects, and work with community programs. Thousands of crumbling homes or vacant lots still blight Detroit's neighborhoods, yet many of these so-called urban prairies are experiencing new life. Both young professionals and investors are buying these abandoned properties for as little as $500, giving the city a chance to revive.

But, Ager recounts, some who live in the Motor City believe that Detroit should be viewed as more than just a rehabilitation project. Ager describes the feelings of Antonio "Shades" Agee, a Detroit native who has gained national fame for his graffiti work:

> *He knows he's part of a now popular brand, a Detroit that's tough, resourceful, proud. He resents that the brand has become a talisman for people who hardly know Detroit but boast its name on their shirts. "This big flourishing," he says, "it's great! I love it. But most people, they wanna save Detroit. You can't save Detroit. You gotta be Detroit."*

Access the full version of "Tough, Cheap, and Real, Detroit Is Cool Again" by Susan Ager through the Resources Menu in MindTap.

THINK ABOUT IT What do you think Antonio Agee means when he says, "You can't save Detroit. You gotta be Detroit"?

the mid-20th century—weakened considerably, and Cleveland saw its iron and steel industries cease to be economic powerhouses. Between 1960 and 2010, both cities lost more than half of their population, due in large part to these economic upheavals.

The growth of suburbs forced municipal governments to find new ways of working together to address issues that transcended city and town borders. It remains a daunting task, considering that an average metropolitan area includes 114 local governments, all of which have their goals and concerns. Public policy experts have encouraged greater collaboration among municipalities to control urban sprawl—the unchecked growth of urbanized areas. This broader metropolitan cooperation can also help promote responsible water use and efficient intercity public transit systems. In the Portland, Oregon, metropolitan area, the country's first elected metropolitan government, named Metro, was formed in 1979. Still, a revolutionary example of regional government, Metro consists of Portland and other cities in a three-county area, all of which work cooperatively to deal with issues that affect the region, including sustainable land use, transportation planning, and preservation of open space.

HISTORICAL THINKING

9. **ANALYZE CAUSE AND EFFECT** What were two factors that led to the growth of the suburbs?
10. **MAKE CONNECTIONS** What were some factors that contributed to the decline of major cities?

LESSON 21.2 County, Township, and Tribal Governments

American government is not simple. You and your family may receive government services from the federal government, from the state, and from a municipality. Your family may pay taxes to all three of those levels of government. If you live in most states, you may also receive services from—and pay taxes to—another level of government, the county. Of course, there are always exceptions. As you'll see, some states have counties but no county government.

County Government

For Americans living in metropolitan areas, the county may be a bit of a mystery, because municipal governments typically take care of most of the services that residents regularly need, such as education. But counties are the main geographic subdivision of states and typically the main political division as well. Counties are found in every single state (although, as you have read, they are called *parishes* in Louisiana and *boroughs* in Alaska).

The services that county government provides vary, depending on the state and the location within a state. County governments tend to be strong in the South and the Far West. In Hawaii, counties are the only form of local government—there are no municipal governments. In most states, county government provides almost all services—from hospitals to road maintenance—in areas where populations are not large enough to require a separate municipal government.

In New England, county government is relatively weak, and towns are the major political subdivision. Rhode Island and Connecticut have abolished county government altogether, relying on only state and local governments. Both still have counties as geographic subdivisions, but the counties in those states have no governing bodies or officials other than some county judicial positions. In Massachusetts, only 6 of the 14 counties have a county government. In the other New England states, government functions are handled by towns or by state offices.

ORGANIZATION OF COUNTY GOVERNMENT There are slightly over 3,000 county governments in the United States. Their structure varies, but most counties are run by a county commission or county board. Commissioners—sometimes called supervisors—are elected and typically hold executive and legislative powers. A county executive may also be elected to manage operations. These officials are similar to strong mayors in municipal government in that they typically have veto power. Some counties have an appointed administrator or manager who typically has less independent power than an elected executive.

Many counties have additional elected officials, such as county clerk, sheriff, prosecutor, clerk of the court, register of deeds, assessor, and coroner. The county clerk provides administrative support to the county commissioners and oversees elections. The sheriff is the chief law enforcement officer. The county prosecutor represents the government in criminal prosecutions, while the clerk of the court maintains official court records. The register, or registrar, of deeds is the official who records the transfer of real estate from one owner to another and may record other official documents as well. The assessor sets the value of real estate in the county, and the coroner records the official cause of death of anyone who dies under suspicious circumstances or from violence. These officials tend to have autonomous power and are not under the control of the county commissioners.

FUNCTIONS OF COUNTY GOVERNMENT Like municipal government, county government derives, or receives, its authority from the state. In other words, a county government has as much power as the state allows it to have. Traditional responsibilities of counties can range from recording deeds and issuing birth and death certificates to running jails and courthouses. Counties also oversee elections. It is counties that set up and run more than 100,000 polling places nationwide and that find and train more than 700,000 people to staff those polling places.

During the 20th century, the movement of the U.S. population from cities to suburbs and semi-rural areas transformed the role of many county governments. Officials suddenly found themselves in charge of functions that used to fall to cities, such as zoning, parking, and garbage collection. Today, county government functions much like a city government in areas where municipal governments have not been established to provide services.

In some counties, specific agencies have responsibility for services that affect millions of people, including utilities, airports, highways, water purification, transportation networks, and hospital systems. In Cook County, Illinois, the county's Forest Preserve District maintains almost 70,000 acres of forest, wetlands, and other preserves—the largest such reserve in the United States. In Los Angeles County, California, the sheriff's department runs the largest jail system in the country, housing between 17,000 and 20,000 inmates every day.

STREAMLINING COUNTY GOVERNMENT As county governments have grown, the lines between their responsibilities and those of municipalities have blurred. Counties and cities may dedicate resources to the same issues, such as emergency management and veteran services. Some states have moved to address this overlap through **consolidation**, a step that joins city and county governments to form one unified government. Supporters of consolidation say it saves money by improving efficiency. They also argue that it strengthens the resulting government by increasing its authority and improving its ability to plan. Finally, consolidation is said to make government officials more accountable by eliminating questions of what government body is responsible for what activity.

About 100 attempts at consolidation of city and county governments have been made in the last 40 or so years, only one fourth of which have gone into effect. The process involves many steps. First, in most cases voters must approve a referendum that says they want a municipality and county to merge. Then the state legislature has to agree. After that, a charter has to be drafted and approved by the affected voters.

While consolidations are few, they include some of the nation's major cities. Boston, Jacksonville, Louisville, New Orleans, New York, Philadelphia, and San Francisco have all consolidated with their respective counties. The administrator of the unified government of Kansas City and Wyandotte County cites such benefits as tax cuts, workforce reduction, and streamlined decision-making. Nashville's mayor has said that consolidation allowed the city to avoid the population loss that other cities have experienced. Even so, some public policy experts have challenged the claim that consolidation results in cost savings.

This densely populated area of Milwaukee, Wisconsin, makes it possible to envision the survey grid in a six-mile-by-six-mile township. This system of dividing land, known as the Public Land Survey System, was first proposed by Thomas Jefferson, who hoped to fairly identify and divide land west of the original 13 states, and was implemented in the Northwest Territory, which included what is now Wisconsin.

HISTORICAL THINKING

1. **DRAW CONCLUSIONS** Why would a county create a special agency to administer its hospital system?
2. **MAKE INFERENCES** Why have relatively few efforts at city and county consolidation gone into effect?

Townships and Special Districts

Modern local government is now primarily within the hands of municipal and county governments. There are two additional government units of local government. They are the township and the special district.

TOWNSHIP GOVERNMENT A **township** is both a form of government and a subdivision of a county. In its nongovernmental sense, *township* refers to a six-mile-by-six-mile piece of land for federal surveying purposes. This type of township—also called a survey township—is found in all states except Maine, Vermont, Kentucky, Tennessee, West Virginia, Texas, and the original 13 states. The remaining states have all been surveyed as part of the Public Land Survey System.

Twenty states also use the township as a unit of local government that appears within a county and provides services to areas that are not incorporated as a municipality. More than 90 percent of townships have fewer than 10,000 people. Townships are prominent in Pennsylvania, New Jersey, and the states of the Midwest. They are typically led by an elected board of trustees and possibly a township clerk and some other officials. Townships generally have responsibility for maintaining roads, making land-use decisions, and overseeing waste management.

SPECIAL DISTRICTS Called a local special purpose government by the U.S. Census Bureau, a **special district** is a state-authorized, specialized body of local government that focuses on one or a few functions and may operate in the jurisdiction of more than one other local government. Special districts were first formed in the western United States in the 19th century to centralize authority regarding water and farm resources. Since then, special districts have been created across the country to tackle common regional issues ranging from education to park and cemetery maintenance to flood control. A special district is typically formed when an existing local government lacks the resources to manage an issue. Most special districts are given the power to levy taxes, collect fees, and qualify for state grants, allowing them to raise needed funds. Special districts are run by a board. Sometimes these board members are elected. In other cases, they are appointed by local government officials.

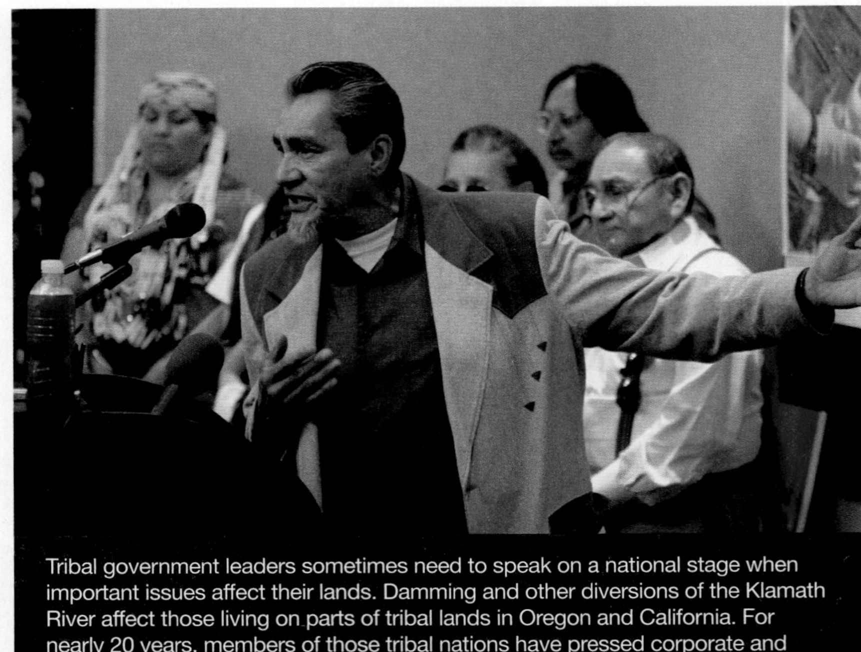

Tribal government leaders sometimes need to speak on a national stage when important issues affect their lands. Damming and other diversions of the Klamath River affect those living on parts of tribal lands in Oregon and California. For nearly 20 years, members of those tribal nations have pressed corporate and government officials to consider the effects of such changes on water levels and endangered salmon populations, both of which are important to their people.

The most common kind of special district is the school district, an autonomous agency that administers public education in a particular area. For example, the Houston Independent School District (HISD), the seventh-largest school district in the country, serves over 200,000 students at approximately 280 schools and has a staff of about 27,000 people. Like many other independent school districts, HISD encompasses more than one municipality.

Many school systems are part of the municipal government. In these cases, the mayor and the city council have some control over school board membership and activities. Major eastern cities such as Boston, New York, and Washington, D.C., follow this model.

HISTORICAL THINKING

3. **IDENTIFY MAIN IDEAS AND DETAILS** In what parts of the country are township governments most likely found?
4. **MAKE GENERALIZATIONS** How can special districts raise the funds needed to administer their areas of responsibility?

Tribal Governments

Tribal governments are another type of government within the United States. **Tribal government** is the self-governing authority of a Native American tribe. Through a series of treaties made during the 18th and 19th centuries, various American Indian tribes agreed to cede millions of acres of their homelands in exchange for certain federal protections and benefits. The result is the federal Indian trust responsibility. In this arrangement, the U.S. government promises to protect tribal lands, resources, and assets and to meet certain obligations to tribes. These obligations include providing federal funding for health care and education on tribal lands. Alaska Natives—indigenous peoples of Alaska—are also part of the federal Indian trust responsibility.

There are about 570 tribal nations within the borders of the United States. Reservations and tribal lands are found in 35 states. Alaska, with 229 official tribal nations, has the most of any state. If combined, the land belonging to these tribal nations would make up the fourth-largest state in the United States. Nineteen of these tribal nations each have more land than Rhode Island.

Each tribal nation is run by its own government, with its own constitution or similar overarching law. Some tribal constitutions are modeled on a constitution created by the U.S. Bureau of Indian Affairs, while others rely on tribal traditions. Tribal governments create, enact, and enforce their own laws. Tribal

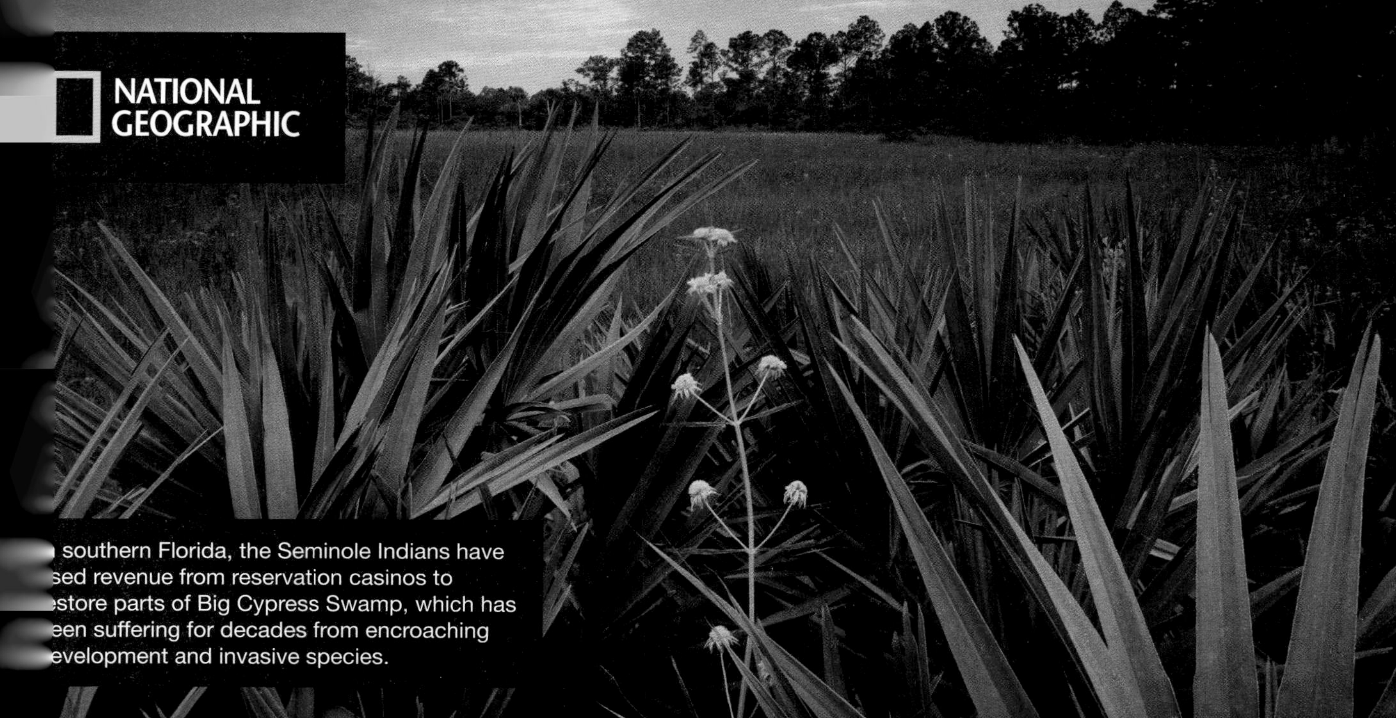

southern Florida, the Seminole Indians have sed revenue from reservation casinos to store parts of Big Cypress Swamp, which has een suffering for decades from encroaching evelopment and invasive species.

Native Lands by Charles Bowden *National Geographic* Magazine, August 2010

As part of the federal Indian trust agreement, Native Americans gave up millions upon millions of acres of land. Many tribes are not happy with the way that the land has been treated. Now they are starting to change the ways in which some of their ancestral lands are managed.

In "Native Lands," Charles Bowden describes ways that tribes have been protecting the land of their reservations and lands previously under the management of the Bureau of Indian Affairs (BIA). Native American reservations comprise 55 million acres of land, and tribes have begun preserving some of this land as protected wilderness. Some tribes have taken back control of ancestral land from the BIA because of their concerns that it has been mismanaged and hurt by modern activity.

Over the past 40 years, Bowden relates, different tribes (often working together) have reclaimed land to focus on conserving the resources that remain. They have undertaken programs to help forests flourish again and to bring back the bison, trout, salmon, and other wildlife once so plentiful on their lands. Activities ranging from livestock grazing to tourism are being re-evaluated or simply halted so that the land can restore itself.

Bowden describes the early success of the efforts of the Santa Clara tribe in this way:

Today the scent of pine and juniper floats in the morning air under a blue sky. The valley rolls out a green tongue of trees in the slot canyon, tracing a path toward the Valles Caldera. The tribe has removed the invasive, exotic tamarisk and Siberian elm and Russian olive from 650 acres along the Rio Grande and restored 75 acres of wetland. . . . Fifteen years ago the last beaver left this canyon. Now the tribe hopes that with the restoration of streamside growth, the beaver will return and once again start the cycle of dams, ponds, and eventually, as silt fills the impoundments, meadows—a rhythm as old as the mountains.

Access the full version of "Native Lands" by Charles Bowden through the Resources Menu in MindTap.

THINK ABOUT IT What challenges might a tribal government face in making a decision to halt activities governments also determine who has the right to claim membership in the tribe. While most tribes elect executive and legislative leaders to their governing councils, others allow elders to appoint leaders. Some tribal governments also include tribal court systems.

Tribal governments provide such services as health care, education, land management, and infrastructure programs. To fund these services, they levy taxes on tribe members, including sales taxes and excise taxes, or taxes on certain products such as alcohol or tobacco. But the extreme poverty of many who live on reservations has made it difficult for tribal governments to rely on an income tax base. In addition, because reservation land is not privately owned, tribal governments cannot draw on property taxes for revenue. American Indians and Alaska Natives have the highest rate of poverty of all racial groups in the United States, at 26.2 percent in 2016, and many native communities were hit especially hard by the COVID-19 pandemic. Many tribes have built casinos to generate income from non-reservation residents. The gaming industry generates jobs and helps fund health clinics, housing, and water and sanitation systems.

In 2020, the Supreme Court issued a ruling that could have far-reaching consequences for Native Americans and tribal governments. The case, *McGirt* v. *Oklahoma*, involved the question of whether a state could prosecute a tribal member for crimes committed on historical tribal land. After Oklahoma became a state in 1907, much of the land once set aside for Native American tribes passed into private hands, and state and local governments asserted jurisdiction. But in its 5–4 decision, the Court declared that, because Congress had not extinguished tribal treaties made in the 19th century, "for purposes of federal criminal law" those lands constituted an Indian reservation. The ruling didn't affect property rights. But it did mean that Native American criminal defendants would need to be tried in tribal courts, or, for more serious offenses, in federal courts, not local or state courts.

HISTORICAL THINKING

5. **MAKE GENERALIZATIONS** Explain the federal Indian trust responsibility.
6. **IDENTIFY MAIN IDEAS AND DETAILS** Why do many tribal governments face financial difficulties?

LESSON 21.3 State and Local Government Finances

Decisions about spending and saving are complex for individuals, families, and governments. Many people borrow funds to complete their education and buy a house. These choices can lead to prosperity, but if the overall economy fails, a student loan and an expensive mortgage might be impossible to repay. State and city governments face similar decisions. New spending might seem necessary to provide services, but at the wrong time it can lead to higher taxes that cut into a state's prosperity. At other times, taxes that allow investment in education and transportation might attract businesses and increase prosperity. It's hard to know when spending is wiser than saving.

Revenues for State and Local Governments

Both state and local governments receive money from other levels of government. About one-third of all state funds—more than $700 billion in fiscal year 2019—comes from the federal government, and about a third of local government money comes from the states. While those hundreds of billions of dollars are substantial, they do not cover all the costs of state and local governments. State and local governments raise additional revenue in a variety of ways, including different kinds of taxes and fees. Even lottery tickets can be a revenue-raising device.

SALES AND PROPERTY TAXES The number one source of tax revenue for state governments is a **general sales tax**, or a tax paid on purchases of goods or services. Forty-five states impose a sales tax—Alaska, Delaware, Montana, New Hampshire, and Oregon are the exceptions. Sales tax rates differ across states, although they average around 5 percent. Most states exempt purchases of food and prescription medicine from the application of their sales tax. Sales taxes are not as important a source of revenue to local governments, but local sales taxes are collected in 38 states.

State Sales Tax Rates, 2019

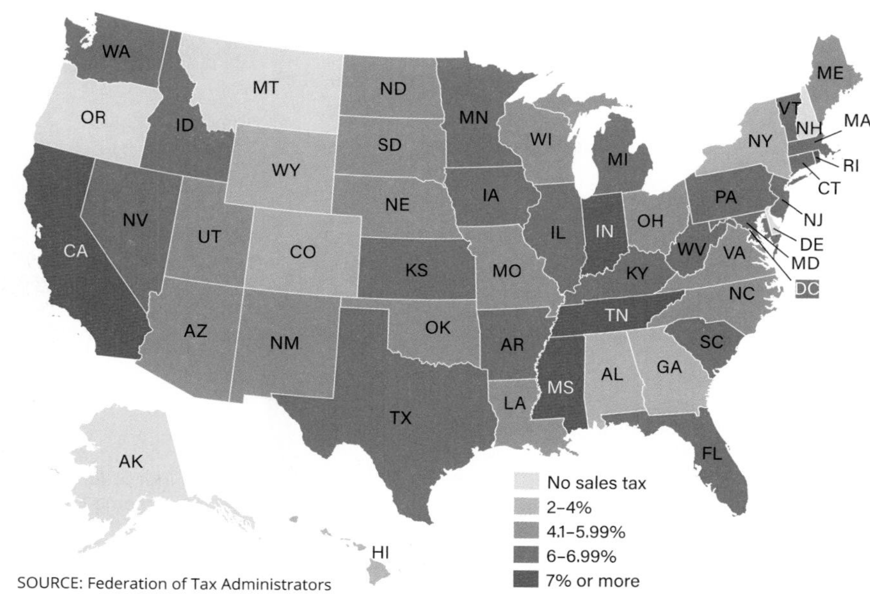

SOURCE: Federation of Tax Administrators

One issue for state lawmakers is how their sales tax compares to the tax of neighboring states. Higher tax rates can lead residents near a border to purchase goods in a state with a lower tax or no tax at all. Recognizing this, New Jersey law allows Salem County, which borders tax-free Delaware, to levy a reduced sales tax rate.

Property tax, a tax levied on homes, other buildings, and land, is the most important source of tax revenue for local governments. Property taxes are based on the tax rate and the estimated value of the property. Many states exempt certain groups, such as the elderly or veterans, from paying property taxes. Property tax rates vary across and within states, from a low of 0.18 percent in Louisiana to a high of 1.89 percent in New Jersey.

INCOME TAXES Most state governments—43 of them—collect taxes on individual income. Alaska, Florida, Nevada, South Dakota, Texas, Washington, and Wyoming rely on other sources of revenue. Two states—New Hampshire and Tennessee—tax only dividend and interest income, not salaries or wages. Tennessee is phasing out its income tax, lowering it by one percent per year until it disappears.

In general, state income taxes are lower than the federal income tax. Most states use a **progressive tax**, a tax plan under which the percentage of income tax a person pays increases with his or her income. A few states employ a **flat tax**, a tax in which all residents pay the same percentage regardless of income level. Several states have reciprocity agreements that apply to people who live in one state but work in another. In states without reciprocity agreements, a person living in one state can request exemption from income tax in another state. These agreements mean that a person who lives in one state and works in another only pays income tax in the state of residence. In 2015, the Supreme Court ruled that a person should never have to pay tax on the same income to more than one state.

Some cities and counties also levy an income tax. Today, 14 states and Washington, D.C., allow for this. School districts and other special districts also have the right to levy an income tax in some of these states. For example, many school districts in Iowa impose an income tax, as do two special districts that provide mass transit in Oregon.

OTHER SOURCES OF REVENUE State and local governments also collect various fees. For example, states collect fees when residents obtain a driver's license or pay tuition to a state university. Local governments collect fees for such services as water and sewage. While some of these fees are small, they add up. Fees account for nearly a fifth of state revenues and almost a quarter of local government funds.

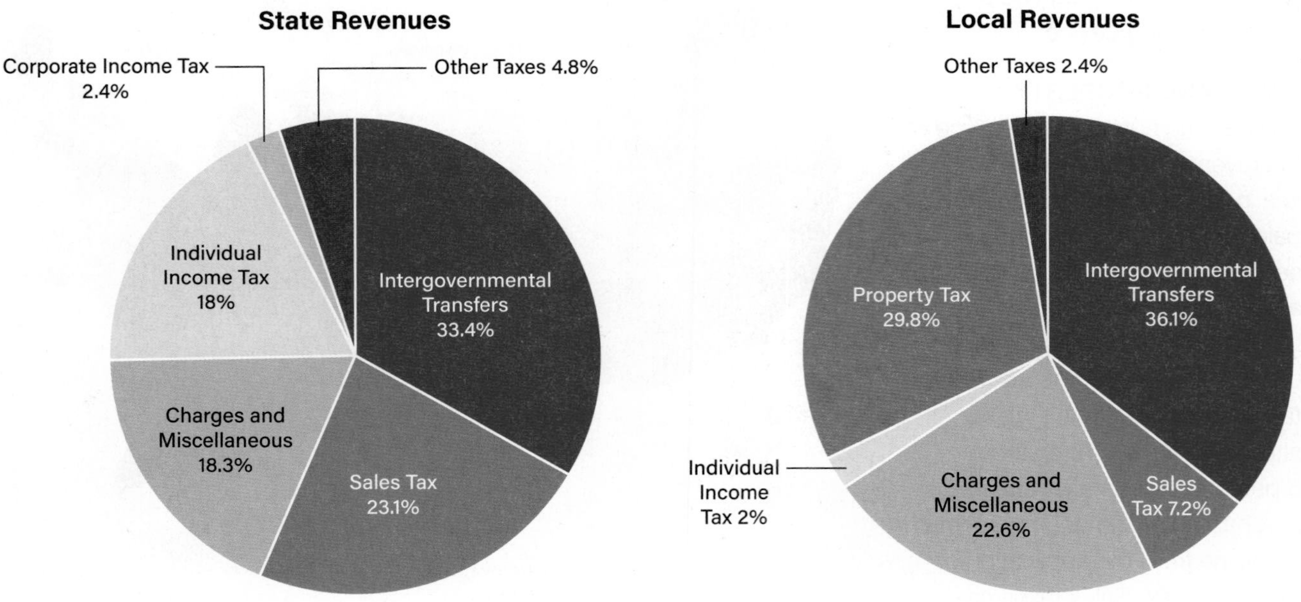

Officials often justify charging fees on the ground that they help people recognize the reality that government services cost money. They also say that fees mean that the burden for funding a service is borne by those who use that service. Critics point out that low-income people who require services pay a disproportionately higher share of their income for fees.

HISTORICAL THINKING

1. **COMPARE AND CONTRAST** How do sources of revenue differ between state and local governments?
2. **INTERPRET GRAPHS** How important are intergovernmental payments to both state and local governments?
3. **MAKE CONNECTIONS** The fees charged by local governments, such as license and parking fees, are often criticized for being unfair to people with less income. Explain this criticism.

Expenditures at State and Local Levels

State and local governments spend a great deal of money. In fiscal year 2018, direct spending by state governments passed $2 trillion for the first time. Local government spending was not far behind. State and local governments often spend in the same areas: health care, education, public assistance, transportation, public safety, environmental services, pensions, and government administration. But the proportion of spending in these categories differs due to different priorities.

STATE GOVERNMENT SPENDING Transfers from states to local government are not counted as part of a state's direct spending. Because the funds are under the control of local governments—although some of it may be earmarked for particular purposes—the funds are really examples of indirect spending by the states.

The biggest category of direct expenditures on the part of states is health care. Most of that money is used to fund Medicaid, health insurance financed by the states and federal government for low-income individuals or those with disabilities. Medicaid spending has increased significantly, nearing 30 percent of state spending in 2018. Some of the money to pay for state Medicaid expenses comes from federal Medicaid funding. Two-thirds of the states have expanded Medicaid enrollment under the Affordable Care Act, with the result that 73 million Americans—about 20 percent of the U.S. population—were covered under the program in 2018. Rising Medicaid costs to the states come from the

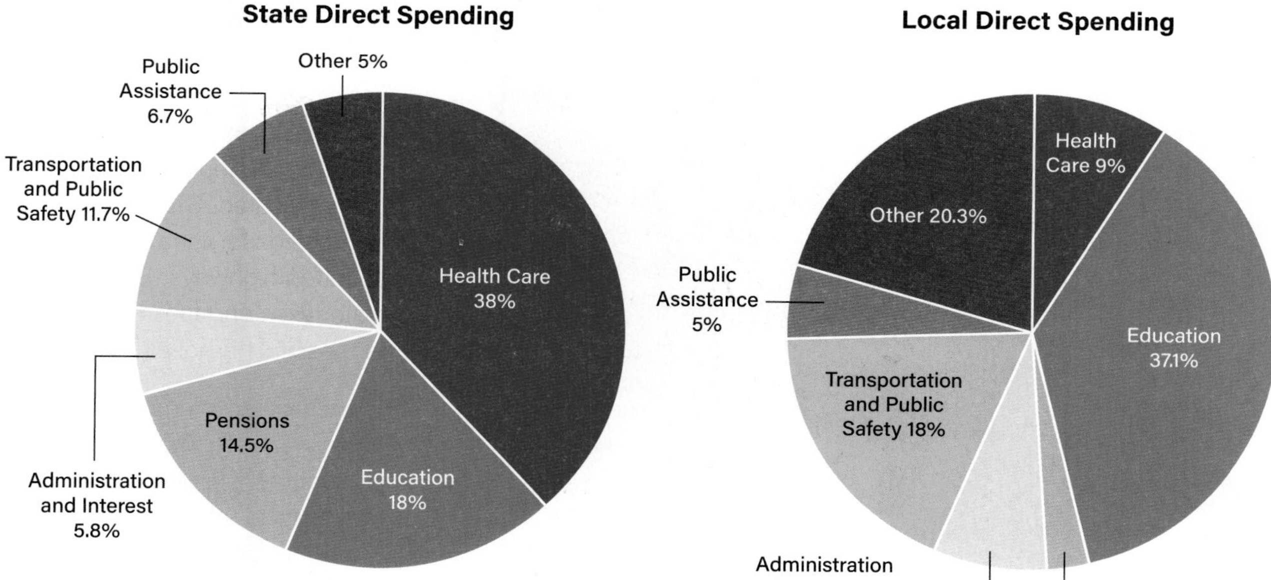

increasing costs of prescription drugs, long-term care, and mental health coverage. They do not come from the greater numbers of people covered by the program, because the costs of most of those increases are covered by the federal government.

Education is a significant share of both state and local government spending. In fiscal year 2016, local governments spent more than twice as much on education as states, however. Local governments devoted nearly all their education dollars to K–12 education. States, in contrast, allocated more than 80 percent of their education spending to higher education.

States contribute more to highway construction and maintenance than do local governments. State pension costs are four times higher than those of local governments—even though local governments employ nearly three times more workers. This is because most local government employees who have a pension receive it through their state government.

State government spending varies widely from state to state and from locality to locality. The top spending states per capita—per person—tend to be states with smaller populations such as Alaska, Delaware, Hawaii, and North Dakota, although Oregon also makes it into the top five. States that spend less per person tend to be traditionally Republican. The low level of government spending reflects the Republican philosophy of smaller government.

LOCAL GOVERNMENT SPENDING Unsurprisingly, local governments typically spend more on local services. For instance, local governments outspend states on public safety and corrections by more than two to one. They also spend far more—about seven times more—than states on utilities such as water, electricity, and sewage systems. The biggest bite of local government spending, though, goes to elementary and secondary education.

Much of the money local governments use for education comes from funds that state governments transfer to them. Education spending in different states is affected by many factors, including the cost of living and student demographics. State population is certainly significant as well. California—the most populous state in the country—spends more than $75 billion in this area, more than double the spending of the six New England states combined. The best way to compare state spending on education is to look at it per pupil, because that measure controls for population size.

Public School Spending per Student by State, 2016

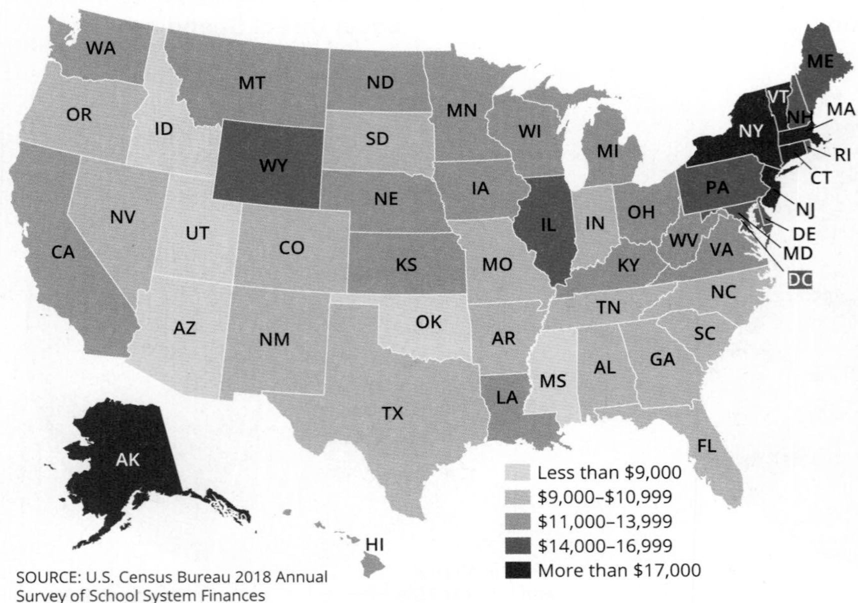

SOURCE: U.S. Census Bureau 2018 Annual Survey of School System Finances

HISTORICAL THINKING

4. **IDENTIFY MAIN IDEAS AND DETAILS** Name the two largest areas of spending for state governments, and explain what these areas have in common.
5. **DRAW CONCLUSIONS** Why do you think the states that spend the most per capita are states with smaller populations?
6. **INTERPRET MAPS** What regional trends can you see in the location of the states with the highest and lowest per-pupil spending?

Balancing State Budgets

Every state except Vermont is mandated by either its constitution, judicial interpretation of the state constitution, or state law to have a balanced budget. In other words, expenses cannot be greater than revenues. Thirty-seven states allow a deficit to carry until the end of the fiscal year, or even from one fiscal year to the next, but require that the deficit end in that second year. To meet the requirement of a balanced budget, states have to raise revenue, cut spending, borrow money, or undertake some combination of these strategies.

States do not have complete freedom in implementing these solutions. Federal grants for programs run by the states have to be used for those programs—and those programs cannot be cut once the federal money has been allocated. State receipts from the gasoline tax must be spent on highways. Some other state taxes and fees are reserved for specific purposes as well.

The federal government typically borrows money when it faces a budget deficit. States have far less freedom to do so. States can sell bonds to fund infrastructure projects or other major expenditures, but state laws generally demand that the legislature provide revenues to repay those bonds. For example, if a state issues bonds to fund construction of a new bridge, it might charge tolls for use of the bridge and use that money to pay off the debt. Because most state legislatures do not meet throughout the year, many states give the governor some authority to reduce spending of appropriated funds if a budget shortfall arises.

States can ask the federal government for financial help, but generally, the president and Congress will not bail out a single state that faces a budget shortfall. During the Great Recession (December 2007 to June 2009), however, a host of states faced such shortfalls. During this nationwide economic crisis, Congress passed the American Recovery and Reinvestment Act, which sent $145 billion to the states to help make up budget deficits.

Job losses during the Great Recession caused consumer incomes and spending to fall, sparking a steep decrease in sales tax revenue and, eventually, income tax. Between the middle of 2008 and 2009, state personal income tax receipts plummeted 27 percent. Most states faced budget deficits, and 40 were forced to raise taxes and fees between 2008 and 2011. In addition, states made massive cuts to essential state programs, including education, higher education, health care, elder services, and state employee salaries. In all, states cut more than 130,000 jobs, and local governments eliminated nearly 440,000 more.

Since the Great Recession, most states have re-examined their budget stabilization funds, better known as rainy-day funds. These reserve accounts are meant to be used in times of unexpected financial pressure and are part of all the budgets of most states. Many states have adjusted rules for depositing and withdrawing money from these funds, and they have been able to replenish their funds during the recovery from the Great Recession. Even so, only four states have been able to reserve close to the 16 percent of their current annual spending level that the national association of state financial officers recommended.

The financial downturn caused by COVID-19 has left states with increased costs and decreased tax revenues. Even states such as California, which had significantly built up its rainy-day fund, is facing severe shortfalls. This situation has left state governors, legislators, and policy makers pleading for federal assistance once again.

HISTORICAL THINKING

7. **IDENTIFY MAIN IDEAS AND DETAILS** Why do balanced budget requirements pose such difficulties for states?

8. **ANALYZE CAUSE AND EFFECT** How did the Great Recession impact state and local governments?

CRITICAL VIEWING In April 2018, Oklahoma teachers went on a nine-day strike, refusing to teach until the state legislature addressed the issue of below-average salaries and cuts in education funding. Thousands of teachers and some of their students crowded into the state capitol building in Oklahoma City to demand attention for their concerns from state legislators. Why do you think teachers from local school districts went to the state capitol to voice their concerns?

CHAPTER 21

LOCAL GOVERNMENTS

Review

VOCABULARY

Complete each sentence below with one of the key vocabulary terms.

1. Cities and towns are both _______, political divisions smaller than counties and run by an incorporated government.
2. When a local government is granted _______ by the state, it is given more freedom and independence over its functions and operations.
3. A municipality or other entity with the right to form its own government must write a(n) _______ that specifies its form of government and the powers of the officials in that government.
4. Local governments use _______ to plan how land should be best used.
5. In general, _______ are not incorporated, are found in rural or semi-rural areas, and perform fewer functions than municipal and county governments.
6. A(n) _______ is a specialized local government body that concentrates on one issue across jurisdictions, such as water treatment.
7. A(n) _______ has the authority to determine which individuals are accepted as official members of its Indian nation.
8. When you consider the cost of many items in most states, you can expect to pay _______ as well as the actual price of the item.
9. The amount of _______ a resident pays is based on the local government's estimate of the value of the land or building being taxed.

MAIN IDEAS

Answer the following questions. Support your answer with evidence from the chapter.

10. How do local governments derive their power to perform certain functions? **LESSON 21.1**
11. What is the most common form of municipal government, and how is it organized? **LESSON 21.1**
12. Explain how the explosion of U.S. suburban growth affected the role of local government. **LESSON 21.1**
13. What are the major differences between county and municipal responsibility? **LESSON 21.2**
14. Why is efficiency a common argument in support of city-county consolidation? **LESSON 21.2**
15. Why are tribal governments not the same as the local governments of the United States? **LESSON 21.2**
16. What are three services that both state and local governments typically provide? **LESSON 21.3**
17. Why do states need to dedicate such a large part of their budget to health-care costs? **LESSON 21.3**
18. How are general sales tax and income tax similar and different in terms of the level of government employing them and the structure of the tax rate? **LESSON 21.3**
19. How do state and local governments absorb the cost of education differently? **LESSON 21.3**

HISTORICAL THINKING

Answer the following questions. Support your answer with evidence from the chapter.

20. **ANALYZE CAUSE AND EFFECT** Why did states allow more municipal governments to adopt home rule in the 20th century than they had previously?
21. **MAKE GENERALIZATIONS** What does zoning try to prevent, and what does it try to encourage?
22. **MAKE PREDICTIONS** Could machine politics ever exist in the current U.S. political system, given the technology Americans can now access? Explain your answer.

23. **COMPARE AND CONTRAST** What are the advantages and disadvantages of having at-large members of a city council compared to having members elected from a particular ward?

24. **FORM AND SUPPORT OPINIONS** Do you think people are typically more or less passionate about politics at the local government level than they are about politics at the state and federal levels? Explain your answer.

25. **IDENTIFY PROBLEMS AND SOLUTIONS** What issue in your region might be best dealt with by a special district? Explain why you think so.

26. **EVALUATE** Why is it particularly important for a state government that is legally required to balance its budget to have a rainy-day fund?

INTERPRET VISUALS

The map shows the communities in San Patricio, Aransas, and Nueces counties served by the San Patricio Municipal Water District in southeastern Texas.

San Patricio Municipal Water District

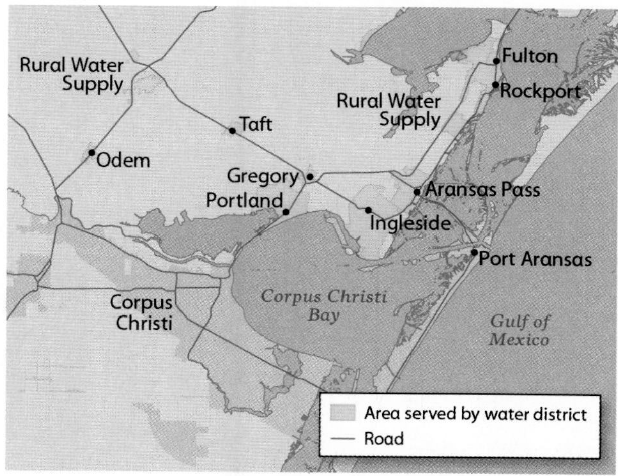

SOURCE: San Patricio Municipal Water District

27. What type of district in terms of government is shown on this map? Explain your answer.

28. Based on the map, what are the advantages of this type of governing body for this resource?

ANALYZE SOURCES

Read the statement from the editor of *Indian Country Today* about the 2018 election of Deb Haaland and Sharice Davids, the first two Native American women to be elected to Congress. Then answer the question that follows.

> "Indian country will see how important it is to have full representation, to show that Americans need to include the first Americans as part of the national discourse."
>
> —Mark Trahant, 2018

29. According to Trahant, why was the election of Haaland and Davids important?

CONNECT TO YOUR LIFE

30. **PERSUASIVE** Visit the website of your local school district. Read the agenda and minutes, if available, of recent school committee or school board meetings. Identify an issue of interest to you, then perform another online search to read more about the issue and its current status according to local media. Then write a brief persuasive essay explaining the issue and your position on it. Be sure to explain what stance you, a student who is affected by the district's actions, take on the issue. Use information you have found in meeting minutes and local media to support your opinion.

TIPS

- Your introduction should clearly summarize the issue being discussed by the school board or committee and should present your opinion on the issue.
- The body of your essay should further explain the issue at hand, using facts and data you found during online research. Be sure to keep the role of a school district as a government body in mind.
- Anticipate the arguments of those who take a different position and respond to them.
- Clearly attribute any data you use, citing authors, publishers, and publication dates.
- Your conclusion should reinforce the explanations and arguments you have made in the body of the essay. As you proofread, be sure to check that each idea mentioned in the body of the essay has been previewed in the introduction and summarized in the conclusion.

STUDENT REFERENCES

Citizenship Handbook R2

Declaration of Independence R3
Excerpts from the Federalist Papers R8
U.S. Constitution and Bill of Rights R14
Citizenship and You R39

Vocabulary Words by Chapter R44
English Glossary R46
English Academic Vocabulary R53
Spanish Glossary R54
Spanish Academic Vocabulary R62
Index R63

U.S. CAPITOL, WASHINGTON, D.C.

CITIZENSHIP HANDBOOK

This Citizenship Handbook will help you take an in-depth look at some of our nation's most important documents: the Declaration of Independence, Essays 10, 39, and 51 from the Federalist Papers, and the U.S. Constitution, which contains the Bill of Rights. The handbook includes notes to help you understand the formal language and difficult concepts contained in the more than 225-year-old documents. The handbook also provides background information and historical context to better help you understand the thinking and motivations of the Framers. At the end of the handbook, you will read about citizenship and the rights and responsibilities that come along with it. You will also find out how you can build and practice citizenship skills in the classroom and beyond.

The Charters of Freedom, as the Declaration of Independence, U.S. Constitution, and Bill of Rights are collectively known, are housed in the National Archives Museum in Washington, D.C.

DECLARATION OF INDEPENDENCE

Introduction

The American colonists wrote the Declaration of Independence in 1776 to formally call for their separation and independence from Britain. Up until then, colonists who were legally British citizens had lived in relative isolation from the king's authority and largely governed themselves. They modeled their colonial governments on Parliament, Britain's legislative body, by forming elected assemblies similar to the House of Commons. Unlike the British legislature, however, elected officials in colonial assemblies lived in the areas they represented. The colonists believed representatives who lived among those who elected them would better understand local interests and needs. At the same time, the colonists had no representatives in Parliament and sometimes resented what they felt to be unfair treatment by Britain.

ROAD TO REVOLUTION

The colonists' resentment grew after they fought alongside the British in the French and Indian War. The Americans had joined the fight so they could expand their settlements westward into Native American territory. But after Britain won the war against the French in 1763, British king George III wanted to keep the peace. To do so, he believed he needed to limit contact between the Native Americans and the colonists. As a result, the British government issued the Proclamation of 1763, which stated that colonists could not settle west of the Appalachian Mountains.

Furthermore, victory in the war had left Britain with overwhelming debt. To help pay it down, King George introduced a series of taxes against the colonists, including customs duties, the Sugar Act of 1764, and the Stamp Act of 1765, which taxed printed materials in the colonies. The Stamp Act was the first direct tax Britain had imposed on the colonists.

The American colonists protested the British legislation with shouts of "No taxation without representation." Angry colonists formed secret groups, such as the Sons of Liberty, and organized demonstrations and boycotts of British goods. As tensions continued to rise, violence erupted. In 1770, the Boston Massacre resulted in the deaths of five colonists at the hands of British soldiers. Three years later, colonists demonstrated their anger over a law on the sale of tea by staging the Boston Tea Party in Boston Harbor.

Finally, in 1775, feelings on both sides reached the boiling point. After British troops learned the colonists had stored weapons in Concord, Massachusetts, the troops marched to the town. Colonial militiamen rushed to face down the British soldiers in nearby Lexington. During the clash, shots rang out at what would later be called the first battle of the American Revolution.

BREAK WITH BRITAIN

American leaders had convened a conference of colonial delegates to respond to British taxation in 1774. At this conference in Philadelphia, known as the First Continental Congress, some delegates had called for the colonies to separate completely from Britain. By 1775, the Second Continental Congress was prepared to take action. The Congress raised an army and formed a committee to write an official document to declare independence from Britain. This "Committee of Five" included Thomas Jefferson, John Adams, Benjamin Franklin, Roger Sherman, and Robert Livingston. Jefferson, the youngest member of the Congress at 33, was chosen to be the principal author of the Declaration of Independence.

Enlightenment thinkers such as John Locke influenced the ideological origins of the American Revolution and the Declaration. Locke argued that humans were born free and equal and that a leader could rule only with the consent of the people. Jefferson was also inspired by the Enlightenment philosophy of unalienable, or natural, rights. The Founding Fathers considered that these rights were "divinely bestowed," or God-given. Unalienable rights, Jefferson insisted, could not be taken away.

On July 4, 1776, the delegates to the Continental Congress adopted the Declaration of Independence. In 1782, seven years after the first shots were fired, the American Revolution officially ended. The American colonists had fought for and won their freedom and independence from Britain.

THE DECLARATION OF INDEPENDENCE

IN CONGRESS, JULY 4, 1776

The Declaration of Independence begins by explaining why the colonists at the Continental Congress want to break away from Britain and become independent. Jefferson and the other Founding Fathers believed it was necessary to explain their motivations.

The unanimous Declaration of the thirteen united States of America, When in the Course of human events, it becomes necessary for one people to dissolve the political bands which have connected them with another, and to assume among the powers of the earth, the separate and equal station to which the Laws of Nature and of Nature's God entitle them, a decent respect to the opinions of mankind requires that they should declare the causes which impel them to the separation.

Here, Jefferson states that people are born equal and have rights, including life, liberty, and the pursuit of happiness, that should be safeguarded by the government. John Locke's idea that government is based on the consent of the people is also established. Jefferson claims that when a government takes away the people's rights, they must overthrow the government. But this step should not be taken lightly.

We hold these truths to be self-evident, that all men are created equal, that they are endowed by their Creator with certain unalienable Rights, that among these are Life, Liberty and the pursuit of Happiness.—That to secure these rights, Governments are instituted among Men, deriving their just powers from the consent of the governed, —That whenever any Form of Government becomes destructive of these ends, it is the Right of the People to alter or to abolish it, and to institute new Government, laying its foundation on such principles and organizing its powers in such form, as to them shall seem most likely to effect their Safety and Happiness. Prudence, indeed, will dictate that Governments long established should not be changed for light and transient causes; and accordingly all experience hath shown, that mankind are more disposed to suffer, while evils are sufferable, than to right themselves by abolishing the forms to which they are accustomed. But when a long train of abuses and usurpations, pursuing invariably the same Object evinces a design to reduce them under absolute Despotism, it is their right, it is their duty, to throw off such Government, and to provide new Guards for their future security.—Such has been the patient sufferance of these Colonies; and such is now the necessity which constrains them to alter their former Systems of Government. The history of the present King of Great Britain is a history of repeated injuries and usurpations, all having in direct object the establishment of an absolute Tyranny over these States. To prove this, let Facts be submitted to a candid world.

The Declaration goes on to explain exactly what King George has done by listing the colonists' grievances against him.

1 **HISTORICAL THINKING** Why do you think Jefferson lists the colonists' grievances against the king?

The king has failed to approve or disapprove laws needed by the people. At the time, colonial laws had to be approved by the king. Britain could also veto colonial legislation.

He has refused his Assent to Laws, the most wholesome and necessary for the public good.

He has forbidden his Governors to pass Laws of immediate and pressing importance, unless suspended in their operation till his Assent should be obtained; and when so suspended, he has utterly neglected to attend to them. He has refused to pass other Laws for the accommodation of large districts of people, unless those people would relinquish the right of Representation in the Legislature, a right inestimable to them and formidable to tyrants only.

The king has ordered his royal governors to block colonial legislation. He has claimed that unless people in the colonies give up the right to have representatives in their own government in America, he will not pass laws those people need.

He has called together legislative bodies at places unusual, uncomfortable, and distant from the depository of their public Records, for the sole purpose of fatiguing them into compliance with his measures.

He has dissolved Representative Houses repeatedly, for opposing with manly firmness his invasions on the rights of the people.

The king has dissolved many colonial lawmaking bodies because they stood up against laws that threatened the rights of Americans. By 1776, many colonial assemblies had been dissolved.

He has refused for a long time, after such dissolutions, to cause others to be elected; whereby the Legislative powers, incapable of Annihilation, have returned to the People at large for their exercise; the State remaining in the mean time exposed to all the dangers of invasion from without, and convulsions within.

After the legislatures were dissolved, some colonies had no laws to protect them. Citizens often created special assemblies to maintain some form of government.

He has endeavored to prevent the population of these States; for that purpose obstructing the Laws for Naturalization of Foreigners; refusing to pass others to encourage their migrations hither, and raising the conditions of new Appropriations of Lands.

He has obstructed the Administration of Justice, by refusing his Assent to Laws for establishing Judiciary powers.

He has made Judges dependent on his Will alone, for the tenure of their offices, and the amount and payment of their salaries.

Some colonial legislatures tried to establish courts, but the king dismissed them. Judges have also been appointed who favored the king's interests.

He has erected a multitude of New Offices, and sent hither swarms of Officers to harass our people, and eat out their substance.

He has kept among us, in times of peace, Standing Armies without the Consent of our legislatures.

He has affected to render the Military independent of and superior to the Civil power.

The king has sent soldiers to America without the consent of colonial legislatures. He has made his soldiers more powerful than the colonists.

DECLARATION OF INDEPENDENCE

The king has allowed others to pass and enforce new laws in the colonies that the colonists consider to be invalid ("pretended").

He has combined with others to subject us to a jurisdiction foreign to our constitution, and unacknowledged by our laws; giving his Assent to their Acts of pretended Legislation:

Jefferson introduces acts of Parliament the colonists considered to be unconstitutional. For example:

- making sure that soldiers who kill colonists are given a fake trial and not held accountable for murder;
- stopping American trade with other countries;
- taxing without permission;
- often refusing the right of trial by jury;
- sending colonists far away to be tried in courts for things they have not done;
- abolishing laws made by the colonies;
- stopping lawmaking groups in America and declaring that only the British government can make laws for people in America.

For Quartering large bodies of armed troops among us:

For protecting them, by a mock Trial, from punishment for any Murders which they should commit on the Inhabitants of these States:

For cutting off our Trade with all parts of the world:

For imposing Taxes on us without our Consent:

For depriving us in many cases, of the benefits of Trial by Jury:

For transporting us beyond Seas to be tried for pretended offences

For abolishing the free System of English Laws in a neighboring Province, establishing therein an Arbitrary government, and enlarging its Boundaries so as to render it at once an example and fit instrument for introducing the same absolute rule into these Colonies:

For taking away our Charters, abolishing our most valuable Laws, and altering fundamentally the Forms of our Governments:

For suspending our own Legislatures, and declaring themselves invested with power to legislate for us in all cases whatsoever.

The colonists claim that the king has essentially given up, or abdicated, his power to govern them. Now the king refuses to protect the colonists and has started a war against them.

He has abdicated Government here, by declaring us out of his Protection and waging War against us.

He has plundered our seas, ravaged our Coasts, burnt our towns, and destroyed the lives of our people.

The king is sending foreign soldiers to fight and suppress the colonists—an act of barbarism unworthy of a civilized nation.

He is at this time transporting large Armies of foreign Mercenaries to complete the works of death, desolation and tyranny, already begun with circumstances of Cruelty & perfidy scarcely paralleled in the most barbarous ages, and totally unworthy the Head of a civilized nation.

He has constrained our fellow Citizens taken Captive on the high Seas to bear Arms against their Country, to become the executioners of their friends and Brethren, or to fall themselves by their Hands.

He has excited domestic insurrections amongst us, and has endeavored to bring on the inhabitants of our frontiers, the merciless Indian Savages, whose known rule of warfare, is an undistinguished destruction of all ages, sexes and conditions.

He has encouraged Native Americans to attack the colonists.

In every stage of these Oppressions We have Petitioned for Redress in the most humble terms: Our repeated Petitions have been answered only by repeated injury. A Prince whose character is thus marked by every act which may define a Tyrant, is unfit to be the ruler of a free people.

The colonists have repeatedly and unsuccessfully made formal requests for this behavior to stop. However, the king has become a tyrant.

Nor have We been wanting in attentions to our British brethren. We have warned them from time to time of attempts by their legislature to extend an unwarrantable jurisdiction over us. We have reminded them of the circumstances of our emigration and settlement here. We have appealed to their native justice and magnanimity, and we have conjured them by the ties of our common kindred to disavow these usurpations, which, would inevitably interrupt our connections and correspondence. They too have been deaf to the voice of justice and of consanguinity. We must, therefore, acquiesce in the necessity, which denounces our Separation, and hold them, as we hold the rest of mankind, Enemies in War, in Peace Friends.

We have appealed to the British people, pointing out the injustice of our treatment and our close ties to them ("consanguinity"), but they have ignored us. We have no choice but to consider them our enemies.

We, therefore, the Representatives of the united States of America, in General Congress, Assembled, appealing to the Supreme Judge of the world for the rectitude of our intentions, do, in the Name, and by Authority of the good People of these Colonies, solemnly publish and declare, That these United Colonies are, and of Right ought to be Free and Independent States; that they are Absolved from all Allegiance to the British Crown, and that all political connection between them and the State of Great Britain, is and ought to be totally dissolved; and that as Free and Independent States, they have full Power to levy War, conclude Peace, contract Alliances, establish Commerce, and to do all other Acts and Things which Independent States may of right do. And for the support of this Declaration, with a firm reliance on the protection of divine Providence, we mutually pledge to each other our Lives, our Fortunes and our sacred Honor.

For all these reasons, Jefferson declares that the United Colonies are free and independent states with no further allegiance to Britain. As free and independent states, they can declare war, negotiate peace, make agreements to work with other countries, establish commerce, and participate in all other activities allowed by independent states.

EXCERPTS FROM THE FEDERALIST PAPERS

Introduction

The Federalist Papers are a series of 85 essays that discuss the rationale behind the United States Constitution. Written in an effort to win New York's ratification for the new framework of government, all but eight were published in New York newspapers from late 1787 to the summer of 1788. The rest were added later. The essays were the brainchild of Alexander Hamilton, who enlisted the help of James Madison of Virginia and John Jay of New York. They were published under the name "Publius," a reference to a man considered a founder of the Roman Republic.

Since the essays were published anonymously, exact authorship is unknown. Hamilton is believed to have written 51 of the essays and Madison 29. Jay wrote only 5 due to illness. The essays explored the weaknesses of the government under the Articles of Confederation, the principles underlying the proposed new government, the structure of that proposed government, and the powers it would grant to the different branches. They are considered a masterful presentation of American political theory. The three essays excerpted here were all penned by Madison.

American statesman, lawyer, military commander, banker, and economist, Alexander Hamilton, used the pen name "Publius" to protect his identity and the identity of James Madison, since they both were serving as delegates to the Constitutional Convention while writing the Federalist Papers.

Hamilton's major collaborator, America's fourth president, and "Father of the Constitution," James Madison wrote at least 29 of the essays that make up the Federalist Papers, although many (including Madison himself) suggested he had written more.

Federalist 10

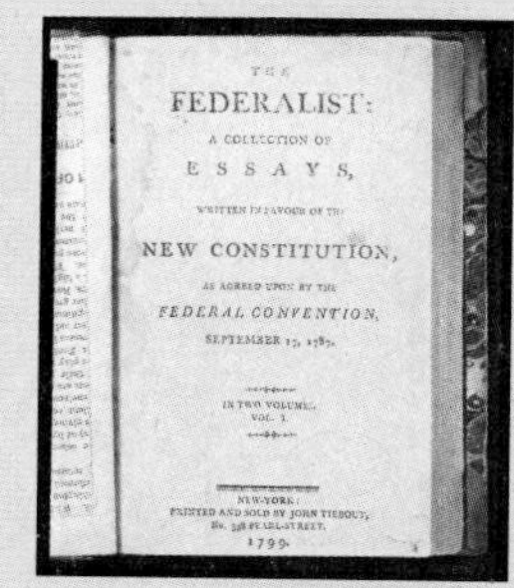

Among the numerous advantages promised by a well-constructed Union, none deserves to be more accurately developed than its tendency to break and control the violence of faction. The friend of popular governments never finds himself so much alarmed for their character and fate, as when he contemplates their propensity to this dangerous vice. . . .

By a faction, I understand a number of citizens . . . who are united and actuated by some common impulse of passion, or of interest, adverse to the rights of other citizens, or to the permanent and aggregate interests of the community.

What Madison calls faction could be a political party, a special interest group, a bloc of like-minded voters, or any other group of people with shared interests.

There are two methods of curing the mischiefs of faction: the one, by removing its causes; the other, by controlling its effects.

After noting the problem, Madison seeks a solution. He does so analytically, looking at all the possible approaches.

There are again two methods of removing the causes of faction: the one, by destroying the liberty which is essential to its existence; the other, by giving to every citizen the same opinions, the same passions, and the same interests. . . .

Neither of these solutions works. Destroying liberty is undesirable. Giving "to every citizen the same opinions" is impossible.

The inference to which we are brought is, that the CAUSES of faction cannot be removed, and that relief is only to be sought in the means of controlling its EFFECTS.

If a faction consists of less than a majority, relief is supplied by the republican principle, which enables the majority to defeat its sinister views by regular vote. . . . When a majority is included in a faction, the form of popular government, on the other hand, enables it to sacrifice to its ruling passion or interest both the public good and the rights of other citizens. To secure the public good and private rights against the danger of such a faction, and at the same time to preserve the spirit and the form of popular government, is then the great object to which our inquiries are directed. . . .

Madison focuses on the key problem. A faction that becomes a majority is the greatest danger because no power could prevent it from having its way.

By what means is this object attainable? . . . Either the existence of the same passion or interest in a majority at the same time must be prevented, or the majority, having such coexistent passion or interest, must be rendered . . . unable to concert and carry into effect schemes of oppression. . . .

EXCERPTS FROM THE FEDERALIST PAPERS

Madison reveals a concern that he and other Framers had about democracy—pure democracy is liable to be swayed by passion.

From this view of the subject it may be concluded that a pure democracy . . . can admit of no cure for the mischiefs of faction. A common passion or interest will, in almost every case, be felt by a majority of the whole . . . and there is nothing to check the inducements to sacrifice the weaker party or an obnoxious individual. . . .

A republic . . . promises the cure for which we are seeking. . . .

The two great points of difference between a democracy and a republic are: first, the delegation of the government, in the latter, to a small number of citizens elected by the rest; secondly, the greater number of citizens, and greater sphere of country, over which the latter may be extended.

Again, Madison is analytical—if the elected representatives are wise, the problem is solved. But what if they aren't?

The effect of the first difference is, on the one hand, to refine and enlarge the public views, by passing them through the medium of a chosen body of citizens, whose wisdom may best discern the true interest of their country, and whose patriotism and love of justice will be least likely to sacrifice it to temporary or partial considerations. . . . . On the other hand, the effect may be inverted. Men of factious tempers, of local prejudices, or of sinister designs, may, by intrigue, by corruption, or by other means, first obtain the suffrages [votes], and then betray the interests, of the people. The question resulting is, whether small or extensive republics are more favorable to the election of proper guardians of the public weal [welfare]. . . .

A republic might be better than a democracy, but a smaller republic is similarly susceptible to a majority faction imposing its will.

. . . The smaller the society, the fewer probably will be the distinct parties and interests composing it; the fewer the distinct parties and interests, the more frequently will a majority be found of the same party; and . . . the more easily will they concert and execute their plans of oppression. Extend the sphere, and you take in a greater variety of parties and interests; you make it less probable that a majority of the whole will have a common motive to invade the rights of other citizens; or if such a common motive exists, it will be more difficult for all who feel it to discover their own strength, and to act in unison with each other. . . .

2 HISTORICAL THINKING Why does Madison think that a large republic is a better defense against faction than a smaller one?

Hence, it clearly appears, that the same advantage which a republic has over a democracy, in controlling the effects of faction, is enjoyed by a large over a small republic. . . .

Federalist 39

[W]e may define a republic to be . . . a government which derives all its powers directly or indirectly from the great body of the people and is administered by persons holding their offices during pleasure, for a limited period, or during good behavior. . . .

On comparing the Constitution planned by the convention with the standard [definition of a republic] here fixed [provided], we perceive at once that it is, in the most rigid sense, conformable to it. The House of Representatives, like that of one branch at least of all the State legislatures, is elected immediately [directly] by the great body of the people. The Senate, like the present Congress, and the Senate of Maryland, derives its appointment indirectly from the people. The President is indirectly derived from the choice of the people, according to the example in most of the States. . . .

Madison explains how each of the elected offices in the planned federal government reflect the republican principle. He says that the Senate and the president are elected indirectly. State legislatures elected senators until 1913. The president is elected by the electoral college.

"But it was not sufficient," say the adversaries of the proposed Constitution, "for the convention to adhere to the republican form. They ought, with equal care, to have preserved the FEDERAL form, which regards the Union as a CONFEDERACY of sovereign states; instead of which, they have framed a NATIONAL government, which regards the Union as a CONSOLIDATION of the States." . . .

Madison recognizes that a strong argument must address counterarguments against it.

Each State, in ratifying the Constitution, is considered as a sovereign body, independent of all others, and only to be bound by its own voluntary act. In this relation, then, the new Constitution will . . . be a FEDERAL, and not a NATIONAL constitution.

The next relation is, to the sources from which the ordinary powers of government are to be derived. The House of Representatives will derive its powers from the people of America; and the people will be represented in the same proportion, and on the same principle, as they are in the legislature of a particular State. So far the government is NATIONAL, not FEDERAL. The Senate, on the other hand, will derive its powers from the States, as political and coequal societies; and these will be represented on the principle of equality in the Senate, as they now are in the existing Congress. So far the government is FEDERAL, not NATIONAL. The executive power will be derived from a very compound source. . . . From this aspect of the government it appears to be of a mixed character, presenting at least as many FEDERAL as NATIONAL features.

The source of executive is compound because the people vote for president, making it national, but electoral votes are awarded by electors named by the state legislatures, making it federal.

If we try the Constitution by its last relation to the authority by which amendments are to be made, we find it neither wholly NATIONAL nor wholly FEDERAL.. . .

The proposed Constitution, therefore, is, in strictness, neither a national nor a federal Constitution, but a composition of both. In its foundation it is federal, not national; in the sources from which the ordinary powers of the government are drawn, it is partly federal and partly national; in the operation of these powers, it is national, not federal; in the extent of them, again, it is federal, not national; and, finally, in the authoritative mode of introducing amendments, it is neither wholly federal nor wholly national.

3 **HISTORICAL THINKING** Why does Madison feel compelled to answer the criticism that the government created by the Constitution is a national one?

Federalist 51

To what expedient, then, shall we finally resort, for maintaining in practice the necessary partition of power among the several departments, as laid down in the Constitution? The only answer that can be given is, that as all these exterior provisions are found to be inadequate, the defect must be supplied, by so contriving the interior structure of the government as that its several constituent parts may, by their mutual relations, be the means of keeping each other in their proper places. . . .

But the great security against a gradual concentration of the several powers in the same department, consists in giving to those who administer each department the necessary constitutional means and personal motives to resist encroachments of the others. . . . Ambition must be made to counteract ambition. The interest of the man must be connected with the constitutional rights of the place [position]. It may be a reflection on human nature, that such devices [systems] should be necessary to control the abuses of government. But what is government itself, but the greatest of all reflections on human nature? If men were angels, no government would be necessary. If angels were to govern men, neither external nor internal controls on government would be necessary. In framing a government which is to be administered by men over men, the great difficulty lies in this: you must first enable the government to control the governed; and in the next place oblige it to control itself.

This is the crux of Madisonian thinking: people are by nature corrupt, and so it is necessary to define the structure and powers of government in such a way as to prevent them from acting in a corrupt way.

. . . But it is not possible to give to each department an equal power of self-defense. In republican government, the legislative authority necessarily predominates. The remedy for this inconveniency is to divide the legislature into different branches; and to render them, by different modes of election and different principles of action, as little connected with each other as the nature of their common functions and their common dependence on the society will admit. It may even be necessary to guard against dangerous encroachments by still further precautions. As the weight of the legislative authority requires that it should be thus divided, the weakness of the executive may require, on the other hand, that it should be fortified.

Note that Madison sees the Congress as the dominant branch.

An absolute negative on the legislature appears, at first view, to be the natural defense with which the executive magistrate should be armed. . . .

Madison here refers to the presidential veto.

There are, moreover, two considerations particularly applicable to the federal system of America, which place that system in a very interesting point of view. First. In a single republic, all the power surrendered by the people is submitted to the administration of a single government; and the usurpations [efforts to seize power] are guarded against by a division of the government into distinct and separate departments. In the compound republic of America, the power surrendered by the people is first divided between two distinct governments, and then the portion allotted to each subdivided among distinct and separate departments. Hence a double security arises to the rights of the people. The different governments will control each other, at the same time that each will be controlled by itself. Second. It is of great importance in a republic not only to guard the society against the oppression of its rulers, but to guard one part of the society against the injustice of the other part. Different interests necessarily exist in different classes of citizens. If a majority be united by a common interest, the rights of the minority will be insecure.

Madison here says that federalism, by dividing power between the federal and state governments, is the first defense against governmental abuse of power.

Madison again returns to a discussion of faction.

There are but two methods of providing against this evil: the one by creating a will in the community independent of the majority that is, of the society itself; the other, by comprehending in the society so many separate descriptions of citizens as will render an unjust combination of a majority of the whole very improbable, if not impracticable. The first method prevails in all governments possessing an hereditary or self-appointed authority. This, at best, is but a precarious security; because a power independent of the society may as well espouse the unjust views of the major, as the rightful interests of the minor party, and may possibly be turned against both parties. The second method will be exemplified in the federal republic of the United States. Whilst all authority in it will be derived from and dependent on the society, the society itself will be broken into so many parts, interests, and classes of citizens, that the rights of individuals, or of the minority, will be in little danger from interested combinations of the majority. . . .

The "will in the community independent of the majority" is, in effect, the idea of the common good.

4 **HISTORICAL THINKING** In addition to federalism, what two principles of the Constitution is Madison describing in his discussion of the structure of the government?

CONSTITUTION OF THE UNITED STATES

Introduction

In 1787, delegates at the Constitutional Convention in Philadelphia engaged in debates for four months as they drafted the Constitution. Among other issues, they debated how the legislative branch should work, how to elect the president, and whether enslaved people should be included in a state's population. After agreeing to a series of compromises, the Framers signed the U.S. Constitution, which, once ratified by the states, became the supreme law of the land in the United States. Considering the size and complexity of the United States today and its position as a world power, the U.S. Constitution is relatively simple. It consists of a Preamble, 7 articles, and currently 27 amendments, based on the 7 key principles below.

1. Popular Sovereignty The phrase means "the authority of the people." The opening words of the Constitution, "We the people" emphasize the idea that people together create a social contract in which they agree to be governed. Government authority is derived from the citizens, who determine how much power the government should have and what rules it must follow.

2. Republicanism This is a form of representational democracy. In a republic, citizens have the power and authority to make decisions as to how they are governed. Citizens elect representatives, who then have the power to write and enforce laws. Most Americans today use the terms *representational democracy* and *republicanism* interchangeably.

3. Federalism Federalism is a form of government in which power is distributed among several levels of government. A federalist system features a strong central government, but states do not lose all rights and power. States pursue and protect their interests as they see fit, while working together as a nation. In American federalism, the federal government's powers are enumerated, or listed. The states have powers that are reserved, or unwritten. Concurrent powers are powers shared by the federal and state governments.

4. Separation of Powers To reduce the potential for abuse of power and to prevent one branch from becoming too powerful, government was divided into three branches: the legislative branch (Congress, consisting of the Senate and the House of Representatives), which writes laws; the executive branch (led by the president), which enforces the laws written by Congress; and the judicial branch (made up of the U.S. Supreme Court and additional lower federal courts), which interprets and applies the laws.

5. Checks and Balances Each branch of government can limit the power of the other two, and so exert a check on the others. As with separation of powers, a system of checks and balances helps prevent one branch from becoming too powerful. For example, the judicial branch can declare a law passed by Congress to be unconstitutional. The president can veto a law written by Congress, but Congress can override the presidential veto. Congress can confirm or reject the president's nominees to his cabinet and the courts.

6. Limited Government The Articles of Confederation had failed because the central government was too weak and lacked the authority to tax or regulate trade. A stronger, stable central government was needed, but the Framers did not want to give it too much power or allow it to abuse what power it had. This principle of limited government seeks to protect rights by restricting the power of the central government. The Framers explicitly outlined the powers of the federal government and set additional limits in the Bill of Rights and other amendments.

7. Individual Rights Amendments, or changes and additions to the Constitution, have become part of the U.S. Constitution over the years. The first 10 amendments, known as the Bill of Rights, were added in 1791. These amendments address many individual rights, such as freedom of religion, freedom of speech, and the right to trial by jury. The Bill of Rights also places strict limits on what the federal government can do. The Bill of Rights was added to the Constitution to ensure that all states would accept and ratify this new plan for government.

THE CONSTITUTION

Preamble We the People of the United States, in Order to form a more perfect Union, establish Justice, insure domestic Tranquility, provide for the common defense, promote the general Welfare, and secure the Blessings of Liberty to ourselves and our Posterity, do ordain and establish this Constitution for the United States of America.

Article I Legislative Branch

SECTION 1: CONGRESS

All legislative Powers herein granted shall be vested in a Congress of the United States, which shall consist of a Senate and House of Representatives.

SECTION 2: THE HOUSE OF REPRESENTATIVES

1 The House of Representatives shall be composed of Members chosen every second Year by the People of the several States, and the Electors in each State shall have the Qualifications requisite for Electors of the most numerous Branch of the State Legislature.

2 No Person shall be a Representative who shall not have attained to the Age of twenty five Years, and been seven Years a Citizen of the United States, and who shall not, when elected, be an Inhabitant of that State in which he shall be chosen.

3 *Representatives and direct Taxes shall be apportioned among the several States which may be included within this Union, according to their respective Numbers, which shall be determined by adding to the whole Number of free Persons, including those bound to Service for a Term of Years, and excluding Indians not taxed, three fifths of all other Persons.* The actual Enumeration shall be made within three Years after the first Meeting of the Congress of the United States, and within every subsequent Term of ten Years, in such Manner as they shall by Law direct. The Number of Representatives shall not exceed one for every thirty Thousand, but each State shall have at Least one Representative; and until such enumeration shall be made, the State of New Hampshire shall be entitled to choose three, Massachusetts eight, Rhode-Island and Providence Plantations one, Connecticut five, New-York six, New Jersey four, Pennsylvania eight, Delaware one, Maryland six, Virginia ten, North Carolina five, South Carolina five, and Georgia three.

4 When vacancies happen in the Representation from any State, the Executive Authority thereof shall issue Writs of Election to fill such Vacancies.

5 The House of Representatives shall choose their Speaker and other Officers; and shall have the sole Power of Impeachment.

NOTE Boldfaced headings, section numbers, margin notes, and questions have been inserted to help you understand and interpret this rich and evolving document. Passages that are no longer part of the Constitution have been printed in italic type.

PREAMBLE
UNDERSTANDING THE CONSTITUTION The Preamble to the Constitution outlines the goals of the U.S. government. With the words, "We the People," the Framers establish that the Constitution's authority comes from the people of the United States.

ARTICLE I
UNDERSTANDING THE CONSTITUTION Sections 1 and 2 The Constitution establishes a bicameral, or two-house, Congress. Representatives in the House serve the members of their districts and are elected every two years. The House provides one of the most direct and effective ways in which citizens can participate in the political process. Constituents can contact their representatives by mail, email, and phone, and by visiting their lawmakers' offices. Representatives must be responsive to the needs and interests of their constituents or face losing their seats.

UNDERSTANDING THE CONSTITUTION 2.3 The number of seats in the House is based on each state's population. Populous states have more representatives than less-populated states.

5 HISTORICAL THINKING How might changes in a state's population affect its political power?

UNDERSTANDING THE CONSTITUTION 2.5 The Speaker of the House presides over sessions of Congress, but the Constitution says nothing about further responsibilities of the Speaker or those of other officers.

UNDERSTANDING THE CONSTITUTION 3.1 Section 3 describes the Senate. Originally, state legislatures chose the senators. With the passage of the 17th Amendment in 1913, senators were elected by voters, which made the process of selecting these federal officials more democratic.

UNDERSTANDING THE CONSTITUTION 3.2 The terms of senators are staggered. One class of senators begins its term in an even-numbered year, the next class begins two years later, and the third class begins two years after that.

As president of the Senate, Vice President Michael Pence is shown here presiding over the daily proceedings of the legislative body in 2019. House Speaker Nancy Pelosi stands beside him.

UNDERSTANDING THE CONSTITUTION 3.6 The House of Representatives has the power to bring impeachment charges, but the Senate conducts the trial and determines if the individual is to be removed from office. The president, vice president, all civil officers, and federal judges can be impeached.

6 **HISTORICAL THINKING** Do you think the power to impeach is essential to the system of checks and balances? Explain why or why not.

SECTION 3: THE SENATE

1 The Senate of the United States shall be composed of two Senators from each State, chosen by the Legislature thereof, for six Years; and each Senator shall have one Vote.

2 Immediately after they shall be assembled in Consequence of the first Election, they shall be divided as equally as may be into three Classes. The Seats of the Senators of the first Class shall be vacated at the Expiration of the second Year, of the second Class at the Expiration of the fourth Year, and of the third Class at the Expiration of the sixth Year, so that one third may be chosen every second Year; and if Vacancies happen by Resignation, or otherwise, during the Recess of the Legislature of any State, the Executive thereof may make temporary Appointments until the next Meeting of the Legislature, which shall then fill such Vacancies.

3 No Person shall be a Senator who shall not have attained to the Age of thirty Years, and been nine Years a Citizen of the United States, and who shall not, when elected, be an Inhabitant of that State for which he shall be chosen.

4 The Vice President of the United States shall be President of the Senate, but shall have no Vote, unless they be equally divided.

5 The Senate shall choose their other Officers, and also a President pro tempore, in the Absence of the Vice President, or when he shall exercise the Office of President of the United States.

6 The Senate shall have the sole Power to try all Impeachments. When sitting for that Purpose, they shall be on Oath or Affirmation. When the President of the United States is tried, the Chief Justice shall preside: And no Person shall be convicted without the Concurrence of two thirds of the Members present.

7 Judgment in Cases of Impeachment shall not extend further than to removal from Office, and disqualification to hold and enjoy any Office of honor, Trust or Profit under the United States: but the Party convicted shall nevertheless be liable and subject to Indictment, Trial, Judgment and Punishment, according to Law.

SECTION 4: CONGRESSIONAL ELECTIONS

1 The Times, Places and Manner of holding Elections for Senators and Representatives, shall be prescribed in each State by the Legislature thereof; but the Congress may at any time by Law make or alter such Regulations, except as to the Places of choosing Senators.

2 *The Congress shall assemble at least once in every Year, and such Meeting shall be on the first Monday in December, unless they shall by Law appoint a different Day.*

SECTION 5: RULES

1 Each House shall be the Judge of the Elections, Returns and Qualifications of its own Members, and a Majority of each shall constitute a Quorum to do Business; but a smaller Number may adjourn from day to day, and may be authorized to compel the Attendance of absent Members, in such Manner, and under such Penalties as each House may provide.

2 Each House may determine the Rules of its Proceedings, punish its Members for disorderly Behavior, and, with the Concurrence of two thirds, expel a Member.

3 Each House shall keep a Journal of its Proceedings, and from time to time publish the same, excepting such Parts as may in their Judgment require Secrecy; and the Yeas and Nays of the Members of either House on any question shall, at the Desire of one fifth of those Present, be entered on the Journal.

4 Neither House, during the Session of Congress, shall, without the Consent of the other, adjourn for more than three days, nor to any other Place than that in which the two Houses shall be sitting.

SECTION 6: PAY AND EXPENSES

1 The Senators and Representatives shall receive a Compensation for their Services, to be ascertained by Law, and paid out of the Treasury of the United States. They shall in all Cases, except Treason, Felony and Breach of the Peace, be privileged from Arrest during their Attendance at the Session of their respective Houses, and in going to and returning from the same; and for any Speech or Debate in either House, they shall not be questioned in any other Place.

2 No Senator or Representative shall, during the Time for which he was elected, be appointed to any civil Office under the Authority of the United States, which shall have been created, or the Emoluments whereof shall have been increased during such time; and no Person holding any Office under the United States, shall be a Member of either House during his Continuance in Office.

SECTION 7: PASSING LAWS

1 All Bills for raising Revenue shall originate in the House of Representatives; but the Senate may propose or concur with Amendments as on other Bills.

2 Every Bill which shall have passed the House of Representatives and the Senate, shall, before it become a Law, be presented to the President of the United States; If he approve he shall sign it, but if not he shall return it, with his Objections to that House in which it shall have originated, who shall enter the Objections at large on their Journal, and proceed to reconsider it. If after such Reconsideration two thirds of that House shall agree to pass the Bill, it shall be sent, together with

UNDERSTANDING THE CONSTITUTION Section 5 This section empowers each house of Congress to make its own rules. The House and Senate have developed different rules over the years that affect how they operate. For example, only members of the Senate can engage in a filibuster, which allows a senator to speak in the chamber as long as it may take to block a piece of legislation. The filibuster gives the minority party in the Senate some power to block or slow the passage of legislation.

UNDERSTANDING THE CONSTITUTION 7.2

How a Bill Becomes a Law in Congress

A The first step in the legislative process is the introduction of a bill to Congress. Although anyone can write a bill or request certain legislation, only a member of Congress can introduce a bill.

B The bill is debated and usually revised. Congressional committees and their subcommittees are the key groups that move bills through the process. Once out of committee, the full House or Senate votes on the bill.

C Each house reviews, debates, and amends the bill, often resulting in different versions. A committee made up of members from both houses then works to resolve differences and create one final version of the bill.

D If both houses accept the compromises, Congress sends the bill to the president.

E The president can either sign the bill—and it becomes law—or veto the bill, which prevents the bill from becoming law. Congress can, however, override the veto with a vote of two-thirds of the members present in each house, in which case the bill becomes law.

the Objections, to the other House, by which it shall likewise be reconsidered, and if approved by two thirds of that House, it shall become a Law. But in all such Cases the Votes of both Houses shall be determined by yeas and Nays, and the Names of the Persons voting for and against the Bill shall be entered on the Journal of each House respectively. If any Bill shall not be returned by the President within ten Days (Sundays excepted) after it shall have been presented to him, the Same shall be a Law, in like Manner as if he had signed it, unless the Congress by their Adjournment prevent its Return, in which Case it shall not be a Law.

3 Every Order, Resolution, or Vote to which the Concurrence of the Senate and House of Representatives may be necessary (except on a question of Adjournment) shall be presented to the President of the United States; and before the Same shall take Effect, shall be approved by him, or being disapproved by him, shall be re-passed by two thirds of the Senate and House of Representatives, according to the Rules and Limitations prescribed in the Case of a Bill.

SECTION 8: POWERS OF CONGRESS

1 The Congress shall have Power To lay and collect Taxes, Duties, Imposts and Excises, to pay the Debts and provide for the common Defense and general Welfare of the United States; but all Duties, Imposts and Excises shall be uniform throughout the United States;

2 To borrow Money on the credit of the United States;

3 To regulate Commerce with foreign Nations, and among the several States, and with the Indian Tribes;

4 To establish an uniform Rule of Naturalization, and uniform Laws on the subject of Bankruptcies throughout the United States;

5 To coin Money, regulate the Value thereof, and of foreign Coin, and fix the Standard of Weights and Measures;

6 To provide for the Punishment of counterfeiting the Securities and current Coin of the United States;

7 To establish Post Offices and post Roads;

8 To promote the Progress of Science and useful Arts, by securing for limited Times to Authors and Inventors the exclusive Right to their respective Writings and Discoveries;

9 To constitute Tribunals inferior to the supreme Court;

10 To define and punish Piracies and Felonies committed on the high Seas, and Offences against the Law of Nations;

11 To declare War, grant Letters of Marque and Reprisal, and make Rules concerning Captures on Land and Water;

UNDERSTANDING THE CONSTITUTION Section 8 Section 8 begins with a list of 18 enumerated powers given to Congress, which cannot be modified by the states. The Constitution includes little detail as to how some of these powers should be carried out. The authority to collect taxes—perhaps the most important power granted to Congress—is often referred to as the "power of the purse."

7 HISTORICAL THINKING Why do you think the authority to collect taxes is an important power?

UNDERSTANDING THE CONSTITUTION 8.3 This clause is generally referred to as the commerce clause. Regulating commerce with foreign nations means controlling imports and exports to provide maximum benefit for U.S. businesses and consumers. Regulating commerce between states means maintaining a common market among the states, with no restrictions.

8 HISTORICAL THINKING Without the commerce clause, what kinds of disputes might arise between states engaged in interstate commerce?

12 To raise and support Armies, but no Appropriation of Money to that Use shall be for a longer Term than two Years;

13 To provide and maintain a Navy;

14 To make Rules for the Government and Regulation of the land and naval Forces;

15 To provide for calling forth the Militia to execute the Laws of the Union, suppress Insurrections and repel Invasions;

16 To provide for organizing, arming, and disciplining, the Militia, and for governing such Part of them as may be employed in the Service of the United States, reserving to the States respectively, the Appointment of the Officers, and the Authority of training the Militia according to the discipline prescribed by Congress;

17 To exercise exclusive Legislation in all Cases whatsoever, over such District (not exceeding ten Miles square) as may, by Cession of particular States, and the Acceptance of Congress, become the Seat of the Government of the United States, and to exercise like Authority over all Places purchased by the Consent of the Legislature of the State in which the Same shall be, for the Erection of Forts, Magazines, Arsenals, dock-Yards, and other needful Buildings;—And

18 To make all Laws which shall be necessary and proper for carrying into Execution the foregoing Powers, and all other Powers vested by this Constitution in the Government of the United States, or in any Department or Officer thereof.

UNDERSTANDING THE CONSTITUTION Section 8 The last of the enumerated powers has been referred to as the "elastic clause" or the "necessary and proper clause." This clause allows Congress "to make all laws which shall be necessary and proper" to support its duties and responsibilities. It is called the "elastic clause" because it allows Congress to expand its authority and handle issues that might not have been anticipated. The vagueness of the phrase "necessary and proper" has created controversy. The Supreme Court provided some guidance in the 1819 case of *McCulloch* v. *Maryland* when it gave Congress wide authority to determine what is "necessary and proper."

SECTION 9: RESTRICTIONS ON CONGRESS

1 *The Migration or Importation of such Persons as any of the States now existing shall think proper to admit, shall not be prohibited by the Congress prior to the Year one thousand eight hundred and eight, but a Tax or duty may be imposed on such Importation, not exceeding ten dollars for each Person.*

2 The Privilege of the Writ of Habeas Corpus shall not be suspended, unless when in Cases of Rebellion or Invasion the public Safety may require it.

3 No Bill of Attainder or ex post facto Law shall be passed.

4 *No Capitation, or other direct, Tax shall be laid, unless in Proportion to the Census or Enumeration herein before directed to be taken.*

5 No Tax or Duty shall be laid on Articles exported from any State.

6 No Preference shall be given by any Regulation of Commerce or Revenue to the Ports of one State over those of another: nor shall Vessels bound to, or from, one State, be obliged to enter, clear, or pay Duties in another.

UNDERSTANDING THE CONSTITUTION Section 9 Section 9 lists specific areas in which Congress may not legislate.

UNDERSTANDING THE CONSTITUTION 9.4 A "capitation tax" is a tax charged on an individual.

UNDERSTANDING THE CONSTITUTION 9.6 Congress cannot pass laws that favor commerce in one state over that in another. For example, Congress cannot pass a law requiring shipping to go through a particular state's port.

UNDERSTANDING THE CONSTITUTION 9.8 This provision, known as the "emoluments clause," is a commitment to transparency and to the prevention of corruption. The clause prohibits federal government officials from benefiting financially from the office they hold by receiving payments from foreign governments.

9 HISTORICAL THINKING Why might a violation of the emoluments clause by a federal government official have significant consequences?

UNDERSTANDING THE CONSTITUTION Section 10 Section 10 limits the power of the states by preventing them from entering into a treaty, coining money, or passing laws that interfere with contracts.

7 No Money shall be drawn from the Treasury, but in Consequence of Appropriations made by Law; and a regular Statement and Account of the Receipts and Expenditures of all public Money shall be published from time to time.

8 No Title of Nobility shall be granted by the United States: And no Person holding any Office of Profit or Trust under them, shall, without the Consent of the Congress, accept of any present, Emolument, Office, or Title, of any kind whatever, from any King, Prince, or foreign State.

SECTION 10: LIMITING THE AUTHORITY OF STATES

1 No State shall enter into any Treaty, Alliance, or Confederation; grant Letters of Marque and Reprisal; coin Money; emit Bills of Credit; make any Thing but gold and silver Coin a Tender in Payment of Debts; pass any Bill of Attainder, ex post facto Law, or Law impairing the Obligation of Contracts, or grant any Title of Nobility.

2 No State shall, without the Consent of the Congress, lay any Imposts or Duties on Imports or Exports, except what may be absolutely necessary for executing its inspection Laws: and the net Produce of all Duties and Imposts, laid by any State on Imports or Exports, shall be for the Use of the Treasury of the United States; and all such Laws shall be subject to the Revision and Control of the Congress.

3 No State shall, without the Consent of Congress, lay any Duty of Tonnage, keep Troops, or Ships of War in time of Peace, enter into any Agreement or Compact with another State, or with a foreign Power, or engage in War, unless actually invaded, or in such imminent Danger as will not admit of delay.

ARTICLE II
UNDERSTANDING THE CONSTITUTION Section 1 Article II establishes an executive branch of government to carry out the laws passed by Congress. Section 1 describes a detailed process for choosing the president, although this process was replaced in 1804 by the 12th Amendment.

10 HISTORICAL THINKING Why might some Americans object to the electoral college?

Article II The Executive Branch

SECTION 1: ELECTING THE PRESIDENT

1 The executive Power shall be vested in a President of the United States of America. He shall hold his Office during the Term of four Years, and, together with the Vice President, chosen for the same Term, be elected, as follows

2 Each State shall appoint, in such Manner as the Legislature thereof may direct, a Number of Electors, equal to the whole Number of Senators and Representatives to which the State may be entitled in the Congress: but no Senator or Representative, or Person holding an Office of Trust or Profit under the United States, shall be appointed an Elector.

3 *The Electors shall meet in their respective States, and vote by Ballot for two Persons, of whom one at least shall not be an Inhabitant of the same State with themselves. And they shall make a List of all the Persons voted for, and of the Number of Votes for each; which List they shall sign and certify, and transmit sealed to the Seat of the Government of the United States, directed to the President of the Senate. The President of the Senate shall, in the Presence of the Senate and House of Representatives, open all the Certificates, and the Votes shall then be counted. The Person having the greatest Number of Votes shall be the President, if such Number be a Majority of the whole Number of Electors appointed; and if there be more than one who have such Majority, and have an equal Number of Votes, then the House of Representatives shall immediately choose by Ballot one of them for President; and if no Person have a Majority, then from the five highest on the List the said House shall in like Manner choose the President. But in choosing the President, the Votes shall be taken by States, the Representation from each State having one Vote; A quorum for this Purpose shall consist of a Member or Members from two thirds of the States, and a Majority of all the States shall be necessary to a Choice. In every Case, after the Choice of the President, the Person having the greatest Number of Votes of the Electors shall be the Vice President. But if there should remain two or more who have equal Votes, the Senate shall choose from them by Ballot the Vice President.*

4 The Congress may determine the Time of choosing the Electors, and the Day on which they shall give their Votes; which Day shall be the same throughout the United States.

5 No Person except a natural born Citizen, or a Citizen of the United States, at the time of the Adoption of this Constitution, shall be eligible to the Office of President; neither shall any Person be eligible to that Office who shall not have attained to the Age of thirty five Years, and been fourteen Years a Resident within the United States.

6 *In Case of the Removal of the President from Office, or of his Death, Resignation, or Inability to discharge the Powers and Duties of the said Office, the Same shall devolve on the Vice President, and the Congress may by Law provide for the Case of Removal, Death, Resignation or Inability, both of the President and Vice President, declaring what Officer shall then act as President, and such Officer shall act accordingly, until the Disability be removed, or a President shall be elected.*

7 The President shall, at stated Times, receive for his Services, a Compensation, which shall neither be increased nor diminished during the Period for which he shall have been elected, and he shall not receive within that Period any other Emolument from the United States, or any of them.

UNDERSTANDING THE CONSTITUTION 1.3 The italicized text refers to how vice presidents were originally elected. In the presidential election of 1800, the top two vote winners (Thomas Jefferson and Aaron Burr) received the same number of electoral votes. The selection of the president then fell to the House of Representatives, which chose Jefferson. Today, presidential candidates select a running mate, and voters cast a single vote for the entire ticket.

UNDERSTANDING THE CONSTITUTION 1.4 The Constitution does not stipulate when federal elections are to be held. Congress determined in 1792 that federal elections should be held in November. In 1845, it established election day as the Tuesday following the first Monday in November in years divisible by four.

UNDERSTANDING THE CONSTITUTION 1.8 Beginning with George Washington, every president has taken the oath of office as it appears in the Constitution.

UNDERSTANDING THE CONSTITUTION Section 2 Section 2 outlines the president's authority. Among other duties, the president serves as commander in chief of the armed forces, has the power to make treaties, and can appoint ambassadors and Supreme Court justices. However, the powers of the presidency increased during the Great Depression, World War II, and the Cold War. For example, although the Constitution states that only Congress can declare war, President Harry Truman began an undeclared war against North Korea in the Cold War.

11 HISTORICAL THINKING Do you think a president is justified to exceed constitutional powers in some situations? Why or why not?

In this photo, President Barack Obama delivers his annual State of the Union address to Congress in 2016. To fulfill the rule in Section 3 on keeping Congress informed "from time to time," presidents present this address every year except in the first year of a new president's term.

UNDERSTANDING THE CONSTITUTION Section 4 In the phrase "high crimes and misdemeanors," the word *high* does not mean "more serious" but rather refers to highly placed public officials.

8 Before he enter on the Execution of his Office, he shall take the following Oath or Affirmation:—"I do solemnly swear (or affirm) that I will faithfully execute the Office of President of the United States, and will to the best of my Ability, preserve, protect and defend the Constitution of the United States."

SECTION 2: EXECUTIVE POWERS

1 The President shall be Commander in Chief of the Army and Navy of the United States, and of the Militia of the several States, when called into the actual Service of the United States; he may require the Opinion, in writing, of the principal Officer in each of the executive Departments, upon any Subject relating to the Duties of their respective Offices, and he shall have Power to grant Reprieves and Pardons for Offences against the United States, except in Cases of Impeachment.

2 He shall have Power, by and with the Advice and Consent of the Senate, to make Treaties, provided two thirds of the Senators present concur; and he shall nominate, and by and with the Advice and Consent of the Senate, shall appoint Ambassadors, other public Ministers and Consuls, Judges of the supreme Court, and all other Officers of the United States, whose Appointments are not herein otherwise provided for, and which shall be established by Law: but the Congress may by Law vest the Appointment of such inferior Officers, as they think proper, in the President alone, in the Courts of Law, or in the Heads of Departments.

3 The President shall have Power to fill up all Vacancies that may happen during the Recess of the Senate, by granting Commissions which shall expire at the End of their next Session.

SECTION 3: THE PRESIDENT AND CONGRESS

He shall from time to time give to the Congress Information of the State of the Union, and recommend to their Consideration such Measures as he shall judge necessary and expedient; he may, on extraordinary Occasions, convene both Houses, or either of them, and in Case of Disagreement between them, with Respect to the Time of Adjournment, he may adjourn them to such Time as he shall think proper; he shall receive Ambassadors and other public Ministers; he shall take Care that the Laws be faithfully executed, and shall Commission all the Officers of the United States.

SECTION 4: IMPEACHMENT

The President, Vice President and all civil Officers of the United States, shall be removed from Office on Impeachment for, and Conviction of, Treason, Bribery, or other high Crimes and Misdemeanors.

Article III The Judiciary Branch

The COVID-19 pandemic made it difficult to safely update the class photo of Supreme Court justices in 2020, but the Court finally gathered in person in April 2021. Top row: Brett Kavanaugh, Elena Kagan, Neil Gorsuch, Amy Coney Barrett. Bottom Row: Samuel Alito, Jr., Clarence Thomas, John Roberts, Jr. (chief justice), Stephen Breyer, Sonia Sotomayor.

SECTION 1: SUPREME COURT AND LOWER COURTS

The judicial Power of the United States, shall be vested in one supreme Court, and in such inferior Courts as the Congress may from time to time ordain and establish. The Judges, both of the supreme and inferior Courts, shall hold their Offices during good Behavior, and shall, at stated Times, receive for their Services, a Compensation, which shall not be diminished during their Continuance in Office.

SECTION 2: AUTHORITY OF THE SUPREME COURT

1 The judicial Power shall extend to all Cases, in Law and Equity, arising under this Constitution, the Laws of the United States, and Treaties made, or which shall be made, under their Authority;—to all Cases affecting Ambassadors, other public Ministers and Consuls;—to all Cases of admiralty and maritime Jurisdiction;—to Controversies to which the United States shall be a Party;*—to Controversies between two or more States;—between a State and Citizens of another State;—between Citizens of different States;—between Citizens of the same State claiming Lands under Grants of different States, and between a State, or the Citizens thereof, and foreign States, Citizens or Subjects.*

2 In all Cases affecting Ambassadors, other public Ministers and Consuls, and those in which a State shall be Party, the supreme Court shall have original Jurisdiction. In all the other Cases before mentioned, the supreme Court shall have appellate Jurisdiction, both as to Law and Fact, with such Exceptions, and under such Regulations as the Congress shall make.

3 The Trial of all Crimes, except in Cases of Impeachment, shall be by Jury; and such Trial shall be held in the State where the said Crimes shall have been committed; but when not committed within any State, the Trial shall be at such Place or Places as the Congress may by Law have directed.

SECTION 3: TREASON

1 Treason against the United States, shall consist only in levying War against them, or in adhering to their Enemies, giving them Aid and Comfort. No Person shall be convicted of Treason unless on the Testimony of two Witnesses to the same overt Act, or on Confession in open Court.

2 The Congress shall have Power to declare the Punishment of Treason, but no Attainder of Treason shall work Corruption of Blood, or Forfeiture except during the Life of the Person attainted.

ARTICLE III

UNDERSTANDING THE CONSTITUTION

Section 1 Article III Section 1 establishes the federal court system. The Supreme Court of the United States is the highest court in the land and the only part of the federal judiciary specifically required by the Constitution. Lower courts were established by Congress by the Judiciary Act of 1789.

UNDERSTANDING THE CONSTITUTION

Section 2 The italicized portion in 2.1 was changed in 1795 by the 11th Amendment. The last part of 2.2 describes the Supreme Court as the final appeals court. As a result of the landmark 1803 case *Marbury* v. *Madison*, the Court is often asked to rule on the constitutionality of a law.

UNDERSTANDING THE CONSTITUTION

Section 3 Treason is the only crime specifically defined in the Constitution. Between 1954 and 2016, one person was charged with treason for collaborating in the production of propaganda videos for the terrorist group al Qaeda. Protesting or opposing U.S. government actions or policies, however, is protected by the free speech clause in Amendment 1.

Article IV States and Citizens

ARTICLE IV
UNDERSTANDING THE CONSTITUTION Section 1 "Full faith and credit" means that states agree to respect and honor each other's laws, court decisions, and documents. For example, a driver's license issued by one state must be honored by all other states. Section 1 was included as a way to create cohesiveness among individual states.

SECTION 1: MUTUAL RESPECT AMONG STATES

Full Faith and Credit shall be given in each State to the public Acts, Records, and judicial Proceedings of every other State. And the Congress may by general Laws prescribe the Manner in which such Acts, Records and Proceedings shall be proved, and the Effect thereof.

SECTION 2: CITIZENS OF STATES AND OF THE UNITED STATES

1 The Citizens of each State shall be entitled to all Privileges and Immunities of Citizens in the several States.

2 A Person charged in any State with Treason, Felony, or other Crime, who shall flee from Justice, and be found in another State, shall on Demand of the executive Authority of the State from which he fled, be delivered up, to be removed to the State having Jurisdiction of the Crime.

3 *No Person held to Service or Labor in one State, under the Laws thereof, escaping into another, shall, in Consequence of any Law or Regulation therein, be discharged from such Service or Labor, but shall be delivered up on Claim of the Party to whom such Service or Labor may be due.*

UNDERSTANDING THE CONSTITUTION 2.3 The text in italics is known as the fugitive slave clause, which barred people who had escaped slavery in the South from living as free people in northern states. It became obsolete with the abolition of slavery. It is interesting to note that the words *slave* and *slavery* do not appear in the Constitution.

12 HISTORICAL THINKING Why might the Framers have chosen not to mention slavery in the Constitution?

SECTION 3: NEW STATES

1 New States may be admitted by the Congress into this Union; but no new State shall be formed or erected within the Jurisdiction of any other State; nor any State be formed by the Junction of two or more States, or Parts of States, without the Consent of the Legislatures of the States concerned as well as of the Congress.

2 The Congress shall have Power to dispose of and make all needful Rules and Regulations respecting the Territory or other Property belonging to the United States; and nothing in this Constitution shall be so construed as to Prejudice any Claims of the United States, or of any particular State.

SECTION 4: PROTECTION OF STATES BY THE UNITED STATES

The United States shall guarantee to every State in this Union a Republican Form of Government, and shall protect each of them against Invasion; and on Application of the Legislature, or of the Executive (when the Legislature cannot be convened), against domestic Violence.

UNDERSTANDING THE CONSTITUTION Section 4 In the "guarantee clause," the Constitution commits the U.S. government to protecting the people of a state from attack by a foreign government as well as from domestic violence or terrorism.

Article V Amending the Constitution

1 The Congress, whenever two thirds of both Houses shall deem it necessary, shall propose Amendments to this Constitution, or, on the Application of the Legislatures of two thirds of the several States, shall call a Convention for proposing Amendments, which, in either Case, shall be valid to all Intents and Purposes, as Part of this Constitution, when ratified by the Legislatures of three fourths of the several States, or by Conventions in three fourths thereof, as the one or the other Mode of Ratification may be proposed by the Congress.

2 Provided that no Amendment which may be made prior to the Year One thousand eight hundred and eight shall in any Manner affect the first and fourth Clauses in the Ninth Section of the first Article; and that no State, without its Consent, shall be deprived of its equal Suffrage in the Senate.

Article VI The Supreme Law of the Land

1 All Debts contracted and Engagements entered into, before the Adoption of this Constitution, shall be as valid against the United States under this Constitution, as under the Confederation.

2 This Constitution, and the Laws of the United States which shall be made in Pursuance thereof; and all Treaties made, or which shall be made, under the Authority of the United States, shall be the supreme Law of the Land; and the Judges in every State shall be bound thereby, any Thing in the Constitution or Laws of any State to the Contrary notwithstanding.

3 The Senators and Representatives before mentioned, and the Members of the several State Legislatures, and all executive and judicial Officers, both of the United States and of the several States, shall be bound by Oath or Affirmation, to support this Constitution; but no religious Test shall ever be required as a Qualification to any Office or public Trust under the United States.

ARTICLE V
UNDERSTANDING THE CONSTITUTION Article V This article describes the process for amending the Constitution but states that the first and fourth clauses in Article 1's ninth section cannot be amended before 1808. These clauses refer to the importation of slaves and to a tax charged on an individual. The Framers realized that the Constitution would need to be amended at some point, but they made the amendment process extremely difficult. U.S. Senate records through January 2019 indicate that approximately 11,770 bills have been proposed as amendments to the Constitution. However, as of 2020, only 27 amendments had been added to the Constitution.

13 HISTORICAL THINKING Do you think the amendment process should be made easier? Explain why or why not.

ARTICLE VI
UNDERSTANDING THE CONSTITUTION Article VI Paragraph 2 is known as the "supremacy clause." The clause establishes the Constitution and all federal laws and treaties as the supreme law of the land. When state law is in conflict with federal law, federal law prevails. The Supreme Court has used the supremacy clause to ensure that federal law pre-empts, or takes priority over, state law. This is known as the doctrine of pre-emption.

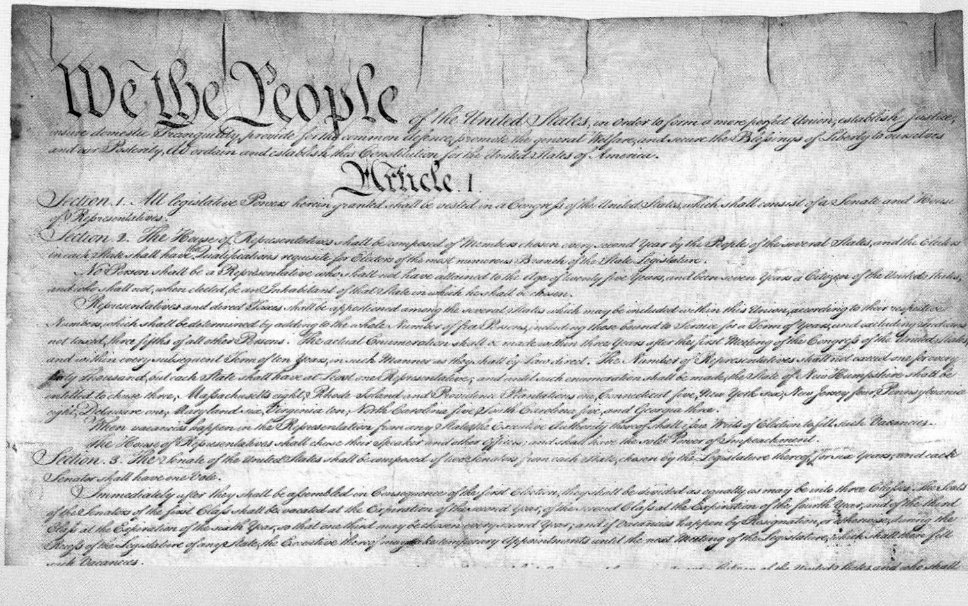

Today, "the people" referred to in the Constitution includes all adult U.S. citizens.

ARTICLE VII

UNDERSTANDING THE CONSTITUTION Article 7 The Framers clearly stated in Article 7 that the Constitution required the approval of only 9 states, not the entire 13. This contrasted with the Articles of Confederation, which required the consent of all 13 states. In addition, the Framers decided to hold a special ratification convention in each state. Delegates to these conventions were chosen by the state's citizens.

On June 21, 1788, New Hampshire became the 9th state to ratify the Constitution and make it the law of the United States. However, the Framers knew that the new nation's survival depended on the populous and wealthy states of Virginia and New York, which were slow to ratify. After lengthy debates, first Virginia and then New York approved the measure, becoming the 11th and 12th states to ratify the Constitution. Rhode Island was the only obstacle to unanimous approval. It officially joined the United States only after being warned that it would be treated like a foreign government if it did not.

14 HISTORICAL THINKING Why did the Framers call for ratification conventions in the 13 states?

Article VII Ratification

The Ratification of the Conventions of nine States, shall be sufficient for the Establishment of this Constitution between the States so ratifying the Same.

[Here appears some text noting corrections that were made on the original copy of the document.]

Done in Convention by the Unanimous Consent of the States present the Seventeenth Day of September in the Year of our Lord one thousand seven hundred and Eighty seven and of the Independence of the United States of America the Twelfth In witness whereof We have hereunto subscribed our Names,

G°. Washington
President and deputy from Virginia

Massachusetts
Nathaniel Gorham
Rufus King

New York
Alexander Hamilton

Delaware
George Read
Gunning Bedford, Jr.
John Dickinson
Richard Bassett
Jacob Broom

Virginia
John Blair
James Madison, Jr.

Pennsylvania
Benjamin Franklin
Thomas Mifflin
Robert Morris
George Clymer
Thomas Fitzsimons
Jared Ingersoll
James Wilson
Gouverneur Morris

New Hampshire
John Langdon
Nicholas Gilman

New Jersey
William Livingston
David Brearley
William Paterson
Jonathan Dayton

Connecticut
William Samuel Johnson
Roger Sherman

North Carolina
William Blount
Richard Dobbs Spaight
Hugh Williamson

South Carolina
John Rutledge
Charles Cotesworth Pinckney
Charles Pinckney
Pierce Butler

Maryland
James McHenry
Daniel of St. Thomas Jenifer
Daniel Carroll

Georgia
William Few
Abraham Baldwin

THE BILL OF RIGHTS AND AMENDMENTS 11–27

Introduction

Individual rights are fundamental to liberty. The Magna Carta, the charter of English liberties granted in 1215, helped inspire the Bill of Rights. Those who sailed to North America from Britain had enjoyed the freedoms granted to them under both the Magna Carta and the English Bill of Rights. They believed they were entitled to these same rights when they settled their colonies.

No one argued whether Americans should have these rights, but there was debate as to whether it was necessary and advisable to include them in the Constitution. At first, James Madison didn't believe the rights needed to be included. He argued that state constitutions already offered the explicit protection of individual liberties. Stating the rights in the Constitution might actually have the effect of limiting them. However, in 1787, Thomas Jefferson wrote to Madison, "[A] bill of rights is what the people are entitled to against every government on earth, general or particular, and what no just government should refuse." After long discussion among the Framers, Madison changed his mind. He drafted 19 amendments. On December 15, 1791, 10 of them were ratified, and the Bill of Rights was added to the Constitution.

The following is a transcription of the Bill of Rights. Over time, as you'll see, more amendments were added to the Constitution to address issues that arose as the nation grew and changed.

The Preamble to the Bill of Rights

Congress of the United States begun and held at the City of New York, on Wednesday the fourth of March, one thousand seven hundred and eighty nine.

THE Conventions of a number of the States, having at the time of their adopting the Constitution, expressed a desire, in order to prevent misconstruction or abuse of its powers, that further declaratory and restrictive clauses should be added: And as extending the ground of public confidence in the Government, will best ensure the beneficient ends of its institution.

RESOLVED by the Senate and House of Representatives of the United States of America, in Congress assembled, two thirds of both Houses concurring, that the following Articles be proposed to the Legislatures of the several States, as amendments to the Constitution of the United States, all, or any of which Articles, when ratified by three fourths of the said Legislatures, to be valid to all intents and purposes, as part of the said Constitution; viz.

UNDERSTANDING THE PREAMBLE *Viz* is Latin for "that is to say" or "namely."

ARTICLES in addition to, and Amendment of the Constitution of the United States of America, proposed by Congress, and ratified by the Legislatures of the several States, pursuant to the fifth Article of the original Constitution.

Amendment 1 (1791)

Congress shall make no law respecting an establishment of religion, or prohibiting the free exercise thereof; or abridging the freedom of speech, or of the press; or the right of the people peaceably to assemble, and to petition the Government for a redress of grievances.

Amendment 2 (1791)

A well regulated Militia, being necessary to the security of a free State, the right of the people to keep and bear Arms, shall not be infringed.

Amendment 3 (1791)

No Soldier shall, in time of peace be quartered in any house, without the consent of the Owner, nor in time of war, but in a manner to be prescribed by law.

Amendment 4 (1791)

The right of the people to be secure in their persons, houses, papers, and effects, against unreasonable searches and seizures, shall not be violated, and no Warrants shall issue, but upon probable cause, supported by Oath or affirmation, and particularly describing the place to be searched, and the persons or things to be seized.

UNDERSTANDING AMENDMENT 1

Amendment 1 protects the free exercise of religious liberty by prohibiting the government from establishing a church, endorsing a particular religion, or favoring one set of religious beliefs over another. Thomas Jefferson's 1786 Statute for Religious Freedom, which he wrote for the Virginia legislature, influenced the protection of religious freedom. In his statute, Jefferson also called for the separation of church and state. This idea is contained—although not explicitly—in the "establishment" clause. The Framers debated the wording of the clause and finally adopted that shown here.

UNDERSTANDING AMENDMENT 2

This amendment has been debated for decades. Many Americans believe the amendment ensures the right to possess guns. Others think gun ownership should be controlled. In 2008, the Supreme Court ruled in *District of Columbia* v. *Heller* that Amendment 2 guarantees the right to possess a firearm for self-defense and hunting. There has been debate as to whether the amendment protects ownership of any type of weapon, however.

15 **HISTORICAL THINKING** Do you think gun ownership should be controlled? Why or why not?

Amendment 5 (1791)

No person shall be held to answer for a capital, or otherwise infamous crime, unless on a presentment or indictment of a Grand Jury, except in cases arising in the land or naval forces, or in the Militia, when in actual service in time of War or public danger; nor shall any person be subject for the same offence to be twice put in jeopardy of life or limb; nor shall be compelled in any criminal case to be a witness against himself, nor be deprived of life, liberty, or property, without due process of law; nor shall private property be taken for public use, without just compensation.

Amendment 6 (1791)

In all criminal prosecutions, the accused shall enjoy the right to a speedy and public trial, by an impartial jury of the State and district wherein the crime shall have been committed, which district shall have been previously ascertained by law, and to be informed of the nature and cause of the accusation; to be confronted with the witnesses against him; to have compulsory process for obtaining witnesses in his favor, and to have the Assistance of Counsel for his defence.

Amendment 7 (1791)

In Suits at common law, where the value in controversy shall exceed twenty dollars, the right of trial by jury shall be preserved, and no fact tried by a jury, shall be otherwise re-examined in any Court of the United States, than according to the rules of the common law.

Amendment 8 (1791)

Excessive bail shall not be required, nor excessive fines imposed, nor cruel and unusual punishments inflicted.

Amendment 9 (1791)

The enumeration in the Constitution, of certain rights, shall not be construed to deny or disparage others retained by the people.

Amendment 10 (1791)

The powers not delegated to the United States by the Constitution, nor prohibited by it to the States, are reserved to the States respectively, or to the people.

UNDERSTANDING AMENDMENTS 4–6 These three amendments protect people who are suspected of a crime or are being tried for one.

Amendment 4 says that police must have "probable cause" (a good reason) before they can seize someone's possessions. It also protects people from unreasonable searches by government officials.

Amendment 5 protects those accused of crimes. The Due Process Clause was the basis for the defense of Fred Korematsu, an American citizen and and the son of Japanese parents, who refused to obey President Franklin Roosevelt's executive order and report to an internment camp during World War II. Under Roosevelt's order, Korematsu's lawyers argued, Japanese Americans were "deprived of life, liberty, or property, without due process of law." The case, *Fred Korematsu* v. *United States of America*, finally went to the Supreme Court, which upheld Korematsu's removal to an internment camp.

Amendment 6 guarantees a speedy public trial to those accused of a crime.

16 **HISTORICAL THINKING** Why do you suppose the Supreme Court upheld Roosevelt's executive order?

UNDERSTANDING AMENDMENTS 9 and 10 Amendment 9 prevents the government from denying rights that are not listed in the Bill of Rights. These are called "unenumerated" rights and include the right to travel and to vote.

The Framers added Amendment 10 to better define the balance of power between the states and the federal government. Each state is given the power to make laws that are not covered by the Constitution.

Amendment 11 (1798)

[**Note:** Article 3, Section 2, of the Constitution was modified by the 11th Amendment.]

The Judicial power of the United States shall not be construed to extend to any suit in law or equity, commenced or prosecuted against one of the United States by Citizens of another State, or by Citizens or Subjects of any Foreign State.

Amendment 12 (1804)

[**Note:** Part of Article 2, Section 1, of the Constitution was replaced by the 12th Amendment.]

The Electors shall meet in their respective states and vote by ballot for President and Vice-President, one of whom, at least, shall not be an inhabitant of the same state with themselves; they shall name in their ballots the person voted for as President, and in distinct ballots the person voted for as Vice-President, and they shall make distinct lists of all persons voted for as President, and of all persons voted for as Vice-President, and of the number of votes for each, which lists they shall sign and certify, and transmit sealed to the seat of the government of the United States, directed to the President of the Senate; —the President of the Senate shall, in the presence of the Senate and House of Representatives, open all the certificates and the votes shall then be counted; —The person having the greatest number of votes for President, shall be the President, if such number be a majority of the whole number of Electors appointed; and if no person have such majority, then from the persons having the highest numbers not exceeding three on the list of those voted for as President, the House of Representatives shall choose immediately, by ballot, the President. But in choosing the President, the votes shall be taken by states, the representation from each state having one vote; a quorum for this purpose shall consist of a member or members from two-thirds of the states, and a majority of all the states shall be necessary to a choice. *And if the House of Representatives shall not choose a President whenever the right of choice shall devolve upon them, before the fourth day of March next following, then the Vice-President shall act as President, as in case of the death or other constitutional disability of the President.* The person having the greatest number of votes as Vice-President, shall be the Vice-President, if such number be a majority of the whole number of Electors appointed, and if no person have a majority, then from the two highest numbers on the list, the Senate shall choose the Vice-President; a quorum for the purpose shall consist of two-thirds of the whole number of Senators, and a majority of the whole number shall be necessary to a choice. But no person constitutionally ineligible to the office of President shall be eligible to that of Vice-President of the United States.

UNDERSTANDING AMENDMENT 12
Amendment 12 established the electoral college. As you know, prior to its passage, the presidential candidate who received the most electoral votes won the presidency. The candidate with the second most votes became the vice president. The amendment changed this system by allowing the delegates of each party to choose its nominees for both president and vice president.

The electoral college was challenged in 2000 and 2016, when the candidates who won the popular vote (Al Gore in 2000 and Hillary Clinton in 2016) lost the elections to George W. Bush and Donald Trump, respectively.

17 **HISTORICAL THINKING** Do you think the electoral college should be abolished? Why or why not?

Amendment 13 (1865)

[**Note:** A portion of Article 4, Section 2, of the Constitution was superseded by the 13th Amendment.]

SECTION 1: Neither slavery nor involuntary servitude, except as a punishment for crime whereof the party shall have been duly convicted, shall exist within the United States, or any place subject to their jurisdiction.

SECTION 2: Congress shall have power to enforce this article by appropriate legislation.

Amendment 14 (1868)

[**Note:** Article 1, Section 2, of the Constitution was modified by Section 2 of the 14th Amendment.]

SECTION 1: All persons born or naturalized in the United States, and subject to the jurisdiction thereof, are citizens of the United States and of the State wherein they reside. No State shall make or enforce any law which shall abridge the privileges or immunities of citizens of the United States; nor shall any State deprive any person of life, liberty, or property, without due process of law; nor deny to any person within its jurisdiction the equal protection of the laws.

SECTION 2: Representatives shall be apportioned among the several States according to their respective numbers, counting the whole number of persons in each State, excluding Indians not taxed. But when the right to vote at any election for the choice of electors for President and Vice-President of the United States, Representatives in Congress, the Executive and Judicial officers of a State, or the members of the *Legislature thereof, is denied to any of the male inhabitants of such State, being twenty-one years of age, and citizens of the United States,* or in any way abridged, except for participation in rebellion, or other crime, the basis of representation therein shall be reduced in the proportion which the number of such male citizens shall bear to the whole number of male citizens twenty-one years of age in such State.

SECTION 3: No person shall be a Senator or Representative in Congress, or elector of President and Vice-President, or hold any office, civil or military, under the United States, or under any State, who, having previously taken an oath, as a member of Congress, or as an officer of the United States, or as a member of any State legislature, or as an executive or judicial officer of any State, to support the Constitution of the United States, shall have engaged in insurrection or rebellion against the same, or given aid or comfort to the enemies thereof. But Congress may by a vote of two-thirds of each House, remove such disability.

UNDERSTANDING AMENDMENTS 13–15 Amendments 13–15 are often referred to as the "civil war" or "reconstruction" amendments because they were created in the aftermath of the war. These post-Civil War amendments laid the foundation for the legal phase of the 20th-century civil rights movement.

UNDERSTANDING AMENDMENT 13
This amendment outlawed slavery.

UNDERSTANDING AMENDMENT 14
Section 1 This section defines citizenship and ensures that all citizens enjoy the same rights and the same protections by the law. The amendment has been continually reinterpreted and applied to different contexts by the courts. For example, sometimes it has been employed as a protection for workers and other times as a protection for corporations. In the 1877 case, *Munn* v. *Illinois*, the Supreme Court upheld the idea that a corporation and its business activities were protected by the 14th Amendment.

UNDERSTANDING AMENDMENT 14
Section 2 This section overrides the three-fifths clause in Article I. As a result of this amendment, each citizen is counted as a whole person. Section 2 also calls for reducing the number of representatives of a state if it denies some citizens the right to vote.

SECTION 4: The validity of the public debt of the United States, authorized by law, including debts incurred for payment of pensions and bounties for services in suppressing insurrection or rebellion, shall not be questioned. But neither the United States nor any State shall assume or pay any debt or obligation incurred in aid of insurrection or rebellion against the United States, or any claim for the loss or emancipation of any slave; but all such debts, obligations and claims shall be held illegal and void.

SECTION 5: The Congress shall have the power to enforce, by appropriate legislation, the provisions of this article.

UNDERSTANDING AMENDMENT 15
The 15th Amendment prohibits federal and state governments from limiting or denying an individual's ability to vote because of "race, color, or previous conditions of servitude." Section 2 of the amendment gives Congress the authority to enforce the amendment by passing federal laws that guarantee voting rights. Note that the amendment granted African-American men voting rights but not women of any race. In addition, some states imposed literacy tests, white primaries, poll taxes, and other barriers to keep African Americans from voting. Almost 100 years would pass before African Americans secured stronger protections through federal legislation and the 24th Amendment.

18 **HISTORICAL THINKING** Why might some states have made it difficult for African-American men to vote?

Amendment 15 (1870)

SECTION 1: The right of citizens of the United States to vote shall not be denied or abridged by the United States or by any State on account of race, color, or previous condition of servitude—

SECTION 2: The Congress shall have the power to enforce this article by appropriate legislation.

In this illustration, a group of men who helped bring about the 15th Amendment, including Abraham Lincoln, Hiram Revels, and Frederick Douglass, watch as President Ulysses S. Grant signs the amendment.

UNDERSTANDING AMENDMENT 16
The 16th Amendment was the first of four "Progressive" amendments. During the Progressive Era (1890–1920), many Americans worked to reform government. Seeking to reduce tariffs and still provide revenue for the federal government, progressives pushed for this amendment, which established an income tax.

Amendment 16 (1913)

[**Note:** Article 1, Section 9, of the Constitution was modified by the 16th Amendment.]

The Congress shall have power to lay and collect taxes on incomes, from whatever source derived, without apportionment among the several States, and without regard to any census or enumeration.

Amendment 17 (1913)

[**Note:** Article 1, Section 3, of the Constitution was modified by the 17th Amendment.]

The Senate of the United States shall be composed of two Senators from each State, elected by the people thereof, for six years; and each Senator shall have one vote. The electors in each State shall have the qualifications requisite for electors of the most numerous branch of the State legislatures.

When vacancies happen in the representation of any State in the Senate, the executive authority of such State shall issue writs of election to fill such vacancies: Provided, That the legislature of any State may empower the executive thereof to make temporary appointments until the people fill the vacancies by election as the legislature may direct.

This amendment shall not be so construed as to affect the election or term of any Senator chosen before it becomes valid as part of the Constitution.

UNDERSTANDING AMENDMENT 17
The 17th Amendment changed the process by which Senators are elected. Through the popular election of senators, the amendment made the process more democratic.

Amendment 18 (1919)

Repealed by the 21st Amendment.

SECTION 1: *After one year from the ratification of this article the manufacture, sale, or transportation of intoxicating liquors within, the importation thereof into, or the exportation thereof from the United States and all territory subject to the jurisdiction thereof for beverage purposes is hereby prohibited.*

SECTION 2: *The Congress and the several States shall have concurrent power to enforce this article by appropriate legislation.*

SECTION 3: *This article shall be inoperative unless it shall have been ratified as an amendment to the Constitution by the legislatures of the several States, as provided in the Constitution, within seven years from the date of the submission hereof to the States by the Congress.*

Philadelphia's Director of Public Safety, Smedley Butler, smashes casks of beer in 1924 to enforce Prohibition.

UNDERSTANDING AMENDMENT 18
Known as the Prohibition Amendment, the 18th Amendment prohibited the production, sale, or transportation of alcoholic beverages in the United States. Many of those who supported the amendment also supported the temperance movement, which advocated for the control of alcohol consumption. Many progressives viewed alcohol abuse as a significant social problem. Congress passed the Volstead Act in 1919, which gave the U.S. Treasury Department the power to enforce Prohibition.

19 **HISTORICAL THINKING** In what way was Amendment 18 different from the preceding amendments?

Following the passage of the 19th Amendment, the women shown here voted for the first time in a 1920 election in New York City.

UNDERSTANDING AMENDMENT 19
Although many states had granted some voting privileges to women before 1920, the 19th Amendment extended equal voting rights to all women in the country. In the 1800s, women's rights leaders such as Elizabeth Cady Stanton and Susan B. Anthony dedicated their lives to securing political and social equality for women. Their actions helped inspire and launch another movement in the 1960s, which called for further rights for women and offered differing perspectives on the roles of women.

20 HISTORICAL THINKING Why does the amendment specify that women's right to vote "shall not be denied or abridged by the United States or by any state"?

UNDERSTANDING AMENDMENT 20
This amendment is often called the "Lame Duck Amendment." In government, a lame duck is an elected official whose term in office is about to end. So, for instance, a president who has already served two terms is a lame duck. Officials who have not won re-election are also considered lame ducks. Congress has little incentive to work with a lame duck president.

Amendment 19 (1920)

The right of citizens of the United States to vote shall not be denied or abridged by the United States or by any State on account of sex.

Congress shall have power to enforce this article by appropriate legislation.

Amendment 20 (1933)

[**Note:** Article 1, Section 4, of the Constitution was modified by Section 2 of the 20th Amendment. In addition, a portion of the 12th Amendment was superseded by Section 3.]

SECTION 1: The terms of the President and the Vice President shall end at noon on the 20th day of January, and the terms of Senators and Representatives at noon on the 3d day of January, of the years in which such terms would have ended if this article had not been ratified; and the terms of their successors shall then begin.

SECTION 2: The Congress shall assemble at least once in every year, and such meeting shall begin at noon on the 3d day of January, unless they shall by law appoint a different day.

SECTION 3: If, at the time fixed for the beginning of the term of the President, the President elect shall have died, the Vice President elect shall become President. If a President shall not have been chosen before the time fixed for the beginning of his term, or if the President elect shall have failed to qualify, then the Vice President elect shall act as President until a President shall have qualified; and the Congress may by law provide for the case wherein neither a President elect nor a Vice President elect shall have qualified, declaring who shall then act as President, or the manner in which one who is to act shall be selected, and such person shall act accordingly until a President or Vice President shall have qualified.

SECTION 4: The Congress may by law provide for the case of the death of any of the persons from whom the House of Representatives may choose a President whenever the right of choice shall have devolved upon them, and for the case of the death of any of the persons from whom the Senate may choose a Vice President whenever the right of choice shall have devolved upon them.

SECTION 5: Sections 1 and 2 shall take effect on the 15th day of October following the ratification of this article.

SECTION 6: This article shall be inoperative unless it shall have been ratified as an amendment to the Constitution by the legislatures of three-fourths of the several States within seven years from the date of its submission.

Amendment 21 (1933)

SECTION 1: The eighteenth article of amendment to the Constitution of the United States is hereby repealed.

SECTION 2: The transportation or importation into any State, Territory, or possession of the United States for delivery or use therein of intoxicating liquors, in violation of the laws thereof, is hereby prohibited.

SECTION 3: This article shall be inoperative unless it shall have been ratified as an amendment to the Constitution by conventions in the several States, as provided in the Constitution, within seven years from the date of the submission hereof to the States by the Congress.

Amendment 22 (1951)

SECTION 1: No person shall be elected to the office of the President more than twice, and no person who has held the office of President, or acted as President, for more than two years of a term to which some other person was elected President shall be elected to the office of the President more than once. But this Article shall not apply to any person holding the office of President when this Article was proposed by the Congress, and shall not prevent any person who may be holding the office of President, or acting as President, during the term within which this Article becomes operative from holding the office of President or acting as President during the remainder of such term.

SECTION 2: This article shall be inoperative unless it shall have been ratified as an amendment to the Constitution by the legislatures of three-fourths of the several States within seven years from the date of its submission to the States by the Congress.

UNDERSTANDING AMENDMENT 21
Amendment 21 repealed Amendment 18 and ended Prohibition. Amendment 21 is the only amendment that was ratified by state conventions rather than state legislatures. Section 2 of the amendment returned the regulation of alcohol to the states, giving them significant control of alcohol within and across their borders. Consequently, alcohol laws vary throughout the states. States also have the power to establish the legal drinking age within their borders. In an effort to prohibit the sale of alcohol to minors, the federal government provides federal funds only to states who set the legal drinking age at 21. All 50 states have done so.

21 **HISTORICAL THINKING** What potential problems or issues might arise when states have different laws regulating people of the same age?

UNDERSTANDING AMENDMENT 22
Democrat Franklin D. Roosevelt served three terms as president of the United States and was elected to a fourth term shortly before he died in 1945. George Washington had declined to run for a third term. All presidents before Roosevelt followed this unwritten custom and served no more than two terms. Within months of Roosevelt's death, Republicans in Congress presented the 22nd Amendment for consideration.

22 **HISTORICAL THINKING** Do you think a president should be able to serve for more than two terms? Explain your answer.

UNDERSTANDING AMENDMENT 23
The District of Columbia is the official seat of the U.S. government, but it is a federal territory, not a state, and has only a nonvoting representative in Congress. Washington, D.C., began as a small community, but by 1960, more than 760,000 people who paid federal taxes and could be drafted into the military lived there. The states ratified Amendment 23 in 1961 to allow residents of the District to vote in presidential elections. The District of Columbia has three electoral votes.

Amendment 23 (1961)

SECTION 1: The District constituting the seat of Government of the United States shall appoint in such manner as the Congress may direct:

A number of electors of President and Vice President equal to the whole number of Senators and Representatives in Congress to which the District would be entitled if it were a State, but in no event more than the least populous State; they shall be in addition to those appointed by the States, but they shall be considered, for the purposes of the election of President and Vice President, to be electors appointed by a State; and they shall meet in the District and perform such duties as provided by the twelfth article of amendment.

SECTION 2: The Congress shall have power to enforce this article by appropriate legislation.

UNDERSTANDING AMENDMENT 24
This amendment abolished poll taxes and election fees charged by states to keep low-income and mostly African-American citizens from voting. The successful push to get the amendment passed was in part based on the support and demands of the civil rights movement. The amendment gave African Americans greater access to the political process. As written, Amendment 24 prohibits poll taxes only in federal elections. The Voting Rights Act of 1965 and a 1966 Supreme Court decision banned poll taxes in state elections as well.

23 HISTORICAL THINKING Why do you think the amendment refers to the "right of citizens of the United States to vote," rather than name specific minority groups?

Amendment 24 (1964)

SECTION 1: The right of citizens of the United States to vote in any primary or other election for President or Vice President, for electors for President or Vice President, or for Senator or Representative in Congress, shall not be denied or abridged by the United States or any State by reason of failure to pay any poll tax or other tax.

SECTION 2: The Congress shall have power to enforce this article by appropriate legislation.

Amendment 25 (1967)

[**Note:** Article 2, Section 1, of the Constitution was affected by the 25th Amendment.]

SECTION 1: In case of the removal of the President from office or of his death or resignation, the Vice President shall become President.

SECTION 2: Whenever there is a vacancy in the office of the Vice President, the President shall nominate a Vice President who shall take office upon confirmation by a majority vote of both Houses of Congress.

SECTION 3: Whenever the President transmits to the President pro tempore of the Senate and the Speaker of the House of Representatives his written declaration that he is unable to discharge the powers and duties of his office, and until he transmits to them a written declaration to the contrary, such powers and duties shall be discharged by the Vice President as Acting President.

SECTION 4: Whenever the Vice President and a majority of either the principal officers of the executive departments or of such other body as Congress may by law provide, transmit to the President pro tempore of the Senate and the Speaker of the House of Representatives their written declaration that the President is unable to discharge the powers and duties of his office, the Vice President shall immediately assume the powers and duties of the office as Acting President.

Thereafter, when the President transmits to the President pro tempore of the Senate and the Speaker of the House of Representatives his written declaration that no inability exists, he shall resume the powers and duties of his office unless the Vice President and a majority of either the principal officers of the executive department or of such other body as Congress may by law provide, transmit within four days to the President pro tempore of the Senate and the Speaker of the House of Representatives their written declaration that the President is unable to discharge the powers and duties of his office. Thereupon Congress shall decide the issue, assembling within forty-eight hours for that purpose if not in session. If the Congress, within twenty-one days after receipt of the latter written declaration, or, if Congress is not in session, within twenty-one days after Congress is required to assemble, determines by two-thirds vote of both Houses that the President is unable to discharge the powers and duties of his office, the Vice President shall continue to discharge the same as Acting President; otherwise, the President shall resume the powers and duties of his office.

UNDERSTANDING AMENDMENT 25

The 25th Amendment was ratified in 1967 to establish procedures to follow if a president becomes disabled while in office. The amendment was proposed after the assassination of President John F. Kennedy in 1963. Following his death, many questioned what would have happened if he had survived the shooting but been unable to govern. Eight presidents have died and one resigned while in office. In addition, seven vice presidents have died while in office and two have resigned. This amendment provides for an orderly transfer of power.

24 **HISTORICAL THINKING** Why is there a plan of succession for the presidency?

Pat Keefer, a leader in advocating for the youth vote in the early 1970s, holds signs urging 18-year olds to vote.

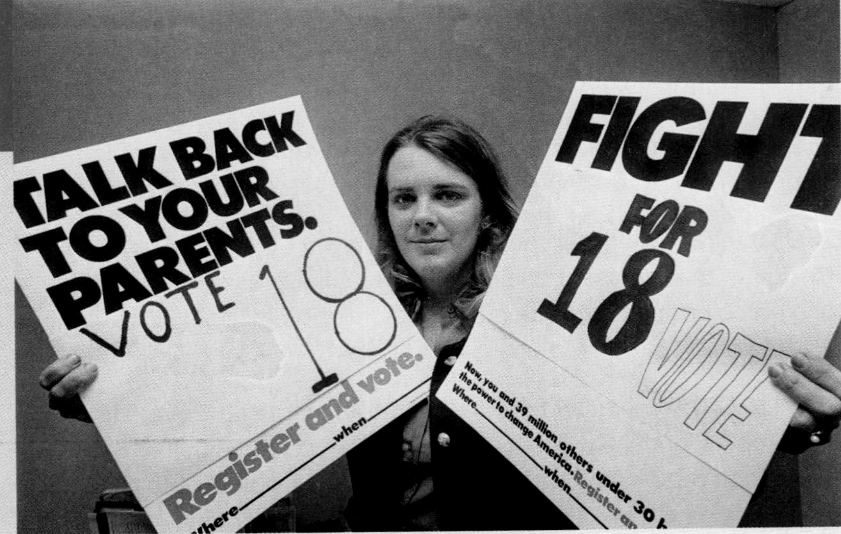

Amendment 26 (1971)

[**Note:** Amendment 14, Section 2, of the Constitution was modified by Section 1 of the 26th Amendment.]

SECTION 1: The right of citizens of the United States, who are eighteen years of age or older, to vote shall not be denied or abridged by the United States or by any State on account of age.

SECTION 2: The Congress shall have power to enforce this article by appropriate legislation.

Amendment 27 (1992)

No law, varying the compensation for the services of the Senators and Representatives, shall take effect, until an election of Representatives shall have intervened.

UNDERSTANDING AMENDMENT 26
Amendment 26 continued the Constitution's expansion of voting rights. In 1954, President Dwight Eisenhower proposed lowering the voting age to 18 years. The movement acquired new momentum in the late 1960s during the Vietnam War. People began to question why 18-year-old men could be drafted to serve in the military but could not vote.

25 **HISTORICAL THINKING** Do you think the voting age should be reduced even more? Explain your answer.

UNDERSTANDING AMENDMENT 27
Amendment 27 defers any congressional pay raise to the next election cycle. The amendment was first proposed in 1789 by James Madison. However, it was ratified more than 200 years later, thanks to a college student's research project. In his research, the student found that a proposed amendment remains pending, no matter how much time passes before action is taken on it. The student decided to see if he could get the amendment passed and found that he was able to gather enough support to do so.

Citizenship and You

For many high school students, getting to a job, meeting with friends, and participating in activities require some source of transportation. Many young adults borrow a car from their parents to get around. To continue to enjoy this privilege, you have to handle responsibilities and prove you are dependable. You have to obey the rules of the road and be a careful, alert driver. Similarly, our responsibilities to our communities, states, and nation balance the rights we receive as citizens. Let's examine some aspects of American citizenship—of being a full member of a country in exchange for certain responsibilities.

STRUGGLE FOR EQUAL RIGHTS

As you have learned by studying the U.S. Constitution and Bill of Rights, privileges and rights such as citizenship and voting have been contested, reshaped, and amended during our country's history. Beginning with freedoms and rights cherished and protected in the Constitution by the Framers, Americans from all walks of life have struggled to expand their own rights and those of others. People gained rights they had been denied through the efforts of the civil rights movement, including the right to participate in government, the right to free expression—in all its forms—and the right to equal treatment under the law. Federal, state, and local governments have responded to these social changes with more equitable laws. For example, in response to demands by the LGBTQIA+ community, the Supreme Court legalized same-sex marriage in 2015. The efforts and sacrifices of rights activists have helped move all Americans forward in our continuing struggle to become a more perfect union—a struggle that continues today.

Individuals act as participatory citizens by exercising their right to vote in local, state, and federal elections.

WE THE PEOPLE

What role do rules play in your life? Have you ever considered what your life would be like if there were no rules? Imagine arriving at school on the first day of your senior year of high school. You discover that there are no schedules. No one knows where to go, what classes to attend, which locker to use. No one understands the processes and procedures that allow a school to operate efficiently.

This is similar to what would happen in a government without clear rules—or laws—that define the rights and responsibilities of citizens. Order, organization, equality, and safety would all be threatened without laws and established procedures and processes. The most concrete example of our society's rules are our laws, and the most fundamental duty of an American citizen is to obey them.

Is it fair that a government makes laws that people must follow? As you learned while studying the Constitution, the United States is a representative democracy, as demonstrated by the phrase "We the people." Your exploration of the Constitution has revealed that the American people hold the power to shape the government and determine its practices. When our government and representatives act in ways that oppose our rules and ideals, we have the means to point the country in the right direction. Americans work to be *good citizens* by obeying laws, *participatory citizens* by voting and serving on juries, and *socially-just citizens* by standing up for the rights of others.

THINK ABOUT IT

1. **SUMMARIZE** Why are rules and laws important, and what would happen without them?

The Rights and Responsibilities of Citizens

Our Constitution defines many of the rights we enjoy as Americans. These rights apply to all citizens, regardless of whether they were born here or immigrated from another country. Knowing your rights can help you better understand the responsibilities that come with being a citizen, and help you determine what you must do to support and protect those rights. Responsibilities include doing what is right, showing good character, and acting in an ethical manner. As you read, think about specific actions you already perform and other steps you might take to be a good, participatory, and socially just citizen.

AMERICAN CITIZENSHIP

Some residents of the United States are citizens because they were born in the country. They are native-born citizens. Others came legally from foreign countries to live in the United States. Our democratic principles have fostered high levels of freedom, political stability, and economic prosperity. These features have attracted people to our nation for hundreds of years. In addition, our political and economic systems have become models for other nations throughout the world. People looking for opportunity and freedom are drawn to our country.

A person who has immigrated to the United States and desires to become a legal citizen goes through a process called **naturalization**. Individuals may qualify for naturalization if they are at least 18 years old and have been a permanent resident in the United States for at least 5 years (or 3 years if they are married to a U.S. citizen). They must learn the laws, rights, and responsibilities of American citizenship.

Following a successful interview with government officials, a prospective citizen must pass a citizenship test. After completing all the steps in this process, a new citizen is sworn in during a naturalization ceremony. As you know, the United States is a country of immigrants. Throughout our country's history, immigrants have helped build our nation, strengthen our economy, and enhance our society. It is a proud day when they become U.S. citizens.

For both native and naturalized citizens, being an American means much more than just living in the United States. After all, Americans living in foreign countries are still citizens of the United States. They are always connected to the United States and other Americans because of their citizenship. Citizenship also encompasses elements of the American tradition, which includes a shared history, customs, and political and cultural beliefs and values. These values include freedom, liberty, and equality—those principles Thomas Jefferson described in the Declaration of Independence.

Rights of Citizens
Right to freedom of religion
Right to freedom of speech (with some limits)
Right to freedom of the press
Right to assemble
Right to trial by jury (in specific types of cases)
Right to vote
Right to buy and sell property
Right to freely travel across the country and to leave and return to the country

RESTRICTIONS ON RIGHTS

By now, you're probably familiar with the basic rights of citizens as guaranteed in the Constitution. These rights also carry responsibilities and are subject to interpretation by the courts. For example, Amendment 1 guarantees the right to free speech—to state one's views or ideas without fear of punishment. Nonetheless, an employer or teacher, for example, can limit speech to what is appropriate in the circumstances. Speech intended to cause harm to others is not protected. For example, crying "Fire!" in a crowded theater when there is no fire is not protected by the right to free speech. The person's "speech" could cause harm to others. The Supreme Court has also placed limits on speech intended to motivate an individual to break the law. Threats of violence are also restricted.

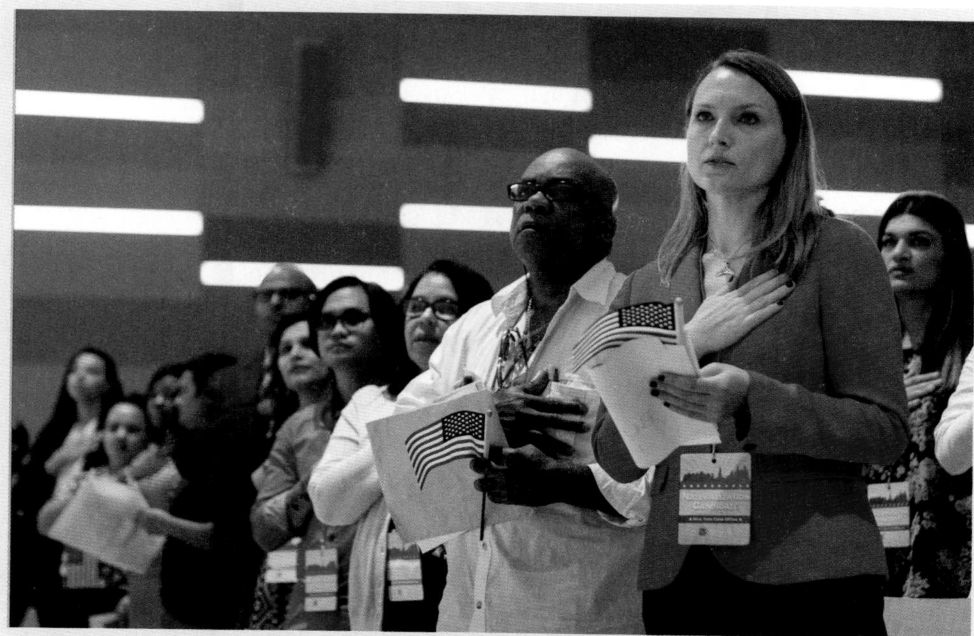

New citizens are sworn in at a naturalization ceremony in 2019 at the 9/11 Memorial & Museum in New York City.

TWO TYPES OF RESPONSIBILITIES

American citizens have two different types of responsibilities: civic and personal. **Civic responsibilities** include voting, paying taxes, and serving on juries. Some of these responsibilities are duties: actions required by law. For example, all citizens must obey laws, pay taxes, and perform jury duty when notified. Neglecting these duties may result in legal penalties. Males over the age of 18 must register with the government in case they are needed for military service.

Personal responsibilities are not required, but they contribute to a more civil society. These include respecting others and their rights, helping in the community, standing up for others, and staying informed about important issues. Personal responsibilities are not as clearly defined as civic duties. They are, however, vital to maintaining an effective government and just society.

All American citizens over the age of 18 have the right to vote. Many people take that right for granted but don't bother to exercise it. Perhaps they don't consider the fact that the right to vote is a privilege that is not granted to people in some countries. These people have no say in how they are governed. Voters also have a responsibility to become informed about issues. They have an obligation to use reliable sources to learn about candidates and their positions on issues. Informed voters can then analyze the credibility of a candidate's claims.

BEING A RESPONSIBLE CITIZEN

When you think of your personal responsibilities as a citizen, consider the choices you make in terms of your actions. Being a responsible citizen means behaving in ways that are right, moral, and just, and acting in a way that benefits you and those around you. Considering the rights of all people, not just the rights of a select few, will help you be a personally responsible citizen.

Citizens have many personal responsibilities, such as being open-minded, respecting the opinions of others, and showing respect for the beliefs and individuality of people with different backgrounds. People of any age can take on personal responsibilities by doing community service projects, standing up for the rights of others, and respecting all people regardless of ethnicity, nationality, gender identity, sexual orientation, or beliefs. Tolerance for others is an important part of being an American citizen.

Tolerance of differences is essential in a democracy, especially one that is as diverse as the United States. Responsible citizens are also willing to give time, effort, and money to improve their communities. Living up to these personal responsibilities helps citizens contribute to an environment of respect and caring and one that protects and promotes the health and welfare of everyone. Responsible citizens work to contribute to the common good.

THINK ABOUT IT

2 **EXPLAIN** How does taking on personal responsibilities as a citizen contribute to the common good?

Building and Practicing Citizenship Skills

Building citizenship skills is like learning to play an instrument. It takes hard work and repetition, but the rewards make the effort worth it. Some citizenship skills, such as helping raise voter participation, will require you to seek out specific opportunities. Others, such as refusing to tolerate unjust behavior, can be exercised whenever appropriate situations arise. Citizenship affords many rights and requires many responsibilities. Enjoying these rights and responsibilities is the reward of being a good citizen.

The following chart includes ways you can build and apply citizenship skills in the classroom and in your community to become an active participant in our democracy. Study the chart, then brainstorm more ways you can be a good, participatory, and socially-just citizen and put them to practice.

THINK ABOUT IT

3 **DESCRIBE** What opportunities for active citizenship appeal to you? Explain what you could do to be involved and engaged in your community and country.

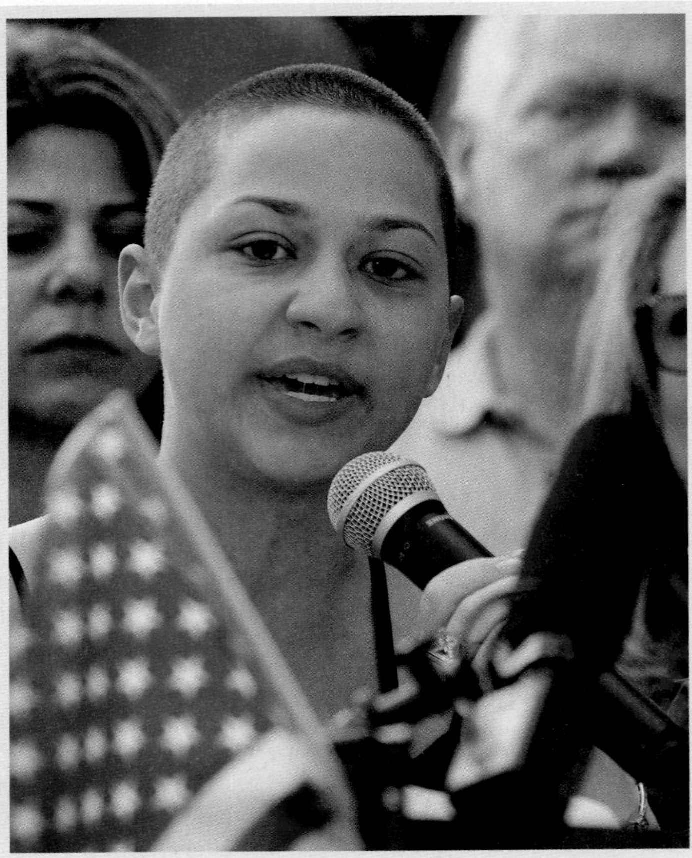

After a gunman terrorized her Parkland, Florida high school on February 14, 2018, killing 17 people and injuring many others, Emma González transformed from a high school student into an activist and gun control advocate. As an engaged citizen, González lobbies for changes to gun legislation, and participates in peaceful protests such as the March For Our Lives, which was held on March 24, 2018, in hundreds of U.S. cities.

ACTIVE CITIZENSHIP

Responsibilities	Citizenship Projects: Ways to Promote Civic Engagement
Become engaged.	• Get information from reliable, unbiased sources. • Ask questions of others who are well informed. • Attend or organize peaceful public demonstrations about issues important to you. • Register to vote, encourage others to vote, and consider becoming an election judge or poll watcher. • Serve your country and your fellow citizens through the military or by participating in organizations such as AmeriCorps, AmeriCorps VISTA, and the Peace Corps. • Participate in citizen journalism by reporting information accurately through blogs, news sites, and social media.

Responsibilities	Citizenship Projects: Ways to Promote Civic Engagement
Do historical research.	• Conduct oral histories with family or community members to better understand historical trends. • Interview citizens who served in the military, took part in social justice movements, or were involved in bringing about social change in schools or the workplace. • Research how you and your classmates can participate in National History Day at a state or national level.
Participate in the democratic process.	• Ask a teacher to organize a trip to a local courtroom to see the legal system in action. • Contact a local political candidate whose ideas you support to see how you might help with his or her campaign. • With the help of a parent or teacher, seek opportunities to witness a naturalization ceremony.
Lobby for change.	• Form a lobbying committee with other students to influence legislation or public policy. • Establish a goal for your lobbying campaign. • Identify whom to lobby. (Who are the people who can help you accomplish your goal?) • Find information and statistics to support your goal. • Get public support for your cause. You might consider gathering signatures on a petition or creating flyers to publicize your campaign. • Present your case to the appropriate individuals.
Volunteer in your community.	• Determine how your skills and interests could help someone else. • Talk with your parents, teachers, and friends to learn what types of volunteer services your community needs. • Make volunteering a regular part of your life. You could consider serving food to the homeless, collecting clothing or canned goods to help a local shelter, cleaning or restoring a local park or playground, or tutoring students who are struggling with their school work.
Pay taxes.	• Read more about your local and state taxes, and what the revenue is used for. • Recognize that you are already paying sales taxes when you purchase many items.
Express political opinions.	• Write a letter or an email to a newspaper editor about an issue that concerns you.
Obey the law.	• Become familiar with the laws in your state, city, and town that apply to people your age.
Stand up for the rights of others.	• Work to stop the discrimination of all people. • Write articles and blog posts about the importance of protecting and supporting the rights of people of different races, religions, and sexual orientations.
Listen to the opinions of others. Discuss differences of opinion in a kind and civil manner.	• When friends or acquaintances express opinions that differ from yours, politely explain why you disagree, if you do.
Respect the value of individuals. Respect differences among people.	• Enjoy and appreciate the differences among people from various backgrounds. • Make friends with people who are different from you. • Volunteer in your community to interact with and help others.
Accept responsibility for your actions.	• If someone asks about a mistake you have made, tell the truth. • Ask what you might do to make up for the mistake.

VOCABULARY WORDS BY CHAPTER

CHAPTER 1 THE PRINCIPLES OF AMERICAN GOVERNMENT

authoritarian
authority
autocracy
Bill of Rights
communism
conservatism
democracy
dictatorship
divine right theory
equality
free enterprise system
government
initiative
liberalism
libertarianism
liberty
limited government
moderate
multiculturalism
pandemic
partisanship
political culture
political ideology
politics
precedent
public services
referendum
republic
social contract theory
socialism
sovereignty
totalitarian

CHAPTER 2 THE BEGINNINGS OF AMERICAN GOVERNMENT

antifederalist
Articles of Confederation
bicameral
coercive
confederation
congress
constitution
Declaration of Independence
delegate
electoral college
elites
federal
federalist
Great Compromise
impeach
inflation
judiciary
legislature
Mayflower Compact
popular sovereignty
Proclamation of 1763
ratify
self-government
separation of powers
slave importation
taxes
Three-Fifths Compromise
unicameral

CHAPTER 3 THE CONSTITUTION

allegiance
amendment
appellate court
checks and balances
commerce
commerce clause
demagogue
electors
establishment clause
executive branch
executive privilege
faction
federalism
Framer
interstate commerce
judicial branch
judicial review
legislative branch
necessary and proper clause
peonage
poll tax
preamble
Progressive Era
republicanism
revenue
suffrage
supermajority
supremacy clause
tariff
term limit
uncodified
unconstitutional
voucher program

CHAPTER 4 FEDERALISM

delegate
devolution
fiscal
grant
judgment
landmark decision
New Deal
nullify
racial discrimination
recession
petition
public policy
secession
special district
welfare

CHAPTER 5 CIVIL LIBERTIES

censorship
civil disobedience
civil liberty
credit rating
cyberbullying
defamation
due process
eminent domain
incorporation
libel
lobby
parochial
polygamy
presumption of innocence
prior restraint
probable cause
search warrant
secular
seditious
slander
surveillance
syndicate
writ of habeas corpus

CHAPTER 6 CITIZENSHIP AND CIVIL RIGHTS

abolition
affirmative action
assimilation
civil rights
civil rights movement
citizenship
compensate
de jure segregation
de facto segregation
disability
doctrine
feminism
freedmen
glass ceiling
green card
immigrant
Jim Crow laws
LGBTQ persons
quota
Reconstruction
separate-but-equal
transgender person
transsexual
undocumented

CHAPTER 7 THE STRUCTURE OF CONGRESS

apportionment
cloture
committee
constituents
earmark
filibuster
general election
gerrymandering
incumbent
jurisdiction
majority party
minority party
nomination
political action
primary election
progressive
redistricting
session
single-member district
standing committee
subcommittee
term

CHAPTER 8 THE POWERS OF CONGRESS

bankruptcy
commerce clause
copyright
deficit
elastic clause
enumerate
expressed powers
implied powers
inherent powers
naturalization
subpoena

CHAPTER 9 THE LEGISLATIVE PROCESS

appropriation
authorization
bill
entitlement program
fiscal year
NATO
omnibus bill
resolution
veto

CHAPTER 10
THE PRESIDENCY

advisor
amnesty
deploy
executive order
ideologue
landslide election
national security
pardon
patronage
pocket veto
signing statement

CHAPTER 11
THE BUREAUCRACY

agency
bureaucracy
civil service
classified
cost-benefit analysis
executive department
federal mandate
Freedom of Information Act (FOIA)
gross domestic product (GDP)
merit system
monopoly
national debt
payroll tax
privatization
regulation
whistleblower

CHAPTER 12
THE AMERICAN COURT SYSTEM

capital crime
civil law
common law
contempt of court
court martial
criminal law
felony
lawsuit
misdemeanor
mistrial
original jurisdiction
senatorial courtesy
statutory law
trial court

CHAPTER 13
THE SUPREME COURT

judicial activism
judicial restraint
oral argument
original intent
statute
stay
swing vote
textualism
written argument

CHAPTER 14
POLITICAL PARTIES AND INTEREST GROUPS

agricultural subsidy
coalition
dealignment
electorate
elite theory
free rider problem
Great Depression
interest group
litigation
lobby
majoritarianism
party platform
pluralist theory
precinct
public interest group
realignment
right-to-work law
rolling realignment
third party
ward

CHAPTER 15
THE ELECTORAL PROCESS

ballot
endorse
establishment
insurgent
mainstream media
nominating convention
plurality
polarization
polls
progressive tax
soft money
Super PAC

CHAPTER 16 VOTING AND VOTING RIGHTS

absentee voting
Australian ballot
confirmation bias
disenfranchise
franchise
opinion leader
political socialization
polling place
push poll
socialization
socioeconomic factors
special election
straw poll
survey sample

CHAPTER 17
GOVERNMENT AND DOMESTIC POLICY

business cycle
discretionary
entrepreneurship
fiscal policy
fracking
government bond
monetary policy
patent
spending
trade-off
Treasuries

CHAPTER 18
GOVERNMENT AND FOREIGN POLICY

Cold War
containment
détente
deterrence
disarmament
economic sanction
foreign policy
free trade
globalization
intellectual property
interventionism
isolationism
Marshall Plan
Monroe Doctrine
moral idealism
neutrality
outsourcing
political realism
terrorism
Truman Doctrine
quarantine
social distancing

CHAPTER 19
GOVERNMENT, POLITICS, AND THE MEDIA

agenda setting
aggregator
broadcast
data mining
disinformation
fairness doctrine
fringe group
mass media
pundit
social media
spin

CHAPTER 20
STATE GOVERNMENTS

discovery
ordinance
parole
per diem
plea bargain
racial gerrymandering
recall
settlement
special district
term limit

CHAPTER 21
LOCAL GOVERNMENTS

charter
consolidation
flat tax
general sales tax
home rule
municipality
progressive tax
property tax
special district
township
tribal government
zoning

GLOSSARY

A

abolition *n.* the ending of slavery (6.2)

absentee voting *n.* a ballot submitted in advance of an election by a voter who cannot be present at the polls (16.2)

affirmative action *n.* a policy that requires employers and educational institutions to take positive steps to remedy past discrimination (6.5)

agency *n.* an organizational unit of government providing a particular service or concerned with a particular category of functions (11.1)

agenda setting *n.* an attempt to focus attention on a favored plan or goal by foreclosing discussion of competing ideas (19.1)

aggregator *n.* a mass or social medium that collects and retransmits news or opinions from other sources (19.3)

agricultural subsidy *n.* financial assistance to farmers and ranchers from the federal government (14.4)

allegiance *n.* the fidelity owed by a subject or citizen to a sovereign or government; loyalty (3.1)

amendment *n.* a formal change to a law or document (such as a constitution) by parliamentary or constitutional procedure (3.1)

amnesty *n.* a pardon bestowed on an entire class of people (10.2)

antifederalists *n.* people who opposed ratification of the U.S. Constitution because of its emphasis on a strong national government (2.5)

appellate court *n.* a court devoted to the hearing of appeals of decisions of lower courts (3.6)

apportionment *n.* the process of distributing House seats among the states based on their respective populations (7.2)

appropriation *n.* the congressional action of determining how many dollars the government will actually spend in a given year on each particular government activity (9.3)

Articles of Confederation *n.* the first constitution of the United States; a set of laws adopted in 1777 that established each state in the Union as a republic, replaced by the U.S. Constitution in 1789 (2.4)

assimilation *n.* a policy of absorption and integration of Native Americans into American society (6.4)

Australian ballot *n.* a secret ballot that is prepared, distributed, and counted by government officials at public expense (16.3)

authoritarian *adj.* refers to governments in which people are required to obey the leaders rather than leaders being required to answer to the people (1.2)

authority *n.* the legitimate, or valid, right to use power (1.1)

authorization *n.* the congressional action that involves specifying the legal basis for government spending (9.3)

autocracy *n.* a government in which power is held by a single person or group of individuals with no accountability to the people (1.2)

B

ballot *n.* a list of candidates that voters mark to indicate their choices in an election (15.1)

bankruptcy *n.* a legal declaration that one is unable to pay all one's debts (8.1)

bicameral *adj.* having two legislative houses (2.5)

bill *n.* a proposed law (9.1)

Bill of Rights *n.* the first 10 amendments to the U.S. Constitution; a list of guarantees to which every person in a country is entitled (1.3)

broadcast *n.* the electronic transmission of information or entertainment to multiple recipients, simultaneously, over a wide area (19.1)

bureaucracy *n.* a large, complex administrative organization that is structured hierarchically (11.1)

business cycle *n.* the alternation between periods of strong economic growth and periods of weak or no growth (17.2)

C

capital crime *n.* a crime punishable by death (12.1)

censorship *n.* the removal of objectionable images or ideas by a person in authority (5.3)

charter *n.* a set of laws that describes the functions of a local government, its organization, and the powers of various officials (21.1)

checks and balances *n.* the system established by the U.S. Constitution that gives each of the branches of government the ability to limit the power of the other two (3.3)

citizenship *n.* the status of owing allegiance to a state and being entitled to its protection (6.1)

civil disobedience *n.* nonviolent refusal to follow a current law or laws (5.4)

civil law *n.* the branch of law that spells out the duties that individuals in society owe to other persons or to their governments, excluding the duty not to commit crimes (12.1)

civil liberty *n.* a legal and constitutional right that protects citizens from government actions (5.1)

civil rights *n.* the rights that enable Americans to participate as equals in public life (6.1)

civil rights movement *n.* a mass movement of the 1950s and 1960s by minorities and concerned Whites to end racial segregation (6.2)

civil service *n.* nonmilitary employees of the government (11.1)

classified *adj.* declared secret by the government (11.4)

cloture *n.* a procedure for closing debate and forcing a vote (7.3)

coalition *n.* an alliance of individuals or groups with a variety of interests and opinions (14.2)

Cold War *n.* a period of hostility without open warfare between the United States and its allies and the Soviet Union and its allies following World War II (18.2)

commerce *n.* business activities; the exchange or buying and selling of commodities on a large scale involving transportation from place to place (3.3)

commerce clause *n.* a clause in section 8, Article I of the Constitution that gives Congress the power to regulate commerce among the states (3.6, 8.1)

common law *n.* the body of law developed from custom and judicial decisions rather than by an act of a legislature (12.1)

communism *n.* a form of government in which all the means of production and transportation are owned by the state (1.4)

compensate *v.* to make amends for past ill treatment (6.4)

confederation n. a voluntary association of independent states (2.4)

confirmation bias *n.* human tendency to interpret experience and information in ways that support what one already believes (16.4)

congress *n.* a conference or meeting held to discuss important issues (2.3)

conservatism *n.* political ideology that holds that government should play a limited role in helping individuals and in economic affairs and supports traditional values and lifestyles (1.4)

consolidation *n.* a step that joins city and county governments to form one unified government (21.2)

containment *n.* an effort to restrict and prevent the spread of communism by offering U.S. military and economic aid to threatened nations (18.2)

contempt of court *n.* a ruling that a person has disobeyed a court order or has shown disrespect to the court or to a judicial proceeding (12.1)

constituents *n.* the voters a member of Congress represents (7.1)

constitution *n.* a set of rules that establishes the framework of a government and the powers of that government (2.1)

copyright *n.* the exclusive legal right to publish, sell, or distribute music or writing (8.1)

cost-benefit analysis *n.* determination of the value of an action by comparison of its total fiscal costs and benefits (11.1)

court-martial *n.* a military court called to try a military service person for crimes (12.3)

credit rating *n.* a numeric score to indicate ability to fulfill financial obligations (5.6)

criminal law *n.* the branch of law that defines and governs actions that constitute crimes; generally, criminal law has to do with wrongful actions committed against society for which society demands redress. (12.1)

cyberbullying *n.* online harassment (5.3)

D

data mining *n.* the practice of using sophisticated analytical methods on large amounts of data to identify patterns (19.3)

dealignment *n.* a political trend in which a large portion of the electorate abandons its previous party affiliation (14.1)

Declaration of Independence *n.* the document declaring U.S. independence from Great Britain, adopted July 4, 1776 (2.3)

de facto segregation *n.* segregation that is present in society even though no laws enforce it (6.2)

defamation *n.* the act of making false statements about a person to hurt his or her reputation (5.3)

deficit *n.* a situation that arises when government expenditures exceed revenues (8.1)

de jure segregation *n.* segregation established by laws (6.2)

delegate *n.* a chosen representative (2.2)

delegate *v.* to assign authority for something (4.1)

demagogue *n.* a leader who makes use of popular prejudices and false claims and promises in order to gain power (3.2)

democracy *n.* a form of government in which the supreme political authority rests with the people (1.2)

deploy *v.* to order troops into action (10.1)

détente *n.* a policy of improved relations with the Soviet Union (18.2)

deterrence *n.* the policy of making the United States and its allies so strong militarily that other countries would be deterred (stopped or discouraged) from attacking (18.2)

devolution *n.* the transfer of powers to political subunits (4.4)

dictatorship *n.* an authoritarian government formed by an individual or group whose power is not supported by tradition (1.2)

disability *n.* a condition that impairs or limits a person's physical or mental abilities, whether it is temporary or permanent (6.4)

disarmament *n.* the reduction of a nation's supply of weapons or the size of its armed forces (18.2)

discovery *n.* the process in legal cases by which the lawyers for the two sides share evidence (20.4)

discretionary spending *n.* government spending that Congress must support each year by an appropriation of funds (17.3)

disenfranchise *v.* to deprive of the right to vote (16.1)

disinformation *n.* false information or propaganda dispersed as part of a plan to deceive or mislead (19.3)

divine right theory *n.* a view of the origin of the state based on the idea that the individual who leads the state is granted the authority to do so by God or gods (1.1)

due process *n.* the right of all persons, not just citizens, to be treated fairly by the judicial system (5.1)

E

earmark *n.* a spending provision inserted into a bill that applies to a small number of constituents (7.1)

economic sanction *n.* a penalty aimed at hurting a country's economy in an effort to get that country to agree to meet certain conditions (18.4)

elastic clause *n.* an alternative name for the "necessary and proper" clause of Article 1, Section 8 of the Constitution because it gives elasticity to the powers of Congress (8.2)

electoral college *n.* a system in which a group of electors selected in each state officially elects the president and vice president; the number of electors for a state is equal to its number of representatives in both chambers of Congress. (2.5)

electorate *n.* the people eligible to vote (14.1)

electors *n.* the people chosen in each state to vote on behalf of that state (3.4)

elites *n.* the most privileged and powerful members of a society (2.5)

elite theory *n.* the view of democracy that contends that the government is controlled by one or more elite groups (14.4)

eminent domain *n.* the power of government to take private land for public use (5.5)

endorse *v.* to express support for publicly (15.2)

entitlement program *n.* government program, such as Social Security, that requires the government to provide specified benefits to persons who qualify (9.3)

entrepreneurship *n.* the willingness to assume the risks of a business or enterprise (17.2)

enumerate *v.* to list one after the other (8.1)

equality *n.* the state of being equal (1.3)

establishment *n.* an elite and powerful group of political and social leaders (15.1)

establishment clause *n.* the clause of the First Amendment that states that Congress cannot establish any national religion (3.5)

executive branch *n.* the part of the government responsible for carrying out the laws (3.1)

executive department *n.* an organization within the executive branch whose head is a member of the Cabinet (11.2)

GLOSSARY

executive order *n.* a presidential order that has the force of law (10.2)

executive privilege *n.* a president's claim to withhold information from Congress and the courts in order to safeguard the internal deliberations of the executive branch (3.2)

expressed powers *n.* the powers specifically assigned to various branches of government in the Constitution (8.1)

F

faction *n.* a group of people with a common interest that might or might not be at odds with the interests of most other people (3.2)

fairness doctrine *n.* a former FCC rule that required television and radio broadcasters to air opposing views on issues of public interest (19.1)

federal *n.* a system of government in which power is shared by a national government and state governments (2.5)

federalism *n.* the distribution of power in an organization (such as a government) between a central authority and the constituent units (3.3)

federalists *n.* people who urged ratification of the U.S. Constitution because of its emphasis on a strong national government (2.5)

federal mandate *n.* an expense required to implement a federal law (11.3)

felony *n.* a serious crime usually involving violence that can be punished by more than a year of imprisonment (12.1)

feminism *n.* a belief or action in support of full political, economic, and social equality for women (6.3)

filibuster *n.* the use of extended debate to delay or block legislation (7.3)

fiscal *adj.* financial (4.4)

fiscal policy *n.* a tool used by the federal government to adjust its spending and taxing in order to influence the economy (17.2)

fiscal year *n.* a 12-month period adopted for accounting purposes (9.3)

flat tax *n.* a tax in which all residents pay the same percentage regardless of income level (21.3)

foreign policy *n.* a systematic plan that guides a country's attitudes and actions toward other countries and international issues (18.1)

fracking *n.* the pumping of a high-pressure mixture of water, sand, and chemicals into oil- or gas-bearing underground rock to release the oil or gas trapped within it (17.4)

Framer *n.* a delegate to the Constitutional Convention (3.1)

franchise *n.* the legally guaranteed right to vote (16.2)

freedmen *n.* formerly enslaved people freed after the U.S. Civil War (6.2)

Freedom of Information Act (FOIA) *n.* a 1967 law establishing the right to request records and information from federal agencies (11.4)

free enterprise system *n.* an economic system in which individuals create private businesses that operate for profit with limited government oversight (1.3)

free rider problem *n.* the existence of persons who benefit from the actions of a group but do not contribute to the group (14.4)

free trade *n.* international commerce with few barriers to trade, like tariffs (18.4)

fringe group *n.* a small group of people who share an uncommon or extreme opinion (19.2)

G

general election *n.* a regularly scheduled election in which all voters choose who will represent them in a public office (7.5)

general sales tax *n.* a tax paid on purchases of goods or services (21.3)

gerrymandering *n.* the shaping of congressional districts for partisan political purposes (7.2)

glass ceiling *n.* an invisible but real discriminatory barrier that prevents women and minorities from rising to top positions of power or responsibility (6.3)

globalization *n.* the development of an integrated, interdependent global exchange of goods, culture, politics, and ideas (18.4)

government *n.* the individuals and groups that make society's rules and also possess the power and authority to guarantee that these rules are followed (1.1)

government bond *n. a* debt issued by the government to raise funds needed to meet expenses (17.2)

grant *n.* a government gift given for a specific purpose (4.4)

Great Compromise *n.* an agreement at the Constitutional Convention that established different methods for apportioning representation in the House and the Senate (2.5)

Great Depression *n.* a worldwide economic depression in the 1930s, marked by poverty and high unemployment (14.1)

green card *n.* a document that grants immigrants permanent resident status that allows them to legally live and work in the United States (6.4)

gross domestic product (GDP) *n.* the total value of all goods and services produced by a country in a year (11.3)

H

home rule *n.* a grant of authority to a local government over certain functions, although the state government still retains overarching authority (21.1)

I

ideologue *n.* an extremely partisan advocate (10.4)

impeach *v.* to formally charge a public official with wrongdoing (2.5)

implied powers *n.* powers indirectly expressed, or implied, by the Constitution (8.2)

incorporation *n.* the inclusion of rights into state and local law (5.1)

incumbent *n.* someone who already holds political office (7.5)

inflation *n.* an overall rise in prices (2.4)

inherent powers *n.* the powers a national government must have by virtue of being a government (8.2)

initiative *n.* a ballot question that allows citizens to vote measures into law or recommend measures to the legislature (1.2)

insurgent *n.* a party member who runs against the party establishment (15.1)

intellectual property *n.* patented, trademarked, and copyrighted inventions and other creations used in commerce (18.4)

interest group *n.* an organized group of people sharing common objectives who attempt to influence government policymakers through direct and indirect methods (14.4)

interstate commerce *n.* the sale, purchase, or trade of goods; transportation of people, money, or goods; navigation of waters between different states (3.6)

interventionism *n.* a policy of direct involvement in foreign affairs (18.2)

isolationism *n.* a policy of avoiding involvement in international affairs (18.2)

J

Jim Crow laws *n.* laws that required segregation, or separation, of the White and Black communities (6.2)

judgment *n.* a court decision (4.2)

judicial activism *n.* the belief that courts should actively use their powers to check the authority of the legislative and executive branches (13.3)

judicial branch *n.* the part of the government responsible for interpreting the laws and resolving controversies (3.1)

judicial restraint *n.* the idea that courts should limit the use of their powers to oppose actions of the legislative and executive branches (13.3)

judicial review *n.* a constitutional doctrine that gives to a court system the power to annul legislative or executive acts judges declare to be unconstitutional (3.6)

judiciary *n.* a system of courts and judges (2.5)

jurisdiction *n.* the authority to interpret and apply the law (7.2)

L

landmark decision *adj.* historic Supreme Court ruling that changes or updates law on a particular topic (4.4)

landslide election *n.* an election in which one candidate receives a notably high majority of the vote (10.3)

lawsuit *n.* a case brought before a court of law (12.1)

legislative branch *n.* the part of the government responsible for making the laws (3.1)

legislature *n.* the lawmaking body of government (2.1)

LGBTQ persons *n.* lesbians, gay men, bisexuals, transgender individuals, and queer or questioning individuals—persons whose sexuality is not easily categorized (6.4)

libel *n.* a published report of a falsehood that is intended to injure a person's reputation or character (5.3)

liberalism *n.* a set of political beliefs that advocate government intervention to promote general well-being and protection of civil rights (1.4)

libertarianism *n.* an ideology that involves opposition to almost all government regulation of the economy (1.4)

liberty *n.* the freedom of individuals to believe, act, and express themselves as they choose so long as doing so does not infringe on the rights of other individuals in the society (1.3)

limited government *n.* a government whose powers and actions are restricted by a system of laws (1.3)

litigation *n.* the act of bringing a lawsuit against another party (14.5)

lobby *v.* seek to influence a government official (5.4)

M

mainstream media *n.* the major television networks and newspapers (15.4)

majoritarianism *n.* a traditional view of American democracy based on the idea that public policy should be set in accordance with the opinions of a majority of the people (14.4)

majority party *n.* the political party that has the majority of members in a legislative body (7.2)

Marshall Plan *n.* a U.S. economic aid program to restore economic stability to Western Europe after World War II (18.2)

mass media *n.* a means of communication designed to reach a mass, or large-scale, audience (19.1)

Mayflower Compact *n.* a social contract signed on the *Mayflower* setting forth rules of government in the new American colony (2.1)

merit system *n.* the hiring and promotion of employees based on demonstrated skills and achievements rather than political loyalty (11.1)

minority party *n.* the party in a legislature with fewer members than the opposing (or majority) party (7.4)

misdemeanor *n.* a crime that is less serious than a felony but is still punishable by a fine or time in jail (12.1)

mistrial *n.* a ruling that a trial has no legal effect due to some error or to a mistake in judicial proceedings (12.1)

moderate *n.* individuals who do not classify themselves as either liberal or conservative but place themselves in or near the center of the political spectrum (1.4)

monetary policy *n.* a tool used by the Federal Reserve System to change the amount of money in circulation in order to influence the economy (17.2)

monopoly *n.* a business that is the sole source of a good or service (11.2)

Monroe Doctrine *n.* a policy of U.S. opposition to intervention in the Western Hemisphere by European powers, announced by President James Monroe in 1823 (18.2)

moral idealism *n.* the belief that the most important goal in foreign policy is to promote the ideals and values of the United States (18.1)

multiculturalism *n.* the belief that the many cultures that make up American society should remain distinct and be protected by laws (1.3)

municipality *n.* a political subdivision, such as a city or town, of a state that is incorporated, or officially recognized as an individual part of the state (21.1)

N

national debt *n.* the total amount of money the federal government owes to investors (11.3)

national security advisor *n.* the president's assistant for national security affairs, who heads the NSC staff and serves as the president's chief in-house advisor on national security (10.4)

NATO *n.* the North Atlantic Treaty Organization, a mutual defense alliance that connects the United States with Canada and more than two dozen other nations, mostly in Europe (9.1)

naturalization *n.* the process by which a person not born in the United States becomes a citizen of the United States (8.1)

necessary and proper clause *n.* often referred to as the elastic clause because it gives elasticity to the constitutional system by stating in Section 8, Article I that Congress can make "all laws which shall be necessary and proper" for carrying out its delegated powers (3.3)

neutrality *n.* a policy of not taking sides in a conflict (18.2)

New Deal *n.* a group of laws, agencies, and programs implemented under President Franklin Roosevelt designed to combat the Great Depression (4.3)

nominating convention *n.* a party meeting to choose candidates (15.1)

nomination *n.* the naming of a candidate to run for elective office on behalf of a political party (7.5)

nullify *v.* to cancel (4.3)

O

omnibus bill *n.* a bill that includes numerous, unrelated issues loaded into the same legislation (9.2)

opinion leader *n.* a well-known person who is able to influence the opinions of others (16.4)

GLOSSARY

oral argument *n.* a presentation by an attorney made in person rather than on paper (13.1)

ordinance *n.* a law passed by a city council or state government (20.4)

original intent *n.* the basic intentions of the Framers of the Constitution (13.3)

original jurisdiction *n.* the power of a court to hear a case for the first time (12.2)

outsourcing *n.* the act of shifting production of goods or services to countries with lower labor costs (18.4)

P

pandemic *n.* an outbreak of disease that affects a large number of people over a wide area (1.1)

pardon *n.* a release from punishment or the legal consequences of a crime that restores the full rights and privileges of citizenship to a person (10.2)

parochial *adj.* church affiliated (5.2)

parole *n.* early release from prison (20.3)

partisan gerrymandering *n.* the drawing of legislative district lines to favor the party drawing the lines (20.2)

partisanship *n.* the strong attachment of people to a political party and the ideals and standards it promotes (1.3)

patent *n.* a license held by an inventor that, for a limited time, excludes anyone else from making, selling, or using his or her invention (17.2)

patronage *n.* the practice of using government or public jobs to reward those who helped victorious candidates win an election (10.1)

party platform *n.* a document drawn up by a political party as a statement of its political positions and principles (14.1)

payroll tax *n.* a tax that employers withhold from an employee's wages and pay on behalf of the employee (11.3)

peonage *n.* the use of laborers bound in servitude because of debt (3.5)

per diem *n.* a payment made to a lawmaker for each day that the legislature is in session (20.2)

petition *n.* a formal written request (4.2)

plea bargain *n.* a plea of guilty to a less serious charge than the original charge (20.4)

pluralist theory *n.* the view that politics is a contest among various interest groups trying to gain benefits for their members (14.4)

plurality *n.* the largest number of votes cast, which may not be a majority when there are more than two options (15.1)

pocket veto *n.* a type of veto that occurs when the president refuses to sign a bill and Congress adjourns within 10 working days after the bill has been submitted to the president (10.2)

polarization *n.* the division into groups holding opposing positions (15.4)

political action committee *n.* an organization formed to raise and spend money to influence elections or legislation (7.5)

political culture *n.* a set of ideas, values, and ways of thinking about government and politics (1.3)

political ideology *n.* a system of political ideas that are rooted in religious or philosophical beliefs about human nature, society, and government (1.4)

political realism *n.* the belief that nations are inevitably selfish (18.1)

political socialization *n.* a social process of acquiring political attitudes, opinions, and beliefs (16.4)

politics *n.* activities aimed at resolving conflicts over the distribution of scarce resources within a society (1.1)

polling place *n.* a location designated for voting (16.3)

polls *n.* the places where people vote in an election (15.1)

poll tax *n.* a tax of a fixed amount per person levied on adults and often linked to the right to vote; abolished by passage of the 24th Amendment in 1964 (3.5)

polygamy *n.* the practice of having more than one spouse simultaneously (5.2)

popular sovereignty *n.* the idea that the people of a country hold the ultimate power (2.3)

preamble *n.* a short introductory statement (3.1)

precedent *n.* an earlier court decision that furnishes an example or authority for deciding later cases (1.3)

precinct *n.* a political district within a city, such as a block or a neighborhood, or a rural portion of a county where a polling place is located (14.2)

presumption of innocence *n.* an expectation or belief that a person is innocent of a crime until proven guilty in a court of law (5.5)

primary election *n.* a preliminary election to choose each party's final candidate for public office (7.5)

prior restraint *n.* the removal of content by a government official prior to broadcast or publication (5.3)

privatization *n.* the hiring or contracting a private business to perform a function on behalf of the government (11.4)

probable cause *n.* a reason for believing that there is a substantial likelihood that a person has committed or is about to commit a crime (5.5)

Proclamation of 1763 *n.* a British law requiring colonists to stay east of the crest of the Appalachian Mountains (2.2)

progressive *n.* a member of a reform movement who seeks to change government and make it more democratic (7.3)

Progressive Era *n.* a period from about 1880 to 1920 in which U.S. reformers sought to correct many social, economic, and political inequalities and injustices (3.5)

progressive tax *n.* a tax with a rate that varies based on the taxpayer's ability to pay (15.2, 21.3)

property tax *n.* a tax levied on homes, other buildings, and land owned by individuals and businesses (21.3)

public interest group *n.* an interest group formed with the broader goal of working for the public good (14.4)

public policy *n.* a plan of action taken by a government to achieve a stated goal (4.1)

public services *n.* services governments provide to all members of a community (1.1)

pundit *n.* someone whose opinions are treated as authoritative (19.2)

push poll *n.* a campaign tactic used to feed false or misleading information to potential voters, under the guise of taking an opinion poll, with the intent to push voters away from one candidate and toward another (16.5)

Q

quarantine *n.* a restraint upon the activities or communication of persons or the transport of goods designed to prevent the spread of disease or pests (18.3)

quota *n.* a fixed number or proportion (6.5)

R

racial discrimination *n.* unjust treatment based on ancestry or physical features (4.3)

racial gerrymandering *n.* drawing legislative district lines to favor one racial group over another (20.2)

ratify *v.* to formally approve (2.5)

realignment *n.* a shift in the relative strength of the political parties as a substantial number of voters shift their political allegiance (14.1)

recall *n.* a procedure in which citizens vote to remove a public official from office (20.2)

recession *n.* economic downturn (4.4)

Reconstruction *n.* the period from 1865 to 1877 when the states that had seceded from the United States were readmitted following the Civil War (6.2)

redistricting *n.* the process of redrawing the boundaries of congressional or legislative districts (7.2)

referendum *n.* a ballot question in which voters have the power to approve a new law or remove an existing law from the books (1.2)

regulation *n.* detailed rules or orders issued by the government and having the force of law (11.1)

republic *n.* a representative democracy with an elected head of state rather than a king or queen (1.2)

republicanism *n.* the belief that a government's power comes from its citizens and the representatives they choose to make their laws (3.2)

resolution *n.* a formal statement of the will or intent of Congress (9.1)

revenue *n.* income (3.5)

right-to-work law *n.* a law that keeps unions from requiring dues or fees from nonunion members, even if they benefit from union-negotiated wages and working conditions in their workplace (14.4)

rolling realignment *n.* a political realignment that occurs over several years as large numbers of legislators as well as voters gradually shift their party loyalties (14.1)

S

search warrant *n.* a document issued by a magistrate or judge indicating the name, address, and possible offense of the person whose property is being searched (5.5)

secession *n.* withdrawal from the Union (4.3)

secular *adj.* having no religious goal or purpose (5.2)

seditious *adj.* urging resistance to lawful authority or overthrow of the government (5.3)

self-government *n.* a government under the control of the people who live in an area rather than that of a distant ruler (2.1)

senatorial courtesy *n.* the practice by which a senator can veto a president's choice for a federal judgeship in that senator's home state (12.2)

separate-but-equal doctrine *n.* the claim that segregated facilities were legal as long as Blacks and Whites were provided separate but equal facilities (6.2)

separation of powers *n.* a political idea from the writings of French philosopher Baron de Montesquieu for dividing power among legislative, executive, and judicial branches (2.3)

session *n.* the period of time in a congressional term during which Congress meets (7.1)

settlement *n.* a mutual agreement by the parties in a lawsuit to end a legal dispute (20.4)

signing statement *n.* a written statement issued by a president at the time he or she signs a bill into law (10.1)

single-member district *n.* an electoral district whose voters elect just one of the members of a legislature (7.2)

slander *n.* a spoken public statement that holds a person up for contempt, ridicule, or hatred (5.3)

slave importation *n.* the business of bringing human beings into the country for the purpose of selling and enslaving them (2.5)

social contract theory *n.* a view of the origin of the state based on the idea that governments began when people agreed to obey a common set of rules, giving up some of their freedom in return for security (1.1)

social distancing *n.* the practice of maintaining substantial physical distance between people in public places to prevent the spread of disease (18.3)

social media *n.* online platforms for communication in which users form communities with which to share information and opinion (19.3)

socialism *n.* an ideology that advocates a system of government in which the welfare of the community, rather than profits, drives the economy (1.4)

socialization *n.* the process of acquiring group characteristics, including norms and the ability to communicate (16.4)

socioeconomic factors *n.* social and economic characteristics that describe individuals and groups in society (16.4)

soft money *n.* money donated to a political party rather than a candidate (15.5)

sovereignty *n.* a characteristic of a state; having the absolute authority to govern itself (1.1)

special district *n.* an independent unit of local government created through state action for a specific purpose, such as a school district; it may operate in the jurisdictions of more than one local government unit (4.1, 20.1, 21.2)

special election *n.* an election held when an issue must be decided before the next general election (16.3)

spin *v.* to attempt to manipulate how an event is interpreted (19.2)

standing committee *n.* a permanent group established in the House or Senate to consider bills that fall within a particular subject area (7.4)

statute *n.* a law enacted by a legislature (13.3)

statutory law *n.* a written law enacted by a legislature (12.1)

stay *v.* to block (13.4)

straw poll *n.* a nonscientific poll that does not ensure that the opinions expressed are representative of the larger population (16.5)

subcommittee *n.* a group composed of members from a standing committee who examine bills or handle certain tasks related to a bill (7.4)

subpoena *n.* a legal order requiring someone to appear to testify or to supply evidence (8.3)

suffrage *n.* the right to vote (3.5)

supermajority *n.* a majority (such as two-thirds or three-fifths) that is significantly greater than a simple majority (3.4)

Super PAC *n.* an independent committee with no limit on the amount of money it can raise to indirectly support a political candidate (15.5)

supremacy clause *n.* the clause in Article VI of the Constitution establishing federal law as the supreme law of the nation, with the power to override state laws (3.1)

surveillance *n.* monitoring actions (5.6)

survey sample *n.* the set, or group, of people who respond to a survey (16.5)

swing vote *n.* a term for a justice who does not vote according to a set ideology but instead decides according to the details of the case at hand (13.4)

syndicate *n.* an organization formed to carry out a particular project (5.4)

T

tariff *n.* a schedule of duties or charges imposed by a government on imported or, in some countries, exported goods (3.5)

taxes *n.* legal requirements for individuals or businesses to pay funds to the government (2.2)

term *n.* the two-year period of time during which a particular Congress meets (7.1)

term limit *n.* a specified maximum number of terms a person is allowed to serve in the same office (3.2, 20.1)

terrorism *n.* the use of planned violence, often against civilians, to achieve political goals (18.3)

textualism *n.* the idea that the plain meaning of the text of a law is all that should be used to review and interpret that law (13.3)

third party *n.* in the United States, any party other than the two major parties (Republican and Democratic) (14.2)

Three-Fifths Compromise *n.* an agreement at the Constitutional Convention to determine representation of enslaved people at the rate of three-fifths of their total population in a state (2.5)

totalitarian *adj.* refers to a government in which a dictatorship sets the goals and controls almost all aspects of a country's social and economic life (1.2)

township *n.* a unit of local government that appears within a county and provides services to areas that are not incorporated as a municipality (21.2)

trade-off *n.* the giving up of one goal to achieve another one (17.1)

transgender person *n.* someone whose internal sense of gender does not match the body with which they were born (6.4)

transsexual *n.* a transgender person who has had or is undergoing sex or gender reassignment surgery (SRS) (6.4)

Treasuries *n.* debt obligations, or IOUs, sold by the U.S. Treasury on behalf of the U.S. government to finance a shortfall in revenue (17.2)

trial court *n.* a court in which issues of fact and law are first heard and determined (12.2)

tribal government *n.* the self-governing authority of a Native American tribe (21.2)

Truman Doctrine *n.* a U.S. Cold War policy, announced by President Truman in 1947, that committed the United States to providing economic and military aid to all countries threatened by a communist takeover (18.2)

U

uncodified *adj.* not collected in a single written code (3.1)

unconstitutional *adj.* in violation of the rules set forth in the Constitution (3.3)

undocumented immigrant *n.* a person who lacks legal documents proving his or her right to live or work in the United States (6.1)

unicameral *adj.* having one legislative house, or chamber (2.4)

V

veto *v.* a president or governor's rejection of a bill passed by the legislative branch (9.2)

voucher program *n.* a government program in which states provide public money to pay for education at private and parochial as well as public schools (3.5)

W

ward *n.* a political division or district within a city (14.2)

welfare *n.* a government program that provides financial support for the needy (4.4)

whistleblower *n.* an insider who reports an agency's or organization's failures or malfeasance to outside authorities (11.4)

writ of *habeas corpus* *n.* an order requiring that an official bring a specified prisoner into court and explain to the judge why the prisoner is being held in jail (5.1)

written argument *n.* a legal brief, or formal written statement, presenting an attorney's position (13.1)

Z

zoning *n.* the legal process of dividing land into specific zones to regulate land development and use (21.1)

ACADEMIC VOCABULARY

acquire *v.* to obtain; to take possession or control of (8.2)

advocate *v.* to support or promote; to argue on behalf of (1.4)

assume *v.* to presume; to take as granted or true (5.1, 5.6)

cite *v.* to quote or mention as proof or evidence (16.1, 16.3)

classic *adj.* serving as an example; definitive or historically notable (8.3)

collapse *v.* to topple or fall; to lose significance or force (1.2, 1.4)

complicated *adj.* involving many steps or parts; difficult to explain or understand (17.1)

comply *v.* to abide by; to conform to or follow as required or requested (12.1, 12.3)

comprehensive *adj.* inclusive; completely or broadly (15.4)

consider *v.* to believe; to think about; to take into account (19.1, 19.2, 19.3)

controversial *adj.* arguable; marked by expressions of opposing views (8.1, 8.2)

convene *v.* to assemble; to meet together in a body (7.1, 7.3)

coordinating *v.* to match efforts; to bring into a common action (14.2)

crucial *adj.* critical, important or essential (2.1)

despite *prep.* regardless, in spite of (16.1, 16.2, 16.3, 16.4, 16.5)

diminish *v.* to lessen, decrease, or reduce (14.4)

diverse *adj.* distinct; made up of elements that differ from one another (20.2, 20.3, 20.4)

dominate *v.* to overpower; to rule or control (11.3)

enhance *v.* to improve; to embellish; to increase in quality or appeal (10.1, 10.2, 15.2)

ensure *v.* to guarantee; to make certain (9.1, 9.2, 9.3)

estimated *adj.* supposed; judged, roughly determined (21.3)

eventuality *n.* possibility; possible event or outcome (3.4)

explicit *adj.* specific; clear, with no vagueness or ambiguity (5.1, 5.4)

facilitate *v.* to assist; to make easier or to help bring about (16.1)

flexibility *n.* the ability to bend without breaking; the quality of being able to adapt to new, different, or changing requirements (3.6)

fundamental *adj.* essential; basic; of central importance (20.4)

generate *v.* to produce; to bring into existence; to cause (21.2)

hierarchical *adj.* ranked; arranged according to levels of power or responsibility; organized according to economic, social, or professional standing (11.1, 11.2)

implement *v.* to enact; to carry out, to accomplish (4.1, 4.3, 4.4)

implicitly *adv.* in a way that is understood but not stated directly (13.3)

imply *v.* to express indirectly (5.4, 5.6)

impose *v.* to dictate; to force upon; to establish or apply by authority (2.1, 2.4, 2.5)

inevitable *adj.* impossible to avoid or escape (1.1)

initiate *v.* to introduce; to cause to begin (6.2)

integral *adj.* essential; a required element for completion (19.3)

intense *adj.* excessive; extreme; marked by great energy, determination, or concentration (14.5)

interpret *v.* to make sense of; to explain or tell the meaning of (12.2)

intervene *v.* to interfere with the outcome; to come between to prevent or change an outcome (18.2)

issue *v.* to put forth; to publish or distribute in an official manner (3.3, 3.6)

justify *v.* to defend; to show to be right or reasonable (13.4)

negotiate *v.* to bargain; to accomplish through discussion and compromise (18.1, 18.2)

normally *adv.* as usual; in a way that is typical or regular (17.1, 17.3)

perceive *v.* to grasp; to attain understanding or awareness; to become aware of (13.3, 13.4)

presumably *adj.* seemingly; by reasonable assumption (7.3)

prospective *adj.* having the quality of potential; likely to become (15.2)

pursue *v.* to seek; to employ measures to accomplish (10.1, 10.2)

radically *adv.* entirely; in essence; in an extreme manner (4.3)

register *v.* to sign up; to enroll formally, for example as a voter or a student (10.2)

relevant *adj.* applicable; significant to the matter being considered (9.1, 9.2, 9.3)

reluctant *adj.* cautious or hesitant; unwilling (17.2)

restrict *v.* to limit or restrain (4.1, 4.3, 4.4)

retain *v.* to hold on to; to keep (7.2)

status *n.* condition or rank in the eyes of the law; position within a hierarchy or in relation to others (6.1)

subsequent *adj.* later; following (6.4)

supplement *v.* to enhance; to add to (19.2)

sustainable *adj.* maintainable; a way of using a resource so that it is neither depleted nor damaged (21.1)

technique *n.* a method of getting something done; a specialized approach to accomplishing an art or a craft (9.1, 9.2)

ultimate *adj.* final or last in a series; eventual; best or most extreme of its kind (18.1, 18.4)

undergo *v.* to experience; to endure or submit to (20.1)

underlying *adj.* fundamental, basic; lying beneath or below (11.4)

valid *adj.* credible, well-grounded; having legal standing; logically correct (12.1, 12.2)

violate *v.* to break an agreement; to disregard, as in a law; to disturb or interrupt (2.1, 2.2, 2.3)

GLOSARIO

A

abolición *s.* el fin de la esclavitud (6.2)

acción afirmativa *s.* política que exige a los empleadores y a las instituciones educativas que adopten medidas positivas para remediar la discriminación del pasado (6.5)

activismo judicial *s.* creencia de que los tribunales deben utilizar activamente su poder para controlar la autoridad de las ramas legislativa y ejecutiva (13.3)

acuerdo de conciliación *s.* acuerdo mutuo entre las partes en un litigio para poner fin a una disputa legal (20.4)

administración pública *s.* empleados no militares del gobierno (11.1)

agencia *s.* unidad organizativa de gobierno que presta un servicio determinado o se ocupa de una categoría particular de funciones (11.1)

agregador *s.* medio de masas o social que recoge y retransmite noticias u opiniones de otras fuentes (19.3)

aislacionismo *s.* política que evita la participación en los asuntos internacionales (18.2)

amnistía *s.* perdón que se concede a toda una clase de personas (10.2)

análisis de costo-beneficio *s.* determinación del valor de una acción mediante la comparación de sus costos y beneficios fiscales totales (11.1)

antifederalistas *s.* personas que se oponían a la ratificación de la Constitución de los Estados Unidos porque el énfasis de esta era un gobierno nacional fuerte (2.5)

año fiscal *s.* período de 12 meses adoptado a efectos contables (9.3)

aplazar *v.* bloquear (13.4)

arancel *s.* una lista de derechos o cargos impuestos por un gobierno a las mercancías importadas o, en algunos países, exportadas (3.5)

argumentación escrita *s.* escrito legal o declaración formal por escrito que presenta la posición de un abogado (13.1)

argumento oral *s.* presentación de un abogado hecha en persona y no en papel (13.1)

Artículos de la Confederación *s.* la primera constitución de los Estados Unidos; un conjunto de leyes adoptadas en 1777 que establecía cada estado de la Unión como una república, reemplazado por la Constitución de los Estados Unidos en 1789 (2.4)

asignación *s.* acción del Congreso por la que se establece cuántos dólares gastará realmente el gobierno en un año determinado en cada actividad gubernamental específica (9.3)

asimilación *s.* política de absorción e integración de los indígenas norteamericanos en la sociedad estadounidense (6.4)

autocracia *s.* gobierno en el que el poder está en manos de una sola persona o grupo de personas sin obligación de rendir cuentas al pueblo (1.2)

autogobierno *s.* gobierno bajo el control de la gente que vive en una zona y no de un gobernante lejano (2.1)

autonomía local *s.* concesión de autoridad a un gobierno local sobre ciertas funciones, aunque el gobierno del Estado sigue conservando la autoridad general (21.1)

autoridad *s.* el derecho legítimo, o válido, de utilizar el poder (1.1)

autoritario *adj.* se refiere a los gobiernos en los que el pueblo está obligado a obedecer a los líderes en lugar de que los líderes rindan cuentas ante el pueblo (1.2)

autorización *s.* acción del congreso que implica especificar la base legal del gasto del gobierno (9.3)

B

bancarrota *s.* declaración legal de que uno no puede pagar todas sus deudas (8.1)

bicameral *adj.* que tiene dos cámaras legislativas (2.5)

bienestar social *s.* programa gubernamental que brinda apoyo financiero a personas necesitadas (4.4)

boleta *s.* lista de candidatos que los votantes marcan para indicar sus preferencias en una elección; papeleta (15.1)

boleta australiana *s.* votación con boleta secreta que es preparada, distribuida y contada por funcionarios del gobierno y financiada con fondos públicos (16.3)

bono del gobierno *s.* deuda emitida por el gobierno para recaudar los fondos necesarios para hacer frente a los gastos (17.2)

bonos del Tesoro *s.* obligaciones de deuda, o pagarés, vendidos por el Tesoro de los Estados Unidos en nombre del gobierno de los Estados Unidos para financiar un déficit de ingresos (17.2)

burocracia *s.* organización administrativa grande y compleja que está estructurada jerárquicamente (11.1)

C

cabildear *v.* tratar de influenciar a un funcionario del gobierno; presionar; *lobby* (5.4)

calificación crediticia *s.* una puntuación numérica que indica la capacidad de una persona de cumplir con sus obligaciones financieras (5.6)

calumnia *s.* declaración pública hablada que califica a una persona con desprecio, ridículo u odio (5.3)

carta *s.* un conjunto de leyes que describe las funciones de un gobierno local, su organización y los poderes de varios funcionarios (21.1)

causa probable *s.* razón para creer que existe una gran probabilidad de que una persona haya cometido o esté a punto de cometer un delito (5.5)

censura *s.* eliminación de imágenes o ideas cuestionables por parte de una persona con autoridad (5.3)

censura previa *s.* retiro de contenido por un funcionario del gobierno antes de la difusión o publicación de cierta información (5.3)

centro de votación *s.* lugar designado para votar (16.3)

ciberacoso *s.* acoso por medios digitales o en línea; ciberbullying (5.3)

ciclo económico *s.* alternancia entre períodos de fuerte crecimiento económico y períodos de crecimiento débil o nulo (17.2)

citación *s.* orden legal que requiere que alguien se presente a testificar o a suministrar evidencia (8.3)

ciudadanía *s.* condición de una persona por la cual debe lealtad a un Estado y tiene el derecho de ser protegida por dicho Estado (6.1)

clasificado *adj.* declarado secreto por el gobierno (11.4)

cláusula de comercio *s.* cláusula en la sección 8, artículo I de la Constitución que otorga al Congreso el poder de regular el comercio entre los estados (3.6, 8.1)

cláusula de establecimiento *s.* cláusula de la Primera Enmienda que declara que el Congreso no puede establecer ninguna religión nacional (3.5)

cláusula de supremacía *s.* cláusula del Artículo VI de la Constitución que establece que la ley federal es la ley suprema de la nación, con el poder de anular las leyes estatales (3.1)

cláusula elástica *s.* nombre alternativo para la cláusula "necesaria y adecuada" del artículo 1, sección 8, de la Constitución porque da elasticidad a los poderes del Congreso (8.2)

cláusula necesaria y adecuada *s.* a menudo llamada cláusula elástica porque da elasticidad al sistema constitucional al declarar en la sección 8, artículo I, que el Congreso puede hacer "todas las leyes que sean necesarias y adecuadas" para ejercer sus poderes delegados (3.3)

clientelismo político *s.* práctica de usar el gobierno o los cargos públicos para recompensar a quienes ayudaron a los candidatos victoriosos a ganar una elección (10.1)

cloture (cierre de debate) *s.* un procedimiento para cerrar el debate y forzar una votación (7.3)

coalición *s.* alianza de individuos o grupos con diversos intereses y opiniones (14.2)

colegio electoral *s.* sistema en el que un grupo de electores seleccionados en cada estado elige oficialmente al presidente y al vicepresidente; el número de electores de un estado es igual a su número de representantes en ambas cámaras del Congreso (2.5)

comentarista *s.* persona cuyas opiniones son consideradas como fidedignas (19.2)

comercio interestatal *s.* venta, compra o intercambio de bienes; transporte de personas, dinero o mercancías; navegación por aguas de diferentes estados (3.6)

comercio *s.* actividades comerciales; intercambio o compra y venta de productos a gran escala que implican el transporte de un lugar a otro (3.3)

comité de acción política *s.* organización formada para recaudar y gastar dinero con el fin de influir en las elecciones o en la legislación (7.5)

comité permanente *s.* grupo permanente establecido en la Cámara o en el Senado para considerar proyectos de ley que caen dentro de un área temática particular (7.4)

compensar *v.* reparar los malos tratos sufridos en el pasado (6.4)

Compromiso de las Tres Quintas Partes *s.* acuerdo de la Convención Constitucional para determinar la representación de las personas esclavizadas a razón de tres quintas partes de su población total en un estado (2.5)

comunismo *s.* forma de gobierno en la que todos los medios de producción y transporte son propiedad del Estado (1.4)

confederación *s.* asociación voluntaria de estados independientes (2.4)

congreso *s.* conferencia o reunión celebrada para discutir cuestiones importantes (2.3)

consejero de seguridad nacional *s.* asistente del presidente para asuntos de seguridad nacional, quien dirige el personal del Consejo de Seguridad Nacional (NSC) y sirve como asesor interno principal del presidente en materia de seguridad nacional (10.4)

conservadurismo *s.* ideología política que sostiene que el gobierno debe desempeñar un papel limitado en la ayuda a los individuos y en los asuntos económicos y apoya los valores y estilos de vida tradicionales (1.4)

consolidación *s.* paso que une los gobiernos de las ciudades y los condados para formar un gobierno unificado (21.2)

constitución *s.* conjunto de reglas que establecen el marco de un gobierno y los poderes de ese gobierno (2.1)

contención *s.* esfuerzo por restringir y prevenir la propagación del comunismo ofreciendo ayuda militar y económica de los Estados Unidos a naciones amenazadas (18.2)

convención de nominación *s.* reunión de un partido para elegir candidatos (15.1)

corte marcial *s.* tribunal militar llamado a juzgar a una persona de las fuerzas armadas por delitos (12.3)

cortesía senatorial *s.* práctica por la cual un senador puede vetar la elección de un presidente para una judicatura federal en su estado natal (12.2)

crimen capital *s.* un delito castigado con la pena de muerte (12.1)

cuarentena *s.* restricción de las actividades o comunicaciones de las personas o del transporte de bienes con el fin de evitar la propagación de enfermedades o plagas (18.3)

cultura política *s.* conjunto de ideas, valores y formas de pensar sobre el gobierno y la política (1.3)

cupo *s.* número o proporción fija; cuota (6.5)

D

debido proceso *s.* el derecho de todas las personas, no solo de los ciudadanos, a recibir un trato justo por parte del sistema judicial (5.1)

decisión histórica *s.* fallo histórico de la Corte Suprema que cambia o actualiza la ley sobre un tema específico (4.4)

Declaración de Derechos *s.* las 10 primeras enmiendas a la Constitución de los Estados Unidos; lista de garantías a las que tienen derecho todas las personas de un país (1.3)

declaración de firma *s.* declaración escrita emitida por un presidente en el momento de ratificar un proyecto de ley (10.1)

Declaración de Independencia *s.* documento que declara la independencia de los Estados Unidos de Gran Bretaña, adoptado el 4 de julio de 1776 (2.3)

déficit *s.* situación que se produce cuando los gastos del gobierno superan los ingresos (8.1)

delator *s.* persona de adentro que informa a las autoridades externas sobre las fallas o malas prácticas de una agencia u organización (11.4)

delegado *s.* representante elegido (2.2)

delegar *v.* asignar autoridad para hacer algo (4.1)

delito grave *s.* delito grave que suele implicar violencia y que puede ser castigado con más de un año de prisión (12.1)

delito menor *s.* delito menos grave que un delito mayor, pero que aún así se castiga con una multa o un tiempo de cárcel (12.1)

demagogo *s.* líder que hace uso de prejuicios populares y de afirmaciones y promesas falsas para ganar poder (3.2)

demanda *s.* caso presentado ante un tribunal de justicia (12.1)

democracia *s.* forma de gobierno en la que la autoridad política suprema recae en el pueblo (1.2)

departamento ejecutivo *s.* organización del poder ejecutivo cuyo jefe es miembro del Gabinete (11.2)

derecho civil *s.* rama del derecho que establece los deberes que los individuos de la sociedad tienen hacia otras personas o hacia sus gobiernos, excluido el deber de no cometer delitos (12.1)

derecho común *s.* cuerpo de leyes elaborado a partir de la costumbre y las decisiones judiciales más que por una ley del poder legislativo (12.1)

derecho penal *s.* rama del derecho que define y rige las acciones que constituyen delitos; en general, el derecho penal tiene que ver con las acciones ilícitas cometidas contra la sociedad por las que esta exige reparación (12.1)

derechos civiles *s.* los derechos que permiten a los estadounidenses participar como iguales en la vida pública (6.1)

GLOSARIO

derechos de autor *s.* el derecho legal exclusivo de publicar, vender o distribuir música o escritos (8.1)

desacato a la corte *s.* fallo de que una persona ha desobedecido una orden judicial o ha mostrado falta de respeto a la corte o a un procedimiento judicial (12.1)

desarme *s.* reducción del suministro de armas de una nación o del tamaño de sus fuerzas armadas (18.2)

desinformación *s.* información falsa o propaganda que se difunde como parte de un plan para engañar o desorientar (19.3)

desobediencia civil *s.* negarse de forma no violenta a seguir una o varias leyes vigentes (5.4)

desplegar *v.* ordenar a las tropas que entren en acción (10.1)

desvinculación *s.* tendencia política en la que una gran parte del electorado abandona su anterior afiliación a un partido político (14.1)

détente *s.* una política de mejora de las relaciones con la Unión Soviética; distensión (18.2)

deuda nacional *s.* cantidad total de dinero que el gobierno federal debe a los inversionistas (11.3)

devolución *s.* la transferencia de poderes a subunidades políticas (4.4)

dictadura *s.* gobierno autoritario formado por un individuo o grupo cuyo poder no cuyo poder no está respaldado por la tradición (1.2)

dietas *s.* pagos hechos a un legislador por cada día que la legislatura está en sesión (20.2)

difamación *s.* el acto de hacer declaraciones falsas sobre una persona para dañar su reputación (5.3)

difusión *s.* transmisión electrónica de información o entretenimiento a múltiples destinatarios, simultáneamente, en un área amplia (19.1)

dinero blando *s.* dinero donado a un partido político en vez de a un candidato (15.5)

discapacidad *s.* condición que perjudica o limita las capacidades físicas o mentales de una persona, ya sea de manera temporal o permanente (6.4)

discriminación racial *s.* tratamiento injusto basado en la ascendencia o en características físicas (4.3)

distanciamiento social *s.* práctica de mantener una distancia física sustancial entre las personas en lugares públicos para evitar la propagación de enfermedades (18.3)

distribución *s.* el proceso de dividir proporcionalmente los escaños de la Cámara de Representantes entre los Estados en función de sus respectivas poblaciones (7.2)

distrito electoral *s.* división política o distrito dentro de una ciudad (14.2)

distrito especial *s.* unidad independiente de gobierno local creada por la acción estatal para un fin específico, como un distrito escolar; puede operar en las jurisdicciones de más de una unidad de gobierno local (4.1, 20.1, 21.2)

distrito unipersonal *s.* distrito electoral cuyos votantes eligen a uno solo de los miembros de una legislatura (7.2)

disuasión *s.* la política de hacer a los Estados Unidos y sus aliados tan fuertes militarmente que otros países se disuadan (se detengan o se desalienten) de atacar (18.2)

Doctrina Monroe *s.* política de oposición de los Estados Unidos a la intervención de las potencias europeas en el Hemisferio Occidental, anunciada por el presidente James Monroe en 1823 (18.2)

doctrina separados pero iguales *s.* afirmación de que las instalaciones segregadas son legales siempre y cuando se provea a negros y blancos de instalaciones separadas pero iguales (6.2)

Doctrina Truman *s.* política estadounidense de la Guerra Fría, anunciada por el presidente Truman en 1947, que comprometía a los Estados Unidos a suministrar ayuda económica y militar a todos los países amenazados por una toma de poder comunista (18.2)

dominio eminente *s.* poder del gobierno de tomar tierras privadas para uso público; expropiación (5.5)

E

earmark (asignación con un fin específico) *s.* disposición de gastos que se incluye en un proyecto de ley que se aplica a un pequeño número de electores (7.1)

elección especial *s.* elección que se realiza cuando una cuestión debe decidirse antes de las próximas elecciones generales (16.3)

elección general *s.* elección programada regularmente en la que todos los votantes eligen quién los representará en un cargo público (7.5)

elección primaria *s.* elección preliminar para elegir al candidato final de cada partido para un cargo público (7.5)

electorado *s.* personas con derecho a voto (14.1)

electores *s.* personas elegidas en cada estado para votar en nombre de ese estado (3.4)

élites *s.* miembros más privilegiados y poderosos de una sociedad (2.5)

emprendimiento *s.* voluntad de asumir los riesgos de un negocio o empresa (17.2)

encuesta de presión *s.* táctica de campaña política que se usa para dar información falsa o engañosa a posibles votantes, bajo la apariencia de una encuesta de opinión, con la intención de alejar a los votantes de un candidato y acercarlos a otro (16.5)

encuesta informal *s.* encuesta no científica que no garantiza que las opiniones expresadas sean representativas de la población en general (16.5)

enmienda *s.* cambio formal en una ley o documento (como una constitución) por parte del parlamento o mediante un procedimiento constitucional (3.1)

enumerar *v.* listar uno tras otro (8.1)

Era Progresista *s.* período de 1880 a 1920 en el que reformadores de los Estados Unidos trataron de corregir muchas desigualdades e injusticias sociales, económicas y políticas (3.5)

establecimiento de la agenda *s.* un intento de centrar la atención en un plan o meta favorecidos excluyendo el debate de ideas en conflicto (19.1)

establishment (poder establecido) *s.* grupo elitista y poderoso de líderes políticos y sociales (15.1)

estatuto *s.* ley aprobada por una legislatura (13.3)

externalización *s.* acto de trasladar la producción de bienes o servicios a países con menores costos laborales; tercerización (18.4)

F

facción *s.* grupo de personas con un interés común que puede o no estar en desacuerdo con los intereses de la mayoría de las otras personas (3.2)

factores socioeconómicos *s.* características sociales y económicas que describen a los individuos y grupos de la sociedad (16.4)

federal *adj.* se dice del sistema de gobierno en el que el poder es compartido por un gobierno nacional y los gobiernos estatales (2.5)

federalismo *s.* la distribución del poder en una organización (como un gobierno) entre una autoridad central y las unidades constitutivas (3.3)

federalistas *s.* personas que apoyaban la ratificación de la Constitución de los Estados Unidos porque el énfasis de esta era un gobierno nacional fuerte (2.5)

feminismo *s.* creencia o acción en apoyo de la plena igualdad política, económica y social de las mujeres (6.3)

fiscal *adj.* financiero (4.4)

fractura hidráulica *s.* bombeo de una mezcla de agua, arena y productos químicos a alta presión en una roca subterránea portadora de petróleo o gas para liberar el petróleo o el gas atrapado en ella; *fracking* (17.4)

Framer (autor de la Constitución) *s.* delegado en la Convención Constitucional (3.1)

franchise *s.* derecho de voto garantizado por ley (16.2)

G

gasto discrecional *s.* gastos del gobierno que el Congreso debe financiar cada año con una asignación de fondos (17.3)

gerrymandering (manipulación de distritos electorales) *s.* conformación de los distritos del Congreso con fines políticos partidistas (7.2)

gerrymandering partidista (manipulación partidista de distritos electorales) *s.* trazado de las líneas de distritos legislativos para favorecer al partido que las traza (20.2)

gerrymandering racial (manipulación de distritos electorales con motivos raciales) *s.* trazado de las líneas de distritos legislativos para favorecer un grupo racial sobre otro (20.2)

globalización *s.* desarrollo de un intercambio mundial integrado e interdependiente de bienes, cultura, política e ideas (18.4)

gobierno *s.* individuos y grupos que hacen las reglas de la sociedad y que también poseen el poder y la autoridad para garantizar que estas reglas se cumplan (1.1)

gobierno limitado *s.* gobierno cuyos poderes y acciones están restringidos por un sistema de leyes (1.3)

gobierno tribal *s.* autoridad de autogobierno de las tribus indígenas norteamericanas (21.2)

Gran Compromiso *s.* acuerdo en la Convención Constitucional que estableció diferentes métodos para la distribución de la representación en la Cámara de Representantes y el Senado (2.5)

Gran Depresión *s.* depresión económica mundial en la década de 1930, caracterizada por la pobreza y el alto desempleo (14.1)

grupo de interés público *s.* grupo de interés formado con el objetivo más amplio de trabajar por el bien público (14.4)

grupo de intereses especiales *s.* grupo organizado de personas que comparten objetivos comunes y que tratan de influir en los responsables de las políticas gubernamentales mediante métodos directos e indirectos (14.4)

grupo de presión *s.* grupo de personas que participan en actividades destinadas a influir en las acciones del gobierno; cabilderos (14.4)

grupo marginal *s.* pequeño grupo de personas que comparten una opinión poco común o extrema (19.2)

Guerra Fría *s.* período de hostilidad sin guerra abierta entre, por un lado, Estados Unidos y sus aliados y, por otro lado, la Unión Soviética y sus aliados después de la Segunda Guerra Mundial (18.2)

I

idealismo moral *s.* creencia de que el objetivo más importante de la política exterior es promover los ideales y valores de los Estados Unidos (18.1)

ideología política *s.* sistema de ideas políticas arraigadas en creencias religiosas o filosóficas sobre la naturaleza humana, la sociedad y el gobierno (1.4)

ideólogo *s.* un activista extremadamente partidario (10.4)

igualdad *s.* el estado de ser igual (1.3)

impeach (someter a juicio político) *v.* acusar formalmente a un funcionario público por mala conducta en el cargo (2.5)

importación de esclavos *s.* negocio de introducir seres humanos en el país con el propósito de venderlos y esclavizarlos (2.5)

impuesto de tasa única *s.* impuesto en el que todos los residentes pagan el mismo porcentaje independientemente de su nivel de ingresos (21.3)

impuesto electoral *s.* impuesto de una cantidad fija por persona que se cobraba a los adultos y que a menudo estaba vinculado al derecho de voto; abolido por la aprobación de la 24a Enmienda en 1964 (3.5)

impuesto general sobre las ventas *s.* impuesto pagado sobre las compras de bienes o servicios (21.3)

impuesto progresivo *s.* impuesto cuya tasa varía según la capacidad de pago del contribuyente (15.2, 21.3)

impuesto sobre la nómina *s.* impuesto que los empleadores retienen del salario de un empleado y lo pagan en su nombre (11.3)

impuesto sobre la propiedad *s.* impuesto aplicado a las casas, otros edificios y terrenos propiedad de individuos y empresas (21.3)

impuestos *s.* requisitos legales para que los individuos o las empresas paguen fondos al gobierno (2.2)

inconstitucional *adj.* que viola las reglas establecidas en la Constitución (3.3)

incorporación *s.* inclusión de derechos en la legislación estatal y local (5.1)

indulto *s.* exoneración de la pena o de las consecuencias legales de un delito que restaura los plenos derechos y privilegios de ciudadanía a una persona (10.2)

inflación *s.* aumento general de los precios (2.4)

ingresos *s.* entradas de fondos públicos (3.5)

iniciativa *s.* pregunta en la boleta electoral que permite a los ciudadanos votar sobre medidas en la ley o recomendar medidas a la legislatura; referendo; plebiscito (1.2)

injuria *s.* informe publicado de una falsedad que tiene por objeto perjudicar la reputación o el carácter de una persona (5.3)

inmigrante indocumentado *s.* persona que carece de documentos legales que prueben su derecho a vivir o trabajar en los Estados Unidos (6.1)

insurgente *s.* miembro del partido que se presenta como candidato contra el poder establecido del partido (15.1)

intención original *s.* intenciones básicas de los autores de la Constitución (13.3)

intervencionismo *s.* política de participación directa en los asuntos exteriores (18.2)

invalidar *v.* cancelar; anular (4.3)

J

judicatura *s.* sistema de tribunales y jueces (2.5)

juicio *s.* una decisión de la corte (4.2)

juicio nulo *s.* decisión de que un juicio no tiene efecto legal debido a algún error o a una equivocación en los procedimientos judiciales (12.1)

jurisdicción original *s.* poder de un tribunal para oír un caso por primera vez (12.2)

jurisdicción *s.* autoridad para interpretar y aplicar la ley (7.2)

L

lealtad *s.* fidelidad que un súbdito o ciudadano debe a un soberano o gobierno; fidelidad (3.1)

legislatura *s.* órgano legislativo del gobierno (2.1)

ley de derecho al trabajo *s.* ley que impide que los sindicatos exijan cuotas o pagos a los miembros no sindicalizados, aunque se beneficien de los salarios y las condiciones laborales en su lugar de trabajo negociados por el sindicato (14.4)

Ley de libertad de información (FOIA) *s.* ley de 1967 que establece el derecho a solicitar registros e información a los organismos federales (11.4)

ley estatutaria *s.* ley escrita aprobada por una legislatura (12.1)

Leyes de Jim Crow *s.* leyes que imponían la segregación, o separación, de las comunidades de personas blancas y negras (6.2)

liberalismo *s.* conjunto de creencias políticas que abogan por la intervención del gobierno para promover el bienestar general y la protección de los derechos civiles (1.4)

libertad *s.* derecho de los individuos de creer, actuar y expresarse como deseen, siempre que al hacerlo no se infrinjan los derechos de los demás individuos de la sociedad (1.3)

libertad civil *s.* derecho legal y constitucional que protege a los ciudadanos de las acciones del gobierno (5.1)

libertad condicional *s.* liberación temprana de la prisión (20.3)

libertarismo *s.* ideología que se opone a casi toda regulación gubernamental de la economía (1.4)

libertos *s.* personas anteriormente esclavizadas liberadas después de la Guerra Civil de los Estados Unidos (6.2)

libre comercio *s.* comercio internacional con pocas barreras a la actividad comercial, como los aranceles (18.4)

líder de opinión *s.* persona conocida capaz de influir en las opiniones de los demás (16.4)

límite de términos *s.* número máximo de períodos que una persona puede servir en el mismo cargo; límite de mandatos (3.2, 20.1)

litigio *s.* el acto de entablar una demanda contra otra parte (14.5)

M

mandato federal *s.* gasto necesario para aplicar una ley federal (11.3)

mayoría cualificada *s.* mayoría (por ejemplo, dos tercios o tres quintos) que es significativamente mayor que la mayoría simple (3.4)

mayoritarismo *s.* visión tradicional de la democracia estadounidense que se basa en la idea de que las políticas públicas deben establecerse de acuerdo con las opiniones de la mayoría del pueblo (14.4)

medios de comunicación de masas *s.* medio de comunicación diseñado para llegar a un público masivo o a gran escala (19.1)

medios de comunicación establecidos *s.* principales cadenas de televisión y periódicos (15.4)

medios sociales *s.* plataformas de comunicación en línea en las que los usuarios forman comunidades con las que compartir información y opiniones (19.3)

minería de datos *s.* la práctica de utilizar métodos analíticos sofisticados en grandes cantidades de datos para identificar patrones (19.3)

moderado *s.* individuos que no se clasifican ni como liberales ni como conservadores, sino que se sitúan en el centro del espectro político o cerca de él (1.4)

monopolio *s.* empresa que es la única fuente de un bien o servicio (11.2)

movimiento por los derechos civiles *s.* un movimiento masivo de las décadas de 1950 y 1960 en el que participaron minorías y personas blancas preocupadas por poner fin a la segregación racial (6.2)

muestra de encuesta *s.* conjunto o grupo de personas que responden a una encuesta (16.5)

multiculturalismo *s.* creencia de que las muchas culturas que componen la sociedad estadounidense deben permanecer diferenciadas y ser protegidas por leyes (1.3)

municipio *s.* subdivisión política, como una ciudad o pueblo, de un estado que está incorporada o reconocida oficialmente como parte individual del estado (21.1)

N

naturalización *s.* proceso mediante el cual una persona que no nació en los Estados Unidos se convierte en ciudadana de este país (8.1)

neutralidad *s.* política de no tomar partido en un conflicto (18.2)

New Deal *s.* leyes, organismos y programas iniciados por el presidente Franklin Roosevelt para combatir la Gran Depresión (4.3)

no codificado *adj.* no recogido en un solo código escrito (3.1)

nominación *s.* designación de un candidato para postularse a un cargo electivo en nombre de un partido político (7.5)

O

obstrucción *s.* uso de extensos debates para retrasar o bloquear la aprobación de una ley (7.3)

orden de *hábeas corpus* *s.* orden que requiere que un funcionario lleve a un prisionero específico a un tribunal y le explique al juez por qué está detenido (5.1)

orden de registro *s.* documento emitido por un magistrado o juez indicando el nombre, la dirección y el posible delito de la persona cuyos bienes o propiedades se están registrando (5.5)

orden ejecutiva *s.* orden presidencial que tiene fuerza de ley (10.2)

ordenanza *s.* ley aprobada por un consejo municipal o un gobierno estatal (20.4)

OTAN *s.* Organización del Tratado del Atlántico Norte, una alianza de defensa mutua que conecta a los Estados Unidos con Canadá y más de dos docenas de otras naciones, principalmente en Europa (9.1)

P

Pacto del Mayflower *s.* contrato social firmado en el *Mayflower* que establece las reglas de gobierno en la nueva colonia americana (2.1)

pandemia *s.* brote de una enfermedad que afecta a un gran número de personas en una amplia área geográfica (1.1)

parroquial *adj.* asociado con la iglesia (5.2)

partidismo *s.* fuerte apego de la gente a un partido político y a los ideales y normas que este promueve (1.3)

partido mayoritario *s.* partido político que tiene la mayoría de miembros en un cuerpo legislativo (7.2)

partido minoritario *s.* partido en una legislatura con menos miembros que el partido opositor (o mayoritario) (7.4)

patente *s.* licencia de un inventor que, por un tiempo limitado, excluye a cualquier otra persona de la fabricación, venta o uso de su invento (17.2)

peonaje *s.* uso de trabajadores en servidumbre hasta cancelar las deudas contraídas (3.5)

persona transgénero *s.* persona cuyo sentido interno del género no coincide con el cuerpo con el que nació (6.4)

personas LGBTQ *s.* lesbianas, gais, bisexuales, transexuales y personas *queer* o que se cuestionan–personas cuya sexualidad no se puede categorizar fácilmente (6.4)

pesos y contrapesos *s.* sistema establecido en la Constitución de los Estados Unidos que da a cada una de las ramas del gobierno la capacidad de limitar el poder de las otras dos (3.3)

petición *s.* solicitud formal por escrito (4.2)

Plan Marshall *s.* programa de ayuda económica de los Estados Unidos para restablecer la estabilidad económica en Europa occidental después de la Segunda Guerra Mundial (18.2)

plataforma del partido *s.* documento redactado por un partido político como declaración de sus posiciones y principios políticos (14.1)

pluralidad *s.* el mayor número de votos emitidos, que puede no ser mayoritario cuando hay más de dos opciones (15.1)

poder ejecutivo *s.* parte del gobierno responsable de que se cumplan las leyes; rama ejecutiva (3.1)

poder judicial *s.* parte del gobierno responsable de interpretar las leyes y resolver disputas; rama judicial (3.1)

poder legislativo *s.* parte del gobierno responsable de hacer las leyes; rama legislativa (3.1)

poderes expresados *s.* poderes específicamente asignados a las distintas ramas del gobierno en la Constitución (8.1)

poderes implícitos *s.* poderes expresados indirectamente, o de manera implícita, por la Constitución (8.2)

poderes inherentes *s.* poderes que un gobierno nacional debe tener en virtud de ser un gobierno (8.2)

polarización *s.* división en grupos que mantienen posiciones opuestas (15.4)

poligamia *s.* práctica de tener más de un cónyuge simultáneamente (5.2)

política *s.* actividades dirigidas a resolver conflictos por la distribución de recursos escasos en una sociedad (1.1)

política exterior *s.* plan sistemático que guía las actitudes y acciones de un país hacia otros países y asuntos internacionales (18.1)

política fiscal *s.* herramienta utilizada por el gobierno federal para ajustar sus gastos e impuestos con el fin de influir en la economía (17.2)

política monetaria *s.* herramienta utilizada por el Sistema de la Reserva Federal para modificar la cantidad de dinero en circulación con el fin de influir en la economía (17.2)

política pública *s.* plan de acción de un gobierno para alcanzar un objetivo declarado (4.1)

poner un sesgo *v.* intentar manipular la interpretación de un acontecimiento (19.2)

preámbulo *s.* breve declaración introductoria (3.1)

precedente *s.* decisión judicial anterior que sirve de ejemplo o autoridad para decidir casos posteriores (1.3)

precinto *s.* división política dentro de una ciudad, como una cuadra o un vecindario, o una porción rural de un condado donde se encuentra un centro de votación (14.2)

presunción de inocencia *s.* expectativa o creencia de que una persona es inocente de un delito hasta que se demuestre su culpabilidad en un tribunal (5.5)

Principio de imparcialidad *s.* una antigua norma de la FCC que obligaba a las emisoras de radio y televisión a emitir puntos de vista opuestos sobre cuestiones de interés público (19.1)

privar del derecho de voto *v.* negar a alguien el derecho de votar (16.1)

privatización *s.* contratación de una empresa privada para desempeñar una función en nombre del gobierno (11.4)

privilegio ejecutivo *s.* facultad del presidente de no divulgar información al Congreso y a los tribunales a fin de salvaguardar las deliberaciones internas del poder ejecutivo (3.2)

problema del *free rider* *s.* existencia de personas que se benefician de las acciones de un grupo pero que no contribuyen al grupo (14.4)

Proclamación de 1763 *s.* ley británica que establecía que los colonos debían mantenerse al este de la línea divisoria de las montañas de los Apalaches (2.2)

producto interno bruto (PIB) *s.* el valor total de todos los bienes y servicios producidos por un país en un año (11.3)

programa de asistencia social *s.* programa gubernamental, como la Seguridad Social, que requiere que el gobierno provea beneficios específicos a las personas que califican (9.3)

programa de cupones *s.* programa gubernamental en el que los estados proveen dinero público para pagar la educación en escuelas privadas y parroquiales, así como en escuelas públicas (3.5)

progresista *s.* miembro de un movimiento de reforma que busca cambiar el gobierno y hacerlo más democrático (7.3)

propiedad intelectual *s.* invenciones patentadas, de marca y con derecho de autor y otras creaciones utilizadas en el comercio (18.4)

proyecto de ley ómnibus *s.* proyecto de ley que incluye numerosas cuestiones no relacionadas entre sí incluidas en la misma legislación (9.2)

proyecto de ley *s.* propuesta de ley (9.1)

R

ratificar *v.* aprobar formalmente (2.5)

realineamiento *s.* cambio en la fuerza relativa de los partidos políticos a medida que un número considerable de votantes cambia su lealtad política (14.1)

realineamiento progresivo *s.* reajuste político que se produce a lo largo de varios años cuando un gran número de legisladores y votantes cambian gradualmente sus lealtades partidistas (14.1)

realismo político *s.* creencia de que las naciones son inevitablemente egoístas (18.1)

recesión *s.* crisis económica (4.4)

Reconstrucción *s.* período de 1865 a 1877 en que los estados que se habían separado de los Estados Unidos fueron readmitidos después de la Guerra Civil (6.2)

redistribución de distritos *s.* proceso de redefinición de los límites de los distritos legislativos o congresionales (7.2)

referendo *s.* pregunta incluida en la boleta electoral sobre la que los votantes tienen el poder de aprobar una nueva ley o eliminar una ley existente de los libros (1.2)

GLOSARIO

reglamento *s.* reglas u órdenes detalladas emitidas por el Gobierno y que tienen fuerza de ley (11.1)

república *s.* democracia representativa con un jefe de estado elegido en lugar de un rey o una reina (1.2)

republicanismo *s.* creencia de que el poder de un gobierno proviene de sus ciudadanos y de los representantes que estos eligen para hacer sus leyes (3.2)

resolución *s.* declaración formal de la voluntad o intención del Congreso (9.1)

respaldar *v.* expresar públicamente el apoyo a un candidato (15.2)

restricción judicial *s.* idea de que los tribunales deben limitar el uso de su poder de oponerse a las acciones de las ramas legislativa y ejecutiva (13.3)

revisión judicial *s.* doctrina constitucional que otorga a un sistema judicial el poder de anular leyes aprobadas en las ramas legislativa o ejecutiva que los jueces declaren inconstitucionales (3.6)

revocatoria *s.* proceso mediante el cual los ciudadanos votan para sacar de su cargo a un funcionario público (20.2)

S

sanción económica *s.* una pena destinada a perjudicar la economía de un país en un esfuerzo por lograr que ese país acepte cumplir ciertas condiciones (18.4)

secesión *s.* separación de la Unión (4.3)

secular *adj.* sin objetivo o propósito religioso (5.2)

sedicioso *adj.* que insta a la resistencia a la autoridad legítima o al derrocamiento del gobierno (5.3)

segregación de facto *s.* segregación que está presente en la sociedad aunque no haya leyes que la establezcan (6.2)

segregación de jure *s.* segregación establecida por la ley (6.2)

sentencia acordada de conformidad *s.* declaración de culpabilidad por un cargo menos grave que el original (20.4)

separación de poderes *s.* idea política de los escritos del filósofo francés Barón de Montesquieu para dividir el poder entre las tres ramas de gobierno: legislativa, ejecutiva y judicial (2.3)

servicios públicos *s.* servicios que los gobiernos prestan a todos los miembros de una comunidad (1.1)

sesgo de confirmación *s.* tendencia humana a interpretar la experiencia y la información de manera que apoye lo que ya se cree (16.4)

sesión *s.* tiempo en que se reúne el Congreso durante un período congresional (7.1)

sindicato *s.* organización formada para llevar a cabo un proyecto particular (5.4)

sistema de libre empresa *s.* sistema económico en el que los individuos crean empresas privadas que operan con fines de lucro con una supervisión gubernamental limitada (1.3)

sistema de méritos *s.* contratación y promoción de empleados basadas en habilidades y logros demostrados, en vez de en la lealtad política (11.1)

soberanía *s.* característica de un estado que tiene la autoridad absoluta para gobernarse a sí mismo (1.1)

soberanía popular *s.* idea de que el pueblo de un país tiene el poder supremo (2.3)

socialismo *s.* ideología que aboga por un sistema de gobierno en el que la economía está impulsada por el bienestar de la comunidad, en vez de por los beneficios (1.4)

socialización *s.* proceso de adquisición de características de grupo, incluidas normas y capacidad de comunicación (16.4)

socialización política *s.* proceso social de adquisición de actitudes, opiniones y creencias políticas (16.4)

solución de compromiso *s.* abandono de un objetivo para lograr otro (17.1)

subcomité *s.* grupo compuesto por miembros de una comisión permanente que examina proyectos de ley o se ocupa de ciertas tareas relacionadas con un proyecto de ley (7.4)

subsidio agrícola *s.* ayuda financiera a los agricultores y ganaderos por parte del gobierno federal (14.4)

subvención *s.* dinero que el gobierno regala para un propósito específico (4.4)

sufragio *s.* derecho a votar (3.5)

Súper PAC *s.* comité independiente que no tiene límites en cuanto a la cantidad de dinero que puede recaudar para apoyar indirectamente a un candidato político (15.5)

T

tarjeta verde *s.* documento que otorga a los inmigrantes el estatus de residente permanente que les permite vivir y trabajar legalmente en los Estados Unidos (6.4)

techo de cristal *s.* barrera discriminatoria invisible pero real que impide que las mujeres y las minorías lleguen a puestos de poder o responsabilidad (6.3)

teoría de la élite *s.* visión de la democracia que sostiene que el gobierno está controlado por uno o más grupos de élite (14.4)

teoría del contrato social *s.* visión del origen del estado basada en la idea de que los gobiernos comenzaron cuando la gente acordó obedecer un conjunto de reglas comunes, renunciando a algunas de sus libertades a cambio de seguridad (1.1)

teoría del derecho divino *s.* una visión del origen del Estado basada en la idea de que la autoridad de un individuo para gobernar en el Estado proviene de Dios o los dioses (1.1)

teoría pluralista *s.* opinión de que la política es una competencia entre varios grupos de interés que tratan de obtener beneficios para sus miembros (14.4)

tercer partido *s.* en los Estados Unidos, cualquier partido que no sean los dos principales (republicano y demócrata) (14.2)

término *s.* período de dos años durante el cual se reúne un Congreso particular; mandato (7.1)

terrorismo *s.* uso de violencia planificada, a menudo contra civiles, para lograr objetivos políticos (18.3)

textualismo *s.* idea de que el significado simple del texto de una ley es todo lo que se debe usar para revisar e interpretar esa ley (13.3)

titular *s.* alguien que ya tiene un cargo político (7.5)

totalitario *adj.* se refiere a un gobierno en el que una dictadura establece los objetivos y controla casi todos los aspectos de la vida social y económica de un país (1.2)

township (subdivisión administrativa) *s.* unidad de gobierno local que aparece dentro de un condado y que presta servicios a áreas que no están incorporadas como municipio (21.2)

transexual *s.* persona transgénero que ha tenido o está pasando por una cirugía de reasignación de sexo o de género (SRS) (6.4)

tribunal de apelación *s.* tribunal dedicado a la audiencia de las apelaciones de las decisiones de los tribunales inferiores (3.6)

tribunal de primera instancia *s.* tribunal en el que se escuchan y determinan por primera vez cuestiones de hecho y de derecho (12.2)

U

unicameral *adj.* que tiene una cámara legislativa (2.4)

urnas *s.* lugares donde la gente vota en una elección (15.1)

V

veto *s.* rechazo del presidente o del gobernador de un proyecto de ley aprobado por el poder legislativo (9.2)

veto de bolsillo *s.* tipo de veto que se produce cuando el presidente se niega a firmar un proyecto de ley y el Congreso levanta la sesión dentro de los 10 días hábiles siguientes a la presentación del proyecto al presidente (10.2)

victoria aplastante *s.* elección en la que un candidato recibe una mayoría muy alta de los votos (10.3)

vigilancia *s.* acciones de monitoreo (5.6)

vista *s.* proceso en los casos legales por el cual los abogados de ambas partes comparten las pruebas; descubrimiento (20.4)

votantes *s.* personas con derecho a voto y que están representadas por un miembro del Congreso (7.1)

voto decisivo *s.* término para un juez que no vota según una ideología establecida, sino que decide según los detalles del caso en cuestión (13.4)

voto en ausencia *s.* boleta presentada antes de una elección por un votante que no puede estar presente en las urnas (16.2)

Z

zonificación *s.* proceso legal de dividir la tierra en zonas específicas para regular el desarrollo y el uso de la tierra (21.1)

VOCABULARIO ACADÉMICO

a pesar de *prep.* pese a; aun así; contra su voluntad (16.1, 16.2, 16.3, 16.4, 16.5)

adquirir *v.* obtener; tomar posesión o control de algo (8.2)

abogar *v.* apoyar o promover; defender en juicio a una de las partes (1.4)

aproximado *adj.* estimado; juzgado, que se acerca más o menos a lo exacto (21.3)

asegurar *v.* garantizar; dar certeza de algo (9.1, 9.2, 9.3)

citar *v.* reproducir palabras de otros; mencionar autores o textos para autorizar o justificar lo que se dice o escribe (16.1, 16.3)

clásico *adj.* que se considera como modelo; que no se aparta de lo tradicional, de las reglas establecidas por la costumbre y el uso (8.3)

colapsar *v.* desplomarse; perder significado o fuerza (1.2, 1.4)

complementar *v.* mejorar; añadir; completar (19.2)

complicado *adj.* compuesto de muchos pasos o múltiples piezas; difícil de explicar o comprender (17.1)

cumplir *v.* obedecer; llevar a efecto o seguir las órdenes de (12.1, 12.2)

comprensivo *adj.* completo; entero, con todas las partes que lo componen (15.4)

considerar *v.* creer; meditar; tener en cuenta (19.1, 19.2, 19.3)

controvertido *adj.* polémico; marcado por posturas o pensamientos contrarios (8.1, 8.2)

convocar *v.* reunirse; juntarse varias personas para tratar un asunto (7.1, 7.3)

coordinar *v.* reunir medios, esfuerzos, personas, para una acción común (14.2)

crucial *adj.* decisivo, importante o esencial (2.1)

disminuir *v.* reducir, aminorar, o acortar (14.4)

diverso *adj.* distinto; compuesto de elementos diferentes (20.2, 20.3, 20.4)

dominar *v.* tener poder sobre personas o cosas; controlar (11.3)

estado *n.* posición social según la ley; situación en relación a la jerarquía de clase (6.1)

eventualidad *n.* posibilidad; suceso o resultado posible (3.4)

expedir *v.* remitir; publicar o distribuir de manera oficial (3.3, 3.6)

explícito *adj.* específico; claro, sin ambigüedad o falta de exactitud (5.1, 5.4)

facilitar *v.* prestar ayuda en; hacer más fácil o ayudar a llevar a cabo (16.1)

flexible *adj.* que se adapta fácilmente a los cambios y a las diversas situaciones o circunstancias (3.6)

fundamental *adj.* esencial; básico; de principal importancia (20.4)

generar *v.* producir; crear; causar (21.2)

implementar *v.* dar validez a una ley; llevar a cabo, cumplir (4.1, 4.3, 4.4)

implícito *adv.* sobreentendido; que se entiende sin decirlo directamente (13.3)

imponer *v.* dictar; obligar a hacer; ejercer poder (2.1, 2.4, 2.5)

inevitable *adj.* imposible de evitar o escapar (1.1)

iniciar *v.* comenzar; introducir a alguien (6.2)

inscribirse *v.* apuntarse; registrarse, por ejemplo, como votante o estudiante (10.2)

insinuar *v.* dar a entender algo expresándolo de modo sutil (13.3)

integral *adj.* esencial; un elemento necesario requerido para cumplir algo (19.3)

intenso *adj.* excesivo; extremo; marcado por energía, determinación o concentración (14.5)

interpretar *v.* explicar el sentido o significado de una cosa (12.2)

intervenir *v.* mediar; interceder para prevenir o cambiar el resultado (18.2)

jerárquico *adj.* clasificado; organizado según nivel de poder o responsabilidad; ordenado según criterio económico, posición social o profesional (11.1, 11.2)

justificar *v.* defender; probar la razón (13.4)

mejorar *v.* perfeccionar algo, haciéndolo pasar de un estado bueno a otro mejor (10.1, 10.2, 15.2)

negociar *v.* regatear; tratar un acuerdo mediante el discurso y el compromiso (18.1, 18.2)

normalmente *adv.* habitualmente; de manera ordinaria (17.1, 17.3)

percibir *v.* notar; darse cuenta; comprender o conocer una cosa (13.3, 13.4)

perseguir *v.* tratar de alcanzar algo; emplear medidas para conseguir un fin (10.1, 10.2)

posible *adj.* que puede ser o suceder, o que se puede realizar (7.3)

presumir *v.* dar por hecho; considerar una cosa verdadera o real sin tener certeza completa (10.1, 10.2)

presuntamente *adj.* supuestamente; por conjetura lógica (7.3)

radicalmente *adv.* completamente; en esencia; de manera radical (4.3)

relevante *adj.* pertinente; que es adecuado u oportuno en un momento o una ocasión determinados (9.1, 9.2, 9.3)

restringir *v.* limitar o frenar (4.1, 4.3, 4.4)

retener *v.* quedarse con; conservar (7.2)

reticente *adj.* cauteloso o indeciso; que muestra oposición o resistencia a hacer algo (17.2)

someterse *v.* experimentar; sufrir (20.1)

sostenible *adj.* que se puede mantener; sin agotar o dañar recursos (21.1)

subsiguiente *adj.* posterior; que sigue inmediatamente a lo expresado o sobreentendido como consecuencia de ello (6.4)

subyacente *adj.* fundamental, básico; por debajo (11.4)

técnica *n.* método de hacer algo; procedimiento especializado de un arte o un oficio (9.1, 9.2)

último *adj.* que acaba o concluye una cosa o serie; el mejor o más extremo de su clase (18.1, 18.4)

válido *adj.* creíble, que tiene una buena base; con valor legal; con base lógica (12.1, 12.2)

violar *v.* romper un acuerdo; desobedecer una ley; molestar o interrumpir (2.1, 2.2, 2.3)

INDEX

A

***Ableman* v. *Booth*,** 11.3 p. 340
absentee voting, 6.1 p. 184, 16.2 p. 484, 16.3 pp. 492–493
ADA Amendments Act, 6.4 p. 218
Adams, John, U1 p. 3, 2.2 p. 47, 2.3 p. 48, p. 51, 2.5 p. 58, 3.6 p. 101, 10.1 p. 295, 10.4 p. 320, 14.1 p. 405, p. 406, 15.1 p. 446
Adams, John Quincy, 10.1 p. 295, 14.1 p. 406, p. 407, p. 446
Adams, Samuel, 2.5 p. 58, p. 64
***Adarand Constructors* v. *Peña*,** 6.5 p. 221
administrative law, 12.1 p. 362, 20.4 p. 615
Administrative Procedure Act of 1946, 11.1 p. 328
affirmative action, 6.5 p. 219–223
Affordable Care Act (2010), 1.4 p. 29, 8.2 p. 263, U8 p. 512, 9.1 p. 279, 9.2 p. 283, 10.1 p. 300, 10.3 p. 312, 13.1 p. 380, 13.4 p. 396, 17.3 pp. 526–529, 18.1 p. 515, 21.3 p. 640
African Americans. *See also civil rights movement*
citizenship, 6.1 p. 179
COVID-19 impacting, 18.3 p. 557
disenfranchised felons, 16.2 p. 484
domestic terrorism against, 18.3 p. 549
during Civil War, 4.3 p. 120
Emancipation Proclamation, 2.3 p. 48
in early colonies, 2.1 p. 37
in politics, 6.2 p. 193, 14.1 p. 408, 16.4 p. 500, 20.2 p. 603, 20.3 p. 609
Jim Crow laws, 6.2 p. 188
law enforcement and, 6.2 p. 194
lynching of, 6.2 p. 188
majority-minority districts, 20.2 p. 602
police-involved deaths, 1.3 pp. 22–23
poll taxes, 3.5 p. 93, 3.5 p. 97, R36
protests and riots, 6.2 p. 194
racial and school segregation, 6.2 pp. 188–191, 12.1 p. 361
separate-but-equal doctrine, 6.2 p. 188, p. 189
Thirteenth, Fourteenth, and Fifteenth Amendments, 3.4 p. 88, 5.1 p. 141, 6.1 p. 179, 16.2 p. 480
Twenty-Fourth Amendment, 3.5 p. 97
voting, 2.5 p. 65, 3.4 p. 88, 4.3 p. 122, 4.4 p. 124, p. 126, 6.2 p. 187, p. 188, p. 193, p. 194, 16.2 pp. 480–482, R32
age, voting rights, 16.4 p. 498
Agricultural Act of 2014, 17.1 pp. 515–516
Agricultural Adjustment Act, 4.3 p. 121
agricultural economy, 11.1 p. 330–331
agricultural subsidies, 14.4 p. 430
Aid to Families with Dependent Children (AFDC), 6.4 p. 208
air-pollution control, 4.1 p. 109
al Qaeda, 10.2 p. 309, 11.3 p. 344, 18.3 pp. 549–550, p. 551
Alaska Natives, 6.4 p. 212, 20.1 p. 599
Albright, Madeleine, 6.3 p. 204, 10.4 p. 321
Alien Registration Act, 5.3 p. 156
allegiance, oath of, 3.1 p. 75
alt-right extremists, 18.3 p. 549
amendments, 3.1 p. 74, 3.4 pp. 86–90, 9.2 p. 280. *See also* Bill of Rights; *specific amendments*
America First, 15.5 p. 473
American Association of Retired Persons (AARP), 14.4 p. 425, p. 426, p. 429, p. 433
American Bar Association (ABA), 12.1 p. 366, 14.4 p. 432
American Civil Liberties Union (ACLU), 5.1 p. 141, 14.4 p. 432
American Federation of Labor–Congress of Industrial Organizations (AFL-CIO), 14.4 pp. 430–431
American Independent Party, 14.1 p. 407, 14.3 p. 422
American Indian Movement, 6.4 p. 214
American Israel Public Affairs Committee (AIPAC), 14.4 p. 434
American labor unions, 14.4 p. 431
American law, 12.1 pp. 359–367
American Recovery and Reinvestment Act, 17.2 p. 520, 21.3 pp. 642–643
American Revolution, U1 p. 52, 2.2 p. 44, pp. 42–48, 6.2 p. 187, 12.1 p. 365
American Samoa, 7.2 p. 233
American Woman Suffrage Association (AWSA), 6.3 p. 197
Americans for Democratic Action (ADA), 14.5 p. 437
Americans with Disabilities Act (ADA), 4.4 p. 127p, 6.4 pp. 217–218, 11.3 p. 342, 13.3 p. 388, 14.4 p. 433, 16.2 p. 484
amnesty, 10.2 pp. 304–305
Anglo-Saxon law, 12.1 p. 359
Anti-Defamation League (ADL), 19.3 p. 588
anti-abortion groups, 5.6 p. 170
Antifederalists, 2.5 pp. 63–64, 14.1 p. 405, 14.1 p. 407
antiwar radicals, 18.3 p. 549
apartheid, 18.4 p. 558
appellate court, 3.6 p. 98, 12.2 p. 368.
appropriation bills, 9.1 pp. 274–275, 9.3 p. 285
appropriation committees, 11.1 p. 330–331
***Arizona* v. *Inter-Tribal Council of Arizona*,** 13.3 p. 388
***Arizona* v. *United States*,** 4.4 p. 126, 14.5 p. 438
Armed Services Committee, 18.1 p. 542
ARPANET, 19.3 p. 583
Article I-VII. *See* Constitution, U.S.
Articles of Confederation, 2.4 pp. 53–57, 3.1 p. 71, 4.1 p. 108, 10.1 p. 298
Asian Americans, 1.3 p. 25, 6.4 pp. 211–212, p. 209, p. 213, 16.2 pp. 481–482, p. 480, 16.4 p. 500, 20.3 p. 609
associate justices, role of, 13.1 p. 379
attorney general, 20.3 p. 613
authoritarian governments, 1.1 p. 7, 1.2 pp. 10–12
autocracy, 1.2 p. 11

B

***Bailey* v. *Alabama*,** 3.5 p. 94
***Baker* v. *Carr*,** 7.2 p. 234, p. 236
ballots, 15.1 p. 445, 15.3 pp. 457–458, 16.3 p. 490, p. 492
banking crisis, Great Depression, 1.4 p. 28
bankruptcy, 8.1 pp. 253–254
Barrett, Amy Coney, 8.3 p. 268, 13.4 p. 396, p. 397, R23
***Barron* v. *Baltimore* (1833),** 5.1 p. 141
***Battle of Gettysburg Cyclorama*,** 20.2 p. 607
biased sample, 16.5 p. 502
bicameral, 2.5 p. 59, 3.1 p. 73, p. 74, 7.1 p. 229–231, R15
Biden, Joseph R., 1.3 pp. 23–24, p. 23, p. 24, 6.3 p. 205, 10.1 p. 297, 10.4 p. 320, 11.4 p. 347, 14.1 p. 409, p. 410, p. 411, 14.2 p. 415, p. 419, 15.2 p. 456, 15.4 p. 468, 16.4 p. 498, p. 500, 16.5 p. 507, 17.3 p. 529, 18.1 p. 541, 18.3 p. 552
big government, 1.4 pp. 28–29, 1.4 p. 31
bill of attainder, 3.2 p. 78
Bill of Rights
American Revolution impacting, 3.5 p. 91
civil liberties in, 5.1 pp. 138–140
Congress approving, 3.3 p. 85
Constitution lacking, 3.3 pp. 85–86
establishment of, 2.5 p. 64, R2, 3.5 p. 91, R14
in colonial constitutions, 2.3 p. 50
in National Archives Building, U2 p. 68
interpreting, 3.5 pp. 91–92
liberty, 1.3 p. 19
limited rights of, 3.5 p. 93
limiting government, 3.2 p. 78
Magna Carta inspiring, R27
of England, 1.3 p. 17
Preamble, R27
provisions of, 3.5 p. 92
ratification of, 3.3 p. 85, 5.1 p. 138
states incorporation of, 5.1 pp. 141–142
states power, 3.3 p. 83
Supreme Court and, 5.1 p. 139, 20.1 p. 595
bills, 9.1 pp. 273–278, p. 277, 9.2 pp. 280–283, 9.3 p. 285, R17
bills of attainder, 5.1 p. 138
bin Laden, Osama, 18.3 p. 549, p. 551, p. 552
Bipartisan Campaign Reform Act (BCRA) of 2002, 5.3 p. 152, 14.5 p. 437, 15.5 pp. 470–472. *See also* McCain-Feingold Act
birthright citizenship, 6.1 pp. 179–180
Black Lives Matter, 1.3 p. 23, 2.3 p. 49, 5.5 p. 162, 6.2 p. 194, p. 195, 14.4 p. 433
Blackstone, William, 1.3 p. 17, 12.1 p. 360
Blaine Amendment, 3.5 p. 92
block grant, 4.4 p. 128
Bloody Sunday, 6.2 p. 191–192
blue states, 14.1 p. 409
Board of Governors, 17.2 p. 517
***Bostock* v. *Clayton County, GA*,** 6.3 p. 203
Bottoms, Keisha Lance, 21.1 p. 630
***Boynton* v. *Virginia*,** 8.1 p. 255
Bracero Program, 6.1 p. 181
Brady Handgun Violence Prevention Act of 1993, 4.4 pp. 124–125, 8.2 p. 262
Brandeis, Louis, 4.1 p. 109, 5.5 p. 160, 13.1 p. 382, 20.1 p. 595
***Brown II*,** 6.2 p. 190
***Brown* v. *Board of Education*,** 6.2 p. 191, 12.1 p. 360, p. 361, 13.1 pp. 382–383
Budget Act, 9.3 p. 287
budget deficit, 8.1 p. 253
budget process, 9.3 pp. 284–288
Bull Moose Progressive Party, 14.1 p. 407, 14.3 p. 422, p. 423, 15.1 p. 445
Bureau of Engraving and Printing, 8.1 p. 254
Bureau of Indian Affairs (BIA), 6.4 p. 214, 21.2 p. 636
Bureau of Land Management (BLM), 8.2 p. 261, 11.4 p. 346
bureaucracy, 11.1 p. 325–330
Burr, Aaron, 3.5 pp. 93–94
***Burwell* v. *Hobby Lobby Stores*,** 5.2 p. 151
Bush, George H.W., 3.6 p. 103, 10.1 p. 295, 10.2 p. 303, p. 309, 13.2 p. 384, p. 386, 13.4 p. 395, 17.2 p. 521, 18.3 p. 550, 19.2 p. 578
Bush, George W., 4.4 p. 126, p. 130, 5.6 p. 170, U5 p. 323, 6.2 p. 192, p. 193, 6.3 p. 204, 8.2 p. 260, p. 268, 10.1 p. 295, p. 296, p. 297, p. 299, p. 301, 10.2 p. 308, p. 309, 10.3 p. 313, 10.4 pp. 320–321, p. 316, p. 320, 11.3 p. 341, p. 342, p. 344, 12.2 p. 369, 12.3 p. 374, 13.4 p. 395, p. 398, 14.1 pp. 408–409, p. 409, 14.2 p. 418, 14.3 p. 423, 14.5 p. 441, 15.3 p. 460, 15.4 p. 461, p. 467, 15.5 pp. 470–472, p. 468, p. 471, 16.3 p. 491, 17.2 p. 516, p. 520, 18.3 pp. 550–551, p. 551, 18.4 p. 560, 20.3 p. 608, p. 610
Bush, John E. (Jeb), 5.3 p. 152, 10.1 p. 297, 15.2 p. 451, p. 454
***Bush* v. *Gore*,** 15.3 p. 460, 15.4 p. 461
***Bush* v. *Vera*,** 20.2 p. 602
Business Administration (SBA), 18.3 p. 555
business cycle, 17.2 p. 517
business interest groups, 14.4 pp. 429–430
busing, 6.2 p. 191
Buttigieg, Pete, 6.4 p. 216, 10.1 p. 297, 15.2 p. 456

C

***California Democratic Party* v. *Jones*,** 15.1 p. 449
campaign contributions, 5.3 pp. 152–153
Canadian Pacific Railway, 17.4 p. 530
Candidates' nomination, 15.1 pp. 445–454, 15.2 p. 454–456
***Caperton* v. *Massey Coal Co.*,** 14.5 pp. 439–440
capital crime, 12.1 p. 364
CARES (Coronavirus Aid, Relief, and Economic Security) Act, 18.3 p. 555, p. 557
***Carpenter* v. *United States*,** 13.1 p. 381
Carter, Jimmy, 10.1 p. 296, 10.2 pp. 304–305, 10.4 p. 320, 14.1 p. 408, 16.4 p. 495, 18.4 p. 558, 19.2 p. 578, 20.3 p. 608

INDEX

case law, 20.4 p. 615
censorship, 5.3 pp. 157–158, p. 153
Center for Disease Control (CDC), 11.2 pp. 333–334, 18.3 p. 555
Central Intelligence Agency (CIA), 1.1 p. 8, 10.4 p. 316, 11.2 p. 335, 18.1 p. 542, 18.3 p. 551
Chamber of Commerce, 14.4 p. 429
Change to Win federation, 14.4 p. 431
Charter of Privileges, 2.1 p. 40
charters, of English colonies, 2.1 p. 37
Chávez, César, 6.4 p. 208, 14.5 p. 438
checks and balances, 3.1 p. 75, 3.3 pp. 83–84, p. 84, 20.1 p. 596, R14
chief executive, 10.1 pp. 297–298, p. 301, 20.3 pp. 608–610
chief justice, role of, 13.1 p. 379
Children's Health Insurance Program (CHIP), 11.3 p. 344, 17.3 p. 525
Chinese Exclusion Act of 1882, 6.1 p. 180, p. 181, 6.4 p. 209
Chinese Exclusion Repeal Act (1943–1946), 6.1 p. 181
Chinese immigrants, 6.1 p. 179, p. 180, p. 181, 6.4 p. 207, p. 209
Christian conservatives, 1.4 p. 29
circuit courts, 3.6 p. 98, 20.4 p. 618, p. 620
***Citizens United* v. *Federal Election Commission*,** 5.3 p. 152, 7.5 p. 248, 12.1 p. 362, 14.5 p. 436, 15.5 pp. 471–473
citizens/citizenship
- active citizenship, 6.1 p. 184, R42–R43
- *Dred Scott v. Sandford,* 6.1 p. 179, p. 180
- Fourteenth Amendment, 3.4 p. 88, 5.1 p. 141, R15
- of Mexican Americans, 6.4 p. 208
- Native Americans, 6.4 p. 212, p. 214
- by naturalization, 6.1 pp. 179–180
- responsibilities of, 6.1 p. 184, R41
- rights and privileges of, 3.1 p. 74, R24, R40
- tolerance of differences, R41
- voting rights, 16.1 p. 477

city government, reforming, 21.1 p. 628
civic responsibilities, 6.1 p. 184, R41
civil disobedience, 5.5 p. 161, 6.2 p. 191, 6.3 p. 197
civil law, 12.1 pp. 363–616
civil law violations, 12.1 p. 363
civil liberties, 5.1 pp. 137–142, 5.2 pp. 142–151, 5.3 pp. 151–156, 5.5 pp. 164–169, 5.6 pp. 169–175, 10.3 p. 313
civil rights
- of Asian Americans, 6.4 p. 209, pp. 211–213
- Fourteenth Amendment, 6.1 pp. 185–186
- for Hispanics, 6.4 pp. 207–208
- interracial marriage, 6.2 p. 193
- of LGBTQ persons, 6.4 pp. 215–217
- of Native Americans, 6.4 p. 212, pp. 214–215
- of persons with disability, 6.4 pp. 217–218
- Twenty-Fourth Amendment, 6.2 p. 192
- Voting Rights Act of 1965, 6.2 p. 193
- women's suffrage, 6.3 pp. 197–198

Civil Rights Act of 1957, 7.3 p. 241, 16.2 p. 482
Civil Rights Act of 1960, 16.2 p. 482
Civil Rights Act of 1964, 3.6 p. 99, 4.3 p. 122, 4.4 p. 128, 5.2 p. 147, 6.2 p. 192, 6.3 p. 200, p. 203, 7.3 p. 241, 8.1 p. 255
Civil Rights Act of 1991, 6.3 p. 202
Civil Rights Division of the Justice Department, 16.2 p. 482
civil rights legislation, 4.4 p. 126
civil rights movement. *See also* National Association for Advancement of Colored People (NAACP)
- Black Power movement, 6.2 pp. 191–192
- *Brown v. Board of Education,* 6.2 p. 191
- civil disobedience, 5.5 p. 161, 6.2 p. 191
- Civil Rights Division, 16.2 p. 482
- civil rights violation protests, U3 p. 178
- equal rights struggle, R39
- Freedom Rider, 16.2 p. 483
- George Floyd protests, U3 p. 136, 18.3 p. 557
- Juneteenth, 2.3 p. 49
- King, Martin Luther, Jr., 6.2 p. 191
- legal protection, 6.2 pp. 192–193
- Liberalism, 1.4 p. 29, p. 31
- March on Washington for Jobs and Freedom, U3 p. 134, 6.2 p. 191, p. 483
- Montgomery bus boycott, 5.5 p. 161, 6.2 p. 191
- nonviolent protests, 6.2 p. 191
- Parks, Rosa, 5.5 p. 161
- Southern Christian Leadership Conference (SCLC), 6.2 p. 191
- U.S. Civil Rights Commission, 16.2 p. 482
- Voting Rights Act of 1965, 16.2 pp. 482–483, p. 482
- Woolworth's sit-in, U3 p. 225, 6.2 p. 191

Civil Rights Restoration Act of 1988, 6.3 p. 199
Civil Service Reform Act of 1978, 11.1 p. 327–328
civil service system, 11.1 p. 327–328
Civil War, 2.3 p. 48, 4.3 p. 119, 6.2 p. 187, 11.3 p. 340, 16.2 p. 484
Clean Air Act, 4.4 p. 125p
climate change, 11.4 p. 353, 17.4 pp. 530–531, p. 531
Clinton, Hillary Rodham, 1.3 p. 22, 3.2 p. 79, 5.3 p. 152, 6.3 p. 204, 10.1 p. 297, 10.2 p. 304, 10.4 p. 316, p. 319, p. 320, 14.1 p. 409, p. 410, 14.2 p. 418, 14.3 pp. 423–424, 14.5 p. 440, 15.2 pp. 455–466, 15.4 p. 468, 15.5 p. 471, 16.4 p. 497, 16.5 p. 506, 17.3 p. 526, 19.2 p. 577, p. 578, 19.3 pp. 587–588
Clinton, William (Bill), 4.4 p. 124, p. 126, U5 p. 323, 6.3 p. 204, 6.4 p. 213, p. 217, 8.3 p. 266, p. 268, 10.1 p. 296, p. 297, p. 300, p. 301, 10.2 p. 304, 10.4 p. 320, 12.2 p. 369, 13.2 p. 384, p. 387, 14.5 p. 440, 17.2 p. 521, 17.3 p. 526, 18.3 pp. 549–550, 19.2 p. 578, 20.3 p. 608
Clinton Foundation, 14.5 p. 440, 15.4 p. 464
***Clinton* v. *City of New York*,** 9.2 p. 282
closed primaries, 15.1 pp. 448–449, 20.2 p. 603
cloture, 7.3 p. 241, 9.1 p. 278, p. 279
Coercive Acts, 2.2 p. 45
coercive diplomacy, 18.4 p. 558
Cold War, 18.2 pp. 544–547, 19.2 p. 577
Collins, Susan, 6.3 p. 205, U8 p. 511, 10.3 p. 312
colonial government, 2.1 pp. 38–44, 2.2 p. 45, p. 46, 2.3 p. 48, p. 49, R3
Colorado Civil Rights Commission, 13.4 p. 399
Commander in Chief, 10.1 p. 299, p. 301, R22
commerce clause
- Congress, 3.3 p. 82, R17
- cooperative federalism, 4.3 pp. 121–124
- implied powers, 8.2 pp. 262–263
- interstate commerce, 3.6 pp. 99–255
- nullification crisis, 4.3 p. 119
- Patient Protection and Affordable Care Act, 4.4 p. 126

Commerce Department, 10.4 p. 315, 11.2 p. 333
Commission on Wartime Relocation and Internment of Civilians, 8.3 p. 269
common law, 1.3 p. 17, 12.1 pp. 359–362, p. 360, 20.4 p. 615
***Common Sense* (Paine),** 2.2 pp. 46–47, p. 46
Communication Workers of America, 14.4 p. 431
Communications Decency Act, 19.1 p. 572
communism, 1.2 p. 11, p. 12, 1.4 p. 32, p. 33, 5.3 p. 156, 18.2 pp. 544–547
competitive federalism, 4.4 p. 131
Comprehensive Test Ban Treaty, 10.2 p. 304
compulsory national service, 6.1 p. 184
Confederate States of America, 4.3 p. 119, 6.2 p. 187
confederate system, 4.1 p. 108
Confederation Congress, 2.4 p. 53
Confederation of States, 2.4 pp. 53–57
confirmation bias, 16.4 p. 495
confirmation process, 8.3 pp. 267–268
conflict resolution, 1.1 pp. 6–7, 1.1 p. 6, p. 7, 1.3 p. 18
Congress. *See also* House of Representatives; Senate
- African Americans in, 6.2 p. 193
- bicameral legislature, 7.1 p. 229–231
- budgeting process, 9.3 pp. 284–288
- central institution of government, 7.1 p. 229
- committees, 7.4 pp. 244–245, p. 245, 9.1 pp. 276–277, p. 277, 9.2 pp. 280–281
- congressional term, 7.1 p. 230
- Constitution Article I, 7.1 p. 229
- creating agencies and bureaus, 11.1 p. 325, p. 326
- earmark spending, 7.1 p. 231
- elastic clause, 3.3 p. 82, 4.2 p. 113, R18
- emolument clause, R19
- enumerated powers of, 8.1 pp. 253–259
- first session, 3.3 p. 85
- foreign policy, 18.1 p. 542
- general elections, 7.5 p. 248
- House of Representatives, 3.1 p. 73, p. 74, 3.3 p. 83, R14, R15
- impeachment power, 8.3 p. 266
- implied powers, 8.2 pp. 261–263
- inherent powers of, 8.2 pp. 259–261
- joint committee, 7.4 p. 245
- lawmaking authority, 10.3 p. 311
- limiting presidential power, 10.3 pp. 311–312
- Native Americans in, 6.4 p. 214
- necessary and proper clause, 3.3 p. 82, 4.2 p. 113, 8.2 p. 262, R18
- non-legislative powers, 8.2 p. 263
- political action committees (PACs), 7.5 p. 248
- pork-barrel legislation, 7.1 p. 231
- powers of, 3.3 p. 82, R17–18
- powers prohibited, 8.1 p. 259
- presidential democracy, 1.2 p. 14
- primary elections, 7.5 p. 246, 7.5 p. 248
- regional constituencies, 10.3 p. 312
- sessions of, 7.1 p. 230
- Supreme Court and, 13.4 p. 398
- term length, 3.3 p. 84, 7.1 p. 230
- war powers, 8.1 p. 258
- War Powers Resolution, 18.1 p. 542
- women in, 1.3 p. 26

Congress of Racial Equality (CORE), 6.2 p. 191
Congressional Budget Office (CBO), 8.3 p. 266, 9.3 pp. 286–287, 17.3 p. 529, 18.3 p. 555
congressional campaigns, 14.2 p. 418, 15.4 pp. 463–472, 15.5 p. 469
congressional election, 7.5 pp. 248–249, p. 246
Congressional Leadership Fund, 15.5 p. 473
congressional oversight, 8.3 p. 265
conservatism/ conservatives, 1.4 pp. 27–29, p. 31, 4.4 p. 124, 11.1 p. 329, 13.4 pp. 395–397, 14.1 p. 411, 15.1 p. 448, 16.4 p. 496
constituents, 7.1 p. 230–231
Constitution, U.S., R2. *See also* Bill of Rights
- amending, 3.1 p. 74, 3.4 pp. 86–90, R25
- Antifederalists view of, 2.5 pp. 63–64
- Article I, 3.1 p. 73, p. 74, 4.2 pp. 111–112, p. 113, p. 115, R15–R19
- Article II, 2.5 p. 62, 3.1 p. 73, p. 74, 4.2 pp. 111–112, p. 113, 12.2 p. 370, R19–R22
- Article III, 3.1 pp. 73–112, 4.2 p. 113, R23
- Article IV, 3.1 p. 74, 4.2 p. 114, p. 115, R24
- Article V, 3.1 p. 74, 3.4 pp. 88–90, R25
- Article VI, 3.1 pp. 73–74, 4.1 p. 107, R25
- Article VII, 3.1 p. 74, R26
- checks and balances, 3.1 p. 75, 3.3 pp. 83–84, R14
- civil liberties in, 5.1 pp. 137–142
- Constitutional Convention, 2.5 p. 58

drafting of, R14
federalism, 3.1 p. 75, 3.3 pp. 82–83, R14
Federalist view of, 2.5 pp. 63–64
Fourteenth Amendment, 4.4 p. 131
Great Compromise, 2.5 pp. 60–61
individual rights, 3.1 p. 75, 3.3 pp. 85–86, R14
judicial branch, 2.5 p. 62
laws must comply with, 12.1 p. 361
limited government, 3.1 p. 75, R14
Native Americans and, 6.4 p. 212
New Jersey Plan, 2.5 p. 60
organization of, 3.1 pp. 73–74,
political culture, 1.3 p. 18
popular sovereignty, 3.1 p. 75, 3.2 p. 76, R14
Preamble, 3.1 pp. 71–72, R14, R15
principles of, 3.1 pp. 74–75
purposes of, 3.1 pp. 71–72
ratification of, U1 p. 67, 2.5 p. 65, 3.3 p. 85
republicanism, 3.1 p. 75, 3.2 p. 76–77, R14
right of habeas corpus, 3.3 p. 85
rule of law, 3.1 p. 75, 3.2 p. 78, p. 80
separation of powers, 3.1 p. 75, 3.3 p. 83, R14
slavery, 6.2 pp. 186–187
Tenth Amendment, 4.4 p. 130

Constitutional Convention, 2.5 p. 57, p. 62, U2 p. 70, R14
constitutional monarchy, 1.2 p. 11
constitutions. *See also* Constitution, U.S.
Articles of Confederation, 2.4 p. 53
of the colonies, 2.3 p. 49
comparing federal and state, 20.1 p. 599
English, uncodified, 3.1 p. 72
Mayflower Compact, 2.1 p. 39
of the states, 20.1 pp. 595–600

Consumer Product Safety Commission (CPSC), 11.2 p. 337
Consumers Union, 14.4 pp. 432–433
Continental Congress First and Second, 2.2 p. 45, p. 46, 2.3 p. 48–49, R3
Continental Convention, 2.5 pp. 60–61
convention system, 15.1 p. 446
Coolidge, Calvin, 14.1 p. 408, 15.2 p. 450, 20.3 p. 608
cooperative federalism, 4.3 pp. 121–124
copyrights, 8.1 p. 256, 17.2 p. 523
Coronavirus Aid Relief, U4 p. 272
corporate income tax, 11.3 p. 343
county government, 20.1 p. 598, 21.2 p. 634
court of appeals, 3.2 p. 80, 3.6 p. 98, 5.2 p. 149, 12.2 p. 368, p. 369, 12.3 p. 373, 13.1 p. 379, 20.4 p. 618, p. 620
COVID-19 pandemic
2020 election impacted, 1.3 p. 22, U7 p. 476, 14.2 p. 419, 15.2 p. 453, p. 456, 15.4 p. 468, 16.2 p. 486, p. 488, 16.3 p. 492, p. 493
Center for Disease Control (CDC), 11.2 p. 334
China and, 18.3 p. 554, 18.4 pp. 562–563
Economic Security (CARES) Act, U4 p. 272, 9.2 p. 284, 17.2 p. 520
federal response to, 1.1 p. 8, 18.3 pp. 554–555, p. 557
foreign policy, 18.3 pp. 554–555
global pandemic, 18.3 pp. 554–555
long term economic effects, 17.2 p. 517–518, 18.4 p. 565, 21.3 p. 643
states response to, 1.1 p. 8, 4.4 pp. 125–126, 6.1 p. 183, 17.2 p. 520, 18.3 pp. 554–555, 20.3 p. 611
stimulus spending, 9.2 p. 284 17.2 p. 522

credit rating, 5.6 p. 172
crime statistics, 1.3 p. 26
criminal law, 12.1 pp. 363–364, 20.4 p. 615
crisis, presidential powers during, 10.3 p. 313
Cuban Americans, 6.4 p. 207–209, 16.4 p. 500
Cuban missile crisis, 18.2 p. 546
Culper Spy Ring, U1 p. 52
Customs Courts Act, 12.3 p. 371
cyberattacks, 1.1 p. 8
cyberbullying, 5.3 p. 158, 5.6 p. 173
cyberspace, 19.3 pp. 585–588

D

Dakota Access oil pipeline, 6.4 p. 214, p. 215, 7.2 p. 239
data analytics companies, 5.6 p. 173
de facto segregation, 6.2 pp. 190–191
de jure segregation, 6.2 p. 190
death penalty, U3 p. 177
debt ceiling, 9.3 p. 288
Declaration of Independence, 1.3 p. 18–20, 2.2 p. 47, R2, U2 p. 68, R3–R7
Declaratory Act, 2.2 p. 44
Defense Department, 1.1 p. 8, 10.4 p. 315, 11.2 p. 332–333
Defense Intelligence Agency, 18.1 p. 542
Defense of Marriage Act (DOMA), 4.2 p. 115
defense spending, 11.3 pp. 344–345
Deferred Action for Childhood Arrivals (DACA), 6.1 p. 183
deficit, 8.1 p. 253
***DeJonge* v. *Oregon*,** 5.5 p. 160
demagogue, 3.2 p. 77
democracy, media in, 19.1 pp. 569–576
Democratic National Committee (DNC), U7 p. 402, 14.2 p. 418, p. 419, p. 453, p. 456, 15.4 p. 464, 15.5 p. 473
Democratic Party
1932 election, 14.1 p. 408
1964 elections, 14.1 p. 408
2000 elections, 14.1 pp. 408–409, 14.3 p. 423
2006 and 2008 elections, 1.3 p. 21
2016 elections, 15.2 pp. 455–456
2020 elections, 1.3 p. 24, 14.1 p. 409–411
African Americans in, 6.2 p. 193, 14.1 p. 408
after Civil War, 14.1 p. 407
blue states, 14.1 p. 409
business interest groups, 14.4 pp. 429–430
centralization of power, 4.4 pp. 125–126
civil rights movement, 1.4 p. 29, p. 31
direct primary elections, 15.1 pp. 446–447
establishment of, 14.1 p. 407, 15.1 p. 446
extreme partisanship, 14.1 p. 411
Latinos, 14.1 p. 412
liberalism, 1.4 p. 27, 14.1 p. 411, 16.4 p. 496
members of, 14.1 p. 410–411
Mexican Americans supporting, 6.4 p. 208
partisan disagreement, 9.1 p. 279
political party of, 1.3 p. 21
presidential caucuses, 15.2 p. 452
Puerto Ricans supporting, 6.4 p. 208
socialism/socialists, 1.4 pp. 32–33
southern Democrats separating from, 14.1 p. 408
state government, 20.2 p. 603
unionized workers, 14.1 p. 408
urban professionals, 14.1 p. 412
U.S. voters (1992–2018), 1.3 p. 22

Democratic Republicans, 14.1 p. 405, 15.1 p. 446
democratic systems, 1.2 pp. 12–14
Department of Commerce, 12.3 p. 372, 18.1 p. 540
Department of Defense, 1.1 p. 8, 5.3 p. 157, 18.1 p. 541, 19.3 p. 583
Department of Energy, 17.4 p. 534, 18.1 p. 540
***Department of Homeland Security* v. *Regents of the University of California*,** 6.1 p. 183
Department of State, 1.1 p. 8, 10.4 p. 315, 11.2 p. 333, 11.3 p. 340, 18.1 pp. 540–541, p. 541, 18.4 p. 557
Department of the Interior, 1.1 p. 6, 10.4 p. 315, 11.2 p. 333
Department of Treasury, 10.4 p. 315, 11.2 p. 332–333, 11.3 p. 340, 17.2 pp. 521–522, R33
Department of Veterans Affairs, 6.3 p. 205, 12.3 p. 374
Department of War, 11.3 p. 340, p. 344
deterrence policy, 18.2 p. 546
devolution, 4.4 p. 124
dictatorships, 1.1 p. 7, 1.2 pp. 11–12
digital age, 11.4 p. 351
digital media, news source, U8 p. 568
diplomacy, 18.4 pp. 558–560
direct democracy, 1.2 p. 12, 3.2 p. 77
direct initiative, 1.2 p. 13, 20.2 p. 606
direct lobbying techniques, 14.5 pp. 435–436
direct primary elections, 15.1 pp. 446–448
direct-mail campaign, 15.4 p. 466
discretionary spending, 17.3 p. 525
disinformation, 19.3 p. 588
dissenting opinions, 13.1 pp. 382–383
district courts, 3.6 p. 98, 12.2 p. 367–368, 12.3 p. 373, 13.1 p. 379
***District of Columbia* v. *Heller*,** 5.1 p. 140, R28
districts, state legislative, 20.2 pp. 601–603
divine right theory, 1.1 pp. 9–11
Division for Public Education, 12.1 pp. 366–367
domestic policy, U8 p. 512–514, 17.1 p. 514, 17.2 pp. 516–535
domestic terrorism, 18.3 pp. 548–549
Dominican Americans, 6.4 p. 207–208
Dominican Republic-Central American Free Trade Agreement, 18.4 p. 565
"don't ask, don't tell" policy, 6.4 p. 217
double jeopardy, 5.1 p. 138
Douglass, Frederick, U2 p. 69
***Dred Scott* v. *Sandford*,** 6.1 p. 179–180
Driver's Privacy Protection Act, 5.6 p. 173
Drug Enforcement Administration (DEA), 11.2 p. 333, 12.1 p. 365
dual federalism, 4.3 pp. 119–120
due process, 3.5 p. 94, 5.1 p. 138, p. 141, 5.5 pp. 164–169, R29
***Dunn* v. *Blumstein*,** 16.1 p. 477

E

early polling, 16.5 p. 502
early voting, 15.2 p. 456, 15.3 p. 457, 16.2 p. 484, 16.3 pp. 492–493
easy-money policy, 17.2 p. 517–518
economic policy, goals of, 17.2 pp. 516–517
Economic Policy Institute, 6.3 p. 201
economic sanctions, 18.4 p. 558, 560–561
Economic Security (CARES) Act, U4 p. 272, 9.2 p. 284, 17.2 p. 520
economy
capitalism, 1.3 p. 20
conservatism, 1.4 p. 29
federal government stimulating, 4.4 p. 130
federal spending impacting, 9.3 p. 285
free enterprise system, 1.3 p. 20, 1.3 p. 21
government involvement in, 1.1 pp. 7–8
Great Depression, 1.4 p. 28
New Deal, 1.4 p. 28
between states, 2.4 p. 55

education
aid to parochial schools, 5.2 p. 144, p. 146–147
busing, 6.2 p. 191
evolution, teaching of, 5.2 p. 147
prayer in, 5.2 p. 144, p. 145, p. 147
racial gaps, 6.2 p. 195
separate-but-equal doctrine, 6.2 pp. 190–191
sexual assault on campus, 6.3 p. 202
Title IX, 6.3 pp. 199–200, 11.3 p. 342

Education Department, 10.4 p. 315, 11.2 p. 333
Eighteenth Amendment, 3.5 p. 93, p. 95, R33
Eighth Amendment, 3.5 p. 92, p. 93, 5.1 p. 139, 5.5 p. 167, p. 169, R29
elastic clause, 3.3 p. 82, 3.6 p. 99, 4.2 p. 113, 8.2 pp. 261–262, R18
election process, U1 p. 35, 3.4 pp. 87–88, 6.1 p. 184, 15.1 pp. 445–473, 16.2 p. 484, 16.3 p. 489, p. 490, pp. 492–493, 19.2 pp. 576–577. *See also* voting process
electoral college, 1.3 p. 21–22, p. 24, 2.5 p. 62, 3.2 p. 79, 3.4 p. 90, 15.2 p. 454, 15.3 pp. 459–460, R30

INDEX

electronic voting machines, 15.3 p. 458, 16.3 pp. 491–492
Eleventh Amendment, 3.5 p. 93, R30
Emancipation Proclamation, 2.3 p. 48, 3.6 p. 102
Emergency Banking Relief Act, 9.2 p. 284
Emergency Economic Stabilization Act of 2008, 9.2 p. 284
Emergency Operations Center, 10.4 p. 320
eminent domain, 5.5 p. 166
emolument clause, R19
energy policy, 17.4 pp. 529–534
***Engel* v. *Vitale*,** 5.2 p. 144, 5.2 p. 145
English colonies, 2.1 pp. 37–43
Enlightenment, 1.1 p. 10, 3.3 p. 85, R3
entitlement programs, 9.3 pp. 285–286, 17.3 p. 525
entrepreneurship, 17.2 p. 523
environmental interest groups, 14.4 p. 434
environmental policy, 17.4 pp. 530–534
Environmental Protection Agency (EPA), 5.5 p. 163, 10.4 p. 316, 11.1 p. 328, 11.2 p. 335, p. 337, 13.4 p. 396, 17.4 p. 532
environmental rights, 20.1 p. 596
Equal Employment Opportunity Commission, 6.3 p. 203, 11.2 p. 337
Equal Pay Act, 6.3 pp. 200–201
equal protection, 1.3 p. 17, 6.1 pp. 185–186
Equal Rights Amendment (ERA), 3.4 p. 87, p. 90, 6.3 p. 199
equality, goal of, 1.3 pp. 19–20
Espionage Act of 1917, 5.3 pp. 154–156, 8.1 p. 259, 11.4 p. 347
establishment clause, 3.5 p. 91, 5.2 pp. 144–147
***ex post facto* law,** 3.2 p. 78, 5.1 p. 138
exclusionary rule, 5.5 p. 169
executive actions, 3.6 pp. 101–102
executive agencies, iron triangle, 11.1 p. 330
executive agreements, 3.6 p. 103
executive branch, 11.2 pp. 332–334
- checks and balances, 3.3 pp. 83–84
- establishment of, 2.5 p. 62, 3.1 p. 73–74, 3.3 p. 83, R14, R19–R22
- in federal bureaucracy, 11.2 p. 332
- organization of, 10.4 pp. 315–321
- presidency, 10.1 pp. 295–321, 11.2 p. 333
- presidential succession order, 10.4 p. 321
- president's cabinet, 10.4 pp. 315–317
- proposing bills, 9.1 p. 273
- selecting judges, 20.4 p. 620–621
- vice president, 10.4 pp. 319–321, 11.2 p. 333
- Virginia Plan, 2.5 p. 59

executive departments, 10.4 p. 315, 11.1 p. 331–334, 11.3 p. 340
Executive Office of the President (EOP), 10.4 pp. 317–318
Executive Order 9066, 6.4 p. 211, 6.4 p. 213
executive orders, 10.2 pp. 307–308
executive privilege, 3.2 p. 80, 8.3 p. 264, 10.3 pp. 313–314
exports, 8.1 p. 259, 18.4 p. 562
expressed powers, 4.2 pp. 111–259

F

fact-checking in media, 19.2 pp. 581–582
fair compensation, right to, 5.1 p. 138
fairness doctrine, 19.1 p. 572, 19.2 pp. 580–581
"fake news" claims, 5.3 p. 159, 15.4 p. 465, 19.2 p. 582, 19.3 p. 588
False Claims Act, 11.4 p. 347
family courts, 20.4 p. 619–620
federal appeals court, 12.2 p. 368
Federal Aviation Administration (FAA), 9.1 p. 273
federal budget, 10.4 p. 318, 17.2 p. 522
Federal Bureau of Investigations (FBI), 1.1 p. 8, 4.3 p. 121, 5.6 p. 174, 11.4 p. 351, 18.3 p. 548
federal bureaucracy, 11.1 p. 325–342, 11.2 p. 333, p. 335, 11.3 p. 342, 11.4 pp. 347–348, p. 345, 12.2 p. 368
Federal Communications Commission (FCC), 11.2 p. 337, 11.3 p. 341, 19.1 p. 572, 19.1 p. 575, 19.2 p. 580–581
federal court system, 3.6 p. 98, 12.1 pp. 364–368, 12.2 p. 369, 12.3 pp. 372–399
federal cybersecurity, 11.1 p. 327
federal deficit, 9.3 p. 285
Federal Deposit Insurance Corporation (FDIC), 11.2 p. 338
Federal Election Campaign Act (FECA), 5.3 p. 152, 15.5 pp. 469–470
Federal Election Commission (FEC), 15.5 pp. 469–470, 19.3 p. 586
***Federal Election Commission* v. *Wisconsin Right to Life, Inc.*,** 15.5 p. 471
Federal Emergency Management Agency (FEMA), 9.3 p. 286, 11.1 p. 325
federal government. *See also* Articles of Confederation
- admitting new states, 4.2 p. 112
- congress and commerce clause, 4.3 p. 122
- domestic policy, 17.1 pp. 513–535
- foreign policy, 18.1 pp. 539–565
- funding for, 11.3 p. 343
- growth to World War I, 11.3 pp. 340–341
- immigration, 4.4 p. 126
- Johnson's Great Society, 4.3 p. 122
- Native American relations, 4.2 p. 112
- organization of, 11.2 p. 333
- policy implementation, 17.1 p. 515
- powers specified and limited, 4.2 pp. 111–263, 5.1 p. 139
- private enterprise, 17.2 p. 523
- Roosevelt's New Deal, 4.3 p. 121
- state government conflicting with, 4.4 pp. 125–126
- state powers within, 20.1 pp. 595–596
- stimulating economy, 4.4 p. 130
- supremacy of national government, 20.1 p. 595

Federal Home Loan Mortgage Corporation (Freddie Mac), 11.2 p. 340
Federal Judicial Center, 12.1 pp. 366–367
federal land, 8.2 p. 261
federal magistrate judges, 12.2 p. 368
federal mandates, 4.4 p. 127, p. 131, 11.3 p. 342
federal minimum wage, 8.2 p. 262
Federal National Mortgage Association (Fannie Mae), 11.2 p. 340
Federal Open Market Committee (FOMC), 17.2 p. 517–518
federal preemption, 4.3 p. 122, 4.3 p. 124
Federal Regulation of Lobbying Act in 1946, 14.5 p. 440
Federal Reserve Banks, 8.1 p. 254, 17.2 p. 517
Federal Reserve System (Fed), 8.1 p. 254, U8 p. 537, 11.2 p. 337, 17.2 p. 517
federal spending, 9.3 pp. 284–349
federal statues, 12.1 pp. 361–362
federal surplus, 9.3 p. 285
federal tax system, 17.2 pp. 520–521
Federal Trade Commission (FTC), 11.1 p. 326, 11.2 p. 337, 11.3 p. 341, 12.2 p. 368
federalism
- advantages of, 4.1 pp. 109–110
- competitive federalism, 4.4 p. 131
- disadvantages of, 4.1 pp. 110–111
- dual federalism, 4.3 p. 120
- in U.S. Constitution, 3.1 p. 75, 3.3 pp. 82–83, R14
- federal mandates, 4.4 p. 127
- fiscal side of, 4.4 pp. 127–131
- new federalism, 4.4 pp. 124–125
- politics of, 4.4 pp. 125–126
- powers specified and limited, U2 p. 106p, 4.1 p. 107
- Supreme Court, 4.3 pp. 117–119

Federalist, 2.5 pp. 63–64, 14.1 p. 405–407, 15.1 p. 446
***Federalist Papers*,** 2.5 p. 63, 3.2 p. 77, 7.3 p. 240, R8–R13, 13.3 p. 389
felonies, 12.1 p. 364, 20.4 p. 615
felons, 16.2 p. 481, p. 484
feminism movement, 6.3 pp. 198–200
Fifteenth Amendment, 3.4 p. 88, 3.5 p. 93, p. 94, 4.3 p. 120, 6.2 p. 187, 7.5 p. 246, 16.1 p. 477, 16.2 p. 480, p. 482, R32
Fifth Amendment, 3.5 p. 92–93, 5.1 p. 138, 5.5 p. 165, p. 167, p. 169, R29
financial crisis, 16.4 p. 496
financing political campaigns, 5.3 p. 152, 7.5 p. 248, U7 p. 475, 14.5 p. 435–436, 15.5 pp. 469–473
First Amendment, 3.5 p. 91, 3.5 pp. 92–93, 5.1 p. 138, 5.2 pp. 142–151, 5.6 p. 169, 14.4 p. 425, 19.1 pp. 571–572, R28
First Step Act, 5.1 p. 139
fiscal federalism, 4.4 p. 127
fiscal policy, 17.2 pp. 519–520
fiscal year, 9.3 p. 285
501c and 527 committees, 15.5 p. 473
flat tax, 21.3 p. 639
***Fletcher* v. *Peck*,** 11.3 p. 340
Flint water crisis, 11.4 p. 353
Floyd, George, 2.3 p. 49, U3 p. 136, 18.3 p. 557
Food and Drug Administration (FDA), 11.2 p. 337
food-insecure households, 9.3 p. 289
Foreign Affairs Committee, 18.1 p. 542
Foreign Agents Registration Act, 14.5 p. 441
Foreign Intelligence Surveillance Court (FISC), 5.6 p. 175, 12.3 p. 372
foreign policy, 1.1 p. 8, 3.6 p. 103, 8.1 pp. 257–258, 10.2 p. 308, 10.3 p. 313, 11.3 p. 344, 18.1 pp. 539–547, 18.3 pp. 548–554, p. 556, 18.4 p. 558. pp. 560–565
Foreign Relations Committee, 8.3 p. 267
foreign terrorist networks, 18.3 pp. 549–550
Founding Fathers, unalienable rights, R3
Fourteenth Amendment, 3.4 p. 88, 3.5 p. 93–94, 4.3 p. 120, 4.4 p. 131, 5.1 pp. 140–142, 5.5 p. 165, 6.1 p. 558, p. 179, pp. 185–186, 6.2 p. 187, 6.4 p. 210, 6.5 pp. 220–221
Fourth Amendment, 3.5 p. 92–93, 5.1 p. 138, 5.5 p. 166–167, 5.6 p. 169, R28
Fox News, 15.2 p. 454–455, 19.1 p. 574, 19.1 p. 575
Franklin, Benjamin, 2.2 p. 42, 2.3 p. 48, 2.5 p. 58, R3
fraud allegations, 2020 elections, 1.3 p. 24
free enterprise system, 1.3 p. 20–21
free exercise clause, 3.5 p. 91, 5.2 p. 147, p. 149, p. 151
free markets, 1.3 p. 20
free press, 5.1 p. 138
free rider problem, 14.4 p. 426
Free Soil Party, 14.1 p. 407, 14.3 pp. 421–423
Free Speech Movement, 5.3 p. 153
free trade, 18.4 p. 563
freedmen, rights of, 6.2 p. 187
Freedmen's Bureau, 4.3 p. 120p
Freedom Caucus, 14.1 p. 412, 14.2 p. 420
freedom from quartering soldiers, 5.1 p. 138
freedom of assembly and petition, 5.1 p. 138, 5.5 pp. 159–162, p. 164
freedom of expression, 5.3 pp. 152–164
Freedom of Information Act (FOIA), 5.6 p. 172, 11.4 pp. 349–350
freedom of press, 3.5 p. 91, 5.3 pp. 157–572, 19.1 p. 571
freedom of religion, 5.1 p. 138, 5.2 pp. 143–151
freedom of speech, 1.3 p. 19, 2.5 p. 64, 5.1 p. 138
Freedom Rider, 16.2 p. 483
freedom to assemble and petition, 5.1 p. 138
free-trade agreements, 4.1 p. 108, 10.2 p. 304, 14.4 p. 431, 18.4 p. 564–565
French and Indian War, 2.2 p. 42, R3
front-loading primaries, 15.2 pp. 452–453

Fry v. *Napoleon Community Schools*, 13.1 p. 380
full faith and credit clause, 4.2 p. 115

G

Gay Activist Alliance, 6.4 p. 216
Gay Liberation Front, 6.4 p. 216
Geary Act (1892), 6.1 p. 180
gender equality, 6.3 pp. 199–201, p. 206, 16.4 p. 498
gender gap, 14.1 p. 414, 16.4 p. 498
gender-based civil rights, 6.1 pp. 185–186
General Agreement on Tariff and Trade (GATT), 18.4 p. 564
General Allotment Act, 6.4 p. 214
general elections, 7.5 p. 248, 15.2 p. 454, 20.2 p. 603
general sales tax, 21.3 p. 639, p. 640
general-fund budget, 4.4 p. 128
gerrymandering, 7.2 p. 235, p. 237, 16.2 p. 481
Gettysburg Address, 3.2 p. 76
Gettysburg National Military Park, 20.2 p. 607
G.I. Bill, 21.1 p. 630
Gibbons* v. *Ogden, 4.3 p. 119, p. 122, p. 123, 8.1 p. 255, 11.3 p. 340
Gideon* v. *Wainwright, 3.5 p. 94, 5.5 p. 168
Ginsburg, Ruth Bader, 6.3 p. 204, 6.5 p. 222, U6 p. 401, 8.1 p. 256, 8.3 p. 268, 13.2 p. 384, p. 385, 13.2 p. 387, 13.4 p. 399, 16.2 p. 485, R23
global challenges, 18.3 pp. 548–557
global pandemics, 18.3 p. 557, pp. 554–555. *See also* COVID-19 pandemic
global warming, 17.4 pp. 530–532, 18.3 p. 556
globalization, 18.4 p. 563–564, p. 565
Goldwater, Barry, 1.4 pp. 28–29, 19.2 p. 577
Gomillion* v. *Lightfoot, 16.2 p. 482
Gore, Al, 10.1 p. 297, 10.4 p. 320, 14.3 p. 423, 15.3 p. 460, 15.4 p. 461, 16.3 p. 491
government, systems of, U2 p. 106p, 4.1 p. 107–108
Government Accountability Office (GAO), 11.4 p. 347
government bonds, 17.2 p. 518
government corporations, 8.1 p. 256, 11.2 p. 333, pp. 338–340
government shutdown, 9.2 pp. 282–288
governors, 6.2 p. 193, 20.1 p. 597, 20.3 pp. 608–612
grand jury, 5.1 p. 138, 12.1 p. 366, 20.4 p. 617
grandfather clauses, 6.2 p. 188, 16.2 p. 481–482
Gray* v. *Sanders, 20.2 p. 602
Great Compromise, 2.5 pp. 60–61, 7.1 p. 229
Great Depression, 1.3 p. 20, 1.4 p. 27–28, 4.3 p. 121, 14.1 pp. 408–520
Great Recession (2008–2009), 1.1 pp. 7–8, 4.4 p. 130, 9.2 p. 283–284, 14.1 p. 409, 17.2 p. 517, p. 520, p. 522, 21.3 pp. 642–643
Great Society, 1.4 p. 29, 4.4 p. 128, 11.3 p. 341
Green New Deal, 17.4 p. 531
Green Party, 14.1 p. 407, 14.2 p. 416, 14.3 pp. 421–423
Greenpeace USA, 14.4 p. 433, 14.4 p. 434
Griswold* v. *Connecticut, 5.5 p. 169, 5.6 p. 171
gross domestic product, 9.3 pp. 284–285, 11.3 p. 342, 17.2 p. 522, 18.4 p. 565
Grove City* v. *Bell, 6.3 p. 199
Grutter* v. *Bollinger, 6.5 p. 221–222
Guantanamo Bay, Cuba, 12.3 p. 374
Gulf of Tonkin Resolution, 3.6 p. 103
gun control, 1.1 p. 7, 5.1 pp. 139–140, 8.2 p. 262, R42
Gun Control Act of 1968, 5.1 p. 140
gun ownership, 3.6 p. 101 p. 7, 5.1 pp. 139–140
Gun-Free School Zones Act of 1990, 4.4 p. 124, 8.1 p. 255

H

Haaland, Deb, 6.4 p. 214, 7.1 p. 229, 7.2 p. 239
***habeas corpus*, writ of**, 5.1 p. 138, 12.2 p. 368
Hamdan* v. *Rumsfeld, 8.2 p. 260
Hamilton, Alexander, 2.3 p. 51, 2.4 p. 57, 2.5 p. 58, p. 63, R8, 13.3 p. 389, 14.1 p. 405
Hannity, Sean, 19.2 p. 580, p. 582
Harding, Warren G., 14.1 p. 408
Harris, Kamala, 1.3 pp. 23, 6.3 p. 205, 6.4 p. 212, 10.1 p. 297, 14.2 p. 419, 16.4 p. 498
Hate Crimes Prevention Act of 2009, 3.5 p. 94
head of state, 1.2 p. 14, 10.1 p. 299, p. 301
Head Start, 4.3 p. 122p
Health and Human Services Department, 10.4 p. 315, 11.2 pp. 333–334
Health Insurance Potability and Accountability Act (HIPAA), 5.6 p. 173
health-care system, 17.3 p. 524, pp. 526–528
Heart of Atlanta Motel* v. *United States, 8.1 p. 255
Help America Vote Act, 16.3 p. 491
Henry, Patrick, 2.1 p. 38, 2.5 p. 58, 2.5 p. 64
Hernandez* v. *Texas, 6.4 p. 208, 6.4 p. 210
HIPAA Privacy Rule, 5.6 p. 173
Hispanics. *See also* Latinos
COVID-19 impacting, 18.3 p. 557
as governors, 20.3 p. 609
origins of, 6.4 p. 208
in politics, 1.3 p. 25, 6.4 pp. 208–209
in state legislature, 20.2 p. 603
Homeland Security Department, 1.1 p. 8, 10.4 p. 315, 11.2 p. 333
home-rule charters, 21.1 p. 626
Honest Leadership and Open Government Act, 14.5 p. 441
Hopwood* v. *State of Texas, 6.5 p. 221
House Appropriations Committee, 6.3 p. 205
House Committee on Agriculture, 11.1 p. 330
House *Journal*, 9.1 p. 275
House Majority PAC, 15.5 p. 473
House of Burgesses, 2.1 p. 38, p. 41, U9 p. 594
House of Commons, 1.3 p. 17
House of Lords, 1.3 p. 17
House of Representatives, 3.2 p. 77, U4 p. 272
2018 midterm elections, U7 p. 443
African Americans in, 6.2 p. 193
Asian Americans in, 6.4 p. 212
bicameral Congress, 7.1 p. 229
congressional districts, 7.2 p. 232–234
congressional election candidates, 7.5 p. 246, pp. 248–249
debate rules, 7.2 p. 238
election of, 15.3 pp. 457–458
establishment of, 3.1 p. 73–74, 3.3 p. 83, R14, R15
floor debate rules, 9.1 p. 276, 9.1 p. 278
general elections, 7.5 p. 248
House membership, 7.2 p. 233
Latinos in, 6.4 p. 209
majority leader, 7.4 p. 243
minority leader, 7.4 p. 243
nonvoting delegates, 7.2 p. 233
patterns of representations, 7.1 p. 230–231
political action committees (PACs), 7.5 p. 248
population-based representation, 2.5 p. 60, 7.2 p. 232–233, R15
primary elections, 7.5 p. 246, 7.5 p. 248
proportional representation, 2.5 p. 60, 7.1 p. 229
qualification for, 7.2 p. 232
redistricting, 7.2 p. 236, 7.2 p. 233–234
roll-call vote, 9.1 p. 278
single-member districts, 7.2 p. 233
Speaker of the House, 7.4 pp. 242–243
sponsoring bills, 9.1 p. 273
standing committees, 7.4 pp. 244–245
tax bills originating from, 9.1 pp. 273–274, 9.2 p. 284
term length, 3.3 p. 84, 7.1 p. 230
trade agreements, 10.2 p. 304
voting process for, 3.2 p. 76
whips, 7.4 p. 243
women in, 6.3 p. 202, 6.3 p. 204
House Rules Committee, 7.2 p. 238, 7.2 p. 237–238, 9.1 p. 276
Housing and Urban Development Department, 10.4 p. 315, 11.2 p. 333
Hughes, Charles Evans, 5.5 p. 160, 15.1 p. 445
hurricanes, 4.2 p. 115p, 11.1 p. 325
Hussein, Saddam, 18.3 pp. 550–551
Husted* v. *A. Philip Randolph Institute, 13.1 p. 380

I

identity/ideological interest groups, 14.4 p. 433–434
ideological party, 14.3 p. 422
ideologues, 10.4 p. 317
illegal immigration, 6.1 pp. 181–183
immigration, 1.3 p. 22, 4.4 p. 126, 6.1 pp. 180–212, 6.4 p. 209, 8.1 p. 256, 11.4 p. 353
Immigration Act (1907/1917), 6.1 p. 181
Immigration and Nationality Act (1965), 6.1 p. 181, 6.4 pp. 211–212
impeachment,
Andrew Johnson, 2.5 p. 62
Donald J. Trump, 8.3 p. 266
of governors, 20.1 p. 596, 20.3 p. 610
power of, 3.2 p. 78, p. 80, R16
of president and vice-president, 2.5 p. 62, 3.1 p. 73–74, 3.2 p. 78, 3.2 p. 80, R22
state legislatures, 20.2 p. 605
Supreme Court justices, 13.2 p. 383
implied powers, 4.2 pp. 113–114, 4.3 p. 117–118, 8.2 pp. 261–263
inauguration, 15.2 p. 454
income tax, 3.5 p. 95, 8.1 p. 253, 17.2 pp. 520–521, 21.3 p. 639–640
incumbency power, 7.5 p. 249
independent regulatory agencies, 11.2 pp. 335–337
Independents, 1.3 p. 22, 14.1 p. 412, 14.2 p. 420
Indian Citizenship Act of 1924, 6.4 p. 214
Indian Gaming Regulatory Act, 6.4 p. 214
Indian Reorganization Act of 1934, 6.4 p. 214
indirect lobbying techniques, 14.5 pp. 436–439
indirect primaries, 15.1 pp. 447–448
indirect taxes, 8.1 p. 253
individual income tax, 11.3 p. 343
individual rights, 2.1 p. 40, 3.1 p. 75, 3.3 pp. 85–86, R14
Individuals with Disabilities Education Act (IDEA), 6.4 p. 217
inflation, 2.4 pp. 55–56, 14.1 p. 407, 17.2 p. 517
inherent powers, 4.2 p. 114, 8.2 p. 260, 10.2 pp. 305–306
initiative, 1.2 p. 13, 20.2 pp. 605–606
insurrection, 1.3 p. 24
interest groups, U7 p. 404, 11.1 p. 330, 11.1 p. 331, 14.4 pp. 424–440, 14.5 p. 436, p. 438, 15.5 pp. 470–471
intermediate scrutiny, 6.1 pp. 185–186
Internal Revenue Service (IRS), 11.3 p. 342, 12.3 p. 373
International Atomic Energy Agency (IAEA), 18.4 p. 560, 18.4 p. 561
international commerce, 18.4 pp. 563–565
international economics, 18.4 pp. 558–564
International Monetary Fund, 18.4 p. 565
internet, 5.3 pp. 158–159, 5.5 p. 162, 11.4 p. 351, 15.4 pp. 466–588, 16.5 pp. 502–503, 19.1 p. 570, 19.3 pp. 583–588
Internet Research Agency (IRA), 19.3 p. 588
interstate commerce, 3.6 pp. 99–100, 4.3 p. 119, 4.3 p. 122, 4.3 p. 123, 8.1 pp. 254–255
Interstate Commerce Commission (ICC), 8.1 p. 255, 11.2 p. 337, 11.3 p. 341
interventionism, 16.4 p. 495, 18.2 p. 543
Iran's nuclear weapons, 18.4 p. 561

INDEX

Iraq, 10.2 p. 309, 18.3 pp. 550–554
iron triangle, 11.1 p. 330–515
Islamic State in Iraq and Greater Syria (ISIS), 1.1 p. 8, 10.2 p. 309, 18.3 pp. 553–554
isolationism, 18.2 p. 543, 18.2 p. 544
Israel, 4.1 p. 108
issue ads, 14.5 p. 437, 19.2 p. 577
issue identification, 17.1 p. 513–514
issue-oriented third party, 14.3 pp. 421–422, 15.5 p. 470

J

Jacksonian Democrats, 14.1 pp. 4–6
***Janus* v. *AFSCME*,** 14.4 p. 432
Japanese Americans, internment of, 5.1 p. 141, 6.4 p. 211, p. 213, 8.3 p. 269
Jefferson, Thomas, 1.3 p. 21, 2.1 p. 38, 2.2 p. 47, 2.3 p. 48, 2.5 p. 58, 3.3 p. 85, pp. 93–94, 3.5 p. 91, 4.3 p. 117, 5.2 p. 143, 5.3 p. 154, 7.3 pp. 240–241, U7 p. 403, 10.2 p. 305, 10.3 p. 311, 14.1 p. 405–407, 15.1 p. 446, 19.2 p. 576, 21.2 p. 635, R3, R27, R28
Jeffersonian Republicans, 14.1 p. 405–407, 15.1 p. 446
Jim Crow laws, 6.2 p. 188
Johnson, Andrew, 8.3 p. 266
Joint Chiefs of Staff (JCS), 10.4 p. 318, 18.1 p. 541
judges, 12.1 p. 366, 12.2 p. 368, 20.4 p. 620–621
judicial appointments, 8.3 p. 267, 12.2 p. 370
judicial branch
- checks and balances, 3.3 pp. 83–84
- establishment of, 2.5 p. 62, 3.1 pp. 73–74, 3.3 p. 83, R14, R23
- organization of, 3.6 pp. 98–99
- Supreme Court, 11.2 p. 333

judicial districts, 12.2 p. 367–368
judicial nominations, 8.3 p. 268
judicial requirements, 12.1 pp. 364–365
judicial restraint, 13.3 p. 390
judicial review, 3.6 p. 100, 13.3 p. 389
judicial system, 5.1 p. 141, 5.5 pp. 165–166
Judiciary Act of 1789, 3.6 p. 98, 3.6 p. 100, R23
Judiciary Committee, 8.3 pp. 267–268, 8.3 p. 267
Juneteenth, 2.3 pp. 48–49
juries, 12.1 p. 366
jurisdiction, 7.2 p. 234, 7.2 p. 236, 12.1 pp. 364–383
Justice Department, 10.4 p. 315–316, 11.2 p. 333–334, 16.2 p. 482

K

***Kelo* v. *New London*,** 5.5 p. 166
Keynesian economics, 17.2 p. 519, 17.2 p. 520
Keystone XL oil pipeline, 10.3 p. 311
King, Martin Luther, Jr., U3 p. 134, 6.2 p. 191–192, 6.5 p. 219, 10.1 p. 300, 16.4 p. 495
***King* v. *Burwell*,** 13.3 p. 389, 13.4 p. 396
***Korematsu* v. *United States*,** 6.4 p. 211, 6.4 p. 213, R29
Kurds, 18.3 p. 551, 18.3 p. 553

L

Labor Department, 10.4 p. 315, 11.2 p. 332–333
labor interest groups, 14.4 pp. 430–432
labor movement, 14.4 p. 431
labor unions, 5.5 p. 164
Latinos, 6.4 pp. 207–209, 14.1 p. 413
Law Day programs, 12.1 p. 367
law enforcement, 6.2 p. 194, 17.1 p. 515
***Lawrence* v. *Texas*,** 13.3 p. 394, 13.4 p. 396
laws, 1.1 pp. 6–7, R17
lawsuits, 3.5 p. 93, 12.1 p. 363
League of Nations, 8.1 p. 258, 18.2 p. 544
League of United Latin American Citizens (LULAC), 6.4 p. 208
***Ledbetter* v. *Goodyear Tire and Rubber Co.*,** 6.3 p. 200
Lee Resolution, 2.3 p. 48
Legal Defense and Education Fund, 6.2 pp. 190–191, 14.5 p. 437
legal interpretation approaches, 13.3 p. 390, p. 392, p. 394
legal summaries, 13.1 p. 382
legislative branch (Congress), 2.5 p. 59, 3.1 p. 73–74, 3.3 pp. 83–84, 11.2 p. 333, R14, R15
legislative plans, 10.3 p. 311
legislative powers, presidential, 10.2 pp. 306–307
legislative process, 7.1 p. 231, 9.1 pp. 273–605
legislative referendum, 1.2 p. 13
legislative strategies, 9.1 pp. 274–275
legislatures of the colonies, 2.1 pp. 40–41, 2.1 p. 38
***Lemon* v. *Kurtzman*,** 5.2 p. 146, 5.2 p. 147
LGBTQ community, 1.4 p. 31, 5.1 p. 141, 6.3 p. 203, 6.4 pp. 215–217, U9 p. 594, 13.3 p. 394, 13.4 p. 396, 14.4 p. 433, 18.3 p. 549
liberalism, 1.4 p. 27, p. 29, 1.4 p. 31, 5.3 p. 152, 10.2 p. 305, 13.4 p. 395, 14.1 p. 411, 15.1 p. 448, 16.4 p. 496
Libertarian Party, 1.4 p. 31, p. 33, 14.1 p. 407, 14.3 p. 422–423, 14.3 p. 424, 15.4 p. 466
Lilly Ledbetter Fair Pay Act, 6.3 p. 200
limited government, 1.3 p. 16–17, 3.1 p. 75, 3.2 p. 78, R14
Lincoln, Abraham, 2.3 p. 48, 3.2 p. 76, p. 81, 3.6 p. 102, 4.3 p. 119, 10.1 p. 299, 10.4 p. 316, 11.4 p. 347, 14.1 p. 406, 15.5 p. 468
Line Item Veto Act, 9.2 p. 282
line-item veto amendment, 3.4 p. 90
literacy tests, 6.2 p. 188, 16.2 p. 480, p. 482
Little Rock Nine, 6.2 p. 190
Livingston, Robert, R3, 4.3 p. 123
***Lloyd Corporation, Ltd.* v. *Tanner*,** 5.5 p. 162
Lobbying Disclosure Act, 14.5 pp. 440–441
lobbying/lobbyists, 1.1 p. 7, 5.1 p. 139, 5.5 p. 160, 11.1 p. 331, 14.4 p. 425, p. 427, p. 428, 14.5 pp. 435–441
local government
- education, 21.3 p. 641, 21.3 p. 642
- federal grants, 4.4 p. 131
- foundation of, 21.1 pp. 625–626
- general-fund budget, 4.4 p. 128
- growth of, 11.3 p. 342
- local elections, 16.3 p. 489
- managing cities, 21.1 pp. 628–630
- municipal government, 21.1 pp. 627–628
- organization of, 20.1 p. 598
- political machines, 21.1 p. 628
- revenue sources, 4.4 p. 128
- revenues for, 21.3 pp. 638–640, 21.3 p. 640
- special district, 20.1 p. 599
- spending of, 21.3 pp. 641–642, 21.3 p. 641

local party organization, 14.2 p. 418
Locke, John, 1.3 p. 17, U1 p. 35, 2.3 p. 48, 3.2 p. 76, p. 78, R3
long-term government bonds, 17.2 p. 518
Louisiana Territory, 10.2 p. 305, 15.1 pp. 449–450
***Loving* v. *Virginia*,** 6.2 p. 193, 13.3 p. 391, 13.3 p. 393

M

Madison, James, 2.1 p. 38, 2.3 p. 50, 2.5 pp. 57–60, 2.5 p. 63, 3.2 p. 77, 3.3 p. 82–83, 3.3 p. 86, 3.5 p. 91, 7.1 p. 229, R8, 10.1 p. 295, 14.1 p. 406, R27, R38
Magna Carta (Great Charter), 1.3 p. 16, 3.1 p. 72, R27
mail-in voting, 1.3 p. 23, 15.2 pp. 456–458, 16.3 p. 492
majoritarianism, 14.4 p. 428
Majority Forward, 15.5 p. 473
majority leader, 7.4 p. 243
majority rule/minority rights, 1.3 p. 17
majority-minority districts, 20.2 p. 602
Malcolm X, 6.2 pp. 191–192
managing cities, 21.1 pp. 629–630
***Manual of Parliamentary Practice*,** 7.3 pp. 240–241
***Mapp* v. *Ohio*,** 5.5 p. 166, p. 169
***Marbury* v. *Madison*,** 3.6 p. 100, 4.3 p. 117, 13.3 p. 389, R23
March for Our Lives, 5.1 p. 140, R42
March on Washington for Jobs and Freedom, U3 p. 134, 6.2 p. 191, 16.2 p. 483
Marshall, John, 2.5 p. 63, 3.6 p. 101, 4.3 p. 117, p. 119, p. 123, 8.2 p. 262, 13.3 p. 389
Marshall, Thurgood, U3 p. 134, 6.2 p. 190, p. 193, 13.2 p. 384, 16.2 p. 482
Marshall Plan, 18.2 pp. 544–545
Mason, George, 2.3 p. 50, 2.5 p. 58, 2.5 p. 62, 3.5 p. 91, 10.1 p. 295
mass media, 19.1 p. 569–570, 19.2 p. 582. *See also* media
Massachusetts Bay Colony, 2.1 pp. 39–40
***Massachusetts* v. *Environmental Protection Agency*,** 4.4 p. 125p
***Masterpiece Cakeshop, Ltd.* v. *Colorado Civil Rights*,** 13.4 p. 399
Mayflower Compact, 2.1 p. 39
McCain-Feingold Act, 7.5 p. 248, 15.5 pp. 470–472
McConnell, Mitch, 7.4 p. 243, 8.3 p. 267–268, 9.1 p. 279, 14.2 p. 420, 17.3 pp. 528–529
***McConnell* v. *Federal Election Commission*,** 15.5 p. 471
***McCulloch* v. *Maryland*,** 4.3 p. 117–118, 4.3 p. 122, 8.2 p. 262, 11.3 p. 340
***McCutcheon* v. *Federal Election Commission*,** 15.5 p. 472
***McGirt* v. *Oklahoma*,** 6.4 p. 215, 13.1 p. 381, 21.2 p. 638
McKinley, William, 10.1 p. 297, 18.2 p. 543
***McLain* v. *Real Estate Board of New Orleans, Inc.*,** 8.2 p. 262
media, 16.4 p. 494, 19.1 pp. 569–582, 19.2 p. 579. *See also* mass media
Medicaid, 4.1 p. 110, 4.3 p. 122, 4.4 p. 126, p. 128, 11.3 p. 344, 17.3 pp. 524–525
Medicare, 1.4 p. 29, 4.3 p. 122, 9.3 p. 286, 11.3 pp. 343–525
MeToo movement, 6.3 p. 202
Metric Act, 8.1 p. 256
Mexican Americans, 6.1 p. 181, 6.4 pp. 207–208, 6.4 p. 210, 16.2 pp. 480–482
Mexican Cession, 6.4 pp. 207–208
military actions, presidential, 10.2 pp. 309–310
military budgets, 18.1 p. 541
military courts, 12.3 pp. 373–374
militia, debate about, 5.1 pp. 139–140
***Miller* v. *Johnson*,** 20.2 p. 602
***Milliken* v. *Bradley*,** 6.2 p. 191
minimum wage, 5.5 p. 164
minorities, population percentage of, 6.4 p. 207
minority party, 7.4 p. 243, 14.2 p. 416
Mint Act of 1792, 8.1 p. 254
***Miranda* v. *Arizona*,** 5.5 p. 167
misdemeanors, 12.1 p. 364, 20.4 p. 615
modern primary system, 15.1 pp. 447–448
modernism, 13.3 p. 392, p. 394
monarchy, 1.2 p. 11
monetary policy, 17.2 pp. 517–518
monopolies, 11.2 p. 337, 19.1 p. 576
Monroe Doctrine, 18.2 p. 543
Montesquieu, Charles de, 2.3 p. 49, 3.3 p. 83
Montgomery bus boycott, 5.5 p. 161, 6.2 p. 191
moral idealism, 18.1 p. 539, 18.2 p. 544
Mothers of the Movement, 5.1 p. 137
MoveOn, 14.4 p. 434
multimember districts, 14.2 p. 421
multinational companies, 18.4 p. 564
municipal courts, 20.4 p. 619–620
municipal government, 20.1 p. 598, 21.1 pp. 625–627
***Munn* v. *Illinois*,** R31
Muslims, 1.3 p. 26, 5.2 p. 149, 7.2 p. 238, 16.4 p. 498, 18.3 p. 551, 18.3 p. 553
mutually assured destruction (MAD), 18.2 p. 546

N

***NAACP* v. *Alabama*,** 5.5 pp. 161–162
NARAL Pro-Choice America, 14.4 p. 434
National Aeronautics and Space Administration (NASA), 11.2 p. 335–336, 17.4 p. 530
National American Woman Suffrage Association (NAWSA), 6.3 p. 197
National Association for Advancement of Colored People (NAACP), 5.5 pp. 161–162, 6.2 p. 190–191, 6.5 p. 219, 12.1 p. 360-361, 14.4 p. 433, 19.3 p. 588
National Association of Letter Carriers, 11.2 p. 339
National Broadcasting Company (NBC), 19.1 p. 570
national census, 7.2 p. 233, 7.2 p. 235
National Center for Educational Statistics, 6.3 p. 200
National Civics & Law Academy, 12.1 p. 366
national committee, 14.2 p. 418–419
National Council of Churches, 14.4 p. 434
National Council on Public Polls, 16.5 p. 507
national crisis, presidential powers during, 10.3 p. 313
national debt, 8.1 p. 253, 9.3 p. 285, 9.3 p. 288, 11.3 p. 345, 17.2 pp. 521–522
national defense, 11.3 p. 344
National Education Association, 14.4 p. 431
***National Federation of Independent Business* v. *Sebelius*,** 4.4 p. 126, 4.4 p. 130, 8.2 p. 263, 17.3 p. 526, 17.3 p. 527
National Geographic Society, U7 p. 404
National Governors Association, 20.3 p. 612
National Guard units, 4.2 p. 115p, 14.4 p. 430, 18.1 p. 541
National Intelligence, 10.4 p. 316, p. 318, 18.1 p. 542
National Labor Relations Board (NLRB), 11.2 p. 337, 12.2 p. 368
national nominating convention, 15.2 pp. 453–454
National Organization for Women (NOW), 6.3 p. 198–199
National Origins Act (1924), 6.1 p. 181
National Park Service, 11.2 p. 333
national party convention, 15.2 p. 452, p. 454
national party organization, 14.2 pp. 418–419
National Popular Vote Interstate Compact, 3.2 p. 79
National Republican Congressional Committee, 15.5 p. 473
National Republican Senatorial Committee, 15.5 p. 473
National Response Plan, 11.1 p. 325
National Rifle Association (NRA), 1.1 p. 7, 5.1 p. 139, 14.4 p. 425, 15.5 p. 471
National Right to Life, 14.4 p. 425, p. 434
national security, 1.1 p. 8, 5.6 pp. 174–175, 11.2 p. 333
National Security Act of 1947, 18.1 p. 541
national security advisor, 10.4 p. 318, 18.1 p. 542
National Security Agency (NSA), 1.1 p. 8, 5.3 p. 156, 5.6 pp. 174–175, 11.4 p. 347, 12.3 p. 372
National Security Council (NSC), 10.4 pp. 317–542
National Woman Suffrage Association (NWSA), 6.3 p. 197
nationalist terrorism, 18.3 p. 548
nationality-based immigration quotas, 6.1 p. 181
Native American Graves Protection and Repatriation Act (NAGPRA), 6.4 pp. 214–215
Native American Languages Act, 6.4 p. 214
Native Americans, 1.1 p. 4, 2.2 p. 42, 2.5 p. 65, R3, 6.4 pp. 214–215, 6.4 p. 212, 7.1 p. 229, 7.2 p. 239, 14.4 p. 433, 16.2 pp. 480–482, 20.2 p. 603, 20.3 p. 609, 21.2 pp. 635–638
Native Lands (Bowden), 21.2 p. 637
naturalization process, 3.1 p. 75, 6.1 pp. 179–180, 8.1 p. 256, 16.1 p. 478, R40, R41
necessary and proper clause, 3.3 p. 82, 4.2 p. 113, 8.2 p. 262, R18
negative campaign ads, 19.2 pp. 576–577
net public debt, 8.1 p. 253
neutrality policy, 18.2 p. 544
New Deal, 1.4 p. 27–28, 1.4 p. 29, 10.1 p. 299, 10.2 p. 306, 11.3 p. 341, 14.1 p. 408, 16.4 p. 500, 17.2 p. 519
New Jersey Plan, 2.5 p. 60
New Strategic Arms Reduction Treaty (New START), 10.2 p. 304
***New York Times Co.* v. *United States*,** 5.3 p. 157
news coverage, 19.1 p. 575, 19.2 pp. 578–585
1964/1980/1984 elections, 1.4 p. 28–30
Nineteenth Amendment, 3.4 p. 88, 3.5 p. 93, p. 95, 6.3 p. 198, 16.1 p. 477, 16.2 pp. 481–482, p. 487, R34
Ninth Amendment, 3.5 p. 92–93, 5.1 p. 139, 5.6 pp. 169–170, R29
No Child Left Behind Act of 2001, 4.4 p. 126, p. 130
non-coercive diplomacy, 18.4 pp. 557–558
nondefense discretionary spending, 11.3 p. 345
non-legislative powers, 8.3 pp. 264–266
nonvoting delegates, 7.2 p. 233
North American Free Trade Agreement (NAFTA), 10.2 p. 304, 14.4 p. 431, 18.4 p. 564
North Atlantic Treaty Organization (NATO), 9.1 p. 275, 18.2 p. 545
North Carolina State Board of Elections and Ethics, 16.3 p. 492
Northwest Ordinances, 2.4 p. 54, 4.2 p. 113, 6.4 p. 212
Northwest Territory, 4.2 p. 114, 8.2 p. 260
nuclear energy, 17.4 p. 534
nuclear option, 8.3 p. 268, 13.2 p. 386
Nuclear Regulatory Commission (NRC), 11.2 p. 336
Nuclear Safety Violations, 11.4 p. 352

O

Obama, Barack, 1.3 p. 18, 4.4 pp. 129–131, 5.2 p. 149, p. 151, 6.1 p. 183, 6.2 p. 192–193, 6.3 p. 200, p. 202, p. 204, 6.4 p. 214, p. 216–217, 7.3 p. 242, 7.5 p. 248, 8.3 p. 268, U8 p. 512, 9.3 p. 288, 10.1 p. 295, p. 297, pp. 300–301, 10.2 pp. 304–310, 10.3 p. 311–312, 10.4 p. 316, pp. 319–320, 11.3 p. 341–342, p. 344, 11.4 p. 347–348, 12.2 p. 370, 12.3 p. 374, 13.2 p. 384, 13.4 p. 395, 14.1 p. 409, 15.4 p. 466–468, 15.5 p. 468, 16.4 p. 497–498, 16.5 p. 506, 17.2 p. 516, p. 520, 17.3 p. 523, p. 527, 17.4 pp. 531–532, 18.3 p. 551–552, 18.4 p. 565, 19.2 p. 578, 19.2 p. 580, R22
Obamacare, 4.4 p. 126, 10.1 p. 300. *See also* Affordable Care Act (2010)
***Obergefell* v. *Hodges*,** 4.2 p. 115, 6.4 p. 217, 13.1 p. 381, 13.3 p. 392, 13.3 p. 394, 13.4 p. 396
obscenity restrictions, 5.3 pp. 158–159
Ocasio-Cortez, Alexandria, 6.3 p. 205, 17.4 p. 531
Occupational Safety and Health Act of 1970, 11.1 p. 328
Occupational Safety and Health Administration (OSHA), 11.1 p. 328
O'Connor, Sandra Day, 5.6 p. 170, 6.3 p. 204, 6.5 p. 222, 13.2 p. 384, 13.4 p. 395
Office of Management and Budget (OMB), 9.3 pp. 286–287, 9.3 p. 285, 10.4 pp. 316–318, 11.1 p. 329
Office of National Drug Control Policy, 10.4 p. 317
Office of Personnel Management (OPM), 11.1 p. 327–328
Office of Science and Technology Policy, 10.4 p. 317
oil imports, 17.4 pp. 529–530
oil production, 17.4 p. 532
Oklahoma bombing, 18.3 p. 549
Olive Branch Petition, 2.2 p. 46
***Olmstead* v. *United States*,** 13.1 p. 382
omnibus bills, 9.2 pp. 282–283
Oneida, 6.4 p. 215
online fund-raising, 15.4 pp. 466–467
online voting, 16.2 p. 484, 16.3 pp. 492–493
open primaries, 15.1 pp. 448–449, 20.2 p. 603
open-ended authorizations, 9.3 pp. 285–286
Operation Warp Speed, 18.3 p. 557
opinion leaders, 16.4 p. 495
opioid epidemic, 17.1 p. 514
opposition research, 15.4 pp. 464–465
opposition to regulation, 11.1 p. 329
oral arguments, 13.1 p. 382
ordinances, 12.1 p. 362, 20.4 p. 615
ordinary scrutiny standard (rational basis test), 6.1 pp. 185–186
Organization of American States, 18.1 p. 540
original intent, 13.3 p. 392
original jurisdiction, 12.2 p. 367, 12.2 p. 368
originalism, 13.3 p. 392, 13.3 p. 394
origination clause, 9.1 pp. 273–274
Oslo Accords, 18.4 p. 559
overriding veto, 9.1 p. 277, 9.2 pp. 281–282

P

Page Act (1875), 6.1 p. 181
Paine, Thomas, 2.2 pp. 46–47, 3.5 p. 91
Pakistan, 18.3 p. 551
Palestine, division of, 18.4 p. 558
Palestine Liberation Organization (PLO), 18.4 p. 558
Palestinian Authority, 18.4 p. 559
Palestinian conflict, 18.4 pp. 558–560
Panama Canal, 18.2 pp. 543–544, 18.2 p. 544
pandemic. *See* Covid-19 pandemic
paper ballots, 15.3 p. 458, 16.3 p. 490
pardon power, 10.2 pp. 304–305, 20.3 p. 612
parental rights, 5.2 p. 149
Paris Convention, 17.4 p. 531, 17.4 p. 532, 18.1 p. 541
parishes, 21.1 p. 625, 21.2 p. 633
Parks, Rosa, 5.5 p. 161, 6.2 p. 191
parliamentary democracy, 1.2 p. 14, 1.3 pp. 16–17, 7.5 p. 249, 14.2 p. 420
parole power, 20.3 p. 612
Partial-Birth Abortion Ban Act, 5.6 p. 170
participatory journalism, 19.3 p. 584
participatory citizens, R39
partisan bias, 19.2 p. 581
partisan disagreement, 9.1 p. 279, 10.3 p. 312
partisan gerrymandering, 7.2 p. 235, 20.2 p. 602
partisan view, 7.1 p. 231
partisanship, 1.3 p. 20, 1.3 p. 21, 14.1 p. 411
party activists, 14.2 p. 417
party bosses, 15.1 p. 446
Party for Socialism and Liberations, 14.3 p. 422
party identification, 14.2 pp. 416–417, 16.4 p. 496
party organization, 14.2 pp. 418–419, 14.2 p. 416
party platforms, 14.1 p. 408, 14.2 p. 419
party system, growth of, 10.1 pp. 300–446
Patient Protection and Affordable Care Act, 4.4 p. 126
pay discrimination, 6.3 pp. 200–201
Payroll Protection Program (PPP), 18.3 p. 555
payroll taxes, 11.3 pp. 343–344
Pelosi, Nancy, U4 p. 272, 6.3 p. 202, 6.3 p. 204, 14.2 p. 414, 14.4 p. 427, R16, 17.3 p. 527
Pence, Mike, 3.5 p. 95, 10.4 p. 320, 10.4 p. 321, 14.2 p. 419, R16
Pendleton Civil Service Act, 11.1 p. 327
Pentagon Papers, 5.3 p. 157, 11.4 p. 352
peonage, 3.5 p. 94
People's Party, 14.1 p. 407
Perot, Ross, 14.1 p. 407, 19.2 p. 578
Persian Gulf War, 18.3 p. 550
persons with disabilities, 6.4 pp. 217–218, 16.2 p. 484
petition, for statehood, 4.2 p. 112
The Pew Research Center for the People and the Press, 19.2 p. 580
physician-assisted suicide law, 4.4 p. 126
***Plessy* v. *Ferguson*,** 6.2 p. 189, 13.1 pp. 382–383

INDEX

Plum Book, 11.1 p. 326, 11.1 p. 327
pluralist theory, 13.1 p. 383, 14.4 p. 428, 15.1 p. 450
pocket veto, 9.2 p. 281, 10.2 p. 305
police misconduct, 2.3 p. 49, U3 p. 136, 18.3 p. 557
police powers, 4.2 pp. 114–115
policy riders, 9.1 pp. 274–275
policymaking process, 11.1 p. 329–573
political action committees (PACs), U4 p. 251, 7.5 p. 248, 7.5 p. 249, 14.5 p. 435, 14.5 p. 436, 15.5 p. 469, 15.5 p. 470
political advertising, 15.4 p. 464
political campaign, modern, U4 p. 228, 15.4 pp. 465–588
political consultants, 15.4 pp. 463–464
political district, 14.2 p. 418
political ideology, 1.4 pp. 27–33, 1.4 p. 31, 1.4 p. 32, 1.4 p. 33, 13.4 pp. 394–397, 14.3 p. 422, 16.4 p. 496
political insurgent, 15.1 p. 448
political left (liberal), 15.1 p. 448
political parties, 1.3 p. 21, U7 p. 403, 14.1 pp. 405–429, 15.4 p. 463
political party leader, 10.1 pp. 300–301
political polarization, 14.1 pp. 411–412, 14.1 p. 414, 15.4 p. 463
political realism, 18.1 p. 539
political right (conservative), 15.1 p. 448
political socialization, 16.4 pp. 493–494
political values, 1.3 pp. 18–20, 2.1 p. 41
poll taxes, 3.5 p. 93, 3.5 p. 97, 6.2 p. 188, 6.2 p. 192, 6.2 p. 193, 16.2 pp. 480–82, R36
poll watchers, 15.3 p. 458, 16.3 p. 489
polling accuracy, 16.5 pp. 504–505
polling places, 15.1 p. 446, 15.3 p. 458, 16.3 p. 489
popular sovereignty, 2.3 p. 50, 3.1 p. 75, 3.2 p. 76, R14, 20.1 p. 596
popular vote, 1.2 p. 13, 1.3 p. 22, 15.3 p. 460
population, 1.1 p. 9, 1.3 pp. 25–26, 2.5 p. 59, 6.4 p. 209, 7.2 pp. 232–233
Populist Party, 14.1 p. 407, 14.3 p. 423
Postal Service, 10.4 p. 316
prayer in schools, 5.2 p. 144, 5.2 p. 145, 5.2 p. 147
Preamble, Bill of Rights, R27
Preamble, U.S. Constitution, 3.1 pp. 71–72, R14, R15
precedent, 1.3 p. 17, 12.1 p. 359, 12.1 p. 360
precinct, 14.2 p. 418, 15.3 p. 458
preclearance, 4.4 p. 126, 16.2 p. 482, 16.2 p. 486
President of the United States
congressional elections and, 7.5 pp. 248–249
constituents of, 10.1 p. 298, 10.3 p. 312
divided government impacting, 10.3 p. 312
election of, 3.2 p. 79, 15.2 p. 454
establishment of, 2.5 p. 62, 3.1 p. 73
executive agreements, 3.6 p. 103
executive orders, 3.6 pp. 101–308
federal bureaucracy head, 11.1 p. 325
federal judicial appointments, 13.2 pp. 383–386
foreign affairs power, 10.2 pp. 308–309
head of state, 1.2 p. 14, 10.1 p. 299, 10.1 p. 301, 18.1 p. 540
impeachment of, 2.5 p. 62, 3.1 p. 73, 3.1 p. 74, 3.2 p. 78, 3.2 p. 80, R16, R22
inauguration of, 15.2 p. 454
Line Item Veto Act, 9.2 p. 282
military actions and, 10.2 pp. 309–310
National Security Agency, 10.4 p. 318
patronage, 10.1 p. 300
political party leader, 10.1 pp. 300–301, 10.1 p. 301
powers of, 3.3 p. 84, 3.6 p. 103, 9.1 p. 273, 9.1 p. 277, 9.2 pp. 281–310, 18.1 p. 540
signing statements, 10.2 pp. 307–308, 10.3 p. 312
signs bills into law, 9.1 p. 277, 9.2 pp. 281–282
State of the Union address, 10.2 p. 303
term limits, 3.2 p. 78, 3.4 p. 88, R35
transfer of power, 3.4 p. 88, 3.5 p. 93, p. 97, R37
voting process for, 3.2 p. 76
presidential campaign, 15.4 pp. 463–464, pp. 469–472
presidential caucuses, 15.2 pp. 450–454
presidential democracy, 1.2 p. 14
presidential elections, 5.6 p. 173, 15.3 pp. 459–460
presidential powers, 10.2 pp. 303–314, 10.4 p. 317
presidential primaries, 15.1 p. 447, 15.2 pp. 450–454
Presidential Succession Act of 1947, 10.4 p. 321
president's cabinet, 10.4 p. 316, p. 321
press, 19.1 pp. 569–570. *See also* mass media
press secretary, 15.4 p. 463
primaries, 15.1 pp. 448–450
primary elections, 7.5 p. 246, p. 248, 14.2 pp. 414–447, 20.2 p. 603
primary voters, 15.1 p. 448
print media, 19.1 p. 570–571, 19.1 p. 574
Privacy Act of 1974, 5.6 p. 172
privacy rights, 5.6 pp. 169–175
private bills, 9.1 p. 274
private contractors, 11.3 pp. 341–342
private enterprise, 17.2 p. 523
pro tempore, 7.4 p. 243, 20.2 p. 604
probable cause, 5.5 p. 166, 5.5 p. 169, R29
procedural due process, 5.5 p. 165
Proclamation of 1763, 2.2 p. 42, R3
Progressive Party, 1.4 p. 31, 14.3 p. 422
progressive Republicans, 14.1 pp. 407–408
progressive taxes, 15.2 p. 455, 17.2 pp. 520–521, 21.3 p. 639, 21.3 p. 640
progressivism, 1.4 p. 31, 7.3 p. 240
Prohibition, 3.5 p. 93, 3.5 p. 95, R33, R35
Prohibition Party, 14.3 p. 421
property rights, natural rights of, 1.3 p. 20
property taxes, 11.3 p. 343, 21.3 p. 639, 21.3 p. 640
proposed law, 9.1 p. 273
protest marches, 5.5 p. 159, 14.5 pp. 438–439
protesting, 1.3 pp. 22–23, 5.5 p. 162, 6.2 pp. 194–195
public bills, 9.1 p. 274
public debt, 17.2 pp. 521–522
public interest, 19.1 p. 575
public policy, 4.1 p. 109
public services, 1.1 pp. 7–8
punch card ballots, 15.3 p. 458, 16.3 p. 491
Pure Food and Drug Act, 3.6 p. 99–100, 11.3 p. 341
push-pull factors of immigration, 6.1 p. 180

Q

Quartering Act of 1765, 2.2 p. 44
quota, affirmative action, 6.5 p. 221

R

R. G. & G. R. Harris Funeral Homes, Inc. v. Equal Employment Opportunity Commission, 6.3 p. 203
racial discrimination
of African Americans, 3.5 p. 94, 4.3 p. 120, p. 124, 4.4 p. 128, 5.5 p. 161, 6.2 pp. 187–223, 12.1 p. 361–362
of Asian Americans, 6.4 p. 209, p. 211, p. 213, 8.3 p. 269
of Hispanics, 6.4 pp. 207–208
racial gerrymandering, 7.2 p. 235, 7.2 p. 237, 20.2 p. 602
racial segregation, 4.1 p. 110, 5.5 p. 161, 6.2 pp. 188–191, 6.4 p. 208, 12.1 p. 360, 12.1 p. 361, 21.1 p. 630
ratification, amendments, 3.4 pp. 89–90
ratification, Constitution, 2.5 p. 65, 3.3 p. 85, R26
recall, 1.2 p. 13, 20.2 pp. 605–606
recession, 4.4 p. 128, 17.2 p. 517
reconciliation bill, 7.3 p. 241
reconciliation rule, 9.1 p. 279
redistricting, 7.2 p. 233–234
referendums, 1.2 p. 13, 20.2 pp. 605–606
Reform and Control Act of 1986, 6.1 pp. 181–182
Reform Party, 14.1 p. 407, 14.3 p. 424
Refugee Act (1980), 6.1 p. 181
***Regents of the University of California* v. *Bakke*,** 6.5 p. 220, 6.5 p. 221
Regents' Prayer Case, 5.2 p. 144, 5.2 p. 145
regulations for campaigns, 15.5 pp. 469–472
regulatory agencies, 11.1 p. 330, pp. 335–337
Rehabilitation Act, 6.4 p. 217
Rehnquist, William, 5.3 p. 156, 6.5 p. 220, p. 222, 8.1 p. 256, 13.4 p. 395, 15.4 p. 461
Religious Freedom Restoration Act of 1993 (RFRA), 5.2 p. 151
renewable energy, 17.4 p. 534
representative democracy, 1.1 p. 7, 1.2 p. 10, p. 14, 1.3 pp. 16–18, 3.1 p. 75, 3.2 p. 76, 3.3 pp. 82–83, R14
republic, 1.2 p. 14, 2.3 pp. 50–51
Republican National Committee (RNC), 10.1 p. 301, 14.2 p. 419, 15.2 p. 453, p. 456
Republican National Convention, U7 pp. 402–403, 14.2 pp. 418–419
Republican Party, 14.2 pp. 419–420
1860 elections, 14.1 p. 406
2000 elections, 1.3 p. 21, 14.1 pp. 408–409, 14.3 p. 423
2010 elections, 1.3 p. 21
2014 mid-terms, 14.1 pp. 409–410
2016 elections, 1.3 pp. 21–455
2020 elections, 1.3 p. 24, 14.1 pp. 409–411
after Civil War, 14.1 p. 407
business interest groups, 14.4 pp. 429–430
conservatism, 1.4 p. 27, 14.1 p. 408, p. 411, 16.4 p. 496
Cuban Americans supporting, 6.4 p. 208
establishment of, 14.1 p. 406
extreme partisanship, 14.1 p. 411
Freedom Caucus Republicans, 14.2 p. 420
gender gap, 14.1 p. 414
gerrymandering, 7.2 p. 235
government shutdown, 9.3 p. 288
Great Depression impacting, 14.1 p. 408
members of, 14.1 p. 410–411
partisan disagreement, 9.1 p. 279
political party of, 1.3 p. 21
presidential caucuses, 15.2 p. 452
state government, 20.2 p. 603
states' rights, 4.4 pp. 125–126
urban workers supporting, 14.1 p. 407
U.S. voters (1992–2018), 1.3 p. 22
white, working class voters, 14.1 p. 412
republicanism, 2.3 p. 50, 3.1 p. 75, 3.2 p. 76–77, R14
resolutions, 9.1 p. 274, 9.3 p. 285, 20.4 p. 616–617
revenue sources, 3.5 p. 95, 4.4 p. 128, 21.3 pp. 639–640, 21.3 p. 640
***Reynolds* v. *Sims*,** 7.5 p. 246–247, 16.2 p. 482, 20.2 p. 602
***Reynolds* v. *United States*,** U4 p. 227, 5.2 p. 147
right of free association, 5.5 pp. 161–162
right of habeas corpus, 3.3 p. 85
right to bear arms, 1.1 p. 7, 5.1 p. 138
right to privacy, 20.1 pp. 596–597.
rights of citizens, R40
rights of the accused, 5.5 pp. 167–169
right-to-work laws, 14.4 pp. 431–432
***Roe* v. *Wade*,** 5.6 pp. 170–426
roll-call vote, 9.1 p. 278
rolling realignment, 14.1 p. 406, p. 408, p. 411
rule of law, 3.1 p. 75, 3.2 p. 78, p. 80, 11.1 p. 325

S

same-sex marriage, 2.5 p. 64, 4.2 p. 115, 6.4 pp. 216–217, 13.1 p. 381, 13.3 p. 392, p. 394, 13.4 p. 399
Sanders, Bernie, 1.4 pp. 32–33, 10.1 p. 297, 15.1 p. 449, 15.2 pp. 455–456, 15.4 p. 466, p. 468, 17.3 p. 529
***Santa Fe Independent School District* v. *Doe*,** 5.2 p. 144, p. 147
***Schenck* v. *United States*,** 5.3 p. 155–156, 5.5 p. 162, 8.1 p. 259
school, voter behavior influenced by, 16.4 p. 494
school segregation, 6.2 pp. 190–191, 12.1 p. 361
science, Congress and, 8.1 p. 256
search warrant, 5.5 p. 166
Second Amendment, 3.5 p. 91–93, 5.1 pp. 139–140, R28
Second Bank of United States, 4.3 p. 118
***The Second Treatise on Government* (Locke),** U1 p. 35
secret ballots, 15.3 p. 458, 16.3 p. 490
secretary of defense, 10.4 p. 318, 18.1 p. 540541
secretary of state, 10.4 p. 318, p. 321, 18.1 p. 539, pp. 540–541, 18.2 p. 546
secretary of the treasury, 10.4 p. 318
Securities and Exchange Commission (SEC), 11.1 p. 326, 11.2 p. 337, 11.3 p. 341
Sedition Act, 5.3 pp. 154–156
seditious libel, 19.1 p. 569
select (special) committees, 7.4 p. 245
Selective Service System, 6.1 p. 184
self-government, of early colonies, 2.1 p. 37
self-incrimination protection, 5.1 p. 138
self-proclaimed candidate, 15.1 p. 445
semi-closed primaries, 15.1 pp. 448–449
Senate
African Americans in, 6.2 p. 193
bicameral Congress, 7.1 p. 229
cloture, 7.3 p. 241, 9.1 p. 278–279
committees, 7.4 pp. 244–245, 8.3 p. 264–265, 9.1 pp. 276–277, 9.2 pp. 280–281, 9.3 p. 285, 11.1 p. 330, 14.2 p. 419
confirmation process, 8.3 pp. 267–268
counting electoral college votes, 15.3 p. 460
discharge resolution, 9.1 p. 275
elections, 7.5 pp. 248–458
establishment of, 2.5 p. 60, 3.1 p. 73–74, 3.2 p. 77, 3.3 p. 83, R14, R15
federal judicial appointments, 13.2 p. 386
filibuster, 7.3 p. 241, 8.3 p. 268, 9.1 p. 279, R17
floor debate, 9.1 pp. 278–279
impeachment trial, 8.3 p. 266
Latinos in, 6.4 p. 209
leadership of, 7.4 pp. 243–244
majority/minority leader, 7.4 p. 243
nuclear option, 8.3 p. 268, 13.2 p. 386
patterns of representations, 7.1 p. 230–231
pork-barrel legislation and earmarks, 7.1 p. 231
powers of, 7.5 p. 249
president of, 7.4 p. 243, R16
president pro tempore, 7.4 p. 243, 10.4 p. 321
Seventeenth Amendment, 3.2 p. 77, 3.5 p. 93, p. 95, R33
sponsoring bills, 9.1 p. 273
term length, 3.3 p. 84, 7.1 p. 230, R16
trade agreements, 10.2 p. 304
treaties, 8.1 p. 258, 10.2 pp. 303–304
vice-president, 7.4 pp. 243–244, 15.3 p. 460
voting process for, 3.2 p. 76
whips, 7.4 pp. 243–244
senatorial holds, 7.3 pp. 241–242, 9.1 p. 279
separate-but-equal doctrine, 6.2 p. 188–189, 12.1 p. 360
separation of church and state, 1.4 p. 31, 5.2 p. 143–144
separation of powers, 2.3 p. 49, 3.1 p. 75, 3.3 p. 83, R14, 20.1 p. 596
September 11, 1.1 p. 8, 5.6 p. 174, 8.1 p. 258, 10.1 p. 296, p. 299, 10.2 p. 309, 10.3 p. 313, 11.2 p. 333, 11.4 p. 349, 15.4 p. 464, 18.1 p. 542, 18.2 p. 547, 18.3 pp. 550–551, p. 548–549
Servicemen's Readjustment Act, 21.1 p. 630
Seventeenth Amendment, 3.2 p. 77, 3.5 p. 93, p. 95, 7.3 p. 240, R33
Seventh Amendment, 3.5 p. 92–93, 5.1 p. 138, R29
sexual harassment, 6.3 pp. 201–202
sexual orientation discrimination, 6.4 p. 216
***Shaw* v. *Reno*,** 20.2 p. 602
Shay's Rebellion, 2.4 p. 56–57
***Shelby County* v. *Holder*,** 4.4 p. 126, 6.2 p. 194, 16.2 p. 485–486
short-term continuing resolutions, 9.3 p. 287
shutdowns, 18.3 p. 555
single issue interest groups, 14.4 p. 434
single-member districts, 7.2 p. 233, 14.2 pp. 420–421
Sixteenth Amendment, 3.5 p. 93, p. 95, 5.1 p. 138, R32
Sixth Amendment, 3.5 p. 92–93, 5.5 p. 167, p. 169, 8.1 p. 253, R29
slavery
abolition of, 4.1 p. 110, 4.3 p. 120, 6.2 p. 187
Body of Liberties, 2.1 p. 40
Civil War and, 4.3 p. 119
dividing Whig Party, 14.1 p. 406
Emancipation Proclamation, 3.6 p. 102
legacy and rebellions, 6.2 pp. 186–187
slave importation, 2.5 p. 61
Three-Fifths Compromise, 2.5 p. 61, R15, R31
small-government conservatism, 14.1 p. 412
***Smith* v. *Allwright*,** 16.2 p. 482
Snowden, Edward, 5.3 p. 156, 5.6 p. 174–175, 11.4 p. 347, p. 353
social contract theory, 1.1 p. 10
social democrats, 1.4 p. 33
social media, 5.1 p. 140, 5.3 pp. 158–159, 5.5 p. 162, 5.6 p. 172–173, 15.4 p. 463, p. 466, 16.4 pp. 494–495, 19.3 p. 583, p. 587
Social Security, 1.1 p. 7, 1.4 p. 29, 9.3 p. 286, 11.2 p. 335, 11.3 p. 341, pp. 343–344, 12.2 p. 368, 17.3 pp. 524–525
socialism/socialists, 1.4 pp. 31–33, 5.3 p. 156
soft money, 15.5 p. 470
Sotomayor, Sonia, 6.3 p. 204, U6 p. 401, 13.2 p. 384–385, 13.4 p. 395, R23
the South, 2.5 p. 59, p. 61, 4.3 p. 119, p. 121
Southern Christian Leadership Conference (SCLC), 6.2 p. 191, 6.5 p. 219, 14.4 p. 433
***Southern Pacific Co.* v. *Arizona*,** 8.1 p. 255
sovereign powers, 1.1 p. 9, 4.3 p. 120
space exploration, U4 p. 252, 10.2 p. 307
Speaker of the House, 6.3 p. 204, 7.2 p. 238, 7.4 pp. 242–243, 10.4 p. 321, R15
special district, 4.1 p. 109, 20.1 p. 599, 21.2 pp. 635–636
special elections, 15.3 p. 457, 16.3 p. 488
Special Railroad Court, 12.3 p. 371
specialized courts, 12.2 p. 369, 12.3 p. 373
***SpeechNOW* v. *Federal Election Commission*,** 15.5 pp. 471–472
spoils system, 11.1 p. 327–328
Stamp Act Congress, 2.2 pp. 43–44
Stamp Act of 1765, 2.2 p. 43, R3
Stanton, Elizabeth Cady, 2.2 p. 47, 6.3 p. 197, 16.2 p. 487, R34
state government
agencies, 12.1 p. 362
Articles of Confederation, 2.4 p. 53–54
Bill of Rights, 5.1 pp. 141–142, 5.3 p. 158, 5.5 p. 160, 5.6 p. 173, 20.1 p. 596
budgets, 4.4 p. 128, p. 130
concurrent powers and supremacy clause, 4.2 p. 116
constitutions, 20.1 pp. 596–600
conventions, 15.2 p. 452, p. 454
cooperative federalism, 4.3 pp. 121–124
courts of, 12.1 pp. 364–620
education, 21.3 p. 641–642
executive branch, 20.1 p. 596–597, 20.3 pp. 608–613
federal government and, 4.3 p. 122, 4.4 pp. 124–126
federal grants, 4.4 pp. 130–131
general-fund budget, 4.4 p. 128
growth of, 11.3 p. 342
health care, 21.3 p. 640
initiative and referendum process, 1.2 p. 13
judicial branch, 20.1 p. 596, 20.1 p. 597, 20.2 p. 605, 20.4 p. 614–618
legislative branch, 20.1 p. 596–597, 20.2 pp. 600–607,
powers of, 3.3 pp. 82–120, 5.1 p. 139, R19, 20.1 p. 595
protection and respect of, 3.1 p. 74, R24
public policy, 4.1 p. 109
redistricting, 7.2 pp. 233–234 p. 236
revenues for, 4.4 p. 128, 21.3 pp. 638–640
special district, 4.1 p. 109
spending and budgets of, 21.3 pp. 640–643
statehood, 4.2 p. 112
statutes, 12.1 pp. 361–362
structure of, 20.1 p. 595–600
supreme court, 12.1 p. 364, 20.4 p. 618
treasurer, 20.3 p. 613
trial court, 12.1 p. 364
State of the Union Address, 9.3 p. 286, 10.2 p. 303, R22
state-centered government, 2.3 p. 51
States' Rights (Dixiecrat) Party, 14.1 p. 407, 14.3 p. 422
Statute for Religious Freedom, R28
statutory laws, 12.1 pp. 361–362, 20.4 p. 614–615
Stonewall Riot and National Monument, 6.4 pp. 215–216
strict construction and textualism, 13.3 p. 390, p. 392
strict scrutiny, 6.1 pp. 185–186, 6.5 p. 221
Student Nonviolent Coordinating Committee (SNCC), 6.2 p. 191
substantive due process, 5.5 p. 165
suburbs, growth of, 21.1 p. 633
subversive speech and sedition, 5.3 pp. 154–156
succession of states, 4.3 pp. 119–120
Sugar Act of 1764, 2.2 p. 43, R3
Sunrise Movement, 14.4 p. 427
Sunshine Act, 11.4 p. 349
Super PACs, 5.3 p. 152, 7.5 p. 248, 14.5 p. 435–436, 15.5 pp. 472–473
Super Tuesday, 15.2 p. 453, p. 455
superdelegates, 15.1 p. 447, 15.2 p. 456
superior court, 20.4 p. 620
supermajority, 3.4 pp. 86–87, 9.1 p. 273, 9.2 p. 281
Supplemental Security Income (SSI), 11.3 p. 344
supremacy of national government, 3.1 pp. 73–74, 4.1 p. 107, 4.2 p. 116, 4.3 pp. 117–120, p. 122, p. 124, 20.1 p. 595, R25
Supreme Court
establishment of, 2.5 p. 62, 3.1 p. 73, 3.3 p. 83, 8.1 p. 257, R14
federal judicial appointments, 10.3 p. 313, 13.2 pp. 383–386
federal-state relationships, 4.3 pp. 117–119
judicial review process, 3.6 p. 100, 4.3 p. 120, 5.1 pp. 139–140, 12.1 p. 360, p. 362, 12.2 p. 370, 13.1 pp. 379–383, 13.3 p. 388–394, 20.1 p. 596
organization of, 3.6 p. 98
political ideology impacting, 13.4 pp. 394–398
power of, 3.3 p. 84
Suspending Act, 2.2 p. 44
***Sweatt* v. *Painter*,** 6.2 p. 190
***Swift and Company* v. *United States*,** 8.1 p. 255
swing vote, 13.4 p. 395

T

Taliban, 11.3 p. 344, 18.3 p. 550–551
Tariff of Abominations, 4.3 p. 119

INDEX

Tax Cuts and Jobs Act, 17.2 p. 521, 17.2 p. 522, 17.3 p. 529
Tax Reform Act, 17.2 p. 521
taxes, 1.1 p. 7, 2.2 pp. 42–45, p. 61, 3.5 p. 95, 6.1 p. 184, 9.1 pp. 273–274, 11.3 p. 343
tax-exempt organizations, 14.5 p. 441
Tea Act, 2.2 p. 45
Tea Party movement, 2.2 p. 45, 5.5 p. 162, 14.1 p. 409, pp. 411–412, , 14.4 p. 434, 16.4 p. 496
Tennessee Valley Authority (TVA), 4.3 p. 121, 11.2 p. 338, 11.3 p. 341
Tenth Amendment, 3.3 p. 83, 3.5 pp. 92–93, 4.1 p. 107, 4.2 p. 114, 4.4 p. 130, 5.1 p. 139, 20.1 p. 595, R29
terrorists, 1.1 p. 8, 5.6 p. 174, 11.2 p. 333, 18.3 pp. 548–550, 18.4 p. 560. *See also* war on terrorism
***Texas* v. *Johnson*,** 5.3 p. 156
Third Amendment, 3.5 p. 91–93, 5.1 p. 138, 5.6 p. 169, R28
third parties, 14.3 pp. 420–424, 15.1 p. 445–446
Thirteenth Amendment, 3.4 p. 88, 3.5 p. 93–94, 4.3 p. 120, 6.2 p. 187, R31
***Thornburg* v. *Gingles*,** 20.2 p. 602
2014 Farm Bill, 17.1 pp. 515–516
Three-Fifths Compromise, 2.5 p. 61, 3.4 p. 88, R15, R31
tight-money policy, 17.2 p. 517–518
***Tinker* v. *Des Moines Independent Community School District*,** 5.3 p. 151
tolerance of differences, R41
totalitarian dictatorships, 1.2 pp. 11–12
township government, 20.1 p. 598, 21.2 p. 635
trade agreements, 10.2 p. 304
trade-offs, 17.1 p. 513
traditional journalism, 19.2 p. 582
traditional political spectrum, 1.4 p. 31
traffic courts, 20.4 p. 619
Trafficking Victims Protection Act, 3.5 p. 94
Trans-Pacific Partnership (TPP), 10.2 p. 304, 18.4 p. 565
Transportation Department, 10.4 p. 315, 11.2 p. 333
travel bans, 13.1 p. 381, 13.4 p. 396, 18.3 p. 554
treason, R23
treasuries, 17.2 p. 522
Treaty of Versailles, 8.1 p. 258
Treaty on the Non-Proliferation of Nuclear Weapons, 18.4 p. 560
treaty power, 10.2 pp. 303–304, 18.1 p. 540
trial by jury, 5.1 p. 138, 12.1 p. 366, R14, 20.4 p. 617
trial courts, U6 p. 377, 12.2 p. 368, 20.4 p. 618
trial system, 20.4 p. 616
tribal government, 21.2 pp. 635–638
Truman Doctrine, 18.2 p. 546
Trump, Donald J., 1.3 p. 18, pp. 21–25, 1.4 p. 29, 3.2 p. 80, 4.4 p. 129, 5.2 p. 151, 5.5 p. 160, 6.1 pp. 182–195, 6.3 p. 202, 6.4 p. 214, p. 217, 7.3 p. 241, 8.3 pp. 265–268, U8 p. 510, 10.1 pp. 296–301, 10.2 p. 304–305, p. 308–310, 10.3 p. 312, p. 314, 10.4 p. 317, p. 320, 11.1 p. 329, 11.4 p. 346–348, 12.2 p. 369, 12.3 p. 374, 13.1 p. 381, 13.2 p. 386, 13.4 p. 395–396 14.1 p. 409–412, 14.2 p. 418–419, 14.3 pp. 423–424, 14.4 p. 431, p. 433, 14.5 p. 439, 15.1 p. 448, 15.2 p. 451, 15.2 p. 453–454, p. 456, 15.4 p. 465–468, 16.3 p. 493, 16.4 p. 496–498, 16.5 p. 506, 17.3 pp. 528–532, 18.1 p. 541, 18.2 pp. 546–554, 18.3 p. 557, 18.4 pp. 559–565, 19.2 p. 577–579, p. 582, 19.3 pp. 587–588
Twelfth Amendment, 3.4 pp. 87–88, 3.5 p. 93, R30
Twentieth Amendment, 3.5 p. 93, p. 96, R34–R35
Twenty-Fifth Amendment, 3.4 p. 88–89, 3.5 p. 93, p. 97, 10.4 p. 321, R37
Twenty-First Amendment, 3.2 p. 78, 3.5 p. 93, p. 95, R35
Twenty-Fourth Amendment, 3.5 p. 93, 3.5 p. 97, 6.2 p. 192, 16.2 p. 480, R36
Twenty-Second Amendment, 3.2 p. 78, 3.4 p. 88, 3.5 p. 93, pp. 96–97, 3.5 p. 93, R35
Twenty-Seventh Amendment, 3.2 p. 78, 3.5 p. 93, pp. 96–97, R38
Twenty-Sixth Amendment, 3.4 p. 88, 3.5 p. 93, p. 97, 7.1 p. 229, 16.2 p. 483, R38
Twenty-Third Amendment, 3.4 p. 88, 3.5 p. 93, 3.5 p. 97, R36
2020 elections, 1.3 pp. 22–25, 6.3 p. 205, 14.1 p. 409–411, 14.2 p. 418–419, 15.2 p. 451, p. 453, p. 456, 16.3 p. 493, 16.4 p. 498
two-party system, 14.1 p. 406, 14.2 pp. 420–421

U

unconstitutional laws, 3.3 p. 84
undemocratic systems, 1.2 pp. 10–14
undocumented immigrants, 6.1 pp. 181–183, 6.4 p. 208, 14.1 p. 412
unemployment compensation, 17.3 p. 525
unemployment rates, 1.1 p. 8, 17.2 p. 517, 18.3 p. 555, 18.4 p. 565
unenumerated rights, R29
Uniform Code of Military Justice, 12.3 p. 373
Uniformed and Overseas Citizens Absentee Voting Act (UOCAVA), 16.2 p. 484
United Farm Workers (UFW) union, 6.3 p. 201, 6.4 p. 208, 14.4 p. 431
United Nations, 6.3 p. 206, 10.4 p. 316, 18.1 p. 540, 18.4 p. 558
United States Department of Agriculture (USDA), 10.4 p. 315, 11.1 p. 330–331, 11.2 p. 333–334, 18.1 p. 540
United States Postal Service (USPS), 8.1 p. 256, 11.2 pp. 338–339
United States Tax Court, 12.3 p. 373
United States trade representative, 10.4 p. 316
***United States* v. *Grace*,** 5.5 p. 162
***United States* v. *Lopez*,** 4.4 p. 124, 8.1 p. 255, 8.1 p. 256, 8.2 p. 262
***United States* v. *Morrison*,** 4.4 p. 125
***United States* v. *Nixon*,** 3.2 p. 80
***United States* v. *Virginia*,** 13.2 p. 387
***United States* v. *Windsor*,** 4.2 p. 115
United States-Mexico-Canada Agreement (USMCA), 10.2 p. 304, 14.4 p. 431, 18.4 p. 565
universal health-care insurance program, 15.2 p. 455
universal health-insurance, 17.3 pp. 526–528
U.S. Capitol, storming of, 1.3, p. 24, 19.3 p. 588
U.S. Civil Rights Commission, 16.2 p. 482
U.S. Commission on Civil Rights, 11.2 p. 335
U.S. Council of Muslim Organizations, 14.4 p. 434
U.S. International Trade Commission, 12.3 p. 372
U.S. Socialist Party, 5.3 p. 155
U.S. voters (1992–2018), 1.3 p. 22
USA Freedom Act, 5.6 p. 175
USA Patriot Act of 2001, 5.6 p. 174, 12.3 p. 372
U.S.-Chinese trade relationship, 18.4 pp. 561–563
U.S.S. *Cole*, 18.3 pp. 549–550
U.S.S. *Connecticut*, 18.3 p. 556

V

Veterans Affairs Department, 10.4 p. 315, 11.2 p. 333
veto power, 3.3 p. 84, 9.1 p. 273, p. 277, 9.2 pp. 281–282, 10.2 p. 305, 20.3 p. 611
veto referendum, 1.2 p. 13
vice-president, 3.1 p. 73, 6.3 p. 205, 10.4 pp. 318–321, R16
Vietnam War, 1.4 p. 31, 3.6 p. 103, 5.5 p. 161–162, 6.1 p. 184, 8.1 p. 258, 10.2 p. 309, 15.1 p. 447, 18.2 p. 546, 19.1 pp. 572–573
Violence Against Women Act of 1994, 4.4 p. 125, 8.2 p. 263
Virginia Plan, 2.5 pp. 59–60
Volstead Act, R33
voting patterns, 14.1 pp. 409–411
voting process, 3.2 p. 76, 6.1 p. 184, U7 p. 476, 15.2 pp. 456–478, 16.2 p. 484, 16.3 pp. 488–493
voting rights. *See also* Voting Rights Act of 1965
- absentee voting, 16.2 p. 484
- age limit, 3.4 p. 88, 3.5 p. 93, pp. 96–97, p. 93, 7.1 p. 229, 16.2 p. 483, R38
- colonial, 2.1 p. 41, 2.3 p. 51
- gerrymandering, 7.2 p. 235, p. 237, 16.2 p. 481
- in the 20th century, 16.2 pp. 481–483
- of Mexican and Native Americans, 16.2 pp. 480–482,
- of 21st century, 16.2 pp. 484–488
- of African Americans, 6.2 p. 187, p. 194, 16.1 p. 477, 16.2 pp. 480–482
- of Asian Americans, 16.2 pp. 480–482
- of women, 4.1 p. 110, 6.3 pp. 197–198, 16.1 p. 477, 16.2 pp. 481–482
- online voting, 16.2 p. 484
- participatory citizens, 6.1 p. 184, R39
- poll taxes, 6.2 p. 188, 16.2 p. 480, p. 482
- racial discrimination, 4.3 p. 124, 6.2 p. 187
- religious restrictions, 16.2 p. 480
- restrictions of, 16.2 p. 486
- Uniformed and Overseas Citizens Absentee Voting Act (UOCAVA), 16.2 p. 484
- voter ID, 16.2 p. 486
- voter suppression, 6.2 p. 188

Voting Rights Act of 1965, 4.3 p. 122, 124, 4.4 p. 126, 6.2 p. 194, 6.4 p. 214, 7.2 p. 234–235, 7.2 p. 237, U7 p. 509, 16.1 p. 477, 16.2 pp. 482–483, 20.2 p. 602

W

war on terrorism, 10.3 p. 313, 18.3 pp. 550–551. *See also* terrorists/terrorist attacks
War Powers Resolution in 1973, 3.6 p. 103, 8.1 p. 258, 10.2 p. 309, 18.1 p. 542
Warren Court, 13.3 p. 390, 13.3 p. 391
Washington, George, U1 p. 52, 2.1 p. 38, 2.2 p. 46, 2.3 p. 51, 2.4 p. 55, 2.5 p. 58–59, 3.3 p. 85, 3.4 p. 88, 3.6 pp. 102–103, 10.1 p. 296, 10.2 p. 303, 10.2 p. 305, p. 308, 10.4 pp. 315–446
Watergate hearings, 8.3 p. 264, 10.3 p. 314, 12.1 p. 367, 19.1 p. 569
welfare reform, 4.4 p. 124
***Wesberry* v. *Sanders*,** 7.2 p. 234, 7.5 p. 246, 16.2 p. 482
Westinghouse Electric, 19.1 p. 575
westward expansion, 2.2 p. 42, R3
Whig Party, 14.1 p. 406, p. 407, 15.1 p. 446
Whistleblower Protection Act of 1989, 11.4 p. 345
whistleblowers, 11.4 pp. 347–353
White supremacists, 5.5 pp. 160–161
WikiLeaks, 5.3 p. 159
Wilderness Act, 10.1 p. 302
***Wisconsin Right to Life*,** 15.5 p. 471
***Wisconsin* v. *Yoder*,** 3.5 p. 91
women, in politics, 1.3 pp. 22–24, 1.3 p. 26, 3.2 p. 79, 5.3 p. 152, 5.6 p. 170, 6.2 pp. 193–194, 6.3 p. 197, p. 202, p. 204–205, 7.5 p. 246, 14.1 p. 414, 20.2 p. 603, 20.3 p. 609, R23. *See also specific women*
women, in the workplace, 6.3 pp. 200–202, p. 204
women's suffrage, 2.5 p. 65, 3.4 p. 88, 3.5 p. 93, p. 95, 4.1 p. 110, 6.2 p. 196, 6.3 pp. 197–482, 16.2 p. 487, R34
women's rights, 6.3 pp. 198–200, p. 202, 13.2 p. 387
workplace discrimination, 5.2 p. 147, p. 149, 6.3 pp. 200–201
Works Project Administration, 1.4 p. 27
World Health Organization (WHO), 18.3 p. 554, 18.4 p. 563
world trade, 18.4 pp. 563–565
World Trade Organization (WTO), 18.4 p. 564

Z

***Zarda* v. *Altitude Express*,** 6.3 p. 203
***Zelman* v. *Simmons-Harris*,** 3.5 p. 92
***Ziglar* v. *Abbasi*,** 13.1 p. 380

ACKNOWLEDGMENTS

Illustration: All illustrations are owned by © Cengage.

iii Collection of the Supreme Court of the United States; **iv** Erik Pronske Photography/Moment/Getty Images; **v** Scott Rothstein/iStock/ Getty Images; **vi** Bruce Davidson/Magnum Photos; **vii** Inge Johnsson/ AGE Fotostock/Superstock; **viii** Glowimages/Getty Images; **ix** RubberBall/Superstock; **x** Jeff Swensen/Getty Images News/Getty Images; **xi** Mark Peterson/Redux; **xii** Robert Daemmrich Photography Inc/Corbis Historical/Getty Images; **xvi** Mark Thiessen/National Geographic Image Collection; **1** Scott Rothstein/iStock/Getty Images; **2-3** (spread) Erik Pronske Photography/Moment/Getty Images; **4** Hilary Swift/The New York Time s/Redux; **5** Robyn Beck/AFP/Getty Images; **6** Ronan Donovan/National Geographic Image Collection; **9** Kenneth Garrett/National Geographic Image Collection; **11** Bhutan Government DIT/Getty Images News/Getty Images; **12** Heritage Images/Hulton Archive/Getty Images; **13** AP Images/Miquel Llop; **14** © Ricardo Thomas/Courtesy Gerald R.Ford Library; **15** Cory Richards/National Geographic Image Collection; **16** King John signing the Magna Carta reluctantly (colour litho), Michael, Arthur C. (d.1945) (after)/The Stapleton Collection/Bridgeman Images; **18** Aaron Huey/National Geographic Image Collection; **19** Justin Sullivan/Getty Images News/ Getty Images; **20** © Gary Huck/Konopacki Cartoons; **21** Verville Alexandra/National Geographic Image Collection; **23** Pool/Getty Images News/Getty Images; **25** AP Images/Evan Vucci; **26** Mandel Ngan/AFP/Getty Images; **27** Library of Congress, Prints & Photographs Division, Reproduction number LC-USZC2-5356 (color film copy slide); **28** Historical/Corbis Historical/Getty Images; **32** AP Images/Alexander Zemlianichenko; **36** T.J. Kirkpatrick/Getty Images News/Getty Images; **38** Ira Block/National Geographic Image Collection; **39** SuperStock/ Getty Images; **41** Matt Purciel/Alamy Stock Photo; **42** Library of Congress, Prints & Photographs Division, Reproduction number LC-USZC4-5315 (color film copy transparency) LC-USZ62-9701 (b&w film copy neg.; **43** Colonial teapot relating to the British Stamp Act of 1765/Don Troiani Collection/Bridgeman Images; **44** Niday Picture Library/Alamy Stock Photo; **45** John Moore/Getty Images News/Getty Images; **46** IanDagnall Computing/Alamy Stock Photo; **49** Angela Weiss/AFP/Getty Images; **50** Mira Oberman/AFP/Getty Images; **51** Pulling Down the Statue of King George III, c.1859 (oil on canvas), Oertel, Johannes Adam Simon (1823-1909)/Collection of the New-York Historical Society, USA/Bridgeman Images; **52** Hulton Archive/ Archive Photos/Getty Images; **56** Bill Bachmann/Alamy Stock Photo; **57** Hulton Archive/Archive Photos/Getty Images; **58** JacobH/E+/Getty Images; **62** Marianne Barcellona/The LIFE Images Collection/Getty Images; **64** Olivier Douliery/Getty Images News/Getty Images; **65** Library of Congress Prints and Photographs Division/The Massachusetts Centinel/Library of Congress Serial and Government Publications Division Washington, D.C. 20540 USA; **68-69** (spread) National Archives Museum; **70** Sean Pavone/Shutterstock.com; **72** Michael Ventura/Alamy Stock Photo; **75** AP/Shutterstock.com; **77** Win McNamee/Getty Images News/Getty Images; **80** Xinhua/Shutterstock. com; **81** (t)Lucidio Studio Inc/Photographer's Choice RF/Getty Images, (cl)National Geographic Image Collection; **87** Bettmann/Getty Images; **88** Library of Congress Prints and Photographs Division; **95** Alex Edelman/AFP/Getty Images; **96** Dirck Halstead/The LIFE Images Collection/Getty Images; **100** North Wind Picture Archives/Alamy Stock Photo; **101** Granger/Shutterstock.com; **102** Doug Meek/ Shutterstock.com; **105** Signe Wilkinson/The Cartoonist Group; **106** Jeff Kowalsky/AFP/Getty Images; **108** Avpics/Alamy Stock Photo; **110** Ken Florey Suffrage Collection/Gado/Archive Photos/Getty Images; **112** AP Images/The Star-Bulletin, Albert Yamauchi; **113** Tom Murphy/National Geographic Image Collection; **115** Erich Schlegel/Getty Images News/ Getty Images; **117** © John Marshall, oil on canvas, Richard Norris Brooke, after William de Hartum Washington 1880, Collection of the U.S. House of Representatives; **118** © Second Bank of the United States; **120** Mathew B. Brady/The LIFE Picture Collection/Getty Image; **121** Library of Congress Prints and Photographs Division; **122** AP Images/ Charles Kelly; **123** Gary Hershorn/Corbis News/Getty Images; **125** Pete Saloutos/Image Source/Getty Images; **127** AP Images/Charles Krupa; **129** Aaron Huey/National Geographic Image Collection; **130** Mike Lester/The Cartoonist Group; **134-135** (spread) Bruce Davidson/ Magnum Photos; **136** Sean Rayford/The New York Times/Redux; **137** Alex Wong/Getty Images News/Getty Images; **139** Aaron P. Bernstein/ Getty Images News/Getty Images; **140** Erin Schaff/The New York Times/Redux; **143** Carlos Osorio/Shutterstock.com; **144** Clay Bennett's Editorial Cartoons/The Cartoonist Group; **145** Bettmann/Getty Images; **146** Eldad Carin/Alamy Stock Photo; **148** Library of Congress/Corbis/ Getty Images; **149** AP Images/Brett Flashnick; **150** © Richard Barnes; **151** Bettmann/Getty Images; **152** Sarah Edwards/Alamy Stock Photo; **153** AP Images; **154** Galerie Bilderwelt/Hulton Archive/Getty Images; **155** Galerie Bilderwelt/Hulton Archive/Getty Images; **157** Bettmann/ Getty Images; **160** Salwan Georges/The Washington Post/Getty Images; **161** Don Cravens/The Life Images Collection/Getty Images; **163** Brian J. Skerry/National Geographic Image Collection; **164** Erik Mcgregor/ Pacific Press/LightRocket/Getty Images; **165** Allen J. Schaben/Los Angeles Times/Getty Images; **167** Joe Burbank-Pool/Pool/Getty Images News/Getty Images; **168** (tl) AP Images, (tr) floridamemory.com; **171** Greggibson/AFP/Getty Images; **172** Al Drago/Bloomberg/Getty Images; **175** Travis P Ball/Getty Images Entertainment/Getty Images; **178** Michael Zagaris/Getty Images Sport/Getty Images; **179** Stephanie Keith/Getty Images News/Getty Images; **182** Historical/Corbis Historical/Getty Images; **183** Drew Angerer/Getty Images News/Getty Images; **184** Andy Cross/Denver Post/Getty Images; **185** Tim Shaffer TS/SV/Reuters; **187** AP Images/Brynn Anderson; **189** Digital Image Library/Alamy Stock Photo; **190** The Commercial Appeal/ZUMApress/ Newscom; **192** AP Images/Jacquelyn Martin; **195** Chip Somodevilla/ Getty Images News/Getty Images; **196** John Stanmeyer/National Geographic Image Collection; **198** AP Images; **199** Mao Siqian Xinhua/ eyevine/Redux; **201** Bill Pugliano/Getty Images News/Getty Images; **203** Saul Loeb/AFP/Getty Images; **204** AP Images/Manuel Balce Ceneta; **205** (tl) Dan Videtich/The Washington Post/Getty Images, (tr) dpa picture alliance/Alamy Stock Photo, (cl) AB Forces News Collection/ Alamy Stock Photo, (bl) Brendan Hoffman/Getty Images Entertainment/Getty Images, (br) Toya Sarno Jordan/Bloomberg/Getty Images; **206** Giacomo Pirozzi/Panos Pictures/Redux; **210** © Dr. Hector P. Garcia Papers, Special Collection, Bell Library, Texas A&M University-Corpus Christi; **211** Ansel Adams/Library of Congress Prints and Photographs Division; **213** Paul J. Richards/AFP/Getty Images; **215** Helen H. Richardson/The Denver Post/Getty Images; **216** Steven Greaves/Lonely Planet Images/Getty Images; **218** Design Pics, Inc./National Geographic Image Collection; **219** Photo Quest/Archive Photos/Getty Images; **220** AP Images; **222** AP Images/Susan Walsh; **225** Bruce Roberts/Science Source/Getty Images; **226-227** (spread) Inge Johnsson/AGE Fotostock/Superstock; **228** Reuters; **229** AP Images/ Susan Walsh; **231** Matt Wuerker/The Cartoonist Group; **233** Tom Williams/CQ-Roll Call Group/Getty Images; **236** The Denver Post/Getty Images; **237** Bettmann/Getty Images; **238** AP Images/J. Scott Applewhite; **239** Danielle Zalcman/National Geographic Image Collection; **241** Library of Congress, Prints & Photographs Division, Reproduction number LC-DIG-ppmsca-29146 (digital file from original print); **242** AP Images/WPS; **243** AP Images/J. Scott Applewhite; **244** AP Images/Senate TV; **247** Bettmann/Getty Images; **248** AP Images/ Tom Reel/San Antonio Express-News/Pool; **252** NASA; **254** Gary Cameron/Reuters; **255** Library of Congress, Prints & Photographs Division, Reproduction number LC-USZ62-51781 (b&w film copy neg. of half stereo); **257** Livio Sinibaldi/DigitalVision/Getty Images; **258** Behrouz Mehri/AFP/Getty Images; **260** Danita Delimont/Gallo Images/ Getty Images; **263** AP Images/Manuel Balce Ceneta; **264** AP Images; **265** Jonathan Ernst TPX Images of The Day/Reuters; **267** Chip Somodevilla/Getty Images News/Getty Images; **269** Department of the Interior/National Archives; **273** Howard Kingsnorth/The Image Bank/ Getty Images; **272** Caroline Brehman/CQ-Roll Call, Inc./Getty Images; **274** AP Images/Evan Vucci; **276** AP Images/Patrick Dodson/The Daily Gazette; **281** Fotosearch/Cengage Learning/AGE Fotostock; **282** Gary Varvel/The Cartoonist Group; **283** Keith Bedford/Reuters; **286** Xinhua/ Zhao Hanrong/Xinhua News Agency/Getty Images; **288** Eduardo Munoz Alvarez/Getty Images News/Getty Images; **289** Amy Toensing/ National Geographic Image Collection; **292-293** (spread) Glowimages/ Getty Images; **294** Arnold Newman/Masters/Getty Images; **296** Eric Draper/Us National A/SIPA/SIPA France/USA/Newscom; **298** © Franklin D. Roosevelt Presidential Library & Museum/FDR Library; **300** PictureLux/The Hollywood Archive/Alamy Stock Photo; **302** Michael Melford/National Geographic Image Collection; **303** Diana Walker/The LIFE Images Collection/Getty Images; **306** Museum of the City of New York/Getty Images; **307** © Cecil Stoughton. White House Photographs. John F. Kennedy Presidential Library and Museum, Boston; **310** AP Images/Hassan Ammar; **311** © Dave Granlund, Minnesota/Cagle Cartoons, Inc.; **313** Ralph Morse/The LIFE Images Collection/Getty Images; **314** Bettmann/Getty Images; **316** AP Images/ Carolyn Kaster; **318** Nicholas Kamm/AFP/Getty Images; **319** Bettmann/ Getty Images; **320** Handout/Getty Images News/Getty Images; **321** Douglas Graham/CQ-Roll Call, Inc./Getty Images; **324** PhotoQuest/ Archive Photos/Getty Images; **326** AP Images/Manuel Balce Ceneta; **328** manine99/Shutterstock.com; **334** Archistoric/Alamy Stock Photo;

336 Al Seib/AFP/Getty Images; **339** W. Robert Moore/National Geographic Image Collection; **341** Library of Congress Prints and Photographs Division; **344** Richard Schoenberg/Corbis News/Getty Images; **346** Aaron Huey/National Geographic Image Collection; **348** Barcroft Media/Barcroft Media/Getty Images; **351** Roberto Schmidt/AFP/Getty Images; **352** Richard Ellis/Alamy Stock Photo; **353** (tr) ZUMA Press Inc/Alamy Stock Photo, (br) AP Images/Uncredited; **356-357** (spread) RubberBall/Superstock; **358** Chip Somodevilla/Getty Images News/Getty Images; **360** Print Collector/Hulton Archive/Getty Images; **361** Carl Iwasaki/The LIFE Images Collection/Getty Images; **362** © Bruce Plante politicalcartoons.com/Cagle Cartoons, Inc.; **365** Ted Psahos/U.S. Immigration and Customs Enforcement/Handout/Getty Images News/Getty Images; **370** Pool/Getty Images News/Getty Images; **371** Rick Friedman/Corbis News/Getty Images; **372** © Monte Wolverton, Battle Ground, WA/Cagle Cartoons, Inc.; **374** AP Images/Lois Silver; **375** Toby Smith/National Geographic Image Collection; **378** MCT/Tribune News Service/Getty Images; **379** David Hume Kennerly/3rd Party - Misc/Getty Images; **381** AP Images/Carolyn Kaster; **382** Bettmann/Getty Images; **384** Pete Souza/The White House/PSG/Newscom; **385** (t) AP Images/Kevin Dietsch/picture-alliance/dpa, (tl) (cl) (c) MCT/Tribune News Service/Getty Images, (tc) (cr) WDC Photos/Alamy Stock Photo, (tr) Universal History Archive/Universal Images Group/Getty Images, (bl) Chip Somodevilla/Getty Images News/Getty Images, (bc) Mandel Ngan/AFP/Getty Images, (br) Rachel Malehorn/ZUMA Press/Indiana/USA/Newscom; **387** The Washington Post/The Washington Post/Getty Images; **388** © Dave Granlund/Cagle Cartoons, Inc.; **389** Bill O'Leary/The Washington Post/Getty Images; **390** George Tames/New York Times Co./Getty Images; **391** AP Images/Uncredited; **392** Mark Wilson/Getty Images News/Getty Images; **393** (tl) (tr) Wayne Lawrence/National Geographic Image Collection, (cl) Robin Hammond/National Geographic Image Collection; **396** Tom Williams/CQ-Roll Call Group/Getty Images; **399** Rick Wilking/Reuters/Newscom; **402-403** (spread) Jeff Swensen/Getty Images News/Getty Images; **404** Art Wolfe/The Image Bank/Getty Images; **405** AP Images/David Dermer; **413** © Karla Gachet; **414** Chip Somodevilla/Getty Images News/Getty Images; **415** Joseph Prezioso/AFP/Getty Images; **417** AP Images/Jae C. Hong; **418** Carolyn Cole/Los Angeles Times/Getty Images; **422** Helen H. Richardson/The Denver Post/Getty Images; **423** Nick Anderson/The Cartoonist Group; **425** Alex Wong/Getty Images News/Getty Images; **426** John Sommers II/Reuters/Newscom; **427** AP Images/Michael Brochstein/Sipa USA; **430** Design Pics, Inc./National Geographic Image Collection; **433** Saul Loeb/AFP/Getty Images; **437** Cornell Capa/The LIFE Picture Collection/Getty Images; **438** Paul Fusco/Magnum Photos New York; **441** Drew Angerer/Getty Images News/Getty Images; **444** Tamir Kalifa/The New York Time s/Redux; **445** Bettmann/Getty Images; **449** Ricky Carioti/The Washington Post/Getty Images; **452** John Schultz/ZUMA Press/Newscom; **455** AP Images/John Minchillo; **457** Chicago History Museum/Archive Photos/Getty Images; **461** Robert King/Hulton Archive/Getty Images; **464** Lucy Nicholson/Reuters/Newscom; **466** Andrew Harrer/Bloomberg/Getty Images; **467** Jim Watson/AFP/Getty Images; **471** Citizens United Productions/Everett Collection, Inc./Alamy Stock Photo; **476** AP Images/Marcio Jose Sanchez; **478** Shannon Stapleton TPX Images of The Day/Reuters; **480** Onsite/Alamy Stock Photo; **483** Alex Wong/Getty Images News/Getty Images; **484** Vicki Beaver/Alamy Stock Photo; **485** Win McNamee/Getty Images News/Getty Images; **487** Library of Congress Prints and Photographs Division; **489** Tasos Katodis/AFP/Getty Images; **490** Francis G. Mayer/Corbis Historical/Getty Images; **494** Barbara Alper/Archive Photos/Getty Images; **495** Jim West/image Broker/Shutterstock.com; **497** ZUMA Press Inc/Alamy Stock Photo; **499** (tl) Jim Watson/AFP/Getty Images; (tr) Mandel Ngan/AFP/Getty Images; **504** Gary Varvel/The Cartoonist Group; **510-511** (spread) Mark Peterson/Redux; **512** Alex Wong/Getty Images News/Getty Images; **514** B Chris(t)her/Alamy Stock Photo; **519** AP Images/Carlos Osorio; **525** Lisa Benson's Editorial Cartoons/The Cartoonist Group; **527** Alex Wong/Getty Images News/Getty Images; **528** Todd Bannor/Alamy Stock Photo; **530** AP Images/Larry MacDougal; **531** NOAA; **534** MediaNews Group/Inland Valley Daily Bulletin/Getty Images; **535** Florian Schulz/National Geographic Image Collection; **538** PJF Military Collection/Alamy Stock Photo; **539** dpa picture alliance archive/Alamy Stock Photo; **540** Keystone-France/Gamma-Keystone/Getty Images; **541** Timothy A. Clary/AFP/Getty Images; **544** AGE Fotostock/Alamy Stock Photo; **545** akg-images/akg-images/Newscom; **547** Agencja Fotograficzna Caro/Alamy Stock Photo; **549** Neville Elder/Corbis/Getty Images; **550** Lynsey Addario/Reportage Archive/Getty Images; **551** Trinity Mirror/Mirrorpix/Alamy Stock Photo; **552** Pete Souza/The White House/Getty Images; **554** Fabrice Coffrini/AFP/Getty Images; **555** Issouf Sanogo/AFP/Getty Images; **556** Louie Palu/National Geographic Image Collection, (cl) National Geographic Image Collection; **559** AP Images/Lefteris Pitarakis; **562** Sean Pavone/Shutterstock.com; **564** Noob Pixel/Shutterstock.com; **568** MediaNews Group/East Bay Times/Getty Images; **569** AP Images; **571** Signe Wilkinson/The Cartoonist Group; **573** CBS Photo Archive/Getty Images; **574** Brendan Smialowski/Getty Images News/Getty Images; **577** (tl) (tr) Library of Congress Prints and Photographs Division; **580** Speed Bump/The Cartoonist Group; **585** Christine Ting/The New York Times/Redux; **587** AP Images/Jon Elswick; **589** Karen Bleier/AFP/Getty Images; **592-593** (spread) Robert Daemmrich Photography Inc/Corbis Historical/Getty Images; **594** AP Images/Steve Helber; **596** David Paul Morris/Bloomberg/Getty Images; **597** D Guest Smith/Alamy Stock Photo; **598** Craig Ruttle/AP/Shutterstock.com; **601** AP Images/Charles Krupa; **606** AP Images/Darin Oswald/Idaho Statesman; **607** Stephen St. John/National Geographic Image Collection; **609** Darryl Oumi/Getty Images Entertainment/Getty Images; **611** Doral Chenoweth III/Dispatch/Tribune News Service/USA/Newscom; **612** Tony Shi Photography/Moment/Getty Images; **614** RoschetzkyIstockPhoto/iStock/Getty Images; **618** Fuse/Corbis/Getty Images; **619** AP Images/Robert Cohen/St. Louis Post-Dispatch; **621** AP Images/Paul Woolverton/The Fayetteville Observer; **624** Robert Gauthier/Los Angeles Times/Getty Images; **625** eye35/Alamy Stock Photo; **626** Darryl Brooks/Shutterstock.com; **628** North Wind Picture Archives/Alamy Stock Photo; **629** (cr) Dermot Conlan/Tetra images/Getty Images, (br) Roschetzky Photography/Shutterstock.com; **631** Emmanuel Dunand/AFP/Getty Images; **632** (tl) (tr) Wayne Lawrence/National Geographic Image Collection, **635** BanksPhotos/E+/Getty Images; **636** AP Images/Nati Harnik; **637** Jack Dykinga/National Geographic Image Collection; **643** Nick Oxford/Reuters/Newscom; **R01** Danita Delimont/Gallo Images/Getty Images; **R02** Kumar Sriskandan/Alamy Stock Photo; **R08** (cl) (cr) National Portrait Gallery, Smithsonian Institution; **R09** Library of Congress Prints and Photographs Division; **R16** Alex Edelman/Alamy Stock Photo; **R22** Win McNamee/Getty Images News/Getty Images; **R23** Kevin Dietsch/Pool via CN/ dpa picture alliance/Alamy Stock Photo; **R25** IanDagnall Computing/Alamy Stock Photo; **R32** Library of Congress, Prints & Photographs Division, Reproduction number LC-DIG-pga-03453 (digital file from original print, D size) LC-DIG-pga-04070 (digital file from original print, C size)LC-USZ62-38251 (b&w film copy neg. of D size)LC-USZ62-36274 (b&w film copy neg. of C size); **R33** Library of Congress Prints and Photographs Division; **R34** Underwood Archives/Archive Photos/Getty Images; **R38** Bettmann/Getty Images; **R39** Blend Images - Hill Street Studios/Brand X Pictures/Getty Images; **R41** Drew Angerer/Getty Images News/Getty Images; **R42** Rhona Wise/AFP/Getty Images.